About the author

Respected wine critic and vigneron James Halliday has a career that spans over forty years, but he is most widely known for his witty and informative writing about wine. As one of the founders of Brokenwood in the Lower Hunter Valley region of New South Wales, Australia, and thereafter founder of Coldstream Hills in the Yarra Valley, Victoria, Australia, James is an unmatched authority on every aspect of the wine industry, from the planting and pruning of vines through to the creation and marketing of the finished product. His winemaking has led him to sojourns in Bordeaux and Burgundy, and he is constantly in demand as a wine judge in Australia and overseas.

James Halliday has contributed to more than 50 books on wine since he began writing in 1979. His books have been translated into Japanese, French, German, Danish and Icelandic, and have been published in the UK, the US, as well as Australia. He is also the author of *James Halliday's Wine Atlas of Australia*.

Wine zones and regions of Australia

N

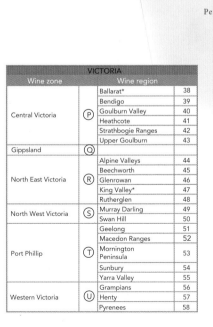

0 _____ 500 km

120°

INDIAN

20°

HAMMERSLEY RA.

Tropic of Capricorn

OCEAN

WESTER

W

AUSTRAL

30°

X

Perth • 61 60

59 V

63

62

66 65 64

Y 67

NEW SOUTH WALES			
Wine zone		Wine region	
Big Rivers	A	Murray Darling	1
		Perricoota	2
		Riverina	3
		Swan Hill	4
Central Ranges	B	Cowra	5
		Mudgee	6
		Orange	7
Hunter Valley	C	Lower Hunter	8
		Upper Hunter	9
Northern Rivers	D	Hastings River	10
Northern Slopes	E	New England*	11
South Coast	F	Shoalhaven Coast	12
		Southern Highlands	13
Southern New South Wales	G	Canberra District	14
		Gundagai	15
		Hilltops	16
		Tumbarumba	17
Western Plains	H		

SOUTH AUSTRALIA			
Wine zone		Wine region	
Adelaide Super Zone includes Mount Lofty Ranges, Fleurieu and Barossa Wine Regions			
Barossa		Barossa Valley	18
		Eden Valley	19
Fleurieu	J	Currency Creek	20
		Kangaroo Island	21
		Langhorne Creek	22
		McLaren Vale	23
		Southern Fleurieu	24
Mount Lofty Ranges		Adelaide Hills	25
		Adelaide Plains	26
		Clare Valley	27
Far North	K	Southern Flinders Ranges	28
Limestone Coast	L	Coonawarra	29
		Mount Benson	30
		Mount Gambier*	31
		Penola*	32
		Padthaway	33
		Robe	34
		Wrattonbully	35
Lower Murray	M	Riverland	36
The Peninsulas	N	Southern Eyre Peninsula*	37

VICTORIA			
Wine zone		Wine region	
Central Victoria	P	Ballarat*	38
		Bendigo	39
		Goulburn Valley	40
		Heathcote	41
		Strathbogie Ranges	42
		Upper Goulburn	43
Gippsland	Q		
North East Victoria	R	Alpine Valleys	44
		Beechworth	45
		Glenrowan	46
		King Valley*	47
		Rutherglen	48
North West Victoria	S	Murray Darling	49
		Swan Hill	50
Port Phillip	T	Geelong	51
		Macedon Ranges	52
		Mornington Peninsula	53
		Sunbury	54
		Yarra Valley	55
Western Victoria	U	Grampians	56
		Henty	57
		Pyrenees	58

*   Regions that have taken, or are likely to take, steps to secure registration.

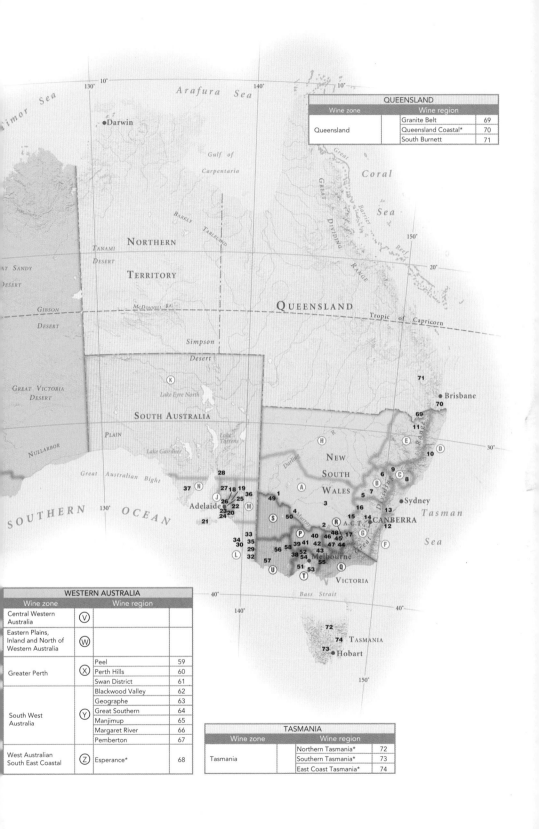

James Halliday
Australian
Wine Companion

2008 Edition

**THE BESTSELLING AND DEFINITIVE GUIDE
TO AUSTRALIAN WINES**

Hardie Grant Books

Published in 2007 by
Hardie Grant Books
85 High Street
Prahran, Victoria 3181, Australia
www.hardiegrant.com.au

ISBN 978 1 74066 515 5
ISSN 1448 3564

Typeset by Megan Ellis
Printed and bound in Australia by McPherson's Printing Group

10 9 8 7 6 5 4 3 2 1

Contents

Introduction

From a feast to a famine, from a world of unlimited opportunity to one clouded with uncertainty, changes have swept across the face of the Australian wine industry with unprecedented speed and power. The 2007 and 2008 calendar years may well prove to be turning points taking grapegrowers, winemakers and wine marketers down paths previously undreamed of.

The dire weather conditions running across Southeast Australia in 2007 (and a bleak outlook for grape production in 2008) were largely caused by the severe El Niño pattern, but it seems certain that there has been and will continue to be a concomitant contribution from climate change.

What is even more certain is a radical change in attitudes to, and allocations of, water, ranging from a city dweller washing the family car to water for all forms of agricultural use, including – of course – growing grapes. Challenges abound, and the vignerons of this country will have to be particularly clever in answering those challenges.

It is thus appropriate that my annual *Australian Wine Companion* should have undergone many changes since its first appearance in 1986. Back then it was published in an A4-sized format, with 325 pages of generously spaced winery and tasting notes; there were four editions in this format. It was then decided to heavily compress the information and page size, resulting in an annual pocket guide in 1991, and from 1992 to 2002 it also included New Zealand. During those 11 years the *Companion*'s size grew remorselessly, both in page size and page numbers, reflecting the ever increasing number of wineries and wines. In 2003 New Zealand was dropped (purely for space reasons), but the offset in Australian winery births meant the page length barely changed (down 19) to 537, growing to 784 in 2007.

It was decided to make a series of changes for this 2008 edition as far reaching as any that preceded it. The most obvious is the introduction of 2-colour printing. This gave birth to 5-star winery ratings printed in red for wineries of outstanding merit. It also led to wine tasting notes of special interest in red. Special interest was usually triggered by special quality, but top-value wines, and those made from unusual varieties and/or unusual techniques have also been highlighted.

Nearly as dramatic has been the consequence of not increasing the number of pages. If I had followed last year's approach of including all wineries I could track down, and rated all wines I tasted during the year, there would have been 2395 wineries (with 218 making their first appearance), over 7200 wines rated and 5962 tasting notes. The consequence would have been a book of over 1000 pages, which was out of the question.

To keep length under control, I have had to delete 665 wineries which were not rated (NR), two-thirds of which did not respond to our 2008 request for updated information, and, more importantly, did not send samples.

Another radical change demanded by word and page length was the deletion of over 1900 wines rated at 86 points or less. It should not be assumed I have become a fairy godmother, treating every wine I taste as worth 87 points or more. Nothing could be further from the truth.

A special complication arose from a never-to-be-repeated attempt to send the update requests by email: spam filters and email fatigue led to a significant number of wineries not reading the request. So, if a winery had responded for the 2007 edition, and had sent samples, its rating was carried over for this edition even though there were no tastings.

In the future, the focus of the *Companion* will increasingly be on the best wineries and best wines. If wineries are unable or unwilling to respond to the form we send annually according to the timelines specified, they will not be included in the 2009 edition. If they respond to the request for updated information, but elect not to submit samples (at all, or by the deadline), they are unlikely to be included.

All is not lost, however. I have an immense database, and at some not-too-distant time, most or all of the material in that database will be put on a new website. At the very least, it will include details of every winery that is in active operation, and a large tasting notes database will likewise be included.

Finally, I would like to express my gratitude to Collins, which – under various names over the years – has published the *Companion* (under its various names) with professionalism and tolerance since the first edition in 1986.

My move to Hardie Grant came in the footsteps of their publication of my *Wine Atlas of Australia*, a book of which I am immensely proud. They gave unflagging support for the *Atlas*, with all the strands of a very complicated and costly publishing project seamlessly woven together, which brought us into close contact at all levels. First and foremost was the Hardie Grant team, led by Sandy Grant, and on my side, by the much smaller team of three: myself, Paula Grey and Beth Anthony.

It led to Hardie Grant putting forward a proposal for a joint venture to take on the *Wine Companion* now, and long into the future, and this 2008 edition is the result. I think I speak for both teams in saying it is the best *Companion* ever published, and establishes a benchmark for subsequent editions.

Australian vintage 2007: a snapshot

The Australian wine industry has experienced a wild ride over the 4 vintages from 2004–07. The first 3 vintages resulted in near identical tonnages of around 1.9 million tonnes. The 2004 vintage was 38% higher than that of 2003, and the yield was recognised as abnormally high. But 2005 and 2006 both produced similar tonnages with only marginal increases in vineyard area between 2002–05 (less than 5%).

The consequence was the massive surplus of wine, expressing itself in the proliferation of cleanskins, discount warehouses operating outside the previously established retail system, a continuing decrease in the FOB value per litre of our exports, and almost all the increase in volume coming from bulk exports. (A note of caution: exports of bottled wine did not decline in value per litre, and bulk exports were in part those of big companies electing to bottle and package their cheaper branded wines in the market in which they were to be sold. Not all bulk exports were at giveaway prices to China or similar markets where control of the wine was lost.)

Working on the basis of a 'normal' vintage of around 1.5 million tonnes, and of a continuing but modest increase in the volume of exports, the projections were for a balance between supply and demand in around 2009–10. But long before spring in calendar 2006 (leading up to the 2007 vintage) the signs were ominous. The ongoing severe drought precipitated by a strong El Niño meant dry soils and night skies without cloud cover, all precursors for severe frosts.

Frosts of unprecedented severity, frequency and geographic spread duly impacted. In parts of the Limestone Coast, 3 frosts over a week apart killed successive budbreaks and shoots, with the certainty of a carry-over impact for the 2008 vintage. The drought also caused severe water shortages, with much discussed options for future water use. The official forecast for 2007 came down from 1.9 million to 1.5 million to 1.3 million tonnes.

Even then, nature still had hail and bushfires up its sleeve, and these duly materialised. The Victorian bushfires in the north and east of the state were the worst ever, with 1 million ha razed as the fires burnt for months, often out of control. Smoke taint, which was first experienced in 2003, will severely impact on the quality of the grapes from the important King Valley region, but its effect spread as far south as the Yarra Valley. The grapes picked will form part of the official crop, but it is no certainty the wine made will be of commercial value.

The discovery of phylloxera in one vineyard in the Yarra Valley (with no secondary sites found despite intensive aerial and ground searches) had no impact on harvest figures for the valley, let along those for Australia as a whole. The parallel is precisely that of cancer: early detection and surgery may prove to be decisive, but the chances of its reappearance elsewhere cannot be dismissed. Stringent protocols have been instituted for vineyards within 5 km of the site of the initial outbreak, resulting in an effective quarantine. It may be a problem for the future; for the time being an uneasy calm prevails.

Finally, there is the climate change debate, and the much shorter influences of the waxing and waning of El Niño. There are corresponding longer term and shorter term challenges for the industry. There can be little doubt the industry of 2028 will be very different to that of today. But how? The flip side of challenge is opportunity, and every part of the winegrowing world will face challenges of similar or greater dimension.

Quite apart from the proposition that the southern hemisphere will face lesser increases in temperature than the northern (because of the greater water to land mass ratio in the southern hemisphere, and the reverse for the northern hemisphere), the so-called New World producers of the south have little or none of the regulations (and subsidies) which will make climate-driven change tortuous and slow in most of Europe, faster and more relevant in the New World. Australia has already demonstrated an ability to quickly respond to changes in market demand for differing wine styles and varieties. There is every reason to suppose it will be equally quick to respond to climate change challenges, the yardstick an unemotional cost/benefit analysis.

The one wild card is the extent to which water resources will be available, and at what cost. It is on this issue alone that Chile and Argentina will prove to be more potent competitors than they have so far. The severity of the drought has led to the Prime Minister's announcement that unless there is heavy and continuous rain along the catchment of the Murray Darling River system, there will be no water available for crop irrigation in 2008, which will massively reduce the theoretical tonnage for the 2008 vintage. But it doesn't stop there: even full restoration of the Murray Darling system (which will take years of 'normal' rainfall) will not provide grapegrowers with the amount of water allocations upon which their sector of the industry has been built.

More water will be used to fill the inadequate dams, which supply all the east coast cities (including Adelaide); more will be retained for environmental flows; and stock watering will be third in line. By the time a longer term balance has been struck, and the amount available for crop irrigation has been determined, it seems highly likely that some grapegrowers will have had no option but to abandon their vines.

How many 'some' means is anyone's guess. Much will depend on what price sharply reduced yields will achieve per tonne, and this in turn on the uncertain quality of the grapes grown under these new conditions. You have to remember that before the irrigation schemes were put in place at the start of the last (20th) century, the land where vines and fruit trees now (or until recently) flourished was – quite literally – desert.

Having said so much about 2007 (and its future implications) I will depart from my usual region-by-region synopsis. There will be some good wines made from an unprecedently early vintage; WA made up for its dismal 2006 red vintage, and those parts of the cooler regions that were not decimated by frost will also make some high-quality wines. Warmer regions, which had access to water and were not affected by bushfires, will produce small crops, but the quality will compensate. It's early days, and the bad news has been given. Only good can follow.

How to use the *Companion*

The *Australian Wine Companion* is arranged with wineries in alphabetical order; the index at the back lists wineries by region, which adds a search facility. The entries should be self-explanatory, but here I will briefly take you through the information provided for each entry using Balnaves of Coonawarra as an example.

Wineries

Balnaves of Coonawarra ★★★★★

Main Road, Coonawarra, SA 5263 **Region** Coonawarra
T (08) 8737 2946 www.balnaves.com.au **Open** Mon–Fri 9–5, w'ends 12–5
Winemaker Pete Bissell **Est.** 1975 **Cases** 10 000
Grapegrower, viticultural consultant and vigneron Doug Balnaves has 52 ha of high-quality estate vineyards. The wines are invariably excellent, often outstanding, notable for their supple mouthfeel, varietal integrity, balance and length; the tannins are always fine and ripe, the oak subtle and perfectly integrated. Coonawarra at its best. Exports to all major markets.

Winery name   Balnaves of Coonawarra

Although it might seem that stating the winery name is straightforward, this is not necessarily so. To avoid confusion, wherever possible I use the name that appears most prominently on the wine label, and do not refer to any associated trading name.

Winery ratings   ★★★★★

The effort to come up with a fair winery rating continues. This year I have looked at the ratings for the last 3 years, including that for this year (the last based on this year's tasting notes). If a winery has been rated at 5 stars in all 3 years, its 5 stars are printed in red; if it has achieved a 5-star rating this year, but not in one or more previous years, it keeps the 5 stars printed in black. In the longer term, the rating will depend on a 5-year track record, although special allowances will be made for new wineries.

The other comment is that, as in prior years (and in the future), the larger wineries tend to have a wide range of products, in a perfect world priced in line with their quality. Thus for both small wineries (which may only make a handful of different wines) and large, the rating is heavily biased by the performance of the best wines of that producer. To do otherwise would be to deny a 5-star rating to any of the 20 or more largest wineries, the most obvious single winery being Penfolds.

The precise meanings attached to the winery star rating is as follows; the percentages at the end of each rating is that of the total number of wineries in the database at the time of going to print.

★★★★★   Outstanding winery regularly producing wines of exemplary quality and typicity. 6.5%

★★★★★   Outstanding winery capable of producing wines of very high quality, and did so this year. 14.9%

★★★★☆   Excellent winery able to produce wines of high to very high quality, knocking on the door of a 5-star rating. 25.1%

★★★★   Very good producer of wines with class and character. 18.4%

★★★☆   A solid, usually reliable, maker of good, sometimes very good wines. 17.8%

★★★   A typically good winery, but often has a few lesser wines. 11.2%

★★☆   Has the potential to, and normally aspires to, improve. 1.8%

NR   A winery, often new, the wines of which I have not tasted in the past 12 months. Will only appear once under this rating. 4.3%

Contact details Main Road, Coonawarra, SA 5263 **T** (08) 8737 2946

The details are usually those of the winery and cellar door, but in a few instances may simply be of the winery; this occurs when the wine is made under contract, and is sold only through retail.

Region Coonawarra

The mapping of Australia into zones, regions and subregions with legally defined boundaries is now largely complete for regions. The registration of subregions is stalled, but there is no fixed date by which all applications for registration of regions or subregions must be completed. A full list of zones, regions and subregions appears on pages 38 to 41. Occasionally you will see 'Warehouse' as the region. This means the wine is made from purchased grapes, in someone else's winery. In other words, it does not have a vineyard or winery in the ordinary way.

www.balnaves.com.au

An increasingly important reference point, containing material not found (for space reasons) in this book.

Open Mon–Fri 9–5, w'ends 12–5

Although a winery might be listed as not open or only open on weekends, some may in fact be prepared to open by appointment. Many will, some won't; a telephone call will establish whether it is possible or not. Virtually every winery that is shown as being open only for weekends is in fact open on public holidays as well. Once again, a telephone call will confirm this.

Winemaker Pete Bissell

In the large companies the winemaker is simply the head of a team; there may be many executive winemakers actually responsible for specific wines.

Est. 1975

A more or less self-explanatory item, but keep in mind that some makers consider the year in which they purchased the land to be the year of establishment, others the year in which they first planted grapes, others the year they first made wine, others the year they first offered wine for sale, and so on. There may also be minor complications where there has been a change of ownership or break in production.

Cases 10 000

This figure (representing the number of cases produced each year) is merely an indication of the size of the operation. Some winery entries do not feature a production figure: this is either because the winery (principally, but not exclusively, the large companies) regards this information as confidential or because the information was not available at the time of going to press.

Summary Grapegrower, viticultural consultant and vigneron Doug Balnaves has 52 ha of high-quality estate vineyards. The wines are invariably excellent, often outstanding, notable for their supple mouthfeel, varietal integrity, balance and length; the tannins are always fine and ripe, the oak subtle and perfectly integrated. Coonawarra at its best. Exports to all major markets.

My summary of the winery. Little needs be said, except that I have tried to vary the subjects I discuss in this part of the winery entry.

New wineries

 The vine leaf symbol indicates the 218 wineries that are new entries in this year's *Companion*.

Tasting notes

Ratings

94–100   ♟♟♟♟♟   **Outstanding.** Wines of the highest quality, usually with a distinguished pedigree.

90–93   ♟♟♟♟♟   **Highly recommended.** Wines of great quality, style and character, worthy of a place in any cellar.

87–89   ♟♟♟♟   **Recommended.** Wines of above-average quality, fault-free, and with clear varietal expression. Due to the necessity of compressing the amount of material in this year's *Companion*, but also to preserve a like-on-like comparison with prior years, the 2.5- to 3.5-glass-rated wines have been dropped (over 1900 in all).

On the other hand, this has enabled the number of tasting notes for wines rated 87 and above to increase from 5200 to 5837.

ŸŸŸŸŸ   **The Tally Reserve Cabernet Sauvignon 2005** Deep purple-red; an incredibly powerful and expressive bouquet, the luscious but tightly framed blackcurrant, cassis and French oak precisely fulfilling the promises of the bouquet. ProCork. 14.5° alc. **Rating** 96 **To** 2025 $80

The tasting note opens with the vintage of the wine tasted. This tasting note will have been made within the 12 months prior to publication. Even that is a long time, and during the life of this book the wine will almost certainly change. More than this, remember the tasting is a highly subjective and imperfect art. NV = non vintage. The price of the wine is listed where information is available.

To 2025

Rather than give a span of drinking years, I have simply provided a (conservative) 'best by' date. Modern winemaking is such that, even if a wine has 10 or 20 years' future during which it will gain much greater complexity, it can be enjoyed at any time over the intervening months and years.

ProCork

This is the closure used for this particular wine. The closures in use for the wines tasted are (in descending order): screwcap 65% (last year 51.5%), one-piece natural cork 22%, Diam 6% (last year not recorded). The remaining 7% (in approximate order of importance) are Twin Top, ProCork, Synthetic, Zork and VinoLock. I believe the percentage of screwcap will continue to rise, as will that of Diam, the latter worthy of explanation: made by Oeneo, the second-largest supplier of closures in the world, it involves grinding cork pieces to the consistency of flour, then treating this to super-critical CO_2 (liquefied at very high pressure and a very low temperature) which, when returned to its normal gaseous form takes with it any contaminant in the cork powder, most importantly including trichloranisole (TCA), the most common form of cork taint (a bitter/earthy/mouldy character that the trained human nose can detect in tiny concentrations of parts per trillion). By sheer chance, Balnaves has chosen screwcaps, ProCork and Cork for its various wines, a typically cautious approach partly driven by the varying demands of export markets.

14.5° alc.

As with closures, I have endeavoured to always include this piece of information, which is in one sense self-explanatory. What is less obvious is the increasing concern of many of Australian winemakers about the rise in levels of alcohol, and much research and practical experiment (picking earlier, higher fermentation temperatures in open fermenters, etc.) is occurring. Reverse osmosis and yeast selection are two of the research fields of particular promise.

Winery of the year

Balnaves of Coonawarra

I'm not too sure that creating this accolade was a good idea; after all, there are over 2400 wineries in Australia, and 370 received a 5-star rating. But which is the best? How many criteria should be used? How do you split dead heats even if you use some complex algebraic formula designed to weigh up all the relevant inputs? My agonising over the choice did lead to one new feature: recognising that some 5-star wineries have a far longer track record of excellence than others. So, for the first time, what I might term 'the classic 5-star wineries' have their stars printed in red.

That achieved, I have chosen Balnaves of Coonawarra as winery of the year. It achieved a perfect score of 6 outstanding table wines (out of a field of 6); only a Sparkling Cabernet (not technically a table wine, which is a 'still' table wine) rated a mere '4.5 glasses – highly recommended'.

The starting point is the 52 ha of vineyards dating back to 1975, when Doug Balnaves realised there might be a dollar or two to be made from selling grapes. After a while, he decided he should have some wine made, and that sold readily enough. But it was the recruitment of Pete Bissell from Wynns Coonawarra Estate in mid-1995 that was the turning point. He persuaded Doug to reduce the yield in the blocks designated for the Balnaves wines, and neither has looked back since.

Great wine does not descend inexplicably and arbitrarily from the sky, like a liquid deus ex machina. Its birthplace is in the terroir of the vineyard, but it has to be treated with ultimate care and respect in the winery. It is a protracted process from fermentation to barrel and to bottle, with literally dozens of key decisions along the way: lengthy books are written about the fundamentals of winemaking, without any consideration of the birthplace of the grapes.

The skills of Pete Bissell were recognised in 2005 when he was acknowledged as *Gourmet Traveller Wine Magazine* Winemaker of the Year, but those skills had long been in place. They say that owners look like their dogs; the quietly spoken, softly smiled, but utterly dedicated Bissell could not help but make wines in the style he does. They are always beautifully balanced and harmonious, the complexity and power there, but encased in the figurative velvet glove. Young or old they beg you to have a second glass, and you don't want to share a bottle with too many others.

While his mastery of red wines across the varietal range is that which gains attention, he is also the foremost maker of chardonnay in Coonawarra, winning successive trophies at the Limestone Coast Wine Show for this wine.

It so happens that 2005 has turned out to be a very good vintage in Coonawarra (and elsewhere) so you should not hesitate to buy these immaculately crafted wines.

Best of the best of Australian wine 2008

I make my usual disclaimer: while there are two periods of intense tasting activity in the 12 months during which the tasting notes for this edition were made, and while some wines are tasted more than once, an over-arching comparative tasting of all the best wines is simply not possible, however desirable it might be.

So the points for the individual wines scoring 94 or above stand uncorrected by the wisdom of hindsight. Nonetheless, the link between variety and region (or, if you prefer, between variety and terroir) is in most instances strikingly evident. It is for this reason that I have shown the region for each of the best wines. While the short-term focus of the export industry is the paramount necessity of reducing stock either in bulk or under the generic bottling of BOB (buyer own brand), medium and longer term prosperity will depend on a sense of place, of regional identity.

Brand Australia has been the foundation upon which the success of the past 20 years has been built, but all recognise it is time to move on. While some naysayers may regard this as marketing rhetoric, the truth is that Australia is blessed with an unmatched range of terroir (including climate in that deceptively simple term) enabling it to make wines ranging from the uniquely complex fortified wines of Rutherglen (fashioned from frontignac and muscadelle, known locally as muscat and tokay), to the 100-year-old Para Liqueur of Seppelt in the Barossa Valley, all the way through to the exceptional sparkling wines of Tasmania, grown in a climate every bit as cool as that of Champagne.

This is one of the principal reasons for the index to be arranged by region, even though the text is alpha-ordered. I should also point out that the cut-off for listing the wines of each variety differs considerably, depending on the strength of the class concerned.

Ten of the best new wineries

I have endeavoured to focus on wineries from different regions making wines of very different styles; this apart, the heading reads 'ten of the best…' not 'the best ten'.

DEISEN Barossa Valley / PAGE 205

Sabine Diesen and Les Fensom are unashamedly artisan winemakers, doing everything possible by hand: making as little as 20 dozen bottles of some of the wines, all open-fermented in small fermenters with hand-plunging and basket pressing through to the painting design for the labels. They then express the terroir of the Barossa at its most opulent, with sweet and luscious fruit, soft, ripe tannins, and a warmth from the alcohol that can reach terrifying levels at times.

FLYNNS WINES Heathcote / PAGE 246

Greg (no relation to the legendary John) Flynn and wife Natala are relative newcomers to Heathcote, planting vines on the vivid red Cambrian soil, and letting that soil work its magic on shiraz (principally), plus sangiovese, cabernet sauvignon, merlot and viognier. For good measure, the wines are modestly priced.

GREENSTONE VINEYARD Heathcote / PAGE 279

Greenstone brings together the multiple talents of David Gleave MW (based in London); Alberto Antonini, in Italy, with degrees from the University of Florence, University of California (Davis) and Bordeaux; and Mark Walpole, manager of Brown Brothers' 700 ha of vineyards. The partners have selected Sandro Mosele as contract winemaker, and planted 17 ha of shiraz, and 1 ha each of mourvedre, sangiovese and tempranillo on a prime vineyard site in Heathcote, the first vintage from 3-year-old vines making one wonder just how exceptional the site is.

PHI Yarra Valley / PAGE 508

The name comes from the 21st letter of the ancient Greek alphabet, symbolising perfect balance and harmony. It is the venture of the Webber and Shelmerdine families, the latter owning the Lusatia Park Vineyard from which the grapes are sourced, the former making the wine (at the De Bortoli Yarra Valley winery). (Stephen's wife Leanne is Darren De Bortoli's sister.) It is an ultimate exercise in site terroir, with specific rows of chardonnay, pinot noir and sauvignon blanc chosen out of the much larger plantings of those varieties, and managed with quality being the sole objective.

POONAWATTA ESTATE Eden Valley / PAGE 523

This is at the same time a testament to the tenacity of 1.8 ha of shiraz planted in 1880, which went through a prolonged period of benign neglect, and the painstaking rehabilitation of that planting by two generations of the Holt family, plus the establishment, row by row, of another 1.8 ha using cuttings taken from the old vines. Almost incidental is a Riesling produced from a single vineyard of 2 ha, hand-planted by the Holt family in the 1970s. The quality of all the wines is exceptional.

POVERTY HILL WINES Eden Valley / PAGE 525

This is the venture of 4 partners, each with decades of experience in the wine industry, and with particular knowledge of the Eden Valley from whence all the wines come. The focus is on the classics of Riesling, Shiraz and Cabernet Sauvignon, with Merlot adding another dimension.

ROOKERY WINES Kangaroo Island / PAGE 555

Garry and Gael Lovering have planted 8.4 ha of vines on their Kangaroo Island vineyard, principally to cabernet sauvignon and shiraz, but with an interesting patch of sangiovese (and other even more exotic varieties). This joins The Islander Estate Vineyards (of Jacques Lurton of Bordeaux) in proving that Kangaroo Island is capable of making wines of the highest quality.

SC PANNELL McLaren Vale / PAGE 573

The twinkle in the dancing eyes of Stephen (Steve) Pannell always meant that, sooner or later, he would forsake the corporate winemaking world, and do his own thing (with wife Fiona). This former Hardys winemaker has immediately come up with quite beautiful Grenache (his secret love) and Shiraz from McLaren Vale, adding a classy Sauvignon Blanc from the Adelaide Hills and a Grenache Rose to make a perfect portfolio.

WILLUNGA 100 WINES McLaren Vale / PAGE 707

This is a joint venture between Blackbilly Wines and Liberty Wines UK, the latter a major importer of quality wines from Australia. By a slightly convoluted route, it gives the joint venture access to the cream of 400 ha of McLaren Vale vineyards, with winemakers Nick Haselgrove and Warren Randall having a direct or indirect interest in the venture, which has opened the batting with 3 outstanding McLaren Vale wines from 2005.

WITCHCLIFFE ESTATE Margaret River / PAGE 715

While Witchcliffe Estate came into its present being in 2003, its 8-ha vineyard was planted in the early 1990s, and when Tony and Maureen Cosby acquired the property in 2000, it was best known as the Margaret River Marron Farm. If you are lucky, you may be able to buy fresh marron, but there is no shortage of high-quality, low-priced wines (only one exceeds $20) made with great skill by contract winemaker Peter Stanlake.

Ten dark horses

This is a highly subjective list of wineries that have excelled over the past 12 months. Some are large, some small; some are old, some quite new. In every case, this year's rating is higher than last year's, with all achieving 5 stars. At the risk or repeating myself, this is not a list of the best wineries; that is to be found at pages 18 to 23.

AUDREY WILKINSON Lower Hunter Valley / PAGE 71

Although the vineyards are barely 10 years old, this is one of the most historic properties in the Hunter Valley, with a beautiful location and cellar door. In 2004 it was acquired by Brian Agnew and family, and the wines have since improved out of all recognition.

BERRYS BRIDGE Pyrenees / PAGE 99

It has been a long road for Roger Milner and Jane Holt stretching over two states and two decades, but the quality of the full-bodied red wines has made it all worthwhile, with three glorious wines from 2004.

BRESS Bendigo / PAGE 123

Adam Marks casts the largest imagineable net around Australia from home base at Bendigo, reaching as far afield as the Margaret River and Yarra Valley, and varieties such as muller thurgau. This year's releases hit the mark.

CARBUNUP CREST VINEYARD Margaret River / PAGE 147

After a dip in quality over 2006 and 2007 (after an earlier spectacular start) Carbunup Crest has returned to its best form, with classic Margaret River wines at thoroughly affordable prices.

CASCABEL McLaren Vale / PAGE 150

Duncan Ferguson and Susana Fernandez just missed out on a 5-star rating in 2006 and 2007, but there was no denying it this year, with a brilliant Eden Valley Riesling and Fleurieu Shiraz leading the way.

DELATITE Upper Goulburn / PAGE 207

Long recognised for the perfume and delicacy of its white wines, but not always hitting the bullseye. There have been a number of changes at home base, and these are reflected in the extreme quality of the current wines.

FONTY'S POOL VINEYARDS Pemberton / PAGE 246

The origins of the property date back 100 years; the name from a huge dam built in the 1920s. These days 110 ha of vineyards allow Fonty's Pool to cherry-pick the best, and it has never been far off the mark. This year it brought home the bacon.

MOUNTADAM Eden Valley / **PAGE 448**

After a relatively brief period of ownership by Moet Hennessy Wine Estates, Mountadam has been purchased by Adelaide businessman-cum-vigneron David Brown, and former Petaluma chief winemaker Con Moshos has been installed. Quite how he has achieved so much in such a short time I don't know, but the results are, to say the least, impressive.

POLLETERS Pyrenees / **PAGE 520**

Polleters has moved from 4 to 4.5 and now to 5 stars. Its full-bodied, supple and succulent red wines, contract-made by Mark Summerfield, are worth every penny of the relatively modest purchase price.

SERAFINO WINES McLaren Vale / **PAGE 582**

Born out of the convulsions in McLaren Vale following the initial financial problems of Andrew Garrett, and then the acquisition of Maglieri Wines by Beringer Blass, Serafino Wines has emerged under the ownership of Steve Maglieri, and with the wizardry of Scott Rawlinson as winemaker. A strong gambit for winery of the year.

Footnote: I was sorely tempted to include Boireann from the Granite Belt, but it has held 5-star status for the last 2 years. In turn, its inclusion would have been in recognition not only of its continuing achievements, but the very marked lift in quality of Queensland's wines, mainly (though not exclusively) in the Granite Belt.

Best wineries of the regions

The nomination of the best wines of the regions has evolved in two ways: the 5 red stars for wineries with a particularly distinguished track record over the past 3 years, and 5 black stars for those which have been consistently at or near the top for this period. While I have deliberately refused to bind myself to this yardstick, the red-starred wineries have in almost all instances achieved 5-star ratings for each of the past 3 years, and most of those with black stars have had maximum ratings in 2 of the past 3 years, including (importantly) this year.

ADELAIDE HILLS
Ashton Hills ★★★★★
Barratt ★★★★★
Bird in Hand ★★★★★
Chain of Ponds ★★★★★
Coobara Wines ★★★★★
Geoff Weaver ★★★★★
Leabrook Estate ★★★★★
Malcolm Creek Vineyard ★★★★★
Mount Torrens Vineyards ★★★★★
Murdoch Hill ★★★★★
Nova Vita Wines ★★★★★
Paracombe Wines ★★★★★
Petaluma ★★★★★
Pfitzner ★★★★★
Setanta Wines ★★★★★
Shaw & Smith ★★★★★
Tilbrook ★★★★★

ADELAIDE PLAINS
Primo Estate ★★★★★

ADELAIDE ZONE
Patritti Wines ★★★★★
Penfolds Magill Estate ★★★★★

ALBANY
Montgomery's Hill ★★★★★
Wignalls Wines ★★★★★

ALPINE VALLEYS
Gapsted ★★★★★

BALLARAT
Nintingbool ★★★★★
Sinclair of Scotsburn ★★★★★
Tomboy Hill ★★★★★

BAROSSA VALLEY
Charles Melton ★★★★★
Cooper Burns ★★★★★
Deisen ★★★★★
Domain Barossa ★★★★★
Dutschke Wines ★★★★★
Grant Burge ★★★★★
Haan Wines ★★★★★
Harbord Wines ★★★★★
Hentley Farm Wines ★★★★★
John Duval Wines ★★★★★
Kaesler Wines ★★★★★
Kalleske ★★★★★
Langmeil Winery ★★★★★
Lanz Thomson Vineyard ★★★★★
Laughing Jack ★★★★★
Leo Buring ★★★★★
Marschall Groom Cellars ★★★★★
Massena Vineyards ★★★★★
McLean's Farm Wines ★★★★★
Murray Street Vineyard ★★★★★
Orlando ★★★★★

Penfolds ★★★★★
Peter Lehmann ★★★★★
Richmond Grove ★★★★★
Rockford ★★★★★
Rosenvale Wines ★★★★★
Saltram ★★★★★
Schild Estate Wines ★★★★★
Seppelt ★★★★★
Sheep's Back ★★★★★
Soul Growers ★★★★★
Spinifex ★★★★★
St John's Road ★★★★★
Teusner ★★★★★
The Willows Vineyard ★★★★★
Thorn-Clarke Wines ★★★★★
Tim Smith Wines ★★★★★
Torbreck Vintners ★★★★★
Trevor Jones/Kellermeister ★★★★★
Turkey Flat ★★★★★
Wolf Blass ★★★★★
Yalumba ★★★★★

BAROSSA VALLEY/HEATHCOTE
Mt Toolleen ★★★★★

BEECHWORTH
battely wines ★★★★★
Smiths Vineyard ★★★★★
Tinkers Hill Vineyard ★★★★★

BENDIGO
Balgownie Estate ★★★★★
Bress ★★★★★
Mount Moliagul ★★★★★
Pondalowie Vineyards ★★★★★
Sandhurst Ridge ★★★★★
Turner's Crossing Vineyard ★★★★★

CANBERRA DISTRICT
Clonakilla ★★★★★
Lark Hill ★★★★★
Shaw Vineyard Estate ★★★★★

CENTRAL RANGES ZONE
Monument Vineyard ★★★★★

CLARE VALLEY
Annie's Lane ★★★★★
Grosset ★★★★★
Inghams Skilly Ridge Wines ★★★★★
Jim Barry Wines ★★★★★
Kilikanoon ★★★★★
Kirrihill Wines ★★★★★
Leasingham ★★★★★
Mintaro Wines ★★★★★
Mitchell ★★★★★
Mount Horrocks ★★★★★
Neagles Rock Vineyards ★★★★★
O'Leary Walker Wines ★★★★★
Paulett ★★★★★
Penna Lane Wines ★★★★★
Pikes ★★★★★
Robertson of Clare Wines ★★★★★
Stephen John Wines ★★★★★
Taylors ★★★★★
Wendouree ★★★★★
Wilson Vineyard ★★★★★

CLARE VALLEY/ HEATHCOTE
Twofold ★★★★★

COONAWARRA
Balnaves of Coonawarra ★★★★★
Brand's of Coonawarra ★★★★★
Jamiesons Run ★★★★★
Katnook Estate ★★★★★
Majella ★★★★★
Murdock ★★★★★
Punters Corner ★★★★★
Wynns Coonawarra Estate ★★★★★

DENMARK
Harewood Estate ★★★★★
Moombaki Wines ★★★★★
West Cape Howe Wines ★★★★★

EDEN VALLEY
Eden Hall ★★★★★
Henschke ★★★★★
Hill Smith Estate ★★★★★
Mountadam ★★★★★
Pewsey Vale ★★★★★

Poonawatta Estate ★★★★★
Poverty Hill Wines ★★★★★
Radford Dale ★★★★★
Torzi Matthews Vintners ★★★★★

FRANKLAND RIVER
Alkoomi ★★★★★
Ferngrove Vineyards ★★★★★
Frankland Estate ★★★★★
Old Kent River ★★★★★

GEELONG
Bannockburn Vineyards ★★★★★
by Farr ★★★★★
Clyde Park Vineyard ★★★★★
Curlewis Winery ★★★★★
Farr Rising ★★★★★
Feehans Road Vineyard ★★★★★
Lethbridge Wines ★★★★★
McGlashan's Wallington Estate ★★★★★
Pettavel ★★★★★
Scotchmans Hill ★★★★★
Shadowfax ★★★★★

GEOGRAPHE
Willow Bridge Estate ★★★★★

GIPPSLAND
Bass Phillip ★★★★★
Caledonia Australis ★★★★★
Narkoojee ★★★★★
Phillip Island Vineyard ★★★★★

GLENROWAN
Baileys of Glenrowan ★★★★★

GRAMPIANS
Best's Wines ★★★★★
Clayfield Wines ★★★★★
Grampians Estate ★★★★★
Mount Cole Wineworks ★★★★★
Mount Langi Ghiran Vineyards ★★★★★
Seppelt ★★★★★
Westgate Vineyard ★★★★★

GRANITE BELT
Boireann ★★★★★
GREAT SOUTHERN
Forest Hill Vineyard ★★★★★
Howard Park ★★★★★

GUNDAGAI
Bidgeebong Wines ★★★★★

HEATHCOTE
Domaines Tatiarra ★★★★★
Downing Estate Vineyard ★★★★★
Flynns Wines ★★★★★
Greenstone Vineyard ★★★★★
Heathcote Estate ★★★★★
Heathcote II ★★★★★
Jasper Hill ★★★★★
Knots Wines ★★★★★
La Pleiade ★★★★★
Munari Wines ★★★★★
Occam's Razor ★★★★★
Shelmerdine Vineyards ★★★★★
Stefani Estate ★★★★★

HENTY
Crawford River Wines ★★★★★
Henty Estate ★★★★★
Tarrington Vineyards ★★★★★

HILLTOPS
Chalkers Crossing ★★★★★

KANGAROO ISLAND
Rookery Wines ★★★★★
The Islander Estate Vineyards ★★★★★

HUNTER VALLEY
Audrey Wilkinson Vineyard ★★★★★
Bimbadgen Estate ★★★★★
Brokenwood ★★★★★
Capercaillie ★★★★★
Chateau Francois ★★★★★
Chateau Pâto ★★★★★
Chatto Wines ★★★★★
De Iuliis ★★★★★
Hungerford Hill ★★★★★

Keith Tulloch Wine ★★★★
Lake's Folly ★★★★★
McWilliam's Mount Pleasant ★★★★★
Meerea Park ★★★★★
Mistletoe Wines ★★★★★
Oakvale ★★★★★
Pepper Tree Wines ★★★★★
Peter Howland Wines ★★★★★
Piggs Peake ★★★★★
Scarborough ★★★★★
Tamburlaine ★★★★★
Tatler Wines ★★★★★
Thomas Wines ★★★★★
Tintilla Wines ★★★★★
Tower Estate ★★★★★
Tulloch ★★★★★
Tyrrell's ★★★★★

LANGHORNE CREEK
Bremerton Wines ★★★★★
Gotham ★★★★★
John's Blend ★★★★★
Lake Breeze Wines ★★★★★

MACEDON RANGES
Bindi Wine Growers ★★★★★
Curly Flat ★★★★★
Granite Hills ★★★★★
Hanging Rock Winery ★★★★★
Rowanston on the Track ★★★★★

MARGARET RIVER
Alexandra Bridge Wines ★★★★★
Arlewood Estate ★★★★★
Ashbrook Estate ★★★★★
Brookland Valley ★★★★★
Cape Mentelle ★★★★★
Celestial Bay ★★★★★
Cullen Wines ★★★★★
Devil's Lair ★★★★★
Flying Fish Cove ★★★★★
Forester Estate ★★★★★
Gralyn Estate ★★★★★
Happs ★★★★★
Howard Park ★★★★★
Leeuwin Estate ★★★★★

Lenton Brae Wines ★★★★★
McHenry Hohnen Vintners ★★★★★
Moss Wood ★★★★★
Preveli Wines ★★★★★
Redgate ★★★★★
Rosabrook Estate ★★★★★
Saracen Estates ★★★★★
Stella Bella Wines ★★★★★
Thompson Estate ★★★★★
Vasse Felix ★★★★★
Voyager Estate ★★★★★
Windance Wines ★★★★★
Witchcliffe Estate ★★★★★
Woodlands ★★★★★
Woodside Valley Estate ★★★★★

MCLAREN VALE
Arakoon ★★★★★
Brini Estate Wines ★★★★★
Cascabel ★★★★★
Coriole ★★★★★
d'Arenberg ★★★★★
Foggo Wines ★★★★★
Geoff Merrill Wines ★★★★★
Gilligan ★★★★★
Hardys ★★★★★
Hoffmann's ★★★★★
Ingoldby ★★★★★
Lazy Ballerina ★★★★★
Mitolo Wines ★★★★★
Mr Riggs Wine Company ★★★★★
Samuel's Gorge ★★★★★
SC Pannell ★★★★★
Serafino Wines ★★★★★
Shingleback ★★★★★
Shottesbrooke ★★★★★
Tapestry ★★★★★
Tatachilla ★★★★★
Willunga 100 Wines ★★★★★
Wirra Wirra ★★★★★

MORNINGTON PENINSULA
Eldridge Estate of Red Hill ★★★★★
Hurley Vineyard ★★★★★
Kooyong ★★★★★
Main Ridge Estate ★★★★★

Merricks Creek Wines ★★★★★
Merricks Estate ★★★★★
Montalto Vineyards ★★★★★
Moorooduc Estate ★★★★★
Paringa Estate ★★★★★
Port Phillip Estate ★★★★★
Prancing Horse Estate ★★★★★
Red Hill Estate ★★★★★
Stonier Wines ★★★★★
Ten Minutes by Tractor Wine Co ★★★★★
The Cups Estate ★★★★★
Tuck's Ridge ★★★★★
Willow Creek ★★★★★
Yabby Lake Vineyard ★★★★★

MOUNT BARKER
Gilberts ★★★★★
Plantagenet ★★★★★

MUDGEE
Huntington Estate ★★★★★

NAGAMBIE LAKES
Tahbilk ★★★★★

ORANGE
Mayfield Vineyard ★★★★★

PADTHAWAY
Stonehaven ★★★★★

PEMBERTON
Bellarmine Wines ★★★★★
Fonty's Pool Vineyards ★★★★★
Merum ★★★★★
Picardy ★★★★★
Smithbrook ★★★★★

PORONGURUP
Castle Rock Estate ★★★★★
Duke's Vineyard ★★★★★

PYRENEES
Amherst Winery ★★★★★
Berrys Bridge ★★★★★
Dalwhinnie ★★★★★

Polleters ★★★★★
Pyrenees Ridge ★★★★★
Summerfield ★★★★★

RIVERINA
De Bortoli ★★★★★
McWilliam's ★★★★★
Nugan Estate ★★★★★

RUTHERGLEN
All Saints Estate ★★★★★
Bullers Calliope ★★★★★
Campbells ★★★★★
Morris ★★★★★
Stanton & Killeen Wines ★★★★★
Warrabilla ★★★★★

SHOALHAVEN COAST
Kladis Estate ★★★★★

SOUTHERN FLEURIEU
Brocks View Estate ★★★★★
Salomon Estate ★★★★★

SOUTHERN HIGHLANDS
Centennial Vineyards ★★★★★

STRATHBOGIE RANGES
Plunkett Fowles ★★★★★

SUNBURY
Craiglee ★★★★★
Galli Estate ★★★★★
Witchmount Estate ★★★★★

SWAN VALLEY
Faber Vineyard ★★★★★
Houghton ★★★★★
Lamont's ★★★★★

TASMANIA
Bay of Fires ★★★★★
Bream Creek ★★★★★
Clover Hill ★★★★★
Domaine A ★★★★★
Freycinet ★★★★★
Home Hill ★★★★★

Hood Wines ★★★★★
Jansz Tasmania ★★★★★
Meure's Wines ★★★★★
Moorilla Estate ★★★★★
Pirie Estate ★★★★★
Providence Vineyards ★★★★★
Stefano Lubiana ★★★★★
Tamar Ridge ★★★★★

UPPER GOULBURN

Delatite ★★★★★
Rocky Passes Wines ★★★★★

WRATTONBULLY

Tapanappa ★★★★★

YARRA VALLEY

Carlei Estate & Carlei Green Vineyards
★★★★★
De Bortoli ★★★★★
Diamond Valley Vineyards ★★★★★
Domaine Chandon/Green Point ★★★★★
Dominique Portet ★★★★★
Gembrook Hill ★★★★★
Hillcrest Vineyard ★★★★★
Labyrinth ★★★★★
Lillydale Estate ★★★★★

macforbes ★★★★★
Metier Wines ★★★★★
Mount Mary ★★★★★
Oakridge ★★★★★
PHI ★★★★★
Punch ★★★★★
Rochford Wines ★★★★★
Seville Estate ★★★★★
Stuart Wines ★★★★★
Tarrawarra Estate ★★★★★
Toolangi Vineyards ★★★★★
Wantirna Estate ★★★★★
William Downie ★★★★★
Yarra Yarra ★★★★★
Yarra Yering ★★★★★
Yarrabank ★★★★★
YarraLoch ★★★★★
Yering Station ★★★★★
Yeringberg ★★★★★

**SOUTHEAST AUSTRALIA/
VARIOUS/WAREHOUSE**

Ainsworth & Snelson ★★★★★
Hewitson ★★★★★
Songlines Estates ★★★★★
Two Hands Wines ★★★★★

Best of the best by variety

Riesling

The most exciting development for this wonderful (though still neglected by too many wine consumers, notwithstanding its outstanding value for money) has been the acceleration in the emergence of low alcohol (8°-10° vol) sweet rieslings with high-balancing acidity. These wines take those of the Mosel, Germany as their model, which are themselves gaining a significantly wider market in Australia. This does not mean the traditional cool-grown, continental climate rieslings are under attack; they are not.

RATING	WINE	REGION
96	2006 Grosset Polish Hill	Clare Valley
96	2005 Mount Horrocks Watervale	Clare Valley
96	2006 Petaluma Hanlin Hill	Clare Valley
96	2006 Pikes The Merle	Clare Valley
96	2006 Tim Adams Reserve	Clare Valley
96	2006 Forest Hill Vineyard Block 1	Great Southern
96	2006 Crawford River	Henty
96	2006 Bellarmine Auslese	Pemberton
96	2006 Castle Rock Estate	Porongurup
96	2005 Bay of Fires Tigress	Tasmania
95	2006 Ashton Hills	Adelaide Hills
95	2006 Domain Day Mt Crawford	Barossa Valley
95	2006 Kilikanoon Mort's Reserve Watervale	Clare Valley
95	2004 Kirrihill Reserve	Clare Valley
95	2006 Neagles Rock Vineyards	Clare Valley
95	2005 Paulett Antonina Polish Hill River	Clare Valley
95	2001 Taylors St Andrews	Clare Valley
95	2006 Wilson Vineyard Polish Hill River	Clare Valley
95	2006 Leo Buring Leonay	Eden Valley
95	2006 Poonawatta Estate The Eden	Eden Valley
95	2001 Poverty Hill Cellar Matured	Eden Valley
95	2006 Ferngrove Vineyards Cossack	Frankland River
95	2006 Frankland Estate Poison Hill Vineyard	Frankland River
95	2006 Howard Park	Great Southern
95	2005 Chalkers Crossing	Hilltops
95	2006 Granite Hills	Macedon Ranges
95	2006 Rowanston on the Track	Macedon Ranges
95	2005 Zig Zag Road	Macedon Ranges
95	2006 Forest Hill Vineyard	Mount Barker
95	2005 Castle Rock Estate	Porongurup

95	2006 Duke's Vineyard	Porongurup
95	2006 Jacob's Creek Reserve	SA
95	2006 Centennial Vineyards Woodside Single Vineyard	Southern Highlands
95	2006 Delatite Sylvia	Upper Goulburn

Chardonnay

Here the news centres around the acceptance by wine shows, sommeliers and knowledgeable consumers of 3 styles of chardonnay. The first takes Chablis as its yardstick, with the emphasis on finely tuned, citrus-tinged fruit, a strongly minerally structure, and minimal oak impact. At the other extreme is the White Burgundy model, with wines of great complexity of flavour and texture, driven by wild yeast, unclarified juice, barrel fermentation at ambient temperatures and prolonged lees contact. The third group is 'modern Australian classic', filling the mid-point between fruit, oak, and all other winemaker inputs, resulting in elegant wines of great purity, and a strong sense of place.

RATING	WINE	REGION
96	2005 Tapanappa Tiers Vineyard	Adelaide Hills
96	2001 Bannockburn Vineyards SRH	Geelong
96	2005 Clyde Park Vineyard Reserve	Geelong
96	2005 Bindi Wine Growers Quartz	Macedon Ranges
96	2004 Leeuwin Estate Art Series	Margaret River
96	2005 Vasse Felix Heytesbury	Margaret River
96	2006 Voyager Estate	Margaret River
96	2005 Kooyong Single Vineyard Selection Farrago	Mornington Peninsula
96	2005 Montalto Vineyards	Mornington Peninsula
96	2005 Moorooduc Estate The Moorooduc Wild Yeast	Mornington Peninsula
96	2005 Principia	Mornington Peninsula
96	2005 Forest Hill Vineyard Block 8	Mount Barker
96	2005 Picardy Pannell Family	Pemberton
96	2005 Providence Vineyards Madame Miguet Reserve	Tasmania
96	2004 Tamar Ridge	Tasmania
96	2004 Hardys Eileen Hardy	Cool-climate blend
96	2005 Hillcrest Vineyard Premium	Yarra Valley
96	2005 Mount Mary	Yarra Valley
96	2005 Oakridge 864	Yarra Valley
96	2005 PHI	Yarra Valley
96	2005 Stefani Estate The View	Yarra Valley
96	2005 Tarrawarra Estate Reserve	Yarra Valley

Semillon

Notwithstanding my love of the variety, a much lower body count than last year, largely explained by the inevitability that the superb Hunter Valley vintage of 2005 could not be repeated in 2006, even though the latter was a high-quality year. What the statistics largely hide is the success of Peter Lehmann wines. It has become the largest producer of semillon in Australia, quietly dropping the alcohol from over 13° to 11°, avoiding skin contact and dropping the use of oak (or oak chips), saving money in so doing, and moving much closer to the fresh Hunter Valley style.

RATING	WINE	REGION
97	1999 Tyrrell's Reserve HVD	Hunter Valley
96	2001 Brokenwood ILR Reserve	Hunter Valley
96	2004 Chatto	Hunter Valley
96	2006 Thomas Braemore	Hunter Valley
96	2001 Tyrrell's Vat 1	Hunter Valley
95	2005 Bimbadgen Estate Signature	Hunter Valley
95	2005 Chateau Francois Pokolbin Mallee	Hunter Valley
95	2006 Chatto	Hunter Valley
95	2006 McWilliam's Mount Pleasant Lovedale Limited Release	Hunter Valley
95	2006 Meerea Park Hell Hole	Hunter Valley
95	2006 Mistletoe Reserve	Hunter Valley
95	2005 (Tulloch) JYT Julia	Hunter Valley
95	2002 Tyrrell's Reserve Stevens	Hunter Valley
95	2006 Warraroong Estate	Hunter Valley
95	2006 Vasse Felix	Margaret River

Sauvignon Blanc

The distribution of points underlines the fact that outstanding sauvignon blancs are as rare as hen's teeth, and the distribution of regions leaves no doubt sauvignon blanc demands a cool climate if it is to produce a wine with clear varietal character and a fresh finish. Fresh finish does not encompass perceptible sweetness, which destroys the whole point and thrust of the variety.

RATING	WINE	REGION
96	2006 Stella Bella	Margaret River
95	2006 Barratt Piccadilly Valley	Adelaide Hills
94	2006 Barristers Block	Adelaide Hills
94	2006 Geoff Hardy K1	Adelaide Hills
94	2006 Geoff Weaver Lenswood	Adelaide Hills
94	2006 Murdoch Hill	Adelaide Hills
94	2006 Paracombe	Adelaide Hills
94	2005 Pfitzner	Adelaide Hills
94	2006 Riposte The Foil	Adelaide Hills
94	2006 SC Pannell	Adelaide Hills
94	2006 Shadowfax	Adelaide Hills
94	2006 Shaw & Smith	Adelaide Hills
94	2006 Tilbrook	Adelaide Hills
94	2006 Wignalls	Albany
94	2006 Alkoomi	Frankland River
94	2006 Willow Bridge Estate Reserve	Geographe
94	2006 West Cape Howe	Great Southern
94	2006 Ashbrook Estate	Margaret River

94	2006 Rosily Vineyard	Margaret River
94	2006 Wolf Blass Gold Label	Mount Gambier
94	2005 Highland Heritage Estate Mount Canobolas	Orange
94	2005 Mayfield Vineyard Icely Road	Orange
94	2006 Jacob's Creek Reserve	SA
94	2006 Plunkett Fowles Blackwood Ridge	Strathbogie Ranges
94	2006 Witchmount Estate	Sunbury
94	2006 Bream Creek	Tasmania
94	2006 Unavale Vineyard Flinders Island	Tasmania
94	2006 De Bortoli Estate Grown	Yarra Valley
94	2006 Green Point	Yarra Valley
94	2006 PHI	Yarra Valley
94	2006 Shelmerdine Vineyards	Yarra Valley

Sauvignon Semillon blends

These wines are the tip of a large iceberg, which has gained great popularity; for once, I am in accord with public opinion. The 2 varieties are synergistic when grown in the southern regions of WA and other cool regions in the east, with a light touch of oak an optional extra. When you move down to the beverage sector at or under $10, regional blends across Southeast Australia can and do produce wines with fresh flavour and a crisp finish. The snake in the garden of Eden is sweetness, which grates horribly with the herbaceous/mineral overall flavour.

RATING	WINE	REGION
95	2006 Grosset Semillon Sauvignon Blanc	Clare Valley
95	2006 Harewood Estate Denmark Sauvignon Blanc Semillon	Denmark
95	2006 Houghton Crofters Sauvignon Blanc Semillon	Great Southern
95	2006 Cullen Mangan Vineyard Sauvignon Blanc Semillon	Margaret River
95	2006 Cullen Margaret River Sauvignon Blanc Semillon	Margaret River
95	2006 Stella Bella Semillon Sauvignon Blanc	Margaret River
95	2006 Merum Pemberton Semillon Sauvignon Blanc	Pemberton
94	2006 Bress Margaret River Semillon Sauvignon Blanc	Bendigo
94	2006 The Lake House Denmark Semillon Sauvignon Blanc	Denmark
94	2006 Henschke Eleanor's Cottage Sauvignon Blanc Semillon	Eden Valley
94	2006 Arlewood Estate Single Vineyard Semillon Sauvignon Blanc	Margaret River
94	2006 Briarose Estate Augusta Semillon Sauvignon Blanc	Margaret River
94	2006 Brookland Valley Verse 1 Semillon Sauvignon Blanc	Margaret River
94	2006 Lenton Brae Margaret River Semillon Sauvignon Blanc	Margaret River
94	2006 Preveli Margaret River Semillon Sauvignon Blanc	Margaret River
94	2006 Redgate Margaret River Sauvignon Blanc Semillon	Margaret River
94	2006 Saracen Estates Margaret River Sauvignon Blanc Semillon	Margaret River
94	2006 Vasse Felix Margaret River Sauvignon Blanc Semillon	Margaret River
94	2006 Voyager Estate Margaret River Sauvignon Blanc Semillon	Margaret River
94	2005 Windance Margaret River Semillon Sauvignon Blanc	Margaret River

94	2006 Serafino McLaren Vale Semillon Sauvignon Blanc	McLaren Vale
94	2006 Fonty's Pool Vineyards Sauvignon Blanc Semillon	Pemberton
94	2006 Wyndham Estate Bin 777 Semillon Sauvignon Blanc	Southeast Australia
94	2004 Yarra Yarra Sauvignon Blanc Semillon	Yarra Valley

Other white wines

A small list, with varieties including aligote, arneis, aucerot, biancone, chasselas, clairette, cortese, fiano, flora, garganega, gouais, kerner, muller thurgau, ondenc, petit manseng, petit meslier, picolit, schonburger, siegerrebe, silvaner, taminga, verduzzo and vermentino also commercially grown and made into varietal white wines: those which follow are by far the most important varieties in this 'other' category.

RATING	WINE	REGION
95	2005 Petaluma Viognier	Adelaide Hills
94	2005 Turkey Flat The Last Straw Marsanne	Barossa Valley
94	2006 Pewsey Vale	
94	Individual Vineyard Selection Gewurztraminer	Eden Valley
94	2005 Yalumba Viognier	Eden Valley
94	2005 by Farr Viognier	Geelong
94	2006 Rochford Pinot Gris	Macedon Ranges
94	2006 (Primo Estate) Joseph Pinot Grigio d'Elena	McLaren Vale
94	2005 Miceli Iolanda Pinot Grigio	Mornington Peninsula
94	2005 Delatite Dead Man's Hill Gewurztraminer	Upper Goulburn
94	2006 Jamsheed Gewurztraminer	Yarra Valley

Sparkling

The best sparkling wines are now solely sourced either from Tasmania or from the coolest sites in the coolest regions in the southern parts of the mainland, with altitude playing a major role. Thus, for example, it is the Upper Yarra Valley (while not an officially recognised subregion) which supplies the Yarra Valley winemakers of these wines.

RATING	WINE	REGION
96	2001 Bay of Fires Arras	Tasmania
96	1998 Yarrabank Late Disgorged	Yarra Valley/ Southern Victoria
95	1996 Petaluma Croser Picadilly Valley Pinot Noir Chardonnay	Adelaide Hills
95	1995 Stefano Lubiana Prestige Pinot Noir Chardonnay	Tasmania
95	2003 Domaine Chandon Vintage Brut	Yarra Valley
95	2003 Domaine Chandon Blanc de Blancs	Yarra Valley
94	NV Gapsted Ballerina Canopy Chardonnay Pinot	Alpine Valleys
94	NV Bindi Wine Growers Chardonnay Pinot Noir	Macedon Ranges
94	1998 Mount William Blanc de Blanc RD	Macedon Ranges
94	2000 Stonier Cuvee	Mornington Peninsula
94	2003 Clover Hill	Tasmania

94	2003 Domaine Chandon Tasmanian Cuvee	Tasmania
94	2002 Dominique Portet Tasmanian Cuvee	Tasmania
94	2002 Jansz Pipers River Vintage Cuvee	Tasmania
94	1999 Stefano Lubiana Vintage Brut	Tasmania
94	2003 Domaine Chandon Z*D Blanc de Blancs	Yarra Valley
94	2004 Yarra Burn Chardonnay Pinot Noir Pinot Meunier	Yarra Valley

A tiny, eclectic group of wines, eagerly sought by the small percentage of wine drinkers who understand the peculiarities of the style and who, better still, are prepared to cellar them for a year or more.

RATING	WINE	REGION
96	1996 Seppelt Show Sparkling Shiraz	Grampians
95	1999 Peter Lehmann The Black Queen Sparkling Shiraz	Barossa Valley
95	1994 Seppelt Show Sparkling Shiraz	Grampians
94	NV Rochford Black Shiraz	Barossa Valley

Sweet

This is an obviously small but particularly interesting group: Noble One requires no introduction, but the others are in a different camp, the di Lusso and Dominique Portet wines taking you well outside the square.

RATING	WINE	REGION
94	2006 Pettavel Evening Star Late Harvest Riesling	Geelong
94	2006 Scarborough Late Harvest Semillon	Hunter Valley
94	2003 di Lusso Appassimento	Mudgee
94	2005 De Bortoli Noble One	Riverina
94	2005 Tamar Ridge Limited Release Botrytis Riesling	Tasmania
94	2005 Delatite Late Picked Riesling	Upper Goulburn
94	2005 Dominique Portet Vendange Tardives Sauvignon Blanc	Yarra Valley

Rose

The number of roses on the market continues to grow, seemingly unabated and unstoppable. There are no rules: they can be bone-dry, slightly sweet, or very sweet. They can be and are made from almost any red variety, red blends or red and white blends. They may be a convenient way of concentrating the red wine left after the rose is run off (bleeding or saignee) from the fermenter shortly after the grapes are crushed, or made from the ground up using grapes and techniques specifically chosen for the purpose. The vast majority fall in the former camp; those listed mainly come from the latter.

RATING	WINE	REGION
95	2006 Charles Melton Rose Of Virginia	Barossa Valley
94	2006 Arrivo Nebbiolo Rose	Adelaide Hills
94	2006 Peter Lehmann Rose	Barossa Valley

94	2006 Brookland Valley Verse 1 Rose	Margaret River
94	2006 Angove's Nine Vines Grenache Shiraz Rose	Riverland
94	2006 Puddleduck Vineyard Rose	Tasmania
94	2006 De Bortoli Pinot Noir Rose	Yarra Valley
94	2006 Yering Station ED Rose	Yarra Valley

Pinot Noir

Pinot noir has emphatically come of age in Australia; equally emphatically it only gives its best in a handful of regions. The very high quality of the 2005 vintage is plain to see.

RATING	WINE	REGION
97	2002 Bannockburn Vineyards Serre Pinot Noir	Geelong
97	2005 Tuck's Ridge Hurley Vineyard Pinot Noir	Mornington Peninsula
97	2005 Punch Close Planted Pinot Noir	Yarra Valley
96	2005 Ashton Hills Reserve Pinot Noir	Adelaide Hills
96	2005 Grosset Pinot Noir	Adelaide Hills
96	2004 Bannockburn Vineyards Pinot Noir	Geelong
96	2004 Curlewis Reserve Pinot Noir	Geelong
96	2005 Bindi Wine Growers Original Vineyard Pinot Noir	Macedon Ranges
96	2005 Kooyong Single Vineyard Selection Haven Pinot Noir	Mornington Peninsula
96	2005 Paringa Estate Reserve Special Barrel Selection Pinot Noir	Mornington Peninsula
96	2005 Brook Eden Vineyard Pinot Noir	Tasmania
96	2005 Home Hill Pinot Noir	Tasmania
95	2005 Nintingbool Pinot Noir	Ballarat
95	2005 by Farr Sangreal	Geelong
95	2005 Farr Rising Pinot Noir	Geelong
95	2005 Bindi Wine Growers Block 5 Pinot Noir	Macedon Ranges
95	2005 Eldridge Estate of Red Hill Single Clone Pinot Noir	Mornington Peninsula
95	2005 Kooyong Single Vineyard Selection Ferrous Pinot Noir	Mornington Peninsula
95	2005 Merricks Creek Pinot Noir	Mornington Peninsula
95	2005 Montalto Vineyards Pinot Noir	Mornington Peninsula
95	2005 Paringa Estate Pinot Noir	Mornington Peninsula
95	2005 The Cups Estate Raimondo Reserve Pinot Noir	Mornington Peninsula
95	2005 Tuck's Ridge Pinot Noir	Mornington Peninsula
95	2005 Yabby Lake Vineyard Pinot Noir	Mornington Peninsula
95	2005 Barringwood Park Mill Block Pinot Noir	Tasmania
95	2005 Tamar Ridge Reserve Pinot Noir	Tasmania
95	2005 Diamond Valley Vineyards Reserve Pinot Noir	Yarra Valley
95	2005 Hillcrest Vineyard Premium Pinot Noir	Yarra Valley
95	2005 macforbes Woori Yallock Pinot Noir	Yarra Valley
95	2005 PHI Pinot Noir	Yarra Valley
95	2004 Tower Estate Pinot Noir	Yarra Valley

Shiraz

Shiraz is grown across the length and breadth of Australia's wine regions (including Tasmania) and any analysis of those regions has little relevance unless one is looking at style and/or domestic and market preferences. Even if one is looking for vines more than 100 years old, they will be found in the Hunter Valley, Goulburn Valley/Nagambie Lakes, Coonawarra, McLaren Vale, Clare Valley, Eden Valley, Langhorne Creek, and, of course, the major repository of the Barossa Valley. It is the most quintessential Australian variety, making its 2 icons, Penfolds Grange and Henschke Hill of Grace.

RATING	WINE	REGION
97	2002 Henschke Hill Of Grace	Eden Valley
97	2002 Penfolds Grange	Barossa Valley
97	2004 Bremerton Old Adam Shiraz	Langhorne Creek
96	2005 Setanta Cuchulain Shiraz	Adelaide Hills
96	2005 Hentley Farm Clos Otto Shiraz	Barossa Valley
96	2004 Kalleske Johann Georg Old Vine Shiraz	Barossa Valley
96	2004 Langmeil Barossa Old Vine Company Shiraz	Barossa Valley
96	2002 Peter Lehmann Stonewell Shiraz	Barossa Valley
96	2004 Rockford Basket Press Shiraz	Barossa Valley
96	2004 The Willows Vineyard Bonesetter Shiraz	Barossa Valley
96	2004 Torbreck Vintners The Factor	Barossa Valley
96	2003 Trevor Jones Wild Witch Reserve Shiraz	Barossa Valley
96	2004 Turner's Crossing Vineyard The Cut Shiraz	Bendigo
96	2004 Jim Barry The Armagh Shiraz	Clare Valley
96	2005 Penna Lane The Willsmore Shiraz	Clare Valley
96	2004 Wendouree Shiraz	Clare Valley
96	2002 Wynns Michael Limited Release Shiraz	Coonawarra
96	2005 Bellbrae Estate Longboard Shiraz	Geelong
96	2004 Lethbridge Indra Shiraz	Geelong
96	2004 Clayfield Shiraz	Grampians
96	2004 Grampians Estate Streeton Reserve Shiraz	Grampians
96	2005 Mount Langi Ghiran Vineyards Langi Shiraz	Grampians
96	2004 Seppelt St Peters Shiraz	Grampians
96	2005 Forest Hill Vineyard Block 9 Shiraz	Great Southern
96	2004 Howard Park Scotsdale Shiraz	Great Southern
96	2005 Bress Unfiltered Shiraz	Heathcote
96	2004 Heathcote II HD Shiraz	Heathcote
96	2004 La Pleiade Shiraz	Heathcote
96	2004 Mt Toolleen Shiraz	Heathcote
96	2004 Shadowfax One Eye Shiraz	Heathcote
96	2004 Brokenwood Graveyard Shiraz	Hunter Valley
96	2005 Coriole Lloyd Reserve Shiraz	McLaren Vale
96	2002 Geoff Merrill Reserve Shiraz	McLaren Vale
96	2004 Hardys Eileen Hardy Shiraz	McLaren Vale
96	2005 Mitolo Savitar Shiraz	McLaren Vale
96	2004 Serafino Sharktooth Shiraz	McLaren Vale

96	2004 Wirra Wirra RSW Shiraz	McLaren Vale
96	2005 Paringa Estate Reserve Special Barrel Selection Shiraz	Mornington Peninsula
96	2005 Port Phillip Estate Rimage Tete de Cuvee Syrah	Mornington Peninsula
96	2001 Tahbilk 1860 Vines Shiraz	Nagambie Lakes
96	2005 Dalwhinnie Southwest Rocks Shiraz	Pyrenees
96	2004 Hewitson The Mad Hatter Shiraz	Southeast Australia
96	2003 Wildwood Shiraz	Sunbury

Shiraz Viognier

In best Australian Tall Poppy Syndrome fashion it has already become fashionable in some quarters to challenge the remarkable synergy obtained by co-fermenting around 5% of viognier with shiraz. The enhancement of colour, aroma and flavour is remarkable, as is the softening and smoothing of texture. Yes, it is not a panacea for lesser quality grapes, and yes, it is and should remain a subtext to the thrust of shiraz simplicity. Nonetheless, the 24 wines in this group offer hedonistic pleasure second to none. There is a wide spread of regions, from cool to temperate, none which I would describe as hot.

RATING	WINE	REGION
97	2005 Spinifex Shiraz Viognier	Eden Valley
96	2006 Clonakilla Shiraz Viognier	Canberra District
96	2005 Yarra Yarra Syrah Viognier	Yarra Valley
96	2005 Yering Station Shiraz Viognier	Yarra Valley
95	2005 (Saltram) Pepperjack Shiraz Viognier	Barossa Valley
95	2005 Turner's Crossing Vineyard Shiraz Viognier	Bendigo
95	2005 Willunga 100 Shiraz Viognier	McLaren Vale
95	2005 De Bortoli Estate Grown Shiraz Viognier	Yarra Valley
95	2004 YarraLoch The Collection Shiraz Viognier	Yarra Valley
94	2005 Mr Riggs Wine Company Shiraz Viognier	Adelaide
94	2004 Uleybury La Vipera Shiraz Viognier	Adelaide Hills
94	2004 Yalumba Hand Picked Shiraz Viognier	Barossa Valley
94	2005 Pondalowie Vineyards Shiraz Viognier	Bendigo
94	2004 Monument Vineyard Cudal Shiraz Viognier	Central Ranges Zone
94	2004 Eden Hall Shiraz Viognier	Eden Valley
94	2005 West Cape Howe Two Steps Shiraz Viognier	Great Southern
94	2005 Galli Estate Shiraz Viognier	Heathcote
94	2004 Gapsted Limited Release Shiraz Viognier	King Valley
94	2005 Cobaw Ridge Shiraz Viognier	Macedon Ranges
94	2004 Tatachilla Keystone Shiraz Viognier	McLaren Vale
94	2004 Mitchelton Parish Shiraz Viognier	Nagambie Lakes
94	2004 Millbrook Shiraz Viognier	Perth Hills
94	2005 Parri Estate Shiraz Viognier	Southern Fleurieu
94	2005 De Bortoli Gulf Station Shiraz Viognier	Yarra Valley

Cabernet Sauvignon

The affinity of cabernet sauvignon with a maritime climate is put beyond doubt by its home in Bordeaux's Medoc region. So it comes as no surprise to find that most (but not all) of Australia's top quality cabernets come from regions with climates similar to Bordeaux (conspicuously Coonawarra) and/or which are within 50 km of the sea with no intervening mountain range). The other feature of the list is the domination of the 2004 vintage.

RATING	WINE	REGION
97	2004 Hardys Thomas Hardy Cabernet Sauvignon	Margaret River
96	2005 Balnaves The Tally Reserve Cabernet Sauvignon	Coonawarra
96	2004 Punters Corner Sovereign Reserve Cabernet Sauvignon	Coonawarra
96	2004 Wynns John Riddoch Cabernet Sauvignon	Coonawarra
96	2004 Faber Vineyard Cabernet Sauvignon	Frankland River
96	2005 Forest Hill Vineyard Block 5 Cabernet Sauvignon	Great Southern
96	2005 Capel Vale Cabernet Sauvignon	Margaret River
96	2004 Houghton Gladstones Cabernet Sauvignon	Margaret River
96	2004 Howard Park Cabernet Sauvignon	Margaret River
96	2004 Woodside Valley Estate Baudin Cabernet Sauvignon	Margaret River
96	2005 Polleters Cabernet Sauvignon	Pyrenees
96	2004 Penfolds Bin 707 Cabernet Sauvignon	Southeast Australia
96	2004 Yarra Yarra The Yarra Yarra	Yarra Valley
95	2002 Chain of Ponds The Amadeus Cabernet Sauvignon	Adelaide Hills
95	2004 Elderton Ashmead Single Vineyard Cabernet Sauvignon	Barossa Valley
95	2003 Glen Eldon Cabernet Sauvignon	Barossa Valley
95	2004 Rockford Rifle Range Cabernet Sauvignon	Barossa Valley
95	2004 Pondalowie Vineyards Special Release Cabernet Sauvignon	Bendigo
95	2004 Annie's Lane Copper Trail Cabernet Sauvignon	Clare Valley
95	2002 Taylors St Andrews Cabernet Sauvignon	Clare Valley
95	2004 (Jamiesons Run) Mildara Rothwell Cabernet Sauvignon	Coonawarra
95	2002 Katnook Estate Odyssey Cabernet Sauvignon	Coonawarra
95	2004 Majella Cabernet Sauvignon	Coonawarra
95	2002 Murdock Cabernet Sauvignon	Coonawarra
95	2000 Jacob's Creek Jacaranda Ridge Cabernet Sauvignon	Coonawarra
95	2005 Windance Reserve Cabernet Sauvignon	Margaret River
95	2004 d'Arenberg The Coppermine Road Cabernet Sauvignon	McLaren Vale
95	2005 Mitolo Serpico Cabernet Sauvignon	McLaren Vale
95	2004 Possums Vineyard Cabernet Sauvignon	McLaren Vale
95	2004 Serafino Cabernet Sauvignon	McLaren Vale
95	2005 Shottesbrooke Punch Cabernet Sauvignon	McLaren Vale
95	2004 Wirra Wirra The Angelus Cabernet Sauvignon	McLaren Vale/ Coonawarra

Cabernet blends

A group which is dominated by cabernet merlot, and in turn by WA's Margaret River, with help from the Great Southern and (back east) the Yarra Valley, with the usual smattering of regional blends.

RATING	WINE	REGION
96	2002 Houghton Jack Mann	Great Southern
96	2004 Lake Breeze Bernoota Shiraz Cabernet	Langhorne Creek
96	2004 Wolf Blass Black Label Cabernet Sauvignon Shiraz Malbec	Langhorne Creek
96	2004 Serafino Sorrento Cabernet Sauvignon Cabernet Franc Merlot	McLaren Vale
96	2004 Yarra Yering Dry Red No. 1	Yarra Valley
95	2003 Henschke Lenswood Abbott's Prayer	Adelaide Hills
95	2004 Haan Wilhelmus	Barossa Valley
95	2005 Robertson of Clare MAX V	Clare Valley
95	2004 (Jamiesons Run) Mildara Cabernet Shiraz	Coonawarra
95	2003 Majella The Malleea	Coonawarra
95	2005 Penfolds Cellar Reserve Cabernet Shiraz	Coonawarra/ Barossa Valley
95	2004 Howard Park Cabernet Merlot	Great Southern
95	2003 Howard Park Cabernet Merlot	Great Southern
95	2004 Stella Bella Cabernet Sauvignon Merlot	Margaret River
95	2004 Vasse Felix Heytesbury	Margaret River
95	2004 Windance Cabernet Merlot	Margaret River
95	2005 Woodlands Margaret Reserve Cabernet Merlot	Margaret River
95	2003 McWilliam's 1877 Cabernet Sauvignon Shiraz	Riverina
95	2002 McWilliam's 1877 Cabernet Sauvignon Shiraz	Riverina
95	2004 Mount Mary Quintet	Yarra Valley

Shiraz and friends

A seemingly motley group, but one which has 2 strands: first, traditional Australian cabernet shiraz blends, and second, varieties and/or styles that emanate from the Rhône Valley, notably grenache and mourvedre, which have had over 150 years of acclimatisation in the regions around Adelaide with a couple of outriders in Heathcote, the Yarra Valley and Margaret River.

RATING	WINE	REGION
97	2005 Hewitson Private Cellar Shiraz Mourvedre	Barossa Valley
96	2002 Jacob's Creek Johann Shiraz Cabernet	Barossa Valley
96	2004 Bremerton B.O.V. Shiraz Cabernet	Langhorne Creek
96	2004 SC Pannell Grenache	McLaren Vale
96	2002 Wolf Blass Black Label Shiraz Cabernet Sauvignon Malbec	South Australia
96	2004 Yarra Yering Dry Red No. 2	Yarra Valley
95	2005 Glaetzer Godolphin	Barossa Valley
95	2005 Hewitson Old Garden Mourvedre	Barossa Valley

95	2005 Jasper Hill Emily's Paddock Shiraz Cabernet Franc	Heathcote
95	2004 SC Pannell Shiraz Grenache	McLaren Vale
94	2003 B3 Grenache Shiraz Mourvedre	Barossa Valley
94	2005 Burge Family Olive Hill Shiraz Mourvedre Grenache	Barossa Valley
94	2004 Kaesler Avignon Grenache Shiraz Mourvedre	Barossa Valley
94	2004 Massena Vineyards The Moonlight Run	Barossa Valley
94	2004 Soul Growers Shiraz Grenache Mourvedre	Barossa Valley
94	2004 Te-aro Estate Two Charlies GSM	Barossa Valley
94	2005 Turkey Flat Mourvedre	Barossa Valley
94	2004 Annie's Lane Copper Trail Shiraz Grenache	Clare Valley
94	2005 Jasper Hill Cornella Vineyard Grenache	Heathcote
94	2005 McHenry Hohnen 3 Amigos Shiraz Grenache Mataro	Margaret River
94	2004 d'Arenberg d'Arry's Original Shiraz Grenache	McLaren Vale
94	2004 Gibson Barossavale Old Vine Collection Grenache	McLaren Vale
94	2005 Gilligan Shiraz Grenache Mourvedre	McLaren Vale
94	2005 Paxton AAA Shiraz Grenache	McLaren Vale
94	2004 Samuel's Gorge Grenache	McLaren Vale

Fortified wines

A relatively small but immensely impressive group of wines, as quintessentially Australian as a Drizabone. I have broken a 25-year rule of refusing to give an Australian wine more than 97 points with the 1907 Seppelt Para Liqueur, and – with the wisdom of hindsight.

RATING	WINE	REGION
100	1907 Seppelt 100 Year Old Para Liqueur	Barossa Valley
97	NV Campbells Isabella Rare Rutherglen Tokay	Rutherglen
97	NV Morris Old Premium Liqueur Tokay	Rutherglen
97	NV Morris Old Premium Liqueur Muscat	Rutherglen
96	NV Penfolds Great Grandfather Rare Old Liqueur Tawny	Barossa Valley
96	NV Seppelt Amontillado DP116	Barossa Valley
96	NV Morris Old Premium Tawny Port	Rutherglen
96	2002 Stanton & Killeen Rutherglen Vintage Port	Rutherglen
95	NV Seppelt Oloroso DP38 NV	Barossa Valley

Special value wines

As always, these are lists of 10 of the best value wines, not the 10 best wines in each price category. There are literally dozens of wines with similar points and prices, and the choice is necessarily an arbitrary one. I have, however, attempted to give as much varietal and style choice as the limited numbers allow.

TEN OF THE BEST VALUE Whites under $10

87	2006 De Bortoli Sacred Hill Traminer Riesling	$6
89	2006 McWilliam's Inheritance Semillon Sauvignon Blanc	$6.99
89	2006 Banrock Station Semillon Chardonnay	$7.20
88	2006 Yalumba Oxford Landing Sauvignon Blanc	$8
88	2006 McPherson Sauvignon Blanc Semillon	$9
94	2006 Jacob's Creek Riesling	$9.95
90	2006 Leasingham Circa 1893 Riesling	$9.95
88	2006 Houghton Sauvignon Blanc Semillon	$9.95
87	2006 Lindemans Bin 65 Chardonnay	$9.95
88	2006 Jacob's Creek Chardonnay	$9.99

TEN OF THE BEST VALUE Reds under $10

88	2005 McWilliams Inheritance Cabernet Merlot	$6.95
90	2006 (Geoff Merrill) Mount Hurtle Grenache Rose	$8
88	2005 Yalumba Oxford Landing Merlot	$8
89	2005 Warburn Estate Premium Merlot	$9
90	2004 McLaren Wines Echidna Grenache Shiraz	$9.25
89	2004 Galli Estate Victoria Shiraz	$9.95
89	2006 Lindemans Bin 50 Shiraz	$9.95
88	2002 Chambers Rosewood Rutherglen Shiraz	$9.95
89	2006 Penfolds Rawson's Retreat Shiraz Cabernet	$9.99
88	2004 Angove's Long Row Cabernet Sauvignon	$9.99

It is in these following two groups that the effect of the wine surplus is most evident, forcing down the price (or upping the quality) of wines that would normally be far more expensive.

TEN OF THE BEST VALUE Whites $10–$15

94	2006 Wyndham Estate Bin 777 Semillon Sauvignon Blanc	$11
94	2005 Moondah Brook Chardonnay	$12.50
94	2004 Rosebrook Estate Chardonnay	$12.95
93	2006 Tahbilk Mrsanne	$12.95
94	2006 Oakvale Semillon	$13
95	2005 Chateau Francois Pokolbin Mallee Semillon	$14
96	2006 Bellarine Pemberton Riesling Auslese	$15
95	2006 Rowanston on the Track Macedon Ranges Riesling	$15
94	2004 Galafrey Mount Barker Riesling	$15
94	2006 Plunkett Fowles Blackwood Ridge Sauvignon Blanc	$15

TEN OF THE BEST VALUE Reds $10–$15

94	2004 Serafino Goose Island McLaren Vale Shiraz	$12
93	2006 Yalumba Limited Release Sangiovese Rose	$12
93	2005 Hardys Oomoo McLaren Vale Shiraz	$12.95
94	2004 Stonehaven Stepping Stone Padthaway Shiraz	$13
93	2004 (Lindemans) Rouge Homme Shiraz Cabernet	$14.95
93	2004 Serafino Sorrento McLaren Vale Cabernet Sauvignon Cabernet Franc Merlot	$15
94	2006 Angove's Nine Vines Grenache Shiraz Rose	$15
94	2006 Peter Lehmann Barossa Rose	$15
93	2005 Old Kent River Backtrack Pinot Noir	$15
93	2005 Amherst Daisy Creek Pyrenees Shiraz Cabernet	$15

Australia's geographical indications

The process of formally mapping Australia's wine regions is all but complete, although will never come to a complete halt – for one thing, climate change is lurking in the wings. The division into states, zones, regions and subregions follows; those regions or subregions marked with an asterisk are variously in an early, late or deadlocked stage of determination. In two instances I have gone beyond the likely finalisation: it makes no sense to me that the Hunter Valley should be a zone, the region Hunter, and then subregions which are all in the Lower Hunter Valley. I have elected to stick with the traditional division between the Upper Hunter Valley on the one hand, and the Lower on the other.

I am also in front of the game with Tasmania, dividing it into Northern, Southern and East Coast, and, to a lesser degree, have anticipated that the coastal hinterland region of Queensland will seek recognition under this or some similar name. Those regions and subregions marked with an asterisk have taken, or are likely to take, steps to secure registration; they may or may not persevere.

State/Zone	Region	Subregion
NEW SOUTH WALES		
Big Rivers	Murray Darling Perricoota Riverina Swan Hill	
Central Ranges	Cowra Mudgee Orange	
Hunter Valley	Hunter	Allandale★ Belford★ Broke Fordwich Dalwood★ Pokolbin★ Rothbury★
Northern Rivers	Hastings River	
Northern Slopes	New England★	

| South Coast | Shoalhaven Coast | |
| | Southern Highlands | |

Southern NSW	Canberra District	
	Gundagai	
	Hilltops	
	Tumbarumba	
Western Plains		

SOUTH AUSTRALIA

Adelaide (Super Zone, includes
Mount Lofty Ranges, Fleurieu
and Barossa)

Barossa	Barossa Valley	
	Eden Valley	
		High Eden
		Springton★

| Far North | Southern Flinders Ranges | |

Fleurieu	Currency Creek	
	Kangaroo Island	
	Langhorne Creek	
	McLaren Vale	Clarendon★
	Southern Fleurieu	

Limestone Coast	Coonawarra	
	Mount Benson	
	Penola★	
	Padthaway	
	Robe	
	Wrattonbully	

| Lower Murray | Riverland | |

Mount Lofty Ranges	Adelaide Hills	Gumeracha★
		Lenswood
		Piccadilly Valley
	Adelaide Plains	Auburn★
	Clare Valley	Clare★
		Hill River★

State/Zone	Region	Subregion
		Polish Hill River★
		Sevenhill★
		Watervale★
The Peninsulas	Southern Eyre Peninsula★	

VICTORIA

State/Zone	Region	Subregion
Central Victoria	Bendigo	
	Goulburn Valley	Nagambie Lakes
	Heathcote	
	Strathbogie Ranges	
	Upper Goulburn	
Gippsland		
North East Victoria	Alpine Valleys	Kiewa Valley★
		Ovens Valley★
	Beechworth	
	Glenrowan	
	King Valley★	Myrrhee★
		Whitlands★
	Rutherglen	Wahgunyah★
North West Victoria	Murray Darling	
	Swan Hill	
Port Phillip	Geelong	
	Macedon Ranges	
	Mornington Peninsula	
	Sunbury	
	Yarra Valley	
Western Victoria	Grampians	
	Henty	
	Pyrenees	

State/Zone	Region	Subregion
WESTERN AUSTRALIA		
Central Western Australia		
Eastern Plains, Inland and North of Western Australia		
Greater Perth	Peel	
	Perth Hills	
	Swan District	Swan Valley
South West Australia	Blackwood Valley	
	Geographe	
	Great Southern	Albany
		Denmark
		Frankland River
		Mount Barker
		Porongurup
	Manjimup	
	Margaret River	
	Pemberton	
WA South East Coastal	Esperance★	
QUEENSLAND		
Queensland	Granite Belt	
	Coastal Hinterland★	
	South Burnett	
TASMANIA		
Tasmania	Northern Tasmania★	
	Southern Tasmania★	
	East Coast Tasmania★	
AUSTRALIAN CAPITAL TERRITORY		
NORTHERN TERRITORY		

Australian vintage chart

Each number represents a mark out of 10 for the quality of vintages in each region.

red wine   white wine

2003	2004	2005	2006

NSW

Lower Hunter Valley

10	8	7	6
7	8	9	7

Upper Hunter Valley

8	6	7	6
8	8	9	7

Mudgee

6	8	7	8
6	7	9	7

Cowra

8	6	7	6
9	5	8	6

Orange

10	9	8	9
9	7	9	8

Riverina/Griffith

7	7	6	6
7	8	6	7

Canberra District

8	8	9	8
7	8	9	9

Southern Highlands

5	8	8
6	9	8

Perricoota

6	7	9	7
6	8	6	8

Gundagai

6	7	9	8
7	7	8	7

Hilltops

5	9	9	10
6	6	8	9

2003	2004	2005	2006

Tumbarumba

5	5	7	7
4	6	9	9

Hastings River

6	7	9	6
6	8	9	7

Shoalhaven

6	7	9	7
7	7	8	8

VIC

Yarra Valley

9	10	9	9
9	8	9	9

Mornington Peninsula

9	10	9	9
8	10	7	8

Geelong

8	8	8	8
9	8	7	8

Macedon

10	8	7	9
9	9	8	8

Sunbury

9	8	7	8
7	7	8	7

Grampians

9	10	10	8
8	6	9	8

Pyrenees

8	10	10	9
6	9	9	8

Henty

7	9	9	8
10	9	8	9

2003	2004	2005	2006

Bendigo

7	9	8	8
6	9	7	8

Heathcote

8	10	8	9
6	9	9	7

Goulburn Valley

8	9	8	9
6	7	8	8

Upper Goulburn

7	7	9	8
6	7	9	8

Strathbogie Ranges

8	8	9	7
7	8	8	8

Glenrowan & Rutherglen

9	9	7	7
7	6	7	7

King Valley

7	8	7	8
8	9	9	7

Alpine Valleys

4	9	8	8
4	9	10	7

Beechworth

8	10	8	8
6	8	8	7

Gippsland

7	10	9	9
6	9	9	8

Murray Darling

7	7	8	8
6	7	8	9

SA

Barossa Valley

2003	2004	2005	2006
7	9	7	8
7	7	8	7

Eden Valley

2003	2004	2005	2006
7	8	8	7
9	9	9	8

Clare Valley

2003	2004	2005	2006
8	9	9	8
10	8	9	7

Adelaide Hills

2003	2004	2005	2006
8	8	7	7
8	7	8	9

Adelaide Plains

2003	2004	2005	2006
6	8	8	7
7	7	9	8

Coonawarra

2003	2004	2005	2006
9	7	8	7
8	6	7	6

Padthaway

2003	2004	2005	2006
8	7	8	8
9	7	7	7

Mount Benson & Robe

2003	2004	2005	2006
8	7	8	7
9	8	9	7

Wrattonbully

2003	2004	2005	2006
7	4	8	9
8	7	8	7

McLaren Vale

2003	2004	2005	2006
8	9	8	8
7	7	8	7

Southern Fleurieu

2003	2004	2005	2006
7	7	8	8
7	8	8	8

Langhorne Creek

2003	2004	2005	2006
8	8	9	8
7	7	8	9

Kangaroo Island

2003	2004	2005	2006
7	8	8	8
7	7	8	7

Riverland

2003	2004	2005	2006
8	8	8	9
9	8	9	8

WA

Margaret River

2003	2004	2005	2006
8	9	9	7
8	8	9	9

Great Southern

2003	2004	2005	2006
7	7	9	6
6	8	9	8

Manjimup

2003	2004	2005	2006
6	9	7	6
6	5	9	8

Pemberton

2003	2004	2005	2006
6	8	9	6
7	8	9	8

Geographe

2003	2004	2005	2006
8	9	7	8
8	9	8	6

Swan District

2003	2004	2005	2006
7	9	9	7
6	7	8	8

Peel

2003	2004	2005	2006
8	8	10	9
8	7	10	9

Perth Hills

2003	2004	2005	2006
7	9	10	8
8	7	9	7

QLD

Granite Belt

2003	2004	2005	2006
8	7	9	8
7	9	9	7

South Burnett

2003	2004	2005	2006
8	6	9	7
8	6	10	8

TAS

Northern Tasmania

2003	2004	2005	2006
7	6	10	8
7	8	9	7

Southern Tasmania

2003	2004	2005	2006
8	7	10	9
7	8	9	8

Grape variety plantings

The Australian Bureau of Statistics produces an annual report on the Australian wine and grape industry. I rely on this report in giving the detailed figures for the area and tonnes produced each year for the major varieties. However, the report is in fact a hybrid: one part of it comes from detailed questionnaires sent to all wineries crushing more than 400 tonnes, a less extensive enquiry to those crushing between 50 and 400 tonnes, and no figures are taken from wineries crushing less than 50 tonnes. Because the scope of the questionnaire sent to the wineries covers a great number of things, the ABS decided long ago that it was unreasonable to ask for a breakdown of the tonnage crushed by variety.

This information comes from a quite separate questionnaire to grapegrowers, sent out by a different department. The net result is a substantial difference between the total tonnage provided by the grapegrowers, and that derived from the wineries. Since the wineries pay a levy on each tonne crushed, there is no reason to imagine that they would ever overstate their crush. Moreover, while the total tonnage crushed by wineries crushing between 50 and 400 tonnes has been calculated by the ABS to be in the region of 34 000 tonnes, the contribution of the very small wineries would be much less than 5% of the total. Nonetheless, it simply underpins the winery information, which in 2006 amounted to 1 901 560 tonnes. The total of that provided by the grapegrowers (and which is reflected in the table on page 45) is 1 781 668 tonnes. (I should also add that I have consistently used the grapegrower numbers in that table, to provide a continuing comparison on a year-by-year basis.)

The two giants in Australian viticulture are shiraz and chardonnay, which between them provided 46% of the total tonnage. Overall, there has been an uneasy calm before the storm, the 2006 crop little changed from the two preceding years, and adding to the already significant wine surplus generated in 2005 and 2004. Nonetheless, for the first time in decades, the hectares planted decreased, not by a large amount, perhaps, but taking them back to where they stood in 2002. Grape production also declined slightly; both of these decreases were the first signs of grapegrowers responding to the lack of demand from the wineries.

As the vintage snapshot of 2007 (page 6) indicates, there will be a dramatically different outcome for 2007, with grape production two-thirds that of 2006. The surplus which was expected to take 3 or 4 years to come back into balance will have virtually disappeared overnight. Because of the lag time between grape harvest and wine sales, the immediate effect on sales may not be as dramatic as the figures might suggest, although wineries are already reacting to the shortfall. The days of massive clearances by cleanskin bottles, of discounts of over 50% of the recommended retail for branded products, and exports in bulk will all sharply diminish.

	2000	2002	2004	2006
CHARDONNAY				
hectares	18,526	21,724	28,008	31,219
tonnes	201,248	256,328	311,273	397,322
RIESLING				
hectares	3,658	3,962	4,255	4,400
tonnes	26,800	27,838	36,404	38,380
SAUVIGNON BLANC				
hectares	2,706	2,914	3,425	4,661
tonnes	21,487	28,567	39,774	40,513
SEMILLON				
hectares	6,832	6,610	6,278	6,236
tonnes	77,506	100,785	99,237	96,934
OTHER WHITE				
hectares	27,873	26,215	23,925	17,683
tonnes	265,196	255,253	266,794	228,311
TOTAL WHITE				
hectares	59,595	61,425	65,891	64,199
tonnes	592,237	666,771	753,482	801,460
CABERNET SAUVIGNON				
hectares	26,674	29,573	29,313	28,103
tonnes	159,358	257,223	319,955	274,350
GRENACHE				
hectares	2,756	2,528	2,292	2,025
tonnes	23,998	26,260	24,987	22,697
MOURVEDRE				
hectares	1,147	1,238	1,040	875
tonnes	10,496	12,452	13,992	10,882
MERLOT				
hectares	8,575	10,101	10,804	10,593
tonnes	51,269	104,423	123,944	123,084
PINOT NOIR				
hectares	3,756	4,414	4,424	4,254
tonnes	19,578	21,341	41,690	33,921
SHIRAZ				
hectares	32,327	37,031	39,182	41,115
tonnes	224,394	326,564	436,691	422,430
OTHER RED				
hectares	11,347	12,284	11,235	7,002
tonnes	57,255	99,467	101,816	92,845
TOTAL RED				
hectares	86,582	97,169	98,290	93,967
tonnes	546,348	847,730	1,063,075	980,209
TOTAL GRAPES				
hectares	146,177	158,594	164,181	158,167
tonnes	1,138,585	1,514,501	1,816,556	1,781,668
PERCENTAGE (TONNES)				
White	52.02%	44.02%	41.48%	44.98%
Red	47.98%	55.98%	58.52%	55.02%

Wine and food or food and wine?

It all depends on your starting point: there are conventional matches for overseas classics such as caviar (Champagne), fresh foie gras (Sauternes, Riesling or Rose), and new season Italian white truffles (any medium-bodied red). Here the food flavour is all important, the wine merely incidental.

At the other extreme come 50-year-old classic red wines: Grange, or Grand Cru Burgundy or, First Growth Bordeaux, or a Maurice O'Shea Mount Pleasant Shiraz. Here the food is, or should be, merely a low-key foil, but at the same time must be of high quality.

In the Australian context I believe not enough attention is paid to the time of year, which – particularly in the southern states – is or should be a major determinant in the choice of both food and wine. And so I shall present my suggestions in this way, always bearing in mind how many ways there are to skin a cat.

Spring

SPARKLING
Oysters, cold crustacea, tapas, any cold hors d'oeuvres

YOUNG RIESLING
Cold salads, sashimi

GEWURZTRAMINER
Asian

YOUNG SEMILLON
Antipasto, vegetable terrine

PINOT GRIS, COLOMBARD
Crab cakes, whitebait

VERDELHO, CHENIN BLANC
Cold smoked chicken, gravlax

MATURE CHARDONNAY
Grilled chicken, chicken pasta, turkey, pheasant

ROSE
Caesar salad, trout mousse

YOUNG PINOT NOIR
Seared kangaroo fillet, grilled quail

MERLOT
Pastrami, warm smoked chicken

YOUNG MEDIUM-BODIED CABERNET SAUVIGNON
Rack of baby lamb

LIGHT- TO MEDIUM-BODIED COOL CLIMATE SHIRAZ
Rare eye fillet of beef

YOUNG BOTRYTISED WINES
Fresh fruits, cake

Summer

CHILLED FINO
Cold consommé

2-3-YEAR-OLD SEMILLON
Gazpacho

2-3-YEAR-OLD RIESLING
Seared tuna

**YOUNG BARREL-FERMENTED
SEMILLON SAUVIGNON BLANC**
Seafood or vegetable tempura

YOUNG OFF-DRY RIESLING
Prosciutto & melon/pear

COOL-CLIMATE CHARDONNAY
Abalone, lobster, Chinese-style prawns

**10-YEAR-OLD SEMILLON OR
RIESLING**
Braised pork neck

MATURE CHARDONNAY
Smoked eel, smoked roe

OFF-DRY ROSE
Chilled fresh fruit

YOUNG LIGHT-BODIED PINOT NOIR
Grilled salmon

AGED PINOT NOIR (5+ YEARS)
Coq au vin, wild duck

YOUNG GRENACHE/SANGIOVESE
Osso bucco

MATURE CHARDONNAY (5+ YEARS)
Braised rabbit

**HUNTER VALLEY SHIRAZ
(5–10 YEARS)**
Beef spare ribs

MERLOT
Saltimbocca, roast pheasant

**MEDIUM-BODIED CABERNET
SAUVIGNON (5 YEARS)**
Barbecued butterfly leg of lamb

ALL WINES
Parmagiana

Autumn

AMONTILLADO
Warm consomme

**BARREL-FERMENTED MATURE
WHITES**
Smoked roe, bouillabaisse

COMPLEX MATURE CHARDONNAY
Sweetbreads, brains

FULLY AGED RIESLING
Chargrilled eggplant, stuffed capsicum

AGED MARSANNE
Seafood risotto, Lebanese

SOUTHERN VICTORIAN PINOT NOIR
Peking duck

AGED PINOT NOIR
Grilled calf's liver, roast kid, lamb or
pig's kidneys

**MATURE MARGARET RIVER
CABERNET MERLOT**
Lamb fillet, roast leg of lamb with garlic
and herbs

COOL CLIMATE MERLOT
Lamb loin chops

**MATURE GRENACHE/RHONE
BLENDS**
Moroccan lamb

**RICH, FULL-BODIED HEATHCOTE
SHIRAZ**
Beef casserole

YOUNG MUSCAT
Plum pudding

Winter

DRY OLOROSO SHERRY
Full-flavoured hors d'oeuvres

SPARKLING BURGUNDY
Borscht

VIOGNIER
Pea and ham soup

AGED (10+ YEARS) SEMILLON
Vichysoisse (hot)

SAUVIGNON BLANC
Coquilles St Jacques, pan-fried scallops

MATURE CHARDONNAY
Quiche Lorraine

CHARDONNAY (10+ YEARS)
Cassoulet

MATURE SEMILLON SAUVIGNON BLANC
Seafood pasta

YOUNG TASMANIAN PINOT NOIR
Squab, duck breast

MATURE PINOT NOIR
Mushroom ragout, ravioli

MATURE MERLOT
Pot au feu

10-YEAR-OLD HEATHCOTE SHIRAZ
Char-grilled rump steak

15–20-YEAR-OLD FULL-BODIED BAROSSA SHIRAZ
Venison, kangaroo fillet

COONAWARRA CABERNET SAUVIGNON
Braised lamb shanks/shoulder

MUSCAT (OLD)
Chocolate-based desserts

TOKAY (OLD)
Creme brûlée

VINTAGE PORT
Dried fruits, salty cheese

Acknowledgements

It is, I suppose, inevitable that the production of a book such as this should involve many people in a long chain of events, some seemingly trivial, others of fundamental importance.

The starting point is the making of the thousands of bottles of wine that I (and no one else) taste each year, and the end point is the appearance of the book on retailers' shelves across Australia on 1 August 2007.

My foremost thanks must go to the winemakers for sending the wines to me at their cost, and in particular those who treat submission dates as serious deadlines rather than an approximate wish list on my part.

Next are those responsible for getting the wine to me, whether by the excellent parcel delivery service of Australia Post, by courier or by hand delivery. I am reliant on the good will and tolerance of many people involved in what may seem as a warped version of trivial pursuits as the wines arrive and are placed in large bins; in due course fork-lifted up one story and removed from those bins; unpacked; listed; entered into the database, with precise names cross-checked; alcohol, price, and closure type recorded (with a reference to second bottles if the wines are not screwcapped); tasting sheets printed for the day's tasting of 150 to 170 wines, initially arranged by producer, but then re-sorted by variety; moved on to a long tasting bench; opened, poured at the same pace I taste; the Riedel glasses returned to washing racks, washed, rinsed and dried (my task each day); the tasting notes dictated; the database now returning the notes to a winery-by-winery sequence; proofed by me (and at least three others at subsequent stages before going to print).

In the meantime, my office team has been busy chasing up new, missing or inconsistent details regarding the wineries, and many of the wines, with special emphasis on new wineries.

Then there is the ever-patient but deadline-conscious team at Hardie Grant, working on the cover design (surely brilliant), page design, paper type, 2-colour printing, which give rise to the galley pages for proofreading again and again.

To my team of Paula Grey, Beth Anthony, Marcus Hutson; Bev and Chris Bailey (Coldstream Post Office); Pam Holmes (and others at Coldstream Hills); John Cook (Programmer); and the Hardie Grant team of Jasmin Chua (Senior Editor) and Megan Ellis (Typesetter), my heartfelt thanks. This is as much their book as it is mine.

Australian wineries
and wines 2008

A note on alphabetical order
Wineries beginning with 'The' are listed under 'T'; for example,
'The Blok Estate'. Winery names that include a numeral are treated
as if the numeral is spelled out; for example, '5 Maddens Lane'
is listed under 'F'.

Abbey Creek Vineyard

2388 Porongurup Road, Porongurup, WA 6324 **Region** Porongurup
T (08) 9853 1044 **F** (08) 9454 5501 **Open** By appt
Winemaker Castle Rock Estate (Robert Diletti) **Est.** 1990 **Cases** 900
This is the family business of Mike and Mary Dilworth, the name coming from a winter creek running alongside the vineyard, and a view of The Abbey in the Stirling Range. The vineyard is only 1.6 ha, equally split between riesling, pinot noir and cabernet sauvignon; the pinot noir and riesling were planted in 1990, the remainder in 1993. The rieslings have had significant show success.

ᵀᵀᵀᵀᵀ   **Porongurup Riesling 2006** Intense lime juice flavours run through to the
         lingering finish; distinguished wine. Screwcap. 12° alc. **Rating** 94 **To** 2016 $19

ᵀᵀᵀᵀ   **Porongurup Sauvignon Blanc 2006** While there is no reduction or sweatiness
         on the bouquet, it is still as closed as a clam shell; the delicate minerally palate may
         offer more over the short term, particularly as the bouquet opens up. Screwcap.
         12.8° alc. **Rating** 88 **To** 2009 $19
         Porongurup Cabernet Merlot 2004 Light but bright red-purple; fresh and
         lively, but needed more hot sun to give greater depth (and higher points). Screwcap.
         13.5° alc. **Rating** 87 **To** 2010 $22

Abbey Rock

1 Onkaparinga Valley Road, Balhannah, SA 5242 **Region** Mount Lofty Ranges Zone
T (08) 8398 0192 **F** (08) 8398 0188 www.abbeyrock.com.au **Open** 7 days 9–5
Winemaker Les Sampson **Est.** 2001 **Cases** 18 000
A recent but expanding business with wines sourced from a number of regions spread across SA. The premium wines are made from pinot noir (2.2 ha) and chardonnay (3.5 ha) near Hahndorf in the Adelaide Hills, and from chardonnay (2 ha), semillon (6.5 ha), shiraz (8 ha) and grenache (2 ha) in the Clare Valley. Plans are afoot to increase the plantings.

ᵀᵀᵀᵀᵀ   **Old School House Coonawarra Riesling 2004** Has begun its development in
         convincing fashion; still shows Coonawarra terroir expressed by the apple, pear and
         citrus aromas and flavours, all with a special delicacy. Screwcap. 12.8° alc. **Rating** 92
         To 2013 $18

ᵀᵀᵀᵀ   **Helmsford Clare Valley Semillon Sauvignon Blanc 2005** A strange decision
         to look to the Clare Valley for this blend; however, it works well, with good balance
         and integration of the varieties, the semillon doing most of the work; expands on
         the finish courtesy of the sauvignon blanc. Screwcap. 13.4° alc. **Rating** 89
         To 2008 $18
         Hahndorf Rise Adelaide Hills Chardonnay 2006 A flowery, aromatic bouquet
         leading to flavours of nectarine and citrus/grapefruit; synthetic closure demands
         immediate consumption, and the wine deserved a better fate. Synthetic. **Rating** 89
         To 2008 $23
         Coonawarra Cabernet Merlot 2004 Medium-bodied, with clear blackcurrant
         varietal fruit, and regional nuances of earth and leaf; slightly austere tannins.
         Screwcap. 14.1° alc. **Rating** 88 **To** 2014 $22

Abercorn

Cassilis Road, Mudgee, NSW 2850 **Region** Mudgee
T 1800 000 959 www.abercornwine.com.au **Open** Thurs–Mon 10.30–4.30
Winemaker Tim Stevens **Est.** 1996 **Cases** 8000
Tim and Connie Stevens acquired the 25-year-old Abercorn Vineyard in 1996. The quality of the red wines has improved over the years to the point where two-thirds of the production is released under the 'A Reserve' banner, led by A Reserve Shiraz and A Reserve Shiraz Cabernet Merlot. These now rank among the best of the region, selling out prior to the next release. A few hundred cases of white wines continue to be made for cellar door release only. In late 2005 the Stevens acquired neighbour Huntington Estate, which they will run as a separate entity.

Acreage Vineyard & Winery

681 Gardner and Holman Road, Drouin South, Vic 3818 **Region** Gippsland
T (03) 5627 6383 **F** (03) 5627 6135 **Open** 7 days 10–5
Winemaker Terry Blundell **Est.** 1997 **Cases** 450
Terry and Jan Blundell commenced the planting of their vineyard in 1997 with chardonnay and pinot noir. In 2003 shiraz, merlot and cabernet sauvignon were added, taking the total plantings to 2.5 ha. Former school principal Terry says 'I am under threat of further pain from Jan if I plant any more of what she calls "your little weeds".' He also points out that the cellar door, with views to the Baw Baw Ranges, is only 65 mins from the Melbourne CBD.

Unwooded Chardonnay 2006 Pleasant nectarine and melon fruit; has enough going for it, including balance, to make it interesting. **Rating** 87 **To** 2009 $15
Chardonnay 2004 A solid wine showing rather more power than the alcohol suggests, with plenty of ripe fruit, although the poor-quality cork is doing the wine no favours. 13° alc. **Rating** 87 **To** 2007 $15
Pinot Noir 2005 Another powerful wine, with dried plum and spice aromas and flavours; does show varietal character, albeit with a tough finish. Screwcap. 13.5° alc. **Rating** 87 **To** 2009 $17

Across the Lake

Box 66, Lake Grace, WA 6353 **Region** Central Western Australia Zone
T (08) 9864 9026 **Open** By appt
Winemaker Dr Diane Miller (Contract) **Est.** 1999 **Cases** 380
The Taylor family has been farming (wheat and sheep) for over 40 years at Lake Grace; a small diversification into grapegrowing started as a hobby, but has developed into a little more than that with 1.6 ha of shiraz. They were motivated to support their friend Bill (WJ) Walker, who had started growing shiraz 3 years previously, and has since produced a gold medal-winning wine. Having learnt the hard way which soils are suitable, the Taylors intend to increase their plantings.

Ada River

2330 Main Road, Neerim South, Vic 3831 **Region** Gippsland
T (03) 5628 1661 **F** (03) 5628 1661 **Open** W'ends & public hols 10–6
Winemaker Peter Kelliher **Est.** 1983 **Cases** 1500
The Kelliher family first planted vines on their dairy farm at Neerim South in 1983, extending the vineyard in 1989 and increasing plantings further by establishing the nearby Manilla Vineyard in 1994. Until 2000, Ada River leased a Yarra Valley vineyard; it has relinquished that lease and in its place established a vineyard at Heathcote in conjunction with a local grower.

Reserve Heathcote Shiraz 2005 Richer, ripe, more succulent and more texture than the varietal, though the alcohol is in no way threatening; long spicy, licorice, black fruits. The use of cork for the longer lived Reserve, and screwcap for the shorter lived varietal is, to put it mildly, quaint. 14° alc. **Rating** 94 **To** 2020 $30

Heathcote Shiraz 2005 Medium-bodied; quite powerful blackberry fruit, with touches of spice and licorice; ripe tannins, good length and balance. Screwcap. 14° alc. **Rating** 92 **To** 2018 $25
Gippsland Chardonnay 2005 Elegant, intense and long; driven by stone fruit and citrus, the oak integrated and balanced. Screwcap. 12.8° alc. **Rating** 91 **To** 2012 $20
Heathcote Merlot 2005 A medium-bodied mix of sweet red fruits, olive and snow peas; fine, persistent tannins, and subtle oak. Screwcap. 13.4° alc. **Rating** 90 **To** 2015 $25

Gewurztraminer 2006 Nicely balanced, not too sweet, and has length; needs more varietal punch for higher points. Screwcap. 12.5° alc. **Rating** 89 **To** 2009 $20

Heathcote Cabernet Sauvignon 2005 Clear cassis and blackcurrant fruit, but unusually light-bodied for the region, possibly picked too early. Screwcap. 14.2° alc. **Rating 88 To** 2015 $25
Gippsland Chardonnay 2006 Lots of flavour, with nectarine and peach, the oak (or some other character) giving a slightly cosmetic character. Screwcap. 13° alc. **Rating 87 To** 2010 $20

Adinfern Estate

Bussell Highway, Cowaramup, WA 6284 **Region** Margaret River
T (08) 9755 5272 **F** (08) 9755 5206 **www**.adinfern.com **Open** 7 days 11–5.30
Winemaker Merv Smith, Matt Thomas, Transview Pty Ltd (Kevin McKay, Michael Langridge) **Est.** 1996 **Cases** 3500
Merv and Jan Smith have farmed their property as a fine wool and lamb producer for over 30 years, but in 1996 diversified by the development of a 25-ha vineyard planted to sauvignon blanc, semillon, chardonnay, pinot noir, merlot, shiraz, cabernet sauvignon and malbec. One hundred tonnes of grapes are sold to other makers, 25 retained for Adinfern Estate. Exports to Belgium, Singapore, Taiwan and China.

ΨΨΨΨ Margaret River Cabernet Sauvignon 2004 Medium-bodied; an elegant, understated style offering blackcurrant, earth and spice flavours supported by gentle tannins. Cork. 14° alc. **Rating 89 To** 2011 $25

Affleck

154 Millynn Road off Bungendore Road, Bungendore, NSW 2621 **Region** Canberra District
T (02) 6236 9276 **F** (02) 6236 9090 **www**.affleck.com.au **Open** Fri–Wed 9–5
Winemaker Ian Hendry **Est.** 1976 **Cases** 500
The cellar door and mail order price list says that the wines are 'grown, produced and bottled on the estate by Ian and Susie Hendry with much dedicated help from family and friends'. The original 2.5-ha vineyard has been expanded to 7 ha.

ΨΨΨΨΨ Canberra District Rose 2006 Bright puce; crisp, clean and fresh red fruits; excellent acidity gives length without sweetness. Very well-made. Screwcap. 12.5° alc. **Rating 90 To** 2008 $14

ΨΨΨΨ Lake George Semillon 2006 Clean; light- to medium-bodied; pleasant fruit doesn't have the crunchy, crisp finish of Hunter Valley semillon, but why should it? Screwcap. 11° alc. **Rating 87 To** 2010 $25
Canberra District Chardonnay 2005 Medium-bodied; gentle nectarine, melon and fig fruit; some vestiges of oak; moderate length. Cork. 12° alc. **Rating 87 To** 2008 $18

Ainsworth & Snelson

22 Gourlay Street, St Kilda East, Vic 3183 **Region** Warehouse
T (03) 9530 3333 **F** (03) 9530 3446 **www**.ainsworthandsnelson.com **Open** Not
Winemaker Brett Snelson **Est.** 2002 **Cases** 5000
Brett Snelson and Gregg Ainsworth take a handcrafted regional approach to the production of their wines. They use traditional techniques which allow the emphasis to remain on terroir, sourcing grapes from the Clare Valley, Yarra Valley, Barossa and Coonawarra. Brett Snelson keeps his winemaking skills sharp with an annual vintage in Rousillon. Exports to the UK, France, Denmark, Norway, Hong Kong and Singapore.

ΨΨΨΨΨ Watervale Riesling 2006 Glowing green-straw; voluminous aromas and flavours of lime and tropical fruit without losing focus or brightness; fabulous drink now (or later). Screwcap. 13° alc. **Rating 94 To** 2016 $22
Barossa Valley Shiraz 2004 Bursting with traditional Barossa Valley black fruits with underlying nuances of licorice; good tannin texture and structure; carries its alcohol with aplomb. Cork. 15° alc. **Rating 94 To** 2024 $28

Albert River Wines

869 Mundoolun Connection Road, Tamborine, Qld 4270 **Region** Queensland Coastal
T (07) 5543 6622 **F** (07) 5543 6627 www.albertriverwines.com.au **Open** Wed–Sun 10–4
Winemaker Contract **Est.** 1998 **Cases** 3000

Albert River is one of the high-profile wineries on the Gold Coast hinterland. David and Janette
Bladin, with a combined 30 years' experience in tourism and hospitality, have acquired and
relocated 2 of Qld's most historic buildings, Tamborine House and Auchenflower House. The
winery itself is housed in a newly constructed annex to Auchenflower House; the Bladins have
established 4 ha of vineyards on the property, and have another 50 ha under contract. All of its
distribution is through cellar door, mail order and local restaurants. Exports to Japan.

Aldgate Ridge

23 Nation Ridge Road, Aldgate, SA 5154 **Region** Adelaide Hills
T (08) 8388 5225 **F** (08) 8388 5856 www.aldgateridge.com.au **Open** By appt
Winemaker Torbreck Vintners **Est.** 1992 **Cases** 500

Jill and Chris Whisson acquired their vineyard property in 1988, when the land was being used
as a market garden. The first vines were planted in 1992 and 1997; further plantings of pinot noir
and a block of sauvignon blanc have been added, taking the total plantings to 1 ha of each variety.
The vineyard is typical of the Adelaide Hills region, on a rolling to steep southeast-facing hillside
at an altitude of 440 m.

▼▼▼▼▽ **Sauvignon Blanc 2006** Fresh, clean apple, gooseberry, pear and passionfruit
aromas and flavours all intermingle. Screwcap. 13° alc. **Rating** 90 **To** 2008 $22
Pinot Noir 2004 Forest floor, plum and spice characters; a long, quite zippy finish.
Screwcap. 13.3° alc. **Rating** 90 **To** 2010 $33

Alexandra Bridge Wines

PO Box 255, South Perth, WA 6951 **Region** Margaret River
T (08) 9368 0099 **F** (08) 9368 0133 www.alexandrabridgewines.com.au **Open** Not
Winemaker Brian Fletcher **Est.** 1999 **Cases** 9000

Alexandra Bridge has become the operating arm of Australian Wine Holdings. The 800-tonne
winery, commissioned in 2000, was the first built in the Karridale area at the southern end of
the Margaret River. The Brockman Vineyard, planted in 3 stages commencing in 1995, is estate-
owned and has a total of 30.5 ha of semillon, sauvignon blanc, chardonnay, shiraz and cabernet
sauvignon. The grapes coming from the Brockman Vineyard are supplemented by long-term
supply agreements with other Margaret River growers. Exports to Europe and South-East Asia.

▼▼▼▼▼ **Margaret River Chardonnay 2005** Pale green-straw; obvious barrel
fermentation inputs on both the bouquet and palate introduce a complex wine, the
fruit coming through strongly on the back-palate and finish; fresh and lively.
Screwcap. 13.5° alc. **Rating** 94 **To** 2013 $19.50
Margaret River Shiraz 2004 Fully ripe shiraz, though not over the top; supple,
velvety black fruits and shafts of spice; good tannin and oak management. Screwcap.
14.5° alc. **Rating** 94 **To** 2024 $24.50

▼▼▼▼▽ **101 Chardonnay 2004** Glowing yellow-green; belies its alcohol; citrus, melon
and nectarine fruit supported by gentle oak throughout; a light, fresh finish.
Screwcap. 14.5° alc. **Rating** 93 **To** 2011 $38

▼▼▼▼ **Margaret River Cabernet Merlot 2004** Light- to medium-bodied; bright
red fruits with some blackcurrant, though not a lot of structure or depth. Screwcap.
14° alc. **Rating** 89 **To** 2014 $24.50
101 Cabernet Sauvignon 2003 Distinctly savoury/earthy overtones to the
medium-bodied blackcurrant fruit; overall, quite austere. Cork. 14.5° alc. **Rating** 89
To 2013 $48

Alkoomi

Wingebellup Road, Frankland, WA 6396 **Region** Frankland River
T (08) 9855 2229 **F** (08) 9855 2284 **www.**alkoomiwines.com.au **Open** 7 days 10–5
Winemaker Michael Staniford, Merv Lange, Ryan Charuschenko **Est.** 1971 **Cases** 90 000
For those who see the wineries of WA as suffering from the tyranny of distance, this most remote
of all wineries shows there is no tyranny after all. It is a story of unqualified success due to sheer
hard work, and no doubt to Merv and Judy Lange's aversion to borrowing a single dollar from
the bank. The substantial production is entirely drawn from the ever-expanding estate vineyards
– now over 100 ha. Wine quality across the range is impeccable, always with precisely defined
varietal character. Exports to all major markets.

ΨΨΨΨΨ **Frankland River Sauvignon Blanc 2006** A clean and strong varietal expression
on the bouquet; classic gooseberry and passionfruit flavours, with a long, lingering
and crisp finish. Screwcap. 12.5° alc. **Rating** 94 **To** 2008 $18

ΨΨΨΨΨ **Frankland River Semillon Sauvignon Blanc 2006** Spotlessly clean; lively and
fresh aromas and flavours; lemon juice, lemon zest with touches of passionfruit and
gooseberry. Screwcap. 11.5° alc. **Rating** 93 **To** 2008 $13
Frankland River Chardonnay 2005 Fine and elegant, still very youthful; crisp
white peach, nectarine and grapefruit flavours supported by good acidity and
seamless oak. Still developing. Screwcap. 11.5° alc. **Rating** 93 **To** 2012 $20

Frankland River Shiraz Viognier 2005 An elegant, medium-bodied spicy wine
without the usual viognier impact, though not necessarily the worse for that. Black
fruits, fine tannins and integrated oak. Screwcap. 14° alc. **Rating** 93 **To** 2018 $20
Frankland River Riesling 2006 Fragrant herb, nettle and lime aromas, then a
crisp, clean and dry palate notwithstanding the low alcohol; lime juice and mineral
flavours. An intriguing wine. Screwcap. 10.4° alc. **Rating** 92 **To** 2015 $18
Frankland River Late Harvest 2006 Complex scented and spicy fruit aromas;
a basically dry finish, with tingling, citrussy acidity. Screwcap. 10° alc. **Rating** 92
To 2010 $13

ΨΨΨΨ **Unwooded Chardonnay 2006** Clean, fresh light-bodied wine, with melon and
grapefruit flavours; well-balanced. Screwcap. 12.5° alc. **Rating** 89 **To** 2008 $13

All Saints Estate

All Saints Road, Wahgunyah, Vic 3687 **Region** Rutherglen
T (02) 6035 2222 **www.**allsaintswine.com.au **Open** Mon–Sat 9–5.30, Sun 10–5.30
Winemaker Dan Crane **Est.** 1864 **Cases** 40 000
The winery rating reflects the fortified wines, but the table wines are more than adequate. The
Terrace restaurant makes this a most enjoyable stop for any visitor to the northeast. The faux castle,
modelled on a Scottish castle beloved of the founder, is classified by the Historic Buildings
Council. All Saints and St Leonards were wholly owned by Peter Brown, tragically killed in a road
accident in late 2005. Ownership has passed to Peter's 3 children, Eliza, Angela and Nicholas, and
it is the intention to keep the business in the family. Exports to the US.

ΨΨΨΨΨ **Rare Rutherglen Tokay NV** Deeper colour than the Grand; completely fills
the mouth with layers of flavour; malt, Christmas cake, butterscotch and
anything else you care to name, but is never cloyingly sweet. Cork. 18° alc.
Rating 96 **To** 2008 $107.50
Rare Rutherglen Muscat NV Deep brown, olive rim; very complex, with a
balance of extreme age and a touch of youthful freshness; raisin, dark chocolate
and Christmas pudding flavours sit within a strong nutty, rancio framework on
the luscious mid-palate, then the touch of youth helps create the cleansing, dry
finish. **Rating** 96 **To** 2008 $110
Grand Rutherglen Tokay NV Deep olive tawny; complex, intense and perfectly
balanced; flavours of malt, toffee and cold tea, the finish lingering on and on.
Rating 94 **To** 2008 $62

ΥΥΥΥΥ **Marsanne 2004** A similar sophisticated touch; 18 months in older oak provides structure rather than flavour; delicate notes of honeysuckle; very good length; 50-year-old vines. Cork. 13.8° alc. **Rating** 93 **To** 2011 $26

Estate Rutherglen Chardonnay 2004 Sophisticated winemaking from vineyard to the bottle overcomes the limitations of the region; cashew, melon and stone fruit, with excellent balance and length. Wild yeast and the works. Cork. 13.8° alc. **Rating** 91 **To** 2010 $26

Estate Rutherglen Durif 2003 A full-bodied, densely layered palate with black fruits, earth and bitter chocolate; a huge mouthful with great structure. A long future if the cork permits. 15° alc. **Rating** 91 **To** 2023 $49

Family Cellar Rutherglen Chardonnay 2004 Well-made; well-balanced fruit and oak, the alcohol under control; nectarine fruit, supported by good acidity, is ageing well. Cork. 13.8° alc. **Rating** 90 **To** 2009 $26

Family Reserve Marsanne 2004 Makes a strongly varietal statement from the outset; almond, pear and honeysuckle aromas and flavours; developing nicely, and should continue to do so. Cork. 13.8° alc. **Rating** 90 **To** 2010 $26.50

Family Cellar Rutherglen Shiraz 2004 Medium-bodied; quite elegant, and strictly counter-cultural to normal Northeast Victoria reds; perhaps slimmed down a little too much. Cork. 14.2° alc. **Rating** 90 **To** 2012 $49

Classic Rutherglen Tokay NV Pale gold; vibrant and fresh apricot, tea-leaf and butterscotch flavours; would not be heretical to serve it on the rocks in the height of summer. Cork. 18° alc. **Rating** 90 **To** 2008 $19.50

ΥΥΥΥ **Limited Release Rutherglen Marsanne Viognier 2006** A gentle synergy between the 2 varieties, the marsanne providing spine and acidity, the viognier apricot and peach flesh. Screwcap. 14° alc. **Rating** 88 **To** 2010 $19

Estate Rutherglen Durif 2004 A typical robust wine, though not entirely muscle-bound; a mix of black fruits and touches of spice, the tannins and extract controlled. Cork. 14° alc. **Rating** 88 **To** 2014 $23

Estate Rutherglen Chardonnay 2006 Ripe but not over the top peachy fruit; unoaked, and a little simple, but has flavour. Cork. 13.6° alc. **Rating** 87 **To** 2008 $18

Allandale ★★★★

132 Lovedale Road, Lovedale, NSW 2321 **Region** Lower Hunter Valley
T (02) 4990 4526 **www.**allandalewinery.com.au **Open** Mon–Sat 9–5, Sun 10–5
Winemaker Bill Sneddon, Rod Russell **Est.** 1978 **Cases** 20 000
Owners Wally and Judith Atallah have overseen the growth of Allandale from a small, cellar door operation to a substantial business. Allandale has developed a reputation for its Chardonnay, but offers a broad range of wines of consistently good quality, including red wines variously sourced from the Hilltops, Orange and Mudgee. Exports to the UK, the US and other major markets.

ΥΥΥΥΥ **Orange Sauvignon Blanc 2006** Light straw-green; totally clean tropical/passionfruit aromas; an attractive, generous style à la Marlborough, finishing with a touch of sweetness. Screwcap. 12.5° alc. **Rating** 91 **To** 2008 $18

Hunter Valley Chardonnay 2004 Nice wine, quite complex and powerful, but with a slightly broken line. Not sweet, however. **Rating** 90 **To** 2010 $18

Allison Valley Wines

RSM 457 North Jindong Road, Busselton, WA 6280 (postal) **Region** Margaret River
T (08) 9368 6370 **F** (08) 9474 1804 **www.**allisonvalley.com.au **Open** Not
Winemaker Harmans Ridge Estate (Paul Green) **Est.** 1997 **Cases** 2000
The Porter family planted 10 ha of semillon, sauvignon blanc, shiraz and cabernet sauvignon with the sole intention of selling the grapes to other winemakers in the region. However, as has been the case with hundreds of other such ventures, the family has decided to have some of the production vinified under the Allison Valley label. Exports to Hong Kong, China and Taiwan.

🍷🍷🍷🍷🍷 **Margaret River Semillon Sauvignon Blanc 2005** Spotlessly clean; a range of flavours, headed by tropical but balanced by herb and grass; good length. Screwcap. 14° alc. **Rating** 90 **To** 2008 $13.50

Margaret River Shiraz 2004 Utterly unexpected richness and weight at this price and provenance; lots of blackberry and spicy black cherry fruit; good, ripe tannins, the oak irrelevant. Twin top. 14.5° alc. **Rating** 90 **To** 2015 $13.50

🍷🍷🍷🍷 **Margaret River Semillon Sauvignon Blanc 2006** The bouquet is clean but closed, the wine opening up on the palate with good length to its citrus and kiwifruit. Screwcap. **Rating** 89 **To** 2008 $13.50

Margaret River Cabernet Merlot 2004 Masses of flavour, just a tad uncomfortably sweet, though balanced on the finish by tannins. Twin top. 14.3° alc. **Rating** 88 **To** 2013 $13.50

Margaret River Cabernet Sauvignon 2004 Something on the bouquet warns you that despite the quite sweet fruit, there are tannins on the prowl which need taming; still, good value. Cork. 14.3° alc. **Rating** 88 **To** 2016 $13.50

Alta Wines ★★★★

PO Box 63, Mt Torrens, SA 5244 **Region** Adelaide Hills
T 0434 077 059 **F** (08) 8389 5193 **Open** Not
Winemaker Sarah Fletcher **Est.** NA **Cases** 6000

Sarah Fletcher comes to Alta with an impressive winemaking background: a degree from Roseworthy, and thereafter 7 years working for Orlando Wyndham as both red and white winemaker. She came face to face with grapes from all over Australia, and developed a particular regard for those coming from the Adelaide Hills. She became financially involved with Alta in 2005, making the '05 Sauvignon Blanc, her first under the Alta brand. The range is being extended with varieties suited to the cool climate of the Adelaide Hills. Exports to the UK and Canada.

🍷🍷🍷🍷🍷 **Adelaide Hills Sauvignon Blanc 2006** Pale straw-green; aromas of nettle, grass and asparagus, the flavours moving more to passionfruit; a lively wine, with lots of interest. Screwcap. 12° alc. **Rating** 93 **To** 2008 $20

🍷🍷🍷🍷 **Pinot Noir for Elsie Rose 2006** Light-bodied, but has unusual textural interest, and is as near to dry as any rose; spicy, almost earthy mouthfeel and flavours which are quite compelling. Screwcap. 12° alc. **Rating** 89 **To** 2008 $18

Amadio Wines ★★★★☆

633 Lower North East Road, Campbelltown, SA 2074 **Region** Adelaide Hills
T (08) 8365 5988 **F** (08) 8336 2462 **www**.movingjuice.com.au **Open** Mon–Wed & Fri 9–5.30, Thurs 9–7, Sat 9–5
Winemaker Danniel Amadio **Est.** 2004 **Cases** 25 000

Danniel Amadio says he has followed in the footsteps of his Italian grandfather, selling wine from his cellar (cantina) direct to the consumer, cutting out wholesale and distribution. He also draws upon the business of his parents, built not in Italy, but in Australia. Amadio Wines has over 100 ha of vineyards, in the Adelaide Hills, Clare Valley and McLaren Vale, covering just about every variety imaginable, and – naturally – with a very strong representation of Italian varieties.

🍷🍷🍷🍷🍷 **Block 2A Reserve Shiraz 2004** Light- to medium-bodied; elegant, attractive spicy/savoury nuances with touches of bitter chocolate; fine tannins and subtle oak; lovely cool-climate style. Cork. 14.5° alc. **Rating** 94 **To** 2012 $25

Sebastien's Adelaide Hills Cabernet Sauvignon 2004 A clean bouquet; more savoury and a little more elegant than the McLaren Vale version; fine tannins and excellent line and length. Cork. 14.5° alc. **Rating** 94 **To** 2019 $20

🍷🍷🍷🍷🍷 **Adelaide Hills Sauvignon Blanc 2006** Spotlessly clean; an intense and firm palate with herb, grass and some gooseberry; excellent length. Screwcap. 12.5° alc. **Rating** 93 **To** 2008 $18

Adelaide Hills Shiraz 2005 Clean, fragrant black fruit aromas; blackberry and plum fruit with a gentle touch of mocha/vanilla oak; fine tannins to close. Great value. Screwcap. 14.5° alc. **Rating** 93 **To** 2015 $15

McLaren Vale Cabernet Sauvignon 2004 A generous, medium- to full-bodied wine, with ripe cassis/blackcurrant fruit and lashings of chocolate; ripe tannins; very attractive style. Screwcap. 14° alc. **Rating** 93 **To** 2024 $18

ŸŸŸŸ **Merlot Rose 2005** Bright fuchsia; clean, fresh red fruits; attractive back-palate and finish; good balance. Screwcap. 12.5° alc. **Rating** 89 **To** 2008 $13

Adelaide Hills Sangiovese 2004 Light red-purple; savoury, spicy, cherry varietal fruit on a light- to medium-bodied palate; good varietal identity. Screwcap. 13.5° alc. **Rating** 89 **To** 2010 $21

Adelaide Hills Semillon Sauvignon Blanc 2006 Overall gently sweet fruit flavours, nicely balanced and welcoming drink now style. Screwcap. 12.5° alc. **Rating** 88 **To** 2008 $16

Rosso Quattro 2005 Not surprisingly, a kaleidoscope of aromas and flavours, mostly in the red fruit spectrum; light- to medium-bodied with minimal tannins. Barbera/Merlot/Sangiovese/Grenache. Screwcap. 14° alc. **Rating** 88 **To** 2010 $18

Clare Valley Riesling 2005 Medium green-straw, showing some development; a generous, full-bodied wine (in riesling terms) with ripe tropical fruit; slightly short finish. Screwcap. 12.5° alc. **Rating** 87 **To** 2009 $18

Adelaide Hills Chardonnay 2005 Light straw-yellow; soft stone fruit and melon, with some creamy notes, and relatively low acidity; easy style. Screwcap. 13.5° alc. **Rating** 87 **To** 2008 $16

Adelaide Hills Pinot Noir 2004 Holding hue well; like the '05, more to dry red, but does have cherry fruit, and the tannins are less assertive. Screwcap. 14.5° alc. **Rating** 87 **To** 2010 $22

Amarillo Vines   NR

27 Marlock Place, Karnup, WA 6176 **Region** Peel
T (08) 9537 1800 **F** (08) 9537 1800 **www**.rockinghamvisitorcentre.com.au/amarillovines
Open 7 days 10–5, or by appt
Winemaker Phil Franzone (Contract) **Est.** 1995 **Cases** NA

Ambar Hill   ★★★

1/57–59 Oxford Street, Bulimba, Qld 4171 (postal) **Region** Granite Belt
T (07) 3899 9146 **F** (07) 3899 9410 **www**.ambarhill.com.au **Open** Not
Winemaker Jim Barnes **Est.** 2001 **Cases** 500
Graham and Judy Dalton have planted just under 2 ha of shiraz, cabernet, merlot, verdelho, chardonnay and semillon, the first wine produced in 2003. Both have varied backgrounds stretching back to Canberra in the Whitlam era. Graham Dalton is an economist-turned-restaurateur to prison reform consultant to running the Queensland Farmer's Federation. The wines, incidentally, are only sold wholesale through Fino Food + Wine of Bulimba, Qld.

Amberley Edge Vineyard   NR

47 Clark Lane, Stanthorpe, Qld 4380 **Region** Granite Belt
T (07) 4683 6203 **F** (07) 4683 6203 **www**.amberleyedge.com.au **Open** 7 days 10–5
Winemaker (Grant Casley) Contract **Est.** 2005 **Cases** NA
Former Victorians Trevor and Carolyn Sharp acquired a 29-ha property at Severnlea after moving to Qld. They have planted 1.5 ha each of shiraz and black muscat, 0.75 ha of chardonnay, 0.25 ha of merlot, and a few vines of cabernet sauvignon; all of the vines are dry-grown. The cellar door has great views of the surrounding country, and complements the stone B&B accommodation.

Amberley Estate

Thornton Road, Yallingup, WA 6282 **Region** Margaret River
T (08) 9755 2288 **F** (08) 9755 2171 **www**1.amberleyestate.com.au **Open** 7 days 10–4.30
Winemaker Paul Dunnewyk **Est.** 1986 **Cases** 120 000
Based on its initial growth on its ultra-commercial, fairly sweet Chenin Blanc, which continues to
provide the volume for the brand. However, the quality of all the other wines has risen markedly
over recent years as the 31 ha of estate plantings have become fully mature. Purchased by Canadian
company Vincor in early 2004. Exports to the UK and the US.

ΨΨΨΨΨ **First Selection Shiraz 2003** Red-purple; a medium-bodied, vibrant, fresh and
elegant palate offering raspberry, black cherry and fine tannins; judicious oak. Cork.
14° alc. **Rating** 94 **To** 2015 $36

ΨΨΨΨΨ **First Selection Chardonnay 2004** Pale, bright straw-green; a restrained, elegant
style; nectarine and citrus within an overall minerally frame; subtle oak. Screwcap.
13.5° alc. **Rating** 92 **To** 2010 $36
Margaret River Shiraz 2003 At the opposite end of the spectrum to the
First Selection Shiraz, strongly coloured, with powerful, complex black fruits
and substantial black tannins. Still gathering pace. Screwcap. 14° alc. **Rating** 91
To 2018 $16.99

ΨΨΨΨ **Chardonnay 2005** Light straw-green; a somewhat gritty/minerally style; touches
of stone fruit and minimal oak. Screwcap. 13.5° alc. **Rating** 87 **To** 2009 $22
Chimney Brush Margaret River Shiraz 2004 More southern than northern
Margaret River style; light, spicy aromas and flavours; lacks concentration. Screwcap.
14° alc. **Rating** 87 **To** 2010 $21.99

Ambrook Wines

Lot 198 West Swan Road, Caversham, WA 6055 **Region** Swan Valley
T (08) 9274 1003 **F** (08) 9379 0334 **www**.ambrookwines.com.au **Open** Wed–Fri 12–5,
w'ends & public hols 10–5
Winemaker Rob Marshall **Est.** 1990 **Cases** 1500
Mickele and Kaz Amonini purchased the property several years ago, and have built a large, low-
slung winery on the site. Some of the vines (grenache and muscat) which still thrive on the
property were planted in 1945 by the Waldeck family, and have been carefully tended by successive
owners since that time. The plantings now extend to 4 acres of chenin blanc, semillon, verdelho,
shiraz, cabernet sauvignon and merlot, the wines being well-made by Rob Marshall.

Amherst Winery

Talbot-Avoca Road, Amherst, Vic 3371 **Region** Pyrenees
T (03) 5463 2105 **www**.amherstwinery.com **Open** W'ends & public hols 10–5
Winemaker Graham Jukes (Red), Paul Lesock (White) **Est.** 1991 **Cases** 1200
Norman and Elizabeth Jones have planted 4 ha of vines on a property with an extraordinarily
rich history, a shorthand reflection of which is seen in the name Dunn's Paddock Shiraz. This
variety dominates the planting, with 3.4 ha; the rest is cabernet sauvignon and chardonnay. Samuel
Knowles was a convict who arrived in Van Diemen's Land in 1838. He endured continuous
punishment before fleeing to SA in 1846 and changing his name to Dunn. When, at the end of
1851, he married 18-year-old Mary Therese Taaffe in Adelaide, they walked from Adelaide to
Amherst pushing a wheelbarrow carrying their belongings. They had 14 children, and Samuel
Dunn died in 1898, a highly respected citizen; his widow lived until 1923. Exports to China.

ΨΨΨΨΨ **Lachlan's Pyrenees Chardonnay 2006** Bright and bursting with nectarine
and grapefruit flavours; great length and vivacity; 30% barrel ferment then
4 months in oak has given the best of both worlds. Major surprise for the
region. Screwcap. 12.5° alc. **Rating** 94 **To** 2011 $18
Dunn's Paddock Pyrenees Shiraz 2005 A deep, rich blackberry, prune and
plum assemblage; a long, balanced finish; no issues with either the alcohol or the
tannins. Screwcap. 14.8° alc. **Rating** 94 **To** 2020 $25

ŢŢŢŢ♀ **Daisy Creek Pyrenees Shiraz Cabernet 2005** Deep colour; rich, ripe, multi-layered black fruits; not extractive, and thoroughly impressive at this alcohol level; ripe tannins in balance. What a bargain; 60%/40%. Screwcap. 13.7° alc. **Rating** 93 **To** 2015 $15

Chinese Gardens Pyrenees Cabernet Sauvignon 2005 Intense blackcurrant and cassis, but also leaf, olive and earth within the varietal spectrum, but overall confronts rather than caresses. Screwcap. 13.7° alc. **Rating** 90 **To** 2020 $25

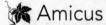 # Amicus

Rifle Range Road, McLaren Vale, SA 5171 **Region** McLaren Vale
T (08) 8373 6811 **F** (08) 8299 9500 **www**.amicuswines.com.au **Open** Not
Winemaker Walter Clappis, Kimberly Clappis **Est.** 2002 **Cases** 2000
Amicus is a venture bred in the purple. Its owners are 30-year industry veteran (and former Ingoldby owner) Walter William Wilfred Clappis (he has always provided his name in full), wife Kerry, plus Amanda and Tony Vanstone and Robert and Diana Hill, known in an altogether different environment. The grapes come in part from the Clappis' McLaren Vale vineyard (run on biodynamic principles) and from grapes purchased from growers in Langhorne Creek.

ŢŢŢŢŢ **Reserve Shiraz 2004** A rich, succulent and seductive marriage of Langhorne Creek shiraz and 18 months in new French oak; those lovely soft tannins of Langhorne Creek bring the wine to a harmonious close. Cork. 14.5° alc. **Rating** 94 **To** 2024 $42

ŢŢŢŢ♀ **Shiraz Cabernet Malbec 2004** A medium-bodied, supple wine; the varietal flavours each make a discernible contribution, without breaking the line of the wine. Even the malbec adds a touch of juiciness to the black fruits, spice and oak of the blend. Screwcap. 14° alc. **Rating** 93 **To** 2019 $22

The Hedonist McLaren Vale Shiraz 2005 Strong colour; powerful regional blackberry, dark chocolate, warm vanilla oak and soft tannins; indeed, the pig satisfied. Screwcap. 14.5° alc. **Rating** 92 **To** 2020 $19

Amietta Vineyard

30 Steddy Road, Lethbridge, Vic 3332 **Region** Geelong
T (03) 5281 7407 **F** (03) 5281 7427 **www**.amietta.com.au **Open** By appt
Winemaker Nicholas Clark, Janet Cockbill **Est.** 1995 **Cases** 450
Janet Cockbill and Nicholas Clark are multi-talented. Both are archaeologists, but Janet manages to combine part-time archaeology, part-time radiography at Geelong Hospital and part-time organic viticulture. Nicholas Clark has nearly completed a viticulture degree at Charles Sturt University, and both he and Janet worked vintage in France at Michel Chapoutier's biodynamic Domaine de Beates in Provence in 2001. Amietta is producing cameo wines of some beauty.

ŢŢŢŢ **Geelong Riesling 2006** Clean, light, fresh, with green apple and citrus aromas; will develop. Screwcap. 11.3° alc. **Rating** 89 **To** 2014 $20

Anakie Ridge Vineyard

2290 Ballan Road, Anakie, Vic 3221 **Region** Geelong
T 0409 418 175 **F** (03) 5222 3157 **Open** W'ends 11–5
Winemaker Ernesto Vellucci **Est.** 1998 **Cases** NFP
Leo and Isobel Gold planted 2 ha of cabernet sauvignon and 0.8 ha of chardonnay in the spring of 1998, leading to the first vintage in 2001. The winemaking techniques are traditional: small vat fermentation, minimum time in oak and minimal filtration. The Pinot Noir comes from the Quarry Vineyard at Waurn Ponds, the Shiraz from Sutherlands Creek Vineyard.

Anderson

Lot 12 Chiltern Road, Rutherglen, Vic 3685 **Region** Rutherglen
T (02) 6032 8111 **F** (02) 6032 7151 **www.**andersonwinery.com.au **Open** 7 days 10–5
Winemaker Howard Anderson, Christobelle Anderson **Est.** 1992 **Cases** 2000
Having notched up a winemaking career spanning over 30 years, including a stint at Seppelt (Great Western), Howard Anderson and family started their own winery, initially with a particular focus on sparkling wine but now extending across all table wine styles. There are 4 ha of estate shiraz, and 1 ha each of durif and petit verdot, with yields controlled at a very low 2.5 tonnes per ha.

🍷🍷🍷🍷🍷 **Cellar Block Durif 2004** Deep colour; layer upon layer of blackberry and plum jam plus chocolate surrounds and a dusting of spice; fine tannins and a bright finish. Cork. 14° alc. **Rating** 94 **To** 2025 $32

🍷🍷🍷🍷🍷 **Cellar Block Petit Verdot 2004** Typical impenetrable colour; marches to the tune of its own big base drum, with thickly textured licorice, prune and dark chocolate flavours, yet the tannins barely evident. Cork. 16° alc. **Rating** 93 **To** 2029 $32

Andrew Harris Vineyards

Sydney Road, Mudgee, NSW 2850 **Region** Mudgee
T (02) 6373 1213 **F** (02) 6373 1296 **www.**andrewharris.com.au **Open** 7 days 9–5
Winemaker Lisa Bray **Est.** 1991 **Cases** 65 000
Andrew and Deb Harris got away to a flying start after purchasing a 300-ha sheep station and planting it with 106 ha of vines. The early red wine releases had considerable show success, but these days the accent seems to be on relatively low prices, rather than on quality. Exports to the UK, the US, Canada, Denmark, Switzerland, Dubai, Malaysia, Thailand, China, Japan and NZ.

🍷🍷🍷🍷🍷 **Personal Selection Hilltops Shiraz 2003** Firm, direct cool-grown blackberry and pepper aromas; long and persistent flavours and tannins; still very youthful. Cork. 14° alc. **Rating** 92 **To** 2023 $24.95
Harvest Road Mudgee Shiraz Cabernet 2005 Bright purple-red; excellent, clear-cut fruit, with blackberry and some cherry; good acidity and length, tannins balanced and oak integrated. Value plus. Cork. 13.5° alc. **Rating** 90 **To** 2015 $11.95
Personal Selection Mudgee Cabernet Sauvignon 2004 As with the other pairs of Andrew Harris wines, has stronger colour, structure and flavours; supple blackcurrant, spice and cedar flavours; fine tannins. Cork. 13.9° alc. **Rating** 90 **To** 2019 $24.95

🍷🍷🍷🍷 **Personal Selection Mudgee Cabernet Merlot 2005** Altogether firmer and more focused than the Harvest Road, moving more to cassis, olive, bracken and briar, with some black fruit lurking; needs time to sort itself out. Cork. 14.5° alc. **Rating** 88 **To** 2020 $24.95
Highfields Mudgee Merlot 2005 Rich, sweet fruit giving a false impression of higher alcohol than that which is present; a nice red wine, with almost no varietal character. Cork. 14° alc. **Rating** 87 **To** 2011 $14.95
Harvest Road Mudgee Cabernet Merlot 2005 Spicy, savoury aromas; medium-bodied; well-balanced and constructed commercial wine, with a little less oak influence better still. Twin top. 13.5° alc. **Rating** 87 **To** 2011 $11.95

Andrew Peace Wines

Murray Valley Highway, Piangil, Vic 3597 **Region** Swan Hill
T (03) 5030 5291 **www.**apwines.com **Open** Mon–Fri 8–5, Sat 12–4, Sun by appt
Winemaker Andrew Peace, Nina Viergutz **Est.** 1995 **Cases** 400 000
The Peace family has been a major Swan Hill grapegrower since 1980, with 100 ha of vineyards, moving into winemaking with the opening of a $3 million winery in 1996. The modestly priced wines are aimed at supermarket-type outlets in Australia and exports to all major markets.

Angas Plains Estate

Lot 52 Angas Plains Road, Langhorne Creek, SA 5255 **Region** Langhorne Creek
T (08) 8537 3159 www.angasplainswines.com.au **Open** W'ends & public hols 10–5
Winemaker Judy Cross (Contract) **Est.** 2000 **Cases** 2000
Angas Plains Estate is 10 mins drive south from the historic town of Strathalbyn, on the banks of
the Angas River. Owners Phillip and Judy Cross employ organic measures to tend their 24 ha
of shiraz, cabernet sauvignon and chardonnay. Exports to the US, China and Malaysia.

ΥΥΥΥΥ **Special Reserve Langhorne Creek Cabernet Sauvignon 2004** Dense black
fruits; very good texture and structure; the fruit has absorbed almost 2 years in new
French oak; impressively long finish. High-quality cork. 14.5° alc. **Rating** 94
To 2019 $28

ΥΥΥΥΥ **PJ's Langhorne Creek Cabernet Sauvignon 2005** Medium red-purple;
attractive, sweet blackcurrant and cassis fruit on the medium-bodied palate, rounded
off with a touch of chocolate and appealing French oak. Cork. 14.5° alc. **Rating** 90
To 2015 $18

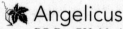 Angelicus   NR

PO Box 723, Manjimup, WA 6258 **Region** Pemberton
T (08) 9772 3003 **F** (08) 9772 3153 www.angelicus.com.au **Open** Not
Winemaker John Ward **Est.** 1997 **Cases** NA
Dr John and Sue Ward moved from Sydney to Middlesex in the Pemberton Region with the
sole aim of establishing a premium quality vineyard, having taken 2 years to select the right site.
It's a busy life; John continues to work as a medical practitioner simultaneously completing a
wine science degree at Charles Sturt University, and Sue manages the vineyard while
undertaking a business degree at Adelaide University following on many years in the hospitality
industry as a caterer and restaurateur. They have planted pinot noir, followed by sauvignon
blanc, merlot, cabernet sauvignon, chardonnay and tempranillo.

Angove's

Bookmark Avenue, Renmark, SA 5341 **Region** Riverland
T (08) 8580 3100 **F** (08) 8580 3155 www.angoves.com.au **Open** Mon–Fri 9–5
Winemaker Warrick Billings, Shane Clohesy, Tony Ingle **Est.** 1886 **Cases** 1.8 million
Exemplifies the economies of scale achievable in the Riverland without compromising
potential quality. Very good technology provides wines which are never poor and sometimes
exceed their theoretical station in life; the white varietals are best. Angove's expansion into
Padthaway has resulted in estate-grown premium wines at the top of the range. Exports to all
major markets.

ΥΥΥΥΥ **Nine Vines Grenache Shiraz Rose 2006** An unusually complex rose, with
more structure than usual; has excellent length and balance; good acidity. Screwcap.
12.5° alc. **Rating** 94 To 2008 $15

ΥΥΥΥΥ **Vineyard Select McLaren Vale Shiraz 2004** Strong red-purple; archetypal
McLaren Vale blackberry and dark chocolate fruit; controlled extract and oak.
Stained cork a worry. 14.5° alc. **Rating** 90 To 2010 $18

ΥΥΥΥ **Vineyard Select Coonawarra Cabernet Sauvignon 2004** Medium- to full-
bodied, with blackcurrant, mulberry and mocha; persistent tannins should soften.
Cork. 13.5° alc. **Rating** 89 To 2012 $18
Long Row Cabernet Sauvignon 2004 Excellent wine at the price; has both
structure and varietal character, with ample length, and not forced. Screwcap. 14° alc.
Rating 88 To 2008 $9.99

Angullong Wines

Four Mile Creek Road, Orange, NSW 2800 (postal) **Region** Orange
T (02) 6366 4300 **F** (02) 6466 4399 **www.**angullong.com.au **Open** Not
Winemaker Jon Reynolds **Est.** 1998 **Cases** 4000
The Crossing family (Bill and Hatty, and third generation James and Ben) have owned a 2000-ha
sheep and cattle station for over half a century. Located 40 km south of Orange on the lower
slopes of the Orange region, overlooking the Belubula Valley, 217 ha of vines have been planted
since 1998. In all, there are 13 varieties, with shiraz, cabernet sauvignon and merlot leading the
way. Most of the production is sold to Hunter Valley wineries. Exports to the UK and Denmark.

ŸŸŸŸŸ **Fossil Hill Orange Shiraz Viognier 2005** Dense purple-red, typical of the
blend; extremely powerful and dense, but not extractive; masses of dark plum,
blackberry and licorice plus that unique lift of viognier. A cellaring special from
this up-and-coming region. Screwcap. 14.5° alc. **Rating** 93 To 2025 $19.95
Orange Shiraz Viognier 2005 Good purple-red; firm, somewhat austere,
uncompromising cool-grown style with spicy black fruits. Screwcap. 14.5° alc.
Rating 90 To 2015 $20

ŸŸŸŸ **Orange Sauvignon Blanc 2006** Good focus and intensity; a long palate, ranging
through citrus to gooseberry/tropical/passionfruit flavours. Just a touch too sweet.
Screwcap. 12.5° alc. **Rating** 89 To 2008 $15
Fossil Hill Orange Pinot Gris 2006 Ripe pear and musk aromas and flavours
provide clear varietal character; a slightly sharper jab of acidity might have been
desirable, but there's no doubting the variety. Screwcap. 13.5° alc. **Rating** 88
To 2008 $19.95
Fossil Hill Orange Viognier 2006 A neutral bouquet; the varietal character
comes as much in the texture as it does in the flavour, but avoids the phenolic trap.
Screwcap. 14° alc. **Rating** 88 To 2010 $19.95
Orange Shiraz Viognier 2004 Youthful, spicy, peppery wine; just a little severe,
perhaps. Screwcap. 14° alc. **Rating** 87 To 2013 $20
Fossil Hill Orange Barbera 2006 Bright red-purple; cedar, black cherry and
spice aromas and flavours; overall, slightly savoury, but nicely made. Screwcap. 14.5°
alc. **Rating** 87 To 2010 $19.95

Angus the Bull

PO Box 3016, South Yarra, Vic 3141 **Region** Southeast Australia
T (03) 9820 4077 **F** (03) 9820 4677 **www.**angusthebull.com **Open** Not
Winemaker Hamish MacGowan **Est.** 2002 **Cases** 20 000
Hamish MacGowan, who describes himself as 'a young Australian wine industry professional', has
taken the virtual winery idea to its ultimate conclusion, with a single wine (Cabernet Sauvignon)
designed to be drunk with premium red meat, or, more particularly, a perfectly cooked steak.

Angus Wines

Captain Sturt Road, Hindmarsh Island, SA 5214 **Region** Southern Fleurieu
T (08) 8555 2320 **www.**anguswines.com.au **Open** W'ends & public hols 11–5
Winemaker Boar's Rock (Mike Farmilo), Angas Buchanan **Est.** 1995 **Cases** 3000
Susan and Alistair Angus are pioneer viticulturists on Hindmarsh Island having established
3.75 ha of shiraz and 1.25 ha of semillon. Part is bottled under the Angus Wines label, some
is sold in bulk to other wineries. Every aspect of packaging and marketing the wine has a
sophisticated touch. Exports to the UK, the US and other major markets.

ŸŸŸŸŸ **A3 Shiraz 2005** Dense, dark blackberry, bitter chocolate and licorice; the
tannins barely evident. Given open-fermentation and plunging, the potential
alcohol at picking would have been over 16°. Nonetheless, one can't argue with
the overall quality of the wine once one accepts the style. Screwcap. 15.5° alc.
Rating 94 To 2029 $40

ΨΨΨΨΨ **Sturt Ridge Shiraz 2004** Medium red-purple; medium-bodied, and much better balance; red and black fruits with spicy components; seamless tannins and oak. Screwcap. 14.5° alc. **Rating** 92 **To** 2020 $24

Sturt Ridge Semillon 2006 Spotlessly clean, lemon, spice and mineral aromas and flavours, with good length, but, as with the '05 A3 Shiraz, I'm not convinced by the late picking/high alcohol approach. Screwcap. 13.5° alc. **Rating** 90 **To** 2013 $16

Annapurna Estate   ★★★

Simmonds Creek Road, Mt Beauty, Vic 3698 **Region** Alpine Valleys
T (03) 5754 1356 **F** (03) 5754 4517 **www**.annapurnaestate.com.au **Open** Wed–Sun, public & school hols 10–5
Winemaker Ezio Minutello **Est.** 1989 **Cases** 25 000
Ezio and Wendy Minutello began the establishment of the 21-ha vineyard at 550 m on Mt Beauty in 1989, planted to pinot noir, chardonnay, pinot gris and merlot. Finally, in 1999, the first wines were released. Annapurna, the second highest mountain after Mt Everest, is Nepalese for 'goddess of bountiful harvest and fertility'.

Annie's Lane

Quelltaler Road, Watervale, SA 5452 **Region** Clare Valley
T (08) 8843 0003 **www**.annieslane.com.au **Open** Mon–Fri 8.30–5, w'ends 11–4
Winemaker Mark Robertson **Est.** 1851 **Cases** 201 000
The Clare Valley portfolio of Fosters is sold under the Annie's Lane label, the name coming from Annie Weyman, a turn-of-the-century local identity. A series of outstanding wines have been produced since 1996, Copper Trail being the flagship release. Exports to the UK, the US and NZ.

ΨΨΨΨΨ **Copper Trail Clare Valley Shiraz 2004** A voluptuous wine, with a Joseph's Coat of flavours, but no dead fruit; blackberry, anise, spice, chocolate and vanilla oak. Has the balance and structure for a long life. Screwcap. 15° alc. **Rating** 95 **To** 2029 $53.95

Copper Trail Clare Valley Cabernet Sauvignon 2004 As expected, uncompromisingly full-bodied, but not over-extracted, the tannins in balance with the layers of black fruits. Indeed, the wine is supple all the way through to the finish. Screwcap. 13° alc. **Rating** 95 **To** 2034 $53.95

Clare Valley Shiraz 2004 The elegance of '04 shines through; while still full of black fruit, spice and licorice, it is not heavy nor extractive; long finish; good oak and tannins. Screwcap. 14.5° alc. **Rating** 94 **To** 2024 $20.95

Copper Trail Clare Valley Shiraz Grenache Mourvedre 2004 A serious wine, the shiraz in no way diluted or unduly softened by its blend mates; the flavours are in the black fruit spectrum, but with splashes of red, which give the wine finesse and interest. Screwcap. 12.5° alc. **Rating** 94 **To** 2019 $36.95

ΨΨΨΨΨ **Copper Trail Clare Valley Shiraz Grenache Mourvedre 2002** As it starts towards maturity, the wine has picked up notes of spice and mocha; also, the cooler vintage always invested it with elegance, a character now emphasised. Screwcap. 12.5° alc. **Rating** 93 **To** 2015 $36.95

Semillon Sauvignon Blanc 2006 A neat combination; semillon leads the band in both flavour and structure terms, the sauvignon blanc very much the junior partner. Long finish. Clare Valley (Semillon)/Adelaide Hills (Sauvignon Blanc). Screwcap. 12° alc. **Rating** 92 **To** 2011 $17

Clare Valley Shiraz 2005 Medium- to full-bodied; richly textured and layered blackberry, spice and plum aromas and flavours; oak a positive contributor, the tannins soft. Screwcap. 14.5° alc. **Rating** 91 **To** 2020 $20.95

Clare Valley Riesling 2006 A subdued bouquet, but the palate guarantees the bouquet will open up in due course; the wine has rich lime, tropical and passionfruit flavours. Screwcap. 12.5° alc. **Rating** 90 **To** 2012 $20.95

Clare Valley Rose 2006 Full puce-pink; abundant flavour across the spectrum from plum to red berries; dry; true food rose. Screwcap. 13.5° alc. **Rating** 90 To 2008 $16.95

♥♥♥♥ Clare Valley Chardonnay 2006 More elegance and complexity than usual; clever use of part barrel fermentation and part mlf adds to the wine without diminishing the varietal character. Screwcap. 13° alc. **Rating** 89 To 2010 $20.95 Clare Valley Cabernet Merlot 2005 Medium-bodied; attractive flavour and texture, supple and soft, with a mix of blackcurrant, licorice and cassis, finishing with soft tannins. Highly likely to improve significantly. Screwcap. 14° alc. **Rating** 89 To 2017 $20.95

🍇 Anniebrook

247 Wildwood Road, Carbunup River, WA 6280 **Region** Margaret River
T (08) 9755 1155 **F** (08) 9755 1138 **Open** Sat–Thurs 9.30–4.30
Winemaker James Pennington (Contract) **Est.** 1986 **Cases** 1350
A long time ago Wally Lewis (no relation to the celebrated rugby league player) and wife Dawn were third-generation graziers and sheep farmers. In 1985 they decided they had to find a much larger property further inland for their sheep farming, or radically change their existing business. They opted for the latter, simultaneously planting vines and flowers; there are now 7 ha of semillon, chardonnay, sauvignon blanc, cabernet franc and shiraz, and 2 ha of flowers. For almost 20 years they sold the grapes to a nearby winemaker, but in 2006 took the plunge and contracted James Pennington to make the wines for them. Ambience and the Anniebrook River (which flows through the centre of the property) are ready attractions for cellar door visitors.

♥♥♥♥ Sun Kissed Margaret River Semillon Sauvignon Blanc 2006 Crisp and clean; light-bodied passionfruit and citrus mix flow evenly on the palate, but the wine needs more intensity. Screwcap. 12.5° alc. **Rating** 87 To 2008 $16 Wildwood Margaret River Rose 2006 Bright fuchsia; has positive cherry and plum fruit, rather than residual sugar, providing the flavour. Screwcap. 13° alc. **Rating** 87 To 2008 $16

Antcliff's Chase

RMB 4510, Caveat via Seymour, Vic 3660 **Region** Strathbogie Ranges
T (03) 5790 4333 **F** (03) 5790 4333 **Open** W'ends 10–5
Winemaker Chris Bennett, Ian Leamon **Est.** 1982 **Cases** 800
A small family enterprise that began with planting the vineyards at an elevation of 600 m in the Strathbogie Ranges in 1982; wine production from the 4-ha vineyard commenced in the early 1990s. After an uncertain start, wine quality has picked up considerably.

♥♥♥♥♡ Riesling 2005 Clean, plenty of citrus-accented fruit; has the length many of the other Strathbogie Ranges rieslings lack. **Rating** 91 To 2012

Anvers Wines

Lot 11 Main Road, McLaren Vale, SA 5171 **Region** Adelaide Hills
T (08) 8323 9603 **F** (08) 8323 9502 www.anvers.com.au **Open** 7 days 10–5
Winemaker Kym Milne **Est.** 1998 **Cases** 7000
Myriam and Wayne Keoghan established Anvers Wines with the emphasis on quality rather than quantity. The first Cabernet Sauvignon was made in 1998, and volume has increased markedly since then. The quality of the wines is exemplary, no doubt underwriting the increase in production and expansion of markets both across Australia and in most major export markets.

♥♥♥♥♡ Adelaide Hills Semillon Sauvignon Blanc 2006 Delicate yet quite complex, thanks to some barrel ferment in French oak; mainstream kiwifruit, apple and citrus flavours; clean finish. Screwcap. 13° alc. **Rating** 91 To 2010 $16 Langhorne Creek Cabernet Sauvignon 2004 Rich, ripe and full-bodied; lush blackcurrant and some dark chocolate; warm finish. Cork. 14.5° alc. **Rating** 91 To 2019 $28

The Warrior Shiraz 2004 Medium-bodied; the delicacy of the wine is at odds with the extraordinary weight of the bottle and the tale of the terrible fight which gave rise to the name; spicy red fruits; ready now or whenever. Cork. 14.5° alc. **Rating** 90 **To** 2012 $45

21 Years Old Rare Tawny NV Red tinges in the colour suggest freshening with younger material (no problem, because the 21 years is an average age). A powerful tawny, with biscuity/Christmas cake spice flavours, and brisk spirit. Cork. 19° alc. **Rating** 90 **To** 2008 $42

ΥΥΥΥ **Langhorne Creek Cabernet Sauvignon 2003** Firm, savoury, earthy medium-bodied wine, with a long palate. Not the tail-wagging sort. Cork. 14° alc. **Rating** 89 **To** 2013 $28

Razorback Road Fortified Shiraz 2005 Spicy red and black fruits and a splash of licorice; clean spirit; modern style, with lower baume. Cork. 19° alc. **Rating** 89 **To** 2012 $25

Brabo Adelaide Hills Cabernet Shiraz 2006 Intense, deep, youthful purple-red; sweet cassis black fruits; either no oak or very little; ideal with a cheap pizza, and doesn't destroy the bank balance. Screwcap. 14° alc. **Rating** 87 **To** 2008 $12

Arakoon   ★★★★★

229 Main Road, McLaren Vale, SA 5171 **Region** McLaren Vale
T (08) 8323 7339 **F** (02) 6566 6288 **Open** Fri–Sun 10–5, or by appt
Winemaker Raymond Jones **Est.** 1999 **Cases** 3500
Ray and Patrik (sic) Jones' first venture into wine came to nothing: a 1990 proposal for a film about the Australian wine industry with myself as anchorman. Five years too early, say the Joneses. In 1999 they took the plunge into making their own wine, and exporting it along with the wines of others. As the quality of the wines has increased, so has the originally zany labelling been replaced with simple, but elegant, labels. Exports to the UK, Germany, Denmark, Belgium, Sweden, Holland, Canada, Singapore and Malaysia.

ΥΥΥΥΥ **Doyen Willunga Shiraz 2005** Absolutely floods the mouth with flavours ranging through blackberry, spice and dark chocolate; no hint of dead fruit or high alcohol, simply good structure. Screwcap. 14.5° alc. **Rating** 95 **To** 2025 $45

Doyen Willunga Shiraz 2004 Deep red-purple; medium- to full-bodied; flooded with rich blackberry, satsuma plum and dark chocolate backed up by quality French oak. Soft tannins. Screwcap. 14.5° alc. **Rating** 95 **To** 2015 $45

Clarendon Shiraz 2005 More spice/dark chocolate/mocha flavours than the Blewitt Springs Shiraz, but not at the expense of black cherry and blackberry fruit; this is unequivocally elegant. Screwcap. 13.5° alc. **Rating** 94 **To** 2020 $30

Sellicks Beach Shiraz 2005 Deep red-purple; plush, velvety, richly textured wine with multi-flavoured black fruits; a long palate with fine tannins and oak in support. Screwcap. 14.5° alc. **Rating** 94 **To** 2025 $20

Blewitt Springs Shiraz 2005 Layers of blackberry fruit and dark chocolate; fine tannins become evident early on the palate; balanced alcohol another plus. Screwcap. 14.5° alc. **Rating** 94 **To** 2025 $30

ΥΥΥΥΥ **Full Bodied Red McLaren Vale Grenache Shiraz Mataro 2004** Abundant black and red fruits; very good structure and texture; the undeniably lurid label features a painting by artist Jennifer England purchased by Ray Jones (Arakoon winemaker). Screwcap. 14.5° alc. **Rating** 93 **To** 2014 $18

Gap Beach Fleurieu Shiraz 2004 Medium-bodied; excellent texture, structure and mouthfeel; spicy edges to black fruit flavours; fine tannins and balanced oak. Screwcap. 14° alc. **Rating** 92 **To** 2014 $20

The Lighthouse McLaren Vale Cabernet Sauvignon 2005 Slightly savoury aromas quickly give way to a palate charged with black fruits, regional chocolate and firm but ripe tannins. Screwcap. 14.5° alc. **Rating** 92 **To** 2017 $20

Good on Ya Fleurieu Viognier 2005 Stacked with varietal apricot fruit, bordering on dried apricot. Rich, but little or no phenolics. Screwcap. 13.5° alc. **Rating** 90 **To** 2008 $22

The Lighthouse McLaren Vale Cabernet Sauvignon 2004 Strong red-purple; an interesting wine; fine, slightly chewy tannins from both the fruit and oak run through the length of the bitter chocolate and blackcurrant fruit flavours. Screwcap. 14.5° alc. **Rating** 90 **To** 2015 $20

Aramis Vineyards ★★★★☆

PO Box 208, Marleston, SA 5033 **Region** McLaren Vale
T (08) 8238 0000 **F** (08) 8234 0485 **www**.aramisvineyards.com **Open** Not
Winemaker Scott Rawlinson **Est.** 1998 **Cases** 4000
The estate vineyards have been planted to just 2 varieties: shiraz (18 ha) and cabernet sauvignon (8 ha). Viticulturist David Mills is a third-generation McLaren Vale resident and has been involved in the establishment of the vineyards from the very beginning. Winemaker Scott Rawlinson was with Mildara Blass for 8 years before joining the Aramis team under the direction of owner Lee Flourentzou. Exports to the UK, the US, Canada, Singapore and Hong Kong.

ɡɡɡɡɡ **The Black Label Shiraz 2004** Deep, inky red-purple; powerful and deep, but supple; a well of black fruits and spices; controlled oak, good tannins. Cork. **Rating** 94 **To** 2019 $28

ɡɡɡɡɡ **The Governor Shiraz 2003** Dense purple-red; potent, powerful, in-your-face black fruits; strong tannins, but in balance. Cork. **Rating** 92 **To** 2013 $45
The Black Label Cabernet Sauvignon 2004 A high-toned bouquet, with a curious mix of mint, blackcurrant and cassis flowing through to the palate; has textural focus and length. Cork. **Rating** 91 **To** 2015 $28

Arimia Margaret River NR

Quininup Road, Wilyabrup, WA 6280 **Region** Margaret River
T (08) 9287 2411 **F** (08) 9287 2422 **www**.arimia.com.au **Open** Not
Winemaker Harmans Ridge **Est.** 1998 **Cases** NA
Anne Spencer and Malcolm Washbourne purchased their 55-ha property overlooking the Indian Ocean, and its northern boundaries marked by the Cape Naturaliste National Park, in 1997. Quininup Creek meanders through the property, providing the water source for its blue-green dam. The name is a combination of daughters Mia and Ariann. They have planted a Joseph's Coat array of varieties, the Short Story wines coming from the traditional range of white varietals (semillon, sauvignon blanc, verdelho, chardonnay), the Full Story wines featuring cabernet sauvignon, merlot, petit verdot, shiraz, grenache, mourvedre and zinfandel.

Arlewood Estate ★★★★★

Harmans Road South, Wilyabrup, WA 6284 **Region** Margaret River
T (08) 9755 6267 **F** (08) 9755 6267 **www**.arlewood.com.au **Open** Sat 11–5 by appt
Winemaker Ian Bell, Mark Messenger **Est.** 1988 **Cases** 7000
The Gosatti and Heydon families acquired Arlewood Estate in 1999, having previously established a small vineyard in Cowaramup in 1995, and have expanded the vineyard to 15 ha. Garry Gosatti has been involved in the boutique brewing and hospitality industries for many years, and the Gosatti family acquired sole ownership in 2005. Exports to the UK and other major markets.

ɡɡɡɡɡ **Single Vineyard Estate Margaret River Semillon Sauvignon Blanc 2006** A powerful and complex, medium- to full-bodied, wine tending to white Bordeaux in style; tangy citrus fruit has stood up to 18 months in French oak; excellent balance; 50/50 blend. Screwcap. 13° alc. **Rating** 94 **To** 2015 $20
Margaret River Chardonnay 2004 At first sight understated, but there is no shortage of fruit, and there is a gentle creamy/nutty substrate, the mlf seeming to have played a significant role. Screwcap. 13.5° alc. **Rating** 94 **To** 2017 $38

ŶŶŶŶŶ **Single Vineyard Estate Margaret River Semillon 2005** Plenty of varietal fruit impact in typical regional style; strong grassy components offset by complex French oak barrel ferment inputs; an extra dimension of texture and flavour. Screwcap. 13° alc. **Rating** 93 **To** 2015 $25

Margaret River Chardonnay 2005 No reduction; a complex blend of stone fruit and balanced oak; the mlf adds creamy/nutty characters to a stylish wine of good length. Screwcap. 14° alc. **Rating** 93 **To** 2018 $38

Single Vineyard Estate Margaret River Sauvignon Blanc Semillon 2006 No reduction whatsoever; harmonious balance and integration of fruit and oak; good length; partial barrel ferment; 60%/40%. Screwcap. 13° alc. **Rating** 92 **To** 2013 $20

Margaret River Cabernet Sauvignon 2003 A stylish, medium-bodied wine built in similar style to the '04, but with slightly more graceful cassis berry fruit. Screwcap. 14° alc. **Rating** 92 **To** 2018 $38

Single Vineyard Estate Margaret River Shiraz 2004 A medium- to full-bodied cascade of red and black fruits plus spice and mocha; good-quality French oak also helps. Screwcap. 14° alc. **Rating** 91 **To** 2014 $20

Margaret River Cabernet Sauvignon 2004 Medium-bodied; savoury/leafy/earthy edges to the blackcurrant fruit open proceedings; long, fine-grained tannins and quality oak help define the wine. Screwcap. 14.5° alc. **Rating** 91 **To** 2019 $40

ŶŶŶŶ **Single Vineyard Estate Margaret River Shiraz 2003** Medium-bodied; some earthy/spicy/savoury notes are consistent with the relatively low alcohol. Screwcap. 13.1° alc. **Rating** 88 **To** 2012 $20

Armstrong Vineyards ★★★★☆

Lot 1 Military Road, Armstrong, Vic 3381 (postal) **Region** Grampians
T (08) 8277 6073 **F** (08) 8277 6035 **www**.winesource.com.au **Open** Not
Winemaker Tony Royal **Est.** 1989 **Cases** 1000
Armstrong Vineyards is the brain- or love-child of Tony Royal, former Seppelt (Great Western) winemaker, former CEO of Seguin Moreau Australia, and now CEO and joint owner of Portavin Integrated Wine Services. Armstrong Vineyards has 6.7 ha of shiraz, the first 2 ha planted in 1989, the remainder in 1995–96. Low yields (4.5–5.5 tonnes per ha) mean the wine will always be produced in limited quantities. Exports to the UK.

Arranmore Vineyard ★★★☆

Rangeview Road, Carey Gully, SA 5144 **Region** Adelaide Hills
T (08) 8390 3034 **F** (08) 8390 0005 **www**.arranmore.com.au **Open** By appt
Winemaker John Venus **Est.** 1998 **Cases** 700
One of the tiny operations which dot the landscape of the beautiful Adelaide Hills. At an altitude of around 550 m, the 2-ha vineyard is planted to clonally selected pinot noir, chardonnay and sauvignon blanc. Exports to the UK.

Arrivo ★★★★☆

22 Kanmantoo Road, Aldgate, SA 5154 (postal) **Region** Adelaide Hills
T (08) 8370 8072 **F** (08) 8303 6621 **Open** Not
Winemaker Peter Godden, Sally McGill **Est.** 1998 **Cases** 120
While the establishment date of Arrivo is 1998, when Peter Godden and partner Sally McGill established a nursery block of 35 vines of nebbiolo, the inspiration goes back to 1990, while Peter was still at Roseworthy College, heading off the following year to become assistant winemaker to Joe Grilli at Primo Estate. In 1995 and 1996 Peter spent much time in Barolo, Italy, working the 1996 vintage at leading producer Vietti. In the meantime, Sally had become a leading Italian wine exporter and importer/distributor with Red+White. By 2001 they had propagated sufficient vines from the original 35 to plant 1 ha of vineyard, using a unique trellis and training system

derived from Barolo, but with an Australian twist. Not only is the trellis complicated and unique, but so are the amazingly complicated fermentation techniques being used by Peter Godden, best known these days for his work with the AWRI. Arrivo means 'arrival' in Italian, the first 100 cases (from 2004) released in 2006. Exports to the UK.

🍷🍷🍷🍷🍷 **Adelaide Hills Nebbiolo Rose 2006** Delicate but clear-cut strawberry and cherry blossom aromas; has structure and length, crisp and vibrant; this is what rose should be about. Screwcap. 12.5° alc. **Rating** 94 **To** 2008 $22

🍷🍷🍷🍷🍷 **Adelaide Hills Nebbiolo 2004** Vibrant flavours in the savoury/briary/lemony end of the spectrum; for the true believers. Screwcap. 14.5° alc. **Rating** 91 **To** 2014 $55

🍷🍷🍷🍷 **Adelaide Hills Nebbiolo 2005** Excellent hue and depth for the variety, with no browning; a crystal-clear bouquet, then an extremely savoury palate with some green bean characters and seemingly high acidity. Screwcap. 14.5° alc. **Rating** 89 **To** 2012 $57

Arrowfield Estate

Golden Highway, Jerrys Plains, NSW 2330 **Region** Upper Hunter Valley
T (02) 6576 4041 **F** (02) 6576 4144 **www**.arrowfieldestate.com.au **Open** 7 days 10–5
Winemaker Barry Kooij, Adrianna Mansueto **Est.** 1968 **Cases** 80 000
Arrowfield continues in the ownership of the Inagaki family, which has been involved in the Japanese liquor industry for over a century. It has 52 ha of low-yielding, old vines in the Upper Hunter Valley, and also buys grapes from other parts of Australia, making varietal wines appropriate to those regions. In 2007 it merged with Mornington Peninsula winery Red Hill Estate, the merged group trading as InWine Group Australia, with Brenton Martin installed as CEO. Exports to all major markets.

🍷🍷🍷🍷🍷 **The Author's Hunter Valley Semillon 2005** Light straw-green; has already developed some richness and complexity; ripe lemon flavours and good length. Screwcap. 11.5° alc. **Rating** 91 **To** 2012 $17
The Author's Cabernet Merlot 2004 Light- to medium-bodied; attractive earthy/savoury edges to well-balanced black fruit; finishes with fine tannins. McLaren Vale/Alpine Valleys/King Valley/Hunter Valley. Screwcap. 14° alc. **Rating** 90 **To** 2013 $17

🍷🍷🍷🍷 **The Author's Shiraz Viognier 2005** Fresh plum, blackberry and black cherry fruit with a spicy, savoury twist; 10% viognier is at the upper level. Orange. Screwcap. 14.5° alc. **Rating** 89 **To** 2015 $17
Sophie's Bridge Shiraz 2005 Light- to medium-bodied; supple, smooth red and black fruits and fine tannins; slightly cosmetic. Screwcap. 13.3° alc. **Rating** 88 **To** 2010 $12
Sophie's Bridge Shiraz 2004 A pleasant, light- to medium-bodied wine; fresh, clean black cherry, plum and blackberry mix. Hunter Valley with a splash of McLaren Vale. Screwcap. 12.5° alc. **Rating** 88 **To** 2008 $13
The Author's Sauvignon Blanc 2005 Some underlying complexity to the ripe, gently tropical, fruit aromas, perhaps in part due to the 15% semillon component. Alpine Valleys/King Valley/Orange. Screwcap. 12.5° alc. **Rating** 87 **To** 2008 $17
The Author's Unwooded Chardonnay 2005 Light straw-green; gentle stone fruit braced by a touch of minerally acidity; some length. Single vineyard Hunter Valley. Screwcap. 13° alc. **Rating** 87 **To** 2008 $17

Arundel

Arundel Farm Estate, PO Box 136, Keilor, Vic 3036 **Region** Sunbury
T (03) 9335 3422 **F** (03) 9335 4912 **www**.arundel.com.au **Open** Not
Winemaker Bianca Hayes **Est.** 1995 **Cases** 1000

Arundel was built around an acre of cabernet and shiraz planted in the 1970s, but abandoned. When the Conwell family purchased the property in the early 1990s, the vineyard was resurrected, and the first vintage made by Rick Kinzbrunner in 1995. Thereafter the cabernet was grafted over to shiraz, the block slowly increased to 1.6 ha, and an additional 4 ha of shiraz and 1.6 ha of viognier and marsanne planted.

ҮҮҮҮҰ **Shiraz 2005** Strongly lifted black cherry and spice aromas and flavours; intense and long. Gives the impression of the inclusion of a touch of viognier. Cork. 13° alc. **Rating** 90 **To** 2015 $28

Ashbrook Estate

379 Harmans Road, Wilyabrup via Cowaramup, WA 6284 **Region** Margaret River
T (08) 9755 6262 **F** (08) 9755 6290 **Open** 7 days 10–5
Winemaker Tony Devitt, Brian Devitt **Est.** 1975 **Cases** 14 000
A fastidious maker of consistently excellent estate-grown table wines which shuns publicity and the wine show system alike and is less well known than it deserves to be, selling much of its wine through the cellar door and by an understandably very loyal mailing list clientele. All of the white wines are of the highest quality, year in, year out. Exports to the UK, Canada, Denmark, Germany, Indonesia, Japan, Singapore and Hong Kong.

ҮҮҮҮҮ **Sauvignon Blanc 2006** Brightly coloured and spotlessly clean; a complex web of gooseberry, spice and tropical fruit runs through a palate with a long finish. Screwcap. 13.5° alc. **Rating** 94 **To** 2008 $20

ҮҮҮҮҰ **Margaret River Semillon 2006** Light straw-green; a complex bouquet of herb, grass and spice; very lively and tangy, with some lemon bolt-on flavours; long finish. Screwcap. 13.5° alc. **Rating** 93 **To** 2015 $19

Margaret River Chardonnay 2005 Light straw-green; tight citrus and stone fruit with a touch of spicy oak; good length; needs – and will repay – time. Screwcap. 14° alc. **Rating** 92 **To** 2015 $28

Margaret River Cabernet Merlot 2002 Savoury, earthy, light- to medium-bodied wine, lifted by a spine of blackcurrant fruit, and, likewise, with a long future. Screwcap. 14° alc. **Rating** 91 **To** 2020 $28

Margaret River Riesling 2006 Pale straw-green; generous aromas and flavours, with ripe, tropical fruit and a pinch of salt. Silver medal Sheraton Wine Awards '06. Screwcap. 13.5° alc. **Rating** 90 **To** 2011 $20

Ashley Wines

392 Redesdale Road, Metcalfe, Vic 3448 **Region** Heathcote
T (03) 5423 2002 **F** (03) 5423 2002 www.ashleywines.com.au **Open** By appt
Winemaker Granite Hills (Llew Knight) **Est.** 1997 **Cases** 450
Steve Ashley planted his vineyard with the help of friends and family in 1997, with 3 ha of shiraz and 0.75 ha each of merlot and cabernet sauvignon. It is situated at the very southern (and coolest) end of the Heathcote region, with picking usually in late April. The quality of the grapes, and the skill of Llew Knight as contract winemaker, has been reflected in the track record of the wines in wine shows, where there has been a 100% success rate with the entries.

ҮҮҮҮҰ **Heathcote Shiraz 2004** A whisper of reduction on the bouquet quickly breathes off; on the palate, a medium-bodied wine with attractive red cherry, plum and blackberry fruit, the restrained alcohol a relief; acid and tannins in balance; good line and length. Screwcap. 14° alc. **Rating** 92 **To** 2017 $35

Ashton Hills ★★★★★

Tregarthen Road, Ashton, SA 5137 **Region** Adelaide Hills
T (08) 8390 1243 **F** (08) 8390 1243 **Open** Fri–Mon 11.30–5
Winemaker Stephen George **Est.** 1982 **Cases** 1500

Stephen George wears 3 winemaker hats: one for Ashton Hills, drawing upon a 3.5-ha estate vineyard high in the Adelaide Hills; one for Galah Wines; and one for Wendouree. It would be hard to imagine 3 wineries with more diverse styles, from the elegance and finesse of Ashton Hills to the awesome power of Wendouree. The Riesling, Chardonnay and Pinot Noir have moved into the highest echelon. Exports to the UK and the US.

TTTTT **Reserve Adelaide Hills Pinot Noir 2005** A complex, intense and long mix of plum, cherry, spice, stem and forest notes; a serious pinot noir with the power to develop over many years. Screwcap. 14° alc. **Rating** 96 **To** 2015 $50

Adelaide Hills Riesling 2006 Highly aromatic, bursting with citrus and apple blossom; the same flavours come through strongly on the well-balanced and long palate. Unusually strong for Ashton Hills. Screwcap. 13° alc. **Rating** 95 **To** 2018 $20

TTTTT **Adelaide Hills Chardonnay 2005** A complex and subtle interweaving of barrel ferment, mlf and lees; stone fruit, melon, cream and nuts; good length. Screwcap. 13.5° alc. **Rating** 92 **To** 2011 $27.50

Burra Burra Lone Star Vineyard Shiraz 2002 Holding its hue well; medium-to full-bodied, with an attractive mix of blackberry, spice and a touch of sweet leather; overall extract well-handled. Screwcap. 14° alc. **Rating** 91 **To** 2017 $25

Three 2006 A synergistic blend of pinot gris, gewurztraminer and riesling which does not obscure the varietal character of any one or more of the components; spice, lychee, apple and citrus flavours are all there; good acidity, dry finish. Screwcap. 13.5° alc. **Rating** 90 **To** 2008 $20

Sparkling Shiraz 2001 A lovely, full-flavoured wine which spends 4 years in old oak before tirage and the second fermentation; sweetness a little over the top for some, perhaps. 13° alc. **Rating** 90 **To** 2010 $37.50

TTTT **Estate Adelaide Hills Pinot Noir 2005** Very stemmy/leafy/spicy/stalky aromas, but comes together better on an intense palate; marches to the tune of its own drum. Screwcap. 14° alc. **Rating** 89 **To** 2011 $37.50

Audrey Wilkinson Vineyard   ★★★★★

Oakdale, De Beyers Road, Pokolbin, NSW 2320 **Region** Lower Hunter Valley
T (02) 4998 7411 **F** (02) 4998 7824 **www.**audreywilkinson.com.au **Open** Mon–Fri 9–5, w'ends & public hols 9.30–5
Winemaker Mark Woods **Est.** 1999 **Cases** 12 500
One of the most historic properties in the Hunter Valley, set in a particularly beautiful location, and with a very attractive cellar door. In 2004 it was acquired by Brian Agnew and family, and is no longer part of the Pepper Tree/James Fairfax wine group. The wines are made from estate-grown grapes; the vines were planted between the 1970s and 1990s.

TTTTT **Museum Reserve Semillon 2006** A lovely young semillon; the expressive bouquet with citrus and lemon aromas which flow into the long palate; an interesting finish with fruit sweetness and acidity. Curious to release a museum reserve in the year of its making. Screwcap. 11° alc. **Rating** 94 **To** 2020 $25

Reserve Hunter Valley Semillon 2002 Crisp, crunchy mineral plus lemon juice flavours; particularly good length and persistence; lovely wine. Cork. 10° alc. **Rating** 94 **To** 2012 $25

Museum Reserve Lake Shiraz 2005 A medium-bodied, plummy, earthy, spicy regional style with ripe tannins and controlled oak. Screwcap. 14° alc. **Rating** 94 **To** 2025 $55

TTTTT **Dessert Semillon 2006** Glowing green-gold; rich, supple and sweet; good length. Cork. 9.5° alc. **Rating** 91 **To** 2009 $25

Museum Reserve Semillon 2001 The low alcohol plays a role in the strong minerally components and bone-dry finish; an austere, seafood style, little changed over the past 6 years. Cork. 10° alc. **Rating** 90 **To** 2009 $25

ŸŸŸŸ   **Pioneer Rose 2006** Good colour; is undeniably sweet, but does have acidity. Screwcap. 13.5° alc. **Rating** 88 **To** 2008 $20

Auldstone

Booths Road, Taminick via Glenrowan, Vic 3675 **Region** Glenrowan
T (03) 5766 2237 **F** (03) 5766 2131 **www**.auldstone.com.au **Open** Thurs–Sat & school hols 9–5, Sun 10–5
Winemaker Michael Reid **Est.** 1987 **Cases** 2000
Michael and Nancy Reid have restored a century-old stone winery and have replanted the largely abandoned 26-ha vineyard around it. All the Auldstone varietal and fortified wines have won medals (usually bronze) in Australian wine shows. Exports to Singapore and China.

ŸŸŸŸ   **Riesling 2005** Perhaps aided by the screwcap, exceeds expectations for (continuing) freshness; apple, pear and citrus flavours; good length; particularly meritorious for the region. Screwcap. 12.2° alc. **Rating** 88 **To** 2011 $15
Chardonnay 2005 Peach and melon fruit is supported by subtle oak, the finish quite crisp and lively. Considerable achievement given the region. Screwcap. 13.4° alc. **Rating** 87 **To** 2010 $18
Cabernet Sauvignon 2001 A big, dry, earthy, chocolatey wine in thoroughly old-fashioned style; the tannins and alcohol have largely exhausted each other, and there's no reason to delay consumption. Cork. 15.2° alc. **Rating** 87 **To** 2008 $20
Sparkling Shiraz 1999 Quite complex, with good base material; it is just a pity that the high level of sweetness has been incorporated for cellar door trade. 14° alc. **Rating** 87 **To** 2008 $30
Late Bottled Vintage Port 1999 Powerful, but the sweetness is even more extreme than the Sparkling Shiraz, and will never dry out enough. Again, a pity. Cork. 18° alc. **Rating** 87 **To** 2008 $30
Liqueur Muscat NV Pleasant raisin muscat varietal fruit; the spirit well-chosen and balanced; it's what you get from 2–4-year-old base. Cork. 18° alc. **Rating** 87 **To** 2008 $25

Austin's Wines

870 Steiglitz Road, Sutherlands Creek, Vic 3331 **Region** Geelong
T (03) 5281 1799 **F** (03) 5281 1673 **www**.austinswines.com.au **Open** By appt
Winemaker Scott Ireland, Richard Austin **Est.** 1982 **Cases** 23 000
Pamela and Richard Austin have quietly built their business from a tiny base, and it has flourished. The vineyard has been progressively extended to 56 ha, and production has soared from 700 cases in 1998 to 23 000 cases in 2007. Scott Ireland is now full-time resident winemaker in the new and capacious onsite winery, and the quality of the wines is admirable. Exports to the UK, Sweden, Denmark, Canada, Dubai, Japan, Hong Kong and Singapore.

ŸŸŸŸŸ   **Shiraz 2004** Medium-bodied; excellent texture, structure and weight; blackberry fruits with touches of spice and chocolate. Screwcap. 15.5° alc. **Rating** 92 **To** 2015 $25
Geelong Sauvignon Blanc 2006 Absolutely clean with no reduction; aromatic, almost flowery bouquet, then a palate offering tropical fruits, citrus and kiwifruit; good acidity and length. Screwcap. 13° alc. **Rating** 91 **To** 2008 $20
Six Foot Six Pinot Noir 2005 Light-bodied but elegant, with gentle spice and fruit notes; good length. Screwcap. 14° alc. **Rating** 90 **To** 2011 $16

ŸŸŸŸ   **Geelong Riesling 2006** Spice, herb and mineral, all cast in a robust frame; lacks the aromatics of continental sites. Screwcap. 13° alc. **Rating** 88 **To** 2011 $20
Six Foot Six Shiraz Viognier 2004 Ripe and lush, with lots of flavour augmented by the viognier; soft tannins. Screwcap. 14° alc. **Rating** 87 **To** 2012 $16

Australian Domaine Wines ★★★★☆

PO Box 13, Walkerville, SA 5081 **Region** Various
T (08) 8340 3807 **F** (08) 8346 3766 **www**.ausdomwines.com.au **Open** By appt
Winemaker Pikes (Neil Pike), Andrew Braithwaite **Est.** 1998 **Cases** 5000
Australian Domaine Wines is the reincarnation of Barletta Bros, who started their own brand business for leading Adelaide retailer Walkerville Cellars, which they then owned. The wines are made at Pikes using tanks and barrels owned by the Barlettas. Grapes are sourced from the Clare Valley, McLaren Vale and the Barossa Valley. Exports to the UK, the US and other major markets.

🍷🍷🍷🍷🍷 **Solitary Block Greenock Creek Shiraz 2004** Full red-purple; has very complex texture, structure and flavour; black fruits, quality oak and extremely fine, persistent tannins all play their part. Zork. 15° alc. **Rating** 95 **To** 2019 $45

Alliance McLaren Vale Shiraz 2004 Full purple-red; a full-bodied, classic regional mix of dark chocolate, blackberry, notes of licorice and ripe spice; fine tannins and good length; handles the alcohol quite well. Extraordinary value. Cork. 15° alc. **Rating** 94 **To** 2024 $15

🍷🍷🍷🍷◯ **Solitary Block Barossa Valley Shiraz 2004** Deep colour; rich, very ripe, full-blown, luscious style headed to the US heartland; a bit less might have been a bit better for Australian tastes, but not for the needs of its market. Cork. 15° alc. **Rating** 92 **To** 2014 $47

Solitary Block Barossa Valley Grenache 2004 Lighter red-purple than the Shiraz; sweet raspberry and cherry fruit; as always, minimal tannins, but it has good length, and carries the alcohol well. Cork. 15.5° alc. **Rating** 90 **To** 2011 $47

🍷🍷🍷🍷 **Barletta Clare Valley Shiraz 2003** Holding good hue; medium-bodied spicy black fruits, with a touch of prune but not jammy or dead fruit; fresh finish; good for the vintage. Cork. 15° alc. **Rating** 89 **To** 2013 $19

Alliance McLaren Vale Cabernet Merlot 2003 Obvious development; the region triumphs (via dark chocolate) over the varietal cassis/blackcurrant, but is still an enjoyable, flavoursome wine, with soft tannins and admirable value. Cork. 15° alc. **Rating** 89 **To** 2013 $15

The Hattrick McLaren Vale Red 2004 Dense red-purple; the ultimate vintage port without the fortifying spirit; this is seriously over the top, and the points are halfway between 70 and 99. Shiraz (49%)/Grenache (46%)/Cabernet Sauvignon (5%). Cork. 16.1° alc. **Rating** 89 **To** 2030 $50

Barletta Clare Valley Grenache 2003 What is it with old vine Clare Valley grenache? It simply doesn't deliver weight or complexity. Pleasant enough but why isn't there more? Cork. 15.3° alc. **Rating** 87 **To** 2008 $19

Australian Old Vine Wine **NR**

Farm 271, Rossetto Road, Beelbangera, NSW 2680 **Region** Riverina
T (02) 6963 5239 **F** (02) 6963 5239 **www**.australianoldvine.com.au **Open** 7 days 10–4
Winemaker Piromit Wines (Dom Piromalli) **Est.** 2002 **Cases** NA

Avalon Vineyard ★★★☆

1605 Bailey Road, Glen Forrest, WA 6071 **Region** Perth Hills
T (08) 9298 8049 **F** (08) 9298 8049 **www**.avalonvineyard.com.au **Open** By appt
Winemaker Rob Marshall (Contract) **Est.** 1986 **Cases** 500
One of the smaller wineries in the Perth Hills, drawing upon 0.75 ha each of chardonnay, semillon and cabernet sauvignon. Plans to open a cellar door sales and tasting area. Exports to Malaysia.

Avalon Wines ★★★☆

RMB 9556 Whitfield Road, Wangaratta, Vic 3678 **Region** King Valley
T (03) 5729 3629 **F** (03) 5729 3635 **www**.avalonwines.com.au **Open** 7 days 10–5
Winemaker Doug Groom **Est.** 1981 **Cases** 1000

Roseworthy graduate Doug Groom and wife Rosa established a 10-ha vineyard, selling part of the grapes, but making inter alia highly rated Shiraz. Non-interventionist winemaking is reflected in the use of indigenous yeasts and unfiltered wines.

Avonmore Estate

Mayreef-Avonmore Road, Avonmore, Vic 3558 **Region** Bendigo
T (03) 5432 6291 **F** (03) 5432 6291 **www**.avonmoreestatewine.com **Open** Wed–Sun & public hols 11–5, or by appt
Winemaker Shaun Bryans, Rob Bryans **Est.** 1996 **Cases** 2000
Rob and Pauline Bryans own and operate a Grade A-certified biodynamic farm, producing and selling beef, lamb and cereals as well as establishing 9 ha of viognier, sangiovese, cabernet sauvignon, cabernet franc and shiraz which produced its first crop in 2000. The winery is also biodynamic-certified and the wines are sold with the worldwide Demeter logo. Exports to the US and Canada.

☙☙☙☙ **Bendigo Shiraz 2003** Medium-bodied; spicy, savoury notes to blackberry fruits; good tannin balance, and the American oak works well. Cork. 14.5° alc. **Rating** 89 To 2008 $20
Bendigo Cabernet Sauvignon 2003 Savoury, spicy, earthy black fruits are a good expression of the variety; medium-bodied, with ripe tannins and controlled oak. Cork. 14° alc. **Rating** 89 To 2013 $20

B'darra Estate

1415 Stumpy Gully Road, Moorooduc, Vic 3933 **Region** Mornington Peninsula
T (03) 5978 8447 **F** (03) 5978 8977 **Open** W'ends 11–5
Winemaker Gavin Perry **Est.** 1998 **Cases** 2000
Gavin and Linda Perry fell in love with Bedarra Island (off the north Qld coast) when they stayed there, hence the name of their property, which they acquired in 1998. They planted 5 ha of vines in 1999, and are progressively developing the 21-ha holding. A revegetation and wetland, of which a lake and 2 big dams form part, are planned. Exports to China.

☙☙☙☙☙ **Shiraz 2004** Lovely richness and suppleness to blackberry, dark plum and licorice fruit; controlled tannins. Diam. **Rating** 94 To 2019 $24

☙☙☙☙ **Pinot Noir 2004** Quite aromatic, with lots of savoury/spicy/stemmy elements to give length to the medium body; needs a touch more sweet fruit/vinosity on the mid-palate. Diam. **Rating** 89 To 2010 $18
Chardonnay 2004 Clean, but showing expected bottle development; nectarine, melon and fig flavours; overall, fairly light-bodied. Screwcap. **Rating** 88 To 2008 $16
Cabernet Sauvignon 2004 An odd mixture of jammy, porty fruit and more savoury characters; possibly a mix of overripe and under-ripe berries. Cork. **Rating** 88 To 2011 $18

✿ B3 Wines

PO Box 648, Kent Town, SA 5071 **Region** South Australia
T (08) 8363 2211 **F** (08) 8363 2231 **www**.b3wines.com.au **Open** Not
Winemaker The B3, Craig Stansborough **Est.** 2001 **Cases** NA
Peter, Michael and Richard Basedow are the 3 Brothers Basedow (as they call themselves), fifth-generation Barossans, with distinguished forefathers. Grandfather Oscar Basedow established the Basedow winery (no longer in family ownership) in 1896, while Martin Basedow established the Roseworthy Agricultural College. Their father, John Oscar Basedow, died in the 1970s, having won the 1970 Jimmy Watson Trophy for his 1969 Cabernet Sauvignon, a high point for the family. This is a virtual winery enterprise, grapes being purchased in Coonawarra, the Barossa Valley, the Adelaide Hills and Eden Valley, and contract-made.

☙☙☙☙☙ **Eden Valley Riesling 2006** Fragrant lemon/lime zest and pith; a fine palate, with both depth and length in the full citrus spectrum. Screwcap. 12.5° alc. **Rating** 94 To 2013 $18

Barossa Grenache Shiraz Mourvedre 2003 Medium-bodied; very good balance, texture and structure; the fruit flavours of the varieties come together seamlessly in a black cherry, red cherry, blackberry stream; fine, ripe tannins. Screwcap. 14.5° alc. **Rating** 94 **To** 2023 $18

♼♼♼♼♀ **Eden Valley Riesling 2005** Moves away from the single citrus family of flavours to include apple, pear and a hint of pineapple, although the citrus foundation remains in place. Screwcap. 12° alc. **Rating** 93 **To** 2011 $18
Adelaide Hills Sauvignon Blanc 2005 A delicate, fragrant passionfruit and gooseberry bouquet; good mouthfeel and balance; the flavours follow the bouquet through to a long, convincing finish. Screwcap. 13.5° alc. **Rating** 92 **To** 2008 $18
Pauline Barossa Cabernet Shiraz 2003 A supple, smooth, medium- to full-bodied palate, with gently sweet black fruits; the tannins are fine and ripe, the oak positive but not over the top. Cork. 13.5° alc. **Rating** 92 **To** 2020 $25
Barossa Semillon 2004 Excellent green-yellow; full of character and flavour, albeit in a traditional Barossa Valley style. Screwcap. 12° alc. **Rating** 90 **To** 2008 $13

♼♼♼♼ **Barossa Semillon 2005** Full-flavoured, multi-layered traditional style; oak seems to have played a role, and the wine has good acidity and length. Screwcap. 12.5° alc. **Rating** 89 **To** 2010 $13
Barossa Chardonnay 2005 Mainstream style; soft, peachy fruit; flavoursome, but not particularly long. Screwcap. 14° alc. **Rating** 87 **To** 2008 $13

Bacchus Hill   ★★★

100 O'Connell Road, Bacchus Marsh, Vic 3340 **Region** Sunbury
T (03) 5367 8176 **F** (03) 5367 8176 **www.**bacchushill.com.au **Open** Wed–Sun 10–5
Winemaker Bruno Tassone **Est.** 2000 **Cases** 3200
Lawyer Bruno Tassone migrated from Italy when he was 8, and watched his father carry on the Italian tradition of making wine for home consumption. Tassone followed the same path before purchasing a 35-ha property with wife, Jennifer. Here they have planted 18 ha of riesling, semillon, sauvignon blanc, chardonnay, pinot noir, merlot, shiraz, cabernet sauvignon, chenin blanc and nebbiolo. A move to screwcaps would be of great advantage for the older wines.

♼♼♼♼ **Le Repaire de Bacchus Sauvignon Blanc 2006** Light gooseberry and kiwifruit flavours; hints of fruit salad, and also a touch of sweetness on the finish. Diam. 14.5° alc. **Rating** 88 **To** 2008 $20
Le Repaire de Bacchus Semillon 2006 Very pale; fresh grassy/lemon cake flavours; a hint of sweetness on the finish; will develop. Diam. 13° alc. **Rating** 87 **To** 2013 $18

☀ BackVintage Wines   ★★★☆

2/177 Sailors Bay Road, Northbridge, NSW 2063 (postal) **Region** Warehouse
T (02) 9967 9880 **F** (02) 9967 9882 **www.**backvintage.com.au **Open** Not
Winemaker Rob Moody (Contract) **Est.** 2003 **Cases** 10 000
BackVintage Wines is a virtual winery with a difference; not only does it not own vineyards, nor a winery, it sells only through its website, or by fax or phone. While Robin Moody is shown as winemaker, his role is limited to sourcing wines (with the assistance of Nick Bulleid in the selection process, blending and bottling where the wine has not already been packaged as a cleanskin). As the tasting notes indicate, the experience of Robin Moody (former long-term Southcorp winemaker) and Nick Bulleid shows, and they have done their job well.

♼♼♼♼♀ **Hunter Valley Semillon 2002** Plenty of length and vitality; lemon and lemon-grass characters; good length and back-palate flavour. Cork. 11° alc. **Rating** 90 **To** 2012 $10.95

♼♼♼♼ **Mornington Peninsula Pinot Noir 2005** Predominantly red cherry with some plum; overall very firm (perhaps low pH) and needs a bit more time. Screwcap. 13.7° alc. **Rating** 89 **To** 2010 $11.95

McLaren Vale Shiraz 2004 Nicely balanced and structured; moderate alcohol helps the gentle blackcurrant fruit express itself along with nuances of chocolate and vanilla oak. Great value. Screwcap. 14° alc. **Rating** 89 **To** 2010 $12

Margaret River Cabernet Merlot 2003 Attractive, medium-bodied well-balanced wine; a mix of blackcurrant, some cassis, fine tannins and a touch of French oak. Screwcap. 14° alc. **Rating** 89 **To** 2009 $11.95

Central Ranges Cabernet Rose 2006 Nicely balanced; has ripe cassis fruit without undue sweetness, and some length. Screwcap. 12.5° alc. **Rating** 88 **To** 2008 $10.95

Barossa Shiraz 2004 An unostentatious wine; earthy shiraz varietal character, with moderate oak and alcohol; ready now, but will hold. Screwcap. 14.5° alc. **Rating** 88 **To** 2010 $11.95

Eden Valley Riesling 2005 Potent, slightly old-fashioned notes of petrol and mineral on the bouquet, the solid palate running along similar lines. Screwcap. 12.3° alc. **Rating** 87 **To** 2010 $10.95

Baddaginnie Run   ★★★☆

PO Box 579, North Melbourne, Vic 3051 **Region** Strathbogie Ranges
T (03) 9348 9310 **F** (03) 9348 9370 **www**.baddaginnierun.net.au **Open** Not
Winemaker Toby Barlow **Est.** 1996 **Cases** 1250

Winsome McCaughey and Professor Snow Barlow (Professor of Horticulture and Viticulture at the University of Melbourne) spend part of their week in the Strathbogie Ranges, part in Melbourne. The business name, Seven Sisters Vineyard, reflects the 7 generations of the McCaughey family associated with the land for over 135 years; Baddaginnie is the nearby township. The vineyard is one element in a restored valley landscape, 100 000 indigenous trees having been replanted. The wines are made by son Toby Barlow, winemaker at Mitchelton.

Badger's Brook   ★★★☆

874 Maroondah Highway, Coldstream, Vic 3770 **Region** Yarra Valley
T (03) 5962 4130 **F** (03) 5962 4238 **www**.badgersbrook.com.au **Open** Wed–Mon 11–5
Winemaker Contract **Est.** 1993 **Cases** 5000

Situated next door to the well-known Rochford, it has a total of 10 ha of vineyard, planted mainly to chardonnay, sauvignon blanc, pinot noir, shiraz and cabernet sauvignon, with a few rows each of viognier, roussanne, marsanne and tempranillo. All of the wines are Yarra Valley–sourced, including the second Storm Ridge label. Now houses the smart brasserie restaurant Bella Vedere Cucina with well-known chef Gary Cooper in charge. Exports to Asia.

 Yarra Valley Shiraz 2005 Has serious weight and very serious tannins, the latter needing to soften, which should happen before the fruit dies. Screwcap. **Rating** 90 **To** 2025 $25

ⓎⓎⓎⓎ **Yarra Valley Chardonnay 2005** An elegant, understated style; melon and stone fruit with negligible new oak influence; may grow in bottle. Screwcap. 13.5° alc. **Rating** 89 **To** 2010 $22

Yarra Valley Pinot Noir 2004 Significantly riper and more complex than the Storm Ridge; spice, plum with some bramble and earth. Screwcap. 14° alc. **Rating** 89 **To** 2011 $25

Storm Ridge Yarra Valley Cabernet Merlot 2002 Not deep, but holding hue well; the flavours are still equally fresh, even if they also reflect the very cool vintage to a degree, holding a kernel of sweet cassis fruit. Screwcap. 13° alc. **Rating** 89 **To** 2010 $18

Baileys of Glenrowan   ★★★★★

Cnr Taminick Gap Road/Upper Taminick Road, Glenrowan, Vic 3675 **Region** Glenrowan
T (03) 5766 2392 **F** (03) 5766 2596 **www**.baileysofglenrowan.com.au **Open** 7 days 10–5
Winemaker Paul Dahlenburg **Est.** 1870 **Cases** 15 000

Just when it seemed that Baileys would remain one of the forgotten outposts of the Fosters group, the reverse has occurred. Since 1998 Paul Dahlenburg has been in charge of Baileys, and has overseen an expansion in the vineyard to 143 ha and the construction of a totally new 2000-tonne winery. The cellar door has a heritage museum, winery viewing deck, contemporary art gallery and landscaped grounds, preserving much of the heritage value. Baileys has also picked up the pace with its Muscat and Tokay, reintroducing the Winemaker's Selection at the top of the tree, while continuing the larger-volume Founder series. Exports to the UK and NZ.

ŶŶŶŶŶ **1904 Block Shiraz 2004** Surprisingly fragrant, suggesting a cooler site, although that's not the case; elegant black fruits with a touch of spice; lovely fine tannins run through the length and finish. Screwcap. 14° alc. **Rating** 95 **To** 2025 $52.95
Winemaker's Selection Old Tokay NV Obvious age showing from its mahogany/olive-green colour; classic tea-leaf, butterscotch and malt flavours; great harmony with the spirit; a long finish, at once sweet yet dry and spicy. Cork. 16.5° alc. **Rating** 95 **To** 2008 $20.95
Winemaker's Selection Old Muscat NV Gloriously rich, luscious and powerful; retains the essence of raisin muscat, but complexed by rancio and oriental spices; again, perfect harmony with the fortifying spirit. Cork. 17° alc. **Rating** 95 **To** 2008 $20.95
1920's Block Shiraz 2005 Dense purple-red; blackberry, licorice and plum fruit on both bouquet and palate; rich, but not jammy; controlled oak; like the 1904 Block, Northeast Victoria at its best. Screwcap. 14° alc. **Rating** 94 **To** 2025 $31.95
Founder Liqueur Muscat NV Intense, lively, grapey varietal character of raisins and plum pudding; acidity gives more lift and intensifies the flavour, yet does not bite; the volatile component of the acidity appears low. Cork. 17° alc. **Rating** 94 **To** 2008 $17

ŶŶŶŶŶ **Founder Liqueur Tokay NV** Moderate age; classic tea-leaf, butterscotch and malt aromas and flavours; a lingering sweetness through the palate, then a final farewell is (commendably) almost dry. Cork. 17° alc. **Rating** 93 **To** 2008 $17

ŶŶŶŶ **Cabernet Sauvignon 2006** Continues the theme of elegance, almost to an extreme; light- to medium-bodied, with quite sweet cassis fruit; minimal tannins and oak. Cork. 14° alc. **Rating** 89 **To** 2013 $21.95
Frontignac 2006 Crushed rose petal and strawberries are the drivers for a fermentation-arrested wine, the residual sweetness balanced by acidity. Adventuresome. Screwcap. 9° alc. **Rating** 87 **To** 2008 $19.95

Baillieu Vineyard ★★★★

'Bulldog Run', RMB 5560 Junction Road, Merricks North, Vic 3926
Region Mornington Peninsula
T (03) 5989 7622 **F** (03) 5989 7199 www.baillieuvineyard.com.au **Open** By appt
Winemaker Rollo Crittenden, Kevin McCarthy (Contract) **Est.** 1999 **Cases** NFP
The 10-ha, north-facing vineyard established by Charlie and Samantha Baillieu on their 64-ha Bulldog Run property is planted to chardonnay, pinot gris, pinot meunier, pinot noir and shiraz, all of the wines using estate-grown grapes.

ŶŶŶŶŶ **Pinot Noir 2004** Still holding excellent hue; a generous palate with plum, black cherry, nice touches of spice, and controlled French oak. Screwcap. 14° alc. **Rating** 90 **To** 2011 $20

Bald Mountain ★★★

41 Hickling Lane, via Wallangarra, Qld 4383 **Region** Granite Belt
T (07) 4684 3186 **F** (07) 4684 3433 **Open** 7 days 10–5
Winemaker Monarch Winemaking Services **Est.** 1985 **Cases** 3500
Denis Parsons is a self-taught but exceptionally competent vigneron who has turned Bald Mountain into one of the viticultural showpieces of the Granite Belt. The sauvignon blanc–based wines, Classic Queenslander and Late Harvest Sauvignon Blanc, are interesting alternatives to the

mainstream wines. Future production will also see grapes coming from new vineyards near Tenterfield just across the border in NSW. Significant exports to The Netherlands.

Bald Rock Vineyard

Alexandersons Road, Locksley, Vic 3665 (postal) **Region** Strathbogie Ranges
T (03) 5798 5277 **F** (03) 5798 5277 **Open** Not
Winemaker Travis Bush (Contract) **Est.** 2000 **Cases** 350
John and Judy Thomson began the establishment of their vineyard in 1999, the first commercial bottling following in 2005. They have 2.4 ha pinot noir, 1.4 ha shiraz and 0.6 ha chardonnay, established under monitored drip irrigation to control berry size. The wines are available through King & Godfrey, Lygon Street, Carlton.

Balgownie Estate

Hermitage Road, Maiden Gully, Vic 3551 **Region** Bendigo
T (03) 5449 6222 **F** (03) 5449 6506 **www.**balgownieestate.com.au **Open** 7 days 11–5
Winemaker Tobias Ansted **Est.** 1969 **Cases** 10 000
Balgownie Estate continues to grow in the wake of its acquisition by the Forrester family. A $3 million upgrade of the winery coincided with a doubling of the size of the vineyard to 35 ha, and in 2004 Balgownie Estate opened a cellar door in the Yarra Valley (see separate entry). Exports to the UK, the US and other major markets.

Bendigo Shiraz 2005 Firm, in classic Balgownie/Bendigo style; rich blackberry fruits, licorice, and splashes of red fruits and allied spices; fine tannins, long finish. Screwcap. 14° alc. **Rating** 94 **To** 2020 $31
Cabernet Merlot 2005 A generously endowed wine which literally fills the mouth with a seamless mix of black and red fruits, savoury/briary notes barely evident. Screwcap. 14° alc. **Rating** 94 **To** 2020 $19.50
Bendigo Cabernet Sauvignon 2004 Deep, bright colour; medium-bodied, mouthfilling soft black fruits with gentle mocha oak; the tannins are likewise very soft, but persistent. Screwcap. 14° alc. **Rating** 94 **To** 2014 $33

Shiraz Viognier 2005 Supple, sensuous black fruits with an aromatic lift from the viognier; medium-bodied, with soft tannins on a fine finish. Screwcap. 14° alc. **Rating** 91 **To** 2020 $19.50

Balgownie Estate (Yarra Valley)

Cnr Melba Highway/Gulf Road, Yarra Glen, Vic 3775 **Region** Yarra Valley
T (03) 9730 0700 **F** (03) 9730 2647 **www.**balgownieestate.com.au **Open** 7 days 10–5
Winemaker Tobias Ansted **Est.** 2004 **Cases** 2500
Balgownie Estate opened a very attractive rammed-earth cellar door in 2004, offering the full range of Balgownie wines. The range of Chardonnay, Pinot Noir, Shiraz and Cabernet Sauvignon are 100% Yarra Valley, using contract-grown grapes from several vineyards.

Balhannah Estate

Lot 100, Johnson Road, Balhannah, SA 5242 **Region** Adelaide Hills
T (08) 8398 0698 **F** (08) 8398 0698 **Open** By appt
Winemaker Rod Short, Rachel Short **Est.** 1997 **Cases** 1000
Rod and Rachel Short began the planting of 3 ha of shiraz, 2 ha of chardonnay, 1.5 ha of merlot and 1 ha of pinot noir in 1997. The first vintage was in 2002, made from 100% estate-grown grapes. Yields are limited to 1.5 to 2 tonnes per acre for the red wines, and 2 to 3 tonnes for the chardonnay. Most of the grapes are sold; the limited production is sold by mail order. Exports to Germany.

Reserve Adelaide Hills Shiraz 2005 Concentrated and focused black cherry, cracked pepper and spice aromas and flavours; long, perfectly balanced palate with fine tannins. Diam. 14.5° alc. **Rating** 94 **To** 2020 $35

🍷🍷🍷🍷 **Adelaide Hills Pinot Noir 2005** The texture is good, but the varietal line blurred somewhat; high alcohol partly to blame, one suspects; gives the impression of much work in the winery. Diam. 14.5° alc. **Rating** 88 **To** 2012 $27

Ballandean Estate ★★★☆

Sundown Road, Ballandean, Qld 4382 **Region** Granite Belt
T (07) 4684 1226 **F** (07) 4684 1288 **www.**ballandeanestate.com **Open** 7 days 9–5
Winemaker Dylan Rhymer, Angelo Puglisi **Est.** 1970 **Cases** 12 000
The senior winery of the Granite Belt, owned by the ever-cheerful and charming Angelo Puglisi, but who is an appalling correspondent. The white wines are of diverse but interesting styles, the red wines smooth and usually well-made. The estate speciality, Sylvaner Late Harvest, is a particularly interesting wine of great character and flavour if given 10 years bottle age.

🍷🍷🍷🍷 **Family Reserve Viognier 2006** Very pale; does have viognier varietal character, albeit in muted fashion, with wisps of apricot blossom; the crisp finish avoids phenolics. Screwcap. 14° alc. **Rating** 87 **To** 2008 $18

Ballast Stone Estate Wines ★★★

Myrtle Grove Road, Currency Creek, SA 5214 **Region** Currency Creek
T (08) 8555 4215 **F** (08) 8555 4216 **www.**ballaststone.com.au **Open** 7 days 10.30–4.30
Winemaker John Loxton **Est.** 2001 **Cases** 15 000
The Shaw family had been grapegrowers in McLaren Vale for 25 years before deciding to establish a large vineyard (250 ha) in Currency Creek in 1994. The vineyard is planted mainly to cabernet sauvignon and shiraz, with much smaller quantities of other trendy varieties. Only a small part of the production is sold under the Ballast Stone Estate label, most is sold in bulk. Exports to the UK and Germany.

🍷🍷🍷🍷 **Shiraz 2004** Good fruit, but the oak pokes out somewhat, and so do the tannins to a lesser degree. Has some potential. **Rating** 87 **To** 2012 $20

Balnaves of Coonawarra

Main Road, Coonawarra, SA 5263 **Region** Coonawarra
T (08) 8737 2946 **www.**balnaves.com.au **Open** Mon–Fri 9–5, w'ends 12–5
Winemaker Pete Bissell **Est.** 1975 **Cases** 10 000
Grapegrower, viticultural consultant and vigneron Doug Balnaves has 52 ha of high-quality estate vineyards. The wines are invariably excellent, often outstanding, notable for their supple mouthfeel, varietal integrity, balance and length; the tannins are always fine and ripe, the oak subtle and perfectly integrated. Coonawarra at its best. Exports to all major markets.

🍷🍷🍷🍷🍷 **The Tally Reserve Cabernet Sauvignon 2005** Deep purple-red; an incredibly powerful and expressive bouquet, the luscious but tightly framed blackcurrant, cassis and French oak precisely fulfilling the promises of the bouquet. ProCork. 14.5° alc. **Rating** 96 **To** 2025 $80
Shiraz 2005 Very deep colour and great hue; a lovely wine, showing Coonawarra back to its best; pure black fruits and superb oak and tannin management; long finish. Screwcap. 14.5° alc. **Rating** 95 **To** 2020 $24
Chardonnay 2005 Glowing yellow-green; a complex bouquet the result of barrel fermentation of cloudy juice in 1- and 2-year-old barriques; in typical Balnaves fashion, the palate is smooth, supple and long, with Burgundian nuances. Screwcap. 13° alc. **Rating** 94 **To** 2012 $28
Cabernet Merlot 2005 Much more richness, texture and weight than Coonawarra usually provides; sophisticated winemaking provides a balance between cassis blackcurrant (cabernet) and touches of olive and spice from the merlot. Cork. 14.5° alc. **Rating** 94 **To** 2015 $24
Cabernet Sauvignon 2005 Generously proportioned and flavoured cabernet sauvignon; the blackcurrant fruit has latent earthy/savoury notes which will emerge with age, thus emphasising terroir. ProCork. 14.7° alc. **Rating** 94 **To** 2020 $31

The Blend 2005 Typical colour; a smooth, supple and vibrant array of blackcurrant, cassis, blueberry and raspberry fruit supported by fine tannins and controlled oak. Cabernet Sauvignon/Merlot/Cabernet Franc. Screwcap. 14.5° alc. **Rating** 94 **To** 2018 $19

Sparkling Cabernet NV Attractive sweet cassis cabernet fruit, with good balance. Composed of 8 vintages of reserve wines, tiraged in Sept '06 and disgorged Feb '07. Having built up the base wines for so many years, the short period on lees is a strange decision. 14° alc. **Rating** 90 **To** 2008 $28

Balthazar of the Barossa

PO Box 675, Nuriootpa, SA 5355 **Region** Barossa Valley
T (08) 8562 2949 **F** (08) 8562 2949 **www**.balthazarbarossa.com **Open** At the Small Winemakers Centre, Chateau Tanunda
Winemaker Anita Bowen **Est.** 1999 **Cases** 870
Anita Bowen announces her occupation as 'a 40-something sex therapist with a 17-year involvement in the wine industry'; she is also the wife of a high-ranked executive with Fosters. Anita undertook her first vintage at Mudgee, then McLaren Vale, and ultimately the Barossa; she worked at St Hallet while studying at Roseworthy College. A versatile lady, indeed. As to her wine, she says, 'Anyway, prepare a feast, pour yourself a glass (no chalices, please) of Balthazar and share it with your concubines. Who knows? It may help to lubricate thoughts, firm up ideas and get the creative juices flowing!' Exports to all major markets.

Banca Ridge ★★★

2 McGlew Street, Stanthorpe, Qld 4380 **Region** Granite Belt
T (07) 4681 5833 **F** (07) 4681 3416 **www**.bancaridge.eq.edu.au **Open** Mon–Fri 9–3
Winemaker Ravens Croft Wines **Est.** 2001 **Cases** 500
Banca Ridge is an initiative of the Stanthorpe State High School, which has established the first commercial school winery in Qld. It has 0.5 ha each of marsanne and merlot, and students are involved in all stages of the grape growing and winemaking process under the direction of Mark Ravenscroft. It is designed to train students in the wine, hospitality and tourism industry, and the wines produced are a credit to the school and the program.

Banks Road

600 Banks Road, Marcus Hill, Vic 3222 **Region** Geelong
T (03) 9822 6587 **F** (03) 9822 5077 **www**.banksroadwine.com.au **Open** W'ends 10–4
Winemaker Darren Burke, William Derham **Est.** 2001 **Cases** 2000
Banks Road, owned and operated by William Derham, has 2 vineyards: the first, 2.5 ha, is on the Bellarine Peninsula at Marcus Hill, planted to pinot noir and chardonnay; the second is at Harcourt in the Bendigo region, planted to 3 ha of shiraz and cabernet sauvignon, the vines ranging from 8 to 12 years of age. Although Darren Burke, with wide-ranging winemaking experience, has replaced Justyn Baker, there will be no change to the style of the wines.

Chardonnay 2005 Medium-bodied and solid, with plenty of oak but enough ripe stone fruit to give balance. Screwcap. 13.5° alc. **Rating** 88 **To** 2008 $25

Banks Thargo Wines

Racecourse Road, Penola, SA 5277 (postal) **Region** Coonawarra
T (08) 8737 2338 **F** (08) 8737 3369 **Open** Not
Winemaker Banks Kidman, Jonathon Kidman **Est.** 1980 **Cases** 900
The unusual name comes from family history. One branch of the Kidman family moved to the Mt Gambier district in 1858, but Thomas Kidman (who had been in the foster care of the Banks family from the age of 2 to 13) moved to Broken Hill/southwest Qld to work for the famous Kidman Bros pastoral interests. When he 'retired' from the outback, he bought this property in 1919. His second son was named Banks Thargomindah Kidman, and it was he and wife Jenny

who decided to diversify their grazing activities by planting vines in the 1980s: 16.5 ha are under contract, leaving 1.3 ha each of merlot and cabernet sauvignon for the Banks Thargo brand.

Bannockburn Vineyards

Midland Highway, Bannockburn, Vic 3331 (postal) **Region** Geelong
T (03) 5281 1363 **F** (03) 5281 1349 **www**.bannockburnvineyards.com **Open** By appt
Winemaker Michael Glover **Est.** 1974 **Cases** 10 000
With the qualified exception of the Cabernet Merlot, which can be a little leafy and gamey, Bannockburn produces outstanding wines across the range, all with individuality, style, great complexity and depth of flavour. The low-yielding estate vineyards play their role. Incoming winemaker Michael Glover brings a wealth of experience to the job, and a determination to enhance the reputation of Bannockburn. Exports to Canada, Dubai, Korea, China, Singapore and Hong Kong.

Serre Pinot Noir 2002 Exceptional deep red-purple; a super-intense and focused array of dark plum and cherry fruit. Is it worth it? Yes. Will it age? Yes. Cork. 14° alc. **Rating** 97 **To** 2017 $120
SRH Chardonnay 2001 Glowing yellow-green; gloriously complex, yet still tight; melon, nectarine and grapefruit flavours have absorbed the oak; very long finish. Cork. 14° alc. **Rating** 96 **To** 2011 $120
Pinot Noir 2004 Highly fragrant and pure; a lovely wine, fine and long, with superb texture and outstanding finesse. Unanimous top wine at the Stonier International Pinot Noir Tasting. Cork. 13.5° alc. **Rating** 96 **To** 2015 $65
Stuart Pinot Noir 2003 An intense wine, with a particularly strong structure; forest floor, spice and black cherry, then a lingering finish. Cork. 14° alc. **Rating** 94 **To** 2011 $65

Banrock Station

Holmes Road (off Sturt Highway), Kingston-on-Murray, SA 5331 **Region** Riverland
T (08) 8583 0299 **F** (08) 8583 0288 **www**.banrockstation.com **Open** 7 days 10–5
Winemaker Mark Zeppel, Paul Kassebaum **Est.** 1994 **Cases** 1.9 million
The $1 million visitor centre at Banrock Station was opened in 1999. Owned by Hardys, the Banrock Station property covers over 1700 ha, with 240 ha of vineyard and the remainder being a major wildlife and wetland preservation area. The wines have consistently offered excellent value for money.

Semillon Chardonnay 2006 A particularly well-made wine at this price; tangy citrus, lemon and nectarine mix; lingering finish. Unoaked, of course. Twin top. 12.5° alc. **Rating** 89 **To** 2008 $7.20
The Reserve Petit Verdot 2003 First tasted at the National Wine Show '04; has developed better than expected since that time; flavours and tannins have come together in a smooth union. Cork. 13.5° alc. **Rating** 89 **To** 2014 $12
The Reserve Chardonnay 2006 A fair whack of oak on ripe, peachy fruit; old-fashioned, but what the public wants at this price point. Cork. 14° alc. **Rating** 87 **To** 2008 $12

Baptista ★★★☆

c/- David Traeger, 139 High Street, Nagambie, Vic 3608 **Region** Heathcote
T (03) 5794 2514 **www**.baptista.com.au **Open** Mon–Fri 10–5, w'ends 12–5
Winemaker David Traeger **Est.** 1993 **Cases** 400
In 1993 David Traeger acquired a vineyard he had coveted for many years, and which had been planted by Baptista Governa in 1891. He had been buying grapes from the vineyard since 1988, but it was in a run-down condition, and required a number of years rehabilitation before he felt the quality of the grapes was sufficient. Is jointly owned by Traeger and the Wine Investment Fund, the latter a majority shareholder in Dromana Estate. Exports to the UK, Singapore and Japan.

ŶŶŶŶ **Heathcote Shiraz 2001** Simply doesn't have the depth and concentration one expects; on the other hand, the palate is long and silky. I have a suspicion that future vintages will be even better. Cork. 14.6° alc. **Rating** 89 **To** 2016 $115

Barambah

GPO Box 799, Brisbane, Qld 4001 **Region** South Burnett
T 1300 781 815 **F** 1300 138 949 **www**.barambah.com.au **Open** Not
Winemaker Peter Scudamore-Smith MW (Contract) **Est.** 1995 **Cases** 1000
Barambah has been purchased by Brisbane couple Jane and Steve Wilson. They live in a historic 19th-century West End home, but have owned a 1600-ha cattle property, Barambah Station, for the past 6 years. This made them near-neighbours of Barambah, and they had ample opportunity to watch the development of the 7-ha estate vineyard and the quality of its wines. When the opportunity came to purchase the winery and vineyard, they obtained consultancy advice from Peter Scudamore-Smith MW. His response was so positive they did not hesitate to buy the property. Under Scudamore-Smith's direction, wine quality has markedly improved, part of a remarkable renaissance in overall quality from Qld noted in this year's *Wine Companion*.

ŶŶŶŶŶ **First Grid Cabernet Sauvignon 2005** Classic, tight cabernet sauvignon with a mix of blackcurrant and cassis on entry then earthy black olive tannins to close; yet another very good Qld wine. Screwcap. 13.5° alc. **Rating** 90 **To** 2018 $29

ŶŶŶŶ **First Grid Chardonnay 2006** Nicely made; not overmuch fruit intensity, but what is there has been very well-handled, partly barrel-fermented and part in stainless steel, preserving the stone fruit flavours. Screwcap. 13.5° alc. **Rating** 89 **To** 2009 $24
First Grid Shiraz 2005 Light- to medium-bodied ripe black and red cherry and blackberry fruit; good line and length, although doesn't assert itself quite enough on the finish. Screwcap. 13.5° alc. **Rating** 89 **To** 2013 $29

Barfold Estate

57 School Road, Barfold, Vic 3444 **Region** Heathcote
T (03) 5423 4225 **F** (03) 5423 4225 **Open** 7 days 10–5
Winemaker Craig Aitken **Est.** 1998 **Cases** 900
Craig and Sandra Aitken acquired their farm property in the southwestern corner of the Heathcote wine region with the specific intention of growing premium grapes. They inspected more than 70 properties over the 18 months prior to purchasing Barfold, and are in fact only the second family to own the property since the 1850s. So far they have planted 3.8 ha of shiraz, and 0.4 ha of cabernet sauvignon; a small planting of viognier is planned.

Barmah Park Wines

945 Moorooduc Road, Moorooduc, Vic 3933 **Region** Mornington Peninsula
T (03) 5978 8049 **F** (03) 5978 8088 **www**.barmahparkwines.com.au **Open** 7 days 10–5
Winemaker Ewan Campbell (Contract) **Est.** 2000 **Cases** 2000
Tony Williams planted 1 ha of pinot gris and 2 ha of pinot noir (using 2 clones, MV6 and G5V15), having the first vintage made in 2003. In 2005 a substantial restaurant was opened, offering breakfast in the vines until 11.30 am, and lunch from noon–5 pm.

Barnadown Run

390 Cornella Road, Toolleen, Vic 3551 **Region** Heathcote
T (03) 5433 6376 **F** (03) 5433 6386 **www**.barnadownrun.com.au **Open** 7 days 10–5
Winemaker Andrew Millis **Est.** 1995 **Cases** 1700
Named after the original pastoral lease of which the vineyard forms part, established on the rich terra rossa soil for which Heathcote vineyards are famous. Owner Andrew Millis carries out both the viticulture and winemaking at the 5-ha vineyard. Exports to the US and the UK.

Barokes Wines

100 Market Street, South Melbourne, Vic 3205 (postal) **Region** Warehouse
T (03) 9698 1349 **F** (03) 9690 8114 **www**.wineinacan.com **Open** Not
Winemaker Steve Barics **Est.** 1997 **Cases** 150 000
Barokes Wines packages its wines in aluminium cans. The filling process is patented, and has been in commercial production since 2003. The wines show normal maturation and none of the cans used since start-up shows signs of corrosion. Wines are supplied in bulk by large wineries in southeast Australia, with Peter Scudamore-Smith acting as blending consultant. The wines are perfectly adequate for the market they serve and do not exhibit reduced characters retailing for $4.59 per can. Remarkably even quality, but, of course, no pretensions to greatness. Exports to all major markets with great success, production rising from 60 000 to 150 000 cases.

Barossa Ridge Wine Estate

Light Pass Road, Tanunda, SA 5352 **Region** Barossa Valley
T (08) 8563 2811 **F** (08) 8563 2811 **Open** By appt
Winemaker Marco Litterini **Est.** 1987 **Cases** 1500
A grapegrower turned winemaker with a small list of interesting red varietals, shunning the more common Rhône varietals and looking to Bordeaux. Increasing retail distribution in Australia; exports to Switzerland, Germany, Malaysia and Thailand.

ᵀᵀᵀᵀᵀ **Bamboo Creek Barossa Valley Merlot 2002** Savoury/earthy/spicy notes reflect both the vintage and the variety; lean and elegant. Screwcap. 14° alc. **Rating** 91 **To** 2015 $24.95
4 in One 2004 Medium red-purple; more density than the '05, but still with finesse and length; unusual for the Barossa to do so well with these varieties. Cabernet Sauvignon/Petit Verdot/Merlot/Cabernet Franc. Screwcap. 13.5° alc. **Rating** 91 **To** 2014 $14.95
Litterini Barossa Valley Cabernet Shiraz 2004 Medium-bodied, with good mouthfeel and balance; blackberry and blackcurrant are backed up by good oak handling and tannin control. Screwcap. 14° alc. **Rating** 90 **To** 2015 $29.95
Litterini Barossa Valley Cabernet Shiraz 2003 Less composed than the '04, the tannins not as round, the fruit slightly less expansive. Nonetheless, nice wine. Screwcap. 14° alc. **Rating** 90 **To** 2015 $29.95
Mardia Classic Red Blend 2005 Light- to medium-bodied; bright, fresh, lively, juicy array of predominantly red fruits; good length, to be enjoyed now or later. Classic Bordeaux blend: Merlot/Petit Verdot/Cabernet Sauvignon/Cabernet Franc. Screwcap. 14° alc. **Rating** 90 **To** 2013 $14.95

ᵀᵀᵀᵀ **Mardia Barossa Valley Shiraz 2005** Strong colour; blackberry, plum and chocolate with over-the-top jammy dead fruit flavours. Some like the style, it must be said. Screwcap. 15° alc. **Rating** 89 **To** 2013 $24.95
Litterini Barossa Valley Shiraz Cabernet 2005 Does show high alcohol courtesy of the sweetness running through both the bouquet and palate; the flavours are strangely attractive, ranging through black fruits and dark chocolate, but the grapes were picked too late. Screwcap. 15.5° alc. **Rating** 89 **To** 2015 $29.95
Barossa Valley Cabernet Franc 2004 Medium red-purple; unusual variety for the Barossa Valley; theoretically needs a much cooler climate such as the Loire Valley; light-bodied cedar/cigar box are varietal characters; clever making, the tannins not green. Screwcap. 13.5° alc. **Rating** 89 **To** 2011 $14.95

Barossa Valley Estate

Seppeltsfield Road, Marananga, SA 5355 **Region** Barossa Valley
T (08) 8562 3599 **F** (08) 8562 4255 **www**.bve.com.au **Open** 7 days 10–4.30
Winemaker Stuart Bourne **Est.** 1984 **Cases** 100 000

Barossa Valley Estate is owned by Hardys, marking the end of a period during which it was one of the last significant cooperative owned wineries in Australia. Across the board, the wines are full flavoured and honest. E&E Black Pepper Shiraz is an upmarket label with a strong reputation and following; the Ebenezer range likewise.

ΨΨΨΨΨ **E&E Black Pepper Shiraz 2003** Leather, prune, licorice, plum and blackberry all intermingle on the supple palate; simply doesn't have the intense focus of the best '04s, but is a pretty good wine. Cork. 15° alc. **Rating** 91 **To** 2013 $80
Ebenezer Barossa Valley Shiraz 2003 Abundant ripe, but not jammy, blackberry and licorice fruit; tannins balanced, as is the oak; good outcome for an indifferent vintage. Poor-quality cork. 14.5° alc. **Rating** 91 **To** 2018 $28.50

Barratt   ★★★★★

Uley Vineyard, Cornish Road, Summertown, SA 5141 **Region** Adelaide Hills
T (08) 8390 1788 **www.**barrattwines.com.au **Open** Fri–Sun & public hols 11.30–5
Winemaker Lindsay Barratt **Est.** 1993 **Cases** 1800
Lindsay and Carolyn Barratt own 2 vineyards at Summertown: Uley Vineyard and Bonython Vineyard. They have 8.4 ha of vines; sauvignon blanc and merlot were added to the wine range from 2002. Part of the production is sold to other makers. Arrangements were finalised for a winery facility at the Adelaide Hills Business and Tourism Centre at Lobethal in time for the 2003 vintage. Limited quantities are sold in the UK, Canada and Asia.

ΨΨΨΨΨ **Piccadilly Valley Adelaide Hills Sauvignon Blanc 2006** A pure and fragrant bouquet of passionfruit and citrus; a very long, very intense lime and lemon palate; bracing finish. Screwcap. 13.5° alc. **Rating** 95 **To** 2016 $21
Piccadilly Valley Adelaide Hills Chardonnay 2005 An elegant wine; seamless integration of nectarine fruit and oak; long, lingering finish with perfect acidity. Screwcap. 13.5° alc. **Rating** 94 **To** 2012 $29

ΨΨΨΨΨ **The Reserve Piccadilly Valley Pinot Noir 2005** Slightly deeper hue than the Bonython; much more intensity and concentration; plum, spice and cherry; firm acidity, and definitely needs time. Cork. 14° alc. **Rating** 92 **To** 2013 $44
Piccadilly Sunrise Adelaide Hills Rose 2006 Fresh, lively strawberry and cherry aromas and flavours; crisp, dry and long finish. Classy style. Screwcap. 12.5° alc. **Rating** 90 **To** 2008 $21

ΨΨΨΨ **The Bonython Piccadilly Valley Pinot Noir 2005** A clean bouquet with no reduction; a light- to medium-bodied spicy/stemmy style, but with sufficient red fruit flavours. Screwcap. 14.5° alc. **Rating** 89 **To** 2010 $24

Barretts Wines   ★★★★☆

Portland-Nelson Highway, Portland, Vic 3305 **Region** Henty
T (03) 5526 5251 **Open** 7 days 11–5
Winemaker Rod Barrett **Est.** 1983 **Cases** 1000
Has a low profile, selling its wines locally, but deserves a far wider audience. The initial releases were made at Best's, but since 1992 all wines have been made (with increasing skill) on the property by Rod Barrett, emulating John Thomson at Crawford River Wines. The 5.5-ha vineyard is planted to riesling, pinot noir and cabernet sauvignon.

ΨΨΨΨΨ **Henty Riesling 2006** Intense lemon and lime zest aromas; very good power, length and intensity; will be long-lived. Screwcap. 12.5° alc. **Rating** 94 **To** 2021 $25

ΨΨΨΨ **Pinot Noir 2004** Ripe plum and spice with a touch of forest on the bouquet; a powerful, long palate with similar plum, spice and forest flavours. Excellent value. Screwcap. 13° alc. **Rating** 92 **To** 2010 $20
Henty Riesling 2005 Interesting wine; intense lime and passionfruit aromas and flavours, with distinct residual sweetness. Screwcap. 11.9° alc. **Rating** 91 **To** 2015 $23

Barrgowan Vineyard

30 Pax Parade, Curlewis, Vic 3222 **Region** Geelong
T (03) 5250 3861 **F** (03) 5250 3840 **Open** By appt
Winemaker Dick Simonsen **Est.** 1998 **Cases** 100
Dick and Dib (Elizabeth) Simonsen began the planting of their 0.5 ha of shiraz (with 5 clones) in 1994, intending to simply make wine for their own consumption. As all of the 5 clones are in full production, the Simonsens expect a maximum production of 200 cases, and have accordingly released small quantities of Shiraz, which sells out very quickly. The vines are hand-pruned, the grapes hand-picked, the must basket-pressed, and all wine movements are by gravity.

Barringwood Park

60 Gillams Road, Lower Barrington, Tas 7306 **Region** Northern Tasmania
T (03) 6492 3140 **F** (03) 6492 3360 **www**.barringwoodpark.com.au **Open** Jan & Feb
7 days, March–Dec Wed–Sun & public hols 10–5
Winemaker Tamar Ridge **Est.** 1993 **Cases** 1600
Judy and Ian Robinson operate a sawmill at Lower Barrington, 15 mins south of Devonport on the main tourist trail to Cradle Mountain, and when they planted 500 vines in 1993 the aim was to do a bit of home winemaking. In a thoroughly familiar story, the urge to expand the vineyard and make wine on a commercial scale came almost immediately, and they embarked on a 6-year plan, planting 1 ha a year in the first 4 years and building the cellar and tasting rooms during the following 2 years.

ŦŦŦŦŦ **Mill Block Pinot Noir 2005** Great colour; fragrant plum aromas, then a long, silky palate with cherry coming into the mix; utterly delicious. Gold medal Tas Wine Show '07. Screwcap. 14° alc. **Rating** 95 **To** 2014 $34

ŦŦŦŦŦ **Forest Raven Pinot Noir 2005** Medium- to full purple-red; powerful and concentrated; lots of structure and character; a lighter touch might have made an even better wine. Screwcap. 13.7° alc. **Rating** 91 **To** 2015 $28
Flagship Chardonnay 2005 Complex and rich, with lots of rumbling power and intensity to the ripe fruit; ultimately submerged by the barrel ferment oak. So near and yet so far. Screwcap. 14.3° alc. **Rating** 90 **To** 2009 $25

ŦŦŦŦ **Pinot Meunier Rose 2006** An unusual pinot noir/meunier rose; cherries, strawberries and spice; just needed a touch more conviction. Screwcap. 13° alc. **Rating** 87 **To** 2008 $19

Barristers Block

6 The Parkway, Leabrook, SA 5068 (postal) **Region** Adelaide Hills
T 0427 076 237 **F** (08) 8364 2930 **www**.barristersblock.com.au **Open** Not
Winemaker Richard Langford, Simon Greenleaf (Contract) **Est.** 2004 **Cases** 2000
Owner Jan Siemelink-Allen has had 20 years in the industry, and 5 years in SA's Supreme Court in a successful battle to reclaim ownership of 10 ha of cabernet sauvignon and shiraz in Wrattonbully after a joint venture collapsed; it is not hard to imagine the origin of the name. In '06 she and her family purchased an 8-ha vineyard planted to sauvignon blanc and pinot noir near Woodside in the Adelaide Hills, adjoining some of Shaw & Smith's vineyards. Jan Siemelink-Allen, as well as having senior management positions with several companies, is currently a member of the SA Premier's Wine Industry Advisory Council; no rose-tinted spectacles here.

ŦŦŦŦŦ **Adelaide Hills Sauvignon Blanc 2006** Clean and fresh; very attractive passionfruit and tropical aromas and flavours, balanced by clean, crisp acidity on the finish. Zork. 13.5° alc. **Rating** 94 **To** 2008 $17
Barossa Shiraz 2004 An elegant, medium-bodied wine with appealing black cherry and blackberry fruit; smooth and supple; fine tannins. Zork. 14.2° alc. **Rating** 94 **To** 2014 $24

ŸŸŸŸ **Eden Valley Riesling 2004** Bright straw-green; the bouquet is complex, but with a slight suggestion of reduction to the gentle mix of citrus, tropical and lime fruit. Screwcap. 12° alc. **Rating** 89 **To** 2010 $16

Wrattonbully Cabernet Sauvignon 2004 Juicy blackcurrant fruit, with touches of mint; controlled extract and oak. Zork. 14° alc. **Rating** 89 **To** 2012 $24

Barton Estate

45 Milford Street, Latham, ACT 2615 (postal) **Region** Canberra District
T (02) 6254 6121 **F** (02) 6254 7606 **www**.bartonestate.com.au **Open** Not
Winemaker Roger Harris, Brindabella Hills, Kyeema Estate **Est.** 1997 **Cases** 900
Bob Furbank and wife Julie Chitty are both CSIRO plant biologists: he is a biochemist (physiologist) and she a specialist in plant tissue culture. In 1997 they acquired the 120-ha property forming part of historic Jeir Station, and have since planted 8 ha to 15 varieties, the most substantial plantings to cabernet sauvignon, shiraz, merlot, riesling and chardonnay, the Joseph's Coat completed with micro quantities of other varieties.

Barwang Vineyard

Barwang Road, Young, NSW 2594 (postal) **Region** Hilltops
T (02) 6382 3594 **F** (02) 6382 2594 **www**.mcwilliams.com.au **Open** Not
Winemaker Jim Brayne, Martin Cooper, Russell Cody **Est.** 1969 **Cases** NFP
Peter Robertson pioneered viticulture in the Young region when he planted his first vines in 1969 as part of a diversification program for his 400-ha grazing property. When McWilliam's acquired Barwang in 1989, the vineyard amounted to 13 ha; today the plantings exceed 100 ha. Wine quality has been exemplary from the word go: always elegant, restrained and deliberately understated, repaying extended cellaring.

ŸŸŸŸŸ **Chardonnay 2006** Typically refined and elegant; citrus and stone fruit, seamless oak; very good acidity and length. Screwcap. 13° alc. **Rating** 94 **To** 2013 $19

ŸŸŸŸŸ **Tumbarumba Chardonnay 2005** An elegant, light- to medium-bodied wine driven by its long, pure palate of grapefruit and nectarine; lively finish. Screwcap. 13° alc. **Rating** 93 **To** 2012 $25

Shiraz 2003 Medium-bodied, with extremely good balance and texture, the black fruits supported by fine, ripe tannins, and to a lesser degree by oak. Cork. 13.5° alc. **Rating** 93 **To** 2019 $22.95

Cabernet Sauvignon 2003 Solidly constructed; blackcurrant and blackberry fruit; emphatic tannins on the finish need to soften over the next 5 years, but the wine has the balance to come out on top. Cork. 13.5° alc. **Rating** 90 **To** 2023 $22.95

Barwick Wines

Yelverton North Road, Dunsborough, WA 6281 **Region** Margaret River
T (08) 9755 7100 **F** (08) 9755 7133 **www**.barwickwines.com **Open** 7 days 11–4
Winemaker Nigel Ludlow **Est.** 1997 **Cases** 120 000
The production gives some guide to the size of the 3 estate vineyards. The first is the 83-ha Dwalganup Vineyard in the Blackwood Valley region; the second, the 38-ha St John's Brook Vineyard in Margaret River; and the third, the 73-ha Treenbrook Vineyard in Pemberton. Taken together, the 3 vineyard holdings place Barwick Estates in the top 10 wine producers in WA. The wines are released under 4 labels: at the bottom, the Crush Label; next the White Label estate range; next the Black Label single vineyard wines from any one of the 3 regions; and at the top the Platinum Label, which, confusingly, is in fact called The Collectables, from small parcels of estate-grown grapes. Exports to the UK, the US and other major markets.

ŸŸŸŸŸ **The Collectables Blackwood Valley Cabernet Sauvignon 2004** Medium-bodied, with attractive cedary overtones to the black fruits, and fine, ripe tannins; good overall content and balance. Screwcap. 14° alc. **Rating** 91 **To** 2015 $24

Sauvignon Blanc Semillon 2006 Plenty of flavour and length; the sauvignon blanc dominant with tropical passionfruit flavours, the semillon providing structure and acidity. Screwcap. 12.5° alc. **Rating** 90 **To** 2009 $15

The Collectables Pemberton Viognier 2005 More life and a greater range of aromas and flavours than most, but avoids phenolics, offering apricot, pear, peach and bright citrussy acidity on the finish. Screwcap. 14° alc. **Rating** 90 **To** 2010 $24

The Collectables Blackwood Valley Shiraz 2004 Fragrant, spicy fruit with lifted aromas; a lively, medium-bodied palate offering red and black cherry fruit, fine tannins aiding the wine's considerable length. Screwcap. 14.5° alc. **Rating** 90 **To** 2015 $24

 Margaret River Shiraz 2005 Potent earthy/spicy black fruit aromas, then a medium-bodied palate following a similar track, needing just a touch more sweet fruit. Screwcap. 13.5° alc. **Rating** 88 **To** 2015 $18

Cabernet Sauvignon 2004 Clean, fresh, direct cassis-accented cabernet fruit; no frills, but good length and balance. Value. Screwcap. 14° alc. **Rating** 88 **To** 2011 $15

Chardonnay 2006 Soft peachy fruit balanced by equally soft oak; easy-access style. Screwcap. 13° alc. **Rating** 87 **To** 2008 $15

Margaret River Cabernet Sauvignon 2005 Light- to medium-bodied; bright, fresh blackcurrant/cassis fruit; direct and well-balanced, but not complex or weighty. Screwcap. 14° alc. **Rating** 87 **To** 2012 $18

Barwite Vineyards ★★★☆

PO Box 542, Mansfield, Vic 3724 **Region** Upper Goulburn
T 0408 525 135 **F** (03) 5776 9800 **www**.barwitevineyards.com.au **Open** Not
Winemaker Delatite (Jane Donat) **Est.** 1997 **Cases** 4000
David Ritchie and a group of fellow grape and wine enthusiasts established their substantial vineyard in 1997 on a slope facing the mouth of the Broken River and thereon to Mt Stirling. A little under 26 ha of pinot noir and 12 ha of chardonnay were planted for Orlando, to be used in sparkling wine. Given the reputation of the region for the production of aromatic white wines, 4.5 ha of riesling were also planted, the intention being to sell the grapes. However, since 2003 some of the best parcels have been kept aside for the Barwite label.

Barwon Plains ★★★

61 Trebeck Court, Winchelsea, Vic 3241 **Region** Geelong
T (03) 5267 2792 **F** (03) 5267 2792 **Open** By appt
Winemaker Phil Kelly **Est.** 1995 **Cases** 300
Phil and Merridee Kelly planted 1.5 ha of pinot noir, 1 ha of chardonnay and 0.2 ha of shiraz between 1995 and 1998. The Kellys personally carry out all of the vineyard and winery operations, selling most of the grape production to Shadowfax. The wines have been medal winners at the Geelong Wine Show.

Basedow ★★★☆

951 Bylong Valley Way, Baerami via Denman, NSW 2333 (postal) **Region** Barossa Valley
T 1300 887 966 **F** (02) 6574 5164 **www**.basedow.com.au **Open** Not
Winemaker Peter Orr, Ian Long **Est.** 1896 **Cases** 30 000
An old and proud label, once particularly well known for its oak-matured Semillon, but which has changed hands on a number of occasions before passing into the ownership of James Estate in 2003. Continues making traditional styles, big in flavour, but not so much in finesse, the alcohol remaining relatively high. Exports to the US and other major markets.

 Barossa Shiraz 2004 Good depth to black fruit flavours typical of '04 Barossa reds; has good length and balance, with perfectly pitched tannins. Twin top. 15.1° alc. **Rating** 91 **To** 2011 $22

♀♀♀♀   **Barossa Valley Semillon 2006** Medium- to full-bodied, but very different to the days of the so-called white burgundy; attractive ripe lemon/lemon custard flavours in a drink now version. Twin top. 11.9° alc. **Rating** 89 **To** 2008 $14

Basket Range Wines   ★★★

PO Box 65, Basket Range, SA 5138 **Region** Adelaide Hills
T 0427 021 915 **F** (08) 8390 1515 **www.**basketrangewine.com.au **Open** By appt
Winemaker Phillip Broderick **Est.** 1980 **Cases** 400
A tiny operation known to very few, run by civil and Aboriginal rights lawyer Phillip Broderick, a most engaging man with a disarmingly laid-back manner. He has recently established a new vineyard with 1.3 ha each of cabernet sauvignon, merlot and pinot noir, plus a splash (0.3 ha) of petit verdot which will see production increase as it comes into bearing. Great to see Phillip is continuing to quietly make and release his wines after a quarter of a century in the saddle.

♀♀♀♀   **Cabernet Sauvignon Cabernet Franc Petit Verdot Malbec Merlot 2002**
Still very fresh and lively, with relatively low pH; some minty overtones, but has appealing red fruit flavours amplified by the cool vintage. Screwcap. 13.2° alc.
Rating 87 **To** 2008 $23
Cabernet Sauvignon Cabernet Franc Petit Verdot Malbec Merlot 2001
Surprisingly similar given the radical difference in vintage conditions ('01 being very warm); slightly less minty and fresh, but has by no means given up the fight. Cork. 13.5° alc. **Rating** 87 **To** 2008 $25

Bass Fine Wines

Upper McEwans Road, Rosevears, Tas 7270 **Region** Northern Tasmania
T (03) 6331 0136 **F** (03) 6331 0136 **Open** Not
Winemaker Guy Wagner **Est.** 1999 **Cases** 4500
Owner/winemaker Guy Wagner had been carrying on the business as a classic negociant (in Burgundian terms), originally buying wine from various vineyards in bottle and/or in barrel, but from 2000 also purchasing grapes, the wines made at other existing wineries. Prior to the 2006 vintage, he completed the construction of a new winery, at which he now makes his own wines, and offers contract winemaking services for others.

♀♀♀♀♀   **Bass Strait Pinot Noir 2005** Complex and intense, with beautifully balanced cherry, spice and plum flavours. Outstanding value. Screwcap. 13.5° alc.
Rating 94 **To** 2012 $22

♀♀♀♀♀   **Bass Strait Pinot Noir 2006** Plenty of depth and power; almost but not over the top; spice, pepper and black cherry. Outstanding value. Screwcap. 14° alc.
Rating 92 **To** 2011 $22
Bass Strait Riesling 1999 Excellent bouquet, with clean, lively blossom aromas; a long and pure palate, with good acidity. **Rating** 91 **To** 2015
Bass Strait Chardonnay 2006 Peachy nectarine fruit, with a subtle touch of oak; good balance and mouthfeel. Screwcap. 13.4° alc. **Rating** 90 **To** 2010 $21

♀♀♀♀   **Strait Sauvignon Blanc 2006** A quiet bouquet, then passionfruit and lemon/citrus flavours are revealed, the touch of sweetness on the finish a pity. Screwcap. 13° alc. **Rating** 87 **To** 2008 $21

Bass Phillip

Tosch's Road, Leongatha South, Vic 3953 **Region** Gippsland
T (03) 5664 3341 **F** (03) 5664 3209 **Open** By appt
Winemaker Phillip Jones **Est.** 1979 **Cases** 1500
Phillip Jones has retired from the Melbourne rat-race to handcraft tiny quantities of superlative Pinot Noir which, at its best, has no equal in Australia. Painstaking site selection, ultra-close vine spacing and the very, very cool climate of South Gippsland are the keys to the magic of Bass Phillip and its eerily Burgundian Pinots. Tastings are sporadic (a mega-tasting in 2006) and the rating is very much that of the best, not the lesser, wines.

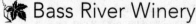 # Bass River Winery   ★★★

1835 Dalyston Glen Forbes Road, Glen Forbes, Vic 3990 **Region** Gippsland
T (03) 5678 8252 **F** (03) 9462 2527 www.bassriverwinery.com **Open** Thurs–Tues 9–5
Winemaker Pasquale Butera, Frank Butera **Est.** 1999 **Cases** NA
The Butera family has established 7 ha of riesling, chardonnay, pinot noir, cabernet sauvignon and merlot, with both the winemaking and viticulture handled by the father and son team of Pasquale and Frank Butera. The small production is principally sold through the cellar door plus some retailers and restaurants in the South Gippsland area.

ŶŶŶŶ **Riesling 2005** Fragrant citrus aromas and flavours; good depth and balance.
Rating 89 **To** 2008 $20
Pinot Noir 2005 Subtle plum and cherry fruit line; not complex. **Rating** 87
To 2011 $15

battely wines   ★★★★★

1375 Beechworth-Wangaratta Road, Beechworth, Vic 3747 **Region** Beechworth
T (03) 5727 0505 **F** (03) 5727 0506 www.battelywines.com.au **Open** By appt
Winemaker Russell Bourne **Est.** 1998 **Cases** 450
Dr Russell Bourne is an anaesthetist and former GP at Mt Beauty, who has always loved the food, wine and skiing of Northeast Victoria. He completed his oenology degree at Charles Sturt University in 2002 following his 1998 acquisition of the former Brown Brothers Everton Hills vineyard. He has since planted 1.6 ha of shiraz and viognier, with further Rhône Valley varietal plantings planned, including counoise. Since 2001 all wines have come from the estate vineyards, which have increased to 2.3 ha. Exports to the US, Denmark and Singapore.

ŶŶŶŶŶ **Syrah 2005** A highly aromatic and very complex bouquet; black fruits with a full range of spices, some oriental, plus cracked pepper; soft, persistent tannins. Cork. 15.5° alc. **Rating** 94 **To** 2020 $52

ŶŶŶŶŶ **Marsanne 2005** Subtle incorporation of oak sits alongside honeysuckle and creamy notes; good balance, though there is some alcohol warmth. Cork. 14.5° alc. **Rating** 90 **To** 2015 $28

Battle of Bosworth   ★★★★☆

Edgehill Vineyards, Gaffney Road, Willunga, SA 5172 **Region** McLaren Vale
T (08) 8556 2441 **F** (08) 8556 4881 www.battleofbosworth.com.au **Open** By appt
Winemaker Joch Bosworth, Ben Riggs (Consultant) **Est.** 1996 **Cases** 4500
The 75-ha Edgehill Vineyard, established many years ago by Peter and Anthea Bosworth, was taken over by son Joch Bosworth in 1996. He set about converting 10 ha of shiraz, cabernet sauvignon and chardonnay to fully certified A-grade organic viticulture. The regime prohibits the use of herbicides and pesticides; the weeds are controlled by soursob, the pretty yellow flower considered a weed by many, which carpets the vineyards in winter, but dies off in early spring as surface moisture dries, forming a natural weed mat. Organic viticulture is never easy, and when Joch moved to make the first wines from the vines, the Battle of Bosworth name was a neat take. Exports to the UK, the US and other major markets.

ŶŶŶŶŶ **McLaren Vale Cabernet Sauvignon 2005** Filled to the gills with blackcurrant fruit and an echo of dark chocolate; good tannin and oak management; will likely outlive its cork closure. 14.5° alc. **Rating** 94 **To** 2020 $25

ŶŶŶŶŶ **McLaren Vale Shiraz 2005** Deep, dense colour; a powerful, layered and structured wine; masses of blackberry fruit with a touch of chocolate; ripe tannins. Screwcap. 14.5° alc. **Rating** 93 **To** 2020 $25
White Boar 2005 Powerful, rich and deep; the prune-like sweetness in Amarone style is the result of cane cutting and up to 2 weeks drying before vinification. Cork. 15.4° alc. **Rating** 90 **To** 2025 $45

ŸŸŸŸ **The War of the Rose 2006** Light red–purple; crisp, lively, vibrant and fresh red cherry/redcurrant fruit; good length. Cabernet Sauvignon. Screwcap. 13.5° alc. **Rating** 89 **To** 2008 $18
McLaren Vale Shiraz Viognier 2005 Rich confit fruit; sweetness (fruit and alcohol) apparent throughout; may settle down and dry out a little with time. Screwcap. 15° alc. **Rating** 89 **To** 2015 $25
McLaren Vale Chardonnay Viognier 2006 Flavoursome wine; stone fruit, especially including apricot, bears testament to the blend; no oak obvious. Screwcap. 13° alc. **Rating** 87 **To** 2009 $18

Bay of Fires ★★★★★

40 Baxters Road, Pipers River, Tas 7252 **Region** Northern Tasmania
T (03) 6382 7622 **F** (03) 6382 7225 **www**.bayoffireswines.com.au **Open** 7 days 10–5
Winemaker Fran Austin **Est.** 2001 **Cases** 3000
In 1994 Hardys purchased its first grapes from Tasmania, with the aim of further developing and refining its sparkling wines, a process which quickly gave birth to Arras. The next stage was the inclusion of various parcels of chardonnay from Tas in the 1998 Eileen Hardy, then the development in 2001 of the Bay of Fires brand, offering wines sourced from various parts of Tas. As one would expect, there is great potential for the brand. The winery was originally that of Rochecombe, then Ninth Island, and now, of course, Bay of Fires.

ŸŸŸŸŸ **Tigress Riesling 2005** Tasmanian riesling at its best; impressed when 7 months old and winning silver at the Tas Wine Show '06, but is now opening up to show its superb mid–palate ripe lemon and citrus fruit; great length. Out-pointed some great classic rieslings to win a trophy at the National Wine Show '06. Screwcap. 11.5° alc. **Rating** 96 **To** 2015 $21.50
Arras 2001 A beautifully balanced wine, with entrancing stone fruit and citrus flavours; great length and persistence. Trophy National Wine Show '06. 12.6° alc. **Rating** 96 **To** 2015 $60
Chardonnay 2006 Has the particular type and finesse which only comes from Tasmania; especially when young, the fruit flavours are subtle and in the nectarine/grapefruit spectrum; hints of cream and subtle, toasty oak. Shades of Chablis. Screwcap. 13.5° alc. **Rating** 94 **To** 2012 $27.50
Tigress Chardonnay 2004 A complex wine, with controlled barrel ferment inputs to nectarine and peach fruit; balanced acidity. Retasted 12 months later, virtually unchanged, once again winning gold (Tas Wine Show '07). Cork. 12.9° alc. **Rating** 94 **To** 2012 $21.50

ŸŸŸŸŸ **Tigress Late Harvest Riesling 2006** Intense riesling flavour; good intensity and length; absolutely certain to flower further with age. Screwcap. 10.3° alc. **Rating** 93 **To** 2013 $21.50
Riesling 2006 Delicate, fresh and crystal clean; a well-balanced palate with gentle citrus offset by nice minerally notes. Has considerable potential for development. Screwcap. 12.4° alc. **Rating** 92 **To** 2016 $21.50
Chardonnay 2005 Light- to medium-bodied; smooth, supple and elegant wine, the fruit expressive, oak in the background. Screwcap. 13.3° alc. **Rating** 92 **To** 2011 $27.50
Tigress Sauvignon Blanc 2006 Lively, citrussy, tangy aromas and flavours; well-balanced acidity; superior to many. Screwcap. 11.7° alc. **Rating** 90 **To** 2009 $21.50
Tigress Pinot Noir 2005 Elegant and fine, with long red cherry/red berry fruit, and delicate but sustained tannins. The only Australian pinot to withstand the NZ blitz on this class at the National Wine Show '06, where it showed far more than at the Tas Wine Show '07. Screwcap. 13.6° alc. **Rating** 90 **To** 2009 $25.50

ŸŸŸŸ **Tigress Rose 2006** Delicate, fragrant rose water, says Bay of Fires, and it's correct; add in a dash of strawberry and a balanced finish, and you have the wine. Screwcap. 13.5° alc. **Rating** 88 **To** 2008 $21.50

Pinot Noir 2005 Very good hue; a complex wine with many shades and nuances yet to harmonise; a child behaving badly today, tomorrow an angel. Screwcap. 13.6° alc. **Rating** 88 **To** 2011 $35

Pinot Gris 2006 A powerful wine, with much more structure than one usually encounters; perhaps some winemaking tricks at work. Screwcap. 13.5° alc. **Rating** 87 **To** 2008 $27.50

Beaumont Estate

Lot 20, 155 Milbrodale Road, Broke, NSW 2330 **Region** Lower Hunter Valley
T 0419 616 461 **F** (07) 5474 3722 **Open** Not
Winemaker Scott Stephens (Contract) **Est.** 1998 **Cases** 1500
The vineyards were planted in 1999 on the river flats of Parson Creek, nestled between the Yengo and Wollemi National Parks. The soils were enhanced with organic preparations; after 17 months the 2.2 ha of semillon and 1.3 ha of merlot produced a substantial crop, the vine growth, equivalent to 3 years under normal conditions. The intention is to eventually become certified biodynamic. Profits from wine sales support a respite and natural therapies centre for life-limited children that is currently being constructed on the property.

Beckett's Flat

49 Beckett Road, Metricup, WA 6280 **Region** Margaret River
T (08) 9755 7402 **F** (08) 9755 7344 **www**.beckettsflat.com.au **Open** 7 days 10–6
Winemaker Belizar Ilic **Est.** 1992 **Cases** 8000
Bill Belizar and Noni Ilic opened Beckett's Flat in 1997. Situated just off the Bussell Highway, midway between Busselton and the Margaret River, it draws upon 14 ha of estate vineyards, first planted in 1992. Since 1998 the wines have been made onsite. Exports to the UK, Singapore and Israel.

Margaret River Sauvignon Blanc 2006 A clean, tangy, lively and fresh bouquet leads into a palate with gooseberry, kiwifruit and touches of grass, finished off with attractive lemony acidity. Quality Margaret River wines do not have to be expensive. Screwcap. 13° alc. **Rating** 92 **To** 2008 $16

Margaret River Shiraz 2004 Medium-bodied blackberry, spice and licorice aromas and flavours in an attractive, cool-grown wine; good finish. Screwcap. 14.5° alc. **Rating** 90 **To** 2013 $23

Belizar's Reserve Justinian 2003 Light- to medium-bodied; notes of herb, leaf, spice and earth play along with black fruits; fine tannins lengthen the finish. Merlot/Cabernet Sauvignon/Malbec. Screwcap. 13° alc. **Rating** 90 **To** 2013 $29

Belizar's Reserve Margaret River Sparkling Shiraz 2003 Some complexity to the spicy red fruit flavours; lesser dosage would have made an even better wine. 12° alc. **Rating** 88 **To** 2011 $25

Beckingham Wines

6–7/477 Warrigal Road, Moorabbin, Vic 3189 **Region** Mornington Peninsula
T (03) 9258 7352 **F** (03) 9360 0713 **www**.beckinghamwines.com.au **Open** W'ends 10–5
Winemaker Peter Beckingham **Est.** 1998 **Cases** 4000
Peter Beckingham is a chemical engineer who has turned a hobby into a part-time business, moving operations from the driveway of his house to a warehouse in Moorabbin. The situation of the winery may not be romantic, but it is eminently practical, and more than a few winemakers in California have adopted the same solution. His friends grow the grapes, and he makes the wine, both for himself and as a contract maker for others.

Semillon 2005 Clean, fresh, crisp and lively; excellent given the fact that only 500 litres (from Goulburn Valley fruit) was made; attractive citrus and mineral notes. Screwcap. 11.5° alc. **Rating** 89 **To** 2010 $13

Cornelia Creek Cabernet Sauvignon 2004 Somewhat rustic oak; powerful black fruit/blackcurrant flavours have both length and depth. Cork. 14° alc. **Rating** 88 **To** 2015 $18

Pas de Deux Pinot Noir Chardonnay 1997 Has complexity, partly from the base wine, partly from the regions, and partly from age in bottle. Yarra Valley/Mornington Peninsula/Strathbogie Ranges. 11.5° alc. **Rating** 88 **To** 2008 $30

Beelgara Estate

Farm 576 Rossetto Road, Beelbangera, NSW 2680 **Region** Riverina
T (02) 6966 0200 **F** (02) 6966 0298 www.beelgara.com.au **Open** Mon–Sat 10–5, Sun 11–3
Winemaker Rod Hooper, Danny Toaldo, Sean Hampel **Est.** 1930 **Cases** 600 000
Beelgara Estate was formed in 2001 after the purchase of the 60-year-old Rossetto family winery by a group of growers, distributors and investors. The new management is placing far greater emphasis on bottled table wine (albeit at low prices), spreading its wings to premium regions, but still maintaining excellent value for money.

♀♀♀♀♀ Regional Reserve Yarra Valley Chardonnay 2006 No reduction whatsoever; fresh and lively melon, nectarine and citrus fruit; no doubting the Yarra Valley origin or character; has length and delicacy; well-made. Screwcap. 13° alc. **Rating** 90 **To** 2013 $20

Regional Reserve Coonawarra Cabernet Sauvignon 2005 Medium-bodied; clear-cut Coonawarra cabernet sauvignon aromas and flavours; blackcurrant fruit, balanced oak and good length. The Regional Reserves are 3 examples of the silver lining in the clouds of excess supply. Screwcap. 14° alc. **Rating** 90 **To** 2015 $20

♀♀♀♀ Regional Reserve Clare Valley Shiraz 2005 Medium-bodied, with good depth to black fruits without over-extraction; fine tannins, good length and subtle oak. Screwcap. 14.5° alc. **Rating** 89 **To** 2017 $20

Winemakers Selection Black Shiraz 2005 Abundant blackberry and plum fruit; good structure, and a clever touch of oak. Screwcap. 15° alc. **Rating** 89 **To** 2015 $16

Winemakers Selection Rose 2006 Neatly balanced; some red fruit, the residual sugar and acidity in balance and in support. Screwcap. 13° alc. **Rating** 87 **To** 2008 $16

Rascal's Prayer Old Vine Shiraz 2005 Light- to medium-bodied; clean plum and black cherry fruit; cheap and cheerful. Neither in Europe nor Australia is there any definition of what constitutes an old vine, but it's possible these could date back to 1930. Screwcap. 14° alc. **Rating** 87 **To** 2008 $11

Belalie Bend

Mannanarie Road, Jamestown, SA 5491 **Region** Southern Flinders Ranges
T (08) 8664 1323 **F** (08) 8664 1923 www.belaliebend.com.au **Open** By appt
Winemaker Emma Bowley **Est.** 2001 **Cases** 350
Emma Bowley obtained her wine science degree from Charles Sturt University, and after a varied career working for large Australian wine companies, and thereafter in the US and Italy, decided to turn her attention to smaller wineries where she could have a hands-on winemaking role. Emma works as a contract winemaker in the Clare Valley, while she and husband Guy have established a vineyard in Jamestown situated beneath Mt Remarkable at an elevation of over 400 m. One ha each of shiraz, cabernet sauvignon and riesling were planted in 2001, followed by 1.5 ha each of mourvedre and shiraz the following year.

♀♀♀♀♀ Southern Flinders Ranges Shiraz 2004 Saturated with blackberry, plum and black cherry fruit, with strands of licorice, spice and chocolate woven through it. Real concern about the long-term performance of the closure. Zork. 14.8° alc. **Rating** 94 **To** 2019 $40

ŶŶŶŶŶ **Southern Flinders Ranges Riesling 2005** An attractive mix of mineral, slate and lime juice; good length and a bracing finish. Screwcap. 12° alc. **Rating** 92 To 2015 $16

Southern Flinders Ranges Riesling 2006 Aromatic crushed lime leaves and apple blossom aromas; similar flavours on the palate; nicely balanced and weighted. Synthetic. 12° alc. **Rating** 91 To 2014 $16

Belgravia Vineyards   ★★★★

84 Byng Street, Orange, NSW 2800 **Region** Orange
T (02) 6361 4441 **www.**belgravia.com.au **Open** Sun–Thurs 10–8, Fri–Sat 10–late
Winemaker David Lowe, Jane Wilson (Contract) **Est.** 2003 **Cases** 6000
Belgravia is an 1800-ha mixed farming property (sheep, cattle and vines) 20 km north of Orange. There are now 190 ha of vineyard with 10 ha devoted to the Belgravia brand. In 2006 Belgravia opened its cellar door at the heritage-listed former Union Bank building in Orange, which also operates as a wine bar with an all-day tapas menu. Exports to the UK and Denmark.

ŶŶŶŶŶ **Union Bank Semillon Sauvignon Blanc 2005** Light straw-green; a clean sunburst of flavours; passionfruit, pineapple and refreshing citrus on the finish. Screwcap. 13° alc. **Rating** 93 To 2008 $13

Platinum Shiraz 2004 Good structure, texture and weight; ripe, not jammy, fruit, with positive oak; good length and balance. Screwcap. 14.7° alc. **Rating** 92 To 2017 $26

Viognier 2005 Clear-cut varietal apricot/fruit pastille aromas; generous flavour, with no alcohol heat. Screwcap. 14.2° alc. **Rating** 90 To 2010 $26

Roussanne 2005 Fresh, clean and well-made; touches of ripe citrus and melon; a blend with the Viognier might have been synergistic. Screwcap. 15.2° alc. **Rating** 90 To 2010 $18

ŶŶŶŶ **Chardonnay 2005** Bright but light yellow-green; gentle peach, nectarine and melon fruit; no obvious oak influence. Screwcap. 14.7° alc. **Rating** 89 To 2009 $18

Platinum Shiraz 2003 Holding hue well; a mix of cool-grown aromas and flavours; leaf, spice, anise and licorice through the black fruits. Cork. **Rating** 89 To 2011 $26

Merlot 2005 Varietal character is well-expressed, but has a slightly hollow structure. Screwcap. 14.1° alc. **Rating** 88 To 2012 $18

Union Bank Rose 2005 A pleasant dry style; light strawberry and raspberry fruit; clean finish. Screwcap. 13.5° alc. **Rating** 87 To 2008 $13

Bella Ridge Estate   ★★★★

78 Campersic Road, Herne Hill, WA 6056 **Region** Swan District
T (08) 9250 4962 **F** (08) 9246 0244 **www.**bellaridge.com.au **Open** By appt
Winemaker Alon Arbel **Est.** 2003 **Cases** 2500
Alon Arbel came to WA from Israel in search of strong, easterly sea breezes to power his passion for windsurfing. Here he met wife-to-be, Jodi, and, after working overseas and travelling, they returned to Perth to live. A year out from completing a degree in engineering, Alon switched to Curtin University's oenology and viticulture course, which he duly completed. Entirely fortuitously, Jodi's parents, Frank and Lois, discovered a 10-ha property (8 ha under vine) on the foothills of the Darling Scarp, with plantings dating back to 1966. The 2003 purchase of the property was a couple of months before the commencement of the 2004 vintage, by which time they had managed to erect a 30-tonne winery, crushing 20 tonnes of fruit for their own label and 10 tonnes for contract clients. Since then they have grafted the plantings to an ultra-eclectic mix, which includes Japanese grapes, kyoho and madonna.

ŶŶŶŶŶ **Semillon 2006** Well-made lemon rind and grass flavours, the barest touch of oak adding an extra dimension. Screwcap. 12.5° alc. **Rating** 90 To 2011 $18

Grenache Shiraz Mourvedre 2005 Light- to medium red-purple; smooth, supple, gently spicy/earthy overtones to the core of sweet red fruits; controlled oak. Screwcap. 14° alc. **Rating** 90 To 2013 $20

Tempranillo 2005 More focus and intensity than many tempranillos; firm red fruits and good acidity, the tannins in balance. Could develop into something quite special. Screwcap. 14° alc. **Rating** 90 **To** 2015 $20

⚑⚑⚑⚑ **Chenin Blanc 2006** A lot of effort into a wine of dubious varietal worth; subtle oak and a long finish sustained by good acidity; does have development potential. Screwcap. 13° alc. **Rating** 89 **To** 2012 $18

Bellarine Estate   ★★★★☆

2270 Portarlington Road, Bellarine, Vic 3222 **Region** Geelong
T (03) 5259 3310 **F** (03) 5259 3393 www.bellarineestate.com.au **Open** 7 days 10–4
Winemaker Scotchmans Hill **Est.** 1995 **Cases** 7000
A substantial business, with 4 ha each of chardonnay and pinot noir, 3 ha of shiraz, 1 ha of merlot and 0.5 ha each of pinot gris and viognier. The wines are made by Robin Brockett at Scotchmans Hill. Bella's restaurant is open for lunch 7 days and dinner Fri/Sat evenings. Wine quality – and consistency – is a testament to Robin Brockett's skill.

⚑⚑⚑⚑⚑ **Sharon's Vineyard Riesling 2006** Aromatic lemon-lime bouquet; has unusual precision and intensity for a maritime region; length and power. Screwcap. 13° alc. **Rating** 94 **To** 2015 $22

⚑⚑⚑⚑⚑ **Two Wives Geelong Shiraz 2005** Deep purple-red; spotlessly clean; despite the supple and smooth mouthfeel, more to full-bodied than medium-bodied; black cherry, plum, licorice and blackberry; fine tannins. Drink now or before the 7-year itch. Screwcap. 13.9° alc. **Rating** 93 **To** 2015 $28
Two Wives Geelong Shiraz 2004 Medium red-purple; a typical cool-grown, aromatic cascade of spices and fine tannins run through the elegant, medium-bodied palate. Screwcap. 14.5° alc. **Rating** 92 **To** 2014 $28
James' Paddock Geelong Chardonnay 2005 Quite complex, particularly given its freshness; stone fruit, melon and citrus married with quality oak and good acidity. Screwcap. 13.5° alc. **Rating** 91 **To** 2012 $26

⚑⚑⚑⚑ **Nine Drives Sauvignon Blanc 2006** Plenty of flavour, ranging from tropical on the bouquet through to more mineral on the palate; subliminal sweetness. Screwcap. 13° alc. **Rating** 89 **To** 2008 $24
Unwooded Chardonnay 2006 Nectarine, stone fruit and melon given presence by lemony acidity on the finish; good example of the style. Screwcap. 13.5° alc. **Rating** 89 **To** 2009 $22
Phil's Fetish Pinot Noir 2005 Generous, rich, medium- to full-bodied with plenty of ripe, varietal fruit; just a touch sweet/alcoholic. **Rating** 88 **To** 2012 $26
Bellatage Shiraz Merlot Pinot Noir 2005 Ripe juicy berry aromas; similar juicy, sweet flavours; it's not entirely clear why the blend was made. Screwcap. 14° alc. **Rating** 88 **To** 2008 $18
Nanna's Garden Rose 2006 Bright colour; fresh, small red berry fruits; good length. **Rating** 87 **To** 2008 $23
Julian's Merlot 2005 Light, clear colour; a mix of savoury and small sweet berry flavours, with more punch than the colour suggests. Screwcap. 13.5° alc. **Rating** 87 **To** 2008 $28

Bellarmine Wines

PO Box 1450, Manjimup, WA 6258 **Region** Pemberton
T (08) 9776 0667 **F** (08) 9776 0657 www.bellarmine.com.au **Open** Not
Winemaker Mike Bewsher, Tam Bewsher, Robert Paul (Consultant) **Est.** 2000 **Cases** 4000
This substantial operation is owned by German residents Dr Willi and Gudrun Schumacher. Long-term wine lovers, the Schumachers decided to establish a vineyard and winery of their own, using Australia partly because of its stable political climate. The venture is managed by Mike and Tam Bewsher, both of whom have extensive knowledge of the wine industry. There are 20 ha of chardonnay, riesling, sauvignon blanc, pinot noir, shiraz, merlot and petit verdot.

ΨΨΨΨΨ **Pemberton Riesling Auslese 2006** The sweetest of the beautiful Bellarmine Rieslings, but – as with the others – maintains impeccable balance (and great length) thanks to its acidity. The development of the wine over the next 20 years will be fascinating to watch. Screwcap. 8° alc. **Rating** 96 To 2026 $15
Pemberton Riesling Dry 2006 Pure, intense Rheingau style; a dry, minerally and long palate, finishing with zesty lemony acidity. Screwcap. 12.5° alc. **Rating** 94 To 2019 $15
Pemberton Riesling 2006 A delicate, gently flowery bouquet; the light-bodied palate is fine and elegant, with wisps of herb and lemon, the sweetness perfectly balanced by acidity. Screwcap. 11° alc. **Rating** 94 To 2016 $15
Pemberton Shiraz 2005 Bright purple-red; a fragrant bouquet leads into a medium-bodied, firm and fresh palate offering black cherry, spice and wisps of smoky/charry oak; fine, firm tannins; good length and aftertaste. Screwcap. 14.5° alc. **Rating** 94 To 2015 $20

ΨΨΨΨΩ **Pemberton Sauvignon Blanc 2006** Spotlessly clean; fresh, very crisp and lively; an interesting conjunction of passionfruit, guava and herb flavours, especially at this low alcohol. Screwcap. 11.5° alc. **Rating** 93 To 2008 $15
Pemberton Chardonnay 2006 Light straw-green; a very tight, restrained and disciplined style; light-bodied nectarine fruit is supported by carefully controlled oak. Screwcap. 13.5° alc. **Rating** 92 To 2011 $15
Pemberton Pinot Noir 2004 Holding hue very well, still bright red-purple; fresh red cherry and plum; silky tannins add to the structure; good acidity suggests a fairly low pH. Screwcap. 13.5° alc. **Rating** 92 To 2011 $15
Bellarmino 2006 Pale blush pink; attractive melon, passionfruit and strawberry flavours; another take on rose style achieved by blending chardonnay and pinot noir. Screwcap. 11.5° alc. **Rating** 90 To 2008 $15

Bellbrae Estate

520 Great Ocean Road, Bellbrae, Vic 3228 **Region** Geelong
T (03) 5264 8480 **F** (03) 5222 6182 **www**.bellbraeestate.com.au **Open** W'ends & public hols 11–5 (winter), 7 days (Jan)
Winemaker Matthew di Sciascio, Peter Flewellyn **Est.** 1999 **Cases** 1800
Bellbrae Estate (and the Longboard Wines brand) is the venture of friends Richard Macdougall and Matthew di Sciascio. Sharing a common love of wine, surf and coastal life, they decided to establish a vineyard and produce their own wine. In 1998 Richard purchased a small sheep grazing property with 8 ha of fertile, sheltered north-facing slopes on the Great Ocean Road near Bellbrae, and with Matthew's help as business associate, Bellbrae Estate was born. Since 2003 all the wines have been Geelong-sourced.

ΨΨΨΨΨ **Longboard Shiraz 2005** Lovely elegant wine; medium-bodied; red and black fruits supported by silky tannins giving lovely line and length. Trophy and gold medal Geelong Wine Show '06. Screwcap. 14° alc. **Rating** 96 To 2015 $19

ΨΨΨΨΩ **Gundry's Shiraz 2005** Light- to medium-bodied; spice, pepper and licorice edges to the core of red fruits; light tannins and nice mouthfeel. Screwcap. 14° alc. **Rating** 90 To 2013 $29

ΨΨΨΨ **Addiscott Pinot Noir 2005** Deep, plummy and rich; big, sweet style; some questions on bacterial status. Screwcap. 14° alc. **Rating** 88 To 2008 $29
Longboard Sauvignon Blanc Semillon 2006 Medium- to full-bodied, with quite complex flavours primarily driven by the semillon. Screwcap. 12.5° alc. **Rating** 87 To 2009 $17
Longboard Chardonnay 2006 Ample white and yellow peach fruit; in a much fuller style than prior vintages. Screwcap. 13.5° alc. **Rating** 87 To 2009 $19
Longboard Pinot Noir 2005 Textured and quite powerful structure with spice and forest flavours. Screwcap. 14° alc. **Rating** 87 To 2011 $19

Bellendena Wines NR

240 Tinderbox Road, Tinderbox, Tas 7054 **Region** Southern Tasmania
T (03) 6229 8264 **F** (03) 6229 8307 www.users.bigpond.com/janeelek/vineyard/vineyard.htm
Open By appt
Winemaker Bryce Bounaccorsi **Est.** 1995 **Cases** NA
Andrew and Jane Elek, the former a consultant in international economic policy, the latter a
biologist and entomologist, have established 0.5 ha of vineyard, planted equally to chardonnay
and pinot noir. The name Bellendena comes from the botanical name of a native Tasmanian
plant, Bellendena montana, commonly known as Mountain Rocket. The label depicts the red
seed capsules of the plant viewed from above.

Bellvale Wines ★★★★☆

95 Forresters Lane, Berrys Creek, Vic 3953 **Region** Gippsland
T (03) 5668 8230 **F** (03) 5668 8230 www.bellvalewine.com.au **Open** By appt
Winemaker John Ellis **Est.** 1998 **Cases** 2500
John Ellis, in this instance, is the third under this name to be actively involved in the wine
industry. His background as a former 747 pilot, and the knowledge he gained of Burgundy over
many visits, sets him apart from the others. He has established 13 ha of pinot noir and
chardonnay on the red soils of a north-facing slope. He chose a density of 7150 vines per ha,
following as far as possible the precepts of Burgundy, but limited by tractor size, which precludes
narrower row spacing and even higher plant density. Exports to the US, Singapore, China, Japan
and Hong Kong.

 The Quercus Vineyard Gippsland Pinot Noir 2005 Very light colour; savoury,
spicy overtones to red cherry/strawberry fruit; elegant and balanced, but needs more
intensity. Diam. 13.5° alc. **Rating** 90 **To** 2011 $40

Belvoir Park Estate ★★★★☆

39 Belvoir Park Road, Big Hill, Vic 3453 **Region** Bendigo
T (03) 5435 3075 www.belvoirparkwines.com.au **Open** W'ends & public hols 11–5
Winemaker Ian Hall, Achilles Kalanis **Est.** 1997 **Cases** 800
Ian and Julie Hall have established 2 ha of shiraz and 0.5 ha of cabernet sauvignon on deep,
granite-based soils. As is common with small winery vineyards, the vines are hand-pruned and all
the grapes hand-picked, followed by small batch processing in the winery via open fermenters
and a basket press. The quality of the wines has improved in leaps and bounds.

 The Symposiarch 2005 Has very good depth to the range of perfectly balanced
and integrated black fruits; the tannins are ripe, the oak integrated. Shiraz/Cabernet
Sauvignon/Merlot. Diam. 14° alc. **Rating** 94 **To** 2025 $25

Shiraz 2005 A rich, velvety tapestry of black fruits, licorice and a dash of dark
chocolate; fine, ripe tannins; overall quite spicy and savoury. Diam. 13° alc. **Rating** 91
To 2019 $25
Merlot 2005 Attractive merlot fruit profile with flavours of raspberry, red cherry
and cassis; the structure is likewise good, light- to medium-bodied, with fine tannins.
Diam. 13.8° alc. **Rating** 90 **To** 2015 $22

Cabernet Sauvignon 2005 Full-bodied; blackcurrant fruit presently held as a
prisoner by the tannins; a reasonable probability of escape in 5 years. Diam. 13.5° alc.
Rating 89 **To** 2020 $22

Ben Potts Wines ★★★★

Step Road, Langhorne Creek, SA 5255 (postal) **Region** Langhorne Creek
T (08) 8537 3029 **F** (08) 8537 3284 www.benpottswines.com.au **Open** Not
Winemaker Ben Potts **Est.** 2002 **Cases** 1000

Ben Potts is the sixth generation to be involved in grapegrowing and winemaking in Langhorne Creek, the first being Frank Potts, founder of Bleasdale Vineyards. Ben completed the oenology degree at Charles Sturt University, and (aged 25) ventured into winemaking on a commercial scale in 2002. Fiddle's Block Shiraz is named after great-grandfather Fiddle; Lenny's Block Cabernet Sauvignon Malbec after grandfather Len; and Bill's Block Malbec after father Bill.

Ben's Run

PO Box 127, Broke, NSW 2330 **Region** Lower Hunter Valley
T (02) 6579 1310 **F** (02) 6579 1370 **Open** Not
Winemaker Pooles Rock (Patrick Auld) **Est.** 1997 **Cases** 900
Ben's Run, say the owners, 'is named for our kelpie dog for graciously allowing part of his retirement run to be converted into a showpiece shiraz-only vineyard'. Norman Marran was the pioneer of the Australian cotton industry, with a long and distinguished career as a former director of both the Australian Wheat Board and the Grains Research Corporation, and is currently chairman of a leading food research company. Exports to the US, Canada, Hong Kong and Malaysia.

Benchmark

135 Paterson Street, Launceston, Tas 7250 **Region** Northern Tasmania
T (03) 6331 3977 **F** (03) 6334 3273 **www**.benchmarkwinegallery.com **Open**
Mon–Thurs 10–6, Fri & Sat 10–7, public hols 11–5
Winemaker Contract **Est.** NA **Cases** NFP
This is a case of poacher and gamekeeper. It is at once a virtual winery and a major outlet for many of Tasmania's leading brands. But in addition to running its wine club, a website and a retail shop, it has wines contract-made, which have had more than a little success in the Tas Wine Show.

♀♀♀♀ **Pinot Noir 2006** Classy plum and cherry aromas, the palate yet to fully reflect the promise of the bouquet, but should do so in time. **Rating** 89 **To** 2012 $21.95
Chardonnay 2006 Good intensity and length; acidity brightens the wine, but will frighten some of the horses. **Rating** 87 **To** 2011 $17.95

Bendbrook Wines

Section 19, Pound Road, Macclesfield, SA 5153 **Region** Adelaide Hills
T (08) 8388 9773 **F** (08) 8388 9373 **www**.bendbrookwines.com.au **Open** By appt
Winemaker Contract **Est.** 1998 **Cases** 2000
John and Margaret Struik have established their vineyard on either side of a significant bend in the Angas River which runs through the property, with cabernet sauvignon on one side and shiraz on the other. The name comes from the bend in question, which is indirectly responsible for the flood which occurs every 4–5 years. The Struiks have restored what was known as the Postmaster's Residence, which is now their home.

♀♀♀♀♀ **Section 19 Grower's Reserve Macclesfield Cabernet Sauvignon 2004** Firm, but slightly sweeter notes to the black fruits and dark chocolate flavours; fine, supple tannins, and controlled oak. Screwcap. 14.5° alc. **Rating** 92 **To** 2020 $25
Goat Track Macclesfield Shiraz 2004 Strong colour; rich, dense, sweet blackberry fruit with a dusting of dark chocolate; ripe tannins and a strong finish. Screwcap. 14.5° alc. **Rating** 90 **To** 2019 $30
Pound Road Macclesfield Cabernet Sauvignon 2004 Strongly savoury, tight, black fruits on both bouquet and palate; a long finish, with firm tannins. Screwcap. 14° alc. **Rating** 90 **To** 2019 $18

Bended Knee Vineyard

PO Box 334, Buninyong, Vic 3357 **Region** Ballarat
T (03) 5341 8437 **F** (03) 5341 8437 **www**.bendedknee.com.au **Open** Not
Winemaker Peter Roche **Est.** 1999 **Cases** 300

Peter and Pauline Roche began the development of their property in 1999. They have 0.5 ha each of chardonnay and pinot noir at moderately high density, and 0.2 ha of ultra-close-planted pinot noir at the equivalent of 9000 vines per ha. Here 4 clones have been used: 114, 115, G5V15 and 777. The Roches say, 'We are committed to sustainable viticulture and aim to leave the planet in better shape than we found it.' Ducks, guinea fowl and chooks are vineyard custodians, and all vine canopy management is done by hand, including – of course – pruning and picking. Although production is tiny, Bended Knee can be found at 4 of Melbourne's best restaurants.

♀♀♀♀♀ **Bowen Hill Riesling 2005** Refreshingly tight and taught citrus and mineral aromas and flavours; a clean, dry finish; developing slowly but surely. Screwcap. 11° alc. **Rating** 92 **To** 2015 $20
Chardonnay 2005 Finely chiselled and shaped; barrel fermentation not too heavy, partial mlf spot on; light-bodied in quasi Chablis style. Screwcap. 12.6° alc. **Rating** 91 **To** 2012 $28
Chardonnay 2004 Fine, elegant grapefruit and melon run through a long palate, augmented by barrel fermentation and partial mlf, the impact perfectly judged. Diam. 12° alc. **Rating** 90 **To** 2012 $28

♀♀♀♀ **Pinot Noir 2005** Clean, firm cherry fruit, with some spice and stem notes; light- to medium-bodied, but has the potential to develop. Screwcap. 13.6° alc. **Rating** 89 **To** 2011 $28
Pinot Noir 2004 Aromatic red fruits with a touch of spice; light-bodied, but clear varietal character, albeit in a foresty mode, and needs just a touch more sweet pinot fruit for top points. Screwcap. 12° alc. **Rating** 89 **To** 2010 $28

Bent Creek Vineyards ★★★★

Lot 10 Blewitt Springs Road, McLaren Flat, SA 5171 **Region** McLaren Vale
T (08) 8383 0414 **www.**bentcreekvineyards.com.au **Open** Sun & public hols 11–5
Winemaker Peter Polson, Tim Geddes **Est.** 2001 **Cases** 5000
Peter Polson is now the sole owner of Bent Creek, which has acquired a second vineyard of 5 ha at McLaren Vale. As a parallel development, Tim Geddes is now assisting Peter in the winemaking.

♀♀♀♀♀ **The Nude McLaren Vale Shiraz 2004** Medium- to full-bodied; smooth and supple texture with blackberry, plum, dark chocolate and mocha oak influences all coalescing; the oak is evident, but in balance. The Nude is censored. Screwcap. 15° alc. **Rating** 93 **To** 2024 $30
McLaren Vale Cabernet Merlot 2005 Very well-made, extracting quality from a region hardly reputed for the blend; good weight and mouthfeel from the powerful blackcurrant fruit and balanced tannins. Screwcap. 14.5° alc. **Rating** 92 **To** 2018 $20
Black Dog McLaren Vale Shiraz 2005 A medium-bodied, lively and fresh mix of red and black fruits; pure and direct. A long story about a prior vintage and a black dog on the back label, and a similarity in the colour of the 2. Screwcap. 14.5° alc. **Rating** 91 **To** 2015 $21
McLaren Vale Chardonnay 2005 Light straw-green; quite elegant stone fruit with a touch of grapefruit; good acidity enlivens the palate, barrel ferment French oak providing the complexity. Screwcap. 13.5° alc. **Rating** 90 **To** 2012 $20

♀♀♀♀ **Adelaide Hills Sauvignon Blanc 2006** A slightly closed/flattened bouquet; a firm river pebble, green apple and citrus palate; will develop. Screwcap. 12.2° alc. **Rating** 89 **To** 2010 $19

Benwarin Wines ★★★★

32 Kings Lane, Darlinghurst, NSW 2010 (postal) **Region** Lower Hunter Valley
T (02) 8354 1375 **F** (02) 8354 1376 **www.**benwarin.com.au **Open** Not
Winemaker Monarch Winemaking Services **Est.** 1999 **Cases** 7000
Allan Bagley and wife Janneke have planted a substantial 18.57-ha vineyard with shiraz, verdelho, sangiovese, chambourcin, semillon and chardonnay. Until 2004 most of the grapes were sold to others, but since then all of the production has gone to the Benwarin label. The yield is restricted to 2 tonnes per acre, and the wines have been consistent medal winners. Exports to Canada.

ŶŶŶŶŶ **Hunter Valley Semillon 2006** Spotlessly clean and well-made; very lively and fresh, reflecting the lower than usual alcohol; grassy/lemongrass/citrus/mineral flavours will allow the wine to grow and mellow with age; good length and acid balance. Screwcap. 9.5° alc. **Rating** 92 **To** 2016 $15
Hunter Valley Verdelho 2006 Good example of the variety; a fruit salad base plus touches of dried apricot and lemon rind. Trophy Best Current Vintage Verdelho Hunter Valley Wine Show '06 and NSW Small Winemakers Wine Show '06. Screwcap. 13.7° alc. **Rating** 91 **To** 2008 $15

ŶŶŶŶ **Hunter Valley Chardonnay 2005** Light straw-green; clean, gentle stone fruit and melon; good balance, unforced. Screwcap. 13.2° alc. **Rating** 88 **To** 2008 $16
Hunter Valley Sangiovese 2005 Many flavours are held within a savoury and tannin net; they need to escape. Screwcap. 14.1° alc. **Rating** 88 **To** 2010 $18
Hunter Valley Shiraz 2004 Bright colour; deceptively light, perhaps, and may surprise with age; but, at this juncture, needs more punch. Screwcap. 12.8° alc. **Rating** 87 **To** 2011 $18

Beresford Wines

26 Kangarilla Road, McLaren Vale, SA 5171 **Region** McLaren Vale
T (08) 8323 8899 **www.**beresfordwines.com.au **Open** Mon–Fri 9–5, w'ends 10–5
Winemaker Scott McIntosh, Rob Dundon **Est.** 1985 **Cases** 130 000
The Beresford brand sits at the top of a range of labels primarily and successfully aimed at export markets in the UK, the US, Hong Kong and China. The intention is that ultimately most, if not all, the wines will be sourced from grapes grown in McLaren Vale.

ŶŶŶŶŶ **McLaren Vale Shiraz 2004** Fractionally hazy red-purple; a strongly regional-varietal display of aromas and flavours: a typical blackberry and dark chocolate mix supported by soft, slightly chewy tannins. Value. Screwcap. 14° alc. **Rating** 92 **To** 2015 $20
McLaren Vale Cabernet Sauvignon 2004 Medium-bodied, with nicely balanced fruit, oak and tannins; flavours of blackcurrant and the omnipresent touch of regional chocolate. Screwcap. 13.5° alc. **Rating** 90 **To** 2014 $20

ŶŶŶŶ **Reserve Shiraz 2004** Plenty of blackberry fruit, but with edgy tannins still needing to resolve themselves. Cork. 14.5° alc. **Rating** 88 **To** 2013 $30

Berrigan Wines

38 Dumfries Road, Floreat, WA 6014 (postal) **Region** Swan District
T (08) 9383 7526 **F** (08) 9383 7516 **www.**berriganwines.com.au **Open** Not
Winemaker Ryan Sudano, Daniel Berrigan **Est.** 1998 **Cases** 500
Berrigan Wines is situated on Creighton Farm, one of the oldest farms in the Swan District, dating back to 1849. The Berrigan family, headed by Thomas John Berrigan, has planted verdelho, merlot, shiraz and cabernet sauvignon, and the wines are principally sold through the website.

ŶŶŶŶ **Creighton Farm Cabernet Merlot 2003** Holding hue well; a ripe style, with plenty of sweet cassis fruit; silver medal WA Wine Show '05. Screwcap. 13.5° alc. **Rating** 89 **To** 2009 $10

Berrys Bridge

633 Carapooee Road, Carapooee, Vic 3478 **Region** Pyrenees
T (03) 5496 3220 **F** (03) 8610 1621 **www.**berrysbridge.com.au **Open** W'ends 10.30–4.30, or by appt
Winemaker Jane Holt **Est.** 1990 **Cases** 1200
While the date of establishment is 1990, Roger Milner purchased the property in 1975. In the mid-1980s, with Jane Holt, he began the construction of the stone house-cum-winery. Planting of the existing 7 ha vineyard commenced in 1990, around the time that Jane began viticulture and oenology studies at Charles Sturt University. Until 1997 the grapes were sold to others; the first vintage (from 1997) was released in 1998. Exports to the US and Switzerland.

⟡⟡⟡⟡⟡ **Pyrenees Shiraz 2004** Has hit the sweet spot, with layers of robed flavours without undue extraction, and gets away with the alcohol; the tannins and oak have good texture and balance. ProCork. 15.5° alc. **Rating** 94 **To** 2024 $40

Pyrenees Merlot 2004 Medium red-purple; savoury black olive and briar notes to the blackcurrant fruit are positively varietal; good balance. Cork. 15° alc. **Rating** 94 **To** 2020 $30

Pyrenees Cabernet Sauvignon 2004 An unusual feature is gossamer-like tannins woven throughout the medium-bodied palate, gently supporting the expressive cassis/blackcurrant fruit. Cork. 14° alc. **Rating** 94 **To** 2024 $30

Berton Vineyard

Boehm Springs Road, Eden Valley, SA 5235 (postal) **Region** Eden Valley
T (02) 6962 9455 **F** (02) 6962 9755 **Open** Not
Winemaker James Ceccato **Est.** 2001 **Cases** 15 000
The Berton Vineyard partners – Bob and Cherie Berton, Paul Bartholomaeus, James Ceccato and Jamie Bennett – have almost 100 years combined experience in winemaking, viticulture, finance, production and marketing. 1996 saw the acquisition of a 30-ha property and the planting of the first vines. It took 2 years for the dam to fill, and the vines struggled on the white rock soil, looking like little bonsais – hence the names of the estate-grown Bonsai Shiraz and White Rock varietals. The business also offers (in descending order of price) the cleverly labelled Head Over Heels range, the Hay Plains range and the Odd Socks range. Exports to the UK and Europe.

Best's Wines

111 Best's Road, Great Western, Vic 3377 **Region** Grampians
T (03) 5356 2250 **F** (03) 5356 2430 **www**.bestswines.com **Open** Mon–Sat 10–5, Sun 11–4
Winemaker Viv Thomson, Adam Wadewitz **Est.** 1866 **Cases** 30 000
Best's winery and vineyards are among Australia's best-kept secrets. Indeed the vineyards, with vines dating back to 1867, have secrets which may never be revealed: for example, certain vines planted in the Nursery Block have defied identification and are thought to exist nowhere else in the world. The cellars, too, go back to the same era, constructed by butcher-turned-winemaker Joseph Best and his family. Since 1920, the Thomson family has owned the property, with father Viv and sons Ben, Bart and Marcus representing the fourth and fifth generations. Consistently producing elegant, supple wines which deserve far greater recognition than they receive. The Bin O Shiraz is a classic, the Thomson Family Shiraz magnificent. Exports to all major markets.

⟡⟡⟡⟡⟡ **Thomson Family Shiraz 2004** More concentration of power and greater structure than Bin O; blackberry with splashes of licorice and spice; will be seriously long-lived, and is not yet showing its best. Cork. 14.5° alc. **Rating** 95 **To** 2010 $99

Bin O Shiraz 2004 Good red-purple; a lovely wine, with great texture and silky mouthfeel; fine, savoury tannins are woven through the blackberry and plum fruit; perfectly judged oak. Cork. 14° alc. **Rating** 95 **To** 2034 $42.50

⟡⟡⟡⟡⟡ **Great Western Pinot Noir 2004** Light- to medium red-purple; no questioning varietal expression, which is very clear; not especially complex, but has plenty of gently spicy, plummy fruit and good length. From vines planted in the 1860s, extended in the 1980s with cuttings from the then 120-year-old vines. A joyous expression of history. Screwcap. 13° alc. **Rating** 93 **To** 2012 $25

Great Western Cabernet Sauvignon 2002 The cool vintage certainly leaves its mark; blackcurrant, earth, black olive; classic severity. The cork will mature well before the wine does. 13.5° alc. **Rating** 92 **To** 2017 $26.50

Great Western Pinot Noir Rose 2006 A crisp, firm, dry style although the strawberry/cherry pinot fruit is clearly present, set against slatey minerality. Serious rose style. Screwcap. 13° alc. **Rating** 90 **To** 2008 $22

Bin No. 1 Great Western Shiraz 2004 Blackberry, plum, pepper and spice all in a relatively warm flavour register; 18 months in French and American oak has produced a balanced and long wine. You get what you pay for in the Best's range. Screwcap. 14° alc. **Rating** 90 **To** 2012 $25

ŶŶŶŶ   **Great Western Riesling 2006** Very pale straw-green; well-crafted, but relatively subdued fruit throughout; some river pebble/mineral notes. Screwcap. 12.5° alc. **Rating** 89 **To** 2012 $22

Shiraz 2004 Light- to medium-bodied; smooth, supple plum and blackberry fruit; gentle tannins, with more than adequate flavour at the price. From the Lake Boga vineyard planted in the 1930s and Salvation Hills in 1995. Screwcap. 14° alc. **Rating** 87 **To** 2010 $15

Bethany Wines   ★★★★☆

Bethany Road, Bethany via Tanunda, SA 5352 **Region** Barossa Valley
T (08) 8563 2086 **F** (08) 8563 0046 **www.**bethany.com.au **Open** Mon–Sat 10–5, Sun 1–5
Winemaker Geoff Schrapel, Robert Schrapel **Est.** 1977 **Cases** 30 000
The Schrapel family has been growing grapes in the Barossa Valley for over 140 years, but the winery has only been in operation since 1977. Nestled high on a hillside on the site of an old quarry, Geoff and Rob Schrapel produce a range of consistently well-made and attractively packaged wines. They have 36 ha of vineyards in the Barossa Valley, 8 ha in the Eden Valley and (recently and interestingly) 2 ha each of chardonnay and cabernet sauvignon on Kangaroo Island. Exports to the UK, the US, Sweden, Switzerland, Denmark, Holland, NZ and Japan.

ŶŶŶŶŶ   **Reserve Shiraz 2004** GR9. Ripe but relatively restrained blackberry and black cherry fruit on the medium-bodied palate; both tannins and oak carefully handled and balanced; Bethany's icon wine made only in the best years, and with less than 700 dozen produced in any year. Cork. 14° alc. **Rating** 94 **To** 2024 $70

ŶŶŶŶŶ   **Reserve Shiraz 2002** GR8. Shows the cool '02 vintage to advantage; medium-bodied, but with intense flavours ranging from spicy to gentle black fruits, with a twist of mocha. Cork. 14° alc. **Rating** 93 **To** 2015 $70

Eden Valley Riesling 2006 Strong scented apple and citrus blossom aromas; the rich, full-flavoured palate is slightly at odds with the finer bouquet; whatever, makes a good glass now. Screwcap. 12° alc. **Rating** 91 **To** 2011 $28

Barossa Shiraz Cabernet 2004 Medium to full red-purple; an abundance of black fruits, licorice, plum and prune, touched off with chocolate and mocha; ripe tannins, good length. Diam. 14° alc. **Rating** 91 **To** 2014 $18

Barossa Semillon 2005 Crisp, clean and fresh; belies its alcohol; a very interesting wine, relying on restrained winemaking, the exclusion of oak, and 45-year-old vines. Screwcap. 13° alc. **Rating** 90 **To** 2012 $18

Barossa Valley Semillon Sauvignon Blanc 2006 No reduction whatsoever; the sauvignon blanc from a neighbour with a cool site; a real surprise packet, offering flavour without phenolics. Screwcap. 12.5° alc. **Rating** 90 **To** 2010 $16

ŶŶŶŶ   **Barossa Chardonnay 2005** Abundant peachy/stone fruit flavours, the oak influence minimal, but evident. Barossa Valley/Eden Valley. Screwcap. 13.5° alc. **Rating** 89 **To** 2010 $16

Barossa Valley Riesling 2005 Notes of canned pineapple and some citrus; good structure and balance for basic Barossa riesling. Screwcap. 13° alc. **Rating** 88 **To** 2010 $15

Steinbruch Riesling 2006 Rich, ripe and luscious from start to finish, unapologetic for its touch of sweetness; ready right now. Screwcap. 11° alc. **Rating** 87 **To** 2008 $14

Barossa Valley Grenache 2005 Ultra-typical light-bodied cherry/raspberry jam fruit; I must be missing something with this style. Screwcap. 14.5° alc. **Rating** 87 **To** 2008 $16

Barossa Cabernet Merlot 2004 A pleasant wine, although this isn't the region for the blend; balance and structure are ok, the oak likewise. Cork. 14° alc. **Rating** 87 **To** 2010 $23

Bettenay's   **NR**

Cnr Harmans South Road/Miamup Road, Wilyabrup, WA 6284 **Region** Margaret River
T (08) 9755 5539 **F** (08) 9755 5539 www.bettenaysmargaretriver.com.au **Open** 7 days 11–5
Winemaker Greg Bettenay, Peter Stanlake (Consultant) **Est.** 1989 **Cases** NA

Bianchet   ★★★

187 Victoria Road, Lilydale, Vic 3140 **Region** Yarra Valley
T (03) 9739 1779 **F** (03) 9739 1277 **Open** Thurs–Fri 10–4, w'ends 10–5
Winemaker Contract **Est.** 1976 **Cases** 2500
Owned by a small Melbourne-based syndicate that acquired the business from the founding
Bianchet family. One of the most unusual wines from the winery is Verduzzo Gold, a late-
harvest sweet white wine made from the Italian grape variety. The wines are sold through the
cellar door.

♀♀♀♀   **Yarra Valley Chardonnay 2004** Medium-bodied peach and nectarine fruit;
oak needed to be less strident and of better quality. Screwcap. 13.5° alc. **Rating** 88
To 2010 $23

Bidgeebong Wines

352 Byrnes Road, Wagga Wagga, NSW 2650 **Region** Gundagai
T (02) 6931 9955 **F** (02) 6931 9966 www.bidgeebong.com **Open** Mon–Fri 9–4
Winemaker Andrew Birks, Keiran Spencer **Est.** 2000 **Cases** 12 000
Encompasses what the founders refer to as the Bidgeebong triangle – between Young, Wagga
Wagga, Tumbarumba and Gundagai – which provides grapes for the Bidgeebong brand. A winery
was completed in 2002, and will eventually be capable of handling 2000 tonnes of grapes for
Bidgeebong's own needs, and those of other local growers and larger producers who purchase
grapes from the region. Exports to the UK, Canada, India, Singapore and China.

♀♀♀♀♀   **The Icon Series Chardonnay 2005** A classic marriage and variety; the bouquet
is highly aromatic, foretelling the grapefruit flavours, creamy texture and oak
seamlessly welded on the palate; long finish; 234 dozen made. Screwcap. 13° alc.
Rating 95 **To** 2015 $31
The Icon Series Shiraz 2004 Red and black cherry fruit, with lots of spice,
licorice and cracked pepper but no green characters whatsoever, but nor does it
exhibit any sign of the 15° alcohol; long and silky tannins and quality oak; 443
dozen made from a single vineyard high in the Tumbarumba region. Screwcap.
15° alc. **Rating** 95 **To** 2020 $35

♀♀♀♀♀   **Tumbarumba Sauvignon Blanc 2006** A highly aromatic bouquet of
passionfruit, kiwifruit and citrus; the palate follows suit, though seems to fade a little
on the back-palate and finish. Screwcap. 13.5° alc. **Rating** 92 **To** 2008 $22

Big Hill Vineyard

Cnr Calder Highway/Belvoir Park Road, Big Hill, Bendigo, Vic 3550 **Region** Bendigo
T (03) 5435 3366 **F** (03) 5435 3311 www.bighillvineyard.com **Open** 7 days 10–5
Winemaker Stuart Auld (Contract) **Est.** 1998 **Cases** 1200
A partnership headed by Nick Cugura began the re-establishment of Big Hill Vineyard on a site
which was first planted to grapes almost 150 years ago. That was in the height of the gold rush,
and there was even a long-disappeared pub, the Granite Rock Hotel. The modern-day plantings
began with 2 ha of shiraz in 1998, followed by 1 ha each of merlot and cabernet sauvignon.

♀♀♀♀♀   **Bendigo Merlot 2004** Deep colour; lots of rich and juicy blackcurrant fruit
giving a supple mouthfeel; not particularly varietal, but that hardly matters. Cork. 13°
alc. **Rating** 91 **To** 2012 $20
Bendigo Shiraz 2003 An elegant, medium-bodied wine reflecting the controlled
alcohol; blackberry and raspberry fruit supported by fine tannins and oak. Diam.
13.5° alc. **Rating** 90 **To** 2013 $20

ΥΥΥΥ **Bendigo Cabernet Sauvignon 2004** Slightly dull colour; tannins take hold early in the mouth, and don't loosen their grip, though there is good fruit underneath. Cork. 14° alc. **Rating** 87 **To** 2011 $20

big shed wines

1289 Malmsbury Road, Glenlyon, Vic 3461 **Region** Macedon Ranges
T (03) 5348 7825 **F** (03) 5348 7825 www.bigshedwines.com.au **Open** 7 days, winter 10–6, summer 10–7
Winemaker Ken Jones **Est.** 1999 **Cases** 1300
Founder and winemaker Ken Jones was formerly a geneticist and molecular biologist at Edinburgh University, and the chemistry of winemaking comes easily. The estate-based wine comes from the 2 ha of pinot noir; the other wines are made from purchased grapes grown in various parts of Central Victoria.

ΥΥΥΥΥ **Cabernets 2004** Clean and abundant sweet cassis/blackcurrant fruit; ripe tannins in balance, supported by good oak. Silver medal Victorian Wines Show '06. Screwcap. 14.7° alc. **Rating** 90 **To** 2015 $23

ΥΥΥΥ **Macedon Ranges Pinot Noir 2004** Plenty of varietal character; a mix of red fruits, some stem, forest and spice; has good length, but is just a little too stemmy/foresty. Screwcap. 14° alc. **Rating** 89 **To** 2010 $25
Reserve Macedon Ranges Shiraz 2004 Very deep colour; a potent, powerful, full-bodied wine in Stygian black fruit mould; fining would have helped; now long-term patience is required. Screwcap. 14.7° alc. **Rating** 88 **To** 2020 $22
Macedon Ranges Chardonnay 2004 Gentle stone fruit, with riper tones than many Macedon Ranges chardonnays; not especially complex, but has flavour. Screwcap. 13.5° alc. **Rating** 87 **To** 2008 $22
Heathcote Shiraz 2004 Medium-bodied; quite complex; a mix of black fruits with a distinctly savoury overcoat; persistent tannins. Screwcap. 14.9° alc. **Rating** 87 **To** 2014 $22

Bimbadeen Estate   NR

Cnr Bimbadeen Road/Mount View Road, Mount View, NSW 2325 **Region** Lower Hunter Valley
T (02) 4990 1577 **F** (02) 4991 3689 www.bimbadeen.com.au **Open** By appt
Winemaker Mark Davidson **Est.** 2000 **Cases** NA
Bimbadeen Estate has 1.2 ha of semillon, shiraz and verdelho, but is primarily driven by its 6 self-contained villas perched high on the side of the Brokenback Range, with panoramic views out across the Hunter Valley, and which deserve the hyperbole often encountered in describing ventures of this kind.

Bimbadgen Estate

790 McDonalds Road, Pokolbin, NSW 2321 **Region** Lower Hunter Valley
T (02) 4998 7585 **F** (02) 4998 7732 www.bimbadgen.com.au **Open** 7 days 9.30–5
Winemaker Simon Thistlewood, Jane Turner **Est.** 1968 **Cases** 60 000
Established as McPherson Wines, then successively Tamalee, Sobels, Parker Wines and now Bimbadgen, this substantial winery has had what might be politely termed a turbulent history. It has 109 ha of estate plantings, mostly with relatively old vines, supplemented by a separate estate vineyard at Yenda for the lower-priced Ridge series, and purchased grapes from various premium regions. Exports to the UK, Hong Kong and Japan.

ΥΥΥΥΥ **Signature Semillon 2005** Intense; great line and length; great clarity of varietal expression. Screwcap. 9.5° alc. **Rating** 95 **To** 2017 $40
Signature Individual Vineyard Shiraz 2005 Light but bright colour; light- to medium-bodied; elegant, earthy regional nuances to fine blackberry fruit; integrated oak and a long finish. Screwcap. 14° alc. **Rating** 94 **To** 2019 $40

Bindi Wine Growers

343 Melton Road, Gisborne, Vic 3437 (postal) **Region** Macedon Ranges
T (03) 5428 2564 **F** (03) 5428 2564 **Open** Not
Winemaker Michael Dhillon, Stuart Anderson (Consultant) **Est.** 1988 **Cases** 1500
One of the icons of Macedon. The Chardonnay is top-shelf, the Pinot Noir as remarkable (albeit
in a very different idiom) as Bass Phillip, Giaconda or any of the other tiny-production, icon
wines. The addition of Heathcote-sourced Shiraz under the Pyrette label confirms Bindi as one
of the greatest small producers in Australia. Notwithstanding the tiny production, the wines are
exported (in small quantities, of course) to the UK, the US and other major markets.

ŦŦŦŦŦ **Quartz Chardonnay 2005** Light straw-green; distinctly finer and racier than
the Composition, but slightly less complex; 6 of one, half a dozen of the other.
Diam. 13.5° alc. **Rating** 96 **To** 2016 $66
Composition Chardonnay 2005 Light straw-green; complex aromas with a
touch of Burgundian funk; elegant, seamless palate with perfect balance and
length. Diam. 13.5° alc. **Rating** 96 **To** 2014 $45
Original Vineyard Pinot Noir 2005 Marginally the best colour of the 3
pinots; similar complexity to Block 5, likewise intensity and length; a lovely mix
of red and black fruits; tight finish. Diam. 13.5° alc. **Rating** 96 **To** 2015 $66
Block 5 Pinot Noir 2005 Complex red and black fruit with touches of spice; a
round, supple and sinuous medium-bodied palate offering plum, cherry and spice,
with very good length. Diam. 13.5° alc. **Rating** 95 **To** 2014 $90
Pyrette Heathcote Shiraz 2005 Bright purple-red; super-elegant, almost silky
flavours suggest some whole bunch component; regardless, could only be made by
Bindi, totally delicious other face of Heathcote. Wild yeast. (Formerly released under
the Bundaleer label.) Diam. 13.5° alc. **Rating** 94 **To** 2018 $40
Macedon Chardonnay Pinot Noir NV Michael Dhillon has gone a long way to
getting this right; citrussy tangy fruit runs through a long palate, complexity from
biscuity, brioche lees flavours and textures. Disgorged Oct '06. 12.5° alc. **Rating** 94
To 2010 $40

ŦŦŦŦŢ **Composition Pinot Noir 2005** A very complex feral bouquet, with forest floor
or other agencies at work; the palate continues to challenge. I'm far from sure what
is going on here. Diam. 13.5° alc. **Rating** 92 **To** 2012 $45

Bird in Hand

Bird in Hand Road, Woodside, SA 5244 **Region** Adelaide Hills
T (08) 8389 9488 **F** (08) 8389 9511 **www**.birdinhand.com.au **Open** 7 days 11–5
Winemaker Andrew Nugent, Kym Milne **Est.** 1997 **Cases** 20 000
This substantial wine and olive oil property, which took its name from a 19th-century gold mine.
It is the venture of the Nugent family, headed by Dr Michael Nugent. Son Andrew Nugent is a
Roseworthy graduate, and his wife, Susie, manages the olive oil side of the business. The family
also has properties on the Fleurieu Peninsula and in the Clare Valley, the latter providing both
riesling and shiraz (and olives from 100-year-old wild olive trees). Exports to the UK, the US and
other major markets.

ŦŦŦŦŦ **Clare Valley Riesling 2006** Fragrant, though delicate, apple/citrus blossom
aromas; the palate is likewise delicate and precise; perfect balance, with citrussy
acidity to close. Screwcap. 13° alc. **Rating** 94 **To** 2015 $25
Adelaide Hills Merlot 2005 Intense flavours of cassis, blackcurrant and a
touch of olive; particularly good mouthfeel, line and length. A rare beast – or,
rather, bird. Screwcap. 14.5° alc. **Rating** 94 **To** 2020 $30
Adelaide Hills Cabernet Sauvignon 2005 A powerful wine; tightly woven,
savoury black fruit, with anise, quality oak and suitably imposing tannins finishing
the picture. ProCork. 14.5° alc. **Rating** 94 **To** 2025 $30

ŦŦŦŦŢ **Adelaide Hills Shiraz 2005** Rich, concentrated dark fruits; velvety mouthfeel,
and considerable potential. Cork. 14.5° alc. **Rating** 92 **To** 2019 $30

Two in the Bush Shiraz 2005 Bright and fresh; a rollicking mix of red and black fruits, spice and lively acidity, and fine but ripe tannins holding the wine together. Sheer enjoyment. Screwcap. 14.5° alc. **Rating** 92 **To** 2020 $20

Two in the Bush Semillon Sauvignon Blanc 2006 Semillon is the dominant player; it creates a gentle fusion between the varieties, with a relatively soft but evenly balanced palate thanks to the sauvignon blanc. Screwcap. 12° alc. **Rating** 90 **To** 2008 $20

Adelaide Hills Chardonnay 2006 Very tight, crisp and citrussy, almost into sauvignon blanc country. A long palate, with strong acidity, and little concession to Australian conventions; little or no oak, and will be long-lived. Screwcap. 13.5° alc. **Rating** 90 **To** 2012 $20

Two in the Bush Chardonnay 2006 Slightly softer and less precise, partly due to some discernible barrel fermentation. What you gain on the swings, you lose on the roundabouts. Screwcap. 13.5° alc. **Rating** 90 **To** 2010 $20

♟♟♟♟ **Two in the Bush Merlot Cabernet 2005** Fragrant; hints of new-mown grass along with black cherry on the bouquet; medium-bodied, with fine, ripe tannins, and good length. Screwcap. 13.5° alc. **Rating** 89 **To** 2012 $20

Nest Egg Cabernet Sauvignon 2004 Faintly hazy colour; sweet cassis and mint fruit with well-integrated oak on the light- to medium-bodied palate; fine tannins. Cork. 13.5° alc. **Rating** 89 **To** 2014 $60

Adelaide Hills Pinot Noir 2005 Deep colour; a very powerful wine more to dry red in character than pinot; picking 1° baume earlier may have made a far better wine. ProCork. 14.5° alc. **Rating** 88 **To** 2011 $30

Adelaide Hills Sparkling Pinot Noir 2006 Pale pink; distinct strawberry flavours; good length, and while delicate and devoid of complexity, has nigh on perfect balance. 12.5° alc. **Rating** 88 **To** 2011 $25

Birrarung Estate ★★★

PO Box 116, Eltham, Vic 3095 **Region** Yarra Valley
T 0412 324 510 **F** (03) 9431 4815 **www.**birrarung.com.au **Open** By appt
Winemaker Chris Seidler **Est.** 1994 **Cases** 1700
One ha each of chardonnay and sauvignon blanc, and 4 ha of pinot noir, have been established using sustainable agriculture headed towards organic grower accreditation. Owners Chris and Joanne Seidler are planning an eco 5-star resort with restaurant, health spa and conference facilities. Early experiments with a revolutionary glass closure have been terminated.

Birthday Villa Vineyard ★★★★

Lot 2, Campbell Street, Malmsbury Street, Vic 3446 **Region** Macedon Ranges
T (03) 5423 2789 **F** (03) 5423 2789 **Open** By appt 10–5
Winemaker Greg Dedman (Contract) **Est.** 1968 **Cases** 350
The Birthday Villa name comes from the 19th-century Birthday Mine at nearby Drummond, discovered on Queen Victoria's birthday. The 1.5 ha of traminer was planted in 1962, the 0.5 ha of cabernet sauvignon following at a later date. The quality of the Gewurztraminer comes as no surprise; the very cool climate is suited to the variety. On the other hand, the Cabernet Sauvignon comes as a major surprise although there are likely to be vintages where the variety will provide a major challenge as it struggles for ripeness.

♟♟♟♟♀ **Malmsbury Cabernet Sauvignon 2005** An elegant wine, with utterly unexpected ripeness to the cassis berry fruit and supple, fine tannins. Screwcap. 12.5° alc. **Rating** 91 **To** 2013 $25

Malmsbury Gewurztraminer 2006 Well-balanced; plenty of varietal fruit flavour absent from the '05. Screwcap. 13° alc. **Rating** 90 **To** 2010 $22

♟♟♟♟ **Malmsbury Gewurztraminer 2005** Clean, crisp and minerally but simply not enough varietal character for higher points. Screwcap. 12° alc. **Rating** 87 **To** 2010 $22

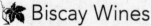 Biscay Wines

Lot 567 Barossa Valley Highway, Tanunda, SA 5352 **Region** Barossa Valley
T (08) 8563 0297 **F** (08) 8563 0187 **Open** By appt
Winemaker John Hongell, Trevor Hongell **Est.** 1998 **Cases** 1000
While John and Carolyn Hongell are the owners, this is very much a family business. Son Trevor
is vineyard manager and budding winemaker; daughter-in-law Daniela is in charge of sales and
marketing; and the Hongell's 3 other children, Geoff, Ian and Jenny, provide their support for the
vineyard. In his various previous lives, John Hongell was a brewer, then production director for
Dalgety Wines, and then manager of Saltram. Long experience in the industry taught him that
sales were far better pulled by demand than pushed by supply, and, despite significant sales in the
US and Canada, production has been deliberately restricted during the establishment phase.

John Hongell Old Vine Barossa Valley Grenache Shiraz 2005 Light, bright
red-purple; excellent structure; light but fine tannins run through the length of the
palate, with no cosmetic fruit, simply cherry and raspberry. Grenache (90%, planted
1942)/Shiraz (10%). Screwcap. 15° alc. **Rating** 91 **To** 2012 $19
John Hongell Barossa Valley Shiraz 2004 Clean blackberry and black cherry
fruit; lower alcohol suits the style much better; precise line, good length and fine
tannins. Screwcap. 14.5° alc. **Rating** 90 **To** 2015 $20
John Hongell Barossa Valley Shiraz 2003 A medium-bodied mix of red and
black fruits which are quite fresh; a long, fruit-driven finish with good acidity. Good
achievement for the vintage. Cork. 14.5° alc. **Rating** 90 **To** 2014 $20

John Hongell Barossa Valley Shiraz Viognier 2004 Dull colour for both
vintage and blend; very ripe fruit, arguably not best suited to the viognier blend;
whatever, has flavour but neither finesse nor intensity. Screwcap. 15.5° alc. **Rating** 88
To 2012 $35

Bishops Rock

RSD Melrose, Cranbrook, Tas 7190 **Region** East Coast Tasmania
T (03) 6257 8531 **F** (03) 6257 8531 **Open** 7 days 10–4
Winemaker Winemaking Tasmania (Julian Alcorso) **Est.** 1998 **Cases** 1350
Bob and Annie Browning have been progressively establishing 3 ha of pinot noir, 1 ha of
sauvignon blanc, a little over 1 ha of riesling and 0.5 ha of chardonnay since 1998. The name
comes from a famous lighthouse 4 miles west of the Scilly Isles which the Brownings felt was
similar to the Oyster Bay area near their vineyard site.

Pinot Noir 2005 Medium-bodied; neatly constructed and weighted; pure pinot
fruit with good length and acidity which does not unduly distract. **Rating** 92
To 2013

Unwooded Chardonnay 2006 Light- to medium-bodied; tangy grapefruit and
nectarine flavours; clean finish. **Rating** 89 **To** 2010
Ice Riesling 2006 Intensely sweet fruit offset by high acidity; whether it is too
high is very much a matter of personal opinion. **Rating** 89 **To** 2011

Bishops Vineyard ★★★★

86 Acton Road, Acton Park, Tas 7170 (postal) **Region** Southern Tasmania
T (03) 6248 7342 **F** (03) 6248 7342 www.bishopsvineyard.com.au **Open** Not
Winemaker Julian Alcorso (Contract) **Est.** 1999 **Cases** 350
Phillip and Maree Bishop planted the first vines on their property in 1999, keeping things under
control with 0.5 ha of each of chardonnay and pinot noir. The property overlooks Frederick
Henry Bay and Ralph's Bay, 15 mins drive from Hobart. Skilled contract winemaking has paid
rewards, and a cellar door is planned to open sometime in 2008.

Chardonnay 2006 White peach, melon and nectarine; medium-bodied, with
good length. **Rating** 90 **To** 2011 $24

Pinot Noir 2005 Lively, medium-bodied spicy/savoury/stemmy style, which makes up for lesser red fruit with excellent length and persistence. **Rating** 90 To 2011 $25

♥♥♥♥ **Chardonnay 2005** Ripe stone fruit flavour, but not over-much elegance. **Rating** 88 **To** 2008 $23

Black Swan Wines

8600 West Swan Road, Henley Brook, WA 6055 **Region** Swan Valley
T (08) 9296 6090 **www**.blackswanwines.com.au **Open** 7 days 10–5
Winemaker Rob Marshall (Contract) **Est.** NA **Cases** 3000
Barry Scrivener and Robyn Meloury have established a little over 3 ha of chardonnay, cabernet sauvignon, cabernet franc and merlot, all made as easy-drinking styles with the emphasis on fresh fruit. The vines are mostly unirrigated, and managed by John Corich, who has over 50 years' vineyard experience.

Blackbilly Wines

Main Street, McLaren Vale, SA 5171 **Region** McLaren Vale
T 0419 383 907 **F** (08) 8323 9747 **www**.blackbilly.com **Open** By appt
Winemaker Nick Haselgrove, Warren Randall **Est.** 2005 **Cases** 5000
Blackbilly has emerged from the numerous changes in the various Haselgrove wine interests. It was founded by Nick Haselgrove, but thereafter joined forces with the Tinlins wine group; these days the people behind Blackbilly are Nick Haselgrove, Warren Randall, Warren Ward and Andrew Fletcher. Blackbilly is able to access the 400 ha of vines owned by Tinlins, along with smaller suppliers in McLaren Vale. The intention is to add tempranillo and grenache-based wines to the existing portfolio of Shiraz, GSM, Pinot Gris and Sauvignon Blanc. Exports to the UK and the US.

♥♥♥♥♀ **Adelaide Hills Sauvignon Blanc 2006** Light straw-green; an expressive bouquet with citrus and gooseberry; the flavours of the light- to medium-bodied palate track the bouquet, and have good length. Screwcap. 13° alc. **Rating** 91 **To** 2008 $18

♥♥♥♥ **Fleurieu Pinot Gris 2006** Crisp and clean, with good balance, length and mouthfeel; limitations – as ever – with the variety. Screwcap. 13° alc. **Rating** 88 **To** 2008 $22

Blackboy Ridge Estate

PO Box 554, Donnybrook, WA 6239 **Region** Geographe
T (08) 9731 2233 **F** (08) 9731 2233 **www**.blackboyridge.com.au **Open** Not
Winemaker David Crawford (Contract) **Est.** 2003 **Cases** 1000
The 22-ha property on which Blackboy Ridge Estate is established was partly cleared and planted to 2.5 ha of semillon, chenin blanc, shiraz and cabernet sauvignon in 1978. When current owners Adrian Jones and Jackie Barton purchased the property in 2000 the vines were already some of the oldest in the region. The vineyard and the owners' house is on gentle north-facing slopes, with extensive views over the Donnybrook area. A cellar door is planned for late 2007/early '08.

♥♥♥♥♀ **Geographe Shiraz 2005** Light-bodied, crisp, spicy/leafy cool-grown style; red cherry fruit picks up intensity; nice finish. Cork. 13.5° alc. **Rating** 90 **To** 2012 $19
Geographe Cabernet Sauvignon 2005 Clear, light purple-red; light- to medium-bodied, with fresh cassis and blackcurrant fruit; light tannins, but enough intensity and length. Cork. 13.5° alc. **Rating** 90 **To** 2012 $17

♥♥♥♥ **Geographe Semillon 2005** Herb, mineral and a touch of citrus; elegant, crisp and dry. Screwcap. 12.5° alc. **Rating** 89 **To** 2013 $14

BlackJack Vineyards

Cnr Blackjack Road/Calder Highway, Harcourt, Vic 3453 **Region** Bendigo
T (03) 5474 2355 **F** (03) 5474 2355 **www**.blackjackwines.com.au **Open** W'ends &
public hols 11–5, when stock available
Winemaker Ian McKenzie, Ken Pollock **Est.** 1987 **Cases** 2500
Established by the McKenzie and Pollock families on the site of an old apple and pear orchard
in the Harcourt Valley and is best known for some very good Shirazs. Ian McKenzie,
incidentally, is not to be confused with Ian McKenzie formerly of Seppelt (Great Western).
Exports to NZ.

ᵀᵀᵀᵀᵀ **Chortle's Edge Bendigo Shiraz 2004** Paradoxically, by far the strongest red-
purple colour; smooth, supple blackberry, licorice and prune fruit; alcohol evident
but not over the top. An altogether surprising outcome. Screwcap. 15° alc. **Rating** 93
To 2019 $18
Block 6 Bendigo Shiraz 2004 More colour and more convincing than the
varietal, albeit still in a light to medium-bodied, elegant spectrum; attractive black
cherry fruit and fine tannins. Screwcap. 14° alc. **Rating** 92 **To** 2012 $35
Bendigo Cabernet Merlot 2004 Medium red-purple; elegant, medium-bodied
wine; flourished in mild weather conditions; cassis and blackberry fruit, silky finish.
Screwcap. 14° alc. **Rating** 91 **To** 2019 $25

ᵀᵀᵀᵀ **Bendigo Shiraz 2004** A light-bodied wine; most surprising, but somehow missed
the boat in a very good vintage. Screwcap. 14° alc. **Rating** 87 **To** 2010 $35

Blackwood Crest Wines

RMB 404A, Boyup Brook, WA 6244 **Region** Blackwood Valley
T (08) 9767 3029 **F** (08) 9767 3029 **Open** 10–5 by appt
Winemaker Max Fairbrass **Est.** 1976 **Cases** 3000
Blackwood Crest has been holding a low profile while developing its vineyards and a new 100-
tonne winery. It is hoped that developments will be complete in 2008 when the family will
celebrate its centenary (Max Fairbrass's grandparents took up the property as virgin bush in 1908).

ᵀᵀᵀᵀᵀ **Kulikup Cabernet Sauvignon 2002** Holding hue very well; a very pure
expression of cabernet sauvignon, with fragrant cassis/blackcurrant fruit; long,
fine tannins and integrated oak; elegant and harmonious. Screwcap. 13.5° alc.
Rating 94 **To** 2022 $22.50

ᵀᵀᵀᵀᵀ **Kulikup Shiraz 2002** Scented black cherry/berry spice and cracked pepper
aromas; the medium-bodied palate follows along the same path, with fine tannins
and good length. Cork. 13.5° alc. **Rating** 93 **To** 2022 $22.50

Blackwood Wines

Kearney Street, Nannup, WA 6275 **Region** Blackwood Valley
T (08) 9756 0077 **F** (08) 9756 0089 **www**.blackwoodwines.com.au **Open** 7 days 10–4
Winemaker Peter Nicholas **Est.** 1996 **Cases** 15 000
Blackwood Wines draws upon 1 ha each of chardonnay, merlot and chenin blanc and 0.5 ha of
pinot noir, supplemented by contract-grown fruit which significantly broadens the product range.
Redevelopment of the cellar door and winery is designed to see production increase significantly
by 2009. Exports to Ireland, Singapore and The Netherlands.

ᵀᵀᵀᵀᵀ **Fishbone Cabernet Shiraz 2005** Red-purple; medium-bodied, with attractive
mouthfeel and structure; blackcurrant fruit with fine, ripe tannins, and good length.
Screwcap. 13.5° alc. **Rating** 90 **To** 2013 $15

ᵀᵀᵀᵀ **Fishbone Shiraz 2005** Clean bouquet; spicy plum and black cherry fruit, with a
savoury cast to the fine tannins. Screwcap. 13.5° alc. **Rating** 89 **To** 2010 $15

Fishbone Classic White 2006 Nicely put together; a clear fruit line of grapefruit, melon and lemon on the light- to medium-bodied palate. Screwcap. 13° alc. **Rating** 88 **To** 2008 $15

Fishbone Unwooded Chardonnay 2006 A clean, fresh and delicate wine, helped by positive stone fruit plus nuances of grapefruit in the background. Screwcap. 13° alc. **Rating** 87 **To** 2008 $15

Blamires Butterfly Crossing

410 Harcourt Road, Sutton Grange, Vic 3448 **Region** Bendigo
T (03) 5474 2567 **www**.butterflycrossing.com.au **Open** W'ends & public hols 11–5, or by appt
Winemaker Bill Blamires **Est.** 2001 **Cases** 800
Bill and Sandra Blamires acquired their property after a 2-year search of the southern Bendigo area for what they considered to be an ideal location. They have firmly planted their faith in shiraz (6 ha) with merlot, cabernet sauvignon, chardonnay and viognier contributing another 0.5 ha. The vineyard is bisected by Axe Creek, and the butterflies that frequent the creek (in the absence of drought) are the source of the name for the property.

Shiraz 2005 Dense colour; potent and concentrated black fruits and licorice, finishing with savoury notes. Open-fermented, hand-plunged, basket-pressed and minimum preservatives. Screwcap. 14° alc. **Rating** 89 **To** 2015 $15

Blanche Barkly Wines

14 Kingower-Brenanah Road, Kingower, Vic 3517 **Region** Bendigo
T (03) 5438 8223 **F** (03) 5438 8223 **www**.bendigowine.org.au **Open** W'ends & public hols 10–5, or by appt
Winemaker David Reimers, Arleen Reimers **Est.** 1972 **Cases** 500
The Reimers are happy with their relatively low profile; yields from the 30+-year-old, dry-grown vines are low, and the quality of the wines is reward in itself. Limited availability makes the mailing list the best way of securing the wines.

Bleasdale Vineyards

Wellington Road, Langhorne Creek, SA 5255 **Region** Langhorne Creek
T (08) 8537 3001 **F** (08) 8537 3224 **www**.bleasdale.com.au **Open** 7 days 10–5
Winemaker Michael Potts, Renae Hirsch **Est.** 1850 **Cases** 100 000
One of the most historic wineries in Australia, drawing upon 63.5 ha of vineyards that are flooded every winter by diversion of the Bremer River, which provides moisture throughout the dry, cool growing season. The wines offer excellent value for money, all showing that particular softness which is the hallmark of the Langhorne Creek region. Production has soared; export markets established in the UK, the US, NZ, Switzerland and Germany.

Frank Potts 2004 Strong colour, clear red-purple; equally strong palate structure; masses of blackcurrant and cassis fruit; soft tannins typical of the region. Cork. 14.5° alc. **Rating** 94 **To** 2010 $28

Langhorne Creek Malbec 2003 Good depth to the colour, holding hue; moderately full-bodied and rich, with ripe raspberry jam flavour typical of the variety; of interest, perhaps. Cork. 14.5° alc. **Rating** 88 **To** 2013 $13

Langhorne Creek Verdelho 2006 Old vines add to the intensity of the fruit salad flavours, and the cool climate of the region gives freshness and acidity to also lift it from the ruck. Screwcap. 13.5° alc. **Rating** 87 **To** 2010 $13.50

Blickling Estate

Green Valley Road, Bendemeer, NSW 2355 **Region** Northern Slopes Zone
T (02) 6769 6786 **F** (02) 6769 6740 **www**.blickling.com.au **Open** 7 days 9–5
Winemaker Monarch Winemaking Services **Est.** 1999 **Cases** 6500

Rolf Blickling has established his 10-ha vineyard, planted to riesling, chardonnay, sauvignon blanc, pinot noir, cabernet sauvignon and shiraz, at an elevation of 950 m. Frosts in spring and April underline how cool the climate is, necessitating careful site selection. The cellar door also operates a lavender and eucalyptus oil distillery.

Blind Man's Bluff Vineyards

Lot 15 Bluff Road, Kenilworth, Qld 4574 **Region** Queensland Coastal
T (07) 5472 3168 **F** (07) 5472 3168 **www**.blindmansbluff.com.au **Open** W'ends & school hols 10–5
Winemaker Peter Scudamore-Smith (Contract) **Est.** 2001 **Cases** 450
Blind Man's Bluff Vineyards is situated 45 mins away from Qld's Sunshine Coast. Noel Evans dream of establishing a vineyard when joined by his partner Tricia Toussaint and family members, turned into reality in 2000, when the property was planted to chardonnay, shiraz and verdelho.

ҰҰҰҰ **Liaisons Chardonnay 2006** Well-made; plenty of gently tropical yellow peach fruit; well-handled lemony acidity. Screwcap. 12° alc. **Rating** 87 **To** 2008 $27
Infatuation 2005 Typical spirit-fortified, early-bottled style; spicy flavours work well, although the spirit is hot. (Fermentation arrested very early by significant spirit addition.) Screwcap. 16° alc. **Rating** 87 **To** 2008 $20

Bloodwood

4 Griffin Road, Orange, NSW 2800 **Region** Orange
T (02) 6362 5631 **F** (02) 6361 1173 **www**.bloodwood.com.au **Open** By appt
Winemaker Stephen Doyle **Est.** 1983 **Cases** 4000
Rhonda and Stephen Doyle are 2 of the pioneers of the burgeoning Orange district. The wines are sold mainly through the cellar door and by an energetically and informatively run mailing list. Bloodwood has done best with elegant but intense Chardonnay and the intermittent releases of super-late-harvest Ice Riesling. Exports to the UK.

ҰҰҰҰҰ **Schubert 2004** Glowing green-yellow; developing into a lovely mature chardonnay with years in front of it on its plateau; stone fruit and citrus, oak a muted bassoon. Screwcap. 13.8° alc. **Rating** 94 **To** 2012 $25

ҰҰҰҰҰ **Riesling 2006** Aromatic with slightly unusual crushed nettle and passionfruit aromas; delightful flavours moving more to citrus and passionfruit; excellent finish. Screwcap. 12.5° alc. **Rating** 93 **To** 2016 $20
Malbec 2004 Typical varietal character, the fruit at once sombre and slightly jammy; despite the description, this is a good wine. Screwcap. 14° alc. **Rating** 90 **To** 2019 $22

ҰҰҰҰ **Chardonnay 2005** Ripe stone fruit and melon; complex, but oak a little over the top for the fruit. Screwcap. 13.5° alc. **Rating** 89 **To** 2010 $24
Pinot Noir 2005 Deep colour; teeters on the edge of dry red, but stays within the bounds of pinot noir, even if on the big side of town. Black cherry, and even a hint of prune and licorice. Patience needed and may reward. Screwcap. 13.5° alc. **Rating** 89 **To** 2013 $35
Cabernet Sauvignon 2003 Has the structure (courtesy of its tannins) which the Merlot Cabernet Franc doesn't have; I wouldn't have hesitated about blending the 2 wines. Screwcap. 13.5° alc. **Rating** 89 **To** 2014 $24
Big Men in Tights 2006 Bloodwood has been making its rose from malbec for many years, and practise makes perfect; a touch of plum jam fruit, with good length and balance. Screwcap. 13° alc. **Rating** 88 **To** 2008 $15
Merlot Cabernet Franc 2003 Light- to medium-bodied; a clean and fragrant mix of spice, leaf, mint and berry; the flavours are good but there is not much depth to the structure. Screwcap. 13.5° alc. **Rating** 88 **To** 2010 $22

Blue Metal Vineyard

Lot 18 Compton Park Road, Berrima, NSW 2025 **Region** Southern Highlands
T 0438 377 727 **www.bluemetalvineyard.com Open** Thurs–Sun 10–5, or by appt
Winemaker Nick Spencer **Est.** 1999 **Cases** 1300
The 10.74-ha Blue Metal Vineyard is situated on part of a cattle station at an elevation of 790 m;
the name comes from the rich red soil that overlies the cap of basalt rock. A wide range of grape
varieties are planted, including sauvignon blanc, pinot gris, merlot, cabernet sauvignon, sangiovese
and petit verdot. The wines have been very competently made. Exports to the UK.

Southern Highlands Sauvignon Blanc 2006 Attractive aromas of passionfruit
and gooseberry; a strong twist of lemon adds to the impact and appeal of the palate.
Screwcap. 11.2° alc. **Rating** 91 **To** 2008 $18.95

Southern Highlands Sangiovese Cabernet Sauvignon 2005 Curiously,
works infinitely better than the varietal cabernet; light-bodied; attractive red cherry
fragrance and flavour from the sangiovese drives the wine; fine tannins, subtle oak.
Screwcap. 13° alc. **Rating** 90 **To** 2012 $25

Blue Poles Vineyard

PO Box 34, Mt Lawley, WA 6929 **Region** Margaret River
T 0408 096 411 **F** (08) 9370 5354 **www.bluepolesvineyard.com.au Open** Not
Winemaker Sharna Kowalczuk (Vasse River Wines) **Est.** 2001 **Cases** 400
Geologists Mark Gifford and Tim Markwell formed a joint venture to locate and develop Blue
Poles Vineyard. Their search was unhurried, and contact with the University of Bordeaux
(supplemented by extensive reading of technical literature) showed that a portion of the
property included a block that mimicked some of the best vineyards in St Emilion and
Pomerol, leading to the planting of merlot and cabernet franc in 2001. Further soil mapping
and topography also identified blocks best suited to shiraz and Rhône Valley white varietals,
which were planted in 2003. The vineyard maintenance has proceeded with minimal irrigation,
and the non-use of fertilisers.

Blue Pyrenees Estate

Vinoca Road, Avoca, Vic 3467 **Region** Pyrenees
T (03) 5465 1111 **F** (03) 5465 3529 **www.bluepyrenees.com.au Open** Mon–Fri 10–4.30,
w'ends & public hols 10–5
Winemaker Andrew Koerner, Chris Smales **Est.** 1963 **Cases** 50 000
Forty years after Remy Cointreau established Blue Pyrenees Estate (then known as Chateau
Remy), it sold the business to a small group of Sydney businessmen led by John Ellis (no relation
to the John Ellis of Hanging Rock). Former Rosemount senior winemaker Andrew Koerner
heads the winery team, and Josephine Rozman (with long-term knowledge of the US market)
has been appointed CEO. The core of the business is the 180-ha estate vineyard, much of it fully
mature. Exports to all major markets.

Estate Reserve Red 2002 Luscious and rich, with lots of texture and structure;
black fruits, bitter chocolate, mocha, spice and savoury tannins; oak in the back seat.
Heavily stained cork. Cabernet Sauvignon (62%)/Shiraz (33%)/Merlot
(3%)/Cabernet Franc (2%). Cork. 14.5° alc. **Rating** 94 **To** 2012 $32

Cabernet Sauvignon 2004 Muted bouquet; a nicely crafted medium-bodied
cabernet; strong varietal character without bitterness or aggression, nor, on the other
hand, over-elaboration. Good length. Cork. 14° alc. **Rating** 93 **To** 2014 $18
Estate Reserve Chardonnay 2004 Glowing yellow-green; a quite elegant mix
of grapefruit, melon and nectarine; minimal barrel ferment impact. Cork. 13.5° alc.
Rating 92 **To** 2011 $28

Chardonnay 2005 Clean bouquet; lively, fresh stone fruit/citrus aromas and
flavours; a brisk, minerally finish; barest touch of oak. Screwcap. 14° alc. **Rating** 89
To 2010 $18

Shiraz 2004 Medium-bodied, with spicy/earthy/savoury overtones to the black fruits, followed by savoury, though not aggressive tannins on the finish. Plenty of substance. Cork. 14.5° alc. **Rating** 89 **To** 2012 $18

Vintage Brut 2001 Has good complexity at this price point; pleasantly tangy fruit; good length and a crisp, lingering finish. 12° alc. **Rating** 89 **To** 2010 $24

Shiraz 2003 Showing some development; earthy, spicy aromas and flavours, plus soft plum fruit on the mid-palate. Cork. 14.5° alc. **Rating** 87 **To** 2009 $18

Blue Wren

433 Cassilis Road, Mudgee, NSW 2850 **Region** Mudgee
T (02) 6372 6205 **F** (02) 6372 6206 www.bluewrenwines.com.au **Open** 7 days 10.30–4.30
Winemaker Various contract **Est.** 1985 **Cases** 2000

James and Diana Anderson have 2 vineyards. The first is Stoney Creek, 20 km north of Mudgee, which was planted in 1985 and has 2 ha each of dry-grown chardonnay and semillon, 1.5 ha of cabernet and 0.5 ha of merlot. The Bombira Vineyard, adjacent to the old Augustine vineyards, has been planted to 3.8 ha of shiraz and verdelho, leaving more than 20 ha unplanted.

ŦŦŦŦ♀ **Mudgee Shiraz 2004** Good hue though faintly hazy; an abundance of well-structured black fruits, with nuances of licorice and earth; good tannins and length to the finish. Screwcap. 15.1° alc. **Rating** 91 **To** 2015 $28

Mudgee Merlot 2005 Fragrant olive, bracken and small red berries; slippery red fruits provide a seductive texture. Screwcap. 14.1° alc. **Rating** 90 **To** 2013 $18

ŦŦŦŦ **Reserve Mudgee Shiraz 2005** Medium-bodied; considerably more depth and structure than the '05 varietal, and is also less sweet; a black cherry/blackberry mix. Screwcap. 15.4° alc. **Rating** 89 **To** 2013 $26

 ## Bluestone Acres Vineyard

PO Box 206, Wandin North, Vic 3139 **Region** Yarra Valley
T (03) 5964 4909 **F** (03) 5964 3936 www.bluestoneacres.com.au **Open** Not
Winemaker Paul Evans **Est.** 2000 **Cases** 700

Graeme and Isabel Ross have 1.2 ha of merlot, 1.15 ha of shiraz and 1 ha of sauvignon blanc on a north-facing slope. The soil is predominantly grey loam in the merlot and shiraz blocks, with a vein of volcanic red clay loam running through part of the shiraz and most of the sauvignon blanc block; a vein of basalt adds spice to the salt of the sauvignon blanc. Integrated pest management is used in the vineyard (no insecticides) and sprays are held to a minimum.

ŦŦŦŦ **Yarra Valley Shiraz 2004** Light- to medium-bodied; cool climate, spice, leaf and berry aromas and flavours; unforced, but needs a touch more weight. Cork. 13.5° alc. **Rating** 88 **To** 2010 $22

Yarra Valley Sauvignon Blanc 2006 Pale straw; clean, not much varietal expression, but well enough made, with modest development potential. Screwcap. **Rating** 87 **To** 2008 $18

Yarra Valley Sauvignon Blanc 2005 Well-made, with no fault; light mineral notes; touches of citrus and grass. Screwcap. 13.5° alc. **Rating** 87 **To** 2008 $18

 ## Bluestone Lane

269 Myers Road, Balnarring, Vic 3926 **Region** Mornington Peninsula
T 0411 862 193 **F** (03) 5948 2311 www.bluestonelane.com **Open** Thurs–Mon 11–5
Winemaker Philip Kettle **Est.** 1997 **Cases** 2000

Bluestone Lane takes its inspiration from the many bluestone-cobbled laneways around Melbourne. From time to time large quantities of bluestone pavings become available for purchase as more modern surfaces are used in the city, and Michael and Pauline Poulter have incorporated these in their much-revitalised and altered property. Wetlands and bush have been rejuvenated, while run-down cattle grazing land now supports the 5 ha of vineyard planted in 1997. The present plantings of pinot noir, chardonnay, shiraz, pinot meunier and sauvignon blanc will be increased by a further 4 ha divided between pinot gris and additional chardonnay. Mark Poulter will also bring his 10 years' experience as a chef on the Mornington Peninsula into play.

▼▼▼▼ **Mornington Peninsula Pinot Noir 2005** Forest, plum and spice flavours on the medium-bodied palate; not particularly long, but the balance is good. Screwcap. 13.9° alc. **Rating** 89 **To** 2010 $24
Mornington Peninsula Shiraz 2005 Fragrant and spicy aromas; medium-bodied, with attractive spicy, almost malt biscuit flavours; low tannins. Screwcap. 13.9° alc. **Rating** 89 **To** 2011 $24
Wooded Mornington Peninsula Chardonnay 2005 Light green-straw; a light- to medium-bodied palate with pleasing stone fruit and a touch of citrus, oak merely a bystander. Screwcap. 13.8° alc. **Rating** 88 **To** 2009 $21
Mornington Peninsula Unwooded Chardonnay 2006 Water white; citrus, grapefruit and a touch of melon fruit; simple but balanced. Screwcap. 12.5° alc. **Rating** 87 **To** 2008 $20

Boat O'Craigo

458 Maroondah Highway, Healesville, Vic 3777 **Region** Yarra Valley
T (03) 5962 6899 **F** (03) 5962 5140 **www.boatocraigo.com.au Open** Thurs–Sun 10–5
Winemaker Al Fencaros, The YarraHill (Contract) **Est.** 1998 **Cases** 3500
Steve Graham purchased the property which is now known as Boat O'Craigo (a tiny place in a Scottish valley where his ancestors lived) in 2003. It has 2 quite separate vineyards: a 12-ha hillside planting on one of the highest sites in the Yarra Valley, and 8 ha at Kangaroo Ground on the opposite side of the valley. Exports to China and Hong Kong.

▼▼▼▼▼ **Rob Roy Kangaroo Ground Pinot Noir 2005** Lively, spiced black cherry fruit; spotlessly clean; very good mouthfeel and length. Twin top. 12.8° alc. **Rating** 94 **To** 2011 $22

▼▼▼▼♀ **Black Cameron Kangaroo Ground Shiraz 2004** A light- to medium-bodied, elegant wine with a mix of red and black fruits, plus splashes of spice; gentle oak, good length. Diam. 14° alc. **Rating** 93 **To** 2014 $24
Dundee Kangaroo Ground Shiraz Viognier 2005 Lively, fresh black cherry and spice fruit; soft, fine tannins and good mouthfeel; nice oak. Twin top. 14.8° alc. **Rating** 92 **To** 2012 $22
Black Spur Reserve Yarra Valley Sauvignon Blanc 2006 Complex and intense; medium- to full-bodied, with the fruit and French oak well-balanced and integrated; gooseberry fruit runs through the long and clean palate. Screwcap. 13° alc. **Rating** 91 **To** 2008 $23
Black Spur Yarra Valley Chardonnay 2005 Nicely balanced, framed and structured, with stone fruit and melon backed by more nutty/creamy notes. Screwcap. 13° alc. **Rating** 91 **To** 2011 $19
Dundee Kangaroo Ground Shiraz Viognier 2006 Light- to medium-bodied, with lively red cherry, black cherry and blackberry fruit; fine tannins, good length. Screwcap. 14.7° alc. **Rating** 91 **To** 2015 $22
Braveheart Yarra Valley Cabernet Sauvignon 2004 Redcurrant/blackcurrant and spice; gentle oak, and fine, persistent tannins. Twin top. 13.5° alc. **Rating** 90 **To** 2014 $22

▼▼▼▼ **Black Spur Yarra Valley Sauvignon Blanc 2006** A clean and fragrant bouquet, the palate a light mix of tropical and more grassy/asparagus/gooseberry flavours; delicate style. Screwcap. 13° alc. **Rating** 89 **To** 2008 $16
Rob Roy Kangaroo Ground Pinot Noir 2004 Spicy, cherry fruit aromas; a light- to medium-bodied palate; fine, spicy tannins, and particularly good length. Cork. 13° alc. **Rating** 89 **To** 2008 $22
Black Spur Yarra Valley Pinot Noir 2005 Light- to medium-bodied, with distinctly foresty/savoury overtones to plum and black cherry fruit. Twin top. 12.5° alc. **Rating** 88 **To** 2009 $22

Bochara Wines

1099 Glenelg Highway, Hamilton, Vic 3300 **Region** Henty
T (03) 5571 9309 **www.**bocharawine.com.au **Open** Fri–Sun 11–5, or by appt
Winemaker Martin Slocombe **Est.** 1998 **Cases** 1000
This is the small business of experienced winemaker Martin Slocombe and former Yalumba viticulturist Kylie McIntyre. They have established 1 ha each of pinot noir and sauvignon blanc, 1.6 ha of shiraz and cabernet sauvignon, and 0.5 ha of pinot meunier, supplemented by grapes purchased from local growers. The modestly priced, but well-made wines are principally sold through the cellar door sales cottage on the property, which has been transformed from a decrepit weatherboard shanty with 1 cold tap to a fully functional 2-room tasting area, and through a number of local restaurants and bottle shops. The label design, incidentally, comes from a 1901 poster advertising the subdivision of the original Bochara property into smaller farms.

🍷🍷🍷🍷🍷 **Picnic Train Rose 2006** Has well above-average intensity, length and character through its strawberry and citrus mix; long, balanced finish. Takes its name from the train running from Hamilton through Bochara to the picnic destination of Wannan Falls at the end of the 19th century. Screwcap. 12.3° alc. **Rating** 92 **To** 2008 $16
Henty Sauvignon Blanc 2006 Spotless bouquet; delicate gooseberry, passionfruit and kiwifruit; a long and fresh finish; great value for quality sauvignon blanc. Screwcap. 12.5° alc. **Rating** 91 **To** 2008 $15

Boggy Creek Vineyards

★★★★

1657 Boggy Creek Road, Myrrhee, Vic 3732 **Region** King Valley
T (03) 5729 7587 **F** (03) 5729 7600 **www.**boggycreek.com.au **Open** 7 days 10–5
Winemaker Graeme Ray, Daniel Balzer **Est.** 1978 **Cases** 15 000
Graeme and Maggie Ray started their vineyard in 1978, planting small quantities of riesling and chardonnay. Since then the vineyard has grown to over 40 ha with the addition of cabernet sauvignon, shiraz, barbera, pinot gris and other experimental lots. It is situated on northeast-facing slopes at an altitude of 350 m, with warm summer days and cool nights. Exports to the US, Canada, Malaysia, China and Hong Kong.

🍷🍷🍷🍷🍷 **King Valley Cabernet Sauvignon 2004** A powerful wine, with considerable depth to the blackcurrant fruit; not over-extracted; impressive. Heavily stained cork a worry. 13.5° alc. **Rating** 93 **To** 2014 $18
King Valley Sangiovese 2006 Very attractive example of sangiovese; fragrant, light- to medium-bodied cherry and spice flavours; balanced, fine tannins. Screwcap. 13° alc. **Rating** 92 **To** 2012 $18
King Valley Barbera 2004 Attractive wine; sweet black and red fruits supported by soft, ripe tannins; plenty of presence. Screwcap. 13.5° alc. **Rating** 90 **To** 2010 $18

🍷🍷🍷🍷 **Barrel Selection King Valley Pinot Gris 2003** Barrel fermentation in old oak works very well; has both richness and texture; thanks to the closure, developing at a leisurely pace. Screwcap. 13.5° alc. **Rating** 89 **To** 2010 $25
King Valley Rose 2005 The blend does work and adds interest to the wine; spicy wild berry fruit notes; has considerable length. Barbera/Sangiovese/Shiraz. Screwcap. 13.5° alc. **Rating** 89 **To** 2008 $15
King Valley Shiraz Cabernet Sauvignon 2004 Medium-bodied; supple blackberry and blackcurrant mix; soft tannins; balanced oak and extract. Screwcap. 13.5° alc. **Rating** 89 **To** 2013 $26
King Valley Riesling 2004 Light-bodied, clean and crisp; not much fruit flesh to the mineral backbone, but has length and a bright finish. Will improve with bottle age. Screwcap. 12.5° alc. **Rating** 88 **To** 2012 $16
King Valley Pinot Gris 2004 Has more fruit weight than most without reliance on residual sugar; picked fully ripe in true gris style. Screwcap. 14.5° alc. **Rating** 87 **To** 2008 $26
King Valley Barbera 2005 Some slightly bitter/reduced notes, but the wine does have intensity and may well come around with time. Screwcap. 13.5° alc. **Rating** 87 **To** 2013 $18

Bogong Estate

Cnr Mountain Creek Road/Damms Road, Mt Beauty, Vic 3699 **Region** Alpine Valleys
T 0419 567 588 **F** (03) 5754 1320 **www**.pinotnoir.com.au **Open** 7 days 11–5
Winemaker Bill Tynan **Est.** 1997 **Cases** 4000

Bill Tynan and family began the establishment of their 10-ha pinot noir vineyard a decade ago
and have been relentless pursuers of different techniques, wine styles and labels. The zany nature
of some of this should not hide the fact that the Tynans are totally committed to their production
of pinot noir in a number of guises. They have 4 clones (D5V12, MV6, 114 and 115) grown in
separate blocks with differing soil and site climate characteristics. Wild/indigenous yeasts are used
in 1-tonne open fermenters, then basket-pressed.

pinotnoir.com.au Rose 2005 Salmon pink; some strawberry fruit, and slightly
more flesh than its white sister; dry finish. Zork. 13° alc. **Rating** 88 **To** 2008 $20
pinotnoir.com.au Red Pinot Noir 2005 Light- to medium red; light, very
savoury/sappy/foresty style, away from the mainstream. Zork. 13° alc. **Rating** 88
To 2008 $20
Alpine Valleys Pinot Noir 2005 Savoury, foresty flavours; fine, almost milky
tannins emphasise the forest floor components, but the wine is clearly varietal.
Screwcap. 13.5° alc. **Rating** 88 **To** 2010 $25
pinotnoir.com.au White Pinot Noir 2005 Bone-dry; a serious attempt with
whole-bunch pressing and 4 weeks cold fermentation; fairly austere, but has some
length. Zork. 13° alc. **Rating** 87 **To** 2008 $20

Boireann

26 Donnellys Castle Road, The Summit Qld 4377 **Region** Granite Belt
T (07) 4683 2194 **Open** 7 days 10–4.30
Winemaker Peter Stark **Est.** 1998 **Cases** 900

Peter and Therese Stark have a 10-ha property set amongst the great granite boulders and trees
which are so much part of the Granite Belt. They have established 1.5 ha of vines planted to no
fewer than 11 varieties, including the 4 Bordeaux varieties which go to make a Bordeaux-blend;
shiraz and viognier; grenache and mourvedre provide a Rhône blend, and there will also be a
straight merlot. Tannat (French) and barbera and nebbiolo (Italian) make up the viticultural
League of Nations. Peter Stark is a winemaker of exceptional talent, making cameo amounts of
red wines which are quite beautifully made and of a quality equal to Australia's best.

The Lurnea Petit Verdot Cabernet Franc Merlot 2005 A very powerful
Bordeaux-style blend, yet in some ways more welcoming and open than the other
'05 reds; predominantly black fruits and generous, firm tannins; 1200 bottles. Diam.
14° alc. **Rating** 94 **To** 2020 $20

Granite Belt Shiraz Viognier 2005 An interesting wine, with vibrant, spicy
aromas and flavours; dark fruits, fine tannins and a fractionally uncompromising
finish. Total wine penetration of the ProCork; 1200 bottles. ProCork. 14° alc.
Rating 93 **To** 2015 $45
Reserve Granite Belt Merlot 2005 A pristine redcurrant/cassis core surrounded
by fine tannins and a passing hint of olive; immaculate handling; 1500 bottles. Diam.
13.5° alc. **Rating** 93 **To** 2015 $25
Granite Belt Grenache Mourvedre Shiraz 2005 A very youthful and tight
array of red and black fruits; no hint of jamminess ex the grenache; crisp acidity, and
needs time to soften and loosen up; 2000 bottles. Diam. 14.5° alc. **Rating** 92
To 2015 $26
Reserve Granite Belt Cabernet Sauvignon 2005 Excellent purple-red; clean,
fresh cassis/blackcurrant fruit; fine tannins on the long finish, but still tight; minimal
oak; 1350 bottles. ProCork. 13.8° alc. **Rating** 91 **To** 2015 $25
Granite Belt Barbera 2005 A vibrant mix of blackcurrant and black cherry fruit;
fine tannins; impressive for barbera; 300 bottles. Diam. 13.8° alc. **Rating** 91
To 2015 $22

Granite Belt Tannat 2005 Deep colour; dense and powerful; pervasive tannins typical of the variety; what you see is what you get; 400 bottles. Diam. 14° alc. **Rating** 91 **To** 2015 $22

♍♍♍♍ **Granite Belt Nebbiolo 2005** Pale red, headed to tawny; strongly varietal, with inimitable sour cherry, tar and bracken characters; for more sophisticated palates than mine; 300 bottles. Diam. 13.5° alc. **Rating** 89 **To** 2010 $22

Booroolite Wines

PO Box 542, Mansfield, Vic 3724 **Region** Upper Goulburn
T (03) 5775 2195 **F** (03) 5779 1636 **www**.booroolitewines.com.au **Open** Not
Winemaker King Valley Wines **Est.** 2004 **Cases** 1000
David and Catherine Ritchie (of Delatite fame) set up Booroolite Wines in 2004 to salvage locally grown, high-quality grapes which could not find an owner. They have started with an Unoaked Chardonnay and a Cabernet Merlot blend, and the product range will vary according to grape supply and pricing. The aim is to provide wines from small vineyards which are competitive price-wise with wines from the big companies.

Borambola Wines

★★★

Sturt Highway, Wagga Wagga, NSW 2650 **Region** Gundagai
T (02) 6928 4210 **F** (02) 6928 4210 **www**.borambola.com **Open** 7 days 11–4 by appt
Winemaker Chris Derrez **Est.** 1995 **Cases** 8000
Borambola Homestead was built in the 1880s, and in the latter part of that century was the centre of a pastoral empire of 1.4 million ha, ownership of which passed to the McMullen family in 1992. It is situated in rolling foothills 25 km east of Wagga Wagga in the Gundagai region. Ten and a half ha of vines surround the homestead (shiraz, cabernet sauvignon and chardonnay).

♍♍♍♍ **Hiraji's Spell Shiraz 2005** Bright, clear purple-red; a medium-bodied, appealing mix of black cherry, plum and blackberry; good structure and length. Cork. 14° alc. **Rating** 89 **To** 2013 $20

Cabernet Sauvignon 2002 A powerful, savoury, earthy wine; the cabernet sauvignon reflects the cool vintage even in this relatively warm area. Cork. 14.4° alc. **Rating** 88 **To** 2012 $16

Borrodell on the Mount

Lake Canobolas Road, Orange, NSW 2800 **Region** Orange
T (02) 6365 3425 **F** (02) 6365 3588 **www**.borrodell.com.au **Open** 7 days 10–5
Winemaker Chris Derrez, Lucy Maddox **Est.** 1995 **Cases** 1300
Barry Gartrell and Gaye Stuart-Nairne have planted 5.25 ha of pinot noir, sauvignon blanc, pinot meunier, traminer and chardonnay adjacent to a cherry, plum and heritage apple orchard and truffiere. It is a 10 mins drive from Orange, and adjacent to Lake Canobolas, at an altitude of 1000 m. The wines have been consistent medal winners at regional and small winemaker shows.

♍♍♍♍♍ **Winemakers Daughter Orange Riesling 2006** Lovely lime, lemon and passionfruit aromas and flavours; smooth line and good length; sheer pleasure. Screwcap. 13.5° alc. **Rating** 93 **To** 2015 $20
Orange Chardonnay 2005 An elegant wine with a seamless fusion of nectarine, stone fruit and citrus plus a modest amount of French oak. Screwcap. 14.3° alc. **Rating** 92 **To** 2012 $22

♍♍♍♍ **Winemaker's Daughter Gewurztraminer 2006** Good balance and flavour, the only lack being of varietal character. Screwcap. 13.5° alc. **Rating** 89 **To** 2008 $20
Orange Sauvignon Blanc 2006 Aromatic and forthcoming; rich, soft gooseberry/tropical fruit; easy style. Screwcap. 12.8° alc. **Rating** 88 **To** 2008 $20
Ruby 2005 Ruby cabernet has proved an unsuccessful cross in quality terms; however, the cabernet sauvignon and merlot in the wine partly compensate; some minty notes, and soft oak. Screwcap. 14.3° alc. **Rating** 87 **To** 2008 $20

Boston Bay Wines

Lincoln Highway, Port Lincoln, SA 5606 **Region** Southern Eyre Peninsula
T (08) 8684 3600 **F** (08) 8684 3637 **www.bostonbaywines.com.au Open** W'ends,
school & public hols 11.30–4.30
Winemaker David O'Leary, Nick Walker **Est.** 1984 **Cases** 3000
A strongly tourist-oriented operation which has extended the viticultural map in SA. It is situated
at the same latitude as Adelaide, overlooking the Spencer Gulf at the southern tip of the Eyre
Peninsula. Say proprietors Graham and Mary Ford, 'it is the only vineyard in the world to offer
frequent sightings of whales at play in the waters at its foot'.

Botobolar

89 Botobolar Road, Mudgee, NSW 2850 **Region** Mudgee
T (02) 6373 3840 **www.botobolar.com Open** Mon–Sat 10–5, Sun 10–3
Winemaker Kevin Karstrom **Est.** 1971 **Cases** 5000
One of the first organic vineyards in Australia, with present owner Kevin Karstrom continuing
the practices established by founder Gil Wahlquist. Preservative Free Dry White and Dry Red
extend the organic practice of the vineyard to the winery. Shiraz is consistently the best wine to
appear under the Botobolar label. Exports to Denmark.

ㅜㅜㅜㅜㅜ **The King Mudgee Cabernet Sauvignon Shiraz 2003** A massive wine high
in extract and tannins, but not alcoholic or jammy; a long, savoury palate. A good
big'un. Cork. 14° alc. **Rating** 91 **To** 2015 $23
KK's Choice Shiraz 2004 A rich and generous wine with abundant black fruits
and ripe, soft, almost fleshy tannins. As honest as they come. Diam. **Rating** 90
To 2011 $23

ㅜㅜㅜㅜ **Low Preservative Marsanne 2006** Unusually flowery and aromatic, with
touches of honeysuckle and abundant tropical fruit; all unexpected. Screwcap.
Rating 89 **To** 2008 $19
Preservative Free Dry Red 2006 A distinctly sweet overall caste to the red
berry fruits; hopefully it has been steril-filtered. Pinot Noir/Shiraz. Screwcap. 14° alc.
Rating 87 **To** 2008 $20

 # Bou-saada   **NR**

Kells Creek Road, Mittagong, NSW 2575 **Region** Southern Highlands
T (02) 4878 5399 **F** (02) 4878 5397 **www.bousaada.com Open** By appt
Winemaker Contract **Est.** 1997 **Cases** NA
The 40-ha property was purchased in 1996, and planting of the vineyard began the following
year with sauvignon blanc, followed by merlot, chardonnay and riesling. There are a little over
5 ha of vines, and all of the wines are estate grown. The name, incidentally, is a pilgrimage town
in Algeria built around an oasis, with 'Bou' meaning father and 'saada' peace and happiness. The
cellar door is made from Sydney blue gum and stringybark grown in the locality.

Bowen Estate

Riddoch Highway, Coonawarra, SA 5263 **Region** Coonawarra
T (08) 8737 2229 **F** (08) 8737 2173 **Open** 7 days 10–5
Winemaker Doug Bowen, Emma Bowen **Est.** 1972 **Cases** 12 000
Bluff-faced regional veteran Doug Bowen, now with daughter Emma at his side in the winery,
presides over one of Coonawarra's landmarks. For reasons I do not begin to understand, the wines
no longer have the edge they once possessed.

ㅜㅜㅜㅜㅜ **Coonawarra Chardonnay 2005** A nicely composed and structured wine with
fig, cashew and melon; backs off a little on the finish. Screwcap. 13.5° alc. **Rating** 90
To 2010 $22
Coonawarra Shiraz 2004 Medium-bodied; blackberry/black cherry fruit in a
restrained, earthy style; ripe tannins and subtle oak. Some questions on bacterial
status. Cork. 13° alc. **Rating** 90 **To** 2015 $26

ŶŶŶŶ   **Coonawarra Cabernet Sauvignon 2004** Medium-bodied blackcurrant fruit with savoury notes and touches of earth. Cork. 14.5° alc. **Rating** 89 **To** 2014 $27

Bowman's Run

1305 Beechworth-Wodonga Road, Wooragee, Vic 3747 **Region** Beechworth
T (03) 5728 7318 **Open** Most w'ends & by appt
Winemaker Fran Robertson, Andrew Doyle **Est.** 1989 **Cases** 250
Struan and Fran Robertson have 1 ha of cabernet sauvignon, 0.5 ha of riesling and small plots of shiraz and traminer dating back to 1989. The tiny winery came on-stream in 2000, part of a larger general agricultural holding.

ŶŶŶŶ   **Seven Springs Beechworth Riesling 2006** Clean, with gentle apple and citrus aromas and flavours; not a lot of intensity, but a pleasant wine. Screwcap. 12.8° alc. **Rating** 87 **To** 2010 $20
Granite Rise Beechworth Cabernet Sauvignon 2004 Light- to medium-bodied; earthy/savoury/briary notes come before the shy blackcurrant fruit, but the wine does end up in balance. Cork. 12.7° alc. **Rating** 87 **To** 2012 $25

Box Stallion   ★★★★

64 Turrarubba Road, Merricks North, Vic 3926 **Region** Mornington Peninsula
T (03) 5989 7444 **F** (03) 5989 7688 **www**.boxstallion.com.au **Open** 7 days 11–5
Winemaker Alex White **Est.** 2001 **Cases** 8000
Box Stallion is the joint venture of Stephen Wharton, John Gillies and Garry Zerbe, who have linked 2 vineyards at Bittern and Merricks North, with 20 ha of vines planted between 1997 and 2003. What was once a thoroughbred stud has now become a vineyard, with the Red Barn (in their words) 'now home to a stable of fine wines'. Exports to the US, Canada and China.

ŶŶŶŶŶ   **Shiraz 2004** A fragrant and elegant light- to medium-bodied palate, with red and black fruits, spicy notes and subtle oak. Stained Diam. 14.2° alc. **Rating** 93 **To** 2014 $35
Red Barn Chardonnay 2004 Light-bodied; ripe melon and apple fruit with subtle oak; crisp, clean finish. Screwcap. 14.5° alc. **Rating** 90 **To** 2009 $19

ŶŶŶŶ   **Sauvignon Blanc 2004** A solid array of passionfruit, gooseberry and citrus flavours, edging past its best-by date. Screwcap. 13.2° alc. **Rating** 89 **To** 2008 $19
Red Barn Pinot Noir 2003 Sweet slightly stewed plum/confit fruit; some spicy notes; well-priced for pinot noir. Stained cork. 14° alc. **Rating** 89 **To** 2008 $19
Tempranillo 2004 Medium red-purple; a distinct skein of sweetness runs throughout spiced black fruits; challenging price. Stained Diam. 15° alc. **Rating** 88 **To** 2011 $39
Moscato 2005 Actually quite a nice soft, gentle summer drink; however, definitely a filly, not a stallion. Screwcap. 11° alc. **Rating** 87 **To** 2008 $19
Arneis 2004 A mirror-image of the Lost Valley Cortese; crisp minerality, some citrus and apple; well-made, but the flavours and mouthfeel are, at best, fleeting. Screwcap. 14.6° alc. **Rating** 87 **To** 2008 $19

Boynton's Feathertop

Great Alpine Road, Porepunkah, Vic 3741 **Region** Alpine Valleys
T (03) 5756 2356 **F** (03) 5756 2610 **www**.boynton.com.au **Open** 7 days 10–5
Winemaker Kel Boynton **Est.** 1987 **Cases** 20 000
Kel Boynton has a beautiful 16-ha vineyard, framed by Mt Feathertop rising into the skies above it. Overall, the red wines have always outshone the whites. The initial very strong American oak input has been softened in more recent vintages to give a better fruit/oak balance. The wines are released under the Boyton Reserve, Feathertop and Paiko labels. The Paiko label is for wines grown near Mildura by business partner and famed nurseryman Bruce Chalmers. Exports to the UK, the US, Canada, Austria and Fiji.

🍷🍷🍷🍷🍷 **Alpine Valleys Cabernet Sauvignon 2003** Particularly good hue; gently sweet cassis, blackcurrant and even a touch of raspberry fruit; fine, savoury tannins and oak an excellent counterbalance. Screwcap. 13.5° alc. **Rating** 92 **To** 2015 $25

Alpine Valleys Pinot Gris 2006 Aromatic and flowery apple blossom, pear and spice; delicate but lively, with good acidity; well above average for a variety which usually keeps itself to itself. Screwcap. 13.5° alc. **Rating** 90 **To** 2008 $20

🍷🍷🍷🍷 **Alpine Valleys Sauvignon Blanc 2006** No reduction whatsoever on the bouquet; gentle apple and passionfruit flavours boosted by crisp acidity on the finish. Screwcap. 13.5° alc. **Rating** 88 **To** 2008 $20

Alpine Valleys Shiraz Viognier 2003 Light- to medium-bodied; fresh and clean, the flavour undoubtedly lifted by the viognier, and not enough without it. Screwcap. 14° alc. **Rating** 87 **To** 2010 $20

Braewattie ★★★☆

351 Rochford Road, Rochford, Vic 3442 **Region** Macedon Ranges
T (03) 9818 5742 **F** (03) 9818 8361 **Open** By appt
Winemaker Hanging Rock Winery **Est.** 1993 **Cases** 300

Maggi Ryan's great-grandfather acquired the Braewattie property in the 1880s, and it remained in the family until 1971. When the property came back on the market in 1990, Maggi and husband Des seized the opportunity to reclaim it, complete with a small existing planting of 300 pinot noir and chardonnay vines. Those plantings now extend to 5 ha; part of the production is sold and a small amount is contract-made. The Macedon Brut is a particularly good wine.

Brand's of Coonawarra ★★★★★

Riddoch Highway, Coonawarra, SA 5263 **Region** Coonawarra
T (08) 8736 3260 **www**.mcwilliams.com.au **Open** Mon–Fri 8–5, w'ends 10–4
Winemaker Jim Brayne, Peter Weinberg **Est.** 1966 **Cases** NFP

Part of a substantial investment in Coonawarra by McWilliam's, which first acquired a 50% interest from the founding Brand family, moved to 100%, and followed this with the purchase of 100 ha of additional vineyard land. Significantly increased production of the smooth wines for which Brand's is known has followed. The estate plantings include the 100-year-old Stentiford block.

🍷🍷🍷🍷🍷 **Stentiford's Reserve Old Vines Shiraz 2002** A restrained yet intense display of old vine Coonawarra shiraz; seamless black cherry and blackberry, spice, oak and tannins. High-quality cork. 14.5° alc. **Rating** 94 **To** 2017 $60

Cabernet Sauvignon 2004 Good structure; firm tannins run throughout, but maintain the line and do not threaten the delicately sweet berry fruit. Gold medal National Wine Show '06. Cork. 14° alc. **Rating** 94 **To** 2020 $23

🍷🍷🍷🍷🍷 **Chardonnay 2005** A richer, riper wine than one would expect from Coonawarra at this early stage, particularly given the screwcap closure; a touch of minerality helps lift the wine. Gold medal National Wine Show '06. Screwcap. 14.5° alc. **Rating** 93 **To** 2011 $20

Shiraz 2004 Medium-bodied, supple and smooth; above all, has length rather than depth. Cork. 14.5° alc. **Rating** 93 **To** 2014 $23

Special Release Merlot 2004 Plenty of depth and structure; an interesting wine dominated by sombre, dark fruits rather than the usual juxtaposition of brighter red fruits and savoury characters. Gold medal National Wine Show '06. Screwcap. 14.5° alc. **Rating** 93 **To** 2019 $22.95

Cabernet Sauvignon 2005 Very youthful and focused; tight red and black berry fruits; brisk finish, the tannin and oak under the usual control. Screwcap. 15° alc. **Rating** 90 **To** 2025 $60

Brandy Creek Wines

570 Buln Buln Road, Drouin East, Vic 3818 **Region** Gippsland
T (03) 5625 4498 **F** (03) 5623 5102 www.brandycreekwines.com.au **Open** Thurs &
public hols 10–5, w'ends 10–late, or by appt
Winemaker Peter Beckingham (Contract) **Est.** 2005 **Cases** 1200
Marie McDonald and Rick Stockdale purchased the property on which they have since
established their vineyard, cellar door and café restaurant in 1997. One ha each of pinot gris and
tempranillo were progressively planted over the 1999, 2001 and 2002 vintages, with other varieties
purchased from local growers in the region. The café (and surrounding vineyard) is situated on a
northeast-facing slope with spectacular views out to the Baw Baw Ranges.

♀♀♀♀♀ **Chardonnay 2005** Elegant and fresh, with harmonious fruit and oak; just lacks the
drive for gold medal points. **Rating** 92 **To** 2013 $21
Bairnsdale Shiraz 2005 Good wine; rich and deep blackberry, licorice and spice;
balanced tannins and oak. **Rating** 92 **To** 2016 $24
Sparkling Pinot Gris 2005 A truly astonishing wine, made from an unlikely
base variety with great skill; the pinot gris must have been picked at exactly the
right point, and treated with kid gloves thereafter. Trophy Gippsland Wine
Show '07. **Rating** 91 **To** 2008 $33

♀♀♀♀ **Menage A Trois Pinot Noir Chardonnay Pinot Meunier 2005** Green-
yellow; excellent mousse, with good balance and length, each of the 3 varieties
making its contribution. **Rating** 88 **To** 2008 $28
Pinot Rose 2006 Pleasing red fruit flavours; well-balanced, and not too sweet.
Rating 87 **To** 2008 $18
Longford Vineyard Gippsland Shiraz 2004 Light- to medium-bodied; some
of the same flavour characteristics as the Bairnsdale Shiraz, but a touch more
herbaceous; good length. Screwcap. 13.8° alc. **Rating** 87 **To** 2011 $24

Brangayne of Orange

837 Pinnacle Road, Orange, NSW 2800 **Region** Orange
T (02) 6365 3229 **F** (02) 6365 3170 www.brangayne.com **Open** Sat 10–4.30, or by appt
Winemaker Simon Gilbert **Est.** 1994 **Cases** 2500
Orchardists Don and Pamela Hoskins decided to diversify into grapegrowing in 1994 and have
progressively established 25.7 ha of high-quality vineyards. Brangayne made an auspicious debut,
underlining the potential of the Orange region. Exports to the UK, Canada and Spain.

♀♀♀♀♀ **Tristan Cabernet Sauvignon Shiraz Merlot 2003** Generous, but not excessive,
blackcurrant, cassis and blackberry fruit; oak and tannins are both perfectly balanced
and integrated. A beautiful wine. Cork. 13.5° alc. **Rating** 94 **To** 2018 $29

♀♀♀♀ **Sauvignon Blanc 2006** A wine with an abundance of varietal aroma and flavour,
all turning around a touch of sweatiness, and which utterly polarises opinions.
Outside the norm for Brangayne. Screwcap. 13° alc. **Rating** 89 **To** 2008 $23
Isolde Reserve Chardonnay 2005 A complex bouquet promises much, but
backs off somewhat on the palate; may be going through a phase of its development.
Screwcap. 13.5° alc. **Rating** 87 **To** 2011 $24

Brave Goose Vineyard

PO Box 633, Seymour, Vic 3660 **Region** Goulburn Valley
T (03) 9593 9421 **F** (03) 9493 9431 www.bravegoosevineyard.com.au **Open** By appt
Winemaker John Stocker, Don Lewis **Est.** 1988 **Cases** 400
Dr John Stocker and wife Joanne must be among the most highly qualified boutique vineyard
and winery operators in Australia. John Stocker is the former chief executive of CSIRO and
chairman of the Grape and Wine Research & Development Corporation for 7 years, and
daughter Nina has completed the Roseworthy postgraduate oenology course. Moreover, they
established their first vineyard (while living in Switzerland) on the French/Swiss border in the

village of Flueh, working in conjunction with friends. On returning to Australia in 1987 they found a property on the inside of the Great Dividing Range with north-facing slopes and shallow, weathered ironstone soils. Here they have established 2.5 ha each of shiraz and cabernet sauvignon, and 0.5 ha each of merlot and gamay, selling the majority of grapes from the 18-year-old vines, but making small quantities of Cabernet Merlot, Merlot and Gamay. The brave goose in question was the sole survivor of a flock put into the vineyard to repel cockatoos and foxes.

ŸŸŸŸŸ **Shiraz 2005** A beautifully balanced and structured wine; blackberry, plum, black cherry, licorice, spice and cedar are interwoven; fine tannins run through the back-palate and finish. Screwcap. 14.7° alc. **Rating** 95 **To** 2025 $20

ŸŸŸŸŸ **Cabernet Merlot 2005** Clean and firm, with crystal-clear blackcurrant and cassis fruit supporting fine, ripe, lingering tannins and good oak. Picked at the perfect point of ripeness. Screwcap. 14.7° alc. **Rating** 93 **To** 2020 $20

Braydon Estate ★★★★
40 Londons Road, Lovedale, NSW 2325 (postal) **Region** Lower Hunter Valley
T (02) 4990 9122 **F** (02) 4990 9133 **Open** Not
Winemaker Pothana (David Hook) **Est.** 1998 **Cases** 500
Peter and Lesley Giles built their idyllically situated home in 1998, completing the idyll (so they thought) by planting 1.25 ha of shiraz and semillon on the paddock in front of the home. The site was a good one, and the wines were well-made, earning consistently high points. However, properly tending to the vineyard became such a millstone around their necks that after the 2006 vintage they removed the vines and returned the block to its original form. Wines made over the 2004, '05 and '06 vintages will remain on sale for some time to come. They add 'This coming season will be full of both joy and sadness with our new situation. We don't regret any of this chapter of our lives – indeed we feel we have accomplished a great deal during our time here.'

Braydun Hill Vineyard ★★★★☆
38–40 Hepenstal Road, Hackham, SA 5163 **Region** McLaren Vale
T (08) 8382 3023 **F** (08) 8326 0033 **www**.braydunhill.com.au **Open** By appt
Winemaker Rebecca Kennedy **Est.** 2001 **Cases** 1500
It is hard to imagine there would be such an interesting (and inspiring) story behind a 4-ha vineyard planted between 1998 and 1999 by the husband and wife team of Tony Dunn and Carol Bradley, wishing to get out of growing angora goats and into grapegrowing. The extension of the business into winemaking was totally unplanned, forced on them by the liquidation of Normans in late 2001. With humour, courage and perseverance, they have met obstacles and setbacks which would have caused many to give up, and have produced wines since 2001 which leave no doubt this is a very distinguished site capable of producing wines of the highest order.

ŸŸŸŸŸ **Handpicked McLaren Vale Shiraz 2004** Extremely rich and concentrated; masses of black fruits, with dark chocolate, oak and tannins singing in the background. Cork. 14.5° alc. **Rating** 95 **To** 2024

ŸŸŸŸŸ **Single Vineyard McLaren Vale Shiraz 2005** A powerful array of black fruit supported by positive oak; the tannins need to settle down and soften, which they will do given time. Cork. 15° alc. **Rating** 92 **To** 2018 $24

Bream Creek ★★★★★
Marion Bay Road, Bream Creek, Tas 7175 **Region** Southern Tasmania
T (03) 6231 4646 **F** (03) 6231 4646 **Open** At Potters Croft, Dunally, tel (03) 6253 5469
Winemaker Winemaking Tasmania (Julian Alcorso) **Est.** 1975 **Cases** 3500
Until 1990 the Bream Creek fruit was sold to Moorilla Estate, but since then the winery has been independently owned and managed under the control of Fred Peacock, legendary for the care he bestows on the vines under his direction. Peacock's skills have seen both an increase in production and also a vast lift in wine quality across the range, headed by the Pinot Noir. The 1996 acquisition of a second vineyard in the Tamar Valley has significantly strengthened the business base of the venture.

Pinot Noir 2005 Medium to full purple-red; rich, complex, multi-layered plum and black cherry fruit on the round and smooth palate; lots of life and spark. Diam. 13.6° alc. **Rating** 94 **To** 2013 $34

Sauvignon Blanc 2006 A delicious wine; gentle tropical aromas and fruit flavours; good acidity and length round off a wine which has real finesse. Screwcap. 13.6° alc. **Rating** 94 **To** 2009 $22

Schonburger 2005 Heather, wild flower aromas; the palate, however, doesn't quite deliver the promise of the bouquet. Screwcap. 12.7° alc. **Rating** 87 **To** 2008 $19

Bremerton Wines   ★★★★★

Strathalbyn Road, Langhorne Creek, SA 5255 **Region** Langhorne Creek
T (08) 8537 3093 **F** (08) 8537 3109 **www.**bremerton.com.au **Open** 7 days 10–5
Winemaker Rebecca Willson **Est.** 1988 **Cases** 30 000
The Willsons have been grapegrowers in the Langhorne Creek region for some considerable time but their dual business as grapegrowers and winemakers has expanded significantly. Their vineyards have more than doubled to over 100 ha (predominantly cabernet sauvignon, shiraz and merlot), as has their production of wine under the Bremerton label. In 2004 sisters Rebecca and Lucy (marketing) took control of the business, marking the event with (guess what) revamped label designs. Exports to the UK, the US and other major markets.

Old Adam Shiraz 2004 Amazingly vivid purple-red; licorice, blackberry, plum, spice and pepper are all present in roughly equal portions on both bouquet and palate, and there are sufficient tannins to provide all the structure needed; oak is the hidden note. Cork. 15° alc. **Rating** 97 **To** 2024 $38

B.O.V. Shiraz Cabernet 2004 Complex aromas of spice, black fruits and licorice; the palate is so flooded with flavour it seems reluctant to leave the mouth; a dry red wine in semi-liqueur fashion (not vintage port); hugely impressive, but I prefer the Old Adam. Cork. 14° alc. **Rating** 96 **To** 2028 $75

Selkirk Shiraz 2005 Very good purple-red; fragrant fruit aromas; soft, supple, round and alluring black fruit flavours; cleverly used oak and perfectly judged tannins. Great value. Cork. 14.5° alc. **Rating** 94 **To** 2020 $22

Selkirk Shiraz 2004 In most ways very similar to the '05, except for a slightly firmer structure and tighter black fruits, lingering savoury tannins. Will take longer to come around. Cork. 14.5° alc. **Rating** 94 **To** 2019 $22

Langhorne Creek Verdelho 2006 Much more personality and life than the vast majority of verdelhos; a really bright lemon twist on top of the fruit salad adds both flavour and length. Screwcap. 13° alc. **Rating** 93 **To** 2009 $18

Reserve Cabernet Sauvignon 2003 Very ripe fruit; a mix of prune, blackcurrant and licorice; doesn't quite have the tannin structure to support all that fruit, but that is a carping criticism. Cork. 15° alc. **Rating** 92 **To** 2019 $40

Special Release Malbec 2005 Good purple-red; Langhorne Creek has had long experience and success with this difficult variety; blackberry jam, chocolate, spice and redeeming tannins. There is, it is true, an element of the dog preaching. Screwcap. 14.5° alc. **Rating** 92 **To** 2018 $24

Langhorne Creek Sauvignon Blanc 2006 A slightly closed, but not reduced bouquet; comes alive with citrussy, zesty, minerally, juicy fruit flavours; Langhorne Creek is cooler than many realise. Screwcap. 12° alc. **Rating** 90 **To** 2011 $18

Tamblyn Cabernet Sauvignon Shiraz Malbec Merlot 2004 Complex flavours reflecting the multi-varietal blend; satsuma plum and spice rather than black fruits; quite juicy overall, with soft tannins. A really strange decision to give this wine a screwcap, but deny the same benefit for the Selkirks. Screwcap. 14.5° alc. **Rating** 90 **To** 2014 $18

Tamblyn Cabernet Sauvignon Shiraz Malbec Merlot 2005 Lots of black and red fruits with a slightly tangy/earthy edge; hadn't come together not long after bottling. Screwcap. 14.5° alc. **Rating** 89 **To** 2015 $18

Wiggy Sparkling Chardonnay 2003 Fresh, tight lemony and crisp; not especially complex, but has length. 12° alc. **Rating** 87 **To** 2008 $25

Bress ★★★★★

3894 Calder Highway, Harcourt, Vic 3453 **Region** Bendigo
T (03) 5474 2262 www.bress.com.au **Open** W'ends & public hols 11–5, or by appt
Winemaker Adam Marks **Est.** 2001 **Cases** 5000
Adam Marks has made wine in all parts of the world since 1991, and made the brave decision (during his honeymoon in 2000) to start his own business. He has selected Margaret River semillon and sauvignon blanc as the best source of white Bordeaux-style wine in Australia; Yarra Valley as the best pinot noir region; and shiraz from Heathcote for precisely the same reason. In early 2005 the Marks family acquired the former Mt Alexander Vineyard and cellar door, expanding the business overnight. Exports to the Maldives and Indonesia.

ΨΨΨΨΨ **Unfiltered Heathcote Shiraz 2005** Not star-bright, but good hue; highly aromatic black cherry/plum/berry; excellent texture and structure with finely meshed tannins – all this achieved at 13.5 baume. Screwcap. 13.5° alc. **Rating** 96 **To** 2025 $39
Margaret River Semillon Sauvignon Blanc 2006 A fresh, lively, flowery bouquet; a lovely array of gentle citrus, passionfruit and gooseberry; perfect line, length and balance; outstanding value. Screwcap. 12.6° alc. **Rating** 94 **To** 2008 $19
Heathcote & Bendigo Shiraz 2005 Abundant flavour, texture and structure; blackberry fruits interwoven with fine, ripe tannins from start to finish; good oak. Bargain. Screwcap. 14° alc. **Rating** 94 **To** 2022 $19

ΨΨΨΨΨ **Harcourt Valley OD Riesling 2006** Orange and lemon zest; the sweetness is evident throughout but not over the top for the style; does need a touch more acidity, perhaps. Screwcap. 10° alc. **Rating** 90 **To** 2012 $19

ΨΨΨΨ **Yarra Valley Pinot Noir 2006** Very light colour; light spice and plum fruit; in reality an upscale rose. Screwcap. 12.5° alc. **Rating** 88 **To** 2008 $19
The Kindest Cane Cut Riesling Muller Thurgau Gewurztraminer 2006 Lots of lolly shop fruit flavours balanced by soft acidity; a designer match for tropical fruit salad or sorbet. Screwcap. 9° alc. **Rating** 88 **To** 2008 $21.95

Briagolong Estate ★★★☆

Valencia–Briagolong Road, Briagolong, Vic 3860 **Region** Gippsland
T (03) 5147 2322 **F** (03) 5147 2341 www.briagolongestate.com.au **Open** By appt
Winemaker Gordon McIntosh **Est.** 1979 **Cases** 400
This is very much a weekend hobby for medical practitioner Gordon McIntosh, who invests his chardonnay and pinot noir with Burgundian complexity. He has made several decisions since 2003. First, having had his best vintage in the 1990s (1998) destroyed by TCA cork taint, he has moved to screwcaps. Next, he has introduced the Foothills of Gippsland range at a lower price point (but still estate-grown). Third, he has increased the price of the Estate Chardonnay and Pinot Noir, limited to exceptional barrels, which will not be released every year.

Brian Barry Wines ★★★★

PO Box 128, Stepney, SA 5069 **Region** Clare Valley
T (08) 8363 6211 **F** (08) 8362 0498 www.brianbarrywines.com **Open** Not
Winemaker Brian Barry, Judson Barry **Est.** 1977 **Cases** 6000
Brian Barry is an industry veteran with a wealth of winemaking and show-judging experience. His is nonetheless in reality a vineyard-only operation, with a substantial part of the output sold as grapes to other wineries and the wines made under contract at various wineries, albeit under his supervision. As one would expect, the quality is reliably good. Exports to the UK and the US.

Briar Ridge

Mount View Road, Mount View, NSW 2325 **Region** Lower Hunter Valley
T (02) 4990 3670 **F** (02) 4990 7802 **www**.briarridge.com.au **Open** 7 days 10–5
Winemaker Karl Stockhausen, Mark Woods **Est.** 1972 **Cases** 18 000
Semillon and shiraz have been the most consistent performers, underlying the suitability of these
varieties to the Hunter Valley. The Semillon, in particular, invariably shows intense fruit and cellars
well. Briar Ridge has been a model of stability, and has the comfort of over 48 ha of estate
vineyards, from which it is able to select the best grapes. Exports to the US and Canada.

ⓎⓎⓎⓎ **Signature Shiraz 2005** Powerful blackberry fruit with slightly aggressive, earthy
tannins; needs time to settle down. Cork. 13.5° alc. **Rating** 87 **To** 2012 $29

Briarose Estate

Bussell Highway, Augusta, WA 6290 **Region** Margaret River
T (08) 9758 4160 **F** (08) 9758 4161 **www**.briarose.com.au **Open** 7 days 10–4.30
Winemaker Cath Oates **Est.** 1998 **Cases** 10 000
Brian and Rosemary Webster began the development of the estate plantings in 1998, which now
comprise sauvignon blanc (2.33 ha), semillon (1.33 ha), cabernet sauvignon (6.6 ha), merlot (2.2
ha) and cabernet franc (1.1 ha). The winery is situated at the southern end of the Margaret River
region, where the climate is distinctly cooler than that of northern Margaret River.

ⓎⓎⓎⓎⓎ **Augusta Margaret River Semillon Sauvignon Blanc 2006** Spotless bouquet;
highly aromatic herb, grass and asparagus aromas; has both weight and length,
finishing with lively, citrussy acidity. Trophy WA Wine Show '06. Screwcap. 13° alc.
Rating 94 **To** 2011 $26.90

ⓎⓎⓎⓎⓎ **Augusta Margaret River Sauvignon Blanc 2006** No reduction or sweaty
characters on the bouquet; elegant and delicate, but with a wide range of flavours
from passionfruit to grass/mineral. Screwcap. 13° alc. **Rating** 93 **To** 2008 $25

Brick Kiln

PO Box 56, Glen Osmond, SA 5064 **Region** McLaren Vale
T (08) 8379 9314 **F** (08) 8338 6652 **www**.brickiln.com.au **Open** Not
Winemaker Branson Coach House Winery **Est.** 2001 **Cases** 1500
This is the venture of Malcolm and Alison Mackinnon, Garry and Nancy Watson, and Ian and
Pene Davey. They purchased the 8-ha Nine Gums Vineyard, which had been planted to shiraz in
1995–96, in 2001. The majority of the grapes are sold with a lesser portion contract-made for the
partners under the Brick Kiln label, which takes its name from the Brick Kiln Bridge adjacent to
the vineyard. Exports to the UK, the US, Canada and Hong Kong.

ⓎⓎⓎⓎⓎ **McLaren Vale Shiraz 2005** A solid, ripe, chewy style with black fruits and
regional chocolate; slightly short, but should build with age. Screwcap. 15° alc.
Rating 91 **To** 2015 $22

🍇 Brimsmore Park Winery   **NR**

40 Merricks Road, Merricks, Vic 3926 **Region** Mornington Peninsula
T (03) 5989 8164 **F** (03) 5989 8046 **www**.brimsmore.com.au **Open** By appt
Winemaker Michael Darch **Est.** 1998 **Cases** NA
Michael and Sheila Darch began the establishment of Brimsmore Park in 1998. Situated on the
rolling hills of Merricks, it overlooks Western Port Bay and Phillip Island. The 8.5-ha property
has been planted with 2.8 ha of pinot noir: MV6 for half of the vineyard, and the Dijon clones
114 and 115 (a quarter each). The benefits of concentrating on one variety are obvious, especially
so when that variety is pinot noir and the region is Mornington Peninsula.

Brindabella Hills

Woodgrove Close, via Hall, ACT 2618 **Region** Canberra District
T (02) 6230 2583 **www.brindabellahills.com.au Open** W'ends & public hols 10–5
Winemaker Dr Roger Harris, Brian Sinclair **Est.** 1986 **Cases** 2000
Distinguished research scientist Dr Roger Harris presides over Brindabella Hills, which increasingly relies on estate-produced grapes, with small plantings of cabernet sauvignon, cabernet franc, merlot, shiraz, chardonnay, sauvignon blanc, semillon and riesling, and a new planting of sangiovese and brunello. Wine quality has been consistently impressive.

Canberra District Riesling 2006 A clean bouquet; intense lime juice and some tropical passionfruit notes; long and lingering finish. Screwcap. 11.5° alc. **Rating** 94 To 2015 $20

Canberra Sauvignon Blanc 2006 Crisp, clean, mineral, herb and grass supported by touches of citrus and gooseberry; a subtle wine which creeps up on re-tasting. Screwcap. 12.3° alc. **Rating** 92 To 2008 $15
Canberra District Shiraz 2005 Lively, cool-grown aromas and flavours; black fruits, licorice, spice and cracked pepper; medium-bodied tannins and good oak. Screwcap. 13.7° alc. **Rating** 92 To 2020 $25
Canberra District Chardonnay Viognier 2006 The addition of 12% viognier and fermentation/maturation in 1-year-old French oak, with 6 months lees contact, are techniques which have worked well; delicate, peachy chardonnay has been enriched by the viognier without losing its character. Screwcap. 13° alc. **Rating** 91 To 2012 $25

Canberra District Cabernet Merlot 2005 Cabernet adds some of the weight the merlot is missing, yet only to a degree; clear redcurrant and blackcurrant fruits but still a lack of flesh. Screwcap. 13.3° alc. **Rating** 89 To 2010 $20
Canberra District Sangiovese Shiraz 2005 I'm not entirely sure what the shiraz is supposed to do, but it's true that the light-bodied wine has pleasant savoury red fruits, and very fine tannins, which will displease no-one. Screwcap. 13.3° alc. **Rating** 88 To 2009 $18

Brini Estate Wines

RSD 600 Blewitt Springs Road, McLaren Vale, SA 5171 (postal) **Region** McLaren Vale
T (08) 8383 0080 **F** (08) 8383 0104 **Open** Not
Winemaker Brian Light (Contract) **Est.** 2000 **Cases** 3000
The Brini family has been growing grapes in the Blewitt Springs area of McLaren Vale since 1953. In 2000 John and Marcello Brini established Brini Estate Wines to vinify a portion of the grape production; up to that time it had been sold to companies such as Penfolds, Rosemount Estate and d'Arenberg. The flagship Sebastian Shiraz is produced from dry-grown vines planted in 1947, the Shiraz Grenache from dry-grown vines planted in 1964. Skilled winemaking, coupled with impeccable fruit sources, has resulted in a new star in the McLaren Vale firmament.

Brocks View Estate

PO Box 396, Yankalilla, SA 5203 **Region** Southern Fleurieu
T (08) 8558 2233 **Open** Not
Winemaker Phillip Christiansen (Contract) **Est.** 1998 **Cases** NA
Peter and Julie Brocksopp have planted a single ha of shiraz at Carrickalinga, with coastal views out over Yankalilla Bay, giving rise to the slogan 'from vines with a view'. The close density planting on gravel loam over red clay soils is managed organically, with minimal irrigation, the vines hand-pruned and hand-picked.

Southern Fleurieu Shiraz 2004 Holding depth and hue; a similar array of flavours to the '05, the fruit perhaps a little more incisive and beautifully ripened; background touches of spice. Cork. 14.5° alc. **Rating** 94 To 2015 $18

Southern Fleurieu Shiraz 2001 Holding hue very well; fragrant black cherry and spice aromas lead into a medium-bodied, smooth and supple palate, still retaining virtually all the joyful primary fruit flavours; fine tannins to close. Cork. 13° alc. **Rating** 94 **To** 2011 $18

Southern Fleurieu Shiraz 2005 Medium- to medium-full-bodied wine; an attractive array of black fruits and dark chocolate, ripe tannins and oak seamlessly integrated; excellent balance. Cork. 14.5° alc. **Rating** 93 **To** 2013 $18

Broke Estate/Ryan Family Wines

Wollombi Road, Broke, NSW 2330 **Region** Lower Hunter Valley
T (02) 6579 1065 **www.**ryanwines.com.au **Open** W'ends & public hols 11–5
Winemaker Matthew Ryan **Est.** 1988 **Cases** 2000
This is the flagship operation of the Ryan family, with 25 ha of largely mature vineyards, the lion's share to chardonnay, but also including meaningful plantings of semillon, sauvignon blanc, shiraz, merlot, barbera, tempranillo, cabernet sauvignon and cabernet franc.

Broke's Promise Wines ★★★★

725 Milbrodale Road, Broke, NSW 2330 **Region** Lower Hunter Valley
T (02) 6579 1165 **www.**brokespromise.com.au **Open** Mon–Fri by appt, w'ends 10–4
Winemaker Margan Family **Est.** 1996 **Cases** 7000
Joe and Carol Re purchased Broke's Promise in 2005 from Jane Marquard and Dennis Karp, and have continued the winemaking arrangements with Andrew Margan. A new cellar door opened Easter 2006. The 3.3-ha vineyard is complemented by 1800 olive trees.

Hunter Valley Shiraz 2005 A complex array of blackberry, plum, spice, licorice and earth flavours; balanced tannins and oak; good development potential and good value. Screwcap. 13.7° alc. **Rating** 93 **To** 2025 $20

Hunter Valley Semillon 2006 Does immediately show the high alcohol, which invests flavour but blunts the rapier-like thrust of quality semillon. No point in cellaring. Screwcap. 12° alc. **Rating** 89 **To** 2008 $18

Hunter Valley Barbera 2005 More structure and flavour than normal; black cherry and plum, with tannins in ideal balance. Screwcap. 14° alc. **Rating** 88 **To** 2013 $18

Hunter Valley Rose 2006 Bright pale pink; has a definite faintly spicy/earthy varietal presence from its barbera base, which adds interest; not reliant only on residual sugar. Screwcap. 14° alc. **Rating** 87 **To** 2008 $15

Broken Gate Wines

57 Rokeby Street, Collingwood, Vic 3066 (postal) **Region** Southeast Australia
T (03) 9417 5757 **F** (03) 9417 5757 **www.**brokengate.com.au **Open** Not
Winemaker Contract **Est.** 2001 **Cases** 5000
Broken Gate is a partnership between Brendan Chapman and Josef Orbach. Chapman has an extensive liquor retailing background, and is presently bulk wine buyer for Swords Wines, responsible for the purchase of 160 000 litres of wine across Australia. Josef Orbach lived and worked in the Clare Valley from 1994 to 1998 at Leasingham Wines, while also leading the restoration of the Clarevale Winery Co-op building.

Leongatha Petite Chardonnay 2004 Has matured beautifully; scented nectarine fruit seamlessly interwoven with French oak; good length, line and finish; ridiculously low price. Screwcap. 13.6° alc. **Rating** 94 **To** 2010 $17

Heathcote Shiraz 2005 Strong colour, though not deep or saturated; medium-bodied; an abundance of black cherry, blackberry and plum intermingle; good balance and finish. Screwcap. 14.5° alc. **Rating** 92 **To** 2020 $17

ŸŸŸŸ **Sunbury Pinot Grigio 2006** Plenty of depth, texture and mouthfeel; some pear and apple, but the main strength of the wine is in the structure, not its fruit flavour. Screwcap. 14.1° alc. **Rating** 89 **To** 2008 $15
Geelong Pinot Noir 2004 Light- to medium-bodied; plum, cherry and spice aromas; medium-bodied, with good length and varietal expression. Screwcap. 13.9° alc. **Rating** 89 **To** 2011 $20
Adelaide Hills Semillon Sauvignon Blanc 2006 Clean, crisp and lively aromas and flavours running through grass, mineral and asparagus characters; good length and finish. Screwcap. 13.5° alc. **Rating** 87 **To** 2008 $15

Brokenwood

401–427 McDonalds Road, Pokolbin, NSW 2321 **Region** Lower Hunter Valley
T (02) 4998 7559 **www.**brokenwood.com.au **Open** Sun–Fri 10–5, Sat 9.30–5
Winemaker Iain Riggs, PJ Charteris **Est.** 1970 **Cases** 100 000
Deservedly fashionable winery producing consistently excellent wines. Has kept Graveyard Shiraz as its ultimate flagship wine, while extending its reach through many of the best eastern regions for its broad selection of varietal wine styles. Its big-selling Hunter Semillon remains alongside Graveyard, and there is then a range of wines coming from regions including Orange, Central Ranges, Beechworth, McLaren Vale, Cowra and elsewhere. A newly built 2-storey tasting facility named the Albert Room (in honour of the late Tony Albert, one of the founders) was opened in 2006. Exports to all major markets.

ŸŸŸŸŸ **ILR Reserve Semillon 2001** Bright, light green-straw; a complex bouquet, still unfurling into the characteristic toast and honey which will grow as the wine ages. Cork. 11° alc. **Rating** 96 **To** 2011 $45
Graveyard Hunter Valley Shiraz 2004 Of brilliant clarity, this medium-bodied wine has perfect texture and structure to its array of black and red cherry fruits, finishing with fine ripe tannins. Carefully judged oak completes a wine of real finesse – and low alcohol. Screwcap. 12.5° alc. **Rating** 96 **To** 2029 $100
Hunter Valley Semillon 2006 Spotlessly clean; a classic young semillon, finely tuned and honed notes of lemon rind, herb, spice and mineral; great acidity and mouthfeel. Screwcap. 11° alc. **Rating** 94 **To** 2017 $17
Indigo Vineyard Beechworth Chardonnay 2005 A complex but not feral bouquet; has considerable structure, with fig, melon and ripe stone fruit; the oak well-balanced and integrated. Screwcap. 14° alc. **Rating** 94 **To** 2012 $30
Hunter Valley Shiraz 2004 Fragrant red fruit aromas; a light- to medium-bodied, vibrant and fresh palate; red fruits with slight mint, leaf and earth notes. Screwcap. 13° alc. **Rating** 94 **To** 2019 $35
Rayner Vineyard McLaren Vale Shiraz 2004 A medium- to full-bodied mainstream varietal style with blackberry, dark chocolate and some savoury/earthy notes; oak in appropriately solid support; good tannins and mouthfeel. Top vintage, top wine. Screwcap. 14.5° alc. **Rating** 94 **To** 2019 $69

ŸŸŸŸŸ **Mt Panorama Vineyard Central Ranges Chardonnay 2005** An elegant, medium-bodied wine with melon and cashew flavours; finely balanced acidity, good length. Screwcap. 14° alc. **Rating** 93 **To** 2011 $30
Forest Edge Vineyard Orange Sauvignon Blanc 2005 Again, spotlessly clean; a firm, clean, minerally framework, with grass, herb, gooseberry and grapefruit all intermingling sotto voce; lemony acidity to close. Screwcap. 12.5° alc. **Rating** 92 **To** 2008 $28
Beechworth Pinot Gris 2006 Has considerable presence, length and grip, with spiced pear flavours; just as long as I don't have to drink it. Screwcap. 14.5° alc. **Rating** 90 **To** 2008 $25
McLaren Vale Padthaway Beechworth Shiraz 2002 Development in colour is entirely appropriate; shows the cool vintage, with attractive savoury/earthy elements; fine tannins and good length. Screwcap. 14° alc. **Rating** 90 **To** 2015 $25

ǏǏǏǏ   **Indigo Vineyard Beechworth Viognier 2005** Powerful, mouthfilling, no compromise style; apricot, peach and pear; bludgeons you into submission in best viognier fashion. Screwcap. 15° alc. **Rating** 89 **To** 2008 $28
Beechworth Pinot Noir 2005 Big, bold style, part dry red, part pinot; has savoury notes, and may evolve in bottle. Screwcap. 14° alc. **Rating** 89 **To** 2011 $24
McLaren Vale Sangiovese 2005 Medium-bodied; red cherry and spice fruit; fine, almost powdery tannins. Rayner Vineyard. Screwcap. 14.5° alc. **Rating** 89 **To** 2010 $24
Beechworth Nebbiolo 2005 Typical light colour; tight, crisp and lean; you need to be a vinous masochist to really like wines such as this, however true to variety they may be. Screwcap. 13.5° alc. **Rating** 88 **To** 2010 $25

Brook Eden Vineyard

Adams Road, Lebrina, Tas 7254 **Region** Northern Tasmania
T (03) 6395 6244 **F** (03) 6395 6211 **www.**brookeden.com.au **Open** 7 days 10–5 (Aug–June)
Winemaker Tamar Ridge **Est.** 1988 **Cases** 900
Peter McIntosh and Sue Stuart purchased Brook Eden from Sheila Bezemer in 2004. At 41° south and at an altitude of 160 m it is one of the coolest sites in Tas, and (in the words of the new owners) 'represents viticulture on the edge'. While the plantings remain the same (1 ha pinot noir, 0.75 ha chardonnay and 0.25 ha riesling), yield has been significantly reduced, resulting in earlier picking and better quality grapes. Exports to Malaysia and Singapore.

ǏǏǏǏǏ   **Pinot Noir 2005** Strong colour; stacked with dark plum and black cherry flavour; excellent structure and length, the oak playing a pure support role. Top gold and trophy Tas Wine Show '07. Screwcap. 13.5° alc. **Rating** 96 **To** 2012 $32

ǏǏǏǏǏ   **Riesling 2006** Citrus blossom and crushed citrus leaf aromas; good length and balance. Screwcap. 12.3° alc. **Rating** 92 **To** 2014 $22
Chardonnay 2005 Light green-straw; abundant nectarine and citrus fruit; a long palate and balanced acidity. Screwcap. 12.7° alc. **Rating** 92 **To** 2011 $25

ǏǏǏǏ   **Pinot Rose 2006** Delicate, fresh strawberry flavours; good length and a dry finish; fraction simple. Screwcap. 12.8° alc. **Rating** 87 **To** 2008 $22

Brookland Valley

Caves Road, Wilyabrup, WA 6280 **Region** Margaret River
T (08) 9755 6042 **F** (08) 9755 6214 **www.**brooklandvalley.com.au **Open** 7 days 10–5
Winemaker Ross Pomment **Est.** 1984 **Cases** 2800
Brookland Valley has an idyllic setting, plus its much enlarged Flutes Café (one of the best winery restaurants in the Margaret River region) and its Gallery of Wine Arts, which houses an eclectic collection of wine and food-related art and wine accessories. After acquiring a 50% share of Brookland Valley in 1997, Hardys moved to full ownership in 2004. Exports to the UK, Germany, Switzerland, Japan and Hong Kong.

ǏǏǏǏǏ   **Reserve Chardonnay 2004** Super-fine and elegant, slightly to one side of the usual Margaret River style; nectarine, white peach and grapefruit are seamlessly interwoven with oak; still very fresh. Screwcap. 13.2° alc. **Rating** 95 **To** 2013 $35
Verse 1 Semillon Sauvignon Blanc 2006 A zesty, fresh, crisp mix of tropical fruit and more herbaceous notes; good line and length and a bright, crisp finish. Screwcap. 12.5° alc. **Rating** 94 **To** 2008 $15.90
Verse 1 Margaret River Rose 2006 Vivid red-purple; a lively, fresh basket of red fruits lifted by perfectly judged acidity. Amazing track record of gold medals at Adelaide, Brisbane and Melbourne Wine Shows '06. Screwcap. 13° alc. **Rating** 94 **To** 2008 $17
Verse 1 Margaret River Shiraz 2005 A rich and structured wine without any semblance of over-extraction. Oak, tannins and black fruits are all seamlessly woven together. Gold medal National Wine Show '06. Screwcap. 13.5° alc. **Rating** 94 **To** 2009 $17

ŢŢŢŢŢ Cabernet Sauvignon Merlot 2004 A slightly more supple wine than the Verse 1 '05, with just a touch more polish, and also reflecting the extra year in bottle. Cork. 14° alc. **Rating** 93 **To** 2018 $15.90
Verse 1 Margaret River Cabernet Merlot 2005 A powerful cabernet merlot which has the balls missing from Pan (playing the flute on the label). Solid, positive blackcurrant, with a passing nod to the merlot component in the red fruit spectrum; serious wine which ages well. Screwcap. 13.5° alc. **Rating** 92 **To** 2020 $15.90

ŢŢŢŢ Margaret River Sauvignon Blanc 2006 Normally a beautiful wine, but this vintage has a touch of reduction, and the palate can't break free of it. Screwcap. 12° alc. **Rating** 87 **To** 2008 $20.50

Brookwood Estate

Treeton Road, Cowaramup, WA 6284 **Region** Margaret River
T (08) 9755 5604 **F** (08) 9755 5870 **www**.brookwood.com.au **Open** 7 days 10–5
Winemaker Lyn Mann **Est.** 1996 **Cases** 2200
Trevor and Lyn Mann began the development of their 50-ha property in 1996, and now have 1.3 ha each of semillon, sauvignon blanc and chenin blanc, 1.2 ha shiraz and 1 ha of cabernet sauvignon. An onsite winery was constructed in 1999 to accommodate the first vintage.

ŢŢŢŢŢ Margaret River Cabernet Sauvignon 2005 Firm, clear-cut cabernet varietal fruit from start to finish; blackcurrant with just a touch of cassis; neatly controlled tannins and oak. ProCork. 14° alc. **Rating** 94 **To** 2025 $35

ŢŢŢŢŢ Margaret River Sauvignon Blanc 2006 Herbaceous, grassy aromas change gear on the palate into an altogether more tropical expression with passionfruit and kiwifruit; good balance and length. Screwcap. 13° alc. **Rating** 91 **To** 2008 $19.95
Margaret River Shiraz 2005 Fresh black cherry and plum fruit with just a dash of blackberry in medium-bodied mode; a nice dusting of spice, plus balanced oak and tannins. ProCork. 14° alc. **Rating** 91 **To** 2012 $28
Margaret River Semillon Sauvignon Blanc 2006 Herb, grass and mineral aromas and flavours, led by semillon, and filled out by touches of tropical fruit from the sauvignon blanc. Screwcap. 12° alc. **Rating** 90 **To** 2009 $19.95

ŢŢŢŢ Margaret River Rose 2006 Quite aromatic small red fruits, the palate in similar vein; has length, and finishes dry. Screwcap. 12.5° alc. **Rating** 88 **To** 2008 $20

Broomstick Estate

4 Frances Street, Mt Lawley, WA 6050 (postal) **Region** Margaret River
T (08) 9271 9594 **F** (08) 9271 9741 **www**.broomstick.com.au **Open** Not
Winemaker Rockfield Estate (Andrew Gaman) **Est.** 1997 **Cases** 750
Robert Holloway and family purchased the property on which the vineyard is now established in 1993 as an operating dairy farm. In 1997, 5.5 ha of shiraz was planted. Over the following years 3.8 ha of merlot and then (in 2004) 5.3 ha of chardonnay and 2 ha of sauvignon blanc were added. The Holloways see themselves as grapegrowers first and foremost, but make a small amount of wine under the Broomstick Estate label.

ŢŢŢŢŢ Witchcliffe Margaret River Merlot 2005 Fragrant red fruit aromas; a delicious merlot, with fine cassis and raspberry fruit on the light- to medium-bodied palate; fine tannins in perfect balance. Value-plus for a cantankerous variety. Screwcap. 13.5° alc. **Rating** 93 **To** 2012 $17

ŢŢŢŢ Witchcliffe Margaret River Shiraz 2004 Relatively light colour; light- to medium-bodied, with spicy/leafy/savoury components along with some black fruits. Screwcap. 13.5° alc. **Rating** 87 **To** 2011 $16

Brothers in Arms

PO Box 840, Langhorne Creek, SA 5255 **Region** Langhorne Creek
T (08) 83537 3182 **F** (08) 8537 3383 **www.brothersinarms.com.au Open** Not
Winemaker Justin Lane **Est.** 1998 **Cases** 33 000
The Adams family has been growing grapes at Langhorne Creek since 1891, when the first vines at the famed Metala vineyards were planted. Guy Adams is the fifth generation to own and work the vineyard, and over the past 20 years has both improved the viticulture and expanded the plantings to the present 40 ha (shiraz and cabernet sauvignon). It was not until 1998 that they decided to hold back a small proportion of the production for vinification under the Brothers in Arms label. Exports to the UK, US, Canada and Singapore.

ﾔﾔﾔﾔﾔ **No. 6 Langhorne Creek Shiraz Cabernet 2004** A big, powerful, robust wine; masses of black and red fruits and bitter chocolate, with firm, almost gritty tannins; considerable length and persistence. Screwcap. 14.8° alc. **Rating** 90 **To** 2024 $20

ﾔﾔﾔﾔ **Formby's Run Langhorne Creek Cabernet Sauvignon 2005** Slightly diffuse red-purple; light- to medium-bodied; blackcurrant with notes of earth, olive and leaf, and not the usual suppleness of Langhorne Creek. Screwcap. 14.8° alc. **Rating** 87 **To** 2012 $16.50

Brown Brothers

Milawa-Bobinawarrah Road, Milawa, Vic 3678 **Region** King Valley
T (03) 5720 5500 **F** (03) 5720 5511 **www.brownbrothers.com.au Open** 7 days 9–5
Winemaker Wendy Cameron, Marc Scalzo, Hamish Seabrook, Joel Tilbrook, Catherine Looney **Est.** 1885 **Cases** 1.1 million
Draws upon a considerable number of vineyards spread throughout a range of site climates, ranging from very warm to very cool. It is known for the diversity of varieties with which it works, and the wines represent good value for money. Deservedly one of the most successful family wineries in Australia. A glitch led to very few tastings this year. Exports to all major markets.

ﾔﾔﾔﾔ **Cellar Door Release Heathcote Petit Verdot 2003** A more restrained version than most; medium- to full-bodied with a mix of dark fruits, spices and herbs. Cork. 14.5° alc. **Rating** 89 **To** 2015 $19.90
Victoria Tempranillo 2004 Medium red; light-bodied, with aromas of cherry, spice and earth; entirely fruit-driven. Still young vines, of course. Twin top. 14° alc. **Rating** 87 **To** 2006 $16

Brown Hill Estate

Cnr Rosa Brook Road/Barrett Road, Rosa Brook, WA 6285 **Region** Margaret River
T (08) 9757 4003 **F** (08) 9757 4004 **www.brownhillestate.com.au Open** 7 days 10–5
Winemaker Nathan Bailey **Est.** 1995 **Cases** 3000
The Bailey family's stated aim is to produce top-quality wines at affordable prices, via uncompromising viticultural practices emphasising low yields per ha, in conjunction with the family being involved in all stages of production with minimum outside help. They have 7 ha each of shiraz and cabernet sauvignon, 4 ha of semillon and 2 ha each of sauvignon blanc and merlot, and by the standards of the Margaret River, the prices are indeed affordable.

ﾔﾔﾔﾔﾔ **Bill Bailey Margaret River Shiraz Cabernet 2005** Plenty of depth to the flavours of blackberry, blackcurrant and a twist of dark chocolate; smooth and supple tannins, good oak; considerable length. Screwcap. 14.8° alc. **Rating** 94 **To** 2025 $40

ﾔﾔﾔﾔﾔ **Fimiston Reserve Margaret River Shiraz 2005** More extract and depth than Chaffers; distinct spice, earth and dark chocolate characters; perhaps pushed a little too hard in the winery. Screwcap. 14.8° alc. **Rating** 92 **To** 2020 $25
Chaffers Margaret River Shiraz 2005 Blackberry, black cherry, dark spice and savoury/earthy notes all intermingle; plenty of fine tannins. Screwcap. 14.5° alc. **Rating** 91 **To** 2015 $18

Ivanhoe Reserve Margaret River Cabernet Sauvignon 2005 Very powerful, assertive blackcurrant fruit; slightly abrasive tannins might have been polished a little more. Top wine potential. Screwcap. 14.8° alc. **Rating** 91 **To** 2020 $25

Charlotte Margaret River Sauvignon Blanc 2006 Crisp and clean, with overall delicacy to gooseberry and passionfruit flavours; pleasing minerally acidity. Screwcap. 13.5° alc. **Rating** 90 **To** 2008 $15

♟♟♟♟ **Lakeview Margaret River Sauvignon Blanc Semillon 2006** A faint trace of reduction, but pleasant apple/pear/citrus/passionfruit flavours. Screwcap. 13.5° alc. **Rating** 89 **To** 2008 $15

Block 45 Paddy's White 2006 Quite lively, tropical sauvignon blanc characters on both bouquet and palate; good balance, a hint of sweetness within style parameters. Screwcap. 13.5° alc. **Rating** 88 **To** 2008 $15

Hannans Margaret River Cabernet Sauvignon 2005 Ripe, full-flavoured, but with a slightly chewy/rustic texture and mouthfeel; more fining needed. References to stewed plums and porty characters on the back label are decidedly curious. Screwcap. 14.5° alc. **Rating** 88 **To** 2015 $18

Croesus Reserve Margaret River Merlot 2005 Fragrant red fruits on the bouquet give no warning of the overly aggressive tannins. Screwcap. 14.8° alc. **Rating** 87 **To** 2012 $25

Block 45 Paddy's Red 2004 No shortage of fruit flavour, but seemingly a few shortcuts in the winery, hardly surprising at the price. Good barbecue red. Screwcap. 14.5° alc. **Rating** 87 **To** 2008 $15

Brown Magpie Wines ★★★★☆

125 Larcombes Road, Modewarre, Vic 3240 **Region** Geelong
T (03) 5261 3875 **F** (03) 5261 3875 **www.**brownmagpiewines.com **Open** 7 days 12–3
Winemaker Shane Breheny, Karen Coulston (Consultant) **Est.** 2000 **Cases** 5000
Shane and Loretta Breheny own a 20-ha property predominantly situated on a gentle, north-facing slope, with cypress trees on the western and southern borders providing protection against the wind. Over 2001 and 2002, 9 ha of vines were planted, with pinot noir (5 ha) taking the lion's share, followed by pinot gris (2 ha), shiraz (1.5 ha) and 0.25 ha each of chardonnay and sauvignon blanc. Viticulture is Loretta Breheny's love; winemaking (and wine) is Shane's.

♟♟♟♟♟ **Pinot Noir 2004** Complex with a fine, elegant and supple mix of savoury and red berry fruits, finishing with fine tannins. Gold and trophy winner Geelong Wine Show '06. Screwcap. 13° alc. **Rating** 94 **To** 2011 $22

♟♟♟♟♟ **Geelong Shiraz 2005** Deep colour; abundant blackberry and licorice flavour supported by equally abundant oak and tannins. Cellaring special. Screwcap. 14° alc. **Rating** 93 **To** 2015 $27

Pinot Noir 2005 Powerful, layered dark fruits with abundant flavour. Screwcap. 14° alc. **Rating** 90 **To** 2012 $22

♟♟♟♟ **Three Brown Magpies Chardonnay Blends 2006** A rich, full-bodied chardonnay reflecting its alcohol; ripe peach, and some warmth on the finish; earlier picking might have paid dividends. Screwcap. 14.5° alc. **Rating** 89 **To** 2010 $22

Geelong Pinot Gris 2006 Pear, musk and talc aromas and flavours; an extra touch of alcohol has worked well. Screwcap. 14° alc. **Rating** 87 **To** 2008 $18

Brown's Farm Winery ★★★

3675 Great North Road, Laguna, NSW 2325 (postal) **Region** Lower Hunter Valley
T (02) 4998 8273 **F** (02) 4998 8273 **www.**wollombivalley.com **Open** Not
Winemaker Frank Geisler, Jarmila Geisler **Est.** 1998 **Cases** 250
Frank and Jarmila Geisler established their 1-ha vineyard with the simple belief that 'the best wine is made in the smallest vineyard'. It is principally planted to cabernet sauvignon and merlot, with a small quantity of chardonnay and pinot gris. It is managed on quasi-organic principles, and both the viticulture and winemaking are carried out by the Geislers 'without too much outside help'. Exports to Taiwan.

Browns of Padthaway

Keith Road, Padthaway, SA 5271 **Region** Padthaway
T (08) 8765 6063 **F** (08) 8765 6083 www.browns-of-padthaway.com **Open** At Padthaway
Estate
Winemaker Contract **Est.** 1993 **Cases** 35 000
The Brown family has for many years been the largest independent grapegrower in Padthaway,
a district in which most of the vineyards were established and owned by Wynns, Seppelt,
Lindemans and Hardys, respectively. Since 1998, after a slow start, Browns has produced
excellent wines and wine production has increased accordingly.

Myra Family Reserve Cabernet Sauvignon 2002 A complex and very
concentrated/savoury wine, but does not go over the top. Cork. 14.3° alc.
Rating 93 **To** 2022 $22

Sauvignon Blanc 2006 Soft, tropical, easy-drinking style; not broad, but needs
more focus. Screwcap. 12.7° alc. **Rating** 87 **To** 2007 $16
Verdelho 2006 Lemony/citrussy overtones points either to early picking or a
touch of sauvignon blanc; either way, the result works well. Screwcap. 12.9° alc.
Rating 87 **To** 2007 $16

Brumby Wines

Sandyanna, 24 Cannon Lane, Wood Wood, Vic 3596 **Region** Swan Hill
T 0438 305 364 **F** (03) 5030 5366 www.brumbywines.com.au **Open** Mon–Fri 9–5
Winemaker Neil Robb, John Ellis, Glen Olsen (Contract) **Est.** 2001 **Cases** 2000
The derivation of the name is even more direct and simple than you might imagine: the owners
are Stuart and Liz Brumby, who decided to plant grapes for supply to others before moving to
having an increasing portion of their production from the 13.5 ha of chardonnay, cabernet
sauvignon, shiraz and durif vinified under their own label.

Bruny Island Wines

4391 Main Road, Lunawanna, Bruny Island, Tas 7150 (postal) **Region** Southern Tasmania
T (03) 6293 1088 **F** (03) 6293 1088 **Open** W'ends & hols, or by appt (closed June–Aug)
Winemaker Bernice Woolley **Est.** 1998 **Cases** 250
Richard and Bernice Woolley have established the only vineyard on Bruny Island, the
southernmost commercial planting in Australia. They have a total of 2 ha of chardonnay and pinot
noir, not all in production. Bernice has a degree in marketing from Curtin University, and she and
Richard have operated budget-style holiday accommodation on the property since 1999.

Pinot Noir 2005 An aromatic and complex mix of spice, stem, plum and forest
aromas; more of the same on the palate, which is not so much intense as it is long
and lingering. Screwcap. 13° alc. **Rating** 92 **To** 2012 $25
Chardonnay 2005 Similarly delicate to the Unwooded, yet is quite intense;
nectarine and citrus fruit, with very subtle French oak adding a dimension to the
texture on the finish. Screwcap. 12.7° alc. **Rating** 91 **To** 2010 $25

Unwooded Chardonnay 2005 Delicate, crisp and lively; the flavours are a
cross between sauvignon blanc and chardonnay; good finish and length. Screwcap.
12.9° alc. **Rating** 87 **To** 2009 $20

Brushwood Wines

Suite 3, 49 Ord Street, West Perth, WA 6005 (postal) **Region** Margaret River
T (08) 9426 6300 **F** (08) 9322 6954 www.brushwoodwines.com.au **Open** Not
Winemaker Peter Stanlake (Contract) **Est.** 2000 **Cases** 2100
This is very much a part-time occupation for owners David van der Walt and Stephen Vaughan.
They have planted 6 ha of cabernet sauvignon, 2 ha of chardonnay and 1 ha of shiraz, limiting
the make of each variety to 700 cases a year and selling the surplus grapes.

Bullers Beverford

Murray Valley Highway, Beverford, Vic 3590 **Region** Swan Hill
T (03) 5037 6305 **F** (03) 5037 6803 **www.**buller.com.au **Open** Mon–Sat 9–5
Winemaker Richard Buller (Jnr) **Est.** 1951 **Cases** 120 000
This is a parallel operation to the Calliope winery at Rutherglen, similarly owned and operated
by third-generation Richard and Andrew Buller. It offers traditional wines which in the final
analysis reflect both their Riverland origin and a fairly low-key approach to style in the winery.

ΨΨΨΨ   **Durif 2003** Retaining strong colour; powerful black fruits, prune, black cherry and
dark chocolate; carries its alcohol; great value. Cork. 15° alc. **Rating** 89 **To** 2010 $13
Cabernet Sauvignon 2003 Good red-purple; surprising depth and structure; ripe
black fruits and positive tannins. Cork. 14.5° alc. **Rating** 88 **To** 2008 $13
Shiraz 2003 Maturing well; an attractive mix of medium-bodied plum and
blackberry fruit supported by ripe tannins. Twin top. 14.5° alc. **Rating** 87
To 2008 $13

Bullers Calliope

Three Chain Road, Rutherglen, Vic 3685 **Region** Rutherglen
T (02) 6032 9660 **F** (02) 6032 8005 **www.**buller.com.au **Open** Mon–Sat 9–5, Sun 10–5
Winemaker Andrew Buller **Est.** 1921 **Cases** 4000
The Buller family is very well known and highly regarded in Northeast Victoria, and the business
benefits from vines that are now 80 years old. The rating is for the superb releases of Museum
fortified wines. Limited releases of Calliope Shiraz and Shiraz Mondeuse can also be very good.
Exports to the UK and the US.

Bullerview Wines

PO Box 457, Reservoir, Vic 3073 **Region** Upper Goulburn
T (03) 9355 7070 **F** (03) 9355 7353 **www.**bullerviewwines.com.au **Open** Not
Winemaker George Apted (Contract) **Est.** 1996 **Cases** 1750
Pasquale 'Charlie' Orrico migrated from his native Calabria in 1956, establishing a successful
commercial building enterprise in Melbourne. Childhood memories of winemaking on his
grandfather's vineyard remained with Charlie, and in 1982 he and his wife, Maria, purchased land
near Mansfield with the intention of establishing a vineyard. This eventuated in 1996, with the
planting of 2 ha of merlot and 0.8 ha of cabernet sauvignon. From 2002 the estate-grown fruit
has been processed onsite. It has to be said that Charlie Orrico has gone where angels fear to tread
by choosing to plant merlot and cabernet sauvignon, rather than earlier ripening varieties.

Bulong Estate

70 Summerhill Road, Yarra Junction, Vic 3797 **Region** Yarra Valley
T (03) 5967 1358 **F** (03) 5967 1350 **www.**bulongestate.com **Open** 7 days 11–5
Winemaker Matt Carter, MasterWineMakers **Est.** 1994 **Cases** 2000
Judy and Howard Carter purchased their beautifully situated 45-ha property in 1994, looking
down into the valley below and across to the nearby ranges with Mt Donna Buang at their peak.
Most of the grapes from the immaculately tended vineyard are sold, with limited quantities made
for the Bulong Estate label. Exports to the UK.

ΨΨΨΨΨ   **Yarra Valley Cabernet Sauvignon 2004** Good colour and depth for the
vintage; a light- to medium-bodied pure evocation of cabernet sauvignon; cassis,
blackcurrant and fine tannins. Cork. **Rating** 90 **To** 2014 $21

ΨΨΨΨ   **Yarra Valley Pinot Noir 2004** A clean, light-bodied mix of plum and cherry;
supple mouthfeel and balance. Cork. 13.5° alc. **Rating** 88 **To** 2011 $21
Yarra Valley Sauvignon Blanc 2006 Clean aromas; a delicate wine, with touches
of passionfruit; needs more depth, but has been well-made. Screwcap. 12.5° alc.
Rating 87 **To** 2008 $16

Bundaleer Wines

41 King Street, Brighton, SA 5048 (postal) **Region** Southern Flinders Ranges
T (08) 8296 1231 **F** (08) 8296 2484 **www**.bundaleerwines.com.au **Open** At North Star
Hotel, Melrose, 7 days 11–5
Winemaker Angela Meaney **Est.** 1998 **Cases** 300
Bundaleer is a joint venture between third-generation farmer Des Meaney and manufacturing
industry executive Graham Spurling (whose family originally came from the Southern Flinders).
Planting of the 8-ha vineyard began in 1998, the first vintage in 2001. It is situated in a region
known as the Bundaleer Gardens, on the edge of the Bundaleer Forest, 200 km north of Adelaide.
This should not be confused with the Bundaleer Shiraz brand made by Bindi.

ҮҮҮҮ **Southern Flinders Ranges Shiraz 2004** Medium to medium-full-bodied;
firm, clear-cut shiraz blackberry and plum fruit; fine-grained tannins, and good
oak. One of several excellent red wines from this new GI. Screwcap. 14° alc.
Rating 93 **To** 2019 $17

ҮҮҮҮ **Eden Valley Riesling 2006** A closed bouquet, the palate also still very shy;
minerally, with some apple and citrus peeping through; needs time. Screwcap. 12°
alc. **Rating** 89 **To** 2013 $15
Southern Flinders Ranges Sparkling Shiraz NV Very full-flavoured and rich
blackcurrant fruit; moderately sweet; does not venture outside the norm; the base
wine was not simply a failed red. 14° alc. **Rating** 87 **To** 2012 $16

Bundaleera Vineyard

449 Glenwood Road, Relbia, Tas 7258 (postal) **Region** Northern Tasmania
T (03) 6343 1231 **F** (03) 6343 1250 **Open** W'ends 10–5
Winemaker Pirie Consulting (Andrew Pirie) **Est.** 1996 **Cases** 1000
David (a consultant metallurgist in the mining industry) and Jan Jenkinson have established 2.5
ha of vines on a sunny, sheltered north to northeast slope in the North Esk Valley. The 12-ha
property on which their house and vineyard are established gives them some protection from the
urban sprawl of Launceston; Jan is the full-time viticulturist and gardener for the immaculately
tended property.

Bungawarra

Bents Road, Ballandean, Qld 4382 **Region** Granite Belt
T (07) 4684 1128 **F** (07) 4684 1128 **www**.bungawarrawines.com.au **Open** 7 days 10–4.30
Winemaker Jeff Harden **Est.** 1975 **Cases** 1500
Now owned by Jeff Harden, Bungawarra draws upon 4 ha of mature vineyards which over the
years have shown themselves capable of producing red wines of considerable character.

ҮҮҮҮ **Thomas Granite Belt Semillon 2005** Clean, quite pronounced varietal fruit
aromas; likewise plenty of ripe and sweet citrus fruit on the palate before a crisp, dry
finish. Commendable. Cork. 12.9° alc. **Rating** 89 **To** 2011 $15
Limited Release Granite Belt Cabernet Sauvignon 2005 Medium-bodied;
fair varietal expression, the plus-side being blackcurrant fruit, touches of mint leaf
attesting to the low baume. Cork. 12.7° alc. **Rating** 88 **To** 2012 $19

Bunnamagoo Estate

Bunnamagoo, Rockley, NSW 2795 (postal) **Region** Central Ranges Zone
T 1300 304 707 **F** (02) 6377 5231 **www**.bunnamagoowines.com.au **Open** Not
Winemaker Printhie Wines (Robert Black) **Est.** 1995 **Cases** 12 000
Bunnamagoo Estate (on one of the first land grants in the region) is situated near the historic
town of Rockley. Here a 6-ha vineyard planted to chardonnay, merlot and cabernet sauvignon
has been established by Paspaley Pearls, a famous name in the pearl industry. Production rose
steeply between 2005 and '06, with frost creating a question mark for the future.

ŦŦŦŦ° **Shiraz 2005** A medium-bodied, lively and fresh array of red and black fruits, not the least jammy or extractive; fruit-driven, with good length. ProCork. 14.5° alc. **Rating** 91 **To** 2013 $25

ŦŦŦŦ **Chardonnay 2006** Medium-bodied; obvious winemaker inputs through barrel ferment, part wild yeast, and lees; sweet nectarine and peach fruit; oak there, but not over the top. Cork. 13.5° alc. **Rating** 89 **To** 2010 $21

Cabernet Shiraz Merlot 2005 A mix of savoury, earthy and black fruits, the touches of vanilla and chocolate helping to sweeten the medium-bodied palate. Cork. 13.6° alc. **Rating** 88 **To** 2011 $20

Pinot Noir Chardonnay Sparkling Rose 2004 Light-bodied, but well-balanced thanks in part to 24 months on lees. 12° alc. **Rating** 87 **To** 2008 $25

Burge Family Winemakers ★★★★☆

Barossa Way, Lyndoch, SA 5351 **Region** Barossa Valley
T (08) 8524 4644 **F** (08) 8524 4444 **www**.burgefamily.com.au **Open** Mon & Thurs–Sat 10–5
Winemaker Rick Burge **Est.** 1928 **Cases** 3800
Rick Burge and Burge Family Winemakers (not to be confused with Grant Burge, although the families are related) has established itself as an icon producer of exceptionally rich, lush and concentrated Barossa red wines. Rick Burge's sense of humour was evident with the Nice Red (a Merlot/Cabernet blend made for those who come to the cellar door and ask 'Do you have a nice red?'). Exports to all major markets.

ŦŦŦŦŦ **Olive Hill Barossa Valley Shiraz Mourvedre Grenache 2005** One of the best examples going around of this blend, albeit shiraz (71%) is by far the dominant partner; offers a complex spray of spicy black fruits with wafts of dark chocolate and mocha. Cork. 14.5° alc. **Rating** 94 **To** 2020 $32

ŦŦŦŦ° **Draycott Barossa Shiraz 2005** A very attractive medium-bodied wine with plum, blackberry and black cherry fruit; good length, restrained alcohol and fine tannins. Cork. 14.5° alc. **Rating** 93 **To** 2015 $36

Garnacha Dry Grown Barossa Valley Grenache 2005 Lots of juicy varietal fruit, but has positive tannin structure to give distinction. Well above the norm for the Barossa. Cork. 15° alc. **Rating** 90 **To** 2012 $25

The Homestead Barossa Valley Cabernet Sauvignon 2005 Solid blackcurrant fruit, with touches of earth and chocolate to a medium- to full-bodied palate; good tannins. Cork. 14° alc. **Rating** 90 **To** 2018 $25

ŦŦŦŦ **D & OH Barossa Valley Shiraz Grenache 2005** Medium-bodied; the juicy berry grenache contribution is evident, but shiraz rules the roost in flavour and structure, though still an easy-drinking style. Screwcap. 14° alc. **Rating** 89 **To** 2010 $22

Olive Hill Barossa Semillon 2006 Relatively deep colour suggests skin contact as there is no oak; power-packed, slightly old-fashioned style, with the ripe fruit given a kick along by the alcohol. Screwcap. 13.5° alc. **Rating** 88 **To** 2009 $17

Burgi Hill Vineyard

290 Victoria Road, Wandin North, Vic 3139 **Region** Yarra Valley
T (03) 5964 3568 **F** (03) 5964 3568 **www**.burgihill.com.au **Open** By appt
Winemaker Christopher Sargeant, Dominique Portet **Est.** 1974 **Cases** 500
The 4.5-ha vineyard now operated by Christopher Sargeant and family was established over 30 years ago and is planted to chardonnay, sauvignon blanc, pinot noir, merlot and cabernet sauvignon. For many years the grapes were sold, but now some are vinified for the Burgi Hill label.

Burk Salter Wines

Lot 5, Paisley Road, Blanchetown, SA 5357 **Region** Riverland
T (08) 8540 5023 **F** (08) 8540 5023 **www**.burksalterwines.com.au **Open** Fri–Sun &
public hols 11–4.30, 7 days during school hols
Winemaker Various contract **Est.** 2002 **Cases** 3000
The husband and wife team of Gregory Burk Salter and Jane Vivienne Salter is the third
generation of the Salter family to grow grapes at their Blanchetown property. They have a little
over 20 ha of chardonnay, semillon, colombard, ruby cabernet, shiraz, merlot, cabernet sauvignon
and muscat gordo blanco; 450 tonnes are sold each year, the remaining 50 tonnes contract-made
at various small Barossa Valley wineries. The cellar door and a self-contained B&B adjoin the
vineyard, which has Murray River frontage.

Burke & Wills Winery

3155 Burke & Wills Track, Mia Mia, Vic 3444 **Region** Heathcote
T (03) 5425 5400 **F** (03) 5425 5401 **www**.wineandmusic.net **Open** By appt
Winemaker Andrew Pattison **Est.** 2003 **Cases** 1500
Andrew Pattison established Burke & Wills Winery in 2003, after selling Lancefield Winery. He is
in the course of establishing 1 ha of shiraz and 0.5 ha of gewurztraminer (and 0.5 ha of merlot,
malbec and petit verdot); also has 1 ha each of chardonnay and cabernets at Malmsbury (in the
Macedon Ranges), plus 0.5 ha of pinot noir, supplemented by contract-grown grapes from a
Macedon Ranges vineyard supplying chardonnay, pinot noir and cabernets. Not to be confused
with Burke & Hills of Orange.

ŸŸŸŸŸ Camp 5 Heathcote Shiraz 2005 Attractive, aromatic plum and black cherry
fruit aromas lead into a medium to medium–full-bodied palate, the fruit flavours
tracking the bouquet. Good French oak, and fine, ripe tannins. Diam. 13.8° alc.
Rating 94 **To** 2025 $24

ŸŸŸŸŸ Heathcote Shiraz 2005 A very different fruit register from the Camp 5; while
only fractionally riper on chemical analysis, the flavours seem significantly riper;
American oak also changes the profile. Overall less finesse, though no less flavour.
Screwcap. 14° alc. **Rating** 92 **To** 2027 $24
Pattison Family Reserve Macedon Ranges Pinot Noir 2005 Light plum
and spice aromas; picks up the pace on the well-structured and balanced plum and
forest floor palate; has length and panache. Diam. 14° alc. **Rating** 91 **To** 2012 $28
Pattison Family Reserve Macedon Ranges Cabernet Merlot 2005 A
medium-bodied, savoury mix of black and red fruits, spice and a touch of earth; fine
tannins, and a good aftertaste; impressive for the region. Diam. 14° alc. **Rating** 90
To 2013 $28
Dig Tree Macedon Ranges Cabernet Sauvignon 2005 Vivid purple-red;
clean, clear cassis and blackcurrant fruit; an exceptional achievement for
Macedon Ranges, normally far too cool for cabernet. An enticing price, too.
Screwcap. 14.3° alc. **Rating** 90 **To** 2013 $18

ŸŸŸŸ Dig Tree Unwooded Chardonnay 2005 Tangy and focused citrussy fruit, with
good intensity and length. **Rating** 89 **To** 2010 $17
Pattison Family Reserve Macedon Ranges Chardonnay 2005 Light- to
medium-bodied; citrus and nectarine flavours, with a light kiss of French oak; good
balance. Screwcap. 12.8° alc. **Rating** 89 **To** 2011 $22
**Pattison Family Reserve Macedon Ranges Malbec Cabernet Sauvignon
2005** Juicy berry malbec; texturally similar to grenache but the flavours are in an
entirely different cassis/raspberry spectrum; has absorbed 18 months in French oak.
Cork. 13.5° alc. **Rating** 89 **To** 2015 $28
Dig Tree Unwooded Chardonnay 2006 Light-bodied; citrus/grapefruit/apple
flavours balanced by a faint hint of sweetness on the finish. Screwcap. 12.5° alc.
Rating 87 **To** 2009 $17

Burrundulla Vineyards

Sydney Road, Mudgee, NSW 2850 **Region** Mudgee
T (02) 6372 1620 **F** (02) 6372 4058 **www**.burrundulla.com **Open** 7 days 10–4
Winemaker Contract **Est.** 1996 **Cases** 3000
The Cox family are multi-generation residents of Burrundulla. In 2006 management of the
60 ha of shiraz, cabernet sauvignon, chardonnay, merlot and semillon passed to the seventh
generation of Jeremy, Vincent, Rowan and Andrew, with Andrew leading the way. The wines
are made in 2 ranges: Heritage at the top, then GX.

Heritage Mudgee Semillon 2006 Pure, youthful, mineral-driven; the fruit is still
locked up but will emerge with time. Screwcap. **Rating** 87 **To** 2013 $15

Burton Premium Wines

PO Box 242, Killara, NSW 2071 **Region** McLaren Vale
T (02) 9416 6631 **F** (02) 9416 6681 **www**.burtonpremiumwines.com **Open** Not
Winemaker Boar's Rock (Mike Farmilo), Pat Tocaciu (Contract) **Est.** 1998 **Cases** 5000
Burton Premium Wines has neither vineyards nor winery, purchasing its grapes from McLaren
Vale and Coonawarra, and having its wines made in various locations by contract winemakers. It
brings together the marketing and financial skills of managing director Nigel Burton, and the
extensive wine experience (as a senior wine show judge) of Dr Ray Healy, who is director in
charge of winemaking. Exports to Canada, Thailand and Vietnam.

McLaren Vale Shiraz 2002 Holding hue well; good mouthfeel; McLaren Vale
terroir to the fore in a wine of length and complex fruit flavours in a black
spectrum. Cork. 14° alc. **Rating** 94 **To** 2019 $32.45
Reserve McLaren Vale Shiraz 2002 Richer than the varietal, a bizarre
situation given the much lower alcohol, more oak being part of the
explanation; black fruits, chocolate, coffee and mocha. Fascinating wine. Cork.
12° alc. **Rating** 94 **To** 2022 $55

McLaren Vale Chardonnay 2005 Crisp and lively melon and stone fruit, plus a
touch of citrus; good length; no oak evident, and doesn't need it. Screwcap. 13° alc.
Rating 89 **To** 2009 $20.95
McLaren Vale Chardonnay 2004 Has similar fruit flavours to the '05, and shows
little sign of ageing; fresh, unoaked, quality fruit. Screwcap. 13.5° alc. **Rating** 89
To 2008 $20.95
McLaren Vale Shiraz 2003 Medium-bodied regional flavours of black fruits,
licorice, dark chocolate and a touch of mocha; overall well-balanced; good finish.
Cork. 14° alc. **Rating** 89 **To** 2018 $32.45

by Farr

PO Box 72, Bannockburn, Vic 3331 **Region** Geelong
T (03) 5281 1979 **F** (03) 5281 1433 **www**.byfarr.com.au **Open** Not
Winemaker Gary Farr, Nick Farr **Est.** 1999 **Cases** 3000
In 1994 Gary Farr and family planted 12 ha of clonally selected viognier, chardonnay, pinot noir
and shiraz at a density of 7000 per ha on a north-facing hill directly opposite the Bannockburn
Winery. The quality of the wines is exemplary, their character subtly different from those of
Bannockburn itself due, in Farr's view, to the interaction of the terroir of the hill and the clonal
selection. Exports to the UK, the US, India, Malaysia, Hong Kong and Singapore.

Geelong Chardonnay 2005 Has exceptional depth and complexity, yet no
particular component stands out; rich stone fruit and barrel ferment underwrite
a long life. Cork. 13.5° alc. **Rating** 95 **To** 2015 $50
Sangreal 2005 Very fine texture, body and flavour; in a young Burgundian
mould, still tied up, but achieves the length of quality pinot without those
touches of green. Pinot Noir. Cork. 13.5° alc. **Rating** 95 **To** 2015 $60

Geelong Viognier 2005 Fragrant, intense and long; has the great balance so difficult to achieve with this variety; opens with apricot and peach, moving to citrussy acidity on the finish. Cork. 14° alc. **Rating** 94 **To** 2011 $50

♀♀♀♀♀ Geelong Pinot Noir 2005 Pure, long and intense; a hint of green/mint lurks under the surface; has the same alcohol as Sangreal, so I'm not sure where the flavour difference emanates from. Cork. 13.5° alc. **Rating** 92 **To** 2015 $55
Geelong Shiraz 2005 Slightly cloudy colour; clear cool-climate shiraz; spicy, peppery overtones, but well off the pace of his best. Cork. 15° alc. **Rating** 90 **To** 2015 $55

Byrne & Smith Wines

PO Box 640, Unley, SA 5061 **Region** South Australia
T (08) 8272 1911 **F** (08) 8272 1944 **www.**byrneandsmith.com.au **Open** Not
Winemaker Duane Coates (Contract) **Est.** 1999 **Cases** 40 000
Byrne & Smith is a substantial business with 2 vineyards totalling 53 ha at Stanley Flat in the northern Clare Valley, and a third vineyard of 106 ha near Waikerie in the Riverland. The majority of the grapes are sold, and the wines being marketed also use purchased grapes from regions as far away as the Margaret River.

Cahills Wines ★★★

PO Box 70, Kingaroy, Qld 4610 **Region** South Burnett
T (07) 4163 1563 **Open** From Sept 2007, 7 days 10–4
Winemaker Crane Winery (Bernie Cooper) **Est.** 1998 **Cases** 200
When Cindy and John Cahill purchased a former 66-ha dairy farm in 1996, they did so with the intention of planting a vineyard. John Cahill worked for Lindemans for 13 years in Sydney, Brisbane and Cairns, and developed marketing skills from this experience. Nonetheless, they have hastened slowly, planting 1.2 ha of shiraz (in 1998) and chardonnay (in 2000), slowly extending the plantings since. An olive grove has also been established. They make the Shiraz onsite, the Unwooded Chardonnay being processed at Crane Winery.

♀♀♀♀ Unwooded Chardonnay 2006 Early picking has kept some freshness and a touch of citrus; well done. Twin top. 12.5° alc. **Rating** 87 **To** 2008 $17
Shiraz 2005 Plenty of black fruits, prunes and licorice with a dusting of chocolate; has abundant flavour, if not finesse. Twin top. 14.5° alc. **Rating** 87 **To** 2013 $20

Caledonia Australis ★★★★★

PO Box 626, North Melbourne, Vic 3051 **Region** Gippsland
T (03) 9416 4156 **F** (03) 9416 4157 **www.**caledoniaaustralis.com **Open** Not
Winemaker MasterWineMakers **Est.** 1995 **Cases** 6000
The reclusive Caledonia Australis is a Pinot Noir and Chardonnay specialist, with a total of 18 ha in 3 separate vineyard locations. The vineyards are in the Leongatha area, on red, free-draining, high-ironstone soils, on a limestone or marl base, and the slopes are east to northeast-facing. Small-batch winemaking has resulted in consistently high-quality wines.

♀♀♀♀ Rose 2006 Clean, light-bodied, quite long, and not sweet. Top-pointed rose Gippsland Wine Show '07. Screwcap. 12.5° alc. **Rating** 88 **To** 2008 $22

Callipari Wine

68–70 Madden Avenue, Mildura, Vic 3500 **Region** Murray Darling
T 1300 633 733 **F** (03) 5021 0988 **www.**callipari.com **Open** Mon–Fri 10–4
Winemaker Michael Callipari **Est.** 1999 **Cases** 14 000
Michael Callipari is among the third generation of the Callipari family, the first members of which left Calabria, Sicily, in 1951. Various members of the family have developed vineyards over the years, with over 25 ha of vines on 2 properties. Mother Giuseppa Callipari makes food products

(from produce grown on the family farm) that are sold through the cellar door (which operates from the winery warehouse in Mildura) and at tourism outlets and shops in the district. Ned Kelly Red, incidentally, is described as a 'premium red wine spritzer with a dash of orange and lemon'.

Cambewarra Estate ★★★☆

520 Illaroo Road, Cambewarra, NSW 2540 **Region** Shoalhaven Coast
T (02) 4446 0170 **www**.cambewarraestate.com.au **Open** Thurs–Sun & public & school hols 10–5
Winemaker Tamburlaine **Est.** 1991 **Cases** 3000
Louise Cole owns and runs Cambewarra Estate, near the Shoalhaven River on the central southern coast of NSW, the wines made at Tamburlaine in the Hunter Valley. Cambewarra continues to produce attractive wines which have had significant success in wine shows.

 John Unwooded Chardonnay 2005 Has a quite unexpected array of stone fruit flavours running through its length; good example of the style. Screwcap. 12.4° alc. **Rating** 88 **To** 2008 $16
Amanda Verdelho 2005 A quiet bouquet, but a quite expressive palate; light-bodied despite the alcohol; fruit salad and a twist of citrus. Screwcap. 14.1° alc. **Rating** 87 **To** 2008 $19
Anniversary Chambourcin 2004 As ever, a head and shoulders wine; sweet red and black fruits on entry fading away on the finish. Enjoyable nonetheless. Screwcap. 13.7° alc. **Rating** 87 **To** 2008 $21

Campania Hills ★★★★

447 Native Corners Road, Campania, Tas 7026 **Region** Southern Tasmania
T (03) 6260 4387 **Open** By appt
Winemaker Winemaking Tasmania (Julian Alcorso) **Est.** 1994 **Cases** 500
This is the former Colmaur, purchased by Jeanette and Lindsay Kingston in 2005. They had just sold a business they had built up over 22 years and thought they were returning to country life and relaxation when they purchased the property with 1.5 ha of vines equally split between pinot noir and chardonnay (plus 700 olive trees). Says Lindsay Kingston, somewhat wryly, 'We welcome visitors. The last lot stayed 3 hours.'

Unwooded Chardonnay 2006 Appealing citrus and nectarine fruit; long and intense; good example of Tasmanian unwooded chardonnay. **Rating** 91 **To** 2010 $15

Campbells ★★★★★

Murray Valley Highway, Rutherglen, Vic 3685 **Region** Rutherglen
T (02) 6032 9458 **www**.campbellswines.com.au **Open** Mon–Sat 9–5, Sun 10–5
Winemaker Colin Campbell **Est.** 1870 **Cases** 40 000
A wide range of table and fortified wines of ascending quality and price, which are always honest. As so often happens in this part of the world, the fortified wines are the best, with the extremely elegant Isabella Rare Tokay and Merchant Prince Rare Muscat at the top of the tree; the winery rating is for the fortified wines. A feature of the Vintage Room at the cellar door is an extensive range of back vintage releases of small parcels of wine not available through any other outlet, other than the Cellar Club members. Exports to the UK, the US, Canada and NZ.

 Isabella Rare Rutherglen Tokay NV Very deep olive-brown; broodingly complex, deep and concentrated aromas, then layer upon layer of flavour in the mouth. Incredibly intense and complex, with the varietal tea-leaf/muscadelle fruit continuity. 18° alc. **Rating** 97 **To** 2008 $94
Grand Rutherglen Tokay NV Deep mahogany, olive rim. An intensely complex bouquet, with hints of smoke, abundant rancio. Glorious malty, tea-leaf flavours linger long in the mouth; great style and balance. 17.5° alc. **Rating** 95 **To** 2008 $73

Merchant Prince Rare Rutherglen Muscat NV Dark brown, with olive-green on the rim; particularly fragrant, with essencey, raisiny fruit; supple, smooth and intense wine floods every corner of the mouth, but yet retains elegance, and continues the house style to perfection. 18° alc. **Rating** 95 **To** 2008 $94

♥♥♥♥♀ **Classic Rutherglen Tokay NV** Medium brown; a complex bouquet with dried muscadelle fruit; deliciously idiosyncratic. The faintly smoky palate has power and depth, again with dried muscadelle grapes reflecting the bouquet. 17.5° alc. **Rating** 93 **To** 2008 $35
Grand Rutherglen Muscat NV Full olive-brown; highly aromatic; a rich and complex palate is silky smooth, supple and long, the raisiny fruit perfectly balanced by the clean, lingering acid (and spirit) cut on the finish. 17.5° alc. **Rating** 93 **To** 2008 $73
Classic Rutherglen Muscat NV Spicy/raisiny complexity starting to build; in typical Campbells style, lively, clearly articulated, with good balance and length. 17.5° alc. **Rating** 92 **To** 2008 $35
Rutherglen Tokay NV Bright, light golden-brown; classic mix of tea-leaf and butterscotch aromas lead into an elegant wine which dances in the mouth; has balance and length. 17.5° alc. **Rating** 92 **To** 2005 $17
Rutherglen Muscat NV Bright, clear tawny-gold; a highly aromatic bouquet, spicy and grapey, is mirrored precisely on the palate, which has nigh-on perfect balance. Trophy at 2005 International Wine Challenge, London. 17.5° alc. **Rating** 91 **To** 2006 $17

♥♥♥♥ **Bobbie Burns Rutherglen Shiraz 2004** Medium to full red-purple; seems much riper than the alcohol suggests, with elements of prune and raisin to the fruits; rugged finish. Cork. 14.5° alc. **Rating** 88 **To** 2012 $22

Camyr Allyn Wines

Camyr Allyn North, Allyn River Road, East Gresford, NSW 2311 **Region** Upper Hunter Valley
T (02) 4938 9576 **F** (02) 4938 9576 **www**.camyrallynwines.com.au **Open** 7 days 10–5
Winemaker James Evers **Est.** 1999 **Cases** 2500
John and Judy Evers purchased the Camyr Allyn North property in 1997, and immediately set about planting 4.4 ha of verdelho, merlot and shiraz. The wines are made at the new Northern Hunter winery at East Gresford by James Evers, who worked for Mildara Blass in Coonawarra for some time. The promotion and packaging of the wines is innovative and stylish.

♥♥♥♥ **Ruins Liqueur Verdelho NV** Very cleverly handled; quality spirit well-integrated, the sweetness utterly deceptive; well-balanced. The ultimate in extravagant packaging; the wine will not improve in the extraordinary bottle, which can be quickly used for whatever decorative or other purpose you can visualise. Diam. 19° alc. **Rating** 89 **To** 2008 $35
Hunter Valley Rose 2006 Attractive, fresh cherry fruit; good acidity and balance; not sweet. Screwcap. 13.4° alc. **Rating** 88 **To** 2008 $16
Hunter Valley Verdelho 2006 Light- to medium-bodied; well-made, with attractive, fresh citrus components to the fruit salad varietal base; good length. Screwcap. 13.8° alc. **Rating** 87 **To** 2009 $18

🍇 Cana Estate

Escort Way, Orange, NSW 2800 (postal) **Region** Orange
T (02) 6365 2306 **F** (02) 6365 2306 **www**.canaestate.com **Open** Not
Winemaker Monarch Winemaking Service **Est.** 1997 **Cases** NFP
Cana Estate is a somewhat unusual venture; it has a strong humanitarian background, with an overlay of religion. The wines are contract-made at Monarch Winemaking Services, up to 2007 by Jim Chatto. The profits from the venture are paid to the Aboriginal Medical Services Fund.

♀♀♀♀♀ **Chardonnay 2005** Attractive stone fruit and citrus aromas and flavours backed by a touch of oak; good length, though not overly intense. Screwcap. **Rating** 90 To 2009
Shiraz 2005 A solid wine, with much going on; dark chocolate, spice, licorice, a touch of green leaf and plenty of oak. Cork. **Rating** 90 To 2015

♀♀♀♀ **Limited Release Pinot Noir 2002** Savoury/foresty aromas, though not much varietal fruit; texture and weight quite good. Has held on remarkably well. Cork. **Rating** 87 To 2008

Candlebark Hill ★★★

Fordes Lane, Kyneton, Vic 3444 **Region** Macedon Ranges
T (03) 9836 2712 **F** (03) 9836 2712 **Open** By appt
Winemaker David Forster, Vincent Lakey, Llew Knight (Consultant) **Est.** 1987 **Cases** 600
Candlebark Hill, established by David Forster at the northern end of the Macedon Ranges, has magnificent views over the Central Victoria countryside north of the Great Dividing Range. The 3.5-ha vineyard is planted to 1.5 ha of pinot noir, 1 ha each of chardonnay and the 3 main Bordeaux varieties, and 0.5 ha of shiraz and malbec. The Reserve Pinot Noir has been especially meritorious.

♀♀♀♀ **Cabernet Merlot 2005** Ripe blackcurrant and cassis fruit, though the tannins are distinctly robust. **Rating** 87 To 2011
Aged Macedon Brut Methode Champenoise 11 NV Glowing yellow-green; very rich, ripe stone fruit/citrus; perhaps a touch heavy handed. **Rating** 87 To 2008

Cannibal Creek Vineyard ★★★★

260 Tynong North Road, Tynong North, Vic 3813 **Region** Gippsland
T (03) 5942 8380 **F** (03) 5942 8202 **www**.cannibalcreek.com.au **Open** 7 days 11–5
Winemaker Patrick Hardiker **Est.** 1997 **Cases** 2000
The Hardiker family moved to Tynong North in 1988, initially only grazing beef cattle, but aware of the viticultural potential of the sandy clay loam and bleached sub-surface soils weathered from the granite foothills of the Black Snake Ranges. Plantings began in 1997, using organically based cultivation methods. The family decided to make their own wine, and a heritage-style shed built from locally milled timber has been converted into a winery and cellar door. Exports to the UK.

♀♀♀♀♀ **Hardiker Pinot Noir 2005** Light- to medium-bodied; cherry and plum, with attractive touches of forest floor and spice; long and supple. Gold medal Gippsland Wine Show '07. Bargain. Diam. 14° alc. **Rating** 93 To 2010 $16
Sauvignon Blanc 2006 Nicely made, with a mix of tropical and citrus fruit; has length and intensity, and a dry finish. Diam. 13.8° alc. **Rating** 90 To 2008 $24
Merlot 2005 Flavoursome, with lots of fruit in a cassis/raspberry spectrum; tannins push the limit for merlot, but are justified by the depth and texture of the fruit. Diam. 13.5° alc. **Rating** 90 To 2011 $28

♀♀♀♀ **Hardiker Chardonnay 2005** Line and length are the strong points, with pronounced nectarine and citrus fruit; any oak used is not evident. Diam. 14° alc. **Rating** 89 To 2010 $16
Vin de Liqueur 2005 Racy spirit adds interest and length to an unusual style. Diam. 19° alc. **Rating** 87 To 2008 $20

Canobolas-Smith ★★★★

Boree Lane, off Cargo Road, Lidster via Orange, NSW 2800 **Region** Orange
T (02) 6365 6113 **www**.canobolassmithwines.com.au **Open** W'ends & public hols 11–5
Winemaker Murray Smith **Est.** 1986 **Cases** 2000

Canobolas-Smith has established itself as one of the leading Orange region wineries, and its blue wraparound labels are distinctive. Much of the wine is sold from the cellar door, which is well worth a visit. Exports to the US and Asia.

 🍷🍷🍷🍷🍷 **Shine Reserve Chardonnay 2002** Great colour; a rich but not heavy wine, with length, intensity and balance. Another of many gold medals to its credit (at the Orange Wine Show '06). Screwcap. 14.5° alc. **Rating** 94 **To** 2009 $35

🍷🍷🍷🍷🍷 **Orange Chardonnay 2004** Complex and very rich; stone fruit and peach flavours are equally ripe; lacks the tension of the great '02, but still very good. Screwcap. 14.5° alc. **Rating** 92 **To** 2012 $35
Orange Pinot Noir 2004 Plenty of depth, with strong, plummy fruit; quite complex, with savoury characters and good length. Screwcap. 13.9° alc. **Rating** 90 **To** 2009 $25

Canonbah Bridge ★★★

Merryanbone Station, Warren, NSW 2824 (postal) **Region** Western Plains Zone
T (02) 6833 9966 **F** (02) 6833 9980 **www.**canonbahbridge.com **Open** Not
Winemaker Hunter Wine Services (John Hordern) **Est.** 1999 **Cases** 25 000
The 29-ha vineyard has been established by Shane McLaughlin on the very large Merryanbone Station, a Merino sheep stud which has been in the family for 4 generations. The wines are at 3 price points: at the bottom is Bottle Tree, from southeast Australia; then Ram's Leap, specific regional blends; and at the top, Canonbah Bridge, either estate or estate/regional blends. Exports to the UK, the US, Canada, Hong Kong and China.

🍷🍷🍷🍷 **Orange Sauvignon Blanc 2005** A fresh, clean and lively bouquet; in the mouth a mix of citrus, herb, spice and grass; long finish. Screwcap. 13.5° alc. **Rating** 89 **To** 2008 $20
Bottle Tree Chardonnay 2006 An elegant wine with delicate but piercing flavours; a rare chardonnay in which the absence of oak is appropriate. Screwcap. 13° alc. **Rating** 88 **To** 2008 $9.95
Drought Reserve Western Plains Shiraz 2002 Dried/desiccated prune, plum and blackberry; drought and alcohol are not necessarily good things, but the wine does have character. Cork. 15.5° alc. **Rating** 88 **To** 2012 $30
Ram's Leap Semillon Sauvignon Blanc 2006 Well-made; has quite distinctive grass/herb/mineral flavours and no reliance on residual sugar; good length. Screwcap. 12.5° alc. **Rating** 87 **To** 2009 $14.95
Ram's Leap Semillon Sauvignon Blanc 2005 Clean and crisp; light-bodied, predominantly mineral, herb and grass; demands time. Western Plains/Orange. Screwcap. 12° alc. **Rating** 87 **To** 2011 $15
Ram's Leap Rose 2006 Surprisingly, not sweet; red fruits with a spicy finish. Screwcap. 12.5° alc. **Rating** 87 **To** 2008 $14.95
Drought Reserve Western Plains Shiraz 2003 A big, rustic red; dark berry fruits with powerful, untamed tannins throughout; pray the scrappy cork holds. 15° alc. **Rating** 87 **To** 2020 $35

Cape Barren Wines ★★★★

Lot 20, Little Road, Willunga, SA 5172 **Region** McLaren Vale
T (08) 8556 4374 **F** (08) 8556 4364 **Open** By appt
Winemaker Brian Light (Contract) **Est.** 1999 **Cases** 3500
Lifelong friends and vignerons Peter Matthews and Brian Ledgard joined forces in 1999 to create Cape Barren Wines. In all they have 62 ha of vineyards throughout the McLaren Vale region, the jewel in the crown being 4 ha of 70-year-old shiraz at Blewitt Springs, which provides the grapes for the Old Vine Shiraz. The McLaren Vale Grenache Shiraz Mourvedre and McLaren Vale Shiraz come from their other vineyards; most of the grapes are sold. Exports to the US, Canada, NZ, Malaysia, Singapore, Hong Kong, Indonesia, Philippines, Dubai, Germany and Switzerland.

🍷🍷🍷🍷🍷 **Old Vine McLaren Vale Shiraz 2004** Deep purple-red; blackberry, plum and bitter chocolate; good control of oak and extract; has balance to go with the abundant fruit flavour. Cork. 14.9° alc. **Rating** 94 **To** 2014 $33

🍷🍷🍷🍷🍷 **McLaren Vale Grenache Shiraz Mourvedre 2005** Light- to medium-bodied; nicely balanced juicy grenache tempered by the other blend components; touches of spice and savoury chocolate; fine tannins. Screwcap. 14.5° alc. **Rating** 90 **To** 2010 $23

🍷🍷🍷🍷 **Native Goose McLaren Vale Shiraz 2005** Medium-bodied; soft red and black plummy fruit; moderate length; easy style. Screwcap. 14.5° alc. **Rating** 88 **To** 2011 $21

Cape Bernier Vineyard ★★★

GPO Box 1743, Hobart, Tas 7001 **Region** Southern Tasmania
T (03) 6253 5443 **F** (03) 6253 6087 **www**.capebernier.com.au **Open** Not
Winemaker Winemaking Tasmania (Julian Alcorso) **Est.** 1999 **Cases** 750

Alastair Christie (and family) has established 2 ha of Dijon clone pinot noir, another 1.5 ha of chardonnay and 0.5 ha of pinot gris on a north-facing slope overlooking historic Marion Bay. The property is not far from the Bream Creek vineyard, and is one of several developments in the region changing the land use from dairy and beef cattle to wine production and tourism.

Cape Grace ★★★★☆

Fifty One Road, Cowaramup, WA 6284 **Region** Margaret River
T (08) 9755 5669 **F** (08) 9755 5668 **www**.capegracewines.com.au **Open** 7 days 10–5
Winemaker Robert Karri-Davies, Mark Messenger (Consultant) **Est.** 1996 **Cases** 2000

Cape Grace Wines can trace its history back to 1875, when timber baron MC Davies settled at Karridale, building the Leeuwin lighthouse and founding the township of Margaret River; 120 years later, Robert and Karen Karri-Davies planted just under 6 ha of vineyard to chardonnay, shiraz and cabernet sauvignon, with smaller amounts of merlot, semillon and chenin blanc. Robert is a self-taught viticulturist; Karen has over 15 years of international sales and marketing experience in the hospitality industry. Winemaking is carried out on the property; consultant Mark Messenger is a veteran of the Margaret River region. Exports to Singapore.

🍷🍷🍷🍷🍷 **Margaret River Chardonnay 2005** Potent fruit in ultra-typical Margaret River and Cape Grace style; long and very well balanced, with integrated oak; melon, nectarine and grapefruit; long finish. Screwcap. 13.5° alc. **Rating** 93 **To** 2014 $29.50

Margaret River Shiraz 2005 Youthful and fresh; vibrant colour and mouthfeel on entry suggest a relatively low pH; blackberry fruits and contrasting savoury finish to the initial fruit vibrancy. Confused? So am I. Screwcap. 14° alc. **Rating** 92 **To** 2020 $29.50

Margaret River Cabernet Sauvignon 2005 Medium-bodied; varietal blackcurrant and cassis, with slightly disassociated tannins; time will certainly cure the issue, but the points are for the wine as it is today, not as it will be in the future. Screwcap. 14.5° alc. **Rating** 90 **To** 2020 $39.50

Cape Horn Vineyard ★★★

Echuca-Picola Road, Kanyapella, Vic 3564 **Region** Goulburn Valley
T (03) 5480 6013 **F** (03) 5480 6013 **www**.capehornvineyard.com.au **Open** 7 days 11–5
Winemaker John Ellis (Contract) **Est.** 1993 **Cases** 3000

The unusual name comes from a bend in the Murray River which was considered by riverboat owners of the 19th century to resemble Cape Horn, which is depicted on the wine label. The property was acquired by Echuca GP Dr Sue Harrison and her schoolteacher husband Ian in 1993. Ian Harrison has progressively planted their 11-ha vineyard to chardonnay, shiraz, cabernet sauvignon, zinfandel, marsanne and durif.

Cape Jaffa Wines

Limestone Coast Road, Cape Jaffa, SA 5276 **Region** Mt Benson
T (08) 8768 5053 **F** (08) 8768 5040 **www**.capejaffawines.com.au **Open** 7 days 10–5
Winemaker Derek Hooper **Est.** 1993 **Cases** 30 000
Cape Jaffa was the first of the Mt Benson wineries and all of the production now comes from the substantial estate plantings of 16.4 ha, which include the 4 major Bordeaux red varieties, plus shiraz, chardonnay, sauvignon blanc and semillon. The winery (built of local paddock rock) has been designed to allow eventual expansion to 1000 tonnes, or 70 000 cases. Exports to the UK, Philippines, Hong Kong, Singapore and China.

Semillon Sauvignon Blanc 2006 Clean and aromatic; complex aromas and flavours running the full gamut from herb/grass through to passionfruit/tropical; a long palate with subliminal sweetness. Screwcap. 12.5° alc. **Rating** 92 **To** 2008 $16
Brocks Reef Shiraz 2004 Strongly accented, cool-grown style; has length and vivacity to its red and black fruits; long finish. Screwcap. **Rating** 91 **To** 2014 $13

Brocks Reef Cabernet Merlot 2004 Spicy/earthy aromas and flavours; controlled tannins and extract, and not dilute. Screwcap. **Rating** 88 **To** 2010 $13
Brocks Reef Chardonnay 2006 Quite complex aromas, a touch of barrel ferment French oak showing through; good flavour depth, with subliminal sweetness fleshing out the finish. Screwcap. 14.5° alc. **Rating** 87 **To** 2008 $13

Cape Landing

PO Box 1441, Margaret River, WA 6285 **Region** Margaret River
T (08) 9757 6418 **F** (08) 9757 6148 **Open** Not
Winemaker Rockfield Estate (Andrew Gaman) **Est.** 1998 **Cases** 650
Larry and Cheryl de Jong planted a total of 12.8 ha of shiraz, cabernet sauvignon, chardonnay, semillon and sauvignon blanc in 1998, adding another 2 ha (chardonnay) in 2003. The intention was to simply be grapegrowers, but in 2003, concerned about the uncertain nature of the industry, they decided to have part of the grapes contract-made. For once Murphy's Law worked favourably; with 3 wineries competing for the grapes, a long-term contract was entered into with one winemaker, allowing the de Jongs to pursue their other aim of making small quantities of wines for sale primarily to friends and through Cheryl's boutique guesthouse in Subiaco.

Margaret River Cabernet Shiraz 2005 Medium- to full-bodied; features both sides of the black fruit divide, blackcurrant on one side, blackberry on the other; tannins and overall balance good, the cabernet giving the line. Screwcap. 14.3° alc. **Rating** 90 **To** 2018 $18

Margaret River Shiraz 2005 An abundance of fully ripe blackberry, prune and plum fruit; not so much regional character, but no shortage of flavour. Radically different from the '03. Screwcap. **Rating** 89 **To** 2013 $19

Cape Lavender

4 Carter Road, Metricup, WA 6280 **Region** Margaret River
T (08) 9755 7552 **F** (08) 9755 7556 **www**.capelavender.com.au **Open** 7 days 10–5
Winemaker Peter Stanlake, Eion Lindsay **Est.** 1999 **Cases** 3500
With 11.5 ha of vines, a much-awarded winery restaurant, and lavender fields which help make unique wines, this is a business with something extra. There are 7 Lavender wines, moving from sparkling through table to port, which have been infused with *Lavandula angustifolia*; the impact isn't overwhelming, but is nonetheless evident, and far from unpleasant. Whether it is a legal additive to wine, I do not know. There is also a conventional estate range of Semillon, Sauvignon Blanc, Chardonnay, Merlot, Shiraz and Cabernet Sauvignon, made without lavender.

Cape Lodge Wines

Caves Road, Yallingup, WA 6282 (postal) **Region** Margaret River
T (08) 9755 6311 **F** (08) 9755 6322 **www.**capelodge.com.au **Open** Not
Winemaker Jan Macintosh **Est.** 1998 **Cases** 1000
Cape Lodge has evolved from a protea farm in the early 1980s, through a small luxury B&B operation in 1993, and now a multimillion dollar investment has propelled it to the top 100 hotels of the world in the *Condé Nast Traveler* magazine gold list of 2005, the fourth-best restaurant in the world for food by the same publication, and the best 5-star resort in Australia and Asia Pacific by a conference of its peers. Since 2001 it has been owned by Malaysians Seng and So Ong, who were responsible for the major expansion to 22 rooms, a new restaurant and a 14 000-bottle wine cellar. In 1998, 1.6 ha each of sauvignon blanc and shiraz were planted, the wine sold exclusively through the Cape Lodge resort.

Cape Mentelle

Wallcliffe Road, Margaret River, WA 6285 **Region** Margaret River
T (08) 9757 0888 **F** (08) 9757 3233 **www.**capementelle.com.au **Open** 7 days 10–4.30
Winemaker Robert Mann, Simon Burnell, Lara Bray **Est.** 1970 **Cases** NFP
Part of the LVMH (Louis Vuitton Möet Hennessy) group. Since the advent of Dr Tony Jordan as Australasian CEO there has been a concerted and successful campaign to rid the winery of the brettanomyces infection which particularly affected the Cabernet Sauvignon. The Chardonnay and Semillon Sauvignon Blanc are among Australia's best, the potent Shiraz usually superb, and the berry/spicy Zinfandel makes one wonder why this grape is not as widespread in Australia as it is in California. Exports to all major markets.

ᵠᵠᵠᵠᵠ **Margaret River Chardonnay 2005** A very elegant and precise wine in typical winery style; melon and nectarine fruit lead the way; good acidity and oak balance and integration. Screwcap. 14.5° alc. **Rating** 94 **To** 2015 $42

ᵠᵠᵠᵠᵠ **Margaret River Sauvignon Blanc Semillon 2006** Spotlessly clean; a carefully crafted and balanced wine, the semillon, as much as the sauvignon blanc, in the driver's seat; good length. Screwcap. 13° alc. **Rating** 93 **To** 2009 $25
Georgiana 2006 Fresh, lively, tangy, juicy style with lemon, nectarine and grass flavours; bright finish. Sauvignon Blanc/Semillon/Chenin Blanc. Screwcap. 13° alc. **Rating** 90 **To** 2008 $18

Cape Naturaliste Vineyard

Lot 77, Caves Road, Yallingup, WA 6282 **Region** Margaret River
T (08) 9755 2538 **www.**capenaturalistevineyard.com.au **Open** Wed–Mon 10.30–5
Winemaker David Moss, Barney Mitchell, Craig Brent-White **Est.** 1997 **Cases** 4000
Cape Naturaliste Vineyard has a long and varied history, going back 150 years when it was a coach inn for travellers journeying between Perth and Margaret River. Later it became a dairy farm, and in 1970 was purchased by a mining company intending to extract the mineral sands. The government stepped in and declared it a national park, whereafter (in 1980) Craig Brent-White purchased the property. In 1997 the 9-ha vineyard was planted to cabernet sauvignon, shiraz, merlot, semillon and sauvignon blanc. The vineyard is run on an organic/biodynamic basis. The quality of the wines would suggest the effort is well worthwhile.

ᵠᵠᵠᵠᵠ **Torpedo Rocks Margaret River Semillon 2005** Still moving from adolescence towards maturity; barrel ferment oak is evident, but not dominant; fruit needs to, and certainly will, develop with time in bottle. Cork. 13° alc. **Rating** 90 **To** 2012 $23

ᵠᵠᵠᵠ **Torpedo Rocks Margaret River Shiraz 2003** Light colour, but holding hue well; light- to medium-bodied spicy red and black cherry fruit; balanced tannins and oak. Cork. 14.1° alc. **Rating** 89 **To** 2013 $32
Torpedo Rocks Margaret River Merlot 2005 Fresh, light, crisp cassis-accented fruit at variance with the alcohol (the flavours should have been riper); easy lunch red. Screwcap. 14° alc. **Rating** 87 **To** 2010 $27

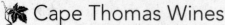 # Cape Thomas Wines ★★★

Southern Ports Highway, Mount Benson, SA 5275 **Region** Mount Benson
T (08) 8768 6155 **F** (08) 8768 7264 **www**.capethomasvineyards.com.au **Open** 7 days
10–4.30, closed Mon May–Dec
Winemaker Kristen McGann, Nigel Westblade (Contract) **Est.** 2006 **Cases** 2000
Cape Thomas vineyards are owned and operated by Maureen, Peter and Tom Andrews, the family
having been farming in the district for 57 years. Peter was a student at Roseworthy Agricultural
College in the early 1960s, but it was not until 1995 that he fulfilled his long-held ambition to
diversify into viticulture. Until 2004 all of the grapes were sold to Cellarmasters and Norfolk Rise,
but since then wines have been made under the Cape Thomas label, the first release coming in
2006. The wines are sold at the Mount Benson Wine & Tourism Centre (along with Guichen
Bay Vineyards' wines), which is owned and operated by a community trust offering a range of
facilities for visitors and community projects.

▼▼▼▼ **The Skipper Mount Benson Shiraz 2004** Clear, bright colour; light-bodied,
with fresh, lively red fruits; not topped up with oak or over-extracted. Screwcap.
14° alc. **Rating** 87 **To** 2008 $18
Bosun's Blend Cabernet Shiraz 2005 A savoury, earthy, spicy array of complex
flavours; needs a touch more depth. Screwcap. **Rating** 87 **To** 2010 $9

Capel Vale ★★★★☆

Lot 5 Stirling Estate, Mallokup Road, Capel, WA 6271 **Region** Geographe
T (08) 9702 1012 **F** (08) 9727 1904 **www**.capelvale.com **Open** 7 days 10–4
Winemaker Justin Hearn, Elizabeth Richardson, Peter Pratten (Consultants) **Est.** 1974
Cases 100 000
Dr Peter Pratten's Capel Vale has expanded its viticultural empire to the point where it is entirely
an estate-run business, with 220 ha of vineyards spread through Mount Barker, Pemberton,
Margaret River and Geographe. Its wines cross every price point and style from fighting varietal
to ultra-premium; always known for its Riesling, powerful red wines are now very much part of
the portfolio. Exports to all major markets.

▼▼▼▼▼ **Margaret River Cabernet Sauvignon 2005** Medium-bodied wine, with fine,
spicy black fruits; excellent oak handling with silky and long tannins; lovely wine.
Gold medal National Wine Show '06. Screwcap. 14.9° alc. **Rating** 96 **To** 2025 $23

Capercaillie ★★★★★

4 Londons Road, Lovedale, NSW 2325 **Region** Lower Hunter Valley
T (02) 4990 2904 **www**.capercailliewine.com.au **Open** Mon–Sat 9–5, Sun 10–5
Winemaker Alasdair Sutherland, Daniel Binet **Est.** 1995 **Cases** 6000
The former Dawson Estate, now run by Hunter Valley veteran Alasdair Sutherland. The
Capercaillie wines are particularly well-made, with generous flavour. Following the example of
Brokenwood, its fruit sources are spread across southeastern Australia. Exports to the UK, NZ,
Japan and Singapore.

▼▼▼▼▼ **The Creel Hunter Valley Semillon 2006** Fresh and delicate, yet with
considerable length; passionfruit nuances are unusual; a clever interplay between
sweetness and acidity. Screwcap. 10° alc. **Rating** 94 **To** 2016 $19
Cuillin Chardonnay 2006 Complex and intense, a cut above the average for a
Hunter Valley chardonnay; a harmonious touch of barrel ferment on intense melon,
stone fruit and citrus; good length. Screwcap. 13.5° alc. **Rating** 94 **To** 2011 $21
The Ghillie Hunter Valley Shiraz 2005 A medium-bodied, finely crafted wine;
black and red fruits, with silky tannins and a long finish. Screwcap. 13.5° alc.
Rating 94 **To** 2019 $45

▼▼▼▼▽ **The Clan 2005** An elegant, savoury wine with the cabernet family flavours coming
through strongly; red fruits with a degree of underlying austerity. Cabernet Sauvignon
(50%, Hilltops)/Petit Verdot (30%, McLaren Vale)/Merlot (20%, Mudgee). Screwcap.
14° alc. **Rating** 91 **To** 2015 $28

ΨΨΨΨ **Slainte Semillon Sauvignon Blanc 2006** Quite fragrant; the blend works well, giving length, but I can't decide whether the sweetness works or not, and how much of it is fruit-derived. Screwcap. 11° alc. **Rating** 88 **To** 2008 $13
Mudgee Merlot 2005 Light- to medium-bodied; gently sweet cassis fruit, and fine, soft tannins, but doesn't excite. Screwcap. 14° alc. **Rating** 88 **To** 2012 $27
Hunter Valley Rose 2006 Bright colour; flavoursome and lengthened by good acidity. Cork. 13.5° alc. **Rating** 87 **To** 2008 $19

Captain's Paddock

18 Millers Road, Kingaroy, Qld 4610 **Region** South Burnett
T (07) 4162 4534 **F** (07) 4162 4502 www.captainspaddock.com.au **Open** 7 days 10–5
Winemaker Luke Fitzpatrick **Est.** 1995 **Cases** 1000
Don and Judy McCallum planted the first ha of vineyard in 1995, followed by a further 3.5 ha in 1996, focusing on shiraz and chardonnay. Their son Stuart built many unusual but practicable objects dotted around the property. In 2002 Maryanne Pidcock and Peter Eaton purchased the property, with business as usual thereafter.

ΨΨΨΨ **Verdelho 2005** While the flavours are essentially neutral, with light fruit salad overtones, the wine does have some structure and length. Screwcap. 13.5° alc. **Rating** 87 **To** 2008 $17

Captains Creek Organic Wines

160 Mays Road, Blampied, Vic 3364 **Region** Ballarat
T (03) 5345 7408 **F** (03) 5345 7408 www.captainscreek.com **Open** W'ends & public hols 11–5, or by appt
Winemaker Norman Latta, Kilchurn Wines (David Cowburn) **Est.** 1994 **Cases** 1000
Doug and Carolyn May are the third generation of farmers at the Captains Creek property, and have been conducting the business for over 20 years without using any chemicals. When they began establishing the vineyard in 1994, with 1.5 ha chardonnay and 0.5 ha pinot noir, they resolved to go down the same path: they use preventive spray programs of copper and sulphur, thermal flame weeding, and beneficial predatory insects to control weeds and mites.

Carbunup Crest Vineyard

PO Box 235, Busselton, WA 6280 **Region** Margaret River
T (08) 9754 2618 **F** (08) 9754 2618 www.carbunupcrestwines.com.au **Open** Not
Winemaker Flying Fish Cove **Est.** 1998 **Cases** 2000
Carbunup Crest is owned by the Meares family with Kris Meares managing the business. Initially it operated as a grapevine rootling nursery, but it has gradually converted to grapegrowing and winemaking. There are 6 ha of vineyard, all of which are all now in production, and plans to extend the plantings to 20 ha (the property is 53 ha in total). The contract-made wines are great value.

ΨΨΨΨΨ **Chardonnay 2005** Elegant; perfectly weighted and proportioned, its melon, apple and nectarine fruit supported and lengthened by very good acidity and subtle oak. Screwcap. 13.6° alc. **Rating** 94 **To** 2010 $18.25
Cella Rage Cabernet Sauvignon Merlot 2001 Ageing impressively; still full of vigour with layers of ripe cassis and blackcurrant fruit; nice oak. **Rating** 94 **To** 2016 $22.75
Cabernet Sauvignon 2002 A powerful wine, developing with grace; blackcurrant and cassis with touches of dark chocolate and mocha, fine tannins, and a long finish. Cork. 13.5° alc. **Rating** 94 **To** 2017 $21.50

ΨΨΨΨႳ **Shiraz 2004** Medium-bodied; elegant, supple and finer style, with red and black cherry fruit, fine tannins and balanced oak. 13.5° alc. **Rating** 92 **To** 2012 $19.75
Cabernet Merlot 2004 Medium-bodied and clean, with ample blackcurrant and spice fruit supported by notes of dark chocolate; fine, ripe tannins and well-judged oak. 13.8° alc. **Rating** 92 **To** 2014 $18.25

Semillon Sauvignon Blanc 2006 Spotlessly clean aromas; bright, fresh cut-grass and herb flavours with notes of lemon and citrus. 12.5° alc. **Rating** 90 **To** 2009 $17.25

Cardinham Estate ★★★★☆

Main North Road, Stanley Flat, SA 5453 **Region** Clare Valley
T (08) 8842 1944 **F** (08) 8842 1955 **Open** 7 days 10–5
Winemaker Scott Smith, Emma Bowley **Est.** 1981 **Cases** 4500
The Smith family has progressively increased the vineyard to its present level of 60 ha, the largest plantings being of cabernet sauvignon, shiraz and riesling. It entered into a grape supply contract with Wolf Blass, which led to an association with then Quelltaler winemaker Stephen John. The joint venture then formed has now terminated, and Cardinham is locating its 500-tonne winery on its Emerald Vineyard and using only estate-grown grapes. This has seen production rise, especially with the staples of Riesling, Cabernet Merlot and Stradbroke Shiraz. Exports to Singapore.

ΨΨΨΨΨ **Clare Valley Shiraz 2004** Plum, prune and blackberry aromas; a supple palate, with some spice added to the mix; fine tannins and good length. Screwcap. 13.5° alc. **Rating** 93 **To** 2019 $19.95
Clare Valley Cabernet Sauvignon 2004 Good varietal expression, with blackcurrant/cassis fruit supported by fine, lingering tannins, and good oak. Screwcap. 13.5° alc. **Rating** 93 **To** 2024 $19.95
Clare Valley Riesling 2006 Lemon/citrus blossom aromas; a long, clean and intense palate, with lingering, fine acidity. Screwcap. 11.7° alc. **Rating** 92 **To** 2016 $17.95

ΨΨΨΨ **Clare Valley Sangiovese 2005** A light- to medium-bodied, classic mix of red and sour cherry, plus spicy notes. Value. Screwcap. 14.3° alc. **Rating** 89 **To** 2008 $18
Clare Valley Chardonnay 2006 Well-made, particularly within the limitations of the Clare Valley; gentle stone fruit and all but invisible oak. Screwcap. 13.5° alc. **Rating** 88 **To** 2009 $17.95
Clare Valley Cabernet Merlot 2004 Medium-bodied; quite rich blackcurrant fruit sweetened further by oak; balanced tannins. Screwcap. 13.5° alc. **Rating** 88 **To** 2012 $17.95

Cargo Road Wines ★★★☆

Cargo Road, Orange, NSW 2800 **Region** Orange
T (02) 6365 6100 **F** (02) 6365 6001 www.cargoroadwines.com.au **Open** W'ends & public hols 11–5, or by appt
Winemaker James Sweetapple **Est.** 1983 **Cases** 3000
Originally called The Midas Tree, the vineyard was planted in 1984 by Roseworthy graduate John Swanson. When he established a 2.5-ha vineyard that included zinfandel, he was 15 years ahead of his time. The property was acquired in 1997 by Charles Lane, James Sweetapple and Brian Walters. Since then they have rejuvenated the original vineyard and planted more zinfandel, sauvignon blanc and cabernet.

ΨΨΨΨ **Orange Sauvignon Blanc 2006** Intriguing aromas of nettle, citrus, grass and mineral; good balance, but needs a touch more intensity. Screwcap. **Rating** 87 **To** 2008 $18

Carindale Wines ★★★☆

Palmers Lane, Pokolbin, NSW 2321 **Region** Lower Hunter Valley
T (02) 4998 7665 **F** (02) 4998 7065 www.carindalewines.com.au **Open** Fri–Mon 10–5
Winemaker Brian Walsh (Contract) **Est.** 1996 **Cases** 1500
Carindale draws upon 2 ha of chardonnay, 1.2 ha of cabernet franc and 0.2 ha of merlot (together with a few muscat vines). Exports to the US, Canada, Singapore and China.

Carlaminda Estate ★★★★

59 Richards Road, Ferguson, WA 6236 **Region** Geographe
T (08) 9728 3002 **F** (08) 9728 3002 www.carlaminda.com **Open** W'ends 11–4
Winemaker Siobhan Lynch **Est.** 2003 **Cases** 800
Quirinus Olsthoorn is primarily a cattle breeder, but has established 6 ha of semillon, shiraz, viognier and tempranillo on his property, the first plantings dating back to 1994. Until 2003 the grapes were sold, but since then district veteran Siobhan Lynch has made the wine.

ŶŶŶŶŶ **Ferguson Valley Geographe Shiraz Viognier 2004** Lively, fresh and vibrant cherry, raspberry and blackberry fruit with that distinctive viognier twist; good length and balance. Diam. 14° alc. **Rating** 92 **To** 2015 $22
Ferguson Valley Geographe Shiraz 2003 Holding hue well; a mix of vanilla/mocha oak, blackberry and plum, and oriental spice and pepper. Good length. Cork. 15° alc. **Rating** 90 **To** 2010 $16

ŶŶŶŶ **Reserve Ferguson Valley Geographe Semillon 2005** Twelve months in new and used French oak takes the process a step further towards the French white burgundy model; demands food. Screwcap. 14.5° alc. **Rating** 89 **To** 2010 $19
Ferguson Valley Geographe Semillon Sauvignon Blanc 2005 A nicely balanced mix of ripe citrus, cut grass and tropical flavours; good length and balance. Screwcap. 13° alc. **Rating** 89 **To** 2009 $16
Ferguson Valley Geographe Shiraz 2004 A pretty wine; an array of sweet red fruits similar to the Shiraz Viognier but on a smaller scale; fine tannins, with little oak evident. Diam. 14° alc. **Rating** 89 **To** 2013 $20
Ferguson Valley Geographe Semillon 2005 Good green-yellow; full-flavoured, but the soft mid-palate and slightly phenolic finish, emphasised by the high alcohol, are far from classic. Screwcap. 14.5° alc. **Rating** 87 **To** 2008 $17

Carlei Estate & Carlei Green Vineyards ★★★★★

1 Albert Road, Upper Beaconsfield, Vic 3808 **Region** Yarra Valley
T (03) 5944 4599 **F** (03) 5944 4599 www.carlei.com.au **Open** W'ends by appt
Winemaker Sergio Carlei **Est.** 1994 **Cases** 10 000
Carlei Estate has come a long way in a little time, with Sergio Carlei graduating from home winemaking in a suburban garage to his own (commercial) winery in Upper Beaconsfield, which falls just within the boundaries of the Yarra Valley. Along the way Carlei acquired a Bachelor of Wine Science from Charles Sturt University, and has established a 2.25-ha vineyard with organic and biodynamic accreditation adjacent to the Upper Beaconsfield winery. His contract winemaking services are now a major part of the business, and are a showcase for his extremely impressive winemaking talents. Exports to the US, Canada, China, Singapore and Malaysia.

ŶŶŶŶŶ **Green Vineyards Heathcote Shiraz 2004** Beautifully rounded, supple and smooth; red and black fruits are supported by fine tannins; flawless balance. Cork. 14.7° alc. **Rating** 95 **To** 2020 $29
Green Vineyards Yarra Valley Pinot Noir 2004 Rich, ripe damson plum fruit on a full, round and fleshy palate; very good balance, structure and length; somehow retains elegance. Diam. 13.5° alc. **Rating** 94 **To** 2011 $29
Estate Heathcote Nord Shiraz 2004 Potent, powerful black fruits, spice and licorice; built-in tannins are unobtrusive but definitely present. Cork. 14° alc. **Rating** 94 **To** 2020 $49
Tre Amici 2005 Notwithstanding the Diam, a whisper of reduction which, however, quickly fades in a rich and succulent array of red fruits; the oak has been cleverly used more to preserve fruit than impart flavour, and the tannins are soft. Sangiovese/Cabernet Sauvignon/Merlot. Diam. 15° alc. **Rating** 94 **To** 2015 $39

ŶŶŶŶŶ **Estate Heathcote Sud Shiraz 2004** More substantial, rounder and sweeter fruit than the Nord, with less evident tannin structure, which perhaps explains why the alcohol seems higher (when it isn't). Screwcap. 14° alc. **Rating** 93 **To** 2020 $49

Estate Tre Rossi 2005 No trace of reduction; a powerful wine with strong character and structure needing time to settle down and soften a little, but should come through with flying colours. Shiraz/Barbera/Nebbiolo. Diam. 14.7° alc. **Rating** 93 **To** 2018 $39

Estate Yarra Valley Chardonnay 2005 A complex wine with sweet nectarine and peach fruit; good length and acidity to balance the sweetness. Diam. 13.5° alc. **Rating** 90 **To** 2011

ŸŸŸŸ   **Tre Bianchi 2006** Clean and bright; abundant flavour featuring tropical through to citrus notes, balanced by a touch of sweetness on the finish which may or may not be accepted within the confines of the style. Screwcap. 13° alc. **Rating** 89 **To** 2011 $26

Green Vineyards Rose 2006 Has flavour with length and balance, not relying on residual sugar. Screwcap. 13.5° alc. **Rating** 88 **To** 2008 $25

Carosa   ★★★☆

310 Houston Street, Mt Helena, WA 6082 **Region** Perth Hills
T (08) 9572 1603 www.carosavineyard.com **Open** W'ends & hols 11–5, or by appt
Winemaker James Elson **Est.** 1984 **Cases** 2000
Many years ago, Jim Elson worked as a winemaker for Seppelt at Rutherglen, Barossa Valley and Great Western, before moving to WA with wife Carol and family. They named Carosa for their 3 daughters (Catherine, Rosemary and Sarah), and the latest range of wines is named after their 6 grandchildren. In 2000 a new café area was built overlooking the vineyard.

ŸŸŸŸ   **Lucian Merlot 2003** Holding hue well; is at the spicy/earthy/savoury edge of the varietal spectrum, the finish distinctly tart. Nonetheless, shows the potential of the Perth Hills, and is undeniably varietal. Diam. 13.5° alc. **Rating** 87 **To** 2010 $17

Casa Freschi

PO Box 45, Summertown, SA 5141 **Region** Langhorne Creek
T 0409 364 569 **F** (08) 8390 3232 www.casafreschi.com.au **Open** Not
Winemaker David Freschi **Est.** 1998 **Cases** 1000
David Freschi graduated with a degree in Oenology from Roseworthy College in 1991 and spent most of the decade working overseas in California, Italy and NZ. In 1998 he and his wife decided to trade in the corporate world for a small family-owned winemaking business, with a core of 2.5 ha of vines established by his parents in 1972; an additional 2 ha of nebbiolo have now been planted adjacent to the original vineyard. Says David, 'the names of the wines were chosen to best express the personality of the wines grown in our vineyard, as well as to express our heritage'. The establishment of a 3-ha vineyard in the Adelaide Hills began in 2004, with further plantings in 2005. Exports to the US and Canada.

ŸŸŸŸŸ   **La Signora 2004** A truly intriguing array of aromas, even more so the flavours; sour black cherries, anise, leather and spice, held together by a firm structure not common in Langhorne Creek. The wine could easily be identified (mistakenly, of course) as Italian in a blind judging, which is no doubt what David Freschi wishes to hear. Nebbiolo/Cabernet Sauvignon/Shiraz/Malbec. Cork. 14° alc. **Rating** 93 **To** 2029 $38

Cascabel

Rogers Road, Willunga, SA 5172 (postal) **Region** McLaren Vale
T (08) 8557 4434 **F** (08) 8557 4435 **Open** Not
Winemaker Susana Fernandez, Duncan Ferguson **Est.** 1997 **Cases** 2500
Cascabel's proprietors, Duncan Ferguson and Susana Fernandez, planted a 5 ha mosaic of southern Rhône and Spanish varieties. The choice of grapes reflects the winemaking experience of the proprietors in Australia, the Rhône Valley, Bordeaux, Italy, Germany and NZ – and also Susana Fernandez's birthplace, Spain. Production has moved steadily towards the style of the Rhône Valley, Rioja and other parts of Spain. Exports to the UK, the US, Switzerland, Japan and Spain.

⟡⟡⟡⟡⟡ **Eden Valley Riesling 2006** Lively, tart, spicy lemon/lemon-rind aromas; excellent minerality and length to the pure, bone-dry finish. Screwcap. 12° alc. **Rating** 94 To 2016 $23
Fleurieu Shiraz 2004 Medium-bodied; strong regional expression through dark chocolate and spice; has finesse; 550 cases. Screwcap. 14.5° alc. **Rating** 94 To 2015 $32

⟡⟡⟡⟡⟡ **Tipico McLaren Vale Grenache Monastrell Shiraz 2004** Savoury, spicy, leathery overtones to the black fruits; excellent texture and structure; fine-grained tannins, long finish. Screwcap. 14° alc. **Rating** 92 To 2014 $25
McLaren Vale Tempranillo Graciano 2004 Light- to medium-bodied; spicy/cedary/savoury characters take it out of the mainstream; super-fine tannins and quality French oak (18 months); 70%/30%. Cork. 14° alc. **Rating** 91 To 2012 $40
McLaren Vale Roussanne Viognier 2006 An interesting wine; a powerful palate with strong structure; some pear and apricot; good length; 50/50 blend. Screwcap. 13.5° alc. **Rating** 90 To 2011 $24

⟡⟡⟡⟡ **McLaren Vale Tempranillo 2006** Light- to medium-bodied; spice, cherry and strawberry fruit to both bouquet and palate; fine, slightly savoury tannins. Screwcap. 13.5° alc. **Rating** 89 To 2008 $20
McLaren Vale Monastrell 2004 Perfumed; in depth and structure more akin to Barossa Valley mourvedre, with juicy flavours and a spicy finish. (Monastrell, mataro and mourvedre are one and the same grape.) Cork. 15° alc. **Rating** 89 To 2011 $40

Casella Wines
★★★☆

Wakely Road, Yenda, NSW 2681 **Region** Riverina
T (02) 6961 3000 **F** (02) 6961 3099 **www**.casellawines.com.au **Open** Not
Winemaker Alan Kennett, Phillip Casella **Est.** 1969 **Cases** 12 million
One of the modern-day fairytale success stories, transformed overnight from a substantial, successful but non-charismatic business shown as making 650 000 cases in 2000. Its opportunity came when the US distribution of Lindemans Bin 65 Chardonnay was taken away from WJ Deutsch & Sons, leaving a massive gap in its portfolio, which was filled by yellow tail. It has built its US presence at a faster rate than any other wine or brand in history. A major plus in 2004 was Casella's capture of 2 most important trophies in Australia, Brisbane's Stodart and Melbourne's Jimmy Watson (both with unbottled wines, however). Exports to all major markets.

⟡⟡⟡⟡⟡ **Yendah Clare Valley Sangiovese 2005** Good, bright red-purple hue; abundant sweet black cherry/sour cherry/spice fruit; fine tannins, well-made. Screwcap. 14.5° alc. **Rating** 90 To 2011 $16
Yendah Goulburn Valley Durif 2005 Layered flavours of blackberry interleaved with chocolate; soft tannins; seductive wine. Screwcap. 14° alc. **Rating** 90 To 2009 $16

⟡⟡⟡⟡ **Yendah Riverina Pinot Grigio 2005** Sophisticated packaging and winemaking; bright acidity helps both length and flavour. Screwcap. 12.5° alc. **Rating** 87 To 2008 $16
Yendah Goulburn Valley Tempranillo 2005 Clear red; fresh, tangy fruit with some herb and mint notes; minimal oak. Screwcap. 14° alc. **Rating** 87 To 2010 $16

Cassegrain
★★★★

764, Fernbank Creek Road, Port Macquarie, NSW 2444 **Region** Hastings River
T (02) 6582 8377 **F** (02) 6582 8378 **www**.cassegrainwines.com.au **Open** 7 days 9–5
Winemaker John Cassegrain, Paul Pudner **Est.** 1980 **Cases** 60 000
In late 2005 Cassegrain and Simon Gilbert Wines merged their businesses. In the outcome, Simon Gilbert holds 70% of Cassegrain, the remainder held by John Cassegrain and associates. Winemaking will shift to Simon Gilbert, but the Cassegrain restaurant and cellar door will continue as before. Exports to Ireland, Germany, Denmark, Sweden, Slovakia, Japan, Thailand, Vanuatu, NZ and Canada.

Castagna

88 Ressom Lane, Beechworth, Vic 3747 **Region** Beechworth
T (03) 5728 2888 **F** (03) 5728 2898 **www.**castagna.com.au **Open** By appt
Winemaker Julian Castagna **Est.** 1997 **Cases** 2000
The elegantly labelled wines of Castagna will ultimately come from 4 ha of biodynamically managed estate shiraz and viognier being established (the latter making up 15% of the total). Winemaker Julian Castagna is intent on making wines which reflect the terroir as closely as possible, and declines to use cultured yeast or filtration. Genesis Syrah deserves its icon status.

Castle Rock Estate

Porongurup Road, Porongurup, WA 6324 **Region** Porongurup
T (08) 9853 1035 **F** (08) 9853 1010 **www.**castlerockestate.com.au **Open** Mon–Fri 10–4, w'ends & public hols 10–5
Winemaker Robert Diletti **Est.** 1983 **Cases** 4000
An exceptionally beautifully sited vineyard, winery and cellar door sales area on a 55-ha property with sweeping vistas from the Porongurups, operated by the Diletti family. The standard of viticulture is very high, and the site itself ideally situated (quite apart from its beauty). The 2-level winery, set on the natural slope, maximises gravity flow, in particular for crushed must feeding into the press. The Rieslings have always been elegant and have handsomely repaid time in bottle; the Pinot Noir is the most consistent performer in the region.

ȚȚȚȚȚ **Riesling 2006** A flowery, aromatic lime blossom bouquet; beautifully delineated varietal character of lime juice and passionfruit on the long palate. Two trophies Sydney Wine Show '07. Screwcap. 12.5° alc. **Rating** 96 **To** 2018 $20
Riesling 2005 A powdery/talcy/spicy bouquet; explodes on the palate with a mix of citrus and more tropical fruit flavours, then crunchy acidity on a long finish. Screwcap. 13° alc. **Rating** 95 **To** 2018 $18

ȚȚȚȚ? **Pinot Noir 2004** Light, bright red–purple; fragrant and elegant red cherry and strawberry fruit; a long, lingering finish, texture around the corner. Screwcap. 12.5° alc. **Rating** 92 **To** 2010 $23
Sauvignon Blanc 2005 An attractive light- to medium-bodied wine with passionfruit and gooseberry flavours, then a bright, dry finish. Screwcap. 14° alc. **Rating** 90 **To** 2008 $17
Shiraz 2004 Clear red–purple; fragrant, almost into blossom, aromas followed by a medium-bodied palate offering black cherry, plum and a nice touch of spice. Cork. 14.5° alc. **Rating** 90 **To** 2012 $19

ȚȚȚȚ **Cabernet Merlot 2001** Light- to medium-bodied; as elegant as always; not forced, and the savoury notes do not overwhelm the latent sweetness in the fruit; balanced finish. Cork. 13.5° alc. **Rating** 89 **To** 2011 $22
Sauvignon Blanc 2006 No reduction; fresh, crisp and well-made, but not enough interest in the fruit flavours. Screwcap. 12.5° alc. **Rating** 88 **To** 2008 $18

 # Casuarina Estate

NR

1014 Hermitage Road, Pokolbin, NSW 2320 **Region** Lower Hunter Valley
T (02) 4998 7888 **F** (02) 4998 7692 **www.**casuarinainn.com.au **Open** 7 days 5–6
Winemaker Mark Davidson (Contract) **Est.** 1980 **Cases** NA
The Casuarina Estate property, including restaurant and accommodation, was established by Peter Meier, well known for his cooking abilities at the Rothbury Estate in the 1970s. It is now owned by Ken and Maureen Brittliff, who now run 5-star luxury accommodation with 9 fantasy theme suites to complement the restaurant.

Catherine Vale Vineyard ★★★★

656 Milbrodale Road, Bulga, NSW 2330 **Region** Lower Hunter Valley
T (02) 6579 1334 **F** (02) 6579 1299 **www**.catherinevale.com.au **Open** W'ends &
public hols 10–5, or by appt
Winemaker Hunter Wine Services (John Hordern) **Est.** 1994 **Cases** 1200
Former schoolteachers Bill and Wendy Lawson have established Catherine Vale as a not-so-idle
retirement venture. Part of the production from the 5.8-ha vineyard is sold to contract winemaker
John Hordern; the remainder is vinified for the Catherine Vale label. Exports to Germany.

ŶŶŶŶŶ   **Hunter Valley Semillon 2005** Bright, clear colour; touches of lemon and herb,
and a long finish. Screwcap. 11.5° alc. **Rating** 91 **To** 2015 $14
Hunter Valley Chardonnay 2005 Considerable weight to the peach, nectarine
and pear fruit, the alcohol intruding just a little; balanced oak. Screwcap. 14° alc.
Rating 90 **To** 2010 $16

ŶŶŶŶ   **Semillon Chardonnay 2005** Round, soft peachy fruit from the chardonnay does
much of the flavour talking, semillon provides the structure and the alcohol balance.
Screwcap. 12.5° alc. **Rating** 88 **To** 2009 $14
Hunter Valley Verdelho 2005 Well-made; typical varietal fruit salad flavours;
well-balanced, and shows the vintage to advantage. Screwcap. 14.5° alc. **Rating** 88
To 2008 $14
Winifred Barbera 2005 Light-bodied, but quite savoury and spicy; enough to
catch and retain interest in the palate. Screwcap. 13.5° alc. **Rating** 87 **To** 2008 $18

Cavalier Crest ★★★★

Davis Road, Rosa Glen, WA 6285 **Region** Margaret River
T (08) 9757 5091 **F** (08) 9757 5091 **www**.cavaliercrest.com.au **Open** 7 days 10–5
Winemaker Andrew Gaman (Contract) **Est.** 1978 **Cases** 3000
The Halcyon Vineyard, as it is known locally, was established in 1978 with the planting of a little
under 5 ha of cabernet sauvignon, merlot, pinot noir, chardonnay and semillon. Graham and Sue
Connell purchased the property in 1991, increasing the plantings to 8 ha with more pinot noir,
cabernet sauvignon and merlot. Exports to Hong Kong.

ŶŶŶŶŶ   **Margaret River Chardonnay 2005** Elegant wine, sharing many of the
characteristics of the '06, but has superior mouthfeel and balance, characters which
the '06 may develop in time. Screwcap. 13.1° alc. **Rating** 93 **To** 2010 $25
Margaret River Semillon 2005 Almost a carbon copy of the '06; developing
slowly but surely; buy some of each. Screwcap. 12° alc. **Rating** 91 **To** 2012 $18
Margaret River Chardonnay 2006 Stone fruit and melon aromas and flavours;
perfectly balanced and integrated French oak comes through on the mid- to back-
palate, the wine finishing with citrussy acidity. Screwcap. 13.3° alc. **Rating** 91
To 2011 $25
Margaret River Semillon 2006 Pronounced herb/lanolin/lemon aromas; good
length, depth, line and balance; no frills, and classic each way bet for drinking now or
cellaring. Screwcap. 12.8° alc. **Rating** 90 **To** 2013 $18

ŶŶŶŶ   **Margaret River Pinot Noir 2004** Strongly varietal aromas of olive, bracken and
leaf plus red fruits; those savoury characters largely dominate the palate and raise the
question whether the grapes were picked a little early, with sharp acidity underlining
that question. Screwcap. 13.5° alc. **Rating** 89 **To** 2013 $28
Margaret River Cabernet Sauvignon 2004 Savoury/leafy/earthy aromas in
apparently typical Cavalier Crest mould; the palate, too, is defiant, daring you to
come and drink me. Screwcap. 13.5° alc. **Rating** 88 **To** 2015 $25

Ceccanti Kiewa Valley Wines ★★★☆

Bay Creek Lane, Mongans Bridge, Vic 3691 **Region** Alpine Valleys
T (03) 5754 5236 **F** (03) 5754 5353 **www**.ceccanti.com.au **Open** 7 days 11-5
Winemaker Angelo, Moya and Danny Ceccanti **Est.** 1988 **Cases** NA

Angelo and Moya Ceccanti, with son Danny, have established 16 ha of vines, and now use all the production for their wines, which are made onsite by the family. Angelo, raised in Tuscany, had extensive exposure to viticulture and winemaking, and Moya and Danny have the technical knowledge.

Cedar Creek Estate

104–144 Hartley Road, Mt Tamborine, Qld 4272 **Region** Queensland Coastal
T (07) 5545 1666 **F** (07) 5545 4762 **www**.cedarcreekestate.com.au **Open** 7 days 10–4
Winemaker Peter Scudamore-Smith **Est.** 2000 **Cases** 1500
Cedar Creek Estate takes its name from the creek which flows through the property at an altitude of 550 m on Mt Tamborine. A 3.7-ha vineyard is planted to chambourcin and verdelho, and is supplemented by grapes grown elsewhere. The focus will always be on general tourism, with a host of facilities for visitors, including a restaurant; it also offers wines from Ballandean Estate.

Celestial Bay

33 Welwyn Avenue, Manning, WA 6152 (postal) **Region** Margaret River
T (08) 9450 4191 **F** (08) 9313 1544 **www**.celestialbay.com.au **Open** Not
Winemaker Bernard Abbott **Est.** 1999 **Cases** 6000
Michael and Kim O'Brien had a background of farming in the Chittering Valley when they purchased their 104-ha property. It is very much a family enterprise, with son Aaron studying Viticulture and Oenology at Curtin University, and daughter Daneka involved in marketing and sales. Under the direction of vineyard manager Sam Juniper, 50 ha of vines have been rapidly planted. The plantings are totally logical: semillon and sauvignon blanc (13 ha); chardonnay (13 ha); shiraz (6 ha); and cabernet sauvignon, merlot, malbec and petit verdot (18 ha). Winemaker Bernard Abbott celebrates his 23rd Margaret River vintage in 2008.

ŸŸŸŸŸ **Margaret River Cabernet Merlot 2003** Clean, pure; medium-bodied blackcurrant/redcurrant mix; excellent balance, length and texture; fine tannins. Cork. 14° alc. **Rating** 94 **To** 2015 $19.99
Margaret River Cabernet Sauvignon 2003 Very much in the vineyard style; medium-bodied, with clear-cut varietal fruit and sustained but ripe tannin support; quality French oak. Cork. 14° alc. **Rating** 94 **To** 2017 $19.99

ŸŸŸŸŸ **Margaret River Semillon Sauvignon Blanc 2005** A voluminous bouquet leads into a powerful mix of slate, grass and lemon; excellent structure. Screwcap. 14° alc. **Rating** 93 **To** 2010 $17
Margaret River Shiraz 2003 Aromatic red and black fruit and spice mix; a vibrant, tangy edge to the palate, yet in no way green; controlled extract. Cork. 14° alc. **Rating** 91 **To** 2012 $20
Margaret River Shiraz 2004 Retaining hue well; medium-bodied, smooth, supple mouthfeel; plum, spice and blackberry flavours; good tannins and length. Screwcap. 14.5° alc. **Rating** 90 **To** 2013 $20
Margaret River Cabernet Sauvignon 2004 Carries the oak far more convincingly than the Cabernet Merlot, though still evident, along with cassis and blackcurrant fruit. Cork. 14.5° alc. **Rating** 90 **To** 2015 $20

ŸŸŸŸ **Margaret River Semillon Sauvignon Blanc 2006** Crisp, clean, lively and delicate; the semillon is dominant, partly reflected in the low alcohol; flavour will grow with age. Screwcap. 11.5° alc. **Rating** 89 **To** 2011 $16
Goose Chase Margaret River Rose 2006 Delicate but precise nuances of cassis and raspberry; good balance and finish; good value. Cabernet Sauvignon. Screwcap. 13.5° alc. **Rating** 88 **To** 2008 $12
Margaret River Cabernet Merlot 2004 Vanillin oak outweighs the fruit, and doesn't look as if it will come into balance. Some won't mind, however. Screwcap. 14.5° alc. **Rating** 88 **To** 2011 $20

Cellante Wines   ★★★☆

8 Willmette Court, Lilydale, Vic 3140 (postal) **Region** Yarra Valley
T 0409 940 188 **F** (03) 9735 5704 **Open** Not
Winemaker Tokar Estate (Paul Evans) **Est.** 1997 **Cases** 900
Dominic and Karen Cellante have established their vineyard on the corner of Melba Highway
and Rudduck Lane, Coldstream. They planted 1 ha each of cabernet sauvignon and chardonnay,
and were content to sell the grapes until prices started falling, which led to the establishment of
the Cellante Wines label, and the retention of Paul Evans as contract winemaker.

♟♟♟♟ **Yarra Valley Chardonnay 2005** Still fresh and bright; fruit-driven by melon,
stone fruit and a touch of fig; long, firm finish. Cork. 13.5° alc. **Rating** 89
To 2012 $15.95

Cellarmasters   ★★★★

Cnr Barossa Valley Way/Siegersdorf Road, Tanunda, SA 5352 **Region** Barossa Valley
T (08) 8561 2200 **F** (08) 8561 2299 **www**.cellarmasters.com.au **Open** Not
Winemaker Nick Badrice, John Schwartzkopff, Sally Blackwell, Neil Doddridge,
Mark Starick **Est.** 1982 **Cases** 800 000
The Cellarmasters Group was acquired by Fosters in 1997. Dorrien Estate is the physical base of
the vast Cellarmasters network which, wearing its retailer's hat, is by far the largest direct-sale
outlet in Australia. It buys substantial quantities of wine from other makers either in bulk or as
cleanskin (unlabelled bottles), or with recognisable but subtly different labels of the producers
concerned. It also makes wine on its own account at Dorrien Estate, many of which are quite
excellent, and of trophy quality. Chateau Dorrien is an entirely unrelated business. Purchased by
private equity firm Archer Capital in April '07.

♟♟♟♟♟ **Black Wattle Vineyard Coonawarra Cabernet Sauvignon 2005** Classic
regional cabernet sauvignon flavour and structure; austere but classy; long finish.
Screwcap. 15° alc. **Rating** 94 **To** 2015 $35.95

Centennial Vineyards   ★★★★★

'Woodside', Centennial Road, Bowral, NSW 2576 **Region** Southern Highlands
T (02) 4861 8700 **F** (02) 4681 8777 **www**.centennial.net.au **Open** 7 days 10–5
Winemaker Tony Cosgriff **Est.** 2002 **Cases** 10 000
Centennial Vineyards is a substantial development jointly owned by wine professional John Large
and investor Mark Dowling, covering 133 ha of beautiful grazing land, with 31 ha planted to
sauvignon blanc, riesling, verdelho, chardonnay, albarino, pinot gris, pinot noir, pinot meunier,
cabernet sauvignon and tempranillo. Production from the estate vineyards is supplemented by
purchases of grapes from other regions, including Orange. Exports to the US, China and Korea.

♟♟♟♟♟ **Woodside Single Vineyard Riesling 2006** Fragrant lemon and lime blossom
aromas; pure and intense, with impeccable line and length; right up there with
the best in Australia. Screwcap. 11° alc. **Rating** 95 **To** 2016 $19

♟♟♟♟♟ **Bowral Extreme Brut NV** No dosage at all; lively pear, apple, citrus and
strawberry flavours vindicate the zero dosage approach; remarkable winemaking
achievement. Pinot Noir/Chardonnay. 11.5° alc. **Rating** 91 **To** 2010 $30
Woodside Single Vineyard Sauvignon Blanc 2006 No sweatiness or
reduction; despite the low alcohol, has more positive fruit than the Reserve; light
tropical passionfruit flavours, and not reliant on residual sugar. Screwcap. 12° alc.
Rating 90 **To** 2008 $20
Woodside Unwooded Chardonnay 2005 Perfectly balanced nectarine, citrus
and melon fruit; good acidity and length. Screwcap. 13° alc. **Rating** 90 **To** 2008 $19
Reserve Single Vineyard Pinot Gris 2006 A long and quite intense flavour,
though far from typical; citrus, pear and melon run through to a lively finish; clever
winemaking. Southern Highlands. Screwcap. 13.4° alc. **Rating** 90 **To** 2008 $23

Bong Bong Sauvignon Blanc Chardonnay 2006 Sauvignon blanc comes through strongly, the blend working well, with the chardonnay adding a substrate of peach and melon; unoaked style. Screwcap. 11° alc. **Rating** 90 **To** 2009 $17

Reserve Single Vineyard Pinot Noir 2005 An aromatic mix of red fruit, with savoury, spicy, briary, foresty components; the palate follows down a similar track; very complex, perhaps a little too much so. Screwcap. 13.4° alc. **Rating** 90 **To** 2011 $27

Reserve Single Vineyard Tempranillo 2004 Has more savoury, earthy characters than most; tobacco isn't far off the mark (Cosgriff's contribution via the back label). The tannins are well above average, though by no means rough. Hilltops. Cork. 14° alc. **Rating** 90 **To** 2011 $30

ＹＹＹＹ **Reserve Single Vineyard Sauvignon Blanc 2006** Spotlessly clean and totally correct in terms of balance, texture and length, but lacks definitive varietal fruit; give it a year or 2 and hope the positive citrussy acidity will hold things together. Orange. Screwcap. 12.7° alc. **Rating** 89 **To** 2008 $25

Woodside Single Vineyard Verdelho 2006 Plenty of fruit salad flavours, and redeeming citrussy acidity. Screwcap. 13° alc. **Rating** 89 **To** 2010 $19

Woodside Single Vineyard Pinot Noir 2005 A very different style to the Reserve, less complex, but also less challenging; fair varietal character overall, and nicely made. Screwcap. 13.5° alc. **Rating** 89 **To** 2009 $22

Woodside Single Vineyard Tempranillo 2005 Light- to medium-bodied, but shows the ever-changing face of tempranillo – one moment sweet cherry, the next tamarillo, the next something quite different again, but always an echo of citrus. Has structure, too. Screwcap. 13.2° alc. **Rating** 89 **To** 2012 $20

Finale Bowral Late Harvest Semillon 2005 Less extreme than some Riverina botrytis semillons; the usual apricot, cumquat, mandarin spectrum; balanced acidity. Screwcap. 11.5° alc. **Rating** 89 **To** 2008 $23

Woodside Single Vineyard Chardonnay 2005 Curiously, while more complex and bigger-bodied than the Woodside unwooded version with riper fruit, comes through as a slightly old-fashioned style. Screwcap. 13.2° alc. **Rating** 88 **To** 2008 $22

Bong Bong Shiraz Tempranillo Cabernet Sauvignon 2006 Brightly coloured light- to medium-bodied and equally brightly flavoured; ideal for lunch at the Bong Bong Picnic Races. Screwcap. 14° alc. **Rating** 87 **To** 2008 $17

Ceravolo Wines

Suite 16, 172 Glynburn Road, Tranmere, SA 5073 (postal) **Region** Adelaide Plains
T (08) 8336 4522 **F** (08) 8365 0538 **www**.ceravolo.com.au **Open** Not
Winemaker Colin Glaetzer, Ben Glaetzer (Contract) **Est.** 1985 **Cases** 20 000
Joe Ceravolo, dental surgeon-turned-vigneron, and wife Heather have been producing single-vineyard wines from their family-owned estate since 1999, centred around Shiraz, but with Chardonnay and Merlot in support. Conspicuous success at the London International Wine Challenge led both to exports and the registration of the Adelaide Plains region under the GI legislation. Wines are released under the Ceravolo, St Andrews Estate and Red Earth labels. Exports to the UK, the US and other major markets.

ＹＹＹＹＹ **Adelaide Plains Petit Verdot 2004** Dense colour; rich, opulent black fruits, ripe tannins and controlled oak. The variety responds very well to warm growing conditions. Cork. 14° alc. **Rating** 91 **To** 2014 $25

Adelaide Plains Shiraz 2004 Strong colour; powerful, earthy blackberry fruits; overall with a certain austerity, but that is a plus rather than a minus. Cork. 13.5° alc. **Rating** 90 **To** 2014 $22

ＹＹＹＹ **Adelaide Hills Pinot Grigio 2006** Elegant and lively; slightly atypical citrus flavours do the talking; dry, crisp, finish. Screwcap. 13.6° alc. **Rating** 89 **To** 2008 $17.95

The Raconteur Reserve Adelaide Hills Late Harvest Shiraz 2006 Deep purple-red; dense, dark depth of richest chocolate and blueberry pudding imaginable; this is enough to turn Sunday communion or mass into a major party. **Rating** 89 **To** 2008 $17.95

Adelaide Plains Sangiovese Rose 2006 Spicy cherry nuances attest to the varietal character; light-bodied, but not sweet; would be enhanced by being chilled as if it were a white wine. Screwcap. 13.5° alc. **Rating** 88 **To** 2008 $17.95

Red Earth Shiraz 2004 A little sharp around the edges, needing more aerative (micro-oxygenation) handling. Twin top. 14° alc. **Rating** 87 **To** 2010 $17

Ceres Bridge Estate ★★★☆

84 Merrawarp Road, Stonehaven, Vic 3221 **Region** Geelong
T (03) 5271 1200 **F** (03) 5271 1200 **Open** W'ends 12–5
Winemaker Challon Murdock **Est.** 1996 **Cases** 500

Challon and Patricia Murdock began the long, slow, and at times very frustrating process of establishing their vineyard in 1996. They planted 1.8 ha of chardonnay in that year, but 50% of the vines died over the next 2 years in the face of drought and inadequate water supply. Instead of turning away and deciding it was all too difficult, they persevered by planting 1.2 ha of pinot noir in 2000, with replanting in '01, and then in '05 signified the intention to become serious by planting between 0.5 ha and 1 ha each of shiraz, nebbiolo, sauvignon blanc, viognier, tempranillo and pinot grigio.

ⵐⵐⵐⵐⵐ **Geelong Chardonnay 2004** Aromatic citrus and stone fruit, with good oak balance and integration on the long palate. Screwcap. 13.2° alc. **Rating** 92 **To** 2011 $16.50

ⵐⵐⵐⵐ **Lightly Oaked Geelong Chardonnay 2004** Light-bodied melon and stone fruit, the oak little more than a whisper; nice finish. Screwcap. 13.2° alc. **Rating** 87 **To** 2009 $15

Chain of Ponds ★★★★★

Adelaide Road, Gumeracha, SA 5233 **Region** Adelaide Hills
T (08) 8389 1415 **Open** Mon–Fri 9.30–4.30, w'ends & public hols 10.30–4.30
Winemaker Greg Clack **Est.** 1993 **Cases** 30 000

Chain of Ponds is the largest grower in the Adelaide Hills, with 100 ha of vines at Gumeracha and 120 ha at Kersbrook, producing 1000 tonnes of grapes a year. Almost all are sold to other wineries, but a significant amount of wine is made under the Chain of Ponds label; these enjoy consistent show success. Exports to the UK, the US, Canada and Singapore.

ⵐⵐⵐⵐⵐ **The Amadeus Cabernet Sauvignon 2002** Rich, juicy cassis and blackcurrant fruit; fine, ripe tannins and good oak; very impressive. Cork. 14° alc. **Rating** 95 **To** 2020 $30

The Red Semi Semillon 2005 Clean, crisp and zesty, with touches of lemon rind and mineral; a particularly long finish; will develop well. Screwcap. 12° alc. **Rating** 94 **To** 2013 $20

ⵐⵐⵐⵐⵐ **Black Thursday Adelaide Hills Sauvignon Blanc 2006** Not a whisper of reduction; attractive passionfruit/tropical/grass mix, with a long finish. Screwcap. 13° alc. **Rating** 93 **To** 2008 $19

Grave's Gate Shiraz 2004 Showing some development; spicy, earthy overtones to raspberry and blackberry fruit on the medium-bodied palate; fine tannins. Adelaide Hills/Kangaroo Island. Screwcap. 14° alc. **Rating** 90 **To** 2012 $19

Adelaide Hills Sangiovese 2004 Has spicy, cherry fruit plus touches of mocha and vanilla; fine, savoury tannins; more interest and length than many examples. Screwcap. 14° alc. **Rating** 90 **To** 2010 $22

ⵐⵐⵐⵐ **Black Thursday Adelaide Hills Sauvignon Blanc 2005** Spotlessly clean, with tropical/gooseberry/passionfruit flavours, but a slight lack of focus and drive. Screwcap. 13° alc. **Rating** 89 **To** 2008 $20

The Corkscrew Road Chardonnay 2003 Rich stone fruit and yellow peach; perfect balance and excellent use of oak; developing slowly; impressive. Cork. 14° alc. **Rating** 89 **To** 2008 $25
Novello Rosso 2006 Intensely perfumed roses and wild flowers; a delicate palate, albeit with fresh-picked fruit flavours. Screwcap. 12.5° alc. **Rating** 89 **To** 2008 $15
Purple Patch Adelaide Hills Riesling 2006 Unusually soft and accessible, with sweetness evident from start to finish running through the tropical citrus fruit. Screwcap. 12.5° alc. **Rating** 88 **To** 2008 $19

Chalice Bridge Estate ★★★★☆

796 Rosa Glen Road, Margaret River, WA 6285 **Region** Margaret River
T (08) 9388 6088 **F** (08) 9382 1887 **www**.chalicebridge.com.au **Open** By appt
Winemaker Bob Cartwright **Est.** 1998 **Cases** 25 000
Planting of the vineyard began in 1998; there are now over 28 ha each of cabernet sauvignon and shiraz, 27 ha of chardonnay, 12.5 ha of semillon, 18 ha sauvignon blanc and 7 ha merlot, making up the total plantings of 122 ha; it is the second-largest single vineyard in Margaret River. The 2006 appointment of former Leeuwin Estate senior winemaker Bob Cartwright was major news, adding thrust to a growing business. Exports to the UK, the US and other major markets.

ŶŶŶŶŶ **Margaret River Sauvignon Blanc 2006** Light green-yellow; delicate and lively bouquet followed by a tangy minerally/grassy/gooseberry-flavoured palate; long finish. Screwcap. 13° alc. **Rating** 93 **To** 2008 $16
Margaret River Semillon Sauvignon Blanc 2006 Lemon zest, grass and spice aromas; long and clean, with a dry, lively finish. Screwcap. 11.5° alc. **Rating** 90 **To** 2010 $16

Chalk Hill

PO Box 205, McLaren Vale, SA 5171 **Region** McLaren Vale
T (08) 8556 2121 **F** (08) 8556 2221 **www**.chalkhill.com.au **Open** Not
Winemaker Emmanuelle Requin-Bekkers **Est.** 1973 **Cases** 5000
Chalk Hill is in full flight again, drawing upon the 3 vineyards (Slate Creek, Wits End and Chalk Hill) of grapegrowing owners John and Di Harvey. There has been considerable work on the Chalk Hill home vineyard: part has been retrellised, and riesling has been replaced by new plantings of shiraz and cabernet sauvignon, plus small amounts of barbera and sangiovese. Exports to all major markets; exports to the US and Canada under the Wits End label.

ŶŶŶŶŶ **The Procrastinator Cabernet Franc 2006** Bright and fresh redcurrant, red cherry and raspberry fruits, and the finest possible tannin support. Screwcap. 14° alc. **Rating** 90 **To** 2008 $15

Chalkers Crossing

285 Grenfell Road, Young, NSW 2594 **Region** Hilltops
T (02) 6382 6900 **F** (02) 6382 5068 **www**.chalkerscrossing.com.au **Open** 7 days 10–4
Winemaker Celine Rousseau **Est.** 2000 **Cases** 7000
Owned and operated by Ted and Wendy Ambler, Chalkers Crossing is near Young, where the first vines were planted at the Rockleigh vineyard in late 1997, with follow-up plantings in 1998 lifting the total to 10 ha. It also purchases grapes from Tumbarumba and Gundagai. Winemaker Celine Rousseau was born in France's Loire Valley, trained in Bordeaux and has worked in Bordeaux, Champagne, Languedoc, Margaret River and the Perth Hills, an eclectic mix of climates if ever there was one. This Flying Winemaker (now an Australian citizen) has exceptional skills and dedication. Exports to the UK, Sweden, France, China, Singapore and Japan.

ŶŶŶŶŶ **Hilltops Riesling 2005** A spotlessly clean bouquet leads into a delicious palate with ripe citrus fruits on entry, flowing through to minerally acidity on the finish; very good length. Screwcap. 12.5° alc. **Rating** 95 **To** 2020 $18

Tumbarumba Chardonnay 2005 Still incredibly pale; very interesting aromas, far from typical, more to melon, apple and nectarine and less grapefruit and citrus; oak invisibly mended with the fruit; will be very long-lived; Chablis style. Screwcap. 14° alc. **Rating** 94 **To** 2020 $22

Hilltops Shiraz 2005 Fragrant blackberry and plum aromas are repeated on the deep and very well-structured palate; ripe and round, with very good tannins and oak; fermentation finished in barrel. Cork. 14.5° alc. **Rating** 94 **To** 2015 $25

ΨΨΨΨΨ **Hilltops Riesling 2006** Lime and apple blossom aromas lead into a firm palate in the citrus spectrum; good length and balance. Screwcap. 12.5° alc. **Rating** 92 **To** 2016 $18

Hilltops Semillon 2005 A clean bouquet with expressive though delicate aromas; a lively, zesty, minerally palate with perfectly integrated oak in the background; lemony fruit to the fore. Screwcap. 13.5° alc. **Rating** 92 **To** 2011 $18

Tumbarumba Pinot Noir 2005 Clean, fresh and moderately intense cherry and plum fruit; crisp acidity, but not particularly complex. Twin top. 13.5° alc. **Rating** 90 **To** 2010 $22

ΨΨΨΨ **Tumbarumba Sauvignon Blanc 2006** Clean, crisp and correct; pleasant tropical fruit flavours, but lacks intensity. Screwcap. 13.5° alc. **Rating** 88 **To** 2020 $18

Chalmers

PO Box 84, Euston, NSW 2737 **Region** Murray Darling
T 0400 261 932 **F** (03) 5026 3228 **www.**murraydarlingcollection.com.au **Open** Not
Winemaker Sandro Mosele (Contract) **Est.** 1989 **Cases** 4000
This is the project of Bruce and Jenny Chalmers, who run the largest vine nursery propagation business in Australia, formerly called Murray Darling Collection. As well as supplying rootlings to vignerons all over Australia, the Chalmers have established substantial plantings of a range of varietals, running from mainstream to rare. By using fine, misty water sprays, Chalmers is able to radically reduce the canopy temperatures in summer, achieving unexpected results with varieties which theoretically require a far cooler climate. A strongly branded Chalmers range has been introduced focusing on cutting-edge Italian varietals; it will be several years yet before definitive quality judgements about these varieties (grown nowhere else in Australia) can be made. The wines are made in the Mornington Peninsula by Sandro Mosele.

ΨΨΨΨΨ **Lagrein 2005** A very deep colour, as expected for the variety; has considerable depth and generosity, with abundant black cherry, prune and plum. Diam. 14.5° alc. **Rating** 90 **To** 2012 $25

ΨΨΨΨ **Project Wine Malvasia Istriana 2005** Has positive fruit flavours; some shades of viognier, almost into dried fruits; of definite interest. Diam. 13.5° alc. **Rating** 87 **To** 2008 $22

Murray Cod Vermentino 2005 Has presence, partly through some bottle development; ripe stone fruit and apple, with a touch of fruit spice; not sweet, and has good length. Diam. 12.5° alc. **Rating** 87 **To** 2008 $22

Aglianico 2004 Light coloured, an expressive bouquet with strawberry flowers, and light-bodied flavours in the same vein. Diam. 12.5° alc. **Rating** 87 **To** 2010 $28

Project Wine Sagrantino 2004 Light, but slightly deeper than Aglianico; wild herbs and oriental spices, plus largely hidden tannins until they bite like a hidden snake. Cork. 13.5° alc. **Rating** 87 **To** 2011 $25

Chambers Rosewood

Barkly Street, Rutherglen, Vic 3685 **Region** Rutherglen
T (02) 6032 8641 **www.**chambersrosewood.com.au **Open** Mon–Sat 9–5, Sun 11–5
Winemaker Bill Chambers, Stephen Chambers **Est.** 1858 **Cases** 20 000
I happen to know that Bill Chambers declines to provide samples of his Rare Muscat and Tokay to Robert Parker, so do not feel the least miffed that I should likewise be deprived, but,

consistently with my (further amended) winery rating system, I only rate the wines I taste, not those I remember or have precious, part-consumed bottles of. Hence the demotion from 5 stars to 3.5 stars. The irony is that the table wines are better than they have ever been previously. Exports to all major markets.

ŶŶŶŶ   **Anton Ruche Rutherglen Shiraz + Mondeuse 2004** A fresh and lively mix of blackcurrant and raspberry fruit; brisk acidity, fine tannins and minimal oak. Anton Ruche was the winemaker whose stocks were acquired by WH Chambers over 100 years ago, and whose name appeared on invoices until quite recently. Screwcap. 14.5° alc. **Rating** 89 **To** 2015 $15
Rutherglen Shiraz 2002 Ample blackberry and plum fruit; good tannin structure, and very good value. Why weren't such table wines made many years ago? Cork. 14.8° alc. **Rating** 88 **To** 2012 $10
Rutherglen Gouais 2004 Lively and fresh, driven by tingling acidity, possibly from the low alcohol. One of only 3 gouais vineyards in the world, having disappeared from France, and one of the parents of chardonnay when on one dark night it had an affair with pinot noir. Screwcap. 11.8° alc. **Rating** 88 **To** 2010 $12

Charles Cimicky   ★★★★☆

Gomersal Road, Lyndoch, SA 5351 **Region** Barossa Valley
T (08) 8524 4025 **F** (08) 8524 4772 **Open** Tues–Sat 10.30–4.30
Winemaker Charles Cimicky **Est.** 1972 **Cases** 15 000
These wines are of very good quality, thanks to the sophisticated use of new oak in tandem with high-quality grapes. It must be said that Charles Cimicky is not a great correspondent, nor liberal with his distribution of samples. Exports to the UK, the US, Switzerland, Canada, Malaysia and Hong Kong.

ŶŶŶŶŶ   **Trumps Barossa Valley Shiraz 2005** Rich, opulent and generous black fruits easily carry the alcohol; blackberry, prune and dark chocolate are all there, tannins and oak controlled. Fantastic value. Cork. 14.5° alc. **Rating** 94 **To** 2015 $16

Channybearup Vineyard   ★★★★

Lot 4, Channybearup Road, Pemberton, WA 6260 (postal) **Region** Pemberton
T (08) 9776 0042 **F** (08) 9776 0043 **www**.channybearup.com.au **Open** Not
Winemaker Larry Cherubino (Contract) **Est.** 1999 **Cases** 13 500
Channybearup has been established by a small group of Perth businessmen who have been responsible for the establishment of 62 ha of vineyards. The leading varieties are chardonnay, merlot, shiraz, cabernet sauvignon and pinot noir, with lesser amounts of verdelho and sauvignon blanc. While principally established as a grape supplier to other makers, the amount of wine being vinified for Channybearup has increased significantly. Exports to the US.

ŶŶŶŶŶ   **Shiraz 2005** Vibrant cool-grown shiraz without any green characters; black cherry, blackberry and plum; fine tannins and acidity. Screwcap. **Rating** 93 **To** 2020 $20
Fly Brook Merlot 2005 An attractive red fruit core, with precise varietal notes of black olive and snow pea; good balance and length. Screwcap. **Rating** 92 **To** 2013 $20

ŶŶŶŶ   **Pemberton Verdelho 2005** Has a spine of acidity to help lift the otherwise normal, slightly bland fruit salad of verdelho; nice wine. Screwcap. 14° alc. **Rating** 89 **To** 2010 $16
Fly Brook Pinot Noir 2005 Light-bodied spice, plum and bramble; not powerful or intense, but does have varietal character. Screwcap. **Rating** 88 **To** 2010 $25

Chanters Ridge   ★★★☆

440 Chanters Lane, Tylden, Vic 3444 **Region** Macedon Ranges
T 0427 511 341 **F** (03) 5424 8140 **www**.chantersridge.com.au **Open** W'ends 10–4 by appt
Winemaker Hanging Rock Winery **Est.** 1995 **Cases** 700

Orthopaedic surgeon Barry Elliott, as well as running the surgery unit at Melbourne's Alfred Hospital has became involved with the Kyneton Hospital. He and his wife acquired the 24-ha property without any clear idea of what they might do with it; later his lifelong interest in wine steered him towards the idea of establishing a vineyard. He retained John Ellis as his consultant, and this led to the planting of 2 ha of pinot noir, and the first tiny make in 2000.

♟♟♟♟♟ **Macedon Ranges Pinot Noir 2005** Black cherry and plum aromas and flavours; while only light- to medium-bodied, has excellent balance, mouthfeel and length, with some appealing savoury notes on the finish. Screwcap. 12.5° alc. **Rating** 92 To 2013 $22

♟♟♟♟ **Macedon Blanc de Noir 2003** Nutty overtones to some red fruit characters, with a typical biscuity edge from the pinot; good balance. **Rating** 89 To 2008 $30
Back Paddock Macedon Ranges Pinot Noir 2005 Clear colour; plum and blackberry fruit; simple and slightly short, but well-priced. Screwcap. 12.5° alc. **Rating** 87 To 2008 $15

Chapel Hill

Chapel Hill Road, McLaren Vale, SA 5171 **Region** McLaren Vale
T (08) 8323 8429 **F** (08) 8323 9245 **www**.chapelhillwine.com.au **Open** 7 days 12–5
Winemaker Michael Fragos **Est.** 1979 **Cases** 50 000
A leading medium-sized winery in the region; in 2000 Chapel Hill was sold to the Swiss Thomas Schmidheiny group, which owns the respected Cuvaison winery in California as well as vineyards in Switzerland and Argentina. Wine quality is as good, if not better, than ever. Exports to the UK, the US, Canada, Germany, Switzerland, NZ, Singapore, Hong Kong and China.

♟♟♟♟♟ **McLaren Vale Shiraz 2004** Superb purple-red colour; a lovely medium-bodied regional wine; luscious black fruits, dark chocolate and fine tannins, then a very long finish. Best for years. Screwcap. 14.5° alc. **Rating** 95 To 2019 $25

♟♟♟♟♟ **McLaren Vale Cabernet Sauvignon 2004** A medium-bodied, elegantly understated wine in contradistinction to many from this region; ripe cassis blackcurrant fruit, and fine tannins. Screwcap. 14.5° alc. **Rating** 92 To 2015 $25

♟♟♟♟ **Il Vescovo 2006** Brilliant pink; a nice attack immediately announcing the presence of savoury, spicy cherry sangiovese; relatively dry. Quality rose. Screwcap. 13° alc. **Rating** 89 To 2008 $14
Il Vescovo Adelaide Hills Pinot Grigio 2006 Tries hard to rise above the ruck, and partially succeeds with the length of the palate and some varietal pear and lychee flavours. Screwcap. 13° alc. **Rating** 88 To 2008 $19

Chaperon Wines

'Grange Hill', Gallaghers Lane, Eastville, Vic 3463 **Region** Bendigo
T (03) 5435 7427 **www**.chaperon.com.au **Open** W'ends & public hols 10–5, or by appt
Winemaker Russell Clarke **Est.** 1994 **Cases** 600
In 1856 English immigrant Edward Bond purchased land in the Maldon area, followed by an adjoining property in 1871. Here he established the 'Grange Hill' winery and vineyard, which flourished in the 1880s, leading to the establishment of a second winery and second vineyard. It disappeared in the 20th century, but in 1994 Russell Clarke and Angelina Chaperon bought the property and began replanting the vineyard and restoring the old winery buildings. They have chosen to bypass irrigation and practise organic viticulture in growing 1.2 ha of bush vine grenache and mourvedre, and 1.8 ha of trellised shiraz.

♟♟♟♟♟ **Shiraz 2004** Masses of ripe blackberry, prune, plum and licorice fruit; supple, ripe tannins; carries alcohol with ease. Screwcap. 15° alc. **Rating** 93 To 2024 $25
Grenache Shiraz Mourvedre 2004 The blend works well in this cooler part of Bendigo; the varietal flavours are very evident, with sweet grenache fruit then a pleasing savoury, dry finish. Screwcap. 14.5° alc. **Rating** 90 To 2011 $20

Charles Melton

Krondorf Road, Tanunda, SA 5352 **Region** Barossa Valley
T (08) 8563 3606 **F** (08) 8563 3422 **www.**charlesmeltonwines.com.au **Open** 7 days 11–5
Winemaker Charlie Melton, Nicola Ormond **Est.** 1984 **Cases** 18 000
Charlie Melton, one of the Barossa Valley's great characters, with wife Virginia by his side, makes
some of the most eagerly sought à la mode wines in Australia. Inevitably, the Melton empire grew
in response to the insatiable demand, with a doubling of estate vineyards to 13 ha (and the
exclusive management and offtake of a further 10 ha) and the erection of a new barrel store in
1996. The expanded volume has had no adverse effect on the wonderfully rich, sweet and well-
made wines. Exports to all major markets.

ƳƳƳƳƳ **Rose of Virginia 2006** Vivid fuchsia, it is spotlessly clean, offering a sunburst of red
fruit flavours ranging from strawberries to cherries to raspberries, with very good
balance and fruit sweetness. Screwcap. 12.5° alc. **Rating** 95 **To** 2008 $20

Charles Sturt University Winery

McKeown Drive (off Coolamon Road), Wagga Wagga, NSW 2650 **Region** Big Rivers Zone
T (02) 6933 2435 **www.**csu.edu.au/winery/ **Open** Mon–Fri 11–5, w'ends 11–4
Winemaker Andrew Drumm **Est.** 1977 **Cases** 15 000
A totally new $2.5 million commercial winery was opened in 2002, complementing the
$1 million experimental winery opened in 2001. The commercial winery has been funded
through the sale of wines produced under the Charles Sturt University brand, which always offer
exceptional value. Following the University's acquisition of the former University of Sydney
campus in Orange, it now has 7.7 ha of estate plantings at Wagga Wagga, 17 ha of mature vineyards
at Orange, the latter planted to chardonnay, sauvignon blanc, shiraz, cabernet sauvignon and
merlot. Interestingly, this teaching facility is using screwcaps for all its wines, white and red,
recalling its pioneering use in 1977. Moreover, since 2005 its sparkling wines have been released
under crown seal.

ƳƳƳƳƳ **Cellar Reserve Cabernet Shiraz 2005** Medium-bodied; a mix of red and black
fruits, the red dominant, partly cassis in the cabernet sauvignon; fine, lingering
tannins and finish. Unstated origins. Screwcap. 14.9° alc. **Rating** 91 **To** 2020 $27
Orange Big Rivers Chardonnay 2006 A very attractive wine; vibrant
nectarine, apple and grapefruit flavours, the percentage of barrel ferment merely
adding texture; mouth-watering bargain. Screwcap. 14.3° alc. **Rating** 90
To 2011 $13
Limited Release Orange Chardonnay 2006 Much more powerful and
complex than its lesser-priced brother; full barrel ferment characters, the long palate
with plenty of drive. Screwcap. 14.6° alc. **Rating** 90 **To** 2010 $18
Limited Release Cabernet Merlot 2004 A supple mix of cassis and
blackcurrant in a medium-bodied frame; ripe fruits and ripe tannins; good length
and balance, the oak subtle. Hilltops/Wagga Wagga. Screwcap. 14.5° alc. **Rating** 90
To 2014 $20

ƳƳƳƳ **Sauvignon Blanc 2006** Spotless, with guava and ripe apple aromas; good
flavour, length and balance, gentle tropical fruit, but not sweet. How can you
resist at this price? Orange/Wagga Wagga/Yarra Valley. Screwcap. 13° alc.
Rating 89 **To** 2008 $13
Gundagai Orange Big Rivers Shiraz 2005 A fragrant and expressive
bouquet; light- to medium-bodied, but has a very well-balanced palate
supported by gentle tannins; great early-drinking style. Screwcap. 14.1° alc.
Rating 89 **To** 2008 $13
Limited Release Pinot Noir Chardonnay 2003 Delicate and very well-
balanced; a young Australian sparkling wine which is dry, and not aggressive; given
extended lees contact. 12.3° alc. **Rating** 89 **To** 2009 $19.80
Limited Release Vintage Sparkling Shiraz 2004 Strong purple-red; spicy red
fruits; the base seems elegant enough to have had a lower dosage; 2 years on lees.
14° alc. **Rating** 87 **To** 2012 $19.80

Chartley Estate

38 Blackwood Hills Road, Rowella, Tas 7270 **Region** Northern Tasmania
T (03) 6394 7198 **F** (03) 6394 7598 **www**.chartleyestatevineyard.com.au **Open** Not
Winemaker Winemaking Tasmania (Julian Alcorso) **Est.** 2000 **Cases** 1200
The Kossman family began the establishment of 2 ha each of pinot gris, sauvignon blanc and
pinot noir, and 1 ha of riesling in 2000. Although the vines are still young, some attractive wines
from each variety have been made.

ΨΨΨΨΨ **Riesling 2006** A wine which caused a massive difference of opinion at the Tas
Wine Show '07; I loved its rich lime and passionfruit blossom aromas, and powerful
palate; others found it altogether too much of a good thing. **Rating** 92 **To** 2009
$19.95

ΨΨΨΨ **Sauvignon Blanc 2006** Plenty of fruit power, but not much finesse; at least
proclaims its varietal identity. **Rating** 87 **To** 2008 $18.95

Chateau Barrosa   **NR**

Cnr Barossa Valley Way/Hermann Thumm Drive, Lyndoch, SA 5351 **Region** Barossa Valley
T (08) 8524 4923 **F** (08) 8524 5663 **www**.chateaubarrosa.com.au **Open** Mon–Sat 10–4.30,
Sun 11–4.30
Winemaker Contract **Est.** 1999 **Cases** NA
Hermann Thumm sold Chateau Yaldara in 1999, and promptly set about recreating an even
more lavish baroque-style chateau surrounded by 30 000 roses and filled with a vast collection
of Meissen porcelain, antique furniture, tapestries and paintings. A wide range of table wines
(vintages going back to 1992), grape liqueurs, ports, grape nectar products are on sale. A variety
of tours are available.

Chateau Dorrien

Cnr Seppeltsfield Road/Barossa Valley Way, Dorrien, SA 5352 **Region** Barossa Valley
T (08) 8562 2850 **F** (08) 8562 1416 **www**.chateaudorrien.com.au **Open** 7 days 10–5
Winemaker Fernando Martin, Ramon Martin **Est.** 1985 **Cases** 3500
The Martin family, headed by Fernando and Jeanette, purchased the old Dorrien winery from the
Seppelt family in 1984; in 1990 the family purchased Twin Valley Estate, and moved the
winemaking operations of Chateau Dorrien to the Twin Valley site. All the Chateau Dorrien
group wines are sold at Chateau Dorrien; Twin Valley is simply a production facility. In 2006 the
Martin family purchased a 32-ha property at Myponga, with over 15 ha of mature vineyards
which will now provide the grapes for San Fernando Estate, as the vineyard has been renamed.

ΨΨΨΨΨ **Cabernet Sauvignon 2002** Shows the beneficial impact of the cool vintage;
blackcurrant, earth and chocolate; fine tannins and controlled oak. Cork. 13.8° alc.
Rating 90 **To** 2012 $20

ΨΨΨΨ **Golden Harvest Riesling 2005** Thoroughly commendable; I'm not sure the
back label comment 'will please the palate of lovers of sweet wine' does the wine
justice, which has much better balance than implied; the only issue is lack of
intensity, as the length is good. Screwcap. 9° alc. **Rating** 89 **To** 2008 $15
San Fernando Estate Expose Pinot Noir 2005 Does have varietal character,
albeit all within a savoury/foresty spectrum; some glimmers of cherry and plum, and
promise for the vineyard in the future. Diam. 14.9° alc. **Rating** 87 **To** 2010 $20
Cabernet Sauvignon 2004 Light- to medium-bodied; gentle black fruits are
accompanied by balanced tannins; no fanfare of trumpets, just easy drinking.
Cork. 13.9° alc. **Rating** 87 **To** 2019 $20

Chateau Francois   ★★★★★

Broke Road, Pokolbin, NSW 2321 **Region** Lower Hunter Valley
T (02) 4998 7548 **F** (02) 4998 7805 **Open** W'ends 9–5, or by appt
Winemaker Don Francois **Est.** 1969 **Cases** 250

I have known former NSW Director of Fisheries Dr Don Francois for almost as long as I have been involved with wine, which is a very long time indeed. I remember his early fermentations of sundry substances other than grapes (none of which, I hasten to add, were the least bit illegal) in the copper bowl of an antiquated washing machine in his laundry. He established Chateau Francois 1 year before Brokenwood, and our winemaking and fishing paths have crossed many times since. Some years ago Don suffered a mild stroke, and no longer speaks or writes with any fluency, but this has not stopped him from producing a range of absolutely beautiful semillons which flourish marvellously with age, none more so than the 1997. All we now have to do is wait for the 2004, a trophy winner at the Hunter Valley Boutique Winemakers Show '05, to develop the same way. I should add that he is even prouder of the distinguished career of his daughter, Rachel Francois, at the NSW bar.

🍷🍷🍷🍷🍷 **Pokolbin Mallee Semillon 2005** Spotlessly clean; starting to develop layers of flavour, the lemongrass/lemon cake of the great '05 vintage a big help; excellent acidity and length. Outstanding value. Screwcap. 11° alc. **Rating** 95 **To** 2017 **$14**

Pokolbin Mallee Semillon 2000 Continues the development theme; citrus dominates, with touches of honey and toast sandwiched between that citrus and the closing acidity. Will the cork serve the wine as well as the screwcaps on the young vintages? 11° alc. **Rating** 94 **To** 2012 **$14**

🍷🍷🍷🍷½ **Pokolbin Mallee Semillon 2004** Hints of straw and toast under an intense layer of crystal lemon and citrus fruit; long finish. Screwcap. 11° alc. **Rating** 93 **To** 2014 **$14**

🍷🍷🍷🍷 **Sparkling Pinot Noir 1999** Light- to medium-bodied; as always, an interesting wine with a niche market; nice dry finish. 13.3° alc. **Rating** 88 **To** 2008 **$18**

Chateau Leamon ★★★★☆

5528 Calder Highway, Bendigo, Vic 3550 **Region** Bendigo
T (03) 5447 7995 **F** (03) 5447 0855 **www**.chateauleamon.com.au **Open** Wed–Mon 10–5
Winemaker Ian Leamon **Est.** 1973 **Cases** 2500

One of the longest-established wineries in the region, with estate and locally grown shiraz and cabernet family grapes providing the excellent red wines. Exports to the UK, Canada and Singapore.

🍷🍷🍷🍷🍷 **Reserve Bendigo Shiraz 2005** Rich and ripe array of black fruits; ripe tannins and quality oak. Screwcap. 15° alc. **Rating** 94 **To** 2025 **$38**

🍷🍷🍷🍷 **Bendigo Cabernet Sauvignon Cabernet Franc Merlot 2005** Savoury/briary/earthy fruit, but the tannins are ripe; a strange conjunction, similar to the '04. Screwcap. 15° alc. **Rating** 88 **To** 2013 **$22**

Strathbogie Ranges Riesling 2006 A slightly unusual touch of musk on the bouquet; a big, rich, tropical fruit style already at its best. Screwcap. 13.4° alc. **Rating** 87 **To** 2008 **$17**

Chateau Mildura ★★★

191 Belar Avenue, Irymple, Vic 3498 **Region** Murray Darling
T (03) 5024 5901 **F** (03) 5024 5763 **www**.chateaumildura.com.au **Open** 7 days 10–4
Winemaker Neville Hudson **Est.** 1888 **Cases** 5000

The history of Chateau Mildura is inextricably bound up with that of winemaking along the Murray River in the northwest corner of Vic. The fathers of irrigation, the founders of Mildura and Renmark (across the border in SA), were the Chaffey Brothers, who built the triple-gable brick winery in 1892. The story of the Chaffeys is an epic one, marked by as many failures as successes. In the outcome, table wine production ceased in 1910, whereafter the building was used for the production of brandy until the '50s. In 2002 it was sold by Beringer Blass to Lance Milne, a local fourth-generation horticulturist. He has incorporated a boutique winery in a small area of the building, the remainder of which will be opened as a museum for the Chaffeys and their pioneering work.

ΨΨΨΨ **Psyche Smuggler Petit Verdot 2005** Rich, sweet blackcurrant and blackberry fruit; once again a testament to the variety's ability to flourish in warm climates. Does have a touch of residual sweetness. Screwcap. 14° alc. **Rating** 88 **To** 2009 $12

Chateau Pâto

67 Thompsons Road, Pokolbin, NSW 2321 **Region** Lower Hunter Valley
T (02) 4998 7634 **F** (02) 4998 7860 **Open** By appt
Winemaker Nicholas Paterson **Est.** 1980 **Cases** 500
Nicholas Paterson took over responsibility for this tiny winery following the death of his father David Paterson during the 1993 vintage. The winery has 2.5 ha of shiraz, 1 ha of chardonnay and 0.5 ha of pinot noir; most of the grapes are sold, with a tiny quantity of shiraz being made into a marvellous wine. David Paterson's inheritance is being handsomely guarded.

ΨΨΨΨΨ **Hunter Wine Country DJP Shiraz 2005** Immediately proclaims its regional identity with nuances of earth and leather on the bouquet; intense black fruits take over on the palate, but terroir will ultimately have its way; finishes with fine tannins. Screwcap. 14.7° alc. **Rating** 94 **To** 2024 $40

Chateau Tanunda

9 Basedow Road, Tanunda, SA 5352 **Region** Barossa Valley
T (08) 8563 3888 **F** (08) 8563 1422 **www.chateautanunda.com Open** 7 days 10–5
Winemaker Tim Smith **Est.** 1890 **Cases** 10 000
This is one of the most imposing winery buildings in the Barossa Valley, built from stone quarried at nearby Bethany in the late 1880s. It started life as a winery, then became a specialist brandy distillery until the death of the Australian brandy industry, whereafter it was simply used as storage cellars. Now completely restored, and converted to a major convention facility catering for groups of up to 400. The large complex also houses a cellar door where the Chateau Tanunda wines are sold; Chateau Bistro and the Barossa Small Winemakers Centre, offering wines made by small independent winemakers in the region. It is a sister winery to Cowra Estate, as both are owned by the Geber family. Exports to the US and other major markets.

ΨΨΨΨΨ **The Chateau Merlot 2005** Big, powerful dark fruits with savoury/foresty/earthy notes, and some black olive; an uncompromising wine. Cork. 14.5° alc. **Rating** 90 **To** 2013 $40

Chatsfield

O'Neil Road, Mount Barker, WA 6324 **Region** Mount Barker
T (08) 9851 1704 **F** (08) 9851 2660 **www.chatsfield.com.au Open** By appt
Winemaker Dr Diane Miller **Est.** 1976 **Cases** 2000
Irish-born medical practitioner Ken Lynch can be proud of his achievements at Chatsfield, as can most of the various contract winemakers who have taken the high-quality estate-grown material and made some impressive wines, notably the Riesling and spicy, licorice Shiraz. Exports to the UK.

ΨΨΨΨΨ **Reserve Mount Barker Shiraz 2004** Plenty of fruit depth, with licorice, spice and blackberry; has taken 18 months in French oak in its stride; 600 cases. Cork. 14.5° alc. **Rating** 92 **To** 2019 $25

Chatto Wines

McDonalds Road, Pokolbin, NSW 2325 **Region** Lower Hunter Valley
T (02) 4998 7293 **F** (02) 4998 7294 **www.chattowines.com.au Open** 7 days 9–5
Winemaker Jim Chatto **Est.** 2000 **Cases** 7000
Jim Chatto spent several years in Tasmania as the first winemaker at Rosevears Estate. He has since moved to the Hunter Valley but has used his Tasmanian contacts to buy small parcels of riesling and pinot noir. Possessed of a particularly good palate, he has made wines of excellent

quality under the Chatto label. He was a star Len Evans Tutorial scholar and is an up-and-coming wine show judge, and recently appointed chief winemaker for Pepper Tree Estate. Exports to the US and Canada.

ＹＹＹＹＹ **Hunter Valley Semillon 2004** Bright green-yellow, glowing as if lit from within; the bouquet well and truly opening up as a prelude to a palate with all the intensity, drive and length one could wish for. Why bother with sauvignon blanc? Screwcap. 10.5° alc. **Rating** 96 **To** 2018 $17
Hunter Valley Semillon 2006 An exceptional example of how much intensity of restrained flavour can come from semillon at this alcohol and youthful age; shades of Mosel Kabinett, with extremely fine intense lemon and wet pebble flavours. Screwcap. 10° alc. **Rating** 95 **To** 2020 $17

ＹＹＹＹＹ **Canberra District Riesling 2006** A relatively subdued bouquet followed by a finely structured palate, with a mix of lime, apple and slate; good balance and length. Screwcap. **Rating** 92 **To** 2016 $17
Hunter Valley Shiraz 2005 Medium- to full-bodied blackberry fruit with some earthy regional characters; fine tannins and controlled oak; will develop. Screwcap. 13.5° alc. **Rating** 92 **To** 2020 $35

Chestnut Grove   ★★★★☆

PO Box 255, South Perth, WA 6951 **Region** Manjimup
T (08) 9368 0099 **F** (08) 9368 0133 **www**.chestnutgrove.com.au **Open** Not
Winemaker Brian Fletcher **Est.** 1988 **Cases** 15 000
A substantial vineyard (18 ha), which is now mature, and the erection of an onsite winery are the most obvious signs of change, but ownership, too, has been passed on from the late founder Vic Kordic to his sons Paul (a Perth lawyer) and Mark (the general manager of the wine business) and thence (in 2002) to Mike Calneggia's Australian Wine Holdings Limited group. Exports to Canada, Denmark, Germany, Hong Kong, Singapore and the UK.

ＹＹＹＹＹ **Manjimup Chardonnay 2005** Aromatic and fragrant citrus and stone fruit; a deliciously lively, fruit-driven wine, oak a subtle but synergistic addition. Screwcap. 13.8° alc. **Rating** 92 **To** 2012 $20
Tall Timber Shiraz Cabernet 2004 Medium-bodied; quality, texture and structure; notes of cedar and spice to the mix of black fruits; long finish, fine tannins. Screwcap. 14.1° alc. **Rating** 90 **To** 2014 $16

ＹＹＹＹ **Manjimup Cabernet Merlot 2005** Spice and pine needle aromas; a firm palate with rather grippy tannins, and a very different profile to the Shiraz Cabernet. Screwcap. 13.8° alc. **Rating** 87 **To** 2012 $20

Chestnut Hill Vineyard   ★★★★

1280 Pakenham Road, Mt Burnett, Vic 3781 **Region** Gippsland
T (03) 5942 7314 **F** (03) 5942 7314 **www**.chestnuthillvineyard.com.au **Open** W'ends & public hols 10.30–5.30, or by appt
Winemaker Charlie Javor **Est.** 1995 **Cases** 1300
Charlie and Ivka Javor started Chestnut Hill with small plantings of chardonnay, sauvignon blanc and pinot noir in 1985 and have slowly increased the vineyards to a little over 3 ha. Less than 1 hour's drive from Melbourne, the picturesque vineyard is situated among the rolling hills in the Dandenongs near Mt Burnett. The label explains, 'liberty is a gift we had never experienced in our homeland', which was Croatia, from which they emigrated in the late 1960s.

ＹＹＹＹＹ **Liberty Mount Burnett Chardonnay 2004** Has developed slowly but very well; has focused varietal expression of nectarine and citrus; intense and long. Cork. 14.4° alc. **Rating** 93 **To** 2011 $27

ＹＹＹＹ **Mount Burnett Sauvignon Blanc 2005** Overall, full-flavoured, but does retain balancing crisp acidity. **Rating** 89 **To** 2008 $24

Mount Burnett Chardonnay 2005 Light-bodied, citrus and stone fruit; does not have the length or intensity of the '04. Cork. **Rating** 87 **To** 2008 $27

Mount Burnett Pinot Noir 2004 Distinctly savoury/stemmy style, which gives considerable length; the lack of sweet fruit will put some off, and the wine should be consumed without further delay. Cork. 14.2° alc. **Rating** 87 **To** 2008 $27

Cheviot Bridge/Long Flat   ★★★

10/499 St Kilda Road, Melbourne, Vic 3004 (postal) **Region** Upper Goulburn
T (03) 9820 9080 **F** (03) 9820 9070 **www**.cheviotbridge.com.au **Open** Not
Winemaker Hugh Cuthbertson **Est.** 1998 **Cases** NFP
Cheviot Bridge/Long Flat brings together a highly experienced team of wine industry professionals and investors who provided the $10 million-plus required to purchase the Long Flat range of wines from Tyrrell's; the purchase took place in the second half of 2003. In 2004 the group acquired the listed vehicle Winepros Limited, changing its name to Cheviot Bridge Limited. The bulk of the business activity is that of virtual winery, acquiring bulk and/or bottled wine from various third party suppliers. The brands include Cheviot Bridge Yea Valley, Cheviot Bridge CB, Kissing Bridge, Thirsty Lizard, Long Flat, The Long Flat Wine Co. and Terrace Vale. Exports to all major markets. Has gone off the boil in 2007.

Chidlow's Well Estate   ★★★★

PO Box 84, Chidlow, WA 6556 **Region** Perth Hills
T (08) 9572 3770 **F** (08) 9572 3750 **www**.chidlowswell.com.au **Open** By appt
Winemaker Rob Marshall, Julie Smith **Est.** 2002 **Cases** 850
Chidlow is around 60 km east of Perth and was originally known as Chidlows Well. The 3-ha vineyard is now owned and managed by Peter Costa and Sandy Gray, who continue to grow the chardonnay, chenin blanc, verdelho and shiraz planted on the vineyard by the former owners.

 Perth Hills Shiraz 2005 Clean, fresh red and black fruit aromas; light- to medium-bodied, with good texture and structure; fine tannins and integrated oak. Screwcap. 13.9° alc. **Rating** 90 **To** 2015 $18

 Perth Hills Chenin Blanc 2006 Clean and fresh; appealing lemon blossom/zest overtones to the fruit; good length and intensity; a surprise packet. Screwcap. 13° alc. **Rating** 88 **To** 2008 $15

Sparkling Shiraz 2005 Provided it is not taken too seriously, this is a commendable wine, to be bought today and consumed as soon as it is chilled, as it does have attractive red fruit flavours (and the obligatory sweetness). **Rating** 87 **To** 2008 $20

Chrismont   ★★★★☆

251 Upper King River Road, Cheshunt, Vic 3678 **Region** King Valley
T (03) 5729 8220 **F** (03) 5729 8253 **www**.chrismont.com.au **Open** 7 days 11–5
Winemaker Warren Proft **Est.** 1980 **Cases** 7500
Arnold (Arnie) and Jo Pizzini have established 83 ha of vineyards in the Whitfield area of the upper King Valley. They have planted riesling, sauvignon blanc, chardonnay, pinot gris, cabernet sauvignon, merlot, shiraz, barbera, marzemino and arneis. The La Zona range ties in the Italian heritage of the Pizzinis and is part of the intense interest in all things Italian.

King Valley Riesling 2005 Fresh, clean and lively aromas and flavours of citrus and green apple; a vibrant, dry finish; developing well, though slowly. Screwcap. 12.5° alc. **Rating** 91 **To** 2018 $15

La Zona King Valley Arneis 2006 Light, fresh apple blossom aromas; good length and balance, the flavours in an apple and pear spectrum. Impressive. Screwcap. 12.4° alc. **Rating** 90 **To** 2010 $20

La Zona Sangiovese 2004 Light red; tangy, savoury and spice aromas and flavours; light tannins, and minimal oak. Screwcap. 14° alc. **Rating** 87 **To** 2008 $20

Christmas Hill

RSD 25C, Meadows, SA 5201 (postal) **Region** Adelaide Hills
T (08) 8388 3779 **F** (08) 8388 3759 **Open** Not
Winemaker Nepenthe Vineyards **Est.** 2000 **Cases** 1000
Christmas Hill is primarily a grapegrower, selling most of its production from the 13 ha of chardonnay, sauvignon blanc, shiraz, cabernet sauvignon and pinot noir, but keeping back the equivalent of around 2000 cases of Sauvignon Blanc. It is primarily sold to Adelaide Cellar Door (www.adelaidecellardoor.com.au), by the case through Christmas Hill's mailing list, with a dribble finding its way onto the Adelaide retail market. Exports to the US, Sweden and Hong Kong.

ȲȲȲȲ   **Adelaide Hills Sauvignon Blanc 2006** A rather closed bouquet, the palate, too, lacking positive varietal expression; paradoxically, the wine has good balance and fair length. Screwcap. 13.5° alc. **Rating** 88 **To** 2008 $14

Churchview Estate

Cnr Bussell Highway/Gale Road, Metricup, WA 6280 **Region** Margaret River
T (08) 9755 7200 **F** (08) 9755 7300 **www.**churchview.com.au **Open** Mon–Sat 9.30–5.30
Winemaker Paul Green **Est.** 1998 **Cases** 20 000
The Fokkema family, headed by Spike Fokkema, immigrated from The Netherlands in the 1950s. Their business success in the following decades led to the acquisition of the 100-ha Churchview Estate property in 1997, and to the progressive establishment of 70 ha of vineyards. Exports to the UK and other major markets.

ȲȲȲȲȲ   **The Bartondale Reserve Margaret River Cabernet Merlot 2004** Medium-to full-bodied, with good structure and mouthfeel; fine-grained tannins run through the cassis and blackcurrant palate; excellent finish. Screwcap. 15° alc. **Rating** 94 **To** 2025 $34

ȲȲȲȲȲ   **The Bartondale Reserve Margaret River Shiraz 2004** Clear blackberry fruit with touches of licorice and quality oak on the bouquet; a medium- to full-bodied palate with an interplay between rich fruit and quality oak; soft tannins. Screwcap. 15° alc. **Rating** 93 **To** 2019 $34
Margaret River Sauvignon Blanc Semillon 2006 Punchy herbaceous/gooseberry/citrus flavours; good intensity and very good length; brisk finish. Screwcap. 12° alc. **Rating** 92 **To** 2009 $18
Premium Range Margaret River Shiraz 2004 Strong colour; typical of the increasing depth of Margaret River shiraz; black fruits and positive but ripe tannins. Cork. 15° alc. **Rating** 91 **To** 2020 $22
Margaret River Cabernet Sauvignon 2005 Medium-bodied; clear-cut, earthy cabernet varietal fruit, with savoury tannins on the finish. Screwcap. 14.5° alc. **Rating** 90 **To** 2015 $22

ȲȲȲȲ   **Reserve Shiraz 2004** Abundant, sweet black fruits, but undermined by tannins which needed more softening. Time may or may not solve the problem. Screwcap. 15° alc. **Rating** 89 **To** 2015 $29
Premium Late Harvest Dessert Margaret River Shiraz 2004 Interesting and unexpected; neutral fortifying spirit; intense and appropriately dry (relatively speaking). Cork. 19.5° alc. **Rating** 88 **To** 2015 $20
Margaret River Riesling 2006 Light-bodied; herb, grass and lemon aromas and flavours; moderate length. This really isn't the right region. Screwcap. 12.5° alc. **Rating** 87 **To** 2010 $18
Margaret River Unwooded Chardonnay 2006 Gentle stone fruit and melon; clean and well-made, but not a lot of drive. Screwcap. 14.5° alc. **Rating** 87 **To** 2008 $18
Margaret River Rose 2006 Strawberry and raspberry fruit, plus nice acidity, balance the sweetness on the finish. Screwcap. 12° alc. **Rating** 87 **To** 2008 $16

Ciavarella   ★★★☆

Evans Lane, Oxley, Vic 3678 **Region** King Valley
T (03) 5727 3384 **F** (03) 5727 3384 **Open** Mon–Sat 9–6, Sun 10–6
Winemaker Cyril Ciavarella, Tony Ciavarella **Est.** 1978 **Cases** 3000
Cyril and Jan Ciavarella's vineyard was planted in 1978, with plantings and varieties being extended over the years. One variety, aucerot, was first produced by Maurice O'Shea of McWilliam's Mount Pleasant 60 or more years ago; the Ciavarella vines have been grown from cuttings collected from an old Glenrowan vineyard before the parent plants were removed in the mid-1980s. Tony Ciavarella left a career in agricultural research in mid-2003 to join his parents at Ciavarella.

Oxley Estate Graciano 2005 Quite powerful and focused red fruits; has held good acidity and tannins. Its main home is in Rioja, although losing ground there. Screwcap. 13.2° alc. **Rating** 88 **To** 2013 $22

Oxley Estate Viognier 2005 Remarkable retention of freshness, though the condition of the cork a worry for the future; light-bodied, with touches of apricot and peach supported by good acidity. Cork. 13.5° alc. **Rating** 87 **To** 2008 $16

Oxley Estate Graciano Merlot 2005 Clear colour; spicy/earthy aromas, then ripe confit/jam fruit flavours, almost into plum cake. A weird liaison between France and Spain. Screwcap. **Rating** 87 **To** 2009 $22

Oxley Estate Late Harvest Semillon Aucerot 2005 Not complex, but has good fruit flavour, the low alcohol, residual sugar and acid balance all commendable. Cork. 8.5° alc. **Rating** 87 **To** 2008 $25

White Port NV Has unexpected character and some complexity coming from the blend of verdelho and aucerot; nutty, moderately luscious and well-balanced. Contrary to the back label, verdelho's ancestral home is Madeira, not the Douro. Cork. 18.3° alc. **Rating** 87 **To** 2008 $18

Cicada Wines ★★★☆

PO Box 808, Riverwood, NSW 2210 **Region** Warehouse
T (02) 9594 4980 **F** (02) 9594 5290 **www.**cicadawines.com **Open** Not
Winemaker Contract **Est.** NA **Cases** NFP
Cicada Wines is an ultimate virtual winery, created by a group of wine lovers and professionals who scour Australia for quality wines which have already been bottled but are, when purchased, cleanskin. They have succeeded in finding some good wines.

Black Emperor Heathcote Shiraz 2004 Rich and bursting with ripe fruit in typical Heathcote style; concentrated plum, blackberry and chocolate; controlled oak, less so the alcohol. Cork. 15° alc. **Rating** 91 **To** 2014

Ciccone Wines NR

Factory Road, Milawa, Vic 3678 **Region** King Valley
T (03) 5727 3860 **F** (03) 5729 8511 **www.**cicconewines.com.au **Open** Thurs–Mon 10–5
Winemaker Pat Ciccone, Joe Ciccone **Est.** 2005 **Cases** NA
With generations of Italian viticulture in their blood (father Antonio was raised among vineyards and olive groves in Calabria, Italy) Pat and Joe Ciccone began the development of their vineyard in 2005, with 8 ha of riesling, sauvignon blanc, merlot, shiraz and cabernet sauvignon.

Cirko V ★★★☆

148 Markwood-Tarrawingee Road, Markwood, Vic 3678 **Region** King Valley
T (03) 5727 0535 **F** (03) 5727 0487 **www.**cirko-v.com.au **Open** At Tinkers Hill
Winemaker Trevor Knaggs (contract) **Est.** 2003 **Cases** 400
The derivation of the name Cirko V is, to put it mildly, eclectic. Cirko is Esperanto for circus, and V is an abbreviation of *vie*, French for life. Inspired partly by Cirque du Soleil and Circus Oz, Kristy Taylor and Peter Lumsden decided to undertake a major seachange, giving up their jobs,

selling the various properties they had acquired and moving to the King Valley, buying an existing vineyard planted to 4 ha of shiraz, 2 ha of merlot, and 1 ha of viognier. They intend to sell most of the wine through the Tinkers Hill cellar door, and a wine club.

🍷🍷🍷🍷🍷 **Viognier 2005** Well-made, with good varietal character coming through on both bouquet and palate; apricot dominant, plus ripe apple and pear. Screwcap. 14° alc. **Rating** 91 **To** 2009 $29

Clair de Lune Vineyard

Lot 8805 South Gippsland Highway, Kardella South, Vic 3951 **Region** Gippsland
T (03) 5655 1032 **www.clairdelune.com.au Open** 7 days 11.30–5.30
Winemaker Brian Gaffy **Est.** 1997 **Cases** 500
Brian Gaffy married a successful 20-year career in civil engineering with a long-term involvement in the Bundaburra Wine & Food Club in Melbourne. His interest in wine grew, leading to studies at the Dookie Agricultural College, with particular input from Martin Williams MW and Denise Miller. He has now planted a total of 4 ha on the rolling hills of the Strzelecki Range to sauvignon blanc, chardonnay, pinot noir and a mixed block of shiraz/merlot/cabernet.

🍷🍷🍷🍷 **South Gippsland Shiraz 2005** Fresh, lively red cherry, raspberry and blackberry fruit; tannins and oak controlled. Saturated twin top cork a worry. 12.4° alc. **Rating** 90 **To** 2012 $25

🍷🍷🍷🍷 **South Gippsland Wooded Chardonnay 2005** Belies its low alcohol, as does the '06 Unwooded; ripe, round stone fruit and apple plus slightly edgy oak; has flavour. Twin top. 11.9° alc. **Rating** 87 **To** 2010 $25

Clairault

Caves Road, Wilyabrup, WA 6280 **Region** Margaret River
T (08) 9755 6225 **F** (08) 9755 6229 **www.clairaultwines.com.au Open** 7 days 10–5
Winemaker Will Shields **Est.** 1976 **Cases** 25 000
Bill and Ena Martin, with sons Conor, Brian and Shane, acquired Clairault several years ago and have expanded the vineyards on the 120-ha property. The 12 ha of vines established by the former owners (up to 30 years old) are being supplemented by another 70 ha of vines, with a ratio of 70% red varieties to 30% white. Brian Martin is moving the vineyard to a 100% chemical-free management, with biodynamic management at the end of the process. Exports to the UK, the US and other major markets.

🍷🍷🍷🍷🍷 **Estate Margaret River Chardonnay 2005** A clean, expressive bouquet showing both fruit and oak; good balance and length; delicate but intense melon, stone fruit and grapefruit with quality oak in the background. Screwcap. 13.5° alc. **Rating** 94 **To** 2015 $29

🍷🍷🍷🍷🍷 **Margaret River Semillon Sauvignon Blanc 2006** Tight, lively and long, with grassy semillon undertones giving both structure and length, the sauvignon blanc that touch of ripe fruit. Screwcap. 12° alc. **Rating** 93 **To** 2011 $19
Margaret River Chardonnay 2005 Shares with the Estate wine an above-average intensity, focus and length; fruit drives the long palate, with melon and grapefruit, the oak subtle. Screwcap. 13.5° alc. **Rating** 93 **To** 2013 $19
Estate Margaret River Cabernet Sauvignon 2004 Oak plays an important role in distinguishing this wine from the regional version, giving it more structure, but (given the alcohol) it is surprising there isn't even more sweet fruit. Screwcap. 15° alc. **Rating** 91 **To** 2019 $36
Estate Margaret River Riesling 2006 Light apple and spice aromas; a fresh, nicely balanced palate; well-made within its geographical limits. Screwcap. 12° alc. **Rating** 90 **To** 2011 $17
Estate Margaret River Chardonnay 2004 A powerful figgy, stone fruit mix; has good flavour but not the finesse of the '05s; it may simply be a stage of its development. Screwcap. 14° alc. **Rating** 90 **To** 2012 $29

Estate Margaret River Cabernet Merlot 2003 More concentrated and focused than the '04 regional version, although sharing some of its austerity; blackcurrant and black olive fruits sustain a longer, more accessible palate. Screwcap. 14° alc. **Rating** 90 **To** 2018 $36

Margaret River Sauvignon Blanc 2006 A clean but suppressed bouquet, the palate likewise yet to express itself; an extra year for good luck. Screwcap. 12.5° alc. **Rating** 88 **To** 2009 $19

Margaret River Cabernet Merlot 2004 Medium-bodied; has blackcurrant fruit with distinct touches of earth and olive giving it overall austerity. Screwcap. 14.5° alc. **Rating** 87 **To** 2011 $19

Margaret River Cabernet Sauvignon 2004 Medium-bodied; clear-cut varietal fruit in a slightly forbidding mode; black fruits and dark olive flavours. Screwcap. 15° alc. **Rating** 87 **To** 2012 $19

Clancy Fuller

PO Box 34, Tanunda, SA 5352 **Region** Barossa Valley
T (08) 8563 0080 **F** (08) 8563 0080 **Open** Not
Winemaker Chris Ringland **Est.** 1996 **Cases** 550
This is the venture of industry veterans who should know better: Paul Clancy, long responsible for the Wine Industry Directory which sits in every winery office in Australia; and Peter Fuller, who has built up by far the largest public relations business for all sectors of the wine industry. They own 2 ha of dry-grown 120-year-old shiraz at Bethany, and 2 ha of shiraz and grenache at Jacob's Creek.

Three Hogsheads Shiraz 2002 A very big, fat wine, swollen with alcohol, but does have fine, ripe, supple tannins and good length; 120-year-old vines. Cork. 15.5° alc. **Rating** 90 **To** 2027 $40

Classic McLaren Wines

Lot B, Coppermine Road, McLaren Vale, SA 5171 **Region** McLaren Vale
T (08) 8323 0115 **F** (08) 8323 9242 **www.**classicmclarenwines.com.au **Open** By appt
Winemaker Andrew Braithwaite **Est.** 1996 **Cases** 7100
Classic McLaren Wines, owned by Mark Picard, is a substantial business, with 57 ha of vineyards planted to shiraz, merlot, cabernet sauvignon, semillon and chardonnay, and has built a new winery and underground cellar. Exports to the UK, the US and other major markets.

Clayfield Wines

Wilde Lane, Moyston, Vic 3377 **Region** Grampians
T (03) 5354 2689 **www.**clayfieldwines.com **Open** Mon–Sat 10–5, Sun 11–4
Winemaker Simon Clayfield **Est.** 1997 **Cases** 1000
Former long-serving Best's winemaker Simon Clayfield and wife Kaye are now doing their own thing. They planted 2 ha of shiraz and merlot between 1997 and 1999. Production is modest, but the quality is high. Exports to the UK, the US and Canada.

Grampians Shiraz 2004 Medium- to full-bodied, with spice, licorice and blackberry running through the long palate; great mouthfeel and fine tannins. Superb cool-climate wine. Runner up Great Shiraz Challenge '06. Screwcap. 14.3° alc. **Rating** 96 **To** 2024 $45

Claymore Wines

Leasingham Road, Leasingham, SA 5452 **Region** Clare Valley
T (08) 8843 0200 **F** (08) 8843 0200 **www.**claymorewines.com.au **Open** Wed–Mon 11–4
Winemaker David Mavor, Ben Jeanneret **Est.** 1998 **Cases** 9000

Claymore Wines is the venture of 2 medical professionals imagining that it would lead the way to early retirement (which, of course, it did not). The starting date depends on which event you take: the first 4-ha vineyard at Leasingham purchased in 1991 (with 70-year-old grenache, riesling and shiraz); 1996, when a 16-ha block at Penwortham was purchased and planted to shiraz, merlot and grenache; 1997, when the first wines were made; or 1998, when the first releases came onto the market, the labels inspired by U2, Pink Floyd and Lou Reed. Exports to the US, Denmark, Malaysia, Taiwan, Singapore and Hong Kong.

ΨΨΨΨΨ **Joshua Tree Watervale Riesling 2005** Fresh, clean and lively, slowly unfurling aromas and flavours of lime and lemon; good finish and balance. Screwcap. 12° alc. **Rating** 94 **To** 2015 $18

ΨΨΨΨΨ **Dark Side of the Moon Clare Valley Shiraz 2004** A powerful, dense wine; an initial flush of rich fruit on entry to the mouth is smartly followed by tannins; patience will richly reward. Screwcap. 14° alc. **Rating** 92 **To** 2024 $25
Walk on the Wild Side Shiraz Viognier 2005 An exotic and expressive bouquet, the viognier making a major impact on the luscious fruit; likewise rich in the mouth. Screwcap. 15° alc. **Rating** 91 **To** 2015 $20
Joshua Tree Clare Valley Riesling 2006 A powerful bouquet with citrus/lime and an overlay of more tropical fruit; similarly rich, sweet fruit on the full-flavoured palate; this is not residual sugar sweetness, however. Screwcap. 13.5° alc. **Rating** 90 **To** 2011 $18

ΨΨΨΨ **You'll Never Walk Alone Clare Valley Grenache Shiraz 2004** As ever, that strangely light-bodied character of Clare grenache; spicy notes and more than a touch of jam. Screwcap. 15° alc. **Rating** 87 **To** 2008 $18

Clearview Estate Mudgee ★★★

Cnr Sydney Road/Rocky Water Hole Road, Mudgee, NSW 2850 **Region** Mudgee
T (02) 6372 4546 **F** (02) 6372 7577 **Open** Mon–Fri 10–3 (Mar–Dec), w'ends 10–4, or by appt
Winemaker Robert Stein Vineyard **Est.** 1995 **Cases** 1500
Paul and Michelle Baguley acquired the 11-ha vineyard from the founding Hickey family in 2006. Paul brings 10 years' experience as a viticulturist, and Paul and Michelle have already introduced new wine styles, although no samples (other than Semillon) were submitted.

ΨΨΨΨ **Church Creek Semillon 2006** Attractive, slightly unusual, lemon citrus aromas and flavours; a bold, but not over the top style for early drinking. Screwcap. 12° alc. **Rating** 89 **To** 2010 $15

Cleggett Wines ★★★☆

'Shalistin', Strathalbyn Road, Langhorne Creek, SA 5255 **Region** Langhorne Creek
T (08) 8537 3133 **F** (08) 8537 3102 **www.**cleggettwines.com.au **Open** 7 days 10–6 (summer), Thurs–Tues 10–6 (winter)
Winemaker Stephen Clark, Chris Day, Duane Coates (Consultant) **Est.** 2000 **Cases** 1500
The Cleggett family first planted grape vines at Langhorne Creek in 1911. In 1977 a sport (a natural mutation) of cabernet sauvignon produced bronze-coloured grapes; cuttings were taken and increasing quantities of the vine were gradually established, and called malian. Ten years later one of the malian vines itself mutated to yield golden-white bunches, and this in turn was propagated with the name shalistin. There are now 4 ha of shalistin and 2 ha of malian in bearing. Shalistin is made as a full-bodied but unoaked white wine; malian produces both an early and a late harvest rose style wine. Exports to the UK.

ΨΨΨΨ **The Two of Us Langhorne Creek Cabernet Merlot 2005** Light- to medium-bodied; clean, fresh, light cassis, raspberry and blackcurrant fruit; minimal tannins and subtle French oak; 56%/44%. Screwcap. 14° alc. **Rating** 89 **To** 2012 $15
Legend Series Langhorne Creek Cabernet Sauvignon 2003 A mix of cassis, blackcurrant and more savoury/minty/earthy notes; has good length. Cork. 14° alc. **Rating** 89 **To** 2015 $19

Clemens Hill

686 Richmond Road, Cambridge, Tas 7170 **Region** Southern Tasmania
T (03) 6248 5985 **F** (03) 6248 5985 **Open** By appt
Winemaker Winemaking Tasmania **Est.** 1994 **Cases** 700
The Shepherd family acquired Clemens Hill in 2001 after selling their Rosabrook winery in the
Margaret River. They also have a shareholding in Winemaking Tasmania, the newly established
contract winemaking facility run by Julian Alcorso, who makes the Clemens Hill wines. The
estate vineyards have now been increased to 2.1 ha. Following the death of Joan Shepherd in
2006, John took John Schuts, an assistant winemaker at Julian Alcorso's Winemaking Tasmania,
into partnership.

ԹԹԹԹԹ **Reserve Pinot Noir 2004** Attractive wine; supple and smooth, with very good
line and clear varietal character; controlled oak and tannins; acidity may upset some,
but not me. Screwcap. **Rating** 94 **To** 2010 $40

ԹԹԹԹ **Pinot Noir 2005** Plentiful, soft, mouthfilling flavour, the fruit in the plum
spectrum. **Rating** 89 **To** 2011 $26.95
Sauvignon Blanc 2006 A touch of reduction on the bouquet, but gooseberry/
passionfruit varietal fruit comes through on the palate. **Rating** 88 **To** 2006 $19.95

Cleveland

Shannons Road, Lancefield, Vic 3435 **Region** Macedon Ranges
T (03) 5429 9000 **F** (03) 5429 2143 **Open** 7 days 9–5
Winemaker Kilchurn Wines (David Cowburn) **Est.** 1985 **Cases** 2500
The Cleveland homestead was built in 1889 in the style of a Gothic Revival manor house, but
had been abandoned for 40 years when purchased by the Briens in 1983. It has since been restored
and 3.8 ha of surrounding vineyard established. In 2002 new owner, Grange Group of Conference
Centres, initiated fast-track development of The Grange at Cleveland Winery, with 22 suites, plus
a large conference room and facilities alongside a new winery.

Clonakilla

Crisps Lane, Murrumbateman, NSW 2582 **Region** Canberra District
T (02) 6227 5877 **F** (02) 6227 5871 **www.**clonakilla.com.au **Open** 7 days 11–5
Winemaker Tim Kirk **Est.** 1971 **Cases** 6500
The indefatigable Tim Kirk, with an inexhaustible thirst for knowledge, is the winemaker and
manager of this family winery founded by father, scientist Dr John Kirk. It is not at all surprising
that the quality of the wines is excellent, especially the highly regarded Shiraz Viognier, which sells
out quickly every year. Exports to all major markets.

ԹԹԹԹԹ **Canberra District Shiraz Viognier 2006** Exceptionally powerful, rich and
concentrated; a full-bodied, lush, velvety texture and mouthfeel; black fruits and spice
seem to subdue the viognier lift, but this is an exception tasted just prior to bottling.
Screwcap. 14° alc. **Rating** 96 **To** 2026 $70
Canberra District Shiraz Viognier 2005 Fragrant and aromatic; a picture of
medium-bodied, silky, satin elegance; if you want a musical analogy, think of
Vivaldi's Four Seasons and Spring. More prosaically, is very different to the '06,
even allowing for the time in bottle, with more finesse and less power.
Screwcap. 14° alc. **Rating** 96 **To** 2025 $68
Canberra District Riesling 2006 Flint, apple, spice and citrus are all to be found
in the bouquet; a particularly smooth and supple mouthfeel, without losing focus or
elegance; good length and aftertaste. Screwcap. 12° alc. **Rating** 94 **To** 2015 $22
Hilltops Shiraz 2006 Spicy/earthy/blackberry/black cherry aromas and flavours;
medium- to full-bodied, with a velvety texture to the mid-palate, firming with
appropriate tannins on the finish. Screwcap. 14.5° alc. **Rating** 94 **To** 2026 $25

Ballinderry 2005 A virtually equal blend of Cabernet Sauvignon/Cabernet Franc/Merlot; has the ripeness, polish and fruit purity which many Canberra cabernet blends lack, and avoids the earthy, gritty characters that those others often exhibit. Screwcap. 14.5° alc. **Rating** 94 **To** 2025 $30

ᵀᵀᵀᵀ℗ Canberra District Viognier 2006 It is only on the back-palate and finish that the wine, and its varietal origin, really starts to talk clearly: apricot, musk and a velvety texture, all enhanced by good acidity. Screwcap. 14.5° alc. **Rating** 90 **To** 2010 $45

Clos Clare

Old Road, Watervale, SA 5452 **Region** Clare Valley
T (08) 8843 0161 **F** (08) 8843 0161 **Open** W'ends & public hols 10–5
Winemaker Various contract **Est.** 1993 **Cases** 1200
Clos Clare is based on a small (2 ha), unirrigated section of the original Florita Vineyard once owned by Leo Buring, and now by Noel Kelly; it produces Riesling of extraordinary concentration and power. Exports to the US, Singapore and Ireland.

Cloudbreak Wines

5A/1 Adelaide Lobethal Road, Lobethal, SA 5241 **Region** Adelaide Hills
T 0431 245 668 **www**.cloudbreakwines.com.au **Open** W'ends & public hols 11–4
Winemaker Simon Greenleaf, William Finlayson **Est.** 2001 **Cases** 300
Owners Will Finlayson and Simon Greenleaf met 16 years ago while both working at Petaluma. A long-term plan to make their own wine came after Simon had done vintages in France, Chile and Spain, and Will in Oregon. In 1998 Simon's parents bought a 7-ha property at which time it was completely overgrown with blackberries. Will says, 'We had limited funds so we did it all ourselves, from clearing the land to growing the cuttings and eventually putting the posts in – it took months of work.' Two varieties were planted first: pinot noir, using Burgundy clones 114 and 115; and pinot gris, followed by sauvignon blanc and chardonnay

ᵀᵀᵀᵀ℗ Adelaide Hills Pinot Noir 2003 Hue still holding well, though not with the brilliance of the '05; seemingly riper, although the alcohol denies this. Certainly more complex, with plummy spicy fruit, and good length; French oak a pure support role. Screwcap. 13.5° alc. **Rating** 93 **To** 2011 $24

Adelaide Hills Pinot Noir 2005 Bright and vividly clear; fresh, crisp and lively, as befits its colour; really only one step up from rose, but has length, and builds on the finish, opening like the proverbial peacock's tail. Screwcap. 13.5° alc. **Rating** 92 **To** 2013 $24

ᵀᵀᵀᵀ Adelaide Hills Pinot Gris 2005 Strong pear/pear skin aromas and flavours; a crisp, clean and long finish. Screwcap. 13.5° alc. **Rating** 89 **To** 2008 $24

Clovely Estate

Steinhardts Road, Moffatdale via Murgon, Qld 4605 **Region** South Burnett
T (07) 3216 1088 **F** (07) 3216 1050 **www**.clovely.com.au **Open** Wed–Sun 10–5
Winemaker Luke Fitzpatrick **Est.** 1998 **Cases** 25 000
Clovely Estate has the largest vineyards in Qld, having established 174 ha of immaculately maintained vines at 2 locations just to the east of Murgon in the Burnett Valley. There are 127 ha of red grapes (including 74 ha of shiraz) and 47 ha of white grapes. The attractively packaged wines are sold in 4 tiers: Clovely Estate at the top (not produced every year); Left Field, strongly fruity and designed to age; Fifth Row, for early drinking; and Queensland, primarily designed for the export market.

Clover Hill ★★★★★

60 Clover Hill Road, Lebrina, Tas 7254 **Region** Northern Tasmania
T (03) 6395 6114 **www**.taltarni.com.au **Open** 7 days 10–5, by appt in winter
Winemaker Loic Le Calvez **Est.** 1986 **Cases** 10 000

Clover Hill was established by Taltarni in 1986 with the sole purpose of making a premium sparkling wine. It has 21 ha of vineyards: 13 ha of chardonnay, 6.76 of pinot noir and 1.24 of pinot meunier. The sparkling wine quality is excellent, combining finesse with power and length. Exports to the UK, the US and other major markets.

ΨΨΨΨΨ **2003** Tight and crisp with stoney/minerally citrus fruit and a relatively low dosage; long finish. Will benefit from time on cork. 13° alc. **Rating** 94 **To** 2012 $41

Clown Fish ★★★★

PO Box 342, Cowaramup, WA 6284 **Region** Margaret River
T (08) 9755 5195 **F** (08) 9755 9441 **www.**cowaramupwines.com.au **Open** Not
Winemaker Naturaliste Vintners (Bruce Dukes) **Est.** 1996 **Cases** 2000
Russell and Marilyn Reynolds run a 17-ha biodynamic vineyard with the aid of sons Cameron (viticulturist) and Anthony (assistant winemaker). Plantings began in 1996, and have been expanded to cover 4.2 ha of merlot, 4 ha of cabernet sauvignon, 2.3 ha each of chardonnay and sauvignon blanc, and 2.1 ha each of shiraz and semillon. Notwithstanding low yields and the discipline which biodynamic grapegrowing entails, wine prices are modest.

ΨΨΨΨΨ **Margaret River Chardonnay 2005** An attractive grapefruit and stone fruit mix; good length, balance and acidity. Biodynamic. Screwcap. 13° alc. **Rating** 92 **To** 2010 $18

ΨΨΨΨ **Margaret River Sauvignon Blanc Semillon 2006** Firm, crisp, grassy, minerally, with the semillon component (40%) driving the style, and just a hint of sauvignon blanc tropical notes; good length. Screwcap. 13° alc. **Rating** 89 **To** 2008 $18
Margaret River Chardonnay 2006 A touch of reduction on the bouquet; citrus, grapefruit, melon and nectarine fruit; the length is a plus. Screwcap. 13.5° alc. **Rating** 89 **To** 2010 $20

Clyde Park Vineyard ★★★★★

2490 Midland Highway, Bannockburn, Vic 3331 **Region** Geelong
T (03) 5281 7274 **www.**clydepark.com.au **Open** W'ends & public hols 11–5
Winemaker Simon Black **Est.** 1979 **Cases** 5500
Clyde Park Vineyard was established by Gary Farr, but sold by him many years ago, and has passed through several changes of ownership. It is now owned by Terry Jongebloed and Sue Jongebloed-Dixon. It has significant mature plantings of pinot noir (3.4 ha), chardonnay (3.1 ha), sauvignon blanc (1.5 ha), shiraz (1.2 ha) and pinot gris (0.9 ha).

ΨΨΨΨΨ **Reserve Chardonnay 2005** A very complex bouquet, with Burgundian funk, but entirely positive and controlled; an intense and tight palate, revelling in its low alcohol and controlled oak. Cork. 13° alc. **Rating** 96 **To** 2012 $41
Chardonnay 2005 A compelling bouquet with melon, fig and cashew plus a touch of funk; a similarly complex palate, both in terms of texture and structure; more to Chablis in style than the Reserve; less new oak, and slightly less intense. Screwcap. 13.5° alc. **Rating** 94 **To** 2015 $24

ΨΨΨΨΨ **Pinot Gris 2006** Particularly lively and fresh palate; lemon zest, apple and pear; a long, clean palate with no phenolics. Gold medal Geelong Wine Show '06. Screwcap. 13.5° alc. **Rating** 93 **To** 2008 $24
Sauvignon Blanc 2006 Spotlessly clean; admirable focus and restraint; grass, herb, gooseberry and citrus mix; dry, fresh finish; good balance. Screwcap. 13° alc. **Rating** 91 **To** 2008 $24
Pinot Noir 2005 Light- to medium-bodied; clear-cut plum varietal fruit throughout; needs more time in bottle. Screwcap. 13.5° alc. **Rating** 90 **To** 2012 $27
Shiraz 2005 A medium-bodied, obvious cool-climate style with spice and licorice overtones to black fruits; nicely worked tannins. Screwcap. 14° alc. **Rating** 90 **To** 2020 $30

Coal Valley Vineyard

257 Richmond Road, Cambridge, Tas 7170 **Region** Southern Tasmania
T (03) 6248 5367 **F** (03) 6248 4175 **www**.coalvalley.com.au **Open** Thurs–Mon 10–5
Winemaker Andrew Hood (Contract) **Est.** 1991 **Cases** 600

Coal Valley Vineyard is the new name for Treehouse Vineyard & Wine Centre, the change brought about by the fact that Treehouse had been trademarked by Pemberton winery, Salitage. Purchased by Todd Goebel and wife Gillian Christian in 1999, the 4.5-ha vineyard comprises riesling, chardonnay, pinot noir, cabernet merlot and tempranillo.

Chardonnay 2005 Light-bodied, but beautifully pure and intense; grapefruit and melon all buoyed by natural acidity, oak a background whisper. Screwcap. 13.3° alc. **Rating** 94 **To** 2013 $25

Riesling 2006 Lemon and lime blossom aromas; unusually rich and ripe by Tasmanian standards, possibly with a bit of botrytis influence; ready when you are. Screwcap. 13.7° alc. **Rating** 90 **To** 2010 $21
Pinot Noir 2005 Medium-bodied, supple and round, with precise and pure pinot fruit in a red spectrum. Screwcap. 13.7° alc. **Rating** 90 **To** 2012 $35

Cabernet Merlot 2005 Light- to medium-bodied; fruit balanced on a knife's edge of greenness, this in a good vintage. Is it worth it? Screwcap. 13° alc. **Rating** 88 **To** 2010 $30

Coates Wines

PO Box 859, McLaren Vale, SA 5171 **Region** McLaren Vale
T 0417 882 557 **F** (08) 8363 9925 **www**.coates-wines.com **Open** Not
Winemaker Duane Coates **Est.** 2003 **Cases** 800

Duane Coates has Bachelor of Science, Master of Business Administration and Master of Oenology degrees from Adelaide University; for good measure he completed the theory component of the Masters of Wine degree in 2005. Having made wine in various parts of the world, and in SA for a number of important brands, he is more than qualified to make and market the Coates Wines. Nonetheless, his original intention was to simply make a single barrel of wine employing various philosophies and practices outside the mainstream, and with no intention of moving to commercial production. The key is organically grown grapes and the refusal to use additives and fining agents. A deliberately low level of new oak (20%) is part of the picture. Exports to the US, Canada, Germany, Sweden and Singapore.

Organically Grown McLaren Vale Shiraz 2005 While relatively light-bodied, has an abundance of sweet fruit in a black confit cherry spectrum, yet light extracted; oak certainly present. Diam. 14.5° alc. **Rating** 91 **To** 2015 $35

The Gimp Shiraz 2005 Very ripe, sweet confit/jam overtones to the fruit; an overall impression of sweetness, but probably as much due to alcohol and fruit flavour as residual sugar. Diam. 14.5° alc. **Rating** 89 **To** 2014 $25

Cobaw Ridge

31 Perc Boyers Lane, East Pastoria via Kyneton, Vic 3444 **Region** Macedon Ranges
T (03) 5423 5227 **www**.cobawridge.com.au **Open** Mon–Fri 10–5, w'ends 12–5.30
Winemaker Alan Cooper **Est.** 1985 **Cases** 1200

Nelly and Alan Cooper established Cobaw Ridge's 6-ha vineyard at an altitude of 610 m in the hills above Kyneton. The plantings of cabernet sauvignon have been removed and partially replaced by lagrein, a variety which sent me scuttling to Jancis Robinson's seminal book on grape varieties: it is a northeast Italian variety typically used to make delicate rose, but at Cobaw Ridge it is made into an impressive full-bodied dry red. This success has prompted Alan Cooper to remove 0.5 ha of chardonnay and plant vermentino in its place. The Cooper's son Joshua is studying Wine Science at Adelaide University and will become the sixth generation of the family on the land. Exports to the UK, the US and France.

♥♥♥♥♥ **Shiraz Viognier 2005** Generous, soft, velvety black cherry, plum and blackberry fruit; fine tannins and supporting oak. Diam. 13.8° alc. **Rating** 94 **To** 2025 $42

♥♥♥♥♀ **Pinot Noir 2005** Powerful, intense dark plum and accompanying black cherry; a long palate sustained by fine tannins; should develop very well with age. Diam. 13.9° alc. **Rating** 93 **To** 2015 $38
Lagrein 2005 Considerable density and structure coming with greater vine maturity and expectations of the variety; black fruits, the only criticism being a fractionally short finish. Diam. 13.3° alc. **Rating** 90 **To** 2015 $48

Cofield Wines   ★★★★☆

Distillery Road, Wahgunyah, Vic 3687 **Region** Rutherglen
T (02) 6033 3798 **www.**cofieldwines.com.au **Open** Mon–Sat 9–5, Sun 10–5
Winemaker Max Cofield, Damien Cofield **Est.** 1990 **Cases** 10 000
District veteran Max Cofield, together with wife Karen and sons Damien (winery) and Andrew (vineyard), has developed an impressively broad-based product range with a strong cellar door sales base. The Pickled Sisters Café is open for lunch Wed–Mon (tel 02 6033 2377). A 20-ha property at Rutherglen was purchased in 2007, which has 5.3 ha already planted to shiraz, and planting of durif and sangiovese is underway.

♥♥♥♥♀ **Rutherglen Shiraz 2005** Medium-bodied, with pleasantly ripe black and red fruits retaining freshness and elegance; restrained oak and tannin extraction. Diam. 14° alc. **Rating** 90 **To** 2015 $19
Sangiovese 2005 Clear varietal expression through a mix of sour cherry, tobacco leaf and spice; fine tannins round off an impressive example of the variety. Cork. 14.2° alc. **Rating** 90 **To** 2010 $19
QVP Vintage Port 2006 Impressive black fruit base and fortifying spirit; touches of black chocolate, spice and licorice; needs a minimum of 5 years; not too sweet. Diam. 19.5° alc. **Rating** 90 **To** 2016 $23

♥♥♥♥ **Rutherglen Shiraz 2002** Attractive, not overripe black fruits; stewed plum and blackberry, round and supple; not over-extracted. Cork. 14.4° alc. **Rating** 89 **To** 2012 $18
Quartz Vein Rutherglen Durif 2005 Deep colour; complex and ripe, showing more spice and development than some durifs of this vintage; great barbecue red. Cork. 15.3° alc. **Rating** 89 **To** 2015 $28
Sauvignon Blanc Semillon 2006 Clean, crisp, fresh grass and mineral flavours; nice dry finish. Screwcap. 12.5° alc. **Rating** 88 **To** 2008 $16
Rutherglen Chardonnay 2006 A particularly crisp, fresh and bright finish is the main strength; light stone fruit and echoes of barrel-ferment on the opening stanzas. Screwcap. 14° alc. **Rating** 88 **To** 2010 $16
Rutherglen Cabernet Sauvignon 2004 A solid wine; blackcurrant and some mocha notes; the sweet fruit reflects the climate, though the alcohol has been kept well in check. Diam. 13.5° alc. **Rating** 87 **To** 2012 $19
T XV Sparkling Shiraz NV Good balance, though as is so common, the dosage sweetness is obvious; some spice helps. Cork. 14.5° alc. **Rating** 87 **To** 2008 $28

Coldstream Hills   **NR**

31 Maddens Lane, Coldstream, Vic 3770 **Region** Yarra Valley
T (03) 5964 9410 **F** (03) 5964 9389 **www.**coldstreamhills.com.au **Open** 7 days 10–5
Winemaker Andrew Fleming, Greg Jarratt, James Halliday (Consultant) **Est.** 1985 **Cases** NA
Founded by the author, who continues to be involved with the winemaking, but acquired by Southcorp in mid-1996, thus now a small part of Fosters. Expansion plans already then underway have been maintained, with well in excess of 100 ha of owned or managed estate vineyards as the base. Chardonnay and Pinot Noir continue to be the principal focus; Merlot came on-stream in 1997, Sauvignon Blanc around the same time. Vintage conditions permitting, these wines are made in both varietal and Reserve form, the latter in restricted quantities. Tasting notes are written by Andrew Fleming. Exports to the UK, the US and Singapore.

Coldstream Hills Chardonnay 2006 Classic, cool-climate style, with fruit intensity and tight mineral acidity. White peach, nectarine and lemon characters dominate, with cashew nut barrel ferment characters, toasty French oak and slatey minerality providing additional complexity. Screwcap. **Rating** NR **To** 2015 $28.90

Coldstream Hills Reserve Chardonnay 2005 Elegant, restrained, and shows wonderful fine acidity. Savoury, toasty oak complements the fruit characters of citrus, pear and white peach, which are further enhanced by underlying minerality. The wine has excellent length and balance. An excellent example of cool-climate chardonnay from the outstanding '05 vintage. Has an extraordinary wine show track record, unequalled in recent times, winning gold medals at Brisbane, Melbourne, Hobart, Perth, Sydney and Melbourne in the same year. In Melbourne it won the trophy for Best Victorian White Wine, and at Adelaide it won 3 trophies, including Best Wine of Show. Screwcap. **Rating** NR **To** 2015 $46.90

Coldstream Hills Pinot Noir 2006 Medium-bodied, with supple texture and a fine tannin finish. Dark red fruit characters of cherry and blueberry dominate, with savoury stalkiness and toasty oak evident in the background. Excellent structure and length; will reward careful cellaring. Screwcap. **Rating** NR **To** 2013 $28.90

Coldstream Hills Reserve Pinot Noir 2005 Great structure and depth, with concentrated cherry and raspberry fruit characters. Exhibits beautifully integrated toasty French oak, with a long, fine, silky finish. Trophy for Best Pinot Noir at the Sydney Wine Show '07. Screwcap. **Rating** NR **To** 2015 $75

Coldstream Hills Limited Release Shiraz 2005 Medium-bodied with concentration and depth. The palate is round and full, with a fine tannin finish. Plums and cherry fruit characters are dominant and are supported by smoky, toasty oak and spice. An excellent example from the mild '05 vintage. Screwcap. **Rating** NR points **To** 2020 $35

Coldstream Hills Merlot 2005 A medium-bodied style with dark fruit characters of cherry and blueberry. The tannins are fine and persistent and give the wine length and structure. Smoky, cedary oak is evident and provides additional complexity. The wine has roundness and texture and is an excellent example of cool-climate merlot. An excellent growing season in '05, with mild conditions throughout the autumn months. Screwcap. **Rating** NR **To** 2018 $28.90

Coldstream Hills Cabernet Sauvignon 2005 Medium-bodied, with fine powdery tannins and great length. The palate exhibits fruit characters of cassis and blueberry, with dark chocolate and vanilla bean adding further complexity. Cedary, toasty oak is evident and integrates harmoniously. This wine exhibits classic cool-climate cabernet characters from the mild '05 vintage. It will reward careful cellaring. Screwcap. **Rating** NR **To** 2025 $28.90

Coliban Valley Wines ★★★★☆

Metcalfe-Redesdale Road, Metcalfe, Vic 3448 **Region** Heathcote
T 0417 312 098 **F** (03) 9813 3895 **www.**heathcotewinegrowers.com.au **Open** W'ends 10–5
Winemaker Helen Miles **Est.** 1997 **Cases** 400

Helen Miles (with a degree in science) and partner Greg Miles have planted 2.8 ha of shiraz, 1.2 ha of cabernet and 0.4 ha of merlot near Metcalfe, in the cooler southwest corner of Heathcote. The granitic soils and warm climate allow organic principles to be used successfully. The shiraz is dry-grown, while the cabernet sauvignon and merlot receive minimal irrigation.

ŸŸŸŸŸ **Heathcote Cabernet Sauvignon 2005** Medium-bodied; succulent cassis blackcurrant fruit with a web of fine, ripe tannins; sensitive oak, and masses of flavour at moderate alcohol. Diam. 13° alc. **Rating** 94 **To** 2015 $20

ŸŸŸŸŸ **Heathcote Merlot 2005** A surprise for the region; has both varietal character and structure; small berry fruits, black olive notes and fine tannins; lingering finish. Diam. 13° alc. **Rating** 91 **To** 2013 $20

Heathcote Rose 2006 Quite intense, savoury, spicy fruit; no reliance on residual sugar but has excellent length; perfect with Italian pasta. Diam. 12.5° alc. **Rating** 90 **To** 2008 $15

Heathcote Shiraz 2005 Radically different to the '04; a medium-bodied mix of black fruits, spice and savoury/earthy notes. One suspects the dry-grown vines may be struggling in the face of persistent drought. Diam. 13.5° alc. **Rating** 90 **To** 2012 $25

Colville Estate   ★★★

PO Box 504, McLaren Vale, SA 5171 **Region** McLaren Vale
T (08) 8323 8973 **F** (08) 8323 8001 **Open** Not
Winemaker Wayne Thomas Wines (Contract) **Est.** 2001 **Cases** 750
Peter Easterbrook has a 25-year career as a professional grapegrower in McLaren Vale, and over an extended period has (with wife Jennie) planted 20 ha of shiraz, 4 ha of cabernet sauvignon and 2 ha each of grenache and merlot. The estate is run using non-chemical regimes, relying on composting and natural fertilisers. Most of the grapes are sold, a small amount retained and made for export to Canada, Ireland and Hong Kong.

 McLaren Vale Shiraz 2003 Light red; a light-bodied, spicy, savoury style, with touches of regional chocolate and gentle tannins. Cork. 14° alc. **Rating** 87 **To** 2009 $15

Colvin Wines   ★★★★

19 Boyle Street, Mosman, NSW 2088 (postal) **Region** Lower Hunter Valley
T (02) 9908 7886 **F** (02) 9908 7885 **www.**colvinwines.com.au **Open** Not
Winemaker Andrew Spinaze, Trevor Drayton (Contract) **Est.** 1999 **Cases** 500
Sydney lawyer John Colvin and wife Robyn purchased the De Beyers Vineyard in 1990, which has a history going back to the second half of the 19th century. By 1967, when a syndicate headed by Douglas McGregor purchased 35 ha of the original vineyard site, no vines remained. The syndicate planted semillon on the alluvial soil of the creek flats and shiraz on the red clay hillsides. When the Colvins acquired the property the vineyard was in need of attention. Up to 1998 all the grapes were sold to Tyrrell's, but since 1999 quantities have been made for the Colvin Wines label. These include Sangiovese, from a little over 1 ha of vines planted by John Colvin in 1996 because of his love of the wines of Tuscany.

 De Beyers Vineyard Hunter Valley Sangiovese 2000 Brick red; light-bodied, earthy, spicy wine; predominantly regional, but some varietal character; the tannins have not outlived the fruit. Cork. 12° alc. **Rating** 87 **To** 2008 $25

Connor Park Winery   ★★★★

59 Connors Road, Leichardt, Vic 3516 **Region** Bendigo
T (03) 5437 5234 **F** (03) 5437 5204 **www.**connorparkwinery.com.au **Open** 7 days 11–5.30
Winemaker Ross Lougoon **Est.** 1994 **Cases** 5000
The original planting of 2 ha of vineyard dates back to the mid-1960s and to the uncle of the present owners. When the present owners purchased the property in 1985 the vineyard had run wild. They resuscitated and expanded the vineyard (which formed part of a much larger mixed farming operation) and until 1994 were content to sell the grapes to other winemakers. Exports to the US, Canada and Asia.

♟♟♟♟♟ **The Honour Bendigo Shiraz 2003** Similarly potent to the '04, but unexpectedly (drought and so forth) expresses its shiraz fruit better, the alcohol less obvious. Nonetheless, for aficionados of 'the biggest is best' theory; 200 cases. Cork. 16° alc. **Rating** 92 **To** 2015 $35
The Honour Bendigo Shiraz 2004 Dense colour; the alcohol is immediately apparent in a massively lush and opulent wine ranging through prune, cassis and blackberry. Aged in French oak. From 1960s planting; a pity it wasn't picked earlier; 200 cases. Cork. 16° alc. **Rating** 90 **To** 2014 $35

♟♟♟♟ **Bendigo Durif 2003** Deep red-purple; typical black fruits, plums, prunes, blackberries with a dusting of bitter chocolate; good barbecue red. Cork. 15.5° alc. **Rating** 88 **To** 2011 $20

Bendigo Shiraz 2004 A light- to medium-bodied mix of red and black fruits, plus lots of vanilla oak and ripe tannins. Cork. 14.5° alc. **Rating** 87 **To** 2010 $20
Bendigo Shiraz 2003 Strong colour; alcohol makes the wine taste sweet from start to finish, which will appeal to some. Cork. 15.5° alc. **Rating** 87 **To** 2012 $20
Bendigo Barbera 2003 Has depth and alcohol-assisted power to the black fruits and solid tannins; some patience may reward. Cork. 15° alc. **Rating** 87 **To** 2010 $20
Bendigo Sparkling Shiraz 2002 Plenty of base fruit flavour in a spice and blackberry range; quite good balance and length. Bottle-fermented, and could improve with a few more years on cork. 14.5° alc. **Rating** 87 **To** 2010 $28

Constable & Hershon   ★★★

205 Gillards Road, Pokolbin, NSW 2320 **Region** Lower Hunter Valley
T (02) 4998 7887 **F** (02) 4998 6555 **www**.constablehershon.com.au **Open** 7 days 10–5
Winemaker Neil McGuigan (Contract) **Est.** 1981 **Cases** 3000
Features spectacular formal gardens: the Rose, Knot and Herb, Secret and Sculpture; a free 30-minute garden tour is conducted Mon–Fri at 10.30 am. The 7-ha vineyard is spectacularly situated under the backdrop of the Brokenback Range. Offers a range of several vintages of each variety.

ΨΨΨΨ   Chardonnay 2005 Plenty of mouthfilling fruit; balanced, but not especially complex. **Rating** 88 **To** 2009

 ## Conte Estate Wines   ★★★★☆

Lot 51 Sand Road, McLaren Flat, SA 5171 **Region** McLaren Vale
T 0414 942 072 **F** (08) 8383 0125 **www**.conteestatewines.com.au **Open** By appt
Winemaker Danial Conte, Steve Conte **Est.** 2003 **Cases** 10 000
Steve and Maria Conte, assisted by son Danial, have a large vineyard, predominantly established since 1960 but with 2.5 ha of shiraz planted 100 years earlier in the 1860s. In all there are 18 ha of shiraz, 12 ha of grenache, 7 ha each of cabernet sauvignon and sauvignon blanc, 6 ha of chardonnay and 1.66 ha of gewurztraminer. While continuing to sell a large proportion of the production, winemaking has become a larger part of the business.

ΨΨΨΨΨ   3 Generations Over The Hill McLaren Vale Shiraz 2005 The 3 generations refers to the Conte family, not the Hardy family which planted the shiraz in the 1860s. Beautifully focused and balanced; the first whiff of the bouquet proclaims its quality and typicity; the palate offers blackberry, plum and a touch of chocolate, followed by a long, fine finish, and subtle oak. Incomprehensibly low price. Cork. 14.5° alc. **Rating** 95 **To** 2025 $18

ΨΨΨΨΨ   McLaren Vale Shiraz 2004 Medium-bodied; more distinctly McLaren Vale, with dark chocolate running right through the wine; does show the higher alcohol, and is fractionally warm in consequence; nonetheless still well within medium-bodied boundaries, and has very good black fruits on the back-palate and finish. Cork. 15° alc. **Rating** 93 **To** 2020 $18
3 Generations Congoli Creek Sauvignon Blanc 2006 Clean, precise and focused; aromas and flavours are in a grass/herb/asparagus spectrum, with no concession to residual sugar; good length and well-made – and great value. Screwcap. 12.5° alc. **Rating** 90 **To** 2008 $13
McLaren Vale Grenache Shiraz 2004 Medium-bodied; considerably more structure than the Grenache, McLaren Vale chocolate coming through for one thing, and plenty of black fruits for another, even if tempered a little by the grenache; good tannins and length. Cork. 15° alc. **Rating** 90 **To** 2012 $18

ΨΨΨΨ   3 Generations The Numb Hand Pruner McLaren Vale Grenache 2004 Light- to medium-bodied; spicy red and black fruits; as so often, doesn't have a lot of structure, but is easy to drink. Vines planted by the Conte family in 1965. Cork. 14.5° alc. **Rating** 87 **To** 2008 $18

Coobara Wines

PO Box 231, Birdwood, SA 5234 **Region** Adelaide Hills
T (08) 8568 5375 **F** (08) 8568 5375 **www.**coobarawines.com.au **Open** By appt
Winemaker David Cook, Mark Jamieson **Est.** 1992 **Cases** 1500
David Cook has worked in the wine industry for over 18 years, principally with Orlando, but also with Jim Irvine, John Glaetzer and the late Neil Ashmead. As well as working full-time for Orlando, he undertook oenology and viticulture courses, and – with support from his parents – planted 4 ha of cabernet sauvignon and merlot on the family property at Birdwood. In 1993 they purchased the adjoining property, planting 2 ha of riesling, and thereafter lifting the plantings of merlot and cabernet sauvignon to 4 ha each, plus 0.4 ha of shiraz. In 2003 David decided to commence wine production, a fortuitous decision given that the following year their long-term grape purchase contracts were not renewed. Coobara means 'place of birds' (Aboriginal).

♟♟♟♟♟ **Adelaide Hills Merlot 2005** A fragrant allspice core of cassis and blackcurrant; lots of structure and substance, with guaranteed cellaring potential. Merlots don't come much better. Screwcap. 14° alc. **Rating** 94 **To** 2019 $18
Adelaide Hills Cabernet Merlot 2005 Another wine of real authority and power; French oak adds an impressive frame for the blackcurrant fruit. Screwcap. 14° alc. **Rating** 94 **To** 2010 $18

♟♟♟♟♟ **Adelaide Hills Shiraz 2005** A bright medium-bodied wine; appealing cool-grown fruit, smooth and supple, yet spicy and talkative; fine, lingering tannins. A lovely wine for drinking now or later. Screwcap. 14° alc. **Rating** 93 **To** 2015 $18

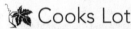 Cooks Lot

Cassilis Road, Mudgee, NSW 2850 **Region** Mudgee
T (02) 9550 3228 **F** (02) 9550 4390 **Open** 7 days 10–5
Winemaker Duncan Cook, Ian McRae **Est.** 2002 **Cases** 2500
Duncan Cook has established his cellar door and café (open Tues–Sat 10–5) at the Parklands Resort. As well as leasing the cellar door and restaurant, he is planting a little over 1 ha of vines, again on a land-lease basis. In the meantime he is producing wines from Mudgee and Orange. Winemaking is split between Miramar Winery and Lowe Family, although Duncan is halfway through his oenology degree at Charles Sturt University, and will gradually take over the winemaking. The cellar door and café has artworks by Amber Subaki, an illustrator who specialises in nudes and portraits, and who designed the Cooks Lot label.

♟♟♟♟♟ **Riesling 2005** Well-balanced and proportioned; generous tropical lime juice flavours; power rather than finesse, but follows in the footsteps of Miramar in winning the trophy for Best White Wine at the Mudgee Wine Show '05. Screwcap. 12.5° alc. **Rating** 92 **To** 2010

Mudgee Shiraz 2004 Medium- to full-bodied, with plenty of upfront blackberry and plum fruit, then savoury tannins; good length. Screwcap. 14.2° alc. **Rating** 91 **To** 2019 $17.95

♟♟♟♟ **Late Harvest Mudgee Semillon Sauvignon Blanc Riesling 2005** Has some merit at intermediate sweetness levels; plenty of fruit flavour. Screwcap. 12° alc. **Rating** 87 **To** 2010 $18

Coolangatta Estate

1335 Bolong Road, Shoalhaven Heads, NSW 2535 **Region** Shoalhaven Coast
T (02) 4448 7131 **F** (02) 4448 7997 **www.**coolangattaestate.com.au **Open** 7 days 10–5
Winemaker Tyrrell's **Est.** 1988 **Cases** 5000
Coolangatta Estate is part of a 150-ha resort with accommodation, restaurants, golf course, etc; some of the oldest buildings were convict-built in 1822. It might be thought that the wines are tailored purely for the tourist market, but in fact the standard of viticulture is exceptionally high

(immaculate Scott Henry trellising), and the contract winemaking is wholly professional. Has a habit of bobbing up with gold medals at Sydney and Canberra wine shows.

ŸŸŸŸŸ **Estate Grown Semillon 2006** A clean and lively wine with mineral, herb, grass and lemon peel flavours; sure to flourish with time. Screwcap. 10.3° alc. **Rating** 91 To 2016 $18
Eileen Chambourcin 2005 Smooth and supple raspberry and mulberry fruit; has far better line than most, exhibiting some length. Screwcap. 13.1° alc. **Rating** 90 To 2008 $19

ŸŸŸŸ **Alexander Berry Chardonnay 2005** A big, full-bodied, peachy chardonnay, with French oak in solid support. Screwcap. 13.5° alc. **Rating** 89 **To** 2010 $22
Estate Grown Sauvignon Blanc Chardonnay 2006 An odd couple which work well here; tangy lemon peel flavours through to a clean finish. Screwcap. 11.4° alc. **Rating** 89 To 2008 $16
Estate Grown Rose 2006 Brilliant fuchsia colour; plenty of red fruit in a strawberry/cherry spectrum; not overly sweet. Chambourcin/Merlot. Screwcap. 13° alc. **Rating** 88 **To** 2008 $16
Estate Grown Verdelho 2006 Well-made; gentle fruit salad varietal character, with a touch of minerality helping the crisp finish. Screwcap. 13.3° alc. **Rating** 87 **To** 2008 $18

Coombend Estate

Coombend via Swansea, Tas 7190 **Region** East Coast Tasmania
T (03) 6257 8881 **F** (03) 6257 8884 **Open** 7 days 10–5
Winemaker Tamar Ridge (Andrew Pirie) **Est.** 1985 **Cases** 3000
In 2005 Tamar Ridge acquired Coombend Estate, including all the assets and the business name. Tamar Ridge has immediately commenced the establishment of a large vineyard which will dwarf the existing 1.75 ha of cabernet sauvignon, 2.25 ha of sauvignon blanc, 0.5 ha of pinot noir and 0.3 ha of riesling. Exports to Sweden.

ŸŸŸŸ **Sauvignon Blanc 2006** Herb, passionfruit and citrus aromas and flavours; has line and length, and is not sweet. **Rating** 89 **To** 2008 $25

Cooper Burns

1 Golden Way, Nuriootpa, SA 5353 (postal) **Region** Barossa Valley
T (08) 8563 9196 **F** (08) 8563 9196 **www**.cooperburns.com.au **Open** Not
Winemaker Mark Cooper, Russell Burns **Est.** 2004 **Cases** 200
Cooper Burns is the winemaking partnership of Mark Cooper and Russell Burns. It is a virtual winery focusing on small batch, handmade wine from the Barossa Valley (grapes are sourced from Kalimna at the northern end of the valley). In 2006 production was increased to add a Shiraz Viognier and Grenache to the existing single-vineyard Shiraz.

ŸŸŸŸŸ **Barossa Valley Shiraz 2005** Rich blackberry, plum, prune and dark chocolate; impressive power, length and overall balance; 200 cases made. Screwcap. 14.5° alc. **Rating** 94 **To** 2025 $30

Cooper Wines

Lovedale Road, Lovedale, NSW 2321 **Region** Lower Hunter Valley
T (02) 4930 7387 **www**.cooperwines.com.au **Open** Mon–Fri 10–5, w'ends 9.30–5
Winemaker Max Cooper **Est.** 2001 **Cases** 3000
Max Cooper is a Qantas pilot who purchased the former Allanmere Winery & Vineyard. The chardonnay is estate-grown; the other wines are made onsite from grapes purchased by growers in the region.

Cooralook Wines

1 Garden Street, South Yarra, Vic 3141 (postal) **Region** Mornington Peninsula
T (03) 9251 5375 **F** (03) 9639 1540 **www**.cooralook.com.au **Open** Not
Winemaker Tod Dexter **Est.** 2000 **Cases** 10 000
Cooralook Wines, owned by Robert and Mem Kirby, has substantial vineyards in the Mornington
Peninsula, Heathcote and Strathbogie Ranges, each vineyard focusing on the varieties most suited
to each region. The wines represent great value. Exports to the US.

ΨΨΨΨΨ **Mornington Peninsula Pinot Noir 2005** Light but bright purple-red; spicy
black and red cherry fruits; quite intense, and also has structure in a forest spectrum.
Screwcap. 14° alc. **Rating** 90 **To** 2011 $22

ΨΨΨΨ **Mornington Peninsula Chardonnay 2005** Light- to medium-bodied; citrus
and melon fruit with nutty/creamy characters, and a slightly fuzzy finish. Screwcap.
13.5° alc. **Rating** 89 **To** 2008 $20
Heathcote Shiraz 2005 Unconvincing colour; seems to have struggled for
ripeness; spicy, but at the savoury/green end of the spectrum. Screwcap. 14.5° alc.
Rating 87 **To** 2011 $22

Cooyal Grove

Lot 9 Stoney Creek Road, Mudgee, NSW 2850 **Region** Mudgee
T (02) 6373 5337 **F** (02) 6373 5337 **Open** 7 days by appt
Winemaker Moore Haszard (Contract) **Est.** 1990 **Cases** 800
In 2002 the 10-ha Cooyal Grove property of vines, pistachio nut trees and olives was purchased
by Sydney publican John Lenard, and Paul and Lydele Walker, a local Mudgee vigneron and his
wife. The partners say, 'We have worked almost every weekend in the vineyard and grove,
undertaking every task from planting, pruning, training, harvesting, bottling and labelling. Given
that all of the partners are only 30 years old and not yet financially able to employ outside labour,
we seem to call on every friend, relative and friend's relatives to assist. This has made for a feeling
of building something from scratch which we are proud of.' The vineyards now total 4.5 ha, with
chardonnay, semillon, sauvignon blanc, merlot, shiraz and cabernet sauvignon.

ΨΨΨΨ **Mudgee Merlot 2004** Light-bodied; has elegance and clear varietal character;
savoury black olives with a splash of sweet berry fruit. Cork. 13.5° alc. **Rating** 87
To 2008 $12

Cope-Williams

Glenfern Road, Romsey, Vic 3434 **Region** Macedon Ranges
T (03) 5429 5428 **F** (03) 5429 5655 **Open** 7 days 11–5
Winemaker David Cowburn **Est.** 1977 **Cases** 7000
One of Macedon's pioneers, specialising in sparkling wines that are full flavoured but also
producing excellent Chardonnay and Pinot Noir table wines in warmer vintages. A traditional
'English Green'-type cricket ground is available for hire and booked out most days from spring
through until autumn.

ΨΨΨΨ **R.O.M.S.E.Y. Brut NV** A funky, but appealing bouquet, and a rich palate; elevated
dosage just a trifle too enthusiastic. Cork. **Rating** 89 **To** 2008 $28

Coriole

Chaffeys Road, McLaren Vale, SA 5171 **Region** McLaren Vale
T (08) 8323 8305 **www**.coriole.com **Open** Mon–Fri 10–5, w'ends & public hols 11–5
Winemaker Grant Harrison **Est.** 1967 **Cases** 34 000
Justifiably best known for its Shiraz, which – in both the rare Lloyd Reserve and standard forms
– is extremely impressive. One of the first wineries to catch on to the Italian fashion with its
Sangiovese, but its white varietal wines lose nothing by comparison. It is also a producer of high-
quality olive oil.

ŸŸŸŸŸ **Lloyd Reserve McLaren Vale Shiraz 2005** An even deeper colour and better hue than the Estate Grown; more profound in every respect; dark blackberry fruit flavours intermingle with chocolate and licorice; a very long, balanced palate. Vines planted 1919. Quality cork. 14.5° alc. **Rating** 96 **To** 2030 $72

Lloyd Reserve McLaren Vale Shiraz 2004 Strong red-purple; a totally delicious wine, opening with blackberry, anise, spice and dark chocolate; abundant flavour without the millstone of high alcohol; good oak in support. Cork. 14° alc. **Rating** 96 **To** 2019 $65

Redstone Shiraz Cabernet 2004 Saturated with black fruits and bitter chocolate with ripe tannins giving very good structure and balance; restrained alcohol a plus. Bargain price. Cork. 14° alc. **Rating** 94 **To** 2015 $19.95

Mary Kathleen Reserve McLaren Vale Cabernet Merlot 2004 Medium-full-bodied; abundant depth to the blackcurrant fruit; high-quality, fine tannins run through the palate giving balance and mouthfeel; long finish. Cork. 13.5° alc. **Rating** 94 **To** 2024 $41.50

ŸŸŸŸ♀ **Estate Grown McLaren Vale Shiraz 2005** Aromatic blackberry, licorice and dark chocolate aromas, then persistent but balanced and ripe tannins on the palate; subtle oak. Cork. 14° alc. **Rating** 93 **To** 2018 $27.95

McLaren Vale Barbera 2005 Exceptional colour for the variety, which is a prelude to the flavours across a silky spectrum of red fruits, ranging from cherry to raspberry; fine tannins and good balance; one of the best yet in Australia for a workhorse variety. Screwcap. 14° alc. **Rating** 93 **To** 2015 $29.95

Fortified Shiraz 2006 Vivid purple-red; history tells us the Hardys and Reynell vintage ports from quality shiraz and with similar spice aged magnificently for 40 years or more; there is no reason why this shouldn't do so in a 750 ml bottle. Cork. 18° alc. **Rating** 93 **To** 2026 $19.95

Redstone Shiraz 2004 A quiet bouquet then latent regional dark chocolate surges to the surface after an initial blackberry and plum impact. Good tannin control and minimal oak flavour. Screwcap. 14° alc. **Rating** 91 **To** 2019 $18

Fortified Shiraz 2005 Deeply coloured, this is a rich and archetypal McLaren Vale vintage-style port, replete with dark chocolate and blackberry fruit. The fortifying spirit is good, as is the balance. 375 ml. Cork. 19° alc. **Rating** 91 **To** 2015 $17.50

McLaren Vale Nebbiolo Rose 2006 A quite aromatic cherry blossom bouquet, the lively and fresh palate with real presence; convincing dry finish; considerable character. Screwcap. 13° alc. **Rating** 90 **To** 2008 $19.95

ŸŸŸŸ **Contour 4 McLaren Vale Sangiovese Shiraz 2005** Medium-bodied; sangiovese drives the wine from start to finish; savoury, spicy cherry/sour cherry flavours; no regional chocolate. Ideal Italian food partner. Screwcap. 14° alc. **Rating** 89 **To** 2015 $16.95

McLaren Vale Sangiovese 2005 Spicy, savoury notes to the core of cherry fruit; light- to medium-bodied and quite long, but needs a touch more intensity. Cork. 14° alc. **Rating** 89 **To** 2010 $19.95

McLaren Vale Adelaide Hills Semillon Sauvignon Blanc 2006 Clean and crisp; a touch of tropical passionfruit from the sauvignon blanc, the semillon providing structure, but also some of the grassy, mineral notes on the finish. Screwcap. 13.5° alc. **Rating** 88 **To** 2009 $18.95

Redstone Cabernet Sauvignon 2004 Dark chocolate and blackcurrant vie with each other from the outset, the first proclaiming the region, the second the variety. Screwcap. 14° alc. **Rating** 88 **To** 2012 $18

Estate Grown McLaren Vale Cabernet Sauvignon 2005 Pure varietal aromas lead into a palate which (unexpectedly) is driven by dry, rough tannins which may soften some day. Cork. 14° alc. **Rating** 87 **To** 2025 $27.95

Adelaide Hills Nebbiolo 2005 Typical light colour; tannins hold whatever fruit there is in a vice-like grip; for nebbiolo masochists. Screwcap. 14° alc. **Rating** 87 **To** 2015 $29.95

Cosham ★★★☆

101 Union Road, Carmel via Kalamunda, WA 6076 **Region** Perth Hills
T (08) 9293 5424 **Open** W'ends & public hols 10–5
Winemaker Julie White (Contract) **Est.** 1989 **Cases** 1000
Has grown significantly from its small base in recent years. The vineyard is planted on an old orchard, and consists of 2 ha of cabernet sauvignon, merlot, shiraz, pinot noir, cabernet franc, chardonnay and petit verdot, established between 1990 and 1995. They grow in gravelly loam with some clay, but overall in a well-drained soil with good rainfall.

 # Counterpoint Vineyard **NR**

107 McAdams Lane, Moonambel, Vic 3478 **Region** Pyrenees
T (03) 5467 2245 **F** (03) 5467 2245 **Open** W'ends & public hols Sept–Apr
Winemaker Campbell McAdam **Est.** 1976 **Cases** NA
Noreen and Campbell McAdam began the establishment of their 3.2-ha vineyard in 1976, with much the same aims as Ewan Jones had for the adjacent Dalwhinnie vineyard. From here on, the ways parted, the McAdams continuing full-time employment, running an unrelated small business, and raising a sporting son. While somewhat neglected, the 1.2 ha of cabernet sauvignon and 0.8 ha of shiraz survived, and since the mid-1990s have produced quality grapes, as have the newer plantings of white varieties. Since 2002 the McAdams have lived full-time on the property, building a winery in '02, and selling their wine by mail order and restricted cellar door sales.

Cowra Estate ★★★★

Boorowa Road, Cowra, NSW 2794 **Region** Cowra
T (02) 9907 7735 **F** (02) 9907 7734 **Open** At The Quarry Restaurant Tues–Sun 10–4
Winemaker Ralph Fowler **Est.** 1973 **Cases** 5000
Cowra Estate was purchased from the family of founder Tony Gray by South African-born food and beverage entrepreneur John Geber in 1995. A vigourous promotional campaign has gained a higher domestic profile for the once export-oriented brand. John Geber is actively involved in the promotional effort and rightly proud of the wines. The Quarry Wine Cellars and Restaurant offer visitors a full range of Cowra Estate's wines, plus wines from other producers in the region. The Geber family, incidentally, also owns Chateau Tanunda in the Barossa Valley. Exports to Switzerland and Denmark.

 Eagle Rock Chardonnay 2005 Plenty of nectarine and peach fruit running through the length of the palate; attractive barrel ferment notes from French oak; the best for years from Cowra Estate. Cork. 13.5° alc. **Rating** 92 **To** 2008 $28
Eagle Rock Cabernet Merlot 2005 Medium-bodied; soft tannins run right through the palate supporting the ample blackcurrant and cassis fruit; another feather in the cap for Cowra Estate this vintage. Cork. 14.5° alc. **Rating** 90 **To** 2013 $22

 Merlot 2005 Way above expectations; spice, cedar, black olive and cassis flavours, all clearly varietal; good length. Cork. 13.5° alc. **Rating** 89 **To** 2008 $15
Chardonnay 2006 Clean, soft, peachy fruit; a pleasant wine, not showing much oak notwithstanding the barrel fermentation; presumably, older oak used. Screwcap. 13° alc. **Rating** 87 **To** 2008 $15

 # Cowrock Vineyards ★★★

28 Dequetteville Terrace, Kent Town DC, SA 5067 (postal) **Region** Margaret River
T (08) 8331 3000 **F** (08) 8331 3377 **Open** Not
Winemaker Jodie Opie **Est.** 2006 **Cases** NFP
Global Wine Ventures Ltd is the phoenix arisen from the ashes of Xanadu Wines Ltd. The wines will be predominantly sourced from the 44 ha Cowrock Vineyard, situated 20 km south of the Margaret River township. Distribution in Australia is through Red+White, and it is anticipated exports will follow in the US, the UK and select parts of Asia.

Crabtree Watervale Wines

North Terrace, Watervale, SA 5452 **Region** Clare Valley
T (08) 8843 0069 **F** (08) 8843 0144 **www**.crabtreewines.com.au **Open** Mon–Sat 11–5
Winemaker Robert Crabtree **Est.** 1979 **Cases** 5000
Best known for producing classic Clare Valley styles, most notably Watervale Riesling, displaying elegance rather than richness. Robert Crabtree has recently handed over the reins to new owners, but remains as a consultant. Exports to Canada and Singapore.

Riesling 2006 Clean, firm, classic Watervale style; stone and slate characters, and a long finish; needs a minimum of 5 years. Screwcap. 12.5° alc. **Rating** 92 **To** 2016 $20

Windmill Vineyard Cabernet Sauvignon 2003 By Clare Valley standards, quite supple; medium-bodied, with fresh fruit flavours, and fine tannins. Screwcap. 13.5° alc. **Rating** 89 **To** 2015 $20
Tempranillo 2006 Light- to medium-bodied; in the mainstream of young tempranillo springing up all around Australia; a blend of red fruits, tamarillo and citrus. Screwcap. 13.5° alc. **Rating** 89 **To** 2012 $20
Picnic Hill Vineyard Shiraz 2004 Slightly hazy colour, though the hue is good; a firm, light- to medium-bodied palate, with fairly brisk acidity to the fresh red fruit flavours. Screwcap. 14° alc. **Rating** 88 **To** 2012 $20

Craig Avon Vineyard

Craig Avon Lane, Merricks North, Vic 3926 **Region** Mornington Peninsula
T (03) 5989 7465 **F** (03) 5989 7615 **Open** By appt
Winemaker Ken Lang **Est.** 1986 **Cases** 1000
The estate-grown wines are produced from 0.9 ha of chardonnay, 0.5 ha of pinot noir and 0.4 ha of cabernet sauvignon. They are competently made, clean and with pleasant fruit flavour. All the wines are sold through the cellar door and by mailing list.

Craiglee

Sunbury Road, Sunbury, Vic 3429 **Region** Sunbury
T (03) 9744 4489 **www**.craiglee.com.au **Open** Sun & public hols 10–5, or by appt
Winemaker Patrick Carmody **Est.** 1976 **Cases** 3000
A winery with a proud 19th-century record which recommenced winemaking in 1976 after a prolonged hiatus. Produces one of the finest cool-climate Shirazs in Australia, redolent of cherry, licorice and spice in the better (warmer) vintages, lighter-bodied in the cooler ones. Mature vines and improved viticulture have made the wines more consistent (and even better) over the past 10 years or so. Exports to the UK, the US and NZ.

Shiraz 2004 Deep, vivid purple-red; super-intense black fruits and powerful tannins, far stronger and deeper than the normally medium-bodied style of Craiglee. Diam. 14.5° alc. **Rating** 95 **To** 2029 $40

Craigow

528 Richmond Road, Cambridge, Tas 7170 **Region** Southern Tasmania
T (03) 6248 5379 **www**.craigow.com.au **Open** 7 days Christmas to Easter (except public hols), or by appt
Winemaker Winemaking Tasmania (Julian Alcorso) **Est.** 1989 **Cases** 1500
Craigow has substantial vineyards, with 5 ha of pinot noir and another 5 ha (in total) of riesling, chardonnay and gewurztraminer. Barry and Cathy Edwards have moved from being grapegrowers with only one wine made for sale to a portfolio of 6 wines, while continuing to sell most of their grapes. Craigow has an impressive museum release program; the best are outstanding, others show the impact of sporadic bottle oxidation. Exports to the UK.

𐂷𐂷𐂷𐂷𐂷 **Chardonnay 2003** Has continued to develop over the past 12 months, and lose none of its freshness. As I noted in last year's *Companion*, 'high natural acidity is the steely structure around which the wine has been built; very Chablis-like'. The acidity is still there, but the overall complexity of the wine is increasing. Cork. 12.8° alc. **Rating** 94 **To** 2012 $23

𐂷𐂷𐂷𐂷𐂷 **Riesling 2005** Attractive style, full of sweet lime juice flavours; long, dry finish; has started to evolve as anticipated. Screwcap. 12.7° alc. **Rating** 91 **To** 2014 $19
Pinot Noir 2005 Savoury, spicy, forest floor underneath cherry and plum fruit; good length, and still developing, as is the excellent '03 Pinot. Cork. 13.6° alc. **Rating** 90 **To** 2012 $28
Dessert Gewurztraminer 2006 Abundant flavour, well-balanced and rich; the gewurztraminer varietal character is, however, muted. Screwcap. 10° alc. **Rating** 90 **To** 2010 $21

𐂷𐂷𐂷𐂷 **Sauvignon Blanc 2006** Soft, tropical fruit; has varietal flavour even if there is a hint of sweetness which really wasn't necessary. Screwcap. 13.6° alc. **Rating** 88 **To** 2008 $19
Easy Rose 2006 Pleasant red fruits, but trembles on the brink of excessive sweetness, which will not worry cellar door visitors one iota. Screwcap. 13.6° alc. **Rating** 87 **To** 2008 $15

Crane Winery

Haydens Road, Kingaroy, Qld 4610 **Region** South Burnett
T (07) 4162 7647 **F** (07) 4162 8381 **www**.cranewines.com.au **Open** 7 days 10–4
Winemaker John Crane, Bernie Cooper **Est.** 1996 **Cases** 2000
Founded by John and Sue Crane, has 8 ha of estate plantings but also purchases grapes from 20 other growers in the region. Sue Crane's great-grandfather established a vineyard planted to shiraz 100 years ago (in 1898) and which remained in production until 1970. The vineyard was sold to Bernard and Judy Cooper on condition that John Crane made the 2005–07 vintages.

𐂷𐂷𐂷𐂷𐂷 **Late Harvest Frontignac NV** Extremely rich and luscious Christmas cake/plum pudding/brandysnap flavours. Cork. 17.8° alc. **Rating** 90 **To** 2008 $20

Craneford ★★★★☆

Moorundie Street, Truro, SA 5356 **Region** Barossa Valley
T (08) 8564 0003 **F** (08) 8564 0008 **www**.cranefordwines.com **Open** Mon–Fri 10–5
Winemaker John Glaetzer (Consultant), Carol Riebcke **Est.** 1978 **Cases** 25 000
Since Craneford was founded in 1978 it has undergone a number of changes of both location and ownership. The biggest change came in 2004 when the winery, by then housed in the old country fire station building in Truro, was expanded and upgraded. In 2006 John Glaetzer joined the team as consultant winemaker, with Carol Riebcke the day-to-day winemaker. Grapes are sourced from a number of small growers, the emphasis on quality. Exports to all major markets.

𐂷𐂷𐂷𐂷𐂷 **Barossa Valley Grenache 2005** Spicy, sweet berry aromas; more structure and less cosmetic flavours than most Barossa grenache; flavours head more towards black fruits, with fine tannins. Screwcap. 15° alc. **Rating** 90 **To** 2013 $25
Barossa Valley Cabernet Sauvignon 2005 I'm not sure why such a high alcohol should be accepted for cabernet; that said, there is enough structure to partially compensate, and to give length. Screwcap. 15.5° alc. **Rating** 90 **To** 2020 $30

𐂷𐂷𐂷𐂷 **Barossa Valley Shiraz 2005** Dense colour; complex licorice, prune, blackberry jam and chocolate aromas; floods the mouth as expected, but paradoxically has less apparent alcohol than Allyson. Screwcap. 15.5° alc. **Rating** 89 **To** 2020 $30
Allyson Parsons Barossa Valley Cabernet Sauvignon 2005 In the super-ripe style of Craneford's '05 wines, although here the strength of the blackcurrant cabernet and associated tannins balances the sweetness. Screwcap. 14.9° alc. **Rating** 89 **To** 2015 $16

Barossa Valley Merlot 2005 A soft, round medium-bodied red wine with substantial vanillin oak and soft tannins; the only problem is the absence of varietal character. Screwcap. 14.5° alc. **Rating** 88 **To** 2010 $30

Allyson Parsons Barossa Valley Shiraz 2005 Almost shockingly sweet, with a viscous entry to the mouth; while sweetness diminishes, it still dominates; what time will do is the $64–question, though only requiring $16. Screwcap. 14.9° alc. **Rating** 87 **To** 2020 $16

Crawford River Wines   ★★★★★

741 Hotspur Upper Road, Condah, Vic 3303 **Region** Henty
T (03) 5578 2267 **F** (03) 5578 2240 **www.**crawfordriverwines.com **Open** By appt
Winemaker John Thomson **Est.** 1975 **Cases** 5000
Time flies, and it seems incredible that Crawford River has celebrated its 30th birthday. Once a tiny outpost in a little-known wine region, Crawford River has now established itself as one of the foremost producers of Riesling (and other excellent wines) thanks to the unremitting attention to detail and skill of its founder and winemaker, John Thomson. His exceptionally talented and (dare I say) attractive daughter Belinda has returned full-time after completing her winemaking degree and working along the way in Marlborough (NZ), Bordeaux, Ribera del Duero (Spain), Bolgheri and Tuscany, and the Nahe (Germany), with Crawford River filling in the gaps. Exports to the UK, Canada, Denmark, Singapore and Japan.

ＹＹＹＹＹ **Riesling 2006** Spotless lime and apple blossom aromas; wonderfully intense, with great line and length, a touch of CO_2 on the lingering aftertaste underwriting the future. Screwcap. 13° alc. **Rating** 96 **To** 2020 $30
Young Vines Riesling 2006 Fragrant, more to green apple than lime on the bouquet; a lovely wine by normal standards, delicate and lively. I am not sure how young the young vines are, and even less sure that it matters. Screwcap. 13.5° alc. **Rating** 94 **To** 2015 $24

ＹＹＹＹＹ **Sauvignon Blanc Semillon 2006** Lemongrass aromas; a firm palate with good length, but not a lot of fruit expression early in its life. Will undoubtedly gain character as it ages. Screwcap. 13° alc. **Rating** 90 **To** 2014 $24
Cabernet Merlot 2004 Light- to medium-bodied; elegant, but minty/leafy notes better if absent; cassis and redcurrant are on the plus side, fine tannins likewise. Screwcap. 13.5° alc. **Rating** 90 **To** 2014 $30

 # Creed of Barossa   ★★★★☆

PO Box 481, Lyndoch, SA 5351 **Region** Barossa Valley
T (08) 8524 4046 **F** (08) 8524 4046 **www.**creedwines.com **Open** Not
Winemaker Daniel Eggleton **Est.** 2005 **Cases** 2160
This is the venture of luxuriantly bearded Mark Creed and business partner (and winemaker) Daniel Eggleton. Their first wine (an intriguing blend of shiraz, cabernet franc and viognier) was made in 2004, with a number of different Shirazs, Merlot, Cabernet Franc and a little Grenache in the pipeline. The partners also own a consulting wing, called C & E Dry Grown Projects Pty Ltd, to make wines for others, and to collaboratively market and distribute those wines.

ＹＹＹＹＹ **The Pretty Miss Shiraz Cabernet Franc Viognier 2004** A light- to medium-bodied, long and tangy wine with the unusual blend giving very good length; fine tannins to close. Screwcap. 14.5° alc. **Rating** 90 **To** 2012 $20

Crittenden at Dromana   ★★★★

25 Harrisons Road, Dromana, Vic 3936 **Region** Mornington Peninsula
T (03) 5981 8322 **F** (03) 5981 8366 **www.**geppettowines.com.au **Open** Dec–Mar 7 days 11–4, Apr–Nov w'ends & public hols 11–4
Winemaker Garry Crittenden **Est.** 2003 **Cases** 6000

Like a phoenix from the ashes, Garry Crittenden has risen again, soon after his formal ties with Dromana Estate were severed (son Rollo remains chief winemaker at Dromana Estate). He took with him the Schinus range; has Sangiovese and Arneis due for progressive release under the Pinocchio label; and, under the premium Crittenden at Dromana label, wines made from the 22-year-old 5-ha vineyard surrounding the family house and cellar door. Exports to the UK, Malaysia and Singapore.

ΨΨΨΨΨ **Mornington Peninsula Chardonnay 2004** Medium-bodied with attractive supple and smooth mouthfeel; perfect integration of oak with nectarine and ripe melon fruit; developing surely. Screwcap. 13.5° alc. **Rating** 92 **To** 2011 $25
Mornington Peninsula Pinot Noir 2004 Fresh cherry and small red fruit aromas and flavours; clear-cut varietal character, but just a little lacking in weight/intensity. Screwcap. 13.5° alc. **Rating** 90 **To** 2010 $25

Crooked River Wines

11 Willow Vale Road, Gerringong, NSW 2534 **Region** Shoalhaven Coast
T (02) 4234 0975 **F** (02) 4234 4477 **www**.crookedriverwines.com **Open** 7 days 10.30–4.30
Winemaker Bevan Wilson **Est.** 1998 **Cases** 10 000
With 14 ha of vineyard planted to riesling, traminer, semillon, sauvignon blanc, chardonnay, verdelho, viognier, arneis, shiraz, cabernet sauvignon, sangiovese and chambourcin, Crooked River Wines has the largest vineyard on the NSW south coast.

Cruickshank Callatoota Estate ★★★☆

2656 Wybong Road, Wybong, NSW 2333 **Region** Upper Hunter Valley
T (02) 6547 8149 **F** (02) 6547 8144 **www**.cruickshank.com.au **Open** 7 days 9–5
Winemaker John Cruickshank, Laurie Nicholls **Est.** 1973 **Cases** 4000
Owned by Sydney management consultant John Cruickshank and family. The Rose continues its good form, but it is with the younger Cabernet Franc and Cabernet Sauvignon wines that the greatest show success is being achieved (mainly in the Hunter Valley Boutique Winemakers Show).

Cullen Wines

Caves Road, Cowaramup, WA 6284 **Region** Margaret River
T (08) 9755 5277 **F** (08) 9755 5550 **www**.cullenwines.com.au **Open** 7 days 10–4
Winemaker Vanya Cullen, Trevor Kent **Est.** 1971 **Cases** 20 000
One of the pioneers of Margaret River which has always produced long-lived wines of highly individual style from the substantial and mature estate vineyards. The vineyard has now progressed beyond organic to biodynamic certification, and, subsequent to that, has become the first vineyard and winery in Australia to be certified carbon neutral. This requires the calculation of all of the carbon used and carbon dioxide emitted in the winery, and then offset by the planting of new trees. Winemaking is now in the hands of Vanya Cullen, daughter of the founders; she is possessed of an extraordinarily good palate. It is impossible to single out any particular wine from the top echelon; all are superb. Exports to all major markets.

ΨΨΨΨΨ **Mangan Vineyard Margaret River Sauvignon Blanc Semillon 2006** Spotlessly clean; long, lingering, minerally/lemony palate, the oak providing a textural, rather than flavour, component; great length, and undoubtedly will be long-lived; 60/40 blend. Screwcap. 12.5° alc. **Rating** 95 **To** 2016 $35
Margaret River Sauvignon Blanc Semillon 2006 Equally clean, but a more expressive palate thanks to the higher percentage of sauvignon blanc (80%) and more oak, though it (the oak) is totally integrated and balanced. Very different from Mangan Vineyard. Screwcap. 12° alc. **Rating** 95 **To** 2013 $35

ΨΨΨΨΨ **Mangan Margaret River Malbec Petit Verdot Merlot 2005** A powerful, very youthful wine; all the components are in flavour and structure balance, but need further time to knit; another long-lived wine in the making. Screwcap. 13.5° alc. **Rating** 93 **To** 2025 $45

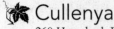 # Cullenya   NR

260 Homebush Road, Avoca, Vic 3467 **Region** Pyrenees
T (03) 5465 3360 **www**.cullenya.com **Open** Thurs–Mon & public hols 10–5
Winemaker Contract **Est.** 1998 **Cases** NA
Andre des Barres and Carol Diggins have established 3.5 ha of chardonnay, shiraz and cabernet sauvignon on their Pyrenees property. The red wines are all priced at $19 per bottle, the Chardonnay at $16. They are available through their Red Barn cellar door and usual mail/website orders.

Cumulus Wines   ★★★★

PO Box 41, Cudal, NSW 2864 **Region** Orange
T (02) 6390 7900 **F** (02) 6364 2388 **www**.cumuluswines.com.au **Open** Not
Winemaker Philip Shaw, Debbie Lauritz, Andrew Bilankij **Est.** 1995 **Cases** 220 000
Cumulus Wines is the reborn Reynolds Wines, purchased by Assetinsure in 2003, with Philip Shaw, previously head of winemaking for Rosemount and Southcorp, as Chief Executive Officer. This is an asset-rich business, with over 500 ha of vineyards planted to all the mainstream varieties, the lion's share going to shiraz, cabernet sauvignon, chardonnay and merlot. The wines are released under 3 brands: Rolling, from the Central Ranges region; Climbing, solely from Orange fruit; and a third, yet to be named, super-premium from the best of the estate vineyard blocks. Exports to the UK and the US.

ŦŦŦŦŦ **Rolling Shiraz 2005** Attractive palate; clear, cool-grown but supple fruit with spice, licorice, pepper and blackberry flavours all intermingling. Screwcap. 13.5° alc. **Rating** 93 **To** 2018 $17
Climbing Cabernet Sauvignon 2005 Powerful blackcurrant, cassis and cedar, with touches of bitter chocolate; fractionally green tannins. Screwcap. 14° alc. **Rating** 93 **To** 2018 $22
Climbing Shiraz 2005 An attractive medium-bodied wine with cherry and blackberry fruit, fine tannins and controlled oak. Screwcap. 14° alc. **Rating** 90 **To** 2015 $22

ŦŦŦŦ **Climbing Chardonnay 2006** Fresh, crisp and youthful; mineral and citrus, with just a touch of oak. Screwcap. 13° alc. **Rating** 89 **To** 2011 $22
Rolling Sauvignon Blanc Semillon 2006 Has plenty of flavour and structure, the flavour components marrying well. Screwcap. 12.5° alc. **Rating** 88 **To** 2009 $17
Rolling Chardonnay 2006 Elegant stone fruit and citrus mix; fruit-driven, with good potential. Screwcap. 13.5° alc. **Rating** 88 **To** 2011 $17
Climbing Orange Pinot Gris 2006 Faint blush-pink; pear and spice aromas and flavours; light- to medium-bodied, and a well-balanced finish. Screwcap. 13.5° alc. **Rating** 88 **To** 2008 $22
Climbing Merlot 2005 Quite firm flavour and structure; green olive and leaf within varietal bounds. Screwcap. 13.5° alc. **Rating** 87 **To** 2011 $22

Curlewis Winery   ★★★★★

55 Navarre Road, Curlewis, Vic 3222 **Region** Geelong
T (03) 5250 4567 **F** (03) 5250 4567 **www**.curlewiswinery.com.au **Open** By appt
Winemaker Rainer Breit **Est.** 1998 **Cases** 2300
Rainer Breit and partner Wendy Oliver purchased their property in 1996 with 1.6 ha of what were then 11-year-old pinot noir vines. Rainer Breit, a self-taught winemaker, uses the full bag of pinot noir winemaking tricks: cold-soaking, hot-fermentation, post-ferment maceration, part inoculated and partly wild yeast use, prolonged lees contact, and bottling the wine neither fined nor filtered. While Rainer and Wendy are self-confessed 'pinotphiles', they have planted a little chardonnay and buy a little locally grown shiraz and chardonnay. Exports to Canada, Sweden, Malaysia, Singapore and Hong Kong.

ŶŶŶŶŶ **Reserve Geelong Pinot Noir 2004** Deep colour and hue; wonderfully rich, potent and complex, with layer upon layer of fruit in a dark spectrum; perfect tannin and oak balance. Diam. 14° alc. **Rating** 96 **To** 2014 $65
Geelong Pinot Noir 2004 Spotlessly pure plum and black cherry fruit; supple mouthfeel although a slightly firm finish. Diam. 13.5° alc. **Rating** 94 **To** 2012 $40
Geelong Syrah 2004 Complex, medium-bodied, cool-grown style; licorice, spice, blackberry and black cherry fruit; good length and acidity. Diam. 14.5° alc. **Rating** 94 **To** 2019 $30

ŶŶŶŶŶ **Bel Sel Geelong Chardonnay 2005** A typically complex and textured wine from this maker; medium-bodied, with creamy/nutty/figgy overtones to gentle nectarine fruit; good balance. Diam. 14° alc. **Rating** 92 **To** 2011 $17
Pinot Saignee 2005 Full-on salmon-pink in European mould; good intensity and length, with texture which might well come from barrel fermentation in old oak; a classy, albeit lateral, version of rose. Diam. 13.5° alc. **Rating** 90 **To** 2008 $25

ŶŶŶŶ **Bel Sel Geelong Pinot Noir 2005** Complex forest floor, and a hint of game; there could possibly be some issues with brett; while the palate is long, it has a slightly hard finish. Diam. 14° alc. **Rating** 89 **To** 2012 $24

Curly Flat ★★★★★

Collivers Road, Lancefield, Vic 3435 **Region** Macedon Ranges
T (03) 5429 1956 **F** (03) 5429 2256 www.curlyflat.com **Open** Sun, or by appt
Winemaker Phillip Moraghan, Jillian Ryan **Est.** 1991 **Cases** 5000
Phillip and Jeni Moraghan began the development of Curly Flat in 1992, drawing in part upon Phillip's working experience in Switzerland in the late 1980s, and with a passing nod to Michael Leunig. With ceaseless help and guidance from the late Laurie Williams (and others), the Moraghans painstakingly established 8.5 ha of pinot noir, 3.4 ha of chardonnay and 0.6 ha of pinot gris, and a multi-level, gravity-flow winery. Exports to the UK.

ŶŶŶŶŶ **Macedon Ranges Chardonnay 2005** Very attractive wine, with great balance, structure and mouthfeel; nectarine and citrus fruit are seamlessly integrated with quality oak. Screwcap. **Rating** 95 **To** 2015 $39
Pinot Noir 2004 Distinctly spicy/foresty overtones to the red fruits; has excellent length and intensity, plus abundant oak. Screwcap. **Rating** 94 **To** 2012 $48

ŶŶŶŶŶ **Williams Crossing Chardonnay 2005** Pleasant melon and nectarine flavours with touches of more creamy/cashew notes; good length. Chablis overtones. Screwcap. 13.8° alc. **Rating** 90 **To** 2010 $15

ŶŶŶŶ **Williams Crossing Pinot Noir 2005** A pleasant, light- to medium-bodied wine with clean fruit and clear varietal expression via black cherries; just a little simple. Screwcap. **Rating** 88 **To** 2009 $22

Currans Family Wines **NR**

PO Box 271 SM, Mildura South, Vic 3501 **Region** Murray Darling
T (03) 5025 7154 **F** (03) 5025 7174 www.curransfamilywines.com.au **Open** Not
Winemaker Olsen Wines (Glenn Olsen) **Est.** 1997 **Cases** NA

Currency Creek Estate

Winery Road, Currency Creek, SA 5214 **Region** Currency Creek
T (08) 8555 4069 **F** (08) 8555 4100 www.currencycreekwines.com.au **Open** 7 days 10–5
Winemaker John Loxton **Est.** 1969 **Cases** 9000
For over 35 years this relatively low-profile winery has produced some outstanding wood-matured whites and pleasant, soft reds selling at attractive prices. Exports to the US and Canada.

Cuttaway Hill Estate

PO Box 2034, Bowral, NSW 2576 **Region** Southern Highlands
T (02) 4871 1004 **F** (02) 4871 1005 **www**.cuttawayhillwines.com.au **Open** Not
Winemaker Mark Bourne, Monarch Winemaking Services **Est.** 1998 **Cases** 15 000
Owned by the O'Neil family, Cuttaway Hill Estate is one of the largest vineyard properties in the
Southern Highlands, with a total of 38 ha on 3 vineyard sites. The original Cuttaway Hill vineyard
at Mittagong has 17 ha of chardonnay, merlot, cabernet sauvignon and shiraz. The Allambie
vineyard of 6.9 ha, on the light sandy loam soils of Ninety Acre Hill, is planted to sauvignon blanc,
pinot gris and pinot noir. The third and newest vineyard is 14.2 ha at Maytree, west of Moss Vale,
in a relatively drier and warmer meso-climate. Here cabernet sauvignon, merlot and pinot noir
(and a small amount of chardonnay) have been planted. The standard of both viticulture and
contract winemaking is evident in the quality of the wines, not to mention the growth in
production and sales. Exports to the UK, the US and Canada.

ΨΨΨΨΨ **Southern Highlands Pinot Gris 2006** An unusually aromatic bouquet with
clove, spice and pear; likewise, the palate has plenty of flavour, and gets away with
just a twitch of residual sugar on the finish. Sophisticated winemaking. Screwcap.
14.5° alc. **Rating** 91 **To** 2010 $20
Southern Highlands Semillon Sauvignon Blanc 2006 Well-made; clean,
intense and long, largely driven by the semillon, sauvignon blanc surreptitiously
adding a touch of sex appeal (passionfruit) to the fruit profile. Excellent value.
Screwcap. 12.5° alc. **Rating** 90 **To** 2010 $15
Family Reserve Merlot 2005 Light, bright red-purple; while only of light- to
medium body, offers herb, olive and cassis all within varietal expectations; lively and
long, but not deep; tangy finish. Screwcap. 12.7° alc. **Rating** 90 **To** 2011 $25

ΨΨΨΨ **Southern Highlands Sauvignon Blanc 2006** A shy bouquet, not giving much
away; the intense, lingering palate with stone/slate and mineral, more than fruit, is
crisp and clean, with considerable drive. Summer shellfish. Screwcap. 12.5° alc.
Rating 89 **To** 2008 $15
Southern Highlands Chardonnay 2005 Light- to medium-bodied; citrus and
some nectarine, with the barest hint of oak; a fresh and zesty finish. Screwcap. 13.5°
alc. **Rating** 89 **To** 2011 $15
Southern Highlands Merlot 2005 Medium-bodied; has good structure
supporting the vibrant cassis fruit; good length and minimal oak. Screwcap. 13° alc.
Rating 88 **To** 2010 $15

Cypress Post ★★★☆

PO Box 1124, Oxley, Qld 4075 **Region** Granite Belt
T (07) 3375 4083 **F** (07) 3375 4083 **www**.cypresspost.com.au **Open** Not
Winemaker Peter Scudamore-Smith MW (Contract) **Est.** 2000 **Cases** 750
The Olsen family – headed by Drs Michael (a consultant botanist) and Catherine Olsen – has a
strong botanical and conservation background continuing over 2 generations. The property has
been registered under the Land for Wildlife program, and will continue to be run on these
principles, blending science and caring for the future.

ΨΨΨΨ **6000 Granite Belt Syrah Rose 2006** Lots of substance, with obvious shiraz
varietal flavour; almost a crossover to light-bodied dry red, the touch of sweetness
carried by the overall fruit flavour. Screwcap. 14.5° alc. **Rating** 87 **To** 2008 $18
6000 Granite Belt Syrah 2006 Clean, light- to medium-bodied, with
attractive red fruits; a touch of sweetness haunts the finish; the other side of the
coin, the rose drinker's red wine. Screwcap. 13.5° alc. **Rating** 87 **To** 2008 $18

D'Angelo Estate ★★★☆

41 Bayview Road, Officer, Vic 3809 **Region** Yarra Valley
T 0417 055 651 **F** (03) 9759 7111 **www**.dangelowines.com.au **Open** By appt
Winemaker Benny D'Angelo **Est.** 1994 **Cases** NA

The business dates back to 1994 when Benny D'Angelo's father planted a small block of pinot noir for home winemaking. One thing led to another, with son Benny taking over winemaking and doing well in amateur wine shows. This led to the planting of more pinot and some cabernet sauvignon, increasing the vineyard to 2.8 ha. Expansion continued with the 2001 acquisition of a 4-ha site at Officer, which has been planted to 6 clones of pinot noir, and small parcels of cabernet sauvignon and shiraz. Grapes are also purchased from a wide range of vineyards stretching from Gippsland to Langhorne Creek.

♀♀♀♀♀ **Lady Chardonnay 2004** Highly fragrant blossom aromas; an elegant, light- to medium-bodied palate, with citrus and nectarine fruit, oak a mere support role. Trophy Best Wine of Show Gippsland Wine Show '07. **Rating 94 To** 2013 $20

♀♀♀♀ **Gin Gin Bin Pinot Noir 2003** Is starting to show its age, but retains some attractive sweet fruit elements; waste no time in drinking it. **Rating 88 To** 2008 $20
Blanc de Noir NV Rich, high-flavoured pinot-based wine works well, albeit fractionally sweet for the purists. **Rating 88 To** 2008 $18

d'Arenberg ★★★★★

Osborn Road, McLaren Vale, SA 5171 **Region** McLaren Vale
T (08) 8323 8206 **F** (08) 8323 8423 **www.**darenberg.com.au **Open** 7 days 10–5
Winemaker Chester Osborn, Phillip Dean **Est.** 1912 **Cases** 250 000
Originally a conservative, traditional business (albeit successful), d'Arenberg adopted a much higher profile in the second half of the 1990s, with a cascade of volubly worded labels and the opening of a spectacularly situated and high-quality restaurant, d'Arry's Verandah. Happily, wine quality has more than kept pace with the label uplifts. The winery has over 100 ha of estate vineyards dating back to the 1890s, 1920 and 1950s, and a Joseph's Coat of trendy new varieties planted in the 1990s. Exports to all major markets.

♀♀♀♀♀ **The Coppermine Road Cabernet Sauvignon 2004** A wine of exceptional concentration and power; very good cassis blackcurrant fruit; luscious, but not over the top. Screwcap. 14.5° alc. **Rating 95 To** 2029 $65
The Laughing Magpie McLaren Vale Shiraz Viognier 2005 Warm, dark fruits, with licorice and plum added to the usual blackberry and dark chocolate; medium- to full-bodied, very complex, and multi-layered texture; ripe, balanced tannins. Screwcap. 15° alc. **Rating 94 To** 2019 $30
The Dead Arm Shiraz 2004 Remarkably elegant and fine in the overall context of Dead Arm; black cherry and blackberry fruit with the mandatory chocolate; fine, soft tannins and controlled oak. Some suggestion of brett, which doesn't spoil the wine for me. Screwcap. 14.5° alc. **Rating 94 To** 2019 $65
d'Arry's Original Shiraz Grenache 2004 Abundant blackberry, plum cake, spice and chocolate flavours, supported by fine, ripe tannins and restrained oak. Screwcap. 14.5° alc. **Rating 94 To** 2014 $19.95

♀♀♀♀♀ **The Footbolt McLaren Vale Shiraz 2004** Rich blackberry and licorice compote, with sweet fruit notes (not residual sugar); good line and texture; controlled oak. Screwcap. 14.5° alc. **Rating 93 To** 2014 $20
The Ironstone Pressings Grenache Shiraz Mourvedre 2004 More elegant than the '03; grenache makes a bigger statement with juicy fruit; finishes with fine tannins. Screwcap. 15° alc. **Rating 93 To** 2015 $65
Sticks & Stones Tempranillo Grenache Souzao 2004 Here the tangy notes of tempranillo are the leaders, and not overtaken by grenache; does have good texture, structure and finish. Screwcap. 14.5° alc. **Rating 93 To** 2017 $30
Vintage Fortified Shiraz 2004 Extremely rich, high-quality shiraz base; has been left with much lesser baume than in bygone years, allowing the blackberry spice fruit full expression; gentle spirit and good length. Ultimate reward for those who are patient. Cork. 17.5° alc. **Rating 93 To** 2024 $34.95
The Lucky Lizard Adelaide Hills Chardonnay 2006 More elegant than the '05; melon, stone fruit and citrus with barrel ferment support; fruit-driven. Screwcap. 13.5° alc. **Rating 92 To** 2010 $25

The Lucky Lizard Adelaide Hills Chardonnay 2005 Radically different to the Olive Grove Chardonnay; elegant and precise citrus, melon and apple; complex bouquet from barrel ferment, but not over the top. Screwcap. 13.5° alc. **Rating** 92 To 2009 $25

The Galvo Garage 2004 A wine with lots of light and shade; juicy cassis berry fruit flavours, and fine, ripe tannins. Cabernet Sauvignon/Merlot/Petit Verdot/Cabernet Franc. Cork. 14.5° alc. **Rating** 92 To 2019 $30

The High Trellis McLaren Vale Cabernet Sauvignon 2005 A very typical outcome of terroir, variety and maker; smooth, supple blackcurrant fruit, a jab of dark chocolate; balanced tannins. Screwcap. 14° alc. **Rating** 91 To 2020 $19.95

The Broken Fishplate Sauvignon Blanc 2006 Extremely rich; tropical gooseberry and passionfruit flavours; just a whisper of oak. Screwcap. 13.5° alc. **Rating** 90 To 2008 $20

The Last Ditch McLaren Vale Adelaide Hills Viognier 2006 Distinctive and quite weighty varietal mouthfeel, but not heavy, oily or phenolic; moderate alcohol is counterbalanced by barrel ferment and 9 months in oak. Screwcap. 13° alc. **Rating** 90 To 2009 $19.95

The Money Spider McLaren Vale Roussanne 2006 Tangy dried citrus-rind aromatics, with grassy undertones; long and particularly well-balanced; hard to pick the variety, perhaps, but not the fault of the winemaker. Screwcap. 13.5° alc. **Rating** 90 To 2010 $19.95

The Hermit Crab McLaren Vale Viognier Marsanne 2005 Attractive texture; minerally, almost gritty, but in the good sense, the marsanne coming to the rescue of the viognier; good fruit flavour balance. Screwcap. 14.5° alc. **Rating** 90 To 2010 $17

The Feral Fox Adelaide Hills Pinot Noir 2005 Notwithstanding the closure, has pleasant development; very good texture and length to the predominantly red fruits of the palate; good acidity and subtle oak. Screwcap. 14.5° alc. **Rating** 90 To 2008 $30

The Cadenzia Grenache Shiraz Mourvedre 2005 Much stronger colour than The Custodian; deeper, richer flavours across the black and red fruit spectrum; balanced tannins and extract. Zork. 14.5° alc. **Rating** 90 To 2015 $25

Sticks & Stones Tempranillo Grenache Souzao 2005 A fragrant array of predominantly red fruit aromas and flavours; medium-bodied, with silky mouthfeel and fine tannins; not noble, but a fun commoner, even if pricey. Screwcap. 14.5° alc. **Rating** 90 To 2014 $30

The Twentyeight Road Mourvedre 2005 Medium-bodied; a nice interplay between the savoury tannin tendencies of the variety, and the richness of McLaren Vale plus that dark chocolate. Has plenty going for it in its own right, but would always add something to a blend. Screwcap. 14.5° alc. **Rating** 90 To 2015 $35

ΨΨΨΨ **The Last Ditch McLaren Vale Adelaide Hills Viognier 2005** Well-made wine, with gentle apricot and nectarine fruit, finishing with fresh, lemony acidity. Screwcap. 14° alc. **Rating** 88 To 2008 $20

The Hermit Crab McLaren Vale Viognier Marsanne 2006 Highly scented; overall driven by viognier's aromas and flavours; plenty happening, including a touch of residual sugar on the finish. Screwcap. 13.5° alc. **Rating** 88 To 2009 $16.95

The Dry Dam McLaren Vale Riesling 2005 About as good as you can get for the region; not too phenolic and has soft, rounded fruit. Screwcap. 13° alc. **Rating** 87 To 2008 $17

The Olive Grove McLaren Vale Adelaide Hills Chardonnay 2005 Some oak obvious; a big wine, with nutty characters and some phenolics; slightly old-fashioned. Screwcap. 14.5° alc. **Rating** 87 To 2008 $17

The Stump Jump Grenache Shiraz Mourvedre 2005 Considerable weight and richness given the price; red and black fruits, with soft tannins adding structure. Screwcap. 14° alc. **Rating** 87 To 2009 $12

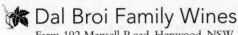 Dal Broi Family Wines   **NR**

Farm 192 Mansell Road, Henwood, NSW 2680 **Region** Riverina
T (02) 6960 3000 **F** (02) 6963 0210 **www.**dalbroiwines.com.au **Open** By appt
Winemaker Michael Slater **Est.** 1991 **Cases** NA
The very substantial wine business of the Dal Broi family is only part of group activities: the family has 250 ha of rice, 1000 ha of wheat, and is also involved in heavy earth moving equipment, transport and real estate in the Riverina and surrounding districts. The family has over 400 ha of mainstream varieties, supplemented by contract purchases both within and without the Riverina region (thus there's a Padthaway Chardonnay and Barossa Valley Shiraz in the Reserve range). At the bottom is Dal Broi Red Hill, then The Red Deer Station and at the top, Yarrenvale Station. The wines are made at the former Miranda winery.

Dal Zotto Estate

Main Road, Whitfield, Vic 3733 **Region** King Valley
T (03) 5729 8321 **F** (03) 5729 8490 **www.**dalzottoestatewines.com.au **Open** 7 days 10–5
Winemaker Otto Dal Zotto, Michael Dal Zotto **Est.** 1987 **Cases** 13 000
The Dal Zotto family are a King Valley institution; ex tobacco growers, then contract grapegrowers and now primarily focused on their Dal Zotto Estate range. Led by Otto and Elena Dal Zotto, and with sons Michael and Christian handling winemaking and sales/marketing respectively, the family are delivering increasing amounts of wine from its 48-ha vineyard. The cellar door has now relocated to a more accessible position in the centre of Whitfield and is also home to Rinaldo's Restaurant. Exports to the UK, Canada, Hong Kong and China.

ŶŶŶŶŶ King Valley Chardonnay 2004 Pleasing texture and structure; stone fruit with creamy/nutty characters; good length and subtle oak. Screwcap. 13.5° alc. **Rating** 90 To 2011 $22
King Valley Arneis 2006 Positive floral aromas; a precise palate, with green apple, pear and citrus flavours, and unexpected length. Screwcap. 12.5° alc. **Rating** 90 To 2010 $22
King Valley Shiraz 2004 Lots of blackberry, licorice and some fine, earthy/savoury tannins; the oak is largely incidental, and the wine has the character and substance to benefit from cellaring. Cork. 14° alc. **Rating** 90 To 2019 $29
King Valley Cabernet Sauvignon 2003 Blackcurrant, blackberry, savoury earthy notes with good length and intensity; fine-grained tannins. Stained cork. 13.5° alc. **Rating** 90 To 2015 $19

ŶŶŶŶ King Valley Merlot 2003 Zingy, zesty merlot with green olive and green leaf before dark fruits with earthy undertones take over. Has hastened slowly. Screwcap. 13.5° alc. **Rating** 87 To 2009 $19
King Valley Cabernet Merlot 2003 Some possible brett issues to a powerful wine with a slightly hard/bitter finish; a Curate's Egg, if ever there was one. Stained cork. Cork. 13.5° alc. **Rating** 87 To 2012 $19
King Valley Prosecco 2005 Bone-dry; a fresh mix of spice and minerally characters; good acidity and length, and a lively finish. A common sparkling wine in Italy, rare in Australia. 12° alc. **Rating** 87 To 2008 $31

Dalfarras

PO Box 123, Nagambie, Vic 3608 **Region** Nagambie Lakes
T (03) 5794 2637 **F** (03) 5794 2360 **Open** At Tahbilk
Winemaker Alister Purbrick, Alan George **Est.** 1991 **Cases** 15 000
The personal project of Alister Purbrick and artist wife Rosa (née Dalfarra), whose paintings adorn the labels of the wines, a redesign in 2004 brilliantly successful. Alister, of course, is best known as winemaker at Tahbilk, the family winery and home, but this range of wines is intended to (in Alister's words) 'allow me to expand my winemaking horizons and mould wines in styles different from Tahbilk'. It now draws upon 23 ha of its own plantings in the Goulburn Valley.

ΨΨΨΨΨ **Cabernet Sangiovese 2005** Bright colour; medium-bodied; very fresh and flavoursome cassis, raspberry and cherry mix, by far the best I have tasted in Australia. Truly delicious, and outstanding value, but drink sooner rather than later. Screwcap. 14.5° alc. **Rating** 94 **To** 2010 $15.95

ΨΨΨΨΨ **Sauvignon Blanc 2005** No reduction whatsoever; remarkably generous varietal flavours in a tropical, passionfruit and stone fruit spectrum. Screwcap. 12.5° alc. **Rating** 90 **To** 2008 $11
Marsanne Viognier 2005 The blend works well; has positive fruit flavours ranging through tropical guava to honeysuckle to peach; good length and balance. Screwcap. 13° alc. **Rating** 90 **To** 2012 $17
Viognier Pinot Gris 2005 A touch of citrus underpins and tightens up the viognier nicely; plenty of flavour. Screwcap. 13° alc. **Rating** 90 **To** 2008 $13
Shiraz Viognier 2004 A big, rich wine with blackberry and dark plum fruit; the viognier influence is obvious, but not over the top. Screwcap. 14.5° alc. **Rating** 90 **To** 2015 $17

ΨΨΨΨ **Viognier Pinot Gris 2006** Fragrant and floral citrus and spice aromas; viognier powers the palate, pinot gris at last put to good use in cutting back the otherwise slightly oily finish of viognier. Screwcap. 14° alc. **Rating** 89 **To** 2008 $15.95
Marsanne Viognier 2006 Continues the theme of freshness across all the Dalfarras wines in this release; the interest lies as much in the texture and mouthfeel as in the flavour, and the varieties are synergistic. Screwcap. 13° alc. **Rating** 89 **To** 2013 $15.95
Cabernet Sangiovese 2004 Quite elegant, with some echoes of Super Tuscan blends; light- to medium-bodied; sweet black and red fruits; minimal tannins and oak. Screwcap. 13.5° alc. **Rating** 89 **To** 2010 $13
Sauvignon Blanc 2006 Fresh and clean; a very delicate wine without any strong varietal markers other than faint apple and gooseberry; clean finish. Screwcap. 13° alc. **Rating** 87 **To** 2008 $15.95

Dalrymple   ★★★★☆

1337 Pipers Brook Road, Pipers Brook, Tas 7254 **Region** Northern Tasmania
T (03) 6382 7222 **F** (03) 6382 7222 **www**.dalrymplevineyards.com.au **Open** 7 days 10–5
Winemaker Dr Bertel Sundstrup **Est.** 1987 **Cases** 6000
A partnership between Jill Mitchell and her sister and brother-in-law, Anne and Bertel Sundstrup, inspired by father Bill Mitchell's establishment of the Tamarway Vineyard in the late 1960s. In 1991 Tamarway reverted to the Sundstrup and Mitchell families and it, too, will be producing wine in the future, probably under its own label but sold ex the Dalrymple cellar door. As production has grown (significantly), so has wine quality across the board.

ΨΨΨΨΨ **Special Bin Reserve Pinot Noir 2004** Rich, full and round, with lots of dark fruit; good line and length; I found no undue problem with brett, others did. Screwcap. 13.2° alc. **Rating** 91 **To** 2012 $35

ΨΨΨΨ **Sauvignon Blanc 2006** Over the years Dalrymple Sauvignon Blanc has been near the forefront; a touch of reduction on the bouquet takes the edge off the fruit on both the bouquet and palate, but there is definite merit in the wine. Screwcap. 13.2° alc. **Rating** 87 **To** 2008 $25

Dalwhinnie   ★★★★★

448 Taltarni Road, Moonambel, Vic 3478 **Region** Pyrenees
T (03) 5467 2388 **F** (03) 5467 2237 **www**.dalwhinnie.com.au **Open** 7 days 10–5
Winemaker David Jones, Gary Baldwin (Consultant) **Est.** 1976 **Cases** 4500
David and Jenny Jones are making wines with tremendous depth of fruit flavour, reflecting the relatively low-yielding but very well-maintained vineyards. It is hard to say whether the Chardonnay, the Cabernet Sauvignon or the Shiraz is the more distinguished. A further 8 ha of shiraz (with a little viognier) were planted in the spring of 1999 on a newly acquired block on

Taltarni Road. A 50-tonne contemporary high-tech winery now allows the wines to be made onsite. Exports to the UK, Sweden, Switzerland, the US, Canada, NZ and Hong Kong.

ƗƗƗƗƗ **Southwest Rocks Shiraz 2005** Slightly more complex, powerful and grainy than the Moonambel, but the swings and roundabouts mean there is less hedonistically luscious fruit. It's all a question of personal taste, I suppose. Cork. 14.2° alc. **Rating** 96 **To** 2025 $60
Moonambel Shiraz 2005 Flooded with perfectly ripened plum and blackberry fruit seamlessly woven with oak and tannins; great mouthfeel, line and length. Cork. 14.3° alc. **Rating** 96 **To** 2025 $52
Eagle Series Pyrenees Shiraz 2004 Intense blackberry fruit with a mix of spice and savoury characters; very powerful, but not over-extracted; good oak and tannins. Worth the price? That's for you to decide. Cork. 14.6° alc. **Rating** 96 **To** 2025 $155
Moonambel Chardonnay 2004 Super-elegant, but intense and long; developing slowly, a compliment to the closure; citrus and stone fruit dominate, oak merely a backdrop. ProCork. 13° alc. **Rating** 95 **To** 2013 $34
Moonambel Cabernet Sauvignon 2005 Medium-full-bodied, but no rough edges to lose; intense blackcurrant fruit backed by finely balanced and integrated tannins; quality French oak. Cork. 13.1° alc. **Rating** 94 **To** 2022 $45

ƗƗƗƗƗ **Pinot Noir 2005** As ever, amazes with its varietal character from a region which shouldn't produce the pinot goods. Spicy red cherry fruit and good length; may not be the world's greatest, but it's a dog preaching well. Cork. 13.7° alc. **Rating** 90 **To** 2010 $38

Darling Estate   NR
Whitfield Road, Cheshunt, Vic 3678 **Region** King Valley
T (03) 5729 8396 **F** (03) 5729 8396 **Open** By appt
Winemaker Guy Darling **Est.** 1990 **Cases** NA

Darling Park   ★★★★☆
232 Red Hill Road, Red Hill, Vic 3937 **Region** Mornington Peninsula
T (03) 5989 2324 www.darlingparkwinery.com **Open** Jan 7 days 11–5, w'ends 11–5
Winemaker Judy Gifford **Est.** 1986 **Cases** 2500
Josh and Karen Liberman and David Coe have energetically expanded the range of Darling Park's wines while maintaining a high-quality standard. The Art of Wine club offers back vintages, as well as previews of upcoming releases. Wine labels feature artworks from the owners' collections, with artists including Sidney Nolan, Arthur Boyd, John Perceval and Charles Blackman.

ƗƗƗƗƗ **Chardonnay 2005** Almost flowery peach blossom aromas; skilled use of all of the winemaker's tricks of whole-bunch pressing, barrel ferment, mlf and lees contact; never big, always elegant. Screwcap. 13.5° alc. **Rating** 93 **To** 2015 $24
Syrah 2005 Excellent colour and hue; a light-footed but flavoursome syrah with a range of red fruits which drive the wine; oak and tannins incidental. Screwcap. 13.9° alc. **Rating** 92 **To** 2012 $28

ƗƗƗƗ **Rose 2006** Distinctly aromatic; attractive spicy, strawberry fruit; has texture, length and a dry finish; worth the effort of 20 hours' skin contact and 20% barrel-fermented in old oak. Screwcap. 14° alc. **Rating** 89 **To** 2008 $20
Pinot Noir 2005 Clear, bright, fresh small red fruits; a simple but enjoyable lunch style. Screwcap. 13.5° alc. **Rating** 89 **To** 2009 $28
Pinot Noir 2004 Fresh and fragrant; a delicate but intense wine with very good length, mixing red fruits and slightly tangy notes; a fraction sweet and sour. Screwcap. 14.2° alc. **Rating** 89 **To** 2012 $28
Viognier 2006 Not particularly strong in varietal terms, but has nice freshness from citrussy acidity, and no residual sugar. Screwcap. 14° alc. **Rating** 88 **To** 2009 $24

Pinot Gris 2006 Some pear and musk aromas and flavours, but this is still an acquired non-taste. Screwcap. 14° alc. **Rating** 87 **To** 2008 $24

Basket Pressed Merlot 2004 Fresh, light and clean, small red fruits with a hint of snow pea; light tannins and minimal oak; a rose/red wine cross. Screwcap. 14.2° alc. **Rating** 87 **To** 2008 $20

Darlington Vineyard ★★★

Holkam Court, Orford, Tas 7190 **Region** Southern Tasmania
T (03) 6257 1630 **F** (03) 6257 1630 **Open** Thurs–Mon 10–5
Winemaker Hood Wines (Andrew Hood) **Est.** 1993 **Cases** 600
Peter and Margaret Hyland planted a little under 2 ha of vineyard in 1993. The first wines were made from the 1999 vintage, forcing retired builder Peter Hyland to complete their home so that the small building in which they had been living could be converted into a cellar door. The vineyard looks out over the settlement of Darlington on Maria Island, the site of Diego Bernacci's attempt to establish a vineyard and lure investors by attaching artificial bunches of grapes to his vines.

♈♈♈♈♀ Sauvignon Blanc 2006 Clean lemon, citrus and passionfruit aromas and flavours; good balance; very attractive wine. **Rating** 92 **To** 2008

♈♈♈♈ Riesling 2005 Apple blossom aromas, and apple and spice flavours; precise line and length. **Rating** 89 **To** 2010 $17

Date Brothers Wines

PO Box 1599, Swan Hill, Vic 3585 **Region** Swan Hill
T (03) 5033 2325 **F** (03) 5033 2325 **www**.datebroswines.com.au **Open** Not
Winemaker Travis Bush (Contract) **Est.** 1997 **Cases** 1500
The brothers in question are Roy, Barry and Tony Date, who, with sister Kerry, run the 42-ha vineyard. They had a background in dryland cereal farming, and in their words 'decided to have a go' at the grape industry, which in turn led them into winemaking. There are 12 ha of shiraz, and 10 ha each of chardonnay, cabernet sauvignon and durif; part of the grape production is sold. Exports to Japan.

David Hook Wines

Cnr Broke Road/Ekerts Road, Pokolbin, NSW 2320 **Region** Lower Hunter Valley
T (02) 4998 7121 **www**.davidhookwines.com.au **Open** 7 days 10–5
Winemaker David Hook **Est.** 1984 **Cases** 5000
David Hook has over 20 years' experience, as a winemaker for Tyrrell's and Lake's Folly, also doing the full Flying Winemaker bit, with jobs in Bordeaux, the Rhône Valley, Spain, the US and Georgia. He and his family began establishing the vineyard in 1984. In 2004 they moved the winery home to the former Peppers Creek Winery. Exports to the US.

♈♈♈♈♀ Pothana Hunter Valley Shiraz 2005 Some earthy regional notes on a foundation of powerful blackberry fruit; needs 10+ years to fully open. Screwcap. 13.5° alc. **Rating** 93 **To** 2020 $30

The Gorge Hunter Valley Shiraz 2005 Exceptional depth of colour, with voluminous aromas of ripe plum and blackberry, and plenty of texture and tannin structure for the spicy black fruit of the palate. Screwcap. 13.5° alc. **Rating** 92 **To** 2018 $16

♈♈♈♈ The Gorge Riesling 2006 Apple and lime aromas, the flavours following suit; distinct residual sugar is well enough balanced with the fruit. Central Highlands. Screwcap. 11.5° alc. **Rating** 89 **To** 2016 $18

The Gorge Mosto 2006 Attractive, sweet lemon and lime juice flavours with a few tropical notes thrown in for good measure; made from freeze-concentrated semillon juice. Screwcap. 10.5° alc. **Rating** 89 **To** 2008 $20

The Gorge Viognier 2006 Light- to medium-bodied; distinct apricot nuances, and finishes clean and clear. Screwcap. 13.5° alc. **Rating** 88 **To** 2008 $18

The Gorge Verdelho 2006 Clean and fresh, with touches of varietal fruit salad flavours; non-pretentious. Screwcap. 13° alc. **Rating** 87 **To** 2008 $18

The Gorge Barbera 2004 Light- to medium-bodied; notwithstanding the complex regional blend, there isn't much to fire the palate or the imagination; just earthy/leafy characters. Orange/Mudgee/Hunter Valley. Screwcap. 13.5° alc. **Rating** 87 **To** 2008 $18

David Traeger Wines

139 High Street, Nagambie, Vic 3608 **Region** Nagambie Lakes
T (03) 5794 2514 **F** (03) 5794 1776 **www**.dromanaestate.com.au **Open** Mon–Fri 10–5, w'ends & public hols 12–5
Winemaker David Traeger **Est.** 1986 **Cases** 10 000
David Traeger learned much during his years as assistant winemaker at Mitchelton and knows Central Victoria well. The red wines are solidly crafted, the Verdelho interesting and surprisingly long-lived. In late 2002 the business was acquired by the Dromana Estate group, but David Traeger has stayed on as winemaker. See also Baptista entry. Exports to the UK, Japan, Italy and Canada.

ΨΨΨΨ **Shiraz 2002** Savoury/cedary/earthy overtones to medium-bodied, strongly spicy black fruits, oak playing a role. Finishes with fine, well-balanced tannins. Cork. 14.5° alc. **Rating** 90 **To** 2017 $22

ΨΨΨΨ **Cabernet Merlot 2003** Quite rich and ripe, reflecting the hot drought vintage perhaps. If so, it has been to the wine's advantage, giving it more substance. Cork. 15° alc. **Rating** 89 **To** 2015 $22

Verdelho 2006 Quite fragrant aromas, the flavours following suit with ultra-typical lively fruit salad. Screwcap. 14° alc. **Rating** 87 **To** 2008 $17.50

 # Dawson & Wills

PO Box 4154, Dandenong South, Vic 3164 **Region** Strathbogie Ranges
T (03) 5790 4259 **F** (03) 9768 5887 **Open** Not
Winemaker Scott McCarthy (Contract) **Est.** 1998 **Cases** 750
This is a weekend and weekday night busman's holiday for Rob Wills and Frank Dawson. Rob is a professional viticulturist with a day job of running a vineyard in the Goulburn Valley, while Frank Dawson is an engineer manufacturing equipment for the farming, mining and construction industries. As neighbours, they first formed a partnership agisting sheep and cattle, and this in turn led to the establishment of their vineyard, which has 3.6 ha of sauvignon blanc, 2.5 ha of pinot noir, 1 ha each of cabernet sauvignon and tempranillo, and a few vines of merlot.

ΨΨΨΨ **Sauvignon Blanc 2006** Spotlessly clean; a distinctly fruity bouquet, with tropical fruit on entry to the mouth, tightening up nicely with a crisp, minerally finish. **Rating** 91 **To** 2008 $17

Tempranillo 2004 A strong mix of red fruits with touches of plum and lemon; harmonious mouthfeel; impressive. **Rating** 91 **To** 2012 $19

Pinot Noir 2006 A marked improvement on the '05, with classy texture, line and length; red fruits with a generous sprinkle of spice; good length. **Rating** 90 **To** 2011 $19

ΨΨΨΨ **Cabernet Merlot 2004** Quite rich blackcurrant fruit with hints of chocolate; doesn't quite deliver the early promise, needing more structure on the finish. **Rating** 88 **To** 2010 $19

Dawson's Patch

71 Kallista-Emerald Road, The Patch, Vic 3792 (postal) **Region** Yarra Valley
T 0419 521 080 **Open** Not
Winemaker Paul Evans (Contract) **Est.** 1996 **Cases** 500

James and Jody Dawson own and manage a 1.2-ha vineyard at the southern end of the Yarra Valley, planted in 1996 to chardonnay. The climate here is particularly cool, and the grapes do not normally ripen until late April. Jody Dawson has completed a degree in viticulture through Charles Sturt University. The tiny hand-crafted production is sold through local restaurants and cellars in the Olinda/Emerald/Belgrave area.

ŸŸŸŸ♀ **Yarra Valley Chardonnay 2004** More elegance than the other chardonnays; citrus and melon fruit, acidity acting to freshen the wine, the oak more subtle. Diam. 13° alc. **Rating** 93 **To** 2011 $30

ŸŸŸŸ **Yarra Valley Chardonnay 2005** Shows strong oak influence from start to finish which goes that little bit too far, and bottle age is unlikely to restore balance. Some nice fruit underneath. Diam. 13.5° alc. **Rating** 89 **To** 2011 $30
Yarra Valley Unwooded Chardonnay 2005 Distinctly nutty/figgy notes have made their appearance, and a slightly flat finish. Diam. 13.5° alc. **Rating** 87 **To** 2009 $17

De Beaurepaire Wines ★★★☆

Main Street, Rylstone, NSW 2849 **Region** Mudgee
T 0427 791 473 **F** (02) 6379 1474 **www**.debeaurepairewines.com **Open** W'ends & public hols 11–4, or by appt
Winemaker David Lowe, Jane Wilson (Contract) **Est.** 1998 **Cases** 1500
This is the substantial retirement business of former clinical psychologist Janet de Beaurepaire and investment banker Richard de Beaurepaire. Beaurepaire Ridge Vineyard is situated on the 200-ha Woodlawn property, one of the oldest properties west of the Blue Mountains, at an altitude of 570–600 m. While part of the Mudgee GI, the Rylstone climate is significantly cooler than other parts of the region. It is planted to 55 ha of shiraz, merlot, cabernet sauvignon, petit verdot, semillon, chardonnay, viognier and verdelho. The property is bounded on by 2 sides by the Cudgegong River which provides irrigation for the vineyard.

ŸŸŸŸ♀ **Victor Mudgee Cabernet Sauvignon 2004** Fresh, medium-bodied cassis, redcurrant and blackcurrant fruit; supple tannins, gentle oak. Cork. 13.6° alc. **Rating** 90 **To** 2011 $25

ŸŸŸŸ **Leopold Mudgee Shiraz Viognier 2005** A light- to medium-bodied wine with pleasant red fruit flavours, and – notwithstanding the alcohol – not particularly deep or intense. Diam. 15° alc. **Rating** 89 **To** 2011 $25
Elyanne Mudgee Semillon 2005 A clean bouquet, then a basically unevolved palate with mineral and talc flavours, finishing somewhat short. The quality of the cork does not inspire confidence. (The '04 Mudgee Semillon was oxidised.) Cork. 11.1° alc. **Rating** 88 **To** 2010 $20
Captain Starlight Series Mudgee Shiraz Viognier 2004 Light-bodied, clean, easy style; doesn't have the vivacity normally adduced by this blend, raising the question of young vines or high yields. Diam. 13.5° alc. **Rating** 87 **To** 2008 $16
Captain Starlight Series Mudgee Merlot Petit Verdot Shiraz 2004 Light-to medium-bodied; savoury black fruits with touches of spice; firm, grippy tannins; an odd blend, but does have length. Cork. 13.3° alc. **Rating** 87 **To** 2011 $16

De Bortoli ★★★★★

De Bortoli Road, Bilbul, NSW 2680 **Region** Riverina
T (02) 6966 0100 **F** (02) 6966 0199 **www**.debortoli.com.au **Open** Mon–Sat 9–5, Sun 9–4
Winemaker Darren De Bortoli **Est.** 1928 **Cases** 3 million
Famous among the cognoscenti for its superb Botrytis Semillon, which in fact accounts for only a minute part of its total production, this winery turns around low-priced varietal and generic wines which are invariably competently made and equally invariably provide value for money. These come in part from 250 ha of estate vineyards, but mostly from contract-grown grapes. The death of founder Deen De Bortoli in 2003 was widely mourned by the wine industry. Exports to all major markets.

ŸŸŸŸŸ **Noble One 2005** A rich, round, bordering on fleshy, basket of tropical fruit flavours plus a dash of honey; oak totally absorbed; acidity spot-on. Screwcap. 11° alc. **Rating** 94 **To** 2018 $29

Black Noble NV A freakish wine; botrytis semillon kept aside and aged for many years in barrel; highly aromatic biscuit, treacle and mandarin flavours; long and very fine. **Rating** 94 **To** 2008 $32

ŸŸŸŸŸ **Show Liqueur Muscat NV** Dark mahogany, with some olive on the rim; powerful yet balanced raisin flavours; lacks the complexity of the very best; nonetheless multiple trophies and gold medals in minor wine shows. **Rating** 93 **To** 2008 $19.95

Old Boys 21 Years Barrel Aged Tawny Port NV Pale, clear, bright tawny colour; a tangy tawny port style, less sweet than many; the age is in fact considerable. **Rating** 90 **To** 2008 $38

ŸŸŸŸ **Deen De Bortoli Vat 8 Shiraz 2005** Light- to medium-bodied, with good balance and line; blackberry and plum fruit uncomplicated by 12 months in oak; utterly exceptional value. Gold medal Sydney Wine Show '07. Screwcap. 14° alc. **Rating** 89 **To** 2010 $11

Deen De Bortoli Vat 4 Petit Verdot 2005 Complex fruit, with some unexpected leaf and olive overtones to the core of red fruit flavours at its heart. Gold medal Melbourne Wine Show '06. Screwcap. 14.5° alc. **Rating** 88 **To** 2008 $11

Montage Semillon Sauvignon Blanc 2006 Clean; a well-balanced wine with a pleasing mix of herb, grass and tropical fruit influences; a relatively dry finish reflecting very competent winemaking. Great price/value. Screwcap. **Rating** 87 **To** 2008 $9

Sacred Hill Semillon Chardonnay 2006 A no-fuss wine, but has balance and length, fruit flavour rather than residual sugar. Don't worry about the points, just the price. Screwcap. 13° alc. **Rating** 87 **To** 2008 $6

Sacred Hill Traminer Riesling 2006 Full-on sweetness, almost spatlese in weight; an altogether surprising spicy varietal impact of traminer; just be aware of the sweetness. Screwcap. 11.5° alc. **Rating** 87 **To** 2008 $6

Wild Vine Shiraz 2005 Light- to medium-bodied; as ever, a high degree of winemaking competence; red cherry fruit and good acidity. Screwcap. 13.5° alc. **Rating** 87 **To** 2008 $8.45

Deen De Bortoli Vat 5 Botrytis Semillon 2005 The botrytis is not strong, but enough, especially at this price; preserved lemon/lemon slice, and gentle acidity. Screwcap. 12° alc. **Rating** 87 **To** 2009 $11

8 Year Old Tawny Port NV Good, middle-aged tawny port with some biscuity/rancio characters; good balance. **Rating** 87 **To** 2008 $11

De Bortoli (Hunter Valley) ★★★☆

532 Wine Country Drive, Pokolbin, NSW 2320 **Region** Lower Hunter Valley
T (02) 4993 8800 **F** (02) 4993 8899 **www.debortoli.com.au Open** 7 days 10–5
Winemaker Steve Webber **Est.** 2002 **Cases** 35 000
De Bortoli extended its wine empire in 2002 with the purchase of the former Wilderness Estate, giving it an immediate and substantial presence in the Hunter Valley courtesy of the 26 ha of established vineyards; this was expanded significantly by the subsequent purchase of an adjoining 40-ha property. Exports to all major markets.

ŸŸŸŸ **Hunter Valley Semillon 2006** Spotlessly clean and crisp; light cut-grass touches to green apple and citrus fruit; still to flower. Screwcap. 11° alc. **Rating** 89 **To** 2016 $16

De Bortoli (Victoria) ★★★★★

Pinnacle Lane, Dixons Creek, Vic 3775 **Region** Yarra Valley
T (03) 5965 2271 **F** (03) 5965 2464 **www.debortoli.com.au Open** 7 days 10–5
Winemaker Steve Webber **Est.** 1987 **Cases** 400 000

The quality arm of the bustling De Bortoli group, run by Leanne De Bortoli and husband Stephen Webber, ex-Lindeman winemaker. The top label (De Bortoli), the second (Gulf Station) and the third label (Windy Peak) offer wines of consistently good quality and excellent value – the complex Chardonnay and the Pinot Noirs are usually of outstanding quality. The volume of production, by many times the largest in the Yarra Valley, simply underlines the quality/value for money ratio of the wines. Exports to all major markets.

ŸŸŸŸŸ **Estate Grown Yarra Valley Shiraz Viognier 2005** Startling depth of colour and hue; a mouth-coating array of flavours featuring spice, anise almost into dried fruits (as opposed to lolly sweet or to dead fruit characters). Excellent tannin texture and structure. Screwcap. 14° alc. **Rating** 95 **To** 2025 $30

Estate Grown Yarra Valley Sauvignon Blanc 2006 A complex wine, sotto voce and all about texture; has very considerable length, with nutty/minerally nuances; very good balance. Screwcap. 13.5° alc. **Rating** 94 **To** 2010 $23

Estate Yarra Valley Chardonnay 2005 Complex flavour and texture with seamlessly woven melon, nectarine and creamy lees notes; oak contributes more to the texture than the flavour. Screwcap. 13.5° alc. **Rating** 94 **To** 2015 $23

Yarra Valley Pinot Noir Rose 2006 Has structure and texture; bone-dry, with spicy components reflecting the wild yeast and barrel fermentation in old oak, followed by 3 months on yeast lees; way left field, its points in part to emphasise how different it is. Screwcap. 13.5° alc. **Rating** 94 **To** 2008 $22

Gulf Station Yarra Valley Pinot Noir 2006 A stylish, light- to medium-bodied but very complex wine, with cherry, plum and spice running through the long finish. Gold medal Sydney Wine Show '07. Great value. Screwcap. 13.5° alc. **Rating** 94 **To** 2010 $19

Gulf Station Yarra Valley Shiraz Viognier 2005 A powerful, yet elegant, wine stacked with black cherry and blackberry flavour, the oak barely evident. Gold medal National Wine Show '06. Screwcap. **Rating** 94 **To** 2020 $19

ŸŸŸŸŸ **Gulf Station Yarra Valley Sauvignon Blanc Semillon 2006** Spotlessly clean; a wine which creeps up on you, at first blush not showing much, then both gooseberry/kiwifruit and touches of creaminess build, all achieved without overt oak. Screwcap. 12.5° alc. **Rating** 93 **To** 2012 $19

Estate Grown Yarra Valley Pinot Noir 2005 A subtle yet complex wine, the structure there from start to finish, though never aggressive; gently spicy overtones to red fruits running through to a long finish. Screwcap. 13° alc. **Rating** 93 **To** 2012 $27

Gulf Station Chardonnay 2005 Typical Yarra Valley melon and nectarine plus a touch of citrus; controlled barrel ferment oak inputs; good length. Screwcap. 13.5° alc. **Rating** 91 **To** 2012 $17

Windy Peak Riesling 2006 Fragrant lemon zest and lemon blossom aromas; a delicate wine, with good balance, but doesn't quite live up to the intensity promised by the bouquet. King Valley/Yarra Valley. Screwcap. 12.5° alc. **Rating** 90 **To** 2011 $14

Estate Grown Yarra Valley Viognier 2005 Abundant, rounded mouthfeel on entry; as much about texture as flavour, but there are apricot/peach nuances. Screwcap. 13.5° alc. **Rating** 90 **To** 2009 $22

Windy Peak Yarra Valley Pinot Noir 2006 Abundant plum and black cherry fruit, with undertones of spice from partial whole-bunch fermentation; shortens slightly, but what more can you ask at the price? Screwcap. 13.5° alc. **Rating** 90 **To** 2010 $14

Gulf Station Yarra Valley Cabernet Sauvignon 2004 Holding hue well; perfectly ripened cassis blackcurrant fruit, the medium-bodied palate finishing with soft, fine tannins; a gentle touch of French oak is in balance. Screwcap. 13° alc. **Rating** 90 **To** 2013 $19

ŸŸŸŸ **Gulf Station Riesling 2006** Spotlessly clean and clear-cut varietal aromas in a citrus spectrum; gentle palate, with good balance, though not particularly intense. Screwcap. 13° alc. **Rating** 89 **To** 2010 $17

Windy Peak Shiraz Viognier 2003 Medium red-purple; fragrant black fruit aromas, then an unexpectedly powerful palate, finishing with strongly built, earthy/grainy tannins. Screwcap. 14° alc. **Rating** 89 **To** 2009 $13

Windy Peak Cabernet Merlot 2004 A medium-bodied, complex array of flavours; soft mouthfeel and some texture from partial barrel fermentation; cassis, black olive and blackcurrant fruit rounded off with good tannins. Screwcap. 13.5° alc. **Rating** 88 **To** 2010 $14

Windy Peak Sauvignon Blanc Semillon 2006 No reduction; light- to medium-bodied, with gently grassy/minerally flavours, and fair length. Screwcap. 13° alc. **Rating** 87 **To** 2008 $14

Windy Peak King Valley Pinot Grigio 2006 Quite aromatic; an impression of riper fruits on entry, then on the back-palate emphatic, dusty grigio characters emerge. Screwcap. 13.5° alc. **Rating** 87 **To** 2008 $14

De Iuliis ★★★★★

21 Broke Road, Pokolbin, NSW 2320 **Region** Lower Hunter Valley
T (02) 4993 8000 **F** (02) 4998 7168 **www.**dewine.com.au **Open** 7 days 10–5
Winemaker Michael De Iuliis **Est.** 1990 **Cases** 10 000
Three generations of the De Iuliis family have been involved in the establishment of their 45-ha vineyard. The family acquired the property in 1986 and planted the first vines in 1990, selling the grapes from the first few vintages to Tyrrell's but retaining increasing amounts for release under the De Iuliis label. Winemaker Michael De Iuliis has completed postgraduate studies in oenology at the Roseworthy campus of Adelaide University and was a Len Evans Tutorial scholar.

♟♟♟♟♟ **Limited Release Hunter Valley Shiraz 2005** Attractive, medium-bodied wine with sweet blackberry/black cherry fruit; subtle mouthfeel and line supported by new French oak; drink now or in 15 years. Screwcap. 14.3° alc. **Rating** 95 **To** 2020 $40

Show Reserve Hunter Valley Shiraz 2005 Riper, denser fruit immediately obvious in both the bouquet and new oak; not as regional as the Charlie version so far, but will become so. Screwcap. 14.3° alc. **Rating** 94 **To** 2020 $28

♟♟♟♟♟ **Hunter Valley Semillon 2006** Crisp, clean, fresh and lively; a lemon and mineral mix, excellent acidity helping to lengthen the palate. Screwcap. 10.5° alc. **Rating** 92 **To** 2016 $16

Charlie Hunter Valley Shiraz 2005 Elegant, distinctively regional style founded on black fruits and fine-grained tannins; subtle oak, good length. Screwcap. 13.2° alc. **Rating** 91 **To** 2015 $25

de Mestre Wines NR

'Inverway', Warrangunyah Road, Ilford, NSW 2850 **Region** Mudgee
T (02) 9221 5711 **F** (02) 9233 6181 **www.**demestrewines.com.au **Open** By appt
Winemaker Paul de Mestre **Est.** 1999 **Cases** NA
de Mestre Wines, with Paul de Mestre at the head, has established 16 ha of low-yielding viognier, shiraz and cabernet sauvignon on a gently sloping, north-facing hill approximately 750 m above sea level. The soil, of volcanic origin, is 460 million years old, that also (intriguingly) includes marine deposits. The wines are made and bottled onsite, with full participation of the 3 young de Mestre children.

Dead Horse Hill ★★★★☆

Myola East Road, Toolleen, Vic 3551 **Region** Heathcote
T (03) 5433 6214 **F** (03) 5433 6164 **Open** By appt
Winemaker Jencie McRobert **Est.** 1994 **Cases** 500
Jencie McRobert (and husband Russell) 'did a deal with Dad' for approximately 65 ha of her parents' large sheep and wheat farm at Toolleen, 20 km north of Heathcote. It took a number of years for the 4-ha dry-grown shiraz vines to achieve reasonable yields, but they are now yielding

between 3.7 and 5 tonnes per ha of high-quality fruit. Jencie's introduction to wine came partly through the family dining table and partly from meeting Steve Webber, then working for Lindemans at Karadoc, when she was working in soil conservation and salinity management in the Mallee. She subsequently completed a course at Charles Sturt University, and makes the wine at De Bortoli in the Yarra Valley with the odd bit of assistance from Webber.

♥♥♥♥♀ **Heathcote Shiraz 2005** A powerful, incisive palate; blackberry and black cherry with spicy notes and crisp acidity; does need to soften with time in bottle. Screwcap. 14° alc. **Rating** 91 **To** 2025 $25

Deakin Estate   ★★★
Kulkyne Way, via Red Cliffs, Vic 3496 **Region** Murray Darling
T (03) 5029 1666 **F** (03) 5024 3316 **www**.deakinestate.com.au **Open** Not
Winemaker Phil Spillman **Est.** 1980 **Cases** 500 000
Part of the Katnook Estate, Riddoch and Deakin Estate triumvirate, which constitutes the Wingara Wine Group, now 60% owned by Freixenet of Spain. The Sunnycliff label is still used for export purposes but no longer appears on the domestic market. Deakin Estate draws on over 300 ha of its own vineyards, making it largely self-sufficient, and produces competitively priced wines of consistent quality and impressive value. Exports to the UK, the US, Canada, NZ and Asia.

Deep Woods Estate
Commonage Road, Yallingup, WA 6282 **Region** Margaret River
T (08) 9756 6066 **www**.deepwoods.com.au **Open** Tues–Sun 11–5, 7 days during hols
Winemaker Travis Clydesdale **Est.** 1987 **Cases** 20 000
The Gould family acquired Deep Woods Estate in 1992, when the first plantings were 4 years old. In 2005, the business was purchased by Perth businessman Peter Fogarty and family, who also own Lake's Folly in the Hunter Valley, and Millbrook in the Perth Hills. The 32-ha property has 16 ha plantings of cabernet sauvignon, shiraz, merlot, cabernet franc, chardonnay, sauvignon blanc, semillon and verdelho. Exports to Switzerland, Belgium Denmark and Ireland.

♥♥♥♥♥ **Block 7 Margaret River Shiraz 2005** Initially medium-bodied, then bolstered by fine, persistent tannins running through the length of the palate; blackberry and plum fruit has very good length and aftertaste; 14 months in French oak barely shows. Screwcap. 13.5° alc. **Rating** 94 **To** 2018 $25

♥♥♥♥♀ **Ivory Margaret River Semillon Sauvignon Blanc 2006** An intense, almost explosive palate, driven by grassy/citrussy semillon; great with Asian foods, spice no limit. Screwcap. 11.5° alc. **Rating** 92 **To** 2009 $14
Reserve Chardonnay 2006 Sophisticated winemaking; a combination of restraint and power, and bred for improvement for 5+ years; citrus, nectarine and oak in balance, albeit still to fully express themselves. Screwcap. 13.5° alc. **Rating** 92 **To** 2016 $35
Margaret River Verdelho 2006 Aromatic tropical fruit salad with contrasting lemon/citrus notes move seamlessly from the bouquet onto the palate; succeeds admirably where most verdelhos fail. Screwcap. 13.5° alc. **Rating** 90 **To** 2010 $17

♥♥♥♥ **Margaret River Semillon Sauvignon Blanc 2006** More conventional than the Ivory, with tropical sauvignon blanc influence; this reduces the exciting drive of the cheaper Ivory. Screwcap. 11.5° alc. **Rating** 89 **To** 2009 $19
Cabernet Merlot 2005 Very powerful, full-bodied wine, with masses of blackcurrant and cassis fruit, and – at this stage – somewhat aggressive tannins. Needs time for war to be waged, and a victor determined. I think the good guys will win. Screwcap. 14° alc. **Rating** 89 **To** 2020 $25
Reserve Cabernet Sauvignon 2005 Another powerful, concentrated, full-bodied wine, with tannins a major strike force amidst the blackcurrant and cassis fruit. Take the quinella with the cabernet merlot. Screwcap. 14° alc. **Rating** 89 **To** 2022 $35

Ebony Margaret River Cabernet Shiraz 2005 Light- to medium-bodied, and distinctly spicy; has just enough red fruits to get away with a fractionally green finish. Screwcap. 13.5° alc. **Rating** 87 **To** 2009 $14

Deetswood Wines ★★★★

Washpool Creek Road, Tenterfield, NSW 2372 **Region** New England
T (02) 6736 1322 **www.**deetswoodwines.com.au **Open** Fri–Mon 10–5, or by appt
Winemaker Contract **Est.** 1996 **Cases** 1500
Deanne Eaton and Tim Condrick established their micro-vineyard in 1996, planting 2 ha of semillon, chardonnay, pinot noir, shiraz, merlot and cabernet sauvignon. At the end of the 19th century German immigrant (Joe Nicoll) planted vines and made wines for family use, and there is still 1 vine surviving on the site today from the original plantings. The wines are are strikingly consistent both in quality and style, offering further proof that this is a very interesting area.

ŢŢŢŢŢ **Semillon 2006** In classic Hunter Valley style; dry, and with relatively low alcohol; lemon, citrus rind and mineral run through the palate to a long finish; still developing. Screwcap. 11.5° alc. **Rating** 90 **To** 2013 $16
Pinot Noir 2005 Spicy forest floor notes to clear-cut pinot varietal character; good length and structure; major surprise. Cork. 12.7° alc. **Rating** 90 **To** 2013 $18

ŢŢŢŢ **Cabernet Merlot 2005** Light- to medium-bodied; a fresh mix of black and red fruits; freshness a major plus, likewise fine tannins. Cork. 13.5° alc. **Rating** 88 **To** 2011 $16
Unwooded Chardonnay 2006 Very interesting given the region; has the tang and intensity of cool-climate ripening so essential for unwooded chardonnay; bright finish. Screwcap. 12.5° alc. **Rating** 87 **To** 2009 $15

Deisen ★★★★★

PO Box 61, Tanunda, SA 5352 **Region** Barossa Valley
T (08) 8563 2298 **F** (08) 8563 2298 **Open** Not
Winemaker Sabine Deisen **Est.** 2001 **Cases** 1000
Deisen (owned by Sabine Deisen and Les Fensom) once again proves the old adage that nothing succeeds like success. In the first year, 3.5 tonnes of grapes produced 5 barrels of shiraz and 2 of grenache. Since that time, production has grown slowly but steadily with bits and pieces of traditional winemaking equipment (small crushers, open tanks and hand-plunging, all housed in a small tin shed, now extended to a slightly larger tin shed). The number of wines made and the tiny quantities of some (20 dozen is not uncommon) is staggering. Space restraints limit my notes to the top 12 out of 17 tasted, but only one (a 16.5° alcohol grenache) scored less than 87 points. The style of all the wines is remarkably similar: sweet and luscious fruit; soft, ripe tannins; and a warmth from the alcohol which can reach terrifying levels at times.

ŢŢŢŢŢ **Barossa Shiraz 2002** Still deep and vibrantly coloured; layer upon layer of flavour; blackberry, spice, licorice and plum, oak only a bit player; excellent balance and length. Cork. 14.5° alc. **Rating** 94 **To** 2019 $56
Barossa Shiraz 2001 Holding colour well; welcoming, softly luscious red and black fruits; soft, ripe tannins with belated touches of chocolate and mocha. While ready now, will hold. Cork. 14.5° alc. **Rating** 94 **To** 2018 $56

ŢŢŢŢŢ **Winter Sun Barossa Shiraz Mataro 02/03** Bright red cherry and blackberry fruit aromas; fresh flavours, fine tannins; a strange wine constituted by a blend of 2002 and '03 vintages; 65%/35%. Cork. 15° alc. **Rating** 93 **To** 2019 $49
Barossa Mataro 2005 As ripe and as luscious as one could expect, achieved at a reasonable alcohol; good length and well-balanced tannins. Includes 10% Shiraz. Cork. 14.5° alc. **Rating** 93 **To** 2019 $36
Barossa Shiraz Cabernet 2004 The blackcurrant of cabernet sauvignon seems to outweigh the blackberry of shiraz; regardless, a wine oozing fruit flavour and carrying the alcohol in doing so; soft tannins to close; 65%/35%. Cork. 15° alc. **Rating** 92 **To** 2020 $48

Barossa Mataro 2004 Savoury, peaty aromas; a powerful palate, with earthy black fruits, controlled tannins, and good depth and weight. Mataro is, of course, old language for mourvedre. Cork. 14.8° alc. **Rating** 92 **To** 2014 $36

Sweetheart Barossa Shiraz 2004 Rich and generous black fruits are supported by soft, ripe tannins and neatly judged oak. Like all the Deisen wines, neither fined nor filtered. Cork. 14.3° alc. **Rating** 91 **To** 2010 $48

Barossa Mataro 2002 Tightly focused, brooding dark fruits from the cool vintage belied by the high alcohol; has considerable length, and the fruit carries that alcohol. Cork. 15.5° alc. **Rating** 90 **To** 2014 $36

ŸŸŸŸ **Barossa Shiraz 2003** Surprising texture and mouthfeel which largely get around the issue of high alcohol; confit fruit and chocolate; good tannins. Cork. 15.5° alc. **Rating** 89 **To** 2010 $56

Winter Sun Barossa Shiraz Mataro 03/04 Rich, ripe/luscious/juicy berry fruit, and an echo of dark chocolate. An unusual 2-vintage blend, '04 to the fore; 85 cases made; 65%/35%. Cork. 15° alc. **Rating** 89 **To** 2012 $49

Barossa Grenache 2004 Significantly more weight and structure than the Autumn Song, though still in a similar flavour spectrum; 15% Shiraz. Cork. 15° alc. **Rating** 89 **To** 2009 $36

Autumn Song Barossa Grenache 2004 Typical juicy/jammy/confection Barossa grenache flavours; 2% Shiraz. Cork. 14.5° alc. **Rating** 87 **To** 2008 $32

del Rios of Mt Anakie   ★★★★☆

2320 Ballan Road, Anakie, Vic 3221 **Region** Geelong
T (03) 9497 4644 **F** (03) 9499 9266 **www**.delrios.com.au **Open** W'ends 10–5
Winemaker Matthew Bowden **Est.** 1996 **Cases** 5000
German del Rio was born in northern Spain (in 1920) where his family owned vineyards. After 3 generations in Australia, his family has established 15 ha of vines on their 104-ha property on the slopes of Mt Anakie, the principal focus being chardonnay, pinot noir and cabernet sauvignon (4 ha each), then marsanne, sauvignon blanc, merlot and shiraz (1 ha each). Planting commenced in 1996, and vintage 2000 was the first commercial release; winemaking moved onsite in 2004.

ŸŸŸŸŸ **Shiraz 2005** Medium- to full-bodied; excellent texture and structure; black fruits, licorice, ripe tannins and good length; flavour with elegance. **Rating** 95 **To** 2015 $23

ŸŸŸŸŸ **Pinot Noir 2005** Medium-bodied; a silky, supple array of red fruits; fine tannins, long finish. **Rating** 93 **To** 2011 $21

Cabernet Sauvignon 2005 Generous blackcurrant and cassis fruit aromas and flavours do the work; tannin and oak are simply props; good ripeness. Screwcap. 13.5° alc. **Rating** 91 **To** 2015 $21

ŸŸŸŸ **Sauvignon Blanc 2006** Elegant and aromatic, ranging through passionfruit, gooseberry and tropical; good length. **Rating** 89 **To** 2008 $18

Marsanne 2005 Very clear varietal character; distinctive, slightly chalky bitterness crying out for a touch of viognier, but nonetheless interesting. **Rating** 87 **To** 2010 $18

Rose 2006 Some gently spicy notes; good length, acidity and balance. **Rating** 87 **To** 2008 $16

Delamere   ★★★★

Bridport Road, Pipers Brook, Tas 7254 **Region** Northern Tasmania
T (03) 6382 7190 **F** (03) 6382 7250 **Open** 7 days 10–5
Winemaker Richard Richardson **Est.** 1983 **Cases** 2000
Richie Richardson produces elegant, rather light-bodied wines that have a strong following. The Chardonnay has been most successful, a textured, complex, malolactic-influenced wine with great, creamy feel in the mouth. Has had a field day with the 2005 vintage.

ŦŦŦŦŦ **Reserve Chardonnay 2005** Much more complex than the varietal, with the oak evident but by no means oppressive; overall melon and creamy nuances adding complexity. Screwcap. 13.1° alc. **Rating** 94 **To** 2015 $28

ŦŦŦŦŶ **Reserve Pinot Noir 2005** Excellent hue; lovely balance and line perfectly exposing cherry and spice varietal character; harmonious and balanced. Screwcap. 13.2° alc. **Rating** 93 **To** 2012 $32

ŦŦŦŦ **Chardonnay 2005** No reduction whatsoever; clean, fresh melon, citrus and grapefruit flavours naturally provide good length and likewise balance in an unoaked wine. Screwcap. 13.2° alc. **Rating** 88 **To** 2009 $18

Delatite ★★★★★

Stoneys Road, Mansfield, Vic 3722 **Region** Upper Goulburn
T (03) 5775 2922 **F** (03) 5775 2911 **www**.delatitewinery.com.au **Open** 7 days 10–5
Winemaker Jane Donat **Est.** 1982 **Cases** 16 000

With its sweeping views across to the snow-clad Alps, this is uncompromising cool-climate viticulture, and the wines naturally reflect that. Light but intense Riesling and spicy Traminer flower with a year or 2 in bottle, and in the warmer vintages the red wines achieve flavour and mouthfeel. In spring 2002 David Ritchie (the viticulturist in the family) embarked on a program to adopt biodynamics, commencing with the sauvignon blanc and gewurztraminer. He says, 'It will take time for us to convert the vineyard and change our mindset and practices, but I am fully convinced it will lead to healthier soil and vines.' Exports to Japan and Malaysia.

ŦŦŦŦŦ **Sylvia Riesling 2006** Beautifully balanced and focused Kabinett style; sweet fruit offset by perfectly judged acidity; 24 g per litre residual sugar. Screwcap. 9° alc. **Rating** 95 **To** 2011 $20

Dead Man's Hill Gewurztraminer 2005 A delicate wine albeit with clear varietal character with spice and rose petal flavours; no phenolics whatsoever, and good balance and length. One of a small handful of gewurztraminers made in Australia. Gold medal National Wine Show '06. Screwcap. 13.8° alc. **Rating** 94 **To** 2009 $20

Late Picked Riesling 2005 In delicious Germanic style; vibrant and fresh lime/lemon juice flavours; crisp acidity, and a long finish. Let there be more of such wine. Screwcap. 11.5° alc. **Rating** 94 **To** 2015 $20

ŦŦŦŦŶ **V.S. Limited Edition Riesling 2005** Firm citrus and apple aromas; the palate does not disappoint, firm, and full of ripe (but not overripe) fruit, and a dry, crisp finish. Screwcap. 13.5° alc. **Rating** 93 **To** 2017 $27

Shiraz 2005 Fully ripened, though still unequivocally cool-grown, with a cascade of red and black spicy fruits; a long, clean finish, and room to grow. Screwcap. 14° alc. **Rating** 92 **To** 2020 $25

Estate Riesling 2006 A powerful bouquet tied to mineral and spice; while the palate is firm to the point of austerity, still has elegance, and will open up with time. Screwcap. 13° alc. **Rating** 91 **To** 2016 $20

Estate Unwooded Chardonnay 2005 Lively, fresh, citrus and stone fruit aromas and flavours; has the intensity often lacking in this style; acidity provides line and length. Screwcap. 13° alc. **Rating** 91 **To** 2008 $18

Dead Man's Hill Gewurztraminer 2006 Varietal character – spice, lychee and a little lime – is there, but partly obscured by the frame and weight of the wine. On the plus side, the finish is not phenolic. Screwcap. 13.5° alc. **Rating** 90 **To** 2010 $20

Sauvignon Blanc 2006 Herb, grass and mineral aromas; more lemon, citrus and passionfruit on the palate; good balance and length. Screwcap. 13° alc. **Rating** 90 **To** 2008 $19

Pinot Gris 2006 Tangy; has some (welcome) bite to announce its presence, plus pear skin varietal flavour; long finish and no shortage of character. Screwcap. 14° alc. **Rating** 90 **To** 2008 $20

Devils River Cabernet Merlot 2004 Medium- to full-bodied; cassis, blackcurrant and a twist of olive, the tannins savoury but not green, notwithstanding the low alcohol. Screwcap. 12.5° alc. **Rating** 90 **To** 2015 $29

 R.J. Limited Edition 2002 The cool vintage shows through with minty/savoury overtones, and while the palate has considerable length, it simply doesn't achieve enough ripeness. Cabernet Sauvignon/Merlot/Malbec. Cork. 14° alc. **Rating** 88 **To** 2012 $49

Tempranillo 2005 Light- to medium-bodied; fresh and vibrant in a tangy/lemony varietal mould; tannins and structure still to appear. Screwcap. 14° alc. **Rating** 88 **To** 2011 $29

Delbard ★★★

'Spring Hill', 577 Springs Road, at the Crystal Brook, Vic 3660 **Region** Strathbogie Ranges
T (03) 5790 4006 **Open** By appt
Winemaker Ross MacLean **Est.** NA **Cases** NFP
Ross and Christine MacLean have established their small vineyard, principally planted to pinot noir, on a rolling granite plateau at an elevation of 600 m, complete with lichen-covered granite boulders and bubbling springs (drought permitting). The wine is made onsite in small, hand-plunged vats and basket-pressed.

 Terip Shiraz 2005 Intense, cool-grown shiraz; red cherry, spice and slightly green tannins to close. **Rating** 89 **To** 2010 $19

Terip Merlot 2005 Elegant, with red fruits, but suffers from an excessively green finish. **Rating** 87 **To** 2009

Dennis ★★★★

Kangarilla Road, McLaren Vale, SA 5171 **Region** McLaren Vale
T (08) 8323 8665 www.denniswines.com.au **Open** Mon–Fri 10–5, w'ends, hols 11–5
Winemaker Peter Dennis **Est.** 1970 **Cases** 7000
Egerton (Ege) was well-known in McLaren Vale, starting his vineyard at McLaren Flat in 1947 after serving in the RAAF during the war. Wine production under the Dennis label began in 1971, and in 1979 winemaking and management passed to son Peter. The 22-ha vineyard is planted to cabernet sauvignon, shiraz, merlot, chardonnay and sauvignon blanc. Exports to the UK, NZ, Singapore and Canada.

Derwent Estate ★★★★☆

329 Lyell Highway, Granton, Tas 7070 **Region** Southern Tasmania
T (03) 6263 5802 **F** (03) 6263 5802 www.derwentestate.com.au **Open** Mon–Fri 10–4 summer, Sun 11–3 Dec–Jan, closed winter
Winemaker Winemaking Tasmania (Julian Alcorso) **Est.** 1993 **Cases** 1200
The Hanigan family established Derwent Estate as part of a diversification program for their 400-ha mixed farming property: 10 ha of vineyard have been planted, since 1993, to riesling, pinot noir, chardonnay, cabernet sauvignon and pinot gris.

 Pinot Noir 2005 On the big side of town, but convincingly so; a supple array of red and black cherry fruit; very good oak and tannin management. Gold medal Tas Wine Show '07. Screwcap. 14.5° alc. **Rating** 94 **To** 2013 $27

Riesling 2006 Apple, citrus and spice aromas; good balance and length; gentle, but pleasing. Screwcap. 13.1° alc. **Rating** 90 **To** 2010 $22

Cabernet Sauvignon 2005 Strong blackcurrant varietal character allied with earth and dark chocolate; lots of oak, but not bitter. Screwcap. 14.2° alc. **Rating** 90 **To** 2013 $25

Rose 2006 Trembles on the brink of excessive sweetness, but does have very attractive cherry flavours, and will be a big hit with the punters. Screwcap. 13.6° alc. **Rating** 88 **To** 2008 $18

Chardonnay 2006 A flavoursome wine which gave rise to a wide divergence of opinion at the Tas Wine Show '07. Screwcap. 13.9° alc. **Rating** 87 **To** 2008 $20

Deviation Road   ★★★★☆

Lobethal–Mount Torrens Road, Charleston, SA 5244 **Region** Adelaide Hills
T (08) 8389 4455 **F** (08) 8389 4407 **www.**deviationroad.com **Open** 7 days 11–5
Winemaker Kate Laurie, Hamish Laurie **Est.** 1999 **Cases** 1000
Deviation Road was created in 1998 by Hamish Laurie, great-great-grandson of Mary Laurie, SA's first female winemaker. He had joined with father Dr Chris Laurie in 1992 to help build the Hillstowe Wines business. The brand was sold to Banksia Wines in 2001, but the Laurie family retained the vineyard, which now supplies Deviation Road with its grapes. Wife Kate Laurie joined the business in 2001, having studied winemaking and viticulture in Champagne, then spending 4 years at her family's Stone Bridge winery in Manjimup. All the wines except the Sangiovese (WA) and Riesling (other Adelaide Hills growers) come from the 16-ha family vineyards, but only account for a small portion of the annual grape production of those vineyards.

Devil's Lair   ★★★★★

Rocky Road, Forest Grove via Margaret River, WA 6285 **Region** Margaret River
T (08) 9757 7573 **F** (08) 9757 7533 **www.**devils-lair.com **Open** Not
Winemaker Stuart Pym **Est.** 1981 **Cases** 220 000
Having rapidly carved out a high reputation for itself through a combination of clever packaging and impressive wine quality, Devil's Lair was acquired by Southcorp in 1996. The estate vineyards have been substantially increased since. An exceptionally successful business, production increasing from 40 000 to 220 000 cases. Exports to the UK, the US and other major markets.

ᵞᵞᵞᵞᵞ **Margaret River Chardonnay 2005** Immaculately balanced and crafted; has the region's depth of mid-palate flavour unmatched by any other; nectarine, melon and white peach are supported by immaculate oak and good acidity. Screwcap. 13.5° alc. **Rating** 95 **To** 2012 $42.95
Margaret River Chardonnay 2004 Outstanding focus and intensity to the melon and nectarine fruit; sure oak handling makes a positive contribution. Screwcap. 13.5° alc. **Rating** 94 **To** 2015 $42.95
Margaret River Cabernet 2003 A complex bouquet and palate; ripples of blackcurrant fruit, spice and quality French oak; tannins and extract perfectly judged. Cork. 14° alc. **Rating** 94 **To** 2017 $58.95

ᵞᵞᵞᵞᵞ **Fifth Leg White 2006** Spotlessly clean bouquet; a crisp, no-frills, minerally style with strong citrus components; ideal for beach/café/casual drinking anywhere, any time. Screwcap. 13.5° alc. **Rating** 90 **To** 2008 $18
Fifth Leg Rose 2006 Very pale pink; clean, brisk splashes of spice, red fruits and mineral; dry style, good length. Screwcap. 13.5° alc. **Rating** 90 **To** 2008 $18.99

ᵞᵞᵞᵞ **Fifth Leg Dry Red 2005** A light- to medium-bodied, no-frills style; clear cabernet merlot varietal origins with savoury olive edges to the blackcurrant fruit; the tannins have been polished almost to the point of removal, no doubt deliberately. Screwcap. 14° alc. **Rating** 89 **To** 2008 $18

Di Fabio Estate   NR

5 Valleyview Drive, McLaren Vale, SA 5171 (postal) **Region** McLaren Vale
T (08) 8383 0188 **F** (08) 8383 0168 **www.**difabioestatewines.com.au **Open** Not
Winemaker Goe Di Fabio **Est.** 1994 **Cases** NA
Di Fabio Estate is the venture of brothers Goe and Tony Di Fabio. Their parents Giovanni and Maria Di Fabio purchased their first vineyard in McLaren Vale in 1966 (with a tradition stretching back further to Italy) and became long-term contract grapegrowers for other winemakers. The business carried on by their sons has a 56-ha property at McLaren Vale, and 8.5 ha at Waikerie. The plantings are dominated by 12.7 ha of grenache, 9.1 ha of shiraz, and 3.6 ha of mourvedre. Cabernet franc, merlot, petit verdot, chardonnay, sauvignon blanc and semillon are also grown.

Goe became senior winemaker with Geoff Merrill Wines in 1987, since moving into the role of consultant winemaker to oversee the production of the Geoff Merrill wines which are in fact made at the Di Fabio Estate winery, which has a 1500-tonne capacity.

di Lusso Wines ★★★★☆

Eurunderee Lane, Mudgee, NSW 2850 **Region** Mudgee
T (02) 6373 3125 **F** (02) 6373 3128 **www**.dilusso.com.au **Open** 7 days 10–5
Winemaker Contract **Est.** 1998 **Cases** 5000
Rob Fairall and partner Luanne Hill have brought to fruition their vision to establish an Italian 'enoteca' operation, offering Italian varietal wines and foods. The plantings of 2.5 ha of barbera and 2 ha of sangiovese are supported by 0.5 ha each of nebbiolo, picolit, lagrein and aleatico. The estate also produces olives for olive oil and table olives, and the range of both wine and food will increase over the years. The decision to focus on Italian varieties has been a major success.

TTTTT **Appassimento 2003** Tawny-brown; an extraordinary wine with dried banana and apricot aromas; intensely sweet, but balanced by acidity. The grapes were dried on racks for 2 months before fermentation, a method used in northern Italy to make semi-sweet and sweet wines. Semillon. Cork. 7° alc. **Rating** 94 **To** 2008 $40

TTTTT **Pinot Grigio 2006** A highly aromatic and flowery bouquet; tangy passionfruit and citrus flavours; a very good example of the variety which beats the odds with positive fruit. Orange. Screwcap. 13.5° alc. **Rating** 90 **To** 2009 $25
Vermentino 2005 Fragrant and flowery; lively and penetrating citrussy/grassy flavours; excellent acidity as befits this warm-area grape. No region stated. Screwcap. 13° alc. **Rating** 90 **To** 2009 $18
Barbera 2004 Has more red fruit characters than often is the case, tempered by notes of spice, leaf and earth; a very good example of a usually ordinary variety in Australia. Estate-grown. Cork. **Rating** 90 **To** 2010 $25
Picolit 2005 Has some real presence, with a mix of citrus, pear and apple; moderately sweet, and good balance. For once, paying for a quality wine, not a rare label. Cork. 10.5° alc. **Rating** 90 **To** 2008 $25

TTTT **Vino Rosato 2006** An attractive melange of strawberries and cherries with a touch of warm spice; good balance; rose with a purpose in life. Estate-grown Sangiovese/Barbera/Lagrein. Screwcap. 13° alc. **Rating** 89 **To** 2008 $18
il Palio 2004 Light-bodied with some red cherry fruit; balance good, but needed more flesh. Sangiovese/Merlot/Shiraz/Cabernet Sauvignon. Cork. 14.5° alc. **Rating** 87 **To** 2010 $25
Sangiovese 2004 Bright light red; some varietal red cherry, a touch of fine tannins ok. Cork. 14.1° alc. **Rating** 87 **To** 2009 $25

Diamond Creek Estate NR

Diamond Fields Road, Mittagong, NSW 2575 **Region** Southern Highlands
T (02) 4872 3311 **F** (02) 4872 3311 **www**.diamondcreekestate.com.au **Open** By appt
Winemaker Eddy Rossi, Nick Spencer (Contract) **Est.** 1997 **Cases** NA
Helen Hale purchased Diamond Creek Estate in late 2002, by which time the chardonnay, sauvignon blanc, riesling, pinot noir and cabernet sauvignon planted in 1997 by the prior owner, had come into bearing. The vineyard is established at 680 m on rich basalt soil, the north-facing slope being relatively frost-free. Since Helen acquired the property, most of the grapes have been sold to Southern Highlands Winery, but small amounts have been retained for release under the Diamond Creek label: these include Riesling, Sauvignon Blanc, Pinot Noir, Cabernet Sauvignon and a highly successful Noble Diamond Botrytis Riesling.

Diamond Valley Vineyards ★★★★★

PO Box 4255, Croydon Hills, Vic 3136 **Region** Yarra Valley
T (03) 9722 0840 **F** (03) 9722 2373 **www**.diamondvalley.com.au **Open** Not
Winemaker James Lance **Est.** 1976 **Cases** 7000

One of the Yarra Valley's finest producers of Pinot Noir and an early pacesetter for the variety, making wines of tremendous style and crystal-clear varietal character. They are not cabernet sauvignon lookalikes but true pinot noir, fragrant and intense. The Chardonnays show the same marriage of finesse and intensity, and the Cabernet family wines shine in the warmer vintages. In early 2005 the brand and wine stocks were acquired by Graeme Rathbone (of SpringLane), the Lances continuing to own the vineyard and winery, and to make the wine. Exports to the UK.

ΤΤΤΤΤ **Reserve Pinot Noir 2005** Slightly deeper colour than the Yarra Valley; the bouquet much riper and sweeter, the palate with abundant plum and black cherry, with years of development. The eternal question: is it worth more than twice as much as the Yarra Valley Pinot? Screwcap. 14° alc. **Rating** 95 **To** 2013 $64
Reserve Chardonnay 2005 Complexity without ostentation; nectarine, melon and fig, the citrus and oak components come together effortlessly; very good length and line. Screwcap. 14° alc. **Rating** 94 **To** 2013 $32
Yarra Valley Pinot Noir 2005 Black cherry and plum aromas; remarkable intensity and length from such an apparently light-bodied wine; very good texture from sophisticated winemaking. Screwcap. 14° alc. **Rating** 94 **To** 2011 $26

ΤΤΤΤΥ **Yarra Valley Chardonnay 2005** Fragrant and fresh; white peach and nectarine fruit; lingering citrussy acidity. Screwcap. 14° alc. **Rating** 92 **To** 2010 $22

 Diggers Bluff ★★★★☆

PO Box 34, Tanunda, SA 5352 **Region** Barossa Valley
T 0419 825 437 **F** (08) 8563 1613 **www**.diggersbluff.com **Open** Not
Winemaker Timothy O'Callaghan **Est.** 1998 **Cases** 1250
Timothy O'Callaghan explains that his family crest is an Irish Hound standing under an oak tree; the Diggers Bluff label features his faithful hound Digger, under a Mallee tree. He is a third-generation O'Callaghan winemaker, and – reading his newsletter – it's not too hard to guess who the second generation is represented by. Diggers Bluff has 2.5 ha of grenache, mataro, shiraz, cabernet sauvignon and alicante, all of it old vines.

ΤΤΤΤΤ **Watchdog 2000** Developing gradually but convincingly; has lush black fruits, fine tannins, and a long finish; great mouthfeel and aftertaste. Quality cork. Cabernet Sauvignon/Shiraz. 14.5° alc. **Rating** 94 **To** 2025 $32

ΤΤΤΤΥ **Watchdog 2001** Rich, ripe, traditional Barossa Valley style, but in no sense overdone. Has sweet black fruits, softly rounded tannins and good length, the oak largely incidental. Quality cork. Cork. 14.5° alc. **Rating** 93 **To** 2021 $32

ΤΤΤΤ **Stray Dog 2004** Light- to medium-bodied; a fresh, spicy array of red and black fruits with fine, silky tannins; clean finish. Does not come from the same litter as the Watchdogs. Grenache/Shiraz/Mataro. Screwcap. 13.4° alc. **Rating** 88 **To** 2008 $16

DiGiorgio Family Wines ★★★☆

Riddoch Highway, Coonawarra, SA 5263 **Region** Coonawarra
T (08) 8736 3222 **F** (08) 8736 3233 **www**.digiorgio.com.au **Open** 7 days 10–5
Winemaker Peter Douglas **Est.** 1998 **Cases** 10 000
Stefano DiGiorgio emigrated from Abruzzi, Italy, arriving in Australia in 1952. Over the years, he and his family gradually expanded their holdings at Lucindale. In 1989 he began planting cabernet sauvignon (99 ha), chardonnay (10 ha), merlot (9 ha), shiraz (6 ha) and pinot noir (2 ha). In 2002 the family purchased the historic Rouge Homme winery, capable of crushing 10 000 tonnes of grapes a year, and its surrounding 13.5 ha of vines, from Southcorp. The enterprise is offering full winemaking services to vignerons in the Limestone Coast Zone. Exports to several major markets.

ΤΤΤΤΥ **Coonawarra Shiraz 2002** Light- to medium-bodied, smooth and supple black fruits, spice and fine tannins; the cool vintage obvious. Creased and stained cork. 14° alc. **Rating** 90 **To** 2010 $23

ŢŢŢŢ **Sterita Semillon Sauvignon Blanc 2006** Attractive wine; good line and length; herb, grass and some fruit plus a touch of sweetness. Screwcap. **Rating** 88 To 2008 $15
Lucindale Pinot Chardonnay NV Quite well-balanced; some citrus and strawberry fruit; balancing acidity. **Rating** 87 **To** 2008 $15

Dindima Wines

Lot 22 Cargo Road, Orange, NSW 2800 **Region** Orange
T (02) 6365 3388 **www**.dindima.com.au **Open** W'ends & public hols 10–5, or by appt
Winemaker James Bell **Est.** 2002 **Cases** 700
David Bell and family acquired the property known as Osmond Wines in 2002, renaming it Dindima Wines, with the first vintage under the new ownership made in 2003 from the 4-ha plantings. It is a retirement occupation for Dave Bell and his wife, but both sons are becoming involved with grapegrowing and winemaking.

ŢŢŢŢ **Chardonnay 2005** Intense and focused, with long grapefruit and nectarine flavours; slightly green acid worries some. Cork. **Rating** 87 **To** 2010 $20

Dinny Goonan Family Estate

880 Winchelsea-Deans Marsh Road, Bambra, Vic 3241 **Region** Geelong
T 0438 408 420 **F** (03) 5288 7100 **www**.dinnygoonan.com.au **Open** 7 days Jan, w'ends & public hols Nov–Apr
Winemaker Dinny Goonan **Est.** 2001 **Cases** 1000
Although the establishment date is given as 2004, the estate dates back to the 1980s when Dinny and Susan Goonan bought a 20-ha property near Bambra, in the hinterland of the Otway Coast. Dinny had recently completed a viticulture diploma at Charles Sturt University, but, as he and Susan were viticultural pioneers in the area, they were not sure what varieties would do well, and which wouldn't. In the early 1990s they planted a wide range of varieties in what they now call their Nursery Block. Dinny also headed back to Charles Sturt University to complete a wine science degree.

ŢŢŢŢ **Cabernets 2004** Light- to medium-bodied; a mix of cassis, redcurrant and blackcurrant backed by subtle oak and fine tannins. Cork. 13.5° alc. **Rating** 89 To 2010 $16

Dionysus Winery

1 Patemans Lane, Murrumbateman, NSW 2582 **Region** Canberra District
T (02) 6227 0208 **F** (02) 6227 0209 **www**.dionysus-winery.com.au **Open** W'ends & public hols 10–5, or by appt
Winemaker Michael O'Dea **Est.** 1998 **Cases** 1000
Michael and Wendy O'Dea are both public servants in Canberra, seeking weekend and holiday relief from their everyday life at work. They purchased their property at Murrumbateman in 1996, and planted 4 ha of chardonnay, sauvignon blanc, riesling, pinot noir, cabernet sauvignon and shiraz between 1998 and 2001. Michael has completed an associate degree in winemaking at Charles Sturt University, and is responsible for viticulture and winemaking; Wendy has completed various courses at the Canberra TAFE and is responsible for wine marketing and (in their words) 'nagging Michael and being a general slushie'.

ŢŢŢŢŢ **Canberra District Merlot 2005** Seems to have the mark of all Canberra District merlots, with a pronounced savoury/earthy accent; does, however, have plenty of red fruit to give the wine balance. Screwcap. 13.5° alc. **Rating** 90 **To** 2013 $20

Disaster Bay Wines
★★★★

133 Oaklands Road, Pambula, NSW 2549 (postal) **Region** South Coast Zone
T (02) 6495 6488 **www**.disasterbaywines.com **Open** Not
Winemaker Dean O'Reilly, Andrew McEwen **Est.** 2000 **Cases** 250

Dean O'Reilly has a 10-year background in the distribution of fine table wines, culminating in employment by Fine Wine Partners. He has accumulated the UK-based WSET Intermediate and Advanced Certificates, completed various other programs and competitions, and has been associate judge and judge at various Canberra district events. He has also travelled through the wine regions of NZ, Champagne, Bordeaux, Chablis, Piedmont and Tuscany. The wines are made at Kyeema with Andrew McEwen overseeing Dean's apprenticeship, coming from small parcels of fruit grown on some of the original vineyards of the Canberra District.

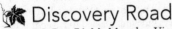 ## Discovery Road   ★★★★

PO Box 76, Mt Macedon, Vic 3441 **Region** Gippsland
T 0408 333 995 **F** (03) 9012 4378 **Open** Not
Winemaker Bruce Dowding **Est.** 1993 **Cases** 1000
Former Macedon vigneron Bruce Dowding, who sold Rochford back in 1998, has returned to the fray. In 2004 he produced a Pinot Noir using predominantly Gippsland fruit (with some Whitlands material) while, from 2005, there are 2 Gippsland wines, a standard release and a premium release, the latter a selection of the best barrels. Of the latter he says, 'It represents my personal preference and, unlike its sibling, is designed to appeal to those who are already familiar with the variety.'

🍷🍷🍷🍷 **Premium Pinot Noir 2005** Light-bodied; despite the same alcohol as the varietal, has more concentration, focus and length, though still for purists. Screwcap. 13.5° alc. **Rating** 90 **To** 2010

🍷🍷🍷🍷 **Pinot Noir 2005** Light-bodied, with a savoury/spicy/forest floor backbone, but there are some notes of varietal cherry fruit. A back label notable for its poetic licence. 13.5° alc. **Rating** 88 **To** 2009

Djinta Djinta Winery   ★★★

10 Stevens Road, Kardella South, Vic 3951 **Region** Gippsland
T (03) 5658 1163 **F** (03) 5658 1928 **www**.djintadjintawinery.com.au **Open** Wed–Sun 10–5
Winemaker Marcus Satchell **Est.** 1991 **Cases** 600
One of a group of wineries situated between Leongatha and Korumburra, the most famous being Bass Phillip. Vines were first planted in 1986 but were largely neglected until Peter and Helen Harley acquired the property in 1991. They set about reviving the 2 ha of sauvignon blanc and a little cabernet sauvignon, and planted an additional 3 ha of merlot, cabernet franc, cabernet sauvignon, semillon, marsanne, roussanne and viognier. The first vintage was 1995, and in late 2004 the property was purchased by Alex and Eleonor Biro. Winemaker Marcus Satchell has 8 years' experience in the Yarra Valley, and vintage experience with Bonnie Doon Vineyard in California.

🍷🍷🍷🍷 **Classique Marsanne Viognier Roussane 2006** Interesting wine; light, clean and crisp; while relatively neutral now, could gain considerable character with bottle age. **Rating** 87 **To** 2012 $21

 ## Doctor's Nose Wines   NR

'Koorooba', Old Racecourse Road, Tenterfield, NSW 2372 **Region** New England
T (02) 6736 3113 **www**.doctorsnosewines.com.au **Open** By appt
Winemaker Mike Hayes (Contract) **Est.** 1997 **Cases** NA
Koorooba has been home to the Reid family since the 1860s, and when the decision was taken in 1997 to establish a vineyard, 3 generations were involved: Max, Peter and Ben Reid. Ben and Janice Reid have since developed the 3.6-ha vineyard planted to sauvignon blanc, semillon, verdelho, grenache, shiraz, mataro, petit verdot, tempranillo. The slightly quaint name comes from John Traill, Tenterfield's first doctor, whose nose was apparently reminiscent of the dominant rocky mountain on the western horizon of the property.

DogRock Winery

114 De Graves Road, Crowlands, Vic 3377 **Region** Pyrenees
T (03) 5354 9201 **www**.dogrock.com.au **Open** W'ends 11–5
Winemaker Allen Hart **Est.** 1999 **Cases** 100

This is the micro-venture (but with inbuilt future growth to something slightly larger) of Allen (winemaker) and Andrea (viticulturist) Hart. Having purchased the property in 1998, planting of 6.4 ha of riesling, chardonnay, shiraz, tempranillo and grenache began in 2000. Given Allen Hart's position as research scientist/winemaker with Fosters Wine Estates, the attitude taken to both viticulture and winemaking is utterly unexpected. Andrea's Vineyard (planted to riesling) is dry-grown, while Pedro's Vineyard (planted to tempranillo and shiraz) receives minimal irrigation from a small dam. The wines are made in an ultra low-tech fashion, without gas cover or filtration. The one concession to technology, say the Harts, is that 'all wine will be sealed with a screwcap and no DogRock wine will ever be released under natural cork bark. Prices are to remain at the lower end as we are intent on making the world's best wine, not the world's best profit'.

ＹＹＹＹＹ **Pyrenees Shiraz 2005** A vibrant mix of blackberry and plum; excellent control of tannin, oak and good acidity. Screwcap. 13.5° alc. **Rating** 93 **To** 2016 $22
Pyrenees Tempranillo 2005 Medium-bodied; a very attractive and supple array of red fruits and spices; distinct echoes of the variety as it performs in Spain; loaded with potential. Screwcap. 13° alc. **Rating** 91 **To** 2012 $19
Riesling 2006 Herb, slate and wild flower aromas; good intensity, length and balance. Grampians/Henty/Pyrenees. Screwcap. 12° alc. **Rating** 90 **To** 2015 $17

Domain Barossa

★★★★★

25 Murray Street, Tanunda, SA 5352 **Region** Barossa Valley
T (08) 8563 2170 **F** (08) 8563 2164 **www**.domainbarossa.com **Open** 7 days 11–6.30
Winemaker Todd Riethmuller **Est.** 2002 **Cases** 2000

Todd Riethmuller and family are long-term residents of the Barossa Valley, and have the inside running, as it were, when it comes to buying grapes from local growers. Thus they have been able to dispense with the expensive and often frustrating business of having their own winery, yet can make wines of exceptional quality.

ＹＹＹＹＹ **Reserve Black Tongue Shiraz 2004** More elegant than most Barossa shirazs, due to the French oak and controlled alcohol; plum, blackberry and raspberry fruits, the oak precisely in tune. Cork. 14.5° alc. **Rating** 94 **To** 2019 $34
Cabernet Sauvignon 2005 Abundant blackcurrant and cassis fruit perfectly tempered by savoury/earthy tannins and good oak. Cork. 14° alc. **Rating** 94 **To** 2022 $34

ＹＹＹＹＹ **Black Tongue Shiraz 2004** Powerful and still very youthful; focused blackberry fruit needing to unwind; controlled oak and firm acidity. Should get there. Screwcap. 14° alc. **Rating** 92 **To** 2024 $27
Toddler GSM 2006 Masses of fresh, juicy berry fruit, but with a little more structure than usual; fine tannins. Screwcap. 15° alc. **Rating** 90 **To** 2008 $18

ＹＹＹＹ **Sticky 2006** Quite elegant and restrained, the sweetness at spatlese level, and offering a tropical, citrus, cumquat mix. Cane-cut. Screwcap. 11.5° alc. **Rating** 89 **To** 2008 $15

Domain Day

★★★★☆

24 Queen Street, Williamstown, SA 5351 **Region** Barossa Valley
T (08) 8524 6224 **F** (08) 8524 6229 **www**.domaindaywines.com **Open** By appt
Winemaker Robin Day Est. 2000 **Cases** NA

This is a classic case of an old dog learning new tricks, and doing so with panache. Robin Day had a long and distinguished career as winemaker, then chief winemaker, then technical director of Orlando; participated in the management buy-out; and profited substantially from the on-sale to Pernod Ricard. He hastened slowly with the establishment of Domain Day, but there is nothing conservative about his approach in establishing his 15-ha vineyard at Mt Crawford, high in the hills (at 450 m) of the southeastern extremity of the Barossa Valley, bordering (on 2 sides of the vineyard) the Eden Valley. While the mainstream varieties are merlot, pinot noir and riesling, he has trawled Italy, France and Georgia for the other varieties: viognier, sangiovese, saperavi, lagrein, garganega and sagrantino. Robin Day says, 'Years of writing descriptions for back labels have left me convinced that this energy is more gainfully employed in growing grapes and making wine.'

ŶŶŶŶŶ **Mt Crawford Riesling 2006** Highly aromatic lime blossom/apple blossom and an illusive whisper of hard-to-pin-down spice; abundant flavour, long and intense, but not heavy. Screwcap. 12° alc. **Rating** 95 **To** 2016 $20

ŶŶŶŶŶ **Mt Crawford Sangiovese 2004** A thoroughly attractive example of sangiovese, with clear black cherry/sour cherry fruit; fine, ripe tannins and good acidity. Screwcap. 13.5° alc. **Rating** 92 **To** 2011 $28
One Serious Pinot Noir 2004 Light- to medium-bodied, with fresh strawberry and raspberry red fruits; good varietal character. Screwcap. 13° alc. **Rating** 91 **To** 2009 $28

ŶŶŶŶ **One Serious Mt Crawford Rose 2006** Has the colour of pinot noir, and overall, closer to light-bodied red wine than rose; not sweetened, just spicy fruit. Screwcap. 12° alc. **Rating** 88 **To** 2008 $16
Mt Crawford Garganega 2006 Faint citrus blossom; a well-made wine, appealing mainly to wine voyeurs or those who don't actually like the taste of wine. Screwcap. 12.5° alc. **Rating** 87 **To** 2008 $20

Domaine A   ★★★★★

Campania, Tas 7026 **Region** Southern Tasmania
T (03) 6260 4174 **www**.domaine-a.com.au **Open** Mon–Fri 9–4, w'ends by appt
Winemaker Peter Althaus **Est.** 1973 **Cases** 5000
The striking black label of the premium Domaine A wine, dominated by the single, multicoloured 'A', signified the change of ownership from George Park to Swiss businessman Peter Althaus many years ago. The wines are made without compromise, and reflect the low yields from the immaculately tended vineyards. They represent aspects of both Old World and New World philosophies, techniques and styles. Exports to the UK, Denmark, Switzerland, Germany, France, Canada, China, Hong Kong, South Korea, Japan and Singapore.

Domaine Chandon/Green Point   ★★★★★

Green Point, Maroondah Highway, Coldstream, Vic 3770 **Region** Yarra Valley
T (03) 9738 9200 **F** (03) 9738 9201 **www**.chandon.com.au **Open** 7 days 10.30–4.30
Winemaker Dr Tony Jordan, James Gosper, Matt Steel, John Harris, Glen Thompson
Est. 1986 **Cases** 150 000
Wholly owned by Möet et Chandon, and one of the 2 most important wine facilities in the Yarra Valley, the Green Point tasting room has a national and international reputation, having won a number of major tourism awards in recent years. The sparkling wine product range has evolved, and there has been increasing emphasis placed on the table wines. The return of Dr Tony Jordan, the first CEO of Domaine Chandon, has further strengthened both the focus and quality of the brand. The table wines are made under the Green Point label, and all of the sparkling wines which are exported are likewise called Green Point. Exports to all major markets.

ŶŶŶŶŶ **Yarra Valley Vintage Brut 2003** Fragrant aromas of fresh citrus and brioche lead into a gently nutty/creamy palate with citrus and melon fruit; perfect balance and length. **Rating** 95 **To** 2008 $36.99
Blanc de Blancs 2003 Medium straw-yellow, again with strong mousse; attractive biscuity, creamy characters; nectarine fruit in a long, fine and excellently balanced palate. **Rating** 95 **To** 2008 $36.99

Green Point Sauvignon Blanc 2006 Particularly well-made; firm and precise sauvignon with backbone and length; a proportion of barrel ferment gives structure reminiscent of white Bordeaux, then a bell-clear finish. Screwcap. 12.5° alc. **Rating** 94 **To** 2010 $22.95

Green Point Reserve Yarra Valley Chardonnay 2004 Light straw-green; still very youthful and elegant, the deliberately low alcohol paying dividends with the stone fruit and grapefruit flavours; a Chablis/New World mix, though with more of the latter. Screwcap. 12.8° alc. **Rating** 94 **To** 2013 $41

Green Point Reserve Yarra Valley Shiraz 2004 Fragrant black cherry and blackberry; medium-bodied, with very good structure and mouthfeel; fine, ripe tannins and quality oak. Screwcap. 13.7° alc. **Rating** 94 **To** 2029 $47

Tasmanian Cuvee 2003 Excellent mousse; the 30% pinot noir contribution more evident than the blend suggests; bready cracked-wheat notes around a spicy core of sweet fruit. **Rating** 94 **To** 2008 $36.99

Z*D Blanc de Blancs 2003 Bright straw-green, with fine, persistent mousse and great balance, it flies in the face of the belief that zero dosage can only work with aged wines. **Rating** 94 **To** 2008 $36.99

Z*D Vintage Brut 2003 Super-fine, persistent mousse; the absence of dosage is evident, but without taking away balance from the vibrantly fresh strawberry and stone fruit palate. **Rating** 94 **To** 2008 $35

♀♀♀♀♀ **Green Point Pinot Noir Rose 2006** Bright, lively and crisp, with an almost citrussy edge to the strawberry fruit; dry finish; perfect antipasto wine picked at exactly the right moment. Screwcap. 12.5° alc. **Rating** 90 **To** 2008 $22

Domaines Tatiarra   ★★★★★

2/102 Barkers Road, Hawthorn, Vic 3124 (postal) **Region** Heathcote
T 0411 240 815 **F** (03) 9822 4108 **www**.cambrianshiraz.com **Open** Not
Winemaker Ben Riggs **Est.** 1991 **Cases** 2000
Domaines Tatiarra Limited is an unlisted public company, its core asset being a 60-ha property of Cambrian earth identified and developed by Bill Hepburn, who sold the project to the company in 1991. It will produce only one varietal wine: Shiraz. The majority of the wine will come from the Tatiarra (Aboriginal word meaning 'beautiful country') property, but the Trademark Shiraz is an equal blend of McLaren Vale and Heathcote wine. The wines are made at the Pettavel Winery in Geelong, with Ben Riggs commuting between McLaren Vale and the winery as required.

♀♀♀♀♀ **Trademark Heathcote McLaren Vale Shiraz 2005** The synergy of the regional blend is immediately apparent; the wine has greater length and more complexity of both texture and flavour; curiously, the alcohol is less obvious and overall there is more elegance. Cork. 15.5° alc. **Rating** 94 **To** 2020 $65

♀♀♀♀♀ **Cambrian Heathcote Shiraz 2005** A very big-framed wine with lots of red and black fruits plus earth, chocolate and mocha. The alcohol slightly strips the fruit on the finish. Cork. 15.5° alc. **Rating** 93 **To** 2019 $45

Caravan of Dreams Heathcote Shiraz Pressings 2005 Denser colour than the Cambrian, though less vibrant, presumably due to the pressings component; an extreme wine, with ultra-ripe fruit providing a potent bouquet and palate, the alcohol accentuating that which needs no emphasis. Cork. 15.5° alc. **Rating** 92 **To** 2024 $55

♀♀♀♀ **Culled Barrel Heathcote Shiraz 2005** Undoubtedly less concentrated and focused than the top releases, but offers excellent value. Cork. 15.5° alc. **Rating** 89 **To** 2015 $20

Dominic Versace Wines   ★★★★☆

Lot 258 Heaslip Road, MacDonald Park, SA 5121 **Region** Adelaide Plains
T (08) 8379 7132 **F** (08) 8338 0979 **www**.dominicversace.com.au **Open** By appt
Winemaker Dominic Versace, Armando Verdiglione **Est.** 2000 **Cases** 1500

Dominic Versace and brother-in-law Armando Verdiglione have a long association with wine, through their families in Italy and in Australia since 1980. In that year Dominic Versace planted 4.5 ha of shiraz, grenache and sangiovese (one of the earliest such plantings in Australia), selling the grapes until 1999. In 2000 the pair decided to pool their experience and resources, using the near-organically grown grapes from the Versace vineyard, and deliberately rustic winemaking techniques.

ΨΨΨΨΨ **Reserve McLaren Vale Cabernet Sauvignon 2004** Vibrant fruit flavours run right down the centre line for quality cabernet from a top vintage; a seamless, effortless flow, supported by full tannins for the long haul. Cork. 14° alc. **Rating** 94 **To** 2019 $53.90

ΨΨΨΨΨ **Reserve McLaren Vale Shiraz 2004** Layers of blackberry, plum, spice and chocolate; savoury but fine tannins; quality oak. Cork. 14° alc. **Rating** 92 **To** 2019 $33
Limited Release Adelaide Plains Shiraz 2003 Dense colour; plum, prune and blackberry mix, with some interesting savoury edges; lingering finish. Cork. 14.5° alc. **Rating** 90 **To** 2015 $50

ΨΨΨΨ **Reserve McLaren Vale Unwooded Chardonnay 2006** There's nothing new under the sun, offering (as per the back label) 'mouthful sensation'. Enters the Guinness Book of Records as the first reserve unwooded chardonnay, and does indeed have pleasant tropical stone fruit and balanced acidity. Screwcap. 13° alc. **Rating** 89 **To** 2008 $17.60
Casalingo Adelaide Plains Sangiovese Grenache Shiraz 2004 Hangs together more convincingly than the blend might suggest, particularly on the bouquet and entry to the mouth; slightly astringent tannins on the finish detract a little. Screwcap. 13.5° alc. **Rating** 88 **To** 2012 $30
Rossino Adelaide Plains Rose 2006 Light-bodied, the low alcohol a plus; does have touches of cherry fruit. Screwcap. 10.8° alc. **Rating** 87 **To** 2008 $15

Dominique Portet   ★★★★★

870–872 Maroondah Highway, Coldstream, Vic 3770 **Region** Yarra Valley
T (03) 5962 5760 **F** (03) 5962 4938 **www**.dominiqueportet.com **Open** 7 days 10–5
Winemaker Dominique Portet, Scott Baker **Est.** 2000 **Cases** 12 000
Dominique Portet was bred in the purple. He spent his early years at Chateau Lafite (where his father was regisseur) and was one of the very first Flying Winemakers, commuting to Clos du Val in the Napa Valley where his brother is winemaker. Since 1976 he has lived in Australia, spending more than 20 years as managing director of Taltarni, and also developing the Clover Hill Vineyard in Tas. After retiring from Taltarni, he moved to the Yarra Valley, a region he had been closely observing since the mid-1980s. In 2001 he found the site he had long looked for, and in a twinkling of an eye built his winery and cellar door, and planted a quixotic mix of viognier, sauvignon blanc and merlot next to the winery; he also undertakes contract winemaking for others. Exports to the UK, the US and other major markets.

ΨΨΨΨΨ **Tasmanian Cuvee 2002** Bracingly fresh and vibrant; a long, lemon-rind palate with some green apple; a fine, fresh finish; very good balance, length and aftertaste. 12.5° alc. **Rating** 94 **To** 2010 $40
Vendange Tardives Yarra Valley Sauvignon Blanc 2005 An amazing wine, bursting with lusciously rich peach and citrus fruit, the sweetness perfectly balanced by acidity. The first high-quality late harvest or botrytised sauvignon blanc to come from Australia. Screwcap. 14.5° alc. **Rating** 94 **To** 2012 $40

ΨΨΨΨΨ **Yarra Valley Shiraz 2005** Medium-bodied; supple, smooth, cool-grown fruit, with touches of licorice and leather; fine, savoury tannins. Screwcap. 14.5° alc. **Rating** 93 **To** 2015 $45

ΨΨΨΨ **Yarra Valley Sauvignon Blanc 2006** Clean, fresh and very tight, much more to the mineral and herb than to the tropical fruit end of the spectrum. Screwcap. 13.5° alc. **Rating** 88 **To** 2008 $22

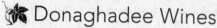 Donaghadee Wines

65 Burrows Road, Lethbridge, Vic 3332 (postal) **Region** Geelong
T (03) 5281 7364 **www**.donaghadeewines.com.au **Open** Not
Winemaker David Warnock **Est.** 2000 **Cases** 200
David and Pam Warnock planted a 0.25-ha plot of shiraz, cabernet and merlot as a hobby, but
with retirement around the corner, and encouragement from their nephew (also a winemaker),
have increased the plantings to 1 ha of chardonnay and 1 ha of shiraz.

ΨΨΨΨ   **Chardonnay 2005** Lots of structure and complexity; ripe stone fruit flavours
balanced by fair acidity. **Rating** 89 **To** 2010 $19

Dookie College Winery ★★★☆

Dookie-Nalinga Road, Dookie, Vic 3647 **Region** Goulburn Valley
T (03) 5833 9296 **F** (03) 5833 9296 **www**.dookie.unimelb.edu.au **Open** Fri–Sun 11–5
Winemaker Sam Scarpari, Wendy Cotter **Est.** 1896 **Cases** 5000
Viticulture and winemaking have been taught at Dookie since 1883; in the 1880s the Dookie
Hills produced a quarter of Australia's total vintage, and included Australia's largest winery, before
being devastated by phylloxera. Exactly 100 years after the Dookie winery was built in 1896, it
was reopened, and since 1996 has been producing campus wine, used in teaching and research,
and providing contract winemaking for boutique winemakers. It has 22 ha of vineyards planted
to cabernet sauvignon, shiraz, sauvignon blanc, semillon and tarango.

ΨΨΨΨ   **360° Rose 2006** Supple light red fruit flavours; good length, the residual sugar
balanced. Screwcap. 13° alc. **Rating** 87 **To** 2008 $14
360° Cabernet Sauvignon 2004 Medium-bodied; fractionally jammy on entry,
but cassis, dark chocolate and gentle tannins do come together well enough. Twin
top. 14° alc. **Rating** 87 **To** 2009 $16

Doonkuna Estate ★★★★☆

Barton Highway, Murrumbateman, NSW 2582 **Region** Canberra District
T (02) 6227 5811 **F** (02) 6227 5085 **www**.doonkuna.com.au **Open** 7 days 11–4
Winemaker Bruce March **Est.** 1971 **Cases** 4000
Following the acquisition of Doonkuna by Barry and Maureen Moran in late 1996, the plantings
have been increased from a little under 4 ha to 20 ha. A wide range of vintages of many of the
wines are available at cellar door at modest prices.

ΨΨΨΨ   **Cian Canberra District Chardonnay Pinot Noir 2001** An elegant style, with
some primary fruit flavours still present; 3 years on yeast lees; 55%/45%. 12.8° alc.
Rating 89 **To** 2010 $30

Dos Rios ★★★

PO Box 343, Nyah, Vic 3594 **Region** Swan Hill
T (03) 5030 3005 **F** (03) 5030 3006 **www**.dosrios.com.au **Open** Fri–Mon 9–9
Winemaker Cobaw Ridge (Alan Cooper) **Est.** 2003 **Cases** 1000
Bruce Hall entered the wine business as a small contract grower for McGuigan Simeon Wines.
From this point on, the story goes in reverse: instead of McGuigan Simeon saying it no longer
required the grapes, it purchased the vineyard outright in 2003. In the meantime, Hall had hand-
picked the grapes left at the end of the rows after the mechanical harvester had passed through,
and had the wines made by Alan Cooper of Cobaw Ridge. In 2004 he purchased a small property
northwest of Swan Hill with plantings of 20-year-old shiraz, which has been extended by small
areas of viognier, tempranillo, durif and merlot. Exports to Spain and Japan.

ΨΨΨΨ   **Swan Hill Pinot Gris 2004** Not, as one might imagine, sweet, but bone-dry; has
largely triumphed over the wildly unsuitable climate (far too warm); nice minerally
notes, with a hint of pear. Screwcap. 13° alc. **Rating** 87 **To** 2008 $15.40

Swan Hill Shiraz Viognier 2005 Fragrant, lifted red fruits; light- to medium-bodied, but has bright, lively flavours and good acidity (no doubt corrected in the winery). Diam. 14° alc. **Rating** 87 **To** 2008 $15.95

Dowie Doole

Cnr McMurtrie Road/Main Road, McLaren Vale, SA 5171 **Region** McLaren Vale
T (08) 8323 8875 **F** (08) 8323 8895 **www**.dowiedoole.com **Open** 7 days 10–5
Winemaker Brian Light (Contract) **Est.** 1996 **Cases** 15 000
Dowie Doole has 3 vineyards owned by individual partners: California Road in McLaren Vale, with 25 ha; the so-called Home Block in the Adelaide Hills with 4.6 ha (sauvignon blanc); and Tintookie at Blewitt Springs, with 12 ha. Steadily increasing amounts of the grapes are used for the Dowie Doole wines. Exports to the UK, the US and other major markets.

ￕￕￕￕￕ Reserve McLaren Vale Shiraz 2004 Another dimension altogether over the varietal version; intense black fruits, a strong streak of regional bitter chocolate, and structure to burn. Diam. 14.5° alc. **Rating** 94 **To** 2024 $50

ￕￕￕￕ Hooley Dooley White 2006 Perhaps a shotgun blend, but the sauvignon blanc/semillon partners are largely oblivious of the viognier cuckoo in the marriage bed; attractive tropical/citrus flavours, and a crisp finish. Screwcap. 13° alc. **Rating** 89 **To** 2008 $15
McLaren Vale Shiraz 2004 Medium-bodied; offers black fruits, hints of earth and dark chocolate with a neat connection of tannins and gentle oak. Diam. 14.5° alc. **Rating** 89 **To** 2014 $23
McLaren Vale Merlot 2005 Light- to medium-bodied; some spicy notes and touches of leaf and olive, but also small, sweet berry fruits of the variety. Diam. 14° alc. **Rating** 87 **To** 2011 $21

Downing Estate Vineyard

19 Drummonds Lane, Heathcote, Vic 3523 **Region** Heathcote
T (03) 5433 3387 **F** (03) 5433 3389 **www**.downingestate.com.au **Open** By appt
Winemaker Don Lewis **Est.** 1994 **Cases** 1300
Bob and Joy Downing purchased 24 ha of undulating land in 1994, and have since established a 9.5-ha dry-grown vineyard planted to shiraz (75%), cabernet sauvignon and merlot. At any one time, a number of vintages of each wine are available for sale. Exports to the US.

ￕￕￕￕￕ Heathcote Shiraz 2004 A complex but seamless web of blackberry fruit, licorice, cracked pepper, oak and tannins; very good length. Oh for a screwcap. Cork. 14° alc. **Rating** 95 **To** 2020 $39
Heathcote Merlot 2004 An expressive bouquet, flooded with cassis/redcurrant fruit, but the relatively low alcohol pulls it well back down from the wannabe cabernet style; fine tannins and good length; just delicious. Cork. 13.5° alc. **Rating** 94 **To** 2018 $39
Heathcote Cabernet Sauvignon 2004 Typical deep, strong colour; dense, rich almost cassis essence plus blackcurrant, but not sweet or alcoholic; supple and long. A thoroughly distinguished trio. Cork. 14° alc. **Rating** 94 **To** 2021 $39

Drayton's Family Wines

Oakey Creek Road, Cessnock, NSW 2321 **Region** Lower Hunter Valley
T (02) 4998 7513 **F** (02) 4998 7743 **www**.draytonswines.com.au **Open** Mon–Fri 8–5, w'ends & public hols 10–5
Winemaker Trevor Drayton **Est.** 1853 **Cases** 90 000
A family-owned and run stalwart of the Hunter Valley, producing honest, full-flavoured wines that sometimes excel themselves and are invariably modestly priced. The size of the production will come as a surprise to many, but it is a clear indication of the good standing of the brand, notwithstanding the low profile of recent years. It is not to be confused with Reg Drayton Wines. Exports to NZ, the US, Japan, Singapore, Taiwan, Samoa and Switzerland.

ŶŶŶŶŶ **Susanne Pokolbin Semillon 2004** Pale straw-green; very fresh and lively; a long, perfectly balanced palate with grass, herb and lemon flavours; 100-year-old vines. Quality cork, but oh for a screwcap. 10.5° alc. **Rating** 94 **To** 2015 $35

ŶŶŶŶŶ **Vineyard Reserve Pokolbin Semillon 2002** Clean, lively and fresh, very much in the winery style of semillon; good balance and a lingering finish. Cork. 11° alc. **Rating** 92 **To** 2011 $19

William Pokolbin Shiraz 1999 Remarkable colour and hue; a strongly savoury, earthy regional style; medium-bodied, but will age and keep the regional characters for decades if the cork permits. 13° alc. **Rating** 91 **To** 2024 $45

Hunter Valley Semillon 2004 Faint reduction on the bouquet in no way marks the intensely crisp and fresh palate, with herb, lemon and vibrant acidity. Screwcap. 11.5° alc. **Rating** 90 **To** 2014 $14

Vineyard Reserve Pokolbin Shiraz 2002 Medium-bodied, supple blackberry, earth and sweet leather; very good regional style, with more to come. Cork. 13° alc. **Rating** 90 **To** 2012 $25

ŶŶŶŶ **Hunter Valley Semillon 2006** Clean; the varietal character is there, but the wine is as yet painfully shy; needs time and patience, which will be rewarded. Screwcap. 10.5° alc. **Rating** 87 **To** 2016 $15

drinkmoor wines

All Saints Road, Wahgunyah, Vic 3687 **Region** Rutherglen
T (02) 6033 5544 **F** (02) 6033 5645 **www**.drinkmoorwines.com.au **Open** 7 days 10–5
Winemaker Damien Cofield **Est.** 2002 **Cases** 2500
This is a separate venture of Max and Karen Cofield (who also own Cofield Wines) and son Damien, with a very clear vision and marketing plan. It is to encourage people to make wine their beverage of choice; in other words, don't drink beer or spirits, drink wine instead, or drink more wines. Thus the wines are made in an everyday, easy-drinking style, with the cost kept as low as possible. The labelling, too, is designed to take the pretentiousness out of wine drinking, and to provide a bit of fun. Although the Cofields don't say so, this is the heartland of Generation X.

ŶŶŶŶ **Durif NV** Inky colour, inky aromas and an inky palate, the latter – however – without undue extraction. Prunes, blackcurrant and plum jam; rollicking barbecue red. Screwcap. 14.7° alc. **Rating** 88 **To** 2008 $15

Sticky NV Positive blackberry and black cherry fruit, with a light touch of American oak; good balance. **Rating** 87 **To** 2008 $15

Dromana Estate

555 Old Moorooduc Road, Tuerong, Vic 3933 **Region** Mornington Peninsula
T (03) 5974 4400 **www**.dromanaestate.com.au **Open** Wed–Sun 11–5, 7 days in summer
Winemaker Rollo Crittenden **Est.** 1982 **Cases** 30 000
Since it was established, Dromana Estate has always been near or at the cutting edge, both in marketing terms and in terms of development of new varietals, most obviously the Italian range under the 'i' label. Rollo Crittenden has taken over winemaking responsibilities after the departure of father Garry, and the business is now majority-owned by investors. The capital provided has resulted in the Yarra Valley Hills and Mornington Estate wines coming under the Dromana Estate umbrella. Exports to the UK, the US, Canada and Singapore.

ŶŶŶŶŶ **Dromana Estate Reserve Chardonnay 2004** Restrained, elegant yet exhibiting lovely nectarine, stone fruit and grapefruit, gently enhanced by barrel ferment and associated inputs. Screwcap. 13° alc. **Rating** 95 **To** 2013 $58

ŶŶŶŶŶ **Dromana Estate Reserve Pinot Noir 2004** A complex mix of red fruits and more foresty/savoury aromas; appropriate tannins aid the structure, as does some oak impact. Screwcap. 14° alc. **Rating** 91 **To** 2011 $58

🍷🍷🍷🍷 **Asciutto 2003** Certainly gives unusual plum cake and spice characters, carrying the alcohol (just). Cabernet sauvignon is left to dry for 4 weeks on bakers' racks before being crushed and fermented. A risky business if it rains. Screwcap. 15° alc. **Rating** 89 **To** 2008 $74

Drummonds Corrina Vineyard ★★★

85 Wintles Road, Leongatha South, Vic 3953 **Region** Gippsland
T (03) 5664 3317 **Open** W'ends 12.30–4.30
Winemaker Bass Phillip **Est.** 1983 **Cases** NA
The Drummond family has 3 ha of vines (1 ha each of pinot noir and sauvignon blanc, and 0.5 ha each of cabernet sauvignon and merlot) which was slowly established without the aid of irrigation. The viticultural methods are those practised by Phillip Jones, who makes the wines for Drummonds: north–south row orientation, leaf plucking on the east side of the rows, low yields, and all fruit picked by hand. Similarly restrained winemaking methods (no pumping, no filters and low SO_2) follow in the winery.

🍷🍷🍷🍷 **South Gippsland Pinot Noir 2003** Should have been bottled and sold much earlier. Cork. 12.5° alc. **Rating** 87 **To** 2008 $35

Ducketts Mill NR

1678, Scotsdale Road, Denmark, WA 6333 **Region** Denmark
T (08) 9840 9844 **F** (08) 9840 9668 www.duckettsmillwines.com.au **Open** 7 days 11–5
Winemaker Harewood Estate **Est.** 1997 **Cases** NA

Dudley Wines ★★★★

Porky Flat Vineyard, Penneshaw, Kangaroo Island, SA 5222 (postal) **Region** Kangaroo Island
T (08) 8553 1509 **F** (08) 8553 1509 **Open** 7 days 11–5
Winemaker Jeff Howard, Brodie Howard **Est.** 1994 **Cases** 5000
Colin Hopkins, Jeff Howard, Alan Willson and Paul Mansfield have formed a partnership to bring together 3 vineyards on Kangaroo Island's Dudley Peninsula: the Porky Flat Vineyard (5 ha), Hog Bay River (2 ha) and Sawyers (4 ha). It is the quirky vineyard names which give the products their distinctive identities. The partners not only look after viticulture, but also join in the winemaking process. Most of the wines are sold through licensed outlets on Kangaroo Island.

🍷🍷🍷🍷🍷 **Porky Flat Kangaroo Island Shiraz 2005** Intense licorice, spice, leather and blackberry aromas and flavours; a striking wine, with a very long finish. Screwcap. 14.9° alc. **Rating** 94 **To** 2020 $18

🍷🍷🍷🍷🍷 **Porky Flat Kangaroo Island Shiraz 2004** Light- to medium-bodied, fragrant and elegant; multi-flavours of red and black fruits, herbs and spices; fine tannins to finish. Screwcap. 14° alc. **Rating** 92 **To** 2019 $18

🍷🍷🍷🍷 **Island Chardonnay 2005** Fine and elegant; acidity is again evident, but in much better balance; the citrussy palate, while not rich, has good length. Screwcap. 13.9° alc. **Rating** 89 **To** 2010 $16
Hog Bay River Kangaroo Island Cabernet Sauvignon 2003 Cassis and blackcurrant fruit aromas and flavours; while light- to medium-bodied, has length and better tannin ripeness than the '04. Screwcap. 14° alc. **Rating** 88 **To** 2013 $18
Grassy Flat Kangaroo Island Sauvignon Blanc 2006 A complex wine; the entry to the mouth has nutty notes suggesting the use of some oak, but there is in fact none; finishes with pointed acidity. Screwcap. 12.5° alc. **Rating** 87 **To** 2008 $16

Duke's Vineyard ★★★★★

Porongurup Road, Porongurup, WA 6324 **Region** Porongurup
T (08) 9853 1107 **F** (08) 9853 1107 www.dukesvineyard.com **Open** 7 days 10–4.30
Winemaker Wineworx (Diane Miller) **Est.** 1998 **Cases** 2500

When Hilde and Ian (Duke) Ranson sold their clothing manufacturing business in 1998 they were able to fulfil a long-held dream of establishing a vineyard in the Porongurup subregion of Great Southern with the acquisition of a 65-ha farm at the foot of the Porongurup Range. They planted 3 ha each of shiraz and cabernet sauvignon and 4 ha of riesling. Hilde Ranson is a successful artist, and it was she who designed the beautiful scalloped, glass-walled cellar door sales area with its mountain blue cladding. Exports to the UK.

ŶŶŶŶŶ **Great Southern Riesling 2006** Fragrant apple and lime blossom aromas; a fine, but intense palate, with crisp, crunchy acidity; beautiful line and length. In 3 or 4 years' time could be a trophy winner (as was the '02 at the same age). Screwcap. 12.5° alc. **Rating** 95 **To** 2016 $18
Magpie Hill Reserve Riesling 2006 More powerful and concentrated than the Great Southern Riesling; curiously, despite the pricing and selection, and despite the greater power, I prefer the Great Southern. Screwcap. 11.3° alc. **Rating** 94 **To** 2016 $30
Great Southern Riesling 2002 Bright straw-green; a wonderful mix of intense fruit and complex maturity; a long palate, with a lingering finish and aftertaste. Multiple trophy winner. Screwcap. 12° alc. **Rating** 94 **To** 2012 $18
Great Southern Shiraz 2004 Complex and substantial, with very good blackberry and spice fruit; seamless oak and ripe tannin integration. Screwcap. 13.9° alc. **Rating** 94 **To** 2015 $24

ŶŶŶŶŶ **Great Southern Cabernet Sauvignon 2004** A sophisticated wine with blackcurrant fruit, the cedary oak just a little over the top. Screwcap. 14.2° alc. **Rating** 90 **To** 2013 $22
Magpie Hill Reserve Cabernet Sauvignon 2004 Very cedary, savoury; some cassis to offset those briary characters, without entirely convincing, although the wine does have extra length. A strange parallel to the 2 rieslings. Screwcap. 14.8° alc. **Rating** 90 **To** 2019 $35

Dulcinea   ★★★☆

Jubilee Road, Sulky, Ballarat, Vic 3352 **Region** Ballarat
T (03) 5334 6440 **F** (03) 5334 6828 www.dulcinea.com.au **Open** 7 days 10–5
Winemaker Rod Stott **Est.** 1983 **Cases** 3000
Rod Stott is a passionate grapegrower and winemaker (with 6 ha of vineyard) who chose the name Dulcinea from *The Man of La Mancha*, where only a fool fights windmills. With winemaking help from various sources, he has produced a series of interesting and often complex wines. Exports to Japan, Fiji and China.

ŶŶŶŶŶ **Bottle Fermented Sparkling Shiraz 2001** Spicy red fruits; long and clean, the apparently low dosage working very well; major surprise. 14.5° alc. **Rating** 90 **To** 2011 $16

ŶŶŶŶ **Ballarat Sauvignon Blanc 2006** Quite intense grass, gooseberry and capsicum flavours; good line and length, finishing with clean acidity. Screwcap. 12.6° alc. **Rating** 89 **To** 2008 $15
Ballarat Chardonnay 2006 A sauvignon blanc–crossover; citrus, lemon and a touch of stone fruit; lingering acidity; all reflecting the low alcohol. Screwcap. 12.8° alc. **Rating** 87 **To** 2009 $15

Dumaresq Valley Vineyard   ★★★☆

Bruxner Highway, Tenterfield, NSW 2372 **Region** New England
T (02) 6737 5281 **F** (02) 6737 5293 www.dumaresqvalleyvineyard.com.au **Open** 7 days 9–5
Winemaker Contract **Est.** 1997 **Cases** 900
Three generations of the Zappa family have been involved in the establishment of what is now a very large mixed farming property on 1600 ha, all beginning when the first generation arrived from Italy in the late 1940s to work as cane-cutters in Qld. Today, Martin and Amelia, with 3 of their sons and their wives, have a property sustaining 120 cattle, 5000 super-fine wool Merino

sheep, 140 ha of fresh produce, 250 ha of cereal crops and a 25-ha vineyard. The vineyard was progressively established between 1997 and 2000, with plantings of chardonnay, semillon, sauvignon blanc, shiraz, merlot, cabernet sauvignon, barbera and tempranillo.

ΨΨΨΨΨ Reserve Shiraz 2005 Light- to medium-bodied, elegant and precise; smooth and supple black cherry, with touches of spice and licorice; finishes with fine, ripe tannins and subtle oak. My premature comment about high-quality cork was based on visual inspection and before it was found the wine was heavily affected by TCA. The tasting note is for the 2nd bottle. Cork. 14° alc. **Rating** 90 **To** 2017 $18

ΨΨΨΨ Merlot 2005 Plenty of flavour through a neat balance of cassis/blackcurrant and more savoury, olive notes; good line and mouthfeel for an often recalcitrant variety. Screwcap. 13° alc. **Rating** 88 **To** 2013 $16
Amelia's Chardonnay 2005 Faintly reduced aromas; a range of stone fruit, nectarine, peach and apricot flavours; crisp acidity. Screwcap. 13° alc. **Rating** 87 **To** 2008 $16

Dunelm Wines

Lot 509 Scotsdale Road, Denmark, WA 6333 **Region** Great Southern
T (08) 9840 9027 **F** (08) 9840 9027 **Open** W'ends, public & school hols 10–4, or by appt
Winemaker Harewood Estate (James Kellie) **Est.** 1999 **Cases** 300
After 35 years as a General Practitioner in Fremantle, Graeme Gargett (and wife Lesley) decided to 'semi-retire' and pursue a career in viticulture. They purchased their beautiful 35-ha property in the Scotsdale Valley in 1997. The north-facing slopes of well-drained karri loam soils were ideal for viticulture, and in 1999 they planted 4 ha of pinot noir, chardonnay, shiraz and cabernet sauvignon. Most of the grapes are sold to Plantagenet, but small quantities have been made each year since 2002, some by Graeme Gargett without the use of preservatives. The Barking Dog label is in honour of the resident bird-scarer, the Gargetts' dachshund Harley.

ΨΨΨΨ Barking Dog Denmark Pinot Noir 2005 Light red, showing some development; spicy and savoury, but not bitter; light-bodied, yet has some length. Just gets over the line. Screwcap. 13.8° alc. **Rating** 87 **To** 2008

Dunns Creek Estate

137 McIlroys Road, Red Hill, Vic 3937 **Region** Mornington Peninsula
T 0413 020 467 **F** (03) 5989 2011 www.dunnscreek.com.au **Open** By appt
Winemaker Sandro Mosele (Contract) **Est.** 2001 **Cases** 1270
This is the retirement venture of Roger and Hannah Stuart-Andrews, a former professional couple whose love of Italian and Spanish wines led them to their eclectic choice of varieties. Thus they have planted a total of 2.7 ha of tempranillo, albarino, arneis and barbera in more or less equal quantities. There seems no reason why these grapes should not produce wines of distinction.

Dusty Hill Wines

Barambah Road, Moffatdale via Murgon, Qld 4605 **Region** South Burnett
T (07) 4168 4700 **F** (07) 4168 4888 www.dustyhill.com.au **Open** 7 days 9.30–5
Winemaker Symphony Hill (Mike Hayes) **Est.** 1996 **Cases** 1500
Joe Prendergast and family have established 2 ha each of shiraz and cabernet sauvignon, 1 ha each of verdelho and semillon and 0.5 ha each of merlot and black muscat. The vines are crop-thinned to obtain maximum ripeness in the fruit and to maximise tannin extract, although the winery's speciality is the Dusty Rose.

Dutschke Wines

PO Box 107, Lyndoch, SA 5351 **Region** Barossa Valley
T (08) 8524 5485 **F** (08) 8524 5489 www.dutschkewines.com **Open** Not
Winemaker Wayne Dutschke **Est.** 1998 **Cases** 6000

Wayne Dutschke spent over 20 years working in Australia and overseas for companies large and small before joining his uncle (and grapegrower) Ken Smellier to form Dutschke Wines. In addition to outstanding table wines, he has a once-yearly release of fortified wines (doubtless drawing on his time at Baileys of Glenrowan); these sell out overnight, and have received the usual stratospheric points from Robert Parker. Exports to the UK, the US and other major markets.

ΥΥΥΥΥ **Oscar Semmler Shiraz 2004** Tightly focused blackberry, plum and spice fruit; has depth and good tannins, the oak well integrated. Carries its alcohol with ease. ProCork. 15° alc. **Rating** 94 **To** 2015 $50
Single Barrel Barossa Valley Shiraz 2004 Layer-upon-layer of rich flavours of blackberry, satsuma plum, licorice and spice; has more or less absorbed the oak in which it spent 24 months; unfined and unfiltered. ProCork. 15° alc. **Rating** 94 **To** 2029 $55

ΥΥΥΥΥ **WillowBend Merlot Shiraz Cabernet 2004** An array of ripe but not jammy blackcurrant and cassis fruit; long palate, fine tannins. ProCork. 14° alc. **Rating** 92 **To** 2019 $22
St Jakobi Shiraz 2004 Fragrant berry aromas; fresh fruit flavours with berry and spice; controlled oak. ProCork. 15° alc. **Rating** 91 **To** 2014 $30

ΥΥΥΥ **Barossa Valley Moscato 2006** Full-on sweet, well into Auslese equivalent; drink stone-cold with chilled fresh fruit on a summer day. Cork. 8° alc. **Rating** 87 **To** 2008 $18

Dyson Wines   ★★★★

Sherriff Road, Maslin Beach, SA 5170 **Region** McLaren Vale
T (08) 8386 1092 **F** (08) 8327 0066 **www.**dysonwines.com **Open** 7 days 10–5
Winemaker Allan Dyson **Est.** 1976 **Cases** 2000
Allan Dyson, who described himself (a few years ago) as 'a young man of 50-odd years', has recently added to his 1.5 ha of viognier with 2.5 ha of cabernet sauvignon and 2 ha of chardonnay, and has absolutely no thoughts of slowing down or retiring. All wines are estate-grown, made and bottled. I'm not too sure about this sudden elevation to Grande Privilege status, but never mind.

ΥΥΥΥΥ **Grande Privilege Reserve Clarice Cabernet Sauvignon 2002** Medium-bodied; has developed well over the past 5 years; cedary, earthy notes alongside blackcurrant supported by fine, ripe tannins; oak merely a vehicle. Cork. 14.5° alc. **Rating** 90 **To** 2012 $22

ΥΥΥΥ **Grande Privilege Reserve Viognier 2005** Well-made; good balance without too much residual sugar; peach, citrus and a hint of apricot. Cork. 14.5° alc. **Rating** 88 **To** 2009 $20
Grande Privilege Reserve Clarice Cabernet Sauvignon 2001 Surprisingly, has a better colour hue than the '02; equally surprisingly, the underlying ripeness is less, leading to a touch of bitterness on the finish, though it has length. Cork. 14° alc. **Rating** 88 **To** 2010 $22
Sparkling Shiraz NV Well-balanced with red fruits not swamped by oak, nor by sweetness on the finish; excellent value for the category. 12.5° alc. **Rating** 87 **To** 2008 $14

Eagle Vale   ★★★★

51 Caves Road, Margaret River, WA 6285 **Region** Margaret River
T (08) 9757 6477 **F** (08) 9757 6199 **www.**eaglevalewine.com **Open** 7 days 10–5
Winemaker Guy Gallienne **Est.** 1997 **Cases** 10 000
Eagle Vale is a joint venture between the property owners, Steve and Wendy Jacobs, and the operator/winemaking team of Guy, Chantal and Karl Gallienne. It is a united nations team: Steve Jacobs was born in Colorado, and has business interests in Bali. The Galliennes come from the Loire Valley, although Guy secured his winemaking degree at Roseworthy College/Adelaide University. The vineyard, now 11.5 ha, is managed on a low-impact basis, without pesticides

(guinea fowls do the work) and with minimal irrigation. All the wines are made from estate-grown grapes. Exports to the UK, the US, Germany, Seychelles, Singapore and Hong Kong.

♀♀♀♀♀ **Margaret River Semillon Sauvignon Blanc 2006** No hint of reduction; the clear-cut drive of the grass and herb semillon provides both length and intensity, filled out just a touch by riper sauvignon blanc fruit. Screwcap. 13.5° alc. **Rating** 90 To 2011 $20

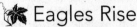 Eagles Rise

310 Russells Bridge Road, Russells Bridge (nr Bannockburn), Vic 3331 **Region** Geelong
T (03) 5281 2040 **www.**wildwine.com.au **Open** By appt
Winemaker David Dillon **Est.** 1996 **Cases** NFP
Erica and David Dillon established Eagles Rise in 1996, on a property 5 km from the township of Bannockburn. In the early years, the grapes were exclusively sold to Southcorp, but (as so often has been the case) that exclusive arrangement no longer continues. Since 2003 Eagles Rise has been making wine in limited but commercial quantities, making Sparkling Pinot Gris, Sparkling Pinot Noir, Pinot Gris, Pinot Noir, Shiraz, Shiraz Cabernet, Cabernet Sauvignon and a Fortified Late Pick Pinot Gris. It has had significant success in both the Geelong Wine Show '05 and '06.

♀♀♀♀♀ **Cabernet Shiraz 2004** Abundant blackcurrant fruit plus a touch of chocolate; good oak and ripe tannin support. **Rating** 92 To 2015

East Arm Vineyard

111 Archers Road, Hillwood, Tas 7250 **Region** Northern Tasmania
T (03) 6334 0266 **F** (03) 6334 1405 **Open** W'ends & public hols, or by appt
Winemaker Bert Sundstrup, Nicholas Butler (Contract) **Est.** 1993 **Cases** 1200
East Arm Vineyard was established by Launceston gastroenterologist Dr John Wettenhall and partner Anita James, who has completed the Charles Sturt University Diploma in Applied Science (winegrowing). The 2 ha-vineyard, which came into full production in 1998, is more or less equally divided among riesling, chardonnay and pinot noir. It is established on a historic block, part of a grant made to retired British soldiers of the Georgetown garrison in 1821, and slopes down to the Tamar River. The property is 25 ha, and there are plans for further planting and, somewhere down the track, a winery. The Riesling is usually excellent. It has been sold, but details not available at the time of going to press.

Eastern Peake

67 Pickfords Road, Coghills Creek, Vic 3364 **Region** Ballarat
T (03) 5343 4245 **F** (03) 5343 4365 **www.**ballaratwineries.com **Open** 7 days 11–5
Winemaker Norman Latta, Owen Latta **Est.** 1983 **Cases** 1150
Norm Latta and Di Pym established Eastern Peake, 25 km northeast of Ballarat on a high plateau overlooking the Creswick Valley, over 20 years ago. In the early years the grapes were sold to Trevor Mast of Mount Chalambar and Mount Langi Ghiran, but the 5 ha of vines are now dedicated to the production of Eastern Peake wines. The Pinot Noir is on the minerally/stemmy side; earlier bottling might preserve more of the sweet fruit. Exports to the UK.

♀♀♀♀ **Chardonnay 2003** High natural acidity has underpinned slow development; citrus and mineral still dominate; will run for many years. Screwcap. 14.5° alc. **Rating** 89 To 2018 $25
Pinot Rose 2005 Pale salmon; a European style, spicy and dry, finishing with crisp acidity. Screwcap. 12.5° alc. **Rating** 87 To 2008 $20
Pinot Noir 2003 Struggled for ripeness; lots of forest floor, leaf and mint, its balance helping it hang in, but there seems little point in waiting for fruit to develop which isn't there in the first place. Screwcap. 13° alc. **Rating** 87 To 2008 $25

Eden Hall ★★★★★

36A Murray Street, Angaston, SA 5353 **Region** Eden Valley
T (08) 8562 4590 **F** (08) 8342 3950 **www.**edenhall.com.au **Open** 7 days 10–5
Winemaker Wine Wise Consultancy **Est.** 2002 **Cases** 1820
David and Mardi Hall purchased the historic Avon Brae property in 1996. The 120-ha property
has been planted to 32 ha of cabernet sauvignon (the lion's share), shiraz, merlot, cabernet franc,
riesling (over 9 ha) and viognier. The majority of the production is contracted to Yalumba, St
Hallett and McGuigan Simeon, with 10% of the best grapes held back for the Eden Hall label.
The Riesling, Shiraz Viognier and Cabernet Sauvignon are all excellent, the red wines
outstanding. Exports to the UK, the US and Asia.

ƟƟƟƟƟ **Shiraz Viognier 2004** Typical deep, bright colour; fragrant, spicy black fruits with
an overlay of viognier perfume on the bouquet; a medium-bodied, fine palate,
with good tannins and length. Screwcap. 14.5° alc. **Rating** 94 **To** 2019 $32
Cabernet Sauvignon 2004 Firm, classic cabernet; blackcurrant, cigar box and
cedar; fine, lingering tannins; blue blood breeding. Screwcap. 14.5° alc. **Rating** 94
To 2024 $32

ƟƟƟƟƟ **Riesling 2006** Floral herb, spice and lime aromas, then abundant flavour firmly in
the citrus spectrum. Screwcap. 12.8° alc. **Rating** 92 **To** 2014 $20
CSV Cabernet Shiraz Viognier 2004 Has undeniable fragrance and flavour
inputs from the viognier, but I am far from convinced the blend is a synergistic one.
Screwcap. 14.5° alc. **Rating** 92 **To** 2019 $32

Edwards Vineyard ★★★★☆

Cnr Caves Road/Ellensbrook Road, Cowaramup, WA 6284 **Region** Margaret River
T (08) 9755 5999 **F** (08) 9755 5988 **www.**edwardsvineyard.com.au **Open** 7 days 10.30–5
Winemaker Michael Edwards **Est.** 1993 **Cases** 14 000
Edwards Vineyard is a family-owned and operated winery, with brothers Michael (formerly a
winemaker at Voyager Estate) and Christo being the winemaker and viticulturist, respectively.
There are 48 ha of chardonnay, semillon, sauvignon blanc, shiraz, cabernet sauvignon and merlot.
The consistency in the quality of the wines is remarkable. Exports to the US, Canada, Denmark,
Spain, Philippines, Indonesia, Singapore and Hong Kong.

ƟƟƟƟƟ **Margaret River Chardonnay 2005** Like all the Edwards' releases, no reduction;
fresh, lively nectarine, citrus and grapefruit set within a frame of perfectly integrated
barrel ferment oak; long finish. Screwcap. 13.5° alc. **Rating** 94 **To** 2015 $24

ƟƟƟƟƟ **Margaret River Sauvignon Blanc 2006** No reduction/sweatiness; an elegant
wine, with intense lemon/lemon rind/tropical flavours, tied together by lemony
acidity; good length. Screwcap. 12.5° alc. **Rating** 93 **To** 2008 $19
Margaret River Semillon Sauvignon Blanc 2006 A touch of barrel ferment
enlivens the bouquet; good structure, balance and length; grassy/herbaceous semillon
drives the wine, but lifted by tropical sauvignon blanc. Screwcap. 12.5° alc.
Rating 92 **To** 2010 $19
Tiger's Tale Margaret River Cabernet Merlot 2005 Medium- to medium-
full-bodied; abundant blackcurrant and cassis fruit; supple mouthfeel and
negligible oak. Fruit forward, uncomplicated, and great value. Screwcap. 14° alc.
Rating 92 **To** 2015 $16
Tiger's Tale Sauvignon Blanc Semillon 2006 An aromatic, herbaceous
bouquet, then a similar palate lifted by touches of more tropical fruit; bright, fresh
finish. Screwcap. 12° alc. **Rating** 90 **To** 2009 $16
Margaret River Shiraz 2005 Medium-bodied; complex interplay between
blackberry fruits, tannins, spice and oak, with savoury tannins on the finish.
Screwcap. 14° alc. **Rating** 90 **To** 2015 $26

ƟƟƟƟ **Margaret River Cabernet Sauvignon 2005** Medium- to full-bodied; solid
black fruits; slightly earthy/rough tannins need to soften, but should do so. Screwcap.
14° alc. **Rating** 89 **To** 2017 $29

Eighteen Forty-Seven

PO Box 918, Rowland Flat, SA 5352 **Region** Barossa Valley
T (08) 8524 5328 **F** (08) 8524 5329 **www**.eighteenfortyseven.com **Open** Not
Winemaker Rod Chapman, John Curnow **Est.** 1996 **Cases** 3000
A youthful John Curnow began his career over 30 years ago buying and selling wines from all over the world. He then moved to Coca-Cola, becoming a senior executive or CEO in Hungary, the Czech Republic, NZ, the US and Australia. In 1996 he and wife Sue began the development of Eighteen Forty-Seven, with 2 vineyards planted to shiraz, semillon, petit verdot and a little sauvignon blanc. The name has a dual source: the original land grant of the Rowland Flat property dates from 1847, and 1–8–47 is John Curnow's birth date. Until 2002 the grapes were sold to other Barossa Valley producers, but in that vintage the first wines were made, and have had much critical acclaim. Exports to Hungary, the Czech Republic, Denmark and Canada.

Elan Vineyard

17 Turners Road, Bittern, Vic 3918 **Region** Mornington Peninsula
T (03) 5983 1858 **F** (03) 5983 2821 **www**.elanvineyard.com.au **Open** First weekend of month, public hols 11–5, or by appt
Winemaker Selma Lowther **Est.** 1980 **Cases** 400
Selma Lowther, fresh from Charles Sturt University (as a mature-age student) made an impressive debut with her spicy, fresh, crisp Chardonnay, and has continued to make tiny quantities of appealing and sensibly priced wines. Most of the grapes from the 2.5 ha of estate vineyards are sold; production remains minuscule.

Elderton

3 Tanunda Road, Nuriootpa, SA 5355 **Region** Barossa Valley
T (08) 8568 7878 **www**.eldertonwines.com.au **Open** Mon–Fri 8.30–5, w'ends, hols 11–4
Winemaker Richard Langford **Est.** 1984 **Cases** 40 000
The wines are based on old, high-quality Barossa floor estate vineyards, but has moved with the times by moving towards French oak, and is reaping the benefits in quality terms. The Command Shiraz is justifiably regarded as its icon wine. Energetic promotion and marketing both in Australia and overseas is paying dividends. Elderton has followed in the footsteps of Cullen by becoming carbon neutral. Exports to all major markets.

ϓϓϓϓϓ **Command Shiraz 2002** Good colour; excellent focus, balance and length; blackberry fruit with lashings of dark chocolate and spice; ripe tannins, controlled oak. Screwcap. 14.5° alc. **Rating** 95 **To** 2022 $95
Ashmead Single Vineyard Barossa Cabernet Sauvignon 2004 Multiple layers of fruit and French oak; blackcurrant, spice, dark chocolate and mocha; serious wine. Screwcap. 14.5° alc. **Rating** 95 **To** 2029 $85

ϓϓϓϓϓ **Ode to Lorraine Cabernet Shiraz Merlot 2002** A powerful, earthy, savoury wine; has considerable length and intensity, finishing with lingering but ripe tannins. I'm far less convinced by the shocking lipstick-pink label. Cork. 14.5° alc. **Rating** 93 **To** 2017 $40
Barossa Shiraz 2004 Elegant, medium-bodied, unforced wine with black fruits, spice and fine, savoury tannins; controlled oak and good length. Cork. 14.5° alc. **Rating** 92 **To** 2011 $27

Eldredge

Spring Gully Road, Clare, SA 5453 **Region** Clare Valley
T (08) 8842 3086 **F** (08) 8842 3086 **Open** 7 days 11–5
Winemaker Leigh Eldredge **Est.** 1993 **Cases** 6000
Leigh and Karen Eldredge have established their winery and cellar door in the Sevenhill Ranges at an altitude of 500 m, above Watervale. Both the Rieslings and red wines have had considerable success in recent years. Exports to the UK, the US, Canada and Hong Kong.

Eldridge Estate of Red Hill

120 Arthurs Seat Road, Red Hill, Vic 3937 **Region** Mornington Peninsula
T (03) 5989 2644 **www**.eldridge-estate.com.au **Open** Mon–Fri 12–4, w'ends & hols 11–5
Winemaker David Lloyd **Est.** 1985 **Cases** 800

The Eldridge Estate vineyard, with 7 varieties included in its 3.5 ha, was purchased by Wendy and David Lloyd in 1995. Major retrellising work has been undertaken, changing to Scott Henry, and all the wines are now estate-grown and made. David Lloyd has also planted several Dijon-selected pinot noir clones (114, 115 and 777) which have made their contribution since 2004, likewise the Dijon chardonnay clone 96. Exports to the US.

ŸŸŸŸŸ **Single Clone 96 Chardonnay 2005** More aromatic and with a higher flavour profile than the other Eldridge Chardonnays, although the differences are not great; here delicacy and overall finesse carry the day. Screwcap. 14° alc. **Rating** 95 **To** 2015 $39

Chardonnay 2005 Elegant, but complex and intense in terms of both flavour and texture; nectarine and grapefruit are the dominant players, the other inputs (barrel ferment, mlf and lees contact) subtle props. Screwcap. 14.3° alc. **Rating** 95 **To** 2015 $35

Single Clone Pinot Noir 2005 Clone 777. Slightly more density, texture and ripeness than the varietal, adding a touch of plum to the bright fruit flavours. Screwcap. 14.3° alc. **Rating** 95 **To** 2013 $50

North Patch Chardonnay 2005 Slightly firmer and longer than the varietal, though obviously the same winemaking philosophy; more tangy, citrussy elements. Screwcap. 14.3° alc. **Rating** 94 **To** 2015 $30

Pinot Noir 2005 Fragrant cherry, strawberry and raspberry fruit in a graceful, light- to medium-bodied and elegant frame. Screwcap. 14° alc. **Rating** 94 **To** 2012 $39

ŸŸŸŸŸ **Single Clone Pinot Noir 2005** Clone MV6. Red and black cherry aromas; has length and focus, though the slightly savoury/green finish is a surprise. Screwcap. 14° alc. **Rating** 93 **To** 2012 $35

Pinot Noir 2004 An elegant, light-bodied but complex wine offers a mix of red and black fruits; fine-grained tannins add gravitas and length. 14° alc. **Rating** 93 **To** 2012 $30

Euroa Creeks Reserve Shiraz 2005 Medium- to full-bodied; abundant black and red confit fruit flavours cut by substantial tannins; made specifically for our American friends. Goulburn Valley. Screwcap. 15.5° alc. **Rating** 90 **To** 2025 $50

ŸŸŸŸ **Sauvignon Blanc Semillon 2006** Clean bouquet and palate; a nicely balanced, easy-drinking style, though not a lot of sparkle. Estate-grown young vines. Screwcap. 13° alc. **Rating** 89 **To** 2009 $20

Gamay 2005 Good red-purple; solid plummy fruit with balancing acidity; the limitations lie with the grape, not the terroir or the maker. Screwcap. 14.3° alc. **Rating** 89 **To** 2008 $30

Eleven Paddocks

PO Box 829, Macleod, Vic 3084 **Region** Pyrenees
T (03) 9458 4997 **F** (03) 9458 5075 **www**.elevenpaddocks.com.au **Open** Not
Winemaker Gabriel Horvat, Gary Mills **Est.** 2003 **Cases** 1000

Eleven partners, under the direction of managing partner Danny Gravell, purchased a small vineyard in 2002, in the foothills of the Pyrenees Ranges near Landsborough. The quality of the first vintage was sufficient to encourage the partners to increase planting to 4 ha of shiraz, 2 ha each of chardonnay and cabernet sauvignon and a dash of petit verdot.

ŸŸŸŸŸ **McKinlay Shiraz 2005** A medium-bodied, lively, cool-grown style, with spicy black fruits, then a very tangy, if not downright challenging, finish. Commands respect. Screwcap. 13.7° alc. **Rating** 92 **To** 2017 $25

Rose 2006 A fresh, lively, almost citrussy tang to the red fruits; excellent length and finish; made from the ground up, with whole-bunch pressing and barrel fermentation of 100% pinot noir. Screwcap. 12.5° alc. **Rating** 91 **To** 2008 $14

ΨΨΨΨ **Shiraz 2005** Bright colour; a fresh and lively but distinctly toned-down version of the McKinlay; shares a bright, thrusting finish with a fair degree of acidity. Screwcap. 13.5° alc. **Rating** 89 **To** 2013 $18

Cabernet Sauvignon 2005 Light- to medium-bodied; spicy, earthy blackcurrant fruit; lacks complexity and depth, but is technically fault-free. Screwcap. 14° alc. **Rating** 87 **To** 2009 $18

Elgee Park

Wallaces Road RMB 5560, Merricks North, Vic 3926 **Region** Mornington Peninsula
T (03) 5989 7338 **F** (03) 5989 7199 **www.elgeeparkwines.com.au Open** 1 day a year –
Sun of Queen's Birthday w'end
Winemaker Contract **Est.** 1972 **Cases** 1600
The pioneer of the Mornington Peninsula in its 20th-century rebirth, owned by Baillieu Myer and family. The wines are made at Stonier and T'Gallant, Elgee Park's own winery having been closed, and the overall level of activity decreased, although the quality has increased.

ΨΨΨΨΨ **Family Reserve Chardonnay 2005** Super-fine elegant style; melon and nectarine, with hints of creamy mlf inputs; gentle oak; good balance and length. Screwcap. 14° alc. **Rating** 94 **To** 2013 $30

ΨΨΨΨΦ **Family Reserve Pinot Gris 2005** It is immediately obvious something more has been done courtesy of French oak fermentation and maturation, old oak ensuring it does not go over the top. Excellent texture is the result. Screwcap. 14° alc. **Rating** 90 **To** 2009 $25

Mornington Peninsula Cuvee Brut 2003 Elegant, fine and long; lemon, citrus and stone fruit with 36 months on lees allow a low dosage and clean finish. Chardonnay (60%)/Pinot Noir (40%). 12° alc. **Rating** 90 **To** 2010 $35

ΨΨΨΨ **Family Reserve Cabernet Merlot 2004** Fragrant red berry aromas and flavours on entry to the mouth, though green notes take away on the finish. Screwcap. 13.5° alc. **Rating** 89 **To** 2012 $25

Elgo Estate

2020 Upton Road, Upton Hill, via Longwood, Vic 3665 **Region** Strathbogie Ranges
T (03) 5798 5563 **F** (03) 5798 5524 **www.elgoestate.com.au Open** By appt
Winemaker Cameron Atkins, Dennis Clarke **Est.** 1999 **Cases** 7000
The second Australian generation of the Taresch family has an 890-ha grazing property, with 55 ha of vines in 3 vineyards: Tarcombe Valley Vineyard (the warmest, planted to shiraz and cabernet); Lakeside Vineyard (planted in the 1970s with chardonnay, merlot and riesling); and the highest at Upton Hill (pinot noir and sauvignon blanc), the last adjacent to the winery built in 2004. Most of the power for the winery comes from a 150 kW wind-powered turbine. Exports to the US.

ΨΨΨΨΨ **Strathbogie Ranges Shiraz 2004** Deep, bright purple-red; rich, fragrant blackberry and spice aromas; absolutely flooded with layers of juicy black fruits and ripe tannins; will live forever. Trophy Best Wine of Show Strathbogie Ranges Wine Show '06. Screwcap. 14.5° alc. **Rating** 95 **To** 2024 $25

ΨΨΨΨ **Strathbogie Ranges Cabernet Sauvignon 2004** Blackcurrant and cedar aromas; an elegant, savoury palate with some notes of black olive; good length. Screwcap. 14° alc. **Rating** 89 **To** 2013 $25

Allira Strathbogie Ranges Chardonnay 2005 A clean, undemanding wine with white and yellow peach flavours, and a fractionally phenolic finish. Nonetheless, good value. Screwcap. 14° alc. **Rating** 88 **To** 2010 $12

Allira Strathbogie Ranges Riesling 2006 Pleasant blossom aromas, and a mix of gentle tropical fruit and a touch of mineral; shortens somewhat on the finish. Screwcap. 13° alc. **Rating** 87 **To** 2009 $12

Eling Forest Winery

Hume Highway, Sutton Forest, NSW 2577 **Region** Southern Highlands
T (02) 4878 9155 **F** (02) 4878 9246 **www**.elingforest.com.au **Open** 7 days 10–5
Winemaker Michelle Crockett **Est.** 1987 **Cases** 6000
Eling Forest's mentally agile and innovative founder Leslie Fritz celebrated his 80th birthday not long after he planted the first vines here in 1987. He celebrated his 88th birthday by expanding the vineyards from 3 to 4 ha, primarily with additional plantings of Hungarian varieties. He also developed a Cherry Port using spinning cone technology to produce various peach-based liqueurs, utilising second-class peach waste. The vineyard has since been expanded to 32 ha.

Ellender Estate

Leura Glen, 260 Green Gully Road, Glenlyon, Vic 3461 **Region** Macedon Ranges
T (03) 5348 7785 **F** (03) 5348 7784 **www**.ellenderwines.com **Open** W'ends & public hols 11–5, or by appt
Winemaker Graham Ellender **Est.** 1996 **Cases** 1000
The Ellenders have established 4 ha of pinot noir, chardonnay, sauvignon blanc and pinot gris. Wine style is now restricted to those varieties true to the ultra-cool climate of the Macedon Ranges: pinot noir, pinot rose, chardonnay and sparkling. Exports to the United Arab Emirates.

Macedon Pinot Noir 2005 Deep red–purple; a solid wine, with ripe plummy fruit; the balance and structure are good, the varietal character in diminuendo. Screwcap. 13.5° alc. **Rating** 89 **To** 2012 $35

Elliot Rocke Estate

Craigmoor Road, Mudgee, NSW 2850 **Region** Mudgee
T (02) 6372 7722 **F** (02) 6372 0680 **www**.elliotrockeestate.com.au **Open** 7 days 9–4
Winemaker Monarch Winemaking Services **Est.** 1999 **Cases** 11 000
Elliot Rocke Estate has 24.2 ha of vineyards dating back to 1987 when the property was known as Seldom Seen. Plantings are made up of around 9 ha of semillon, 4.3 ha of shiraz and chardonnay, 2.2 ha of merlot and 2 ha each of cabernet sauvignon and traminer, with 0.5 ha of doradillo. Exports to South Korea and Japan.

Mudgee Semillon 2005 Crisp lemon and herb; lively but firm, with good length and minerally structure. Screwcap. 12.5° alc. **Rating** 92 **To** 2015 $17.95
Reserve Shiraz 2005 Medium-bodied; elegantly framed and balanced, with length and finesse; black and red cherry fruit supported by fine tannins. Screwcap. 14.6° alc. **Rating** 91 **To** 2020 $29.95
Mudgee Semillon Sauvignon Blanc 2006 Has good focus and intensity, with tropical fruit stiffened by the semillon, especially on the crisp finish. Screwcap. 12° alc. **Rating** 90 **To** 2010 $17.95
Semillon Ice Wine 2006 Cleverly made; good balance between residual sugar and acidity, the fruit flavours in a citrus/lemon/mandarin spectrum. Part of the water in the juice is removed by freezing prior to fermentation, and the fermentation itself stopped at low alcohol levels. Cork. 8.5° alc. **Rating** 90 **To** 2008 $24.95
Semillon Ice Wine 2005 Richer and sweeter than the '06; peachy apricot flavours; more isn't necessarily better. Cork. 9° alc. **Rating** 90 **To** 2008 $24.95

Mudgee Cabernet Sauvignon 2005 While light- to medium-bodied, has surprising cassis fruit, with some blackcurrant, and the tannins, though light, are ripe. Screwcap. 13.4° alc. **Rating** 88 **To** 2015 $21.95
Mudgee Rose 2006 Red fruits are on the cusp; residual sugar is (just) sufficiently balanced by the fruit and acidity. Screwcap. 13° alc. **Rating** 87 **To** 2008 $15.95

Mudgee Shiraz 2004 Typical regional quasi-Hunter style; medium-bodied, with distinct earthy/savoury/leathery notes; balanced tannins. Screwcap. 14° alc. **Rating** 87 **To** 2014 $21.95

Mudgee Merlot 2005 Strongly varietal; slightly minty though does have red fruits and snow pea flavours; fresh and bright. Screwcap. 13.5° alc. **Rating** 87 **To** 2010 $21.95

Elmslie

Upper McEwans Road, Legana, Tas 7277 **Region** Northern Tasmania
T (03) 6330 1225 **F** (03) 6330 2161 **Open** By appt
Winemaker Bass Fine Wines (Guy Wagner) **Est.** 1972 **Cases** 600
Since Kevin French acquired this long-established vineyard and appointed Guy Wagner as winemaker, quality has improved greatly, with further gains in sight.

ŸŸŸŸŸ **3 Mountain View Pinot Noir 2005** Medium- to full-bodied; lots of cherry plum fruit, mouthfilling, but not too heavy. High on the hedonistic scale. **Rating** 92 **To** 2012

ŸŸŸŸ **3 Mountain View Pinot Noir 2004** Light- to medium-bodied; a savoury, spicy wine with just enough red fruits to satisfy. **Rating** 87 **To** 2008

Elmswood Estate

75 Monbulk-Seville Road, Wandin East, Vic 3139 **Region** Yarra Valley
T (03) 5964 3015 **F** (03) 5964 3405 **www.elmswoodestate.com.au Open** 7 days 10–5
Winemaker Paul Evans **Est.** 1981 **Cases** 2000
Elmswood Estate has 9.5 ha of vineyard, planted in 1981 on the red volcanic soils of the far-southern side of the Yarra Valley. The cellar door offers spectacular views across the Upper Yarra Valley to Mt Donna Buang and Warburton. Exports to China.

ŸŸŸŸŸ **Yarra Valley Cabernet Sauvignon 2005** Strong colour; admirable varietal character ranging through blackcurrant, black olive and earth flavours; considerable length and structure. Diam. **Rating** 94 **To** 2025 $40

ŸŸŸŸŸ **Yarra Valley Merlot 2005** Medium-bodied; a good varietal mix of blackcurrant and black olive flavours; fine tannins and good length; well above average. Diam. **Rating** 90 **To** 2015 $25

Yarra Valley Cabernet Merlot 2005 More blackcurrant than the Merlot, but – surprisingly – a slightly softer mid-palate before authoritative tannins on the finish. Controlled oak. Diam. **Rating** 90 **To** 2017 $25

ŸŸŸŸ **Yarra Valley Unoaked Chardonnay 2006** Has some brightness to the grapefruit and melon; in typical Elmswood style, has more structure and mouthfeel than the usual bland, anonymous offering. Diam. **Rating** 89 **To** 2010 $20

Elsewhere Vineyard

42 Dillons Hill Road, Glaziers Bay, Tas 7109 **Region** Southern Tasmania
T (03) 6295 1228 **F** (03) 6295 1591 **www.elsewherevineyard.com Open** Not
Winemaker Andrew Hood, Steve Lubiana (Contract) **Est.** 1984 **Cases** 4000
Kylie and Andrew Cameron's evocatively named Elsewhere Vineyard used to jostle for space with a commercial flower farm. The estate-produced range comes from the 6 ha of pinot noir, 3 ha of chardonnay and 1 ha of riesling, which constitute the immaculately tended vineyard.

Elysium Vineyard ★★★

393 Milbrodale Road, Broke, NSW 2330 **Region** Lower Hunter Valley
T 0417 282 746 **F** (02) 9664 2368 **www.winecountry.com.au Open** W'ends 10–5, or by appt
Winemaker Tyrrell's (Nick Paterson) **Est.** 1990 **Cases** 500

Elysium was once part of a much larger vineyard established by John Tulloch. Tulloch (not part of the Tulloch operation previously owned by Southcorp) continues to look after the viticulture, with the 1 acre of verdelho. The Elysium Cottage has won a number of tourism awards. Proprietor Victoria Foster, in partnership with Ben Moechtar (Vice-President of the Australian Sommeliers Association), conducts wine education weekends on request, with meals prepared by a chef brought in for the occasion. Exports to the US, Canada and China.

Emmetts Crossing Wines   ★★★

PO Box 84, Dwellingup, WA 6213 **Region** Peel
T (08) 9538 4110 **F** (08) 9538 4110 **Open** Not
Winemaker Frank Kittler **Est.** 1996 **Cases** 3000
The Ganfield family has established its 4.5-ha vineyard and winery in a pristine area of the Darling Range. There is a 4-generation family history of farming, and the development has been planned with the maximum possible respect for the environment. Chardonnay, Verdelho, Shiraz, Cabernet Malbec and Cabernet Sauvignon are produced.

Empress Vineyard   NR

Drapers Road, Irrewarra, Vic 3250 (postal Amberley House, 391 Sandy Bay Road, Hobart, Tas 7005) **Region** Western Victoria Zone
T (03) 6225 1005 **F** (03) 6225 0639 **www**.empress.com.au **Open** By appt
Winemaker Robin Brockett, Cate Looney, Lisa Togni **Est.** 1998 **Cases** NA

Eppalock Ridge   ★★★★☆

633 North Redesdale Road, Redesdale, Vic 3444 **Region** Heathcote
T (03) 5443 7841 **www**.eppalockridge.com **Open** By appt
Winemaker Rod Hourigan **Est.** 1979 **Cases** 1500
Sue and Rod Hourigan gave up their careers in fabric design and television production at the ABC in 1976 to chase their passion for fine wine. This took them first to McLaren Vale, Sue working in the celebrated Barn Restaurant, Rod starting at d'Arenberg, and over the next 3 years did vintages at Pirramimma and Coriole while undertaking the first short course for winemakers at what is now Charles Sturt University. After 3 hectic years they moved to Redesdale in 1979 and established Eppalock Ridge on a basalt hilltop overlooking Lake Eppalock. The 10 ha of shiraz, cabernet sauvignon, cabernet franc and merlot are capable of producing wines of high quality. Exports to the UK, the US, Canada, Hong Kong, Singapore and NZ.

 Heathcote Shiraz 2004 Medium- to full-bodied; spicy blackberry fruits, with touches of mocha and licorice; fine-grained, persistent tannins on a long, gently savoury finish. Screwcap. 14.5° alc. **Rating** 94 **To** 2024 $28

♥♥♥♥ **Heathcote Cabernet Merlot 2004** Medium-bodied; blackcurrant and cassis fruit is surrounded by a wall of French and American oak, and soft tannins. The suspicion is that merlot is the Trojan Horse which will let the oak take over completely. Screwcap. 15° alc. **Rating** 89 **To** 2014 $28

Ernest Hill Wines   ★★★★

307 Wine Country Drive, Nulkaba, NSW 2325 **Region** Lower Hunter Valley
T (02) 4991 4418 **F** (02) 4991 7724 **www**.ernesthillwines.com.au **Open** 7 days 10–5
Winemaker Mark Woods **Est.** 1999 **Cases** 1400
The Wilson family has owned the Ernest Hill property since 1990; the vineyard has 3 ha of semillon, and 1 ha each of chardonnay, traminer and verdelho; an additional ha of shiraz is leased. The business has had show success with the wines so far released.

 Over The Hill Unwooded Chardonnay 2005 Fine and elegant; a tightly focused and fine palate with citrus and melon fruit; good length. Utterly admirable unwooded chardonnay. **Rating** 94 **To** 2010 $18

'ese Vineyards

1013 Tea Tree Road, Tea Tree, Tas 7017 **Region** Southern Tasmania
T 0417 319 875 **F** (03) 6234 2015 **Open** By appt
Winemaker Winemaking Tasmania (Julian Alcorso) **Est.** 1994 **Cases** 3000
Elvio and Natalie Brianese are an architect and graphic designer couple whose extended family have centuries-old viticultural roots in the Veneto region of northern Italy. They have 2.5 ha of bearing vineyard. The Pinot Noir can be outstanding. Exports to China.

♟♟♟♟　**Non Oaked Chardonnay 2006** Fresh, lively, citrussy; light to medium-bodied; what is there is appealing, but lacks intensity. Screwcap. 13° alc. **Rating** 87 To 2009 $20

　　　　Pinot Rose 2006 While the cellar door customers will love it, a really nice wine spoilt by unnecessary sweetness. Screwcap. 13.5° alc. **Rating** 87 To 2008 $18

Eurabbie Estate ★★★★

251 Dawson Road, Avoca, Vic 3467 **Region** Pyrenees
T (03) 5465 3799 **Open** 7 days 10–5
Winemaker John Higgins **Est.** 2000 **Cases** 1500
John and Kerry Higgins have established Eurabbie Estate in an 80-ha forest property overlooking a 4-ha natural lake. Two separate blocks of cabernet sauvignon, shiraz and merlot, with a dash of pinot noir, give rise to the Eurabbie Estate range. Since 2004 grapes have been purchased from 3 small Pyrenees growers to produce the Pyrenees Villages range: Percydale Chardonnay, Percydale Cabernet Franc, Amherst Shiraz, Stuart Mill Shiraz and Avoca Cabernet Sauvignon. The wines are made in a mudbrick winery powered by solar energy.

Evans & Tate

Cnr Metricup Road/Caves Road, Wilyabrup, WA 6280 **Region** Margaret River
T (08) 9755 2199 **F** (08) 9755 4362 **www**.evansandtate.com.au **Open** 7 days 10.30–5
Winemaker Richard Rowe **Est.** 1970 **Cases** 450 000
From its Swan Valley base 30 years ago, Evans & Tate became the largest Margaret River winery and producer. Having increased its estate vineyard holdings with the establishment of a large planting in the Jindong area, it raised substantial capital by listing on the Stock Exchange. It then turned its attention eastwards, with the acquisition of Oakridge Estate in the Yarra Valley, followed by Cranswick Wines (since sold). It became a casualty of the downturn in the market in 2005, its future direction uncertain, a merger with a US company aborted in March '07. Throughout all this turmoil, the high quality of its Margaret River wines has been maintained, although the pricing of some is ambitious. Exports to all major markets.

♟♟♟♟♟　**The Reserve Margaret River Chardonnay 2003** An elegant wine developing and unfurling its sails at an unhurried pace; fine citrus and melon fruit; very good oak balance. Screwcap. 14.5° alc. **Rating** 95 To 2013 $30

♟♟♟♟♀　**Margaret River Chardonnay 2006** Well-made; nectarine and melon fruit complexed by carefully controlled barrel fermentation and other winemaker inputs; good mouthfeel and weight. Screwcap. 13.5° alc. **Rating** 92 To 2011 $19
　　　　The Reserve Margaret River Chardonnay 2002 Obvious barrel ferment inputs dominate the bouquet, but the wine comes together better on the palate, with ripe peach, fig, nuts and cream; has developed remarkably slowly but surely. Screwcap. 14° alc. **Rating** 92 To 2012 $30
　　　　The Reserve Margaret River Shiraz 2004 Aromatic, spicy black fruits; good structure and texture despite the burden of alcohol; has length. Screwcap. 15° alc. **Rating** 92 To 2018 $30
　　　　The Reserve Margaret River Cabernet Sauvignon 2002 Medium-bodied; good texture and structure, with quality spicy oak woven through gentle black fruits; fine tannins to close. Screwcap. 14.5° alc. **Rating** 92 To 2012 $30

X&Y Vineyards Margaret River Chardonnay 2006 Flavoursome melon, nectarine and grapefruit give plenty of depth and power; little or no oak. Screwcap. 14.5° alc. **Rating** 90 **To** 2010 $17

Wildberry Springs Estate Margaret River Chardonnay 2005 A Chablis-like exercise in extreme restraint; fine and long. Screwcap. 14.5° alc. **Rating** 90 **To** 2012 $45

X&Y Vineyards Margaret River Shiraz 2004 An appealing array of red fruits, cherries, plums and raspberries; fine tannins, controlled oak; alcohol not too hot. Screwcap. 15° alc. **Rating** 90 **To** 2014 $17

ΨΨΨΨ **Stellar Ridge Vineyard Margaret River Chardonnay 2005** Clean and fresh, with light melon, stone fruit and citrus backed by a touch of cashew; neat balance. To put it politely, I'm confused about the price. Screwcap. 14.5° alc. **Rating** 89 **To** 2010 $45

X&Y Vineyards Margaret River Cabernet Merlot 2004 Light- to medium-bodied; firm, fractionally green flavours and mouthfeel; needs to soften and loosen up. Screwcap. 14.5° alc. **Rating** 89 **To** 2014 $17

Margaret River Cabernet Merlot 2004 Medium-bodied; shows the Margaret River synergy between the 2 varieties, even if on a modest scale; black fruits with hints of olive and earth; fine tannins, good length. Screwcap. 14.5° alc. **Rating** 89 **To** 2010 $19

Margaret River Classic White 2006 Clean, fresh and crisp; no varieties are stated, but it is in a citrus spectrum, with good acidity. Screwcap. 12.5° alc. **Rating** 88 **To** 2008 $18

The Reserve Margaret River Cabernet Sauvignon 2003 Unconvincing colour; spicy/cedary/savoury aromas are offset by some fruit and oak sweetening. Screwcap. 14.5° alc. **Rating** 88 **To** 2010 $30

X&Y Vineyards Margaret River Sauvignon Blanc 2006 Light straw-green; clean, no reduction; slightly amorphous mouthfeel and flavours; ripe, but not particularly distinctive. Screwcap. 12.5° alc. **Rating** 87 **To** 2008 $17

Margaret River Shiraz 2004 A pleasant wine; spicy edges to black fruits, but lacks concentration. Screwcap. 14.5° alc. **Rating** 87 **To** 2009 $19

Evans Family Wines ★★★★

97 Palmers Lane, Pokolbin, NSW 2320 **Region** Lower Hunter Valley
T (02) 4998 7237 **F** (02) 4998 7201 **Open** Thurs–Mon 10–5
Winemaker Andrew Thomas, Michael De Iuliis **Est.** 1979 **Cases** 2500
In the wake of the acquisition of Rothbury by Mildara Blass, Len Evans' wine interests focused on Evans Family (estate-grown and produced from vineyards around the family home), the Evans Wine Company (a quite different, part-maker, part-negotiant business) and, most recently, Tower Estate (see separate entry). The family is considering the future of the business in the wake of Len Evans' untimely death in early 2007. Exports to the US.

ΨΨΨΨ **Hunter Valley Shiraz 2005** Light- to medium-bodied; some mint and green leaf characters, but good balance and length. Cork. 13.2° alc. **Rating** 88 **To** 2010 $28.50

Evelyn County Estate ★★★★☆

55 Eltham-Yarra Glen Road, Kangaroo Ground, Vic 3097 **Region** Yarra Valley
T (03) 9437 2155 **F** (03) 9437 2188 **www**.evelyncountyestate.com.au **Open** Mon–Thurs 11–5, Fri 11–10, Sat 11–midnight, Sun 9–6
Winemaker Robyn Male, Diamond Valley Vineyards (James Lance) **Est.** 1994 **Cases** 2000
The 8-ha Evelyn County Estate has been established by former Coopers & Lybrand managing partner Roger Male and his wife, Robyn, who has completed a degree in Applied Science (wine science) at Charles Sturt University. An architect-designed cellar door, gallery and restaurant opened in 2001. A small planting of tempranillo bore its first crop in 2004 and this wine is made onsite by Robyn Male. Exports to France, Malaysia, Macau, Singapore and Hong Kong.

ΨΨΨΨΨ Black Paddock Pinot Noir 2005 Strong colour; abundant dark plum and spice aromas and flavours; a wine of real substance and future development, without going over the top. ProCork. 14° alc. **Rating** 94 **To** 2012 $32

ΨΨΨΨΨ Black Paddock Merlot 2005 An attractive medium-bodied wine with clear-cut varietal flavours and texture; cassis, raspberry and plum supported by fine tannins. Cork. 15° alc. **Rating** 92 **To** 2015 $29
Black Paddock Sauvignon Blanc 2006 A faintly sweaty bouquet, but acceptable; lively, fresh, crisp herb/grass/gooseberry flavours throw off the bouquet; bright finish. Screwcap. 11° alc. **Rating** 91 **To** 2008 $23
Black Paddock Chardonnay 2005 A light- to medium-bodied, elegant, relatively understated style; good length to the nectarine fruit and minerally finish. Twin top. 14° alc. **Rating** 91 **To** 2010 $29

ΨΨΨΨ Black Paddock Chardonnay 2004 Obvious bottle development; plenty of fruit, but not as much structure as the '05. Cork. 13.5° alc. **Rating** 89 **To** 2008 $29
Black Paddock Merlot Rose 2006 Nicely made, with adequate red berry fruit flavours and no reliance on residual sugar; all-purpose food style. Screwcap. 13° alc. **Rating** 88 **To** 2008 $23
Black Paddock Cabernet Sauvignon 2005 Faintly reduced bitter aromas and flavours; perhaps left to hang for too long on the vine. ProCork. 15.5° alc. **Rating** 87 **To** 2009 $29

Faber Vineyard ★★★★★

233 Haddrill Road, Baskerville, WA 6056 (postal) **Region** Swan Valley
T (08) 9296 0619 **F** (08) 9296 0681 **Open** Not
Winemaker John Griffiths **Est.** 1997 **Cases** 800
Former Houghton winemaker, and now university lecturer and consultant, John Griffiths teamed with wife, Jane Micallef, to found Faber Vineyard. They have established 4 ha of shiraz, chardonnay, verdelho, cabernet sauvignon, petit verdot and brown muscat. Says John, 'It may be somewhat quixotic, but I'm a great fan of traditional warm-area Australia wine styles – those found in areas such as Rutherglen and the Barossa. Wines made in a relatively simple manner that reflect the concentrated ripe flavours one expects in these regions. And when one searches, some of these gems can be found from the Swan Valley.' Possessed of an excellent palate, and with an impeccable winemaking background, the quality of John Griffiths' wines is guaranteed.

ΨΨΨΨΨ Frankland River Cabernet Sauvignon 2004 A fragrant mix of blackcurrant, cedar and spice on the bouquet; outstanding texture and mouthfeel, matching equally seductive fruit in a classic profile; fine tannins and oak. Cork. 14° alc. **Rating** 96 **To** 2029 $35
Dwellingup Chardonnay 2006 A fine and fragrant bouquet; a beautifully restrained palate, with melon and nectarine fruit; whole-bunch pressed, barrel-fermented and 10 months on lees, but still towards Chablis in style. Screwcap. 13.5° alc. **Rating** 95 **To** 2014 $19.50

ΨΨΨΨΨ Riche Swan Valley Shiraz 2006 The unusually cool vintage has partially tamed the usual Alaskan bear style; blackberry fruits, with quality French and American oak. Cork. 14.5° alc. **Rating** 92 **To** 2019 $16.50

ΨΨΨΨ Swan Valley Petit Verdot 2006 Winemaker John Griffiths has used a gentle approach to the variety, backed up by the cool vintage; the result is a positively elegant wine, almost too much so for the variety. Cork. 14° alc. **Rating** 89 **To** 2009 $19.50
Swan Valley Shiraz Cabernet 2005 A deliberately light-bodied, early-drinking style; low tannins, fresh fruit; don't wait. Cork. 14° alc. **Rating** 87 **To** 2008 $12

Fairview Wines

422 Elderslie Road, Branxton, NSW 2335 **Region** Lower Hunter Valley
T (02) 4938 1116 **F** (02) 9383 8609 **www**.fairviewwines.com.au **Open** By appt
Winemaker Rhys Eather (Contract) **Est.** 1997 **Cases** 500
Greg and Elaine Searles purchased the property on which they have established Fairview Wines
in 1997. For the previous 90 years it had sustained an orchard, but since that time 2 ha of shiraz,
1 ha each of barbera and semillon and 0.5 ha of chambourcin and verdelho have been established,
using organic procedures wherever possible.

Farmer's Daughter Wines

791 Cassilis Road, Mudgee, NSW 2850 **Region** Mudgee
T (02) 6373 3177 **F** (02) 6373 3759 **www**.farmersdaughterwines.com.au **Open** 7 days 9–5
Winemaker Jim Chatto **Est.** 1995 **Cases** 9000
The intriguingly named Farmer's Daughter Wines is a family-owned vineyard, run by the
daughters of a feed-lot farmer. Much of the production from the substantial vineyard of 20 ha,
planted to shiraz (7 ha), merlot (6 ha), chardonnay and cabernet sauvignon (3 ha each) and
semillon (1 ha), is sold to other makers, but increasing quantities are made for the Farmer's
Daughter label.

ΨΨΨΨΨ **Reserve Mudgee Shiraz 2005** Medium-bodied, with attractive cherry, plum and
blackberry fruit supported by gentle oak, light tannins and balanced acidity; 3
trophies including Best Dry Red at Mudgee Wine Show '06. For those with a
knowledge of an earlier show raises an uncomfortable feeling of deja vu. Screwcap.
14.8° alc. **Rating** 92 **To** 2015 $39

Farr Rising

27 Maddens Road, Bannockburn, Vic 3331 **Region** Geelong
T (03) 5281 1733 **F** (03) 5281 1433 **www**.byfarr.com.au **Open** By appt
Winemaker Nicholas Farr **Est.** 2001 **Cases** 2000
Nicholas Farr is the son of Gary Farr, and with encouragement from his father he has
launched his own brand. He learned his winemaking in France and Australia, and has access
to some excellent base material, hence the quality of the wines. Exports to Denmark, Hong
Kong and Japan.

ΨΨΨΨΨ **Geelong Chardonnay 2005** Like father, like son; shares many attributes with
the by Farr Chardonnay, perhaps a little less complex and powerful, but also
more lively with piercing citrus and nectarine fruit. Cork. 13.3° alc. **Rating** 95
To 2015 $33
Geelong Pinot Noir 2005 Elegant and fresh; the fruit profile is sweeter than
the by Farr, but no hint of anything amiss; beautiful weight and length;
understated but stylish. Cork. 13.5° alc. **Rating** 95 **To** 2015 $35
Geelong Shiraz 2005 Classic regional shiraz; black fruits, licorice, spice and
pepper; good balance and length. Cork. 14.5° alc. **Rating** 94 **To** 2020 $35

Farrell Estate Wines

PO Box 926, Mildura, Vic 3502 **Region** Murray Darling
T (03) 5022 7066 **F** (03) 5022 7066 **www**.farrellestate.com.au **Open** Not
Winemaker Janel Farrell **Est.** 2000 **Cases** 700
This is an extended family-owned business, dating back to 1982 when John and Janette
Carruthers established the vineyard. In 2000 their daughter Janel Farrell and husband Chad built
the winery, and the business moved into its second phase. All have experience in various aspects
of the wine industry, from logistics and planning through to wine science and winemaking.
Indeed, their combined experience covers every base in the most impressive manner imaginable.
The first wines were made in 2004; the estate vineyards have chardonnay and cabernet sauvignon
in full production, with sauvignon blanc, sangiovese and viognier scheduled for full production in
'08. In the meantime, grapes are sourced through family and friends in the region.

ŸŸŸŸ   **Block 181 Circle of Friends Cabernet Shiraz Merlot 2006** Bright, light red-purple; light- to medium-bodied, with fresh, juicy berry fruits; early-drinking style. Twin top. 13.4° alc. **Rating** 87 **To** 2009 $15

Feehans Road Vineyard

50 Feehans Road, Mt Duneed, Vic 3216 **Region** Geelong
T (03) 5264 1706 **F** (03) 5264 1307 www.feehansroad.com.au **Open** W'ends 10–5
Winemaker Ray Nadeson **Est.** 2000 **Cases** 350
Peter Logan's interest in viticulture dates back to a 10-week course run by Denise Miller (at Dixons Creek in the Yarra Valley) in the early 1990s. This led to further formal studies, and the planting of a 'classroom' vineyard of 500 chardonnay and shiraz vines. A move from Melbourne suburbia to the slopes of Mt Duneed led to the planting of a 1.2-ha vineyard of shiraz in 2000, and, through long-term friend Nicholas Clark of Amietta, to the appointment of Ray Nadeson as winemaker. Plans include the planting of chardonnay and sauvignon blanc to extend the range.

ŸŸŸŸŸ   **Geelong Shiraz 2005** Very good colour; pure varietal expression; long and highly focused. Screwcap. 13.5° alc. **Rating** 94 **To** 2015 $23

Feet First Wines

32 Parkinson Lane, Kardinya, WA 6163 (postal) **Region** Southeast Australia
T (08) 9314 7133 **F** (08) 9314 7134 **Open** Not
Winemaker Contract **Est.** 2004 **Cases** 5000
This is the business of Ross and Ronnie (Veronica) Lawrence, who have been fine wine wholesalers in Perth since 1987, handling top-shelf Australian and imported wines. It is a virtual winery, with both grapegrowing and winemaking provided by contract, the aim being to produce easy-drinking, good-value wines under $20; the deliberately limited portfolio includes Semillon Sauvignon Blanc, Cabernets Merlot and Cabernet Merlot.

ŸŸŸŸŶ   **Geographe Frankland Sauvignon Blanc Semillon 2006** Crisp green apple aromas, gooseberry joining on the palate; good balance and mouthfeel. Screwcap. 11.5° alc. **Rating** 90 **To** 2008 $15

ŸŸŸŸ   **Geographe Cabernet Merlot 2005** Clean, full-on luscious cassis fruit drives the medium-bodied palate, finishing with super-fine tannins. Screwcap. 14° alc. **Rating** 89 **To** 2010 $15

Fenwick Wines

180 Lings Road, Wallington, Vic 3221 **Region** Geelong
T (03) 5250 1943 **F** (03) 5250 1943 www.fenwickwines.com **Open** By appt
Winemaker Robin Brockett (Contract) **Est.** 1997 **Cases** 350
When, in 1988, Madeleine and Dr David Fenwick purchased a 20-ha property between Ocean Grove and Wallington, it was pure chance that it had first been settled by Fairfax Fenwick, no relative. The Fenwicks planted 2 ha of pinot noir in 1997 and have since added 2 ha of chardonnay and 1 ha of shiraz, and increased the pinot noir plantings slightly with 3 clones (114, 115 and MV6). The first 5 vintages were contracted to Scotchmans Hill Winery, the 6th (2005) split between Scotchmans Hill and Fenwick Wines, giving rise to their very first, very creditable wine.

ŸŸŸŸŶ   **Pinot Noir 2005** Light- to medium-bodied; high-toned, high-flavoured plum, cherry and spice; controlled oak. **Rating** 90 **To** 2012

Fergusson   ★★★★

Wills Road, Yarra Glen, Vic 3775 **Region** Yarra Valley
T (03) 5965 2237 **F** (03) 5965 2405 www.fergussonwinery.com.au **Open** 7 days 11–5
Winemaker Christopher Keyes, Peter Fergusson **Est.** 1968 **Cases** 5000
One of the very first Yarra wineries to announce the rebirth of the Valley, now best known as a favoured destination for tourist coaches, offering hearty fare in comfortable surroundings and

wines of both Yarra and non-Yarra Valley origin. For this reason the limited quantities of its estate wines are often ignored, but they should not be. Exports to the UK.

Fermoy Estate

Metricup Road, Wilyabrup, WA 6280 **Region** Margaret River
T (08) 9755 6285 **F** (08) 9755 6251 **www**.fermoy.com.au **Open** 7 days 11–4.30
Winemaker Michael Kelly **Est.** 1985 **Cases** 30 000
A long-established estate-based winery with 14 ha of semillon, sauvignon blanc, chardonnay, cabernet sauvignon and merlot. Notwithstanding its substantial production, it is happy to keep a relatively low profile. Exports to the UK, the US, Holland and Switzerland.

ŶŶŶŶŶ **Nebbiolo 2005** Far more colour than most; now, this really is something, with a richness and depth beyond any nebbiolo previously made in Australia; intense black cherry, herb and spice; has tannins, but these are surprisingly fine in the overall context. Cork. **Rating** 94 **To** 2025 $26

ŶŶŶŶŶ **Margaret River Sauvignon Blanc 2006** The bouquet is closed, but no hint of reduction; springs into life on the palate, with citrus, green apple and gooseberry flavours running through to a long, bright finish. Screwcap. 12.5° alc. **Rating** 92 **To** 2009 $18
Margaret River Cabernet Sauvignon 2004 Bright, firm blackcurrant fruit; positive, ripe tannins will underwrite the development, oak in further support. Cork. 14° alc. **Rating** 91 **To** 2019 $26
Margaret River Semillon 2005 Good structure and texture, suggesting fermentation in old oak; totally dry, but not the least heavy; needs patience to see the best. Screwcap. 13° alc. **Rating** 90 **To** 2010 $18
Margaret River Chardonnay 2005 A very tight bouquet and palate in marked contrast to the usual Margaret River style; citrus and stone fruit, with the oak barely visible; will grow slowly but surely in bottle. Screwcap. 13.5° alc. **Rating** 90 **To** 2015 $25

Fern Hill Estate

2 Chalk Hill Road, McLaren Vale, SA 5171 **Region** McLaren Vale
T (08) 8323 9666 **F** (08) 8323 9600 **Open** At Marienberg Limeburners Centre, 7 days 10–5
Winemaker Peter Orr **Est.** 1975 **Cases** 5000
Fern Hill Estate, along with Marienberg and Basedow, became part of the James Estate empire in 2003. The wines are made under the direction of Peter Orr and sold through the Marienberg cellar door. A recent revamping of the packaging and labelling, plus acquisition of grapes from the Adelaide Hills to supplement that of McLaren Vale, has been accompanied by a move away from retail to restaurant/on-premises sales. Exports to Hong Kong.

ŶŶŶŶ **McLaren Vale Chardonnay 2006** Clean; medium-bodied; ripe stone fruit and fig with a background whisper of oak. Screwcap. 14° alc. **Rating** 89 **To** 2009 $16
Adelaide Hills Merlot 2004 Light- to medium-bodied; good varietal character, even if it is a little lean and savoury; a neat mix of green olive and red fruits. Screwcap. 14° alc. **Rating** 87 **To** 2010 $16
Adelaide Hills Cabernet Sauvignon 2004 Light- to medium-bodied; not a lot of depth, but what is there is clearly defined cool-grown cabernet sauvignon. Screwcap. 14° alc. **Rating** 87 **To** 2010 $16

Ferngrove Vineyards

Ferngrove Road, Frankland, WA 6396 **Region** Frankland River
T (08) 9855 2378 **F** (08) 9855 2368 **www**.ferngrove.com.au **Open** 7 days 10–4
Winemaker Kim Horton **Est.** 1997 **Cases** 50 000
After 90 years of family beef and dairy farming heritage, Murray Burton decided in 1997 to venture into premium grapegrowing and winemaking. Since that time he has moved with exceptional speed (and equal success), establishing 414 ha of grapes on 3 vineyards in the

Frankland River subregion, and a fourth at Mount Barker. The operation centres around the Ferngrove Vineyard, where a large rammed-earth winery and tourist complex was built in 2000. Part of the vineyard production is sold as grapes; part is sold as juice or must; part is sold as finished wine; and part is made under the Ferngrove Vineyards label. Exports to the UK and the US.

ΨΨΨΨΨ **Cossack Frankland River Riesling 2006** Spotlessly clean; floral apple blossom and lime aromas lead into a palate of exceptional length and intensity to its citrus and green apple flavours. A classic in its own lifetime. Screwcap. 12° alc. **Rating** 95 **To** 2021 $20

Diamond Frankland River Chardonnay 2005 A complex wine with a multitude of winemaker inputs which don't overwhelm the fruit; very good balance. Screwcap. 14° alc. **Rating** 94 **To** 2011 $22

The Stirlings 2004 Manages to not only blend 57% Shiraz with 43% Cabernet Sauvignon, but also power with finesse; the power from the tannins (still needing to soften a little), helped by finesse from the array of balanced, black fruits. A winner of a trophy and 2 gold medals. Cork. 14.5° alc. **Rating** 94 **To** 2024 $40

Majestic Cabernet Sauvignon 2005 Ripe, dense blackcurrant fruit, with soft, ripe tannins and good supporting oak. Gold medal National Wine Show '06. Cork. 15° alc. **Rating** 94 **To** 2029 $26

ΨΨΨΨΨ **Dragon Shiraz 2005** A lush array of black fruits, blackberry, plum, black cherry and a touch of licorice; powerful but smooth and long; good oak and tannins. Indifferent-quality cork. 14.5° alc. **Rating** 93 **To** 2020 $25.95

Frankland River Chardonnay 2006 Tightly focused grapefruit and nectarine has swallowed up the French oak; good length. Screwcap. 13.5° alc. **Rating** 91 **To** 2010 $18

Symbols Frankland River Sauvignon Blanc Semillon 2006 Spotlessly clean, fresh and lively aromas; a light-bodied mix of citrus, tropical and mineral notes; nice balance and length. Screwcap. 13° alc. **Rating** 90 **To** 2010 $15

Symbols Shiraz Viognier 2006 Medium-bodied at best, but still shows the synergies viognier unlocks when fermented with shiraz; supple blackberry and plum; minimal tannins. Maximum value. Screwcap. 13.5° alc. **Rating** 90 **To** 2012 $14.95

Symbols Shiraz Viognier 2005 Light- to medium-bodied, but with abundant aroma and plum and raspberry flavours, together with a touch of viognier lift; soft tannins. Screwcap. 14.5° alc. **Rating** 90 **To** 2010 $15

King Malbec 2005 Sweet, smooth, supple blackberry, mulberry and plum; just avoids the jamminess the variety is prone to; this wine always interesting, always good. Cork. 14° alc. **Rating** 90 **To** 2015 $25.95

ΨΨΨΨ **Merlot 2006** Light- to medium-bodied, with maximum emphasis on red fruits, making it an early-drinking proposition. Screwcap. 13.5° alc. **Rating** 89 **To** 2008 $17.95

Frankland River Sauvignon Blanc 2006 Clean; good structure and mouthfeel, although the varietal character/fruit is subdued; expected more. Screwcap. 12.5° alc. **Rating** 88 **To** 2008 $18

🍃 Ferraris Vineyard ★★★

428 Hermitage Road, Pokolbin, NSW 2321 **Region** Lower Hunter Valley
T (02) 9958 8728 **F** (02) 9958 6724 **www**.ferrarisvineyard.com.au **Open** 7 days 10–5
Winemaker Rhys Eather **Est.** 2001 **Cases** 650

Claude and Paula Ferraris purchased their property in the Hunter Valley in 2000, guided from the outset by Rhys Eather of Meerea Park. They were also following in the footsteps of their grandparents and parents who had arrived in Australia at the turn of last century, and became pioneers of the sugar industry in Far North Qld. From sugar cane to vines, and to the establishment of 3.2 ha of shiraz on sandy loam with a light clay loam topsoil, has paid dividends.

ŶŶŶŶ   Shiraz 2004 A quite powerful and concentrated structure, tannins running through the black fruits; the other side of saignee employed to make the rose. 13.5° alc. **Rating** 88 **To** 2014 $15

Finestra   ★★★★

PO Box 120, Coldstream, Vic 3770 **Region** Yarra Valley
T (03) 9739 1690 **Open** Not
Winemaker Alan Johns, Bruce Lang **Est.** 1989 **Cases** 500
Owners Bruce and Jo-Anne Lang have combined professional careers and small-scale winemaking for over 30 years. In the early 1970s they gained vacation employment with Yarra Valley wineries, and at the end of that decade they joined with friends in acquiring the old Brown Brothers' Everton Hills vineyard near Beechworth, bringing them into contact with Rick Kinzbrunner. In 1987 they acquired their property adjacent to Yeringberg, overlooking Domaine Chandon, beginning the establishment of the vineyard in 1989, and extending it in 1996. With a total of 2.9 ha of pinot noir, chardonnay, shiraz and cabernet sauvignon, it is small, and until 2002 all of the grapes were sold to 2 major Yarra Valley wineries. Since then 50% of the grapes have been used for the Finestra label, with considerable success.

ŶŶŶŶŶ   Dalla Mia Yarra Valley Pinot Noir 2004 Black cherry, plum and a touch of spice; a supple palate with good fruit and oak balance. Diam. 13.2° alc. **Rating** 90 **To** 2012 $17

ŶŶŶŶ   Dalla Mia Yarra Valley Cabernet Sauvignon 2004 Sweet cassis blackcurrant fruit, the light tannins not providing quite enough structure. Diam. 13.2° alc. **Rating** 89 **To** 2014 $20

Finniss Hills Wines

RSD 455 Braeside Road, Finniss, SA 5255 (postal) **Region** Southern Fleurieu
T (08) 8536 0061 **Open** Not
Winemaker O'Leary Walker **Est.** 1996 **Cases** 1000
Owner Nigel Wood traces his interest in wine back to 1971, and the time he spent in Bordeaux that year. The germ took some time to hatch, but in 1996 he selected an outstanding 15-ha property in the southern Mount Lofty Ranges, looking out over the Finniss River, Lake Alexandrina and the coast of Goolwa. The focus is on cabernet sauvignon and shiraz, with a skilled contract winemaking team.

Fire Gully

Metricup Road, Wilyabrup, WA 6280 **Region** Margaret River
T (08) 9755 6220 **F** (08) 9755 6308 **Open** By appt
Winemaker Dr Michael Peterkin **Est.** 1998 **Cases** 5000
The Fire Gully vineyard has been established on what was first a dairy and then a beef farm. A 6-ha lake created in a gully ravaged by bushfires gave the property its name. In 1998 Mike Peterkin, of Pierro, purchased the property and manages the vineyard in conjunction with former owners Ellis and Margaret Butcher. He regards the Fire Gully wines as entirely separate from those of Pierro, being estate-grown: just under 9 ha is planted to cabernet sauvignon, merlot, shiraz, semillon, sauvignon blanc, chardonnay and viognier. Exports to all major markets.

ŶŶŶŶŶ   Reserve Margaret River Cabernet Sauvignon 2003 Medium-bodied; fine, elegant, perfectly ripened/balanced cabernet fruit, with long and silky tannins woven through the cassis and blackcurrant flavours. Cork. 13.5° alc. **Rating** 94 **To** 2023 $40

ŶŶŶŶŶ   Margaret River Sauvignon Blanc Semillon 2006 Clean, fresh and expressive aromas offer a mix of herbaceous through to more tropical fruit, setting the scene for the medium-bodied, harmonious palate. Screwcap. 12.5° alc. **Rating** 92 **To** 2011 $23

Margaret River Chardonnay 2006 No reduction; a clean, fresh light- to medium-bodied wine with a citrus and stone fruit mix, and minimal oak influence. Screwcap. 13.5° alc. **Rating** 90 **To** 2012 $25

ΨΨΨΨ **Cabernet Sauvignon Merlot 2003** Medium-bodied, with a firm fruit palate and equally firm tannins on the finish; needs a few years to soften the edges. Cork. 13.5° alc. **Rating** 89 **To** 2013 $24

Margaret River Shiraz 2004 Unconvincing colour; light- to medium-bodied; savoury, almost lemony overtones throughout attesting to the cool site. Cork. 13.5° alc. **Rating** 87 **To** 2011 $23

No 1 Reserve Margaret River Shiraz Blend 2003 A clean, fresh array of red and black fruits is the centrepiece, oak and tannins providing a pure support role; nice finish. Shiraz/Cabernet Sauvignon/Merlot/Cabernet Franc/Malbec. Cork. 14.1° alc. **Rating** 87 **To** 2011 $40

Fireblock

St Vincent Street, Watervale, SA 5452 **Region** Clare Valley
T 0414 441 925 **F** (02) 9144 1925 **Open** Not
Winemaker O'Leary Walker **Est.** 1926 **Cases** 3000
Fireblock (formerly Old Station Vineyard) is owned by Alastair Gillespie and Bill and Noel Ireland, who purchased the 6-ha, 70-year-old vineyard in 1995. Watervale Riesling, Old Vine Shiraz and Old Vine Grenache are skilfully contract-made, winning trophies and gold medals at capital-city wine shows. Exports to the US, Sweden and Malaysia.

ΨΨΨΨŸ **Watervale Riesling 2006** Clean, gentle citrus and apple aromatics; good length and balance; a twist of lemony acidity lifts the finish. Screwcap. 12.5° alc. **Rating** 91 **To** 2012 $20

First Creek Wines

Cnr McDonalds Road/Gillards Road, Pokolbin, NSW 2321 **Region** Lower Hunter Valley
T (02) 4998 7293 **F** (02) 4998 7294 **www.**firstcreekwines.com.au **Open** 7 days 9.30–5
Winemaker Monarch Winemaking Services **Est.** 1984 **Cases** 25 000
First Creek is the shopfront of Monarch Winemaking Services, which has acquired the former Allanmere wine business and offers a complex range of wines under both the First Creek and the Allanmere labels. The quality is very reliable.

ΨΨΨΨΨ **Hunter Valley Semillon 2006** A spotless bouquet, albeit not yet singing; intense lemon, citrus and grass flavours are followed by a crisp, dry and lingering finish. Screwcap. 9.5° alc. **Rating** 94 **To** 2020 $17

ΨΨΨΨŸ **Orange Cabernet Sauvignon 2004** Spotlessly clean; perfectly ripened cassis and blackcurrant fruit; silky, ripe tannins; well-integrated and balanced oak. Screwcap. 14.1° alc. **Rating** 92 **To** 2014 $24

Durham Hunter Valley Chardonnay 2006 Very well-made; a proportion of barrel ferment in new and used barrels, but the wine is predominantly driven by its nectarine and fig fruit; bright finish. Screwcap. 13° alc. **Rating** 91 **To** 2010 $20

Hunter Valley Shiraz 2005 Firm and clean blackberry and plum fruit; a medium-bodied wine with well-balanced oak and tannins; certain to develop well and merit higher points down the track. Screwcap. 13.3° alc. **Rating** 90 **To** 2015 $24

ΨΨΨΨ **Canberra District Shiraz Viognier 2005** A pleasant, light- to medium-bodied wine which, however, lacks the usual visual and flavour impact of viognier; red fruits and fine tannins. Screwcap. 13.1° alc. **Rating** 88 **To** 2011 $35

Five Geese

RSD 587 Chapel Hill Road, Blewitt Springs, SA 5171 (postal) **Region** McLaren Vale
T (08) 8383 0576 **F** (08) 8383 0629 **www.**fivegeese.com.au **Open** Not
Winemaker Boar's Rock (Mike Farmilo) **Est.** 1999 **Cases** 3200
Sue Trott is passionate about her Five Geese wine, which is produced by Hillgrove Wines. The
wines come from 32 ha of vines planted in 1927 and 1963. The grapes were sold for many years,
but in 1999 Sue decided to create her own label and make a strictly limited amount of wine from
the pick of the vineyards. Exports to the UK, the US, Canada, Singapore and NZ.

McLaren Vale Shiraz 2004 Medium-bodied; very good texture and structure;
ripe tannins run throughout the blackberry and cherry fruit; overall elegance.
Screwcap. 14.5° alc. **Rating** 94 **To** 2024 $23

McLaren Vale Grenache Shiraz 2005 An ultra-attractive blend bringing black
and red cherry, raspberry and blackberry together; very soft tannins, and no cerebral
demands. Cork. 14.5° alc. **Rating** 91 **To** 2010 $20

572 Richmond Road

572 Richmond Road, Cambridge, Tas 7170 (postal) **Region** Southern Tasmania
T 0418 889 477 **Open** Not
Winemaker Hood Wine (Andrew Hood) **Est.** 1994 **Cases** 450
John and Sue Carney have decided not to sell 572 Richmond Road, acknowledging they enjoyed
the masochism of owning a vineyard and winery more than they realised. Tony Scherer (of
Frogmore Creek) has taken over the day-to-day management allowing the Carneys some free
time. The wines are available for sale at Wellington cellar door.

5 Maddens Lane

PO Box 7001, McMahons Point, NSW 2060 **Region** Yarra Valley
T 0401 145 964 **www.**5maddenslane.com.au **Open** Not
Winemaker Mac Forbes (Contract) **Est.** 2005 **Cases** 1000
5 Maddens Lane has been developed over a number of years. The existing 4 ha of cabernet
sauvignon were planted between 1988 and '97, and the 2 ha of sauvignon blanc were planted in
'87. Owner Marc de Cure lives in Sydney, and has secured the services of up-and-coming
winemaker Mac Forbes as contract maker, and John Evans of Yering Station as vineyard manager.
However, de Cure has his own qualifications, with a Master of Wine Quality (with distinction)
from the University of Western Sydney. Sophisticated winemaking techniques have been used for
the initial releases, which will come onto the market progressively over 2007 and '08.

Yarra Valley Sauvignon Blanc 2006 Spotlessly clean; vibrant and crisp at the
grassy end of the spectrum, without any concessions to residual sugar on the long
finish. Screwcap. 13.5° alc. **Rating** 91 **To** 2008 $28

Five Oaks Vineyard

60 Aitken Road, Seville, Vic 3139 **Region** Yarra Valley
T (03) 5964 3704 **www.**fiveoaks.com.au **Open** W'ends & public hols 10–5, or by appt
Winemaker Wally Zuk **Est.** 1997 **Cases** 2000
Wally Zuk and wife Judy run all aspects of Five Oaks – far removed from Wally's background in
nuclear physics. He has, however, completed his wine science degree at Charles Sturt University,
and is thus more than qualified to make the Five Oaks wines. Exports to Canada.

Yarra Valley Merlot 2005 Fairly typical light- to medium-bodied weight and
structure; savoury/earthy/olive overtones, but red fruits are there, as is the length.
Screwcap. 14° alc. **Rating** 90 **To** 2013 $30

Yarra Valley Cabernet Sauvignon Merlot 2005 A distinctly savoury medium-
bodied wine, the flavour largely through the agency of slightly green tannins poking
through the red fruits. Screwcap. 14° alc. **Rating** 88 **To** 2012 $25

Five Sons Estate

85 Harrisons Road, Dromana, Vic 3936 **Region** Mornington Peninsula
T (03) 5987 3137 **F** (03) 5981 0572 **www.**fivesonsestate.com.au **Open** W'ends & public
hols 11–5, 7 days in Jan
Winemaker Rollo Crittenden (Contract) **Est.** 1998 **Cases** 2700
Bob and Sue Peime purchased the most historically significant viticultural holding in the
Mornington Peninsula in 1998. Development of the 68-ha property began in the early 1930s,
and was sold to a member of the Seppelt family, who planted riesling in 1948. Two years later the
property was sold to the Broadhurst family, close relatives of Doug Seabrook, who persisted with
growing and making riesling until a 1967 bushfire destroyed the vines. Since 1998 approximately
19 ha of vines have been planted to (in descending order) pinot noir, chardonnay, shiraz, pinot gris
and cabernet sauvignon.

ΨΨΨΨΨ **Mornington Peninsula Shiraz 2005** Fragrant and pure cool-grown shiraz fruit
aromas and flavours in a classic red and black cherry spectrum plus plenty of spice;
smooth and supple; long finish. Screwcap. 13.5° alc. **Rating** 93 **To** 2020 $26
Mornington Peninsula Pinot Noir 2005 A pure line of plum and black cherry;
firm, with a hint of spice on the finish but needs time. Screwcap. 13.5° alc.
Rating 90 **To** 2012 $26

ΨΨΨΨ **Mornington Peninsula Chardonnay 2005** Medium yellow-green; a soft peach
and stone fruit mix, gentle oak evident in support. Screwcap. 13.5° alc. **Rating** 88
To 2009 $24
The Boyz Mornington Peninsula Pinot Noir 2005 Slightly lighter in body
and concentration with more development; ready now. Screwcap. 13.5° alc.
Rating 88 **To** 2009 $18
The Boyz Mornington Peninsula Chardonnay 2006 Nectarine, white peach
and passionfruit aromas; the palate trails along behind the bouquet, adding a touch
of citrus. Screwcap. 13.5° alc. **Rating** 87 **To** 2008 $15
The Boyz Mornington Peninsula Rose 2006 Pale pink; crisp, fresh and small
red fruits; good acidity rather than residual sugar. Screwcap. 13.5° alc. **Rating** 87
To 2008 $15

Flaxman Wines

Lot 535 Flaxmans Valley Road, Angaston, SA 5353 **Region** Eden Valley
T 0411 668 949 **F** (08) 8565 3299 **www.**flaxmanwines.com.au **Open** By appt
Winemaker Colin Sheppard, Tim Smith **Est.** 2005 **Cases** 500
After visiting the Barossa Valley over a decade, and working during vintage with Andrew
Seppelt at Murray Street Vineyards, Melbourne residents Colin and Fiona Sheppard decided on
a seachange, and found a small, old vineyard overlooking Flaxmans Valley. It consists of 1 ha of
40+-year-old riesling, 1 ha of 50+-year-old shiraz and a small planting of 40+-year-old
semillon. The vines are dry-grown, hand-pruned and hand-picked, and treated – say the
Sheppards – as their garden. Yields are restricted to under 4 tonnes per ha, and small amounts
of locally grown grapes are also purchased.

ΨΨΨΨΨ **The Stranger Barossa Shiraz Cabernet 2005** Medium- to full-bodied,
blackcurrant and blackberry coalescing with smooth, ripe tannins; a coherent
and seductive blend. Screwcap. 14° alc. **Rating** 94 **To** 2020 $35

ΨΨΨΨΨ **Eden Valley Riesling 2006** A quiet bouquet, the palate delicate and ranging
across crisp apple, citrus and passionfruit flavours. Certain to develop well. Screwcap.
12° alc. **Rating** 93 **To** 2015 $25
Eden Valley Dessert Semillon 2006 Works well; picked at normal maturity
and fermented to leave 40+ g per litre of unfermented residual sugar, the
semillon equivalent to Mosel Kabinetts. Screwcap. 10° alc. **Rating** 90 **To** 2010
$18

Flinders Bay

Bussell Highway, Metricup, WA 6280 **Region** Margaret River
T (08) 9757 6281 **F** (08) 9757 6353 **Open** 7 days 10–4
Winemaker O'Leary Waker, Flying Fish Cove **Est.** 1995 **Cases** 10 000

A joint venture between Alastair Gillespie and Bill and Noel Ireland, the former a grapegrower and viticultural contractor in the Margaret River region for over 25 years, the latter 2 Sydney wine retailers for an even longer period. The wines are made from grapes grown on the 50-ha Karridale Vineyard (planted between 1995 and 1998), with the exception of a Verdelho, which is purchased from the northern Margaret River. Part of the grape production is sold, and part made under the Flinders Bay and Dunsborough Hills brands. Exports to the UK and the US.

Margaret River Sauvignon Blanc Semillon 2006 Clean and lively, with apple/citrus/passionfruit blossom aromas; the palate is not powerful, but has length and good flavour on the finish. Screwcap. 13° alc. **Rating** 90 **To** 2009 $17
Dunsborough Hills Margaret River Shiraz 2005 Plenty of weight and texture; an attractive mix of black fruits, then spice, closing with vibrant red fruits. Screwcap. 14° alc. **Rating** 90 **To** 2015 $17
Dunsborough Hills Margaret River Cabernet Sauvignon 2005 Light- to medium-bodied; nicely balanced, with good blackcurrant varietal fruit at near-perfect ripeness. Screwcap. 13.5° alc. **Rating** 90 **To** 2015 $17

Margaret River Chardonnay 2006 Clean, fresh, fruit-driven mix of nectarine and grapefruit; good length, though far from complex. Screwcap. 13° alc. **Rating** 89 **To** 2011 $17
Margaret River Shiraz 2004 Elegant light- to medium-bodied wine, with predominantly cherry and warm spice flavours, then darker fruit notes; good oak and tannin management. Screwcap. 15° alc. **Rating** 89 **To** 2013 $17
Dunsborough Hills Geographe Margaret River Verdelho 2006 More flavour and personality than many verdelhos; has structure, and some fruit definition. Screwcap. 13.5° alc. **Rating** 88 **To** 2010 $15
Margaret River Cabernet Sauvignon 2005 The fragrant bouquet leads into a light- to medium-bodied palate with notes of mint and leaf as well as cassis/blackcurrant; although the alcohol is higher, is less flavour-ripe than the Dunsborough Hills. Screwcap. 14° alc. **Rating** 88 **To** 2013 $17
Dunsborough Hills Margaret River Sauvignon Blanc Semillon 2006 Structure and length driven by the semillon component, with some gentle tropical fruit from the sauvignon blanc. Screwcap. 12.5° alc. **Rating** 87 **To** 2009 $15
Margaret River Verdelho 2006 Well-made and finely sculpted, but in a more conventional, whack-it-down style. Screwcap. 13.5° alc. **Rating** 87 **To** 2008 $17
Margaret River Merlot 2004 Clean and fresh, has varietal character, but is very light-bodied; a rose on steroids. Screwcap. 14.5° alc. **Rating** 87 **To** 2008 $17

Flint's of Coonawarra

PO Box 8, Coonawarra, SA 5263 **Region** Coonawarra
T (08) 8736 5046 **F** (08) 8736 5146 **www.**flintsofcoonawarra.com.au **Open** Not
Winemaker Majella **Est.** 2000 **Cases** 1700

Six generations of the Flint family have lived and worked in Coonawarra since 1840. Damian Flint and his family began the development of 20 ha of cabernet sauvignon, shiraz and merlot in 1989, but it was not until 2000 that they decided to have a small portion of cabernet sauvignon made at Majella, owned by their lifelong friends the Lynn brothers. The wine had immediate show success another 10 tonnes were diverted from the 2001 vintage, and the first wines were released in 2003. Exports to the UK.

Rostrevor Coonawarra Shiraz 2004 Dense, deep purple-red; medium- to full-bodied, with layers of flavour; great structure and texture, with excellent tannins. Trophy Best Shiraz Limestone Coast Wine Show '06. Screwcap. **Rating** 95 **To** 2024 $23

♟♟♟♟♀ **Gammon's Crossing Cabernet Sauvignon 2004** Complex wine with very good texture courtesy of slightly grainy tannins and some savoury blackcurrant fruit. **Rating** 93 **To** 2014 $23

Fluted Cape Vineyard

28 Groombridge Road, Kettering, Tas 7155 **Region** Southern Tasmania
T (03) 6267 4262 **Open** 7 days 10–5
Winemaker Andrew Hood **Est.** 1993 **Cases** 170
For many years Val Dell was the senior wildlife ranger on the central plateau of Tasmania, his wife Jan running the information centre at Liawenee. I met them there on trout fishing expeditions, staying in one of the park huts. They have now retired to the Huon Valley region, having established 0.25 ha each of pinot noir and chardonnay overlooking Kettering and Bruny Island, said to be a spectacularly beautiful site. The wines are made for them by Andrew Hood and are sold through the cellar door and Hartzview Cellars in Gardners Bay.

♟♟♟♟♀ **Chardonnay 2006** Good intensity and length; ultra-typical citrus and nectarine fruit; clean finish. **Rating** 93 **To** 2011
Pinot Noir 2005 Abundant black and red fruits with the supple and round mouthfeel, which is the marker of this lovely Tasmanian vintage; a very pretty wine. **Rating** 90 **To** 2012

♟♟♟♟ **Pinot Noir 2006** Medium-bodied; an attractive array of spicy black fruits; good texture and mouthfeel. **Rating** 89 **To** 2009

Flying Duck Estate

3838 Wangaratta–Whitfield Road, King Valley, Vic 3678 **Region** King Valley
T (03) 9819 7787 **F** (03) 9819 7789 **Open** By appt
Winemaker Trevor Knaggs, Paul Burgoyne **Est.** 1998 **Cases** 850
Wayne and Sally Burgoyne, with John and Karen Butler, purchased the 3-year-old vineyard in 2001, with 2 ha of shiraz which had been planted by Paul Burgoyne, who continues to be involved with the operation as assistant winemaker. In 2001 2.3 ha of merlot and 1 ha of viognier were planted, with Shiraz Viognier, Merlot and Viognier first made in 2005.

Flying Fish Cove

Caves Road, Wilyabrup, WA 6284 **Region** Margaret River
T (08) 9755 6600 **F** (08) 9755 6788 **www.**flyingfishcove.com **Open** 7 days 11–5
Winemaker Damon Eastaugh, Liz Reed **Est.** 2000 **Cases** 18 000
A group of 20 shareholders acquired the 130-ha property on which the Flying Fish Cove winery was subsequently built. It has 2 strings to its bow: contract winemaking for others, and the development of 3 product ranges (Upstream, Prize Catch and Margaret River varietals), partly based on 25 ha of estate plantings, with another 10 ha planned. Exports to the US, Italy, West Indies, Indonesia, Singapore, Japan and Hong Kong.

♟♟♟♟♟ **Margaret River Shiraz 2005** Excellent texture and structure from the mid-palate onwards, with red and black fruits seamlessly woven through the supporting oak and tannins. Gold medal National Wine Show '06. Screwcap. 14.5° alc. **Rating** 94 **To** 2025 $20
Margaret River Cabernet Sauvignon Merlot 2005 Dense red-purple; abundant cassis and blackcurrant; supple, ripe tannins add to the structure; minimal oak. Value plus. Fully deserves its distinguished show record. Gold National Wine Show '06. Screwcap. 14.5° alc. **Rating** 94 **To** 2015 $20

♟♟♟♟♀ **Wildberry Estate Shiraz 2005** A solid wine with lots of extract and richness to the array of spicy black fruits. Screwcap. 14.5° alc. **Rating** 91 **To** 2015 $20

♟♟♟♟ **Margaret River Sauvignon Blanc Semillon 2006** A clean but closed bouquet; all about structure rather than fruit; tight slate and mineral flavours; may evolve. Screwcap. 12° alc. **Rating** 87 **To** 2009 $20

Cuttlefish Margaret River Classic White 2006 Neat café style; a nice interplay between the sauvignon blanc, semillon and chardonnay components; good balance. Screwcap. 12.5° alc. **Rating** 87 **To** 2008 $14

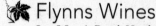 # Flynns Wines   ★★★★★

Lot 5 Lewis Road, Heathcote, Vic 3523 **Region** Heathcote
T (03) 5433 6297 **F** (03) 5433 6297 www.flynnswines.com **Open** W'ends 11–5, or by appt
Winemaker Greg Flynn, Natala Flynn **Est.** 1999 **Cases** 1800
The Flynn name has a long association with Heathcote. In the 1970s John Flynn and Laurie Williams established a 2-ha vineyard next door to Mount Ida Vineyard, on the rich, red Cambrian soil. It produced some spectacular wines before being sold in 1983. Greg and Natala Flynn are no relation to John Flynn, but did spend 18 months searching for their property, 13 km north of Heathcote on the same red Cambrian soil. They have established 4 ha of shiraz, sangiovese, cabernet sauvignon, merlot and viognier. Greg Flynn is a Roseworthy graduate from the marketing course, and has had 22 years working on the coal-face of retail and wholesale businesses, interweaving 8 years of vineyard and winemaking experience, supplemented by the 2-year Bendigo TAFE winemaking course. Just for good measure, wife Natala joined Greg for the last 8 years of vineyard and winemaking, and likewise completed the Bendigo TAFE course.

🍷🍷🍷🍷🍷 **MC Heathcote Shiraz 2004** At this moderate alcohol level (for Heathcote) it is not surprising to find a fragrant, medium-bodied wine with blackberry and black cherry fruit sustained by fine tannins; a long and harmonious finish. Cork. 14.5° alc. **Rating** 94 **To** 2024 $29.90
Heathcote Cabernet Merlot 2004 Medium-bodied; fragrant and elegant; has great length and balance, the red and black fruit flavours very fresh, the oak seamless. Basket-pressed, the components separately matured for 14 months in French oak. Cork. 14° alc. **Rating** 94 **To** 2024 $25

🍷🍷🍷🍷🍷 **Lewis Road Heathcote Shiraz 2005** Similar weight to the Shiraz Viognier, the fruit slightly more savoury and spicy; long, fine tannins give the wine outstanding structure, firm but without hardness or bitterness. Screwcap. 14.5° alc. **Rating** 93 **To** 2025 $19.90
Lewis Road Heathcote Shiraz Viognier 2005 Medium-bodied; abundant blackberry fruit, spice and licorice, the viognier less obvious than most, though at the commonly adopted level of 5%. Good balance and tannin structure. Screwcap. 14.9° alc. **Rating** 91 **To** 2020 $19.90
Heathcote Sangiovese 2004 Excellent medium-bodied texture, structure and mouthfeel; the sour cherry and red cherry fruit woven through with tannins; good typicity. Cork. 14° alc. **Rating** 90 **To** 2010 $29.90

Foggo Wines   ★★★★★

Lot 21 Foggos Road, McLaren Vale, SA 5171 **Region** McLaren Vale
T (08) 8323 0131 **F** (08) 8323 7626 www.foggowines.com.au **Open** Mon–Fri 10.30–4.30, w'ends & public hols 11–5
Winemaker Herb Van De Wiel **Est.** 1999 **Cases** 3000
Herb and Sandie Van De Wiel have been grapegrowers in McLaren Vale for 16 years, and in 1999 they were able to purchase the former Curtis winery. They have 3 vineyards: the oldest (Foggos Road) is 9 ha of shiraz dating back to 1915; 80-year-old grenache, 45-year-old cinsaut and 20-year-old chardonnay and sauvignon blanc come from their other vineyards, totalling 25 ha in all. They have established a formidable reputation for their Shiraz, Grenache, Grenache Shiraz Cinsaut and Cabernet Sauvignon equal to the best. Exports to the US, Canada and Taiwan.

Fonty's Pool Vineyards   ★★★★★

Seven Day Road, Manjimup, WA 6258 **Region** Pemberton
T (08) 9777 0777 **F** (08) 9777 0788 www.fontyspoolwines.com.au **Open** 7 days 10–4.30
Winemaker Eloise Jarvis, Melanie Bowater **Est.** 1989 **Cases** 30 000

The Fonty's Pool vineyards are part of the original farm owned by pioneer settler Archie Fontanini, who was granted land by the government in 1907. In the early 1920s a large dam was created to provide water for the intensive vegetable farming which was part of the farming activities. The dam became known as Fonty's Pool, and to this day remains a famous local landmark and recreational facility. The first grapes were planted in 1989, and at 110 ha the vineyard is now one of the region's largest, supplying grapes to a number of leading WA wineries. An increasing amount of the production is used for Fonty's Pool. Exports to all major markets.

ႣႣႣႣႣ **Pemberton Sauvignon Blanc Semillon 2006** Lively aromas and a touch of spicy oak; a very long and beautifully balanced palate with lemon and citrus; great finish and aftertaste. Immaculate winemaking. Screwcap. 12.5° alc. **Rating** 94 **To** 2008 $15.95

Pemberton Shiraz 2004 Elegant and vibrant fruit aromas and flavours, with red cherry and raspberry at the core; fine tannins in a wonderfully fresh finish. Screwcap. 13° alc. **Rating** 94 **To** 2015 $20.75

ႣႣႣႣ♀ **Pemberton Chardonnay 2005** Fragrant grapefruit and white peach aromas, with just a hint of oak, the palate providing an instant replay, the texture spot-on. Screwcap. 14° alc. **Rating** 93 **To** 2012 $20.75

Pemberton Pinot Noir 2005 A stylish wine, with strong foresty/savoury notes carried by plum and black cherry fruit. Screwcap. 14° alc. **Rating** 91 **To** 2012 $20.75

Pemberton Rose 2006 Some salmon colour; spicy, strawberry, pinot-based wine; crisp, clean finish; superior example. Screwcap. 13° alc. **Rating** 90 **To** 2008 $15.95

ႣႣႣႣ **Pemberton Cabernet Merlot 2005** Cool-grown influences obvious in the savoury/leafy/olive tones to the underlying blackcurrant fruit; fine tannins to close. Screwcap. 13° alc. **Rating** 89 **To** 2012 $15.95

Pemberton Viognier 2005 The mouthfeel and texture of the wine are its strongest points (barrel ferment), citrus/apricot (just), and spice/musk (just) its flavours. Screwcap. 13° alc. **Rating** 88 **To** 2010 $20.75

Forest Hill Vineyard   ★★★★★

South Coast Highway, Denmark, WA 6333 **Region** Great Southern
T (08) 9848 2199 **F** (08) 9848 3199 **www**.foresthillwines.com.au **Open** 7 days 10–5
Winemaker Clemenc Haselgrove **Est.** 1965 **Cases** 10 000
This is one of the oldest 'new' winemaking operations in WA, and was the site for the first grape plantings for Great Southern in 1965. The Forest Hill brand became well known, aided by the fact that a 1975 Riesling made by Sandalford from Forest Hill grapes won 9 trophies. In 1997 the property was acquired by interests associated with Perth stockbroker Tim Lyons, and a program of renovation and expansion of the vineyards commenced. The minuscule release of the wines made from the oldest vines on the property is awesome. Exports to the UK, the US and China.

ႣႣႣႣႣ **Block 1 Great Southern Riesling 2006** A spotlessly clean, floral bouquet; wonderfully fine and intense; a delicate rainbow of citrus, apple and passionfruit flavours, with lingering acidity. From dry-grown vines planted in 1965. Screwcap. 12.2° alc. **Rating** 96 **To** 2021 $35

Block 8 Mount Barker Chardonnay 2005 Still very pale colour; refined and restrained power; a sinuous palate of nectarine and grapefruit interwoven with French oak, finishing with low acidity. Hand-pruned and hand-picked; restrained alcohol. Screwcap. 13° alc. **Rating** 96 **To** 2018 $35

Block 9 Great Southern Shiraz 2005 An elegant fusion of wonderfully focused black cherry and blackberry fruit with quality oak; only medium-bodied, but has effortless length and super-fine tannins. Screwcap. 14° alc. **Rating** 96 **To** 2025 $45

Block 5 Great Southern Cabernet Sauvignon 2005 Fine-grained tannins underpin a classically restrained medium-bodied wine, helping its considerable length. Fine, pure blackcurrant fruit, with quality oak in the background. Screwcap. 14° alc. **Rating** 96 **To** 2025 $45

Riesling 2006 Wonderfully fragrant apple and citrus blossom aromas and flavours; a tight spine of acidity will hold the wine for many years. Gold medal National Wine Show '06. Screwcap. 13° alc. **Rating** 95 **To** 2021 $19

Great Southern Shiraz 2005 High-quality wine; fine, ripe but persistent tannins run through the length of the palate, surrounded by a mix of red cherry, black cherry, blackberry, licorice and spice. Screwcap. 14° alc. **Rating** 94 **To** 2020 $22

ŸŸŸŸŸ **Great Southern Cabernet Merlot 2005** Medium-bodied, with good, firm structure and texture; keeps its line better than many such blends, blackcurrant and citrussy cassis in a courtly dance around each other. Value plus. Screwcap. 14.5° alc. **Rating** 91 **To** 2015 $17

Great Southern Cabernet Sauvignon 2005 Excellent varietal bouquet, and equally classic varietal fruit; however, the assertive tannins still need to learn their place, the saving grace is that they are ripe. Screwcap. 14° alc. **Rating** 91 **To** 2025 $22

Forester Estate

1064 Wildwood Road, Yallingup, WA 6282 **Region** Margaret River
T (08) 9755 2788 **F** (08) 9755 2766 **www.**foresterestate.com.au **Open** By appt
Winemaker Kevin McKay, Michael Langridge **Est.** 2001 **Cases** 20 000
The Forester Estate business partners are Kevin McKay and Redmond Sweeny. Winemaker Michael Langridge has a Bachelor of Arts (Hons) in Psychology and a Bachelor of Applied Science (wine science, Charles Sturt). As Kevin McKay says, 'He is the most over-qualified forklift driver in Australia.' They have built and designed a 500-tonne winery, half devoted to contract winemaking, the other half for the Forester label. Part of the intake comes from the 4.5-ha estate plantings of sauvignon blanc, cabernet and shiraz, the remainder from nearby growers, one of whom is the operating viticulturist at Forester Estate. Exports to Hong Kong and China.

ŸŸŸŸŸ **Margaret River Chardonnay 2005** A clean bouquet; complex and rich, medium- to full-bodied regional style; ripe stone fruit, melon and fig flavours, with good oak integration; lots happening. Diam. 13.5° alc. **Rating** 94 **To** 2012 $25

Yelverton Reserve Margaret River Cabernet Sauvignon 2001 Interesting wine; classic, slightly austere cabernet sauvignon in a Bordeaux mould; ripe tannins and good oak support; blackcurrant and cigar box flavours. Cork. 14° alc. **Rating** 94 **To** 2016 $47

ŸŸŸŸŸ **Margaret River Sauvignon Blanc 2006** Pale straw-green; a clean, flowery bouquet, then a tight, intense and long palate with grass, gooseberry and notes of mineral. Screwcap. 13.5° alc. **Rating** 93 **To** 2009 $21

Margaret River Semillon Sauvignon Blanc 2006 A clean, fresh style ranging through citrus, herb and grass flavours; refreshing, dry finish. Screwcap. 13° alc. **Rating** 93 **To** 2009 $19

Margaret River Shiraz 2004 Fragrant cherry fruit plus touches of spice; the palate precisely follows the bouquet in an elegant, medium-bodied mode. Bargain. Screwcap. 14° alc. **Rating** 93 **To** 2014 $18

Margaret River Cabernet Sauvignon 2004 Bright, clear red-purple; very much in winery style, elegant and finely structured cassis fruit and silky tannins. Diam. 14° alc. **Rating** 92 **To** 2014 $29

Margaret River Semillon 2005 Picks up expression and power from the mid-palate through to the finish and aftertaste; classic lemon/lemongrass/herb flavours. Screwcap. 13.5° alc. **Rating** 90 **To** 2012 $26

Home Block Margaret River Shiraz 2004 Clear red-purple; light- to medium-bodied; fresh and bright red and black fruits, quite tangy; fine tannins and subtle oak. Diam. 14° alc. **Rating** 90 **To** 2014 $29

Margaret River Cabernet Merlot 2005 Enters the mouth quietly, but builds both structure and flavour through to the finish with a mix of briar, olive and blackcurrant fruit. Screwcap. 13.5° alc. **Rating** 90 **To** 2015 $18

Fosters Wine Estates

77 Southbank Boulevard, Southbank, Vic 3006 **Region** Australia
T 1300 651 650 **F** (03) 8626 3450 **www.fosters.com.au Open** Not
Winemaker Chris Hatcher **Est.** 2005 **Cases** 40 million

Fosters Wine Estates has 2 main streams of brands: those which it had prior to the amalgamation with Southcorp, and those that came with Southcorp. Alphabetically, in the former category are: Andrew Garrett, Annie's Lane, Baileys of Glenrowan, Cartwheel, Early Harvest, Eye Spy, Half Mile Creek, Ingoldby, Jamiesons Run, Maglieri Lambrusco, Maglieri of McLaren Vale, Metala, Mildara, Mount Ida, Pepperjack, Robertson's Well, Saltram, Shadowood, St Huberts, T'Gallant, The Rothbury Estate, Wolf Blass, Yarra Ridge and Yellowglen. The Southcorp originated brands are Blues Point, Coldstream Hills, Devil's Lair, Edwards & Chaffey, Fisher's Circle, Glass Mountain, Kaiser Stuhl, Killawarra, Kirralaa, Leo Buring, Lindemans, Matthew Lang, Minchinbury, Penfolds, Queen Adelaide, Rosemount Estate, Rouge Homme, Seaview, Seppelt, the Little Penguin, Tollana and Wynns Coonawarra. Those which have dedicated vineyards wholly or partially within their control and/or have separate winemaking facilities will be found under their separate entries. Those which are brands without, as it were, an independent existence are covered within this entry. Exports to all major markets.

 Cartwheel Margaret River Chardonnay 2005 A well-made wine; while unambiguously light-bodied, has length and balance to stone fruit and citrus flavours, a flick of French oak to help it along the way. Screwcap. 13.5° alc. **Rating** 89 **To** 2010 $22.95
Fishers Circle Shiraz Merlot Cabernet 2004 Fragrant and aromatic red and black fruits; a fresh medium-bodied palate, albeit with minimal tannin and oak contribution. Screwcap. 14° alc. **Rating** 88 **To** 2010 $13.95
Early Harvest Semillon Sauvignon Blanc 2006 The low alcohol is extremely interesting in the context of this style (as opposed to riesling); while self-evidently and inevitably light-bodied, has gooseberry and passionfruit flavours. Ideal for BYO Chinese. Screwcap. 9.5° alc. **Rating** 87 **To** 2008 $15.95
Shadowood Eden Valley Chardonnay 2005 A wine which neatly underlines the special qualities of Eden Valley chardonnay; this is nicely made, not sweet, subtly oaked, but is not in the same class. Screwcap. 13.5° alc. **Rating** 87 **To** 2008 $17.95

Four Walls Wines

6/231 Roden Street, West Melbourne, Vic 3003 (postal) **Region** Yarra Valley
T (03) 9329 1146 **F** (03) 9646 6977 **www.fourwallswines.com.au Open** Not
Winemaker Tokar Estate (Paul Evans) **Est.** 2003 **Cases** 800

This is the partnership of Robert, Rebecca, David, Shelley and Daniel Walls, who decided the time was right to start a virtual winery business in the Yarra Valley. Thus they buy grapes from specific subregions, and have the wines made by Paul Evans at Tokar Estate. Whether the 2007 frosts will serve to dry up the underlying surplus remains to be seen, the discovery of phylloxera in the Yarra Valley adding another uncertainty. However, if production is kept around the present level of 800–1000 cases, the problems should not prove too difficult to solve.

Yarra Valley Sauvignon Blanc 2006 Firm, but not enough varietal zip; minerally, the balance ok. Screwcap. 13° alc. **Rating** 87 **To** 2008 $15

Fox Creek Wines ★★★★☆

Malpas Road, Willunga, SA 5172 **Region** McLaren Vale
T (08) 8556 2403 **F** (08) 8556 2104 **www.foxcreekwines.com Open** 7 days 10–5
Winemaker Chris Dix, Scott Zrna **Est.** 1995 **Cases** 35 000

Fox Creek has made a major impact since coming on-stream late in 1995. It is the venture of the Watts family: Jim (retired surgeon), wife Helen and son Paul Watts (viticulturist); and the Roberts family: John (retired anaesthetist) and wife Lyn. Kristin McLarty (nee Watts) is marketing manager and Paul Rogers (married to Georgy, nee Watts) is general manager. The wines have enjoyed considerable show success. Exports to the UK, the US and other major markets.

ŶŶŶŶ⁥ **Red Baron McLaren Vale Shiraz 2005** Complex regional style with blackberry, dark chocolate and spice; controlled alcohol and likewise oak make for a thoroughly enjoyable wine at a modest price. Screwcap. 13.5° alc. **Rating** 93 **To** 2012 $17

ŶŶŶŶ **JSM Shiraz Cabernet Franc 2004** Distinctly savoury/earthy overtones to the bouquet, the flavours following much the same track with an earth, olive and black fruit mix. Includes some cabernet sauvignon. Screwcap. 14.5° alc. **Rating** 89 **To** 2015 $22
Vixen NV Better than many; a spicy array of black fruits, and not too sweet. Cabernet Sauvignon/Shiraz/Cabernet Franc. Cork. 13.5° alc. **Rating** 87 **To** 2008 $22

Fox Gordon   ★★★★

PO Box 62, Kent Town, SA 5071 **Region** Barossa Valley
T (08) 8361 8136 **F** (08) 8361 9521 **www**.foxgordon.com.au **Open** Not
Winemaker Natasha Mooney **Est.** 2000 **Cases** 4000
This is the venture of 3 very well known figures in the wine industry: Jane Gordon, Rachel Atkins (nee Fox) and Natasha Mooney. Natasha Mooney (Tash) has had first-class experience in the Barossa Valley, particularly during her time as chief winemaker at Barossa Valley Estate. She and her partners wanted to produce small quantities of high-quality wine which would allow them time to look after their children, the venture planned in the shade of the wisteria tree in Tash's back garden. The grapes come from dry-grown vineyards farmed under biodiversity principles which, says Mooney, makes the winemaker's job easy. Classy packaging adds the final touch. Exports to the UK, the US, Canada, The Netherlands, Singapore and Hong Kong.

ŶŶŶŶ⁥ **By George Barossa Valley Adelaide Hills Cabernet Tempranillo 2004** An unusual array of aromas of spice, lavender and heather persist into the palate; good texture, line and flow; demonstrably unusual. Screwcap. 14° alc. **Rating** 92 **To** 2014 $20

ŶŶŶŶ **Abby Barossa Valley Viognier 2006** Undoubtedly varietal, showing both the strengths (apricot and dried fruits) and weakness (tendency to phenolics) of the variety. Food style. Screwcap. 14° alc. **Rating** 88 **To** 2008 $20

Foxeys Hangout   ★★★★☆

795 White Hill Road, Red Hill, Vic 3937 **Region** Mornington Peninsula
T (03) 5989 2022 **www**.foxeys-hangout.com.au **Open** W'ends & public hols 11–5
Winemaker Tony Lee **Est.** 1998 **Cases** 3000
Michael and Tony Lee spent 20 years in the hospitality business, acquiring a considerable knowledge of wine through the selection of wine lists for 2 decades, then opting for a change of lifestyle and occupation when they planted 4.7 ha of pinot noir, chardonnay and pinot gris on the northeast-facing slopes of an old farm. The name (and the catchy label) stems from the tale of 2 fox-hunters who began a competition with each other in 1936, hanging their kills on the branches of an ancient eucalypt tree to keep count. The corpses have gone, but not the nickname for the area.

ŶŶŶŶŶ **Reserve Pinot Noir 2004** Very good depth to plum and black cherry fruit, and likewise great length; you have to be quick – 75 dozen made. Stained Diam. 13.5° alc. **Rating** 94 **To** 2011 $45

ŶŶŶŶ⁥ **Mornington Peninsula Chardonnay 2005** Very pale straw-green; clean, crisp lemon and grapefruit flavours; bright, fresh finish and aftertaste. All bought by Qantas after it accumulated several trophies. Screwcap. 13.5° alc. **Rating** 93 **To** 2012 $26
Mornington Peninsula Late Harvest Pinot Gris 2006 Very late-picked, with Auslese sweetness; tropical fruit plus pear and musk; good acidity; fermentation stopped at 10.5° alc. Diam. 10.5° alc. **Rating** 90 **To** 2008 $25

Mornington Peninsula Pinot Gris 2006 Crisp and clean, with no reduction; some pear/pear skin flavours; good acidity lengthens the finish. Screwcap. 13.5° alc. **Rating** 88 **To** 2009 $25

Mornington Peninsula Rose 2006 Expressive strawberry-accented bouquet, the palate with similar small red fruit flavours. Pinot Noir/Shiraz. Screwcap. 13° alc. **Rating** 88 **To** 2008 $18

Frankland Estate ★★★★★

Frankland Road, Frankland, WA 6396 **Region** Frankland River
T (08) 9855 1544 **F** (08) 9855 1549 **Open** Mon–Fri 10–4, public hols & w'ends by appt
Winemaker Barrie Smith, Judi Cullam **Est.** 1988 **Cases** 15 000
A significant Frankland River operation, situated on a large sheep property owned by Barrie Smith and Judi Cullam. The 29-ha vineyard has been established progressively since 1988. The recent introduction of an array of single-vineyard Rieslings has been a highlight. The venture into the single vineyard wines is driven by Judi's conviction that terroir is of utmost importance, and the soils are indeed different. The climate is not, and the difference between the wines is not as clear-cut as theory might suggest. In the vernacular, they are all bloody good. Frankland Estate has held several important International Riesling tastings and seminars over recent years. Exports to the UK, the US and other major markets.

Poison Hill Vineyard Riesling 2006 Different from the other Frankland Estate releases; distinctly spicy nuances; the most elegant, lighter-bodied and crisper wine, with apple and citrus; subliminal sweetness in Germanic style. Screwcap. 11° alc. **Rating** 95 **To** 2018 $27

Isolation Ridge Vineyard Riesling 2006 The most expressive bouquet, highly floral and lime/citrus accented; the palate follows along the same track, with lingering lime/citrus fruit; has excellent structure. This was the one which started the terroir search. Screwcap. 12° alc. **Rating** 95 **To** 2016 $27

Cooladerra Vineyard Riesling 2006 Rather closed, with more mineral than fruit, but changes radically on the palate, with generous, mouthfilling sweet citrus fruit, and a lingering, dry finish. Screwcap. 12° alc. **Rating** 94 **To** 2012 $27

Isolation Ridge Vineyard Chardonnay 2004 A complex wine with barrel ferment and some mlf inputs into the medium-bodied, fig and stone fruit palate. Screwcap. 14.5° alc. **Rating** 89 **To** 2008 $22

Isolation Ridge Vineyard Cabernet Sauvignon 2003 Very savoury/earthy style; strong black olive overtones and austere tannins; needs great patience and a degree of faith. Screwcap. 14° alc. **Rating** 88 **To** 2015 $22

Frankland Grange Wines ★★★☆

Lot 71 Frankland/Kojonup Road, Frankland, WA 6396 **Region** Frankland River
T (08) 9388 1288 **F** (08) 9388 1020 www.franklandgrange.com **Open** By appt
Winemaker Alkoomi (Michael Staniford) **Est.** 1995 **Cases** 600
Frank Keet used shiraz cuttings from Alkoomi when he planted 2.5 ha of the variety in 1995, followed by 1.5 ha of chardonnay (also locally sourced) in 1998. Given the quality of fruit coming from the Frankland River subregion, it seems highly likely that the number of wine producers will steadily increase in the years ahead, notwithstanding the excess production blues of 2006.

Chardonnay 2004 In radically different style to the funky, quite sweet '05; firm grapefruit, melon and stone fruit flavours with good balance and length; subtle oak. Screwcap. 13.5° alc. **Rating** 90 **To** 2011 $23

Freeman Vineyards ★★★★

RMB 101, Prunevale, NSW 2587 (postal) **Region** Hilltops
T (02) 6384 4299 **F** (02) 6384 4299 www.freemanvineyards.com.au **Open** Not
Winemaker Dr Brian Freeman **Est.** 2000 **Cases** 500

Dr Brian Freeman has spent much of his long life in research and education, in the latter role as head of Charles Sturt University's viticulture and oenology campus. In 2004 he purchased the 30-year-old vineyard previously known as Demondrille. He has also established a new vineyard next door, and in all has 14 varieties totalling 40.5 ha; these range from staples such as shiraz, cabernet sauvignon, semillon and riesling through to the more exotic, trendy varieties such as tempranillo, and on to corvina and rondinella. He has had a long academic interest in the effect of partial drying of grapes on the tannins, and (living at Prunevale) was easily able to obtain a prune dehydrator to partially raisin the 2 varieties.

ŸŸŸŸ **Fortuna 2006** I wasn't clear whether this was an ultra-sophisticated, carefully planned, eclectic blend, or one that happened by inheritance. In fact, it was inspired, says Brian Freeman, 'by the multiple white varietal wines from the Alto Adige region of northern Italy'. Pinot Gris/Riesling/Sauvignon Blanc/Chardonnay/Aleatico. Screwcap. 13.5° alc. **Rating** 88 **To** 2008 $30

Freycinet   ★★★★★

15919 Tasman Highway via Bicheno, Tas 7215 **Region** East Coast Tasmania
T (03) 6257 8574 **F** (03) 6257 8454 www.freycinetvineyard.com.au **Open** 7 days 9.30–4.30
Winemaker Claudio Radenti, Lindy Bull **Est.** 1980 **Cases** 5000
The original 9-ha Freycinet vineyards are beautifully situated on the sloping hillsides of a small valley. The soils are brown dermosol on top of jurassic dolerite, and the combination of aspect, slope, soil and heat summation produces red grapes with ·unusual depth of colour and ripe flavours. One of Australia's foremost producers of Pinot Noir, with a wholly enviable track record of consistency – rare with such a temperamental variety. The Radenti (sparkling), Riesling and Chardonnay are also wines of the highest quality. Exports to the UK.

ŸŸŸŸŸ **Chardonnay 2005** An elegant and fine wine; nectarine and citrus fruit running through a long palate, the oak taking a back seat. **Rating** 94 **To** 2013 $28

ŸŸŸŸ♀ **Louis Unwooded Chardonnay 2005** Lots of nectarine and grapefruit; a stylish wine with satisfying flavour and texture. **Rating** 92 **To** 2011 $18
Riesling 2006 A clean, expressive bouquet; opens well, with appealing citrus and apple, but falters ever so slightly on the finish; will likely fill out with time in bottle. Screwcap. 13° alc. **Rating** 90 **To** 2015 $26
Pinot Noir 2005 Light- to medium-bodied; clean, fresh perfectly articulated varietal fruit, with good length but a strange lack of intensity. Screwcap. 14° alc. **Rating** 90 **To** 2011 $70

Frog Choir Wines   ★★★

PO Box 515, Margaret River, WA 6285 **Region** Margaret River
T (08) 9757 6510 **F** (08) 9757 6501 www.frogchoir.com **Open** Not
Winemaker Swings & Roundabouts (Mark Lane) **Est.** 1997 **Cases** 550
Eddie Sawiris and partner Sharon Martin have a micro vineyard of 1.5 ha, equally split between shiraz and cabernet sauvignon. It has immaculate address credentials: adjacent to Leeuwin Estate and Voyager Estate, 6 km from the Margaret River township. The hand-tended vines are grown without the use of insecticides.

Frog Island   ★★★

PO Box 423, Kingston SE, SA 5275 **Region** Limestone Coast Zone
T (08) 8768 5000 **F** (08) 8768 5008 www.frogisland.com.au **Open** At Ralph Fowler
Winemaker Sarah Squire **Est.** 2003 **Cases** 4000
Sarah Squire (née Fowler) has decided to do her own thing, with full support from father Ralph (see separate entry for Ralph Fowler Wines). The quixotic name is taken from a small locality inland from the seaside town of Robe, and the wine is deliberately made in a fresh, fruit-forward style. Exports to Europe and Asia.

Frog Rock Wines

Edgell Lane, Mudgee, NSW 2850 **Region** Mudgee
T (02) 6372 2408 **F** (02) 6372 6924 **www.frogrockwines.com Open** 7 days 10–5
Winemaker David Lowe, Jane Wilson (Contract) **Est.** 1973 **Cases** 25 000

Frog Rock is the former Tallara Vineyard, established over 30 years ago by leading Sydney chartered accountant Rick Turner. There are now 60 ha of vineyard, with 22 ha each of shiraz and cabernet sauvignon, and much smaller plantings of chardonnay, semillon, merlot, petit verdot and chambourcin. Exports to the UK, Canada, Singapore, Hong Kong, Fiji, China and NZ.

ƔƔƔƔƔ Premium Shiraz 2002 Has continued to develop well, with supple, smooth and ripe blackberry and black cherry fruit, plus a touch of chocolate; fine, ripe tannins. Cork. 14° alc. **Rating** 90 **To** 2012 $35

ƔƔƔƔ Petit Verdot 2004 Strong purple-red; a spotlessly clean bouquet, then a powerful, intense and mouth-puckering palate, true to variety with black fruits; the tannins are not coarse, but do need to soften. Screwcap. 13.5° alc. **Rating** 89 **To** 2019 $25

Cabernet Sauvignon 2003 Medium-bodied; a regional style which it shares to a degree with the Hunter Valley; leather and earth along with soft black fruits; gentle finish. Cork. 13.5° alc. **Rating** 87 **To** 2013 $25

Sticky Frog 2006 Very rich, luscious, vanilla and cumquat balanced by acidity; just a tad simple, but should grow in bottle. I'm not clear how the wine was made. 12.5° alc. **Rating** 87 **To** 2010 $30

Frogmore Creek ★★★★☆

208 Denholms Road, Cambridge, Tas 7170 **Region** Southern Tasmania
T (03) 6248 5844 **F** (03) 6248 5855 **www.hoodwines.com.au Open** W'ends 10–5
Winemaker Andrew Hood, Alain Rousseau **Est.** 1997 **Cases** 4000

Frogmore Creek is a Pacific Rim joint venture, the owners being Tony Scherer of Tasmania, and Jack Kidwiler of California. They have commenced the establishment of the only organically certified commercial vineyard in Tas, and plan to take the area under vine to 80 ha over the next 4 years. A winery will be constructed; when completed, the development will offer a visitor centre and cellar door sales area; an environmental centre with walking trails and lakeside picnic areas; an organic garden; and a restaurant, accommodation and event facilities. The name is taken from the creek which runs through the property. In late 2003 the Frogmore Creek owners acquired the Wellington wine business of Andrew Hood, and for the foreseeable future will run the operations in tandem, handling all organically grown fruit at the Frogmore Creek winery, and the remainder at the Wellington winery. Exports to the US, South Korea and Indonesia.

ƔƔƔƔƔ Sauvignon Blanc 2006 Clean bouquet; an attractive mix of citrus, herb, gooseberry and mineral; very long finish. Screwcap. 13.8° alc. **Rating** 92 **To** 2009 $25

Reserve Pinot Noir 2005 Lightly framed, and quite stemmy, but carries that note in a pleasing fashion on the long, intense palate. Screwcap. 14.8° alc. **Rating** 91 **To** 2012 $50

ƔƔƔƔ Pinot Noir 2005 A forceful wine, with masses of aroma and flavour; when it calms down in a couple of years, should be a real treat. Screwcap. 14.1° alc. **Rating** 89 **To** 2013 $30

Iced Riesling 2006 Bold and luscious, the mouthfeel softened by comparatively low acidity. Screwcap. 8.6° alc. **Rating** 89 **To** 2010 $26

Riesling 2006 Apple and lime aromas; the fruit line is slightly faint, but does continue through to the finish. Screwcap. 12.7° alc. **Rating** 87 **To** 2011 $24

 Fuddling Cup

18 Purdie Avenue, Ardross, WA 6153 (postal) **Region** Geographe
T (08) 9364 6165 **F** (08) 9364 6165 **www.fuddlingcup.com Open** Not
Winemaker Wine Net (Robert Paul) **Est.** 2000 **Cases** 600

Colin and Gail Higgins have shown admirable restraint by focusing on a single variety, planting 2 ha of cabernet sauvignon on their property near Bunbury, within sight of the Pacific Ocean. They somewhat ambiguously say, 'We ask that you consider the following when you enjoy your first taste of Fuddling Cup: a kiss or a sip are sensual acts, full of information about how the world feels, and what we feel about the feeling.'

ŸŸŸŸ **Geographe Cabernet Sauvignon 2004** A mix of ripe blackcurrant and cassis fruit plus elements of mint, spice and leaf; finishes with slightly sticky tannins. Screwcap. 13.9° alc. **Rating** 88 **To** 2012 $17

FUSE

PO Box 441, South Melbourne, Vic 3205 **Region** Clare Valley & Adelaide Hills
T (03) 9696 7018 **F** (03) 9686 4015 **Open** Not
Winemaker Neil Pike, John Trotter **Est.** 2004 **Cases** 3000
FUSE is a joint venture of the Pikes (Clare Valley), Pike & Joyce (Adelaide Hills) and well-known Melbourne wine distributors Trembath & Taylor. It takes low-cropped grape varieties from terroir that best suits them: riesling, cabernet, merlot, shiraz, grenache and mourvedre from the Clare Valley; and semillon, sauvignon blanc, chardonnay and pinot noir from the Adelaide Hills. Distinctive packaging, and a simple price range, makes the proposition easy to understand.

Galafrey

Quangellup Road, Mount Barker, WA 6324 **Region** Mount Barker
T (08) 9851 2022 **F** (08) 9851 2324 **www**.galafreywines.com.au **Open** 7 days 10–5
Winemaker Vincent Lignac **Est.** 1977 **Cases** 10 000
Relocated to a purpose-built but utilitarian winery after previously inhabiting the exotic surrounds of the old Albany wool store, Galafrey makes wines with plenty of robust, if not rustic, character, drawing grapes in the main from nearly 13 ha of estate plantings. Following the death of husband/father/founder Ian Tyrer, Kim and Linda Tyrer have taken up the reins, announcing, 'There is girl power happening at Galafrey Wines!' There is a cornucopia of back vintages available, some superb and underpriced, at the cellar door. Exports to Belgium, Holland, Japan and Singapore.

ŸŸŸŸŸ **Mount Barker Riesling 2004** Still as fresh as a daisy, a lovely crisp wine; plenty of citrus and passionfruit, and has evolved splendidly over the past 18 months. Screwcap. 13° alc. **Rating** 94 **To** 2015 $15

ŸŸŸŸŸ **Reserve Mount Barker Riesling 2006** Similar flavours to the varietal version, but more length and intensity, and a fraction more apple-accented flavours. Screwcap. 11.5° alc. **Rating** 93 **To** 2016 $20

Mount Barker Riesling 2003 Still pale green-straw; a slow, leisurely but sure development; tangy citrus and mineral flavours; a long, balanced finish. Screwcap. 12° alc. **Rating** 92 **To** 2013 $15

Mount Barker Riesling 2006 An intriguing mix of apple, citrus and a hint of lavender on the bouquet; the light to medium-bodied palate is clean and crisp, bordering on delicate; very good acidity. Value plus. Screwcap. 12° alc. **Rating** 91 **To** 2016 $16

Mount Barker Riesling 2005 Crisp, firm spice, mineral and citrus; good balance and length is slightly closed and needs time. Screwcap. 12° alc. **Rating** 90 **To** 2015 $15

ŸŸŸŸ **Mount Barker Riesling 2001** Bright green-yellow; has a blast of flavour from a touch of volatile acidity lift, but is nonetheless interesting. Cork. 12° alc. **Rating** 89 **To** 2009 $15

Mount Barker Cabernet Sauvignon 2002 Savoury, earthy blackcurrant fruit plus a touch of olive; good texture and length; ripe tannins. Screwcap. 13.5° alc. **Rating** 89 **To** 2010 $22

Mount Barker Sauvignon Blanc 2006 A clean, grassy/herbal/gooseberry mix, though not overmuch intensity. Screwcap. 13° alc. **Rating** 88 **To** 2008 $16

Mount Barker Chardonnay 2006 Clean, fresh, very delicate citrus and nectarine fruit; needs to build in bottle. Screwcap. 12.5° alc. **Rating** 87 **To** 2010 $16

Reserve Chardonnay 2003 Yellow-gold; very developed, complex, medium-bodied wine with a slightly phenolic finish. Quality cork. 14° alc. **Rating** 87 **To** 2008 $22

Mount Barker Muller 2005 Muller thurgau is a German workhorse, but this wine has been cunningly made, the touch of residual sugar complementing the passionfruit and citrus flavours; may well improve in bottle, though that is not the raison d'être. Screwcap. 11.5° alc. **Rating** 87 **To** 2009 $15

Galah ★★★★

Tregarthen Road, Ashton, SA 5137 **Region** Adelaide Hills
T (08) 8390 1243 **F** (08) 8390 1243 **Open** At Ashton Hills
Winemaker Stephen George **Est.** 1986 **Cases** 500
Over the years Stephen George has built up a network of contacts across SA from which he gains some very high-quality small parcels of grapes or wine for the Galah label. These are all sold direct at low prices given the quality. Exports to the UK and the US.

ㅇㅇㅇㅇㅇ **Clare Valley Cabernet Malbec 2001** A solid wine, but the sometimes ferocious tannins are nowhere to be seen; this is medium- to full-bodied, well-balanced, and will mature gracefully. Cork. 13.5° alc. **Rating** 92 **To** 2016 $25

ㅇㅇㅇㅇ **Clare Valley Shiraz 2001** Holding hue well; a typical full-bodied robust wine with particularly robust tannins; the barbecue, or patience, or both. Cork. 13.5° alc. **Rating** 88 **To** 2020 $25

Gallagher Wines ★★★☆

2770 Dog Trap Road, Murrumbateman, NSW 2582 **Region** Canberra District
T (02) 6227 0555 **F** (02) 6227 0666 **www**.gallagherwines.com.au **Open** W'ends & public hols 10–5
Winemaker Greg Gallagher **Est.** 1995 **Cases** 2000
Greg Gallagher was senior winemaker at Taltarni for 20 years, working with Dominique Portet. He began planning a change of career at much the same time as did Portet, and started establishing a small vineyard at Murrumbateman in 1995, now planted to 2 ha each of chardonnay and shiraz.

ㅇㅇㅇㅇ **Canberra District Riesling 2006** A clean bouquet leads into a relatively soft palate, with a gentle tropical/citrus mix; pleasant wine. Screwcap. 11.8° alc. **Rating** 88 **To** 2012 $17

Galli Estate ★★★★★

1507 Melton Highway, Rockbank, Vic 3335 **Region** Sunbury
T (03) 9747 1444 **F** (03) 9747 1481 **www**.galliestate.com.au **Open** 7 days 11–5
Winemaker Stephen Phillips **Est.** 1997 **Cases** 12 000
Galli Estate may be a relative newcomer to the scene, but it is a substantial one. The late Lorenzo, and Pam, Galli first planted 34.5 ha of vines at Rockbank, the lion's share to cabernet sauvignon and shiraz, but with 1.5–2.5 ha of semillon, sauvignon blanc, pinot grigio, chardonnay, sangiovese and pinot noir. This was followed by an even larger vineyard at Heathcote, with 106 ha of an even more diverse spread once 55 ha had been allotted for shiraz. A large underground cellar has been constructed; already 50 m long, it may be extended in the future. Exports to Japan.

 Heathcote Shiraz Viognier 2005 Usual vivid red colour; a fragrant and aromatic bouquet then a medium-bodied palate, as lively and vibrant as the bouquet suggests; vivid red and black fruits, with a fine tannin finish. Screwcap. 14.7° alc. **Rating** 94 **To** 2015 $16

Camelback Vineyard Heathcote Shiraz 2005 Full-bodied, potent, powerful and concentrated blackberry and satsuma plum fruit; oak and tannins controlled. Cork. 14.4° alc. **Rating** 94 **To** 2015 $25

ŸŸŸŸŸ **Heathcote Chardonnay 2006** Attractive wine, with very good balance and integration of fruit and oak; nectarine and stone fruit; good acidity and length; fresh finish. Screwcap. 13.2° alc. **Rating** 92 **To** 2011 $16

Rockbank Vineyard Sunbury Sauvignon Blanc Semillon 2006 Firm but distinctly complex texture; a mix of herb, grass, asparagus and gooseberry; good length. Screwcap. 13.4° alc. **Rating** 91 **To** 2009 $20

Camelback Vineyard Dos Rojo Tempranillo Grenache Mourvedre 2005 A substantial wine with more unusual flavours from tangy, almost lemony, overtones from the tempranillo; long finish. Screwcap. 14° alc. **Rating** 91 **To** 2016 $20

ŸŸŸŸ **Camelback Vineyard Heathcote Viognier 2006** Clean though light apricot, musk and pear aromas; good balance and mouthfeel; not phenolic, and has some length. Screwcap. 14° alc. **Rating** 89 **To** 2008 $22

Victoria Shiraz 2004 A remarkable wine at the price; medium-bodied cherry and blackberry, with a seasoning of spice; good tannins, minimal oak. Cork. 14.2° alc. **Rating** 89 **To** 2012 $10

Camelback Vineyard Heathcote Sangiovese 2005 Light- to medium-bodied cherry, spice and cigar box aromas and flavours are undoubtedly varietal; simply needs more intensity and length for top points. Screwcap. 14° alc. **Rating** 88 **To** 2008 $22

Rockbank Vineyard Sunbury Pinot Grigio 2006 Has some texture and weight, but (unsurprisingly) minimal positive fruit; balance ok. Screwcap. 14.1° alc. **Rating** 87 **To** 2008 $20

Gapsted

★★★★★

Great Alpine Road, Gapsted, Vic 3737 **Region** Alpine Valleys
T (03) 5751 1383 **F** (03) 5751 1368 **www.**gapstedwines.com.au **Open** 7 days 10–5
Winemaker Michael Cope-Williams, Shayne Cunningham **Est.** 1997 **Cases** 50 000
Gapsted has emerged from the shadows of the Victorian Alps winery, which started life (and continues) as large-scale contract winemaking facilities. However, the quality of the wines it made for its own brand (Gapsted) has led to not only the expansion of production under that label, but under a raft of cheaper, subsidiary labels including Tobacco Road, Coldstone, Buckland Gap, Snowy Creek and doubtless others in the pipeline.

ŸŸŸŸŸ **Limited Release King Valley Alpine Valleys Shiraz Viognier 2004** A lovely example of the symbiotic and synergistic nature of the blend; vibrant plum, blackberry and cherry fruit; good structure. Screwcap. 13.5° alc. **Rating** 94 **To** 2019 $27

Ballerina Canopy Chardonnay Pinot NV Fine and persistent mousse; a very elegant and perfectly balanced wine; gently creamy surroundings for the nectarine and citrus fruit; long, fine finish; 3 years on yeast lees. Macedon Ranges/King Valley/Tumbarumba. Cork. 12.5° alc. **Rating** 94 **To** 2008 $30

ŸŸŸŸŸ **Tobacco Road Semillon Sauvignon Blanc 2006** Spotlessly clean, it has an attractive mix of citrus, stone fruit and grapefruit over a base of herb and mineral from the semillon. Screwcap. 12.5° alc. **Rating** 92 **To** 2008 $12

Limited Release King Valley Tempranillo 2004 Medium red-purple; fine, light- to medium-bodied, persistent flavour and structure; classic cool-climate red cherry version; good length and silky mouthfeel. Screwcap. 14° alc. **Rating** 91 **To** 2010 $25

Ballerina Canopy King Valley Sauvignon Blanc 2006 A spotless bouquet, then gentle tropical lime fruit with good balance and mouthfeel; fresh finish. Screwcap. 13° alc. **Rating** 90 **To** 2008 $18

ŸŸŸŸ **Ballerina Canopy King Valley Cabernet Sauvignon 2002** An elegant, light to medium-bodied wine, with a mix of cassis, and more savoury notes; good length. Cork. 14° alc. **Rating** 89 **To** 2012 $25

Coldstone Brut NV Fine, persistent mousse; delicate citrus and strawberry flavours; good dosage and balance; 100% pinot noir. Value plus. 12° alc. **Rating** 89 **To** 2010 $13

Ballerina Canopy King Valley Merlot 2002 Light- to medium-bodied; some savoury/astringency which is varietal, but does not have enough sweet fruit remaining; better younger, when it won a gold medal at the Melbourne Wine Show '03. Cork. 14.5° alc. **Rating** 88 **To** 2008 $23

Garbin Estate ★★★

209 Toodyay Road, Middle Swan, WA 6056 **Region** Swan Valley
T (08) 9274 1747 **F** (08) 9274 1747 **Open** Tues–Sun & public hols 10.30–5.30
Winemaker Peter Garbin **Est.** 1956 **Cases** 4500
Peter Garbin, winemaker by weekend and design draftsman by week, decided in 1990 that he would significantly upgrade the bulk fortified winemaking business commenced by his father in 1956. The 11-ha vineyards were replanted, 2 ha of chardonnay was planted at Gingin, the winery was re-equipped, and the first of the new-generation wines was produced in 1994.

♥♥♥♥ **Semillon 2006** I'm not convinced that the touch of French oak provides a net benefit, with more complexity but less precision; however, well-made in its style; will grow thanks to the appropriate alcohol. Screwcap. 11° alc. **Rating** 88 **To** 2012 $15

Garden Gully ★★★★☆

1477 Western Highway, Great Western, Vic 3377 **Region** Grampians
T (03) 5356 2400 **F** (03) 5356 2405 **www.**gardengully.com.au **Open** 7 days 11–4
Winemaker Contract **Est.** 1987 **Cases** 1000
In mid-2005 a team of local families purchased Garden Gully. They have renovated and reopened the cellar door, selling Garden Gully, Grampians Estate and Westgate Wines, various olive oils and other local produce. The 50-year-old 5.5-ha vineyard is being rejuvenated.

♥♥♥♥♥ **St Ethel's Grampians Shiraz 2005** Medium-bodied; supple and round in the mouth, with an abundance of blackberry, cherry, plum, licorice and spice flavours; fine tannins, quality oak; 60-year-old vines. Screwcap. 14° alc. **Rating** 95 **To** 2025 $40

♥♥♥♥♡ **Grampians Shiraz 2005** Strong purple-red; ripe black cherry, clove and spice aromas, then a medium-bodied, elegant palate, driven by blackberry fruit. Screwcap. 14° alc. **Rating** 92 **To** 2018 $22

Grampians Riesling 2006 Finely structured, still wound up and tight, though the ripe apple and citrus flavours do soften slightly on the finish. Screwcap. 12.8° alc. **Rating** 90 **To** 2012 $20

Sparkling Shiraz 2004 A sweet array of red and black fruits; slightly elevated/sweet dosage, but at least the wine is not too oaky; 12 months on lees, disgorged June 2006. 14.5° alc. **Rating** 90 **To** 2014 $28

Gardner's Ground NR

444 Rivers Road, Canowindra, NSW 2804 **Region** Cowra
T (02) 6344 3135 **Open** Not
Winemaker Graeme Kerr, Chris Derrez (Contract) **Est.** 2001 **Cases** NA
Jenny and Herb Gardner chose their property, situated on the southern bank of the Belubula River, back in 1996. It was the culmination of an extensive search over southeastern Australia, meeting the requirements of appropriate soil structure as well as natural beauty. It was always their intention that the vineyard would be run organically, and the use of chemicals ceased in 1996 before planting began. Chardonnay and Shiraz are made by contract winemakers Graeme Kerr (at Canowindra) and Chris Derrez (at Orange). Most of the wine, labelled under the Hawkewind brand, is exported to Japan.

Garlands

Marmion Street off Mount Barker Hill Road, Mount Barker, WA 6324 **Region** Mount Barker
T (08) 9851 2737 **F** (08) 9851 1062 **www**.garlandswines.com.au **Open** 7 days 10.30–4.30, winter Thurs–Sun 10.30–4.30, or by appt
Winemaker Michael Garland **Est.** 1996 **Cases** 5000
Garlands is a partnership between Michael and Julie Garland and their vigneron neighbours, Craig and Caroline Drummond and Patrick and Christine Gresswell. Michael Garland came to grapegrowing and winemaking with a varied background (in biological research, computer sales and retail clothing) and now has a Charles Sturt University degree in Oenology. The winery has a capacity of 150 tonnes, and will continue contract-making for other small producers in the region as well as making the wine from the 9.25 ha of estate vineyards (planted to shiraz, riesling, cabernet sauvignon, cabernet franc, chardonnay, sauvignon blanc and semillon). Cabernet Franc is the winery speciality, but the quality of all the wines has risen. Exports to the UK, Switzerland, Trinidad, Hong Kong and Singapore.

ΨΨΨΨΨ **Saros 2003** In typical elegant Garland medium-bodied style; fresh cassis/berry fruit, fine tannins and quality French oak seamlessly woven together. Cabernet Franc (80%)/Cabernet Sauvignon (20%). Diam. 13.5° alc. **Rating** 93 **To** 2015 **$25**
Reserve Mount Barker Chardonnay 2005 A complex wine with carefully controlled winemaker inputs, although the exclusion of the partial mlf portion might have left the wine with more precision; 400 cases made. Screwcap. 14.5° alc. **Rating** 90 **To** 2009 **$20**
Mount Barker Shiraz 2004 Medium-bodied; fine, spicy tannins are interwoven with blackberry, plum, spice and pepper, followed by a pleasantly savoury finish. Screwcap. 14° alc. **Rating** 90 **To** 2012 **$20**

ΨΨΨΨ **Mount Barker Merlot 2004** Clean, fresh, light- to medium-bodied clearly articulated varietal character; has length, and makes no apologies for the savoury/olivaceous characters of the variety. Screwcap. 14.2° alc. **Rating** 89 **To** 2011 **$18**
Beltaine 2005 Has plenty of amorphous fruit flavour and fair balance, but I don't understand the pricing rationale. Cork. **Rating** 88 **To** 2010 **$25**

Gartelmann Hunter Estate   ★★★★☆

701 Lovedale Road, Lovedale, NSW 2321 **Region** Lower Hunter Valley
T (02) 4930 7113 **F** (02) 4930 7114 **www**.gartelmann.com.au **Open** 7 days 10–5
Winemaker Jorg Gartelmann, Jim Chatto **Est.** 1970 **Cases** 4000
In 1996 Jan and Jorg Gartelmann purchased what was previously the George Hunter Estate – 16 ha of mature vineyards; most established by Sydney restaurateur Oliver Shaul in 1970, the merlot in 1997. Diedrich Shiraz is the flagship, and is consistently good. Exports to UK and Germany.

ΨΨΨΨΨ **Benjamin Semillon 2006** A spotlessly clean but closed bouquet; the precise and long palate reveals at least some of the secrets locked up in the bouquet; lemongrass, lemon (and unusually) some lime. Will richly repay cellaring. Screwcap. 10.5° alc. **Rating** 94 **To** 2015 **$20**

ΨΨΨΨΨ **Chardonnay 2005** Plenty of peachy stone fruit flavours, backed up by quality oak; smooth and supple mouthfeel; long finish; 35-year-old vines. Screwcap. 13.5° alc. **Rating** 90 **To** 2010 **$26**

Gembrook Hill   ★★★★★

Launching Place Road, Gembrook, Vic 3783 **Region** Yarra Valley
T (03) 5968 1622 **F** (03) 5968 1699 **www**.gembrookhill.com.au **Open** By appt
Winemaker Timo Mayer **Est.** 1983 **Cases** 2000
The 6-ha Gembrook Hill Vineyard is situated on rich, red volcanic soils 2 km north of Gembrook in the coolest part of the Yarra Valley. The vines are not irrigated, with consequent natural vigour control, and low yields. Harvest usually spans mid-April, 3 weeks later than the traditional northern parts of the valley, and the style is consistently elegant. Exports to the UK and Denmark.

ŸŸŸŸŸ **Yarra Valley Chardonnay 2005** A restrained and elegant wine; chardonnay fruit in a tapestry of barrel ferment, lees and creamy mlf influences on nectarine fruit; perfect balance. Diam. 13° alc. **Rating** 94 **To** 2011 $36
Yarra Valley Pinot Noir 2005 Light to medium purple-red; vibrant, fragrant, stemmy, spicy aromas; light- to medium-bodied, but has great length and style; graceful. Diam. 13° alc. **Rating** 94 **To** 2012 $40

ŸŸŸŸŸ **Yarra Valley Sauvignon Blanc 2005** Strongly expressed varietal character throughout, but marred by slightly sweaty/reduced aromas; some are much more tolerant of those characters than I. The points are a compromise. Screwcap. 13° alc. **Rating** 90 **To** 2008 $32

ŸŸŸŸ **Fume Blanc Sauvignon Blanc Semillon 2005** A solid, quite complex wine with ripe fruit, but does tend to wander around a bit in the mouth. Screwcap. 13.2° alc. **Rating** 87 **To** 2008 $23

Gemtree Vineyards

PO Box 164, McLaren Vale, SA 5171 **Region** McLaren Vale
T (08) 8323 8199 **F** (08) 8323 7889 www.gemtreevineyards.com.au **Open** Not
Winemaker Mike Brown **Est.** 1998 **Cases** 10 000
The Buttery family, headed by Paul and Jill, and with the active involvement of Melissa as viticulturist, have been grapegrowers in McLaren Vale since 1980, when they purchased their first vineyard. Today the family owns a little over 130 ha of vines. The oldest block, of 25 ha on Tatachilla Road at McLaren Vale, was planted in 1970. Exports to the US, Canada, the UK, The Netherlands, Switzerland and Singapore.

ŸŸŸŸŸ **Bloodstone Tempranillo 2005** Excellent colour; abundant depth and texture to the black cherry flavour and its regional wisp of chocolate; perfectly judged tannins in support. Screwcap. 14.5° alc. **Rating** 93 **To** 2015 $25
Uncut Shiraz 2005 Smooth, ripe but not jammy fruit; slightly down on structure perhaps, though with a nice touch of chocolate and good length. Screwcap. 14.5° alc. **Rating** 90 **To** 2012 $20
Cadenzia Grenache Tempranillo Shiraz 2005 Much more focus and power than the blend might suggest; an array of black fruits with a firm, though not tannic, core; 60%/20%/20%. Screwcap. 15° alc. **Rating** 90 **To** 2015 $25

Gentle Annie

★★★☆

455 Nalinga Road, Dookie, Vic 3646 **Region** Central Victoria Zone
T (03) 5828 6333 **F** (03) 9602 1349 www.gentle-annie.com **Open** By appt
Winemaker David Hodgson, Tony Lacy **Est.** 1997 **Cases** 8000
Gentle Annie was established by Melbourne businessman Tony Cotter; wife Anne and 5 daughters assist with sales and marketing. The name Gentle Annie refers to an early settler renowned for her beauty and gentle temperament. The vineyard is substantial, with 4 ha of verdelho, 31 ha of shiraz and 23 ha of cabernet sauvignon planted on old volcanic ferrosol soils, similar to the red Cambrian loam at Heathcote. The winemaking team is headed by David Hodgson, who also heads up the Oenology faculty at Dookie College. The increasing production of Gentle Annie wines has a substantial export component, likely to grow in the future.

Geoff Hardy

Tynan Road, Kuitpo, SA 5172 **Region** Adelaide Hills
T (08) 8388 3700 **F** (08) 8388 3564 www.k1.com.au **Open** W'ends & public hols 11–5
Winemaker Geoff Hardy, Ben Riggs **Est.** 1980 **Cases** 18 000
The ultra-cool Kuitpo vineyard in the Adelaide Hills was begun in 1987 and now supplies leading makers such as Fosters and Petaluma. Geoff Hardy wines come from 20 ha of vines, with a large percentage of the grape production being sold to other makers. The new premium K1 range is impressive in both quality and value. Exports to Germany, Denmark, Canada and Hong Kong.

�w♀♀♀♀ **K1 Adelaide Hills Sauvignon Blanc 2006** Quality wine; an intense combination of herbs, grass and more tropical passionfruit flavours; good acidity to close. Screwcap. 12.5° alc. **Rating** 94 **To** 2008 $20

♀♀♀♀♀ **K1 Adelaide Hills Cabernet Sauvignon 2005** Potent, powerful black fruits with a sombre backdrop; the tannins, however, are fine and verging on sweet, making an excellent finish. Cork. 14.5° alc. **Rating** 92 **To** 2015 $28

K1 Adelaide Hills Shiraz 2005 Intense, almost aggressive display of fruit and tannins. Firm, and more spicy/leafy than expected at this alcohol level. Curate's egg with more good than bad parts. Cork. 14.5° alc. **Rating** 91 **To** 2020 $28

K1 Adelaide Hills Chardonnay 2005 Tight and carefully constructed; firm nectarine fruit, with subtle oak; good length and acidity. Screwcap. 13.5° alc. **Rating** 90 **To** 2011 $28

K1 Adelaide Hills Merlot 2004 Strongly savoury/earthy expression of the variety; no wannabe cabernet here, yet is in no way green. Cork. 13.5° alc. **Rating** 90 **To** 2015 $28

♀♀♀♀ **K1 Adelaide Hills Pinot Noir 2005** Has plenty of presence, power and length, the texture and weight appropriate for pinot noir; the finish is particularly good, where pinot character really asserts itself. Surprise packet. Screwcap. 13° alc. **Rating** 89 **To** 2011 $28

K1 Adelaide Hills Rose 2006 Attractive red cherry fruit drives the wine, rather than residual sugar; good balance, just a touch off-dry. Screwcap. 13.5° alc. **Rating** 87 **To** 2008 $15

Geoff Merrill Wines   ★★★★★

291 Pimpala Road, Woodcroft, SA 5162 **Region** McLaren Vale
T (08) 8381 6877 **www.**geoffmerrillwines.com **Open** Mon–Fri 10–5, w'ends 12–5
Winemaker Geoff Merrill, Scott Heidrich **Est.** 1980 **Cases** 75 000
If Geoff Merrill ever loses his impish sense of humour or his zest for life, high and not-so-high, we shall all be the poorer. The product range consists of 3 tiers: premium (varietal); reserve, being the older (and best) wines, reflecting the desire for elegance and subtlety of this otherwise exuberant winemaker; and at the top, Henley Shiraz. Mount Hurtle wines are sold exclusively through Vintage Cellars/Liquorland. Exports to all major markets.

♀♀♀♀♀ **Reserve McLaren Vale Shiraz 2002** The most focused and intense of the 4 Shirazs, with lovely black fruits, touches of licorice, spice and bitter chocolate; long finish; carries its high alcohol well; 30 months in oak. Trophy Great Australian Shiraz Challenge '06. Cork. 15.5° alc. **Rating** 96 **To** 2017 $45

Reserve McLaren Vale Shiraz 2004 A clean, elegant, medium-bodied wine; supple red and black fruits with a touch of regional chocolate, and fine tannins; 23 months in French and American oak, which still intrudes a little. Winner Jimmy Watson '06. Cork. 15° alc. **Rating** 94 **To** 2009 $45

Reserve McLaren Vale Shiraz 2001 An attractive, medium-bodied wine, with a complex amalgam of black fruits, dark chocolate, spice and earth; the oak is well-integrated; 34 months in French and American oak. Cork. 15° alc. **Rating** 94 **To** 2013 $45

♀♀♀♀♀ **Reserve McLaren Vale Shiraz 2003** Medium-bodied, sweet, ripe cassis/confit fruit flavours, the oak woven through seamlessly; just a little sweet overall; 33 months in oak. Cork. 15° alc. **Rating** 93 **To** 2015 $45

Henley Shiraz 2000 Still very potent and strong, with deep fruit notes; will be long-lived. Cork. 14° alc. **Rating** 93 **To** 2020 $150

Reserve Chardonnay 2003 Has that unmistakable aroma and taste of cork (similar to oak, and not a fault per se); has hung in well, aided by good acidity. Cork. 14° alc. **Rating** 90 **To** 2010 $25

Mount Hurtle Grenache Rose 2006 Attractive nuances of oriental spices; good balance and, in particular, a long, dry finish. Great value. Screwcap. 14° alc. **Rating** 90 **To** 2008 $8

McLaren Vale Shiraz Grenache Mourvedre 2003 Elegant medium-bodied wine; a full array of flavours including blackberry, raspberry and red cherries; fine tannins. McLaren Vale can do with ease what the Barossa finds difficult. Screwcap. 14.5° alc. **Rating** 90 **To** 2012 $18.50

Cabernet Sauvignon 2003 Tannins underpin the structure and character of the wine from start to finish; flavours of black fruits, earth and chocolate; controlled oak. McLaren Vale (58%)/Coonawarra (42%). Screwcap. 14.5° alc. **Rating** 90 **To** 2013 $22.50

ⵜⵜⵜⵜ **McLaren Vale Grenache Rose 2006** Bright pink; an attractive red fruit basket with neatly judged acidity, and – best of all – is not sweet. Screwcap. 14.5° alc. **Rating** 89 **To** 2008 $18.50

Jacko's Blend McLaren Vale Shiraz 2003 Black fruits, earth, licorice, pepper and dark chocolate coalesce on both bouquet and the medium-bodied palate; good length, with a slightly savoury bite on the finish. Screwcap. 14.5° alc. **Rating** 89 **To** 2015 $22.50

McLaren Vale Merlot 2003 Light- to medium-bodied; strongly varietal cassis, blackcurrant and black olive fruit, with a little regional dusting of spice and chocolate. Screwcap. 14.5° alc. **Rating** 89 **To** 2011 $22.50

Pimpala Vineyard Cabernet Merlot 2002 Colour not bright, but is holding its hue; shows the cool '02 vintage right from the outset; a wine of length and finesse, but no cleavage. Cork. 14° alc. **Rating** 89 **To** 2012 $30

Wickham McLaren Vale Sauvignon Blanc 2006 A neutral bouquet, the light-bodied palate fresh, with some nuances of gooseberry; easy summer drinking. Screwcap. 13.5° alc. **Rating** 87 **To** 2008 $19.50

McLaren Vale Shiraz Grenache Viognier 2004 Juicy, slurpy style, with grenache and viognier doing most of the talking, exhorting you to sock it down now. Screwcap. 14.5° alc. **Rating** 87 **To** 2008 $15

Geoff Weaver ★★★★★

2 Gilpin Lane, Mitcham, SA 5062 (postal) **Region** Adelaide Hills
T (08) 8272 2105 **F** (08) 8271 0177 **www**.geoffweaver.com.au **Open** Not
Winemaker Geoff Weaver **Est.** 1982 **Cases** 5000
This is the full-time business of former Hardys chief winemaker Geoff Weaver. He draws upon a little over 11 ha of vineyard established between 1982 and 1988, and invariably produces immaculate Riesling and Sauvignon Blanc, and one of the longest-lived Chardonnays to be found in Australia, with intense grapefruit and melon flavour. The beauty of the labels ranks supreme with Pipers Brook. Exports to the UK and the US.

ⵜⵜⵜⵜⵜ **Lenswood Chardonnay 2005** Ultimate elegance and restraint; wild yeast, mlf and no added acidity; all the inputs seamlessly moulded in the light stone fruit, cashew and cream palate. Screwcap. 13° alc. **Rating** 95 **To** 2015 $35

Lenswood Sauvignon Blanc 2006 Excellent mouthfeel and balance; acidity insinuates itself rather than standing out among the passionfruit, gooseberry and guava flavours. Screwcap. 13.5° alc. **Rating** 94 **To** 2009 $23

Ferus Lenswood Sauvignon Blanc 2005 A very interesting wine; barrel-fermented in French oak, and spending 12 months on yeast lees, it has absorbed the oak yet retains the elegance of the Geoff Weaver style; no added acidity, but still has a long, firm, fresh finish. Screwcap. 13° alc. **Rating** 94 **To** 2008 $35

Lenswood Sauvignon Blanc 2005 Vibrant and fresh, with crisp lemon juice, apple and gooseberry flavours; lively finish. Screwcap. 13.5° alc. **Rating** 94 **To** 2008 $23

ⵜⵜⵜⵜⵜ **Lenswood Pinot Noir 2004** Holding hue well; has developed complexity with some savoury/foresty characters, with particularly good length; medium-bodied within the context of the variety. Screwcap. 14° alc. **Rating** 93 **To** 2011 $38

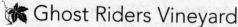 # Ghost Riders Vineyard

NR

535 Hermitage Road, Pokolbin, NSW 2320 **Region** Lower Hunter Valley
T (02) 6574 7171 **F** (02) 6574 7171 **www.**ghostriderswines.com.au **Open** 7 days 10–5
Winemaker Rhys Eather (Contract) **Est.** 1999 **Cases** NA
Ian and Ildi Kalnins have established Ghost Riders Vineyard in association with their
accommodation business, Hermitage Hideaway. Their 2.5-ha vineyard produced its first Shiraz
in 2002, and following the grafting of some of the shiraz, a Chardonnay has followed, with a
Shiraz Viognier released in 2007.

Ghost Rock Vineyard

★★★☆

PO Box 311, Devonport, Tas 7310 **Region** Northern Tasmania
T (03) 6428 4005 **F** (03) 6428 4330 **Open** Wed–Sun 11–5 (7 days Jan–Feb)
Winemaker Tamar Ridge **Est.** 2001 **Cases** 450
Cate and Colin Arnold purchased the former Patrick Creek Vineyard (planted in 1989) in 2001.
They run a printing and design business in Devonport, and were looking for a suitable site to
establish a vineyard. The 3-ha vineyard (chardonnay, pinot noir, sauvignon blanc and pinot gris) is
planted on a northeasterly aspect on a sheltered slope.

Catherine Sparkling 2003 Very fine fruit aromas; still very fresh, although the
period on lees not disclosed; excellent length and finesse. Pinot Noir/Chardonnay.
12.5° alc. **Rating** 90 **To** 2010 $32

Pinot Noir 2005 Lighter colour than many of the Tasmanian vintage; good
balance and proportion, but unequivocally on the light side. **Rating** 87 **To** 2010 $27

Giant Steps

★★★★☆

336 Maroondah Highway, Healesville, Vic 3777 **Region** Yarra Valley
T (03) 5962 6111 **www.**giant-steps.com.au **Open** Mon–Fri 10–10, w'ends 8–10
Winemaker Phil Sexton, Steve Flamsteed **Est.** 1997 **Cases** 35 000
Phil Sexton made his first fortune as a pioneer micro-brewer, and invested a substantial part of
that fortune in establishing Devil's Lair. Late in 1996 he sold Devil's Lair to Southcorp, which had
purchased Coldstream Hills earlier that year. Two years later he and Allison Sexton purchased a
hillside property less than 1 km from Coldstream Hills, and sharing the same geological structure
and aspect. The name Giant Steps comes in part from their love of jazz and John Coltrane's album
of that name, and in part from the rise and fall of the property across a series of ridges ranging
from 120 m to 360 m. The 35-ha vineyard is predominantly planted to pinot noir and chardonnay,
but with significant quantities of cabernet sauvignon and merlot, plus small plantings of cabernet
franc and petit verdot. Innocent Bystander is a successful second label. Exports to the UK, the US,
Sweden and Denmark.

Tarraford Vineyard Yarra Valley Chardonnay 2005 At once elegant, complex
and silkily powerful; sophisticated barrel ferment and maturation; melon, nectarine
and a touch of citrus. Screwcap. 13.5° alc. **Rating** 94 **To** 2013 $39.95

Tarraford Vineyard Yarra Valley Pinot Noir 2005 Highly aromatic, fruit-
driven bouquet and palate featuring wild cherry, plum and fruit spice; medium-
bodied, well-balanced, and good oak handling. Screwcap. 13.3° alc. **Rating** 92
To 2011 $39.95

Innocent Bystander Pinot Gris 2006 Fresh and lively, has real attitude, grainy
acidity supporting the long, lingering finish. Screwcap. 14.2° alc. **Rating** 90 **To** 2008
$19.95

Innocent Bystander Yarra Valley Pinot Noir 2005 Light- to medium-bodied;
a savoury mix of red and black fruits; has length and a firm finish, the acidity
pronounced but not excessive. Screwcap. 13.3° alc. **Rating** 90 **To** 2012 $19.95

Innocent Bystander Shiraz Viognier 2005 Grapes from 5 Yarra Valley vineyards
and McLaren Vale, skilfully chosen, made and blended; no clue where or how the

co-fermentation took place; spiced plum/plum pudding flavours running through a firm, long finish. Screwcap. 14.5° alc. **Rating** 90 **To** 2015 $19.95

Yarra Valley Shiraz 2005 Gentle black cherry and blackberry fruit on the medium-bodied palate is lengthened by fine tannins and neatly judged oak; 6% viognier has been seamlessly interwoven. Screwcap. 14° alc. **Rating** 90 **To** 2013 $30

ȲȲȲȲ **Innocent Bystander Yarra Valley Chardonnay 2005** Generous flavour and structure in nectarine, peach and fig spectrum; subdued oak; does chop off slightly on the finish. Screwcap. 13.5° alc. **Rating** 89 **To** 2010 $19.95

Innocent Bystander Bleeding Heart Sangiovese Merlot 2005 An honoured Tuscan blend, and actually works well here. An intriguing multi-regional, multi-varietal blend with fine but typically dry tannins. Sangiovese (King Valley/McLaren Vale)/Merlot (Yarra Valley). Screwcap. 14.5° alc. **Rating** 89 **To** 2012 $19.95

Gibraltar Rock

Woodlands Road, Porongurup, WA 6324 **Region** Porongurup
T (08) 9481 2856 **F** (08) 9481 2857 **www**.gibraltarrockwines.com.au **Open** By appt
Winemaker Forest Hill Vineyard (Shane McKerrow) **Est.** 1979 **Cases** 800
A once-tiny Riesling specialist in the wilds of the Porongurups, forced to change its name from Narang because Lindemans felt it could be confused with its (now defunct) Nyrang Shiraz brand. This beautifully sited vineyard was acquired by Perth orthopaedic surgeon Dr Peter Honey in 2001. The vineyard now has 23 ha of riesling, chardonnay, merlot, pinot noir, sauvignon blanc and shiraz. Most of the grapes are sold, but Dr Honey intends to slowly increase production from the older vines under the Gibraltar Rock label. Exports to the UK, China and Japan.

ȲȲȲȲȲ **Porongurup Chardonnay 2006** Light- to medium-bodied, crisp and clean with grapefruit, stone fruit and passionfruit; any oak (if used) is irrelevant; a long finish, and will develop further given time. Screwcap. 12.5° alc. **Rating** 91 **To** 2013 $26

Porongurup Pinot Noir 2006 Cherry and plum drive the bouquet and palate; medium- to full-bodied and pure, but needs time to show some secondary characters developing; full of promise. Screwcap. 13° alc. **Rating** 90 **To** 2014 $28

Gibson Barossavale

Willows Road, Light Pass, SA 5355 **Region** Barossa Valley
T (08) 8562 3193 **F** (08) 8562 4490 **www**.barossavale.com **Open** Fri–Mon & public hols 11–5
Winemaker Rob Gibson **Est.** 1996 **Cases** 3500
Rob Gibson spent much of his working life as a senior viticulturist for Penfolds. While at Penfolds he was involved in research tracing the characters that particular parcels of grapes give to a wine, which left him with a passion for identifying and protecting what is left of the original vineyard plantings in wine regions around Australia. This led to the acquisition of an additional 8 ha of old shiraz, mourvedre and grenache, plus some of the oldest chardonnay vines in the Barossa (recent arrivals in comparison with shiraz, but planted in 1982). Exports to the UK and Hong Kong.

ȲȲȲȲȲ **Old Vine Collection Shiraz 2004** Medium- to full-bodied, but smooth to the point of silkiness; supple, juicy plum and blackberry fruit; fine oak and tannin management; long finish; 100–150-year-old vines. High-quality cork. 14.5° alc. **Rating** 95 **To** 2019 $106

Shiraz 2004 Deep colour; abounds with blackberry, dark plum, chocolate and licorice fruit; restrained oak; delicious finish. Screwcap. 14.5° alc. **Rating** 94 **To** 2024 $39

Wilfreda Blend 2004 Generously, deeply flavoured, with none of the jammy/confectionary characters often encountered with this blend in the Barossa; has length, balance and good structure. Grenache/Shiraz/Merlot. Screwcap. 14.2° alc. **Rating** 94 **To** 2019 $27

Old Vine Collection McLaren Vale Grenache 2004 A very pure bouquet, the palate no less so; unmistakable grenache sweetness, but doesn't descend into jammy confectionery mode; oak and tannins are afterplay to the main action. Vines planted 1908. Cork. 14.5° alc. **Rating** 94 **To** 2017 $80

ŶŶŶŶŶ **Reserve Merlot 2004** Deep colour; as befits the very complex blend, powerful and complex, yet retains suppleness through the array of red and blackcurrant fruit. Barossa Valley (48%)/Adelaide Hills (42%)/Coonawarra (10%). Cork. 14.8° alc. **Rating** 93 **To** 2017 $36

Loose End Shiraz 2005 Fragrant bouquet thanks in part to viognier; the palate has more authority than the bouquet might suggest, with blackberry plus touches of chocolate and earth. Screwcap. 14.5° alc. **Rating** 92 **To** 2015 $20

Loose End GSM 2005 A fragrant and expressive array of predominantly red fruits; good structure, fine tannins. Screwcap. 14.5° alc. **Rating** 92 **To** 2011 $17

Isabelle Blend 2004 Lots of blackcurrant fruits, with seriously earthy undertones, possibly from the petit verdot; challenging wine. Merlot/Cabernet Sauvignon/Petit Verdot. Screwcap. 14.3° alc. **Rating** 91 **To** 2024 $25

ŶŶŶŶ **Loose End Grenache Rose 2006** Cleverly made; gets away with quite obvious sweetness thanks to the bright cherry fruit and acidity. Screwcap. 12.8° alc. **Rating** 88 **To** 2008 $15

Gibson Estate   ★★★★☆

57 Tubbarubba Road, Merricks North, Vic 3926 **Region** Mornington Peninsula
T (03) 5989 7501 **www.**gibsonestate.com.au **Open** By appt
Winemaker Phil Kerney **Est.** 2001 **Cases** 400
Kate and Stuart Gibson say they spent 15 years searching for the perfect site to grow classic pinot noir. They ultimately settled on a north-facing slope of the Red Hill area of Mornington Peninsula. It is 110 m above sea level, and is on a moderate (15°) incline picking up maximum sun interception, which allows them to pick a little earlier than vineyards further up the Red Hill hillsides. The 2.5 ha of pinot noir is planted in 3 equal blocks of MV6, 114 and 115 clones, two-thirds planted on vigour reducing rootstocks, thus limiting the yield to 2 tonnes to the acre.

ŶŶŶŶŶ **Mornington Peninsula Pinot Noir 2004** Fragrant plum and spice aromas; an elegant palate with precise balance and good length. Screwcap. 14° alc. **Rating** 92 **To** 2011 $25

Gilberts   ★★★★★

RMB 438 Albany Highway, Kendenup via Mount Barker, WA 6323 **Region** Mount Barker
T (08) 9851 4028 **F** (08) 9851 4021 **Open** 7 days 10–5
Winemaker Plantagenet **Est.** 1980 **Cases** 3500
A part-time occupation for sheep and beef farmers Jim and Beverly Gilbert, but a very successful one. The mature vineyard, coupled with contract winemaking at Plantagenet, has produced small quantities of high-quality Riesling and Chardonnay. The wines sell out quickly each year. Exports to the US, the UK, Singapore and The Netherlands.

ŶŶŶŶŶ **Mount Barker Riesling 2006** Elegant, crisp, dry and long; a mix of fragrant apple and citrus fruit, followed by a long, dry finish. One of a long series of rieslings bringing Gilberts many trophies and gold medals. Screwcap. 11° alc. **Rating** 94 **To** 2016 $19

Reserve Mount Barker Shiraz 2004 Dense, bright red-purple; scented herb, spice and licorice aromas; the medium-bodied palate carries on similar vein with blackberry fruit, mocha and good tannin structure. Quality oak seals the deal. Cork. 15° alc. **Rating** 94 **To** 2024 $27

ŶŶŶŶŶ **Mount Barker Shiraz Cabernet 2004** Some of the same elusive scents as the Reserve Shiraz, a more robust palate with black fruits, dark chocolate and flecks of spice and earth; well worth cellaring. Screwcap. 14.5° alc. **Rating** 91 **To** 2019 $20

Alira 2006 Light straw-green; a fine, delicate but clear bouquet; springs into life on the palate with rich tropical/citrus fruit, the touch of sweetness making it a now or later proposition. Riesling. Screwcap. 11.5° alc. **Rating** 90 **To** 2010 $16

♟♟♟♟ **Three Devils Mount Barker Chardonnay 2006** Light, crisp, fresh citrus and stone fruit flavours; not a great deal of depth, but having no need of oak. Screwcap. 13° alc. **Rating** 87 **To** 2009 $17

Gilead Estate ★★★

1868 Wanneroo Road, Neerabup, WA 6031 (postal) **Region** Swan District
T (08) 9407 5076 **F** (08) 9407 5187 **Open** Not
Winemaker Gerry Gauntlett **Est.** 1995 **Cases** 400
A retirement – but nonetheless serious – venture for Judy and Gerry Gauntlett, who planted 1.2 ha on the Tuart sands of Wanneroo in 1990. The name comes from the Balm of Gilead produced from trees on the hills northeast of Galilee in Biblical times, and was said to have had healing and purifying qualities. The tiny production is mainly sold by mail order.

♟♟♟♟ **Shiraz 2005** Medium-bodied; gently spicy overtones to black and red cherry fruit; fine tannins, gentle oak and good balance. Diam. **Rating** 89 **To** 2013 $15
Cabernet Merlot 2005 Aromas of mint and pine needle; a firm palate, with positive cassis fruit, but also with some of the curious characters of the bouquet; Quo Vadis? Diam. **Rating** 88 **To** 2015 $15

Gilligan ★★★★★

PO Box 235, Willunga, SA 5172 **Region** McLaren Vale
T (08) 8323 8379 **F** (08) 8323 8379 **www**.gilligan.com.au **Open** Not
Winemaker Mark Day, Leigh Gilligan **Est.** 2001 **Cases** 1000
Leigh Gilligan is a 20-year marketing veteran, mostly with McLaren Vale wineries (including Wirra Wirra). The Gilligan family have 6 ha of shiraz and 2 ha of grenache on their Old Rifle Range Vineyard, selling the lion's share. In 2001 they persuaded next-door neighbour Drew Noon to make a barrel of Shiraz, which they drank and gave away. Realising they needed more than 1 barrel they moved to Maxwell Wines, with help from Maxwell winemaker Mark Day and have now migrated to Mark's new Koltz Winery at Blewitt Springs. The longer-term plan is to take all the fruit when the Southcorp contract terminates; they have also planted more grenache, and small parcels of mourvedre, marsanne and roussanne on another property they have acquired in the heart of McLaren Vale. Exports to the UK, the US and other major markets.

♟♟♟♟♟ **McLaren Vale Shiraz Grenache Mourvedre 2005** Supple, succulent blackberry and plum fruit, the texture and flavour led by the shiraz, but with the strength of McLaren Vale coming through on the other 2 varieties. Diam. 14.5° alc. **Rating** 94 **To** 2025 $21

Gipsie Jack Wine Co NR

PO Box 128, Langhorne Creek, SA 5255 **Region** Langhorne Creek
T (08) 8537 3029 **F** (08) 8537 3284 **www**.gipsiejack.com **Open** Not
Winemaker John Glaetzer, Ben Potts **Est.** 2004 **Cases** NA
One might have thought the partners of Gipsie Jack have enough wine on their plate already, but some just can't resist the temptation, it seems. The 2 in question are John Glaetzer and Bill Potts, who made a little over 500 cases from 2 growers in their inaugural vintage in 2004. The 2007 vintage produced 11 000 cases from 15 growers, and the intention is to increase the number growers each year. Glaetzer and Potts say, 'We want to make this label fun, like in the "old days". No pretentiousness, no arrogance, not even a back label. A great wine at a great price, with no discounting.' Tasting notes for the wines will follow in the 2009 edition.

Gisborne Peak

69 Short Road, Gisborne South, Vic 3437 **Region** Macedon Ranges
T (03) 5428 2228 **F** (03) 5428 4816 **www**.gisbornepeakwines.com.au **Open** 7 days 11–5
Winemaker Hanging Rock (John Ellis) **Est.** 1978 **Cases** 1800
Bob Nixon began the development of Gisborne Peak way back in 1978, planting his dream
vineyard row-by-row. (Bob is married to Barbara Nixon, founder of Victoria Winery Tours.) The
tasting room has wide shaded verandahs, plenty of windows and sweeping views. The 4.5-ha
vineyard is planted to chardonnay, pinot noir, semillon and riesling.

ΨΨΨΨΩ   **Mawarra Vineyard Riesling 2006** A range of herb, lemon, lime and tropical
aromas; brisk, bright, lively and long, with Tasmanian-like acidity. Screwcap. 11° alc.
Rating 93 **To** 2014 $17.50
Mawarra Vineyard Pinot Rose 2006 Aromatic and fragrant red fruits; good line,
and not sweet. Quality rose. Screwcap. 13.6° alc. **Rating** 90 **To** 2008 $19.50

ΨΨΨΨ   **Mawarra Vineyard Riesling 2005** Very fine, tight and minerally; still unevolved
thanks to SO$_2$ which will dissipate with further time in bottle. Screwcap. 11° alc.
Rating 87 **To** 2012 $15
Mawarra Vineyard Unwooded Chardonnay 2006 Light-bodied; a sauvignon
blanc/chardonnay cross in terms of aroma and flavour; some sweeter light peach and
tropical fruits on the finish. Screwcap. 12° alc. **Rating** 87 **To** 2008 $17.50
Mawarra Vineyard Reserve Pinot Noir 2003 Plenty of flavour but firm and
slightly lifted on the finish. Screwcap. 12.2° alc. **Rating** 87 **To** 2008 $38.50
Mawarra Vineyard Allegro 2006 Well-balanced and good length; gentle citrus
fruit, acid and residual sugar precisely balanced. A semi-sweet semillon. Screwcap.
12° alc. **Rating** 87 **To** 2010 $20

Glaetzer Wines

34 Barossa Valley Way, Tanunda, SA 5352 (postal) **Region** Barossa Valley
T (08) 8563 0288 **F** (08) 8563 0218 **www**.glaetzer.com **Open** Not
Winemaker Colin Glaetzer, Ben Glaetzer **Est.** 1996 **Cases** 15 000
Colin and son Ben Glaetzer are almost as well known in SA wine circles as Wolf Blass winemaker
John Glaetzer, Colin's twin brother. Glaetzer Wines purchases its grapes from 3rd- and 4th-
generation Barossa Valley growers and makes an array of traditional Barossa styles. The Shiraz
comes predominantly from vines that are 80+ years old. The winery has a very large contract
winemaking business. Exports to all major markets.

ΨΨΨΨΨ   **Godolphin 2005** Deep purple-red; achieves lusciousness, length and intensity
of flavour without resorting to excessive alcohol; great balance and mouthfeel;
very good length and equally well-balanced oak. Unfiltered. Shiraz/Cabernet
Sauvignon. Cork. 14.5° alc. **Rating** 95 **To** 2020 $50

ΨΨΨΨΩ   **Amon-Ra Unfiltered Shiraz 2005** Rich and voluptuous wine, with lots of soft
mocha/vanilla influence on layers of soft, black fruits. Cork. 14.5° alc. **Rating** 93
To 2020 $150
Wallace Barossa Valley Shiraz Grenache 2005 In typical Glaetzer style, and
better than many; juicy, fruity grenache does not undo the flavour or structure
of the shiraz with a positive black and red fruit mix; silky tannins, balanced oak.
Screwcap. 14.5° alc. **Rating** 92 **To** 2010 $19

GlenAyr

Back Tea Tree Road, Richmond, Tas 7025 **Region** Southern Tasmania
T (03) 6260 2388 **F** (03) 6260 2691 **Open** Mon–Fri 8–5
Winemaker Andrew Hood **Est.** 1975 **Cases** 500
The substantial and now fully mature Tolpuddle Vineyard, managed by Warren Schasser, who is
completing a Bachelor of Applied Science (viticulture) at Charles Sturt University, provides the
grapes that go to make the GlenAyr wines. The major part of the grape production continues

to be sold to Domaine Chandon and Hardys, with most going to make premium table wine, and a lesser amount to premium sparkling.

🍷🍷🍷🍷 **Tolpuddle Vineyards Chardonnay 2005** Good intensity and length; grapefruit and stone fruit flavours do the talking, oak well in the background. **Rating** 92 To 2010 $23

🍷🍷🍷🍷 **Tolpuddle Vineyards Pinot Noir 2005** Bright but light hue; fine, intense and very long; elegance and delicacy in a year more noted for its power. **Rating** 89 To 2011 $24
Riesling 2006 Shows some development in colour; overall, more power than finesse. **Rating** 87 **To** 2010 $19
Shiraz 2005 Spice, herb and licorice cool climate characters; just needs a little more richness to the fruit. **Rating** 87 **To** 2008 $25

Glen Eldon Wines

Cnr Koch's Road/Nitschke Road, Krondorf, SA 5235 **Region** Barossa Valley
T (08) 8568 2996 **www.**gleneldonwines.com.au **Open** Mon–Fri 8.30–5, w'ends 11–5
Winemaker Richard Sheedy **Est.** 1997 **Cases** 4000
The Sheedy family – brothers Richard and Andrew, and wives Mary and Sue – have established their base at the Glen Eldon property in the Eden Valley, which is the home of Richard and Mary. The riesling is planted here; the shiraz and cabernet sauvignon come from their vineyards in the Barossa Valley. Exports to the UK, the US and Canada.

🍷🍷🍷🍷🍷 **Barossa Cabernet Sauvignon 2003** Intense cassis and blackcurrant fruit; a very long palate with silky fruit, good tannins and fine oak. If this wine was previously labelled 'Dry Bore' it has improved out of sight. Screwcap. 14.5° alc. **Rating** 95 **To** 2022 $25

🍷🍷🍷🍷 **Eden Valley Riesling 2005** A potent, powerful bouquet with lime, herbs and a touch of spice; the firm palate has mineral and lime running through the long finish; will flower with time in bottle. Screwcap. 12.5° alc. **Rating** 92 **To** 2013 $16
Dry Bore Barossa Shiraz 2003 Rich, juicy, jammy blackberry fruit; controlled extract and fine tannins; a long future. Screwcap. 14.5° alc. **Rating** 90 **To** 2018 $25

🍷🍷🍷🍷 **Barossa Merlot 2003** Medium-bodied, powerful and ripe, but does retain some savoury varietal characters offset by vanillin oak; plenty of structure. Barossa Zone not Barossa Valley region. Screwcap. 14.5° alc. **Rating** 89 **To** 2013 $25

Glen Erin Vineyard Retreat

Rochford Road, Lancefield, Vic 3435 **Region** Macedon Ranges
T (03) 5429 1041 **www.**glenerinretreat.com.au **Open** W'ends & public hols 10–6
Winemaker Hanging Rock Winery **Est.** 1993 **Cases** 400
Brian Scales acquired the former Lancefield Winery and renamed it Glen Erin. Wines are contract-made from Macedon and other grapes, and sold only through the cellar door and restaurant; conferences and events are the major business activity, supported by 24 accommodation rooms.

Glenalbyn

84 Halls Road, Kingower, Vic 3517 **Region** Bendigo
T (03) 5438 8255 **F** (03) 5438 8255 **Open** 10.30–4.30 most days
Winemaker Lee (Leila) Gillespie **Est.** 1997 **Cases** 500
When Leila Gillespie's great-grandfather applied for his land title in 1856, he had already established a vineyard on the property (in 1853). A survey plan of 1857 shows the cultivation paddocks, one marked the Grape Paddock, and a few of the original grapevines have survived in the garden which abuts the National Trust and Heritage homestead. In 1986 Leila and husband John decided on a modest diversification of their sheep, wool and cereal crop farm, and began the establishment of 4 ha of vineyards. 2003 commemorated 150 years of family ownership of the property; ironically, the 2003 drought meant that no grapes were picked.

ＹＹＹＹＹ **Gold Sauvignon Blanc 2006** Clear varietal expression; gentle tropical/gooseberry fruit with some offsetting grassy notes; good length, and a very good price. Screwcap. 12° alc. **Rating** 90 **To** 2008 $16

ＹＹＹＹ **Gold Sauvignon Blanc 2005** Good structure and definition; not effusive, but does have ripe gooseberry and passionfruit flavours. Screwcap. 11.9° alc. **Rating** 89 **To** 2008 $16

Glendonbrook   ★★★★☆

Lot 2 Park Street, East Gresford, NSW 2311 **Region** Upper Hunter Valley
T (02) 4938 9666 **F** (02) 4938 9766 **www**.glendonbrook.com **Open** Mon–Fri 9–5, w'ends & public hols 10.30–4.30
Winemaker Geoff Broadfield **Est.** 2000 **Cases** 25 000
Sydney businessman Tom Smith and wife Terese purchased the Bingleburra homestead at East Gresford in the mid-1990s. The 600-ha property raises beef cattle, but in 1997 12.5 ha of vines were planted (8.3 ha shiraz, 4.2 ha verdelho). This in turn led to the construction (in 2001) of a $2 million, 300-tonne capacity winery. The estate production is supplemented by contract-grown grapes, and the winery offers contract winemaking facilities for others. It marks a major return to the Gresford area, where Dr Henry Lindeman established his Cawarra vineyards in the mid-1800s.

ＹＹＹＹ **Reserve Chardonnay 2003** Quite powerful and tight; developing well with nectarine, melon and neatly balanced oak. **Rating** 89 **To** 2008

Glenguin   ★★★★

Milbrodale Road, Broke, NSW 2330 **Region** Lower Hunter Valley
T (02) 6579 1009 **F** (02) 6579 1009 **Open** At Boutique Wine Centre, Pokolbin
Winemaker Robin Tedder MW **Est.** 1993 **Cases** 5000
Glenguin's vineyard has been established along the banks of the Wollombi Brook by Robin and Rita Tedder; Robin is a grandson of Air Chief Marshal Tedder, made Baron of Glenguin by King George VI in recognition of his wartime deeds. The Glenguin wines come solely from the 19 ha of estate plantings at Wollombi, and the Maestro label matches grape varieties and site climates in regions as diverse as Orange and the Adelaide Hills. Exports to the UK, Germany and NZ.

ＹＹＹＹＹ **The Old Broke Block Semillon 2006** Said to be later-picked, but that does not reflect in the alcohol, although there is a touch of citrus and even stone fruit; good finish. Screwcap. 10.5° alc. **Rating** 93 **To** 2012 $19

ＹＹＹＹ **Pokolbin Vineyard Shiraz 2004** The vibrant colour and freshness, plus evident acidity, suggest a low pH, and considerable acid adjustment which may have got a little out of hand; needs time to get its act together. Screwcap. 13.5° alc. **Rating** 89 **To** 2020 $40

River Terrace Chardonnay 2005 Medium-bodied; yellow peach and melon fruit; the flavour has more depth than length. Screwcap. 13.5° alc. **Rating** 87 **To** 2009 $25

Glenhoya Wines   ★★★

Uralla Road, Armidale, NSW 2350 **Region** Northern Slopes Zone
T (02) 6771 1874 **F** (02) 6771 1874 **Open** Sat 11–4, or by appt
Winemaker MacLean Vineyards (Cameron Webster) **Est.** 1997 **Cases** 500
David and Margaret Graf planted an experimental plot of 320 shiraz and riesling vines in the back garden of their 0.7-ha house property in 1997 and 1998. The first wine was produced in 2000, and in 2001 the Grafs successfully applied for an off-license, the first in the region. In the meantime they have planted a further 1.4 ha on a 4-ha property directly across the road.

ＹＹＹＹ **Armidale Shiraz 2005** Fragrant blackberry, cherry and plum aromas; a lively, medium-bodied palate driven by clean, zesty fruit, rather than oak or tannins. Screwcap. 13.5° alc. **Rating** 89 **To** 2015 $20

Glenmaggie Wines

McLachlans Road, Maffra, Vic 3860 **Region** Gippsland
T (03) 5145 1131 **F** (03) 5145 1131 **Open** Sun & public hols 10–5, or by appt
Winemaker Tony Dawkins, Fleur Dawkins **Est.** 1998 **Cases** 1500
The origins of Glenmaggie go back to 1983, when trial plantings of shiraz and cabernet were sufficiently encouraging to prompt the extension of the vineyard to 3 ha (0.5 ha each of chardonnay, semillon, sauvignon blanc, pinot noir, shiraz and cabernet sauvignon). It is the venture of Fleur and Tony Dawkins, with occasional assistance from their young son Jack (who at the age of 8 has graduated to supervision and grape quality assessment, other vineyard tasks being too menial).

Glenmore

PO Box 201, Yallingup, WA 6282 **Region** Margaret River
T (08) 9755 2330 **F** (08) 9755 2331 **Open** Not
Winemaker Ian Bell **Est.** 1990 **Cases** NFP
Ian Bell started his career as a cellar and vineyard hand at Moss Wood; he was encouraged to study viticulture at the then Roseworthy College in 1987, and returned in 1989 to work for Moss Wood. Between 1990 and 1999 he established 3.6 ha of cabernet sauvignon and 1.2 ha of merlot, petit verdot and malbec on the Glenmore property, which has been in the family's ownership since 1895. Between 1997 and '01 all of the Glenmore Vineyard grapes were sold to Moss Wood, and made under the Glenmore Vineyard Cabernet Sauvignon label. Since then, Ian Bell has developed the Glenmore label in its own right, but continues to sell grapes to Moss Wood, the wine now being called Amy's Vineyard, named after Ian's grandmother Amy Beers who still owns and runs beef cattle at the age of 84.

￥￥￥￥ **Margaret River Cabernet Sauvignon 2003** Light, slightly hazy colour; savoury earthy cabernet on the medium-bodied palate, has length, but not enough depth or richness of fruit. Screwcap. 14.5° alc. **Rating** 88 **To** 2015 $42.50

Glenwillow Vineyard

40 McIntyre Street, White Hills, Vic 3550 (postal) **Region** Bendigo
T 0428 461 076 **F** (03) 5434 1340 **www**.glenwillow.com.au **Open** Not
Winemaker Matt Hunter (Contract) **Est.** 1999 **Cases** 400
Peter and Cherryl Fyffe began their vineyard in 1999, planting 2 ha of shiraz, 0.3 ha of cabernet sauvignon, branching out with 0.6 ha of nebbiolo and 0.2 ha of barbera. The choice of Cyclone Gully for the basic wines (the Reserve wines are not made every year) might be considered a little ghoulish. In Jan 1978 a cyclone moved up Sandon-Yandoit Creek Road, causing much property damage, and killing 2 elderly travellers pulled from their car by the cyclone.

￥￥￥￥￥ **Reserve Bendigo Shiraz 2005** Excellent full purple-red colour; rich and luscious black berry fruits; a long, silky palate showing no signs of overripeness. Screwcap. 14° alc. **Rating** 94 **To** 2020 $27

￥￥￥￥￥ **Cyclone Gully Bendigo Shiraz 2004** Much deeper colour than the '05; more depth to the cherry and plum fruit; tannins and oak balanced. Screwcap. 14.3° alc. **Rating** 92 **To** 2020 $17
Reserve Bendigo Cabernet Sauvignon 2005 Very firm, austere black fruits, and a tannic backbone; the components are in balance; simply needs time. Screwcap. 15° alc. **Rating** 90 **To** 2024 $22

￥￥￥￥ **Cyclone Gully Bendigo Shiraz 2005** Light- to medium-bodied savoury, spicy black fruits; not particularly rich, but has some length. Screwcap. 14.5° alc. **Rating** 87 **To** 2011 $17

Gloucester Ridge Vineyard

Lot 7489 Burma Road, Pemberton, WA 6260 **Region** Pemberton
T (08) 9776 1035 **F** (08) 9776 1390 **www.gloucester-ridge.com.au Open** 7 days 10–5
Winemaker West Cape Howe Wines (Gavin Berry) **Est.** 1985 **Cases** 6000
Gloucester Ridge is the only vineyard located within the Pemberton town boundary. It is owned
and operated by Don and Sue Hancock. The wines are distributed in 3 ranges: at the bottom the
Back Block range, the Mid range, and the Premium Estate range.

Gnadenfrei Estate

Seppeltsfield Road, Marananga via Nuriootpa, SA 5355 **Region** Barossa Valley
T (08) 8562 2522 **F** (08) 8562 3470 **Open** Tues–Sun 11–5.30
Winemaker Malcolm Seppelt **Est.** 1979 **Cases** 750
A strictly cellar door operation, which relies on a variety of sources for its wines but has a core of
2 ha of estate shiraz and 1 ha of grenache. The red wines are from the old estate dry-grown vines,
and are not filtered.

Goaty Hill Wines

PO Box 991, Kings Meadows, Tas 7249 **Region** Northern Tasmania
T (03) 6344 1119 **F** (03) 6344 1119 **www.goatyhill.com Open** Not
Winemaker Francine Austin (Contract) **Est.** 1998 **Cases** 1000
The partners in Goaty Hill are 6 friends from 2 families who moved from Vic to Tasmania who,
they say, 'were determined to build something for the future while having fun'. The partners in
question are Markus Maislinger, Natasha and Tony Nieuwhof, Kristine Grant, and Margaret and
Bruce Grant, and in 1998 they began the planting of 18 ha of pinot noir, riesling and chardonnay.
Part of the grapes are sold to Bay of Fires, and, in return, the highly talented Bay of Fires
winemaker, Fran Austin, makes the Goaty Hill wines from that part of the annual crop retained
by the partners. Goaty Hill's first wine show entries have yielded a string of medals, a gold medal
for the 2006 Riesling at the Sydney Wine Show '07 being a highlight, but with the 2006 Pinot
Noir and '06 Chardonnay also winning medals at the International Cool Climate Wine Show '07.

ΨΨΨΨΨ **Riesling 2006** Lime, herb, green apple and slate aromas; light-bodied, but very tight
and intense with typical Tasmanian acidity woven through the lime and green apple
flavours of the palate; long finish. Screwcap. 12.4° alc. **Rating** 92 **To** 2016 $19.95
Pinot Noir 2006 Smooth, supple, plum and cherry; a fraction one-dimensional,
but has balance and flavour. Screwcap. 14° alc. **Rating** 90 **To** 2012 $27.95

ΨΨΨΨ **Chardonnay 2006** Extremely tight citrus/grapefruit/nectarine aromas and
flavours; at this point, the oak is well and truly hidden by the tight fruit and acidity,
but the wine should open up in time. Screwcap. 13.6° alc. **Rating** 89 **To** 2012
$24.95

Golden Ball

1175 Beechworth-Wangaratta Road, Beechworth, Vic 3747 **Region** Beechworth
T (03) 5727 0284 **F** (03) 5727 0294 **www.goldenball.com.au Open** By appt
Winemaker James McLaurin **Est.** 1996 **Cases** 450
The Golden Ball vineyard is established on one of the original land grants in the Beechworth
region. The 2.4-ha vineyard was planted by James and Janine McLaurin in 1996, mainly to
cabernet sauvignon, shiraz and merlot, with lesser plantings of grenache and malbec. The wines
are vinified separately and aged in one-third new French oak, the remainder 2–3 years old. The
low yields result in intensely flavoured wines which are to be found in a Who's Who of
Melbourne's best restaurants and a handful of local and Melbourne retailers, including Randall's
at Albert Park.

ΨΨΨΨΨ **Beechworth Shiraz 2004** A range of highly spicy, savoury, earthy aromas and
flavours; a medium-bodied palate with elegance, and a quite particular character and
style. Cork. 13.8° alc. **Rating** 92 **To** 2014 $40

Gallice Beechworth Cabernet Merlot Malbec 2004 Bright, light red-purple; in the Golden Ball style, light- to medium-bodied, complex and with spicy dark fruit flavours finished off with fine tannins. Cork. 13.8° alc. **Rating** 92 **To** 2015 $40

Golden Grove Estate ★★★★

Sundown Road, Ballandean, Qld 4382 **Region** Granite Belt
T (07) 4684 1291 **F** (07) 4684 1247 **www**.goldengrovee.com.au **Open** 7 days 9–5
Winemaker Raymond Costanzo **Est.** 1993 **Cases** 3000
Golden Grove Estate was established by Mario and Sebastiana Costanzo in 1946, producing stone fruits and table grapes for the fresh fruit market. The first wine grapes (shiraz) were planted in 1972, but it was not until 1985, when ownership passed to son Sam and wife Grace, that the use of the property started to change. In 1993 chardonnay and merlot joined the shiraz, followed by cabernet sauvignon, sauvignon blanc and semillon. Wine quality has steadily improved.

ΨΨΨΨΫ Granite Belt Chardonnay 2005 Bright green-gold; a major surprise, with positive nectarine and melon fruit driving the long palate; French oak neatly integrated and balanced. Cork. 13.7° alc. **Rating** 90 **To** 2011 $16

ΨΨΨΨ Granite Belt Tempranillo 2005 Definite varietal character as it exhibits in most parts of Australia; fresh red fruits with tangy feijoa, citrus and lemon nuances; still to find structure. Zork. 14° alc. **Rating** 89 **To** 2012 $20
Granite Belt Durif 2005 Strong colour, but not impenetrable; ripe prune, plum and blackberry; not over-extracted. Zork. 13.9° alc. **Rating** 89 **To** 2015 $20
Granite Belt Sauvignon Blanc 2006 Well-made; not a lot of fruit varietal character, but has fair to good length and balance; 100% estate-grown. Zork. 12.5° alc. **Rating** 87 **To** 2008 $16

Golders Vineyard ★★★☆

Bridport Road, Pipers Brook, Tas 7254 **Region** Northern Tasmania
T (03) 6395 4142 **F** (03) 6395 4142 **www**.geocities.com/goldersvineyard **Open** By appt
Winemaker Richard Crabtree **Est.** 1991 **Cases** 400
Richard Crabtree continues to make the Golders Vineyard wines at the Delamere winery as he has in the past. The 2.5-ha vineyard established by Crabtree has in fact been sold, and since 2006, grapes have been purchased from the nearby White Rock Vineyard.

Golding Wines

Western Branch Road, Lobethal, SA 5241 **Region** Adelaide Hills
T (08) 8389 5120 **F** (08) 8389 5290 **www**.goldingwines.com.au **Open** By appt
Winemaker Justin McNamee **Est.** 2002 **Cases** 1500
The Golding family has lived in the Lobethal area of the Adelaide Hills for several generations, and is one of the larger vignerons, owning and operating 3 separate vineyards with around 40 ha planted to pinot noir, chardonnay, sauvignon blanc, cabernet franc and merlot. In 2002 the Golding Wines brand was created, the owners being Darren and Lucy Golding, together with Darren's parents, Connie and Greg. In 2006 Darren secured some Marlborough sauvignon blanc through his brother-in-law, who happens to be managing director of NZ's largest independent contract winemaking company. This has resulted in 3 wines: The Local (100% estate-grown); The Tourist (100% Marlborough); and The Leap (51% estate/49% Marlborough).

ΨΨΨΨΫ The Leap Lenswood Marlborough Sauvignon Blanc 2006 Spotlessly clean; a nice array of tropical through to herbal aromas and flavours are synergistic; not power-packed, but has more length and intensity than its sisters. Screwcap. 13.3° alc. **Rating** 91 **To** 2008 $27
The Tourist Marlborough Sauvignon Blanc 2006 Clean, crisp, light- to medium-bodied; gentle passionfruit and gooseberry flavours plus touches of herb and mineral to close. Screwcap. 13.1° alc. **Rating** 90 **To** 2008 $23

ŸŸŸŸ **The Local Lenswood Sauvignon Blanc 2006** Clean; some ripe apple works its way into the system; well-balanced, but not intense. Screwcap. 13.5° alc. **Rating** 89 To 2008 $23

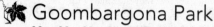 # Goombargona Park ★★★☆

Near Nug Nug, Vic 3737 (postal) **Region** Alpine Valleys
T (03) 5754 2224 **Open** Not
Winemaker Ian Black **Est.** 1996 **Cases** 400
What a tale to tell. Co-owner Ian Black (with wife Clare Leeuwin-Clark) has a myriad of connections with wine growers (and consumers) going back to a family relationship with Francois de Castella, one of the heroes in the development of the Yarra Valley in the 19th century. Since then, the contacts have become rather more direct, firstly through his 2 sons completing oenology degrees at Charles Sturt University, and – prior to that time – an on-again, off-again career as an occasional weekend grapegrower. Goombargona Park (with its wonderful address, no fax, no email and only a postcode to direct the delivery of mail) is his third and most serious wine venture.

ŸŸŸŸ **Sangiovese 2004** Light- to medium red-purple; spicy cherry/sour cherry fruit is assisted by fine tannins; distinct touches of Tuscany. Screwcap. 13.5° alc. **Rating** 89 To 2010 $25

Pinot Noir 2004 Medium-bodied; sweet plum fruit is offset by fine tannins; tenuous varietal character, just gets there. Screwcap. 13.5° alc. **Rating** 87 To 2010

Goona Warra Vineyard ★★★★

Sunbury Road, Sunbury, Vic 3429 **Region** Sunbury
T (03) 9740 7766 **F** (03) 9744 7648 **www**.goonawarra.com.au **Open** 7 days 10–5
Winemaker John Barnier, Adam McCallum **Est.** 1863 **Cases** 3000
A historic stone winery, established under this name by a 19th-century Vic premier. A brief interlude as part of The Wine Investment Fund in 2001 is over, the Barniers having bought back the farm. Excellent tasting facilities, an outstanding venue for weddings and receptions, and lunch on Sunday. Exports to Canada.

ŸŸŸŸŸ **Sunbury Chardonnay 2004** Light- to medium-bodied; developing slowly but surely, with nectarine and grapefruit supported by crunchy, minerally acidity and subtle oak. Screwcap. 14° alc. **Rating** 91 To 2012 $25
Sunbury Pinot Noir 2005 Firm red cherry fruit with some spice in the background, then a long, clean finish; needs another 2–3 years minimum. Screwcap. 13.5° alc. **Rating** 90 To 2012 $25

ŸŸŸŸ **Sunbury Chardonnay 2005** An austere, if elegant, style, with citrus and mineral flavours; meets you on its terms, not yours. Screwcap. 14° alc. **Rating** 89 To 2010 $23
Sunbury Cabernet Franc 2002 A long-term speciality of the winery; spicy, savoury, tobacco-leaf aromas and flavours give clear varietal expression to the light- to medium-bodied palate; good length. Screwcap. 13° alc. **Rating** 89 To 2013 $25
Sunbury Roussanne 2005 Well-made, though no particular distinction to the fruit flavours; some pear, apple and talc, the gentle infusion of oak primarily directed to texture. Screwcap. 14° alc. **Rating** 88 To 2012 $25

Goorambath ★★★☆

103 Hooper Road, Goorambat, Vic 3725 **Region** Glenrowan
T (03) 5764 1380 **F** (03) 5764 1320 **www**.goorambath.com.au **Open** By appt
Winemaker Dookie College (David Hodgson) **Est.** 1997 **Cases** 750
Lyn and Geoff Bath have had a long association with the Vic wine industry. Since 1982 Geoff has been senior lecturer in viticulture with the University of Melbourne at Dookie campus; he and wife Lyn also owned (in conjunction with 2 other couples) a vineyard at Whitlands for 18 years.

In 2000 they sold their interest in that vineyard to focus on their small vineyard at Goorambat, hence the clever name. Planting had begun in 1998 with 1 ha of shiraz, subsequently joined by 1 ha of verdelho, 0.5 ha of orange muscat and 0.2 ha of tannat. Exports to Canada.

ꝶꝶꝶꝶꝶ **Shiraz 2005** Clear medium-bodied blackberry and black cherry fruit, with a nice touch of spice; fine tannins and integrated oak; fruit-accented style. Screwcap. 14° alc. **Rating** 90 **To** 2015 $18

ꝶꝶꝶꝶ **Shiraz 2004** Medium-bodied; ripe, soft black fruits; balanced tannins and a touch of vanillin oak. Cork. 13.9° alc. **Rating** 87 **To** 2012 $20
Late Harvest 2006 Does show the lifted citrus/orange/fruit salad characters of the orange muscat from which it is made; others may have done better with it, but it won't frighten the horses. Screwcap. 10.8° alc. **Rating** 87 **To** 2008 $15

Gordon Parker Wines
PO Box 109, Cottesloe, WA 6911 **Region** Geographe
T 0439 913 039 **www.**gordonparkerwines.com **Open** Not
Winemaker Gordon Parker **Est.** 2005 **Cases** 2500
In 1992 Gordon 'Gordo' Parker left the retail wine business in Perth, and headed south to gain winemaking experience, working at Plantagenet Wines, Forest Hill Vineyards, Cape Clairault and Amberley Estate, before spreading his wings by working at Coldstream Hills and Domaine Chandon in the Yarra Valley. He added to this a Flying Winemaker stint in 1998 in the south of France. He returned to work as a winemaker in WA before deciding to set up his own business in early 2005. He leases a 3.8-ha vineyard in Geographe, and buys grapes from other vineyards in the Frankland River, Geographe, Margaret River and Mount Barker regions.

ꝶꝶꝶꝶꝶ **Black Label Margaret River Shiraz 2005** Excellent texture, structure and mouthfeel; a slightly richer palate, with more line to the blackberry, licorice and spice flavours; quality tannins and oak. Screwcap. 13.5° alc. **Rating** 94 **To** 2020 $25

ꝶꝶꝶꝶꝶ **White Label Margaret River Shiraz 2005** Fully ripe, sweet red and black cherry plus blackberry, all achieved at a moderate alcohol level; nice touches of licorice, leather and spice also present. Screwcap. 13.5° alc. **Rating** 92 **To** 2017 $20
Margaret River Cabernet Sauvignon 2005 Deep, bright purple-red; has a strong and pure varietal expression courtesy of sweet cassis/blackcurrant fruit, and fine, silky tannins. Screwcap. 13.5° alc. **Rating** 92 **To** 2020 $25
Pemberton Sauvignon Blanc Semillon 2006 Clean, fresh and crisp lemon, herb and citrus, more towards semillon than sauvignon blanc; has good length and finish. Value plus. Screwcap. 12.5° alc. **Rating** 90 **To** 2009 $15

ꝶꝶꝶꝶ **Geographe Merlot 2005** Bright purple-red; a slightly milky texture, but the fruit flavours are good; dark berries with nuances of olive and bracken. Screwcap. 13.5° alc. **Rating** 88 **To** 2013 $18

Gotham
PO Box 343, Mona Vale, NSW 1660 **Region** Langhorne Creek
T 0412 124 811 **F** (02) 9973 3586 **Open** Not
Winemaker Bruce Clugston **Est.** 2004 **Cases** 600
Bruce Clugston, with a long involvement in the wine industry purchases grapes from various vineyards; the 2005 Shiraz was made from 5 tonnes of premium shiraz from Jon Pfeiffer's outstanding vineyard at Marananga in the Barossa Valley. Troy Kalleske identified the fruit for Bruce, keeping things within the family, as Pfeiffer is Kalleske's uncle.

ꝶꝶꝶꝶꝶ **Langhorne Creek Shiraz 2005** Saturated with totally delicious satsuma plum, cherry and blackberry fruit; against all the odds 18 months' maturation in Hungarian and American oak has not gone over the top. Striking label provides the polish. Cork. 14.5° alc. **Rating** 95 **To** 2030 $30

Goulburn Terrace

340 High Street, Nagambie, Vic 3608 **Region** Goulburn Valley
T (03) 5794 2828 **F** (03) 5794 1854 **www**.goulburnterrace.com.au **Open** Sat 10–5, Sun
& most public hols 11–5
Winemaker Dr Mike Boudry, Greta Moon **Est.** 1993 **Cases** 1000
Dr Mike Boudry and Greta Moon have established their 7-ha vineyard on the west bank of the
Goulburn River, 8 km south of Lake Nagambie. Planting began in 1993; chardonnay on the
alluvial soils (10 000 years old, adjacent to the river), and cabernet sauvignon on a gravelly rise
based on 400-million-year-old Devonian rocks. The wines are made in small volumes, with open
fermentation and hand-plunging of the reds; all are basket-pressed. Exports to Canada.

ȚȚȚȚ   **Midnight Shiraz 2002** A solid, medium- to full-bodied wine, with slightly rustic
tannins girdling blackberry fruits; needs longer time in the bottle than the cork is
likely to give it. 14.5° alc. **Rating** 88 **To** 2012 $28
Moon Sparkling Marsanne 2002 An interesting wine; the base wine is quite
delicate, the 2.5 years on yeast lees adding complexity without taking away the
crisp fruit. The first sparkling marsanne in Australia, but should not cause a
stampede. 13° alc. **Rating** 88 **To** 2008 $35

Goundrey

Muirs Highway, Mount Barker, WA 6324 **Region** Mount Barker
T (08) 9892 1777 **F** (08) 9851 1997 **www**.goundreywines.com.au **Open** 7 days 10–4.30
Winemaker David Martin, Michael Perkins, Stephen Craig **Est.** 1976 **Cases** 375 000
Jack Bendat acquired Goundrey when it was on its knees; through significant expenditure on
land, vineyards and winery capacity, it became the House that Jack Built. In late 2002 it was
acquired by Vincor, Canada's largest wine producer, for a price widely said to be more than $30
million, a sum which would have provided Bendat with a very satisfactory return on his
investment. Exports to all major markets.

ȚȚȚȚȚ   **Offspring Riesling 2005** Crisp citrus, slate and spice; very good length and
aftertaste; dry finish. Screwcap. 13° alc. **Rating** 91 **To** 2012 $19.95
Offspring Sauvignon Blanc 2005 Fragrant herb and cut-grass aromas lead into
a pungent palate with grass, asparagus and mineral flavours. Screwcap. 13° alc.
Rating 90 **To** 2008 $19.95

ȚȚȚȚ   **Offspring Shiraz 2004** Medium-bodied; quite elegant and fresh blackberry and
black cherry, plus touches of spice and licorice, make for an attractive, early-drinking
style. Screwcap. 14° alc. **Rating** 89 **To** 2010 $19.95
Homestead Unwooded Chardonnay 2006 One of the right regions for
unwooded chardonnay; clean melon and citrus flavours, with some length. Screwcap.
13.5° alc. **Rating** 87 **To** 2008 $14.95

Governor Robe Selection

Waterhouse Range Vineyards, Lot 11, Old Naracoorte Road, Robe, SA 5276 **Region**
Limestone Coast Zone
T (08) 8768 2083 **www**.waterhouserange.com.au **Open** At The Attic House, Robe
Winemaker Cape Jaffa Wines (Nigel Westblade) **Est.** 1998 **Cases** 1500
Bill and Mick Quinlan-Watson, supported by a group of investors, began the development of
Waterhouse Range Vineyards Pty Ltd in 1995, planting 15 ha of vines, with further plantings over
the following few years lifting the total area under vine to just under 60 ha. The majority of the
grapes are sold. The name comes from the third Governor of SA, Frederick Holt Robe, who in
1845 selected the site for a port and personally put in the first survey peg at Robe.

Grace Devlin Wines

53 Siddles Road, Redesdale, Vic 3444 **Region** Heathcote
T (03) 5425 3101 **Open** By appt
Winemaker Brian Paterson, Lee Paterson **Est.** 1998 **Cases** 200
Brian and Lee Paterson have 2 ha of cabernet sauvignon and 0.5 ha of merlot at Redesdale, one of the most southerly vineyards in the Heathcote region. The name comes from the middle names of Brian Paterson's grandmother, mother and daughters. The small production is available from a number of local outlets.

 Heathcote Shiraz 2005 A quite fragrant bouquet; the firm opening to the palate is not expected, nor the continuance of that firmness through savoury black fruits, then fine-grained tannins. Diam. 14° alc. **Rating** 90 **To** 2015 $20

 Heathcote Cabernet Sauvignon 2004 Very savoury, minty, earthy aromas and flavours, but does have a certain left-of-centre appeal. Cork. 13.5° alc. **Rating** 88 **To** 2010 $20
Heathcote Merlot 2005 The cool, southern end of the Heathcote region shows through in the minty notes and fractionally green tannins of the wine. Diam. 13.5° alc. **Rating** 87 **To** 2009 $20

Gracebrook Vineyards ★★★☆

4446 Wangaratta-Whitfield Road, King Valley, Vic 3678 **Region** King Valley
T (03) 5729 3562 **F** (03) 5729 8015 **Open** 7 days 10–5
Winemaker David Maples **Est.** 1989 **Cases** 2500
David and Rhonda Maples' 37.5-ha vineyard in 1989 is planted to merlot, shiraz, riesling, cabernet sauvignon, sangiovese, chardonnay, dolcetto and alborino. Their cellar door is housed in stables built in the 1880s, with panoramic views of the King Valley, and they cater for functions/weddings for up to 100 people.

Gracedale Hills Estate ★★★★☆

770 Healesville-Kooweerup Road, Healesville, Vic 3777 **Region** Yarra Valley
T (03) 5967 3403 **F** (03) 5967 3581 **www.**gracedalehills.com.au **Open** Not
Winemaker Gary Mills **Est.** 1996 **Cases** 450
Dr Richard Gutch established 1.2 ha of chardonnay and 2 ha of shiraz at a time when most would be retiring from active business, but it represents the culmination of a lifelong love of fine wine, and Richard has no hard feelings towards me – it was I who encouraged him, in the mid-1990s, to plant vines on the north-facing slopes of his property. Here, too, the grapes have been sold to others, but he is now retaining sufficient to make around 450 cases a year.

 Yarra Valley Rose 2006 This is real wine: hand-picked pinot noir, barrel-fermented with wild yeast and lees-stirred; vivid colour notwithstanding the barrel ferment; very stylish, more into light-bodied pinot than rose, perhaps; perfect balance; 250 cases made. Screwcap. 12.5° alc. **Rating** 92 **To** 2008 $15
Hill Paddock Yarra Valley Chardonnay 2005 Attractive wine; ripe melon and white peach fruit; the winemaker inputs obvious (wild yeast, barrel ferment, new and old French oak) but not excessive; the wine does finish fractionally short. Screwcap. 12.8° alc. **Rating** 90 **To** 2013 $25
Hill Paddock Yarra Valley Shiraz 2005 Light- to medium-bodied, with spicy/peppery overtones to the black and red cherry fruits; elegant and balanced, still building mid-palate weight. Cork. 13.5° alc. **Rating** 90 **To** 2012 $30

Graham Cohen Wines ★★★★☆

PO Box 195, Bannockburn, Vic 3331 **Region** Geelong
T (03) 5281 7438 **F** (03) 5281 7387 **Open** Not
Winemaker Simon Black **Est.** 1985 **Cases** 100

Graham and Jan Cohen have established 1 ha of pinot noir, which produces a sole wine called Captains Birchwood. The unusual name was chosen by the Cohens' 4 sons, each one in turn House Captain of Birchwood House at their school.

🍷🍷🍷🍷🍷 **Captains Birchwood Pinot Noir 2005** Light- to medium-bodied; fine, elegant and delicate small red fruits with a nice touch of spice to add interest; good length. **Rating** 92 **To** 2011

Gralaine Vineyard

65 Feehan's Road, Mount Duneed, Vic 3216 (postal) **Region** Geelong
T 0429 009 973 **F** (03) 9886 7377 **Open** At Hanging Rock Winery
Winemaker Hanging Rock Winery **Est.** 1983 **Cases** NA
Graeme and Elaine Carroll have gradually established 4 ha of low-yielding merlot (with a few cabernet sauvignon vines). There are no cellar door sales, but the wine can be tasted at Hanging Rock Winery.

Gralyn Estate

Caves Road, Wilyabrup, WA 6280 **Region** Margaret River
T (08) 9755 6245 **F** (08) 9755 6136 www.gralyn.com.au **Open** 7 days 10.30–4.30
Winemaker Graham Hutton, Merilyn Hutton, Dr Bradley Hutton **Est.** 1975 **Cases** 3000
The move from primarily fortified wine to table wine production has been completed, and with considerable success. The red wines are made in a distinctively different style from most from Margaret River, with an opulence which is reminiscent of some of the bigger wines from McLaren Vale. The age of the vines (30+ years) and the site are significant factors. Exports to the US.

🍷🍷🍷🍷🍷 **Margaret River Chardonnay 2005** Considerable fruit intensity and varietal character; nectarine and grapefruit not compromised by too much oak; good length and finish. Excellent chardonnay from a red wine specialist. Screwcap. 13.2° alc. **Rating** 94 **To** 2017 $35

🍷🍷🍷🍷🍷 **Margaret River Cabernet Shiraz 2005** Has the usual power and concentration of Gralyn, but not quite the depth of sweet fruit of its best vintages. Nonetheless, impressive and will develop in bottle. Cork. 14.3° alc. **Rating** 93 **To** 2025 $90
Reserve Margaret River Shiraz 2004 Medium-bodied; savoury, spicy overtones to blackberry fruit; well-integrated oak and tannins; good length. Cork. 14.8° alc. **Rating** 92 **To** 2024 $90

Grampians Estate ★★★★★

366 Mafeking Road, Willaura, Vic 3379 **Region** Grampians
T (03) 5354 6245 **F** (03) 5354 6257 www.grampiansestate.com.au **Open** By appt
Winemaker Contract **Est.** 1989 **Cases** 1000
Local farmers and graziers Sarah and Tom Guthrie diversified their activities, while continuing to run their fat lamb and wool production with 2 ha of shiraz and 1.2 ha of chardonnay. In 2006, 90% of the vineyard was devastated by bushfire; various wineries from across Vic donated grapes and wine ensuring the production of wine for the year.

🍷🍷🍷🍷🍷 **Streeton Reserve Shiraz 2004** A typically complex wine in both texture and flavour; blackberry with touches of licorice and chocolate; excellent silky tannins and oak, likewise length. Cork. 15° alc. **Rating** 96 **To** 2024 $55

🍷🍷🍷🍷🍷 **Rutherford Sparkling Shiraz 2004** A superior example, well-balanced, fine and long with plenty of flavour. Hand-picked and estate-grown; however, I am far from convinced this is the best use for the grapes. 14.6° alc. **Rating** 93 **To** 20214 $28

Grancari Estate Wines

50 Northumberland Road, Onkaparinga Hills, SA 5163 **Region** McLaren Vale
T (08) 8382 4465 **F** (08) 8382 4465 **www**.grancariwines.com.au **Open** By appt
Winemaker Rino Ozzella, Greta Ozzella, James Hastwell (Consultant) **Est.** 1999
Cases 2000
In 1983 Rino and Greta Ozzella purchased a small vineyard in McLaren Vale which had been planted in the early 1940s to a little under 3 ha of grenache; the grapes were sold to other winemakers. Later, they planted a further 3 ha of shiraz on a westerly slope facing the sea, and decided to establish their own brand. At the same time they began the conversion to organic production, which has now been certified (in conversion). Exports to Denmark.

ŸŸŸŸŸ **Old Vine McLaren Vale Grenache 2004** Juicy black fruits in abundance ranging through plum, blackberry and raspberry; soft tannins, long finish; vines planted 1943; high-quality cork. 15° alc. **Rating** 90 **To** 2015 $28

ŸŸŸŸ **Organic McLaren Vale Shiraz 2005** Very typical McLaren Vale Shiraz, with high-octane alcohol, rich, dark berry fruits, and a coating of chocolate, oak essentially a bystander. Cork. 15.5° alc. **Rating** 89 **To** 2025 $32
Organic McLaren Vale Shiraz 2004 Strong colour; extremely ripe fruit with essency/jammy overtones, almost into Italian Amarone style; for aficionados of such. Cork. 16° alc. **Rating** 89 **To** 2019 $32

Granite Hills

1481 Burke and Wills Track, Baynton, Kyneton, Vic 3444 **Region** Macedon Ranges
T (03) 5423 7264 **www**.granitehills.com.au **Open** Mon–Sat 10–6, Sun 12–6
Winemaker Llew Knight, Ian Gunter **Est.** 1970 **Cases** 7000
Granite Hills is one of the enduring classics, pioneering the successful growing of riesling and shiraz in an uncompromisingly cool climate. It is based on 11 ha of riesling, chardonnay, shiraz, cabernet sauvignon, merlot and pinot noir (the last also used in its sparkling wine). After a quiet period in the 1990s, it has been reinvigorated, with its original 2 icons once again to the fore. The Rieslings age superbly, and the Shiraz is at the forefront of the cool-climate school in Australia. Exports to the UK, the US and Canada.

ŸŸŸŸŸ **Macedon Ranges Riesling 2006** The bouquet is slightly closed, though not reduced; the pure and piercing palate is driven by apple and citrus fruit, with faint echoes of spice and mineral leading into a long, vibrant finish. Screwcap. 13° alc. **Rating** 95 **To** 2016 $20
Macedon Ranges Shiraz 2003 Very good, full purple-red; fragrant and spicy aromas lead into a vibrant and intense palate of blackberry, licorice and spice; destined for a very long life under the protection of its screwcap. **Rating** 95 **To** 2028 $32

ŸŸŸŸŸ **Reserve Chardonnay 2004** Fragrant, fine, cool-climate style; citrus, almost into mineral/wet pebble characters; delicate winemaking; good length; will be long-lived. Screwcap. 13.5° alc. **Rating** 93 **To** 2015 $30

ŸŸŸŸ **Macedon Ranges Pinot Noir 2004** Light red; a sappy, spicy, stemmy style; has considerable length, and is not green, but does need more sweet fruit. Screwcap. 14° alc. **Rating** 88 **To** 2010 $24

Granite Range Estate

183 Wilson Road, Wangandary, Vic 3678 **Region** Glenrowan
T (03) 5725 3292 **F** (03) 5725 3292 **www**.graniterangeestate.com.au **Open** Tues–Sun 10–5
Winemaker Peter Long **Est.** 1998 **Cases** 2000
This is the retirement venture of Peter and Maureen Long, who acquired a 16-ha bare-paddock in 1997, with the Warby Ranges behind and a panoramic view of the Australian Alps. The following year they established 2.3 ha each of shiraz and merlot, and a grape purchase contract with Baileys of Glenrowan. Since 2003 production has been split between sales to other

producers, and wine under the Granite Range Estate label. The modern building complex comprises the Longs' house, cellar door, barrel store and self-contained accommodation.

Granite Ridge Wines

Sundown Road, Ballandean, Qld 4382 **Region** Granite Belt
T (07) 4684 1263 **F** (07) 4684 1250 **Open** 7 days 9–5
Winemaker Dennis Ferguson, Juliane Ferguson **Est.** 1995 **Cases** 2000
Formerly known as Denlana Ferguson Estate Wines, Granite Ridge had considerable success in the mid-1990s. Its Goldies Unwooded Chardonnay was the first Qld wine to be chosen as the official Parliamentary Wine of the Qld Government. Most of the production comes from its 5-ha vineyard, which is planted to pinot gris, chardonnay, verdelho, merlot, shiraz, petit verdot, tempranillo and cabernet sauvignon. Exports to Singapore.

Grant Burge

Jacobs Creek, Barossa Valley, SA 5352 **Region** Barossa Valley
T (08) 8563 3700 **F** (08) 8563 2807 **www**.grantburgewines.com.au **Open** 7 days 10–5
Winemaker Grant Burge **Est.** 1988 **Cases** 320 000
As one might expect, this very experienced industry veteran makes consistently good, full-flavoured and smooth wines chosen from the pick of the crop of his extensive vineyard holdings, which total an impressive 440 ha; the immaculately restored/rebuilt stone cellar door sales buildings are another attraction. The provocatively named The Holy Trinity (Grenache/Shiraz/Mourvedre) joins Shadrach and Meshach at the top of the range. In 1999 Grant Burge repurchased the farm from Mildara Blass by acquiring the Krondorf winery in Tanunda (not the brand) in which he made his first fortune. He has renamed it Barossa Vines and has opened a cellar door offering casual food, featuring local produce wherever possible. A third cellar door (Illaparra) is open at Murray Street, Tanunda. Exports to all major markets.

ΨΨΨΨΨ **Thorn Vineyard Riesling 2005** Abundant flavour without compromising the fine and elegant style; lime, passionfruit, apple and spice; excellent line and balance. Screwcap. 12° alc. **Rating** 94 **To** 2015 $16
Filsell Barossa Valley Shiraz 2004 Great colour; a magical mix of fleshy and firmer fruit, great balance and mouthfeel; savoury tannins provide discipline. Cork. 14.5° alc. **Rating** 94 **To** 2019 $30

ΨΨΨΨΨ **East Argyle Eden Valley Pinot Gris 2006** Classic apple, pear, spice and musk aromas; the lively palate has good length and a crisp finish; a particularly good example of pinot gris. Screwcap. 13° alc. **Rating** 90 **To** 2008 $15.95
Hillcot Merlot 2004 Great colour; attractive redcurrant and blackcurrant mix; good control of alcohol, oak and tannins all help a stylish wine, particularly given the region. Cork. 14° alc. **Rating** 90 **To** 2011 $16

ΨΨΨΨ **Kraft Sauvignon Blanc 2005** Light straw-green; full-on high-flavoured, tropical fruit bouquet and palate; small part barrel-fermented; in precisely the same style slot as previous vintages. Screwcap. 12.5° alc. **Rating** 89 **To** 2008 $15
Adelaide Hills and Barossa Viognier 2005 Big, bold, rich style with apricot fruit in abundance; seamless oak and fruit fusion. Screwcap. 14.5° alc. **Rating** 89 **To** 2008 $20
Lily Farm Frontignac 2005 Gently floral, spice and grape aromas; fruit, not residual sugar sweetness; Asian food special. Screwcap. 11.5° alc. **Rating** 89 **To** 2008 $11

Grassy Point Wines

Coatsworth Farm, 145 Coatsworth Road, Portarlington, Vic 3223 **Region** Geelong
T 0409 429 608 **www**.grassypointwines.com.au **Open** By appt
Winemaker Provenance (Scott Ireland) **Est.** 1997 **Cases** 800
Partners David Smith, Robert Bennett and Kerry Jones purchased this 32-ha undeveloped grazing property in 1997. Coatsworth Farm now has 8 ha of vines (chardonnay, sauvignon blanc,

pinot noir, shiraz, merlot, malbec and cabernet franc), South Devon beef cattle and Perendale/White Suffolk-cross lambs.

 Bellarine Peninsula Chardonnay 2005 Very aromatic; high-quality chardonnay varietal expression throughout; long finish. **Rating** 93 **To** 2012 $20
Bellarine Peninsula Pinot Noir 2005 Attractive varietal character, with savoury/spicy edges to bright cherry and plum fruit; good length and balance; value from a little-known producer. **Rating** 90 **To** 2011 $18
Bellarine Peninsula Shiraz 2005 Fine, elegant, spicy black cherry aromas; medium-bodied, with the flavours tracking the bouquet; pleasing silky finish. Cork. **Rating** 90 **To** 2015 $18

 Bellarine Peninsula Sauvignon Blanc 2006 A closed bouquet, but no hint of sweatiness; on the palate, a light mix of grassy/herbal and gently tropical fruit. Screwcap. 12.8° alc. **Rating** 87 **To** 2008 $15
Bellarine Peninsula Cabernets 2004 Firm, quite attractive blackcurrant fruit within a complex structure. Cabernet Franc/Malbec. **Rating** 87 **To** 2011 $14

Greatstone Wines ★★☆

PO Box 245, Lonsdale, SA 5160 **Region** Limestone Coast Zone
T (08) 8357 2999 **F** (08) 8373 5917 **www.**greatstone-wines.com **Open** Not
Winemaker Ulrich Grey-Smith **Est.** NA **Cases** NFP
This is a very large grapegrowing and winemaking enterprise, with industry veteran (and politician) Dale Baker on the board assisting Chief Executive Ken Waldron. Its major asset is the largest independent contract winery in the Coonawarra region, with a capacity of 3.5 million litres, and as well as handling fruit grown throughout the Limestone Coast takes grapes from as far away as the Riverland. The home vineyard is The Eliza Lawson Vineyard, with 150 ha of chardonnay, shiraz, cabernet, merlot and sauvignon blanc. It has 4 quite separate series of wines in its portfolio, the best known being Padthaway Estate (see separate entry). Much of the sales and marketing business is focused on Asia.

Green Valley Vineyard ★★★☆

3137 Sebbes Road, Forest Grove, WA 6286 **Region** Margaret River
T (08) 9757 7510 **F** (08) 9757 7510 **www.**greenvalleyvineyard.com.au **Open** 7 days 10–5
Winemaker Moss Wood **Est.** 1980 **Cases** 3000
Owners Ed and Eleanore Green began developing Green Valley Vineyard in 1980; though still a part-time operation, production has grown steadily from the 7.7 ha of vines, and the Cabernet Sauvignon has been a consistent medal winner. Exports to the US and Singapore.

Greenbrier Park Vineyard ★★★☆

Old South Road, Mittagong, NSW 2575 **Region** Southern Highlands
T (02) 4862 2028 **F** (02) 4862 2028 **Open** Fri–Sun & public hols 10–4
Winemaker Eddy Rossi **Est.** 1999 **Cases** 700
Industry veteran Robert Constable, former director of Hungerford Hill, has established Greenbrier Park Vineyard at an altitude of 740 m on north-facing basalt soils, with cool winds and low frost risk. The original plantings of 0.35 ha of cabernet sauvignon, 0.48 ha of sauvignon blanc and 0.21 ha of pinot noir were extended with the planting of 0.35 ha of pinot noir in 2005.

Greenstone Vineyard ★★★★★

319 Whorouly South Road, Whorouly South, Vic 3735 (postal) **Region** Heathcote
T (03) 5727 1434 **F** (03) 5727 1434 **www.**greenstoneofheathcote.com **Open** Not
Winemaker Sandro Mosele (Contract), Alberto Antonini **Est.** 2002 **Cases** 3000
This is one of the most interesting new ventures to emerge over the past few years, bringing together David Gleave MW, born and educated in Canada, but now a long-term UK resident, managing an imported wine business and writing widely about the wines of Italy; Alberto Antonini, a graduate of the University of Florence, with postgraduate degrees from Bordeaux and

University of California (Davis), and Italian Flying Winemaker; and Mark Walpole, a 20-year veteran with Brown Brothers and now manager of their 700 ha of vineyards. The partners have chosen what they consider an outstanding vineyard on the red soil of the Heathcote region, planted to 17 ha of shiraz, and 1 ha each of monastrell (mourvedre), sangiovese and tempranillo. The quality of the wines is not in doubt.

�♟♟ **Shiraz 2005** A very complex and highly fragrant bouquet with oriental spice aromas; a beautifully fine-grained palate, long, fine and gently savoury. Screwcap. 13.5° alc. **Rating** 95 **To** 2012 $35

🍇 Greg Cooley Wines ★★★★

Lot 2 & 4 Seipelt Lane, Penwortham, SA 5453 (postal) **Region** Clare Valley
T (08) 8843 4284 **Open** Not
Winemaker Greg Cooley **Est.** 2002 **Cases** 1200
Greg Cooley says, 'I followed the traditional path to winemaking via accountancy, fraud squad, corporate investigations, running a Wendy's Supa Sundaes franchise and then selling residential property. I left the property market in Brisbane just as the boom started in 2001 and moved to the beautiful Clare just about when the wine glut started. Things didn't look overly promising when my first wine entered into the Clare Show in 2003. The Riesling came 97th of a total of 97, a platform on which I have since built, having sought loads of advice from local winemakers and subsequently winning a medal the following year.' He explains, 'All my wines are named after people who have been of influence to me in my 45 years and their influence is as varied as the wine styles – from pizza shop owners, to my greyhound's vet and, indeed, my recently departed greyhound Tigger.' I have to confess that I am taken by Greg Cooley's path to glory because my move through law to wine was punctuated by the part-ownership of 2 greyhounds that always wanted to run in the opposite direction to the rest of the field.

♟♟♟♟♡ **Bennett & Byrne Reserve Clare Valley Shiraz 2004** Rich, ripe (but not jammy) black cherry and blackberry fruit on a medium- to full-bodied palate; quiescent tannins and oak. Screwcap. 14.5° alc. **Rating** 91 **To** 2019 $27

♟♟♟♟ **Glynn & Pini Clare Valley Merlot 2004** Medium-bodied, with fresh cassis, raspberry and cherry fruits; gentle oak and tannin handling appropriate. Screwcap. 14.5° alc. **Rating** 89 **To** 2013 $18
Terry & Suzy Clare Valley Cabernet Shiraz 2004 Medium-bodied; very much in the Greg Cooley style; balanced, ripe fruit (even at 13.2° alcohol), tannins and oak, the last certainly adding a touch of sweetness. An easily enjoyed wine. Screwcap. 13.2° alc. **Rating** 89 **To** 2015 $18
Dan & Braschie Clare Valley Chardonnay 2006 Well-made, but proves once again Clare Valley and chardonnay are incompatible bed-mates, even with a dash of viognier as a lubricant. Screwcap. 14.5° alc. **Rating** 88 **To** 2008 $16
Dopity Brownhill Clare Valley Sparkling Shiraz 2004 Well-constructed, with no pretence; not too sweet, and not overtly oaked. These wines improve in bottle over many years if they start off with the appropriate balance, as this one does. 13.5° alc. **Rating** 87 **To** 2012 $20

Gregory's Wines ★★★☆

1 Lizard Park Drive, Kilkerran, SA 5573 **Region** The Peninsulas Zone
T (08) 8834 1258 **F** (08) 8834 1287 **Open** 7 days 10–4.30
Winemaker John Zilm **Est.** 1997 **Cases** 2500
Rod and Toni Gregory have 11 ha of vineyard near Maitland, on the western side of the York Peninsula planted to chardonnay, viognier, shiraz and cabernet sauvignon. The site has facilities to cater for concerts or festivals, and tours by arrangement. Exports to the US and Canada.

Grey Sands

Cnr Kerrisons Road/Frankford Highway, Glengarry, Tas 7275 **Region** Northern Tasmania
T (03) 6396 1167 **www**.greysands.com.au **Open** Last Sun of month 10–5, or by appt
Winemaker Bob Richter **Est.** 1989 **Cases** 800
Bob and Rita Richter began the establishment of Grey Sands in 1989, slowly increasing the
plantings to the present total of 2.5 ha. The ultra-high density of 8900 vines per ha reflects the
experience gained by the Richters during a 3-year stay in England, when they visited many
vineyards across Europe, and Bob Richter's graduate diploma from Roseworthy College.

Pinot Noir 2005 Great colour; a medium-bodied wine offering a smooth and
subtle interplay between red and black fruits; balanced and elegant; there is a
question of brett, however. **Rating** 92 **To** 2012

Griffin Wines

PO Box 221, Clarendon, SA 5157 **Region** Adelaide Hills
T (08) 8377 1300 **F** (08) 8377 3015 **www**.griffinwines.com **Open** Not
Winemaker Phil Christiansen, Shaw & Smith, Kangarilla Road, Di Fabio Estate **Est.** 1997
Cases 1500
The Griffin family (Trevor, Tim, Mark and Val) planted 26 ha of pinot noir, chardonnay, sauvignon
blanc, merlot and shiraz in 1997, having owned the property for over 30 years. It is situated 3 km
from Kuitpo Hall; its 350 m elevation gives sweeping views south down the valley below.

Adelaide Hills Shiraz 2004 Medium-bodied; lovely focus and definition to
the spicy black and red fruits; fine tannins and a vibrant finish; super-elegant.
Screwcap. 14° alc. **Rating** 94 **To** 2019 $20

Adelaide Hills Sauvignon Blanc 2006 A faint touch of reduction on the
bouquet, but the palate pulls the wine through, with herbaceous, lime and
gooseberry flavours; good length. Screwcap. 13° alc. **Rating** 90 **To** 2008 $18
Adelaide Hills Merlot 2004 Medium-bodied; olive, earth and spice varietal
characters sit adjacent to ripe blackcurrant fruit; good balance and length. Cork.
14° alc. **Rating** 90 **To** 2013 $22

Grosset

King Street, Auburn, SA 5451 **Region** Clare Valley
T (08) 8849 2175 **F** (08) 8849 2292 **www**.grosset.com.au **Open** Wed–Sun 10–5 from
1st week of September for approx 6 weeks
Winemaker Jeffrey Grosset **Est.** 1981 **Cases** 9200
Jeffrey Grosset served part of his apprenticeship at the vast Lindeman Karadoc winery, moving
from the largest to one of the smallest when he established Grosset Wines in its old stone winery.
He crafts the wines with the utmost care from grapes grown to the most exacting standards; all
need a certain amount of time in bottle to achieve their ultimate potential, not the least the
Rieslings and Gaia, which are among Australia's best examples of their kind. He is also a passionate
advocate of the use of screwcaps on all wines. Exports to all major markets.

Polish Hill Riesling 2006 Bell-clear apple and lime blossom aromas lead into
a precise palate with a magical combination of delicacy and extreme length.
Screwcap. 12.5° alc. **Rating** 96 **To** 2021 $40
Adelaide Hills Pinot Noir 2005 Outstanding clarity and hue; the usual spotless
bouquet of plum, cherry and spice; flawless structure and balance, the flavours
tracking the bouquet. Unfairly lives in the shadow of the rieslings, when the wine
is, if anything, better. Screwcap. 14° alc. **Rating** 96 **To** 2015 $60
Semillon Sauvignon Blanc 2006 As ever, totally immaculate handling of oak and
fruit alike; a seamless flow of gentle citrus and herb flavours through the long palate
and finish. Screwcap. 13° alc. **Rating** 95 **To** 2011 $30
Piccadilly Adelaide Hills Chardonnay 2005 A glorious, though finely framed,
bouquet; perfectly balanced and seamless palate with melon, nectarine and grapefruit
plus a touch of cashew. Screwcap. 14° alc. **Rating** 95 **To** 2015 $50

Watervale Riesling 2006 More powerful and complex than the Polish Hill, but with slightly less purity of line; mineral, herb and citrus notes. Screwcap. 13° alc. **Rating** 94 **To** 2016 $30

Gaia 2004 Excellent, bright purple-red; in typical fashion, medium-bodied – even light- to medium-bodied – but very fresh and harmonious, with fruit, oak and tannins precisely fashioned and balanced. Will live far longer than one might imagine. Cabernet Sauvignon/Cabernet Franc/Merlot. Screwcap. 13.5° alc. **Rating** 94 **To** 2029 $53

Grove Estate Wines ★★★★☆

Murringo Road, Young, NSW 2594 **Region** Hilltops
T (02) 6382 6999 **www**.groveestate.com.au **Open** W'ends 10–5, or by appt
Winemaker Clonakilla (Tim Kirk), Madrez Wine Services (Chris Derrez) **Est.** 1989
Cases 3000
A partnership of Brian Mullany, John Kirkwood and Mark Flanders has established a 30-ha vineyard planted to semillon, chardonnay, merlot, shiraz, cabernet sauvignon and zinfandel. Some of the grapes are sold (principally to Fosters), but an increasing amount of very good and interesting wine is contract-made for the Grove Estate label. Exports to the UK.

ҮҮҮҮҮ **Reserve Nebbiolo 2006** Has lovely cherry fruit running through the palate, its oft-quoted similarity to pinot easy to see. One of a small handful of nebbiolos to succeed in Australia. Screwcap. 15° alc. **Rating** 92 **To** 2013 $40

Cellar Block Shiraz 2005 Bright, deep purple-red; a medium-bodied mix of black pepper, spice, blackberry and plum fruit supported by firm, fine tannins; subtle oak. Screwcap. 14° alc. **Rating** 91 **To** 2025 $35

The Partners Cabernet Sauvignon 2005 A spicy, earthy edge to the aromas; light- to medium-bodied, with a pleasing marriage of blackcurrant, cassis and cedar oak; fine, almost fluffy, tannins. Screwcap. 13.9° alc. **Rating** 90 **To** 2015 $25

ҮҮҮҮ **The Partners Cabernet Sauvignon 2006** Cassis as much as blackcurrant drives the bouquet; the medium-bodied palate has bright fruit and fine tannins; miraculously, the wine has not been emasculated by the alcohol. Screwcap. 16° alc. **Rating** 89 **To** 2016 $25

The Partners Reserve Sangiovese Nebbiolo Petit Verdot Barbera 2004 Just about the most weird Franco-Italian blend imaginable; quite fragrant, the flavours lively but otherwise impossible to describe coherently. Screwcap. 14.5° alc. **Rating** 89 **To** 2010 $25

Growlers Gully NR

354 Shaws Road, Merton, Vic 3715 **Region** Upper Goulburn
T (03) 5778 9615 **F** (03) 5778 9615 **Open** W'ends & public hols 10–5, or by appt
Winemaker MasterWineMakers **Est.** 1997 **Cases** NA

GrumbleBone Estate Vineyard ★★★☆

PO Box 989, Bowral, NSW 2576 **Region** Southern Highlands
T (02) 4878 5335 **F** (02) 4862 3383 **Open** Not
Winemaker Suzanne Little (Contract) **Est.** 1998 **Cases** 2000
Dr Paul Sibraa, and wife Pamela, purchased a former grazing property in 1992. It is situated at an elevation of 600 m on the ranges between Bowral and Mittagong, and planting of the 22.5 ha of vines began in 1998. In descending order of area, the varieties are chardonnay, merlot, pinot noir, cabernet sauvignon, pinot gris, shiraz and sauvignon blanc. In 2005 Paul Sibraa decided to produce single vineyard wines under the GrumbleBone label, his inspiration going back to '78 when he first met Max Lake in his Hunter Valley winery.

ҮҮҮҮ **Chardonnay 2006** Clean, citrussy edge to stone fruit and melon flavours; any oak present is not obvious; the wine does have weight and mouthfeel. Screwcap. **Rating** 88 **To** 2010 $18

Guichen Bay Vineyards

PO Box 582, Newport, NSW 2106 **Region** Mount Benson
T (02) 9997 6677 **F** (02) 9997 6177 **www**.guichenbay.com.au **Open** At Mount Benson
Tourist & Wine Information Centre
Winemaker Cape Jaffa Wines (Derek Hooper), Ralph Fowler Wines (Sarah Squires)
Est. 2003 **Cases** 850
Guichen Bay Vineyards is one of 3 adjacent vineyards known collectively as the Mount Benson
Community Vineyards. Between 1997 and 2001, 120 ha of vines were planted to chardonnay,
sauvignon blanc, shiraz, merlot and cabernet sauvignon. While the major part of the production
is sold, the owners have obtained a producer's licence, and a small quantity of grapes is held
back and made by local winemakers under the Guichen Bay Vineyards label.

ΨΨΨΨΨ **Mount Benson Shiraz 2005** Dark colour; massively rich and potent prune
and blackberry jam flavours; better picked earlier, but you cannot deny the
richness, and the US market will adore it. Screwcap. 15.5° alc. **Rating** 91
To 2025 $20

ΨΨΨΨ **Mount Benson Cabernet Sauvignon 2005** Very powerful, focused and intense
cassis and blackcurrant supported by solid tannins. Has more varietal flavour than the
thunderous merlot. Screwcap. 14.5° alc. **Rating** 88 **To** 2015 $20

Gundowringla Wines

161 Boyd Road, Gundowring, Vic 3691 **Region** Alpine Valleys
T (02) 6028 9302 **F** (02) 6028 9302 **Open** Fri–Tues 10–5
Winemaker Mark Adams **Est.** 1996 **Cases** 600
Ian and Gertrud Adams began the establishment of their vineyard with the planting of cabernet
sauvignon in 1996, shiraz in 1997, and viognier in 2001, a total of 3 ha; subsequent grafting of
part of the cabernet sauvignon to merlot, cabernet franc and malbec has not increased the area.
It is very much a family affair, winemaking done by their 'chef-aspiring vigneron son, Mark'.
Situated on the snow road to Mt Beauty and Falls Creek running through the Kiewa Valley, it is
beautifully located. Mark handles private functions at Trudi's Kitchen Door.

ΨΨΨΨΨ **Kiewa Valley Cabernet Sauvignon 2002** Perfectly modulated cabernet
varietal fruit; blackcurrant with just a splash of cassis; medium-bodied, smooth
and supple, with controlled oak and tannins; impressive for the region. Cork.
14° alc. **Rating** 91 **To** 2017 $30
Kiewa Valley Shiraz Viognier 2004 A potent, rich wine, crammed with dark,
savoury fruits and bitter chocolate; a masculine version of the normally pretty
shiraz viognier blend; black cherry and licorice flavours. I wish I was certain
where the masculinity comes from. Cork. 14° alc. **Rating** 90 **To** 2014 $35

ΨΨΨΨ **Kiewa Valley Viognier 2004** Light straw-green; has developed slowly but
impressively in bottle with gently ripe pear, apricot and peach; a faint echo of
French oak; good balance and acidity. Screwcap. 14.3° alc. **Rating** 89 **To** 2009 $20
Kiewa Valley Cabernet Sauvignon 2004 The oak is very evident and, perhaps,
sweeter than desirable; blackcurrant, mocha and vanilla; soft tannins. Cork.
Rating 88 **To** 2019

Gypsy Creek Winery

43 School Road, Labertouche, Vic 3816 (postal) **Region** Gippsland
T (03) 5628 7679 **F** (03) 5628 7679 **Open** Not
Winemaker Jeff Wright **Est.** 1997 **Cases** 800
Sam Dardha arrived in Australia 35 years ago with wine in his veins from growing up in the
Macedonia/Northern Greece/Albania sector of Europe. He and wife Mary purchased the
property in 1995, planting 1 ha each of chardonnay and cabernet sauvignon and 0.5 ha each of
shiraz and pinot noir in 1997. The first commercial vintage was in 2004.

♟♟♟♟♗ **Shiraz 2005** Well-made; despite the relatively low alcohol, has appealing sweet cherry and blackberry fruits; fine tannins and good length; overall elegance. Diam. 13° alc. **Rating** 90 **To** 2013 $18

♟♟♟♟ **Chardonnay 2005** Rich, complex barrel ferment surrounds ripe stone fruit and good balance. Perhaps just a little heavy-footed. Screwcap. 13° alc. **Rating** 88 **To** 2010 $18

Haan Wines   ★★★★★

Siegersdorf Road, Tanunda, SA 5352 **Region** Barossa Valley
T (08) 8562 4590 **F** (08) 8562 4590 **www**.haanwines.com.au **Open** Not
Winemaker Mark Jamieson (Contract) **Est.** 1993 **Cases** 4500
Hans and Fransien Haan established their business in 1993 when they acquired a 19-ha vineyard near Tanunda (since extended to 36.7 ha). The primary focus is on merlot, in particular the luxury Merlot Prestige, supported by Semillon, Viognier and Shiraz. These are wines which polarise opinion; the issue is not alcohol, but the amount of oak used, and the way it is used. I think the outcome is very successful, but have never, and would never, seek to make wines in this style. Exports to all major markets.

♟♟♟♟♟ **Wilhelmus 2004** It is no surprise the Cabernet Sauvignon/Merlot/Cabernet Franc/Petit Verdot/Malbec should be so seamlessly welded, nor that there is synergy in the blend to give this wine the greatest fruit expression. Cork. 14.5° alc. **Rating** 95 **To** 2020 $49.95
Shiraz Prestige 2004 In typical style; partial barrel ferment invests the wine with particularly well-integrated oak and a silky texture; whether this places full emphasis on the varietal fruit is a matter of opinion, as, for that matter, is the overall style of Haan. Cork. 14.5° alc. **Rating** 94 **To** 2024 $47.50
Merlot Prestige 2004 As ever, a skein of tightly knit fruit, oak and tannins with the stamp of the maker (and oak) figuring large. It is a unique style; here sweet merlot fruit is there to be seen if you look for it. Cork. 14.5° alc. **Rating** 94 **To** 2020 $45

♟♟♟♟♗ **Viognier Prestige 2006** Full-throated, no holds barred wine; ripe apricot and peach fruit, but warms up on the finish more than usual; 150 cases made. Screwcap. 14.5° alc. **Rating** 90 **To** 2008 $35

Hackersley

Ferguson Road, Dardanup, WA 6236 **Region** Geographe
T (08) 9384 6247 **F** (08) 9383 3364 **www**.hackersley.com.au **Open** Thurs–Sun 10–4
Winemaker Tony Davis (Contract) **Est.** 1997 **Cases** 1200
Hackersley is a partnership between the Ovens, Stacey and Hewitt families, friends since their university days, and with (so they say) the misguided belief that growing and making their own wine would be cheaper than buying it. They found a 'little piece of paradise in the Ferguson Valley just south of Dardanup', and in 1998 they planted a little under 8 ha, extended since then to 11.5 ha of the mainstream varieties; interestingly, they turned their back on chardonnay. Most of the crop is sold to Houghton, but a small quantity is made for the Hackersley label.

♟♟♟♟♗ **Ferguson Valley Semillon 2006** Tight, minerally, grassy semillon with precise varietal character; fine, long and intense, the Ferguson Valley's response to the Hunter Valley; similar approach, but different terroir, and a different wine. Screwcap. 11° alc. **Rating** 92 **To** 2014 $22
Ferguson Valley Shiraz 2005 A light to medium-bodied wine with lively herbs, spices and cracked pepper sprinkled over the base of red and black fruits; a long, even finish; fine, savoury tannins. Screwcap. 14.5° alc. **Rating** 90 **To** 2020 $25
Victor Ferguson Valley Shiraz Cabernet 2005 Light to medium-bodied, but with plenty of flavour in the typical elegant Hackersley style; the sweeter fruit flavours of the shiraz (cherry and plum) prevail over the cabernet (blackberry and olive), but both sides seem content with their lot in life. Screwcap. 14° alc. **Rating** 90 **To** 2015 $25

Ferguson Valley Merlot 2005 Small red berry fruit flavours with just a hint of spice and olive; both texture and weight very good for merlot. Screwcap. 13.5° alc. **Rating** 90 **To** 2013 $25

Ferguson Valley Cabernet Sauvignon 2005 Quite fragrant; the aromas are predominantly in the cassis/red spectrum, the tannins fine and ripe, the oak balanced. Screwcap. 13.5° alc. **Rating** 90 **To** 2018 $25

♀♀♀♀ **Ferguson Valley Sauvignon Blanc 2006** A spotlessly clean, but relatively closed bouquet; tight and minerally; very similar to the Semillon, with only a touch of gooseberry; low alcohol either due to early picking or the cool summer (or both). Screwcap. 11.5° alc. **Rating** 89 **To** 2009 $18

Ferguson Valley Verdelho 2006 The varietal fruit needs to be very good in the first place, and then aged in bottle for 3–5 years like chenin blanc, chardonnay and so forth. This has the acid balance to the fruit salad counterpoint to succeed, but you're left to wonder whether it is all worth it. Screwcap. 12.5° alc. **Rating** 87 **To** 2011 $18

Hahndorf Hill Winery ★★★★☆

Lot 10 Pains Road, Hahndorf, SA 5245 **Region** Adelaide Hills
T (08) 8388 7512 **F** (08) 8388 7618 **www.**hahndorfhillwinery.com.au **Open** 7 days 10–5
Winemaker Geoff Weaver (Consultant) **Est.** 2002 **Cases** 4000
Larry Jacobs and Marc Dobson, both originally from South Africa, purchased Hahndorf Hill Winery in 2002. Jacobs gave up a career in intensive-care medicine in 1988 when he purchased an abandoned property in Stellenbosch, and proceeded to establish one of Capetown's best-known sauvignon blanc producers, Mulderbosch. When Mulderbosch was purchased at the end of 1996, the pair migrated to Australia and eventually found their way to Hahndorf Hill. Rare German varieties trollinger and lemberger were planted by the prior owners. In 2006, the investment by the owners in the winery and cellar door was rewarded by induction into the SA Great Tourism Hall of Fame, having won the award for Best Tourism Winery for 3 consecutive years. Exports to the UK, the US, Poland, Hong Kong and Malaysia.

♀♀♀♀♀ **Adelaide Hills Pinot Grigio 2006** Excellent mouthfeel and balance a major plus, likewise a twist of lemony acidity; an impressive example of an unimpressive variety. Screwcap. 12.5° alc. **Rating** 93 **To** 2009 $22

Adelaide Hills Sauvignon Blanc 2006 Spotlessly clean; a delicate style with gooseberry, herb and grass aromas on entry, then a long finish with some tropical notes making their appearance. Screwcap. 12.5° alc. **Rating** 91 **To** 2008 $19

♀♀♀♀ **Adelaide Hills Shiraz 2004** An elegant, light-bodied wine with pleasing black fruits, but not quite enough depth and structure. Cork. 14.6° alc. **Rating** 89 **To** 2012 $26

Adelaide Hills White Mischief 2006 An uncomplicated, flavoursome, quaffing wine with astute acidity giving a fresh finish and aftertaste. Chardonnay/Sauvignon Blanc/Pinot Gris. Screwcap. 12.5° alc. **Rating** 87 **To** 2008 $18

Halifax Wines ★★★★

Lot 501 Binney Road, McLaren Vale, Willunga, SA 5172 **Region** McLaren Vale
T 0412 257 149 **F** (08) 8367 0333 **www.**halifaxwines.com.au **Open** By appt
Winemaker Peter Butcher **Est.** 2000 **Cases** 1000
Owned and operated by Elizabeth Tasker (background in advertising and marketing) and Peter Butcher (20+ years in the wine industry, in marketing, sales, distribution, education and winemaking). A passionate proponent of wine's 'sense of place', Peter has worked with some of Australia's most well-known winemakers – Jeffrey Grosset, Peter Leske, Mike Farmilo and Peter Gago – and has also been influenced by visits to France and Italy. Produces a single-vineyard Shiraz from 4 ha of estate plantings, supplemented by small quantities of grenache (50-year-old vines) and cabernet sauvignon (40-year-old vines). Exports to the US, Hong Kong and Belgium.

ŸŸŸŸŸ **McLaren Vale Shiraz 2005** Very sweet, rich, plush plummy fruit; whether this is too much of a good thing is a matter of opinion. Cork. 13.5° alc. **Rating** 90 To 2012 $35

Hamelin Bay   ★★★★☆

McDonald Road, Karridale, WA 6288 **Region** Margaret River
T (08) 9758 6779 **F** (08) 9758 6779 **www.hbwines.com.au Open** 7 days 10–5
Winemaker Julian Scott **Est.** 1992 **Cases** 15 000
The 25-ha Hamelin Bay vineyard was established by the Drake-Brockman family. The initial releases were contract-made, but a winery with cellar door sales facility was opened in 2000; this has enabled an increase in production. Exports to all major markets.

ŸŸŸŸŸ **Five Ashes Reserve Margaret River Chardonnay 2005** No hint of reduction; a lovely wine, creamy texture the opening impression, then layers of stone fruit and controlled quality oak; a long, fresh finish thanks to the modest alcohol. Screwcap. 13° alc. **Rating** 95 **To** 2017 $43

ŸŸŸŸŸ **Rampant White 2006** No reduction; lively, fresh and crisp, citrus, lime and grass establishing the theme, chardonnay a passenger; excellent balance and length; even better price. Semillon/Sauvignon Blanc/Chardonnay. Screwcap. 12° alc. **Rating** 90 **To** 2010 $18
Five Ashes Reserve Margaret River Shiraz 2004 Quite potent earthy/spicy overtones to the fruit; tannins in the same spectrum; stares you down. Cork. 14.5° alc. **Rating** 90 **To** 2014 $43

ŸŸŸŸ **Five Ashes Vineyard Margaret River Cabernet Sauvignon 2005** Medium-bodied; distinctly savoury/earthy nuances to black fruits, partially reflecting the moderately low alcohol; damned if you do, damned if you don't. Screwcap. 13.5° alc. **Rating** 89 **To** 2014 $29
Rampant Red 2005 A full-flavoured assemblage of red and black fruits; not for analysis, but for strictly informal consumption with hearty fare. Shiraz/Cabernet Sauvignon/Merlot. Screwcap. 13.5° alc. **Rating** 88 **To** 2010 $20
Five Ashes Vineyard Margaret River Semillon Sauvignon Blanc 2006 Some reduction issues, though less than with the Sauvignon Blanc, partly overcome by the drive of semillon through to a long, lingering finish. Screwcap. 12° alc. **Rating** 87 **To** 2009 $20
Five Ashes Vineyard Margaret River Shiraz 2004 Some eucalypt/menthol aromas with a slightly smoky edge; light to medium-bodied cherry/raspberry fruit; a slightly awkward wine. Cork. 14.5° alc. **Rating** 87 **To** 2009 $29

Hamilton's Ewell Vineyards

Siegersdorf Vineyard, Barossa Valley Way, Nuriootpa, SA 5355 **Region** Barossa Valley
T (08) 8231 0088 **F** (08) 8231 0355 **www.**hamiltonewell.com.au **Open** 7 days 10–5
Winemaker Robert Hamilton **Est.** 1837 **Cases** 11 000
Mark Hamilton, an Adelaide lawyer by profession, is a sixth-generation direct descendant of Richard Hamilton, who arrived in SA in 1838 (a year after the State was proclaimed) and made his first wine in 1841. Hamilton's Ewell Vineyards remained in the family until 1979, when it was acquired by Mildara Blass, much to Mark Hamilton's dismay. Since 1991 he has set about building another Hamilton wine business by a series of astute vineyard acquisitions, and by buying back the name Hamilton's Ewell from Mildara. Most of the grapes are sold, but there is scope to increase production. Exports to the UK, the US and other major markets.

Hamiltons Bluff

Longs Corner Road, Canowindra, NSW 2804 **Region** Cowra
T (02) 6344 2079 **F** (02) 6344 2165 **www.**hamiltonsbluff.com.au **Open** By appt
Winemaker Alasdair Sutherland (Contract) **Est.** 1995 **Cases** 2000

Hamiltons Bluff is owned and operated by the Andrews family, which planted 45 ha of vines in 1995, with the first crop in 1998. Cellar door sales opened in early 1999, heralding a new stage of development for the Cowra region. Exports to the US.

ƟƟƟƟ   **Sangiovese 2004** A spicy bouquet with fairly savoury, almost lemony, characters on the palate; fine tannins, good length. Screwcap. 15.2° alc. **Rating** 88 **To** 2008 $18

Hanging Rock Winery   ★★★★★

88 Jim Road, Newham, Vic 3442 **Region** Macedon Ranges
T (03) 5427 0542 **F** (03) 5427 0310 **www.**hangingrock.com.au **Open** 7 days 10–5
Winemaker John Ellis **Est.** 1982 **Cases** 40 000
The Macedon area has proved very marginal in spots, and the Hanging Rock vineyards, with their lovely vista towards the Rock, are no exception. John Ellis has thus elected to source additional grapes from various parts of Vic to produce an interesting and diverse range of varietals at different price points. Exports to the UK and other major markets.

ƟƟƟƟƟ   **Heathcote Shiraz 2004** The usual deep and bright colour; a multi-layered complex wine in both flavours and tannin texture; blackberry, spice and cracked pepper; magically controlled alcohol. Diam. 13° alc. **Rating** 95 **To** 2019 $60

ƟƟƟƟƟ   **Rowbottoms Heathcote Shiraz 2004** Despite the higher (but still moderate) alcohol has more aromas than the Heathcote Shiraz; fine-grained, savoury – almost lemony – tannins round off an unusual wine. Diam. 14° alc. **Rating** 92 **To** 2019 $33
Macedon Cuvee (Late Disgorged) NV VII. Very good mousse; a complex and high-quality wine, relatively full-bodied, and by dint of its age, yellow-gold. 12° alc. **Rating** 92 **To** 2008 $110
Macedon Brut Rose NV Full-on rose colour; fresh, crisp, with good length and an appealing, dry finish. 12.5° alc. **Rating** 92 **To** 2008 $27
Kilfara Pinot Noir 2005 A powerful wine, with its varietal character not in question; black cherry, with some stemmy forest floor notes; will improve. Bendigo/Yarra Valley/Macedon Ranges. Screwcap. 14° alc. **Rating** 90 **To** 2012 $24

ƟƟƟƟ   **Tarzali Strathbogie Ranges Riesling 2006** A solid wine, medium- to full-bodied in the context of riesling; ripe apple, citrus and pear fruit. Screwcap. 11.5° alc. **Rating** 88 **To** 2010 $18
The Jim Jim Sauvignon Blanc 2006 Firm and tight, with no sweaty characters, the downside being a fairly neutral flavour profile. 12° alc. **Rating** 87 **To** 2008 $27
Gralaine Merlot 2003 Strong green olive/savoury/earthy varietal fruit; just a little too uncompromising. 12.5° alc. **Rating** 87 **To** 2010 $27
Yin Barun Cabernet Franc 2004 Despite its alcohol, has some leaf and mint characters reflected in a slightly green finish; a difficult variety at the best of times. Diam. 15° alc. **Rating** 87 **To** 2010 $27

Hanging Tree Wines

Lot 2 O'Connors Road, Pokolbin, NSW 2325 **Region** Lower Hunter Valley
T (02) 4998 6601 **F** (02) 4998 6602 **www.**hangingtreewines.com.au **Open** By appt
Winemaker Andrew Thomas (Contract) **Est.** 2003 **Cases** 1250
Hanging Tree Wines is the former Van De Scheur Estate. A little under 3 ha of semillon, chardonnay, shiraz and cabernet sauvignon provide the grapes for the wines.

ƟƟƟƟƟ   **HVT Limited Release Hunter Valley Semillon Sauvignon Blanc 2006** Driven by Tumbarumba sauvignon blanc, even though semillon is the major component; plenty of tropical fruit, semillon acting to brace the finish. Screwcap. 12.4° alc. **Rating** 90 **To** 2010 $19

Hanson-Tarrahill Vineyard   ★★★★

49 Cleveland Avenue, Lower Plenty, Vic 3093 (postal) **Region** Yarra Valley
T (03) 9439 7425 **F** (03) 9439 4217 **Open** Not
Winemaker Dr Ian Hanson **Est.** 1983 **Cases** 1300
Dental surgeon Ian Hanson planted his first vines in the late 1960s, close to the junction of the
Yarra and Plenty Rivers; in 1983 those plantings were extended (with 3000 vines), and in 1988
the Tarrahill property at Yarra Glen was established with a further 4 ha. Exports to the UK.

ŶŶŶŶ   **Tarra's Block Cabernet Franc Cabernet Sauvignon 2004** Austere; strong
echoes of traditional Bordeaux-style red; slightly reduced, but has length and should
come around with more time in bottle. Diam. 13.5° alc. **Rating** 89 **To** 2019 $22
Pinot Noir 2004 Slightly hazy colour; some unusual hay/earth aromas, suggesting
it may have been slightly oxidised at some point in the transition to bottle. Diam.
13.5° alc. **Rating** 87 **To** 2010 $22

Happs   ★★★★★

571 Commonage Road, Dunsborough, WA 6281 **Region** Margaret River
T (08) 9755 3300 **F** (08) 9755 3846 **www.**happs.com.au **Open** 7 days 10–5
Winemaker Erl Happ, Mark Warren **Est.** 1978 **Cases** 20 000
Former schoolteacher turned potter and winemaker Erl Happ is an iconoclast and compulsive
experimenter. Many of the styles he makes are unusual, and the future is likely to be even more
so: the Karridale vineyard planted in 1994 has no less than 28 different varieties established.

ŶŶŶŶŶ   **Three Hills Chardonnay 2005** Light straw-green; elegant and fine; citrus and
stone fruit are integrated with perfectly judged oak; excellent length. Cork.
14° alc. **Rating** 94 **To** 2013 $27

ŶŶŶŶŶ   **Merlot 2004** A wine which offers well above-average power and
concentration without compromising varietal character, although it does need
patience; black olives, blackcurrant, controlled oak and tannins are all there; just
give them time. Cork. 14.5° alc. **Rating** 92 **To** 2019 $20
Fortis 2004 Intense red-purple; shows Happs' long experience with this
vintage port style; lots of black fruits, the baume not too high; savoury, fine
tannins. Cork. 18.5° alc. **Rating** 92 **To** 2015 $19
Margaret River Cabernet Merlot 2004 Cabernet plays the lead role in every
respect, autocratic and authoritarian; blackcurrant fruit with an earthy edge. Cork.
14.5° alc. **Rating** 91 **To** 2015 $20
Margaret River Sauvignon Blanc 2006 Medium-bodied; on the
asparagus/grassy side of the hill, but a nice, clean finish with a twist of
passionfruit. Well-priced. Cork. 12° alc. **Rating** 90 **To** 2008 $16
Margaret River Shiraz 2003 The colour doesn't promise much, but this light-
bodied wine has a spicy red fruit palate and vibrant finish. Cork. 14° alc. **Rating** 90
To 2013 $20

ŶŶŶŶ   **Margaret River Semillon Sauvignon Blanc 2006** Crisp, clean,
grassy/herbaceous bouquet, then a mix of gooseberry, asparagus and grass on the
palate. Twin top. 13° alc. **Rating** 89 **To** 2008 $16
Margaret River Chardonnay 2005 Melon and grapefruit plus obvious barrel
ferment oak; stalls slightly on the finish. Twin top. 14° alc. **Rating** 89 **To** 2011 $20
Margaret River Viognier 2005 Quite weighty and mouthfilling; rich, tropical
viognier with a not uncommon slightly congested finish; food style. Cork. 14.5° alc.
Rating 88 **To** 2008 $18
Marrimee Margaret River Unwooded Chardonnay 2006 Some melon and
stone fruit; good balance, and just creeps over the line. Twin top. 13.5° alc. **Rating** 87
To 2008 $16
Margaret River Cabernets 2003 Savoury, earthy, austere cabernet blend; slightly
old-fashioned, but does have length, and the tannins are controlled. Cork. 14° alc.
Rating 87 **To** 2011 $20

Harbord Wines

PO Box 41, Stockwell, SA 5355 **Region** Barossa Valley
T (08) 8562 2598 **F** (08) 8562 2598 **www**.harbordwines.com.au **Open** Not
Winemaker Roger Harbord **Est.** 2003 **Cases** 1000
Roger Harbord is a well-known and respected Barossa winemaker, with over 20 years'
experience, the last 10 as chief winemaker for Cellarmasters Wines, Normans and Ewinexchange.
He has set up his own virtual winery as a complementary activity; the grapes are contract-grown,
and he leases winery space and equipment to make and mature the wines. Exports to the UK,
the US, Canada and Singapore.

ΨΨΨΨΨ **The Tendril Barossa Valley Shiraz 2004** More elegant and restrained than
typical Barossa Valley shiraz, throwing the accent on bright red and black fruits
supported by fine tannins and controlled oak. A pleasure to drink. Screwcap.
14° alc. **Rating** 94 **To** 2019 $25

Harcourt Valley Vineyards

3339 Calder Highway, Harcourt, Vic 3453 **Region** Bendigo
T (03) 5474 2223 **www**.bendigowine.org.au **Open** 7 days 11–5 (11–6 during
daylight saving)
Winemaker Barbara, Kye and Quinn Livingstone **Est.** 1976 **Cases** 1500
Established by Ray and Barbara Broughton, the vineyard was handed over to John and Barbara
Livingstone in 1988. Barbara's Shiraz was created by Barbara Broughton, but with the arrival of the
'new' Barbara it lives on as the flagship of the vineyard. The Livingstones planted a further 2 ha of
shiraz on north-facing slopes with the aid of 2 sons, who, says Barbara, 'have since bolted, vowing
never to have anything to do with vineyards, but having developed fine palates'. John Livingstone
died in mid-2004, but Barbara continues her role of viticulturist; winemaking is now in the hands
of Barbara Livingstone and sons Kye and Quinn (who have returned to the fold after all).

ΨΨΨΨΨ **Riesling 2005** Clean, and full of flavour; the touch of sweetness is neatly balanced
by minerally acidity, leaving a dry aftertaste. Headed in the direction of the Mosel.
Surprise packet. Screwcap. 11.5° alc. **Rating** 90 **To** 2010 $16

ΨΨΨΨ **Barbara's Shiraz 2004** A lighter style than one might expect from this label –
perhaps a shadow of drought; light- to medium-bodied red and black fruits, with
good length and balance. Screwcap. 13.3° alc. **Rating** 89 **To** 2012 $25
Cabernet Sauvignon 2004 Light- to medium-bodied; distinctly earthy (varietal,
nonetheless) edges to the fruit; has length, but not depth. Screwcap. 13.5° alc.
Rating 87 **To** 2011 $25

Hardys

PPPPP

Reynell Road, Reynella, SA 5161 **Region** McLaren Vale
T (08) 8392 2222 **www**.hardys.com.au **Open** Mon–Fri 10–4.30, Sat 10–4, Sun 11–4
Winemaker Peter Dawson, Paul Lapsley, Ed Carr, Tom Newton **Est.** 1853 **Cases** 16 000
The 1992 merger of Thomas Hardy and the Berri Renmano group may well have had some of
the elements of a forced marriage when it took place, but the merged group prospered mightily
over the next 10 years. So successful was it that a further marriage followed in early 2003, with
Constellation Wines of the US the groom, and BRL Hardy the bride, creating the largest wine
group in the world. The Hardys wine brands are many and various, from the lowest price point
to the highest, and covering all the major varietals. They also make outstanding Vintage Port and
fine, wood-aged Brandy.

ΨΨΨΨΨ **Thomas Hardy Cabernet Sauvignon 2004** A rarely encountered fusion of
finesse, length and intensity; a remarkable wine for its varietal purity and
presence. From Margaret River, not Coonawarra. Multiple trophies National
Wine Show '06. Cork. 14° alc. **Rating** 97 **To** 2024 $110

Eileen Hardy Chardonnay 2004 Super-fragrant and flowery, it is fruit, rather than oak, forward, the long and intense palate with sweet citrus and nectarine fruit, plus a light web of creamy notes and fine French oak. Screwcap. 13.5° alc. **Rating** 96 **To** 2014 $38

Eileen Hardy Shiraz 2004 A towering style, yet in great balance; lovely black fruits woven through with quality oak and ripe tannins. Gold medal National Wine Show '06. Cork. 14.1° alc. **Rating** 96 **To** 2029 $110

Eileen Hardy Chardonnay 2005 The colour is a fraction more developed than expected when tasted in March '07; nectarine, grapefruit and melon set within creamy, nutty mlf and oak inputs; the length is exceptional. Tasmania/Tumbarumba. Screwcap. 13.5° alc. **Rating** 95 **To** 2014 $60

Reynell Basket Pressed McLaren Vale Shiraz 2004 A beautifully silky wine, with black fruits and dark chocolate interwoven with perfectly balanced oak and tannins. Gold medal National Wine Show '06. Cork. 14.2° alc. **Rating** 95 **To** 2024 $40

Starvedog Lane Adelaide Hills Chardonnay 2003 Developing with grace; excellent texture and structure; fine nectarine fruit and balanced barrel ferment oak. Gold medal National Wine Show '06. Screwcap. 13.2° alc. **Rating** 94 **To** 2012 $27

Chateau Reynella Shiraz 2004 Rich and ripe, with a supple cascade of red and black fruits supported by fine tannins; no semblance of dead fruit. All exported. Gold medal National Wine Show '06. **Rating** 94 **To** 2024

Thomas Hardy Cabernet Sauvignon 2001 Strong colour for age; enters the mouth quietly, then rapidly builds flavour; blackcurrant, spice, earth and vanilla are set alongside imposing tannins. Will likely outlive the quality cork. 13.5° alc. **Rating** 94 **To** 2031 $96

ŶŶŶŶŶ **Oomoo McLaren Vale Shiraz 2005** An elegant, medium-bodied wine with a ripple of flavours through blackberry, black cherry and dark chocolate, fine tannins and a touch of oak. Cork. 14° alc. **Rating** 93 **To** 2009 $12.95

Tintara Shiraz 2002 Blackberry, dark plum, chocolate and spice are all typical of the region and vintage; fine tannins and good oak; somehow falls a little short of expectations. Cork. 14.4° alc. **Rating** 93 **To** 2012 $42

Tintara Grenache 2003 Neatly encapsulates the difference between McLaren Vale and Barossa grenache; attractive, savoury, dark chocolate flavours surround the core of varietal juicy black fruit; has the structure Barossa often lacks. Cork. 14.5° alc. **Rating** 93 **To** 2011 $35

Oomoo McLaren Vale Grenache Shiraz Mourvedre 2005 Vibrantly sweet fruit, in the best sense – not jammy/confection; overall, fresh and zesty, with minimal tannins and oak. Screwcap. 14° alc. **Rating** 91 **To** 2008 $14

Sir James Vintage 2003 Light straw-green; fine and intense, with excellent focus and balance; citrus and stone fruit, plus a touch of biscuity lees character. 12.9° alc. **Rating** 90 **To** 2010 $25

ŶŶŶŶ **Padthaway Botrytis Riesling 2006** While needs time to open up and develop complexity, has both intensity and the requisite sweetness. Cork. 10° alc. **Rating** 88 **To** 2012 $21

Nottage Hill Cabernet Sauvignon 2005 Cleverly composed commercial wine; dark blackcurrant, mocha and vanilla; soft texture; ready to rip. Cork. 13.6° alc. **Rating** 87 **To** 2008 $8.20

Hare's Chase   ★★★★☆

PO Box 46, Melrose Park, SA 5039 **Region** Barossa Valley
T (08) 8277 3506 **F** (08) 8277 3543 **www.**hareschase.com **Open** Not
Winemaker Peter Taylor **Est.** 1998 **Cases** 2500

Hare's Chase is the creation of 2 families who own a 100-year-old vineyard in the Marananga Valley area of the Barossa Valley. The simple, functional winery sits at the top of a rocky hill in the centre of the vineyard, which has some of the best red soil available for dry-grown viticulture. The winemaking arm of the partnership is provided by Peter Taylor, a senior red winemaker with Penfolds for over 20 years, and now Fosters chief winemaker. Exports to the UK, the US and Switzerland.

🍷🍷🍷🍷🍷 **Barossa Red Blend 2005** A bright and fresh array of fruit aromas from the Joseph's Coat blend of Shiraz (61%)/Merlot (23%)/Cabernet Franc (9%)/Cabernet Sauvignon (4%)/Tempranillo (3%). Soft tannins and an appealing aftertaste. Screwcap. 14.5° alc. **Rating** 90 **To** 2011 $14

Harewood Estate   ★★★★★

Scotsdale Road, Denmark, WA 6333 **Region** Denmark
T (08) 9840 9078 **F** (08) 9840 9053 **www**.harewoodestate.com.au **Open** 7 days 10–4
Winemaker James Kellie **Est.** 1988 **Cases** 5000
In 2003 James Kellie, who for many years was a winemaker with Howard Park, and was responsible for the contract making of Harewood Wines since 1998, purchased the estate with his father and sister as partners. Events moved quickly thereafter: a 300-tonne winery was constructed, offering both contract winemaking services for the Great Southern region, and the ability to expand the Harewood range to include subregional wines that showcase the region. Exports to the UK, Thailand, Vietnam, Hong Kong and Singapore.

🍷🍷🍷🍷🍷 **Denmark Sauvignon Blanc Semillon 2006** Aromas from snow peas to gooseberry and passionfruit are mirrored on the palate, which has an outstanding finish and lingering aftertaste. Screwcap. 12° alc. **Rating** 95 **To** 2008 $19
Denmark Chardonnay 2005 Intense nectarine and grapefruit flavours run through the long palate; exemplary oak handling. Screwcap. 13.5° alc. **Rating** 94 **To** 2012 $25
Museum Release Chardonnay 2002 Has developed with the surety expected of the closure; still fresh and bright, with a lingering citrus and apple finish; minimal oak push. Screwcap. 13.5° alc. **Rating** 94 **To** 2008 $25
Frankland River Shiraz 2005 An attractive bouquet with blackberry, cracked pepper, and spice to the blackberry and cherry fruit; a rich palate, with excellent structure, ripe tannins and long finish. Screwcap. 15° alc. **Rating** 94 **To** 2025 $30

🍷🍷🍷🍷 **Denmark Riesling 2006** Clean, bracing crisp lime and lemon, plus pear and apple nuances; a long finish. Screwcap. 11.5° alc. **Rating** 92 **To** 2013 $21
Great Southern Cabernet Sauvignon 2005 An elegant wine on the entry and mid-palate, then an intense and challenging finish courtesy of the tannins; a roller-coaster ride which will almost certainly come together on the finish. Screwcap. 14.5° alc. **Rating** 91 **To** 2025 $30
Great Southern Shiraz Cabernet 2005 A substantial wine from start to finish; predominantly black fruits, with earthy, savoury edges; will evolve in bottle. Screwcap. 14.5° alc. **Rating** 90 **To** 2018 $21

Harmans Ridge Estate   ★★★★☆

Cnr Bussell Highway/Harmans Mill Road, Wilyabrup, WA 6284 **Region** Margaret River
T (08) 9755 7409 **F** (08) 9755 7400 **www**.harmansridge.com.au **Open** 7 days 10.30–5
Winemaker Paul Green **Est.** 1999 **Cases** 5000
Harmans Ridge Estate, with a crush capacity of 1600 tonnes, is primarily a contract maker for larger producers in the Margaret River region which do not have their own winery/winemaker. It does, however, have 2 ha of shiraz, and does make wines under the Harmans Ridge Estate label from grapes grown in Margaret River. Exports to the UK and the US.

🍷🍷🍷🍷 **Margaret River Semillon Sauvignon Blanc 2006** Tangy, lively and long citrus and grass flavours drive a vibrant, zesty palate. Screwcap. 12° alc. **Rating** 93 **To** 2010 $17

Margaret River Chardonnay 2006 Aromatic and lively; stone fruit, melon and citrus flavours; exceptional unoaked chardonnay, so often bland and boring. Screwcap. 14° alc. **Rating** 92 **To** 2013 $17

ŶŶŶŶ **Margaret River Chenin Blanc 2006** Chenin is simply a verdelho variant or substitute; easy-going fruit salad flavours; hard to fathom the line pricing of these wines. Screwcap. 12.5° alc. **Rating** 87 **To** 2008 $17

Harmony Row Vineyard   NR

362 Pastoria East Road, Pipers Creek near Kyneton, Vic 3444 **Region** Macedon Ranges
T (03) 5423 5286 www.harmonyrowvineyard.com.au **Open** W'ends 10–5
Winemaker Alison Cash, John Ellis, Llew Knight (Contract) **Est.** 1999 **Cases** NA
Originally known as Loxley Vineyard, this was the brainchild of Andrew Pattison, live music doyen, and banker Dennis Cartwright. The vision was to have a wine and music venue dedicated to blues, roots and country live music together with the production of high-quality wine. After a search, the property, with its great views and breathtaking sunsets, was acquired; around 20 music devotees and wine buffs invested in the venture. The property was renamed Harmony Row after a restructure of the ownership interests (Andrew Pattison having moved on early in the piece). Dennis and Alison Cartwright now manage the property, which offers concerts every Sunday, the music ranging across country, blues, roots, acoustic, folk, jazz and classical styles.

Harrington Glen Estate   ★★★★

88 Townsend Road, Glen Aplin, Qld 4381 **Region** Granite Belt
T (07) 4683 4388 **F** (07) 4683 4388 **Open** 7 days 10–4, Sat & public hols 10–5
Winemaker Jim Barnes, Stephen Oliver **Est.** 2003 **Cases** 1200
The Ireland family planted 2.8 ha of cabernet sauvignon, shiraz, merlot and verdelho vines in 1997. Red grapes not required for cellar door production are sold to local wine producers, and some white grapes are purchased from other Granite Belt grape producers. Overall wine quality is very good, putting it in the top echelon of Qld wineries.

ŶŶŶŶŶ **Reserve Shiraz 2005** Good purple-red; an attractive, lively and fresh varietal fruit mix of plum, blackberry and black cherry; good tannins and oak. Screwcap. 13.5° alc. **Rating** 90 **To** 2013 $18

ŶŶŶŶ **Reserve Cabernet Sauvignon 2005** Ripe black fruit, with a generous dollop of dark chocolate; rich and full in the mouth; very soft tannins. Screwcap. 14.5° alc. **Rating** 89 **To** 2014 $30
Shiraz Cabernet 2005 A fractionally reduced bouquet; medium-bodied, with blackcurrant/blackberry/earthy fruit slightly unfinished work in progress. Screwcap. 13.8° alc. **Rating** 87 **To** 2010 $20

Hartley Estate   ★★★★☆

260 Chittering Valley Road, Lower Chittering, WA 6084 **Region** Perth Hills
T (08) 9481 4288 **F** (08) 9481 4291 **Open** By appt
Winemaker Steve Hagan (Contract) **Est.** 1999 **Cases** 1700
While driving through the Chittering Valley one Sunday with his daughter Angela, and reminiscing about the times he had spent there with his father Hartley, Bernie Stephens saw a 'For Sale' sign on the property, and later that day the contract for sale was signed. Planting of 17 ha of vines began, with Cabernet Sauvignon and Shiraz released in 2003. They form part of the Generations Series, recognising the involvement of 3 generations of the family. The major part of the crop goes to Western Range Wines; the remainder made for the Hartley Estate label.

ŶŶŶŶŶ **Hannah's Hill Shiraz 2005** Youthful, but has elegance; a long, supple palate with blackberry, licorice and spice; good line and length. Cork. 14.5° alc. **Rating** 93 **To** 2025 $50

Hartz Barn Wines

1 Truro Road, Moculta, SA 5353 **Region** Eden Valley
T (08) 8563 9002 **F** (08) 8563 9002 **www**.hartzbarnwines.com.au **Open** By appt
Winemaker David Barnett **Est.** 1997 **Cases** 2300
Hartz Barn Wines was formed in 1997 by Penny Hart (operations director), David Barnett
(winemaker/director), Katrina Barnett (marketing director) and Matthew Barnett
(viticulture/cellar director), which may suggest that the operation is rather larger than it in fact is.
The business name and label have an unexpectedly complex background, too, involving elements
from all the partners. The grapes come from the 11.5-ha Dennistone Vineyard, which is planted
to merlot, shiraz, riesling, cabernet sauvignon, chardonnay and lagrein. Exports to NZ.

Haselgrove

150 Main Road, McLaren Vale, SA 5171 **Region** McLaren Vale
T (08) 8323 8706 **F** (08) 8323 8049 **www**.haselgrove.com.au **Open** 7 days 11–4
Winemaker Simon Parker **Est.** 1981 **Cases** 50 000
Changes in ownership throughout the late 1990s and early '00s have led to some confusion, and,
in particular, arising from the coexistence of Haselgrove and James Haselgrove Wines (Haselgrove
Vignerons). They are separately owned, and have no business relationship or dealings with each
other. Haselgrove is principally distributed in Australia through Liquorland and Vintage Cellars,
but does have a cellar door in McLaren Vale. Wines are released in 3 brands: at the top, the
Haselgrove Reserve Series (HRS); next the McLaren Vale series (MVS); and at the bottom the
Sovereign series. Exports to Europe and Asia.

MVS Chardonnay 2005 A lively wine; sophisticated winemaking pays
dividends at this price point; stone fruit and a certain citrussy tang; mlf, partial
barrel ferment, and stainless steel fermentation all employed. Screwcap.
13.5° alc. **Rating** 90 **To** 2010 $15

MVS Shiraz 2004 Elegant but light-bodied wine, with gentle blackberry fruit; fair
price. **Rating** 88 **To** 2011 $15
Sovereign Series Chardonnay 2005 Underlines the quality of the fruit
available in these years of abundance; quite fresh and lively stone fruit; good length
and an airbrush of oak. Screwcap. 13.5° alc. **Rating** 87 **To** 2008 $9.99
HRS Adelaide Hills Viognier 2006 Hard to see the justification for the price;
delicate, varietal character just makes its presence felt; paying more for the label than
the wine. Screwcap. 13° alc. **Rating** 87 **To** 2008 $25

Hastwell & Lightfoot

Foggos Road, McLaren Vale, SA 5171 (postal) **Region** McLaren Vale
T (08) 8323 8692 **F** (08) 8323 8098 **www**.hastwellandlightfoot.com.au **Open** By appt
Winemaker Goe DiFabio (Contract) **Est.** 1990 **Cases** 2500
Hastwell & Lightfoot is an offshoot of a rather larger grapegrowing business, with the majority of
the grapes from the 16 ha of vineyard being sold to others; the vineyard was planted in 1988 and
the first grapes produced in 1990. Varieties planted are shiraz, cabernet sauvignon, chardonnay,
cabernet franc, viognier, tempranillo and barbera. Incidentally, the labels are once seen, never
forgotten. Exports to the UK, the US, Canada, Norway, Germany, Singapore and NZ.

McLaren Vale Shiraz 2004 A totally delicious blend of blackberry and dark
chocolate; oak and tannins perfectly judged and integrated. Screwcap. 14.5° alc.
Rating 95 **To** 2024 $22

McLaren Vale Cabernet Sauvignon 2004 Big, rustic earthy/chocolatey
McLaren Vale cabernet, these regional flavours travelling alongside varietal
blackcurrant fruit. Screwcap. 14.5° alc. **Rating** 89 **To** 2015 $22

Hat Rock Vineyard   ★★★

2330 Portarlington Road, Bellarine, Vic 3221 (postal) **Region** Geelong
T (03) 5259 1386 **F** (03) 9833 1150 **www**.hatrockvineyard.com.au **Open** Not
Winemaker Contract **Est.** 2000 **Cases** NFP
Steven and Vici Funnell began the development of Hat Rock in 2000, planting pinot noir and
chardonnay. The vineyard derives its name from a hat-shaped rocky outcrop on the Corio Bay
shore, not far from the vineyard, a landmark named by Matthew Flinders when he mapped the
southern part of Australia. The wines are available through the website.

♟♟♟♟   **Pinot Noir 2005** Some cherry and sarsparilla notes, overall pleasant flavour, albeit
with fairly simple structure. **Rating** 87 **To** 2008 $22

Hawkers Gate   ★★★★

Lot 31 Foggo Road, McLaren Flat, SA 5171 **Region** McLaren Vale
T 0403 809 990 **F** (08) 8323 9981 **www**.hawkersgate.com.au **Open** By appt
Winemaker James Hastwell **Est.** 2000 **Cases** 500
James Hastwell (son of Mark and Wendy Hastwell of Hastwell & Lightfoot) decided he would
become a winemaker when he was 9 years old, and duly obtained his wine science degree from
the Adelaide University, working each vintage during his degree course at Haselgrove Wines and
later Kay Bros. It is a long way from Hawkers Gate, which takes its name from the gate at the
border of Australia's dog fence between SA and NSW, 250 km north of Broken Hill. A few rows
of saperavi have been planted. Exports to the US.

Hay Shed Hill Wines   ★★★★

Harmans Mill Road, Wilyabrup, WA 6280 **Region** Margaret River
T (08) 9755 6046 **F** (08) 9755 6083 **www**.hayshedhill.com.au **Open** 7 days 10.30–5
Winemaker Michael Kerrigan **Est.** 1987 **Cases** 35 000
The changes continue at Hay Shed Hill. Highly regarded former winemaker at Howard Park,
Mike Kerrigan has acquired the business (with co-ownership by the West Cape Howe syndicate)
and is now the full-time winemaker. He has every confidence he can dramatically lift the quality
of the wines, and there is no reason to doubt his ability to do so; these notes are for wines made
before the change.

♟♟♟♟♟   **Pitchfork Chardonnay 2005** Light straw-green; light- to medium-bodied stone
fruit and citrus with some creamy nuances; fine structure, good length. Screwcap.
13.8° alc. **Rating** 90 **To** 2011 $16

♟♟♟♟   **Pitchfork Semillon Sauvignon Blanc 2005** Light straw-green; a clean bouquet;
a tropical, mineral mix which builds in intensity on the back palate and finish.
Screwcap. 12.7° alc. **Rating** 89 **To** 2008 $16
Margaret River Cabernet Merlot 2004 Light- to medium-bodied; an ultra-
savoury, earthy varietal style, and requires a certain amount of vino-masochism.
Screwcap. 13.9° alc. **Rating** 87 **To** 2010 $22

Haywards of Locksley   ★★★☆

RMB 6365, Locksley, Vic 3665 (postal) **Region** Strathbogie Ranges
T 0432 914 747 **Open** Not
Winemaker David Hayward, Jane Sandilands **Est.** NA **Cases** 500
David Hayward and Jane Sandilands have established a patchwork quilt vineyard of shiraz, riesling,
viognier, cabernet franc, petit verdot and cabernet sauvignon, totalling 2.2 ha. By 2006 they had
been practising organic growing for 5 years, and biodynamic for 1 year. The Shiraz is estate-
grown, the Merlot organically grown at Strath Creek and purchased by Haywards. The Vintage
Port comes from Goulburn Valley fruit.

Hazyblur Wines

Lot 5, Angle Vale Road, Virginia, SA 5120 **Region** Adelaide Plains
T (08) 8380 9307 **F** (08) 8380 8743 **Open** By appt
Winemaker Ross Trimboli **Est.** 1998 **Cases** 2000
Robyne and Ross Trimboli hit the jackpot with their 2000 vintage red wines, sourced from various regions in SA, including one described by Robert Parker as 'Barotta, the most northerly region in SA' (it is in fact Baroota, and is not the most northerly), with Parker points ranging between 91 and 95. One of the wines was a Late Harvest Shiraz, tipping the scales at 17° alcohol, and contract-grown at Kangaroo Island. It is here that the Trimbolis have established their own 4.7-ha vineyard, planted principally to cabernet sauvignon and shiraz (first vintage 2004). Needless to say, almost all the wine is exported to the US (lesser amounts to Canada).

Heafod Glen Winery

8691 West Swan Road, Henley Brook, WA 6055 **Region** Swan Valley
T (08) 9296 3444 **F** (08) 9296 3555 www.heafodglenwine.com.au **Open** Wed–Sun 10–5
Winemaker Neil Head **Est.** 1999 **Cases** NFP
A combined vineyard and restaurant business, each sustaining the other. The estate plantings are shiraz (2.5 ha), cabernet sauvignon (1 ha), viognier (0.75 ha) and chenin blanc, chardonnay and verdelho (0.25 ha each). The wines are made by vineyard owner Neil Head. Chesters restaurant, created by Paul Smith (famed for establishing Dear Friends restaurant in Perth), is run by Duncan Head and sister Anna, and is situated in a former stable which has been restored with all of the tables, cabinet works and feature walls crafted from the original timber.

Healesville Wine Co

189–191a Maroondah Highway, Healesville, Vic 3777 **Region** Yarra Valley
T (03) 5962 1800 **F** (03) 5962 1833 www.healesvillewine.com.au **Open** 7 days 11–6
Winemaker Paul Evans (Contract) **Est.** 2002 **Cases** 700
John Reith and Roger Hocking have a small vineyard, planted with chardonnay in 1997, off Don Road, Healesville, plus pinot noir and chardonnay at the Kiah Yallambee Vineyard in Old Don Road. Small amounts of shiraz, cabernet sauvignon, cabernet franc and merlot are obtained from Yarra Valley vineyards managed or controlled by the Healesville Wine Co.

Heartland Vineyard

PO Box 78, Greta, NSW 2334 **Region** Lower Hunter Valley
T (02) 4938 6272 **F** (02) 4938 6004 www.heartlandvineyard.com.au **Open** Not
Winemaker David Hook **Est.** 1998 **Cases** 1500
Duncan and Libby Thomson, cardiac surgeon and cardiac scrub nurse respectively, say Heartland Vineyard is the result of a sea change that got a little out of hand. 'After looking one weekend at some property in the Hunter Valley to escape the Sydney rat-race, we stumbled upon the beautiful 90 acres that has become our vineyard.' They have built a rammed-earth house on the property, and the vineyard is now a little over 5 ha, with shiraz, semillon, merlot, barbera, verdelho and viognier.

Heartland Wines

229 Greenhill Road, Dulwich, SA 5065 **Region** Limestone Coast Zone
T (08) 8357 9344 **F** (08) 8357 9388 www.heartlandwines.com.au **Open** Not
Winemaker Ben Glaetzer **Est.** 2001 **Cases** 80 000
This is a joint venture of 4 industry veterans: winemakers Ben Glaetzer and Scott Collett, viticulturist Geoff Hardy and wine industry management specialist Grant Tilbrook. It draws upon grapes grown in the Limestone Coast, Barossa Valley and McLaren Vale, predominantly from vineyards owned by the partners. Its sights are firmly set on exports and it has already had impressive results. The wines are principally contract-made at Barossa Vintners and represent excellent value for money. Exports to all major markets.

♟♟♟♟♟ **Directors' Cut Langhorne Creek Shiraz 2005** Medium to full red-purple; supple, rich, ripe blackberry and black cherry fruit; ripe tannins, controlled oak, and good length. Cork. 14.5° alc. **Rating** 94 **To** 2019 $30

♟♟♟♟♀ **Langhorne Creek Cabernet Sauvignon 2005** Medium purple-red; soft, ripe, juicy blackcurrant fruit; touches of chocolate and mocha; ripe tannins. Enticing price. Screwcap. 14° alc. **Rating** 92 **To** 2015 $17

♟♟♟♟ **Langhorne Creek Limestone Coast Shiraz 2005** Fragrant aromas with some minty notes, the palate with a mix of red and black fruits, finishing with savoury tannins in a medium-bodied frame. Screwcap. 14.5° alc. **Rating** 89 **To** 2012 $17
Langhorne Creek Dolcetto Lagrein 2005 Red-purple; a medium-bodied palate with red, black and sour cherry flavours plus a dusting of spice and a sprinkle of French oak. Screwcap. 14.5° alc. **Rating** 89 **To** 2012 $20
Langhorne Creek Viognier Pinot Gris 2006 A clean bouquet; quite aromatic apricot and ripe apple aromas and flavours; good length, albeit an odd blend. Screwcap. 13.5° alc. **Rating** 88 **To** 2008 $20

Heathcote Estate ★★★★★

1 Garden Street, South Yarra, Vic 3141 (postal) **Region** Heathcote
T (03) 9251 5375 **F** (03) 9639 1540 **www**.heathcoteestate.com **Open** Not
Winemaker Tod Dexter, Larry McKenna (Consultant) **Est.** 1988 **Cases** 8500
Heathcote Estate is a thoroughly professional venture, a partnership between Louis Bialkower, founder of Yarra Ridge, and Robert G. Kirby, owner of Yabby Lake Vineyards, Director of Escarpment Vineyards (NZ) and Chairman of Village Roadshow Ltd. They purchased a prime piece of Heathcote red Cambrian soil in 1999, and have an experienced and skilled winemaking team in the form of Tod Dexter (ex-Stonier) and Larry McKenna (of NZ) as consultant. They have planted 30 ha of vines, 85% shiraz and 15% grenache, the latter an interesting variant on viognier. The wines are matured exclusively in French oak (50% new).

♟♟♟♟♟ **Shiraz 2004** Bright red-purple; a substantial wine in every respect, with masses of dark fruits and tannins to match; well-handled French oak; has a dash of grenache. Cork. 14° alc. **Rating** 95 **To** 2019 $45
Shiraz 2005 A medium-bodied wine, retaining substantial natural acidity, thereby investing it with elegance; a mix of blackberry, cherry and plum fruit; fine tannins and restrained oak. Diam. **Rating** 94 **To** 2020 $45

♟♟♟♟♀ **Grenache Noir 2005** So-called in some parts of Europe to distinguish it from grenache blanc; the wine also has 7% syrah which has come in handy. Jasper Hill has also placed its stamp of approval on the variety, but I am far from convinced it is worthy of the best soil of Heathcote. Colour and flavour are a given, and the wine avoids cosmetic/lolly characters. Diam. 14.5° alc.
Rating 90 **To** 2015 $45

Heathcote II ★★★★★

290 Cornella-Toolleen Road, Toolleen, Vic 3551 **Region** Heathcote
T (03) 5433 6292 **F** (03) 5433 6293 **www**.heathcote2.com **Open** W'ends 10–5
Winemaker Peder Rosdal **Est.** 1995 **Cases** 500
This is the venture of Danish-born, French-trained, Flying Winemaker (California, Spain and Chablis) Peder Rosdal and Lionel Flutto. The establishment of the vineyard dates back to 1995, new plantings in 2004 lifted the total to a little over 5 ha, shiraz (with the lion's share of 2.2 ha), cabernet sauvignon, cabernet franc, merlot and tempranillo. The vines are dry-grown on the famed red Cambrian soil, and since 2004 the wines made onsite. Open fermentation, hand-plunging, basket press and (since 2004) French oak maturation are the techniques used. Exports to the US, Switzerland, Denmark, Japan and Singapore.

♟♟♟♟♟ **HD Shiraz 2004** Deep colour; totally formidable concentration, but without bitterness or over-extraction; multi-layered blackberry, prune, plum and dark chocolate, oak and tannins in subdued support, alcohol rather less subdued, but not hot. High-quality cork (and price to match). Cork. 15.5° alc. **Rating** 96 To 2029 $80
HD Shiraz 2005 Substantially more weight and concentration; black fruits, with robust, but not too dry, tannins; very much for the long term. Cork. 15° alc. **Rating** 94 To 2020 $80

♟♟♟♟♟ **Shiraz 2005** Fragrant and complex; medium- to full-bodied, but not muscle-bound; splashes of spice, chocolate and blackberry fruits run across a long, balanced palate. Cork. 15° alc. **Rating** 93 To 2020 $55
Myola 2004 Dense, inky colour; jam-packed with hyper-ripe flavour and extract, all in the upper register of ripeness. Doesn't get away with it as does the HD Shiraz, but 25 years might begin to tame it. Cabernet Franc/Cabernet Sauvignon/Merlot. Cork. 16° alc. **Rating** 93 To 2029 $45

Heathcote Winery

183-185 High Street, Heathcote, Vic 3523 **Region** Heathcote
T (03) 5433 2595 **F** (03) 5433 3081 **www**.heathcotewinery.com.au **Open** 7 days 10–5
Winemaker Rachel Brooker **Est.** 1978 **Cases** 10 000
The Heathcote Winery was one of the first to be established in the region. The wines are produced predominantly from the 16-ha estate vineyard (shiraz, chardonnay and viognier), and some from local and other growers under long-term contracts; the tasting room facilities have been restored and upgraded. Exports to the UK.

♟♟♟♟♟ **Curagee Shiraz 2005** Elegant, lively and young, the 3% viognier making a pronounced impact; spicy black fruits, with tangy notes from the viognier; long finish. Screwcap. 15° alc. **Rating** 93 To 2015 $50
Mail Coach Shiraz 2003 There has been little change over the 2 years since last tasted; blackberry fruits still powerful, the tannins still softening, but on an upwards trajectory. Screwcap. 15° alc. **Rating** 92 To 2018 $29.95
Mail Coach Shiraz 2005 Potent, concentrated wine; predominantly black fruits and a touch of spice, the 'splash of viognier' noted on the back label doing as much for the colour as anything else. Screwcap. 14.9° alc. **Rating** 91 To 2016 $26
Craven's Place Shiraz 2005 A substantial, medium- to full-bodied wine with a range of blackberry, mocha and dark chocolate; good tannin structure. Sensible/affordable price. Screwcap. 14.9° alc. **Rating** 90 To 2012 $17.50

♟♟♟♟ **Mail Coach Chardonnay 2006** A powerful wine; ripe melon and stone fruit are overtaken on the finish by the oak, causing a certain toughness. Screwcap. 14.5° alc. **Rating** 87 To 2010 $19.50

Heathvale

Saw Pit Gully Road, via Keyneton, SA 5353 **Region** Eden Valley
T (08) 8564 8248 **F** (08) 8564 8248 **www**.heathvalewines.com.au **Open** By appt
Winemaker Trevor March **Est.** 1987 **Cases** 2000
The origins of Heathvale go back to 1865, when William Heath purchased the property, building the home and establishing the fruit orchard and 8 ha of vineyard. The property is now 65 ha and has 10 ha of vineyard in production, with future plantings planned. The wine was made in the cellar of the house which still stands on the property (now occupied by owners Trevor and Faye March). The vineyards were re-established in 1987, and consist of shiraz, cabernet sauvignon, chardonnay and riesling, with a 1000-vine sagrantino trial planted in 2004. Exports to the UK and the US.

♟♟♟♟♟ **Eden Valley Barossa Riesling 2006** Lime, lavender and apple aromas; excellent intensity, line and length, flavours largely as promised by the bouquet; lots of content. Screwcap. 12° alc. **Rating** 94 To 2016 $16

ŸŸŸŸ **Eden Valley Barossa Shiraz 2004** A pleasant wine, without the depth and precision most '04s show. Sweet fruit, but not enough structure to give it authority, however pleasing the flavours are. Screwcap. 14° alc. **Rating** 88 **To** 2013 $25

Hedberg Hill

Forbes Road, Orange, NSW 2800 **Region** Orange
T (02) 6365 3428 **F** (02) 6365 3428 **Open** By appt
Winemaker Contract **Est.** 1998 **Cases** NFP
Peter and Lee Hedberg have established their hilltop vineyard 4 km west of Orange. It has great views of Mt Canobolas and the surrounding valleys, and visitors are welcome by appointment.

ŸŸŸŸŸ **Chardonnay 2005** Fine, elegant and long; harmonious fruit and fine oak. Screwcap. **Rating** 91 **To** 2009

Heggies Vineyard

Heggies Range Road, Eden Valley, SA 5235 **Region** Eden Valley
T (08) 8565 3203 **F** (08) 8565 3380 **www**.heggiesvineyard.com **Open** At Yalumba
Winemaker Peter Gambetta **Est.** 1971 **Cases** 13 000
Heggies was the second of the high-altitude (570 m) vineyards established by S Smith & Sons (Yalumba). Plantings on the 120-ha former grazing property began in 1973, and 62 ha is now under vine. Plantings of both chardonnay and viognier were increased in 2002. Exports to all major markets.

Heidenreich Estate   NR

PO Box 99, Tanunda, SA 5352 **Region** Barossa Valley
T (08) 8563 2644 **F** (08) 8563 1554 **www**.heidenreichvineyards.com.au **Open** Not
Winemaker Noel Heidenreich **Est.** 1998 **Cases** NA
The Heidenreich family arrived in the Barossa since 1857, with successive generations growing grapes ever since, and is now owned and run by Noel and Cheryl Heidenreich. Having changed the vineyard plantings, and done much work on the soil, they were content to sell the grapes from the 4.5 ha of shiraz, cabernet sauvignon, cabernet franc, viognier and chardonnay until 1998, when they and friends crushed a tonne in total of shiraz, cabernet sauvignon and cabernet franc. Since that time, production has increased to around 1000 tonnes, most exported to San Diego in the US, a little sold locally.

Helen's Hill Estate

16 Ingram Road, Lilydale, Vic 3140 **Region** Yarra Valley
T (03) 9739 1573 **www**.helenshill.com.au **Open** Thurs–Mon & public hols 10–5
Winemaker Scott McCarthy **Est.** 1984 **Cases** 5000
Helen's Hill Estate is named after the previous owner of the property, Helen Fraser. Allan Nalder, Roma and Lewis Nalder, and Andrew and Robyn McIntosh, with backgrounds in banking and finance, grazing and medicine respectively, are the partners in the venture. A small planting of pinot noir and chardonnay dating from the mid-1980s is retained for the Helen's Hill Estate wines; the grapes from the newer plantings are either used for other Helen's Hill wines or sold to Domaine Chandon and Coldstream Hills. The plantings now cover chardonnay, pinot noir, shiraz, merlot and cabernet sauvignon. A very elegant and relatively large restaurant, with a private function room, looks out over the Yarra Valley.

ŸŸŸŸŸ **Sauvignon Blanc 2006** Spotlessly clean; a lean, grassy style, with the barrel fermentation adding as much to texture as to flavour; long finish. **Rating** 92 **To** 2008 $19.50
Yarra Valley Chardonnay 2004 Faintly cheesy aromas, probably from the French oak; the palate redeems the wine, with lingering nectarine and melon flavours running through the fine and long finish. Screwcap. 14.1° alc. **Rating** 92 **To** 2010 $22

Cinq 2005 A fresh bouquet of the 5 Bordeaux varieties in a medium-bodied, fruit-forward frame; fine tannins and minimal oak. Diam. 13.5° alc. **Rating** 91 To 2013 $28

Yarra Valley Viognier 2006 Well-made; the Yarra Valley may yet prove itself highly suited to viognier; has the flavour of ripe apricot-tinged fruit, the 100% barrel fermentation in no way compromising the varietal character. In particular, no phenolics on the finish. Screwcap. 13.5° alc. **Rating** 90 To 2011 $18

Yarra Valley Pinot Noir 2006 Excellent colour; quite firm plum and black cherry fruit with notes of spice and stem; balanced finish. Screwcap. 13.5° alc. **Rating** 90 To 2012 $25

♥♥♥♥ **Little Rascal 2006** A crisp mix of green apple and pear; nice texture and structure on the back palate, but will never be a giant killer, just a little rascal. Arneis is known as 'the little rascal'. Screwcap. 13.8° alc. **Rating** 87 To 2009 $22

Helm ★★★★

Butt's Road, Murrumbateman, NSW 2582 **Region** Canberra District
T (02) 6227 5953 **F** (02) 6227 0207 **www.**helmwines.com.au **Open** Thurs–Mon 10–5
Winemaker Ken Helm **Est.** 1973 **Cases** 3000
Ken Helm is well known as one of the more stormy petrels of the wine industry and is an energetic promoter of his wines and of the Canberra District generally. His wines have been consistent bronze medal winners, with silvers and golds dotted here and there.

♥♥♥♥♀ **Premium Canberra District Riesling 2006** More precision and focus than the Classic; lime and passionfruit; good line and length. Screwcap. 11.8° alc. **Rating** 91 To 2015 $39

♥♥♥♥ **Classic Dry Canberra District Riesling 2006** Rich, quite soft tropical fruit with touches of citrus; moderate length. Screwcap. 12° alc. **Rating** 88 To 2010 $25

🍇 Henry Holmes Wines ★★★★☆

Gomersal Road, Tanunda, SA 5352 **Region** Barossa Valley
T (08) 8563 2059 **F** (08) 8563 2581 **www.**woodbridgefarm.com **Open** By appt
Winemaker Robin Day **Est.** 1998 **Cases** 1400
The Holmes family's background dates from Samuel Henry Holmes (whose parents William Henry and Penelope Jane Holmes are co-owners of the property) to Samuel Henry's great-great-grandparents, whose son (and great-grandfather) Henry Holmes was born en route to Australia from England. A further distinction is that the property today owned by the Holmes' was first planted by the Henschke family in the 1860s. The label denotes the division of opinion between Bill and Penny (as they are known) on the merits of viticulture on the one hand and White Suffolk sheep on the other. 25.7 ha of shiraz, cabernet sauvignon and grenache are on one side of the property, sheep on the other (held at bay by a fence). The plan is to grow the volume made to 2000 cases over the next 5 years, selling the surplus grapes. The (relatively) low alcohol of the wines is as commercial as it is refreshing. Exports to the US and NZ.

♥♥♥♥♀ **Barossa Valley Cabernet Sauvignon 2005** Has achieved lush blackcurrant fruit with ease at this alcohol level; fine, ripe tannins and quality oak; long finish. Screwcap. 13.5° alc. **Rating** 93 To 2025 $24

Barossa Valley Cabernet Sauvignon 2004 In similar style to the Shiraz, elegant and medium-bodied, but with a trifle more structure to the blackcurrant fruit. Cork. 13.6° alc. **Rating** 91 To 2016 $26

Barossa Valley Shiraz 2005 There is such a thing as elegant Barossa Valley shiraz; light- to medium-bodied, with bright red cherry, black cherry and blackberry fruit; fine tannins. Screwcap. 13.5° alc. **Rating** 90 To 2011 $24

Barossa Valley Shiraz 2004 An interesting take on lower-alcohol Barossa shiraz; light- to medium-bodied, with fresh red fruits and fine tannins; an element of swings and roundabouts. Cork. 13.5° alc. **Rating** 90 To 2014 $26

Henry's Drive ★★★☆

Hodgsons Road, Padthaway, SA 5271 **Region** Padthaway
T (08) 8765 5251 **F** (08) 8765 5180 **www**.henrysdrive.com **Open** 7 days 10–4
Winemaker Kim Johnston, Chris Ringland (Consultant) **Est.** 1998 **Cases** 100 000
The Longbottom families have been farming in Padthaway since the 1940s, with a diverse
operation ranging from sheep and cattle to growing onions. In 1992 they decided to plant a few
vines, and now have almost 300 ha of vineyard consisting mainly of shiraz and cabernet
sauvignon, plus some chardonnay, merlot, verdelho and sauvignon blanc. Henry's Drive is owned
and operated by Brian and Kay Longbottom. Exports to all major markets.

ⓎⓎⓎⓎⓎ **Parson's Flat Padthaway Shiraz Cabernet 2005** Good weight and
concentration; ripe black fruits with touches of spice, licorice and chocolate.
Cork. 14.5° alc. **Rating** 90 To 2014 $35

Henschke ★★★★★

Henschke Road, Keyneton, SA 5353 **Region** Eden Valley
T (08) 8564 8223 **F** (08) 8564 8294 **www**.henschke.com.au **Open** Mon–Fri 9–4.30,
Sat 9–12, public hols 10–3
Winemaker Stephen Henschke **Est.** 1868 **Cases** 50 000
Regarded as the best medium-sized red wine producer in Australia, and has gone from strength
to strength over the past 3 decades under the guidance of winemaker Stephen and viticulturist
Prue Henschke. The red wines fully capitalise on the very old, low-yielding, high-quality vines
and are superbly made with sensitive but positive use of new small oak: Hill of Grace is second
only to Penfolds Grange as Australia's red wine icon. Exports to all major markets.

ⓎⓎⓎⓎⓎ **Hill of Grace 2002** Holding its hue well; fragrant black fruits with touches of
licorice and spice run through the bouquet, with oak in the background. The
medium-bodied palate is feline and focused; very long, finishing with
exceptionally fine-grained tannins. Harmonious and elegant, there is no
intrusion whatsoever from the alcohol; effortless power. While retail prices
always have a degree of elasticity, this wine has overtaken the price of the '02
Penfolds Grange, released at the same time. Screwcap. 14.5° alc. **Rating** 97
To 2035 $550
Mount Edelstone 2004 Excellent purple-red; a mix of blackberry and black
cherry aromas lead into a medium- to full-bodied palate; the structure is more
evident than on the Hill of Grace (but, then, the wine is 2 years younger); with
hints of bitter chocolate, the palate moves decisively to the blackberry
spectrum, the screwcap guaranteeing a very long life; 90-year-old ungrafted
vines. Screwcap. 14.5° alc. **Rating** 95 To 2029 $93
Lenswood Abbott's Prayer 2003 Fragrant, red berry fruits with some
accompanying spices on the bouquet; a medium-bodied palate, with elegant,
fresh cherry and cassis fruit; very fine tannins run through a great finish and
aftertaste. Screwcap. 14.5° alc. **Rating** 95 To 2025 $75
Eleanor's Cottage Eden Valley Sauvignon Blanc Semillon 2006 A clean,
fresh and lively bouquet and palate with herb and ripe citrus; good length and
aftertaste. Screwcap. 12° alc. **Rating** 94 To 2008 $23
Cranes Eden Valley Chardonnay 2006 The same freshness as all the '06
whites from Henschke; grapefruit and nectarine mix with a gentle touch of
oak; elegant wine, fine finish. Screwcap. 13° alc. **Rating** 94 To 2012 $31
Croft Lenswood Chardonnay 2005 Has started to build complexity, with layers
of fig, nectarine and white peach interwoven with high-quality barrel-ferment oak.
Screwcap. 13.5° alc. **Rating** 94 To 2012 $45
Keyneton Estate Euphonium 2004 A lively wine with plenty of interaction
between the varietal components; appealing spices with a silky texture and fine
balance. Shiraz/Cabernet Sauvignon/Merlot. Screwcap. 14.5° alc. **Rating** 94
To 2024 $43

Cyril Henschke Eden Valley Cabernet Sauvignon 2003 Blackcurrant fruit with touches of mint and leaf lead into a medium- to medium-full-bodied palate; lively and long, it has abundant cassis and blackcurrant fruit, a touch of mint again apparent, but not excessive; has absorbed the new oak, and has very good structure. Screwcap. 14.5° alc. **Rating** 94 **To** 2030 $114

ᵺᵺᵺᵺᵺ **Julius Eden Valley Riesling 2006** Extremely fine and floral blossom aromas; a delicately poised palate with good balance, simply needing time. Screwcap. 12.5° alc. **Rating** 93 **To** 2016 $27

Johann's Garden 2005 Excellent clear purple colour; has lift and focus to the vibrantly fresh berry fruits, finishing with fine tannins. Screwcap. 15° alc. **Rating** 93 **To** 2013 $36

Tappa Pass Barossa Shiraz 2003 Very good for the vintage; a mix of red and black fruits, without jammy characters; fine, ripe tannins. Screwcap. 15° alc. **Rating** 92 **To** 2013 $50

Peggy's Hill Eden Valley Riesling 2006 Apple and spice aromas; good overall depth of flavour, and ample length. Screwcap. 13° alc. **Rating** 91 **To** 2011 $20

Coralinga Adelaide Hills Sauvignon Blanc 2006 Highly focused and intense, more so than many from the vintage; a lovely interplay of citrus, tropical and mineral notes. Screwcap. 12° alc. **Rating** 91 **To** 2011 $24

Henry's Seven 2005 Supple, spicy, juicy berry style; light- to medium-bodied, and easy going. Grenache/Shiraz/Mourvedre. Screwcap. 15° alc. **Rating** 90 **To** 2012 $31

Hentley Farm Wines ★★★★★

PO Box 246, Tanunda, SA 5352 **Region** Barossa Valley
T (08) 8562 8427 **F** (08) 8562 8427 **www.hentleyfarm.com.au Open** Not
Winemaker Reid Bosward (Contract) **Est.** 1999 **Cases** 2000
Keith and Alison Hentschke purchased the Hentley Farm in 1997, then an old vineyard and mixed farming property. Keith had thoroughly impressive credentials at the time of the purchase, having studied agricultural science at Roseworthy College, then studying wine marketing, and obtaining an MBA. During the 1990s he had a senior production role with Orlando, before moving on to manage one of Australia's largest vineyard management companies, and from 2002–2006 with Nepenthe. Just under 15 ha of shiraz, 5 ha of grenache, 2 ha of cabernet sauvignon, 0.8 ha of zinfandel and 0.1 ha of viognier are now in production. The vineyard is situated among rolling hills on the banks of Greenock Creek, with red clay loam soils overlaying shattered limestone, lightly rocked slopes and little top soil. It hardly needs to be said the emphasis is on quality.

ᵺᵺᵺᵺᵺ **Clos Otto Barossa Valley Shiraz 2005** Impenetrable colour; an intense bouquet with licorice, plum, prune, blackberry and oak; dark chocolate adds to the fruit array on the palate; dreadnought bottle, wine and price to match. Cork. 16° alc. **Rating** 96 **To** 2020 $100

Barossa Valley Shiraz 2005 Medium- to full-bodied, redolent with blackberry and satsuma plum fruit, with very good oak integration, balance and length. Screwcap. 14.5° alc. **Rating** 95 **To** 2025 $30

The Beauty Barossa Valley Shiraz 2005 A highly perfumed bouquet, followed by an ultra-succulent array of red and black fruits, the 4% viognier present sneaking through with its little bit of magical lift. Cork. 15° alc. **Rating** 95 **To** 2020 $45

The Beast Barossa Valley Shiraz 2004 Powerful, potent, focused full-bodied wine with blackberry, licorice and earth; a very long palate, with inbuilt acidity and tannins. Cork. 14.5° alc. **Rating** 95 **To** 2022 $70

The Beast Barossa Valley Shiraz 2005 A massive wine, whether beastly or not is for the consumer to decide, but informed, consenting adults who pay the price obviously think it is not. Difficult to imagine how much more could be crammed into the dreadnought-weighted bottle. Pointed on the basis of acceptance of the style. Cork. 16° alc. **Rating** 94 **To** 2030 $70

ΨΨΨΨΨ **Barossa Valley Grenache Shiraz Zinfandel 2005** A big, ripe, luscious uplift bra style, full of sweet juicy fruit, best enjoyed sooner than later. Zinfandel adds to the illusion more than the reality; 52%/41%/7%. Screwcap. 14.5° alc. **Rating** 90 **To** 2010 $28

ΨΨΨΨ **Fools Bay Dusty's Desire Shiraz 2005** High-toned aromas and flavours, but does chop off on the finish. Screwcap. 14.5° alc. **Rating** 88 **To** 2015 $20
Barossa Valley Zinfandel 2005 Reminiscent of very ripe zinfandel from Lodi in California's Central Valley, verging on viscous on the tongue, and with hyper-ripe fruit characters. For others to enjoy. Screwcap. 15.5° alc. **Rating** 88 **To** 2012 $28

Henty Estate   ★★★★★

657 Hensley Park Road, Hamilton, Vic 3300 (postal) **Region** Henty
T (03) 5572 4446 **F** (03) 5572 4446 **www.**henty-estate.com.au **Open** Not
Winemaker Peter Dixon **Est.** 1991 **Cases** 1000
Peter and Glenys Dixon have hastened slowly with Henty Estate. In 1991 they began the planting of 4.5 ha of shiraz, 1 ha each of cabernet sauvignon and chardonnay, and 0.5 ha of riesling. In their words, 'we avoided the temptation to make wine until the vineyard was mature', establishing the winery in 2003. Encouraged by neighbours John Thomson and Tamara Irish, they have limited the yield to 3 to 4 tonnes per ha on the VSP-trained, essentially dry-grown, vineyard.

ΨΨΨΨΨ **Hamilton Riesling 2006** Ripe, lime/passionfruit aromas; a very well-balanced palate thanks to good acidity, but still at the big end of town. Screwcap. 12.8° alc. **Rating** 94 **To** 2016 $20
Hamilton Shiraz 2005 Strong purple-red; spicy, leafy nuances on the bouquet unexpectedly foreshadow a deep and powerful palate, with pure blackberry essence fruit (no jammy characters) supported by the excellent use of French oak. Screwcap. 14° alc. **Rating** 94 **To** 2019 $22

ΨΨΨΨΨ **Hamilton Shiraz Cabernet 2005** Herb and spice edges to the aromas; once again, almost lusciously sweet and ripe fruit catches you by surprise; very good balance and length. Screwcap. 14° alc. **Rating** 93 **To** 2019 $22

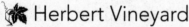 # Herbert Vineyard   ★★★★

Bishop Road, Mount Gambier, SA 5290 **Region** Mount Gambier
T 0408 849 080 **F** (08) 8724 9512 **Open** By appt
Winemaker David Herbert **Est.** 1996 **Cases** 200
David and Trudy Herbert have planted 2 ha of pinot noir, and a total of 0.4 ha of cabernet sauvignon, merlot and pinot gris. The majority of the pinot noir is sold to Fosters for sparkling wine, but the Herberts have built a 2-level (mini) winery, which overlooks a 1600-sq metre maze planted in 2000, and which is reflected in the label logo.

ΨΨΨΨΨ **Mount Gambier Cabernet+ 2005** Excellent colour; a major surprise packet; swathed in sweet berry fruit, with fine, ripe tannins and incidental oak. Cabernet Sauvignon (85%)/Shiraz (15%). Cork. 13.9° alc. **Rating** 92 **To** 2018 $16
Frosted Mount Gambier Pinot Noir 2005 Light, bright colour; light-bodied, savoury, spicy red cherry and plum fruit; tenacious finish. Made from second-crop in the wake of the frost. Cork. 12.2° alc. **Rating** 90 **To** 2011 $27

ΨΨΨΨ **Mount Gambier Pinot Noir 2005** Riper but simpler fruit than the Frosted alternative; plum and cherry, with some spice. Screwcap. 12.8° alc. **Rating** 88 **To** 2009 $18
Mount Gambier Pinot Noir 2004 Light- to medium-bodied; again shows clear varietal character with cherry, plum and savoury/spicy nuances. Cork. 13° alc. **Rating** 88 **To** 2009 $18

Heritage Estate

Granite Belt Drive, Cottonvale, Qld 4375 **Region** Granite Belt
T (07) 4685 2197 **F** (07) 4685 2112 **www.**heritagewines.com.au **Open** 7 days 9–5
Winemaker John Handy **Est.** 1992 **Cases** 7000

Bryce and Paddy Kassulke operate a very successful winery, with many awards in recent years. It also showcases its wines through its cellar door at Mt Tamborine (tel (07) 5545 3144) in an old church converted into a tasting and sales area, which has views over the Gold Coast hinterland, and includes a restaurant, barbecue area and art gallery. The estate plantings, established in 1993, are chardonnay (2.5 ha), merlot (1 ha), shiraz (0.4 ha) and cabernet sauvignon (0.1 ha). The quality of the wines has been consistently good, in the top 10 of the now innumerable Qld wineries.

Heritage Wines

106a Seppeltsfield Road, Marananga, SA 5355 **Region** Barossa Valley
T (08) 8562 2880 **F** (08) 8562 2692 **www.**heritagewinery.com.au **Open** Mon–Fri 10–5, w'ends & public hols 11–5
Winemaker Stephen Hoff **Est.** 1984 **Cases** 6000

A little-known winery which deserves a far wider audience, for Stephen Hoff is apt to produce some startlingly good wines. At various times the Riesling (from old Clare Valley vines), Cabernet Sauvignon and Shiraz (now the flag-bearer) have all excelled. Exports to the UK, the US, The Netherlands, Malaysia, Singapore and Hong Kong.

Rossco's Shiraz 2004 Strong colour; powerful, concentrated black fruits with bitter chocolate, spice and earth; still a little locked up, despite the cork closure. Cork. 15° alc. **Rating** 92 **To** 2019 $38

Steve Hoff Cabernet Sauvignon 2005 Deep red-purple; absolutely in the Heritage slot, with rich and generous blackcurrant and dark chocolate aromas and flavours; ripe tannins; soft and welcoming. Cork. 14.5° alc. **Rating** 91 **To** 2015 $26

Steve Hoff Cabernet Malbec 2004 Has the same blackcurrant base as the Cabernet, and some of the same chocolate, adding mocha and savoury notes plus the particular sweetness of malbec; just a little down on intensity. Screwcap. 14.8° alc. **Rating** 89 **To** 2014 $22

Heron Lake Estate

Loc 27, Rendezvous Road, Vasse, WA 6280 **Region** Margaret River
T (08) 9381 9993 **www.**heronlake.com.au **Open** 7 days 10–4
Winemaker Sharna Kowalc.zuk **Est.** 1984 **Cases** 2000

Di and Rob Goodwin (plus children Hannah and Callum) purchased the Heron Lake Vineyard from its founders, Mike and Faith Sparrow, in 2001, at which time the vineyard was 20 years old. There is a little over 6 ha of vines, chardonnay accounting for 2.6 ha, the remainder verdelho, semillon, sauvignon blanc, cabernet and merlot. Both Rob and Di are involved in postgraduate viticulture studies at various WA campuses. Exports to the UK, Canada and Singapore.

Margaret River Merlot 2003 Clearly varietal, with a silky/savoury texture, but not enough fruit depth for higher points. Twin top. 13° alc. **Rating** 87 **To** 2010 $23

Herons Rise Vineyard ★★★☆

Saddle Road, Kettering, Tas 7155 **Region** Southern Tasmania
T (03) 6267 4339 **F** (03) 6267 4245 **www.**heronsrise.com.au **Open** By appt
Winemaker Andrew Hood **Est.** 1984 **Cases** 250

Sue and Gerry White run a small stone country guesthouse in the D'Entrecasteaux Channel area and basically sell the wines produced from the surrounding hectare of vineyard to those staying at the 2 self-contained cottages.

ŸŸŸŸ   Muller Thurgau 2005 Good muller thurgau is scarcer than hen's teeth, but there is at least 1 tooth here; actually has some life to the fruit, lengthened by good acidity. **Rating** 88 **To** 2008 $17.50

Pinot Noir 2005 Medium purple-red; a pretty wine, with a nice array of red and black fruits, and just a touch of forest floor. **Rating** 88 **To** 2011 $20

Hewitson

The Old Dairy Cold Stores, 66 London Road, Mile End, SA 5031 **Region** Southeast Australia
T (08) 8443 6466 **F** (08) 8443 6866 **www**.hewitson.com.au **Open** By appt
Winemaker Dean Hewitson **Est.** 1996 **Cases** 22 000
Dean Hewitson was a winemaker at Petaluma for 10 years, and during that time managed to do 3 vintages in France and 1 in Oregon as well as undertaking his Masters at UC Davis, California. It is hardly surprising that the wines are immaculately made from a technical viewpoint. He has also managed to source 30-year-old riesling from the Eden Valley and 70-year-old shiraz from McLaren Vale, and makes a Barossa Valley Mourvedre from vines planted in 1853 at Rowland Flat and a Barossa Valley Shiraz and Grenache from 60-year-old vines at Tanunda. Exports to the UK, the US and other major markets.

ŸŸŸŸŸ   Private Cellar Barossa Valley Shiraz Mourvedre 2005 Deep colour; super-intense black fruits and dark chocolate, the mourvedre contributing to the texture as it should; an exciting wine with a great future. Screwcap. 14.5° alc. **Rating** 97 **To** 2030 $69

The Mad Hatter McLaren Vale Shiraz 2004 A classy wine, with great depth of fruit and bitter chocolate bolstered by 2 years in new French oak; great length and balance; lingering finish. Screwcap. 14.5° alc. **Rating** 96 **To** 2029 $50

Old Garden Barossa Valley Mourvedre 2005 Medium-bodied, yet endlessly complex; has the dark fruits and the fine, savoury tannins which the variety is supposed to have, but which in Australia often seems to lack. The plantings are believed to be the oldest in the world. Even in the 1880s the vineyard was called 'The Old Garden' (Garden being the then name for vineyard). Screwcap. 14.5° alc. **Rating** 95 **To** 2020 $59

ŸŸŸŸ̄   Eden Valley Riesling 2006 Clean, fresh and crisp, with a classic twist of lime on a minerally base; long, dry finish. Screwcap. 12.5° alc. **Rating** 93 **To** 2015 $23

LuLu Adelaide Hills Sauvignon Blanc 2006 Spotlessly clean; nicely balanced, weighted and constructed; positive varietal character at the tropical end of the spectrum, but neither sweet nor phenolic. Screwcap. 12.5° alc. **Rating** 92 **To** 2008 $23

Ned & Henry's Barossa Valley Shiraz 2005 Strong, slightly opaque colour; an array of black fruits, prunes and some chocolate; why so ripe? Screwcap. 15° alc. **Rating** 91 **To** 2019 $26

LuLu-V Viognier 2006 Has positive apricot and musk flavours without becoming ponderous; good length and balance. Screwcap. 13.5° alc. **Rating** 90 **To** 2008 $23

Miss Harry Dry Grown and Ancient 2005 Light but bright red; vibrantly fresh brasserie style (especially Italian) not forced into something bigger and larger. Screwcap. 15° alc. **Rating** 90 **To** 2010 $23

Hickinbotham of Dromana

Nepean Highway (near Wallaces Road), Dromana, Vic 3936 **Region** Mornington Peninsula
T (03) 5981 0355 **F** (03) 5987 0692 **www**.hickinbotham.biz **Open** 7 days 11–5
Winemaker Andrew Hickinbotham **Est.** 1981 **Cases** 3000
After a peripatetic period and a hiatus in winemaking, Hickinbotham established a permanent vineyard and winery base at Dromana. It now makes only Mornington Peninsula wines, drawing in part on 6.5 ha of estate vineyards, and in part on contract-grown fruit.

Hidden Creek ★★★★☆

Eukey Road, Ballandean, Qld 4382 **Region** Granite Belt
T (07) 4684 1383 www.hiddencreek.com.au **Open** Mon & Fri 11–3, w'ends 10–4
Winemaker Jim Barnes **Est.** 1997 **Cases** 1000
A beautifully located vineyard and winery on a 1000m-high ridge overlooking the Ballandean township and the Severn River Valley. The granite boulder-strewn hills mean that the 70-ha property only provides a little over 6 ha of vineyard, in turn divided into 6 different blocks. The business has been leased to winemaker Jim Barnes (formerly of Mountview Wines) who is contract winemaker for 10 clients, as well as making the Hidden Creek wines. The latter in turn has 3 labels: Hidden Creek, Red Bird and Rooklyn. Rooklyn is made from Granite Belt grapes which are either of outstanding quality, unusual styles, or are emerging varieties, and have had overwhelming success in wine shows. One of the top wineries in Qld.

♀♀♀♀♀ **Rooklyn Granite Belt Shiraz 2005** The colour is as good as the Shiraz Viognier (unusual in itself); very well-made, with abundant blackberry and plum fruit, seamless French oak and good tannins. Challenges Boireann at the top of the Qld tree. Screwcap. 15° alc. **Rating** 93 **To** 2018 $35
Rooklyn Granite Belt Shiraz Viognier 2005 An impressive achievement; excellent colour, and a totally harmonious interaction between shiraz, viognier and new French oak; plenty of flavour and length. Screwcap. 14° alc. **Rating** 90 **To** 2013 $28

♀♀♀♀ **Rooklyn Granite Belt Merlot 2005** Like all the Rooklyn reds, particularly well-made; that said, it doesn't show as much merlot varietal fruit as it does French oak. Screwcap. 13.5° alc. **Rating** 89 **To** 2011 $25

Hidden River Estate ★★★★

Mullineaux Road, Pemberton, WA 6260 **Region** Pemberton
T (08) 9776 1437 **F** (08) 9776 0189 www.hiddenriver.com.au **Open** 7 days 9–4
Winemaker Brenden Smith, Phil Goldring **Est.** 1994 **Cases** 2000
Phil and Sandy Goldring spent 10 years operating farm chalets in the Pemberton area before selling the business and retiring to become grapegrowers, with the intention of selling the grapes. However, they found old habits hard to kick, so opened a cellar door and café/restaurant. A renovated 1901 Kalgoorlie tram (the streetcar named Desire) has been installed to provide more seating for the award-winning restaurant. I hope the Goldrings did not pay too much for the tram.

♀♀♀♀♀ **Premium Pemberton Chardonnay 2005** A beautifully crafted wine, with lively nectarine/stone fruit/citrus doing almost all the talking, although quality barrel ferment oak is there. Trophy Best Chardonnay WA Wine Show '06. Screwcap. 14.1° alc. **Rating** 95 **To** 2013 $35

♀♀♀♀ **Pinot Noir 2004** Bound to cause controversy because of its apparent sweetness albeit mixed with more savoury notes; sustained finish. Cork. **Rating** 89 **To** 2008 $26

High Valley Wines ★★★☆

137 Cassilis Road, Mudgee, NSW 2850 **Region** Mudgee
T (02) 6372 1011 **F** (02) 6372 1033 www.highvalley.com.au **Open** 7 days 10–5
Winemaker Ian MacRae, David Lowe (Contract) **Est.** 1995 **Cases** 2000
The Francis family, headed by Ro and Grosvenor Francis, have operated a sheep, wheat and cattle property at Dunedoo for several generations. When they handed over the property to their sons in 1995, Ro and Grosvenor subdivided and retained a 40-ha block on which they have since established 11 ha of shiraz, 6 ha of cabernet sauvignon and 5 ha of chardonnay.

♀♀♀♀ **Premium Chardonnay 2006** Surprisingly delicate given the alcohol; the oak is subtle and in balance with the light-bodied fruit; good length and finesse. Screwcap. 14.1° alc. **Rating** 89 **To** 2010 $30

Premium Chardonnay 2003 Sweet stone fruit and melon of moderate intensity; well-handled oak via partial barrel fermentation; ageing slowly but surely. Screwcap. 14° alc. **Rating** 88 **To** 2009 $23

Higher Plane Wines

Location 1077, Wintarru Rise via Warner Glen Road, Forrest Grove, WA 6286 (postal)
Region Margaret River
T (08) 9336 7855 **F** (08) 9336 7866 www.higherplanewines.com.au **Open** Not
Winemaker Keith Mugford (Contract) **Est.** 1997 **Cases** 6000
Plastic and hand surgeon Dr Craig Smith, and wife Cathie, left nothing to chance in planning and establishing Higher Plane. As a prelude, Cathie obtained a Master of Business in wine marketing from Edith Cowan University, and Craig began the wine marketing course at the Adelaide University. An exhaustive search for the right property ended in 1997, and 7.13 ha of vines were planted, followed by a further 6.58 ha in late 2004, covering all the classic varieties. Its eastern and northern boundaries adjoin Devil's Lair, and they have similar gravelly, loamy, sandy soil.

ҸҸҸҸ⅑ Margaret River Chardonnay 2005 Light-bodied; more focused and precise than the Bellibone, with melon, nectarine and fig perfectly integrated with gentle oak. Screwcap. 13° alc. **Rating** 91 **To** 2012 $31

ҸҸҸҸ Bellibone Margaret River Chardonnay 2005 Soft, peach and nectarine fruit; not particularly complex, though has length. Screwcap. 13.5° alc. **Rating** 87 **To** 2009 $22

Highland Heritage Estate

Mitchell Highway, Orange, NSW 2800 **Region** Orange
T (02) 6361 3612 **F** (02) 6361 3613 **Open** Mon–Fri 9–3, w'ends 9–5
Winemaker Hunter Wine Services (John Hordern), Rex D'Aquino **Est.** 1984 **Cases** 3500
The estate plantings have increased from 4 ha to over 15 ha, with 1995 and 1997 plantings now in full production. The tasting facility is unusual: a converted railway carriage overlooking the vineyard. Exports to all major markets.

ҸҸҸҸҸ Mount Canobolas Sauvignon Blanc 2005 Zesty, crisp and lively, with a mix of herbaceous/citrus/passionfruit flavours; great length, lovely wine. Screwcap. 12.5° alc. **Rating** 94 **To** 2008 $20

ҸҸҸҸ⅑ Mount Canobolas Riesling 2005 Spotlessly clean; a bright, crisp and fresh bouquet with sweet citrus fruit on the mid-palate, then a relatively dry finish. Typical continental climate style. Screwcap. 13.2° alc. **Rating** 92 **To** 2015 $20

Mount Canobolas Merlot 2003 Spicy/savoury/olivaceous tones to the core of red fruits; fine-grained tannins, long finish. Cork. 13.5° alc. **Rating** 90 **To** 2010 $25

ҸҸҸҸ Mount Canobolas Cabernet Sauvignon 2003 Developed colour despite the screwcap; possibly aged before bottling. Savoury, leafy, earthy edges to the blackcurrant fruit; does have length. Screwcap. 13° alc. **Rating** 88 **To** 2010 $25

Highlander Wines   NR

PO Box 1833, Orange, NSW 2800 **Region** Orange
T (02) 6361 9898 **F** (02) 6361 9898 www.highlanderwines.com.au **Open** Not
Winemaker David Cumming, Contract **Est.** 2005 **Cases** NA
The origins of Highlander Wines date back to 1977 when Don Cumming and his family established Mountilford Wines at Ilford in one of the highest sites in Mudgee. The new business at Orange is run by son David Cumming and produces Riesling, Sangiovese and Chardonnay Viognier.

Hill Smith Estate ★★★★★

Flaxmans Valley Road, Eden Valley, SA 5235 **Region** Eden Valley
T (08) 8561 3200 **F** (08) 8561 3393 **www**.hillsmithestate.com **Open** At Yalumba
Winemaker Louisa Rose **Est.** 1979 **Cases** 5000
Part of the Yalumba stable, drawing upon estate plantings, including 15 ha of sauvignon blanc.
Over the years has produced some excellent wines, but the style (and perhaps quality) does seem
to vary significantly with vintage.

Hillbillé ★★★★☆

Blackwood Valley Estate, Balingup Road, Nannup, WA 6275 **Region** Blackwood Valley
T (08) 9481 0888 **F** (08) 9486 1899 **www**.hillbille.com **Open** W'ends & hols 10–4
Winemaker Woodlands Wines (Stuart Watson) **Est.** 1998 **Cases** 3000
Gary Bettridge has 19 ha of shiraz, cabernet sauvignon, merlot, chardonnay and semillon. The
vineyard is situated in the Blackwood Valley between Balingup and Nannup, which the RAC
describes as 'the most scenic drive in the southwest of WA'. A significant part of the grape
production is sold to Goundrey, Vasse Felix, Plantagenet and Evans & Tate, but since 2003, part has
been vinified for the Hillbillé label. Exports to Japan and Singapore.

ŸŸŸŸŸ **Reserve Shiraz 2005** Brilliant clarity and hue; medium-bodied, clean and fresh,
smooth and supple; a seamless fruit/oak/tannin line. Screwcap. 14.4° alc. **Rating** 93
To 2015 $35
Signature Series James Brittain 2005 Brilliant purple-red hue; a lively, fresh,
brightly flavoured medium-bodied wine; fine tannins and an appropriately firm
finish. Shiraz/Viognier. Screwcap. 14° alc. **Rating** 92 **To** 2013 $35

ŸŸŸŸ **Reserve Merlot 2005** Light- to medium-bodied, with fresh red berry, green olive
and leaf, simply needing more mid-palate presence. Screwcap. 13.7° alc. **Rating** 89
To 2013 $35
Shiraz 2005 Leafy, spicy, minty edges to juicy blackberry fruit on both bouquet
and palate. Screwcap. 14.3° alc. **Rating** 88 **To** 2012 $15
Merlot 2005 Savoury olive and earth aromas and flavours speak of the variety, but
the wine would have been better had the grapes been riper. Screwcap. 13.6° alc.
Rating 87 **To** 2008 $15

Hillcrest Vineyard ★★★★★

31 Phillip Road, Woori Yallock, Vic 3139 **Region** Yarra Valley
T (03) 5964 6689 **F** (03) 5961 5547 **www**.hillcrestvineyard.com.au **Open** By appt
Winemaker David Bryant, Tanya Bryant, Phillip Jones (Consultant) **Est.** 1971 **Cases** 500
The small, effectively dry-grown, vineyard was established by Graeme and Joy Sweet, who
ultimately sold it to David and Tanya Bryant. The pinot noir, chardonnay, semillon and cabernet
sauvignon grown on the property have always been of the highest quality, and, when Coldstream
Hills was in its infancy, was a particularly important resource for it. The Bryants have developed
the Hillcrest label and, under the guiding hand of Phillip Jones, are progressively taking control of
making these excellent wines.

ŸŸŸŸŸ **Premium Yarra Valley Chardonnay 2005** The epitome of Yarra Valley
chardonnay; has length, intensity and flavour at 12.8° alcohol; nectarine and
grapefruit, with lingering acidity; doubtless has oak, but it's not obvious. Cork.
12.8° alc. **Rating** 96 **To** 2012 $48
Premium Yarra Valley Pinot Noir 2005 Deeper colour again than the Estate
Pinot; a rich and profoundly aromatic bouquet, the palate offering another
dimension of fruit power albeit at the same modest alcohol; give it more time.
Cork. 13.4° alc. **Rating** 95 **To** 2016 $48
Estate Yarra Valley Pinot Noir 2005 Deep colour for the variety; plenty of
strong dark plum fruit with touches of oriental spice; very good line throughout, and
a long finish. Cork. 13.4° alc. **Rating** 94 **To** 2012 $33

Premium Yarra Valley Cabernet Sauvignon 2005 Much stronger colour than the Estate, and likewise far more structure and concentration; a Peter and Paul exercise perhaps; regardless, this is pure cabernet in an austere garb with persistent tannins. For the long haul. Cork. 13.4° alc. **Rating** 94 **To** 2020 $48

Estate Yarra Valley Cabernet Sauvignon 2005 A clean, light- to medium-bodied palate with blackcurrant, notes of olive and earth, fine tannins and subtle oak. Cork. 13.4° alc. **Rating** 89 **To** 2015 $33

Hills of Plenty ★★★

370 Yan Yean Road, Yarrambat, Vic 3091 **Region** Yarra Valley
T (03) 9436 2264 **F** (03) 9436 2264 **www**.hillsofplenty.com.au **Open** Last Sun of month 11–6, or by appt
Winemaker Karen Coulston **Est.** 1998 **Cases** 200
Hills of Plenty is just outside the Melbourne metropolitan area, north of Greensborough. There is a tiny 0.2-ha vineyard of riesling, chardonnay and cabernet sauvignon around the winery, but most of the fruit is purchased from other regions, notably Geelong, Gippsland and Swan Hill. The limited production means that the cellar door only opens once a month, but these are festive occasions, with live music, and picnics welcome.

Hillwood Vineyard ★★★

55 Innocent Street, Kings Meadows, Tas 7249 (postal) **Region** Northern Tasmania
T 0418 500 672 **Open** Not
Winemaker Geoff Carr **Est.** NA **Cases** NA
Geoff Carr, owner, viticulturist and winemaker, has established his vineyard on the east bank of the Tamar River, looking out over the river. He supplements his estate-grown grapes by purchasing some chardonnay and pinot gris from local growers.

 Sauvignon Blanc 2006 Has appealing, gentle fruit salad varietal flavour; needs a touch more drive, perhaps. **Rating** 87 **To** 2008

Hirsch Hill Estate ★★★★

2088 Melba Highway, Dixons Creek, Vic 3775 **Region** Yarra Valley
T (03) 8622 0118 **F** (03) 9640 0370 **www**.hirschhill.com **Open** Not
Winemaker MasterWineMakers, Yering Farm (Alan Johns) **Est.** 1998 **Cases** 3250
The Hirsch family has planted a 14.5-ha vineyard to pinot noir (predominantly), cabernet sauvignon, chardonnay, shiraz, merlot, cabernet franc, sauvignon blanc and viognier. The vineyard is part of a larger racehorse stud, situated in a mini-valley at the northern end of the Yarra Valley.

 Yarra Valley Chardonnay 2006 Light straw-green; clean, fragrant, fruit-driven melon and citrus; a subtle French oak infusion; good length and balance. Screwcap. 13.5° alc. **Rating** 92 **To** 2013 $19

Hochkirch Wines ★★★★☆

Hamilton Highway, Tarrington, Vic 3301 **Region** Henty
T (03) 5573 5200 **F** (03) 5573 5200 **Open** 11–5 by appt
Winemaker John Nagorcka **Est.** 1997 **Cases** 2000
Jennifer and John Nagorcka have developed Hochkirch in response to the very cool climate: growing season temperatures are similar to those in Burgundy. A high-density planting pattern was implemented, with a low fruiting wire taking advantage of soil warmth in the growing season, and the focus was placed on pinot noir (4.5 ha), with lesser quantities of riesling, cabernet sauvignon, semillon and shiraz. The vines are not irrigated, and no synthetic fungicides, pesticides or fertilisers are used; the Nagorckas have moved to certified biodynamic viticulture.

Hoddles Creek Estate ★★★★☆

505 Gembrook Road, Hoddles Creek, Vic 3139 **Region** Yarra Valley
T (03) 5967 4692 **F** (03) 5967 4692 **www.**hoddlescreekestate.com.au **Open** By appt
Winemaker Franco D'Anna **Est.** 1997 **Cases** 10 000
In 1997, the D'Anna family decided to establish a vineyard on the property which had been in
the family since 1960. There are now 2 vineyard blocks totalling 18.5 ha, which are hand-pruned
and hand-harvested. A 300-tonne, split-level winery was completed in 2003. Son Franco D'Anna
is the viticulturist and winemaker, having started to work in the family liquor store at 13,
graduating to chief wine buyer by the time he was 21, then completing a Bachelor of Commerce
degree at Melbourne University before studying viticulture at Charles Sturt University. A vintage
at Coldstream Hills, then consulting help from Peter Dredge of Red Edge and Mario Marson (ex
Mount Mary) has put an old head on young shoulders. Together with his uncle Bruno and one
other worker, he is solely responsible for the vineyard and winery.

ŸŸŸŸŸ **Yarra Valley Chardonnay 2005** Light straw-green; a spotlessly clean bouquet;
tightly focused and vibrant cool-grown chardonnay fruit characters of
nectarine, melon and grapefruit; oak purely a support role. Screwcap. 13.2° alc.
Rating 94 **To** 2013 $17

ŸŸŸŸŸ **Yarra Valley Pinot Noir 2005** Bright colour; an aromatic and complex display
of cherry, strawberry, stalk and spice; the palate follows on, though shortens
fractionally on the finish. Nonetheless, an enticing price. Screwcap. 13.2° alc.
Rating 93 **To** 2011 $18
Yarra Valley Sauvignon Blanc 2005 Crisp, clean, fresh and lively aromas and
flavours; a mineral frame clothed with gentle passionfruit and tropical fruit. Screwcap.
12.9° alc. **Rating** 91 **To** 208 $18
Yarra Valley Pinot Gris 2006 Lively bouquet; has the vivacity and crispness so
often lacking with this variety; good length and balance. Screwcap. 13° alc.
Rating 90 **To** 2009 $18

Hoffmann's ★★★★★

Ingoldby Road, McLaren Flat, SA 5171 **Region** McLaren Vale
T (08) 8383 0232 **F** (08) 8383 0232 **www.**hoffmannswine.com.au **Open** 7 days 11–5
Winemaker Nick Holmes, Hamish McGuire (Consultant) **Est.** 1996 **Cases** 2500
Peter and Anthea Hoffmann have been growing grapes at their property since 1978, and Peter
Hoffmann has worked at various wineries in McLaren Vale since 1979. Both he and Anthea have
undertaken courses at the Regency TAFE Institute in Adelaide, and (in Peter's words), 'in 1996
we decided that we knew a little about winemaking and opened a small cellar door'.

ŸŸŸŸŸ **McLaren Vale Shiraz 2005** A rich array of blackberry, black cherry and
chocolate aromas and flavours; very good tannin, alcohol and oak balance
management. Screwcap. 14.5° alc. **Rating** 94 **To** 2025 $22
McLaren Vale Shiraz Cabernet 2005 An elegant, medium-bodied wine;
black fruits, dark chocolate, controlled oak, and – the high point – positively
silky tannins. The swap to screwcaps will pay big dividends. Screwcap. 14.5° alc.
Rating 94 **To** 2025 $22

ŸŸŸŸŸ **McLaren Vale Cabernet Sauvignon 2005** A medium-bodied mix of black
currant, cassis and regional chocolate; fine tannins, and has absorbed 16 months in
French oak. Screwcap. 14° alc. **Rating** 92 **To** 2025 $22

ŸŸŸŸ **McLaren Vale Chardonnay 2005** Gentle stone fruit and white peach with
integrated and balanced French oak. Screwcap. 14° alc. **Rating** 89 **To** 2010 $17

Holley Hill ★★★★☆

140 Ronalds Road, Willung, Vic 3847 **Region** Gippsland
T (03) 5198 2205 **F** (03) 5198 2205 **Open** Thurs–Sun & public hols 10–6
Winemaker David Packham **Est.** 1998 **Cases** 300

David Packham has used his background as a Master of Applied Science, formerly a research scientist with the CSIRO, and more recently with the Bureau of Meteorology, to plan the establishment of Holley Hill. He served his apprenticeship with Sergio Carlei at Green Vineyards for 2 years before acquiring the then 2-year-old vineyard. The small 1.7-ha vineyard is planted to chardonnay, sauvignon blanc and pinot noir; supplemented by purchased grapes.

ŶŶŶŶŶ **East Gippsland Shiraz 2005** Slightly gamey/peppery aspects – Cote Rotie or a touch of brett? Has intensity and length, and I'll go for Cote Rotie. Diam. 14.7° alc. **Rating** 93 **To** 2015 $20

Tambo Upper Gippsland Pinot Noir 2005 Deep colour; a potent, powerful wine which does, however, retain clear varietal character in a black fruit/plum spectrum. The tannins are not too aggressive. Diam. 14.2° alc. **Rating** 92 **To** 2014 $20

Rubicon Cabernet Sauvignon 2004 Fresh and breezy cassis fruit; fine but persistent tannins; subtle oak. Cork. 13° alc. **Rating** 92 **To** 2014 $20

Gippsland Sauvignon Blanc 2006 Clean, well-made with gentle tropical/kiwifruit flowing into citrussy acidity on the finish. Diam. 12.9° alc. **Rating** 90 **To** 2008 $16

Hollick   ★★★★☆

Riddoch Highway, Coonawarra, SA 5263 **Region** Coonawarra
T (08) 8737 2318 **F** (08) 8737 2952 **www**.hollick.com **Open** 7 days 9–5
Winemaker Ian Hollick, Matthew Caldersmith **Est.** 1983 **Cases** 45 000
A family business owned by Ian and Wendy Hollick, and winner of many trophies (including the most famous of all, the Jimmy Watson), its wines are well crafted and competitively priced. A $1 million cellar door and restaurant complex opened in 2002. The Hollicks have progressively expanded their vineyard holdings: the first is the 12-ha Neilson's Block vineyard, one of the original John Riddoch selections, but used as a dairy farm between 1910 and 1975 when the Hollicks planted cabernet sauvignon and merlot. The second is the 80-plus ha Wilgha vineyard, purchased in 1987 with already established dry-grown cabernet sauvignon and shiraz; total area under vine is 45 ha. The last is the Red Ridge vineyard in Wrattonbully, where 24 ha have been planted including trial plantings of tempranillo and sangiovese. Exports to most major markets.

ŶŶŶŶŶ **Ravenswood Coonawarra Cabernet Sauvignon 2002** An elegant wine moving into the secondary phase of its development with cedar and earth notes starting to appear yet without the loss of blackcurrant fruit in its core. Cautious drinking span due to cork closure. Cork. 13.5° alc. **Rating** 93 **To** 2012 $60

The Nectar 2006 Good wine; the varietal character has not been overwhelmed by botrytis, but there is considerable richness; good balance. Botrytis Riesling. Screwcap. 13° alc. **Rating** 91 **To** 2009 $24

Reserve Coonawarra Chardonnay 2005 Melon, stone fruit and fig, plus evident oak, run through to a long finish. Screwcap. 14° alc. **Rating** 90 **To** 2012 $22

Shiraz Cabernet Sauvignon 2005 An attractive medium-bodied combination of blackberry and blackcurrant fruit, complexed by notes of spice; good tannins and balance. Excellent value. Screwcap. 14° alc. **Rating** 90 **To** 2015 $19

ŶŶŶŶ **Hollaia 2005** The blend works well (as it does in Italy); the plum and cherry sangiovese component tempered by quite austere cabernet, the latter punching above its weight. Sangiovese (65%)/Cabernet Sauvignon (35%). Screwcap. 13° alc. **Rating** 89 **To** 2011 $20

Coonawarra Sauvignon Blanc Semillon 2006 A spotlessly clean bouquet, with faint tropical/blossom aromas, expanding into passionfruit and gooseberry flavours on the palate. Screwcap. 12° alc. **Rating** 88 **To** 2009 $18

Shiraz Cabernet Sauvignon 2004 A light- to medium-bodied wine; fresh red and black fruits, with hints of mint and leaf; minimal tannins. Screwcap. 13.5° alc. **Rating** 87 **To** 2009 $19

Holm Oak

RSD 256 Rowella, West Tamar, Tas 7270 **Region** Northern Tasmania
T (03) 6394 7577 **F** (03) 6394 7350 **www.**holmoakvineyards.com.au **Open** 7 days 10–5
Winemaker Rebecca Catlin **Est.** 1983 **Cases** 2500

Holm Oak takes its name from its grove of oak trees, planted around the turn of the 20th century, and originally intended for the making of tennis racquets. In 2004 Ian and Robyn Wilson purchased the property. The 7-ha vineyard is planted to pinot noir, cabernet sauvignon, riesling and sauvignon blanc (the latter not yet bearing), with small quantities of merlot and cabernet franc. In 2006 the Wilson's daughter Rebecca (with extensive winemaking experience both in Australia and California) and Stuart Catlin took over the lease. While there is no intention to radically extend the vineyard, a new winery is under construction with a capacity of 100 tonnes; it is expected that 50 tonnes will be processed for the Holm Oak label and the remainder for contract clients.

ΨΨΨΨΨ **Riesling 2005** Herb and crushed citrus leaf aromas; a tangy, citrussy palate has both balance and length, the extra year in bottle having hugely benefited the wine. Screwcap. 11.7° alc. **Rating** 94 **To** 2012 $25

ΨΨΨΨΨ **Riesling 2006** Some colour development; plenty of tropical fruit, with balancing acidity; there may be some (inexplicable) bottle variation with this wine. Screwcap. 12.3° alc. **Rating** 90 **To** 2016 $20

ΨΨΨΨ **Cabernet Sauvignon 2004** Hue good, though slightly cloudy; clear-cut cabernet sauvignon, but not a wine for cool Tasmanian vintages; does have length (and, of course, acidity). Cork. 13° alc. **Rating** 87 **To** 2014 $25

Home Hill

38 Nairn Street, Ranelagh, Tas 7109 **Region** Southern Tasmania
T (03) 6264 1200 **F** (03) 6264 1069 **www.**homehillwines.com.au **Open** 7 days 10–5
Winemaker Peter Dunbaven **Est.** 1994 **Cases** 3000

Terry and Rosemary Bennett planted their first 0.5 ha of vines in 1994 on gentle slopes in the beautiful Huon Valley. The plantings were quickly extended to 3 ha, with another ha planted in 1999. The varieties planted are pinot noir, chardonnay and sylvaner, and the quality of the chardonnay and pinot noir in particular is exemplary.

ΨΨΨΨΨ **Pinot Noir 2005** Perfect red-purple hue; a beautiful wine with a cascade of plum, spice and cherry fruit; perfect composition, balance, line and length. Gold medal Tas Wine Show '07. Screwcap. 14° alc. **Rating** 96 **To** 2014 $30
Kelly's Reserve Pinot Noir 2005 Medium to full purple-red; a complex, layered array of ripe plum fruit with splashes of spice, all with finely interwoven tannins giving great structure. Gold medal Tas Wine Show '07. Screwcap. 14° alc. **Rating** 94 **To** 2013 $35

ΨΨΨΨ **Kelly's Sticky 2004** Remarkable effort for sylvaner; good length, intensity and balance for a variety which seldom delivers. Screwcap. **Rating** 87 **To** 2008 $19

Honeytree Estate

16 Gillards Road, Pokolbin, NSW 2321 **Region** Lower Hunter Valley
T (02) 4998 7693 **www.**honeytreewines.com **Open** Wed–Fri 11–4, w'ends 10–5
Winemaker Monarch Winemaking Services **Est.** 1970 **Cases** 2400

The Honeytree Estate vineyard was first planted in 1970, and for a period of time wines were produced. It then disappeared, but the vineyard has since been revived by Dutch-born Henk Strengers and family. Its 10 ha of vines are of shiraz, cabernet sauvignon, semillon and a little clairette, known in the Hunter Valley as blanquette, a variety which has been in existence there for well over a century. Jancis Robinson comments that the wine 'tends to be very high in alcohol, a little low in acid and to oxidise dangerously fast', but in a sign of the times, the first Honeytree Clairette sold out so quickly (in 4 weeks) that 2.2 ha of vineyard has been grafted over to additional clairette. Exports to The Netherlands.

ΨΨΨΨ♀ **Veronica Hunter Valley Semillon 2006** A bouquet as clear as a spring day; well above-average fruit flavour and depth for such a young wine, but no heaviness; drink now or in 15 years. Screwcap. 11° alc. **Rating** 93 **To** 2020 $15
Hunter Valley Cabernet Sauvignon 2005 Has more varietal character than the majority of Hunter cabernets with blackcurrant and cassis, fine tannins, and a positive touch of oak. Screwcap. 13.6° alc. **Rating** 91 **To** 2015 $25

ΨΨΨΨ **Paul Alexander Hunter Valley Shiraz 2004** Regional earthy/leathery/spicy characters are highlighted by the relatively low alcohol. Which way will the cat jump? Screwcap. 13° alc. **Rating** 89 **To** 2012 $25

Hood Wines
★★★★★

208 Denholms Road, Cambridge, Tas 7170 **Region** Southern Tasmania
T (03) 6248 5844 **F** (03) 6248 5855 **www**.hoodwines.com.au **Open** W'ends 10–5
Winemaker Andrew Hood, Alain Rousseau **Est.** 1990 **Cases** 50 000
In 2003 the former Wellington winery was acquired by Tony Scherer and Jack Kidwiler of Frogmore Creek and renamed Hood Wines. It will continue to operate as previously, making both its own label wines and wines for its other contract customers while a new winery is constructed on the Frogmore Creek property. The latter will be exclusively devoted to organically grown wines. Exports to the US, Trinidad/Tobago, Indonesia and Japan.

ΨΨΨΨ♀ **Wellington Iced Riesling (375 ml) 2005** Vibrant lemon tingle flavours, fresh and zingy; a great aperitif style, or serve with fresh fruit. Screwcap. 8.5° alc. **Rating** 93 **To** 2015 $26
Wellington Riesling 2006 A highly aromatic display of citrus, apple blossom, followed by a long and intense palate which finishes strongly, perhaps a little too much so for some. Screwcap. 13.9° alc. **Rating** 91 **To** 2016 $22
Wellington Reserve Chardonnay 2005 A powerful, big and lusciously rich wine, full of interest, though far from typical. Screwcap. 14.4° alc. **Rating** 90 **To** 2011 $50
FGR Riesling 2006 Has all the requisites, but really needs to be held for another 2–3 years before it opens up. FGR stands for 40 grammes residual sugar, the wine made in the style of Mosel, Germany. Screwcap. 9.3° alc. **Rating** 90 **To** 2012 $22

ΨΨΨΨ **Wellington Gewurztraminer 2006** A relatively soft mouthfeel, but does have attractive spicy nuances typical of the variety. Screwcap. 13.4° alc. **Rating** 88 **To** 2009 $23.50
Roaring 40s Rose 2006 Well-handled cabernet sauvignon, with sweetness off-set by appropriate savoury nuances. Cabernet Sauvignon (50%)/Merlot (25%)/Pinot Noir (25%). Screwcap. 13° alc. **Rating** 87 **To** 2008 $19
Wellington Pinot Noir 2005 An elegant, but very savoury style, needing a touch more red fruit for higher points. Screwcap. 14.1° alc. **Rating** 87 **To** 2009 $32

Hope Estate
★★★★☆

Broke Road, Broke, NSW 2330 **Region** Lower Hunter Valley
T (02) 4993 3555 **F** (02) 4993 3556 **www**.hopeestate.com.au **Open** 7 days 10–5
Winemaker James Campkin **Est.** 1996 **Cases** 40 000
Hope Estate has, in the manner of a hermit crab, cast off its older, smaller shell, and moved into a resplendent new home. New in the sense for Hope Estate, for it is in fact the former Rothbury Estate winery. The timing was serendipitous, the giant miner Xstrata found a rich coal seam under the Saxonvale winery previously owned by Michael Hope, and made an offer he couldn't refuse. It will be interesting to watch the future development of Hope Estate, made more complex by the acquisition of quality vineyards in WA. It has also brought Virgin Hills under its umbrella, the once distinctive white and gold label gone forever.

ΨΨΨΨΨ **Virgin Hills 2003** Spotless; medium-bodied, with supple mouthfeel; a seamless flow of varietal influences, and no hint of green; fine tannins, quality oak. Cabernet Sauvignon (76%)/Shiraz/Merlot/Malbec. Cork. 13.5° alc. **Rating** 94 To 2023 $60

ΨΨΨΨΨ **Hunter Valley Shiraz 2005** Flush with ripe blackcurrant plum fruit; a generous splash of oak and tannins in support; impressive quality – and price. Cork. 13.5° alc. **Rating** 93 **To** 2018 $20
Virgin Hills 2001 Medium-bodied; much softer and sweeter cassis red berry fruit than the '02, only to be expected given the 'hot' vintage; ripe tannins. Cork. 13° alc. **Rating** 93 **To** 2015 $60
Virgin Hills 2002 The cool vintage should have made the wine greener and while there is an element of that, the wine is a major achievement; should last. It is also the last vintage to be labelled with the distinctive gold on white, bold Virgin Hills name. Cork. 13° alc. **Rating** 90 **To** 2012 $60

ΨΨΨΨ **Estate Grown Hunter Valley Semillon 2006** Clean and fresh; not particularly long or intense; perhaps picked a fraction too late. Screwcap. 11.5° alc. **Rating** 89 To 2009 $18
Margaret River Sauvignon Blanc Semillon 2005 A fresh, clean bouquet not ageing; the light- to medium-bodied palate has gentle tropical and passionfruit flavours, aided by some structure from the semillon. Screwcap. 12.5° alc. **Rating** 89 To 2008 $22
The Ripper Shiraz 2004 Sourced from Great Southern, with a slightly astringent bouquet, but coming through strongly on the palate and finish. **Rating** 89 **To** 2015 $25
Hunter Valley Merlot 2005 Light red fruits; has not been over-extracted or over-oaked, but this is the wrong place for the variety. Cork. 13.5° alc. **Rating** 87 To 2008 $18
The Cracker Estate Grown Cabernet Merlot 2004 A vibrant wine, providing an Indian arm wrestle between the ripe fruit notes and the green tannins and acidity. Comes from Pope's WA vineyard, but the back label statement 'grown, produced and bottled at Hope Estate' is interesting. Cork. 13° alc. **Rating** 87 **To** 2014 $22

Hopwood ★★★

887 Murray Valley Highway, Echuca, Vic 3564 **Region** Goulburn Valley
T (03) 5480 7090 **F** (03) 5480 7096 **www**.hopwood.com.au **Open** Mon–Fri 9–5
Winemaker Don Buchanan, Rohan Stewart **Est.** 2000 **Cases** 10 000
Previously known first as Echuca Estate Wines, and then by its corporate owner, New Glory Pty Ltd. Since taking the reins, industry veteran Don Buchanan has focused on retrellising and training the 38-ha vineyard planted to verdelho, viognier, shiraz, cabernet sauvignon, durif, sangiovese and petit verdot. The wines are released in 2 price levels: Charlotte's Farm the entry point, and the Hopwood Single Vineyard premium range. Exports to the UK, Canada, Singapore and Hong Kong.

Horndale ★★★☆

41-45 Fraser Avenue, Happy Valley, SA 5159 **Region** McLaren Vale
T (08) 8387 0033 **F** (08) 8387 0033 **Open** Mon–Sat 9–5, Sun & public hols 10–5.30
Winemaker Phil Albrecht (fortified), Bleasdale, Patritti **Est.** 1896 **Cases** 1200
Established in 1896 and has remained continuously in production in one way or another since that time, though with a number of changes of ownership and direction. My father used to buy Horndale Brandy 70 years ago, but it no longer appears on the extensive price list.

ΨΨΨΨΨ **Old Horndale Limited Release Centenary Fine Old Tawny Port NV**
Obvious age shown by the mahogany-olive colour; quite complex and well-balanced rancio, spice, biscuit and Christmas cake flavours; gentle spirit. Cork. 18.5° alc. **Rating** 90 **To** 2008 $25

ΨΨΨΨ **Old Horndale Shiraz 2005** The typical soft, rounded fruit profile of Langhorne Creek shiraz; good wine at the price. Cork. 14° alc. **Rating** 87 **To** 2008 $12.90

Old Horndale Achtzehn Fortified Cabernet Frontignac NV A strange and wondrous blend, which works much better than expected; it has length and quite good balance, with underlying notes of vanilla and mocha Cork. 18° alc. **Rating** 87 **To** 2008 $9

Horvat Estate   ★★★★☆

2444 Ararat-St Arnaud Road, Landsborough, Vic 3384 **Region** Pyrenees
T (03) 5356 9208 **F** (03) 5356 9208 **Open** 7 days 10–5
Winemaker Andrew Horvat, Gabriel Horvat **Est.** 1995 **Cases** 1500
The Horvat family (including Janet, Andrew and Gabriel) began developing their 5-ha vineyard of shiraz in 1995, supplementing production with contract-grown grapes. The wines are made using traditional methods and ideas, deriving in part from the family's Croatian background.

ΨΨΨΨΨ **Premium Family Reserve Pyrenees Shiraz 2004** Healthy colour; similar to its lesser brother; no greater alcohol, but more silky red fruits before strengthening tannins come on the finish. Cork. 13° alc. **Rating** 92 **To** 2014 $25

Grampians Shiraz 2004 Crammed with regional shiraz characters; bramble, licorice, blackberry and mint all take turns to express themselves; overall good balance, low to moderate alcohol no issue. Twin top. 13° alc. **Rating** 90 **To** 2012 $15

🍂 Hotham Ridge Winery   ★★☆

586 Wandering-Pingelly Road, Wandering, WA 6308 **Region** Central Western Australia Zone
T (08) 9884 1521 **www**.hothamridge.com.au **Open** W'ends & public hols 12–5
Winemaker Wouter Denig **Est.** 1987 **Cases** 2050
Hotham Ridge Winery started life as Hotham Valley Estate, and after several changes of ownership, during which time the vineyards suffered a degree of neglect, the property was purchased by Leonard Bruin and Wouter Denig in 2002. By this time the winery had been stripped of all equipment, and had to be re-equipped for the '03 vintage. The patchwork quilt vineyard is planted to chardonnay, chenin blanc, riesling, semillon, cabernet franc, cabernet sauvignon, merlot, shiraz, tempranillo and zinfandel. Grafting of some of the riesling to viognier and verdelho is also underway. Exports to Singapore and The Netherlands.

ΨΨΨΨ **Semillon 2005** Plenty of flavour; a big-framed wine, not in the classic slow-developing style of the Hunter Valley, or elsewhere. Screwcap. 12.9° alc. **Rating** 87 **To** 2008 $12.50

Houghton   ★★★★★

Dale Road, Middle Swan, WA 6056 **Region** Swan Valley
T (08) 9274 9450 **F** (08) 9274 5372 **www**.houghton-wines.com.au **Open** 7 days 10–5
Winemaker Robert Bowen **Est.** 1836 **Cases** 280 000
The 5-star rating was once partially justified by Houghton White Burgundy (now called White Classic), one of Australia's largest-selling white wines: it was almost entirely consumed within days of purchase, but is superlative with 7 or so years' bottle age. The Jack Mann, Gladstones Shiraz, Houghton Reserve Shiraz, the Margaret River reds and Frankland Riesling are all of the highest quality, and simply serve to reinforce the rating. To borrow a saying of the late Jack Mann, 'There are no bad wines here.'

ΨΨΨΨΨ **Gladstones Margaret River Cabernet Sauvignon 2004** A veritable powerhouse, as the wine usually is. This is deadly serious cabernet sauvignon, like a knight in full-body armour. Inside there is a wealth of blackcurrant/blackberry fruit, and tannins as a second line of defence. When and how to attack is the question. Cork. 15° alc. **Rating** 96 **To** 2030 $60

Jack Mann 2002 The usual mega-style which manages to avoid being elephantine, simply needing the 20 years or so which Jack believed any red wine worthy of the name required. Layer upon layer of blackberry, blackcurrant and plum fruit, the new oak long since swallowed up, the tannins rendered mute by the thunder of the wine. Cork. 14° alc. **Rating** 96 **To** 2037 $110

Crofters Sauvignon Blanc Semillon 2006 Spotlessly clean and fresh bouquet; lively passionfruit, gooseberry and lemon flavours; excellent mouthfeel and length; delicious. Screwcap. 12.9° alc. **Rating** 95 **To** 2008 $17

Pemberton Chardonnay 2005 Elegance is the essence of this wine; grapefruit and nectarine are meshed with quality French oak; the full winemaker's bag of tricks has left no visible thumbprints. Cork. 12.9° alc. **Rating** 95 **To** 2015 $27.50

Gladstones Frankland River Shiraz 2003 Powerful but not aggressive; very complex layers of black fruits, licorice and pepper, the tannins and oak playing a mere support role. Its life is limited only by the cork. Cork. 14.1° alc. **Rating** 95 **To** 2030 $60

Frankland River Shiraz 2004 Firm, but not hard, fruit expression, ranging through blackberry, licorice, spice and black pepper; the tannin structure is especially well-executed. Cork. 15.4° alc. **Rating** 94 **To** 2029 $30

Margaret River Cabernet Sauvignon 2004 Another powerful wine, but significantly more accessible. Certainly, the fruit is classic blackcurrant, and the tannins are there for the long haul, but it will welcome those who open the bottle many years before the Gladstones. Cork. 13.9° alc. **Rating** 94 **To** 2020 $30

ɥɥɥɥɥ **Pemberton Sauvignon Blanc 2006** Fragrant passionfruit and gooseberry aromas (no sweatiness or reduction); lively, fresh and zesty palate, with a long finish. Screwcap. 12° alc. **Rating** 93 **To** 2008 $25

Crofters Cabernet Merlot 2004 Medium- to full-bodied; a complex wine with strong fruit and strong oak inputs immediately apparent; blackcurrant and a touch of licorice with firm, ripe tannins in support. Cork. 14.5° alc. **Rating** 93 **To** 2024 $23

ɥɥɥɥ **Sauvignon Blanc Semillon 2006** Fresh, lively, tangy/citrussy aromas; lemon juice and lemon sherbet flavours; lively and fresh, good finish. Cork. 12.5° alc. **Rating** 88 **To** 2008 $10

Chardonnay Verdelho 2006 Has quite high aromatics to its tropical fruit; these 2 varieties were and are key components of White Classic, and may develop equally well with time in bottle. Cork. 13.5° alc. **Rating** 88 **To** 2011 $10

Cabernet Shiraz Merlot 2005 Ripe fruits, some components suggesting over-ripeness, but at this price one shouldn't quibble; plenty of honest, overall flavour. Twin top. 13.5° alc. **Rating** 88 **To** 2011 $11

Chardonnay 2005 Fruit-driven; a nice balance between tropical and more citrus flavours, simply lacking intensity and complexity, though fresh. Twin top. 13.5° alc. **Rating** 87 **To** 2008 $11

House of Certain Views   ★★★★

1238 Milbrodale Road, Broke, NSW 2330 **Region** Lower Hunter Valley
T (02) 6579 1317 **F** (02) 6579 1267 **www.**margan.com.au **Open** 7 days 10–5
Winemaker Andrew Margan **Est.** 2001 **Cases** 1000
A stand-alone business owned by Andrew and Lisa Margan, with a fascinating portfolio of wines based on exclusive or fairly new winegrowing regions on the western side of the Great Dividing Range. The selection of the vineyard sites (via contract growers) involves a careful correlation of latitude, altitude, soil type and variety – the French catch it all in the single word 'terroir'. The packaging of the wines, incidentally, is brilliant.

Howard Park (Denmark)

★★★★★

Scotsdale Road, Denmark, WA 6333 **Region** Great Southern
T (08) 9848 2345 **F** (08) 9848 2064 **www**.howardparkwines.com.au **Open** 7 days 10–4
Winemaker Tony Davis, Andy Browning **Est.** 1986 **Cases** NFP
All the Howard Park wines are made here at the new, large winery. There are 3 groups of wines:
those sourced from either Great Southern or Margaret River; the icon Howard Park Riesling and
Cabernet Sauvignon Merlot; and the multi-regional MadFish range. All are very impressive.
Exports to all major markets.

♈♈♈♈♈ **Scotsdale Great Southern Shiraz 2004** Brightly coloured and clean, this is a
super-elegant and refined wine with great length and intensity. Spice and black
fruits have absorbed the French oak, the tannins perfect. Screwcap. 14.5° alc.
Rating 96 **To** 2024 $35
Riesling 2006 Vibrant and fragrant aromas of apple, passionfruit and lime juice
lead into a palate of wonderful intensity and lusciousness balanced by crisp
acidity. Screwcap. 12° alc. **Rating** 95 **To** 2026 $25
Chardonnay 2005 Spotlessly clean; as ever, a very pure, beautifully and
meticulously crafted wine, using high-quality grapes to start with; grapefruit
and nectarine flavours are as fresh and lively as is possible, having absorbed
12 months in French oak, and been subjected to virtually no mlf. Screwcap.
13.5° alc. **Rating** 95 **To** 2020 $38
Cabernet Merlot 2004 The typical velvet fist, with a panoply of blackcurrant
and cassis aromas and flavours and flavours; a supple finish, and fine tannins.
Screwcap. 13.5° alc. **Rating** 95 **To** 2019 $75
Cabernet Merlot 2003 An even better colour than the '04; more powerful
texture and structure, tannins to the fore; no velvet glove, just fist, demanding
patience; great length. Screwcap. 14° alc. **Rating** 95 **To** 2028 $75

Howard Park (Margaret River)

★★★★★

Miamup Road, Cowaramup, WA 6284 **Region** Margaret River
T (08) 9756 5200 **F** (08) 9756 5222 **www**.howardparkwines.com.au **Open** 7 days 10–5
Winemaker Tony Davis, Matt Burton **Est.** 1986 **Cases** NFP
In the wake of its acquisition by the Burch family, and the construction of a large state-of-the-art
winery at Denmark, a capacious cellar door (incorporating Feng Shui principles) has opened in
the Margaret River, where there are also significant estate plantings. The Margaret River flagships
are the Leston Shiraz and Leston Cabernet Sauvignon, but the Margaret River vineyards routinely
contribute to all the wines in the range, from MadFish at the bottom, to the icon Cabernet
Sauvignon Merlot at the top. Exports to all major markets.

♈♈♈♈♈ **Cabernet Sauvignon 2004** Flooded with ripe, gently sweet blackcurrant
fruit, it has a lovely silky texture and grain on the long palate and finish. Mount
Barker Cabernet Sauvignon (81%)/Margaret River Cabernet Sauvignon (17%)
/Margaret River Merlot (2%). Screwcap. 14.5° alc. **Rating** 96 **To** 2024 $35
Leston Margaret River Shiraz 2004 Medium red-purple; radically different
to the Scotsdale Shiraz; warm aromas, and a mix of predominantly black fruits
(blackberry) and some red cherry; French oak obvious. Screwcap. 14.5° alc.
Rating 94 **To** 2014 $35
MadFish Gold Turtle Shiraz 2004 Medium purple-red; fragrant, supple and
elegant; the touch of viognier may be small in percentage terms, but it infuses the
palate; delicious spice and apricot nuances. Screwcap. 14.5° alc. **Rating** 94
To 2015 $24

♈♈♈♈♉ **MadFish Chardonnay 2005** The price has steadily risen for this wine, simply in
recognition of the quality, which has always been good, and remains so; a mix of
melon and grapefruit, with positive barrel ferment characters; good length. Screwcap.
13.5° alc. **Rating** 93 **To** 2011 $25

MadFish Riesling 2006 Pale straw; clean, crisp and fresh; delicate citrus and passionfruit flavours, finishing with lemony acidity. Screwcap. 12° alc. **Rating** 92 **To** 2016 $16

MadFish Sauvignon Blanc Semillon 2006 While light-bodied and relatively delicate, has positive fruit expression with gentle tropical notes, ripe apple, and a hint of citrus from the semillon. Screwcap. 12.5° alc. **Rating** 91 **To** 2008 $18

MadFish Premium White 2006 Zesty, and with abundant character for an unoaked white; stone fruit and citrus; good length and finish. Screwcap. 13° alc. **Rating** 91 **To** 2010 $18

MadFish Premium Red 2004 Fresh, firm, medium-bodied wine with clear-cut blackcurrant and cassis fruit, with supporting tannins. Cabernet Sauvignon/Merlot. Screwcap. 14.5° alc. **Rating** 90 **To** 2012 $18

Howards Lane Vineyard

Howards Lane, Welby, Mittagong, NSW 2575 **Region** Southern Highlands
T (02) 4872 1971 **www.**howardslane.com.au **Open** 7 days 10–5
Winemaker Michelle Crockett (Contract) **Est.** 1991 **Cases** 600
Tony and Mary Betteridge migrated to Australia in 2002 with the dual objectives of finding an attractive place to live and a worthwhile occupation for their retirement. They say 'The beautiful view we chose came with the vineyard, thus determining our occupation. Within a year we had mastered the tractor, pruned our first vines, chosen a name, logo and label ..., planted a second vineyard, built a rustic cellar door, and added considerably more knowledge of wine culture to our limited experience of simply enjoying Cape (South African) wines.'

Southern Highlands Sauvignon Blanc 2006 Fresh, and no hint of reduction; gentle tropical, apple and gooseberry fruit aromas and flavours; not intense, but has good balance and length. Screwcap. 11.4° alc. **Rating** 90 **To** 2008 $18

Southern Highlands Merlot 2005 Fragrant spice, leaf and olive aromas lead into a savoury, medium-bodied wine with some length and clear varietal character; doesn't show its low alcohol on the palate nearly as much as the bouquet. Screwcap. 11.9° alc. **Rating** 87 **To** 2009 $20

Hugh Hamilton

McMurtrie Road, McLaren Vale, SA 5171 **Region** McLaren Vale
T (08) 8323 8689 **F** (08) 8323 9488 **www.**hughhamiltonwines.com.au **Open** Mon–Fri 10–5.30, w'ends & public hols 11–5.30
Winemaker Hugh Hamilton **Est.** 1991 **Cases** 19 000
Hugh Hamilton is the most recent member of the famous Hamilton winemaking family to enter the business with a label of his own. Production comes from 18.2 ha of estate plantings, supplemented by contract-grown material. Recent plantings go beyond the mainstream to sangiovese, tempranillo, petit verdot and saperavi. Exports to the UK, the US, Canada, Denmark and Malaysia.

The Loose Cannon McLaren Vale Viognier 2006 Goes close to the perfect midpoint between over-the-top oily flavour on the one hand, and anonymity on the other; stone fruit and apricot are precisely as they should be. Screwcap. 14.5° alc. **Rating** 90 **To** 2008 $19

The Villain McLaren Vale Cabernet Sauvignon 2005 Plenty of depth and structure consistent with the alcohol; blackcurrant fruits and earthy tannins, with a whisper of chocolate. Screwcap. 15° alc. **Rating** 90 **To** 2025 $24

The Scoundrel McLaren Vale Tempranillo 2005 A medium-bodied mix of varietal and regional influences; red fruits with a slightly lemony twist, and a core of dark chocolate; more flavour than structure, perhaps. Cork. 14.5° alc. **Rating** 90 **To** 2011 $24

ꟼꟼꟼꟼ   **Jekyll & Hyde McLaren Vale Shiraz Viognier 2005** A very big wine with a profusion of flavours; blackberry, blackcurrant and too much viognier (7%); may settle down with time. Cork. 15° alc. **Rating** 89 **To** 2018 $28

The Odd Ball McLaren Vale Saperavi 2005 A medium-bodied mix of predominantly black fruits, with some red cherry nuances, is supported by fine but ripe tannins. Simply needs a little more generosity. Cork. 13.5° alc. **Rating** 89 **To** 2015 $39

The Scallywag McLaren Vale Unwooded Chardonnay 2006 Clean, fresh, light nectarine and melon fruit; good length and balance; well above average. Screwcap. 13.5° alc. **Rating** 88 **To** 2009 $17

The Rascal Shiraz 2005 Firm, but slightly green tinges to the fruit are distracting. Screwcap. 14.5° alc. **Rating** 87 **To** 2012 $24

The Ratbag McLaren Vale Merlot 2004 Black olive components play a major role, blackberry fruit a minor one; tannins are firm but balanced. Screwcap. 14° alc. **Rating** 87 **To** 2012 $19

Hugo   ★★★☆

Elliott Road, McLaren Flat, SA 5171 **Region** McLaren Vale
T (08) 8383 0098 **F** (08) 8383 0446 **www**.hugowines.com.au **Open** Mon–Fri 9.30–5, Sat 12–5, Sun 10.30–5
Winemaker John Hugo **Est.** 1982 **Cases** 12 000
A winery which came from relative obscurity to prominence in the late 1980s with some lovely ripe, sweet reds which, while strongly American oak-influenced, were quite outstanding. Has picked up the pace again after a dull period in the mid-1990s. There are 32 ha of estate plantings, with part of the grape production sold to others. Exports to the UK, the US and Canada.

ꟼꟼꟼꟼꟼ   **Reserve McLaren Vale Shiraz 2004** Bright purple-red; medium-bodied, but intensely flavoured; cherry, plum and blackberry with chocolate and vanilla in support; controlled alcohol. Screwcap. 14.5° alc. **Rating** 94 **To** 2019

ꟼꟼꟼꟼ   **McLaren Vale Shiraz 2004** Curious aromas, possibly from the oak; a medium-bodied palate, with some of the intensity of the Reserve, though not the depth. Screwcap. 14.5° alc. **Rating** 89 **To** 2014

Dry Grown McLaren Vale Grenache Shiraz 2004 Driven by dry-grown, bush-pruned grenache; slightly jammy fruit characters unexpected for the region and vintage. Screwcap. 14.5° alc. **Rating** 89 **To** 2012

McLaren Vale Sauvignon Blanc 2006 Grass, herb and mineral notes are offset by the illusion of sweetness, perhaps from the alcohol, perhaps some residual sugar. Screwcap. 14° alc. **Rating** 87 **To** 2008

Humbug Reach Vineyard

72 Nobelius Drive, Legana, Tas, 7277 **Region** Northern Tasmania
T (03) 6330 2875 **F** (03) 6330 2739 **www**.humbugreach.com.au **Open** Not
Winemaker Winemaking Tasmania (Julian Alcorso) **Est.** 1988 **Cases** 450
The Humbug Reach Vineyard was established in the late 1980s on the banks of the Tamar River, with plantings of pinot noir; riesling and chardonnay followed thereafter. Owned by Paul and Sally McShane since 1999, who proudly tend the 5000 or so vines on the property.

ꟼꟼꟼꟼꟼ   **Riesling 2006** Good wine; nice balance and length, with nicely moderated citrus fruit running through to a long finish. 12° alc. **Rating** 90 **To** 2013 $23

Pinot Noir 2005 Silky, supple and fine, with an intense and long finish. Perhaps needs a little more sweet fruit. 12.7° alc. **Rating** 90 **To** 2011 $32

ꟼꟼꟼꟼ   **Chardonnay 2006** Apple, pear and stone fruit flavours; has length, though not overmuch intensity. 13° alc. **Rating** 87 **To** 2008 $21

Hundred Tree Hill

Redbank Winery, 1 Sally's Lane, Redbank, Vic 3478 **Region** Pyrenees
T (03) 5467 7255 www.sallyspaddock.com.au **Open** Mon–Sat 9–5, Sun 10–5
Winemaker Scott Hutton, Sasha Robb **Est.** 1973 **Cases** 3000
The next generation of the Robb family (Emily, Huw and Sasha) have established their own vineyard, with 6 ha each of shiraz, cabernet sauvignon and cabernet franc, plus 2 ha of pinot noir. Hundred Tree Hill was so named to commemorate the 100 trees which went into the building of the Hundred Tree Homestead. Exports to the US, Canada, Germany and Philippines.

Pyrenees Cabernet Sauvignon 2002 Savoury, earthy style; good structure and balance; not flamboyant, but has presence and length. Diam. 14° alc. **Rating** 89 To 2013 $14.50
Pyrenees Shiraz 2003 A solid, workmanlike wine with depth of flavour and structure; black fruits, fine tannins and just a hint of sweetness. Cork. 14° alc. **Rating** 88 **To** 2015 $14.50
Pyrenees Pinot Noir 2004 A pleasant, dry red wine with good balance; simply shows no vestige of pinot noir varietal character. Cork. 13.5° alc. **Rating** 87 To 2010 $14.50

Hungerford Hill

1 Broke Road, Pokolbin, NSW 2320 **Region** Lower Hunter Valley
T 1800 187 666 **F** (02) 4998 7375 www.hungerfordhill.com.au **Open** 7 days 10–5
Winemaker Phillip John, Andrew Thomas **Est.** 1967 **Cases** 50 000
Hungerford Hill, sold by Southcorp to the Kirby family in 2002, has emerged with its home base at the impressive winery previously known as One Broke Road. The development of the One Broke Road complex proved wildly uneconomic, and the rationalisation process has resulted in Hungerford Hill becoming the sole owner. The quality of the wines has seen production soar from 20 000 cases to 50 000 cases, reversing the pattern under prior Southcorp ownership. Terroir Restaurant and Wine Bar are run by award-winning chef Darren Ho. Exports to all major markets.

Hunter Valley Semillon 2006 A spotlessly clean bouquet; the palate is very expressive for young semillon, with a delicious mix of grass, herb and citrus; good balance and length; assured future. Screwcap. 11° alc. **Rating** 94 **To** 2021 $23
Tumbarumba Chardonnay 2005 Light straw-green; fragrant grapefruit and nectarine aromas; an elegant, intense, fruit-driven style; good length and focus, likewise oak handling. Screwcap. 13.5° alc. **Rating** 94 **To** 2011 $28

Tumbarumba Pinot Noir 2005 Quite complex plum and spice flavours with good mouthfeel and length; strong varietal character throughout. Screwcap. 13.5° alc. **Rating** 93 **To** 2012 $28
Coonawarra Cabernet Sauvignon 2004 Attractive blackcurrant and mulberry fruit; good line without the cabernet doughnut structure; French oak integrated and balanced. Screwcap. 14.5° alc. **Rating** 93 **To** 2024 $38
Tumbarumba Chardonnay 2006 Spotlessly clean; quite ripe nectarine/citrus fruit, with more depth than is usual for Tumbarumba; the substantial amount of new French oak has been absorbed by the fruit. **Rating** 92 **To** 2012 $30
Tumbarumba Sauvignon Blanc 2006 Clean, crisp, citrus, tropical and pear aromas and flavours; good length and intensity. Screwcap. 13° alc. **Rating** 91 To 2008 $23
FishCage Sauvignon Blanc Semillon 2006 Pale straw-green; clean and fragrant, with lively herb, grass, lime and tropical notes; good structure. A lateral-thinking bargain blend of Currency Creek Semillon/Tumbarumba Sauvignon Blanc. Screwcap. 13° alc. **Rating** 90 **To** 2008 $14
Pinot Gris 2006 Has more than average attitude and flavour, with notes of pear, lychee and strawberry. Screwcap. 13.5° alc. **Rating** 90 **To** 2008 $23

FishCage Shiraz Viognier 2005 Aromatic, with viognier punching above its 5% contribution, as does the wine above its price; black cherry, plum and blackberry, with some spicy components. Screwcap. 13.5° alc. **Rating** 90 To 2015 $13.95

Orange Merlot 2004 Fragrant, spicy aromas; medium-bodied, with good structure although overall dominated by French oak. Blue Gold medal Sydney International Wine Competition '06. Screwcap. 14° alc. **Rating** 90 To 2012 $28

ΨΨΨΨ   **Hilltops Cabernet Sauvignon 2005** Fractionally hazy colour; savoury blackcurrant fruit with hints of earth, leaf and olive; needs a few years to soften. Screwcap. 14.5° alc. **Rating** 89 To 2013 $25

FishCage Chardonnay Viognier 2006 A slightly quixotic blend; light- to medium-bodied, with gentle tropical fruit; hard to dislike. Screwcap. 13° alc. **Rating** 88 To 2008 $14

Huntington Estate   ★★★★★

Cassilis Road, Mudgee, NSW 2850 **Region** Mudgee
T (02) 6373 3825 **F** (02) 6373 3730 www.huntingtonestate.com.au **Open** Mon–Fri 9–5, Sat 10–5, Sun 10–3
Winemaker Tim Stevens **Est.** 1969 **Cases** 20 000
In late 2005 the Stevens (of Abercorn) acquired Huntington from the founders Bob and Wendy Roberts. There is no reason to suppose the quality will change, and the Roberts family intend to remain involved, with the renowned Huntington Music Festival a major annual event. The red wines are outstanding and sell for relatively low prices. Tim Stevens is still getting his act together about sending samples under commercial labels, but have no fear for the quality of the wines.

Huntleigh Vineyards   ★★★★

38 Tunnecliffes Lane, Heathcote, Vic 3523 **Region** Heathcote
T (03) 5433 2795 www.heathcotewinegrowers.com.au **Open** 7 days 10–5.30
Winemaker Leigh Hunt **Est.** 1975 **Cases** 500
The wines are made at the winery by former stockbroker Leigh Hunt from 5 ha of estate-grown grapes; the last-tasted Cabernet Sauvignon was of exemplary quality.

Hurley Vineyard   ★★★★★

101 Balnarring Road, Balnarring, Vic 3926 **Region** Mornington Peninsula
T (03) 5931 3000 **F** (03) 5931 3200 www.hurleyvineyard.com.au **Open** By appt
Winemaker Kevin Bell **Est.** 1998 **Cases** 600
It's never as easy as it seems. Though Kevin Bell is now a Vic Supreme Court judge, and his wife Tricia Byrnes has a busy legal life as a family law specialist in a small Melbourne law firm, they have done most of the hard work in establishing Hurley Vineyard themselves, with family and friends. Most conspicuously, Kevin Bell has completed the Applied Science (Wine Science) degree at Charles Sturt University, and has drawn on Nat White for consultancy advice, and occasionally from Phillip Jones of Bass Phillip, and Domaine Fourrier in Gevrey Chambertin.

ΨΨΨΨΨ   **Homage Mornington Peninsula Pinot Noir 2005** Fractionally deeper colour than the Garamond; distinctly more complexity in both texture and structure; longer finish. Amazing that the wines should have the same alcohol. Diam. 13.4° alc. **Rating** 94 To 2012 $44

ΨΨΨΨΨ   **Garamond Mornington Peninsula Pinot Noir 2005** Light red-purple; clean, fragrant, red cherry aromas; a pretty wine, best enjoyed sooner than later. Diam. 13.4° alc. **Rating** 90 To 2009 $48

Hutton Vale Vineyard   ★★★★☆

Stone Jar Road, Angaston, SA 5353 **Region** Eden Valley
T (08) 8564 8270 **F** (08) 8564 8385 www.huttonvale.com **Open** By appt
Winemaker Torbreck Vintners, Rockford **Est.** 1960 **Cases** 600

John Howard Angas (who arrived in SA in 1843, aged 19, charged with the responsibility of looking after the affairs of his father, George Fife Angas) named part of the family estate Hutton Vale. It is here that John Angas, John Howard's great-great-grandson, and wife Jan tend a little over 26 ha of vines. Almost all the grapes are sold, but a tiny quantity has been made by the Who's Who of the Barossa Valley, notably David Powell of Torbreck and Chris Ringland of Rockford. Exports to the US, Singapore and Malaysia.

ŦŦŦŦŦ **Eden Valley Cabernet Sauvignon 2004** Aromatic, pure cassis and blackcurrant aromas; medium-bodied, smooth and supple; the flavours track the bouquet, with great length and balance; flavour with elegance. Screwcap. 14° alc. **Rating** 94 **To** 2029 $29

ŦŦŦŦ **Eden Valley Riesling 2005** Some lime citrus on the bouquet; a fraction heavy-footed, developing awkwardly, although it has no shortage of flavour. Screwcap. 12° alc. **Rating** 89 **To** 2013 $19
Eden Valley Grenache Mataro 2003 Light-bodied red; has elements of savoury structure, otherwise more towards rose territory; for those who like light reds. Screwcap. 14.5° alc. **Rating** 88 **To** 2012 $29

Ibis Wines

239 Kearneys Drive, Orange, NSW 2800 **Region** Orange
T (02) 6362 3257 **www**.ibiswines.com.au **Open** W'ends & public hols 11–5, or by appt
Winemaker Phil Stevenson **Est.** 1988 **Cases** 500
Ibis Wines is located just north of Orange on what was once a family orchard. Planting of the vineyard commenced in 1988, and a new winery was completed in 1998. The grapes are sourced from the home vineyards (at an altitude of 800 m), the Habitat Vineyard (at 1100 m on Mt Canobolas) (pinot noir and merlot) and the Kanjara Vineyard (shiraz).

Idle Hands Wines

Kurrajong Vineyard & Cottages, 614 Hermitage Road, Pokolbin, NSW 2320 **Region**
Lower Hunter Valley
T (02) 6574 7117 **F** (02) 6574 7006 **www**.kv.com.au **Open** By appt
Winemaker Letitia Cecchini (Contract) **Est.** 2005 **Cases** 800
Brothers Michael (a Sydney-based hand surgeon) and brother Peter Tonkin bought their 4.85 ha vineyard in 2004; 2.15 ha of verdelho had been planted in 1991, the shiraz (1.5 ha) and semillon (1.2 ha) following in 1994. Idle Hands is a self-deprecating acknowledgement that Tish Cecchini makes the wines, Ken Bray is viticultural consultant, and Chris Burgoyne is vineyard manager. But, then, none of those 3 would presume to start up a small hand surgery business.

ŦŦŦŦ **Reserve Hunter Semillon 2006** Clean and fresh; more weight than the alcohol would suggest; a herb, lanolin and lemon mix; part picked early, part late; perhaps more of the former would have been better. Screwcap. 11° alc. **Rating** 89 **To** 2014
Reserve Hunter Verdelho 2005 A complex wine, almost as if oak had been used; an array of tropical flavours bursts through on the long palate; has character. Screwcap. 14.5° alc. **Rating** 89 **To** 2010
Reserve Hunter Semillon 2005 Unusual Hunter Valley style, with much higher alcohol; needs time to move from ugly duckling to swan; the acidity is there. Screwcap. 12.7° alc. **Rating** 88 **To** 2012
Reserve Hunter Shiraz 2005 Clear and bright light red-purple; fresh, predominantly red fruits, with some darker notes; not particularly concentrated; minimal tannin inputs. **Rating** 88 **To** 2012
Reserve Hunter Verdelho 2006 Unusual aromas of overripe rock melon all the way through to grass, with a touch of banana on the way through; crisp acidity helps. Screwcap. 12.5° alc. **Rating** 87 **To** 2008

Idlewild

70 Milbrodale Road, Broke, NSW 2330 **Region** Lower Hunter Valley
T (02) 6574 5188 **F** (03) 6574 5199 **www**.wildbrokewines.com.au **Open** At Broke Estate
Winemaker Matthew Ryan **Est.** 1999 **Cases** 1000
Idlewild is a spin-off from Broke Estate/Ryan Family Wines; it is a partnership between Matthew
Ryan (who continues as viticulturist for Ryan Family Wines on Broke Estate and Minimbah
Vineyards) and wife Tina Ryan (who continues to run Wild Rhino PR Marketing & Events in
Sydney). It shares the 25 ha of vineyards with Broke Estate/Ryan Family Wines, although the
product range is different.

Indigo Ridge

★★★☆

Icely Road, Orange, NSW 2800 **Region** Orange
T (02) 6362 1851 **F** (02) 6362 1851 **www**.indigowines.com.au **Open** First & second
w'end of the month, public hols & w'ends 12–5, or by appt
Winemaker Contract **Est.** 1994 **Cases** 1800
Paul Bridge and Trish McPherson describe themselves as the owners, labourers and viticulturists
at Indigo Ridge; they planted and tend every vine on the 4-ha vineyard. The plantings are of
cabernet sauvignon, sauvignon blanc, merlot and a few riesling vines.

Inghams Skilly Ridge Wines

Gillentown Road, Sevenhill via Clare, SA 5453 **Region** Clare Valley
T (08) 8843 4330 **F** (08) 8843 4330 **Open** W'ends 10–5, or tel 0418 423 998
Winemaker Clark Ingham, O'Leary Walker **Est.** 1994 **Cases** 2000
Clark Ingham has established a substantial 25-ha vineyard of shiraz, cabernet sauvignon, merlot,
chardonnay, riesling, tempranillo and primitivo. Part of the production is made by contract
winemaker David O'Leary (with input from Clark Ingham); the remaining grape production is
sold. Exports to the UK and Germany.

🍷🍷🍷🍷🍷 Clare Valley Riesling 2006 Bright green-yellow; an intense and powerful
bouquet and palate with rich lime juice, spice and ripe apple; good length.
Screwcap. 12.5° alc. **Rating** 94 **To** 2016 $20

Ingoldby

Ingoldby Road, McLaren Flat, SA 5171 **Region** McLaren Vale
T (08) 8383 0005 **F** (08) 8383 0790 **www**.ingoldby.com.au **Open** 7 days 10–4
Winemaker Matt O'Leary **Est.** 1983 **Cases** 170 000
Part of the Fosters group, with the wines now having a sole McLaren Vale source. Over the past
few years, Ingoldby has produced some excellent wines which provide great value for money.

🍷🍷🍷🍷🍷 Golden Vine McLaren Vale Shiraz 2003 A mix of black and red fruits, more
supple and smooth than many; excellent tannin structure really lifts the wine;
the extended period of oak maturation likewise. Cork. 15° alc. **Rating** 94
To 2023 $43.95
McLaren Vale Cabernet Sauvignon 2004 Nicely weighted and structured;
delicious blackcurrant and cassis fruit; fine tannins, good length, oak in a pure
support role. The quality of '04 shines through once again. Cork. 14° alc.
Rating 94 **To** 2019 $18.95

🍷🍷🍷🍷🍷 McLaren Vale Chardonnay 2006 Demonstrates the subtlety of touch and
sophistication the wine has shown in recent vintages; nectarine and stone fruit
supported by quality French oak. Screwcap. 13.5° alc. **Rating** 92 **To** 2012 $18.95
McLaren Vale Shiraz 2004 Bright, fresh fruit in usual McLaren Vale style; a mix
of blackberry fruit, chocolate and a dash of licorice; a little red fruit is a flavour bolt-
on. Poor-quality cork. 14° alc. **Rating** 90 **To** 2014 $18.95

McLaren Vale Semillon Sauvignon Blanc 2005 Quite rich, and a seamless balance between the varieties; citrus, grass and herb elements dominate; good length. Screwcap. 12.5° alc. **Rating** 89 **To** 2009 $18.95
McLaren Vale Rose 2006 Vivid purple-red; a robust wine, almost into light dry red, but is fresh and not sweet, just lots of cherry fruit. Screwcap. 14° alc. **Rating** 89 **To** 2008 $18.95

Inneslake Vineyards ★★★

The Ruins Way, Inneslake, Port Macquarie, NSW 2444 **Region** Hastings River
T (02) 6581 1332 **F** (02) 6581 1954 www.inneslake.com.au **Open** 7 days 10–5
Winemaker Nick Charley, Cassegrain **Est.** 1988 **Cases** 1500
The property upon which the Inneslake vineyard is established has been in the Charley family's ownership since the turn of the 20th century, but had been planted to vines by a Major Innes in the 1840s. After carrying on logging and fruit growing at various times, the Charley family planted vines in 1988 with the encouragement of John Cassegrain. Around 4.5 ha of vines have been established.

Iron Pot Bay Wines ★★★

766 Deviot Road, Deviot, Tas 7275 **Region** Northern Tasmania
T (03) 6394 7320 **F** (03) 6394 7346 www.ironpotbay.com.au **Open** Thurs–Sun 11–5 Sept–May, June–Aug by appt
Winemaker Andrew Pirie **Est.** 1988 **Cases** 2100
Iron Pot Bay is now part of the syndicate which established Rosevears Estate, with its large, state-of-the-art winery on the banks of the Tamar. The vineyard takes its name from a bay on the Tamar River (now called West Bay) and is strongly maritime-influenced, producing delicate but intensely flavoured unwooded white wines. It has 4.58 ha of vines, over half being chardonnay, the remainder semillon, sauvignon blanc, pinot gris, gewurztraminer and riesling.

 # Ironbark Hill Estate ★★★★☆

694 Hermitage Road, Pokolbin, NSW 2321 **Region** Lower Hunter Valley
T (02) 4964 4028 **F** (02) 4964 4957 www.ironbarkhill.com.au **Open** 7 days 10–5
Winemaker Trevor Drayton **Est.** 1990 **Cases** 5000
Ironbark Hill Estate is owned by Peter Drayton and his accountant, Michael Dillon. His father Max Drayton, and brothers John, Trevor and Greg, run Drayton's Family Wines. There are 15 ha of estate plantings of semillon, chardonnay, verdelho, shiraz, cabernet sauvignon and merlot. Peter Drayton is a commercial/industrial builder, and constructing the cellar door was a busman's holiday. The hope is that the striking building and landscape surrounds will bring more wine tourists to the Hermitage Road end of Pokolbin. The quality of the wines, too, is commendable.

 Shiraz 2003 Bright, clear purple-red; an excellent regional-varietal symbiosis; elegant and medium-bodied, with a long, clear finish. Cork. 13.5° alc. **Rating** 94 **To** 2018 $25

Semillon 2004 Light straw-green; evolving slowly but surely; attractive varietal fruit in a traditional spectrum of aromas and flavours; good acidity and balance. Screwcap. 10.5° alc. **Rating** 93 **To** 2019 $20
Chardonnay 2004 Light straw-green; firm and tight style; melon and citrus flavours are fresh and lively; long finish, the oak largely incidental. Cork. 12.5° alc. **Rating** 90 **To** 2010 $25

 Merlot 2003 A savoury mix of red fruits, olive and earth; well-made, but the climate simply doesn't suit the variety. Cork. 13° alc. **Rating** 88 **To** 2008 $20

Ironwood Estate ★★★★☆

RMB 1288, Porongurup, WA 6234 **Region** Porongurup
T (08) 9853 1126 **F** (08) 9853 1172 **Open** By appt
Winemaker Dianne Miller, Bill Crappsley (Consultant) **Est.** 1996 **Cases** 2000

Ironwood Estate was established in 1996; the first wines were made from purchased grapes. In the same year, chardonnay, shiraz and cabernet sauvignon were planted on a northern slope of the Porongurup Range. The first estate-grown grapes were vinified at the Porongurup Winery, co-owned with Jingalla, Chatsfield and Montgomery's Hill.

Irvine

PO Box 308, Angaston, SA 5353 **Region** Eden Valley
T (08) 8564 1046 **F** (08) 8564 1314 **www.**irvinewines.com.au **Open** At Eden Valley Hotel
Winemaker James Irvine, Joanne Irvine **Est.** 1980 **Cases** 8000
Industry veteran Jim Irvine, who has successfully guided the destiny of so many SA wineries, quietly introduced his own label in 1991. The vineyard from which the wines are sourced was planted in 1983 and now comprises a patchwork quilt of 10 ha of vines. The flagship is the rich Grand Merlot. Exports to all major markets.

ρρρρρ **Barossa Valley Merlot Cabernet Franc 2004** As always, Irvine plays the oak
game with great skill, weaving oak through the fruit from start to finish; sweet
cassis and plum fruit, and fine, ripe tannins provide a delicious drink, even if it's
not Chateau Ausone. Screwcap. 14.5° alc. **Rating** 92 **To** 2014 $25
Reserve Eden Valley Zinfandel 2004 A spicy, sweet, aromatic bouquet leads
into a cherry, raspberry palate; judging the ripeness of zinfandel is extremely
difficult, and Irvine has got it spot-on. ProCork. 14° alc. **Rating** 90 **To** 2012 $39

ρρρρ **Barossa Valley Pinot Gris 2006** No reduction; powerful structure and weight,
but its difficult to say much about the flavour. Screwcap. 14° alc. **Rating** 89
To 2008 $24
Barossa Merlot 2004 Undoubtedly varietal, but very stemmy/spicy/leafy/green
olive overtones to the red fruit core are a little confronting. Screwcap. 14.5° alc.
Rating 88 **To** 2010 $25
Barossa Merlot Brut MV NV An acquired taste, I'm afraid, and one which I
haven't (acquired); at least the wine is not excessively sweet. 14° alc. **Rating** 87
To 2010 $26

Island Brook Estate

Bussell Highway, Metricup, WA 6280 **Region** Margaret River
T (08) 9755 7501 **F** (08) 9755 7008 **www.**islandbrook.com.au **Open** 7 days 10–5
Winemaker Flying Fish Cove **Est.** 1985 **Cases** 2000
Island Brook Estate is a small boutique winery situated in the middle of the Margaret River. Owners Peter and Linda Jenkins have begun the process of seeking certification as organic grapegrowers. Luxurious accommodation set among 45 acres of forest is available.

Ivanhoe Wines

Marrowbone Road, Pokolbin, NSW 2320 **Region** Lower Hunter Valley
T (02) 4998 7325 **F** (02) 4998 7848 **www.**ivanhoewines.com.au **Open** 7 days 10–5
Winemaker Stephen and Tracy Drayton **Est.** 1995 **Cases** 7000
Stephen Drayton is the son of the late Reg Drayton and, with wife Tracy, is the third branch of the family to be actively involved in winemaking in the Hunter Valley. The property on which the vineyard is situated has been called Ivanhoe for over 140 years, and 25 ha of 30-year-old vines provide high-quality fruit for the label. The plans are to build a replica of the old homestead (burnt down, along with much of the winery, in the 1968 bushfires) to operate as a sales area.

ρρρρ **SGD Shiraz Pressings 2004** Strangely elegant, given its pressings name; has both
length and balance. **Rating** 89 **To** 2014 $24
Late Picked Gewurztraminer 2005 Curiously lacking in varietal character,
though there is a touch of spice, and the balance is good. **Rating** 87 **To** 2008 $23

Izway Wines ★★★☆

31 George Street, North Adelaide, SA 5006 (postal) **Region** Barossa Valley
T 0423 040 385 **Open** Not
Winemaker Craig Isbel, Brian Conway **Est.** 2002 **Cases** 800
Izway Wines is the venture of business partners Craig Isbel and Brian Conway, both of whom have significant Australian and international wine industry experience. It is a virtual winery, purchasing small quantities of grenache from 80-year-old vines in Greenock, mourvedre from 30-year-old vines in Gomersal, and shiraz from 5-year-old vines in Ebenezer.

🍷🍷🍷🍷 **Bruce Barossa Valley Shiraz 2004** Powerful and dense, but hijacked by the alcohol; black fruits, prune and some confit plum, the apparent sweetness from the alcohol. High-quality cork. 15.5° alc. **Rating** 88 **To** 2015 $35
Mates 2006 Pleasant, fresh, lively fruit; an early-drinking style, but has good structure nonetheless. Grenache/Shiraz/Mataro. Screwcap. 14.5° alc. **Rating** 88 **To** 2008 $24

Jackson's Hill Vineyard ★★★☆

Mount View Road, Mount View, NSW 2321 **Region** Lower Hunter Valley
T 1300 720 098 **F** 1300 130 220 **www**.jacksonshill.com.au **Open** By appt
Winemaker Christian Gaffey **Est.** 1983 **Cases** 1500
One of the low-profile operations on the spectacularly scenic Mount View Road, making small quantities of estate-grown (3 ha) wine sold exclusively through the cellar door and Australian Wine Selectors.

🍷🍷🍷🍷½ **Reserve Semillon 2005** Fine, pure, intense and focused; long and lively; lemon/mineral flavours. **Rating** 93 **To** 2018

🍷🍷🍷🍷 **The Underblock Semillon 2005** Firm, slightly closed; perhaps a touch of reduction or just a phase in development. Headed for much better things. **Rating** 89 **To** 2015

Jacob's Creek ★★★★★

Jacob's Creek Visitor Centre, Barossa Valley Way, Rowland Flat, SA 5352 **Region** Barossa Valley
T (08) 8521 3000 **F** (08) 8521 3003 **www**.jacobscreek.com **Open** 7 days 10-5
Winemaker Philip Laffer, Bernard Hicken **Est.** 1973 **Cases** NFP
Jacob's Creek is one of the largest selling brands in the world and is almost exclusively responsible for driving the fortunes of this French-owned (Pernod Ricard) company. A colossus in the export game, chiefly to the UK and Europe, but also to the US and Asia. Wine quality across the full spectrum from Jacob's Creek upwards has been exemplary, driven by the production skills of Philip Laffer. The global success of the basic Jacob's Creek range has had the perverse effect of prejudicing many critics and wine writers who fail (so it seems) to objectively look behind the label and taste what is in fact in the glass. Jacob's Creek now has 4 ranges, with all the wines having a connection, direct or indirect, with Johann Gramp, who built his tiny stone winery on the banks of the creek in 1847. The 4-tier range consists of Icon (Johann Shiraz Cabernet); then Heritage (Steingarten Riesling, Reeves Point Chardonnay, Centenary Hill Barossa Shiraz and St Hugo Coonawarra Cabernet); then Reserve (all of the major varietals); and finally Traditional (ditto).

🍷🍷🍷🍷🍷 **Johann Shiraz Cabernet 2002** Very good colour; extremely potent, powerful and long, the back palate enriched with fine tannins and dark fruits; outstanding wine; French oak; 65%/35%. Cork. 14.5° alc. **Rating** 96 **To** 2022 $75
Reserve Riesling 2006 Lime juice special; very intense, very long and with great flavour. Clare Valley/Adelaide Hills. Screwcap. 13° alc. **Rating** 95 **To** 2016 $15.95
Centenary Hill Shiraz 2002 Colour still strong and vibrant; has all the flavour and structure expected from a top-quality Barossa Valley shiraz in '02: blackberry, plum and a touch of prune supported by soft but persistent tannins and quality oak. Multiple gold medals, mainly from lesser shows. Cork. 15° alc. **Rating** 95 **To** 2022 $39.95

Riesling 2006 An exceptional achievement; lots of citrus and lime fruit; good balance and length; gold medal Sydney Wine Show '07. Screwcap. 11.5° alc. Rating 94 To 2010 $9.95

Reserve Sauvignon Blanc 2006 Clean and highly aromatic; exceptionally rich and tropical, yet not heavy. Adelaide Hills/Limestone Coast 50/50. Screwcap. 13° alc. Rating 94 To 2008 $15.95

♥♥♥♥♡ **St Hugo Coonawarra Cabernet Sauvignon 2003** Substantial wine; blackcurrant, with distinctly earthy regional notes starting to show; positive tannin contribution through the length of the palate; almost Italianate. Cork. 14.2° alc. Rating 93 To 2018 $29.95

St Hugo Coonawarra Cabernet Sauvignon 2002 Potent, intense and concentrated wine with black fruits, somewhat akin to a black hole in space. Screwcap. 14.2° alc. Rating 93 To 2022 $41.95

Reserve Shiraz 2004 Plenty of black fruits enhanced by good tannins and controlled oak; length a feature. Cork. 15° alc. Rating 92 To 2014 $16

Steingarten Riesling 2003 Relatively soft and round on entry, with ripe, tropical, citrus fruits; strengthened by crisp, bright acidity on the finish. Rating 91 To 2013 $29.95

Reserve Chardonnay 2005 Elegant wine; the Limestone Coast components give a touch of grapefruit and white peach; French oak well-integrated, but positive. Excellent value. Cork. Rating 90 To 2010 $15.95

♥♥♥♥ **Chardonnay 2006** Generous yellow peach and fig fruit flavours, with a vague suggestion of oak influence; will not sell you short. Screwcap. 13.2° alc. Rating 88 To 2008 $9.99

Reserve Shiraz Rose 2006 Attractive cherry fruit; good line and balance; dry finish. A Reserve Rose; how quickly the world changes. Screwcap. 13° alc. Rating 88 To 2008 $16

JAG Wines   ★★★★☆

72 William Street, Norwood, SA 5067 (postal) **Region** Warehouse
T (08) 8364 4497 **F** (08) 8364 4497 **www.**jagwines.com **Open** By appt
Winemaker Grant Anthony White **Est.** 2001 **Cases** 700

The name is doubtless derived from that of owners Julie and Grant White, but might cause raised eyebrows in clothing circles. The project developed from their lifelong love of wine; it started with a hobby vineyard (along with friends) in the Adelaide Hills, then more formal wine studies, then highly successful amateur winemaking. The Whites obtained their producers' licence (and trade-mark) in 2001, purchasing grapes from the major SA regions, bringing them to their suburban house to be fermented and pressed, and then storing the wine offsite in French and American oak until ready for sale.

♥♥♥♥♥ **Josef Shiraz 2004** Medium- to full-bodied, but carries the same lamp of elegance as the others in the stable; blackberry and plum lead the way, tannins and oak in a pure support role. Screwcap. 14.5° alc. Rating 94 To 2029 $44.95

♥♥♥♥♡ **Barossa Shiraz 2004** Light- to medium-bodied; a savoury/spicy/earthy style, the black fruits supported by fine, ripe tannins; 2 years in American oak; 30-year-old vines, and a modest price. Screwcap. 14.5° alc. Rating 91 To 2015 $19.95

McLaren Vale Shiraz 2004 Light- to medium-bodied; fragrant, and for whatever reason the American oak (24 months) seems more prominent; has good texture, with a typical touch of dark chocolate and licorice. Screwcap. 14.6° alc. Rating 90 To 2014 $19.95

James Estate   ★★★☆

951 Bylong Valley Way, Baerami via Denman, NSW 2333 **Region** Upper Hunter Valley
T (02) 6547 5168 **F** (02) 6547 5164 **www.**jamesestatewines.com.au **Open** 7 days 10–4.30
Winemaker Peter Orr, Deane Rose **Est.** 1997 **Cases** 30 000

In 1997 the Cecchini family sold the assets of Serenella (but not the name) to David James, resulting in the change of name to James Estate. It is a large property, planted to 11 different white and red varieties, and with substantial production. In 2005 the business became even more complicated, when Tish Cecchini (winemaker at James Estate prior to its sale) sold the Serenella brand and assets to James Estate. Exports to Asia.

ŸŸŸŸ **Reserve McLaren Vale Barossa Valley Shiraz 2004** A medium-bodied mix of blackberry, mocha and chocolate aromas and flavours; well-balanced, but not intense or particularly long. Twin top. 14° alc. **Rating** 88 **To** 2012 $20

James Haselgrove

PO Box 271, McLaren Vale, SA 5171 **Region** McLaren Vale
T (08) 8332 0618 **F** (08) 8332 0638 **www.**haselgrovevignerons.com **Open** Not
Winemaker James Haselgrove **Est.** 1981 **Cases** 500
While in one sense this is now a virtual winery, Nick Haselgrove is quick to point out that it has access to substantial vineyards and winemaking resources. He and James Haselgrove (who founded this winery) are reluctant to see the business disappear, and intend to continue making and releasing wines under the James Haselgrove label. In terms of both price and style they will differ from Blackbilly (see separate entry). Exports to the US.

ŸŸŸŸŸ **Fleurieu Sauvignon Blanc 2006** No reduction whatsoever; crisp, punchy citrus/grass/tropical mix; a dry, lively finish. Screwcap. 13° alc. **Rating** 90 **To** 2008 $15

ŸŸŸŸ **10 Year Old Tawny NV** Some genuine tawny hues, and does show expected rancio; brandy snap biscuit flavours; good balance and length. Screwcap. 19° alc. **Rating** 89 **To** 2008 $16

 # Jamieson Valley Estate   **NR**

52 Stanhope Street, Malvern, Vic 3144 (postal) **Region** Upper Goulburn
T (03) 5777 0616 **F** (03) 9322 4699 **Open** Not
Winemaker Helen's Hill (Scott McCarthy) **Est.** 2003 **Cases** NA
Anna and Chris Dunphy began the development of their vineyard in 1990. They elected to focus solely on pinot noir, and have planted 1.8 ha of clones 114, 115, MV6 and 777. The vineyard is situated on a north-facing slope near the historic gold mining town of Jamieson, and benefits from the hot days and cool nights, which are especially suited to pinot. They say their aim is to make an 'approachable wine at a realistic price. We want Jameaux (their pinot) to be a signature that is a mixture of French sensibility and Australian larrakin-is'.

Jamiesons Run

Coonawarra Wine Gallery, Riddoch Highway, Penola, SA 5277 **Region** Coonawarra
T (08) 8737 3250 **www.**jamiesonsrun.com.au **Open** 7 days 10–5
Winemaker Andrew Hales **Est.** 1987 **Cases** 150 000
The wheel has turned a full 360° for Jamiesons Run. It started out as a single label, mid-market, high volume brand developed by Ray King during his time as CEO of Mildara. It grew and grew until the point where (Mildara having many years since been merged with Wolf Blass) decided to rename the Mildara Coonawarra winery as Jamiesons Run, with the Mildara label just one of a number of falling under the Jamiesons Run umbrella. Now the Jamiesons Run winery is no more, Fosters has sold it, but retained the brand, the cellar door moving to shared accommodation at the Coonawarra Wine Gallery. Exports to the UK.

ŸŸŸŸŸ **Mildara Rothwell Coonawarra Cabernet Sauvignon 2004** A lovely combination of finesse and flavour; perfect structure and the clearest possible cabernet varietal fruit in a blackcurrant mould. Gold medal National Wine Show '06. Cork. 14.5° alc. **Rating** 95 **To** 2019 $80

Mildara Coonawarra Cabernet Shiraz 2004 Supple and rich texture and structure; full and satisfying black fruits and ripe tannins; very good length. Screwcap. 14.5° alc. **Rating** 95 **To** 2019 $28.95

Winemaker's Reserve Shiraz Cabernet 2003 Plenty of weight, richness and structure; ripe fruit and ripe tannins. Cork. 14° alc. **Rating** 94 **To** 2015 $56.95

ΨΨΨΨ♀ Limestone Coast Sauvignon Blanc 2006 Very pleasant wine, with plenty of flavour at the commercial end, bolstered by a hint of sweetness. Screwcap. 12.5° alc. **Rating** 90 **To** 2008 $17.95

Mildara Coonawarra Shiraz 2004 Powerful, deep structure; layers of earthy black fruits supported by ripe tannins. Good value. Screwcap. 15° alc. **Rating** 90 **To** 2015 $28.95

Coonawarra Shiraz 2004 Medium-bodied with gentle blackberry fruit, with distinct spicy, savoury nuances; good length. Cork. 13.5° alc. **Rating** 90 **To** 2010 $16.95

ΨΨΨΨ Coonawarra Merlot 2004 Light- to medium-bodied; pleasing texture, and more cassis fruit than many of the merlots of the vintage. Cork. 14.5° alc. **Rating** 89 **To** 2010 $19.95

Coonawarra Cabernet Sauvignon 2004 Firm, uncluttered cabernet fruit; will build some earthy regional complexity over the next few years. Cork. 14° alc. **Rating** 88 **To** 2014 $19.95

Jamsheed

157 Faraday Street, Carlton, Vic 3053 (postal) **Region** Yarra Valley
T 0409 540 414 **F** (03) 5967 3581 **www**.jamsheed.com.au **Open** Not
Winemaker Gary Mills **Est.** 2003 **Cases** 200

Jamsheed is the venture of Gary Mills, proprietor of Simpatico Wine Services, a boutique contract winemaking company established at the new Hill Paddock Winery in Healesville. The wines are sourced from a 30-year-old, low-yielding vineyard, and are made using indigenous/wild yeasts and minimal handling techniques. For the short-term future the business will focus on old vine sites in the Yarra Valley, but plans are to include a Grampians and Heathcote Shiraz along with a Strathbogie Gewurztraminer. The name, incidentally, is that of a Persian king recorded in the Annals of Gilgamesh.

ΨΨΨΨΨ Yarra Valley Gewurztraminer 2006 Fragrant, spicy lychee varietal aromas are particularly impressive; there is far more varietal character than usual, yet it is still light on its feet, a graceful ballerina. Perfect acidity. Screwcap. 13° alc. **Rating** 94 **To** 2010 $25

Jane Brook Estate

229 Toodyay Road, Middle Swan, WA 6056 **Region** Swan Valley
T (08) 9274 1432 **F** (08) 9274 1211 **www**.janebrook.com.au **Open** Mon–Fri 10–5, w'ends & public hols 12–5
Winemaker Adam Barton **Est.** 1972 **Cases** 25 000

Beverley and David Atkinson have worked tirelessly to build up the Jane Brook Estate wine business over the past 30-plus years. The most important changes during that time have been the establishment of a Margaret River vineyard, and sourcing grapes from other southern wine regions in WA. Exports to the UK, the US and other major markets.

ΨΨΨΨ♀ Pemberton Margaret River Sauvignon Blanc 2006 Clean and bright; plenty of impact from the aroma through to the palate and finish; a mix of herbaceous, citrus and tropical fruit characters. Screwcap. 12° alc. **Rating** 93 **To** 2008 $20.50

Shovelgate Vineyard Margaret River Cabernet Sauvignon 2004 Bright red-purple; fresh, almost crisp, cassis/redcurrant/blackcurrant, fine tannins and gentle oak. Screwcap. 14.1° alc. **Rating** 92 **To** 2019 $25

🍷🍷🍷🍷 **Margaret River Chardonnay 2005** Light- to medium-bodied; clean and fresh stone fruit, nectarine and peach flavours supported by subtle, toasty oak. Screwcap. 13.5° alc. **Rating** 89 **To** 2011 $22.50
Margaret River Merlot 2004 Light- to medium-bodied, clean and fresh with quite vibrant red fruits; a little simple, perhaps. Screwcap. 13.9° alc. **Rating** 88 **To** 2011 $24.50

Jansz Tasmania

1216b Pipers Brook Road, Pipers Brook, Tas 7254 **Region** Northern Tasmania
T (03) 6382 7066 **F** (03) 6382 7088 www.jansztas.com **Open** 7 days 10–5
Winemaker Natalie Fryar **Est.** 1985 **Cases** 35 000
Jansz is part of the S Smith & Son/Yalumba group, and was one of the early sparkling wine labels in Tasmania, stemming from a short-lived relationship between Heemskerk and Louis Roederer. Its 15 ha of chardonnay, 12 ha of pinot noir and 3 ha of pinot meunier correspond almost exactly to the blend composition of the Jansz wines. It is the only Tas winery entirely devoted to the production of sparkling wine, which is of high quality. Exports to all major markets.

🍷🍷🍷🍷🍷 **Pipers River Vintage Cuvee 2002** A potent, complex wine showing the concentration of the base wine from the unusual vintage (very small berries); 30 months on lees has partially tamed the fruit; unusual style for Jansz. 13° alc. **Rating** 94 **To** 2010 $37

🍇 Jardine Wines

1 Mugsies Road, Moonambel, Vic 3478 **Region** Pyrenees
T (03) 5467 2376 www.jardinewines.com.au **Open** W'ends & public hols 11–5
Winemaker Col Jardine **Est.** 1999 **Cases** 600
Colin and Cynthia Jardine began the development of their 8.5-ha vineyard in 1999, planting 4 ha of shiraz, 3 ha of cabernet sauvignon and 1.5 ha of pinot noir. Col Jardine, who doubles up as viticulturist and winemaker, uses sustainable management practices, and limits the yield to no more than 2 tonnes to the acre.

🍷🍷🍷🍷🍷 **Moonambel Shiraz 2005** Deep, dense purple-red; lovely depth and texture to the seamless mix of black and red fruits, spice, licorice and cracked pepper; oak and tannins in perfect balance. Diam. 14.2° alc. **Rating** 95 **To** 2025 $35

🍷🍷🍷🍷🍷 **Red Block Moonambel Cabernet Sauvignon 2005** Sweet cassis blackcurrant fruit is the first and last impression; there is a slight hole in the mid-palate of an otherwise delicious wine. Diam. 13.5° alc. **Rating** 91 **To** 2020 $29

🍷🍷🍷🍷 **Moonambel Shiraz 2004** Light- to medium red-purple; clean, fresh red and black fruits; high acid and firm tannins provide a formidable finish, but should soften with time. Stained cork. Cork. 13.5° alc. **Rating** 89 **To** 2019 $35

Jarretts of Orange

Annangrove Park, Cargo Road, Orange, NSW 2800 **Region** Orange
T (02) 6364 3118 **F** (02) 6364 3048 **Open** By appt
Winemaker Chris Derrez **Est.** 1995 **Cases** 2000
Justin and Pip Jarrett have established a very substantial vineyard (140 ha), planted to chardonnay, cabernet sauvignon, shiraz, sauvignon blanc, merlot, pinot noir, riesling, marsanne, cabernet franc and verdelho. As well as managing the vineyard, they provide management and development services to growers of another 120 ha in the region. Most of the grapes are sold, with a limited amount produced for local distribution and by mail order. The wines are modestly priced.

🍷🍷🍷🍷 **Row 72 Sauvignon Blanc 2006** Spotlessly clean citrus, grass and mineral interwoven with some passionfruit flavours; needs a touch more length, perhaps. Screwcap. 13.5° alc. **Rating** 88 **To** 2008 $15

Jarvis Estate

Lot 13, Wirring Road, Margaret River, WA 6285 **Region** Margaret River
T (08) 9758 7526 **F** (08) 9758 8017 **www.**jarvisestate.com.au **Open** By appt
Winemaker Naturaliste Vintners (Bruce Dukes) **Est.** 1995 **Cases** 3000
Matt and Jackie Jarvis carefully researched the Margaret River region, and in particular the
Bramley locality, before purchasing their property, where they now live. It is planted to cabernet
sauvignon, shiraz, merlot, chardonnay and cabernet franc (8.4 ha). Exports to Taiwan, Greece and
Ireland.

Jasper Hill

Drummonds Lane, Heathcote, Vic 3523 **Region** Heathcote
T (03) 5433 2528 **F** (03) 5433 3143 **Open** By appt
Winemaker Ron Laughton, Emily Laughton **Est.** 1975 **Cases** 3500
The red wines of Jasper Hill are highly regarded and much sought after, invariably selling out at
the cellar door and through the mailing list within a short time of release. These are wonderful
wines in admittedly Leviathan mould, reflecting the very low yields and the care and attention
given to them by Ron Laughton. The oak is not overdone, and the fruit flavours show Heathcote
at its best. There has been comment (and some criticism) in recent years about the alcohol level
of the wines. Laughton responds by saying he picks the grapes when he judges them to be at
optimum ripeness, and is in no way chasing high alcohol, whether to suit the US market or
otherwise. Exports to the UK, the US and other major markets.

ȲȲȲȲȲ **Emily's Paddock Heathcote Shiraz Cabernet Franc 2005** Similar colour
to Georgia's; a firmer structure, resting on slightly more evident tannins, and the
fruit more towards black cherry and blackberry; a long, balanced finish. Cork.
13.5° alc. **Rating** 95 **To** 2020 $95

Georgia's Paddock Heathcote Shiraz 2005 Far lighter than previous
vintages; a medium–bodied, elegant wine; red cherry, black cherry and spice
intermingle with balanced oak; silky finish. Cork. 13.5° alc. **Rating** 94
To 2020 $72

Cornella Vineyard Heathcote Grenache 2005 Brilliant light purple-red;
lovely grenache, succulent and round, with spice and raspberry flavours; fine
tannins, long finish. Cork. 15° alc. **Rating** 94 **To** 2015 $48

ȲȲȲȲȲ **Georgia's Paddock Heathcote Riesling 2006** Powerful riesling; not
particularly fragrant, but has strong citrus and mineral strands, and a long finish.
Seems quite different to the '05. Cork. 12.5° alc. **Rating** 92 **To** 2013 $36

⚘ Jean Pauls Vineyard

RMB 6173, Yea, Vic 3717 (postal) **Region** Upper Goulburn
T (03) 5797 2235 **www.**jeanpaulsvineyard.com.au **Open** Not
Winemaker William de Castella **Est.** 1995 **Cases** 50
This is a cameo exercise, with all the detail portrayed in finest detail. It is owned by William and
Heather de Castella, a direct descendant of the famous de Castella family of the Yarra Valley.
Hubert de Castella established St Huberts, while brother Paul had the even larger Yering Vineyard
in his care. The full name of today's vigneron is William Jean Paul de Castella, hence the indirect
reference to William's distinguished forebears. His 3-ha vineyard has been run on full biodynamic
principles since the first 0.5 ha of shiraz was planted in 1994/95. The vineyard is NASAA
Certified Organic/Biodynamic and uses minimal irrigation. Even though copper and sulphur
sprays are permitted, they have never been used, and the yields are tiny. To add a further degree of
difficulty to an already difficult project, no sulphur dioxide is added to the wine either during
fermentation or prior to bottling.

ȲȲȲȲȲ **Yea Shiraz 2004** Plenty of blackberry and plum fruit, with no suggestion of
unripe fruit despite the low alcohol, nor of oxidation or mousiness despite the
absence of SO_2. Cork. 12.8° alc. **Rating** 90 **To** 2010 $26

Jeanneret Wines

Jeanneret Road, Sevenhill, SA 5453 **Region** Clare Valley
T (08) 8843 4308 **F** (08) 8843 4251 **Open** Mon–Fri 11–5, w'ends & public hols 10–5
Winemaker Ben Jeanneret **Est.** 1992 **Cases** 10 000
Jeanneret's winery has a most attractive outdoor tasting area and equally attractive picnic facilities, on the edge of a small lake surrounded by bushland. While the business did not open until 1994, its first wine was in fact made in 1992 (Shiraz) and it had already established a loyal following. National distribution; exports to the UK, Canada, Malaysia and Japan.

 Clare Valley Riesling 2006 Ripe citrus aromas; generous flavours, with considerable sweetness both from the fruit and residual sugar; now or later. Screwcap. 13° alc. **Rating** 91 **To** 2015 $18

Okey Dokey Clare Valley Chardonnay 2006 Within the limitations of Clare Valley chardonnay, Ben Jeanneret has done a good job; the oak is obvious, needless to say, but has abundant soft, peachy fruit to set it against. Screwcap. 14° alc. **Rating** 87 **To** 2008 $18
Dickie Clare Valley Rose 2006 Bright pink; small red fruit flavours give ample impact, and the wine is not too sweet. Screwcap. 13.5° alc. **Rating** 87 **To** 2008 $18

Jeir Creek ★★★★

Gooda Creek Road, Murrumbateman, NSW 2582 **Region** Canberra District
T (02) 6227 5999 **www.**jeircreekwines.com.au **Open** Thurs–Mon & hols 10–5
Winemaker Rob Howell **Est.** 1984 **Cases** 4500
Rob Howell came to part-time winemaking through a love of drinking fine wine, and is intent on improving both the quality and the consistency of his wines. It is now a substantial (and still growing) business, with the vineyard plantings increased to 11 ha by the establishment of more cabernet sauvignon, shiraz, merlot and viognier.

Riesling 2005 Very crisp, lively, fresh and elegant; lime juice and bright acidity revelling in the low alcohol. Screwcap. 11.2° alc. **Rating** 92 **To** 2013 $20

Jenke Vineyards ★★★★

Barossa Valley Way, Rowland Flat, SA 5352 **Region** Barossa Valley
T (08) 8524 4154 **F** (08) 8524 5044 **Open** 7 days 11–5
Winemaker Kym Jenke **Est.** 1989 **Cases** 8500
The Jenke family have been vignerons in the Barossa since 1854 and have over 45 ha of vineyards; a small part of the production is now made and marketed through a charming restored stone cottage cellar door. Exports to the US.

Reserve Barossa Shiraz 2002 Excellent retention of red-purple hue; the spicy, savoury bouquet is no guide to the sweet, supple black cherry and blackberry fruit which flows through to a long, slippery finish. Screwcap. 14° alc. **Rating** 94 **To** 2022 $35

 Golf Links VIneyard Barossa Cabernet Franc 2005 Nicely balanced and composed; perhaps the warmth of the Barossa Valley gets rid of the green/tobacco notes of cabernet franc as grown in the Loire Valley; more sweet and spicy than savoury, with good length. Screwcap. 14° alc. **Rating** 90 **To** 2014 $18

Barossa Shiraz 2005 Medium-bodied; a well-made traditional style; sweet blackberry and plum fruit, soft tannins and controlled mocha oak. Screwcap. 14.5° alc. **Rating** 89 **To** 2015 $28
Barossa Chardonnay 2005 A clean bouquet; peachy fruit has largely absorbed the 12 months in French oak; a solid, well-balanced wine. Screwcap. 14° alc. **Rating** 88 **To** 2009 $15

Barossa Merlot 2005 Light- to medium-bodied; savoury/olive/earth aromas and flavours are distinctly varietal; good length, and not too bitter on the finish. Screwcap. 14° alc. **Rating** 88 **To** 2013 $20

Barossa Cabernet Franc Rose 2006 Has some positive red berry fruit expression and length; this is drinking wine, not coloured water with incidental alcohol. Screwcap. 12.5° alc. **Rating** 87 **To** 2008 $13

Jeremiah One   ★★★★☆

PO Box 718, Surry Hills, NSW 2010 **Region** Warehouse
T (02) 9699 2124 **F** (02) 9699 3354 **www**.jeremiahone.com **Open** Not
Winemaker Jonathon Hyams, Pikes, Chain of Ponds **Est.** 2004 **Cases** 2000
Jeremiah One is a name borne of owner Jonathon Hyams' 20 years' experience in the wine industry. He has set up a virtual winery business, precisely sourcing contract-grown grapes and winemakers to match, spanning Clare Valley Riesling; Adelaide Hills Sauvignon Blanc, Pinot Grigio and Chardonnay; Lenswood Pinot Noir; and Adelaide Hills/Clare Valley Merlot.

Jerusalem Hollow   ★★★★

6b Glyde Street, East Fremantle, WA 6158 (postal) **Region** Margaret River
T (08) 9339 6879 **F** (08) 9339 5192 **www**.jerusalemhollowwines.com.au **Open** Not
Winemaker Harold Osborne, Frank Kittler (Contract) **Est.** 2000 **Cases** 500
Perth eye surgeon Bill Ward, wife (and former nurse) Louise and family began planting their 5.8-ha vineyard in 2000. Bill, a long term admirer of Champagne, was inspired by an article by Max Allen in the *Weekend Australian Magazine* in which Californian sparkling winemaker Harold Osborne (maker of Pelorus for Cloudy Bay in NZ) expressed the view that Margaret River was a good region for sparkling wine. This remains the main thrust of the business, with a side bet on Cabernet Sauvignon and a small amount of Roussanne Chardonnay to follow in due course. The name, incidentally, is a local one, but it so happens that Bill worked at the St John's eye hospital in Jerusalem as a surgical fellow in the late 1980s to early '90s.

Jim Barry Wines   ★★★★★

Craig's Hill Road, Clare, SA 5453 **Region** Clare Valley
T (08) 8842 2261 **F** (08) 8842 3752 **Open** Mon–Fri 9–5, w'ends, hols 9–4
Winemaker Mark Barry **Est.** 1959 **Cases** 80 000
The patriarch of this highly successful wine business, Jim Barry, died in 2004, but the business continues under the active management of various of his many children. There is a full range of wine styles across most varietals, but with special emphasis on Riesling, Shiraz and Cabernet Sauvignon. The ultra-premium release is The Armagh Shiraz, with the McCrae Wood red wines not far behind. Jim Barry Wines is able to draw upon 247 ha of mature Clare Valley vineyards, plus a small holding in Coonawarra. Worldwide distribution.

♛♛♛♛♛ **The Armagh Shiraz 2004** As ever, very dense purple-red; full-bodied, but nonetheless is disciplined, and holds its line and structure well; blackberry, licorice and dark chocolate with vanilla oak all coalesce; the wine should long outlive the cork (which is of good quality, it must be said). Cork. 15° alc. **Rating** 96 **To** 2034 $200

The McCrae Wood Shiraz 2004 Deep colour; abundant flavour fills the mouth; black fruits, licorice, dark chocolate, prune and plum. The tannins are excellent, fine and ripe, the oak well-handled; best for some years. Do you buy this wine, or pay almost 5 times as much for The Armagh? An invidious question, perhaps. Cork. 15° alc. **Rating** 95 **To** 2024 $45

Lodge Hill Riesling 2006 Aromas of lime blossom, herb and mineral lead into a direct line of pure lime flavours; excellent length; finesse with power. This or Florita as twice the price? Screwcap. 13.5° alc. **Rating** 94 **To** 2016 $19.95

The Florita Riesling 2005 Abundant lime/tropical fruit; while rich, it avoids heaviness; excellent structure, length and aftertaste. Fully priced. Screwcap. 13.5° alc. **Rating** 94 **To** 2020 $45

ΨΨΨΨΨ **The Lodge Hill Shiraz 2005** Strong colour; blackberry, spice plus touches of prune and mint; a typical Jim Barry shiraz: big, dense, chewy and ripe. Cork. 15° alc. **Rating** 93 **To** 2020 $19.95
Watervale Riesling 2006 A clean, but slightly closed bouquet; abundant flavour in the citrus spectrum; perks up on a delicate, refreshing finish. Screwcap. 13° alc. **Rating** 90 **To** 2014 $14.95
The McCrae Wood Shiraz 2003 As usual, slightly outside the mainstream Clare style; soft, black cherry-accented fruit with touches of mint, chocolate and vanilla/mocha oak. Cork. 15.5° alc. **Rating** 90 **To** 2015 $45

ΨΨΨΨ **The Cover Drive Clare Valley Coonawarra Cabernet Sauvignon 2005** Minty, earthy overtones to berry fruit aromas of cassis and blackcurrant, flowing through to the palate with persistent tannins; needs 2+ years to get its eye in. Screwcap. 15° alc. **Rating** 89 **To** 2015 $19.95
Silly Mid On Sauvignon Blanc Semillon 2006 Clean, fresh, gentle citrus fruit nuances revolving around tropical and passionfruit notes. Screwcap. 12.5° alc. **Rating** 87 **To** 2008 $20

Jimbour Wines

86 Jimbour Station Road, Jimbour, Qld 4406 **Region** Queensland Zone
T (07) 3878 8909 **F** (07) 3878 8920 **www**.jimbourwines.com.au **Open** 7 days 10–4.30
Winemaker Peter Scudamore-Smith MW (Consultant) **Est.** 2000 **Cases** 15 000
Jimbour Station was one of the first properties opened in the Darling Downs, the heritage-listed homestead built in 1876. The property has been owned by the Russell family since 1923, which has diversified by establishing a 22-ha vineyard and opening a cellar door on the property. Increasing production is an indication of its intention to become one of Qld's major wine producers. Exports to the UK, Canada Taiwan and Japan.

ΨΨΨΨΨ Jimbour Station Ludwig Leichhardt Reserve Granite Belt Chardonnay 2005 Sophisticated winemaking; melon and nectarine with creamy/nutty aromas; very good length and balance plus quality oak. The same cannot be said of the cork. 14° alc. **Rating** 93 **To** 2010 $25

ΨΨΨΨ Jimbour Station Ludwig Leichhardt Reserve Granite Belt Chardonnay Pinot Noir 2003 Full-on rose; 8 months in oak before tirage; plenty of flavour, and balanced dosage. 13.5° alc. **Rating** 88 **To** 210 $25

Jindalee Estate

265 Ballan Road, Moorabool, North Geelong, Vic 3221 **Region** Geelong
T (03) 5276 1280 **F** (03) 5276 1537 **www**.jindaleewines.com.au **Open** 7 days 10–5
Winemaker Andrew Byers, Chris Sargeant **Est.** 1997 **Cases** 500 000
Jindalee is part of the Littore Group, which currently has 550 ha of premium wine grapes in production and under development in the Riverland. Corporate offices are now at the former Idyll Vineyard, acquired by Jindalee in 1997. Here 14 ha of estate vineyards have been retrellised and upgraded, and produce the Fettlers Rest range. The Jindalee Estate Chardonnay can offer spectacular value. Exports to the UK, Sweden, the US and Canada.

ΨΨΨΨ Fettlers Rest Shiraz 2005 A complex wine with sweet fruit and some slightly feral notes; needs time to gain coherence. **Rating** 87

Jingalla

49 Bolganup Dam Road, Porongurup, WA 6324 **Region** Porongurup
T (08) 9853 1023 **F** (08) 9853 1023 **www**.jingallawines.com.au **Open** 7 days 10.30–5
Winemaker Dr Diane Miller, Bill Crappsley (Consultant) **Est.** 1979 **Cases** 3000
Jingalla is a family business, owned and run by Geoff and Nita Clarke and Barry and Shelley Coad, the latter the ever-energetic wine marketer of the business. The 8 ha of hillside vineyards are low-yielding, with the white wines succeeding best, but they also produce some lovely red

wines. A partner in the new Porongurup Winery, which means it no longer has to rely on contract winemaking.

ㅇㅇㅇㅇㅇ **Vignerons Select Porongurup Riesling 2006** An aromatic apple and lime blossom bouquet; the intense palate has high natural acidity, but enough citrus fruit to sustain the balance. Screwcap. 11.5° alc. **Rating** 91 **To** 2016 $16

ㅇㅇㅇㅇ **Shimmer Porongurup Shiraz Merlot 2005** Bright, fresh, light- to medium-bodied; an interesting wine, the red fruit dominant, supported by subtle, fine tannins. Screwcap. 13.5° alc. **Rating** 89 **To** 2012 $25

Jinglers Creek Vineyard

288 Relbia Road, Relbia, Tas 7258 (postal) **Region** Northern Tasmania
T (03) 6344 3966 **www**.jinglerscreekvineyard.com.au **Open** Thurs–Sun 11–5
Winemaker Tamar Ridge (Michael Fogarty, Andrew Pirie) **Est.** 1998 **Cases** 800
Irving Fong came to grapegrowing later in life, undertaking the viticulture course at Launceston TAFE when 67 years old (where he also met his second wife). They have 1.8 ha of pinot noir, with small plantings of pinot gris and chardonnay.

ㅇㅇㅇㅇㅇ **Pinot Noir 2005** Superb purple-red; intense, racy mix of black fruits, spice and forest; authoritative mouthfeel and palate; great length. Screwcap. 13.6° alc. **Rating** 93 **To** 2012 $25

Jinks Creek Winery

Tonimbuk Road, Tonimbuk, Vic 3815 **Region** Gippsland
T (03) 5629 8502 **F** (03) 5629 8551 **www**.jinkscreekwinery.com.au **Open** By appt
Winemaker Andrew Clarke **Est.** 1981 **Cases** 1000
Jinks Creek Winery is situated between Gembrook and Bunyip, bordering the evocatively named Bunyip State Park. While the winery was not built until 1992, planting of the 3.64-ha vineyard started back in 1981 and all the wines are estate-grown. The 'sold out' sign goes up each year. Exports to the US and Singapore.

ㅇㅇㅇㅇㅇ **Heathcote Shiraz 2005** Redolent with plush, lush fruit in a blackberry, plum, licorice spectrum; good tannins and oak. Diam. 14.5° alc. **Rating** 94 **To** 2020 $32

ㅇㅇㅇㅇㅇ **Yarra Valley Shiraz 2005** Medium-bodied; spicy, savoury notes surround the blackberry fruit; good balance and length. Diam. 14° alc. **Rating** 93 **To** 2015 $28
Chardonnay 2005 Bright green-yellow; an elegant and harmonious wine, with seamless fruit and oak integration; good balance. Diam. 13.5° alc. **Rating** 91 **To** 2012 $28
Sauvignon Blanc 2006 Aromatic herb, grass, asparagus and gooseberry; lively and fresh, crammed full of flavour without phenolics or sweetness. Screwcap. 13.5° alc. **Rating** 90 **To** 2008 $24

ㅇㅇㅇㅇ **Pinot Gris 2006** Aromatic; classic pear/pear drop and musk aromas; good acidity underlines the flavours. Screwcap. 13.8° alc. **Rating** 89 **To** 2008 $24
Sangiovese 2005 Light- to medium-bodied; savoury, spicy sour cherry fruit; good varietal expression and length to the finish. Cork. 13.5° alc. **Rating** 89 **To** 2010 $30

John Duval Wines

9 Park Street, Tanunda, SA 5352 (postal) **Region** Barossa Valley
T (08) 8563 2591 **F** (08) 8563 0372 **www**.johnduvalwines.com **Open** Not
Winemaker John Duval **Est.** 2003 **Cases** 3500
John Duval is an internationally recognised winemaker, having been the custodian of Penfolds Grange for almost 30 years as part of his role as chief red winemaker at Penfolds. He remains involved with Penfolds as a consultant, but these days is concentrating on establishing his own brand, and providing consultancy services to other clients in various parts of the world. On the

principle of if not broken, don't fix, he is basing his business on shiraz and shiraz blends from old-vine vineyards in the Barossa Valley. The brand name Plexus, incidentally, denotes a network in an animal body that combines elements into a coherent structure. Exports to the UK, the US, NZ, Hong Kong and Switzerland.

ŦŦŦŦŦ Entity Barossa Valley Shiraz 2005 Harmonious fruit, alcohol and oak handling; very considerable length; old vine fruit has soaked up 17 months in French oak. High-quality wine. Cork. 14.5° alc. **Rating** 95 **To** 2025 $43

John Gehrig Wines ★★★★

Oxley-Milawa Road, Oxley, Vic 3678 **Region** King Valley
T (03) 5727 3395 **F** (03) 5727 3699 **www**.johngehrigwines.com.au **Open** 7 days 9–5
Winemaker Ross Gehrig **Est.** 1976 **Cases** 5600
In the manner of Burgundian wineries, where many are owned by families with identical or similar family names, so it is the case with Gehrig in Northeast Victoria. Or, at least, that is my excuse. Ross Gehrig has taken over management of John Gehrig Wines from his parents, John and Elizabeth, and the business has nothing to do with Gehrig Estate at Barnawartha, owned and managed by Ross's uncle Bernard. Having got that off my chest, I will not complicate the matter further about individual wine entries in prior vintages.

ŦŦŦŦŦ RG King Valley Riesling 2005 Spicier edges to the aromas than the varietal, the palate tighter and far less sweet; has good length; all in all, quite an achievement. Screwcap. 13° alc. **Rating** 90 **To** 2011 $22
RG King Valley Durif 2005 Typical impenetrable purple colour; the texture and flavour are equally typical, with massive black fruits more juicy than tannic, however. The only place to drink it is a BBQ, with Jayne Mansfield to help. Screwcap. 15.5° alc. **Rating** 90 **To** 2010 $38

ŦŦŦŦ King Valley Riesling 2006 Abundant, ripe tropical lime flavours; if picked a little earlier might have been better still; early-drinking style. Screwcap. 13° alc. **Rating** 89 **To** 2009 $15
Fossil Hill King Valley Shiraz 2005 A full-bodied, robust shiraz with blackberry/black fruits/prune, the extract controlled, the alcohol less so. Screwcap. 15.5° alc. **Rating** 88 **To** 2020 $30
King Valley Chenin Blanc 2005 Has managed to keep some of the gentle fruit salad flavour in this high-yielding variety without undue reliance on residual sugar (although it is certainly present). Screwcap. 13° alc. **Rating** 87 **To** 2008 $15

John's Blend ★★★★★

18 Neil Avenue, Nuriootpa, SA 5355 (postal) **Region** Langhorne Creek
T (08) 8562 1820 **F** (08) 8562 4050 **www**.johnsblend.com.au **Open** Not
Winemaker John Glaetzer **Est.** 1974 **Cases** 3000
John Glaetzer was Wolf Blass' right-hand man almost from the word go, the power behind the throne of the 3 Jimmy Watson trophies awarded to Wolf Blass Wines in 1974, '75 and '76, and a small matter of 11 Montgomery trophies for the Best Red Wine at the Adelaide Wine Show. This has always been a personal venture on the side, as it were, by John and wife Margarete Glaetzer, officially sanctioned of course, but really needing little marketing effort.

ŦŦŦŦŦ Margarete's Shiraz 2004 No. 10. Very good purple-red; a medium-bodied mix of black fruits, dark chocolate and mocha/vanilla oak; supple mouthfeel and texture; fine tannins. Langhorne Creek (95%)/McLaren Vale. Cork. 14.5° alc. **Rating** 94 **To** 2014 $50
Margarete's Shiraz 2003 No. 9. Holding hue very well; a rigorous selection of grapes has paid big dividends in a difficult year; medium-bodied, with red and black berry flavours, and a strong undertow of dark chocolate – plus oak of course. Langhorne Creek (94%)/McLaren Vale. Cork. 14.5° alc. **Rating** 94 **To** 2017 $50

ŶŶŶŶŶ **Individual Selection Langhorne Creek Cabernet Sauvignon 2003** No. 30. While the oak is very evident, barrel fermentation (and 3 years in oak) has meant it is well integrated; for all that, the fruit is beaten into second place. Cork. 15° alc. **Rating** 90 **To** 2013 $50

Johnston Oakbank

18 Oakwood Road, Oakbank, SA 5243 **Region** Adelaide Hills
T (08) 8388 4263 **F** (08) 8388 4278 **www**.johnston-oakbank.com.au **Open** Mon–Fri 8–5
Winemaker David O'Leary (Contract), Geoff Johnston **Est.** 1843 **Cases** 4000
The origins of this business, owned by the Johnston Group, date back to 1839, making it the oldest family-owned business in SA. The vineyard at Oakbank is substantial, with 49 ha chardonnay, pinot noir, sauvignon blanc, shiraz, merlot and cabernet sauvignon.

ŶŶŶŶŶ **Adelaide Hills Sauvignon Blanc 2006** Power and presence on both bouquet and palate; an attractive combination of herb, gooseberry and tropical fruit, the latter persisting on the long finish. Screwcap. 12.5° alc. **Rating** 91 **To** 2008 $18

ŶŶŶŶ **Adelaide Hills Shiraz 2003** Medium-bodied; spicy, savoury, earthy with some echoes of the Hunter Valley in structure as well as style; good length. Screwcap. 14° alc. **Rating** 89 **To** 2013 $20

Jones Road

133 Jones Road, Somerville, Vic 3912 (postal) **Region** Mornington Peninsula
T (03) 5977 7795 **F** (03) 5977 9695 **www**.jonesroad.com.au **Open** Not
Winemaker Sticks (Rob Dolan) **Est.** 1998 **Cases** 5000
It's a long story, but after establishing a very large and very successful herb-producing business in the UK, Rob Frewer and family migrated to Australia in 1997. By a circuitous route they ended up with a property on the Mornington Peninsula, promptly planting pinot noir and chardonnay, then pinot gris, sauvignon blanc and merlot, and have since leased another vineyard at Mt Eliza. Production is set to increase significantly from its already substantial level. Exports to the UK.

ŶŶŶŶŶ **Sauvignon Blanc 2006** A powerful bouquet, with punchy grass/asparagus/ kiwifruit aromas; the palate mirrors the bouquet, a hint of oak barely evident. Long finish. Screwcap. 15.5° alc. **Rating** 91 **To** 2008 $20

ŶŶŶŶ **Chardonnay 2005** A clean bouquet leading into a nectarine and melon palate, with some cashew nuances; minerally finish. Screwcap. 13.5° alc. **Rating** 89 **To** 2010 $17
JR Jones Pinot Noir 2006 A tangy, stemmy edge to light- to medium-bodied red fruits; good balance and length; well-priced. Screwcap. 13.6° alc. **Rating** 89 **To** 2012 $17
JR Jones Chardonnay 2005 Light- to medium-bodied; smooth stone fruit with a touch of citrus; good acidity lengthens the finish. Screwcap. 13.5° alc. **Rating** 88 **To** 2011 $29
Pinot Gris 2006 Faint blush colour; above-average aromas and flavours of pear, apple and citrus. Screwcap. 14.5° alc. **Rating** 88 **To** 2008 $22
Pinot Noir 2005 Relatively pale colour; light-bodied, with touches of forest floor, mineral and savoury notes. Screwcap. 13.5° alc. **Rating** 87 **To** 2008 $29

Jones Winery & Vineyard

Jones Road, Rutherglen, Vic 3685 **Region** Rutherglen
T (02) 6032 8496 **www**.joneswinery.com **Open** Fri–Sun & public hols 10–5
Winemaker Mandy Jones **Est.** 1864 **Cases** 1500
Late in 1998 the winery was purchased from Les Jones by Leanne Schoen and Mandy and Arthur Jones (nieces and nephew of Les). The cellar door sales area is in a building from the 1860s, still with the original bark ceiling and walls made of handmade bricks fired onsite. Exports to France.

�♟♟♟♟ **The Winemaker Rutherglen Durif 2005** As durifs go, almost achieves the impossible of elegance. Of course it can't really do so, but does have lovely purple-red colour and the flavour, while full-throated, doesn't assault the senses. Cork. 16.5° alc. **Rating** 94 **To** 2012 $25

♟♟♟♟♀ **LJ Rutherglen Shiraz 2004** Powerful, medium- to full-bodied blackberry, leather, licorice and earth. Despite the power, all the components are in good balance. ProCork. 14.8° alc. **Rating** 93 **To** 2024 $42
Rutherglen Shiraz 2004 A full-bodied, strongly structured wine with blackberry and plum fruit, the tannins like built-in cupboards. Cork. 14.5° alc. **Rating** 92 **To** 2025 $25

♟♟♟♟ **The Winemaker Rutherglen Marsanne 2005** An interesting wine, which has distinct varietal character and flavour without oak or residual sugar to help; spice, apple, honeysuckle and mineral; good acidity and length; will age well. Cork. 13.2° alc. **Rating** 88 **To** 2010 $18
The Winemaker Rutherglen Merlot 2004 Clean, black cherry aromas; masses of fruit, albeit varietally anonymous. Simply a good Aussie dry red. ProCork. 14.6° alc. **Rating** 88 **To** 2015 $18

Josef Chromy Wines   ★★★★

370 Relbia Road, Relbia, Tas 7258 **Region** Northern Tasmania
T (03) 6335 8700 **F** (03) 6335 8777 **www.**josefchromy.com.au **Open** 7 days 10–5
Winemaker Jeremy Dineen **Est.** 2004 **Cases** 4500
Joe Chromy just refuses to lie down and admit the wine industry in Tasmania is akin to a financial black hole in space. Since escaping from Czechoslovakia in 1950, establishing Blue Ribbon Meats, using the proceeds of sale of his shares in that large company to buy Rochecombe and Heemskerk Vineyards, then selling those and establishing Tamar Ridge before it, too, was sold Joe Chromy is at it again, this time investing $40 million in a wine-based but multifaceted business. If this were not remarkable enough, Joe Chromy is 76, and spent much of 2006 recovering from a major stroke. Foundation of the new business was the purchase of the large Old Stornoway Vineyard at a receivership sale in 2003; in all, there are 80 ha of 10-year-old vines, the lion's share to pinot noir and chardonnay. He has retained Jeremy Dineen (for many years winemaker at Hood/Wellington) as winemaker, the winery completed prior to the 2007 vintage. Chromy's grandson Dean Cocker is guiding the development of a restaurant, function and equestrian centre, the latter on a scale sufficient to accommodate the Magic Millions yearling sales.

♟♟♟♟♀ **PEPIK Chardonnay 2005** A highly aromatic bouquet of stone fruit blossom; a long palate follows, the acidity too much for some, but not for me. **Rating** 91 **To** 2012
Reserve Riesling 2006 A clean, slightly subdued bouquet, then a lively, fresh palate with delicious lemony acidity to close. Screwcap. **Rating** 90 **To** 2012

♟♟♟♟ **Riesling 2006** Has power and presence, but not the crystal-bright purity of the best rieslings. Screwcap. 11.6° alc. **Rating** 87 **To** 2011 $24
Gewurztraminer 2006 Aromatic and flowery; lychee and rose petal flavours, albeit slightly light. **Rating** 87 **To** 2009
Sauvignon Blanc 2006 Moderately intense flavour in a tropical/gooseberry spectrum; a degree of volatile acidity has to be accepted. **Rating** 87 **To** 2008
Pinot Noir 2005 Light, savoury/stemmy undertones to the red fruits; outclassed in a great vintage. Screwcap. **Rating** 87 **To** 2009 $26
PEPIK Pinot Noir 2004 Light- to medium-bodied; savoury/spicy/earthy/foresty aromas and flavours throughout. **Rating** 87 **To** 2008

Journeys End Vineyards   ★★★★☆

248 Flinders Street, Adelaide, SA 5000 (postal) **Region** Southeast Australia
T 0431 709 305 **www.**journeysendvineyards.com.au **Open** Not
Winemaker Ben Riggs (Contract) **Est.** 2001 **Cases** 10 000

A particularly interesting business in the virtual winery category which, while focused on McLaren Vale shiraz, also has contracts for other varieties in the Adelaide Hills and Langhorne Creek. The shiraz comes in 4 levels, and, for good measure, uses 5 different clones of shiraz to amplify the complexity which comes from having grapegrowers in many different parts of McLaren Vale. Exports to the US, the UK, Canada, Sweden, Switzerland, Germany, Netherlands, Korea and Singapore.

ΨΨΨΨΨ **Arrival McLaren Vale Shiraz 2004** Bright red-purple; a medium-bodied but complex mix of chocolate, mocha, blackberry and raspberry; ripe tannins and good length; 5 clones of shiraz incorporated. Cork. 14.5° alc. **Rating** 94 **To** 2016 $45

ΨΨΨΨΨ **Beginning Shiraz 2004** Powerful but not heavy or extractive; blackberry, bitter chocolate and oak seamlessly welded together, the alcohol relatively restrained. Exceeds expectations and its station in life. Cork. 14.5° alc. **Rating** 93 **To** 2018 $25
Ascent McLaren Vale Shiraz 2004 Very similar style to the Arrival, the flavours in much the same spectrum, just a little less intense. Cork. 14.5° alc. **Rating** 91 **To** 2012 $30
The Return Watervale Riesling 2006 Slightly closed bouquet; a solid regional style, offering citrus with some slate/river pebble notes. Screwcap. 12.5° alc. **Rating** 90 **To** 2016 $22

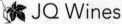 JQ Wines

NR

743 Slopes Road, Tharbogang, NSW 2680 (postal) **Region** Riverina
T (02) 6963 6222 **F** (02) 6963 6473 **www.jqwines.com.au Open** Not
Winemaker John Quarisa **Est.** 2005 **Cases** NA
JQ Wines was established by John and Josephine Quarisa (plus their 3 young children). John Quarisa has had a distinguished career as a winemaker spanning 22 years, working for some of Australia's largest wineries including McWilliam's, Casella and Nugan Estate. He was also chiefly responsible for winning the Jimmy Watson Trophy in 2004 (Melbourne) and the Stodart Trophy (Adelaide). In a busman's holiday venture, they have set up a small family business using grapes from various part of Australia and made in leased space. The quality of the initial releases from the '06 vintage suggests there is a lot of work to be done.

Juniper Estate

★★★★☆

Harmans Road South, Cowaramup, WA 6284 **Region** Margaret River
T (08) 9755 9000 **F** (08) 9755 9100 **www.juniperestate.com.au Open** 7 days 10–5
Winemaker Mark Messenger **Est.** 1973 **Cases** 14 000
This is the reincarnation of Wrights, which was sold by founders Henry and Maureen Wright in 1998. The 10-ha vineyard has been retrellised, and the last 1.5 ha of plantable land has seen the key plantings of shiraz and cabernet sauvignon increase a little. Juniper Crossing wines use a mix of estate-grown and purchased grapes from other Margaret River vineyards. The Juniper Estate releases are made only from the 28-year-old estate plantings. Immaculate packaging and background material. Exports to the US, the UK, Denmark, Germany, Hong Kong and Japan.

ΨΨΨΨΨ **Margaret River Shiraz 2004** A strong wine; has the focus and depth which the Juniper Crossing lacks, even though it is only still medium-bodied; spicy, black cherry and blackberry fruits; fine tannins, good length. Screwcap. 14° alc. **Rating** 94 **To** 2024 $29

ΨΨΨΨΨ **Margaret River Cabernet Sauvignon 2004** Flowery aromas of berry, spice and a touch of mint; a fine, medium-bodied palate, with powdery, fine tannins sprinkled throughout its length in estate style; restrained fruit and extract. Screwcap. 14° alc. **Rating** 93 **To** 2017 $32
Margaret River Semillon 2005 While the barrel ferment oak is quite obvious, the strength of the semillon carries that oak, with complexity the outcome. Screwcap. 13° alc. **Rating** 91 **To** 2013 $22

Margaret River Shiraz 2003 Fragrant earthy/spicy aromas; medium-bodied with savoury, spicy tannins running through the length of the palate, but do not strip or obscure the equally spicy black fruits. Cork. 14.5° alc. **Rating** 91 **To** 2018 $29
Juniper Crossing Margaret River Shiraz 2004 Light- to medium-bodied; spicy/earthy notes intermingle with black cherry and plum fruit; a moderately long finish. Double gold winner at the Sydney International Wine Competition '06, but keenly priced. Screwcap. 14° alc. **Rating** 90 **To** 2014 $16.95
Cane Cut Margaret River Riesling 2005 Tangy and citrussy, with good intensity and balance; not particularly complex (no botrytis) but a nice wine, even if somewhat expensive. Screwcap. 11° alc. **Rating** 90 **To** 2011 $24

ŶŶŶŶ **Juniper Crossing Margaret River Semillon Sauvignon Blanc 2006** Complex tropical aromas, then rich and ripe flavours tracking the bouquet; mouthfilling and fleshy. Screwcap. 12.5° alc. **Rating** 89 **To** 2008 $16
Juniper Crossing Margaret River Geographe Chardonnay 2005 Fresh and lively; an attractive mix of ripe citrus, melon and stone fruit supported by appropriately subtle oak. Screwcap. 13.5° alc. **Rating** 89 **To** 2008 $19
Juniper Crossing Margaret River Cabernet Sauvignon Merlot 2004 Bright hue; a light- to medium-bodied palate with attractive red fruits and a touch of blackcurrant; gentle tannin and oak backing. Screwcap. 13.5° alc. **Rating** 88 **To** 2009 $16
Juniper Crossing Margaret River Rose 2006 Light red and black fruits; uncompromising dry style, using the saignee (bleeding) method; constructed for food. Screwcap. 14° alc. **Rating** 87 **To** 2008 $16

Just Red Wines ★★★☆

2370 Eukey Road, Ballandean, Qld 4382 **Region** Granite Belt
T (07) 4684 1322 www.justred.com.au **Open** W'ends & public hols 10–5, or by appt
Winemaker Michael Hassall **Est.** 1998 **Cases** 1500
Tony, Julia and Michael Hassall have planted 2 ha of shiraz and 1 ha of merlot at an altitude of just under 900 m in the Granite Belt. They run the vineyard minimising the use of chemicals wherever possible, but do not hesitate to protect the grapes if weather conditions threaten an outbreak of mildew or botrytis. The names of the first wines to be released are bittersweet, though more of the former than the latter. The Hassalls' daughter Nikki was very much involved in the creation of the vineyard, and was driving back from university to be there for the first day of picking. By the ultimate cruel finger of fate, the car crashed and she was killed. The Hassalls went on to pick the grapes 'with our hearts broken'; hopefully the quality of the wines will provide some solace.

Jylland Vineyard ★★★

77 Ashby Road, Gingin, WA 6503 **Region** Perth Hills
T (08) 9575 1442 **Open** Tues–Sun 10–5
Winemaker Bella Ridge Wines (Alon Arbel) **Est.** 1999 **Cases** 2000
Jylland is the Danish spelling for Jutland (the Jutland Peninsula divides the North Sea from the Baltic Sea and is home to mainland Denmark and the northern part of Germany). Co-owner Edel Grocke (with Terry Grocke) brought her Viking heritage with her to Australia, with a particular liking for sunshine, fine food and fresh, fruity wine. They have established a total of 4 ha of vines, the lion's share to chardonnay (1.5 ha), the remainder spread across chenin blanc, verdelho, carnelian, shiraz and cabernet sauvignon.

Kabminye Wines ★★★★☆

Krondorf Road, Tanunda, SA 5352 **Region** Barossa Valley
T (08) 8563 0889 **F** (08) 8563 3828 www.kabminye.com **Open** 7 days 11–5
Winemaker Rick Glastonbury **Est.** 2001 **Cases** 3500
Richard and Ingrid Glastonbury's cellar door is on land settled in the 1880s by Ingrid's ancestor Johann Christian Henschke. Kabminye is an Aboriginal word meaning 'morning star', and was given to the hamlet of Krondorf as a result of the anti-German sentiment during the Second

World War (since changed back to the original Krondorf). The cellar door and café opened in 2003; SA Tourism has since used the building as a sustainable tourism case study. Rick makes the wines using 100% Barossa fruit, and has planted some unusual grape varieties, including kerner, clairette, zinfandel and pinot blanc. Exports to the UK, the US and Malaysia.

ŶŶŶŶŶ **Three Posts Eden Valley Riesling 2005** A rich bouquet of tropical and lime fruit leading into a palate bursting with life; a distinct mineral/slate backbone to the citrus fruit. Screwcap. 12° alc. **Rating** 94 To 2015 $19

ŶŶŶŶŶ **Shiraz Cabernet 2004** Rich blackberry and blackcurrant fruit, plus a touch of bitter chocolate; good structure and balance. Screwcap. 15° alc. **Rating** 92 To 2019 $24

Grenache Carignan 2005 For some strange reason, seems to work better than grenache/shiraz/mourvedre, with more direct fruit in both flavour and structure terms; good feel and finish. Screwcap. 15° alc. **Rating** 91 To 2012 $27

Barossa Valley Shiraz 2003 Medium-bodied, with mainstream black fruits plus nuances of mocha and vanilla; fine, ripe tannins. Cork. 14.5° alc. **Rating** 90 To 2013 $24

Barossa Valley Cabernet Sauvignon 2004 Interesting wine, and not typical of the Barossa Valley; intense blackcurrant with some spice, licorice and earth, and pronounced black olive nuances to the tannins. Screwcap. 15.1° alc. **Rating** 90 To 2019 $26

Vintage Fortified Shiraz 2005 A huge wine with masses of flavour; needs decades to mature, but the balance is inherently good, and, in particular, not too sweet. Screwcap. 19° alc. **Rating** 90 To 2025 $37

ŶŶŶŶ **Pinot Blanc 2006** An interesting combination of chalky notes along with gently persistent citrus and stone fruit, then crisp acidity to close. One of very few pinot blancs made in Australia. Screwcap. 10.5° alc. **Rating** 89 To 2010 $24

Barossa Valley White Frontignac 2006 Intensely grapey aromas and flavours; excellent acidity provides balance; good example. Screwcap. 13° alc. **Rating** 89 To 2008 $17 .

Irma Adeline 2003 Fractionally dull colour; the usual magimix array of sweet fruit flavours (not helped by the '03 vintage); the major problem lies with the lack of line and structure, rather than any want of flavour. Shiraz/Mataro/Grenache. Screwcap. 15° alc. **Rating** 88 To 2012 $23

Schliebs Block 2004 Big, alcoholic ripe fruit style, with a slightly hot finish. Screwcap. 15.5° alc. **Rating** 87 To 2008 $27

Barossa Valley White Frontignac 2005 Fruity and flowery, but, like other '05 frontignacs, not with the normally explosive grapiness. Screwcap. 11.5° alc. **Rating** 87 To 2008 $17

Kaesler Wines   ★★★★★

Barossa Valley Way, Nuriootpa, SA 5355 **Region** Barossa Valley
T (08) 8562 4488 **F** (08) 8562 4499 **www**.kaesler.com.au **Open** Mon–Sat 10–5, Sun & public hols 11.30–4
Winemaker Reid Bosward **Est.** 1990 **Cases** 20 000
The Kaesler name dates back to 1845, when the first members of the family settled in the Barossa Valley. The Kaesler vineyards date back to 1893, but the Kaesler ownership ended in 1968. After several changes, the present (much-expanded) Kaesler Wines was acquired by a Swiss banking family in conjunction with former Flying Winemaker Reid Bosward and wife Bindy. Bosward's experience shows through in the wines, which now come from 37 ha of estate vineyards, two-thirds adjacent to the winery, and one-third in the Marananga area. The latter includes shiraz planted in 1899, with both blocks seeing plantings in the 1930s, '60s, then each decade through to the present. Exports to the US, Canada, Switzerland, Denmark, Sweden, Japan, Hong Kong, Singapore, Malaysia and NZ.

ϾϾϾϾϾ **Old Vine Barossa Valley Shiraz 2005** Deep colour; excellent blackberry and satsuma plum fruit; finely balanced and integrated oak; supple tannins; 45-year-old vines. Cork. 16° alc. **Rating** 95 **To** 2025 $60

The Bogan Barossa Valley Shiraz 2005 Like all the Kaesler wines, carries the extreme alcohol with surprising ease; black fruits and a bright finish; from 1899 and 1965 plantings. Cork. 16° alc. **Rating** 95 **To** 2025 $50

Stonehorse Barossa Valley Shiraz 2005 A clean, firm array of black fruits, dark chocolate and ripe tannins; minimal oak influence. Cork. 15.5° alc. **Rating** 94 **To** 2017 $30

The Bogan Barossa Valley Shiraz 2004 Deep colour; a complex mix of blackberry fruits, earth and spice; the alcohol doesn't burn, and the overall extract only medium-bodied, the tannins in restraint. High-quality cork. 15° alc. **Rating** 94 **To** 2015 $50

Avignon Grenache Shiraz Mourvedre 2004 A very attractive array of spicy red and black fruits and dark chocolate; much more stuffing than usual for this type of blend; good tannins; vines up to 105 years old. Cork. 15.5° alc. **Rating** 94 **To** 2016 $30

ϾϾϾϾϿ **Old Bastard Shiraz 2003** Dense colour; massively concentrated black fruits, dark chocolate, oak, tannins and the kitchen sink; a heroic Parker style. Cork. 15.5° alc. **Rating** 93 **To** 2015 $160

Old Vine Barossa Valley Shiraz 2003 Strong colour and hue; big black fruits, with some dark chocolate and licorice, the alcohol evident. A success for the vintage. Cork. 15° alc. **Rating** 92 **To** 2015 $60

Old Vine Riesling 2004 Still very fresh, bright and lively; crisp citrus and mineral flavours; excellent length. Screwcap. 13° alc. **Rating** 91 **To** 2012 $15

Stonehorse Barossa Valley Grenache Shiraz Mourvedre 2004 Sweet blackberry and raspberry fruits; gentle but positive tannins; excellent balance between fruit and oak. Cork. 15.5° alc. **Rating** 90 **To** 2010 $30

Barossa Valley Cabernet Sauvignon 2005 Lots of blackcurrant fruit with some notes of earth and chocolate; solid, slightly rustic tannins; good French oak. Cork. 15.5° alc. **Rating** 90 **To** 2015 $25

Touriga Nacional 2002 Very interesting vintage port style; the varietal character comes through in spiced black fruits; just a fraction too sweet, but will age well. Cork. 19.5° alc. **Rating** 90 **To** 2022 $20

ϾϾϾϾ **The Bogan Barossa Valley Shiraz 2003** Dense colour; powerful and concentrated, and here the alcohol does make life slightly uncomfortable; certainly an abundance of black fruits, chocolate and earth. Cork. 15.5° alc. **Rating** 89 **To** 2012 $50

Barossa Valley Cabernet Sauvignon 2003 Developed colour; typical ripe fruit and chocolate nuances of Barossa Valley cabernet in many vintages; easy-going style; warm oak and soft tannins. Cork. 15° alc. **Rating** 89 **To** 2013 $25

Old Vine Semillon 2005 Rich, ripe fruit in a medium to full-bodied spectrum yet somewhat amorphous; alcohol does not help its cause; 45-year-old vines. Screwcap. 13° alc. **Rating** 87 **To** 2008 $12

Canadian Lead Mudgee Barossa Shiraz 2005 An easy style; soft blackberry and plum fruit with some mocha oak notes; Mudgee (70%)/Barossa (30%). Screwcap. 14.5° alc. **Rating** 87 **To** 2008 $15

Stonehorse Barossa Valley Grenache Shiraz Mourvedre 2005 A light (despite the alcohol), fresh, fruity wine; best slightly chilled in summer to suppress that alcohol. Screwcap. 15° alc. **Rating** 87 **To** 2008 $17

Kalleske

Vinegrove Road, Greenock, SA 5360 **Region** Barossa Valley
T 0403 811 433 **F** (08) 8562 8118 **www.kalleske.com Open** Not
Winemaker Troy Kalleske **Est.** 1999 **Cases** 7000

The Kalleske family has been growing and selling grapes on a mixed farming property at Greenock for over 100 years. Fifth-generation John and Lorraine Kalleske embarked on a trial vintage for a fraction of the grapes in 1999. It was an immediate success, and led to the construction of a small winery with son Troy Kalleske as winemaker. The vineyards, with an average age of 50 years, see no chemical fertilisers or pesticides; some blocks are certified organic. The density of the flavour of the Shiraz and Grenache is awesome. Exports to all major markets.

🍷🍷🍷🍷🍷 **Johann Georg Old Vine Barossa Valley Shiraz 2004** Strong red-purple; flooded with blackberry, black cherry fruit, luscious but not jammy; carries its alcohol amazingly well, and has absorbed the oak; 1875 vineyard. Cork. 15.5° alc. **Rating** 96 **To** 2024 $100

Greenock Shiraz 2005 Ripe colour hue; a Joseph's Coat array of flavours ranging through blackberry, satsuma plum, black cherry, spice and chocolate; supple mouthfeel; soft, ripe tannins, with oak providing appropriate support. Cork. 15.5° alc. **Rating** 94 **To** 2025 $40

🍷🍷🍷🍷½ **Old Vine Barossa Valley Grenache 2004** Has the high-toned confection character so frequent in Barossa Valley grenache; confit and plum fruit, the alcohol very evident. Others will enjoy the wine far more. Cork. 15.5° alc. **Rating** 90 **To** 2015 $47

🍷🍷🍷🍷 **Clarry's Barossa Valley Red 2005** A light- to medium-bodied mix of red fruits, spices and more leafy notes; an interesting, fruit-tingle finish. Grenache/Shiraz. Screwcap. 14.5° alc. **Rating** 89 **To** 2010 $19

Lorraine Barossa Valley Late Harvest Semillon 2006 Clean, fresh and well-made; gentle sweetness balanced by acidity, and refreshingly low alcohol. Screwcap. 9° alc. **Rating** 88 **To** 2008 $10

Kamberra ★★★★☆

Cnr Northbourne Ave/Flemington Rd, Lyneham, ACT 2602 **Region** Canberra District
T (02) 6262 2333 **F** (02) 6262 2300 **www**.kamberra.com.au **Open** 7 days 10–5
Winemaker Alex McKay **Est.** 2000 **Cases** 18 000

Kamberra was part of the Hardys group, established in 2000 with the planting of 40 ha of vines and a winery in the ACT, only a few hundred metres from the showground facilities where the National Wine Show is held every year. Riesling and Shiraz are fully estate-grown, and most of the wines have a Kamberra component. In March '07 Kamberra was sold to a Canberra company, part of the Elvin Group, leaving the business intact.

🍷🍷🍷🍷½ **Meeting Place Canberra District Riesling 2005** Striking sweet fruit in a ripe apple, passionfruit and citrus spectrum; good balance, and a long finish. Screwcap. 12° alc. **Rating** 93 **To** 2015 $15

Meeting Place Canberra District Viognier 2005 Flush with varietal flavour, yet isn't phenolic; abundant apricot and dried peach fruit; long finish. Screwcap. 13.5° alc. **Rating** 93 **To** 2015 $15

Canberra District Shiraz 2003 Light to medium-bodied; clear, bright and fresh fruit offering a mix of black cherry, blackberry and spice; fine, silky tannins. Cork. 13.5° alc. **Rating** 91 **To** 2013 $30

Meeting Place Sparkling 2004 The relative youth of the wine is part of its entirely fruit-driven charm; the bouquet has fragrant lemon zest and spice aromas and the fresh, crisp and long palate is a seamless replay of those aromas. Tumbarumba Pinot Noir/Chardonnay/Pinot Meunier. **Rating** 90 **To** 2008 $15

🍷🍷🍷🍷 **Meeting Place Shiraz 2003** Bright colour; fresh, light to medium-bodied spicy black fruits; gentle oak; not forced. Cork. 13.5° alc. **Rating** 89 **To** 2010 $15

Kangarilla Road Vineyard ★★★★

Kangarilla Road, McLaren Vale, SA 5171 **Region** McLaren Vale
T (08) 8383 0533 **www**.kangarillaroad.com.au **Open** Mon–Fri 9–5, w'ends 11–5
Winemaker Kevin O'Brien **Est.** 1997 **Cases** 42 000

Kangarilla Road was formerly known as Stevens Cambrai. Long-time industry identity Kevin O'Brien and wife Helen purchased the property in 1997, and have now fully established the strikingly labelled Kangarilla Road brand in place of Cambrai, steadily increasing production. Exports to all major markets.

ΨΨΨΨ **McLaren Vale Shiraz Viognier 2005** A highly aromatic bouquet and palate strongly influenced by viognier; carries its alcohol until the aftertaste when warmth comes through. Screwcap. 15° alc. **Rating** 89 To 2015 $25
McLaren Vale Cabernet Sauvignon 2005 A curious mix of tea leaf and black fruit aromas, although the palate is less quixotic, offering classic blackcurrant, earth and bitter chocolate flavours running through to a long finish. Screwcap. 14.5° alc. **Rating** 89 To 2018 $18
McLaren Vale Chardonnay 2006 A fresh, fruit-driven mix of stone fruit, fig and citrus; slightly simple, but has length. Screwcap. 13.5° alc. **Rating** 88 To 2008 $16
McLaren Vale Sangiovese 2005 Smoky, spicy, red and sour dark cherry fruit; fine, dusty tannins. Screwcap. 14.5° alc. **Rating** 87 To 2010 $18

Kangaroo Island Trading Co

633 Lower North East Road, Campbelltown, SA 2074 **Region** Kangaroo Island
T (08) 8365 5988 **F** (08) 8336 2462 **Open** Not
Winemaker Danniel Amadio **Est.** 1990 **Cases** NA
Kangaroo Island is another venture of Caj and Genny Amadio. The Amadios have been the focal point of the development of vineyards on Kangaroo Island, producing the wines from their own plantings, and from grapes from other vignerons on the island.

ΨΨΨΨ **Cygnet River Cabernet Sauvignon Cabernet Franc Merlot 2002** Very intense and savoury, with some olive-leaf/green notes from the cool vintage. Austere style. High-quality cork. 13° alc. **Rating** 89 To 2015

 Kangaroo Ridge Wine Co   NR

PO Box 81, Seaforth, NSW 2082 **Region** Southeast Australia
T (02) 9907 7735 **F** (02) 9907 7734 **Open** At Chateau Tanunda
Winemaker Thomas Jung, Ralph Fowler, Helen Fargo **Est.** 2000 **Cases** NA
This is the export business of John Geber, long-term owner of Cowra Estate, and, more recently, Chateau Tanunda in the Barossa Valley. The wines are produced from grapes grown in the Riverland area, and are exported to 33 countries, market leaders (by volume) in Switzerland, Russia and Belgium/Luxembourg. Substantial markets have also been established in Germany, Finland and Holland.

Kangderaar Vineyard

Wehla-Kingower Road, Rheola, Vic 3517 **Region** Bendigo
T (03) 5438 8292 **F** (03) 5438 8292 **Open** Mon–Sat 9–5, Sun 10–5
Winemaker James Nealy **Est.** 1980 **Cases** 800
The 4.5-ha vineyard is near the Melville Caves, said to have been the hideout of the bushranger Captain Melville in the 1850s, and surrounded by the Kooyoora State Park. It is owned by James and Christine Nealy.

ΨΨΨΨ **Chardonnay 2006** Attractive wine; rich melon and white peach flavours drive the palate, which has good length. Despite the low alcohol, shows no unripe characters. Screwcap. 12.5° alc. **Rating** 89 To 2010 $13

Kara Kara Vineyard

99 Edelsten Road, St Arnaud, Vic 3478 (10 km sth St Arnaud) **Region** Pyrenees
T (03) 5496 3294 **F** (03) 5496 3294 **www**.pyrenees.org.au/karakara **Open** Mon–Fri 10.30–6, w'ends 9–6
Winemaker Steve Zsigmond, Hanging Rock Winery **Est.** 1977 **Cases** 1500

Hungarian-born Steve Zsigmond comes from a long line of vignerons and sees Kara Kara as the eventual retirement occupation for himself and wife Marlene. He is a graduate of the Adelaide University (Roseworthy) wine marketing course, and worked for Yalumba and Negociants as a sales manager in Adelaide and Perth. He looks after sales and marketing from the Melbourne premises of Kara Kara, and the wine is made at Hanging Rock, with consistent results. Draws upon 9 ha of estate plantings.

ŸŸŸŸŸ **Pyrenees Chardonnay 2005** An expressive bouquet, promising melon, nectarine and a touch of citrus, duly delivered by the palate; good mouthfeel and length; the oak influence is appropriately subtle. Screwcap. 14° alc. **Rating** 90 **To** 2010 $18

ŸŸŸŸ **Pyrenees Sauvignon Blanc 2006** A clean, but closed, bouquet; citrus, apple and gooseberry, with fair length and a pleasingly dry finish. Screwcap. 12.7° alc. **Rating** 88 **To** 2008 $16

Karatta Wine

43/22 Liberman Close, Adelaide, SA 5000 (postal) **Region** Mount Benson
T (08) 8215 0250 **F** (08) 8215 0450 **www**.karattawines.com.au **Open** W'ends 11–4, or by appt tel (08) 8735 7255
Winemaker Coates Wines **Est.** 1994 **Cases** 1720
This is the former Anthony Dale vineyard, planted to 12 ha of shiraz, cabernet sauvignon, pinot noir, malbec, and more recently sauvignon blanc and chardonnay. It is owned by Karatta Wine Company in association with the Tenison Vineyard. Since the change of ownership, the volume and weight of flavour in the wines has increased dramatically, due in part to very low yields.

ŸŸŸŸŸ **The 12 Mile Vineyard Reserve Robe Shiraz 2005** An aromatic bouquet, the medium- to full-bodied palate flooded with blackberry, raspberry and a touch of chocolate; fine tannins. Screwcap. 14.5° alc. **Rating** 93 **To** 2015 $25
The 12 Mile Vineyard Robe Shiraz Cabernet 2005 Strong colour; much more richness and depth than many previous red wines from Robe, except Black Wattle Vineyard; luscious plum, blackberry and raspberry fruit; ripe tannins, low price. Screwcap. 14.5° alc. **Rating** 93 **To** 2020 $20
The 12 Mile Vineyard Shiraz Cabernet Sauvignon 2005 Good colour; aromatic black fruits on the bouquet, the a range of red and black fruits and some cassis; controlled oak and tannins. Screwcap. 14.5° alc. **Rating** 90 **To** 2013 $15

ŸŸŸŸ **The 12 Mile Vineyard Shiraz 2005** Dense, inky purple-red; a thick, dense palate with prune, blackberry, spice and some chocolate; a lighter touch might have helped. Screwcap. 14.5° alc. **Rating** 89 **To** 2020 $17

Karina Vineyard

35 Harrisons Road, Dromana, Vic 3936 **Region** Mornington Peninsula
T (03) 5981 0137 **F** (03) 5981 0137 **Open** W'ends 11–5, 7 days in Jan
Winemaker Gerard Terpstra **Est.** 1984 **Cases** 2000
A typical Mornington Peninsula vineyard, situated in the Dromana/Red Hill area on rising, north-facing slopes, just 3 km from the shores of Port Phillip Bay, immaculately tended and with picturesque garden surrounds. Fragrant Riesling and cashew-accented Chardonnay are usually its best wines. Retail distribution in Vic; exports to Japan and Canada.

ŸŸŸŸŸ **Savoir-Faire Sauvignon Blanc 2006** Spotlessly clean; quite powerful, full-flavoured tropical fruit which, however, avoids going over the top. Screwcap. 12.5° alc. **Rating** 91 **To** 2008 $19

ŸŸŸŸ **Mornington Peninsula Riesling 2006** As ever, defies the no-seaside rule; gentle apple, citrus and tropical mix; nicely balanced. Screwcap. 13.5° alc. **Rating** 89 **To** 2012 $17

Karra Yerta Wines ★★★★☆

Lot 534 Flaxman's Valley Road, Wilton, SA 5353 **Region** Eden Valley
T 0438 870 178 **www**.karrayertawines.com.au **Open** By appt
Winemaker Tim Smith, Simon Adams, James Linke **Est.** 2006 **Cases** 350

The name Karra Yerta is derived from the local Aboriginal language, 'karra' the name for the majestic red gum trees, and 'yerta' meaning country or ground. The landscape has changed little (other than the patches of vineyard) since the ancestors of James and Marie Linke arrived (separately) in SA in 1847. Both James and Marie were born in Angaston, but moved to the Flaxmans Valley in 1985, and in 1987 purchased one of the old stone cottages in the region. Much time has been spent in reviving the vineyard which provides most of their grapes; the 2 ha of riesling, shiraz and semillon had been largely abandoned. While most of the grapes were sold, they indulged in home winemaking for many years, but have now moved into commercial winemaking on a micro scale. Quantities will be tiny, the wine selling by word of mouth (and the ubiquitous website).

🍷🍷🍷🍷🍷 **Limited Release Barossa Shiraz 2004** Light- to medium-bodied; a nicely restrained style; multiple flavours of black and red fruits, with touches of cedar and mocha; fine tannins, and good length. Screwcap. 14.3° alc. **Rating** 94 **To** 2024 $30

🍷🍷🍷🍷 **Eden Valley Riesling 2006** Gentle regional lime aroma and flavours, with a nice touch of minerality to provide balance; should develop very well. Screwcap. 13° alc. **Rating** 90 **To** 2015 $20

Eden Valley Riesling 2005 A subdued bouquet, possibly due to subliminal reduction; much more power and length on the palate, with lime fruit and lemony acidity. Screwcap. 11.8° alc. **Rating** 90 **To** 2014 $20

Karrak Estate NR

Cnr Perks Road/Cundinup South Road, Nannup, WA 6275 **Region** Margaret River
T (08) 9756 2141 **F** (08) 9756 2151 **www**.karrakestate.com.au **Open** 7 days 10–5
Winemaker Ian McMahon, Gail McMahon **Est.** 1999 **Cases** NA

Ian and Gail McMahon purchased the property which was to become Karrak Estate in 1999, planting shiraz and cabernet in that year and merlot in the following year. Both had had some prior experience in vineyard establishment (with a friend in Margaret River) and, likewise, winemaking. Gail backed up with a boutique winemaking course and, with a few hiccups, the business was underway. The problems of marauding kangaroos (kangaroo fences) and birds (netting) finally dealt with; the first wine was made in 2002, and sold out quickly. It continues to be a family and friends business, with all winemaking and bottling done in the small onsite winery. It takes its name, incidentally, from the red-tailed cockatoos that come to drink in the dam late each afternoon, which were called karraks by the Aboriginal people of the southwest.

Kassebaum Wines ★★★★☆

Nitschke Road, Marananga, SA 5355 **Region** Barossa Valley
T (08) 8562 2731 **F** (08) 8562 4751 **Open** By appt
Winemaker Rod Chapman (Contract) **Est.** 2003 **Cases** 460

David and Dianne Kassebaum are third-generation grapegrowers. David has been involved in the wine industry for 20 years, working first with Penfolds in bottling, microbiology and maturation laboratories, and most recently in the Vinpac International laboratory. They have 5.4 ha of shiraz and 1.5 ha of semillon, most of which is sold. Yields vary from 1 to 1.5 tonnes per acre. The small amount of shiraz retained for the Kassebaum Magdalena label is matured in new French and American oak for 12 months. Exports to the US.

🍷🍷🍷🍷 **Magdalena Barossa Valley Shiraz 2005** Dark colour; a big, rich, slightly chunky palate, with blackberry and touches of licorice and earth; the oak also needs to settle down. Plenty of potential. Cork. 14.8° alc. **Rating** 90 **To** 2015 $32.50

Katnook Estate   ★★★★★

Riddoch Highway, Coonawarra, SA 5263 **Region** Coonawarra
T (08) 8737 2394 www.katnookestate.com.au **Open** Mon–Sat 10–5, Sun 11–4
Winemaker Wayne Stehbens, Michael Marcus **Est.** 1979 **Cases** 125 000
One of the largest contract grapegrowers and suppliers in Coonawarra, selling more than half its grape production to others. The historic stone wool shed in which the second vintage in Coonawarra (1896) was made, and which has served Katnook since 1980, is being restored. The 1997 launch of the flagship Odyssey and the 2000 follow-up of Prodigy Shiraz point the way to a higher profile for the winemaking side of the venture. Freixenet, the Spanish Cava producer, owns 60% of the business. Exports to the UK, the US and other major markets.

♀♀♀♀♀ **Odyssey Coonawarra Cabernet Sauvignon 2002** Here the wine spends 38 months in oak, in the manner of the super-cuvees of Guigal; in the same way, it achieves miraculous balance, the fruit supple and sinuous; delicious blackcurrant flavours intermingle with cedar, mocha and cigar box; fine tannins to close. Cork. 14.5° alc. **Rating** 95 **To** 2025 $100
Prodigy Coonawarra Shiraz 2003 Well above-average fruit concentration for the vintage; spends several years in oak, but the fruit carries that oak, obvious though the latter may be. Overall quite luscious compared to previous vintages. Cork. 14° alc. **Rating** 94 **To** 2025 $100
Coonawarra Cabernet Sauvignon 2003 Medium-bodied; very elegant, in the earthy/cedary/cigar box style of Katnook; fine, ripe tannins. Cork. 14° alc. **Rating** 94 **To** 2013 $45

♀♀♀♀♀ **Coonawarra Cabernet Sauvignon 2004** Medium-bodied; clean, firm, classic blackcurrant fruit, with fine tannins and touches of cedar and earth. Screwcap. 14.5° alc. **Rating** 92 **To** 2024 $45
Coonawarra Chardonnay 2004 Slightly dissonant French oak sits on top of the fruit on the bouquet, but the palate has more stone fruit flavours, good structure and length. Screwcap. 13.5° alc. **Rating** 90 **To** 2012 $32
Coonawarra Merlot 2004 Shows strong varietal character throughout in an olive/cedar/spice spectrum; medium-bodied, with fine, silky tannins and a long finish. Cork. 13.5° alc. **Rating** 90 **To** 2010 $45

♀♀♀♀ **Founder's Block Shiraz 2004** Light colour; an elegant, light-bodied wine, reflecting the vintage; spicy/savoury notes and fine tannins. Screwcap. 14° alc. **Rating** 88 **To** 2010 $20
Founder's Block Coonawarra Merlot 2004 Fresh, with some savoury/minty overtones to small berry fruits; fine tannins. Screwcap. 14° alc. **Rating** 88 **To** 2012 $20
Founder's Block Coonawarra Cabernet Sauvignon 2004 Slightly more advanced; light to medium-bodied, with clear varietal fruit in easy-drinking style. Screwcap. 14° alc. **Rating** 88 **To** 2014 $20
Sauvignon Blanc 2006 Pleasant, medium-bodied style; gentle tropical fruit with a drizzle of lemon juice. Screwcap. **Rating** 87 **To** 2008 $27
Coonawarra Shiraz 2004 Attractive albeit fairly light fruit in a wraparound of seductive chocolate/mocha oak. Cork. 14° alc. **Rating** 87 **To** 2011 $45
Chardonnay Brut 2005 The price is daunting for a wine with attractive but light flavours (100% chardonnay) and certainly little complexity. Cork. 13° alc. **Rating** 87 **To** 2008 $32

Kay Bros Amery   ★★★★

Kay Road, McLaren Vale, SA 5171 **Region** McLaren Vale
T (08) 8323 8211 **F** (08) 8323 9199 www.kaybrothersamerywines.com **Open** Mon–Fri 9–5, w'ends & public hols 12–5
Winemaker Colin Kay **Est.** 1890 **Cases** 14 000

A traditional winery with a rich history and nearly 20 ha of priceless old vines; while the white wines have been variable, the red wines and fortified wines can be very good. Of particular interest is Block 6 Shiraz, made from 100-year-old vines; both vines and wine are going from strength to strength. Exports to the UK, the US and other major markets.

Keith Tulloch Wine

Hunter Ridge Winery, Hermitage Road, Pokolbin, NSW 2320 **Region** Lower Hunter Valley
T (02) 4998 7500 **www**.keithtullochwine.com.au **Open** Wed–Sun 10–4, or by appt
Winemaker Keith Tulloch **Est.** 1997 **Cases** 6500
Keith Tulloch is, of course, a member of the Tulloch family which has played such a lead role in the Hunter Valley for over a century. Formerly a winemaker at Lindemans and then Rothbury Estate, he has developed his own label since 1997. I cannot remember being more impressed with an initial release of wines than those under the Keith Tulloch label. The only problem is the small scale of their production. There is the same almost obsessive attention to detail, the same almost ascetic intellectual approach, the same refusal to accept anything but the best. Exports to the UK, the US, Canada, Sweden and Singapore.

ΨΨΨΨΨ **Hunter Valley Semillon 2006** Ultra-classic and ultra-refined; the quality now
is in the marvellously long finish and aftertaste, which will build on the mid-
palate with age. Screwcap. 10.5° alc. **Rating** 94 **To** 2021 $26
Hunter Valley Chardonnay 2006 Pale, bright green-straw; a typical elegant
and refined style; long nectarine and melon palate, the oak perfectly integrated.
Screwcap. 13° alc. **Rating** 94 **To** 2012 $26
Kester Hunter Valley Shiraz 2003 Very much in Keith Tulloch style;
medium-bodied, but with fruit ripeness perfectly judged; an array of
predominantly red fruits, fine tannins and oak. Screwcap. 14.5° alc. **Rating** 94
To 2023 $45

ΨΨΨΨΨ **Hilltops Merlot 2004** A serious and substantial merlot; good texture and structure
around redcurrant/cassis fruit, finishing with fine tannins. Well-priced. Screwcap.
14° alc. **Rating** 92 **To** 2017 $22
Forres Blend 2004 Bright red-purple; powerful and tightly focused; a distinct
touch of herb and olive ex the cabernet sauvignon; oak also a contributor; needs
time. Cabernet Sauvignon/Shiraz/Merlot. Coonawarra/Hunter Valley. Cork.
13.5° alc. **Rating** 91 **To** 2015 $30
Botrytis Semillon 2005 Golden yellow; some cumquat and mandarin
complexity; subtle oak, and good overall balance. Screwcap. 12.5° alc. **Rating** 91
To 2010 $30

ΨΨΨΨ **Hunter Valley Shiraz Viognier 2004** A blend and technique which works to
a degree in warmer climates, here giving spicy and aromatic flavours but not the
startling intensity from cooler regions. Screwcap. 13.5° alc. **Rating** 89 **To** 2010 $23
Per Diem Bloodhorse Hunter Valley Viognier 2006 Clean and fresh; well-
made and balanced, but lacks varietal personality. Screwcap. 13.5° alc. **Rating** 87
To 2008 $14

Kellybrook

Fulford Road, Wonga Park, Vic 3115 **Region** Yarra Valley
T (03) 9722 1304 **F** (03) 9722 2092 **www**.kellybrookwinery.com.au **Open** Mon 11–5,
Tues–Sat 9–6, Sun 11–6
Winemaker Philip Kelly, Darren Kelly **Est.** 1960 **Cases** 4000
The 8.5-ha vineyard is at Wonga Park, one of the gateways to the Yarra Valley, and has a picnic area and a full-scale restaurant. As well as table wine, a very competent producer of both cider and apple brandy (in Calvados style). When it received its winery licence in 1960, it became the first winery in the Yarra Valley to open its doors in the 20th century, a distinction often ignored or forgotten (by this author as well as others). Exports to the UK and Denmark.

Kelman Vineyards

Cnr Oakey Creek Road/Mount View Road, Pokolbin, NSW 2320 **Region** Lower
Hunter Valley
T (02) 4991 5456 **F** (02) 4991 7555 www.kelmanvineyards.com.au **Open** 7 days 10–4.30
Winemaker Stephen Hagan (Contract), David Lowe (Consultant) **Est.** 1999 **Cases** 3000
Kelman Vineyards is a California-type development on the outskirts of Cessnock. A 40-ha
property has been subdivided into 80 residential development lots, but with 8 ha of vines wending
between the lots, which are under common ownership. Part of the chardonnay has already been
grafted across to shiraz before coming into full production, and the vineyard has the potential to
produce 8000 cases a year. In the meantime, each owner receives 12 cases of wine a year.

Kelvedon

PO Box 126, Swansea, Tas 7190 **Region** Southern Tasmania
T (03) 6257 8283 **F** (03) 6257 8179 **Open** Not
Winemaker Winemaking Tasmania (Julian Alcorso) **Est.** 1998 **Cases** 260
Jack and Gill Cotton began the development of Kelvedon by planting 1 ha of pinot noir in 1998.
The plantings were extended in 2000/01 by an additional 5 ha, half to pinot noir and half to
chardonnay; all the production from this is under contract to Hardys. The Pinot Noirs can be of
outstanding quality.

ŸŸŸŸŸ **Pinot Noir 2005** A complex bouquet with 1 or 2 offbeat aromas; the quality
of the wine bursts through on the palate, supple, savoury and long, with
particularly fine-grained tannins. **Rating** 93 **To** 2014 $25

Kersbrook Hill

Lot 102 Bagshaw Road, Kersbrook, SA 5231 **Region** Adelaide Hills
T 0419 570 005 www.kersbrookhill.com.au **Open** By appt
Winemaker Ben Jeanneret **Est.** 1998 **Cases** 1500
Paul Clark purchased what is now the Kersbrook Hill property, then grazing land, in 1997,
planting 0.4 ha of shiraz on a reality check basis. Encouraged by the results, 2 years later the
plantings were lifted to 3 ha of shiraz and 1 ha of riesling. Mark Whisson is consultant viticulturist
(Whisson has been growing grapes in the Adelaide Hills for 20 years) and Ben Jeanneret chosen
as winemaker because of his experience with riesling. Exports to China and NZ.

ŸŸŸŸŸ **Adelaide Hills Riesling 2006** Ripe apple dominates the bouquet; citrus and
passionfruit join in on the palate, finishing with slippery acidity. Screwcap. 12.5° alc.
Rating 91 **To** 2013 $25
Adelaide Hills Shiraz 2005 Fragrant red and black fruit aromas immediately
proclaim an early-picked, elegant style, crisp and fresh; a little more depth needed
for top points. Screwcap. 13° alc. **Rating** 90 **To** 2015 $27

Kies Family Wines

Barossa Valley Way, Lyndoch, SA 5381 **Region** Barossa Valley
T (08) 8524 4110 **F** (08) 8524 4544 www.kieswines.com.au **Open** 7 days 9.30–4.30
Winemaker Wine Wise Consultancy **Est.** 1969 **Cases** 4000
The Kies family has been resident in the Barossa Valley since 1857, with the present generation of
winemakers being the fifth, their children the sixth. Until 1969 the family sold almost all the grapes
to others, but in that year they launched their own brand, Karrawirra. The coexistence of Killawarra
forced a name change in 1983 to Redgum Vineyard; this business was subsequently sold. Later still,
Kies Family Wines opened for business, drawing upon vineyards (up to 100 years old) which had
remained in the family throughout the changes, offering a wide range of wines through the 1880
cellar door. Exports to the UK, Canada, Singapore, Hong Kong, China and Japan.

ŸŸŸŸŸ **SSB 2006** Plenty of lively aromas and flavours ranging through gooseberry, kiwifruit and citrus, a spine of acidity from the semillon. A rare accomplishment from the
Barossa Valley. Semillon/Sauvignon Blanc. Screwcap. 12° alc. **Rating** 90 **To** 2010 $15

Klauber Block Shiraz 2004 Medium-bodied; quite complex sweet fruit and vanilla oak; easy style. Cork. 14.5° alc. **Rating** 90 **To** 2015 $25

Hill Block Barossa Valley Riesling 2006 Some complexity to both bouquet and palate; a mix of citrus, spice and canned fruits; plenty of flavour, but finishes a little short. Screwcap. 12° alc. **Rating** 89 **To** 2010 $15
Deer Stalker Barossa Valley Merlot 2006 Overall impression of sweetness from start to finish on a supple and smooth cellar door special. Screwcap. 13.5° alc. **Rating** 87 **To** 2011 $15
Monkey Nut Tree Barossa Valley Merlot 2005 Slightly more structure than the Deer Stalker, but still sweet (and unashamedly so). Cork. 14.5° alc. **Rating** 87 **To** 2012 $25

Kilgour Estate ★★★★

85 McAdams Lane, Bellarine, Vic 3223 **Region** Geelong
T (03) 5251 2223 **www**.kilgourestate.com.au **Open** Tues–Sun 10.30–6, 7 days in Jan
Winemaker Alister Timms **Est.** 1989 **Cases** 3500
Kilgour Estate is a family-owned venture, with just over 10 ha of vines. The beautifully situated cellar door has a restaurant and barbecue facilities. The consistency of the quality of the large portfolio of wines is remarkable.

Kilgour Views Bellarine Peninsula Shiraz 2005 A powerful wine, though not alcoholic or jammy, rather resting on perfectly ripened fruit: cherry and blackberry, plus a twist of spice; ripe tannins. Cork. 13.8° alc. **Rating** 91 **To** 2018 $23

Bellarine Peninsula Oaked Chardonnay 2005 Generously proportioned and flavoured wine; ripe stone fruit and yellow peach; the oak not overdone. Diam. 13.5° alc. **Rating** 89 **To** 2010 $40
Bellarine Peninsula Merlot 2005 Light to medium-bodied; typical cool-grown merlot; savoury/olive/grassy notes establish its varietal character but will leave some looking for more sweet fruit; fine tannins; good length. Diam. 13.5° alc. **Rating** 89 **To** 2013 $25
Kilgour Views Bellarine Peninsula Sauvignon Blanc 2006 A clean bouquet; not particularly intense, but gently tropical flavours will have broad appeal; dry finish a plus. Diam. 13.5° alc. **Rating** 88 **To** 2008 $25
Bellarine Peninsula Rose 2006 Some salmon tinges; a touch of warm spice adds to the attraction of the fruit, which, once again, is not too sweet. Diam. 13° alc. **Rating** 88 **To** 2008 $20
Bellarine Peninsula Cabernet Sauvignon 2004 Nicely balanced medium-bodied wine with similar direct and pure cool-grown cabernet fruit to the Kilgour Views; the acidity is better balanced. Diam. 13.5° alc. **Rating** 88 **To** 2017 $30
Bellarine Peninsula Pinot Gris 2006 Fresh, crisp and lively aromas; the palate is likewise citrussy and crisp, and not particularly varietal (an oxymoron if ever there was one). Screwcap. 13.5° alc. **Rating** 87 **To** 2008 $25
Kilgour Views Bellarine Peninsula Pinot Gris 2006 Very similar; perhaps a little more weight and concentration. Cork. 13° alc. **Rating** 87 **To** 2008 $23
Bellarine Peninsula Pinot Noir 2005 Bright red fruits with an unusual twist of lemon to lengthen the finish. Diam. 13.3° alc. **Rating** 87 **To** 2010 $20
Kilgour Views Bellarine Peninsula Cabernet Sauvignon 2005 Medium-bodied; firm, clean and direct cassis/blackcurrant varietal character, with slightly peaky acidity needing time to settle down. Diam. 13.8° alc. **Rating** 87 **To** 2015 $25

Kilikanoon ★★★★★

Penna Lane, Penwortham, SA 5453 **Region** Clare Valley
T (08) 8843 4377 **F** (08) 8843 4246 **www**.kilikanoon.com.au **Open** Thurs–Mon & public hols 11–5, or by appt
Winemaker Kevin Mitchell **Est.** 1997 **Cases** 50 000

Kilikanoon has over 300 ha of vineyards, predominantly in the Clare Valley, but spreading to all regions around Adelaide and the Barossa Valley. It had the once-in-a-lifetime experience of winning 5 of the 6 trophies awarded at the Clare Valley Wine Show '02, spanning Riesling, Shiraz and Cabernet, and including Best Wine of Show. Exports to all major markets.

ŸŸŸŸŸ **Mort's Reserve Watervale Riesling 2006** Fragrant citrus blossom and citrus leaf aromas; excellent structure and line, combining delicacy and power. The screwcap worked, unlike that of the varietal which remained unopened after a 10-minute multi-pronged attack. Screwcap. 12.5° alc. **Rating** 95 **To** 2017 $30

R Barossa Valley Shiraz 2004 Dense, complex, ultra-concentrated black fruits, leather, licorice and bitter chocolate; good structure, mouthfeel and length. High-quality cork, and a high quality price to match. Cork. 15° alc. **Rating** 94 **To** 2029 $120

M McLaren Vale Shiraz 2004 Strongly regional, though once again the moderating influence of the vintage suppresses the alcohol impact; black fruits, dark chocolate and a spicy/savoury finish. Cork. 15° alc. **Rating** 94 **To** 2024 $69

Baroota Reserve Southern Flinders Shiraz 2004 Abounds with blackberry, plum, prune, licorice and spice; the alcohol doesn't show through unduly; an interesting new region. Cork. 15° alc. **Rating** 94 **To** 2019 $32

Covenant Clare Valley Shiraz 2004 A fragrant array of red and black fruits plus oak on the bouquet; a powerful palate; ripe, glossy black cherries and blackberries; firm tannins, long finish. Cork. 15° alc. **Rating** 94 **To** 2024 $40

ŸŸŸŸŸ **Oracle Clare Valley Shiraz 2004** An immensely powerful, challenging wine which will take at least a decade to settle down, and will live for decades thereafter. Cork. 15° alc. **Rating** 93 **To** 2029 $69

Block's Road Clare Valley Cabernet Sauvignon 2004 A scented, aromatic bouquet; in the usual powerful Kilikanoon style, but there are nice savoury edges to the mainstream of blackcurrant and cassis fruit. Cork. 14.5° alc. **Rating** 93 **To** 2015 $29

Testament Shiraz 2004 In the powerful mode for which Kilikanoon is famous; a mix of rich fruit, cedary tannins plus oak need to come together; will do so; the wine does have length. Cork. 15° alc. **Rating** 91 **To** 2024 $40

The Duke Clare Valley Grenache 2004 Has a much firmer structure, is less lolly-sweet, and has more length than most Clare grenache, all in all closer to the McLaren Vale style; spicy red fruits with some sombre darker notes adding appeal. Cork. 15° alc. **Rating** 90 **To** 2014 $69

The Medley 2004 Medium-bodied; the regional and varietal mix is synergistic; the shiraz seems to provide some backbone, the other varieties supple and smooth; the oak not overdone. Barossa Valley/Clare Valley Grenache/Shiraz Mourvedre. Screwcap. 15° alc. **Rating** 90 **To** 2014 $25

ŸŸŸŸ **Killerman's Run Shiraz 2005** Strong, full purple-red; lush, round, mouthfilling plum, prune and blackberry extract; just gets away with the alcohol and extraction. Screwcap. 15° alc. **Rating** 89 **To** 2015 $18.95

Greens Vineyard Barossa Valley Shiraz 2004 Aggressive, raspy tannins run through what would otherwise have been a very good wine; it is doubtful that tannins will soften before the fruit dies. Cork. 15° alc. **Rating** 89 **To** 2024 $80

Killerman's Run Shiraz Grenache 2004 Medium-bodied; some minty/eucalypt notes run along with the red fruits; soft tannins. Screwcap. 15° alc. **Rating** 88 **To** 2010 $18.95

Prodigal Clare Valley Grenache 2004 Ultra-typical regional style which I simply don't get; there's no fault in the winemaking, I just don't like the taste. ProCork. 15° alc. **Rating** 87 **To** 2008 $27

Killerman's Run Cabernet Sauvignon 2005 Light- to medium-bodied; a well-balanced wine with varietal expression but little or no complexity. Screwcap. 14.5° alc. **Rating** 87 **To** 2010 $18.95

Killara Park Estate

773 Warburton Highway, Seville East, Vic 3139 **Region** Yarra Valley
T (03) 9790 1255 **F** (03) 9790 1633 **www.killarapark.com.au Open** 7 days 11–5
Winemaker Michael Kyberd **Est.** 1997 **Cases** 9000
The striking label design hints at the involvement of the Palazzo family (the owners) in winemaking in Lombardia (Italy) since the 16th century. It also tells you that this is a highly-focused, modern, wine-producing company. With just over 60 ha of vineyard, Killara Park is one of the larger grape suppliers in the Yarra Valley, capable of producing fruit of high quality from its steeply sloping vineyards. Around 90% of the grapes are sold to companies such as McWilliam's, but 10% is now being vinified for the label. Exports to the UK and Hong Kong.

ṬṬṬṬṬ **Yarra Valley Shiraz 2005** Has another dimension of weight and intensity, though still retains elegance; plums, licorice, blackberry and spice chase each other across the palate. Screwcap. 14.5° alc. **Rating** 94 **To** 2015 $20

ṬṬṬṬṬ **Yarra Valley Chardonnay 2005** Light- to medium-bodied; a gently complex blend of melon, fig, stone fruit and cashew reflect barrel ferment and mlf inputs, simultaneously adding creamy notes. Screwcap. 13.5° alc. **Rating** 92 **To** 2011 $22
Racers & Rascals Yarra Valley Chardonnay 2005 A pretty distinguished wine at its price (and a quixotic, though apparently historic, label); typical regional melon and citrus fruit are seemingly unoaked, but it doesn't matter, there is enough happening. Screwcap. 13.5° alc. **Rating** 90 **To** 2011 $15
Yarra Valley Pinot Noir 2005 A firm, fresh, relatively uncomplicated wine with black cherry and plum fruit, and minimal oak; the lovely colour and brilliant hue get it over the line. Screwcap. 13.5° alc. **Rating** 90 **To** 2012 $20
Yarra Valley Merlot 2005 Clear varietal character in the small red berry fruit spectrum, rather than earthy/olive; light- to medium-bodied, finishing with fine tannins. Nicely pitched. Screwcap. 13.5° alc. **Rating** 90 **To** 2011 $20

ṬṬṬṬ **Yarra Valley Sauvignon Blanc 2006** A clean fusion of herb, green pea and tropical fruit; good balance and length; easy style. Screwcap. 13.5° alc. **Rating** 89 **To** 2008 $17
Yarra Valley Rosetta 2006 Filled with delicate strawberry flavours from the pinot noir base; good balance and length, not too sweet. Screwcap. 11.5° alc. **Rating** 89 **To** 2008 $17
Racers & Rascals Yarra Valley Shiraz 2005 Light to medium-bodied; a fresh red and black plum and cherry mix, with attractive, slightly savoury tannins, and a complementary touch of oak. Like the other Racers & Rascals, is hard to resist at this price. Screwcap. 14.5° alc. **Rating** 89 **To** 2011 $15
Racers & Rascals Yarra Valley Pinot Noir 2005 Savoury spice and herb overtones to the fruit; a distinctly stemmy style, but has its good points at the price. Screwcap. 13.5° alc. **Rating** 88 **To** 2008 $15

Killerby ★★★☆

Caves Road, Wilyabrup, WA 6280 **Region** Margaret River
T 1800 655 722 **F** 1800 679 578 **www.killerby.com.au Open** Not
Winemaker Simon Keall **Est.** 1973 **Cases** 15 000
Has moved from Geographe to Margaret River following the acquisition of a vineyard with 25-year-old chardonnay vines on Caves Road. It has kept its substantial mature vineyards in Geographe, where the wines are still made. Exports to the US and Denmark.

ṬṬṬṬ **Semillon Sauvignon Blanc 2005** Tangy citrus, herb and mineral aromas and flavours; crisp and clean, just a little light-on. Screwcap. 13° alc. **Rating** 87 **To** 2008 $19

Killibinbin Wines

PO Box 108, Crafers, SA 5152 **Region** McLaren Vale
T (08) 8339 8664 **F** (08) 8339 8664 **www**.killibinbin.com.au **Open** Not
Winemaker Rolf Binder, Kym Teusner, Phil Christiansen, Justin Lane **Est.** 1998 **Cases** 4000
Business partners Liz Blanks and Wayne Anderson embarked on their virtual winery (with, they say, 'no money, no winemaker, no vineyard and no winery') with the inaugural 1997 Langhorne Creek Shiraz. Robert Parker promptly gave it 92 points, which meant that all of the production, and all of the subsequent growth, went to the US. A challenging set of new labels straight from the early 1940s have gained (and will gain) much attention.

ŸŸŸŸŸ Langhorne Creek Blend 2004 Neatly blends the characters of the shiraz and cabernet; the riper fruit components seem enhanced, but without the perils of jamminess/confit fruit, etc. Screwcap. 14.5° alc. **Rating** 92 **To** 2020 $20
Langhorne Creek Shiraz 2004 Medium-bodied blackberry, plum, prune and chocolate at the ripe end of the flavour spectrum; fine, savoury tannins. Screwcap. 14.5° alc. **Rating** 91 **To** 2019 $23
Langhorne Creek Cabernet Sauvignon 2004 Powerful, savoury/earthy/black olive style, with bitter chocolate nuances; persistent cabernet tannins. Screwcap. 14.5° alc. **Rating** 90 **To** 2020 $23

Kiltynane Estate

Cnr School Lane/Yarra Glen-Healesville Road, Tarrawarra, Vic 3775 **Region** Yarra Valley
T 0418 339 555 **F** (03) 5962 1897 **www**.kiltynane.com.au **Open** By appt
Winemaker Kate Kirkhope **Est.** 2000 **Cases** 300
Kate Kirkhope has owned and run Kiltynane Estate since 1994. Having completed a local viticulture course in 1997, she began the development of the 3.8-ha vineyard, planted to 7 clones of pinot noir, in 2000. Her son's education at a Rudolf Steiner School had given her an interest in biodynamics, and biodynamic practices are followed wherever possible: the vines are not irrigated, and no pesticides are used. The winemaking has been carried out with help from Frederic Blanck, of the highly regarded Alsace winery Paul Blanck et Fils, who has been a regular visitor to Australia and the Yarra Valley over the years.

ŸŸŸŸŸ Yarra Valley Pinot Noir 2006 Slightly odd fern/bracken nuances to the bouquet quickly give way to the powerful cherry and plum fruit of the palate; has time to go and for the components to come together. Diam. 13.5° alc. **Rating** 90 **To** 2014 $40

Kimbarra Wines

422 Barkly Street, Ararat, Vic 3377 **Region** Grampians
T (03) 5352 2238 **F** (03) 5342 1950 **www**.kimbarrawines.com.au **Open** Mon–Fri 9–4.30
Winemaker Peter Leeke, Ian MacKenzie **Est.** 1990 **Cases** 600
Peter and David Leeke have established 21 ha of riesling, shiraz and cabernet sauvignon, varieties which have proved best suited to the Grampians region. The particularly well-made wines deserve a wider audience.

ŸŸŸŸŸ Great Western Shiraz 2004 Spice, licorice, blackberry and earth aromas; an intense and lively palate has good acidity and presence. Screwcap. 13.6° alc. **Rating** 92 **To** 2019 $24
Great Western Riesling 2006 A firm, spotlessly clean bouquet with touches of herb and mineral which flow through to the palate; good balance and length. Screwcap. 13° alc. **Rating** 90 **To** 2012 $18

ŸŸŸŸ Great Western Cabernet Sauvignon 2004 A medium-bodied, restrained style, reflecting its low alcohol in notes of spice, black olive and leaf, yet avoids outright greenness; the tannins are sensibly fined to a minimum. Screwcap. 12.5° alc. **Rating** 88 **To** 2011 $22

Kimber Wines

Chalk Hill Road, McLaren Vale, SA 5171 **Region** McLaren Vale
T (08) 8323 9773 **F** (08) 8323 9773 **Open** 7 days Dec–Apr 9–6, or by appt
Winemaker Reg Wilkinson **Est.** 1996 **Cases** 350
Kimber Wines is primarily a grapegrower, selling its production from 2.5 ha each of chardonnay and cabernet sauvignon, and 1.2 ha of petit verdot to larger producers. A very small amount of its grapes are vinified under the Kimber Wines label which sell out within a few months of release. An added attraction is pick-your-own fruit (peaches, apricots and plums) during the summer months.

King River Estate

3556 Wangaratta-Whitfield Road, Wangaratta, Vic 3678 **Region** King Valley
T (03) 5729 3689 **F** (03) 5729 3688 **www**.kingriverestate.com.au **Open** W'ends, or by appt
Winemaker Trevor Knaggs **Est.** 1996 **Cases** 6000
Trevor Knaggs, with the assistance of his father Collin (sic), began the establishment of King River Estate in 1990, making the first wines in 1996. The initial plantings were of 3.3 ha each of chardonnay and cabernet sauvignon, followed by 8 ha of merlot and 3 ha of shiraz. More recent plantings have extended the varietal range with verdelho, viognier, barbera and sangiovese, lifting the total plantings to a substantial 24 ha. Exports to Canada.

ŶŶŶŶŶ   **Reserve King Valley Viognier 2004** Powerful and concentrated; much more about texture and structure than varietal fruit; nutty, creamy overtones, and the subliminal hint of maturation in old French oak. Diam. 14.5° alc. **Rating** 91 To 2010 $45
King Valley Rose 2006 Vivid fuchsia; good balance and length; pleasant red fruits with good acidity and length; quality well above the average, price below. Diam. 14° alc. **Rating** 90 To 2008 $15
King Valley Merlot 2004 Clear red-purple; equally clear varietal character on the light- to medium-bodied palate; bright, small red fruits with tangy olive notes, spice and fine tannins. Creeps up on you with retasting. Diam. 13.7° alc. **Rating** 90 To 2010 $19
Reserve King Valley Merlot 2004 Medium-bodied, with savoury/olive/earthy varietal fruit; fine tannins, good length. Diam. 14° alc. **Rating** 90 To 2011 $45

ŶŶŶŶ   **Reserve King Valley Chardonnay 2003** Bright green-yellow; light- to medium-bodied; well-made, gently complex fig, nut and melon. A daunting price. Diam. **Rating** 89 To 2008 $40
King Valley Verdelho 2006 The variety expresses itself as much in texture and structure as in flavour; more than simple fruit salad. Diam. 14.5° alc. **Rating** 89 To 2010 $22
Reserve King Valley Viognier 2003 A powerful, complex wine with a mix of apricot, nuts and spices; heats up on the finish, which is a pity. Diam. 14° alc. **Rating** 89 To 2008 $45
King Valley Barbera 2004 Medium-bodied; spicy, savoury edges to sweet red fruits; a very different style to the Boggy Creek Barbera, this wine with more power and structure but less fruit brightness. A question of style. Cork. 14° alc. **Rating** 89 To 2010 $22
King Valley Riesling 2004 Light straw-green; a spicy, minerally wine, citrus/lime fruit leaving it to the last second to appear on the finish and aftertaste. Cork. 13.5° alc. **Rating** 88 To 2012 $15
King Valley Chardonnay 2006 Medium-bodied, with ripe stone fruit; the French oak is evident, and perhaps responsible for a fraction of bitterness on the finish. Screwcap. 14.9° alc. **Rating** 88 To 2001 $19
King Valley Shiraz Viognier 2005 Slightly cloudy colour; a massive wine proclaiming its high alcohol and very ripe fruit; not at all typical of the blend. Diam. 15.5° alc. **Rating** 88 To 2013 $22

King Valley Shiraz Viognier 2003 A highly aromatic bouquet typical of shiraz viognier; light-bodied, with expressive, sweet berry fruit. Diam. 14° alc. **Rating** 88 To 2008 $22

King Valley Shiraz 2005 The colour is indistinguishable from the Shiraz Viognier; again, a very powerful and aggressive stance, with black fruits over the top. Diam. 15.5° alc. **Rating** 88 To 2013 $19

King Valley Sangiovese 2005 Light- to medium-bodied; lemony/leafy/ strawberry/earthy, all spinning around the sangiovese core. Definitely ethnic. Diam. 14.5° alc. **Rating** 87 To 2009 $22

Kings Creek Vineyard   ★★★★☆

237 Myers Road, Bittern, Vic 3918 **Region** Mornington Peninsula
T (03) 5983 1802 **F** (03) 5983 1807 **Open** W'ends 11–5
Winemaker Sandro Mosele (Contract) **Est.** 1980 **Cases** 750
In the wake of the implosion of the original Kings Creek winery, Graham and Dorothy Turner purchased the name Kings Creek, and acquired the original home vineyard block, taking the decision to radically change the trellis system from lyre to vertical spur. The vines have taken time to recover (as is normal in such circumstances), and winemaker Sandro Mosele forecast at the time that it would take until 2006 for the vines to regain balance and produce their best fruit.

Chardonnay 2005 Light straw-green; typical vibrancy of cool-grown chardonnay; grapefruit, citrus and nectarine, with subtle creamy mlf influences and equally subtle oak. Diam. 13° alc. **Rating** 91 To 2015 $18

Reserve Pinot Noir 2005 A tight, reserved style, like a young Burgundy not wanting to be opened; has length, but the question is how much fruit will it ultimately reveal? I may be doing it a grave injustice. Diam. 13.5° alc. **Rating** 90 To 2013 $30

Kings of Kangaroo Ground   ★★★★

15 Graham Road, Kangaroo Ground, Vic 3097 **Region** Yarra Valley
T (03) 9712 0666 **F** (03) 9712 0566 **www**.kkg.com.au **Open** Mon–Sat 10–6, Sun 12–6
Winemaker Ken King, Geoff Anson, Neil Johannesen **Est.** 1990 **Cases** 600
Ken King's involvement in wine began back in 1984 as an amateur member of the Eltham and District Winemakers Guild. Around that time, the Guild was asked to manage a tiny (0.13 ha) experimental vineyard planted on the rich volcanic soil of Kangaroo Ground. In 1988 Ken King purchased a little under 3 ha of similar land, which he describes as 'chocolate cake', and established 1 ha of chardonnay and 0.6 ha of pinot noir in 1990. Until 2000, the grapes were sold to Diamond Valley, but each year King retained sufficient grapes to produce a barrel or 2 of Pinot Noir, and began experimenting with multi-vintage blends of pinot with up to 5 years of continuous ageing in French barriques.

 Di Paolo Block Yarra Valley Cabernet Sauvignon 2004 Intense cassis/ blackcurrant varietal fruit; a long palate and finish with ripe tannins and well-integrated oak. Cork. 13.5° alc. **Rating** 94 To 2020 $40

Yarra Valley Pinot Noir 2003 As expected, showing some colour development; attractive foresty/spicy nuances to the plum and black cherry fruit; long finish. Cork. 13.5° alc. **Rating** 90 To 2010 $22

Kingsley Grove   ★★★

49 Stuart Valley Drive, Kingaroy, Qld 4610 (postal) **Region** South Burnett
T (07) 4162 2229 **F** (07) 4162 2201 **www**.kingsleygrove.com **Open** 7 days 10–5
Winemaker Michael Berry, Patricia Berry, Simon Berry **Est.** 1998 **Cases** 4000
Michael and Patricia Berry have established a substantial vineyard of 8.8 ha near Kingaroy. It is planted to verdelho, chardonnay, semillon, shiraz, merlot, sangiovese, chambourcin and cabernet sauvignon, and the wines are made in a winery built in 2001 and extended in 2003, Michael Berry having undertaken viticulture studies at Melbourne University.

Kingston Estate

Sturt Highway, Kingston-on-Murray, SA 5331 **Region** Southeast Australia
T (08) 8130 4500 **F** (08) 8130 4511 **www.**kingstonestatewines.com **Open** By appt
Winemaker Bill Moularadellis **Est.** 1979 **Cases** 2.5 million
Kingston Estate, under the direction of Bill Moularadellis, has its production roots in the
Riverland region, but it has also set up long-term purchase contracts with growers in the Clare
Valley, the Adelaide Hills, Coonawarra, Langhorne Creek and Mount Benson. It has also spread
its net to take in a wide range of varietals, mainstream and exotic, under a number of different
brands at various price points. Exports to Europe.

ŶŶŶŶ **Shiraz 2005** Medium-bodied plum and black cherry fruit with vanilla oak; a hint
of sweetness will appeal to some. Cork. 14.5° alc. **Rating** 87 **To** 2008 $13
Baritone Limestone Coast Cabernet Shiraz 2003 Gently spicy, savoury fruit
on a light- to medium-bodied palate with fair balance. Great value; 1-litre bottle.
Screwcap. 14° alc. **Rating** 87 **To** 2008 $11

Kinloch Wines

Kainui, Wairere Road, Booroolite, Vic 3723 **Region** Upper Goulburn
T (03) 5777 3447 **F** (03) 5777 3449 **www.**kinlochwines.com.au **Open** W'ends &
public hols 10–5, or by appt
Winemaker Al Fencaros (Contract) **Est.** 1996 **Cases** 2000
In 1996 Susan and Malcolm Kinloch began the development of their vineyard, at an altitude of
400 m on the northern slopes of the Great Dividing Range, 15 mins from Mansfield. One of the
unusual varieties in the portfolio is Pinot Meunier. The grapes are hand-picked and taken to the
Yarra Valley for contract making.

ŶŶŶŶŶ **Wild Ferment Chardonnay 2005** Plenty of depth of ripe stone fruit; only
2 barrels made, but the oak not overplayed; quite complex. Screwcap. 14.2° alc.
Rating 90 **To** 2012 $34

ŶŶŶŶ **Mansfield Sauvignon Blanc 2006** Clear-cut, though not boisterous, varietal
character; gentle tropical fruit, with some additional herbal/grassy/mineral notes.
Screwcap. 13° alc. **Rating** 89 **To** 2008 $22
Don Kinloch Chardonnay Pinot Noir Pinot Meunier 2004 Crisp, clean and
lively stone fruit and citrus; good mousse, and finishes with good acidity. 11.5° alc.
Rating 89 **To** 2010 $28
Mansfield Chardonnay 2003 Still very fresh and flavoursome, driven by ripe,
sweet, stone fruit; good length. **Rating** 88 **To** 2008 $20
Mansfield Merlot 2005 The dominant red fruits(cassis/redcurrant) are strange
bedfellows to find with such persistent tannins. Cork. 13.8° alc. **Rating** 87
To 2010 $24
Mary Friend 2004 Bright colour; fresh and lively, but has had to struggle for
organaleptic ripeness; minty, green leaf flavours. Cabernet Franc/Cabernet
Sauvignon. Cork. 12.8° alc. **Rating** 87 **To** 2011 $50

Kirrihill Wines

Wendouree Road, Clare, SA 5453 **Region** Clare Valley
T (08) 8842 4087 **F** (08) 8842 4089 **www.**kirrihillwines.com.au **Open** 7 days 10–4
Winemaker David Mavor **Est.** 1998 **Cases** 20 000
A large development, with a 7000-tonne, $10 million, winery designed for modular expansion to
20 000 tonnes, and currently storing 3 million litres of wine. It is associated with the Kirribilly
Wine Group, which has developed and now manages 1300 ha of vineyards in the Clare Valley,
Adelaide Hills and Langhorne Creek. Small parcels of its managed vineyards' grapes are taken for
the Kirrihill Estates wine range, with a Cabernet Sauvignon from Clare and Langhorne Creek,
plus a Sauvignon Blanc from the Adelaide Hills completing the range. The quality of the wines is
thus no surprise. Exports to the UK, the US and other major markets.

ŶŶŶŶŶ **Reserve Clare Valley Riesling 2004** Glorious, glowing green-yellow; similar lime/lemon/apple aromas to the '05, with just a touch of toast starting to emerge; crisp, punchy acidity on the lingering finish. Screwcap. 13.1° alc. **Rating** 95 **To** 2008 $29.95

Reserve Clare Valley Riesling 2005 Lovely expression in a lime juice/lemon blossom spectrum on the bouquet; a vibrant and intense palate running along the citrus rail tracks; long, lively finish. Screwcap. 12° alc. **Rating** 94 **To** 2015 $29.95

ŶŶŶŶŶ **Clare Valley Shiraz 2004** Blackberry and cherry aromas; a firm but classy palate, typical of '04; sweet fruit on the mid- to back-palate, with a firm, dry finish. Screwcap. 14° alc. **Rating** 93 **To** 2024 $23.95

Adelaide Hills Sauvignon Blanc 2006 No hint of reduction; a delicate entry to the mouth with melon, grass and mineral flavours, building intensity on the finish and aftertaste. Screwcap. 13.5° alc. **Rating** 92 **To** 2008 $18.95

Clare Valley Riesling 2006 A clean but closed bouquet; a relatively soft citrus and green apple palate is well-balanced; good acidity gives length and will underwrite future development. Screwcap. 12.5° alc. **Rating** 91 **To** 2016 $18.95

Clare Valley Cabernet Sauvignon 2004 Good structure and mouthfeel; medium-bodied, elegant cabernet fruit intermingles with oak, and fine, but gently persistent, tannins; good balance and length. Screwcap. 14° alc. **Rating** 91 **To** 2019 $21.95

Companions Clare Valley Shiraz Cabernet 2004 Medium-bodied; a synergistic blackberry, blackcurrant and spice mix; supple mouthfeel and lingering flavours; soft tannins. Great value. Screwcap. 14° alc. **Rating** 90 **To** 2014 $14.95

ŶŶŶŶ **Companions Clare Valley Adelaide Hills Semillon Sauvignon Blanc 2006** The regional-varietal match works well; fresh, juicy aromas and flavours; good structure, good value. Screwcap. 12.5° alc. **Rating** 89 **To** 2008 $13

Langhorne Creek Shiraz 2003 The opposite of the Clare Valley Shiraz, with rounder, softer, fleshier mid-palate fruit; this wine does have slightly more obvious tannins on the finish, though not to its detriment. Screwcap. 15° alc. **Rating** 89 **To** 2015 $21.95

Companions Clare Valley Cabernet Merlot 2006 Medium-bodied; while fresh, the fruit flavours and structure are quite substantial; blackcurrant and cassis are the usual companions, and there is no departure from the norm. Screwcap. 14.5° alc. **Rating** 89 **To** 2016 $14.95

Clare Valley Riesling Brut 2004 Works well enough, indeed better than many earlier attempts by other makers, including even Petaluma at the dawn of time; tangy riesling provides a long palate; a pleasant, nostalgic surprise. 13.5° alc. **Rating** 88 **To** 2008 $21.45

Kithbrook Estate   ★★★☆

RMB 4480, Strathbogie, Vic 3666 (postal) **Region** Strathbogie Ranges
T (03) 5790 8627 **F** (03) 5790 8630 **Open** Not
Winemaker Contract **Est.** 1994 **Cases** NA
Kithbrook Estate (formerly Gemleigh Meadows) has 2 vineyards at Strathbogie: the first and larger is at an altitude of 480–500 m, the second is higher up the hillside at the 560–580 m contour lines. By far the most important part of the business is grapegrowing for others, coming from 30 ha of sauvignon blanc, 27 ha of merlot, 15 ha of pinot noir and 14 ha of chardonnay, plus a dash of shiraz. Some of the wines have scored well at the Strathbogie Ranges Wine Show.

ŶŶŶŶŶ **Pinot Noir Chardonnay 1998** Deep yellow-bronze; complex nutty/biscuity characters with some aldehydes; the finish is fractionally short, perhaps. Trophy Strathbogie Ranges Wine Show '06. 12° alc. **Rating** 93 **To** 2008 $16

Kladis Estate

Princes Highway, Wandanian, NSW 2540 **Region** Shoalhaven Coast
T (02) 4443 5606 **www**.kladisestatewines.com.au **Open** W'ends & public hols 10–5
Winemaker Briar Ridge (Steve Dodd) **Est.** 1996 **Cases** 10 000
Jim and Nikki Kladis have developed 11 ha of shiraz, cabernet sauvignon, grenache, verdelho,
merlot and muscadelle at their Shoalhaven property, and 4 ha of gewurztraminer and cabernet
sauvignon in the Hunter Valley. Additional grapes are also sourced from the Adelaide Hills. The
inspiration has been the medium-bodied red wines Jim Kladis grew up with on the Greek island
of Zante. Dion is the Kladis' son, who suffers from cerebral palsy. The winery has recently had a
$1.5 million upgrade to include a conference centre, restaurant and cellar door. Exports to China
and Hong Kong.

Dion Hunter Valley Cabernet Sauvignon 2005 Good purple-red; as the
back label acknowledges, not a region known for its cabernet sauvignon (pacé
Lake's Folly). Fine cassis and blackberry fruit; an exceptionally pure wine with
perfect structure. The story behind the wine and the label is genuinely
touching. Cork. 13.5° alc. **Rating** 94 **To** 2019 $95

Knappstein Wines

2 Pioneer Avenue, Clare, SA 5453 **Region** Clare Valley
T (08) 8842 2600 **F** (08) 8842 3831 **www**.knappsteinwines.com.au **Open** Mon–Fri 9–5,
Sat 11–5, Sun & public hols 11–4
Winemaker Paul Smith **Est.** 1969 **Cases** 35 000
Very much part of Lion Nathan's stable, with Paul Smith having taken over from Andrew Hardy,
who has returned to Petaluma headquarters. The 115 ha of mature estate vineyards in prime
locations supply grapes both for the Knappstein brand and for wider Petaluma use. It doesn't
know how not to make seriously good wines, yet can't get across the line to greatness. Exports to
all major markets.

Ackland Vineyard Watervale Riesling 2006 Spicy floral blossom aromas; a
long, lingering and powerful palate has considerable drive right through to the finish.
Screwcap. 13.5° alc. **Rating** 93 **To** 2019 $30
Enterprise Cabernet Sauvignon 2004 An extremely powerful take-no-
prisoners style; forbidding black fruits and tannins, but the wine is in balance and
simply needs 10-15 years in bottle. Cork. 14.5° alc. **Rating** 93 **To** 2024 $42.95
Thr3e Clare Valley Gewurztraminer Riesling Pinot Gris 2006 Works
surprisingly well; lovely juicy flavours, seemingly anchored on riesling and
gewurztraminer; I would never have guessed the origin. Screwcap. 13.5° alc.
Rating 91 **To** 2008 $23
Single Vineyard Clare Valley Fortified Shiraz 2002 Big and powerful; still brash
and youthful despite the 375 ml (half-size) bottle; black fruits, spice, hints of dark
chocolate and good fortifying spirit. Cork. 18.5° alc. **Rating** 91 **To** 2017 $21.95
Hand Picked Clare Valley Riesling 2006 Unusually soft and generous when
12 months old; tropical lime and spice flavours developing early. Screwcap. 13° alc.
Rating 90 **To** 2011 $23
Yertabulti Vineyard Clare Valley Shiraz 2004 Medium red-purple; a medium-
bodied palate with distinct touches of earth and spice to the foundation of black
fruits and controlled oak. Cork. 14.5° alc. **Rating** 90 **To** 2015 $42
Clare Valley Shiraz 2004 Medium-bodied; distinctly savoury, earthy components
to dark fruits; instead of tapering off, has surprising length. Screwcap. 14.5° alc.
Rating 90 **To** 2014 $23
Clare Valley Cabernet Merlot 2004 Supple and very ripe blackberry, plum and
prune flavours, but avoids outright dead fruit characters; touches of chocolate and
vanilla, finishing with soft tannins. Screwcap. 14.5° alc. **Rating** 90 **To** 2015 $23
Clare Valley Sparkling Shiraz NV A distinctly elegant style; gently spicy red and
black cherry fruits; good length and balance, neither sweet nor phenolic. 14° alc.
Rating 90 **To** 2012 $23

ŶŶŶŶ **Clare Valley Semillon Sauvignon Blanc 2006** An attractive light-bodied wine; easy access fruit with gentle tropical notes, surprising given that semillon is (in percentage terms) the dominant partner, and that Clare Valley sauvignon blanc is not meant to be expressive. Screwcap. 13.5° alc. **Rating** 89 **To** 2009 $19

Knots Wines

A8 Shurans Lane, Heathcote, Vic 3552 **Region** Heathcote
T (03) 5441 5429 **F** (03) 5441 5429 **www**.thebridgevineyard.com.au **Open** By appt
Winemaker Lindsay Ross **Est.** 1997 **Cases** 1000
This is the venture of former Balgownie winemaker Lindsay Ross and wife Noeline, and is part of a broader business known as Winedrops, which acts as a wine production and distribution network for the Bendigo wine industry. The Knots wines are sourced from long-established Heathcote and Bendigo vineyards, providing 0.5 ha each of semillon and chardonnay, and 4 ha each of shiraz and cabernets. The viticultural accent is on low-cropping vineyards with concentrated flavours, the winemaking emphasis on flavour, finesse and varietal expression.

ŶŶŶŶŶ **The Bridge Heathcote Shiraz 2004** Strong colour; full-bodied, with masses of blackberry fruit and touches of licorice; the tannins are plentiful, but not excessive; will be very long-lived. Cork. 15° alc. **Rating** 94 **To** 2025 $50
Sheepshank Bendigo Shiraz 2004 Strong colour; a potent, earthy blackberry and licorice bouquet; strong Bendigo regional expression throughout; blackberry and a positive touch of spice; fine, persistent tannins, and a long finish. Cork. 15° alc. **Rating** 94 **To** 2020 $25

ŶŶŶŶŶ **Top Knot Cabernet Sauvignon 2004** Medium-bodied; good texture and structure; blackcurrant fruit supported by persistent, fine tannins and compatible oak. Cork. 14° alc. **Rating** 92 **To** 2015 $80

Koltz ★★★☆

5 Adams Road, Blewitt Springs, SA 5171 (postal) **Region** McLaren Vale
T (08) 8383 0023 **F** (08) 8383 0023 **Open** Not
Winemaker Mark Day **Est.** 1994 **Cases** 2000
Mark Day and Anna Koltunow released their first wine in 1995, using grapes from the Bottin Vineyard in McLaren Vale. Mark Day had worked as winemaker at Maxwell Wines and Wirra Wirra in McLaren Vale, and has been a Flying Winemaker for 6 consecutive vintages in Europe. Day and Koltunow decided to specialise in Shiraz and Shiraz blends from the McLaren Vale region, but added Sangiovese and Mourvedre to the mix in 2002. Exports to the UK, the US and can be ordered by mail.

Kominos Wines ★★★★☆

27145 New England Highway, Severnlea, Qld 4352 **Region** Granite Belt
T (07) 4683 4311 **F** (07) 4683 4291 **www**.kominoswines.com **Open** 7 days 9–5
Winemaker Tony Comino **Est.** 1976 **Cases** 4000
Tony Comino is a dedicated viticulturist and winemaker and, with wife Mary, took over ownership of the winery from his parents on its 21st vintage. Comino is proud of the estate-grown, made and bottled heritage of the winery and is content to keep a relatively low profile in Australia, although the proud show record of the wines might suggest otherwise. Another Qld producer to make seriously good wines, capable of holding their own against all comers from the south (as Qlders refer to anyone not born in the state). Exports to the US and Asia.

ŶŶŶŶŶ **Reserve Shiraz 2005** While medium-full-bodied, has a finer tannin structure than the varietal, with more expression of both red and black fruits; a little more oak is also evident. Diam. 13.5° alc. **Rating** 94 **To** 2022 $30

ŶŶŶŶŶ **Estate Shiraz 2005** Medium- to full-bodied, with strong texture and structure; fine but insistent tannins run through the blackberry fruit of the palate; a serious, well-made, wine. Diam. 13.5° alc. **Rating** 91 **To** 2020 $24

Estate Merlot 2005 Strong purple-red; medium-to full-bodied; rich black fruits with lots to commend it as a red wine, except for that ever-elusive varietal character. Diam. 13.5° alc. **Rating** 90 To 2015 $25

♀♀♀♀ Nouvelle 2005 Must be served ice-cold on a warm day, and will then go with almost anything. Pink Frontignan/Shiraz. Diam. 11° alc. **Rating** 87 **To** 2008 $15

Kongwak Hills Winery ★★★

1030 Korumburra–Wonthaggi Road, Kongwak, Vic 3951 **Region** Gippsland
T (03) 5657 3267 **F** (03) 5657 3267 **Open** W'ends & public hols 10–5
Winemaker Peter Kimmer **Est.** 1989 **Cases** 500
Peter and Jenny Kimmer started the development of their vineyard in 1989 and now have 0.5 ha each of cabernet sauvignon, shiraz and pinot noir, together with lesser quantities of malbec, merlot and riesling. Most of the wines are sold at the cellar door.

Koonara ★★★★☆

Skinner Road, Coonawarra, SA 5263 **Region** Coonawarra
T (08) 8737 3222 **F** (08) 8737 3220 **www**.koonara.com **Open** By appt
Winemaker Dru Reschke, Peter Douglas (Consultant) **Est.** 1988 **Cases** 3000
Koonara is a sister, or, more appropriately, brother company to Reschke Wines. The latter is run by Burke Reschke, Koonara by his brother Dru. Both are sons of Trevor Reschke, who planted the first vines on the Koonara property in 1988. The initial planting was of cabernet sauvignon, followed by shiraz in 1993 and additional cabernet sauvignon in 1998. Peter Douglas, formerly Wynns' chief winemaker before moving overseas for some years, has returned to the district and is consultant winemaker. Exports to the US, Taiwan and China.

♀♀♀♀♀ The Celestial Promise Coonawarra Cabernet Sauvignon 1998 Ripe blackcurrant, cassis, chocolate and mocha aromas and flavours; the tannins are in balance on a long finish; holding well; 60 cases made. Cork. 13.5° alc. **Rating** 93 To 2013 $100
Ambriel's Gift Coonawarra Cabernet Sauvignon 2004 Fine texture and structure; cassis with some olive, fine tannins lingering on the finish. Screwcap. 13.5° alc. **Rating** 90 To 2015 $27
Ambriel's Gift Coonawarra Cabernet Sauvignon 2002 Has developed well; a low-yielding, cool vintage has aided the wine's development; blackberry, a touch of olive, and good tannins. **Rating** 90 To 2012

♀♀♀♀ Ezra's Gift Shiraz 2004 Lively and vivacious as befits the blend, but not particularly rich. Shiraz/Viognier. Screwcap. **Rating** 89 To 2012 $24
Ambriel's Gift Coonawarra Cabernet Sauvignon 1999 Holding well; tangy, earthy, olive overtones to medium-bodied blackberry fruit; supple tannins. Cork. 13.5° alc. **Rating** 89 To 2010 $27
Angels Footsteps Sauvignon Blanc 2006 Gentle tropical fruit; fair balance and length; pleasant commercial style. Screwcap. **Rating** 88 To 2008 $19
Emily May Coonawarra Rose 2006 Pale bright fuchsia; has far more flavour intensity than most; lingering strawberry and cherry fruit. Screwcap. 13.4° alc. **Rating** 88 To 2008 $14.50
Ambriel's Gift Coonawarra Cabernet Sauvignon 2003 Light- to medium-bodied; elegant, gently savoury/earthy style; the tannins are fine, and the wine has length. Screwcap. 13.5° alc. **Rating** 88 To 2010 $27
Ambriel's Gift Coonawarra Cabernet Sauvignon 2000 Unconvincing colour; light- to medium-bodied cedary/savoury/earthy flavours now dominant; fine tannins. Cork. 13.5° alc. **Rating** 88 To 2008 $28

Koonowla Wines ★★★★☆

PO Box 45, Auburn, SA 5451 **Region** Clare Valley
T (08) 8849 2080 **F** (08) 8849 2293 **www**.koonowla.com **Open** Not
Winemaker O'Leary Walker Wines (Contract) **Est.** 1997 **Cases** 3000

It's not often that a light as large as this can be hidden under a bushel. Koonowla is a historic Clare Valley property; situated just east of Auburn, it was first planted with vines in the 1890s, and by the early 1900s was producing 60 000 litres of wine annually. A disastrous fire in 1926 destroyed the winery and wine stocks, and the property was converted to grain and wool production. Replanting of vines began in 1985, and accelerated after Andrew and Booie Michael purchased the property in 1991; there are now 40 ha each of riesling and cabernet sauvignon, 16 ha of shiraz, and 2 ha each of merlot and semillon. In an all too familiar story, the grapes were sold until falling prices forced a change in strategy, and now part of the grapes are made by the infinitely experienced David O'Leary and Nick Walker, with the remainder sold. Most of the wines are exported.

ⓎⓎⓎⓎⓎ **Clare Valley Riesling 2006** An abundance of flavour and depth; ripe lime and citrus aromas and flavours, almost verging on tropical; lingering finish. Trophy Best Current Vintage Riesling Clare Valley Wine Show '06. Screwcap. 12.5° alc. **Rating** 94 **To** 2010 $22

ⓎⓎⓎⓎⓎ **Clare Valley Shiraz 2003** Considerable depth and richness; svelte black fruits with nuances of licorice and spice; good length, and carries the alcohol effortlessly. Screwcap. 15° alc. **Rating** 91 **To** 2023 $25
Clare Valley Riesling 2005 Glowing green-straw; a clean bouquet, then a powerful, slightly introspective style, with a firm, dry finish. Screwcap. 13.2° alc. **Rating** 90 **To** 2012 $22
Clare Valley Cabernet Sauvignon 2002 Firm black fruits and bitter chocolate offset by touches of mocha oak; interesting style. Screwcap. 15° alc. **Rating** 90 **To** 2022 $25

ⓎⓎⓎⓎ **Clare Valley Shiraz 2002** A tight, severe style, with a hint of reduction; black fruits and earth; needs further time to loosen up. Screwcap. 14.8° alc. **Rating** 89 **To** 2018 $25
Clare Valley Cabernet Sauvignon 2003 Some sweet and sour aspects, opening with sweet cassis berry on to the mid-palate, then herb, olive and earth on the finish and aftertaste. Screwcap. 15° alc. **Rating** 89 **To** 2015 $25

Kooyong
★★★★★

PO Box 153, Red Hill South, Vic 3937 **Region** Mornington Peninsula
T (03) 5989 7355 **F** (03) 5989 7677 **www**.kooyong.com **Open** At Port Phillip Estate
Winemaker Sandro Mosele **Est.** 1996 **Cases** 5000
Kooyong, owned by Giorgio and Dianne Gjergja, released its first wines in 2001. The 34-ha vineyard is planted to pinot noir and chardonnay. Winemaker Sandro Mosele is a graduate of Charles Sturt University, having previously gained a science degree, and has a deservedly high reputation. He also provides contract winemaking services for others. The outstanding wines he has made in 2005 stand as an awesome record. Exports to the UK, the US, Canada, Sweden, Korea and Singapore.

ⓎⓎⓎⓎⓎ **Single Vineyard Selection Farrago Chardonnay 2005** Perfumed grapefruit/citrus overtones and a touch of barrel ferment; a fine, elegant palate faithfully reflecting the bouquet; a gloriously fine, fresh finish. Diam. 13.5° alc. **Rating** 96 **To** 2015 $58
Single Vineyard Selection Haven Pinot Noir 2005 As deeply coloured as Ferrous; the ripest (apparently) and most powerful, especially in terms of structure; some foresty tannins just make their presence felt, and add to the character of the wine. Diam. 13.5° alc. **Rating** 96 **To** 2015 $66
Single Vineyard Selection Faultline Chardonnay 2005 Stone fruit with a touch of fig; nectarine flavours, then a lively, fresh and long finish with citrussy acidity. Diam. 13.5° alc. **Rating** 95 **To** 2015 $58
Single Vineyard Selection Faultline Chardonnay 2004 Light straw-green; super-elegant, focused and long; the winemaking inputs perfectly judged; stone fruit, grapefruit, cashew and mineral all merge; crisp, lingering acidity. Diam. 13.5° alc. **Rating** 95 **To** 2014 $52

Single Vineyard Selection Ferrous Pinot Noir 2005 Deeper colour than the Estate; supple, silky plum, black cherry and spice; a long palate, fruit-driven from start to finish. Diam. 13.5° alc. **Rating** 95 **To** 2013 $58

Estate Mornington Peninsula Chardonnay 2005 Refined, elegant and beautifully crafted; seamless integration of fruit, oak, lees and mlf influences; supple and smooth. Diam. 13° alc. **Rating** 94 **To** 2015 $39

Massale Mornington Peninsula Pinot Noir 2005 Strong purple-red; powerful, potent plum fruit and lingering, persistent tannins; not yet ready, but will flower with a few years in bottle. Get in on the ground floor price. Diam. 13.5° alc. **Rating** 94 **To** 2013 $25

Estate Mornington Peninsula Pinot Noir 2005 Bright colour; fragrant and pure plum, cherry and strawberry; feather-light intensity, yet long and lingering. Diam. 13.5° alc. **Rating** 94 **To** 2012 $39

Single Vineyard Selection Haven Pinot Noir 2004 Similar colour to the Ferrous Pinot; light to medium-bodied, but smooth and supple; despite the lower alcohol, has sweeter and more vibrant fruit than Ferrous. Diam. 13° alc. **Rating** 94 **To** 2011 $60

Single Vineyard Selection Meres Pinot Noir 2004 Again, similar colour to Ferrous and Haven; fragrant and fresh red fruits, then a fine and long finish; best drunk sooner than later. Diam. 13° alc. **Rating** 94 **To** 2011 $52

♟♟♟♟♟ **Single Vineyard Selection Ferrous Pinot Noir 2004** Light red, with just a touch of purple; light- to medium-bodied; good structure underpins the wine with savoury nuances to the red and black fruits. Diam. 13.5° alc. **Rating** 93 **To** 2011 $52

Single Vineyard Selection Meres Pinot Noir 2005 Lighter colour; distinctly the lightest of the 4 pinots in terms of its aromas; positively delicate, and can't make up the ground. Diam. 13° alc. **Rating** 92 **To** 2010 $58

Kopparossa Wines   ★★★★☆

PO Box 26, Coonawarra, SA 5263 **Region** Coonawarra
T (08) 8736 3268 **F** (08) 8736 3363 **Open** By appt
Winemaker Gavin Hogg, Mike Press **Est.** 1996 **Cases** 5000
Of the many complicated stories, this is one of the most complicated of all. It was founded by Gavin Hogg and Mike Press in 1996, based on an 80-ha vineyard in the Wrattonbully region, and the Kopparossa label was born in 2000. The vineyard was sold in 2002, and Mike Press retired to pursue separate interests in his Adelaide Hills family vineyard. Various wine releases and events occurred until 2005 when a joint venture between Stentiford Pty Ltd (Kopparossa's parent company) and Estate Licensing Pty Ltd (Olivia Newton John's wine-naming rights company) was entered into. Says Gavin Hogg's newsletter, 'Put simply, Stentiford produces and packages wine for the Olivia Label, which is then marketed and sold by Estate Licensing'. Reading on, we are told there are also Kopparossa wines and the possibility of a premium platinum release in the future under the Olivia banner. Please don't ask me to explain this any further. Exports to the UK, the US, Canada, China and Korea.

♟♟♟♟♟ **Olivia's Coonawarra Cabernet Sauvignon 2002** Medium- to full-bodied; well-balanced; strong regional/varietal expression. Screwcap. 13.6° alc. **Rating** 93 **To** 2022 $20

Kouark Vineyard

300 Thompson Road, Drouin South, Vic 3818 **Region** Gippsland
T (03) 5627 6337 **F** (03) 5627 6337 **www**.gourmetgippsland.com **Open** W'ends 12–5
Winemaker Phil Gray **Est.** 1997 **Cases** 1000
Dairy farmers Phil and Jane Gray decided to diversify with the establishment of a 4-ha vineyard on part of their farm. They have planted 1.3 ha each of chardonnay and pinot noir, and 0.7 ha each of shiraz and cabernet sauvignon (and a few vines of pinot gris and viognier) on a northeasterly slope, bordered on the east by a 2.4-ha lake. As well as their general farming background, they have undertaken various Charles Sturt University grape and wine production

courses, and similar short courses from other education facilities. A simple but appropriately equipped winery has been established, and the wines are sold through local stores and cafés. The name is believed to be the word for kookaburra in the language of the local Kurnai people.

ŶŶŶŶ   **Gippsland Cabernet Sauvignon 2005** Balanced blackcurrant fruit and oak; medium-bodied, with some length. Screwcap. 13.8° alc. **Rating** 89 **To** 2012 $22

Krinklewood   ★★★★☆

712 Wollombi Road, Broke, NSW 2330 **Region** Lower Hunter Valley
T (02) 6579 1322 **www**.krinklewood.com **Open** W'ends, long w'ends & by appt
Winemaker Monarch Winemaking Services **Est.** 1981 **Cases** 5000
A boutique, family-owned biodynamic vineyard, Krinklewood produces 100% estate-grown wines reflecting the terroir of the Broke-Fordwich area of the Hunter Valley. The cellar door is set amongst Provencal-style gardens that overlook the vineyard, with the Wollombi Brook and Brokenback range providing a spectacular backdrop.

ŶŶŶŶŶ   **Hunter Valley Semillon 2006** Light straw-green; a quiet bouquet, then a massively expressive palate with all forms of citrus, even a touch of sauvignon-blanc-like passionfruit; delicious wine, very good acidity. Screwcap. 10.4° alc. **Rating** 94 **To** 2015 $20

ŶŶŶŶŶ   **Hunter Valley Verdelho 2006** The bouquet is subdued, possibly by the screwcap; fresh, lively, lemony acidity from the early picking works very well here, and the wine actually has a future. Gold medal Hunter Valley Wine Show '06. Screwcap. 12.9° alc. **Rating** 93 **To** 2010 $20
Hunter Valley Dessert Semillon 2005 Botrytis sweetness balanced and enhanced by excellent acidity; for immediate enjoyment. Trophy Hunter Valley Boutique Winemakers Show. Screwcap. 9° alc. **Rating** 93 **To** 2008 $28
Hunter Valley Chardonnay 2005 Yellow peach and fig; rich and complex, with barrel ferment inputs; doesn't cloy. Screwcap. 13° alc. **Rating** 90 **To** 2011 $22

ŶŶŶŶ   **Hunter Valley Basket Press Shiraz 2005** Ripe black fruits and nicely balanced oak; fractionally short. Screwcap. 12.5° alc. **Rating** 89 **To** 2013 $25
Hunter Valley Tempranillo 2005 Nice fresh colour; cherry and lemon fruit with what seems to be an element of adjusted acidity. Screwcap. 13.5° alc. **Rating** 88 **To** 2009 $28

Kurabana   ★★★★

580 Hendy Main Road, Mt Moriac, Vic 3240 **Region** Geelong
T 0438 661 273 **F** (03) 5266 1116 **www**.kurabana.com **Open** Not
Winemaker Ray Nadeson, Lee Evans **Est.** 1987 **Cases** 2000
The development of the quite extensive Kurabana Vineyard, west of Geelong in the foothills of Mt Moriac, began in 1987. Pinot noir (7.5 ha) is the largest portion, followed by (in descending order) shiraz, chardonnay, sauvignon blanc and pinot gris. While some of the grapes are sold, there are also limited purchases from the Geelong area.

ŶŶŶŶŶ   **Shiraz 2005** Blackberry fruit, firm and fresh; good acidity adds to the considerable length of the wine. For extended cellaring. Screwcap. 13.5° alc. **Rating** 94 **To** 2020 $20

ŶŶŶŶ   **Chardonnay 2005** Generous style; ripe melon and stone fruit supported by controlled oak. ProCork. 13° alc. **Rating** 87 **To** 2008 $20
Mount Moriac Pinot Noir 2006 Light- to medium-bodied; plum and warm spice aromas; moderate intensity and length; well-priced. Screwcap. 13.5° alc. **Rating** 87 **To** 2008 $16

Kurrajong Downs

Casino Road, via Tenterfield, NSW 2372 **Region** New England
T (02) 6736 4590 **www**.kurrajongdownswines.com **Open** Thurs–Mon 9–4
Winemaker Ravens Croft Wines (Mark Ravenscroft), Symphony Hill (Mike Hayes)
Est. 2000 **Cases** 2400

Jonus Rhodes arrived at Tenterfield in 1858, lured by the gold he mined for the next 40 years, until his death in 1898. He was evidently successful, for the family now runs a 2800-ha cattle grazing property on which Lynton and Sue Rhodes have planted a 5-ha vineyard at an altitude of 850 m. Development of the vineyard started in the spring of 1996, and continued the following year.

♈♈♈♈ **Classic Dry White 2006** Clean bouquet, no reduction; light and fresh with a nice touch of herbaceousness; does fall a fraction short, though may fill out a little with age. Screwcap. 11.5° alc. **Rating** 88 **To** 2014 $16
All Nations Tenterfield Pinot Noir 2005 Medium red; firm, fresh, clean, cherry-accented wine; a little angular in the mouth, not silky, but creditable, nonetheless. Diam. 13.3° alc. **Rating** 88 **To** 2011 $19
Darcy's Hill Tenterfield Merlot 2005 Has the restraint shown by most of the Kurrajong wines; perhaps early picking, but works for those with a European bent to their taste. Diam. 13° alc. **Rating** 88 **To** 2012 $15
Sunset Rose 2006 Nicely balanced; has that touch of cabernet austerity to balance the raspberry/cherry red fruits; good balance, though does fall away a little on the finish. Screwcap. 12° alc. **Rating** 87 **To** 2008 $14
Black Duck Tenterfield Shiraz 2005 Light but bright hue; a light-bodied palate, with vibrant, fresh red fruits; needed a little softening of the acidity. Diam. 13° alc. **Rating** 87 **To** 2012 $21

Kyneton Ridge Estate

90 Blackhill School Road, Kyneton, Vic 3444 **Region** Macedon Ranges
T (03) 5422 7377 **F** (03) 5422 3747 **www**.kynetonridge.com.au **Open** W'ends & public hols 10–5, or by appt
Winemaker John Boucher **Est.** 1997 **Cases** 500

Kyneton Ridge Estate has been established by a family team of winemakers with winemaking roots going back 4 generations in the case of John and Ann Boucher. Together with Pauline Russell they found what they believe is a perfect pinot noir site near Kyneton, and planted 2.5 ha of pinot noir in 1997; 1.5 ha of chardonnay and 0.5 ha of shiraz were added in 2002.

♈♈♈♈ **Macedon Sparkling 2004** Attractive ripe nectarine fruit with a hint of strawberry; good balance and length, though not especially complex. 12.5° alc. **Rating** 89 **To** 2012 $28
Macedon Ranges Shiraz 2005 Light colour; a light-bodied and fresh mix of red cherry, plum, spice and fine tannins. Cork. 13.3° alc. **Rating** 88 **To** 2011 $23

La Curio

11 Sextant Avenue, Seaford, SA 5169 (postal) **Region** McLaren Vale
T (08) 8327 1442 **F** (08) 8327 1442 **www**.lacuriowines.com **Open** Not
Winemaker Adam Hooper, Elena Golakova **Est.** 2003 **Cases** 650

La Curio has been established by Adam Hooper and partner Elena Golakova, who purchase small parcels of grapes from 5 vineyards in McLaren Vale with an average age of 40 years, the oldest 80 years. They make the wines at Redheads Studio, a boutique winery in McLaren Vale which caters for a number of small producers. The manacles depicted on the striking label are those of Harry Houdini, and the brand proposition is very cleverly worked through. Winemaking techniques, too, are avant-garde, and highly successful. Exports to the UK and the US.

♈♈♈♈♈ **Reserve McLaren Vale Shiraz 2005** An array of black and red fruits, licorice and dark chocolate on both bouquet and palate; finishes with spicy/savoury tannins. Cork. 15° alc. **Rating** 92 **To** 2025 $28

Reserve Bush Vine McLaren Vale Grenache 2005 In texture and overall flavour terms, hangs together better than the The Nubile; a complex array of raspberry, cherry and redcurrant fruit; appealing tannins. Cork. 15° alc. **Rating** 91 To 2019 $24

▼▼▼▼ **The Nubile McLaren Vale Grenache Shiraz 2005** Savoury red fruits, a mix of earth and confection; the 30% shiraz confers vitality on the finish. Cork. 15° alc. **Rating** 89 To 2017 $19

🍃 La Fontaine

295 Manks Road, Fiveways, Vic 3977 **Region** Gippsland
T (03) 5998 1133 **F** (03) 5998 1144 **Open** By appt
Winemaker Wild Dog (Mal Stewart) **Est. Cases** 800
Brett Glover has established 6 ha of vines, and had a dream start when he entered the first vintage wines at the Gippsland Wine Show '07. The wines are available at local establishments in Cranbourne and Berwick, with the cellar door and restaurant scheduled to open in Nov 2007.

▼▼▼▼▼ **Unwooded Chardonnay 2006** Nectarine and a touch of citrus run through a palate with plenty of character and length, unusual in unwooded chardonnay. **Rating** 90 To 2009

▼▼▼▼ **Pinot Noir Chardonnay 2004** Quite firm, with some hard edges throughout, but has good length, and would repay further time on cork. **Rating** 87 To 2009 **Liqueur Chardonnay 2006** Clean spirit; fair balance and length. **Rating** 87 To 2008

La Pleiade

c/- Jasper Hill, Drummonds Lane, Heathcote, Vic 3523 **Region** Heathcote
T (03) 5433 2528 **F** (03) 5433 3143 **Open** By appt
Winemaker Ron Laughton, Michel Chapoutier **Est.** 1998 **Cases** NFP
This is the joint venture of Michel and Corinne Chapoutier and Ron and Elva Laughton. In the spring of 1998 a vineyard using Australian shiraz clones and imported French clones was planted. The vineyard is run biodynamically, and the winemaking is deliberately designed to place maximum emphasis on the fruit quality.

▼▼▼▼▼ **Heathcote Shiraz 2004** Dense, impenetrable purple-red; crammed with black fruit/anise/plum; bitter chocolate and oak complete the flavours, all locked together by persistent but fine, ripe tannins. A virtually unlimited life span. Cork. 15° alc. **Rating** 96 To 2039 $69

Laanecoorie

4834 Bendigo/Maryborough Road, Betley, Vic 3472 **Region** Bendigo
T (03) 5468 7260 **F** (03) 5468 7388 **Open** W'ends & public hols 11–5, Mon–Fri by appt
Winemaker Graeme Jukes, John Ellis (Contract) **Est.** 1982 **Cases** 1000
John McQuilten's 7.5-ha vineyard produces grapes of high quality, and competent contract-winemaking has done the rest.

▼▼▼▼▼ **McQuilten's Reserve Shiraz 2005** Floods the mouth with blackberry, dark chocolate, plum and prune; the alcohol is obvious, but the tannins are soft, and the wine remains in overall balance, helped by good oak. Cork. 15° alc. **Rating** 93 To 2024 $39.50

Labyrinth

PO Box 7372, Shepparton, Vic 3632 **Region** Yarra Valley
T 0438 312 793 **F** (03) 5831 2982 **www.labyrinthwine.com Open** Not
Winemaker Rick Hill **Est.** 2000 **Cases** 8500

Rick Hill is running a unique wine business, the name Labyrinth being well chosen. While it is a Pinot Noir-only specialist, one is produced in the southern hemisphere (from the Yarra Valley) and one from the northern hemisphere (Santa Barbara, California) each year. The wines come from individual vineyards: the Bien Nacido Vineyard has a deserved reputation as one of the best sources of pinot noir in California. Rick Hill uses leased space in California and at Long Gully Estate to make the wines, and also has active consultancy work in California.

ŶŶŶŶŶ **Bien Nacido Vineyard Santa Maria Valley Pinot Noir 2003** Deep red-purple, though clear; rich, but not the least porty or jammy; plush plum and blackberry fruit with good structure. Cork. 13.6° alc. **Rating** 95 **To** 2014 $61.50

Viggers Vineyard Yarra Valley Pinot Noir 2004 Some smoky/foresty characters throughout a lengthy palate, which finishes with good acidity. Cork. 13.8° alc. **Rating** 94 **To** 2011 $40

Bien Nacido Vineyard Santa Maria Valley Pinot Noir 2004 Brilliantly clear colour with a perfect hue; fresh precise and youthful cherry with a touch of strawberry needing to build texture with further time in bottle. Cork. 13° alc. **Rating** 94 **To** 2012 $61.50

ŶŶŶŶŶ **Valley Farm Vineyard Yarra Valley Pinot Noir 2004** Bright, clear colour; slightly more foresty notes to the aroma, though the structure is similar, fresh, crisp and direct. Cork. 13.4° alc. **Rating** 93 **To** 2011 $36.50

Ladbroke Grove ★★★★

Riddoch Highway, Coonawarra, SA 5263 **Region** Coonawarra
T (08) 8737 3777 www.ladbrokegrove.com.au **Open** Wed–Sun 10–5, or by appt
Winemaker Contract **Est.** 1982 **Cases** 5000
Established in 1982, Ladbroke Grove is a relatively old Coonawarra brand. However, while the vineyards remained, winemaking and marketing lapsed until the business was purchased by John Cox and Marie Valenzuela, who have quietly gone about the re-establishment and rejuvenation of the label and were rewarded by a string of wine show results. It has extensive grape sources, including the Killian vineyard (10 ha), planted in 1990 to cabernet sauvignon, merlot and chardonnay. It also leases a little over 1 ha of dry-grown shiraz planted in 1965 in the centre of the Coonawarra township. In 2002 it planted another 11 ha at the northern end of Coonawarra to cabernet sauvignon, shiraz, viognier, riesling and merlot.

ŶŶŶŶŶ **Compadres Blend Cabernet Merlot 2004** A medium-bodied, attractive array of spicy red and black fruits; fine tannins. Cork. 14° alc. **Rating** 91 **To** 2014 $26

Lady Bay Vineyard NR

42-44 Davis Street, Wingfield, SA 5013 (postal) **Region** Southern Fleurieu
T (08) 8445 1533 **F** (08) 8445 1561 www.ladybay.com.au **Open** Not
Winemaker Contract **Est.** 1996 **Cases** NA
Lady Bay has 9 ha of viognier, pinot gris, cabernet sauvignon and shiraz a mere 500 m from the waters of the Gulf of St Vincent. On the inland side it is protected by the Great Gorge, part of the southern Mt Lofty Ranges. Cool days and warm nights provide good ripening conditions even for varieties such as cabernet sauvignon.

Lake Breeze Wines

Step Road, Langhorne Creek, SA 5255 **Region** Langhorne Creek
T (08) 8537 3017 **F** (08) 8537 3267 www.lakebreeze.com.au **Open** 7 days 10–5
Winemaker Greg Follett **Est.** 1987 **Cases** 15 000
The Folletts have been farmers at Langhorne Creek since 1880, grapegrowers since the 1930s. Since 1987, increasing amounts of their grapes have been made into wine. The quality of the releases has been exemplary, with the red wines particularly appealing. Lake Breeze also owns and makes the False Cape wines from Kangaroo Island. Exports to the UK, the US and other major markets.

ŢŢŢŢŢ Bernoota Shiraz Cabernet 2004 Medium- to full-bodied, with a seamlessly integrated array of black fruits, oak and ripe tannins; great length. Max Schubert Trophy for Best Red at Adelaide Wine Show '06; gold medal Sydney Wine Show '07. Screwcap. 14.5° alc. **Rating** 96 **To** 2024 $22

Langhorne Creek Cabernet Sauvignon 2004 Deep purple-red; fragrant cassis, redcurrant and blackcurrant aromas; a pure wine, with fine-grained tannins part of its strength; quality oak as well. Gold medal Sydney Wine Show '07. Screwcap. 14.5° alc. **Rating** 94 **To** 2019 $23

False Cape The Captain Cabernet Sauvignon 2004 Beautiful silky mouthfeel a perfect adjunct to the pure cassis and blackcurrant varietal fruit; seamless oak and tannins. Screwcap. 14.5° alc. **Rating** 94 **To** 2019 $28

ŢŢŢŢŢ Winemaker's Selection Shiraz 2004 Strong purple-red; quite aromatic plum and cherry fruit on the bouquet; medium-bodied, with supple mouthfeel, controlled oak and silky tannins. Cork. 14.5° alc. **Rating** 92 **To** 2014 $38

Arthur's Reserve Cabernet Petit Verdot 2003 An austere style, though no more than medium-bodied; has good length, with savoury but ripe tannins, the result of extended maceration. Cork. 14° alc. **Rating** 92 **To** 2018 $29

False Cape Unknown Sailor Cabernet Merlot 2004 Positive flavour and varietal character; blackcurrant, spice and olive with a touch of bitter chocolate, finishing with ripe tannins. Another bargain. Screwcap. 14.5° alc. **Rating** 91 **To** 2014 $18

ŢŢŢŢ False Cape Silver Mermaid Sauvignon Blanc 2006 Clean, fresh and crisp; light tropical fruit is balanced by citrussy acidity which also adds length. Screwcap. 13° alc. **Rating** 88 **To** 2008 $18

False Cape Montebello Rose 2006 Cellar door special; positive sweet red fruits then residual sugar on the finish. Screwcap. 13.5° alc. **Rating** 87 **To** 2008 $18

🍇 Lake Cairn Curran Vineyard ★★★★☆

'Park Hill', Lethbridge Road, Welshman's Reef, Vic 3462 **Region** Bendigo
T (03) 5476 2523 **F** (03) 5476 2523 **www.**lakecairncurranvineyard.com.au **Open** By appt
Winemaker Sarah Ferguson, Ron Snep, Rick McIntyre, David Cowburn (Contract)
Est. 1987 **Cases** 800

When Ross and Sarah Ferguson purchased what is now known as Lake Cairn Curran Vineyard in 1999, they acquired not only 4.5 ha of chardonnay, pinot noir and shiraz, but also a slice of history, evoked by the beautiful labels. The Park Hill homestead dates back to the establishment of the Tarrengower Run in the 1840s, and the mudbrick cellar door is located adjacent to the homestead, overlooking the Cairn Curran Reservoir and Loddon River Valley. Notwithstanding that Sarah has almost completed a wine science (oenology) degree at Charles Sturt University, and husband Ross has invested much time in training his palate, winemaking duties are spread around specialists in handling the various varieties.

ŢŢŢŢŢ Sur Lees Chardonnay 2005 Shows barrel ferment and lees complexity; medium-bodied, with creamy/nutty overtones to ripe stone fruit; good acidity to close. Screwcap. 13.5° alc. **Rating** 92 **To** 2010 $22

Pinot Noir 2004 Light but distinctly savoury/foresty aromas and flavours; also touches of spice, earth and rose petal testifying to the varietal character. Screwcap. 13.5° alc. **Rating** 90 **To** 2010 $22

ŢŢŢŢ Chardonnay 2004 Bright green-straw; richer and deeper than the alcohol would suggest, with abundant stone fruit/peach/melon, and rather more subtle French oak. Screwcap. 13.5° alc. **Rating** 89 **To** 2009 $19

Shiraz 2005 A light-bodied wine, fully reflecting the cool vineyard site; elements of spice and earth with light black fruits. Screwcap. 13° alc. **Rating** 88 **To** 2009 $20

Lake Cooper Estate

1608 Midland Highway, Corop, Vic 316 **Region** Heathcote
T (03) 9397 7781 **www**.lakecooperestate.com.au **Open** W'ends & public hols 11–5
Winemaker Peter Kelliher, Donald Risstrom **Est.** 1998 **Cases** 1000
Lake Cooper Estate is another substantial venture in the burgeoning Heathcote region, set on the side of Mt Camel Range, with panoramic views of Lake Cooper, Greens Lake and the Corop township. Planting began in 1998 with 12 ha of shiraz, and has since been extended to 18 ha of shiraz, 10 ha of cabernet sauvignon and small plantings of merlot and chardonnay; additional small blocks of more exotic varieties will follow.

ᵠᵠᵠᵠᵠ **Reserve Heathcote Shiraz 2005** Deeper colour than the varietal, though not quite as bright; significantly more power, flavour and complexity thanks to satsuma plum, licorice and spice matched with quality oak; 60 cases made. Get on the mailing list for next year. This is a bargain price for a wine made in such tiny volumes. Cork. 15° alc. **Rating** 93 **To** 2015 $25

Heathcote Shiraz 2005 Ripe plum and blackcurrant fruit on the medium-bodied palate; soft tannins and controlled oak. Screwcap. 14.2° alc. **Rating** 90 **To** 2013 $20

ᵠᵠᵠᵠ **Heathcote Merlot 2005** Quite fragrant; juicy cassis with a neat varietal twist of olive; almost there. Screwcap. 13.8° alc. **Rating** 89 **To** 2011 $20

Heathcote Cabernet Sauvignon 2005 Light to medium-bodied; savoury/briary flavour components along with the blackcurrant fruit. Not entirely convincing. Screwcap. 14.4° alc. **Rating** 89 **To** 2010 $20

Lake George Winery

Federal Highway, Collector, NSW 2581 **Region** Canberra District
T (02) 4848 0039 **F** (02) 4848 0039 **www**.lakegeorgewinery.com.au **Open** By appt
Winemaker Sam Karelas **Est.** 1971 **Cases** 1000
Lake George Winery was sold by founder Dr Edgar Riek some years ago. The 3.5 ha of 36-year-old chardonnay, pinot noir, cabernet sauvignon, semillon and merlot have now been joined by shiraz and tempranillo, and more plantings of pinot gris, viognier, pinot noir and malbec. The winemaking techniques are exactly those one would expect with a small winery, including basket pressing and small batch barrel maturation.

ᵠᵠᵠᵠ **Viognier 2005** Faint reduction; still very youthful, with apricot, tropical varietal character; good balance, and time to grow and become even more complex. Screwcap. 13.5° alc. **Rating** 88 **To** 2011 $25

Cabernet Sauvignon 2004 Light- to medium-bodied; slightly leafy, but enough blackcurrant to satisfy; moderate length. Screwcap. 14° alc. **Rating** 87 **To** 2011 $28

Botrytis Semillon 2003 Headed to orange in colour; malt, butterscotch and some less than entirely noble rot; is, however, complex and has good acidity. Screwcap. 12.5° alc. **Rating** 87 **To** 2008 $35

Lake Moodemere Vineyards

McDonalds Road, Rutherglen, Vic 3685 **Region** Rutherglen
T (02) 6032 9449 **F** (02) 6032 9449 **www**.moodemerewines.com.au **Open** W'ends & public hols 10–5, Mon, Thurs, Fri 10–3.30
Winemaker Michael Chambers **Est.** 1995 **Cases** 2500
Michael, Belinda, Peter and Helen Chambers are members of the famous Chambers family of Rutherglen. They have 22 ha of vineyards (tended by Peter), with the Italian grape variety biancone a vineyard speciality, made in a light-bodied late-harvest style. The cellar door sits high above Lake Moodemere, and gourmet hampers can be arranged with 24 hours' notice.

Lake's Folly

★★★★★

Broke Road, Pokolbin, NSW 2320 **Region** Lower Hunter Valley
T (02) 4998 7507 www.lakesfolly.com.au **Open** 7 days 10–4 while wine available
Winemaker Rodney Kempe **Est.** 1963 **Cases** 4500
The first of the weekend wineries to produce wines for commercial sale, long revered for its
Cabernet Sauvignon and thereafter its Chardonnay. Very properly, terroir and climate produce a
distinct regional influence and thereby a distinctive wine style. The winery continues to enjoy an
incredibly loyal clientele, with much of each year's wine selling out quickly by mail order. Lake's
Folly no longer has any connection with the Lake family, having been acquired some years ago
by Perth businessman Peter Fogarty. Peter's family company previously established the Millbrook
Winery in the Perth Hills, so is no stranger to the joys and agonies of running a small winery.

ΨΨΨΨΨ **Hunter Valley Chardonnay 2005** Deeper green-yellow than the '06; intense,
rich, deep and long; ripe nectarine and a touch of citrus reflects the top
vintage. Cork. 14° alc. **Rating** 95 **To** 2015 $50
Hunter Valley Chardonnay 2006 Bright green-yellow; the usual excellent
balance and structure; melon and nectarine fruit, barrel ferment oak inputs
perfectly judged. Cork. 13.5° alc. **Rating** 94 **To** 2015 $50
Hunter Valley Cabernets 2005 A medium-bodied wine, spotlessly clean, with
fresh cassis/blackcurrant fruit; oak a pure support role to a wine of elegance
and finesse. Cork. 13° alc. **Rating** 94 **To** 2015 $50

Lambert Vineyards

★★★★☆

810 Norton Road, Wamboin, NSW 2620 **Region** Canberra District
T (02) 6238 3866 www.lambertvineyards.com.au **Open** Thurs–Sun 10–5, or by appt
Winemaker Steve Lambert, Ruth Lambert **Est.** 1998 **Cases** 6000
Ruth and Steve Lambert have established 8 ha of riesling, chardonnay, pinot gris, pinot noir,
cabernet sauvignon, merlot and shiraz. Steve Lambert makes the many wines onsite, and does so
with skill and sensitivity. Definitely a winery to watch.

ΨΨΨΨΨ **Canberra District Chardonnay 2004** Bright green-yellow; lots of toasty barrel
ferment French oak inputs dominate the bouquet; the palate makes a partial
comeback thanks to the length of the fruit, but 20 months in oak is just too long.
Screwcap. 14° alc. **Rating** 91 **To** 2012 $20
Canberra District Pinot Gris 2005 Abundant pear and musk varietal aromas;
the palate follows suit in a rich and flavoursome mould, not far short of Alsace.
If you must have pinot gris, this is the way to go. Screwcap. 14.3° alc.
Rating 90 **To** 2008 $20
Canberra District Merlot 2004 Fragrant red and black fruits; medium-bodied
with a quite silky texture, and good length; maintains its varietal profile
throughout. Screwcap. 14.7° alc. **Rating** 90 **To** 2015 $22
Canberra District Cabernet Merlot 2004 Attractive fruit-driven bouquet;
overall fragrance to the fruit; fine-grained tannins to close. Screwcap. 14.8° alc.
Rating 90 **To** 2017 $22

ΨΨΨΨ **Canberra District Riesling 2006** A clean but muted bouquet; much more
expression on the palate with sweet citrus and tropical flavours; early-developing
style. Screwcap. 13° alc. **Rating** 89 **To** 2011 $18
Reserve Canberra District Shiraz 2004 Moderate colour; similar to the
varietal version, except those edges are even more pronounced; spicy, earthy,
blackberry fruits, but doesn't rest easy in the mouth. Time may help. Screwcap.
14.8° alc. **Rating** 89 **To** 2014 $30
Cellar Door Canberra District Rose 2006 Brilliant colour; custom-tailored for
the cellar door as the label acknowledges; lots of sweet strawberry fruit and some
appreciable sweetness on the finish. Merlot/Cabernet Sauvignon/Cabernet Franc.
Screwcap. 12.8° alc. **Rating** 88 **To** 2008 $20

Canberra District Shiraz 2004 Some lifted fruit aromas and a slightly edgy mouthfeel with earthy notes. I'm not too sure what's going on here. Screwcap. 14.5° alc. **Rating** 88 **To** 2012 $25

Lamont's   ★★★★★

85 Bisdee Road, Millendon, WA 6056 **Region** Swan Valley
T (08) 9296 4485 **F** (08) 9296 1663 **www.**lamonts.com.au **Open** 7 days 10–5
Winemaker Digby Leddin, Rachael Robinson **Est.** 1978 **Cases** 8000
Corin Lamont is the daughter of the late Jack Mann, and oversees the making of wines in a style which would have pleased her father. Lamont's also boasts a superb restaurant run by granddaughter Kate Lamont. The wines are going from strength to strength, utilising both estate-grown and contract-grown (from southern regions) grapes. There are 2 cellar doors, the second (open 7 days) in the Margaret River at Gunyulgup Valley Drive, Yallingup.

🍷🍷🍷🍷🍷 **Frankland River Riesling 2006** Light straw-green; a clean and fresh bouquet leads into an excellent palate, lime juice and mineral driving through to a very long finish. Screwcap. 12.5° alc. **Rating** 94 **To** 2016 $25
Margaret River Cabernet Sauvignon 2004 Medium- to full-bodied blackcurrant fruit with a touch of cassis; very good tannin structure and length; quality oak. Screwcap. 14.5° alc. **Rating** 94 **To** 2024 $35

🍷🍷🍷🍷🍷 **Family Reserve 2004** Medium to full purple-red; tannins soon take control as the wine enters the mouth, but the fruit fights back towards the finish; savoury style, and cabernet and shiraz must figure in the undisclosed blend; 20 months oak maturation. Screwcap. 14.5° alc. **Rating** 92 **To** 2024 $40
Semillon 2005 In a style category of its own; baroque and full of flavour, particularly oak, but doesn't hit too hard. Good length. Barrel-fermented in new French oak. Screwcap. 13.7° alc. **Rating** 90 **To** 2011 $30
Chardonnay 2005 An understated wine notwithstanding 100% barrel fermentation; melon and fig at the riper end of the scale, though not all from the Swan Valley; good balance and length. Screwcap. 13.9° alc. **Rating** 90 **To** 2011 $25
Family Reserve 2003 Medium red-purple; starting to show some development; gentle earth, cedar and leather overtones to black fruits; good length, nice oak and fine tannins. Multi-region, multi-varietal blend. Screwcap. 14.3° alc. **Rating** 90 **To** 2015 $40

🍷🍷🍷🍷 **Quartet 2006** Rich and full in the best Jack Mann style; these were the base blocks of Houghton White Burgundy, although there was no chardonnay until later in the piece; a great example of ripeness without high alcohol. Verdelho/Semillon/Chenin Blanc/Chardonnay. Screwcap. 13.4° alc. **Rating** 89 **To** 2013 $14
Shiraz 2004 Powerful, very ripe, fractionally jammy/dead fruit characters; certainly has abundant flavour. Screwcap. 14.9° alc. **Rating** 88 **To** 2014 $25
Shiraz 2003 A very big, rather rustic, full-bodied wine with some alcohol-derived sweetness to the earthy/blackberry fruit; American oak as an incidental. Screwcap. 14.9° alc. **Rating** 88 **To** 2009 $25
Verdelho 2006 Rich, full-throated traditional Swan style; ripe fruit salad flavours; Jack Mann would approve. Screwcap. 13.5° alc. **Rating** 87 **To** 2010 $18

Landsborough Valley Estate   ★★★★☆

850 Landsborough-Elmhurst Road, Landsborough, Vic 3385 **Region** Pyrenees
T (03) 5356 9390 **F** (03) 5356 9130 **Open** Mon–Fri 10–4, w'ends by appt
Winemaker Vicki Henning, Trevor Mast (Consultant) **Est.** 1996 **Cases** 6000
LVE (for short) originated in 1963, when civil engineering contractor Wal Henning was engaged to undertake work at Chateau Remy (now Blue Pyrenees). He was so impressed with the potential of the region for viticulture that he began an aerial search for sites with close friend Geoff Oliver. Their first choice was not available; they chose a site which is now Taltarni,

developing 40 ha. Taltarni was then sold, and the pair (with Geoff's brother Max) moved on to establish Warrenmang Vineyard. When it, too, was sold the pair was left without a vineyard, but in 1996 they were finally able to purchase the property they had identified 33 years previously, which is now partly given over to LVE and part to the giant Glen Kara vineyard. They have established 20 ha on LVE, the lion's share to shiraz, with lesser amounts of cabernet sauvignon, pinot noir, chardonnay and riesling.

ΨΨΨΨΨ **Geoff Oliver Pyrenees Ranges Shiraz 2005** A complex array of aromas and flavours, ranging through black fruits, mint, plum and spice; the tannins lengthen the finish though need to soften a little Screwcap. 14° alc. **Rating** 94 **To** 2020 $25

ΨΨΨΨΨ **Pyrenees Ranges Shiraz 2005** Ripe blackberry and plum fruit with touches of chocolate and spice; overall the wine veers towards the savoury end of the spectrum, rather than the lush or overripe. Screwcap. 13.9° alc. **Rating** 90 **To** 2018 $15

ΨΨΨΨ **Vinoteca Dimattina Grand Riserva Pyrenees Ranges Shiraz 2004** Blackberry fruit and dark chocolate aromas and flavours, but a slightly green edge to the finish. Screwcap. 13.9° alc. **Rating** 89 **To** 2015 $14

Landscape Wines ★★★★

383 Prossers Road, Richmond, Tas 7025 **Region** Southern Tasmania
T (03) 6260 4216 **F** (03) 6260 4016 **Open** By appt
Winemaker Andrew Hood, Jeremy Direen, Alain Rousseau (Contract) **Est.** 1998 **Cases** 120
Knowles and Elizabeth Kerry run the Wondoomarook mixed farming and irrigation property in the heart of the Coal River Valley. In 1998/99 they decided to undertake a small scale diversification, planting 0.5 ha each of riesling and pinot noir. The labels, depicting Antarctic scenes by Jenni Mitchell, hark back to the Kerrys' original occupation in Antarctic scientific research.

ΨΨΨΨ **Pinot Noir 2006** Firm, direct black cherry; some length, though still to build complexity, which will follow. Screwcap. 13.5° alc. **Rating** 88 **To** 2010 $20

Lane's End Vineyard ★★★★

885 Mount William Road, Lancefield, Vic 3435 (postal) **Region** Macedon Ranges
T (03) 5429 1760 **F** (03) 5429 1760 **www**.lanesend.com.au **Open** Not
Winemaker Howard Matthews **Est.** 1985 **Cases** 450
Pharmacist Howard Matthews and family purchased the former Woodend Winery in 2000, with 1.8 ha of chardonnay and pinot noir (and a small amount of cabernet franc) dating back to the mid-1980s. Subsequently, the cabernet franc has been grafted over to pinot noir (with a mix of 4 clones), the chardonnay now totalling 1 ha. After working with next-door neighbour Ken Murchison of Portree Wines for 2 years gaining winemaking experience, Howard made the first wines in 2003.

ΨΨΨΨΨ **Macedon Ranges Chardonnay 2005** An elegant, light- to medium-bodied wine; has good balance of fruit, barrel ferment and mlf influences to the gentle nectarine fruit, giving background creamy/nutty notes; an exercise in restraint. Gold medal Cool Climate Show '06. Screwcap. 13.7° alc. **Rating** 93 **To** 2012 $28

ΨΨΨΨ **Macedon Ranges Cabernet Franc 2005** Really falls outside Australian expectations of red wine; if made in Chinon, Loire Valley (its home) there would be no issues. As it is, very light-bodied, albeit varietal. Screwcap. 13° alc. **Rating** 88 **To** 2009 $23

Langanook Wines ★★★★☆

91 McKittericks Road, Sutton Grange, Vic 3448 **Region** Bendigo
T (03) 5474 8250 **F** (03) 5474 8250 **www**.bendigowine.org.au **Open** W'ends & public hols 11–5, or by appt
Winemaker Matt Hunter **Est.** 1985 **Cases** 1500

The Langanook vineyard was established back in 1985 (the first wines came much later), at an altitude of 450m on the granite slopes of Mt Alexander. The climate is much cooler than in other parts of Bendigo, with a heat summation on a par with the Yarra Valley. The 20-tonne winery allows minimal handling of the wines. Exports to Belgium and Canada.

ΨΨΨΨΨ **Syrah 2005** Deep, dense colour; a similarly rich and dense plum, blackberry, prune, licorice and chocolate, yet doesn't cloy or heat up on the finish; excellent within the parameters of style; interesting decision to bypass viognier. Screwcap. 15.5° alc. **Rating** 94 **To** 2030 $29

ΨΨΨΨ **Chardonnay Viognier 2005** Chardonnay is the dominant partner providing peachy fruit with just a hint of apricot from the viognier, then a subtle twist of oak. Screwcap. 14° alc. **Rating** 89 **To** 2011 $18

Langmeil Winery   ★★★★★

Cnr Para Road/Langmeil Road, Tanunda, SA 5352 **Region** Barossa Valley
T (08) 8563 2595 **F** (08) 8563 3622 **www.**langmeilwinery.com.au **Open** 7 days 11–4.30
Winemaker Paul Lindner **Est.** 1996 **Cases** 15 000
Vines were first planted at Langmeil in the 1840s, and the first winery on the site, known as Paradale Wines, opened in 1932. In 1996, cousins Carl and Richard Lindner with brother-in-law Chris Bitter formed a partnership to acquire and refurbish the winery and its 5-ha vineyard (planted to shiraz, and including 2 ha planted in 1846). Another vineyard was acquired in 1998, taking total plantings to 14.5 ha and including cabernet sauvignon and grenache. Exports to the UK, the US and other major markets.

ΨΨΨΨΨ **Barossa Old Vine Company Shiraz 2004** Very well-made; very precise and beautifully balanced gentle black fruits against a background of French and American oak; has great length. Vines over 100 years old. Cork. 14.5° alc. **Rating** 96 **To** 2024 $100
The 1843 Freedom Barossa Valley Shiraz 2004 In many ways a halfway house between Orphan Bank and the Barossa Old Vine Company; smooth, supple and mouthfilling plum, prune and blackberry fruit; excellent oak, tannin and structure. Cork. 14.5° alc. **Rating** 95 **To** 2020 $100

ΨΨΨΨΨ **Valley Floor Barossa Valley Shiraz 2005** Most attractive effortless, almost lazy, flavour development; shiny black cherry fruit with touches of spice and licorice. Cork. 14.5° alc. **Rating** 93 **To** 2020 $24.95
Orphan Bank Barossa Valley Shiraz 2004 Serves to point out – or up – the grace of very old vines; much more conventional and honest Barossa Valley fruit, full and ripe. Screwcap. 14.5° alc. **Rating** 93 **To** 2025 $45
Eden Valley Riesling 2006 Apple blossom and crushed citrus leaves; delicate and crisp, with a pleasantly dry finish; quite different to the '05. Screwcap. 12.5° alc. **Rating** 91 **To** 2014 $20
Hangin' Snakes Barossa Valley Shiraz Viognier 2005 Medium- to full-bodied, filled with black cherry and blackberry fruit which does, however, go slightly over the top; that said, good length. Screwcap. 14.5° alc. **Rating** 90 **To** 2020 $20
Barossa Valley Sparkling Shiraz NV A surprise packet; good flavour, with appropriate base material avoiding the phenolics which would in turn require high dosage, hence sweetness; 18 months on lees and several years in bottle have paid dividends with this well-balanced example. 13° alc. **Rating** 90 **To** 2012 $35

ΨΨΨΨ **GWH Barossa Valley Viognier 2006** Rich, viscous and strongly varietal expression thanks to apricot and peach fruit; phenolics on the finish are, as ever, the issue. GWH stands for Great White Hope. Screwcap. 14° alc. **Rating** 89 **To** 2010 $20
Barossa Old Vine Company Shiraz 2003 A medium-bodied, luscious, sweet fruit style, certainly made from fully ripe grapes; carries the oak well (71% French/ 29% American), the alcohol less convincingly. Cork. 15° alc. **Rating** 89 **To** 2013 $100

Three Gardens Barossa Valley Shiraz Grenache Mourvedre 2005 A very typical mix with sweet, slightly jammy varietal character of grenache dominant; soft and supple, with fine tannins. Screwcap. 14.5° alc. **Rating** 89 **To** 2014 $20

Jackaman's Barossa Valley Cabernet 2004 Minty notes to both the bouquet and palate, but also substantial cassis/blackcurrant engine doing the work; fine tannins to close. Cork. 14° alc. **Rating** 89 **To** 2019 $45

Fifth Wave Barossa Valley Grenache 2004 Strongly varietal in both flavour and structure terms; it's simply a style which, try as I can, I can't relate to. Cork. 16° alc. **Rating** 87 **To** 2012 $30

Lankeys Creek Wines

River Road, Walwa, Vic 3709 **Region** North East Victoria Zone
T (02) 6037 1577 **www.**lankeyscreekwines.com.au **Open** By appt
Winemaker Steve Thompson **Est.** 2002 **Cases** NA
Lankeys Creek is the former Upper Murray Estate crushing 70 tonnes a year, making wine both for its own label and for other growers in the Tumbarumba region, from which most of the Lankeys Creek grapes come. The white wines are made in Flexitank plastic bags which winemaker Steve Thompson believes prevent oxidation and enhance flavour components, particularly with small batches.

LanzThomson Vineyard

Lot 1 Rosedale Scenic Road, Lyndoch, SA 5351 **Region** Barossa Valley
T (08) 8524 9227 **F** (08) 8524 9269 **www.**lanzthomson.com **Open** By appt
Winemaker Jamieson's Wine Consulting (Mark Jamieson) **Est.** 1998 **Cases** 1300
The friendship of the Lanz and Thomson families stretches back for 30 years, although it was the 2 (future) wives who first became friends through Rotary International in the 1970s. In their words 'Brian and Thomas came on the scene over the next few years, sharing stories and bottles of wine'. One thing led to another, and in 1998 they began the establishment of the 15-ha Outlook Vineyard and the 16.5-ha Moolanda Vineyard, each planted predominantly to shiraz, each with around 2 ha of mourvedre and viognier, splitting only with grenache (1.44 ha) on Outlook and cabernet (3.25 ha) on Moolanda. The lion's share of the grapes is sold.

ŸŸŸŸŸ **Shattered Rock Barossa Valley Shiraz 2005** Plums, blackberries, chocolate, mocha and vanilla all contribute to excellent balance and mouthfeel; abundant content, but no excess extraction; balanced tannins, long finish. Screwcap. 14.5° alc. **Rating** 94 **To** 2020 $24

Shattered Rock Barossa Valley Cabernet Sauvignon 2005 An elegant wine with aromas of cassis, herb and earth; the palate is only medium-bodied, but has considerable length, the finish brightened by fresh acidity. Screwcap. 14.5° alc. **Rating** 94 **To** 2025 $24

Lark Hill ★★★★★

521 Bungendore Road, Bungendore, NSW 2621 **Region** Canberra District
T (02) 6238 1393 **F** (02) 6238 1393 **www.**larkhillwine.com.au **Open** Wed–Mon 10–5
Winemaker Dr David Carpenter, Sue Carpenter **Est.** 1978 **Cases** 4000
The 7-ha Lark Hill vineyard is situated at an altitude of 860 m, level with the observation deck on Black Mountain Tower, and offers splendid views of the Lake George escarpment. The Carpenters have made wines of real quality, style and elegance from the start, but have defied all the odds (and conventional thinking) with the quality of their Pinot Noirs.

ŸŸŸŸŸ **Canberra District Cabernet Merlot 2003** Medium-bodied; a smooth and supple blend of blackcurrant and cassis; fine tannins plus well-handled and integrated oak; exceptional length and mouthfeel. Screwcap. 13.5° alc. **Rating** 94 **To** 2018 $34

ŶŶŶŶŶ **Canberra District Auslese Riesling 2006** Some colour development; plenty of flavour and depth to the sweet citrus and stone fruit; perhaps more Spatlese than Auslese richness; a twitch more acidity may have helped, but the decision was taken to add none to preserve the full biodynamic status of the wine. Screwcap. 10.5° alc. **Rating** 92 **To** 2016 $40

Exaltation Canberra District Pinot Noir 2003 Light-bodied, but a convincing varietal display of spice, forest and small red fruits; good length and persistence. Screwcap. 14° alc. **Rating** 92 **To** 2010 $50

Canberra District Chardonnay 2005 Attractive wine; supple stone fruit flavours balanced by barrel ferment oak, the slight suggestion of sweetness a minor distraction; 100% wild yeast barrel ferment. Screwcap. 13.5° alc. **Rating** 91 **To** 2012 $34

Canberra District Shiraz Viognier 2005 Typical strong colour; rich blackberry and spice fruit with the viognier lift from the 5% co-fermentation; soft tannins, lush wine. Screwcap. 13° alc. **Rating** 91 **To** 2015 $34

Lashmar   ★★★★☆

c/- 24 Lindsay Terrace, Belair, SA 5052 **Region** Kangaroo Island
T (08) 8278 3669 **F** (08) 8278 3998 **www**.lashmarwines.com **Open** Not
Winemaker Colin Cooter **Est.** 1996 **Cases** 1000
Colin and Bronwyn Cooter (who are also part of the Lengs & Cooter business) are the driving force behind Antechamber Bay Wines. The wines are in fact labelled and branded Lashmar; the Kangaroo Island Cabernet Sauvignon comes from vines planted in 1991 on the Lashmar family property, which is on the extreme eastern end of Kangaroo Island overlooking Antechamber Bay. The Three Valleys and Sisters wines (from other regions including McLaren Vale and Adelaide Hills) give the business added volume. Exports to the US, Canada, Singapore and Japan.

ŶŶŶŶŶ **Clarendon Shiraz 2002** Extremely powerful and long; very much typical of the cool vintage; tangy, savoury blackberry flavours, but with sweet fruit and vinosity still much in evidence on the mid-palate. Screwcap. **Rating** 93 **To** 2022

Sister's Blend 2003 A smooth, harmonious, medium-bodied wine; redcurrant contributes more than the blackberry component; fine tannins, and good oak use. Cabernet Sauvignon (50%)/Shiraz (40%)/Merlot (10%). From a block on the southern edge of suburban Adelaide, hand-pruned and hand-picked by 2 sisters for the last 30 years. Screwcap. **Rating** 92 **To** 2018

ŶŶŶŶ **Adelaide Hills Viognier 2004** Well-balanced and constructed; flavour without phenolics or residual sugar, just nicely balanced apricot and peach fruit in a medium-bodied frame. Screwcap. **Rating** 89 **To** 2010

McLaren Vale Nebbiolo 2002 Good colour for the variety; although only medium-bodied, fine, sandpaper tannins run throughout what is strictly a food style. Screwcap. **Rating** 87 **To** 2010

Laughing Jack   ★★★★★

Cnr Parbs Road/Boundry Road, Greenock, SA 5360 **Region** Barossa Valley
T 0427 396 928 **F** (08) 8562 8607 **www**.laughingjackwines.com **Open** By appt
Winemaker Mick Schroeter, Shawn Kalleske **Est.** 1999 **Cases** 1200
The Kalleske family has many branches in the Barossa Valley. Laughing Jack is owned by Shawn, Nathan and Helen, Ian and Carol Kalleske, and Mick and Linda Schroeter. They have just under 35 ha of vines, the lion's share to shiraz (22 ha), with lesser amounts of semillon, chardonnay, riesling and grenache. Vine age varies considerably, with old dry-grown shiraz the jewel in the crown. A small part of the shiraz production is taken for the Laughing Jack Shiraz. As any Australian knows, the kookaburra is known as the laughing jackass, and there is a resident flock of kookaburras in the stands of blue and red gum eucalypts surrounding the vineyards.

Laurance of Margaret River   ★★★★

Lot 549 Caves Road, Wilyabrup, WA 6290 **Region** Margaret River
T (08) 9755 6199 **F** (08) 9755 6276 **www**.laurancewines.com **Open** 7 days 11–5
Winemaker Naturaliste Vintners (Bruce Dukes) **Est.** 2001 **Cases** 4000
Dianne Laurance is the driving force of this family business, with husband Peter and son Brendon (and wife Kerrianne) also involved. Brendon is vineyard manager, living on the property with his family. The 40-ha property had 21 ha planted when it was purchased, and since its acquisition it has been turned into a showplace, with a rose garden to put that of Voyager Estate to shame. While the wine is made offsite, a substantial wine storage facility has been built. But it is the tenpin bowling-shaped bottles which will gain the most attention – and doubtless secondary use as lamp stands. The way-out packaging does tend to obscure the quality of the wines in the eyes of intolerant geriatrics such as myself. Exports to Singapore and Japan.

ΨΨΨΨΩ   **Rose 2006** Pale, bright fuchsia; an upscale version of Aussie Jeans Rock Pink; again highly focused, intense and long; unusual. Cork. 13° alc. **Rating** 91 **To** 2008 $25
Red 2004 Medium-bodied; blackcurrant, cassis and redcurrant; fine tannins and controlled oak; good length. Dodgy cork. 13.5° alc. **Rating** 90 **To** 2008 $30

ΨΨΨΨ   **Chardonnay 2005** Light straw-green; gentle melon, nectarine and fig flavours; controlled oak. Cork. 13.5° alc. **Rating** 89 **To** 2010 $30
Aussie Jeans Rock White 2006 A tight, minerally, citrussy wine, with good length, and no hint of residual sugar. Semillon/Sauvignon Blanc. Screwcap. 13° alc. **Rating** 89 **To** 2008 $21
Aussie Jeans Rock Pink 2006 Has a good backbone of lemony acidity giving both intensity and length. Shiraz. Screwcap. 13.5° alc. **Rating** 89 **To** 2008 $17

Laurel Bank   ★★★☆

130 Black Snake Lane, Granton, Tas 7030 **Region** Southern Tasmania
T (03) 6263 5977 **F** (03) 6263 3117 **Open** By appt
Winemaker Winemaking Tasmania (Julian Alcorso) **Est.** 1987 **Cases** 900
Laurel (hence Laurel Bank) and Kerry Carland began planting their 3-ha vineyard in 1986. They delayed the first release of their wines for some years and (by virtue of the number of entries they were able to make) won the trophy for Most Successful Exhibitor at the Hobart Wine Show '95. Things have settled down since; wine quality is solid and reliable.

ΨΨΨΨ   **Cabernet Sauvignon Merlot 2005** Quite powerful cassis and blackcurrant, offset by a touch of oak sweetening, though green tannins slightly nip your heels. Screwcap. 13.6° alc. **Rating** 89 **To** 2012 $28
Sauvignon Blanc 2006 Plenty of attractive tropical fruit flavours, but seems to fall into the all too common trap of a little sweetness on the finish, which is a pity. Screwcap. 12.7° alc. **Rating** 87 **To** 2008 $20
Pinot Noir 2005 Abundant, sweet ripe plummy fruit; better still if picked a little earlier. Screwcap. 13.6° alc. **Rating** 87 **To** 2009 $24

Lawrence Victor Estate   ★★★★

Riddoch Highway, Nangwarry, SA 5277 **Region** Coonawarra
T (08) 8739 7276 **F** (08) 8739 7344 **www**.lawrencevictorestate.com.au **Open** Not
Winemaker Contract **Est.** 1994 **Cases** 1500
Lawrence Victor Estate is part of a large SA company principally engaged in harvesting and transport of plantation softwood. The company was established by Lawrence Victor Dohnt in 1932, and the estate has been named in his honour by the third generation of the family. Though a small part of the group's activities, the plantings are substantial, with 11 ha of shiraz and 20 ha of cabernet sauvignon established between 1994 and 1999. An additional 12 ha of cabernet sauvignon and 6 ha of pinot noir were planted in 2000.

ΨΨΨΨΩ   **Coonawarra Sparkling Shiraz 2005** Big, bold style with classic licorice, shoe leather and spice flavours of quality sparkling shiraz. **Rating** 90 **To** 2015

Lazy Ballerina

26 Vine Street, McLaren Vale, SA 5171 **Region** McLaren Vale
T (08) 8556 8753 **F** (08) 8556 8753 **www.lazyballerina.com Open** By appt
Winemaker James Hook **Est.** 2004 **Cases** 600
James Hook, a leading viticulturist, and father Paul have set up a small – perhaps very small is a
better description – winery in a converted McLaren Vale garage. The equipment extends to
shovels, buckets, open fermenters and a small basket press, and enough French and American oak
barrels to allow 20 months maturation. The grapes come from micro-selections from a number
of vineyards in McLaren Vale.

McLaren Vale Shiraz 2005 Stacked full of flavour, but not showing its 15%
alcohol; a mix of predominantly black fruits, with some splashes of red;
medium- to full-bodied, with smooth tannins and controlled oak. Cork.
15° alc. **Rating** 94 **To** 2025 $24

McLaren Vale Shiraz 2004 Dense purple-red; full-bodied, extremely powerful
and concentrated; more flavour but less polish than that of the '05; still a
commendable wine. Cork. 15° alc. **Rating** 92 **To** 2028 $24

Le Poidevin ★★★☆

11 Elizabeth Street, Evandale, SA 5069 (postal) **Region** Mount Lofty Ranges Zone
T (08) 8363 3991 **F** (08) 8363 0905 **www.sublimewines.net Open** Not
Winemaker Kellermeister (Trevor Jones, Matt Reynolds) **Est.** 2005 **Cases** 2000
The name Le Poidevin is derived from the French, literally meaning the weight of wine. His
great, great-grandfather Daniel Le Poidevin emigrated from Guernsey, arriving in Adelaide in
1850; various generations of the family retained links to the wine industry, that of Greg
manifested as a devoted consumer during his 35 years as a lawyer. Just as I divorced my wife (law)
and made my mistress (wine) my new wife, so did Greg Le Poidevin in 2005 when he obtained
his producer's licence and severely curtailed his legal practice. He has established a virtual winery,
sourcing the grapes for his white wine from the Adelaide Hills, the red wines from dry-grown
vineyards in the Barossa Valley. A lifelong friendship with Barossa winemaker Trevor Jones has
not only secured contract red winemaking of the highest standard, but also assisted in ferreting
out small parcels of high quality fruit. In the outcome, the price of the wines has a most
unlawyerly ring of modesty.

Adelaide Hills Sauvignon Blanc Semillon 2006 Clean, fresh and well-
balanced, though not particularly intense gooseberry, apple, melon and citrus.
Adelaide Hills Sauvignon Blanc (85%)/Barossa Valley Semillon (15%). Screwcap.
13° alc. **Rating** 88 **To** 2008 $14
Gun Barossa Shiraz 2004 Light to medium-bodied; far from typical Barossa,
especially '04. It is not clear how far this represents the pursuit of lower alcohol.
Screwcap. 13.5° alc. **Rating** 87 **To** 2009 $18

Leabrook Estate ★★★★★

4/3 Rochester Street, Leabrook, SA 5068 (postal) **Region** Adelaide Hills
T (08) 8331 7150 **F** (08) 8364 1520 **www.leabrookestate.com Open** By appt
Winemaker Colin Best **Est.** 1998 **Cases** 4500
With a background as an engineer, and having dabbled in home winemaking for 30 years, Colin
Best took the plunge and moved into commercial winemaking in 1998. His wines are found in
a Who's Who of restaurants, and in some of the best independent wine retailers on the east coast.
Best says, 'I consider that my success is primarily due to the quality of my grapes, since they have
been planted on a 1.2 x 1.2 m spacing and very low yields.' I won't argue with that; he has also
done a fine job in converting the grapes into wine. Exports to the UK, the US and Singapore.

Reserve Chardonnay 2005 Complex texture and structure; a nutty/creamy
overlay to intense nectarine fruit leads into a long finish. Screwcap. 13.4° alc.
Rating 94 **To** 2015 $30

Adelaide Hills Pinot Noir 2005 Light to medium red-purple; clear varietal expression from the word go; pure plum and black cherry fruit with just a hint of stem and forest floor; will undoubtedly build complexity with age. Screwcap. 13.9° alc. **Rating** 94 **To** 2015 $35

🍷🍷🍷🍷🍷 **Three Region Shiraz 2005** Complex aromas suggesting some fruit shrivel; a similarly complex palate, with licorice, blackberry, prune and spice. Adelaide Hills/Langhorne Creek/Adelaide Plains. Screwcap. 14.1° alc. **Rating** 90 **To** 2020 $30

Adelaide Hills Cabernet Franc 2005 Tobacco leaf and dark berry mix in a light- to medium-bodied frame; a spare wine in fruit terms, but with good structure, balance and length. Give it time. A quality variety outside of WA (and, of course, in France's Loire Valley). Screwcap. 14.3° alc. **Rating** 90 **To** 2013 $27

🍷🍷🍷🍷 **Adelaide Hills Sauvignon Blanc 2006** Fully ripe style in tropical fruit spectrum; does catch up slightly on the finish, and might have been better if picked earlier. Screwcap. 14° alc. **Rating** 89 **To** 2008 $20

Adelaide Hills Pinot Gris 2006 Faint pink colour; plenty of flavour, but, oh, so sweet. Screwcap. 13° alc. **Rating** 87 **To** 2008 $25

🌿 Leaky Door   ★★★★☆

61 Jones Avenue, Mt Clear, Vic 3350 **Region** Ballarat
T (03) 5330 1611 **F** (03) 5330 1851 **Open** By appt
Winemaker Michael Unwin (Contract) **Est.** 1999 **Cases** 200
John Weinrich, a local GP, doubtless shares much of the cost of runnng the vineyard, but it is wife Jay Mitchell (having completed a viticultural course with the South East Institute of TAFE in SA) who calls the shots and runs the vineyard. Their then teenage children helped the development of the vineyard, which has been a hands-on affair from start to finish. Currently a winery building is nearing completion; the widespread frost of 2006 means the '07 vintage will have been a test run only, with the first real vintage coming in '08. The vineyard is close-planted, primarily to 2.5 ha of chardonnay and 0.5 ha of pinot noir, and is a favourite haunt of birds, wallabies and foxes most of which pay little attention to the netting put on 2 months before vintage.

🍷🍷🍷🍷🍷 **Ballarat Chardonnay 2004** Fragrant and intense; Chablis-like citrus and mineral flavours run through a long palate. Screwcap. 13° alc. **Rating** 92 **To** 2012 $33

Ballarat Chardonnay 2005 Elegant white peach, nectarine and citrus; tight acidity, but has attained full ripeness. Screwcap. 13° alc. **Rating** 90 **To** 2011 $33

Leasingham

7 Dominic Street, Clare, SA 5453 **Region** Clare Valley
T (08) 8842 2555 **F** (08) 8842 3293 **www.**leasingham-wines.com.au **Open** Mon–Fri 8.30–5.30, w'ends 10–4
Winemaker Simon Osicka **Est.** 1893 **Cases** 70 000
Successive big-company ownerships and various peregrinations in labelling and branding have not resulted in any permanent loss of identity or quality. With a core of high-quality, aged vineyards to draw on, Leasingham is in fact going from strength to strength under Hardys' direction. The stentorian red wines take no prisoners, compacting densely rich fruit and layer upon layer of oak into every long-lived bottle; the Bin 7 Riesling often excels.

🍷🍷🍷🍷🍷 **Classic Clare Shiraz 2002** Last tasted at the National Wine Show '04; now approaching its long plateau of maturity, and shows even greater potential than it did 3 years ago. Cork. 14.5° alc. **Rating** 94 **To** 2022 $47

Bin 61 Clare Valley Shiraz 2004 Cascades of fruit as much in the red spectrum as black; moderate alcohol a blessed relief. Good tannins and oak; even better price. Cork. 13.5° alc. **Rating** 94 **To** 2024 $22

Classic Clare Cabernet Sauvignon 2003 Uncompromising full-bodied wine; masses of black fruits, but even more tannins; needs a minimum of 10 years before approaching; pray for the cork. 14.5° alc. **Rating** 94 **To** 2033 $47

Bin 56 Clare Valley Cabernet Sauvignon 2002 Medium-bodied; much more refined than the Magnus, but certainly no more depth of flavour; has a fine mix of red and black fruits, and good oak handling. Top vintage. Cork. 14° alc. **Rating** 94 **To** 2022 $22

ΨΨΨΨΩ **Bin 7 Clare Valley Riesling 2006** In the mainstream of Clare style; a balanced display of lime juice, spice, passionfruit and slatey minerals; good length, and will only get better in the years ahead. Screwcap. 12.5° alc. **Rating** 93 **To** 2016 $20

Magnus Clare Valley Cabernet Sauvignon 2004 Some smoky/charry aromas; very powerful blackcurrant fruit on a long palate; ridiculously low price but will in all probability be discounted even further. Cork. 13° alc. **Rating** 92 **To** 2019 $14

Magnus Clare Valley Riesling 2006 Spicy, slatey lime aromas and flavours; scores for its length of palate, finish and aftertaste. A full sister of Magnus Cabernet Sauvignon and Magnus Shiraz, and offers the same exceptional value. Screwcap. 13° alc. **Rating** 90 **To** 2012 $14

Circa 1893 Riesling 2006 Light- to medium-bodied; some citrus fruit with a light touch of sweetness making for everyday drinking. Good value; some would regard the name as thoroughly misleading, as it has nothing whatsoever to do with this wine, which doesn't even point out it was the year in which Leasingham itself was founded. Screwcap. 12.5° alc. **Rating** 90 **To** 2012 $10

Magnus Clare Valley Shiraz 2005 Rich, multi-layered, multifaceted wine, black fruits, with oak in restraint and tannins balanced. Deserved a screwcap. Cork. 14° alc. **Rating** 90 **To** 2015 $14

Leconfield

Riddoch Highway, Coonawarra, SA 5263 **Region** Coonawarra
T (08) 8737 2326 **F** (08) 8737 2385 www.leconfieldwines.com **Open** Mon–Fri 9–5, w'ends & public hols 10–4.30
Winemaker Paul Gordon, Tim Bailey (Assistant) **Est.** 1974 **Cases** 17 000
A distinguished estate with a proud history. Long renowned for its Cabernet Sauvignon, its repertoire has steadily grown with the emphasis on single-variety wines. The style overall is fruit- rather than oak-driven. Exports to the UK, the US and other major markets.

ΨΨΨΨΩ **Coonawarra Cabernet Sauvignon 2004** Medium-bodied; ripe cassis and blackcurrant fruit supported by good tannins and oak; has length. Successful outcome for the year. Screwcap. 13.5° alc. **Rating** 92 **To** 2015 $30

McLaren Vale Shiraz 2004 Medium red; medium-bodied, with spicy/earthy/savoury notes throughout; fine tannins; overall a touch of austerity, no bad thing. Screwcap. 14° alc. **Rating** 90 **To** 2019 $30

Coonawarra Merlot 2004 Good colour; punch and drive to the black olive/savoury varietal fruit. Screwcap. **Rating** 90 **To** 2012

ΨΨΨΨ **Synergy Chardonnay 2005** Light straw-green; nectarine, melon and a touch of fig; light- to medium-bodied, but has length, and without undue oak. Screwcap. 13.5° alc. **Rating** 89 **To** 2008 $20

LedaSwan

179 Memorial Avenue, Baskerville, WA 6065 **Region** Swan Valley
T (08) 9296 0216 www.ledaswan.com.au **Open** 7 days 11–4.30
Winemaker Duncan Harris **Est.** 1998 **Cases** 250
LedaSwan claims to be the smallest winery in the Swan Valley. It uses organically grown grapes, partly coming from its own vineyard, and partly from contract-grown grapes; the intention is to move to 100% estate-grown in the future, from the 2 ha of estate vineyards. Tours of the underground cellar are offered, and there is an extensive range of back vintages on offer.

Leeuwin Estate

Stevens Road, Margaret River, WA 6285 **Region** Margaret River
T (08) 9759 0000 **F** (08) 9759 0001 **www.**leeuwinestate.com.au **Open** 7 days 10–4.30
Winemaker Paul Atwood **Est.** 1974 **Cases** 60 000

Leeuwin Estate's Chardonnay is, in my opinion, Australia's finest example, based on the wines of the last 20-odd vintages, and it is this wine alone which demands a 5-star rating for the winery. The Cabernet Sauvignon can be an excellent wine with great style and character in warmer vintages, and Shiraz made an auspicious debut. Almost inevitably, the other wines in the portfolio are not in the same Olympian class, although the Prelude Chardonnay and Siblings Sauvignon Blanc are impressive at their lower price level. Exports to all major markets.

ɣɣɣɣɣ **Art Series Margaret River Chardonnay 2004** The fruit literally sings, appropriate given Leeuwin's annual concerts; white peach, nectarine and grapefruit are the sopranos, barrel ferment and mlf the orchestra behind, the result seamless but synergistic. Screwcap. 14.5° alc. **Rating** 96 **To** 2024 $92
Prelude Vineyards Margaret River Chardonnay 2005 Fine, intense nectarine and grapefruit with seamless oak; as fresh as a daisy, the oak perfectly balanced and integrated. No hint of reduction at any stage. Screwcap. 14° alc. **Rating** 94 **To** 2015 $30
Art Series Margaret River Shiraz 2004 Classic medium-bodied shiraz, the blackberry fruit with nuances of spice and earth; greater vibrancy and purity than prior releases as the vines become older; fine tannins and quality oak. Screwcap. 14° alc. **Rating** 94 **To** 2024 $35

ɣɣɣɣɣ **Siblings Margaret River Sauvignon Blanc Semillon 2006** Immaculately crafted and balanced wine, rightly unadorned by oak; crisp, clean lemon, herb and grass aromas and flavours reflecting the coolest vintage yet for Margaret River; 62%/38%. Screwcap. 12.5° alc. **Rating** 93 **To** 2011 $24
Art Series Margaret River Cabernet Sauvignon 2002 The hue is good, though not deep; basically in the mainstream of Leeuwin cabernet style, good length and balance to the savoury black fruits, oak a positive contributor. Cork. 13.5° alc. **Rating** 92 **To** 2022 $54
Art Series Margaret River Riesling 2006 Bright straw-green; fresh, crisp, bright and lively; citrus and mineral flavours with good length; the best-seller in the Leeuwin stable. Screwcap. 12° alc. **Rating** 91 **To** 2011 $24

Leland Estate

PO Lenswood, SA 5240 **Region** Adelaide Hills
T (08) 8389 6928 **www.**lelandestate.com.au **Open** Not
Winemaker Robb Cootes **Est.** 1986 **Cases** 950

Former Yalumba senior winemaker Robb Cootes, with a Master of Science degree, opted out of mainstream life when he established Leland Estate, living in a split-level, 1-roomed house built from timber salvaged from trees killed in the Ash Wednesday bushfires. The Sauvignon Blanc is usually good. Exports to Singapore.

Lengs & Cooter

24 Lindsay Terrace, Belair, SA 5042 **Region** Southeast Australia
T (08) 8278 3998 **F** (08) 8278 3998 **www.**lengscooter.com.au **Open** Not
Winemaker Contract **Est.** 1993 **Cases** 8000

Karel Lengs and Colin Cooter began making wine as a hobby in the early 1980s. Each had (and has) a full-time occupation outside the wine industry, and it was all strictly for fun. One thing has led to another, and although they still possess neither vineyards nor what might truly be described as a winery, the wines graduated to big-boy status, winning gold medals at national wine shows and receiving critical acclaim from writers across Australia. Exports to the UK, Canada, Singapore and Malaysia.

ŢŢŢŢŢ **Reserve McLaren Vale Shiraz 2003** Strong colour; finer and even more focused than the Clare Valley version; smooth blackberry, earth and dark chocolate flavours; fine tannins and a long finish. Once again, a heavily stained cork. 14.5° alc. **Rating** 94 **To** 2015 $45

ŢŢŢŢŢ **Old Vines Clare Valley Shiraz 2003** Rich, succulently ripe but not overripe black fruits; ripe tannins and good use of American oak; the heavily stained cork a major worry for long-term cellaring. Cork. 14.5° alc. **Rating** 93 **To** 2015 $25
McLaren Vale Shiraz Viognier 2004 An interesting and complex interplay between varietal characters and regional influence; blackberry, red cherry fruit and chocolate with the subtle viognier lift. Screwcap. 14.5° alc. **Rating** 92 **To** 2019 $22
Watervale Riesling 2006 Clean, albeit slightly closed bouquet, opening into a powerful palate with ripe citrus and apple fruit, even bordering on stone fruit. Screwcap. 12.5° alc. **Rating** 90 **To** 2014 $19

ŢŢŢŢ **The Victor Shiraz 2005** Soft and gentle mix of spicy and sweeter fruit aromas and flavours, finishing with a hint of sweetness. Screwcap. 14.5° alc. **Rating** 88 **To** 2012 $18

Lenton Brae Wines   ★★★★★
Wilyabrup Valley, Margaret River, WA 6285 **Region** Margaret River
T (08) 9755 6255 **F** (08) 9755 6268 **www**.lentonbrae.com **Open** 7 days 10–6
Winemaker Edward Tomlinson **Est.** 1983 **Cases** NFP
Former architect and town planner Bruce Tomlinson built a strikingly beautiful winery which is now in the hands of winemaker son Edward, who makes elegant wines in classic Margaret River style. Exports to the UK, the US, Canada and Singapore.

ŢŢŢŢŢ **Margaret River Semillon Sauvignon Blanc 2006** In winery tradition, plays the 2 varieties off against each other to give complexity without oak; gentle tropical fruits with a strong twist of lemon from the semillon; very good balance and length. Coolest vintage in 50 years. Screwcap. 12.5° alc. **Rating** 94 **To** 2011 $21

ŢŢŢŢŢ **Margaret River Cabernet Sauvignon 2003** Fragrant and stylish; medium-bodied blackcurrant and cassis, fine-grained tannins giving structure and balance; includes Petit Verdot (10%)/Merlot (3%)/Cabernet Franc (2%). Screwcap. 14° alc. **Rating** 93 **To** 2023 $40

Leo Buring   ★★★★★
Tanunda Road, Nuriootpa, SA 5355 **Region** Barossa Valley
T (08) 8560 9408 **F** (08) 8563 2804 **www**.leoburing.com.au **Open** Not
Winemaker Glenn James **Est.** 1931 **Cases** 15 000
Australia's foremost producer of Rieslings over a 35-year period, with a rich legacy left by former winemaker John Vickery. After veering away from its core business with other varietal wines, has now been refocused as a specialist riesling producer.

ŢŢŢŢŢ **Leonay Eden Valley Riesling 2006** DWJ17. Finer, tighter, more intense lime, mineral and spice than the varietal Eden Valley Riesling; very long finish, the flavours complex. Screwcap. 13° alc. **Rating** 95 **To** 2021 $36.95
Mount Barker Riesling 2006 A distinctly more aromatic bouquet than either of the Eden Valley wines; the lime and citrus fruit runs through the palate and into the long finish. The mountain (Eden Valley) comes to Mahomet (Mount Barker). Screwcap. 12.5° alc. **Rating** 94 **To** 2016 $28.95

ŢŢŢŢŢ **Eden Valley Riesling 2006** Excellent regional and varietal expression; light to medium-bodied, with lime blossom aromas followed by a smooth and supple palate with citrus, lemon and slate flavours; long finish. Screwcap. 13° alc. **Rating** 93 **To** 2016 $18.95

Lerida Estate

The Vineyards, Old Federal Highway, Lake George, NSW 2581 **Region** Canberra District
T (02) 6295 6640 **F** (02) 6295 6676 **www**.leridaestate.com **Open** 7 days 10–5, or by appt
Winemaker Malcolm Burdett **Est.** 1999 **Cases** 3000
Lerida Estate continues the planting of vineyards along the escarpment sloping down to Lake
George. It is immediately to the south of the Lake George vineyard established by Edgar Riek 36
years ago. Inspired by Edgar Riek's success with pinot noir, Lerida founder Jim Lumbers planted
3.75 ha of pinot noir together with lesser amounts of pinot gris, chardonnay, shiraz, merlot,
viognier and cabernet franc (7.4 ha total). The Glenn Murcutt-designed winery, barrel room and
cellar door complex has spectacular views over Lake George. Exports to Taiwan and Bangladesh.

TTTTT **Lake George Merlot 2004** Powerful and intense; strongly varietal savoury
black olive nuances; lingering, ripe, savoury tannins; no shrinking violet.
Screwcap. **Rating** 91 **To** 2014 $24
Lake George Pinot Noir 2004 Plenty of depth to the colour; complex dark
plum, spice and bramble flavours; ripe, but not to the point of dry red; great
texture. Screwcap. **Rating** 90 **To** 2009 $28

TTTT **Lake George Chardonnay 2005** Has developed complexity over and above
the inclusion of oak; figgy/peachy fruit, with a slightly congested finish. Screwcap.
14.8° alc. **Rating** 89 **To** 2009 $30
Canberra District Pinot Noir Chardonnay 2001 Elegant; fresh yet complex
nutty/bready/yeasty overtones to the citrus and strawberry fruit; appealing dry finish.
Rating 89 **To** 2011 $26
Lake George Pinot Rose 2006 Light, fresh and lively strawberry and red cherry
fruits; crisp, clean finish. Screwcap. 13.9° alc. **Rating** 88 **To** 2008 $18
Lake George Late Harvest Pinot Gris 2006 Quite luscious, and shows varietal
pear and varietal character with a faint musky overtone; slightly less alcohol, more
residual sugar and more acidity could result in an excellent wine. Screwcap. 13.2° alc.
Rating 88 **To** 2008 $19
Lake George Pinot Gris 2006 Spice, pear skin and apple aromas; the apparent
sweetness on the finish will appeal to cellar door visitors. Screwcap. 13.9° alc.
Rating 87 **To** 2008 $28

Lethbridge Wines ★★★★★

74 Burrows Road, Lethbridge, Vic 3222 **Region** Geelong
T (03) 5281 7279 **F** (03) 5281 7221 **www**.lethbridgewines.com **Open** Thurs–Sun &
public hols 10.30–5, or by appt
Winemaker Ray Nadeson, Maree Collis **Est.** 1996 **Cases** 2500
Lethbridge was founded by scientists Ray Nadeson, Maree Collis and Adrian Thomas. In Ray
Nadeson's words, 'Our belief is that the best wines express the unique character of special places'.
As well as understanding the importance of terroir, the partners have built a unique straw-bale
winery, designed for its ability to recreate the controlled environment of cellars and caves in
Europe. Winemaking is no less ecological: hand-picking, indigenous yeast fermentations, small
open fermenters, pigeage (foot-stamping) and minimal handling of the wine throughout the
maturation process are all part and parcel of the highly successful Lethbridge approach.

TTTTT **Indra Shiraz 2004** Great colour; totally harmonious fruit, tannins and oak;
plum, cherry and blackberry within a silky web of texture. Diam. 13° alc.
Rating 96 **To** 2020 $48
Allegra Chardonnay 2004 Has developed out of all recognition over the past
18 months; very complex, powerful and intense, with long and penetrating
flavours, yet retaining class. Trophy and gold medal Geelong Wine Show '06.
Screwcap. 13° alc. **Rating** 95 **To** 2012 $38

TTTTT **Menage Que Syrah 2005** Generous, rich; opulent though not jammy fruit; good
length and balance. Brett issues for some tasters. Screwcap. 13.5° alc. **Rating** 90
To 2012 $20

Shiraz 2005 Medium-bodied; attractive plum, black cherry and blackberry fruit; fine tannins, balanced oak. Diam. 13.5° alc. **Rating** 90 **To** 2014 $28

♟♟♟♟   **Menage a Noir Pinot Noir 2005** Attractive, smooth and supple red cherry fruit, though lacking textural complexity. Screwcap. 13.5° alc. **Rating** 88 **To** 2010 $20

Leura Park Estate

1400 Portarlington Road, Curlewis, Vic 3222 **Region** Geelong
T (03) 5253 3180 **F** (03) 5251 1262 **Open** W'ends 11–5
Winemaker De Bortoli (Steve Webber) **Est.** 1995 **Cases** 600
Stephen and Lisa Cross gained fame as restaurateurs in the 1990s, first at Touché and then at the outstanding Saltwater at Noosa Heads. They have established a substantial vineyard, with 8 ha of chardonnay, over 3 ha each of pinot gris, pinot noir and sauvignon blanc, and 1 ha of shiraz. Most of the production is sold to De Bortoli.

♟♟♟♟   **25 d'Gris Pinot Gris 2006** A solid wine; while not having much varietal character (common enough with the variety), it does finish well. **Rating** 87 **To** 2008

Liebich Wein ★★★★

Steingarten Road, Rowland Flat, SA 5352 **Region** Barossa Valley
T (08) 8524 4543 **F** (08) 8524 4543 www.liebichwein.com.au **Open** Wed–Mon 11–5
Winemaker Ron Liebich **Est.** 1992 **Cases** 3000
Liebich Wein is Barossa Deutsch for 'Love I wine'. The Liebich family have been grapegrowers and winemakers at Rowland Flat since 1919, with CW 'Darkie' Liebich one of the great local characters. His nephew Ron began making wine in 1969, but it was not until 1992 that he and wife Janet began selling wine under the Liebich Wein label. Exports to the UK, Mexico, Germany, Switzerland, Malaysia and Singapore.

♟♟♟♟   **Riesling Of The Valleys 2006** More varietal precision; perhaps the Clare Valley, perhaps fruit selection; mineral, herb and lime flavours with a clean finish. Barossa Valley (80%)/Clare Valley (20%). Screwcap. 13° alc. **Rating** 89 **To** 2012 $15
Riesling 2006 Clean and fresh; light-bodied, gentle apple and citrus mix; impressive for the region and price. Cork. 13° alc. **Rating** 87 **To** 2008 $10
Tempranillo Rose 2006 Interesting variation, though common in Spain; crisp and lively with small red fruit flavours. Screwcap. 12.8° alc. **Rating** 87 **To** 2008 $18
Barossa Valley Fortified Shiraz 2004 Interesting style; still has some fruit freshness and spice; very clean fortifying spirit. 18° alc. **Rating** 87 **To** 2008 $14

Lightfoot & Sons ★★★

Myrtle Point Vineyard, 717 Calulu Road, Bairnsdale, Vic 3875 (postal) **Region** Gippsland
T (03) 5156 9205 **Open** Not
Winemaker Dr Robert Brownlee (Contract) **Est.** 1995 **Cases** 300
Brian and Helen Lightfoot have established just under 30 ha of pinot noir, shiraz, chardonnay, cabernet sauvignon and merlot, the lion's share to pinot noir and shiraz. The soil bears a striking resemblance to that of Coonawarra, with terra rossa over limestone. The vines are irrigated courtesy of a licence allowing the Lightfoots to pump water from the Mitchell River, and most of the grapes are sold (as originally planned) to other Gippsland winemakers.

♟♟♟♟   **Myrtle Point Vineyard Shiraz 2005** A robust wine, full of ripe fruit, its Achilles heel being robust/astringent tannins on the finish. 15.3° alc. **Rating** 89 **To** 2013 $22

Lilac Hill Estate ★★★

55 Benara Road, Caversham, WA 6055 **Region** Swan Valley
T (08) 9378 9945 **F** (08) 9378 9946 www.lilachillestate.com.au **Open** Tues–Sun 10.30–5.00
Winemaker Stephen Murfit **Est.** 1998 **Cases** 15 000

Lilac Hill Estate is part of the renaissance which is sweeping the Swan Valley. Just when it seemed it would die a lingering death, supported only by Houghton, Sandalford and the remnants of the once Yugoslav-dominated cellar door trade, wine tourism has changed the entire scene. Lilac Hill Estate, drawing in part upon 4 ha of estate vineyards, has built a substantial business; considerable contract winemaking fleshes out the business even further.

Lillian

Box 174, Pemberton, WA 6260 **Region** Pemberton
T (08) 9776 0193 **F** (08) 9776 0193 **Open** Not
Winemaker John Brocksopp **Est.** 1993 **Cases** 400
Long-serving (and continuing consultant) viticulturist to Leeuwin Estate John Brocksopp established 3-ha of the Rhône trio of marsanne, roussanne and viognier and the South of France trio of shiraz, mourvedre and graciano. The varietal mix may seem à la mode, but it in fact comes from John's early experience working for Seppelt at Barooga in NSW, and his formative years in the Barossa Valley. Exports to the UK.

ＹＹＹＹＹ **Pemberton Marsanne Roussanne 2005** An extremely interesting Rhone Valley-inspired blend; great length and intensity, with almost floral aromas, hint of spice and honeysuckle, and tangy, citrussy acidity to close. Guaranteed to flourish in bottle. Screwcap. 14° alc. **Rating** 94 **To** 2011 $19

ＹＹＹＹＹ **Pemberton Viognier 2005** Excellent mouthfeel, length and finish; lively fruit salad and apricot, finishing with squeaky, lemony acidity. Way above average for the variety. Screwcap. 14° alc. **Rating** 92 **To** 2010 $25

Lillico Wines ★★★

297 Copelands Road, Warragul, Vic 3820 **Region** Gippsland
T (03) 5623 4231 **F** (03) 5623 4231 **www**.lillicowines.com.au **Open** Thurs–Sun & public hols 10–6, or by appt
Winemaker Marie Young **Est.** 1998 **Cases** 700
Cattle farmer Robert and senior nurse Marie Young impulsively planted 1.7 ha of cabernet sauvignon on their property in 1998. Two years later they added 1.3 ha of pinot noir, and in the meantime Marie had completed a diploma of horticulture, specialising in viticulture, at Dookie College. The first commercial vintage of cabernet was sold, and encouraged by the quality of the wine made from their grapes, Marie and Rob decided to produce some of their own wine. She promptly enrolled in the diploma of wine technology course, and now makes the wines. The vineyard is run on a no-pesticide and non-residual chemical regime, and the vines are not irrigated.

ＹＹＹＹ **Unwooded Chardonnay 2006** Excellent green-yellow; smooth nectarine and melon fruit; good line and balance. **Rating** 88 **To** 2009 $17

Lilliput Wines ★★★

Withers Road, Springhurst, Vic 3602 **Region** Rutherglen
T (03) 5726 5055 **www**.lilliputwinesofrutherglen.com.au **Open** Fri–Sun, public hols or by appt
Winemaker Angelica Hellema **Est.** 2001 **Cases** 2000
Angelica and Pieter Hellema have painstakingly developed an 8-ha vineyard planted to cabernet sauvignon, merlot, shiraz, viognier and petit verdot, using organic principles. Correspondingly, in the winery, only a small quantity of SO_2 is added. The name 'Lilliput Wines' dates back to the original crown land allotments (which were extremely small) and the presence of a large family headed by James Gullifer (9 of 16 children survived). In the 1870s there was a Lilliput Winery on the other side of the nearby creek.

Lillydale Estate

45 Davross Court, Seville, Vic 3139 **Region** Yarra Valley
T (03) 5964 2016 **F** (03) 5964 3009 **www**.mcwilliams.com.au **Open** 7 days 11–5
Winemaker Jim Brayne, Max McWilliam **Est.** 1975 **Cases** NFP
Acquired by McWilliam's Wines in 1994; Max McWilliam is in charge of the business. With a number of other major developments, notably Coonawarra and Barwang, on its plate, McWilliam's has adopted a softly, softly approach to Lillydale Estate.

ＹＹＹＹＹ **Yarra Valley Chardonnay 2005** Light straw-green; complex aromas driven in part by barrel ferment oak; the extremely elegant and fine palate does a U-turn, moving towards Chablis in style. The future face of quality Australian chardonnay. Screwcap. 13.5° alc. **Rating** 94 **To** 2020 $19.99
Yarra Valley Pinot Noir 2005 A complex array of red cherry, plum, spice and hints of forest floor; silky mouthfeel, and good balance. Screwcap. 13.5° alc. **Rating** 94 **To** 2013 $26

ＹＹＹＹＹ **Yarra Valley Shiraz 2004** Lively, fresh red and black cherry plus a touch of blackberry fruit; fine, silky tannins. Screwcap. 13.5° alc. **Rating** 90 **To** 2020 $26

ＹＹＹＹ **Yarra Valley Gewurztraminer 2005** Faint spice and rose petal aromas and flavours run through a delicate wine ideal for Chinese food. Screwcap. 12.5° alc. **Rating** 89 **To** 2010 $20
Cabernet Merlot 2003 An elegant, light to medium-bodied wine; the flavours are correct, but lack depth and conviction. Screwcap. 12.5° alc. **Rating** 87 **To** 2010 $23

Lillypilly Estate

Lillypilly Road, Leeton, NSW 2705 **Region** Riverina
T (02) 6953 4069 **www**.lillypilly.com **Open** Mon–Sat 10–5.30, Sun by appt
Winemaker Robert Fiumara **Est.** 1982 **Cases** 18 000
Botrytised white wines are by far the best from Lillypilly, with the Noble Muscat of Alexandria unique to the winery; these wines have both style and intensity of flavour and can age well. However, table wine quality is always steady. Exports to the UK, the US and Canada.

ＹＹＹＹＹ **Show Reserve Noble Harvest 2002** Glowing yellow-green; another quantum of intensity, complexity, length and flavour, with cumquat and mandarin, a girdle of honey, with balancing acidity on the long finish. Screwcap. **Rating** 93 **To** 2008 $38.50

ＹＹＹＹ **Noble Muscat Of Alexandria 2006** Not especially, or obviously, affected by botrytis; certainly muscat varietal character is still there; between spatlese and auslese sweetness, the balance good. Screwcap. **Rating** 89 **To** 2008 $18.50
Noble Blend 2005 Brighter fruit flavours than the Muscat of Alexandria, although the varieties are not specified; similar weight and balance, perhaps a little more length. Screwcap. 11° alc. **Rating** 89 **To** 2008 $22.50
Sauvignon Blanc 2006 As well-made as is possible, varietal fruit inevitably suppressed by the warm climate, but with a tangy, citrussy finish. Screwcap. 13° alc. **Rating** 87 **To** 2008 $15.50

Lilyvale Wines

8 Canara Street, Benowa, Qld 4217 **Region** Darling Downs
T 0405 132 507 **F** (07) 5597 2507 **www**.lilyvalewines.com **Open** Not
Winemaker Hunter Wine Services (John Hordern), Peter Scudamore-Smith MW
Est. 1997 **Cases** 4000
Another fast-moving entrant into the Qld wine scene. John Beale and Darryl McCarthy sold their 13.5-ha vineyard established on their substantial cattle property in April 2006. Wines from the 2005 and '06 vintages will be sold under the Lilyvale brand, with subsequent vintages coming from what they hope will prove to be new distinguished Qld sites.

♟♟♟♟♀ **Texas Gold Late Harvest Semillon & Riesling 2005** Very well-made; these wines are not as simple as they may appear; sweet lime juice and cumquat, the oak barely visible on a long palate, the sweetness balance by acidity. Ideal for fresh fruit dessert. **Rating** 90 **To** 2008 $20

Limbic

295 Morrison Road, Pakenham Upper, Vic 3810 **Region** Port Phillip Zone
T (03) 5942 7723 **F** (03) 5942 7723 **www**.limbicwines.com.au **Open** By appt
Winemaker Michael Pullar **Est.** 1997 **Cases** 750
Jennifer and Michael Pullar have established a vineyard on the hills between Yarra Valley and Gippsland, overlooking the Mornington Peninsula and Westernport Bay (thus entitled only to the Port Phillip Zone GI). They have planted 3.1 ha of pinot noir, 1.8 ha of chardonnay and 1.3 ha of sauvignon blanc, increasingly using organic and thereafter biodynamic practices. Trial vintages under the Limbic label commenced in 2001, followed by the first commercial releases in 2003. 'Limbic' is the word for a network of neural pathways in the brain that link smell, taste and emotion.

 # Linda Domas Wines

PO Box 1988, McLaren Flat, SA 5171 **Region** McLaren Vale
T (08) 8383 0195 **F** (08) 8383 0178 **www**.ldwines.com.au **Open** Not
Winemaker Linda Domas **Est.** 2003 **Cases** 3000
Linda Domas, Steve Brunato and Markus Domas have their fingers in many vinous pies in many parts of the world. The venture came into being in 2001, made by Linda Domas and Steve Brunato while they were holidaying in Australia. At that time both were employed by Casa Vinicola Calatrasi in Sicily, Linda in charge of winemaking and Steve head viticulturist for the company's vineyards in Tunisia, Sicily and Puglia. After 3 vintages with Calatrasi, they decided to head home to McLaren Vale to start their own label, making both the Linda Domas wines and other contract-made wines in leased space at Daringa Cellars. To keep them in touch with the rest of the world, they say, they have done both winemaking and viticulture work in Slovenia, Bulgaria, and are currently undertaking a project with Sula Wines in Nashik, India. It can safely be said they are very busy. Exports to the UK, the US, Singapore, and Chile.

♟♟♟♟♀ **Brunato Vineyard McLaren Vale Shiraz 2005** Strong red-purple; abundant blackberry with touches of chocolate and spice; soft tannins, and gentle vanilla oak. Screwcap. 13.5° alc. **Rating** 92 **To** 2013 $20
Salience Southern Fleurieu Sauvignon Blanc 2006 Straw-green; complex aromas and flavours of gooseberry, grass and herb; bone-dry finish. Screwcap. 12° alc. **Rating** 90 **To** 2008 $20

♟♟♟♟ **Shot Bull Southern Fleurieu Shiraz 2004** Spicy overtones to the light-bodied palate; pursues commendably low alcohol with greater access, the cooler climate doubtless helping the red and black fruits. Screwcap. 12.5° alc. **Rating** 89 **To** 2012 $25
Shot Bull Southern Fleurieu Rose 2006 Crisp, small red fruit flavours; dry finish, good length. Shiraz. Screwcap. 13° alc. **Rating** 88 **To** 2008 $16
Top Hat McLaren Vale Grenache 2005 Light to medium red-purple; pleasant juicy/jammy grenache varietal character, though not as much structure as McLaren Vale provides at its best. Screwcap. 14° alc. **Rating** 88 **To** 2008 $22
Egidio McLaren Vale Shiraz 2004 Light-bodied; seems to have pushed the lower alcohol envelope a little too far; a touch of regional chocolate. Screwcap. 13.5° alc. **Rating** 87 **To** 2012 $25
Boycat McLaren Vale Merlot 2005 Strong colour; sweet blackcurrant fruit, with riper flavour than the alcohol suggests; suppressed varietal character. Screwcap. 13.5° alc. **Rating** 87 **To** 2009 $22

Lindemans (Coonawarra/Padthaway) ★★★★☆

Coonawarra Wine Gallery, Riddoch Highway, Penola, SA 5277 **Region** Coonawarra
T (08) 8737 3250 **www**.lindemans.com.au **Open** 7 days 10–5
Winemaker Brett Sharpe **Est.** 1908 **Cases** 7 million
Lindemans' Limestone Coast vineyards are of increasing significance because of the move towards regional identity in the all-important export markets, which has led to the emergence of a range of regional/varietal labels. Exports to the UK, the US, Canada and NZ.

ⓎⓎⓎⓎⓎ **Rouge Homme Shiraz Cabernet 2004** Medium-bodied; a classic mix of blackberry, blackcurrant, spice and leaf; very much in cool-climate style, and being sold at a cool price. Cork. 13.5° alc. **Rating** 93 **To** 2015 $14.95
St George Cabernet Sauvignon 2004 A quite powerful, earthy, regional style; slightly austere blackcurrant fruit on a long palate with fine tannins running throughout. Classic style. Cork. 13° alc. **Rating** 93 **To** 2014 $52.95
Pyrus 2001 Medium-bodied; savoury/earthy flavours, but has a delicacy of texture and structure which allow red fruit flavours to kick in on the finish. Cork. 13.5° alc. **Rating** 91 **To** 2016 $52.95

ⓎⓎⓎⓎ **Reserve Padthaway Shiraz 2005** Medium-bodied, with smooth plum, black cherry and raspberry fruit, though not over-much texture and structure. Screwcap. 14° alc. **Rating** 89 **To** 2012 $12.95
Limestone Ridge 2003 Quite good balance; spicy black fruits; good length. Cork. 13.5° alc. **Rating** 88 **To** 2010 $52.95
Reserve Padthaway Chardonnay 2006 Light- to medium-bodied; typical stone fruit/grapefruit flavours of the region have been given a touch of American oak; I think the wine would have been better without it. Cork. 13.5° alc. **Rating** 87 **To** 2008 $12.95
Limestone Ridge 2004 Pleasant red and black fruits, but not a great deal of depth. Cork. 13° alc. **Rating** 87 **To** 2011 $52.95

Lindemans (Hunter Valley) ★★★☆

McDonalds Road, Pokolbin, NSW 2320 **Region** Lower Hunter Valley
T (02) 4998 7684 **F** (02) 4998 7324 **www**.lindemans.com.au **Open** 7 days 10–5
Winemaker Wayne Falkenberg, Greg Clayfield **Est.** 1843 **Cases** 7 million
One way or another, I have intersected with the Hunter Valley in general and Lindemans in particular for over 50 years. The wines are no longer made in the Lower Hunter, and the once mighty Semillon is a mere shadow of its former self. However, the refurbished historic Ben Ean winery (while no longer making wine) is a must-see for the wine tourist. Exports to the UK, the US and other major markets.

ⓎⓎⓎⓎ **Limited Release Hunter River Semillon 2005** Bin 0555. Has plenty of flavour and impact, but lacks the finesse of a wine of say 10.5° alcohol. A strange decision to use up semillon from 80-year-old vines in this fashion. Screwcap. 12.5° alc. **Rating** 89 **To** 2010 $19.95
Reserve Hunter Valley Verdelho 2006 Well-made; typical fruit salad braced by citrus notes and crisp acidity. Screwcap. 13.5° alc. **Rating** 88 **To** 2011 $12.95

Lindemans (Karadoc) ★★★

Edey Road, Karadoc via Red Cliffs, Vic 3496 **Region** Murray Darling
T (03) 5051 3333 **F** (03) 5051 3390 **www**.lindemans.com.au **Open** 7 days 10–4.30
Winemaker Wayne Falkenberg **Est.** 1974 **Cases** 7 million
Now the production centre for all the Lindemans and Leo Buring wines, with the exception of special lines made in Coonawarra. The very large winery allows all-important economies of scale, and is the major processing centre for Fosters beverage wine sector (casks, flagons and low-priced bottles). Its achievement in making several million cases of Bin 65 Chardonnay a year is extraordinary given the quality and consistency of the wines. Exports to all major markets.

ΥΥΥΥ **Bin 50 Shiraz 2006** Altogether surprisingly deep and supple black fruits; not much structure or oak input, but at the price, you can't expect more. Gold medal and trophy (Best Early Drinking Red) Perth Wine Show '06. Screwcap. 13.5° alc. **Rating** 89 **To** 2008 $9.95

Bin 95 Sauvignon Blanc 2006 Light-bodied, crisp and clean; some citrussy acidity adds interest to the gentle tropical fruit. Screwcap. 11.5° alc. **Rating** 87 **To** 2008 $10.95

Bin 65 Chardonnay 2006 Light-bodied; gentle stone fruit has an airbrush of well-handled oak; needs a touch more mid-palate fruit, but in no way, shape or form relies on residual sugar. Utterly true to itself. Screwcap. 13.5° alc. **Rating** 87 **To** 2008 $9.95

Bin 35 Rose 2006 A rose for all seasons, just enough red fruits, just enough sweetness, just enough acidity. Screwcap. 12.5° alc. **Rating** 87 **To** 2008 $10.95

Bin 55 Shiraz Cabernet 2006 Light- to medium-bodied; well-crafted with expected fruit flavours; a whisk of oak and some structure. Cork. 13.5° alc. **Rating** 87 **To** 2008 $10.95

Lindenton Wines ★★★★

102 High Street, Heathcote, Vic 3523 **Region** Heathcote
T (03) 5433 3246 **F** (03) 5433 3246 **Open** 7 days 10–4 by appt
Winemaker Adrian Munari, Greg Dedman (Contract) **Est.** 2003 **Cases** 2000
Jim Harrison's Lindenton Wines is a semi-retirement occupation. His business plan is based on the purchase of grapes from smaller growers in the region who do not have access to winemaking facilities or outlets for their fruit. From the word go there has been an extensive range of wines available, running through Verdelho, Chardonnay, Viognier, Marsanne, Merlot, Shiraz, Shiraz Viognier and top-of-the-tree Melange. Harrison's longer range plan is to make the wines himself.

ΥΥΥΥΥ **Heathcote Shiraz 2005** A mix of spice, licorice, forest floor and blackberry fruits; medium-bodied, with controlled oak, and gains intensity on the finish. Screwcap. 14.9° alc. **Rating** 90 **To** 2015 $20

Heathcote Vintage Port 2005 Good colour and balance; licorice, blackberry and spice; worth waiting for. One doesn't expect to find vintage fortified wines from Heathcote. Screwcap. 18.4° alc. **Rating** 90 **To** 2015 $15

ΥΥΥΥ **Heathcote Merlot 2005** Light- to medium-bodied; a fresh mix of red berries and snow peas/green olives; fine tannins. Screwcap. 14.5° alc. **Rating** 87 **To** 2010 $25

Heathcote Late Picked Marsanne Viognier NV A curious and cunning wine; doesn't show obvious spirit, but has been fortified, as a glance at the alcohol on the label will tell you. Screwcap. 17.5° alc. **Rating** 87 **To** 2008 $18

Lindsays ★★★☆

Cowra Road, Young, NSW 2594 **Region** Hilltops
T (02) 6382 2972 **F** (02) 6382 2972 **Open** 7 days 9–5
Winemaker Jill Lindsay **Est.** 1986 **Cases** 4000
A subtle name change and radical label redesign coincide with the release of a series of well-made wines, perseverance paying appropriate dividends. The estate vineyards have always been dry-grown, with low yields the consequence, but Bill Lindsay (talking of the prolonged drought which has affected so much of eastern Australia) wrote in Jan 2007, 'The vineyard's oldest blocks are almost 30 years old, and I don't believe they have ever looked so threatened.' But the redesigned labels, and the move to using Diam corks are all signs they intend to continue to fight the elements.

ΥΥΥΥΥ **Hilltops Shiraz 2004** Spicy, earthy nuances to blackberry and black cherry fruit; good length, balance and finish. Cork. 13.1° alc. **Rating** 90 **To** 2019 $21

ΥΥΥΥ **Hilltops Riesling 2006** Apple, nashi pear and citrus aromas; a lively palate follows in the tracks of the bouquet, perhaps just a fraction diffuse. Diam. 11.2° alc. **Rating** 89 **To** 2013 $19

Hilltops Chardonnay 2005 Clean, fresh, light melon and nectarine fruit on both bouquet and palate; a dash of French oak through barrel fermentation of part of the wine has worked well. Diam. 13° alc. **Rating** 89 **To** 2011 $18

Hilltops Merlot 2004 Light- to medium-bodied; appropriate texture and weight, and is distinctly varietal in flavour, with savoury elements throughout. How to keep these, but add some sweet notes, is the question many makers of merlot have pondered over. Cork. 13.5° alc. **Rating** 88 **To** 2013 $20

Hilltops Botrytis Semillon 2001 Glowing gold; mandarin and cumquat aromas and flavours; starting to dry out, and will continue to do so, thus drink immediately. Cork. 11.3° alc. **Rating** 87 **To** 2008 $19

Hilltops Touriga Port NV Attractive cedary, spicy fruit flavours, the spirit a little fierce. Cork. **Rating** 87 **To** 2015 $20

Linfield Road Wines

PO Box 6, Williamstown, SA 5351 **Region** Barossa Valley
T (08) 8524 6140 **F** (08) 8524 6427 **www**.annandalevineyards.com.au **Open** Not
Winemaker Rod Chapman (Contract), Steve Wilson, Deb Wilson **Est.** 2002 **Cases** 2000
The Wilson family has been growing grapes at their estate vineyard for over 100 years; Steve and Deb Wilson are fourth generation vignerons. The vineyard is in one of the coolest parts of the Barossa Valley, in an elevated position near the Adelaide Hills boundary. The estate's 19 ha are planted to riesling, cabernet sauvignon, semillon, shiraz, merlot, grenache and chardonnay. In 2002 the Wilsons decided to vinify part of the production. Within 12 months of the first release, the wines had accumulated 3 trophies and 5 gold medals.

Lirralirra Estate

15 Paynes Road, Chirnside Park, Vic 3116 **Region** Yarra Valley
T (03) 9735 0224 **F** (03) 9735 0224 **Open** W'ends & hols 10–6
Winemaker Alan Smith **Est.** 1981 **Cases** 400
Alan Smith started Lirralirra with the intention of specialising in a Sauternes-style blend of botrytised semillon and sauvignon blanc. It seemed a good idea – in a sense it still does on paper – but it simply didn't work. He has changed direction to a more conventional mix with dignity and humour, challenged by the mysterious removal of winery direction signs in 2006, and by the combination of drought and frost which meant no grapes at all in '07. The 2006 Sauvignon Blanc may last until Christmas, but the 'sold out' signs are likely to be up until July '08.

♟♟♟♟ **Sauvignon Blanc 2006** Clean mineral, herb and grass aromas which carry through to the palate, where some asparagus notes join the band. Nicely made. Screwcap. 13° alc. **Rating** 89 **To** 2008 $19

Lister Wines

c/- 16 Charles Street, Norword, SA 5067 (postal) **Region** Adelaide Hills/Langhorne Creek
T 0401 524 539 **F** (08) 8361 2399 **Open** Not
Winemaker Cate Lister **Est.** 2001 **Cases** 200
This is a micro-virtual winery run by Cate Lister, drawing upon 2 ha of cabernet sauvignon and 1 ha of merlot in the Adelaide Hills and Langhorne Creek. The tiny production means the wines are mainly sold through word of mouth and mail order, and 2 small retail outlets in SA.

♟♟♟♟ **Soliloquy 2003** Light-bodied; elegant flavours are at the savoury end, but the texture is supple; what there is is very good, simply needing more depth. Merlot (70%)/Cabernet Sauvignon (30%). Cork. 13° alc. **Rating** 88 **To** 2015

Little Brampton Wines   ★★★★

PO Box 61, Clare, SA 5453 **Region** Clare Valley
T (08) 8843 4201 **F** (08) 8843 4244 **www**.littlebramptonwines.com.au **Open** By appt
Winemaker Contract **Est.** 2001 **Cases** 800

Little Brampton Wines is a boutique, family-owned business operated by Alan and Pamela Schwarz. They purchased their 24-ha property in the heart of the Clare Valley in the early 1990s (Alan graduated from Roseworthy in 1981). The property has produced grapes since the 1860s, but the vineyard had been removed during the Vine Pull Scheme of the 1980s. The Schwarzes have replanted 10 ha to riesling, shiraz and cabernet sauvignon on northwest slopes at 520 m; a small proportion of the production is vinified for the Little Brampton label.

ΥΥΥΥ   **Clare Valley Riesling 2006** A clean, but closed aroma; mineral and slate flavours, but slightly diffuse citrus components; good length. Hard to reconcile with the brilliant '05. Screwcap. 13.1° alc. **Rating** 89 **To** 2012 $19
Clare Valley Rose 2006 A lively wine, with cassis and redcurrant fruit, then prolonged, refreshing acidity. Screwcap. 11.8° alc. **Rating** 88 **To** 2008 $19

Little Bridge
PO Box 499, Bungendore, NSW 2621 **Region** Canberra District
T (02) 6251 5242 **F** (02) 6251 4379 **www**.littlebridgewines.com.au **Open** Not
Winemaker Canberra Winemakers (Greg Gallagher, Rob Howell) **Est.** 1996 **Cases** 1000
Little Bridge is a partnership between long-term friends John Leyshon, Rowland Clark, John Jeffrey and Steve Dowton. Two ha of chardonnay, pinot noir, riesling and merlot were planted in on Rowland Clark's property at Butmaroo, near Bungendore, at an altitude of 860 m. In 2004 a further 2.5 ha of shiraz, cabernet sauvignon, sangiovese, grenache and gamay were planted on John Leyshon's property near Yass (560m). Canberra Winemakers make the white wines, and the reds are made by the partners at Bungendore.

Little Valley   ★★★★
RMB 6047, One Chain Road, Merricks North, Vic 3926 **Region** Mornington Peninsula
T (03) 5989 7564 **F** (03) 5989 7564 **Open** By appt
Winemaker Moorooduc Estate **Est.** 1998 **Cases** 270
Wesley College teacher Sue Taylor and part-time Anglican minister husband Brian have planted 0.8 ha each of chardonnay and pinot noir on their Little Valley property, and built their house there. Ian MacRae is consultant viticulturist, and Rick McIntyre makes the wines. The Mornington Peninsula is a beautiful place, and the Little Valley property itself a prime example of that beauty, providing a return which cannot be measured in dollars and cents.

ΥΥΥΥΥ   **Mornington Peninsula Chardonnay 2005** A moderately complex bouquet to an elegant, tangy cool-grown style; grapefruit and nectarine flavours; balanced finish. Screwcap. 14° alc. **Rating** 90 **To** 2010 $20

ΥΥΥΥ   **Mornington Peninsula Pinot Noir 2005** Light but bright red-purple; firm, fresh varietal fruit but tending a little simple/one-dimensional; time may well help. Screwcap. 14° alc. **Rating** 88 **To** 2010 $18

Littles
Cnr Palmers Lane/McDonalds Road, Pokolbin, NSW 2321 **Region** Lower Hunter Valley
T (02) 4998 7626 **F** (02) 4998 7867 **www**.littleswinery.com.au **Open** Fri–Mon 10–4.30
Winemaker Peter Orr (Contract) **Est.** 1984 **Cases** 6000
Littles is managed by the Kindred family, the ownership involving a number of investors. The winery has mature vineyards planted to shiraz (3.3 ha), semillon (3.1 ha), chardonnay (2.4 ha), pinot noir (1.5 ha), cabernet sauvignon (1.3 ha) and marsanne (1 ha). Exports to Germany, Vietnam and Japan.

ΥΥΥΥΥ   **Hunter Valley Reserve Shiraz 2003** Holding hue very well; an elegant wine which has actually gained in intensity over the past 2 years; black and red cherry fruit with good tannins and a long finish. **Rating** 92 **To** 2018 $24

ΥΥΥΥ   **Fusions Marsanne Chardonnay Viognier 2006** The varieties are indeed fused; a fair volume of somewhat amorphous flavour, the best feature being its rejection of residual sugar. Screwcap. **Rating** 87 **To** 2008 $16

Llangibby Estate ★★★☆

Old Mount Barker Road, Echunga, SA 5153 **Region** Adelaide Hills
T (08) 8398 5505 **F** (08) 8398 5505 www.llangibbyestate.com **Open** By appt
Winemaker Chris Addams Williams, John Williamson, James Hastwell **Est.** 1998 **Cases** 500
Chris Addams Williams and John Williamson have established a substantial vineyard cresting a
ridge close to Echunga, at an altitude of 360m. The vineyard plantings have morphed since the
outset; there are now 7.09 ha of sauvignon blanc, 4.67 ha pinot gris, 1.85 tempranillo and 0.17
ha pinot gris, with most of the grapes sold to other producers. Exports to the UK.

Lloyd Brothers NR

34 Warners Road, McLaren Vale, SA 5171 **Region** McLaren Vale
T (08) 8323 8792 **F** (08) 8323 8833 www.lloydbrothers.com.au **Open** 7 days 10–5
Winemaker Sam Temme **Est.** 2002 **Cases** NA
The business is owned by David Lloyd, son of Mark Lloyd of Coriole fame (itself founded by
Mark's father Dr Hugh Lloyd). Lloyd Brothers owns 12 ha of shiraz planted 10–12 years ago,
and shares a property with a planting of old olive trees, which produces high-quality table olives
and extra-virgin olive oil sold through The Olive Grove at McLaren Vale. Lloyd Brothers sells
a significant part of its grape production (inter alia to d'Arenberg and Coriole) and sells the
entire crop in years where the standard is not considered high enough to warrant an estate
release. Thus Shiraz was made in 2002 and 2004, but not 2003. Lloyd Brothers also has an
Adelaide Hills vineyard planted to 5 ha of chardonnay, verdelho, pinot noir and sauvignon
blanc; their Adelaide Hills cellar door is at 94 Main St, Hahndorf.

Lochmoore ★★★☆

PO Box 430, Trafalgar, Vic 3824 **Region** Gippsland
T 0402 216 622 **Open** Not
Winemaker Lyre Bird Hill, Narkoojee **Est.** 1997 **Cases** 300
The 2 ha of chardonnay, pinot noir, pinot gris and shiraz at Lochmoore are tended by one of the
most highly qualified viticulturists one is ever likely to meet. Sue Hasthorpe grew up in Trafalgar,
and went on to obtain a Bachelor of Science (Hons) and Doctor of Philosophy in Physiology at
the University of Melbourne; thereafter working and travelling as a medical research scientist in
Australia, the UK, the US and Europe, and after returning to Australia studied viticulture via the
University of Melbourne, Dookie College campus (distance education). If this were not enough,
she has now completed a Masters of Agribusiness at the University of Melbourne.

▼▼▼▼ **Trafalgar Chardonnay 2005** Quite warm peach and butterscotch flavours belie
the moderate alcohol; some barrel ferment characters evident adding to the
complexity. Diam. 13.5° alc. **Rating** 89 **To** 2010 $18
Trafalgar Pinot Noir 2005 Very tangy, almost citrussy, edge to cherry fruit;
minimal oak; clean, lively finish. Screwcap. 13.5° alc. **Rating** 87 **To** 2008 $18

Logan Wines ★★★☆

Castlereagh Highway, Apple Tree Flat, Mudgee, NSW 2850 **Region** Mudgee
T (02) 6373 1333 **F** (02) 6373 1390 www.loganwines.com.au **Open** 7 days 10–5
Winemaker Peter Logan, Andrew Ling **Est.** 1997 **Cases** 40 000
Logan is a family-owned and operated business with emphasis on cool climate wines from
Orange and Mudgee. The business is run by husband and wife team Peter (winemaker) and
Hannah (sales and marketing). Wines are released from 3 ranges: Logan (from Orange), Weemala
and Apple Tree Flat. Exports to the UK, the US and other major markets.

▼▼▼▼ **Weemala Central Ranges Shiraz Viognier 2005** Medium-bodied; a touch
of lift from the viognier is very evident on both bouquet and palate; appealing
blackberry, cherry and spice fruit; offers more flavour than structure, but that is no
sin. Screwcap. 13.5° alc. **Rating** 89 **To** 2012 $16

Orange Cabernet Merlot 2004 Light- to medium-bodied, but has good intensity and length; blackcurrant, black olive, cassis, earth and spice are all interwoven through the long palate. Cork. 15° alc. **Rating** 89 **To** 2012 $25
Orange Sauvignon Blanc 2006 Abundant fruit and varietal expression; grapefruit, citrus and tropical flavours offering touches of bitterness and sweetness at the same time. Screwcap. 14° alc. **Rating** 88 **To** 2008 $20
Hannah Rose 2006 Fragrant red fruits; light, dry and fresh. Cork. 13.5° alc. **Rating** 88 **To** 2008 $20
Orange Shiraz 2004 Light- to medium-bodied; spicy/earthy overtones to black cherry fruit; pleasant, but lacks depth and body. Cork. 14.5° alc. **Rating** 87 **To** 2008 $25
Weemala Central Ranges Merlot 2004 Spice, hay and red berry aromas; the very ripe fruit on the palate reflects the alcohol, or vice versa; finishes short. Screwcap. 15° alc. **Rating** 87 **To** 2009 $16

Long Gully Estate

Long Gully Road, Healesville, Vic 3777 **Region** Yarra Valley
T (03) 9510 5798 **F** (03) 9510 9859 **www**.longgullyestate.com **Open** 7 days 11–5
Winemaker Luke Houlihan **Est.** 1982 **Cases** 12 000
One of the larger Yarra Valley producers to have successfully established a number of export markets, doubtless due to its core of mature vineyards. Recent vineyard extensions underline Long Gully's commercial success. Exports to the UK, Switzerland and Singapore.

🍷🍷🍷🍷🍷 **Heathcote Shiraz 2004** An elegant, light- to medium-bodied wine more in the style of the Yarra Valley than new-generation Heathcote; fine, sweet, red and black fruits on entry, then lovely fine-grained tannins on the back-palate, with subtle oak. From 50-year-old vines grown by an Italian family; akin to winning Tattslotto. Diam. 13° alc. **Rating** 94 **To** 2019 $24

🍷🍷🍷🍷🍷 **Irma's Cabernet 2004** Tight, earthy blackcurrant fruit shot through with fine, persistent tannins in an overall savoury mode; helped by a touch of French oak. Screwcap. 13° alc. **Rating** 91 **To** 2017 $20
Yarra Valley Shiraz 2005 Clean, medium-bodied; attractive blackberry, plum and cherry mix; a smooth and supple finish. Screwcap. 13.4° alc. **Rating** 90 **To** 2015 $20
Cattleyard Cabernet Merlot 2004 A pleasing, supple medium-bodied mix of red and black fruits, fine tannins, controlled oak. Diam. 13.3° alc. **Rating** 90 **To** 2015 $30

🍷🍷🍷🍷 **Yarra Valley Sauvignon Blanc 2006** Soft, but quite complex, doubtless stemming from the 18% barrel fermentation with wild yeast; gentle tropical fruit; balanced finish. Screwcap. 13.9° alc. **Rating** 89 **To** 2008 $20
Reserve Merlot 2004 Strong green bean and leaf aromas; the palate adds cassis and raspberry flavours; all in all a creditable effort. Diam. 12.5° alc. **Rating** 89 **To** 2014 $30
Reserve Yarra Valley Ice Riesling 2005 Sweet citrus/lemon flavours balanced by good acidity; as is so often the case with freeze-concentrated riesling, lacks complexity. Cork. 12.5° alc. **Rating** 88 **To** 2008 $23
Yarra Valley Riesling 2006 Distinctly soft and fruity; flavoursome, early-drinking style. Screwcap. 12.8° alc. **Rating** 87 **To** 2010 $20

🍇 Longview Creek Vineyard

150 Palmer Road, Sunbury, Vic 3429 **Region** Sunbury
T (03) 9740 2448 **F** (03) 9740 2495 **www**.longviewcreek.com.au **Open** W'ends & public hols 11–5, or by appt
Winemaker Roland Kaval (Contract) **Est.** 1988 **Cases** 900
Bill and Karen Ashby purchased the Longview Creek Vineyard from founders Dr Ron and Joan Parker in 2003. It is situated on the brink of the spectacular Longview Gorge, the bulk of the plantings of chardonnay (0.8 ha), pinot noir (0.6 ha) and chenin blanc (0.4 ha) being made

between 1988 and 1990. Thereafter a little cabernet franc (0.3 ha) and riesling (0.1 ha) were planted. Simon Glover oversees viticulture, and Roland Kaval the contract winemaker.

🍷🍷🍷🍷 **Pinot Noir 2005** Strong foresty/savoury/gamey underbrush to plum and black cherry fruit; overall light-bodied. French oak. Screwcap. 13.8° alc. **Rating** 88 **To** 2010 $20

Riesling 2006 Light straw-green; a gently spicy bouquet with light citrus fruit flavours; slightly short finish. Screwcap. 12.4° alc. **Rating** 87 **To** 2010 $18

Chardonnay 2006 The oak input is very subtle, and doesn't lift the fruit, simply changing the texture to a small degree. Screwcap. 14.4° alc. **Rating** 87 **To** 2010 $18

Longview Vineyard ★★★★☆

Pound Road, Macclesfield, SA 5153 **Region** Adelaide Hills
T (08) 8388 9694 **F** (08) 8388 9693 **www**.longviewvineyard.com.au **Open** Sun–Fri 11–5
Winemaker Shaw & Smith, Kangarilla Road, O'Leary Walker **Est.** 1995 **Cases** 15 000
In a strange twist of fate, Longview Vineyard came to be through the success of Two Dogs, the lemon-flavoured alcoholic drink created by Duncan MacGillivray and sold in 1995 to the Pernod Ricard Group (also the owners of Orlando). Over 60 ha have been planted: shiraz and cabernet sauvignon account for a little over half, and there are significant plantings of chardonnay and merlot, and smaller plantings of viognier, semillon, riesling, sauvignon blanc, zinfandel and nebbiolo. The majority of the production is sold, but $1.2 million has been invested in a cellar door and function area, barrel rooms and an administration centre for the Group's activities. All the buildings have a spectacular view over the Coorong and Lake Alexandrina. Exports to the UK, the US and Canada.

🍷🍷🍷🍷🍷 **Devils Elbow Adelaide Hills Cabernet Sauvignon 2005** Perfectly pitched cabernet sauvignon, picked at exactly the right time; it is not heavy or jammy, but nor is it too green or savoury; oak and tannin management are also spot-on. Cork. 14.5° alc. **Rating** 94 **To** 2025 $22.95

🍷🍷🍷🍷½ **Red Bucket Adelaide Hills Chardonnay 2006** Riper stone fruit, melon and peach aromas and flavours; mouthfilling, but no more than light- to medium-bodied; good length and finish. Screwcap. 13.5° alc. **Rating** 92 **To** 2013 $16

Yakka Adelaide Hills Shiraz 2005 Medium- to full-bodied; blackberry, licorice and black pepper aromas and flavours; firm tannins knit the wine together, oak filling in any cracks; will be long-lived, cork permitting. 14.5° alc. **Rating** 91 **To** 2025 $21.95

Iron Knob Adelaide Hills Riesling 2006 A complex bouquet, with tangy lime, lemon and the first hint of toast; the powerful palate has as much depth as length to the quite ripe fruit. Screwcap. 12.5° alc. **Rating** 90 **To** 2012 $19.50

Red Bucket Adelaide Hills Semillon Sauvignon Blanc 2006 A bracing, intense wine, in part reflecting the low alcohol and in part the semillon component; capsicum and asparagus flavours dominate; a clean, lively finish; for summer seafood. Screwcap. 11.5° alc. **Rating** 90 **To** 2008 $16

Blue Cow Adelaide Hills Chardonnay 2006 Fresh, crisp and lively grapefruit and nectarine providing drive and length; a fresh, breezy finish. Screwcap. 13° alc. **Rating** 90 **To** 2011 $19.50

🍷🍷🍷🍷 **The Boat Shed Adelaide Hills Nebbiolo Rose 2006** Nebbiolo flavours are quite apparent, and the wine has texture and length; spicy sour cherry notes, and a dry finish. Thoroughly commendable. Screwcap. 14.5° alc. **Rating** 89 **To** 2008 $22

Two Still Standing Adelaide Hills Pinot Noir 2005 Light- to medium-bodied, with predominantly savoury/forest floor characters, but does have black and red cherry components. Screwcap. 12.5° alc. **Rating** 89 **To** 2010 $22

The Mob Adelaide Hills Zinfandel 2005 Has that cherry conserve character of zinfandel, plus a few splashes of spice, and a nuance of lemon zest; for when you want something different or are eating Italian. Cork. 17.6° alc. **Rating** 88 **To** 2008 $30

Longwood Wines

RMB 2750 Longwood-Gobur Road, Longwood East, Vic 3665 **Region** Strathbogie Ranges
T (03) 5798 5291 **F** (03) 5798 5437 www.longwoodwine.com.au **Open** W'ends &
public hols 10–5, or by appt
Winemaker Andrew Cameron **Est.** 1969 **Cases** 1000
The Falls Vineyard was planted by Andrew and Elly Cameron way back in 1969, as a minor
diversification for their pastoral company. Two ha of shiraz provides both the Longwood Shiraz
and the Longwood Reserve Shiraz. The exceptionally beautiful property was sold at the end of
2005, but wine sales are continuing.

Loom Wines NR

PO Box 162, McLaren Vale, SA 5171 **Region** McLaren Vale
T (08) 8323 8623 **F** (08) 8323 8694 www.loomwine.com **Open** Not
Winemaker Steve Grimley **Est.** 2005 **Cases** NA
Steve Grimley runs an offsite winemaking business, which includes the Loom Wine and
Willundry Road brands of Shiraz, primarily designed for export into Europe and the US, and
contract winemaking services for others. The estate vineyards comprise 10 ha of shiraz in
McLaren Vale; other varieties are contract-grown.

Lost Lake NR

Lot 3 Vasse Highway, Pemberton, WA 6260 **Region** Pemberton
T (08) 9776 1251 **F** (08) 9776 1919 www.lostlake.com.au **Open** 7 days 10–4
Winemaker Mark Aitken **Est.** 1990 **Cases** NA

Lost Valley Winery

PO Box 4123, Wishart, Vic 3189 **Region** Upper Goulburn
T (03) 9592 3531 **F** (03) 9551 7470 www.lostvalleywinery.com **Open** Not
Winemaker Alex White (Contract) **Est.** 1995 **Cases** 5000
Dr Robert Ippaso planted the Lost Valley vineyard at an elevation of 450 m on the slopes of Mt
Tallarook, with 13 ha of merlot, shiraz, cortese and sauvignon blanc. This cortese is the only
planting in Australia. It pays homage to Dr Ippaso's birthplace: Savoie, in the Franco-Italian Alps,
where cortese flourishes. Exports to the UK, the US and other major markets.

ŸŸŸŸŸ **Thousand Hills Shiraz 2003** Some notes of mint and spice on the bouquet join
with plenty of black cherry and plum on the palate; supple tannins. Cork. 14° alc.
Rating 91 **To** 2010 $32

ŸŸŸŸ **Upper Goulburn Sauvignon Blanc 2006** A straightforward, unpretentious style;
a mix of grass, mineral and a touch of tropical fruit, with just a hint of residual sugar.
Screwcap. 13° alc. **Rating** 88 **To** 2008 $25
Upper Goulburn Cortese 2006 A crisp, clean, slightly more citrussy version
of pinot gris and/or arneis; its chief virtues are its rarity and Italian restaurant
wine lists in Australia. Screwcap. 13° alc. **Rating** 88 **To** 2009 $30
Hazy Mountain Merlot 2005 Strong, cool-grown flavour characteristics, but gets
over the line (just); savoury/spicy/earthy/olivaceous flavours are all varietal; what is
missing are red fruit notes. Cork. 14° alc. **Rating** 88 **To** 2015 $32

Lou Miranda Estate

Barossa Valley Way, Rowland Flat, SA 5352 **Region** Barossa Valley
T (08) 8524 4537 www.loumirandaestate.com.au **Open** Mon–Fri 10–4, w'ends 11–4
Winemaker Lou Miranda **Est.** 2005 **Cases** 15 000
Lou Miranda has joined with his wife and other members of the Miranda family to acquire
Miranda Rovalley vineyard and winery in the Barossa Valley. Thirty ha of predominantly shiraz
(14 ha, including 5 ha of old vines), cabernet sauvignon (7 ha), merlot (6 ha), with lesser amounts
of chardonnay, pinot grigio, mataro and a small patch of old vine grenache provide the grapes for

the venture. The cellar door works on the principle that there should be a wine for every conceivable taste. Exports to Germany, Singapore, Thailand and Japan.

ŢŢŢŢŢ **Leone Adelaide Hills Sauvignon Blanc 2005** No reduction, and the screwcap has helped retain freshness; aromas and flavours in a gentle tropical spectrum; don't delay drinking it. Screwcap. 13° alc. **Rating** 90 **To** 2008 $17

ŢŢŢŢ **Primo Amore Cordon Cut Barossa Shiraz 2000** Interesting wine, with some Amarone characters; an abundance of earthy black fruits balanced by a twist of acidity. Cork. 15° alc. **Rating** 89 **To** 2010 $36

Primo Amore Old Vine Barossa Shiraz 2001 Very ripe, savoury fruit mix; some mocha, vanilla and cedar notes; ripe, fine tannins. As with all the Lou Miranda wines, the quality and condition of the cork is not reassuring. 15° alc. **Rating** 88 **To** 2010 $26

Leone Barossa Cabernet Sauvignon 2004 Light- to medium-bodied, but has some authentic blackcurrant/cassis fruit allowed to speak its mind. Cork. 14.5° alc. **Rating** 88 **To** 2009 $17

Leone Adelaide Hills Pinot Grigio 2005 Not much character or fruit personality, but has good length and balance courtesy of a twist of lemony acidity. Screwcap. 14° alc. **Rating** 87 **To** 2008 $17

Leone Barossa Cabernet Sauvignon 2005 A medium-bodied mix of mint, eucalypt, leaf and blackcurrant on both bouquet and palate; a faint residual bitterness. Screwcap. 14° alc. **Rating** 87 **To** 2013 $16.95

Leone Riverina Botrytis Semillon NV Well-constructed; a moderately sweet palate, the botrytis influence controlled. Cork. 12.5° alc. **Rating** 87 **To** 2008 $17

Louee ★★★★

Cox's Creek Road, Rylstone, NSW 2849 **Region** Mudgee
T (02) 6379 0928 **www**.louee.com.au **Open** Mon–Sat 10–4, Sun & public hols 11–2
Winemaker David Lowe, Jane Wilson (Contract) **Est.** 1998 **Cases** 4000
Jointly owned by Rod James and Tony Maxwell, Louee is a substantial operation. Its home vineyard is at Rylstone with 10 ha, led by shiraz, cabernet sauvignon, petit verdot and merlot, with chardonnay, cabernet franc, verdelho and viognier making up the balance. The second vineyard is on Nullo Mountain, bordered by the Wollemi National Park, at an altitude of 1100 m, high by any standards. Here 4.45 ha of cool-climate varieties (riesling, sauvignon blanc, pinot noir, pinot gris and nebbiolo) have been planted.

ŢŢŢŢŢ **Nullo Mountain Rylstone Riesling 2005** Flowery blossom aromas; a light, clean and crisp palate with gentle lime and tropical fruit; good balance and length. Gold medal Mudgee Wine Show '05. Screwcap. 13.6° alc. **Rating** 91 **To** 2013 $18

Rylstone Petit Verdot 2004 Plenty of depth and richness without any distracting sweetness; smoky/spicy/savoury black fruits; good tannins. Grown in an appropriate climate, allowing natural varietal expression. Cork. 14.8° alc. **Rating** 90 **To** 2014 $19

ŢŢŢŢ **Tongbong Rylstone Chardonnay 2005** Abundant texture, structure and flavour; barrel ferment and oak wrapped around ripe melon and stone fruit; moderate length. Screwcap. 14.5° alc. **Rating** 89 **To** 2010 $18

Nullo Mountain Rylstone Riesling 2006 Pale green-straw; a subdued but clean bouquet, the palate has good length, aided by lemony acidity. Screwcap. 13° alc. **Rating** 88 **To** 2014 $18

Five Peaks 2003 The varieties come together well in a low alcohol environment; light- to medium-bodied, with leaf, mint and spice edges to blackcurrant fruit. Cabernet Sauvignon/Merlot/Cabernet Franc/Petit Verdot/Shiraz. Cork. 12.8° alc. **Rating** 88 **To** 2010 $20

Nullo Mountain Rylstone Nebbiolo 2005 Particularly good colour for the variety, with positive hue; the flavour, too, is positive, ranging – however gently – through rose petals, cherries and spices, the tannins in no way abrasive. Screwcap. 13.5° alc. **Rating** 88 **To** 2011 $24

Nullo Mountain Rylstone Pinot Gris 2006 Has some length; nice acidity and the absence of residual sugar are both distinct pluses; light green apple flavours. Screwcap. 14° alc. **Rating** 87 **To** 2008 $18

Nullo Mountain Rylstone Pinot Gris 2005 A solid wine; well-made, and simply underlining the limitations of the variety; not too sweet. Screwcap. 14° alc. **Rating** 87 **To** 2005 $18

Cox's Crown Rylstone Verdelho 2005 Intense honeysuckle/lantana aromas; the palate backs off a little, but has good acidity; interesting wine. Screwcap. 14° alc. **Rating** 87 **To** 2008 $15

Nullo Mountain Rylstone Pinot Noir 2005 Shows more dry red characters than pinot noir until the finish, when pinot does make a fleeting but definite appearance; better than any previous vintages. Screwcap. 14° alc. **Rating** 87 **To** 2011 $19

Rumkers Peak Shiraz 2004 Developed colour; light to medium-bodied spicy/earthy/savoury regional style, which belies its alcohol. Cork. 14.9° alc. **Rating** 87 **To** 2008 $18

Lowe Family Wines   ★★★★☆

Tinja Lane, Mudgee, NSW 2850 **Region** Mudgee
T (02) 6372 0800 **www.**lowewine.com.au **Open** Fri–Mon 10–5, or by appt
Winemaker David Lowe, Jane Wilson **Est.** 1987 **Cases** 6000
Former Rothbury winemaker David Lowe and Jane Wilson have consolidated their operations in Mudgee, moving back from their cellar door in the Hunter Valley. They have started a new Mudgee business, Mudgee Growers, at the historic Fairview winery (see separate entry). The main business is here, and they have spread their wings, successfully introducing less well-known varieties, and looking to other regions more suited for both mainstream styles (e.g. Orange for pinot gris and sauvignon blanc) and outre varieties (e.g. Orange roussanne). Exports to the UK, Japan and Denmark.

♀♀♀♀♀ **Tinja Orange Pinot Gris 2006** Considerable vivacity and life for a usually boring variety; tangy citrus, pear and musk aromas and flavours. Screwcap. 14.5° alc. **Rating** 91 **To** 2009 $18

Reserve Mudgee Shiraz 2005 Slightly less bright hue than the varietal; a more complex wine, particularly with ripe tannins and length; longer cellaring future. Stained cork. Cork. 13.4° alc. **Rating** 91 **To** 2016 $40

Tinja Orange Sauvignon Blanc 2006 A neutral bouquet, but there is much more action on the palate, with a vibrant tropical fruit and asparagus mix; good acidity, long finish. Screwcap. 13.1° alc. **Rating** 90 **To** 2008 $18

Mudgee Shiraz 2005 An attractive, soft, rounded, medium-bodied palate with good mouthfeel; ripe plum, blackberry and licorice fruit supported by soft tannins. Stained cork. Cork. 14.5° alc. **Rating** 90 **To** 2011 $28

Mudgee Zinfandel 2005 Attractive spicy, small berry fruits (red and black) are apt to make this wine a better proposition than tempranillo, even though it is difficult to grow and manage. However, the Lowe Family seems to have found the key, this following on an equally impressive '04. Cork. 14.3° alc. **Rating** 90 **To** 2015 $40

♀♀♀♀ **Mudgee Merlot 2005** Red fruits with spice, briar and olive aromas; the texture, structure and weight are appropriate for merlot, the palate finishing with fine tannins. Merlot is not easy to love, or even understand. Cork. 13° alc. **Rating** 89 **To** 2013 $25

Tinja Mudgee Botrytis Semillon 2006 Abundant flavour and well-balanced (even though a gram more acidity might not have gone astray) wine. Lots of honey and citrus flavours with a softly sweet finish. Screwcap. 12.5° alc. **Rating** 88 **To** 2008 $18

Tinja Orange Riesling 2006 Slightly blurred varietal expression, possibly due to a touch of reduction; soft, ripe fruit, but not incisive. Screwcap. 14° alc. **Rating** 87 **To** 2010 $18

Tinja Orange Roussanne 2006 Even the back label disclosure of the presence of gunpowder in the taste profile fails to excite the palate; however, these wines have a track record in the Northern Rhone Valley of improving with age, and this is an interesting little-tested variety in Australia. Screwcap. 14.3° alc. **Rating** 87 **To** 2009 $18

Lucas Estate

329 Donges Road, Severnlea, Qld 4352 **Region** Granite Belt
T (07) 4683 6365 **F** (07) 4683 6356 **www**.lucasestate.com.au **Open** 7 days 10–5
Winemaker Colin Sellers, Jim Barnes **Est.** 1999 **Cases** 1300
Louise Samuel and husband Colin Sellers purchased Lucas Estate in 2003. The wines are made from the 2.5-ha estate vineyard (at an altitude of 825 m) which is planted to chardonnay, verdelho, cabernet sauvignon, shiraz, merlot and muscat, and also from purchased grapes. The contemporary cellar door houses an art gallery featuring Louise's work. One of the new stars in the Qld firmament; the consistency of the quality of the '05 wines is truly admirable.

 The Gordon Shiraz 2005 Deep colour and hue; a rich and quite dense mix of blackberry, licorice and plum; well above-average intensity, and a worthy winner of a number of awards. Cork. 14.5° alc. **Rating** 92 **To** 2018 $35
Jamie's Block Merlot 2005 Medium-bodied, with abundant red fruits and a wholly appropriate texture and structure; on slightly less sure ground with its varietal flavour, but impressive overall. Cork. 14.2° alc. **Rating** 90 **To** 2012 $25
Merlot 2005 Deep, bright purple-red; similar to Jamie's Block; likewise medium-bodied, with similar structure and texture; perhaps a little stronger, though not necessarily better. Cork. 13.8° alc. **Rating** 90 **To** 2012 $25
Cabernet Sauvignon 2005 Clear varietal blackcurrant fruit with a touch of black olive; good texture and structure; ripe tannins. Cork. 13.9° alc. **Rating** 90 **To** 2014 $25

Chardonnay 2005 Light- to medium-bodied; firm, with a touch of green running throughout possibly partly from the oak (new French) or perhaps from early picking. Screwcap. 13° alc. **Rating** 87 **To** 2009 $25

Lucy's Run ★★☆

1274 Wine Country Drive, Rothbury, NSW 2335 **Region** Lower Hunter Valley
T (02) 4938 3594 **F** (02) 4938 3592 **www**.lucysrun.com **Open** 7 days 10–5
Winemaker David Hook (Contract) **Est.** 1998 **Cases** 1000
The Lucy's Run business has a variety of offerings of wine, cold-pressed extra virgin olive oil and self-catered farm accommodation. The wines are made from 4.2 ha of verdelho, merlot and shiraz. The feisty label design is the work of local artist Paula Rengger, who doubles up as the chef at the nearby Shakey Tables Restaurant, itself the deserving winner of numerous awards.

Rose 2006 Well-made, nicely balanced red fruit along with residual sugar and acidity. **Rating** 87 **To** 2008 $20

Luke Lambert Wines NR

PO Box 403, Yarra Glen, Vic 3775 (postal) **Region** Yarra Valley
T 0448 349 323 **www**.lukelambertwines.com.au **Open** By appt
Winemaker Luke Lambert **Est.** 2003 **Cases** NA

Lyre Bird Hill ★★★☆

370 Inverloch Road, Koonwarra, Vic 3954 **Region** Gippsland
T (03) 5664 3204 **F** (03) 5664 3206 **www**.lyrebirdhill.com.au **Open** Wed–Mon 10–5
Winemaker Owen Schmidt **Est.** 1986 **Cases** 2500
Former Melbourne professionals Owen and Robyn Schmidt make small quantities of estate-grown wine (the vineyard is 2.4 ha). Various weather-related viticulture problems have seen the

Schmidts supplement their estate-grown intake with grapes from contract growers in Gippsland and the Yarra Valley, and also provide contract winemaking services for others.

🍷🍷🍷🍷 **Reserve Pinot Noir 2004** A tangy, spicy wine which has good length and presence. Cork. 12.8° alc. **Rating** 88 **To** 2009 $25

Lyrebird Ridge Organic Winery   NR

270 Budgong Road, Budgong via Nowra and Kangaroo Valley, NSW 2541 **Region** Shoalhaven Coast
T (02) 4446 0648 **www**.lyrebirdridge.com **Open** Fri–Sun & public hols 10–5
Winemaker Larry Moreau **Est.** 1993 **Cases** NA

M. Chapoutier Australia

PO Box 437, Robe, SA 5276 **Region** Mount Benson
T (03) 5433 2411 **F** (03) 5433 2400 **www**.chapoutier.com **Open** Not
Winemaker Benjamin Darnault, Anthony Terlato **Est.** 1998 **Cases** 10 000
M. Chapoutier Australia is the offshoot of the famous Rhône Valley producer. It has established 3 vineyards in Australia: Domaine Tournon at Mount Benson (17 ha shiraz, 10 ha cabernet sauvignon, 4 ha marsanne, 3 ha viognier), Domaine Terlato Chapoutier in the Pyrenees (30 ha shiraz, 2 ha viognier) and a third at Heathcote (10 ha shiraz). It seems likely that increasing emphasis will be placed on the Victorian vineyards. The business has also established operations in Heathcote. The Domaine Terlato and Chapoutier wines are made by Anthony Terlato, a Napa Valley winemaker. Exports to all major markets.

Macaw Creek Wines

Macaw Creek Road, Riverton, SA 5412 **Region** Mount Lofty Ranges Zone
T (08) 8847 2237 **www**.macawcreekwines.com.au **Open** Sun & public hols 11–4
Winemaker Rodney Hooper **Est.** 1992 **Cases** 5000
The property on which Macaw Creek Wines is established has been owned by the Hooper family since the 1850s, but development of the estate vineyards did not begin until 1995 (30 ha have since been planted). The Macaw Creek brand was established in 1992 with wines made from grapes from other regions, including the Preservative-Free Yoolang Cabernet Shiraz. Rodney Hooper is a highly qualified and skilled winemaker with experience in many parts of Australia and in Germany, France and the US. Exports to the US, Canada and Malaysia.

macforbes

c/- Sticks, Glenview Road, Yarra Glen, Vic 3775 **Region** Yarra Valley
T (03) 9818 8099 **F** (03) 9818 8299 **www**.macforbes.com **Open** Not
Winemaker Mac Forbes **Est.** 2004 **Cases** 3000
Mac Forbes cut his vinous teeth at Mount Mary, where he was winemaker for several years before heading overseas in 2002. He spent 2 years in London working for Southcorp in a marketing liaison role, before heading to Portugal and Austria to gain further winemaking experience. He returned to the Yarra Valley prior to the '05 vintage, purchasing grapes for the 2-tier portfolio: first, the Victorian range (employing unusual varieties or unusual winemaking techniques) and, second, the Yarra Valley range of multiple terroir-based offerings of Chardonnay and Pinot Noir.

🍷🍷🍷🍷🍷 **Woori Yallock Pinot Noir 2005** In similar style to the Coldstream, showing some whole-bunch characters; slightly more fruit weight and length, with beguiling spicy/savoury nuances to the core of plum fruit. Beautiful wine. Screwcap. 13.5° alc. **Rating** 95 **To** 2016 $44
Woori Yallock Chardonnay 2005 While still classic Yarra in terms of fruit flavour and length, has an added layer of barrel ferment oak neatly built into the wine; excellent length. Screwcap. 13.5° alc. **Rating** 94 **To** 2020 $32

🍷🍷🍷🍷🍷 **Coldstream Pinot Noir 2005** Best colour of the 3 pinots, though not by much; spotlessly clean and balanced, with great purity of line and length. Not for lovers of Barossa shiraz. Screwcap. 13.5° alc. **Rating** 93 **To** 2012 $35

Coldstream Chardonnay 2005 Classic light to medium-bodied Yarra chardonnay; melon and stone fruit run through to a long finish with appealing squeaky acidity; oak irrelevant. Screwcap. 13° alc. **Rating** 92 **To** 2015 $24

Yarra Valley Pinot Noir 2005 A pretty wine, seemingly effortlessly achieved; brightly flavoured red fruits, with good line and balance; made with a gentle touch. Screwcap. 14° alc. **Rating** 92 **To** 2012 $28

Hugh Cabernet Sauvignon 2005 Relatively light hue; despite the low alcohol and light to medium-bodied weight, avoids green characters on the long, taught palate; for the serious, not the frivolous. Screwcap. 12.5° alc. **Rating** 91 **To** 2020 $38

RS16 Strathbogie Ranges Riesling 2006 Clean bouquet; in off-dry Kabinett/Mosel style; well-balanced sugar and acidity; 16 g/l residual sugar. Screwcap. 9° alc. **Rating** 90 **To** 2011 $23

Yarra Valley Rose 2006 An ultra-fresh bouquet of strawberries and cherries; delicate, perfectly balanced palate. Screwcap. 13° alc. **Rating** 90 **To** 2008 $18

 Moonambel Syrah 2005 Fresh, bright predominantly red fruits; a touch of spice, but not really enough depth for a wine coming from Moonambel. Screwcap. 13.5° alc. **Rating** 89 **To** 2011 $27

Macquariedale Estate ★★★☆

170 Sweetwater Road, Rothbury, NSW 2335 **Region** Lower Hunter Valley
T (02) 6574 7012 **www**.macquariedale.com.au **Open** Fri–Mon, school & public hols 10–5
Winemaker Ross McDonald **Est.** 1993 **Cases** 4000
Macquariedale is an acorn to oak story, beginning with a small hobby vineyard in Branxton many years ago, and now extending to 3 certified organic (in conversion) vineyards around the Lower Hunter with a total 13 ha of semillon, chardonnay, pinot noir, shiraz, merlot, mataro and cabernet sauvignon. This has led to Ross McDonald (and his family) leaving a busy Sydney life to be full-time grapegrower and winemaker. Exports to the US, Canada and Japan.

 Hunter Valley Unwooded Chardonnay 2004 Bright, pale green-straw; relatively early picking gives the wine brightness and zest in an overall citrus frame, stone fruit making a belated appearance on the finish. Excellent example of unwooded chardonnay from a region not really suited for this style. Screwcap. 13° alc. **Rating** 88 **To** 2009 $15

Hunter Valley Chardonnay 2006 A big, soft peachy wine; controlled oak and good balance. **Rating** 87 **To** 2008

Matthew Hunter Valley Merlot 2005 Light- to medium-bodied; a mix of red fruits, with some notes of green olive; achieves greater varietal character than most from the Hunter. Cork. 13° alc. **Rating** 87 **To** 2011 $22

Mad Dog Wines ★★★★☆

7a Murray Street, Tanunda, SA 5352 (postal) **Region** Barossa Valley
T (08) 8563 1551 **F** (08) 8563 0754 **Open** Not
Winemaker Jeremy Holmes **Est.** 1999 **Cases** 500
Geoff (aka Mad Dog) Munzberg is a third-generation grapegrower who has joined with Jeremy and Heidi Holmes, Aaron and Kirsty Brasher and son Matthew to create Mad Dog Wines. The principal wine, Shiraz, comes from 5 ha of vines with an average age of 35 years. The major portion of the grapes are sold, the best kept for the Mad Dog label. The acquisition of a neighbouring vineyard in 2006 has led to the inclusion of some 100-year-old vine fruit, and the range will be slightly extended with small quantities of Moscato and a few bottles of Sangiovese. Exports to the UK and US.

Maglieri of McLaren Vale ★★★★☆

Douglas Gully Road, McLaren Flat, SA 5171 **Region** McLaren Vale
T (08) 8383 0177 **www**.maglieri.com.au **Open** Mon–Sat 9–4, Sun 12–4
Winemaker Alex Mackenzie **Est.** 1972 **Cases** 10 000

Was one of the better-kept secrets among the wine cognoscenti, but not among the many customers who drink thousands of cases of white and red Lambrusco every year, an example of niche marketing at its profitable best. It was a formula which proved irresistible to Beringer Blass, which acquired Maglieri in 1999. Its dry red wines are invariably generously proportioned and full of character, the Shiraz particularly so.

ŶŶŶŶŶ **Shiraz 2005** Dense, almost viscous palate, laden with blackberry, bitter chocolate and licorice; the finish is surprisingly balanced, and not over the top. Cork. 15° alc. **Rating** 93 **To** 2028 $21.95

Magpie Estate ★★★★☆

PO Box 126, Tanunda, SA 5352 **Region** Barossa Valley
T (08) 8562 3300 **F** (08) 8562 1177 **Open** Not
Winemaker Rolf Binder, Noel Young **Est.** 1993 **Cases** 6000
This is a partnership between Rolf Binder and Cambridge (England) wine merchant Noel Young. It came about in 1993 when there was limited demand for or understanding of Southern Rhône-style blends based on shiraz, grenache and mourvedre. Initially a small, export-only brand, the quality of the wines was such that it has grown substantially over the years, although the intention is to limit production. The majority of the wines are very reasonably priced, the super-premiums (The Gomersal Grenache and The Election Shiraz) are more expensive. The labelling is strongly reminiscent of Torbreck and other subsequent ventures, but the quality of the wine needs no assistance. Exports to the UK, the US and other major markets.

ŶŶŶŶŶ **The Election Barossa Valley Shiraz 2004** Deep colour; hyper-intense and ripe, suggesting far higher alcohol than is in fact the case, with flavours of prunes, plums and confit fruit and licorice; has swallowed up 22 months in French and American oak. High-quality cork. 14.5° alc. **Rating** 91 **To** 2024

 # Magpie Springs ★★★★

RSD 1790 Meadows Road, Hope Forest, SA 5172 **Region** Adelaide Hills
T (08) 8556 7351 **www**.magpiesprings.com.au **Open** Fri–Sun & public hols 10–5
Winemaker James Hastwell, Reg Wilkinson **Est.** 1991 **Cases** 1000
Stuart Brown and Rosemary (Roe) Gartelmann purchased the property on which Magpie Springs is now established in 1983, growing flowers commercially and grazing cattle. Chardonnay was planted experimentally, and were among the earliest vines in the area. In 1991 the commencement of the vineyard proper led to the planting of a little over 16 ha of semillon, chardonnay, sauvignon blanc, riesling, shiraz, pinot noir and merlot. Roe Gartelmann began painting professionally from the Magpie Springs studio in the late 1980s, and many classes and workshops have been held over the years. Her studio can be visited during cellar door hours.

ŶŶŶŶŶ **Adelaide Hills Riesling 2004** Still very pale; tight citrus, herb and mineral aromas and flavours, but fractionally dull. One can only imagine what a screwcap might have revealed. Twin top. 12° alc. **Rating** 91 **To** 2009 $18
Lenore Adelaide Hills Chardonnay 2004 Light to medium yellow-green; gentle fig, melon and stone fruit flavours; good texture and controlled oak handling. Twin top. 13.5° alc. **Rating** 90 **To** 2008 $22

ŶŶŶŶ **Adelaide Hills Merlot 2004** Light-bodied; does show clear varietal character, albeit on a slightly diminished scale; tangy fruit and a long finish. Screwcap. 14° alc. **Rating** 87 **To** 2008 $16

Main Ridge Estate ★★★★★

80 William Road, Red Hill, Vic 3937 **Region** Mornington Peninsula
T (03) 5989 2686 **F** (03) 5931 0000 **www**.mre.com.au **Open** Mon–Fri 12–4, w'ends 12–5
Winemaker Nat White **Est.** 1975 **Cases** 1200

Nat White gives meticulous attention to every aspect of his viticulture and winemaking, doing annual battle with one of the coolest sites on the Peninsula. The same attention to detail extends to the winery and the winemaking. Despite such minuscule production, exports to the UK and Singapore.

ҮҮҮҮҮ **Mornington Peninsula Chardonnay 2005** A full-bodied chardonnay flooded with character; stone fruit, melon, fig, barrel ferment and mlf all making major contributions. Screwcap. 14° alc. **Rating** 94 **To** 2014 $50

Half Acre Mornington Peninsula Pinot Noir 2004 Has fulfilled the promise it showed as a very young wine, with a savoury, spicy overlay to the array of small, red fruits of the palate; controlled oak. Screwcap. 14° alc. **Rating** 94 **To** 2011 $48

Majella ★★★★★

Lynn Road, Coonawarra, SA 5263 **Region** Coonawarra
T (08) 8736 3055 **F** (08) 8736 3057 **www**.majellawines.com.au **Open** 7 days 10–4.30
Winemaker Bruce Gregory **Est.** 1969 **Cases** 15 000
Majella is one of the foremost grapegrowers in Coonawarra, with 61 ha of vineyard, principally shiraz and cabernet sauvignon, and with a little riesling and merlot. The Malleea is one of Coonawarra's best wines, The Musician one of Australia's most outstanding red wines selling for less than $20. Exports to the UK, the US and other major markets.

ҮҮҮҮҮ **Coonawarra Cabernet Sauvignon 2004** A delicious wine, with an abundance of blackcurrant and cassis fruit, supple mouthfeel and tannins; plenty of depth. Screwcap. 14.5° alc. **Rating** 95 **To** 2025 $28

The Malleea 2003 A potent, intense wine with black fruit aromas, and some spice; very good structure; persistent but integrated and fine tannins. Cork. 14° alc. **Rating** 95 **To** 2028 $66

The Musician Coonawarra Cabernet Shiraz 2005 Supple, smooth and classy blackcurrant and blackberry mix; excellent touch of oak. Trophy Limestone Coast Wine Show '06. Phenomenal value. Screwcap. 14° alc. **Rating** 94 **To** 2020 $17

ҮҮҮҮҮ **Coonawarra Merlot 2004** Medium red-purple; very different to the Katnook style, with riper cassis-like notes, but still within varietal bounds, in part due to touches of green olive and earth. Screwcap. 13.5° alc. **Rating** 92 **To** 2015 $28

Coonawarra Riesling 2006 A herb, mineral and apple blossom mix on the bouquet, the lively and fresh palate a reprise; good length. Screwcap. 12° alc. **Rating** 91 **To** 2016 $16

ҮҮҮҮ **Coonawarra Shiraz 2004** Strong, clear red-purple; blackberry, black plum and cherry fruit; touches of spice, supple tannins and good oak. Screwcap. 14° alc. **Rating** 89 **To** 2024 $28

Majors Lane Wines ★★★★☆

64 Majors Lane, Lovedale, NSW 2320 **Region** Lower Hunter Valley
T (02) 4930 7328 **F** (02) 4930 7023 **www**.majorslane.com **Open** Fri–Mon 9.30–5
Winemaker Alasdair Sutherland (white), David Hook (red) **Est.** 1987 **Cases** NFP
Sydney lawyers Ivan and Susan Judd, specialising in contract and industrial law, purchased the Majors Lane vineyard in 2001. Fourteen years earlier Alan and Rosemary MacMillan had planted 3 ha each of semillon, chardonnay and shiraz, plus 1 ha of chambourcin, adding 700 olive trees a decade later. Susan Judd has retired from legal practice to run the cellar door and help in the restaurant, with husband Ivan commuting to and from Sydney.

ҮҮҮҮҮ **Semillon 2005** A fresh, slatey bouquet leads into a tightly focused, lemon-accented palate, the long finish and lingering aftertaste revolving around bright acidity. Screwcap. 10.3° alc. **Rating** 93 **To** 2015 $17

Chardonnay 2005 Unambiguously good wine; plenty of depth and concentration to the fig and melon fruit; subtle barrel ferment oak infusion helps the texture; finishes with good acidity. Screwcap. 13° alc. **Rating** 91 To 2009 $21

ȚȚȚȚ   Oliver Shiraz 2005 An elegant wine reflecting its relatively low alcohol; spicy, earthy regional nuances. Screwcap. 12° alc. **Rating** 88 To 2010 $21

Malcolm Creek Vineyard

Bonython Road, Kersbrook, SA 5231 **Region** Adelaide Hills
T (08) 8389 3235 **F** (08) 8389 3235 **www**.malcolmcreekwines.com.au **Open** W'ends & public hols 11–5, or by appt
Winemaker Reg Tolley **Est.** 1982 **Cases** 700
Malcolm Creek is the retirement venture of Reg Tolley, and he keeps a low profile. However, the wines are invariably well-made and develop gracefully; they are worth seeking out, and are usually available with some extra bottle age at a very modest price. Exports to the UK.

ȚȚȚȚȚ   Adelaide Hills Cabernet Sauvignon 2004 Ripe and supple, with pure blackcurrant/cassis fruit and silky tannins. Best for some years. Screwcap. 13.5° alc. **Rating** 94 To 2024 $20

Mandurang Valley Wines   ★★★★☆

77 Fadersons Lane, Mandurang, Vic 3551 **Region** Bendigo
T (03) 5439 5367 **www**.mandurangvalleywines.com.au **Open** Fri–Tues 11–5
Winemaker Wes Vine, Steve Vine **Est.** 1994 **Cases** 2300
Wes and Pamela Vine planted their first vineyard at Mandurang in 1976 and started making wine as a hobby. Commercial production began in 1993, and an additional vineyard was established in 1997. Wes (a former school principal) has been full-time winemaker since 1999, with son Steve becoming more involved each vintage, the two now forming a formidable marketing team.

ȚȚȚȚȚ   Bendigo Shiraz 2004 Fragrant and sweet, but not jammy, fruit; spicy, peppery cool climate components. Screwcap. 14.2° alc. **Rating** 90 To 2014 $22
Bendigo Shiraz 2003 Riper and richer than the '04, with plum and blackberry fruit; good length and tannins; an altogether different style. Screwcap. 14.6° alc. **Rating** 90 To 2015 $22
Old Vine 2003 Consistently with the other wines, more weight and richness than the '04, but also more tannin structure, bordering on toughness. Cabernet Sauvignon/Shiraz/Merlot. Screwcap. 14.6° alc. **Rating** 90 To 2015 $30

ȚȚȚȚ   Old Vine 2004 Hazy colour; distinctly in the earthy/leafy/briary spectrum, but there are notes of sweet berry fruit to be found. Cabernet Sauvignon/Shiraz/Merlot. Screwcap. 14.1° alc. **Rating** 89 To 2014 $30
Bendigo Cabernet Sauvignon 2003 Medium-bodied; riper than the '04, though the drought doesn't always mean this occurs; still has some slight notes of green tannins. Screwcap. 14.5° alc. **Rating** 88 To 2015 $22
Bendigo Riesling 2005 A clean, but not particularly expressive bouquet; the light-bodied palate has gentle apple and citrus flavours, the finish slightly hard. Screwcap. 12.5° alc. **Rating** 87 To 2010 $18
Bendigo Cabernet Sauvignon 2004 Light- to medium-bodied; fresh, but with some olive/green/mint aspects to the blackcurrant fruit; moderate tannins. Screwcap. 14° alc. **Rating** 87 To 2014 $22

Mansfield Wines

204 Eurunderee Lane, Mudgee, NSW 2850 **Region** Mudgee
T (02) 6373 3871 **F** (02) 6373 3708 **Open** Thurs–Tues & public hols 10–5, or by appt
Winemaker Bob Heslop **Est.** 1975 **Cases** 2000

Mansfield Wines has moved with the times, moving the emphasis from fortified wines to table wines (though still offering some fortifieds) and expanding the product range to take in new generation reds such as Touriga and Zinfandel.

ŸŸŸŸŸ **Touriga 2005** Attractive wine; multi-berry fruit flavours in a rounded palate; the oak and tannins are positive, but do not threaten the fruit expression. Diam. 13.5° alc. **Rating** 90 **To** 2014 $18

ŸŸŸŸ **Merlot 2005** A ripe, medium-bodied wine with plenty of blackcurrant fruit, the merlot varietal character almost inevitably suppressed. Diam. 14° alc. **Rating** 87 **To** 2012 $18

Mantons Creek Vineyard ★★★★

240 Tucks Road, Main Ridge, Vic 3928 **Region** Mornington Peninsula
T (03) 5989 6264 **F** (03) 5989 6348 **www.**mantonscreekvineyard.com.au **Open** 7 days 11–5
Winemaker Alex White (Contract) **Est.** 1990 **Cases** 3500
The 19-ha property was originally an orchard, herb farm and horse stud. After the vineyard was established, the grapes were sold to other wineries in the region until 1998, when the first Mantons Creek wines were made from the 10-ha vineyard planted in 1994. The property was purchased by Dr Michael Ablett, a retired cardiologist, and his wife Judy in 2001. Exports to Hong Kong and Japan.

Margan Family ★★★★

1238 Milbrodale Road, Broke, NSW 2330 **Region** Lower Hunter Valley
T (02) 6579 1317 **F** (02) 6579 1267 **www.**margan.com.au **Open** 7 days 10–5
Winemaker Andrew Margan **Est.** 1997 **Cases** 30 000
Andrew Margan followed in his father's footsteps by entering the wine industry over 20 years ago and has covered a great deal of territory since, working as a Flying Winemaker in Europe, then for Tyrrell's. Andrew and wife Lisa now have over 80 ha of fully yielding vines at their Ceres Hill property at Broke, and lease the nearby Vere Vineyard. Wine quality, is consistently good. Exports to the UK, the US and other major markets.

ŸŸŸŸŸ **White Label Hunter Valley Shiraz 2005** Extremely powerful black fruits; masses of flavour; heroically built for the long haul. Screwcap. 14.5° alc. **Rating** 90 **To** 2025 $30

ŸŸŸŸ **Hunter Valley Botrytis Semillon 2006** Very rich cumquat and marmalade flavours; a touch more acidity might have made a great wine. Screwcap. 10.5° alc. **Rating** 88 **To** 2008 $25

Marienberg ★★★★

2 Chalk Hill Road, McLaren Vale, SA 5171 **Region** McLaren Vale
T (08) 8323 9666 **F** (08) 8323 9600 **Open** 7 days 10–5
Winemaker Peter Orr **Est.** 1966 **Cases** 25 000
A long-established business (founded by Australia's first female owner/vigneron, Ursula Pridham) acquired by James Estate in 2003. Exports to Canada, Guam, Switzerland, Tonga, Singapore and Fiji.

ŸŸŸŸŸ **Clifton Cabernet Sauvignon 2004** Medium-bodied; good cabernet sauvignon varietal expression, fruit and tannins well-integrated and balanced, as is the oak; good acidity provides the length. Cork. **Rating** 90 **To** 2014 $30

ŸŸŸŸ **Reserve Chardonnay 2006** Nectarine, stone fruit and a touch of citrus; well-handled oak is not too assertive. Screwcap. 13.5° alc. **Rating** 89 **To** 2010 $20
Reserve Cabernet Sauvignon 2004 Solid blackberry/earthy fruit with a touch of chocolate and savoury tannins; minimal oak influence. Twin top. **Rating** 88 **To** 2011 $22

Reserve Shiraz 2004 A pleasant, light- to medium-bodied wine, the fruit unable to withstand the challenge of the American oak. Cork. 14° alc. **Rating** 87 **To** 2011 $22

Marinda Park Vineyard   ★★★★☆

238 Myers Road, Balnarring, Vic 3926 **Region** Mornington Peninsula
T (03) 5989 7613 www.marindapark.com **Open** Thurs–Mon 11–5, 7 days in Jan
Winemaker Sandro Mosele (Contract) **Est.** 1999 **Cases** 2000
Mark and Belinda Rodman have established 18.7 ha of chardonnay, sauvignon blanc, pinot noir and merlot on their vineyard on the outskirts of Balnarring. They operate the business in conjunction with American partners Norm and Fanny Winton.

ΨΨΨΨΨ **Mornington Peninsula Chardonnay 2005** Excellent length and intensity; fine nectarine and grapefruit flavours seamlessly woven with oak; good acidity and length. Diam. 13.5° alc. **Rating** 94 **To** 2013 $25

ΨΨΨΨΨ **Mornington Peninsula Chardonnay 2004** Developing slowly; the same balance and structure as in the '05, but less intense; still very good. Diam. 13.6° alc. **Rating** 92 **To** 2011 $25
Mornington Peninsula Pinot Noir 2005 Vivid colour; a light- to medium-bodied, stemmy/earthy style; considerable length, though doesn't go out of its way to charm. Diam. 13.5° alc. **Rating** 91 **To** 2010 $38
Mornington Peninsula Sauvignon Blanc 2006 No reduction on the clear bouquet; a powerful, multi-flavoured wine, with some of the many flavours tending to fall over each other; wild yeast and barrel ferment characters are outside the mainstream, but none the worse for that. Diam. 13.5° alc. **Rating** 90 **To** 2009 $21

ΨΨΨΨ **Mornington Peninsula Rose 2006** Lively, fresh and long; driven by crisp acidity rather than sugar; abundant cherry and strawberry flavours. Diam. 13.5° alc. **Rating** 89 **To** 2008 $19
Mornington Peninsula Merlot 2004 Fresh, lively/minty/leafy/red berry fruits; typical of the Peninsula at its best for this variety. Cork. **Rating** 89 **To** 2014 $26

Maritime Estate   ★★★★☆

Tucks Road, Red Hill, Vic 3937 **Region** Mornington Peninsula
T (03) 9848 2926 **Open** W'ends & public hols 11–5, 7 days Dec 27–Jan 26
Winemaker Sandro Mosele **Est.** 1988 **Cases** 1000
John and Linda Ruljancich and Kevin Ruljancich have enjoyed great success since their first vintage in 1994, no doubt due in part to skilled winemaking but also to the situation of their vineyard, looking across the hills and valleys of the Red Hill subregion.

ΨΨΨΨΨ **HS Mornington Peninsula Pinot Noir 2005** A long, intense and quite racy palate; black cherry, spice and a touch of forest floor. Cork. 13.7° alc. **Rating** 94 **To** 2012 $40

ΨΨΨΨΨ **JR Mornington Peninsula Chardonnay 2005** Some colour change raises the proverbial eyebrow; this to one side, the wine has plenty of focus and power to the nectarine and grapefruit flavours of the long palate; fruit is the major influence, oak distinctly less. Diam. 13.8° alc. **Rating** 90 **To** 2012 $33

Marius Wines   ★★★★☆

PO Box 545, Willunga, SA 5172 **Region** McLaren Vale
T 0402 344 340 **F** (08) 8556 4839 www.mariuswines.com.au **Open** Not
Winemaker Mark Day **Est.** 1994 **Cases** 800
Roger Pike says he has loved wine for over 30 years; that for 15 years he has had the desire to add a little bit to the world of wine; and that over a decade ago he decided to do something about it, ripping the front paddock and planting 1.6 ha of shiraz in 1994. He sold the grapes from the

1997–99 vintages, but when the 1998 vintage became a single-vineyard wine (made by the purchaser of the grapes) selling in the US at $40, the temptation to have his own wine became irresistible. Exports to the US and Denmark.

ΨΨΨΨΨ Symphony Single Vineyard McLaren Vale Shiraz 2004 Medium-to full-bodied; dense, succulent, ripe blackberry fruit and dark chocolate; excellent oak balance and integration; good tannins. A special selection from the 1.8-ha home block vineyard which provides both single vineyard wines. Screwcap. 14.5° alc. **Rating** 94 **To** 2019 $35

ΨΨΨΨΨ Symposium McLaren Vale Shiraz Mourvedre 2005 Medium red-purple; an attractive blend, the shiraz providing the structure and an important part of the quite complex flavours; spice, blackberry, cherry and licorice running through to a long finish. A 50/50 blend. Screwcap. 14.5° alc. **Rating** 93 **To** 2018 $29
Simpatico Single Vineyard McLaren Vale Shiraz 2004 Medium-bodied; black and red fruits, with some regional chocolate; fine tannins. Screwcap. 14.5° alc. **Rating** 90 **To** 2012 $25

Marlargo Wines

PO Box 371, Glenside, SA 5065 **Region** Warehouse
T 0438 987 255 **F** (08) 8379 0596 **www**.marlargowines.com **Open** Not
Winemaker Various contract **Est.** 2003 **Cases** 3000
This is the ultimate virtual winery, with virtual homes in Yarra Glen, McLaren Vale, Adelaide Hills and the Clare Valley. Each of the garishly-labelled wines is contract-made by a different winemaker at a different winery, and the range is being extended further. The partners in the venture are Simon Austerberry, a sixth-generation farmer in the Pyrenees, and Mark Gibbs, a financial adviser from Melbourne. I'm far from convinced by the labels and purple prose (the Latina Cabernet says 'be seduced … sultry, seductive, sensual' and assures us the wine is matured in 'charismatic oak'). Both prices and production volume aspirations have been significantly – and sensibly – reduced. Exports to the US, Canada and Singapore.

ΨΨΨΨΨ Bolero Riesling 2006 Lime and herb aromas; well-made, with excellent tension on the palate blending citrussy fruit with minerally acidity. Clare Valley. Screwcap. 11.4° alc. **Rating** 91 **To** 2014 $19.95

ΨΨΨΨ Simple Pleasures Sauvignon Blanc 2006 Very crisp and crunchy; all about structure, with little to say (yet) on the fruit side. Nonetheless, very fresh in the mouth. Adelaide Hills. Screwcap. 12.9° alc. **Rating** 89 **To** 2008 $21
Gypsy Spirit Chardonnay 2006 An elegant, light- to medium-bodied palate with typical Yarra Valley length, but achieved sotto voce; melon, nectarine and white peach with no evident sign of oak. Screwcap. 13.8° alc. **Rating** 89 **To** 2010 $21
Temptation Rose 2006 Most purchasers will assume it's sweet, when it's not; good length, though not so much depth. McLaren Vale. Screwcap. 12.5° alc. **Rating** 87 **To** 2008 $18

Marri Wood Park

Cnr Caves Road/Whittle Road, Yallingup, WA 6282 **Region** Margaret River
T 0438 525 580 **F** (08) 9386 5087 **www**.marriwoodpark.com.au **Open** Thurs–Sun 11–5
Winemaker Di Miller, Ian Bell **Est.** 1993 **Cases** 2000
With plantings commencing in 1993, Marri Wood Park has 7 ha of vineyards: 1.6 ha semillon and 1.7 each of sauvignon blanc and cabernet sauvignon; part of the grape production is sold to other makers. The budget-priced Guinea Run range takes its name from the guinea fowl which are permanent vineyard residents, busily eating the grasshoppers, weevils and bugs which cluster around the base of the vines, thus reducing the need for pesticides. The premium Marri Wood Park range takes its name from the giant Marri gum tree depicted on the label.

ΨΨΨΨΨ Margaret River Sauvignon Blanc 2006 Piercing, pungent asparagus and cut grass aromas and flavours; no mistaking the variety, although it is at one end of the spectrum of sauvignon blanc. Screwcap. 13° alc. **Rating** 91 **To** 2010 $18

Margaret River Semillon Sauvignon Blanc 2006 Curiously, this wine is fractionally softer with slightly sweeter fruit flavours; difficult to know whether it is the semillon, or the selection of the sauvignon blanc component. Screwcap. 13° alc. **Rating** 91 **To** 2011 $18

Marribrook

5 Tudor Avenue, Shelley, WA 6148 **Region** Mount Barker
T (08) 9457 9959 **F** (08) 9457 9959 **Open** Not
Winemaker Harewood Estate (James Kellie) **Est.** 1990 **Cases** 1000
The Brooks family purchased the former Marron View 5.6-ha vineyard from Kim Hart in 1994 and renamed the venture Marribrook Wines; they have also purchased an additional property north of Mount Barker and immediately south of Gilberts. Exports to the UK and Singapore.

ΨΨΨΨ **Frankland River Cabernet Malbec Merlot 2005** Medium to full red-purple; youthful, still firm and closed, though there is an array of red and black fruits waiting to express themselves; balanced oak; simply needs time. Screwcap. 14.5° alc. **Rating** 89 **To** 2015 $20

Marschall Groom Cellars

28 Langmeil Road, Tanunda, SA 5352 (postal) **Region** Barossa Valley
T (08) 8563 1101 **F** (08) 8563 1102 **www**.groomwines.com **Open** Not
Winemaker Daryl Groom **Est.** 1997 **Cases** 3500
This is a family venture involving Daryl Groom, former Penfolds but now long-term Geyser Peak winemaker in California, Jeannette Marschall and David Marschall. It is an export-focused business, the principal market being the US.

ΨΨΨΨΨ **Barossa Valley Shiraz 2005** Rich blackberry, plum, licorice and a touch of spice; oak and tannin management spot-on. Cork. 14.4° alc. **Rating** 95 **To** 2020 $48

ΨΨΨΨ♀ **Adelaide Hills Sauvignon Blanc 2006** No hint of sweatiness or reduction; a pleasing array of citrus, passionfruit and gooseberry; good length and intensity. Screwcap. 12.8° alc. **Rating** 93 **To** 2009 $24

Marsh Estate

Deasy's Road, Pokolbin, NSW 2321 **Region** Lower Hunter Valley
T (02) 4998 7587 **F** (02) 4998 7884 **Open** Mon–Fri 10–4.30, w'ends 10–5
Winemaker Andrew Marsh **Est.** 1971 **Cases** 6000
Through sheer consistency, value for money and unrelenting hard work, the Marsh family (who purchased the former Quentin Estate in 1978) has built up a sufficiently loyal cellar door and mailing list clientele to allow all the considerable production to be sold direct. Wine style is always direct, with oak playing a minimal role, and prolonged cellaring paying handsome dividends.

ΨΨΨΨ♀ **Private Bin Shiraz 2005** Immediately proclaims its regional origin, and also its moderate alcohol; spice, earth and leather on bright red fruits; has particularly good line and length. Cork. 12° alc. **Rating** 91 **To** 2015 $36.50

ΨΨΨΨ **Holly's Block Semillon 2006** Intense aromas of herb and lemon essence/lemon oil; the palate is softer than the bouquet suggests, full in the mouth, reflecting the late-picked style. Cork. 12° alc. **Rating** 88 **To** 2011 $27.50

Mason Wines

★★★☆

27850 New England Highway, Glen Aplin, Qld 4381 **Region** Granite Belt
T (07) 4684 1341 **F** (07) 4684 1342 **www**.masonwines.com.au **Open** 7 days 11–4
Winemaker Jim Barnes **Est.** 1998 **Cases** 2500

Robert and Kim Mason set strict criteria when searching for land suited to viticulture: a long history of commercial stone fruit production with well-drained, deep soil. The first property was purchased in 1997, the vines planted thereafter. A second orchard was purchased in 2000, and a cellar door was constructed. They have planted 25 ha of chardonnay, verdelho, sauvignon blanc, viognier, semillon, cabernet sauvignon, shiraz, merlot and petit verdot. The wines are released under 2 labels: Rees Road for the top-of-the-range wines, and Booth Lane for slightly cheaper offerings, although the choice of names does not necessarily reflect the vineyard origin. Yet another Qlder on the ascendant.

 TTTTT **Rees Road Granite Belt Shiraz 2005** Strong purple-red; medium-bodied blackberry fruit supported by fine tannins and oak; good length and mouthfeel. Screwcap. 13.5° alc. **Rating** 90 **To** 2012 $20

TTTT **Rees Road Granite Belt Merlot 2005** Surprising weight and varietal character; does have some green olive edges to the tannins, but nonetheless impressive for the region. Screwcap. 13.5° alc. **Rating** 88 **To** 2013 $16
Rees Road Granite Belt Shiraz 2004 Holding good hue; light to medium-bodied, with some green leaf/earth notes to the mainframe of blackberry fruit; brisk finish. Screwcap. 13.5° alc. **Rating** 87 **To** 2015 $20

Massena Vineyards ★★★★★

PO Box 54, Tanunda, SA 5352 **Region** Barossa Valley
T (08) 8564 3037 **F** (08) 8564 3038 **www**.massena.com.au **Open** By appt
Winemaker Dan Standish, Jaysen Collins **Est.** 2000 **Cases** 3000
Massena Vineyards draws upon 4 ha of grenache, shiraz, mourvedre, durif and tinta amarella at Nuriootpa. It is an export-oriented business although the wines can be purchased by mail order, which, given both the quality and innovative nature of the wines, seems more than ordinarily worthwhile. Exports to the UK, the US and other major markets.

TTTTT **The Eleventh Hour Barossa Valley Shiraz 2004** Medium-bodied; rounded, supple blackberry fruit; positive but integrated and balanced oak; overall elegance. Cork. 14.5° alc. **Rating** 94 **To** 2019 $32
The Moonlight Run 2004 Offers so much more than the usual Barossa Valley blend of these varieties; rich, but not the least jammy; an array of black and red fruits, ripe tannins and good oak. Grenache/Shiraz/Mataro/Cinsaut. Cork. 14.5° alc. **Rating** 94 **To** 2015 $25

TTTTT **The Howling Dog Barossa Valley Durif 2004** Typical impenetrable purple, even after 3 years in bottle; a massive wine in typical monolithic fashion, Chambourcin on steroids. Should I give a best-by date of 2014 or 2034? I don't know. Cork. 14.5° alc. **Rating** 90 **To** 2024 $35

TTTT **Barossa Valley Barbera Dolcetto 2005** On the face of it, has more convention than the shiraz dolcetto blend developed by Peter Lehmann so many years ago; the blend gives a softer palate and elevated fruit flavours, but not a lot of structure; for the Italian wine buffs. Cork. 14.5° alc. **Rating** 89 **To** 2012 $23

Matilda's Estate ★★★★☆

RMB 654 Hamilton Road, Denmark, WA 6333 **Region** Denmark
T (08) 9848 1951 **F** (08) 9848 1957 **www**.matildasestate.com **Open** Tues–Sun 10–5,
7 days during school hols
Winemaker Gavin Berry, Dave Cleary **Est.** 1990 **Cases** 4500
In 2003 the founders of Matilda's Meadow (as it was then known), Don Turnbull and Pamela Meldrum, sold the business to former citizen of the world Steve Hall. It is a thriving business based on 10 ha of estate plantings of chardonnay, semillon, sauvignon blanc, pinot noir, cabernet sauvignon, cabernet franc, merlot and shiraz.

Maximilian's Vineyard

Main Road, Verdun, SA 5245 **Region** Adelaide Hills
T (08) 8388 7777 **www**.maximilians.com.au **Open** Wed–Sun & public hols Mon
Winemaker Grant Burge, Paul Hruska **Est.** 1994 **Cases** 2500
Maximilian and Louise Hruska opened Maximilian's Restaurant in 1976 in a homestead built in 1851, and planted 2 ha of chardonnay and 6 ha of cabernet sauvignon in 1994, surrounding the restaurant. The Cabernet Sauvignon is made by Grant Burge, the Chardonnay at Scarpantoni Estate under the direction of the Hruskas' eldest son, Paul. Since graduating from Roseworthy, Paul Hruska has completed vintages in Burgundy, Bordeaux, Spain, Margaret River and the Clare Valley; he was winemaker/vineyard manager at The Islander on Kangaroo Island.

Maxwell Wines

Olivers Road, McLaren Vale, SA 5171 **Region** McLaren Vale
T (08) 8323 8200 **F** (08) 8323 8900 **www**.maxwellwines.com.au **Open** 7 days 10–5
Winemaker Mark Maxwell, Elena Golakova **Est.** 1979 **Cases** 12 000
Maxwell Wines has come a long way since opening for business in 1979 using an amazing array of Heath Robinson equipment in cramped surroundings. A state-of-the-art and much larger winery was built in 1997. The brand has produced some excellent white and red wines in recent years; it is also sourcing grapes from Kangaroo Island. Exports to all major markets.

ΨΨΨΨΨ **First Colony Kangaroo Island Shiraz 2004** Has no shortage of flavour, but also has elegance; spicy/peppery black cherries and plums; fine tannins, good length. Screwcap. 14.5° alc. **Rating** 93 **To** 2024 $25
Little Demon McLaren Vale Cabernet Merlot 2004 Medium-bodied, with a very strong regional overlay of dark chocolate fruit to the spicy red and blackcurrant core; fine tannins; typical for the top '04 vintage. Screwcap. 14.5° alc. **Rating** 90 **To** 2014 $19

Mayer

66 Miller Road, Healesville, Vic 3777 **Region** Yarra Valley
T (03) 5967 3779 **Open** By appt
Winemaker Timo Mayer **Est.** 1999 **Cases** 700
Timo Mayer, also winemaker at Gembrook Hill Vineyard, teamed with partner Rhonda Ferguson to establish Mayer Vineyard on the slopes of Mt Toolebewoong, 8 km south of Healesville. The steepness of those slopes is presumably self-apparent from the name given to the wines (Bloody Hill). There is just under 2.5 ha of vineyard, the lion's share to pinot noir, and smaller amounts of shiraz and chardonnay – all high-density plantings. Mayer's winemaking credo is minimal interference and handling, and no filtration.

ΨΨΨΨΨ **Big Betty Yarra Valley Shiraz 2005** Fragrant, aromatic cherry fruit; a supple and smooth palate, with beautifully integrated fruit, oak and tannins; totally delicious. Diam. 14.2° alc. **Rating** 95 **To** 2015 $25

ΨΨΨΨΨ **Bloody Hill Yarra Valley Chardonnay 2005** Fine, elegant and intense, with all the length for which Yarra Valley chardonnay is known; citrus, nectarine and melon, oak incidental. Diam. 13.2° alc. **Rating** 93 **To** 2015 $25
Bloody Hill Yarra Valley Pinot Noir 2005 Light, bright and clear colour; similarly bright and direct cherry and plum fruit; pure and uncomplicated pinot. Diam. 13.2° alc. **Rating** 91 **To** 2010 $25

Mayfield Vineyard

Icely Road, Orange, NSW 2800 **Region** Orange
T (02) 6365 9295 **www**.mayfieldvineyard.com **Open** Thurs–Sun 10–5, or by appt
Winemaker Jon Reynolds (Contract) **Est.** 1998 **Cases** 10 000
The property – including the house in which owners Richard and Kathy Thomas now live, and its surrounding arboretum – has a rich history as a leading Suffolk sheep stud, founded upon the

vast fortune accumulated by the Crawford family via its biscuit business in the UK. The Thomases planted the 40-ha vineyard in 1998, with merlot (15.3 ha) leading the way, followed (in descending order) by cabernet sauvignon, sauvignon blanc, chardonnay, pinot noir, riesling and sangiovese. The wines are marketed under the Icely Road brand. Exports to the UK.

ŶŶŶŶŶ **Icely Road Orange Riesling 2006** A mix of flowery and more minerally aromas and flavours; rich and layered tropical and citrus fruit; considerable length. Trophy and gold medal winner Orange Wine Show '06. Screwcap. 12.8° alc. **Rating** 94 **To** 2016 $18
Icely Road Orange Sauvignon Blanc 2005 A complex wine, with almost honeysuckle aromas; considerable depth and power, but not sweet. Trophy and gold medal winner Orange Wine Show '06. Screwcap. 12.5° alc. **Rating** 94 **To** 2008 $18
Pinot Noir 2005 A pretty wine, with light but wonderfully attractive red fruits; the balance is good, but this is an early-drinking style. Trophy and gold medal winner Orange Wine Show '06. Screwcap. 14° alc. **Rating** 94 **To** 2008 $35

ŶŶŶŶŶ **Single Vineyard Orange Chardonnay 2005** The bouquet immediately proclaims the quality of the wine; a subtle interaction of melon and stone fruit with French oak; good mouthfeel and length. Screwcap. 14° alc. **Rating** 93 **To** 2012 $24
Cabernet Sauvignon 2005 Quite complex, with cedar, spice and blackcurrant fruit; fine tannins. Screwcap. 14.5° alc. **Rating** 91 **To** 2018 $25
Icely Road Sangiovese 2005 Pale red-purple; aromatic cherry blossom and spice, the fresh and lively palate filled with sweet cherry fruit; fine tannins; now or later. Screwcap. 14° alc. **Rating** 90 **To** 2012 $20

ŶŶŶŶ **Icely Road Orange Sauvignon Blanc 2006** Clean, but powerful and long; regional citrus, herb, mineral and gooseberry flavours; if it follows in the footsteps of the '05, will improve significantly over the '07 calendar year. Screwcap. 12° alc. **Rating** 88 **To** 2008 $18
Pinot Noir Chardonnay 2004 Good intensity, focus and length; positive fruit and good balance. 12.5° alc. **Rating** 88 **To** 2008 $26
Icely Road Orange Merlot 2005 A solid wine with lots of extract and oak, just staying within the merlot field of play. Screwcap. **Rating** 87 **To** 2011 $20
Icely Road Orange Cabernet Merlot 2005 Generous wine, with plenty of black and red fruits; strong structure ends up just a tad aggressive. Screwcap. **Rating** 87 **To** 2012 $20

Maygars Hill Winery ★★★★

53 Longwood-Mansfield Road, Longwood, Vic 3665 **Region** Strathbogie Ranges
T (03) 5798 5417 **F** (03) 5798 5457 **www.**strathbogieboutiquewines.com **Open** By appt
Winemaker Plunkett Wines (Sam Plunkett) **Est.** 1997 **Cases** 1200
Jenny Houghton purchased this 8-ha property in 1994, planting 1.6 ha of shiraz and 0.8 ha of cabernet sauvignon, and has established a stylish B&B cottage. The name comes from Lieutenant Colonel Maygar, who fought with outstanding bravery in the Boer War in South Africa in 1901, where he won the Victoria Cross. In World War I he rose to command the 8th Light Horse Regiment, winning yet further medals for bravery. He died on 1 November 1917.

McCrae Mist Wines ★★★★☆

21 Bass Street, McCrae, Vic 3938 (postal) **Region** Mornington Peninsula
T 0416 008 630 **F** (03) 5986 6973 **Open** Not
Winemaker Brien Cole **Est.** 2003 **Cases** 1250
The McCrae Mist vineyard was acquired by Dr Stephen Smith after the Kings Creek business was broken up in 2003. He thus inherited 15.5 ha of pinot grigio, pinot noir, shiraz and sangiovese, adding another 4 ha of chardonnay in 2005.

McGlashan's Wallington Estate

225 Swan Bay Road, Wallington, Vic 3221 **Region** Geelong
T (03) 5250 5760 **F** (03) 5250 5760 **Open** By appt
Winemaker Robin Brockett (Contract) **Est.** 1996 **Cases** 1500
Russell and Jan McGlashan began the establishment of their 10-ha vineyard in 1996. Chardonnay and pinot noir make up the bulk of the plantings, with the remainder shiraz and pinot gris, and the wines are made by Robin Brockett, with his usual skill and attention to detail. Local restaurants around Geelong and the Bellarine Peninsula take much of the wine.

♀♀♀♀♀ **Bellarine Peninsula Chardonnay 2005** Light straw-green; pure nectarine, melon and grapefruit; subtle French oak merges well into the background; a particularly long finish. Screwcap. 13.5° alc. **Rating** 94 **To** 2015 $19
Bellarine Peninsula Pinot Noir 2005 Attractive pinot varietal character right from the outset; spicy cherry and plum fruit; fine tannins and subtle oak. Screwcap. 13.5° alc. **Rating** 94 **To** 2012 $19

McGuigan Wines

★★★★

Cnr Broke Road/McDonald Road, Pokolbin, NSW 2321 **Region** Lower Hunter Valley
T (02) 4998 7700 **F** (02) 4998 7401 **www.**mcguiganwines.com.au **Open** 7 days 9.30–5
Winemaker Peter Hall **Est.** 1992 **Cases** 1.2 million
A public-listed company which was the ultimate logical expression of Brian McGuigan's marketing drive and vision, on a par with that of Wolf Blass in his heyday; has been particularly active in export markets, notably the US and more recently China. The overall size of the company has been measurably increased by the acquisition of Simeon Wines; Yaldara and Miranda are now also part of the business, which in 2006 made wine industry headlines when it terminated a large number of grape purchase contracts. In 2007 McGuigan Simeon acquired Nepenthe Vineyards, a move which surprised many. Exports to all major markets.

♀♀♀♀♀ **Vineyard Select Semillon 2005** Fine, elegant lemon juice; beautiful balance, almost like a Mosel with a carefully planned touch of sweetness. Controversial but seductive Screwcap. 12.5° alc. **Rating** 92 **To** 2010 $17.50
Personal Reserve Botrytis Semillon 2005 Bright pale green-straw; elegant and moderately sweet; good line and length. Cork. 10° alc. **Rating** 92 **To** 2009 $26

♀♀♀♀ **Personal Reserve Hunter Valley Chardonnay 2006** Complex, funky barrel ferment aromas are too strong for some; the palate is vibrant and fresh, with good length. Cork. 13° alc. **Rating** 89 **To** 2011 $30
Personal Reserve Hunter Valley Shiraz 2005 Powerful blackberry and dark chocolate, with a solid, tannic backbone; aggressive tannins on the finish need to soften. Cork. 13.5° alc. **Rating** 89 **To** 2015 $50
Bin 9000 Semillon 1997 Deep, bright golden colour; aged varietal character is clear enough, but is drifting past its use-by date. Cork. 11° alc. **Rating** 87 **To** 2008 $35

McHenry Hohnen Vintners

PO Box 1480, Margaret River, WA 6285 **Region** Margaret River
T (08) 9758 7777 **F** (08) 9758 7777 **www.**mchv.com.au **Open** Not
Winemaker David Hohnen, Freya Hohnen **Est.** 2004 **Cases** 6500
McHenry Hohnen is a substantial business owned by the McHenry and Hohnen families, sourcing grapes from 4 vineyards owned by various members of the families. In all, 120 ha of vines have been established on the McHenry's, Calgardup Brook, Rocky Road and McLeod Creek properties. A significant part of the grape production is sold to others (including Cape Mentelle) but McHenry Hohnen have 18 varieties to choose from in fashioning their wines. The family members with direct executive responsibilities are leading Perth retailer Murray McHenry, Cape Mentelle founder and former long-term winemaker David Hohnen, and Freya Hohnen, who shares the winemaking duties with father David. Exports to the UK, the US and NZ.

ƯƯƯƯƯ **3 Amigos Shiraz Grenache Mataro 2005** Excellent hue and clarity; a spotlessly clean, aromatic bouquet with a spray of red and black fruits; the light-to medium-bodied palate fulfills the promise of the bouquet; soft but lingering tannins. Screwcap. 14° alc. **Rating** 94 **To** 2012 $27
Rocky Road Zinfandel 2005 An impressively rich and structured wine with dark, small berry fruits and spices; good structure and texture. David Hohnen has had over 20 years' experience in growing and making this difficult variety. Cork. 14.5° alc. **Rating** 94 **To** 2010 $37

ƯƯƯƯƯ **Calgardup Brook Chardonnay 2005** Light straw-green; a particularly restrained and elegant wine in the context of Margaret River; melon, apple and nectarine with touches of cashew and cream; controlled barrel ferment inputs. Screwcap. 13.5° alc. **Rating** 93 **To** 2015 $37
3 Amigos Marsanne Chardonnay Roussanne 2005 Complex aromas (fractionally reduced) and texture; a minerally, chalky underlay to the gentle stone fruit and touches of cashew. Screwcap. 13° alc. **Rating** 90 **To** 2012 $27

McIvor Estate

80 Tooborac-Baynton Road, Tooborac, Vic 3522 **Region** Heathcote
T (03) 5433 5266 **F** (03) 5433 5358 **www**.mcivorestate.com.au **Open** W'ends & public hols 10-5, or by appt
Winemaker Cobaw Ridge (Alan Cooper) **Est.** 1997 **Cases** 2000
McIvor Estate is situated at the base of the Tooborac Hills, at the southern end of the Heathcote wine region, 5 km southwest of Tooborac. Gary and Cynthia Harbor have planted 5.5 ha of marsanne, roussanne, shiraz, cabernet sauvignon, merlot, nebbiolo and sangiovese.

ƯƯƯƯƯ **Shiraz 2005** Bright, deep purple-red; succulent blackberry, plum and bitter chocolate flavours; good tannin structure and balance, likewise oak; great future. Diam. **Rating** 94 **To** 2025 $30

ƯƯƯƯƯ **Shiraz 2004** Elegant medium-bodied wine with black fruits and some spicy notes; neatly controlled extract. Cork. **Rating** 93 **To** 2015 $30
Cabernet Merlot 2004 Ample blackcurrant and mulberry fruit with hints of dark chocolate; very ripe fruit and tannins tremble on the brink. Cork. **Rating** 90 **To** 2012 $26
Sangiovese 2005 Light- to medium-bodied, but quite intense black cherry/sour cherry/briar flavours, and good length; has clear varietal character, but also stands on its own feet as a wine regardless of its variety. Diam. **Rating** 90 **To** 2012 $35

ƯƯƯƯ **Marsanne Roussanne 2005** Substantial wine with lots of weight and texture to the fig and honeysuckle fruit. Diam. **Rating** 88 **To** 2009 $22
Marsanne Roussanne 2004 Developed aromas; powerful nutty cashew and dried fruit flavours; a fractionally thick finish. Diam. **Rating** 88 **To** 2009 $22
Reserve Sangiovese 2004 Light- to medium-bodied; some leaf, red cherry and cigar box aromas and flavours, then persistent tannins. A difficult variety to grow and handle well, though nebbiolo is even more difficult. Cork. 13.5° alc. **Rating** 87 **To** 2009 $35
Nebbiolo 2005 Typical pale colour; light- to medium-bodied; mint, raspberry and cherry; plenty of acidity, but not much tannin structure. Truly, this is the ultimate bitch of a variety. Diam. **Rating** 87 **To** 2010 $30

McKellar Ridge Wines

Point of View Vineyard, 2 Eureka Avenue, Murrumbateman, NSW 2582 **Region** Canberra District
T (02) 6258 1556 **F** (02) 6258 9770 **www**.mckellarridgewines.com.au **Open** By appt
Winemaker Dr Brian Johnston **Est.** 2000 **Cases** 300

Dr Brian Johnston and his wife Janet are the partners in McKellar Ridge Wines. Brian has been undertaking a post-graduate diploma in science at Charles Sturt University, focusing on wine science and wine production techniques. The wines come from low-yielding, mature vines and have had significant show success. They are made using a combination of traditional and new winemaking techniques, the emphasis being on fruit-driven styles.

�♀ **Canberra District Shiraz Viognier 2005** Usual vivid colour; the blackberry/ black cherry fruit is in a darker spectrum than normal, though well-suited to the French oak and savoury, fine tannins. Screwcap. 14° alc. **Rating** 93 **To** 2020 $20
Canberra District Cabernet Sauvignon Cabernet Franc 2005 Firm blackcurrant/savoury fruit, with plenty of integrity and length; controlled oak and fine, ripe tannins. Screwcap. 14° alc. **Rating** 93 **To** 2025 $20
Canberra District Sauvignon Blanc 2006 Grass, herb and lemon aromas lead into a similar range of flavours plus slightly sweeter, more tropical, fruit; good length. Screwcap. 12° alc. **Rating** 91 **To** 2008 $14

McLaren Ridge Estate ★★★☆

Whitings Road, McLaren Vale, SA 5171 **Region** McLaren Vale
T (08) 8383 0504 **F** (08) 8383 0504 **www.**mclarenridge.com **Open** 7 days 11–5
Winemaker Brian Light (Contract) **Est.** 1997 **Cases** 3000
Peter and Heather Oliver have 5 ha of shiraz and 1 ha of grenache, planted over 50 years ago on the ridge which now gives their estate its name. The cellar door opened in February 2007, and luxury vineyard accommodation is available.

� **McLaren Vale Shiraz 2004** Medium red-purple; a strongly structured and flavoured wine, although some sweetness is distracting. ProCork. 14.5° alc. **Rating** 87 **To** 2002 $20

McLaren Vale III Associates ★★★★☆

130 Main Road, McLaren Vale, SA 5171 **Region** McLaren Vale
T 1800 501 513 **www.**associates.com.au **Open** Mon–Fri 9–5, tasting by appt
Winemaker Brian Light **Est.** 1999 **Cases** 14 000
The 3 associates in question all have a decade or more of wine industry experience; Mary Greer is managing partner, Reginald Wymond chairing partner, and Christopher Fox partner. The partnership owns 34 ha of vines spanning 2 vineyards, one owned by Mary and John Greer, the other by Reg and Sue Wymond. An impressive portfolio of affordable quality wines has been the outcome, precisely as the partners wished. Exports to the US, Canada, Germany and China.

McLaren Wines ★★★★☆

PO Box 488, McLaren Vale, SA 5171 **Region** McLaren Vale
T 0408 575 200 **F** (08) 8557 4363 **www.**mclarenwines.com **Open** Not
Winemaker Matthew Rechner **Est.** 2001 **Cases** 2000
Matt Rechner entered the wine industry in 1988, spending most of the intervening years at Tatachilla Winery in McLaren Vale, starting as laboratory technician and finishing as operations manager. Frustrated by the constraints of large winery practice, he decided to strike out on his own in 2001 via the virtual winery option. His long experience has meant he is able to buy grapes from high-quality producers. The success of McLaren Wines in the Great Australian Shiraz Challenge '06 is testimony enough to the quality of the wines.

♀♀♀♀♀ **Linchpin Shiraz 2004** Lots and lots of winemaking inputs, with black fruits, dark chocolate and a hint of herb all adding up to a highly flavoursome wine which will flower with more time. Runner up Great Shiraz Challenge '06. Great value. **Rating** 94 **To** 2019 $19

♀♀♀♀♀ **Echidna Grenache Shiraz 2004** Spicy red and black fruit aromas and flavours; has good structure, balance and particularly good length; a standout red wine under $10. Screwcap. 14.6° alc. **Rating** 90 **To** 2011 $9.25

ΥΥΥΥ   Pinot Gris 2006 Pinot gris at the correct price, a rarity; little essential fruit flavour, but finishes with nice citrussy acidity. Screwcap. 13.8° alc. **Rating** 87 To 2008 $9.25

McLean's Farm Wines   ★★★★★

PO Box 403, Tanunda, SA 5352 **Region** Barossa Valley
T (08) 8564 3340 **F** (08) 8564 3340 **www.**mcleansfarm.com **Open** At barr-Vinum, Angaston, tel (08) 8564 3688
Winemaker Bob McLean **Est.** 2001 **Cases** 2500
At various times known as the Jolly Green Giant and Sir Lunchalot, Bob McLean has gone perilously close to being a marketing legend in his own lifetime, moving from Orlando to Petaluma and then (for longer and more importantly) St Hallett. The farm shed on the home property will house the winery to handle the estate-grown red grapes, which amount to 30 tonnes (or less) a year. Contract makers make the Grenache Shiraz Mourvedre and Eden Valley Riesling. Farm gate sales will be by appointment for personalised tasting. Exports to the UK and US.

ΥΥΥΥΥ   Eden Valley Riesling 2006 The bouquet is still a little shy, but the wine opens up powerfully on a long and intense palate; lively, tangy lemon citrus flavours on the crisp finish. Screwcap. 12.5° alc. **Rating** 94 To 2016 $18.95
Schubert McLean Shiraz Cabernet 2004 Clear purple-red; attractive medium-bodied wine, with good structure and texture; blackberry/ black-currant fruit, fine tannins, subtle oak and a long finish. Screwcap. 14.5° alc. Rating 94 To 2019 $18
Kalimna Eden Valley Shiraz Cabernet 2003 Supple mouthfeel and good line to the blackberry, dark chocolate, licorice and spice flavours; good oak and extract. A classic blend of regions much beloved of the late Max Schubert. Cork. 14.5° alc. **Rating** 94 To 2023 $45

ΥΥΥΥΥ   Shiraz Cabernet 2004 An elegant, medium-bodied, seamless mix, bringing together blackberry and blackcurrant fruit; 12 months in American oak has all but disappeared; 51%/49%. Screwcap. 14.5° alc. **Rating** 92 To 2019 $18
Eden Valley Riesling 2005 Delicate floral blossom aromas with sweet citrus and passionfruit flavours; overall delicacy. Screwcap. 12.5° alc. **Rating** 90 To 2015 $18
Reserve Barossa 2003 A mix of ripe, gently sweet plum and blackcurrant fruit, with mocha/vanilla nuances. Shiraz (55%)/Cabernet Sauvignon (45%). Screwcap. 14.5° alc. **Rating** 90 To 2015 $28

ΥΥΥΥ   Barossa Chardonnay 2006 Nice, unoaked chardonnay at the right alcohol level; lees stirring of the fresh stone fruit and citrus flavours has given texture; good winemaking. Screwcap. 13° alc. **Rating** 89 To 2010 $18.95
Trinity Corner Barossa Shiraz 2003 Medium red-purple; ripe and fleshy, with some mocha notes to an essentially soft wine; light tannins. Cork. 14° alc. **Rating** 89 To 2010 $28
Shiraz Cabernet 2002 Development showing; pleasing light- to medium-bodied style, with early/savoury notes around the fruit core; not forced or extracted. Screwcap. 14.5° alc. **Rating** 89 To 2012 $18

McLeish Estate   ★★★★

Lot 3 De Beyers Road, Pokolbin, NSW 2320 **Region** Lower Hunter Valley
T (02) 4998 7754 **www.**mcleishhunterwines.com.au **Open** 7 days 10–5, or by appt
Winemaker Andrew Thomas **Est.** 1985 **Cases** 3500
Bob and Maryanne McLeish began planting their vineyard in 1985, and now have 11 ha. They have also opened their cellar door, having accumulated a number of gold medals for their wines.

ΥΥΥΥΥ   Hunter Valley Semillon Sauvignon Blanc 2006 Some passionfruit and a touch of gooseberry; good weight and mouthfeel; convincing line. An interesting development for the Hunter Valley. Screwcap. 12.5° alc. **Rating** 92 To 2008 $15

McPherson Wines

PO Box 767, Hawthorn, Vic 3122 **Region** Nagambie Lakes
T (03) 9832 1700 **F** (03) 9832 1750 **www**.mcphersonwines.com **Open** Not
Winemaker Andrew McPherson, Geoff Thompson **Est.** 1993 **Cases** 400 000
McPherson Wines is not well known in Australia but is, by any standards, a substantial business.
Its wines are largely produced for the export market, with some sales in Australia. The wines are
made at various locations from 250 ha of estate vineyards, supplemented with contract-grown
grapes, and represent very good value. For the record, McPherson Wines is a joint venture
between Andrew McPherson and Alister Purbrick (Tahbilk), both of whom have had a lifetime
of experience in the industry. Exports to all major markets.

ΨΨΨΨΨ **Basilisk Shiraz Mourvedre 2005** Medium-bodied blackberry and plum shiraz
is tempered by the savoury tannins of mourvedre; works very well. Compelling
value. Screwcap. 14.5° alc. **Rating** 90 **To** 2011 $15

ΨΨΨΨ **Sauvignon Blanc Semillon 2006** Clean, fresh, gentle tropical fruit offset by
perfectly judged acidity on the finish. What more at this price? Screwcap.
11.5° alc. **Rating** 88 **To** 2008 $9
Merlot 2005 Light- to medium-bodied, in keeping with the range; has distinct
varietal character in a savoury/olive spectrum; good length and persistence.
Cork. 14° alc. **Rating** 88 **To** 2008 $9
Basilisk Cabernet Balzac 2005 Medium- to full-bodied; powerful but not
aggressive; dry cedar cigar box notes introduced into cabernet via the balzac.
Balzac is a synonym for mourvedre, and if McPherson wished to add a touch
of mystery, esparte might have done the job as well (it was the term used by
the late Colin Preece at Seppelt Great Western). Screwcap. 14.5° alc. **Rating** 88
To 2010 $15
Verdelho 2006 Well-made, typical fruit salad flavours, but has a fresh finish, neither
sweet nor dry. Screwcap. 12.5° alc. **Rating** 87 **To** 2008 $9
Murray Darling Shiraz Cabernet 2005 Light- to medium-bodied; positive red
and black fruits in a plum and blackberry spectrum; little or no oak obvious, and not
overmuch structure. Cork. 13.5° alc. **Rating** 87 **To** 2008 $9

McVitty Grove

Wombeyan Caves Road, Mittagong, NSW 2575 **Region** Southern Highlands
T (02) 4878 5044 **www**.mcvittygrove.com.au **Open** Wed–Fri 8–5, w'ends 10–5
Winemaker High Range Vintners (Nick Spencer) **Est.** 1998 **Cases** 1500
Notwithstanding his 20-year career in finance, Mark Phillips also had 6 years of tertiary
qualifications in horticulture when he and wife Jane began the search for a Southern Highlands
site suited to premium grapegrowing and olive cultivation. In 1998 they bought 42 ha of farm
land on Wombeyan Caves Road, just out of Mittagong. They have now established 5.5 ha of pinot
noir and pinot gris on deep, fertile soils at the front of the property. In addition, a 1.5-ha olive
grove has been planted, which provides the backdrop for the cellar door and café.

ΨΨΨΨΨ **Black Label Southern Highlands Pinot Gris 2006** Very well-made; pear,
honeysuckle and citrus aromas; lively acidity, with good length and a dry finish.
Screwcap. 12.9° alc. **Rating** 90 **To** 2008 $24

ΨΨΨΨ **Cut Arm Southern Highlands Pinot Gris 2006** Don't try to learn too much
from the bouquet; the cane-cut (leaving the bunches to dehydrate and concentrate)
has introduced considerable sweetness and balancing acidity, but it won't make the
earth move. Screwcap. 13.2° alc. **Rating** 88 **To** 2008 $25
Southern Highlands Rose 2006 Bright colour; vibrant fruit, but the nippy,
lemony acidity may frighten some. Screwcap. 12.5° alc. **Rating** 87 **To** 2008 $16
Southern Highlands Pinot Noir 2005 Spice, fern and bracken allied with
cherries, raspberries and strawberries; brisk acidity. Screwcap. 13.2° alc. **Rating** 87
To 2008 $25

McWilliam's ★★★★★

Jack McWilliam Road, Hanwood, NSW 2680 **Region** Riverina
T (02) 6963 0001 **F** (02) 6963 0002 **www**.mcwilliams.com.au **Open** Mon–Sat 9–5
Winemaker Jim Brayne, Russell Cody **Est.** 1916 **Cases** NFP
The best wines to emanate from the Hanwood winery are from other regions, notably the
BarwangVineyard at Hilltops (see separate entry), Coonawarra (Brand's of Coonawarra) and Eden
Valley. As McWilliam's viticultural resources have expanded, they have been able to produce
regional blends from across southeastern Australia in the last few years, these have been startlingly
good.The 2006 sale of McWilliam'sYenda winery to Casella has led to a major upgrade in both
the size and equipment at the Hanwood winery, now the nerve centre for the business. Exports
to many countries via a major distribution joint venture with Gallo.

ΨΨΨΨΨ **1877 Cabernet Sauvignon Shiraz 2003** Very long, elegant and penetrating; a
spicy, cool-grown style with some Rhone-like characters.Top gold medal in its
class National Wine Show '06. Cork. 14° alc. **Rating** 95 **To** 2020 $80
1877 Cabernet Sauvignon Shiraz 2002 Powerful and profound, in part due
to the '02 vintage, in part the complex blending and winemaking philosophy.
This is not a show wine style, its 3 gold medals notwithstanding; blackberry,
blackcurrant, licorice and spice are seamlessly backed up by high-quality oak
and fine tannins; its real quality will emerge in 20-30 years time. Cork.
14.5° alc. **Rating** 95 **To** 2037 $80
Show Reserve Liqueur Muscat NV The viscosity, and olive-brown mahogany
colour, immediately attest to its age; swimming with raisin, toffee and cake flavours,
the spirit is very soft, the finish remarkably round and luscious, yet doesn't cloy. A
very different style to NortheastVictoria; 8 trophies, 44 gold medals 1991-'03. Cork.
18° alc. **Rating** 94 **To** 2008 $79.95

ΨΨΨΨΨ **Hanwood Special Reserve 12 Years Old Tawny Port NV** Complex and
intense; nutty, biscuity flavours, with obvious rancio; a long, lingering finish and
aftertaste. Cork. 19° alc. **Rating** 92 **To** 2008 $21.95
Regional Collection Eden Valley Riesling 2005 Lime and apple juice aromas
and flavours; restrained minerally acidity; will develop marvellously well. Screwcap.
12.5° alc. **Rating** 91 **To** 2015 $16
Hanwood Estate Shiraz Viognier 2005 Clear and bright purple-red;
punches way above its price weight from the word go; supple black cherry,
spice and blackberry, then the viognier lift to both bouquet and palate.
Screwcap. 13.5° alc. **Rating** 91 **To** 2010 $11.95
Limited Release Riverina Botrytis Semillon 2005 Lively, fresh and crisp, with
very good balance from the botrytis and acidity; needs 2-3 years to fully flaunt its
wares. Screwcap. 11° alc. **Rating** 91 **To** 2010 $20
Hanwood Estate Chardonnay 2005 As usual, over-delivers dramatically; fruit-
driven with melon and citrus notes ex cool-climate components; the barest hint of
oak. Screwcap. 13.5° alc. **Rating** 90 **To** 2008 $12
Hanwood Estate Merlot 2005 An attractive, medium-bodied mix of savoury
and red fruits with strong varietal expression; on the finish slightly darker
flavours appear.Top gold Qld Wine Show '06. Screwcap. 14° alc. **Rating** 90
To 2011 $11.95

ΨΨΨΨ **Inheritance Semillon Sauvignon Blanc 2006** Spotlessly clean, crisp and fresh
with touches of gooseberry and lychee through to a lively finish. Screwcap. 11° alc.
Rating 89 **To** 2008 $6.99
Inheritance Cabernet Merlot 2005 Arguably the best in the Inheritance
range, with greater depth of ripe fruit and clear varietal characters; lack of
tannins is as much a positive as a negative; a wholly exceptional range at this
price point. Screwcap. 14° alc. **Rating** 88 **To** 2008 $6.95
Hanwood Estate Cabernet Sauvignon 2005 Bright, fresh and uncomplicated,
but purely expressed, cabernet sauvignon; good balance and length. Screwcap.
14° alc. **Rating** 88 **To** 2008 $12

Inheritance Riesling 2006 Clean, crisp and lively with gentle citrus flavours; good length and balance, the sweetness subliminal. How can you expect more at this price? Screwcap. 11.5° alc. **Rating** 87 **To** 2010 $7

Hanwood Estate Sauvignon Blanc 2006 Clean, fresh, light-bodied; citrus/kiwifruit/stone fruit flavours; bright finish. Screwcap. 12.5° alc. **Rating** 87 **To** 2008 $11.95

Hanwood Estate Semillon Sauvignon Blanc 2006 Very similar to the Sauvignon Blanc, though curiously seeming to show more tropical/passionfruit characters. Screwcap. 11.5° alc. **Rating** 87 **To** 2008 $11.95

Hanwood Estate Verdelho 2006 Plenty of activity; fruit salad aromas and flavours with a twist of acidity giving good length. Screwcap. 12.5° alc. **Rating** 87 **To** 2008 $12

Inheritance Shiraz Merlot 2005 Elegant, light to medium-bodied mix of red and black fruits, with a twist of licorice and spice, finishing with fine tannins. A ludicrous price for a wine of this quality. Screwcap. 14° alc. **Rating** 87 **To** 2008 $6.95

McWilliam's Mount Pleasant ★★★★★

Marrowbone Road, Pokolbin, NSW 2320 **Region** Lower Hunter Valley
T (02) 4998 7505 **F** (02) 4998 7761 www.mountpleasantwines.com.au **Open** 7 days 10–5
Winemaker Phillip Ryan, Andrew Leembruggen **Est.** 1921 **Cases** NFP
McWilliam's Elizabeth and the glorious Lovedale Semillon are generally commercially available with 4–5 years of bottle age and are undervalued treasures with a consistently superb show record. The individual vineyard wines, together with the Maurice O'Shea memorial wines, add to the lustre of this proud name. Exports to many countries, the most important being the UK, the US, Germany and NZ.

ΨΨΨΨΨ **Lovedale Limited Release Hunter Valley Semillon 2006** As finely bred and strung as a champion yearling race horse; effortless length and intensity to the special lemon and citrus flavours of great young semillon. Screwcap. 10.5° alc. **Rating** 95 **To** 2030 $38

Elizabeth Semillon 2001 Glowing yellow-green; very good bottle-developed combination of freshness and complexity; excellent length and acidity. Cork. 11° alc. **Rating** 95 **To** 2011 $17

Lovedale Limited Release Hunter Valley Semillon 2001 Light straw-green; a classic Lovedale in the making, with supple citrus, lemon, herb and grass flavours intermingling; as ever, good balance. Pray the cork won't let it down. 11.5° alc. **Rating** 94 **To** 2021 $50

Maurice O'Shea Shiraz 2004 Strong colour, especially for '04; a mix of earthy regional and strong, bright blackberry/raspberry/cherry fruit; immaculate oak and tannin management. Screwcap. 14.5° alc. **Rating** 94 **To** 2029 $60

Maurice O'Shea Shiraz 2003 Fresh plum and blackberry fruit supported by much more structure than usual; firm, though ripe tannins. Cork. 14.5° alc. **Rating** 94 **To** 2023 $60

ΨΨΨΨΨ **Elizabeth Semillon 2002** Light green-yellow; fresh as a daisy, with some remnants of CO_2 spritz; lemongrass and a hint of lemon zest before a minerally finish. Cork permitting, will only get better over the next 5 years. 10.5° alc. **Rating** 92 **To** 2012 $17

ΨΨΨΨ **Sparkling Pinot Noir 2005** The cork came out softly, without any warning that one-third of the contents would gently but insistently follow it; luckily, opened over a bucket and not a white carpet. Abundant flavour in a cherry spectrum, but essentially simple. 14° alc. **Rating** 87 **To** 2010 $18.95

Meadowbank Estate

699 Richmond Road, Cambridge, Tas 7170 **Region** Southern Tasmania
T (03) 6248 4484 **F** (03) 6248 4485 **www**.meadowbankwines.com.au **Open** 7 days 10–5
Winemaker Hood Wines (Andrew Hood) **Est.** 1974 **Cases** 10 000
An important part of the Ellis family business on what was once a large grazing property on the banks of the Derwent. Increased plantings are under contract to Hardys, and a splendid winery has been built to handle the increased production. The winery has expansive entertainment and function facilities, capable of handling up to 1000 people, and offering an arts and music program, plus a large restaurant. Exports to Hong Kong, Germany and Denmark.

ΨΨΨΨΨ **Grace Elizabeth Chardonnay 2005** Smooth and supple citrus and nectarine fruit; good length and balance, the oak present but not oppressive. Screwcap. 13.8° alc. **Rating** 94 **To** 2013 $33

ΨΨΨΨΨ **Chardonnay 2006** Highly aromatic and spotlessly clean stone fruit and citrus aromas; medium-bodied, again fruit-driven, the flavours following the pattern of the bouquet; long finish. Screwcap. 13.5° alc. **Rating** 93 **To** 2015 $25
Pinot Noir 2005 A silky skein of bright cherry and plum fruit runs through the middle of the palate and into the long finish; from a golden pinot noir vintage for Tasmania. Screwcap. 13.5° alc. **Rating** 92 **To** 2013 $28

ΨΨΨΨ **Unwooded Chardonnay 2005** Complex and rich; teeters on the edge of sweetness, but certainly has flavour. Screwcap. 13.7° alc. **Rating** 88 **To** 2008 $25.50

Medhurst

24-26 Medhurst Road, Gruyere, Vic 3770 **Region** Yarra Valley
T (03) 9821 4846 **F** (03) 9592 5435 **www**.medhurstwines.com.au **Open** Fri–Mon 10–5
Winemaker Dominique Portet **Est.** 2000 **Cases** 1500
The wheel has come full circle for Ross and Robyn Wilson; in the course of a very distinguished corporate career, Ross Wilson was CEO of Southcorp during the time it brought the Penfolds, Lindemans and Wynns businesses under the Southcorp banner. For her part, Robyn spent her childhood in the Yarra Valley, her parents living less than a kilometre away as the crow flies from Medhurst. Immaculately sited and tended vineyard blocks, most on steep, north-facing slopes, promise much for the future. In all there are 13 ha planted to sauvignon blanc, chardonnay, pinot noir, cabernet sauvignon and shiraz, all run on a low-yield basis. Red Shed is the newly introduced second label, taking its name from the recently opened café.

ΨΨΨΨΨ **Yarra Valley Pinot Noir 2005** An extremely complex bouquet and palate, with spice, rhubarb and plum aromas; a potent, intense and long palate with stem/forest/spice notes underlying clear pinot fruit; impressive. ProCork. 13.5° alc. **Rating** 94 **To** 2012 $30

ΨΨΨΨΨ **Yarra Valley Chardonnay 2005** A major step up in intensity and complexity from the Red Shed; while the barrel ferment is evident, the wine is essentially driven by citrus, melon and stone fruit; good acidity and length; bright finish. Screwcap. 14° alc. **Rating** 91 **To** 2011 $20
Yarra Valley Rose 2006 Pale pink; very fragrant and aromatic red fruits; has intensity and length; a serious rose, very well-made. Shiraz/Cabernet Sauvignon. Screwcap. 14° alc. **Rating** 90 **To** 2008 $16

ΨΨΨΨ **Red Shed Pinot Noir 2006** A clean and highly aromatic bouquet; a fresh and lively palate with quite intense cherry and plum follows on logically; slightly simple, but a clean finish. Screwcap. 13.5° alc. **Rating** 89 **To** 2010 $17.50
Red Shed Chardonnay 2005 Spotlessly clean; light-bodied melon and stone fruit flavours; gentle acidity; shows the young vines. Screwcap. 14° alc. **Rating** 87 **To** 2009 $15
Red Shed Cabernet Shiraz 2005 Light- to medium-bodied; fresh black fruits and gentle touches of spice; minimal oak, with fine, but slightly green, tannins. Screwcap. 13° alc. **Rating** 87 **To** 2008 $17.50

Meerea Park

Lot 3 Palmers Lane, Pokolbin, NSW 2320 **Region** Lower Hunter Valley
T (02) 4998 7474 www.meereapark.com.au **Open** At The Boutique Wine Centre, Pokolbin
Winemaker Rhys Eather **Est.** 1991 **Cases** 10 000
All the wines are produced from grapes purchased from growers, primarily in the Pokolbin,
Broke-Fordwich and Upper Hunter regions, but also from as far afield as Orange and Young. It
is the brainchild of Rhys Eather, a great-grandson of Alexander Munro, a leading vigneron in the
mid-19th century; he makes the wine at the former Little's Winery at Palmers Lane in Pokolbin.
Exports to the UK, The Netherlands, Germany, Canada and Singapore.

ŶŶŶŶŶ **Hell Hole Semillon 2006** A spotless bouquet, then a super-precise and focused
palate offering intense mineral, herb and lemon flavours; very long finish; 150
dozen made. Rhys Eather is a big man (all dimensions) and doesn't enjoy
extreme vintage-time heat. Screwcap. 10° alc. **Rating** 95 **To** 2026 $25
Hell Hole Shiraz 2004 Medium red-purple; an elegant, medium-bodied wine;
good texture and structure; plum, cherry and blackberry fruit, with fine
tannins. Has soaked up the French oak in which it spent 2 years; 150 dozen
made. Screwcap. 13.5° alc. **Rating** 94 **To** 2029 $55
Terracotta Hunter Valley Shiraz 2004 The aroma and flavour complexity is
enhanced by the 6% viognier; blackberry, dark chocolate and that touch of
apricot; soft and satisfying finish. Controlled use of French oak. Screwcap.
14° alc. **Rating** 94 **To** 2024 $55

ŶŶŶŶŶ **Epoch Semillon 2006** Spotlessly clean; tightly wound, but crisp and balanced,
with very good length; notes of grass and spice are very different to the '05, but do
not suffer in comparison. Screwcap. 10.5° alc. **Rating** 93 **To** 2017 $19
Shiraz Viognier 2005 Typical vivid colour; a medium-bodied, fruit-driven wine
with soft, almost silky, red fruits and viognier lift; minimal tannin and oak inputs.
Screwcap. 14° alc. **Rating** 90 **To** 2012 $19
The Aunts Shiraz 2004 A nicely constructed medium-bodied wine, with neat
red fruits and fine tannins. Screwcap. 13.5° alc. **Rating** 90 **To** 2014 $26

ŶŶŶŶ **Alexandra Munro Individual Vineyard Hunter Valley Shiraz 2004** Neither
the colour or palate are entirely convincing; really needs more intensity at this price,
although there is no fault. Screwcap. 14° alc. **Rating** 89 **To** 2014 $50

Mermerus Vineyard

60 Soho Road, Drysdale, Vic 3222 **Region** Geelong
T (03) 5253 2718 **F** (03) 5251 1555 www.mermerus.com.au **Open** First Sun of month
11–4; every Sun in Jan
Winemaker Paul Champion **Est.** 2000 **Cases** 600
In 1996, Paul Champion established 1.5 ha of pinot noir, 1 ha of chardonnay and 0.2 ha of riesling
at Mermerus. He also acts as contract winemaker for small growers in the region.

ŶŶŶŶŶ **Pinot Noir 2005** An elegant wine; some stem and forest notes run through the
red fruits but do not overwhelm them; long, fine finish. **Rating** 94 **To** 2012 $20

ŶŶŶŶ **Riesling 2006** Solid, showing some bottle-developed fruit characters in a
tropical/lime juice spectrum. **Rating** 88 **To** 2009 $16
Chardonnay 2005 Well-integrated fruit and barrel ferment inputs, though is a
trifle congested on the mid-palate; less winemaker inputs might have been better.
Screwcap. **Rating** 87 **To** 2008 $20

Merops Wines

5992 Caves Road, Margaret River, WA 6825 **Region** Margaret River
T (08) 9757 9195 **F** (08) 9757 3193 www.meropswines.com.au **Open** By appt
Winemaker Flying Fish Cover (Damon Eastough) **Est.** 2000 **Cases** 3000

Jim and Yvonne Ross have been involved in horticulture for over 25 years, in production, retail nurseries and viticulture. They established a nursery and irrigation business in the Margaret River township in 1985 on a 3-ha property before establishing a rootstock nursery. In 2000 they removed the nursery and planted 6.3 ha of cabernet sauvignon, cabernet franc, merlot and shiraz on the laterite gravel over clay soils. They use the practices developed by Professor William Albrecht in the US 50 years ago, providing mineral balance and thus eliminating the need for insecticides and toxic sprays. Organic pre-certification was completed in July 2007, which will result in the 2008 vintage being certified organic. Exports to the US and Indonesia.

ΨΨΨΨΨ **Margaret River Shiraz 2004** More depth, ripeness and power than many Margaret River shirazs; luscious black fruits are supported by persistent, fine tannins. Fine price, too. Cork. 13.9° alc. **Rating** 92 **To** 2014 $19
Margaret River Shiraz 2005 Medium-bodied; bright red and black fruits; fine tannin structure underpins the flavours; subtle oak. Screwcap. 13.6° alc. **Rating** 90 **To** 2012 $20
Margaret River Merlot 2005 Good varietal aromas of red fruit, snow pea and olive, the red fruit components coming through strongly on the palate; fine tannins with echoes of olive on the finish. Screwcap. 13.6° alc. **Rating** 90 **To** 2015 $20
Margaret River Cabernet Sauvignon 2005 Has more texture and weight than the colour and alcohol might suggest; ripe blackcurrant, and soft, balanced tannins. Screwcap. 13.6° alc. **Rating** 90 **To** 2018 $20

ΨΨΨΨ **Margaret River Merlot 2004** Good purple-red; plenty of texture and structure; red fruits with soft, persistent tannins and controlled oak. Stained cork. 13° alc. **Rating** 89 **To** 2010 $19
Ornatus Margaret River Cabernet Franc Cabernet Sauvignon Merlot 2005 Light but clear colour and hue; distinctly foresty/briary/earthy overtones, and the same sweet fruit of the cabernet underpinning the other components. Screwcap. 13.6° alc. **Rating** 88 **To** 2015 $20
Ornatus Margaret River Cabernet Franc Cabernet Sauvignon Merlot 2004 Savoury black fruits, and persistent, lingering tannins in house style. A Bordeaux blend; consistent bronze medal winner. Cork. 14.1° alc. **Rating** 88 **To** 2012 $19

Merricks Creek Wines ★★★★★

44 Merricks Road, Merricks, Vic 3916 **Region** Mornington Peninsula
T (03) 5989 8868 **F** (03) 5989 9070 **www.**pinot.com.au **Open** By appt
Winemaker Nick Farr **Est.** 1998 **Cases** 650
Peter and Georgina Parker retained Gary Farr as viticultural consultant before they began establishing their 2-ha pinot noir vineyard. They say, 'He has been an extraordinarily helpful and stern taskmaster. He advised on clonal selection, trellis design and planting density, and visits the vineyard regularly to monitor canopy management.' (Son Nick Farr completes the circle as contract winemaker.) The vineyard is planted to a sophisticated and rare collection of new pinot noir clones, and is planted at ultra-high density of 500 mm spacing. Exports to the UK, the US and Canada.

ΨΨΨΨΨ **Mornington Peninsula Pinot Noir 2005** Deeper colour than the Close Planted; richer in all respects (though not alcohol) but less spicy; plum and black cherry fruit, with good line, length and depth. Diam. 13.5° alc. **Rating** 95 **To** 2013 $42
Close Planted Mornington Peninsula Pinot Noir 2005 Moderate hue and depth; complex aromas and flavours, with distinct warm spice overtones to the predominantly red cherry fruits. Diam. 13.5° alc. **Rating** 94 **To** 2012 $52

Merricks Estate ★★★★★

Thompsons Lane, Merricks, Vic 3916 **Region** Mornington Peninsula
T (03) 5989 8416 **F** (03) 80803885 **www.**merricksestate.com.au **Open** 1st w'end of month, each w'end in Jan & public hol w'ends 12–5
Winemaker Paul Evans **Est.** 1977 **Cases** 750

Melbourne solicitor George Kefford, with wife Jacquie, runs Merricks Estate as a weekend and holiday enterprise. Right from the outset it has produced distinctive, spicy, cool-climate Shiraz which has accumulated an impressive array of show trophies and gold medals.

ŶŶŶŶŶ **Chardonnay 2004** Finer, more intense and (seemingly) younger than the '05; precise nectarine and stone fruit, the oak and mlf components in the background. Screwcap. 14° alc. **Rating** 94 **To** 2012 $25
Shiraz 2005 Deep, clear purple-red; medium- to full-bodied; abundant blackberry, plum, licorice, spice and black pepper; ripe tannins; 30-year-old vines. Diam. 13.5° alc. **Rating** 94 **To** 2019 $25

ŶŶŶŶŶ **Chardonnay 2005** Very typical Mornington Peninsula style; fruit softened but complexed by mlf and barrel fermentation (no new oak); creamy texture, and a good finish. Screwcap. 13.5° alc. **Rating** 91 **To** 2010 $25
Shiraz 2004 Light- to medium-bodied; more spicy and savoury than the '05, but still with a core of fine fruit; light tannins and oak. Diam. 14° alc. **Rating** 90 **To** 2015 $25

ŶŶŶŶ **Pinot Noir 2005** Slightly hazy colour; a big-framed wine, both the colour and palate suggesting the need for fining to brighten up the undoubted fruit. Screwcap. 14° alc. **Rating** 88 **To** 2011 $27
Cabernet 2003 Medium-bodied; blackcurrant, cassis, mint and leaf are all present, no one prevailing over the other. Diam. 14° alc. **Rating** 88 **To** 2010 $25
Pinot Noir 2004 A light- to medium-bodied wine with complex savoury/foresty/spicy notes suggesting the possibility of some brettanomyces; long finish. Screwcap. 14° alc. **Rating** 87 **To** 2009 $27

Merum   ★★★★★

Hillbrook Road, Quinninup, WA 6258 **Region** Pemberton
T (08) 9776 6011 **F** (08) 9776 6022 **www**.merum.com.au **Open** W'ends & public hols
Winemaker Jan McIntosh (Contract) **Est.** 1996 **Cases** 1400
Merum is owned and managed by viticulturist Mike Melsom and partner Julie Roberts. The 10-ha vineyard, planted in 1996, consists of semillon, shiraz and chardonnay. Its wines, led by the Semillon and Shiraz, have been outstanding since the word go.

ŶŶŶŶŶ **Pemberton Semillon Sauvignon Blanc 2006** Has that immediate and marked lift in intensity and character of so many of the Merum wines; perfect balance and seamless integration of the varieties, some tropical, some citrus and some grass add up to great length. Screwcap. 12° alc. **Rating** 95 **To** 2011 $19
Pemberton Chardonnay 2006 Elegant and perfectly balanced; a melon, nectarine and grapefruit mix, with a very long, lingering finish. Screwcap. 13° alc. **Rating** 94 **To** 2013 $29

ŶŶŶŶŶ **Pemberton Shiraz 2005** Medium-bodied, with attractive spicy plum, black cherry and blackberry fruit; silky tannins and texture; long finish. Screwcap. 13.5° alc. **Rating** 92 **To** 2015 $29

ŶŶŶŶ **Pemberton Shiraz Viognier 2005** Where did the usual depth of colour go? Elegant, spicy, cracked pepper with lively red fruits, but little of the flavour intensity expected of this blend. Screwcap. 13.5° alc. **Rating** 89 **To** 2011 $39
Amphora Pemberton Shiraz 2006 Fresh and light-bodied; plenty of finely constructed flavour, a rose on steroids, but none the worse for that (the wine is unoaked). Screwcap. 12° alc. **Rating** 87 **To** 2009 $19

Metcalfe Valley   ★★★★

283 Metcalfe-Malmsbury Road, Metcalfe, Vic 3448 **Region** Macedon Ranges
T (03) 5423 2035 **F** (03) 5423 2035 **Open** By appt
Winemaker Kilchurn Wines (David Cowburn) **Est.** 1994 **Cases** 1000

Ian Pattison, who has a PhD in metallurgy, and a Diploma in horticultural science and viticulture from Melbourne University/Dookie College, purchased Metcalfe Valley from the Frederiksens in 2003. He has 7.3 ha of shiraz and sauvignon blanc, and production is increasing.

ŶŶŶŶ **Shiraz 2005** Light- to medium-bodied; spicy cherry fruit and fine tannins. **Rating** 87 **To** 2008
Sparkling Shiraz Pinot Noir 2004 A big wine, with powerful base material; not oaky, but slightly phenolic. **Rating** 87 **To** 2009

Metier Wines

Tarraford Vineyard, 440 Healesville Road, Yarra Glen, Vic 3775 (postal) **Region** Yarra Valley **T** 0419 678 918 **F** (03) 5962 2194 **www**.metierwines.com.au **Open** Not
Winemaker Martin Williams MW **Est.** 1995 **Cases** 2000
Metier is the French word for craft, trade or profession; the business is that of Yarra Valley-based Martin Williams, who has notched up an array of degrees and had winemaking stints in France, California and Australia which are, not to put too fine a word on it, extraordinary. The focus of Metier is individual vineyard wines, initially based on grapes from the Tarraford and Schoolhouse Vineyards. Exports to the UK, the US and Hong Kong.

ŶŶŶŶŶ **Tarraford Vineyard Yarra Valley Pinot Noir 2003** Slightly darker hue and colour than the Schoolhouse; similar overall impression, but a bit more forceful; again, a range of potent foresty bottle-developed characters. Screwcap. **Rating** 94 **To** 2012 $30

ŶŶŶŶŶ **Schoolhouse Vineyard Yarra Valley Pinot Noir 2003** Obvious development in colour; a long, intensely savoury, spicy palate; definitely not Beaujolais in drag, and demands serious attention with braised squab to accompany it. Screwcap. **Rating** 93 **To** 2011 $30

Manytrees Vineyard Central Victorian High Country Shiraz Viognier 2003 Usual vibrant purple-red, though not especially deep; elegant, light to medium-bodied palate, with soft cherry, plum and blackberry fruit; soft, ripe tannins. Screwcap. **Rating** 93 **To** 2013 $30

Meure's Wines

16 Fleurtys Lane, Birchs Bay, Tas 7162 **Region** Southern Tasmania
T (03) 6267 4483 **F** (03) 6267 4483 **Open** Not
Winemaker Dirk Meure **Est.** 1991 **Cases** 300
Dirk Meure has established 1 ha of vineyard on the shores of D'Entrecasteaux Channel, overlooking Bruny Island. He says he has been heavily influenced by his mentors, Steve and Monique Lubiana. The philosophy is to produce low yields and to interfere as little as possible in the winemaking and maturation process. The vines are planted with an ultra high density of 8000 vines per ha, and are dry-farmed. No chemicals are used in the viticulture or winemaking, and the wines are bottled without fining or filtering. This is the ultimate challenge.

ŶŶŶŶŶ **d'Meure Chardonnay 2005** A complex, intense, yet elegant array of grapefruit and melon flavours plus barrel ferment and mlf inputs; very good length. Diam. 13.8° alc. **Rating** 95 **To** 2015 $45
d'Meure Pinot Noir 2004 Some development showing; an attractive wine with clear-cut varietal fruit ranging through spice, plums and a touch of forest; fine tannins and good length. Cork. 12.8° alc. **Rating** 94 **To** 2011 $75

ŶŶŶŶ **d'Meure Chardonnay 2003** Some colour development; not in the same class as the '05, with a much shorter palate; the cork may be the culprit. Cork. 13.3° alc. **Rating** 88 **To** 2008 $49

Mia Creek

365 Wickhams Lane, Glenhope East, Vic 3522 **Region** Heathcote
T (03) 5433 5324 **Open** By appt
Winemaker David McKenzie **Est.** 2001 **Cases** 50
David and Dianne McKenzie have planted 2 ha of shiraz and 1 ha of merlot on a mix of granitic soil and rock, 16 km southwest of Heathcote at an elevation of 340m. The dry-grown vines are low-yielding, and it is not expected that production will exceed 150 cases. The windy site means that sprays are seldom required, but the growth of the merlot has been savaged by local wildlife.

Miceli ★★★★☆

60 Main Creek Road, Arthurs Seat, Vic 3936 **Region** Mornington Peninsula
T (03) 5989 2755 **F** (03) 5989 2755 **Open** First w'end each month 12–5, public hols, & every w'end & by appt in Jan
Winemaker Anthony Miceli **Est.** 1991 **Cases** 3500
This may be a part-time labour of love for general practitioner Dr Anthony Miceli, but that hasn't prevented him taking the whole venture very seriously. He acquired the property in 1989 specifically to establish a vineyard, planting 1.8 ha in 1991, followed by a further ha of pinot gris in 1997. Between 1991 and 1997 Dr Miceli completed the Wine Science course at Charles Sturt University and now manages both vineyard and winery.

ŸŸŸŸŸ Iolanda Pinot Grigio 2005 An extremely attractive example; verging on citrussy, with touches of spice and musk; has great line and length, but no phenolics of residual sugar. Right up there. Screwcap. 13.5° alc. **Rating** 94 To 2008 $20

ŸŸŸŸŸ Iolanda Pinot Grigio 2006 Miceli has a special touch with this variety; a long and quite intense mix of citrus, nashi pear, apple and musk; dry finish to a serious wine. Screwcap. 13.5° alc. **Rating** 92 To 2009 $20
Lucy's Choice Pinot Noir 2004 A mix of spice and black and red fruits; good structure, but needs a touch more vinosity. Screwcap. **Rating** 90 To 2011 $26

ŸŸŸŸ **Dry Pinot Noir Rose 2006** Strawberry/cherry aromas; light, fresh and crisp, precisely as described on the label. Screwcap. 13.5° alc. **Rating** 87 To 2008 $20

Michael Unwin Wines

2 Racecourse Road (Western Highway), Beaufort, Vic 3373 **Region** Grampians
T (03) 5349 2021 **F** (03) 5349 2032 **www**.michaelunwinwines.com.au **Open** Mon–Fri 8.30–5, w'ends 11–4.30
Winemaker Michael Unwin **Est.** 2000 **Cases** 2000
Established by winemaker Michael Unwin and wife and business partner Catherine Clark. His track record as a winemaker spans 26 years, and includes extended winemaking experience in France, NZ and Australia; he has found time to obtain a postgraduate degree in oenology and viticulture at Lincoln University, Canterbury, NZ. He also does contract winemaking and consulting; the winemaking takes place in a converted textile factory. The grapes come in part from the estate plantings of 2 ha shiraz, and 1 ha each of cabernet sauvignon, sangiovese, barbera, durif, riesling and chardonnay, plus contracts with a handful of local growers.

ŸŸŸŸŸ Tattooed Lady Shiraz 2002 Strong purple-red; medium- to full-bodied; a rich tapestry of black fruits, licorice, spice and supporting oak; good tannins and a long finish; 130 cases from 30-year-old vines at Great Western. Screwcap. 14° alc. **Rating** 94 To 2022 $45

ŸŸŸŸŸ Acrobat Riesling 2006 A clean, tight, minerally bouquet; citrus, apple and spice flavours on the entry and mid-palate, then a long, citrussy/minerally finish adds significantly to the potential of the wine. From Portland (Henty). Screwcap. 12° alc. **Rating** 93 To 2016 $19

Acrobat Shiraz 2003 Aromatic, spicy plum, black cherry and blackberry aromas; light- to medium-bodied, fresh flavours are more in the red spectrum; good balance and length. Particularly good outcome for the drought vintage. Grampians/Pyrenees. Screwcap. 14° alc. **Rating** 91 **To** 2018 $25

 Acrobat Chardonnay 2005 A light-bodied wine, with a clean bouquet; crisp stone fruit, nectarine and citrus flavours provide length rather than depth; little or no oak. Western Vic. Screwcap. 12.5° alc. **Rating** 89 **To** 2011 $25
Acrobat Cabernet Sauvignon 2003 Light- to medium-bodied; a pretty wine, but seems to have been deprived of body by the difficult growing conditions. Grampians/Pyrenees. Screwcap. 13° alc. **Rating** 88 **To** 2012 $25
Acrobat Sauvignon Blanc 2006 No reduction; plenty of tropical gooseberry fruit, but an unfortunately sweet finish. Screwcap. 12.5° alc. **Rating** 87 **To** 2008 $19

Michelini Wines   ★★★☆

Great Alpine Road, Myrtleford, Vic 3737 **Region** Alpine Valleys
T (03) 5751 1990 **F** (03) 5751 1410 **www**.micheliniwines.com.au **Open** 7 days 10–5
Winemaker Greg O'Keefe **Est.** 1982 **Cases** 8000
The Michelini family are among the best-known grapegrowers in the Buckland Valley of Northeast Victoria. Having migrated from Italy in 1949, the Michelinis originally grew tobacco, diversifying into vineyards in 1982. They now have a little over 42 ha of vineyard on terra rossa soil at an altitude of 300 m, mostly with frontage to the Buckland River. The major part of the production is sold (to Orlando and others), but since 1996 an onsite winery has permitted the Michelinis to vinify part of their production. The winery has the capacity to handle 1000 tonnes of fruit, which eliminates the problem of moving grapes out of a declared phylloxera area.

 Emo Selection Merlot 2004 An extremely tight, savoury style; olive, herb and redcurrant fruit which is strongly varietal, but needs to relax its grip. Plenty of potential. Cork. 14° alc. **Rating** 88 **To** 2012 $50

Midhill Vineyard   ★★★☆

PO Box 30, Romsey, Vic 3434 **Region** Macedon Ranges
T (03) 5429 5565 **Open** Not
Winemaker Contract **Est.** 1993 **Cases** 200
The Richards family has been breeding Angus cattle for the past 35 years, and diversified into grapegrowing in 1993. The vineyard has been planted on a northeast-facing slope on red volcanic clay loam which is free-draining and moderately fertile. There are 2 ha of chardonnay and 0.5 ha each of pinot noir and gewurztraminer.

 Gewurztraminer 2006 Floral spice and rose petal varietal aromas; lively, crisp acidity is offset by just a touch of residual sugar. Clever making. **Rating** 92 **To** 2008

🍇 Millamolong Estate   ★★★

Millamolong Road, Mandurama, NSW 2792 **Region** Orange
T (02) 6367 4088 **F** (02) 6367 4088 **www**.millamolong.com **Open** 7 days 9–4
Winemaker Contract (Madrez Wine Services, Lowe Family Wines) **Est.** 2000 **Cases** 450
This is a book about wine, not polo, but it so happens that Millamolong Estate has been the centrepiece of Australian polo for over 80 years. For an even longer period, generations of James Ashton (differentiated by their middle Christian name) have been at the forefront of a dynasty to make Rawhide or McLeod's Daughters seem tame. In the context of this 28 ha of chardonnay, riesling, cabernet, shiraz and merlot may seem incidental, but it happens to add to the luxury accommodation at the main homestead, which caters for up to 18 guests.

Shiraz 2005 Spice, herb and leaf gives a slightly green overall effect, but the texture and mouthfeel is good, incomparably better than the '04. Cork. **Rating** 87 **To** 2011 $18

Millbrook Winery

Old Chestnut Lane, Jarrahdale, WA 6124 **Region** Perth Hills
T (08) 9525 5796 **F** (08) 9525 5672 **www**.millbrookwinery.com.au **Open** 7 days 10–5
Winemaker Damian Hutton, Andrew Milbourne **Est.** 1996 **Cases** 20 000
The strikingly situated Millbrook Winery is owned by the highly successful Perth-based entrepreneur Peter Fogarty and wife Lee. They also own Lake's Folly in the Hunter Valley, and Deep Woods Estate in Margaret River, and have made a major commitment to the quality end of Australian wine. Millbrook draws on 7.5 ha of vineyards in the Perth Hills, planted to sauvignon blanc, semillon, chardonnay, viognier, cabernet sauvignon, merlot, shiraz and petit verdot. The wines (Millbrook and Barking Owl) are of consistently high quality. Exports to Ireland, Belgium, Germany, Denmark, Singapore and Hong Kong.

ＹＹＹＹＹ **Shiraz Viognier 2004** Deep and clear; flush with blackberry and plum fruit plus the viognier lift; does need time; fleshy, but still with a bite. Cork. 14.5° alc. **Rating** 94 **To** 2024 $35

ＹＹＹＹＹ **Sauvignon Blanc 2006** Good length and intensity; tropical passionfruit flavours dominate, but with some herbaceous notes. Seemingly an excellent vintage for the Perth Hills. Screwcap. 12.5° alc. **Rating** 91 **To** 2008 $20
Cabernet Malbec 2004 Medium-bodied; quite bright and fresh flavours, predominantly in the red fruit spectrum, but blackcurrant still to be felt in the background; overall elegance a plus. Screwcap. 14.5° alc. **Rating** 90 **To** 2014 $25

ＹＹＹＹ **Barking Owl Semillon Sauvignon Blanc 2006** Clean, fresh aromas; considerable flavour and mouthfeel, with sweet fruit in the tropical spectrum, drying off on the finish. Geographe (70%)/Margaret River (30%). Screwcap. 12.5° alc. **Rating** 89 **To** 2008 $16.50
Viognier 2006 Quite weighty in typical viognier style; the flavours, too, are in the expected apricot/ginger/peach spectrum. Screwcap. 14° alc. **Rating** 89 **To** 2009 $22
Barking Owl Shiraz Viognier 2004 Vibrant, penetrating fruit aromas and flavours, with a lingering finish. Edgy rather than the supple feel one expects from this blend. Screwcap. 14.5° alc. **Rating** 89 **To** 2014 $17

Miller's Dixons Creek Estate

1620 Melba Highway, Dixons Creek, Vic 3775 **Region** Yarra Valley
T (03) 5965 2553 **F** (03) 5965 2320 **www**.graememillerwines.com.au **Open** 7 days 10–5
Winemaker Graeme Miller, Reon Vuglar **Est.** 1988 **Cases** 7000
Graeme Miller is a Yarra Valley legend in his own lifetime, having established Chateau Yarrinya (now De Bortoli) in 1971, and as a virtual unknown winning the Jimmy Watson Trophy in 1978 with the 1977 Chateau Yarrinya Cabernet Sauvignon. He sold Chateau Yarrinya in 1986, and, together with wife Bernadette, began establishing a new vineyard which has steadily grown to over 30 ha with chardonnay, cabernet sauvignon, pinot noir, shiraz, sauvignon blanc, petit verdot, pinot gris and merlot. A significant part of the production is sold, but the opening of the winery in 2004, and a cellar door thereafter, has seen production increase.

ＹＹＹＹＹ **Quatrain 2005** This blend of Cabernet Sauvignon/Petit Verdot/Merlot/Cabernet Franc comes together very well; with vibrant, alternating red and black red fruit flavours as the wine travels across the palate; a little on the lean side, but then so were the Bordeauxs of yesteryear. Cork. 13.5° alc. **Rating** 90 **To** 2020 $25

ＹＹＹＹ **Yarra Valley Chardonnay 2006** Light- to medium-bodied; winemaker inputs (whole-bunch pressing, 100% new French oak and partial mlf) have partially subdued the fruit, which needed to be more intense to sustain those inputs. However, the overall flavour is balanced. Poor-quality cork. 13.2° alc. **Rating** 89 **To** 2011 $24
Pinot Noir 2005 Early-picked style with touches of leaf and mint; light-bodied, but not forced; summer drinking. Cork. 13.3° alc. **Rating** 87 **To** 2008 $25

Yarra Valley Shiraz 2005 Firm, cool-grown light- to medium-bodied wine; the acidity is prominent on black cherry fruit and a touch of mint. Cork. 13.5° alc. Rating 87 To 2015 $25

Milton Vineyard ★★★★☆

14635 Tasman Highway, Cranbrook, Tas 7190 **Region** Southern Tasmania
T (03) 6257 8298 **www.**miltonvineyard.com.au **Open** From Dec 2007, 7 days 10–5
Winemaker Julian Alcorso (Contract) **Est.** 1992 **Cases** 780
Michael and Kerry Dunbabin have one of the most historic properties in Tasmania, dating back to 1826. The property is 1800 ha, meaning the 2.7 ha of pinot noir and 1 ha each of riesling and pinot gris (and a touch of traminer) have plenty of room for expansion. Michael Dunbabin says, 'I've planted some of the newer pinot clones in 2001, but have yet to plant what I reckon will prove to be some of the best vineyard sites on the property.' Initially the grapes were sold to Hardys, but in 2005 part of the production was retained; if the climate change Jeremiah's are correct, this small beginning could grow into something good.

 Freycinet Coast Riesling 2006 A fragrant and spotlessly clean bouquet leads into a palate with delicious lime and passionfruit flavours; line, length and balance, are very good, particularly the acidity. Screwcap. 12° alc. Rating 94 To 2016 $20

 Freycinet Coast Pinot Noir 2005 Lots of plum and cherry fruit, the stalky characters adding to length, though not to everyone's liking. Rating 90 To 2012 $27
Freycinet Coast Pinot Noir Chardonnay 2002 Powerful fruit aromas and flavours, the base wine must have been amazing before spending over 3 years on yeast lees; the dosage just a fraction high, perhaps. 12° alc. Rating 90 To 2010 $29

ᵀᵀᵀᵀ Freycinet Coast Rose 2006 Bright puce; light cherry fruit on a long palate with acidity and residual sugar neatly balanced. Screwcap. 13.5° alc. Rating 88 To 2008 $17

Milvine Estate Wines ★★★★

108 Warren Road, Heathcote, Vic 3523 **Region** Heathcote
T (03) 5433 2772 **F** (03) 5433 2769 **Open** W'ends & public hols 11–5
Winemaker Graeme Millard **Est.** 2002 **Cases** 300
Jo and Graeme Millard planted 2 ha of clonally selected shiraz in 1995, picking their first grapes in 1998; in that and the ensuing 4 vintages the grapes were sold to Heathcote Winery, but in 2003 part of the production was vinified by Heathcote Winery for the Millards. Production will increase in the years ahead, and the Millards have a carefully thought-out business plan to market the wine.

Minko Wines ★★★

13 High Street, Willunga, SA 5172 **Region** Southern Fleurieu
T (08) 8556 4987 **F** (08) 8556 2688 **www.**minkowines.com **Open** Wed–Sun 11–5
Winemaker Hawkers Gate (James Hastwell), Mark Day (Consultant), Landara Park (James Little) **Est.** 1997 **Cases** 1600
Mike Boerema (veterinarian) and Margo Kellet (ceramic artist) established the Minko vineyard on their cattle property at Mt Compass. The vineyard is planted to pinot noir, merlot, cabernet sauvignon, chardonnay and pinot gris and managed using sustainable eco-agriculture; 60 ha of the 160-ha property is heritage listed. Exports to the UK.

ᵀᵀᵀᵀ Mount Compass Pinot Grigio 2006 Strong pear skin/apple skin aromas; the palate is not as intense, but in similar vein. Screwcap. 12.5° alc. Rating 89 To 2008 $18
Mount Compass Merlot 2004 Briary/leaf/olive tones; some blackcurrant fruit; strongly varietal, and unforced by oak. Screwcap. 14.5° alc. Rating 88 To 2012 $19

Minot Vineyard

Lot 4 Harrington Road, Margaret River, WA 6285 **Region** Margaret River
T (08) 9757 3579 **F** (08) 9757 2361 **Open** By appt 10–5
Winemaker Harmans Estate (Paul Green) **Est.** 1986 **Cases** 3000
Minot, which takes its name from a small chateau in the Loire Valley in France, is the husband and wife venture of the Miles family, and produces just 2 wines from the 4.2-ha plantings of semillon, sauvignon blanc and cabernet sauvignon. Exports to the UK and Singapore.

ooooo **Margaret River Cabernet Sauvignon 2004** Medium-bodied; and has the precise focus and grip of cool-grown yet ripe cabernet; the tannins are not green, but need to soften and allow the blackcurrant fruit more freedom to move; an interesting wine. Screwcap. 14.4° alc. **Rating** 92 **To** 2024 $25

oooo **Margaret River Semillon Sauvignon Blanc 2006** Fresh and lively citrus and herb aromas and flavours, though a fraction down on intensity. Screwcap. 12° alc. **Rating** 88 **To** 2008 $15

Mintaro Wines

Leasingham Road, Mintaro, SA 5415 **Region** Clare Valley
T (08) 8843 9150 **F** (08) 8843 9050 **Open** 7 days 10–4.30
Winemaker Peter Houldsworth **Est.** 1984 **Cases** 4000
Has produced some very good Riesling over the years, developing well in bottle. The red wines, too, have improved significantly. The labelling is nothing if not interesting, from the depiction of a fish drinking like a fish, not to mention the statuesque belles femmes. Exports to Singapore.

ooooo **Clare Valley Riesling 2006** Aromatic lime and apple blossom, with a touch of slate; intensely focused lime and passionfruit flavours, with a fine, elegant and crisp finish. May be it doesn't reflect its terroir in the usual way, but is a lovely wine. Screwcap. 13° alc. **Rating** 94 **To** 2019 $20
Leckie Window Clare Valley Cabernet Sauvignon 2002 Clear red-purple; excellent blackberry and cassis fruit, bright and focused; a long palate, with good tannins and oak. Slightly sentimental points, perhaps, but only slightly. The story of the Leckie Window is too long to tell here, but it's a remarkable one. Cork. 14.5° alc. **Rating** 94 **To** 2022 $28

oooo **Clare Valley Cabernet Sauvignon 2003** A medium-bodied mix of black and red fruits, with some savoury/earthy overtones; tannin and oak balance good. Screwcap. 14.5° alc. **Rating** 88 **To** 2013 $23

Miramar

Henry Lawson Drive, Mudgee, NSW 2850 **Region** Mudgee
T (02) 6373 3874 **F** (02) 6373 3854 **www**.miramarwines.com.au **Open** 7 days 9–5
Winemaker Ian MacRae **Est.** 1977 **Cases** 6000
Industry veteran Ian MacRae has demonstrated his skill with every type of wine over the decades, ranging from Rose to Chardonnay to full-bodied reds. All have shone under the Miramar label at one time or another; in 2005 there was a marked swing to white wines, with which Ian MacRae has always had a special empathy. The majority of the production from the 35 ha of estate vineyard is sold to others, the best being retained for Miramar's own use.

ooooo **Semillon 2005** Bright, fresh and crisp, with appealing delicacy; flavours of ripe red apple and a touch of stone fruit. Appropriate alcohol a major plus. Screwcap. 11° alc. **Rating** 93 **To** 2015 $15
Riesling 2005 Clean bouquet; powerful and rich, with sweet citrus and apple aromas and flavours; dry finish. Trophy Best Other White Mudgee Wine Show '05. Screwcap. 12.5° alc. **Rating** 90 **To** 2012 $20

Mistletoe Wines

771 Hermitage Road, Pokolbin, NSW 2320 **Region** Lower Hunter Valley
T (02) 4998 7770 **F** (02) 4998 7792 **www.**mistletoewines.com **Open** 7 days 10–6
Winemaker Nick Paterson **Est.** 1989 **Cases** 5000
Mistletoe Wines, owned by Ken and Gwen Sloan, can trace its history back to 1909, when a substantial vineyard was planted on what was then called Mistletoe Farm. The Mistletoe Farm brand made a brief appearance in the late 1970s. The wines are made onsite by Nick Paterson, who has had significant experience in the Hunter Valley. Exports to Japan.

ΨΨΨΨΨ **Reserve Hunter Valley Semillon 2006** High quality Hunter semillon; although youthful, already has citrus characters which will progressively deepen with age, adding toasty notes as they do so. Screwcap. 10° alc.
Rating 95 **To** 2010 $20
Reserve Hunter Valley Chardonnay 2006 Beautifully made wine; quite intense nectarine fruit; barrel ferment in a mix of new and older French oak is carried out by seamless line and flow; good acidity. Screwcap. 13° alc.
Rating 94 **To** 2014 $24
Reserve Hunter Valley Shiraz 2005 Same alcohol as the varietal, but infinitely better colour – strong red-purple; blackberry, plum and a whisper of licorice, earthy Hunter somewhere in the depths and will emerge as the wine matures. Screwcap. 13° alc. **Rating** 94 **To** 2025 $26

ΨΨΨΨΨ **Hunter Valley Chardonnay 2006** Light- to medium-bodied; clean gentle peach and melon fruit; barrel fermentation in older French oak has worked well; good acidity. Screwcap. 13.5° alc. **Rating** 92 **To** 2011 $20
Gold Hunter Valley Botrytis Semillon 2006 Less overwhelmingly sweet than most; well-balanced and by no means short on flavour – indeed, a full-on dessert wine. Screwcap. 10.6° alc. **Rating** 91 **To** 2008 $18.50

ΨΨΨΨ **Hunter Valley Shiraz 2005** Dusty, earthy, regional overtones to red fruits on the light- to medium-bodied palate; overall oak and extract well controlled. Screwcap. 13° alc. **Rating** 89 **To** 2011 $20
Home Vineyard Semillon 2006 Plenty of sweet citrus flavours; full-bodied for such a young wine. Screwcap. 10° alc. **Rating** 87 **To** 2008 $17

Mitchell ★★★★★

Hughes Park Road, Sevenhill via Clare, SA 5453 **Region** Clare Valley
T (08) 8843 4258 **F** (08) 8843 4340 **www.**mitchellwines.com **Open** 7 days 10–4
Winemaker Andrew Mitchell **Est.** 1975 **Cases** 30 000
One of the stalwarts of the Clare Valley, producing long-lived Rieslings and Cabernet Sauvignons in classic regional style. The range now includes very creditable Semillon, Grenache and Shiraz. A lovely old stone apple shed provides the cellar door and upper section of the compact winery. Exports to the US.

ΨΨΨΨΨ **McNicol Riesling 2005** Good texture and depth; won't be exceptionally long-lived, but will certainly have lots of flavour and texture as it matures giving lime, honey, toast, mineral and perhaps a touch of kerosene (the latter not a negative in the case of riesling). Screwcap. **Rating** 94 **To** 2015 $32
Clare Valley Semillon 2005 The characteristic richness and complexity of Mitchell Semillon, but in this instance the fruit and oak are well-balanced and integrated. A high-quality example of barrel-fermented semillon using indigenous/wild yeasts. Screwcap. 13° alc. **Rating** 94 **To** 2012 $21

ΨΨΨΨΨ **Watervale Riesling 2006** Classic regional flavour and structure; also has the tightness often seen with Mitchell Riesling, but with plenty of citrussy flavours and a bright future. Screwcap. 13.5° alc. **Rating** 93 **To** 2016 $21

McNicol Clare Valley Shiraz 1999 Holding its hue particularly well; medium-to full-bodied; a mix of predominantly black fruits with touches of licorice and mocha, the tannins fine but firm; will continue to improve. Cork. 14.5° alc.
Rating 93 **To** 2015 $45

Peppertree Vineyard Sparkling Shiraz NV Particularly good mousse; one of the better sparkling reds, which has picked up elegance from 4 years on lees, and is in no way too sweet. Good length, too. Disgorged May '06. **Rating** 91 **To** 2010 $31

♟♟♟♟ **GSM 2003** An interesting blend, the 'S' normally denoting shiraz, but in this instance sangiovese to go along with the grenache and mourvedre. It comes through with more structure and flavour than expected from the Clare Valley; good balance and length to the spicy red fruits. Screwcap. **Rating** 89 **To** 2010 $20

Sevenhill Cabernet Sauvignon 2003 A strong, indeed formidable, structure; black earthy fruits and firm tannins; needs gentle persuasion and time to temper its aggression. Screwcap. **Rating** 89 **To** 2015 $26

Mitchelton

Mitchellstown via Nagambie, Vic 3608 **Region** Nagambie Lakes
T (03) 5736 2222 **F** (03) 5736 2266 **www.**mitchelton.com.au **Open** 7 days 10–5
Winemaker Toby Barlow **Est.** 1969 **Cases** 220 000
Acquired by Petaluma in 1994 (both now part of Lion Nathan), having already put the runs on the board in no uncertain fashion with gifted winemaker Don Lewis (who retired in 2004). Boasts an array of wines across a broad spectrum of style and price, each carefully aimed at a market niche. Exports to all major markets.

♟♟♟♟♟ **Parish Shiraz Viognier 2004** Excellent colour, and no reduction on the bouquet; rich, multi-layered flavours of spice, licorice and blackberry plus the jab of viognier; not over-extracted, nor over-oaked; impressive wine. Screwcap. 14.5° alc. **Rating** 94 **To** 2019 $29

♟♟♟♟♟ **Heathcote Shiraz 2004** From Jasper and Ironstone rather than Cambrian soils, but still has the same intensity to the black cherry, blackberry, plum and chocolate fruit; very good tannin structure and mouthfeel. Screwcap. 14.5° alc. **Rating** 93 **To** 2024 $14.95

Cigale Barossa Valley Grenache Mourvedre Shiraz 2005 Excellent, supple mouthfeel, with the richness often lacking from the Barossa Valley; a vibrant array of red fruits; begging to be drunk now. Cork. 14.5° alc. **Rating** 93 **To** 2010 $22

Airstrip Marsanne Roussanne Viognier 2004 An interesting wine, with a complex mix of developed and more primary fruit plus the Rhone Valley-inspired varietal mix; should continue to develop typical honeyed/nutty/honeysuckle characters of full maturity. Screwcap. 14° alc. **Rating** 91 **To** 2012 $27

Blackwood Park Riesling 2006 Quite rich and ripe citrus/tropical aromas; plenty of flavour, depth and, above all, length; touches of mineral throughout. Screwcap. 13.5° alc. **Rating** 90 **To** 20146 $16

Viognier 2005 An interesting wine, the colour suggesting more development than there in fact is; apricot and apricot kernel notes, then a clean, crisp finish. Screwcap. 14° alc. **Rating** 90 **To** 2010 $21

♟♟♟♟ **Preece Shiraz 2005** Impressive colour; abundant blackberry, plum and licorice fruit supported by neatly judged tannin and oak inputs; good finish and aftertaste. Screwcap. 14.5° alc. **Rating** 89 **To** 2015 $14.95

Preece Rose 2006 Vivid pink; nicely balanced, with positive cherry/raspberry/strawberry fruit, then a bright, crisp finish. Screwcap. 13° alc. **Rating** 88 **To** 2008 $14.95

Preece Merlot 2005 Plenty of fruit power, though varietal character on the cusp; Sideways fans don't touch it, others enjoy the savoury power. Screwcap. 14.5° alc. **Rating** 88 **To** 2013 $14.95

Preece Sauvignon Blanc 2006 A solid commercial wine, the varietal character blunted but with plenty of presence and overall flavour. Screwcap. 13.5° alc. Rating 87 To 2008 $14.95

Preece Cabernet Sauvignon 2005 Undoubtedly varietal, particularly as it puckers the mouth on the finish; bring on the lamb. Screwcap. 14.5° alc. **Rating** 87 To 2010 $14.95

Blackwood Park Botrytis Riesling 2006 Gently sweet and pleasant; once a bookmark, but others have now passed it by. Screwcap. 12.5° alc. **Rating** 87 To 2009 $17.95

Mitolo Wines   ★★★★★

PO Box 520, Virginia, SA 5120 **Region** McLaren Vale
T (08) 8282 9012 **F** (08) 8282 9062 **www.mitolowines.com.au Open** Not
Winemaker Ben Glaetzer **Est.** 1999 **Cases** 20 000
Frank Mitolo began making wine in 1995 as a hobby, and soon progressed to undertaking formal studies in winemaking. His interest grew year by year, but it was not until 2000 that he took the plunge into the commercial end of the business, retaining Ben Glaetzer to make the wines for him. Since that time, a remarkably good series of wines have been released. Imitation being the sincerest form of flattery, part of the complicated story behind each label name is pure Torbreck, but Mitolo then adds a Latin proverb or saying to the name. Exports to all major markets.

♀♀♀♀♀ **Savitar McLaren Vale Shiraz 2005** Saturated with aromas and flavours; some savoury notes along with blackberry fruits and dark chocolate, lingering tannins; good oak. Cork. 14.5° alc. **Rating** 96 To 2030 $73

Reiver Barossa Valley Shiraz 2005 Very good deep purple-red; intense flavour of black fruits, spices and some red and black cherry; relative control is part of skilled winemaking with such material. Screwcap. 14.5° alc. **Rating** 95 To 2030 $56

G.A.M. McLaren Vale Shiraz 2005 Proclaims its terroir from the first whiff; layer-upon-layer of blackberry and plum fruit, high-quality oak and tannin management. Screwcap. 14.5° alc. **Rating** 95 To 2030 $56

Serpico McLaren Vale Cabernet Sauvignon 2005 Full red-purple; uncompromising varietal character which speaks louder (for once) than the region; savoury blackcurrant and earth fruit, with unexpected elegance. Screwcap. 14.5° alc. **Rating** 95 To 2028 $73

Jester McLaren Vale Cabernet Sauvignon 2005 Potent, rich fruit aromas, then a full, round palate with loads of juicy blackcurrant and cassis fruit; ripe tannins, good oak. Screwcap. 14.5° alc. **Rating** 94 To 2015 $28

♀♀♀♀♀ **Jester McLaren Vale Shiraz 2005** Abundant plum, blackberry, dark chocolate and spice aromas and flavours; soft but adequate tannins; controlled oak. Screwcap. 14.5° alc. **Rating** 93 To 2019 $28

Molly Morgan Vineyard   ★★★☆

Talga Road, Lovedale, NSW 2321 **Region** Lower Hunter Valley
T (02) 9807 4555 **F** (02) 9807 4544 **www.mollymorgan.com Open** By appt
Winemaker John Baruzzi (Consultant) **Est.** 1963 **Cases** 3000
Molly Morgan has been acquired by Andrew and Hady Simon, who established the Camperdown Cellars Group in 1971, which became the largest retailer in Australia, before moving on to other pursuits. They have been recently joined by Grant Breen, their former general manager at Camperdown Cellars. The property has 6.5 ha of 42-year-old unirrigated semillon, which goes to make the Old Vines Semillon, 1 ha for Joe's Block Semillon, 2.4 ha of chardonnay and 3.2 ha of shiraz. Exports to Japan and China.

♀♀♀♀ **Partner's Reserve Shiraz 2004** Fresh, almost juicy berry flavours in a red cherry and plum spectrum; bright finish, good length. Cork. **Rating** 89 To 2015 $38

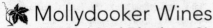

Mollydooker Wines

8/938 South Road, Edwardstown, SA 5039 (postal) **Region** South Australia
T (08) 8179 6500 **F** (08) 8179 6555 www.mollydookerwines.com.au **Open** Not
Winemaker Sarah Marquis, Sparky Marquis **Est.** 2005 **Cases** 65 000
As Sarah and Sparky Marquis wound their way through Fox Creek, Henry's Drive, Parsons Flat,
Marquis Philips and Shirvington, they left a vivid trail of high-flavoured, medal-winning wines in
their wake. After 10 years they took the final step, launching Mollydooker Wines with Robert
Parker their number one ticket holder. Everything about their wines and their business is bigger
than life, with a 65 000-case virtual winery having no credible challenge from within Australia.
They draw grapes from McLaren Vale, Padthaway and Langhorne Creek, restricting themselves to
verdelho, merlot, cabernet sauvignon and – most importantly, of course – shiraz. Oh, and
incidentally, 'mollydooker' is Australian slang for left-handed, an attribute shared by Sarah, Sparky
and Robert Parker. As the tasting notes will make clear, the primary market for the wines will be
the US, and that market should add 5 points to each of my scores.

ΨΨΨΨ   **The Boxer Shiraz 2005** Generous black fruits and lots of dark chocolate in full-
on McLaren Vale style, rich and satisfying. **Rating** 89 **To** 2015 $20
Enchanted Path McLaren Vale Shiraz Cabernet 2005 A massive wine,
although a relatively soft structure to the lashings of dark chocolate, prune and
blackberry jam; the tannins are balanced, but the alcohol shows through on the hot
finish and aftertaste. Cork. 16° alc. **Rating** 89 **To** 2015 $70
Two Left Feet 2005 Another intimidating wine, seemingly higher than 15.5°
alcohol. It seems to sit in the mouth and dares you to swill it, the flavours all of
preserved fruit. Screwcap. 15.5° alc. **Rating** 89 **To** 2015 $23
The Maitre D' Cabernet Sauvignon 2005 There is the impression of sweetness
throughout, emanating not from residual sugar but (one assumes) the alcohol; a
curious wine, offering lots of flavour without much structure. Screwcap. 15° alc.
Rating 88 **To** 2012 $23
Carnival Love McLaren Vale Shiraz 2005 Absurd alcohol completely
dominates the flavour and texture of the wine rather like an Amarone gone off the
rails; in the midst of all of this, a curious touch of bitterness on the finish. Cork.
16.5° alc. **Rating** 87 **To** 2010 $70

Monahan Estate

319 Wilderness Road, Rothbury, NSW 2320 **Region** Lower Hunter Valley
T (02) 4930 9070 **F** (02) 4930 7679 www.monahanestate.com.au **Open** Wed–Sun 10–5
Winemaker Monarch Winemaking Services, Tower Estate **Est.** 1997 **Cases** 2000
Monahan Estate is bordered by Black Creek in the Lovedale district, an area noted for its high-
quality semillon; the old bridge adjoining the property is displayed on the wine label; the wines
themselves have been consistent silver and bronze medal winners at the Hunter Valley Wine Show.

ΨΨΨΨΨ   **Old Bridge Hunter Valley Semillon 2005** Very good green-yellow colour; lots
of flavour in a juicy style, if a fraction broad; a problem, perhaps, for the future.
Screwcap. 12.3° alc. **Rating** 91 **To** 2010 $15

ΨΨΨΨ   **Semillon 1998** Bright gold; toasty/buttery varietal characters have emerged, but
are cut by fairly fierce acidity. **Rating** 89 **To** 2010

Mongrel Creek Vineyard

Lot 72, Hayes Road, Yallingup Siding, WA 6281 **Region** Margaret River
T 0417 991 065 **F** (08) 9755 5708 **Open** W'ends, school & public hols 10–5
Winemaker Michael Kerrigan, Matt Burton **Est.** 1996 **Cases** 900
Larry and Shirley Schoppe both have other occupations, Larry as vineyard supervisor at Howard
Park's Leston Vineyard, Shirley as a full-time nurse. Thus the 2.8-ha vineyard, planted to shiraz,
semillon, sauvignon blanc in 1996, is still a weekend and holiday business. Given the viticultural
and winemaking expertise of those involved, it is hardly surprising that the wines have been
consistent show medal winners.

🍷🍷🍷🍷 **Margaret River Sauvignon Blanc Semillon 2006** A clean but very subdued bouquet, the palate a total contrast; a long, complex interplay of grassy and tropical flavours. Attractive price, as is that for the Shiraz. Screwcap. 12.6° alc. **Rating** 93 **To** 2010 $16
Margaret River Shiraz 2005 Medium-to full-bodied; ripe plum and blackberry fruit supported by soft but persistent tannins and good oak. Screwcap. 14° alc. **Rating** 90 **To** 2015 $18

🍷🍷🍷🍷 **Margaret River Premium White 2005** A clean, fresh and lively blend of semillon, sauvignon blanc and chenin blanc, but not quite enough concentration. Screwcap. 12.4° alc. **Rating** 87 **To** 2008 $14

Monichino Wines

1820 Berrys Road, Katunga, Vic 3640 **Region** Goulburn Valley
T (03) 5864 6452 **www**.monichino.com.au **Open** Mon–Sat 9–5, Sun 10–5
Winemaker Carlo Monichino, Terry Monichino **Est.** 1962 **Cases** 10 000
This winery was an early pacesetter for the region, with clean, fresh wines in which the fruit character was (and is) carefully preserved; also showed a deft touch with its Botrytis Semillon. It has moved with the times, introducing an interesting range of varietal wines while preserving its traditional base.

🌿 Monkey Rock Winery

Wentworth Road, Denmark, WA 6333 **Region** Denmark
T (08) 9840 9353 **F** (08) 9841 6727 **www**.monkeyrockwinery.com.au **Open** W'ends & hols 11–4, or by appt
Winemaker Angelo Scifoni, Hermann Fehr **Est.** 2003 **Cases** 350
Hermann Fehr, a renowned architect, and wife Regula, a retail business owner, left Zurich, Switzerland in 1982 to make their home in Australia. After 7 months travelling they acquired an 80-ha property near Denmark, built their home, began raising cattle, and built 3 self-contained holiday units. In 2000 they planted a small vineyard with sauvignon blanc, pinot noir, merlot and cabernet sauvignon, making the first vintage in 2004, bringing Angelo Scifoni in as partner in the winemaking business. Preservative-free fruit-based wines are also made. The wines are exported (in very small quantities) to Switzerland and Germany, selling into specialist markets offering preservative-free wines. Preservative-free wines are extremely difficult to make; sulphur dioxide not only acts as a preservative (antioxidant) but also as a bacteriacide.

Montalto Vineyards

33 Shoreham Road, Red Hill South, Vic 3937 **Region** Mornington Peninsula
T (03) 5989 8412 **F** (03) 5989 8417 **www**.montalto.com.au **Open** 7 days 11–5
Winemaker Robin Brockett **Est.** 1998 **Cases** 4000
John Mitchell and family established Montalto Vineyards in 1998, but the core of the vineyard goes back to 1986. There are 5.6 ha pinot noir, 3 ha chardonnay, 1 ha pinot gris, and 0.5 ha each of semillon, riesling and pinot meunier. Intensive vineyard work opens up the canopy, with yields ranging between 1.5 and 2.5 tonnes per acre. Wines are released under 2 labels, the flagship Montalto and Pennon, the latter effectively a lower-priced, second label.

🍷🍷🍷🍷🍷 **Mornington Peninsula Chardonnay 2005** Fragrant and intense, with nectarine, grapefruit and white peach all driving the very long palate; the winemaker inputs have all been absorbed by the fruit. Screwcap. 13.1° alc. **Rating** 96 **To** 2018 $32
Mornington Peninsula Pinot Noir 2005 Deeper colour than the Pennon Hill, and has another dimension of depth of flavour; satsuma plum and black cherry; good balance, and a long future; leave it for 3 years, then take your time. Screwcap. 13.2° alc. **Rating** 95 **To** 2014 $37
Pennon Hill Pinot Noir 2005 Typically aromatic and flavoursome, stacked with cherry, plum and spice varietal fruit, oak irrelevant. An impressive second-label wine. Screwcap. 13.2° alc. **Rating** 94 **To** 2010 $25

🍷🍷🍷🍷🍷 **Mornington Peninsula Riesling 2006** A clean and vibrant bouquet with strong apple blossom and wild herb aromas; apple, citrus and pear make their mark on the palate. Has the usual limitations of maritime riesling. Screwcap. 12.5° alc. **Rating** 90 To 2011 $23

Pennon Hill Chardonnay 2006 Fragrant, clean bouquet driven by grapefruit and nectarine, French oak wandering by. Screwcap. 13° alc. **Rating** 90 To 2012 $21

🍷🍷🍷🍷 **Pennon Hill Rose 2006** Has some texture, often missing in rose, and found in Europe; good length and not sweet. Pinot Noir/Pinot Meunier. Screwcap. 13° alc. **Rating** 89 To 2008 $18.50

Pennon Hill Shiraz 2005 Uncompromisingly cool climate; light- to medium-bodied red and black cherry laced with spice and pepper; assertive acidity. Screwcap. 13.5° alc. **Rating** 89 To 2012 $25

Montara ★★★

76 Chalambar Road, Ararat, Vic 3377 **Region** Grampians
T (03) 5352 3868 **F** (03) 5352 4968 **www**.montara.com.au **Open** 7 days 11–4
Winemaker Leigh Clarnette **Est.** 1970 **Cases** 7000
Achieved considerable attention for its Pinot Noirs during the 1980s, but other regions (and other makers) have come along since. It continues to produce wines of distinctive style. One of the most engaging promotions in the entire wine industry is the annual Montara Scarecrow Competition held in the vineyard at the end of April. Even Cirque du Soleil might gain inspiration. I hope the Stapleton family, who have purchased the winery from the founding McRae family, will not evict the scarecrows. Exports to the UK, Switzerland, Canada and Hong Kong.

🍷🍷🍷🍷🍷 **Riesling 2006** Spice, apple, pear and lime aromas; in a taste spectrum all on its own, very different to either the Clare Valley or Great Southern; has length and balance. Screwcap. 13.5° alc. **Rating** 90 To 2013 $17

Montgomery's Hill ★★★★★

South Coast Highway, Upper Kalgan, Albany, WA 6330 **Region** Albany
T (08) 9844 3715 **F** (08) 9844 3819 **www**.montgomeryshill.com.au **Open** 7 days 11–5
Winemaker Dianne Miller, Bill Crappsley (Consultant) **Est.** 1996 **Cases** 6000
Montgomery's Hill is 16 km northeast of Albany on a north-facing slope on the banks of the Kalgan River. Previously used as an apple orchard; it is a diversification for the third generation of the Montgomery family. Chardonnay, cabernet sauvignon, cabernet franc, sauvignon blanc, shiraz and merlot were planted in 1996–97. The wines are made with a gentle touch.

🍷🍷🍷🍷🍷 **Albany Chardonnay 2005** Medium-bodied, cool-grown white peach and melon, with gentle oak woven into the wine; good length and aftertaste. Screwcap. 14.5° alc. **Rating** 94 To 2020 $19

Albany Shiraz 2005 A classy bouquet of black cherry, blackberry and spice; the medium-bodied palate fulfils the promise of the bouquet in its range of flavours, with seamless, ripe tannins. Screwcap. 14° alc. **Rating** 94 To 2020 $19

🍷🍷🍷🍷 **Albany Sauvignon Blanc 2006** Aromatic, attractively delicate style; lemongrass, citrus, passionfruit and gooseberry; long, lingering finish. Different flavour array to the '05. Screwcap. 12° alc. **Rating** 92 To 2008 $17

🍷🍷🍷🍷 **Appleshed Red 2005** Bracingly bright and fresh array of red fruit flavours which are just flavour-ripe; tannin structure a little frail. Screwcap. 14° alc. **Rating** 89 To 2015 $16

Albany Cabernet Sauvignon 2005 Distinctly cool-grown cabernet, with some pretty berry flavours, which are just flavour-ripe; tannin structure a little frail. Screwcap. 13.5° alc. **Rating** 88 To 2013 $19

Albany Cabernet Franc 2005 Quite fragrant, and again proves that WA has better clones of cabernet franc than the eastern states. The wine is a little sharp-edged, but does have sweet berry fruit flavours. Screwcap. 13.5° alc. **Rating** 88 To 2014 $17

Montvalley

150 Mitchells Road, Mount View, NSW 2325 (postal) **Region** Lower Hunter Valley
T (02) 4991 1936 **F** (02) 4991 7994 **www**.montvalley.com.au **Open** Not
Winemaker Monarch Winemaking Services **Est.** 1998 **Cases** 2000
Having looked at dozens of properties over the previous decade, John and Deirdre Colvin purchased their 80-ha property in 1998. They chose the name Montvalley in part because it reflects the beautiful valley in the Brokenback Ranges of which the property forms part, and in part because the name Colvin originates from France, 'col' meaning valley and 'vin' meaning vines. They have planted 5.7 ha of vines, the lion's share to shiraz, with lesser amounts of chardonnay and semillon.

ŶŶŶŶŶ **Hunter Valley Semillon 2003** Bright, light green-straw; introduces a youthful theme, long and lively; crisp lemon, lime and grass flavours. I have never said a good cork can't do the job, and it certainly does so here. 10.2° alc. **Rating** 94 To 2012 $18.75

ŶŶŶŶŶ **Hunter Valley Semillon 2006** Pale straw-green; lemon and lemon zest/lemon peel aromas; lively, with slippery acidity; long and intense. Screwcap. 10.3° alc. **Rating** 93 To 2016 $18.75
Hunter Valley Semillon 2005 Very similar to the '06; perhaps a little richer, and showing the first hints of development. Screwcap. 10.9° alc. **Rating** 93 To 2015 $18.75
Hunter Valley Semillon 2004 A trace of reduction, but the flavour and acidity are very similar to the '06; still very youthful. Screwcap. 10.2° alc. **Rating** 91 To 2014 $18.75

ŶŶŶŶ **Hunter Valley Chardonnay 2006** Light- to medium-bodied; gently peachy fruit, with a well-integrated touch of oak; no horses being frightened here. Screwcap. 13.3° alc. **Rating** 88 To 2008 $19.25
Hunter Valley Shiraz 2003 Obvious colour development; the earthy characters promised by the '04 are starting to show through a wine with somewhat greater persistence. Cork. 12.4° alc. **Rating** 88 To 2012 $19.75
Hunter Valley Shiraz 2004 A pleasant light- to medium-bodied mix of red and black fruits; regional character will develop quickly, but not depth. Screwcap. 12.8° alc. **Rating** 87 To 2011 $19.75

Monument Vineyard

Cnr Escort Way/Manildra Road, Cudal, NSW 2864 **Region** Central Ranges Zone
T (02) 9686 4605 **F** (02) 9686 4605 **www**.monumentvineyard.com.au
Open At Underwood Lane Wines tel (02) 6365 2221
Winemaker Alison Eisermann **Est.** 1998 **Cases** 1500
In the early 1990s 5 mature-age students at Charles Sturt University, successful in their own professions, decided to form a partnership to develop a substantial vineyard and winery After a lengthy search, a large property at Cudal was identified, with ideal terra rossa basalt-derived soil over a limestone base. The property has 110 ha under vine, planted in 1998 and 1999.

ŶŶŶŶŶ **Cudal Shiraz Viognier 2004** Strong colour; abundant blackberry and dark plum base to viognier's polish and fragrance; silky texture. Screwcap. 14.1° alc. **Rating** 94 To 2014 $18
Cudal Cabernet Sauvignon 2004 Attractive blackcurrant and cassis fruit plus mocha oak; excellent mouthfeel, line and flow; equally impressive aftertaste. Screwcap. 15.5° alc. **Rating** 94 To 2024 $16

ŶŶŶŶŶ **Cudal Viognier 2006** Highly scented, positively-accented varietal character; apricot blossom aroma and flavour; not the least phenolic. Screwcap. 14.5° alc. **Rating** 90 To 2009 $18

ŶŶŶŶ **Cudal Sangiovese 2004** Good colour; cigar box and cherry jam characters; perhaps a touch of reduction. Screwcap. 14.5° alc. **Rating** 88 To 2010 $18

Pinot Noir 2004 Deep colour; very strong wine with dark blackberry and plum fruit; long on flavour, but not varietal character. Cork. **Rating** 87 **To** 2011 $14
Cudal Nebbiolo 2004 Typical, very pale, colour; light-bodied, but assertive spicy, savoury hints of forest; enough to tantalise. Screwcap. 14.2° alc. **Rating** 87 **To** 2010 $18

Moojelup Farm ★★★☆

Thompson Road, Cookernup, WA 6220 **Region** Geographe
T (08) 9733 5166 **F** (08) 9733 5490 **www**.moojelup.com.au **Open** By appt
Winemaker Peter Stanlake **Est.** 1997 **Cases** 1000
Moojelup Farm is a historic 40-ha property dating back to the 1870s. The family of present owners, Stephanie and Simon Holthouse, have owned the property for more than half its history. In 1997 they began planting 3.2 ha of semillon, cabernet sauvignon and shiraz; most of the grapes are sold to Millbrook Wines in the Perth Hills, with increasing amounts made for them.

♥♥♥♥ **Thompsons Block Shiraz 2004** Medium red; leaf, mint and herb aromas; the light- to medium-bodied palate offers similar overall flavours; theoretically should taste unripe, but, curiously, the components work quite well. Cork. 14° alc. **Rating** 88 **To** 2012 $18

Moombaki Wines ★★★★★

341 Parker Road, Kentdale via Denmark, WA 6333 **Region** Denmark
T (08) 9840 8006 **F** (08) 9840 8006 **www**.moombaki.com **Open** Thurs–Mon 11–5,
7 days school hols, or by appt
Winemaker Harewood Estate (James Kellie) **Est.** 1997 **Cases** 1200
David Britten and Melissa Boughey (with 3 young sons in tow) established 2 ha of vines on a north-facing gravel hillside with a picturesque Kent River frontage. Not content with establishing the vineyard, they put in significant mixed tree plantings to increase wildlife habitats. It is against this background that they chose Moombaki as their vineyard name: a local Aboriginal word meaning 'where the river meets the sky'. Exports to the UK, Switzerland, Japan and Singapore.

♥♥♥♥♥ **Chardonnay 2005** Delicate, crisp aromas and flavours; grapefruit, melon and nectarine seamlessly woven with French oak; almost fairy-like in its transparency. Screwcap. 13.5° alc. **Rating** 94 **To** 2012 $28
Shiraz 2005 Medium- to full-bodied; abundant black cherry, licorice and spice on both bouquet and palate; the latter has complex texture, with ripe, slightly chewy, but not bitter, tannins. Screwcap. 14.5° alc. **Rating** 94 **To** 2025 $25

♥♥♥♥♀ **Cabernet Sauvignon Cabernet Franc Malbec 2005** A smooth and supple array of sweet red fruits, with some darker berry influences; light- to medium-bodied, the balance good and there is (just) enough structure. Screwcap. 14° alc. **Rating** 90 **To** 2015 $25

Moondah Brook ★★★★☆

c/- Houghton, Dale Road, Middle Swan, WA 6056 **Region** Swan Valley
T (08) 9274 5172 **F** (08) 9274 5372 **www**.moondahbrook.com.au **Open** Not
Winemaker Ross Pamment **Est.** 1968 **Cases** 80 000
Part of the Hardys wine group which has its own special character, as it draws part of its fruit from the large Gingin vineyard, 70 km north of the Swan Valley, and part from the Margaret River and Great Southern. From time to time it has excelled even its own reputation for reliability with some quite lovely wines, in particular honeyed, aged Chenin Blanc, generous Shiraz and finely structured Cabernet Sauvignon.

♥♥♥♥♥ **Chardonnay 2005** Light- to medium-bodied; elegant and crisp stone fruit/grapefruit flavours; just a whisper of oak. Surprise top gold Class 38, National Wine Show '06. Cork. 13.6° alc. **Rating** 94 **To** 2010 $12.50

ƳƳƳƳƳ **Cabernet Sauvignon 2005** Shows why it is regularly rated, year in, year out, as one of the best value cabernets going; medium-bodied, with gentle but unmistakable varietal fruit supported by balanced tannins and oak. Drink now or in 10 years. Cork. 14° alc. **Rating** 91 **To** 2017 $12.50
Cabernet Rose 2006 Vivid red-purple; fresh cassis and raspberry fruit; long and a quite dry finish. Gold medals (at lesser shows) no surprise. Screwcap. 12.5° alc. **Rating** 90 **To** 2008 $12.50

ƳƳƳƳ **Verdelho 2006** Gentle fruit salad helped by lively but not excessive acidity; ever popular. Screwcap. 13.5° alc. **Rating** 87 **To** 2008 $12.50

Moondarra ★★★★☆

Browns Road, Moondarra, Vic 3825 (postal) **Region** Gippsland
T (03) 9598 3049 **F** (03) 9598 0677 **Open** Not
Winemaker Neil Prentice **Est.** 1991 **Cases** 3200
In 1991 Neil Prentice and family established their Moondarra Vineyard in Gippsland, eventually focusing on the 2 ha of low-yielding pinot noir. Subsequently, they began planting their Holly's Garden vineyard at Whitlands in the King Valley, where they have 4 ha of pinot gris and 3 ha of pinot noir. It is from this vineyard that all but 200 cases of their wines come, sold under the Holly's Garden label. Exports to the US and Japan.

ƳƳƳƳƳ **Conception Pinot Noir 2003** Bright and clear colour, the hue still vivid; the palate delivers the promise of the colour, with fresh cherry and raspberry red fruits; good length. The price is awesome. Cork. 12.5° alc. **Rating** 93 **To** 2012 $90
Conception Pinot Noir 2005 Lighter-bodied than Samba Side, but far more complex, with some spicy, savoury notes along with red and black fruits. Cork. 12.5° alc. **Rating** 92 **To** 2012 $100
Samba Side Pinot Noir 2005 Potent plum and black cherry; varietal character is not in doubt, but needs time to open up and reveal its complexity. Cork. 12.5° alc. **Rating** 90 **To** 2013 $120
Holly's Garden Whitlands Pinot Noir 2004 Light to medium red-purple; bright, clean and fresh red berry fruits; good length and balance; just a little light-on. Cork. 13.5° alc. **Rating** 90 **To** 2009 $28

🍇 Moorabool Estate ★★★

45 Dog Rocks Road, Batesford, Vic 3221 (postal) **Region** Geelong
T (03) 5276 1536 **F** (03) 5276 1665 **Open** Not
Winemaker Graham Bonney, Doug Neal **Est.** 1988 **Cases** 1000
Moorabool Estate is established on the site of the original Paradise Vineyard planted in 1848 by Swiss vigneron Jean Henri Dardel, and now owned by Ruth and Graham Bonney. Moorabool Estate re-established grapegrowing in the Moorabool Valley in 1988 with plantings of 0.75 ha each of chardonnay, shiraz and cabernet sauvignon. Doug Neal is a fanatical wine lover, with fingers in many vinicultural pies, and is a particular lover of Burgundy and the Rhone Valley.

🍇 Moorabool Ridge

23 Spiller Road, Lethbridge, Vic 3332 **Region** Geelong
T (03) 5281 9240 **F** (03) 5281 9240 **Open** W'ends & public hols 11–5
Winemaker Peter Flewellyn, Ray Nadeson **Est.** 1991 **Cases** 250
Tim Harrop and Katarina Romanov-Harrop planted their first vines in 1990, and the first olive trees in 2001 (the latter now extended to 800 trees and a commercial olive oil and olive business). Despite the name, the vines are planted on the floor of the Moorabool Valley on the bank of Moorabool River; there are 2 ha of shiraz and 1 ha each of semillon, chardonnay, cabernet sauvignon, cabernet franc and merlot. For the first 10 years the grapes were sold, but thereafter part of the production was retained for the Moorabool Ridge label, sold through the cellar door situated in the historic Sheppard's Hut dating from 1856.

♀♀♀♀♀ Geelong Shiraz 2003 Full red-purple; generous blackberry, licorice and spice fruit; ripe, lingering tannins; controlled oak. Screwcap. 14° alc. **Rating** 92 **To** 2018 $18

Oscar Geelong Cabernet Merlot 2005 Medium red-purple; a light to medium-bodied wine with clean cassis, redcurrant and spice fruit aromas and flavours; unforced and elegant. This wine and the Chardonnay, are at mouth-watering prices. Screwcap. 14° alc. **Rating** 91 **To** 2012 $16

Geelong Chardonnay 2005 A subdued bouquet, but an intense and precise palate has nectarine and citrus fruit, touches of mineral and a whisper of oak, all coming together well. Screwcap. 13° alc. **Rating** 90 **To** 2010 $15

♀♀♀♀ Geelong Semillon 2004 A very generous and rich wine, almost as if some old oak may have been used, though non stated; the screwcap holds the wine together. A fractionally short finish. Screwcap. 13.5° alc. **Rating** 88 **To** 2010 $15

Moores Hill Estate

3343 West Tamar Highway, Sidmouth, Tas 7270 **Region** Northern Tasmania
T (03) 6394 7649 **www**.mooreshill.com.au **Open** Oct–June Wed–Sun 10–5
Winemaker Tamar Ridge **Est.** 1997 **Cases** 3000
Rod and Karen Thorpe established Moores Hill Estate in 1997 on the gentle slopes of the West Tamar Valley. The vineyard has 4.9 ha of riesling, chardonnay, pinot noir, merlot and cabernet sauvignon. The vineyard represents a full circle for the Thorpes, who bought the farm nearly 30 years ago and ripped out a small vineyard. The Wine Centre (built in 2002 mainly from timber found on the property) overlooks the vineyard.

♀♀♀♀♀ Riesling 2006 Ironically, an ever-so-slightly reduced bouquet, but springs into life on the palate, having the power, intensity, drive and length missing from many otherwise good Tasmanian rieslings of the vintage. Screwcap. 13.1° alc. **Rating** 94 **To** 2016 $20

♀♀♀♀♀ Pinot Noir 2005 Medium purple-red; supple, smooth and round plum and black cherry fruit; overall elegance, with a gently savoury finish. Screwcap. 13.9° alc. **Rating** 93 **To** 2012 $22

♀♀♀♀ Unwooded Chardonnay 2006 Nectarine and melon fruit; nicely balanced, but not particularly intense. Screwcap. 13.4° alc. **Rating** 88 **To** 2010 $18

Moorilla Estate

655 Main Road, Berriedale, Tas 7011 **Region** Southern Tasmania
T (03) 6277 9900 **F** (03) 6249 4093 **www**.moorilla.com.au **Open** 7 days 10–5
Winemaker Alan Ferry **Est.** 1958 **Cases** 16 000
Moorilla Estate is an icon in the Tasmanian wine industry and is thriving. Wine quality continues to be unimpeachable, and the opening of the museum in the marvellous Alcorso House designed by Sir Roy Grounds adds even more attraction for visitors to the estate, which is a mere 15–20 mins from Hobart. Five-star self-contained chalets are available, with a stylish, high quality restaurant open for lunch 7 days. A microbrewery, fastidiously equipped and surgically clean, also operates onsite. Exports to the US and Singapore.

♀♀♀♀♀ Riesling 2006 Lime blossom aromas; has considerable power, length and drive; apple, citrus and even peach offset against a minerally backbone. Screwcap. 12° alc. **Rating** 94 **To** 2016 $28

Reserve Cloth Label Syrah 2005 Outstanding colour; great richness and supple mouthfeel; a cascade of spicy black fruits; long finish. Gold medal Tas Wine Show '07. Cork. 14° alc. **Rating** 94 **To** 2015 $60

♀♀♀♀♀ Single Vineyard Chardonnay 2005 Shows colour development, but well within bounds; obvious barrel ferment inputs are carried by the fruit; lots of good things happening here. Screwcap. 13.5° alc. **Rating** 90 **To** 2011 $34

Pinot Noir 2006 Generous plum and cherry fruit; supple and smooth; as yet, not especially complex, but should develop complexity. Screwcap. 14° alc. **Rating** 90 To 2012 $23.50

ᵀᵀᵀᵀ **Vintage Brut 2003** Cuvee 1. Has what can only be described as cleansing penetration; 3 years on lees (disgorged Aug '06), counterbalanced by high acidity. 12.5° alc. **Rating** 88 To 2011 $35

Gewurztraminer 2006 A nice wine; just creeps over the line on varietal character; gentle fruit, with a hint of spice. Screwcap. 13.2° alc. **Rating** 87 To 2008 $34

Claudio's Reserve Cloth Label Pinot Noir 2005 Radically different to the varietal, much more savoury, tangy and stemmy; while long, it is hard to see how sweet pinot fruit will ever escape from the bushes. Cork. 12.5° alc. **Rating** 87 To 2010 $95

Moorooduc Estate

501 Derril Road, Moorooduc, Vic 3936 **Region** Mornington Peninsula
T (03) 5971 8506 **www**.moorooducestate.com.au **Open** W'ends 11–5, 7 days in Jan
Winemaker Dr Richard McIntyre **Est.** 1983 **Cases** 2500
Richard McIntyre has taken Moorooduc Estate to new heights as he has completely mastered the difficult art of gaining maximum results from wild yeast fermentations. While the Chardonnays remain the jewels in the crown, the Pinot Noirs and other wines are also impressive. Exports to Hong Kong and Singapore.

ᵀᵀᵀᵀᵀ **The Moorooduc Wild Yeast Chardonnay 2005** A similar bouquet to the varietal, but overall has slightly more weight and complexity, in particular to the texture and to the creamy notes on the mid- to back-palate. Screwcap. 13.5° alc. **Rating** 96 To 2015 $57.50

Chardonnay 2005 Bright green-yellow; beautifully fashioned and sculpted wine; a multitude of flavours include nectarine, fig, cream and nuts; great length and intensity. Screwcap. 13.5° alc. **Rating** 95 To 2015 $30

Devil Bend Creek Chardonnay 2005 Fine, elegant and pure; gentle inputs to a long and lingering melon and grapefruit palate; only Moorooduc could have a second label of this quality. Screwcap. 13.5° alc. **Rating** 94 To 2012 $21.50

ᵀᵀᵀᵀ **Pinot Noir 2005** Very light colour; light and distinct stemmy/green notes under red fruits. Screwcap. 13.5° alc. **Rating** 90 To 2013 $35

🍃 Mopoke Ridge Wines   **NR**

45B Mopoke Close, Longreach via Nowra, NSW 2541 **Region** Shoalhaven Coast
T (02) 4422 0049 **www**.mopokeridge.com.au **Open** Sept–Mar w'ends 11–5, or by appt
Winemaker Bevan Wilson (Contract) **Est.** 1998 **Cases** NA
Bob and Margaret Torrens began the development of Mopoke Ridge Wines with the planting of cabernet sauvignon in 1998 (0.4 ha), followed by 1 ha of merlot, verdelho and sangiovese in 2000. The most recent addition has been the planting of a few vines of chambourcin. It is a beautifully situated vineyard, in bushland overlooking the Shoalhaven River.

Morambro Creek Wines

Riddoch Highway, Padthaway, SA 5271 (postal) **Region** Padthaway
T (08) 8765 6043 **F** (08) 8765 6011 **Open** Not
Winemaker Nicola Honeysett **Est.** 1994 **Cases** 6000
The Bryson family has been involved in agriculture for more than a century, moving to Padthaway in 1955 as farmers and graziers. In the early 1990s they established 125 ha of vines, principally chardonnay, shiraz and cabernet sauvignon; further plantings are planned. The wines have been consistent winners of bronze and silver medals.

ᵀᵀᵀᵀ **Jip Jip Rocks Chardonnay 2006** Good length; citrus and stone fruit flavours; subtle oak. Screwcap. **Rating** 90 To 2009

ŢŢŢŢ   **Mt Monster Chardonnay 2006** Attractive stone fruit flavours with little, if any, oak evident; good length. Screwcap. **Rating** 89 **To** 2008
Jip Jip Rocks Shiraz 2005 Sweet fruit with nice touches of dark chocolate, a gently ripe finish and fine tannins. **Rating** 89 **To** 2015 $15
Shiraz 2004 Medium-bodied, with plenty of flavour activity through notes of leather, licorice and earth. Zork. **Rating** 88 **To** 2011

Moranghurk Vineyard

1516 Sturt Street, Ballarat, Vic 3350 (postal) **Region** Geelong
T (03) 5331 2105 **F** (03) 5332 9244 **Open** Not
Winemaker Dan Buckle (Contract) **Est.** 1996 **Cases** 340
Ross and Liz Wilkie have established a tiny vineyard on the historic Moranghurk property, which was first settled in 1840. They have planted 0.6 ha of clonally selected pinot noir and 0.5 ha of chardonnay on volcanic soil overlying shale and clay. The vineyard is mulched, and is in the course of being converted to organic, with yields of less than 5 tonnes per ha.

ŢŢŢŢ   **Moorabool Valley Chardonnay 2005** Elegant, fresh and delicate, with the best of its life still to come. Screwcap. 13° alc. **Rating** 89 **To** 2012 $19

Morgan Simpson

PO Box 39, Kensington Park, SA 5068 **Region** McLaren Vale
T 0417 843 118 **F** (08) 8364 3645 **www**.morgansimpson.com.au **Open** Not
Winemaker Richard Simpson **Est.** 1998 **Cases** 2000
Morgan Simpson was founded by SA businessman George Morgan (since retired) and winemaker Richard Simpson, who is a graduate of Charles Sturt University. The grapes are sourced from the Clos Robert Vineyard (where the wine is made) established by Robert Allen Simpson in 1972. The aim is to provide drinkable wines at a reasonable price; it succeeds admirably.

Morgan Vineyards ★★★☆

30 Davross Court, Seville, Vic 3139 **Region** Yarra Valley
T (03) 5964 4807 **www**.morganvineyards.com.au **Open** Mon–Fri 11–4, w'ends & public hols 11–5
Winemaker Roger Morgan **Est.** 1987 **Cases** 1000
Roger Morgan purchased the Kara Gola vineyard (Aboriginal for 'distant views') in 1987. The original 1971 plantings (cabernet sauvignon and pinot noir) were extended in 1989 (pinot noir), 1991 (cabernet sauvignon and merlot) and 1994 (chardonnay) and now total 4.8 ha. Roger completed a wine science degree at Charles Sturt University in 1997 and wife Ally retired from teaching in 2004 to become the marketing and events manager. Heathcote Shiraz was recently added to the product range, and they continue to make elegant and distinctive wines.

ŢŢŢŢŢ   **Heathcote Shiraz 2004** Full of controlled flavours of blackberry, plum, licorice, chocolate and spice; soft but balanced tannins. Cork. 14.3° alc. **Rating** 93 **To** 2019 $30

ŢŢŢŢ   **Yarra Valley Chardonnay 2006** All aspects are under tight wraps, including fruit and oak; how it will evolve is not certain, but the balance is there; worth waiting for. Cork. 14.5° alc. **Rating** 89 **To** 2012 $24
Yarra Valley Pinot Noir 2005 Relatively light in colour and body, but has very good length; red fruits, stem and forest floor interplay; a touch more intensity needed for higher points. Cork. 14.5° alc. **Rating** 89 **To** 2011 $28

MorganField

104 Ashworths Road, Lancefield, Vic 3435 **Region** Macedon Ranges
T (03) 5429 1157 **www**.morganfield.com.au **Open** W'ends & public hols 10–5
Winemaker John Ellis (Contract) **Est.** 2003 **Cases** 800

The vineyard (then known as Ashworths Hill) was first planted in 1980 to pinot noir, shiraz, pinot meunier and cabernet sauvignon. When purchased by Mark and Gina Morgan, additional pinot noir and chardonnay plantings increased the area under vine to 4 ha. The wines are deliberately made in a light-bodied, easy-access fashion.

Morialta Vineyard ★★★★

195 Norton Summit Road, Norton Summit, SA 5136 **Region** Adelaide Hills
T (08) 8390 1061 **F** (08) 8390 1585 **Open** By appt
Winemaker Jeffrey Grosset **Est.** 1989 **Cases** 500
Morialta Vineyard was planted in 1989 on a site first planted to vines in the 1860s by John Baker. The Bunya pine depicted on the label is one of the few surviving trees from that era, and indeed one of the few surviving trees of that genus. The 20-ha property has 11 ha under vine, planted to chardonnay, pinot noir, cabernet sauvignon, sauvignon blanc, shiraz and merlot. Most of the grapes are sold. Given the age of the vineyard and winemaking by Jeffrey Grosset, it is not surprising that the wines have done well in the Adelaide Hills Wine Show.

Morningside Vineyard ★★★☆

711 Middle Tea Tree Road, Tea Tree, Tas 7017 **Region** Southern Tasmania
T (03) 6268 1748 **F** (03) 6268 1748 **Open** By appt
Winemaker Peter Bosworth **Est.** 1980 **Cases** 600
The name Morningside was given to the old property on which the vineyard stands because it gets the morning sun first; the property on the other side of the valley was known as Eveningside. Consistent with the observation of the early settlers, the Morningside grapes achieve full maturity with good colour and varietal flavour. Production will increase as the 2.9-ha vineyard matures, and as recent additions of clonally selected pinot noir (including 8104, 115 and 777) come into bearing.

ŦŦŦŦ **Pinot Noir 2005** Powerful, focused and concentrated; seems to have been picked a little too late, the finish lacking conviction. **Rating** 89 **To** 2012
Riesling 2006 Apple and spice aromas, with pleasant citrus flavours joining on the delicate palate. **Rating** 88 **To** 2011

Morris

Mia Mia Road, Rutherglen, Vic 3685 **Region** Rutherglen
T (02) 6026 7303 **www**.morriswines.com **Open** Mon–Sat 9–5, Sun 10–5
Winemaker David Morris **Est.** 1859 **Cases** 100 000
One of the greatest of the fortified winemakers, ranking with Chambers Rosewood. Just to confuse matters a little, Morris has decided to move away from the 4-tier classification structure used by other Rutherglen winemakers (other than Chambers, that is) and simply have 2 levels: varietal and Old Premium. The oldest components of the Old Premium are entered in a handful of shows, but the trophies and stratospheric gold medal points they receive are not claimed for the Old Premium wines. The art of all of these wines lies in the blending of very old and much younger material. They have no equivalent in any other part of the world.

ŦŦŦŦŦ **Old Premium Liqueur Tokay NV** Much deeper aged olive-brown colour; the wine viscous when poured; while rich and lusciously mouthfilling, the richness is balanced to perfection by nutty/smoky rancio characters highlighting the array of spices, burnt toffee and tea-leaf; exceptional length. A national treasure. 18° alc. **Rating** 97 **To** 2008 $64.95
Old Premium Liqueur Muscat NV Deep olive-brown, coating the sides of the glass briefly when it is swirled; needless to say, is exceptionally rich and luscious, but – even more – complex, with a dense array of oriental sweet spices, dried raisins, and (for me) childhood memories of mother's Christmas pudding laced with brandy. And, yes, this really does go with dark, bitter chocolate in any form. 17.5° alc. **Rating** 97 **To** 2008 $64.95

Old Premium Tawny Port NV Medium depth to the colour, true tawny and not liqueur; a vibrant palate, with rich and luscious fruit, then extreme rancio provides perfect balance, the acidity neither biting nor volatile. Great texture. 18° alc. **Rating** 96 **To** 2008 $44.95

Liqueur Tokay NV Pale golden-brown; classic toffee (dominant), tea-leaf, honey, butterscotch and cake run through the long palate; good spirit is, as ever, beautifully balanced and composed. Marvellous aftertaste and pricing. Screwcap. 18° alc. **Rating** 94 **To** 2008 $16.95

Liqueur Muscat NV More touches of red-brown than the Liqueur Tokay, precisely as it should be; fragrant raisin varietal fruit luring you into the second glass; perfect balance. Screwcap. 18° alc. **Rating** 94 **To** 2008 $16.95

ŸŸŸŸ **Rutherglen Shiraz 2004** Solid traditional style; blackberry fruit, dark plum and touches of earth and chocolate; oak not obvious; ripe tannins. Cork. **Rating** 88 **To** 2012 $14.95

Mortimers of Orange

'Chestnut Garth', 786 Burrendong Way, Orange, NSW 2800 **Region** Orange
T (02) 6365 8689 **F** (02) 6365 8689 **www.**mortimerwine.com.au **Open** W'ends 11–5
Winemaker Simon Gilbert **Est.** 1996 **Cases** 4000
Peter and Julie Mortimer began the establishment of their vineyard (named after a quiet street in the Humberside village of Burton Pidsea in the UK) in 1996. They now have just over 4 ha of chardonnay, shiraz, cabernet sauvignon, merlot and pinot noir. Exports to the UK.

ŸŸŸŸ **Chestnut Garth Chardonnay 2005** In dramatically different style to Autumn Chardonnay, with rich, mouthfilling butterscotch flavours, but short on elegance. Screwcap. **Rating** 87 **To** 2009 $21

Mosquito Hill Wines ★★★☆

18 Trinity Street, College Park, SA 5069 (postal) **Region** Southern Fleurieu
T 0411 661 149 **F** (08) 8222 5896 **Open** Not
Winemaker Glyn Jamieson, Nepenthe **Est.** 2004 **Cases** 2000
In 1994, Glyn and Elizabeth Jamieson brought their small property on Mosquito Hill Road at Mt Jagged on the Fleurieu Peninsula. Glyn Jamieson is yet another of the innumerable tribe of doctors who combine 2 professions; he just happens to be the prestigious Dorothy Mortlock Professor and Chairman of the Department of Surgery of the University of Adelaide. He and wife Elizabeth's interest in wine goes back for decades, and in 1990 they lived in France for a year where he received both vinous and medical recognition. In 1994 Glyn commenced the part-time (distance) degree at Charles Sturt University and says that while he never failed an exam, it did take him 11 years to complete the course. His year in France directed him to Burgundy, rather than Bordeaux, hence the planting of 2.6 ha of chardonnay and 1.8 ha pinot noir on the slopes of Mt Jagged. Just where the future winemaking responsibilities will lie remains to be seen in the wake of Peter Leske's departure from Nepenthe, but Glyn has picked up a lot along the way.

ŸŸŸŸ **Southern Fleurieu Chardonnay 2005** Aromatic, and distinctly more lively and – surprisingly – fresher than the same wine under screwcap; a citrussy tang to the stone fruit, and a lively finish. Comprehensively proves the exception to the rule, and one of the few times I have seen a cork version of a white wine better than a screwcap. Cork. 13.1° alc. **Rating** 89 **To** 2012

Alexandrina Hills The Hawthorns Pinot Noir 2005 Respectable plum and cherry fruit within the parameters for pinot noir; give it time to develop complexity. **Rating** 88 **To** 2011

Moss Brothers

3857 Caves Road, Wilyabrup, WA 6280 **Region** Margaret River
T (08) 9755 6270 **F** (08) 9755 6298 **www.**mossbrothers.com.au **Open** 7 days 10–5
Winemaker David Moss, Navneet Singh **Est.** 1984 **Cases** 20 000

Established by long-term viticulturist Jeff Moss and his family, notably sons Peter and David and Roseworthy graduate daughter Jane. A 100-tonne rammed-earth winery was constructed in 1992 and draws upon both estate-grown and purchased grapes. Exports to the US, Canada, Germany and Singapore.

ŶŶŶŶŶ **Single Vineyard Margaret River Chardonnay 2005** No reduction; an elegant wine, with very good balance and integration of nectarine and white peach fruit, with cashew/smoky oak. Excellent line, length and finish. Screwcap. 13.5° alc. **Rating** 94 **To** 2014 $30

ŶŶŶŶŶ **Jane Moss Semillon Sauvignon Blanc 2006** Clean and fragrant; gentle fruit expression in total contract to Moses Rock; gooseberry and kiwifruit with a balanced, dry, crisp finish. Screwcap. 13° alc. **Rating** 90 **To** 2010 $22

ŶŶŶŶ **Jane Moss Pinot Noir 2004** Not a lot of volume, but has undoubted varietal character in a region which struggles to express this; spice/bramble/forest nuances to plummy fruit; all in all, quite an achievement. Screwcap. 14.5° alc. **Rating** 89 **To** 2010 $22

Moses Rock Shiraz 2004 An attractive mix of spicy black cherry, plum and blackberry fruit; soft tannins, good length. Screwcap. 14.5° alc. **Rating** 89 **To** 2013 $17

Cabernet Sauvignon Merlot 2003 Light- to medium-bodied; has savoury components, but also sweet fruit helped along by nicely balanced French and American oak; soft tannins to finish. Cork. 14.5° alc. **Rating** 89 **To** 2014 $30

Margaret River Sauvignon Blanc 2006 The bouquet is closed, but not reduced as is the Semillon; moderate gooseberry and kiwifruit with some notes of herb. Screwcap. 12.5° alc. **Rating** 88 **To** 2008 $22

Moses Rock Margaret River Sauvignon Blanc Semillon 2006 A tightly wound wine with some mineral overlay to the citrus flavours, seemingly wishing to hide its fruit under the Rock. Screwcap. 12.5° alc. **Rating** 87 **To** 2008 $17

Moss Wood   ★★★★★

Metricup Road, Wilyabrup, WA 6284 **Region** Margaret River
T (08) 9755 6266 **F** (08) 9755 6303 **www.**mosswood.com.au **Open** By appt
Winemaker Keith Mugford, Josh Bahen, Amanda Shepherdson **Est.** 1969 **Cases** 15 000
Widely regarded as one of the best wineries in the region, capable of producing glorious Semillon in both oaked and unoaked forms, unctuous Chardonnay and elegant, gently herbaceous, superfine Cabernet Sauvignon which lives for many years. In 2000 Moss Wood acquired the Ribbon Vale Estate; the Ribbon Vale wines are now treated as vineyard-designated within the Moss Wood umbrella. Exports to all major markets.

ŶŶŶŶŶ **Ribbon Vale Vineyard Semillon Sauvignon Blanc 2006** A clean bouquet; an unusually supple mouthfeel, yet not flabby; the usual complex array of flavours all the way from herb and mineral to tropical passionfruit. Screwcap. 13° alc. **Rating** 92 **To** 2009 $24

Amy's Margaret River Cabernet Sauvignon 2005 Light- to medium-bodied; gentle fruit impact on entry, with some earthy undertones; fine tannins and a restrained style with grows on you each time you return to the glass. Screwcap. 14° alc. **Rating** 92 **To** 2019 $26

Margaret River Cabernet Sauvignon 2003 Bright, clear red-purple; lots of varietal fruit in a typical blackcurrant/cassis spectrum, but the abrupt and slightly dry tannins come as a shock on the back-palate; time should see these soften. Screwcap. 14.5° alc. **Rating** 92 **To** 2028 $95

ŶŶŶŶ **Ribbon Vale Vineyard Cabernet Sauvignon Merlot 2004** Not entirely convincing; despite the alcohol, there are underlying touches of green and mint which diminish an otherwise well-balanced, medium-bodied wine. Screwcap. 14.5° alc. **Rating** 89 **To** 2014 $35.50

Margaret River Pinot Noir 2004 As ever, well-made, and is precisely as Keith Mugford would have it; for me it is no more than a nice, medium-bodied red wine of no particular varietal distinction. Screwcap. 13° alc. **Rating** 87 **To** 2012 $45

Mount Avoca ★★★★

Moates Lane, Avoca, Vic 3467 **Region** Pyrenees
T (03) 5465 3282 **F** (03) 5465 3544 **www**.mountavoca.com **Open** 7 days 10–5
Winemaker Matthew Barry **Est.** 1970 **Cases** 20 000
A substantial winery which has long been one of the stalwarts of the Pyrenees region, and is steadily growing, with 23.7 ha of vineyards. There has been a significant refinement in the style and flavour of the red wines over the past few years. I suspect a lot of worthwhile work has gone into barrel selection and maintenance. Reverted to family ownership in 2003 after a short period as part of the ill-fated Barrington Estates group. Exports to Asia.

ȚȚȚȚ˚ **Shiraz 2003** A smooth, supple, clean medium-bodied wine; predominantly red and black cherry fruits; fine tannins and good length. Cork. 14.5° alc. **Rating** 92 **To** 2013 $22
Semillon Sauvignon Blanc 2006 An undemonstrative bouquet, but the palate has both life and intensity in a citrus, herb and grass spectrum; long finish. Screwcap. 12.5° alc. **Rating** 90 **To** 2011 $16

ȚȚȚȚ **Merlot 2002** Medium red; strongly varietal savoury, black olive and spice accents to the fruit; fine tannins. Procork. 13.5° alc. **Rating** 89 **To** 2012 $22
Sauvignon Blanc 2006 Minerally/slatey aromas; a fleeting nuance of sugar on entry, then gentle passionfruit and gooseberry flavours run through to the finish. Screwcap. 13° alc. **Rating** 88 **To** 2008 $18
Cabernet Sauvignon 2002 Light- to medium-bodied; savoury/earthy wine with touches of green from the cool vintage. ProCork. 13.5° alc. **Rating** 87 **To** 2010 $22

Mount Broke Wines ★★★★☆

130 Adams Peak Road, Broke, NSW 2330 **Region** Lower Hunter Valley
T (02) 6579 1314 **F** (02) 6579 1314 **www**.mtbrokewines.com.au **Open** W'ends 12–3
Winemaker First Creek Winemaking Services **Est.** 1997 **Cases** 500
Phil and Jo McNamara began planting 9.6-ha vineyard to shiraz, merlot, verdelho, barbera, semillon, chardonnay and cabernet sauvignon in 1997 on the west side of Wollombi Brook. Over the years since coming into production, the wines have been prolific medal winners in regional and boutique wine shows.

ȚȚȚȚȚ **River Bank Shiraz 2005** Strong blackberry fruit; has both line and length; oak and tannins controlled. Superb winemaking. **Rating** 94 **To** 2020 $25

ȚȚȚȚ˚ **Quince Tree Paddock Hunter Valley Semillon 2006** Lively, bright flavours almost crossing over into young riesling territory; lemon and mineral drive the long finish. Screwcap. 10.5° alc. **Rating** 93 **To** 2016 $18
Adam's Peak Chardonnay 2006 Particularly expressive and vibrant fruit for the region; nectarine and melon run through to a long finish and clean aftertaste. Screwcap. 13.4° alc. **Rating** 92 **To** 2011 $22

ȚȚȚȚ **Quince Tree Paddock Barbera 2005** Well-made, with firm but bright black cherry and plum fruit; firm acidity gives the wine an impressive finish. Screwcap. 14° alc. **Rating** 89 **To** 2015 $28

Mount Buffalo Vineyard ★★★★☆

6300 Great Alpine Road, Eurobin, Vic 3739 **Region** Alpine Valleys
T (03) 5756 2523 **F** (03) 5756 2523 **Open** 7 days 9–5
Winemaker Cyril Ciavarella **Est.** 1998 **Cases** 450
Colin and Lorraine Leita have a substantial horticultural property (Bright Berry Farms) in the foothills of Mt Buffalo. They have diversified into viticulture with 1 ha each of viognier, shiraz and

cabernet sauvignon, and 4 ha of merlot. The Great Alpine Road provides a steady stream of visitors to the cellar door.

ᵠᵠᵠᵠᵠ **Shiraz Viognier 2004** Fragrant aromas so typical of the blend, as is the rich and juicy fruit, and good structure. Cork. **Rating** 92 **To** 2011 $25
Shiraz 2005 While only medium-bodied, has excellent flavour and structure, showing no green/unripe flavours; smooth, silky tannins and a fresh finish. Screwcap. **Rating** 92 **To** 2015 $25

ᵠᵠᵠᵠ **Shiraz Viognier 2002** Holding hue well enough; elegant, though light-bodied, with some spice, but the viognier not as obvious as it is in the '04, perhaps the very cool vintage. Cork. 13.6° alc. **Rating** 89 **To** 2010 $28
Merlot 2002 Distinctly savoury/earthy characters reflecting both the vintage and bottle age; does not have a lot of flesh, but the spice and olive give varietal appeal. Cork. 13.2° alc. **Rating** 88 **To** 2010 $20

Mount Burrumboot Estate ★★★★☆

3332 Heathcote-Rochester Road, Colbinabbin, Vic 3559 **Region** Heathcote
T (03) 5432 9238 **F** (03) 5432 9238 **www**.burrumboot.com **Open** W'ends & public hols 11–5, or by appt
Winemaker Cathy Branson **Est.** 1999 **Cases** 1500
To quote, 'Mount Burrumboot Estate was born in 1999, when Andrew and Cathy Branson planted vines on the Home Block of the Branson family farm, Donore, on the slopes of Mt Burrumboot, on the Mt Camel Range, above Colbinabbin. Originally the vineyard was just another diversification of an already diverse farming enterprise. However, the wine bug soon bit Andrew and Cathy, and so a winery was established. The first wine was made in 2001 by contract – however, 2002 vintage saw the first wine made by Cathy in the machinery shed, surrounded by headers and tractors. Very primitive, and the appearance of the new 50-tonne winery in 2002 was greeted with great enthusiasm!' And then you taste the wines. Amazing.

Mount Camel Ridge Estate ★★★★☆

473 Heathcote Rochester Road, Heathcote, Vic 3523 **Region** Heathcote
T (03) 5433 2343 **Open** By appt
Winemaker Ian Langford, Gwenda Langford **Est.** 1999 **Cases** 350
Commencing in 1999, Ian and Gwenda Langford planted 18 ha of vines, the majority to shiraz (8.5 ha), cabernet sauvignon (3.8 ha) and merlot (3 ha), with a little over 0.5 ha each of petit verdot, viognier and mourvedre. The land has been developed using organic principles, using composted chicken manure every 3 years, the application of seaweed fertiliser and mulching of the prunings. The vineyard is dry-grown, and no copper, lime or sulphur fungicide has been used. The Langfords say, 'As a result, worms have reappeared, and there is now an extensive frog population, ladybirds and other invertebrates and a range of beautiful spiders.' The very attractive red wines are made in open half-tonne vats, basket-pressed and matured in French oak.

ᵠᵠᵠᵠᵠ **Heathcote Cabernet Sauvignon 2005** Medium-bodied; good blackcurrant fruit supported by fine, almost sweet, tannins and appropriate oak; excellent mouthfeel and balance. Cork. 13.3° alc. **Rating** 94 **To** 2020 $40

ᵠᵠᵠᵠ **Heathcote Shiraz 2005** Light- to medium-bodied, well away from the usual full-blooded alcohol style; has elegant red fruits, but the mid-palate falters before dusty tannins on the finish. Cork. 13.6° alc. **Rating** 89 **To** 2014 $40

Mount Charlie Winery ★★★

228 Mount Charlie Road, Riddells Creek, Vic 3431 **Region** Macedon Ranges
T (03) 5428 6946 **www**.mountcharlie.com.au **Open** Most w'ends 11–3 or by appt
Winemaker Trefor Morgan **Est.** 1991 **Cases** 800
Mount Charlie's wines are sold principally by mail order and through selected restaurants. A futures program encourages mailing list sales with a discount of over 25% on the release price.

Owner/winemaker Trefor Morgan is perhaps better known as Professor of Physiology at Melbourne University. He also acts as a contract maker for others in the region.

ＹＹＹＹ   **Chardonnay 2005** Clean, crisp and fresh; very light-bodied and delicate, the barrel ferment and mlf challenging the depth of the fruit. Screwcap. 14.1° alc. **Rating** 88 To 2013 $19.95

Mount Coghill Vineyard ★★★

Clunes-Learmonth Road, Coghills Creek, Vic 3364 **Region** Ballarat
T (03) 5343 4329 **F** (03) 5343 4329 **Open** W'ends 10–5
Winemaker Norman Latta **Est.** 1993 **Cases** 420
Ian (an award-winning photographer) and Margaret Pym began planting their tiny vineyard in 1995 with 1280 pinot noir rootlings, and added 450 chardonnay rootlings the next year. Since 2001 the wine has been made and released under the Mount Coghill Vineyard label.

ＹＹＹＹ   **Ballarat Pinot Noir 2004** Light but bright colour; fresh, crisp strawberry and cherry flavours; more to rose/Beaujolais; the alcohol tells the tale. Screwcap. 12.2° alc. **Rating** 87 To 2008

 ## Mount Cole Wineworks ★★★★★

197 Mount Cole Road, Warrail, Vic 3377 **Region** Grampians
T (03) 5352 2311 **F** (03) 5354 3279 **www.**mountcolewineworks.com.au **Open** By appt
Winemaker Dr Graeme Bertuch **Est.** 1998 **Cases** 800
Dr Graeme Bertuch's involvement in grapegrowing and winemaking goes back far further than the establishment of Mount Cole Wineworks. In 1977 he established Cathcart Ridge, but found the time demands on a rural doctor-cum-vigneron were too much. He sold Cathcart Ridge in 1993, but did not sell the itch to grow grapes and make wine. In 1998 he and wife Carolyn purchased a property at the foot of Mount Cole State Forest and began planting 3.5 ha of shiraz, adding 1 ha of viognier and 0.5 ha each of nebbiolo and riesling by 2004, the same year that he made his first wine. He chose well, for the quality of his shiraz has already netted him trophies at the Ballarat Wine Show and the Ararat Wine Challenge – and deservedly so.

ＹＹＹＹＹ   **Collectors Edition Shiraz 2004** Very good purple; an elegant, finely structured wine with a gently spicy array of red fruits; not the style which normally catches the judge's eye, but did so at the Ballarat Wine Show '06, winning 2 trophies. Screwcap. 13.5° alc. **Rating** 94 To 2019 $37

ＹＹＹＹＹ   **Off the Beaten Track Shiraz 2004** Despite the lower alcohol, seems to have marginally riper fruit flavours than the Collectors Edition; abundant spice and pepper; good length; good price. Screwcap. 13° alc. **Rating** 92 To 2015 $23

Mount Eyre Vineyards ★★★★☆

173 Gillards Road, Pokolbin, NSW 2321 **Region** Lower Hunter Valley
T 0438 683 973 **F** (02) 6842 4513 **www.**mounteyre.com **Open** By appt
Winemaker Stepehn Hagan, Aniello Iannuzzi **Est.** 1970 **Cases** 5000
Mount Eyre draws on 2 vineyards, the first a 24-ha estate at Broke, planted to semillon, chardonnay, shiraz, chambourcin, cabernet franc and cabernet sauvignon, and the second, Holman Estate, in Gillards Road, Pokolbin, with 4 ha of shiraz and 1.8 ha of merlot. Exports to the US, Canada and other major markets.

ＹＹＹＹＹ   **Three Ponds Hunter Valley Chardonnay 2005** Pale green-straw; fresh, delicate and restrained nectarine and stone fruit aromas and flavours; good length, and the 15 months in oak has not gone over the top. Screwcap. 13.5° alc. **Rating** 91 To 2012 $25

ＹＹＹＹ   **Three Ponds Hunter Valley Shiraz 2005** Light- to medium-bodied; strongly, stridently regional with marked earth and leather characters; good length. Screwcap. 14° alc. **Rating** 88 To 2015 $30

Mount Gisborne Wines

83 Waterson Road, Gisborne, Vic 3437 **Region** Macedon Ranges
T (03) 5428 2834 **F** (03) 5428 2834 **Open** W'ends 10–5
Winemaker David Ell, Stuart Anderson **Est.** 1986 **Cases** 1000
Mount Gisborne Wines is very much a weekend and holiday occupation for proprietor David
Ell, who makes the wines from the 7-ha vineyard under the watchful and skilled eye of industry
veteran Stuart Anderson, now living in semi-retirement high in the Macedon Hills. Exports to
the UK, Canada, Singapore and Malaysia.

ŢŢŢŢŢ **Macedon Ranges Chardonnay 2005** A clean, tangy, citrussy bouquet, with
incisive fruit and acidity in the mouth; long and racy, oak largely irrelevant; at
the far extreme of the Chablis model. Diam. 13° alc. **Rating** 90 **To** 2015 $25

ŢŢŢŢ **Macedon Ranges Pinot Noir 2004** Fresh red fruits in a plum spectrum; quite
tangy (rather than savoury); good length and a brisk finish; needs to soften, and will
do so. Diam. 14° alc. **Rating** 89 **To** 2012 $26.25

Mount Horrocks

The Old Railway Station, Curling Street, Auburn, SA 5451 **Region** Clare Valley
T (08) 8849 2243 www.mounthorrocks.com **Open** W'ends & public hols 10–5
Winemaker Stephanie Toole **Est.** 1982 **Cases** 4500
Mount Horrocks has well and truly established its own identity in recent years, aided by positive
marketing and, equally importantly, wine quality which has resulted in both show success and
critical acclaim. Stephanie Toole has worked long and hard to achieve this, and I strongly advise
you (or anyone else) not to get in her way. Exports to all major markets.

ŢŢŢŢŢ **Watervale Riesling 2005** Bright, light glowing green-straw; a pure expression
of varietal fruit on the bouquet, the gorgeous palate starting to flower with an
extra year in the bottle; multifaceted layers of lime, tropical fruit, spice and
mineral notes. Screwcap. 13° alc. **Rating** 96 **To** 2025 $28
Watervale Riesling 2006 Light straw-green; clean, supple tropical lime juice
flavours run right through the length of the palate to the finish; utterly
delicious now or in 10 years time. Screwcap. 13° alc. **Rating** 94 **To** 2016 $28
Watervale Shiraz 2004 Spotlessly clean aromas; a very supple and smooth
palate with gently sweet red and black fruits; excellent control of extract and
alcohol. Screwcap. 14° alc. **Rating** 94 **To** 2015 $32
Cabernet Sauvignon 2004 Offers sweet cassis berry fruit without undue
tannin or extraction; sympathetic oak plays a role in an overall finely crafted
wine. Screwcap. 14° alc. **Rating** 94 **To** 2024 $35

ŢŢŢŢŢ **Semillon 2005** Light straw-green; remarkably elegant given the alcohol; tight
mineral and citrus rind, plus a touch of passionfruit. Screwcap. 14° alc. **Rating** 93
To 2012 $27
Cordon Cut Riesling 2006 Intensely sweet lime/lemon/crystallised fruit
characters; a lingering finish, albeit with relatively soft acidity. Screwcap. 10.5° alc.
Rating 93 **To** 2016 $32

Mount Langi Ghiran Vineyards

Warrak Road, Buangor, Vic 3375 **Region** Grampians
T (03) 5354 3207 **F** (03) 5354 3277 www.langi.com.au **Open** Mon–Fri 9–5, w'ends 12–5
Winemaker Dan Buckle **Est.** 1969 **Cases** 60 000
A maker of outstanding cool-climate peppery Shiraz, crammed with flavour and vinosity, and very
good Cabernet Sauvignon. The Shiraz points the way for cool-climate examples of the variety. The
business was acquired by the Rathbone family group in 2002, and hence has been integrated with
the Yering Station product range, a synergistic mix with no overlap. Exports to all major markets.

ioioioioio **Langi Shiraz 2005** Powerful purple colour; the same seamless flow of fruit, oak and tannins as in the preceding vintages; the flavours range through red cherry, blackberry, spice, pepper, tamed by lively acidity and fine tannins. Screwcap. 14.5° alc. **Rating** 96 **To** 2020 $60
Langi Shiraz 2004 Shares with the '03 and the '05 vivid flavours, yet has seamless fruit and oak integration on both the bouquet and palate. The flavours range through the expected spectrum of blackberry, spice, cracked pepper and licorice; long and vibrant mouthfeel, with good acidity. Screwcap. 15° alc. **Rating** 95 **To** 2020 $55
Chardonnay 2006 An elegant, understated wine which certainly doesn't show any sign of warm alcohol; stone fruit and citrus are seamlessly integrated with the barrel ferment oak; long finish. Screwcap. 14° alc. **Rating** 94 **To** 2011 $28
Nowhere Creek Shiraz 2005 Strong red-purple; medium-bodied, with multifaceted cherry, blackberry and licorice fruits; more elegant than Moyston Hills. Screwcap. 15° alc. **Rating** 94 **To** 2020 $25

ioioioioio **The Gap Vineyard Shiraz 2005** Vibrant purple-red, clear and vivid; abundant sweet fruit conspicuously lacking from earlier vintages of The Gap; medium-bodied, with good acidity and length. Screwcap. 14° alc. **Rating** 93 **To** 2015 $25
Cliff Edge Shiraz 2005 Even stronger colour than the Billi Billi; a fragrant, elegant bouquet with fresh red and black fruits, gentle oak and a long finish. Screwcap. 14.5° alc. **Rating** 93 **To** 218 $25
Moyston Hills Vineyard Shiraz 2005 Bright colour; medium- to full-bodied; ripe plum, prune and blackberry fruit flavours; a linear style, with intensity running through to the finish. Screwcap. 15° alc. **Rating** 93 **To** 2020 $25
Billi Billi Shiraz 2005 Strong, deep purple-red; abundant blackberry fruits; good structure, combining elegance with power; long finish. Screwcap. 14° alc. **Rating** 91 **To** 2015 $15
Robinson Vineyard Shiraz 2004 Typical deep colour; powerful and focused, the medium- to full-bodied palate with layers of black fruits; long travel and finish. Subsequent vintages labelled Moyston Hills Vineyard. Screwcap. 13.5° alc. **Rating** 91 **To** 2020 $25
The Gap Vineyard Shiraz 2004 A quite perfumed blackberry and raspberry bouquet, then a similarly vibrant array of fruits on the palate; oak and tannins very much in the back row. Screwcap. 13.5° alc. **Rating** 91 **To** 2014 $25

ioioioio **Bradach Vineyard Moyston Pinot Noir 2006** Strong colour; very ripe plum, prune and cherry conserve aromas; the abundant flavour comes as no surprise, but does take the wine close to dry red country; hairy chest pinot. Screwcap. 14.5° alc. **Rating** 89 **To** 2012 $28

Mount Macedon Winery   ★★★

433 Bawden Road, Mount Macedon, Vic 3441 **Region** Macedon Ranges
T (03) 5427 2735 **F** (03) 5427 1071 **www**.mountmacedonwinery.com.au **Open** 7 days 10–6 (10–5 winter)
Winemaker KIlchurn Wines (David Cowburn) **Est.** 1989 **Cases** 1200
The property on which Mount Macedon Winery is situated was purchased by David and Ronda Collins in 2003. The 32-ha property, at an altitude of 680 m, has 8 ha of gewurztraminer, chardonnay, pinot noir and pinot meunier.

ioioioioio **Reserve Pinot Noir 2005** Attractive, ripe plum and black cherry fruit; good length and flavour-stacked. **Rating** 92 **To** 2011

Mount Majura Vineyard   ★★★★☆

RMB 314 Majura Road, Majura, ACT 2609 (postal) **Region** Canberra District
T (02) 6262 3070 **F** (02) 6262 4288 **www**.mountmajura.com.au **Open** Thurs–Mon 10–5
Winemaker Dr Frank van de Loo **Est.** 1988 **Cases** 2000

The first vines were planted in 1988 by Dinny Killen on a site on her family property which had been especially recommended by Dr Edgar Riek; its attractions were red soil of volcanic origin over limestone, with reasonably steep east and northeast slopes providing an element of frost protection. The 1-ha vineyard was planted to pinot noir, chardonnay and merlot in equal quantities. The syndicate which purchased the property in 1999 has extended the plantings and built a new winery and cellar door.

ŢŢŢŢŢ **Canberra District Riesling 2006** Bright straw-green; good varietal expression, without a trace of reduction; harmonious, sweet citrus fruit and a touch of minerality; has excellent balance and length. Screwcap. 12.5° alc. **Rating** 93 **To** 2016 $16
Canberra District Shiraz 2004 Bright red-purple; light- to medium-bodied, clean and fresh with good mouthfeel and balance; a mix of red and black fruits, spice and subtle oak; finishes with fine tannins. Screwcap. 14.1° alc. **Rating** 90 **To** 2014 $20
Canberra District Tempranillo 2005 Fragrant aromas, then a delicate, light- to medium-bodied palate with an attractive lemon twist to the red fruit flavours; fine tannins. Screwcap. 13.2° alc. **Rating** 90 **To** 2010 $25

ŢŢŢŢ **Canberra District Merlot 2004** Bright red-purple; a medium-bodied mix of spice, black olive, small red fruits and savoury tannins; should soften over the next 2-3 years. Screwcap. 13.8° alc. **Rating** 89 **To** 2011 $16
Canberra District Pinot Gris 2006 Light apple and pear aromas and flavours; no reduction, but there is a faint touch of bitterness on the finish. Screwcap. 13.5° alc. **Rating** 87 **To** 2008 $18

Mount Mary   ★★★★★

Coldstream West Road, Lilydale, Vic 3140 **Region** Yarra Valley
T (03) 9739 1761 **F** (03) 9739 0137 **Open** Not
Winemaker Rob Hall **Est.** 1971 **Cases** 3500
Superbly refined, elegant and intense Cabernets and usually outstanding and long-lived Pinot Noirs fully justify Mount Mary's exalted reputation. The Triolet blend is very good; more recent vintages of Chardonnay are even better. Founder and long-term winemaker Dr John Middleton was one of the great, and truly original, figures in the Australian wine industry. He liked nothing more to tilt at windmills, and would do so with passion. His annual newsletter grew longer as each year passed, although the paper size did not. The only change necessary was a reduction in font size, and ultimately very strong light or a magnifying glass (or both) to fully appreciate the barbed wit and incisive mind of this great character. The determination of the family to continue the business is simply wonderful. Limited quantities of the wines are sold through the wholesale/retail distribution system in Vic, NSW, Qld and SA.

ŢŢŢŢŢ **Yarra Valley Chardonnay 2005** A lovely wine, combining delicacy and power; fruit and oak are perfectly balanced and integrated; typical Yarra Valley melon, stone fruit and a touch of citrus, great length. Diam. 13.5° alc. **Rating** 96 **To** 2015 $43
Quintet 2004 Excellent hue though not particularly deep; a classic, understated Mount Mary style, beautiful fruit/oak/tannin balance; cassis and blackcurrant dominate, then silky tannins on a very long finish. Cabernet Sauvignon/Merlot/Cabernet Franc/Malbec/Petit Verdot. Cork. 13° alc. **Rating** 95 **To** 2024 $85
Triolet 2005 Light straw-green; a true synergy from the blend; understated only because there is such inherent compatibility between the way the sauvignon blanc, semillon and muscadelle have been brought together. Diam. 13° alc. **Rating** 94 **To** 2012 $43

ŢŢŢŢŢ **Yarra Valley Pinot Noir 2004** Light but bright hue; delicate, perfumed and pure; lovely fruit flavours and good length; needs just a touch more intensity. Diam. 12.5° alc. **Rating** 93 **To** 2011 $85

Mount Moliagul

Clay Gully Lane, Moliagul, Vic 3472 **Region** Bendigo
T (03) 9809 2113 **www**.mountmoliagulwines.com.au **Open** By appt, tel 0427 221 641
Winemaker Terry Flora **Est.** 1991 **Cases** 400
Terry and Bozenka Flora began their tiny vineyard in 1991, gradually planting 0.5 ha each of shiraz and cabernet sauvignon, and 0.2 ha of chardonnay. Terry Flora has completed 2 winemaking courses, one with Winery Supplies and the other at Dookie College, and has learnt his craft very well.

🍷🍷🍷🍷🍷 **Bendigo Shiraz 2005** A nicely balanced, medium-bodied wine with an array of red and black flavours and aromas; fine, ripe tannins, supple texture, balanced oak, and particularly good length. Cork. 14.5° alc. **Rating** 94 **To** 2020 $25

Mount Ophir Estate

★★★★

Stillards Lane, Rutherglen, Vic 3685 **Region** Rutherglen
T (02) 6032 8920 **Open** W'ends 11–5, or by appt
Winemaker Andersons Winery (Howard Anderson) **Est.** 1891 **Cases** 270
When it was built in 1891 by English wine merchant Peter Burgoyne, Mount Ophir Estate was said to be the largest state-of-the-art winemaking facility in the world, and its brick buildings are as impressive today as they were 116 years ago. While the buildings have survived well, the 300-ha vineyard had shrunk to a poorly-tended 4 ha of shiraz when Ruth Hennessy acquired the property and began the refurbishment of the vineyards, discontinuing the use of chemical sprays, and having the Shiraz made with minimal preservatives to organic winemaking standards. The National Trust and Heritage Victoria listed buildings provide B&B in the main homestead, with 2 self-contained farmhouses also available.

Mount Pierrepoint Estate

271 Pierrepoint Road, Tarrington, Vic 3301 (postal) **Region** Henty
T (03) 5572 5558 **F** (03) 5572 5558 **www**.mountpierrepoint.com **Open** Not
Winemaker Jennifer Lacey **Est.** 1997 **Cases** 400
Mount Pierrepoint Estate has been established by Andrew and Jennifer Lacey on the foothills of Mt Pierrepoint between Hamilton and Tarrington. The initial planting of pinot noir in 1998 was followed by plantings of pinot gris in 1999, chardonnay in 2003 and further plantings of pinot gris in 2005.

🍷🍷🍷🍷🍷 **Pinot Noir 2005** Plum, black cherry and touches of spice and forest floor; a long, brisk finish; time still to go. Screwcap. 14° alc. **Rating** 91 **To** 2013 $30

Mount Prior Vineyard

1194 Gooramadda Road, Rutherglen, Vic 3685 **Region** Rutherglen
T (02) 6026 5591 **F** (02) 6026 5590 **www**.rutherglenvic.com **Open** 7 days 9–5
Winemaker Brian Devitt **Est.** 1860 **Cases** 5000
A full-scale tourist facility, with yet more in the pipeline. Full accommodation packages at the historic Mount Prior House; a restaurant operating weekends; picnic and barbecue facilities; and a California-style gift shop. The 112 ha of vineyards were expanded in 1998 by a further 5 ha of durif, a mark both of the success of Mount Prior and of interest in durif.

Mount Torrens Vineyards

PO Box 1679, Mount Torrens, SA 5244 **Region** Adelaide Hills
T (08) 8389 4229 **F** (08) 8389 4528 **www**.solstice.com.au **Open** Not
Winemaker Torbreck (David Powell) **Est.** 1996 **Cases** 500
Mount Torrens Vineyards has 2.5 ha of shiraz and viognier, and the distinguished team of Mark Whisson as viticulturist and David Powell as contract winemaker. The wines are available by mail order, but are chiefly exported to the UK and the US.

Mount Trio Vineyard ★★★★☆

2534 Porongurup Road, Mount Barker WA 6324 **Region** Porongurup
T (08) 9853 1136 **F** (08) 9853 1120 **www**.mounttriowines.com.au **Open** By appt
Winemaker Gavin Berry **Est.** 1989 **Cases** 6000
Mount Trio was established by Gavin Berry and Gill Graham shortly after they moved to the
Mount Barker district in late 1988. They have slowly built up the Mount Trio business, based in
part on estate plantings of 2 ha of pinot noir and 0.5 ha of chardonnay and in part on purchased
grapes. An additional 6 ha was planted in the spring of 1999. Exports to the UK, Denmark and
Singapore.

ŶŶŶŶŶ **Gravel Pit Porongurup Riesling 2006** Apple and lime blossom aromas; a very
pure, almost piercing, palate, with lingering, cleansing acidity. Needs a minimum
of 5 years. Screwcap. 11° alc. **Rating** 94 **To** 2016 $20

ŶŶŶŶŶ **Great Southern Sauvignon Blanc 2006** Clean, firm asparagus, herb and a
touch of nettle; vibrant but quite austere; great with fresh oysters. Screwcap. 12° alc.
Rating 92 **To** 2008 $16
Great Southern Semillon Sauvignon Blanc 2006 Has a rapier-like thrust
from the semillon, and perhaps a small percentage of barrel ferment which certainly
adds to the back-palate; long finish. Screwcap. 12° alc. **Rating** 91 **To** 2010 $20
Great Southern Cabernet Merlot 2005 Cassis/raspberry/blackcurrant
aromas; a medium-bodied palate more to blackcurrant and without the red
fruits of the bouquet. Sunglasses recommended when looking at the label.
Screwcap. 14° alc. **Rating** 91 **To** 2018 $16
Gravel Pit Porongurup Pinot Noir 2005 Light red; a light to medium-bodied,
savoury/foresty/minty style, but does have varietal expression; some spice and
balanced tannins. Screwcap. 13° alc. **Rating** 90 **To** 2011 $20
Gravel Pit Porongurup Shiraz Viognier 2005 Typical deep colour; a powerful,
highly aromatic bouquet with the presence of viognier very obvious, as it is on the
palate. Bursting with flavour, though the structure is a little unsure. Screwcap. 14° alc.
Rating 90 **To** 2015 $20

Mount Tully Vines NR

PO Box 1461, Toombul, Qld 4061 **Region** Granite Belt
T 0419 709 416 **F** (07) 3266 9384 **www**.mtvines.com.au **Open** Not
Winemaker Jim Barnes (Contract) **Est.** 1995 **Cases** NA
The Wellings and Spowart families began developing the Mount Tully vineyard in 1995 as
contract growers for other Granite Belt producers. They now have 3.5 ha of semillon, chardonnay,
cabernet sauvignon, merlot, malbec, shiraz, cabernet franc and tannat, and since 2002 have made
a limited number of wines under the Mount Tully label. A sideline is the Mother in Law's Tongue
which, despite the name, is a sweet red.

Mount View Estate ★★★★☆

Mount View Road, Mount View, NSW 2325 **Region** Lower Hunter Valley
T (02) 4990 3307 **F** (02) 4991 1289 **www**.mtviewestate.com.au **Open** 7 days 10–5
Winemaker Andrew Thomas (Consultant) **Est.** 1971 **Cases** 3000
John and Polly Burgess became the owners of Mount View Estate in 2000, and astutely appointed
former Tyrrell's winemaker Andrew Thomas as consultant winemaker. Since that time the wines
have been of consistently good quality.

ŶŶŶŶŶ **Flagship Shiraz 2005** Youthful intense black fruits with a savoury, regional cast;
ripe tannins; long finish. 14.3° alc. **Rating** 92 **To** 2010 $35
Limestone Creek Chardonnay 2005 Good colour; direct, linear style, stone
fruit supported by subtle oak. 14° alc. **Rating** 90 **To** 2010 $25

Mount William Winery

Mount William Road, Tantaraboo, Vic 3764 **Region** Macedon Ranges
T (03) 5429 1595 **F** (03) 5429 1998 **www**.mtwilliamwinery.com.au **Open** 7 days 11–5
Winemaker Kilchurn Wines (David Cowburn) **Est.** 1987 **Cases** 3000
Adrienne and Murray Cousins established 7.5 ha of vineyards, planted to pinot noir, cabernet
franc, merlot and chardonnay, between 1987 and 1999. The wines are sold through a stone cellar
door, and through a number of fine wine retailers around Melbourne.

ŢŢŢŢŢ **Macedon Blanc de Blanc RD 1998** Elegant, intense and fine; very good
length and balance; freshness with complexity. 12° alc. **Rating** 94 **To** 2010 $50

ŢŢŢŢŢ **Pinot Noir Chardonnay NV** Good mousse; fine, fresh citrus and strawberry fruit;
dosage at the upper end of the scale, but not over the top. 12.5° alc. **Rating** 90
To 2008 $14

ŢŢŢŢ **Abligne Unwooded Chardonnay 2006** Has length and enough citrus and
stone fruit flavour without having to rely on residual sugar. At $100 a case ex
the winery you are down in cleanskin country, but with significantly better
quality. Screwcap. 13.7° alc. **Rating** 88 **To** 2009 $8.50

Mountadam

High Eden Road, Eden Valley, SA 5235 **Region** Eden Valley
T (08) 8564 1900 **F** (08) 8564 1999 **www**.mountadam.com.au **Open** By appt
Winemaker Con Moshos **Est.** 1972 **Cases** 30 000
Founded by the late David Wynn for the benefit of winemaker son Adam. Mountadam was
(somewhat surprisingly) purchased by Cape Mentelle (doubtless under the direction of Moet
Hennessy Wine Estates) in 2000. Rather less surprising has been its sale in 2005 to Adelaide
businessman David Brown, who has extensive interests in the Padthaway region. The arrival of
Con Moshos (long-serving senior winemaker at Petaluma) has already made a significant impact
in lifting the quality of the wines. Exports to the UK, the US, Poland and Japan.

ŢŢŢŢŢ **Eden Valley Riesling 2006** Floral blossom aromas, then a light-bodied and
crisp palate, with apple, citrus, pear and some mineral/talc. components;
long finish. Very good development potential. Screwcap. 12° alc. **Rating** 94
To 2021 $26

Eden Valley Chardonnay 2004 Light straw-green; super-intense stone fruit and
grapefruit aromas and flavours, barrel ferment purely a background beat; great
length. Screwcap. 14° alc. **Rating** 94 **To** 2014 $32

Patriarch Eden Valley Shiraz 2004 More intensity than the Barossa Shiraz;
lots of licorice, spice and dark chocolate immersed in blackberry fruit; good
oak and tannin management. Screwcap. **Rating** 94 **To** 2020 $38

Patriarch Eden Valley Shiraz 2002 Obvious bottle-developed colour; firm,
savoury blackberry fruit; extremely long palate, with good tannin support.
Cork. 14.5° alc. **Rating** 94 **To** 2017 $35

ŢŢŢŢŢ **The Red 2002** Not unexpectedly, has savoury/earthy overtones, but the focused,
concentrated fruit is there; fine tannins. Cork. 14.5° alc. **Rating** 92 **To** 2015 $35

Barossa Shiraz 2004 Medium-bodied; a completely natural wine, unforced by
alcohol, extract or oak; a lingering, slippery, spicy finish. Screwcap. 14.5° alc.
Rating 90 **To** 2014 $18

Barossa Cabernet Merlot 2004 Ripe but not over the top; a mix of
blackcurrant, mocha and a hint of licorice; supple and smooth; controlled oak.
Screwcap. 14.5° alc. **Rating** 90 **To** 2018 $18

ŢŢŢŢ **The Red 2004** Very firm, austere style; quite grippy, slightly green tannins; does
have length and intensity, but by no means clear where it is headed. Screwcap.
Rating 89 **To** 2020 $38

Mr Riggs Wine Company ★★★★★

Ingleburne, Willunga Road, McLaren Vale, SA 5171 **Region** McLaren Vale
T (08) 8556 4460 **F** (08) 8556 4462 **www.**mrriggs.com.au**Open** 7 days 10–5
Winemaker Ben Riggs **Est.** 2001 **Cases** 19 500
After 14 years as winemaker at Wirra Wirra, and another 6 at various Australian wineries as well as numerous northern hemisphere vintages, Ben Riggs established his own business. His major activity is as consultant winemaker to Penny's Hill, Pertaringa, Coriole, Geoff Hardy and others, offering a 'grape-to-plate' service, plus keeping his hand in consulting for Cazal Viel in the south of France. He also makes wine for his Mr Riggs label, initially buying select parcels of grapes from old vines in McLaren Vale, also using grapes from his own vineyard at Piebald Gully, where he has planted shiraz, viognier and petit verdot. Exports to all major markets.

♥♥♥♥♥ **Adelaide Shiraz Viognier 2005** Dense purple-red; a full-bodied, black, dense wine with lots of regional dark chocolate; shiraz blackberry in no way subverted by viognier; persistent tannins. McLaren Vale (80%)/Langhorne Creek (20%); Viognier (5%). Screwcap. 15° alc. **Rating** 94 **To** 2020 $27
The Gaffer McLaren Vale Shiraz 2005 Strong purple-red; full-bodied, potent, powerful and long; a full but supple mouthfeel; lingering tannins and quality oak. Screwcap. 15° alc. **Rating** 94 **To** 2020 $22
McLaren Vale Shiraz 2005 Comes in one of those bottles needing a forklift; strong purple-red hue; smooth, supple, blackberry and plum fruit; just a whisper of dark chocolate along with positive French and American oak. Pointed within the context of the style, and given a maturity span with a prayer for the cork. 15° alc. **Rating** 94 **To** 2025 $40

♥♥♥♥♡ **Watervale Riesling 2006** More conventional than the VOR-GS; well-structured citrus and herb flavour mix; good balance, length and abundant total flavour. Screwcap. 12.5° alc. **Rating** 92 **To** 2016 $22
Adelaide Hills Riesling VOR-GS 2006 Clean apple blossom and a touch of pineapple on the bouquet; the wine's obvious sweetness is nowhere directly acknowledged on the label; good acidity, but some warning preferable unless you are able to interpret VOR-GS as meaning 'voice of riesling, German style'. Mr Riggs is on to something. though is far from being alone on this. Screwcap. 11° alc. **Rating** 90 **To** 2010 $22

♥♥♥♥ **Adelaide Viognier 2006** A big, rich and powerful wine, always outstripping the apparent alcohol; offers texture and structure more than fruit flavours, and reaches its high point when co-fermented with shiraz. Screwcap. 13.5° alc. **Rating** 88 **To** 2008 $25

🍃 Mt Bera Vineyards ★★★★☆

PO Box 372, Gumeracha, SA 5233 **Region** Adelaide Hills
T (08) 8389 2433 **F** (08) 8389 2433 **www.**mtberavineyards.com.au **Open** Not
Winemaker Jeanneret Wines **Est.** 1997 **Cases** 800
Louise Warner began the development of Mt Bera Vineyards in 1997 with her late partner Peter Hall, who died after a short illness in 2003. The temptation to give up and leave was more than offset by the beauty of the vineyard and quality of the grapes which had already been found by Peter Gago, senior Penfolds red winemaker. These grapes come from 12 ha of merlot, cabernet sauvignon and pinot noir. Most of the grapes continue to be sold, with the Clare Valley's Ben Jeanneret taking over as contract winemaker since 2005.

♥♥♥♥♡ **Boundless Horizons Adelaide Hills Merlot 2004** Bright and clear colour; a light- to medium-bodied, elegant, very clear and totally enjoyable expression of the variety; impressive balance between sweet fruit and more savoury/olive notes. Cork. 14° alc. **Rating** 90 **To** 2014 $16.50

Mt Billy

18 Victoria Street, Victor Harbor, SA 5211 (postal) **Region** Southern Fleurieu
T 0416 227 100 **F** (08) 8552 8333 **www**.mtbillywines.com.au **Open** Not
Winemaker Dan Standish, Peter Schell **Est.** 2000 **Cases** 2000
Having been an avid wine collector and consumer since 1973, John Edwards (a dentist) and wife
Pauline purchased a 3.75-ha property on the hills behind Victor Harbor, planting of 1.2 ha each
of chardonnay and pinot meunier. The original intention was to sell the grapes, but low yields
quickly persuaded Edwards that making and selling a bottle-fermented sparkling wine was the
way to go. Additionally, in 1999 1 tonne each of grenache and shiraz were purchased in the
Barossa Valley, and David Powell of Torbreck agreed to make the wine. Mt Billy was born. Exports
to the UK, the US, Canada and Japan.

ҶҶҶҶҶ **Antiquity 2004** Lashings of black fruits, licorice and spice; a long, lively finish
with high-quality tannins and good oak. Barossa Valley Shiraz. Screwcap.
14.5° alc. **Rating** 94 **To** 2024 $42

ҶҶҶҶҶ **Circe 2005** Strong colour; licorice, blackberry and spice all attest to the cool,
maritime growing conditions; very long, persistent finish. Southern Fleurieu
Shiraz. Screwcap. 14.5° alc. **Rating** 93 **To** 2018 $22
Harmony 2004 A typical blend of juicy berry, mocha, jam and confit fruits; fully
ripe, perhaps just a little too much so, although the alcohol is moderate. Barossa
Valley Shiraz/Mataro/Grenache. Screwcap. 14.5° alc. **Rating** 90 **To** 2011 $22

ҶҶҶҶ **Southern Fleurieu Chardonnay 2006** Clean, crisp, citrus aromas, almost into
mineral, as if it were a sauvignon blanc/chardonnay cross; has length and precision;
no oak obvious. Screwcap. 12.2° alc. **Rating** 89 **To** 2012 $20

🍇 Mt Franklin Estate

2 Whybrow Street, Franklinford, Vic 3461 **Region** Macedon Ranges
T (03) 5476 4473 **F** (03) 5476 4473 **www**.mtfranklinwines.com.au **Open** By appt
Winemaker Scott McGillivray, Colin Mitchell, Graeme Leith (Contract) **Est.** 2000
Cases 300
Owner Lesley McGillivray was well in front of her time when, in 1988, she planted 2 test rows
of Italian varieties on rich volcanic soil situated near the foothills of Mt Franklin. The varieties to
succeed best were dolcetto and pinot gris, and with family and friends they planted the first third
of their 4-ha vineyard with dolcetto and pinot gris in 2000. Since then, the vineyard has been
completed with more dolcetto, pinot gris and a little nebbiolo.

ҶҶҶҶҶ **Pinot Grigio 2006** Pushes the envelope with phenolic extract (as does Alsace),
but invests the wine with well above-average character, complexity and weight.
Screwcap. 13° alc. **Rating** 90 **To** 2009 $20

ҶҶҶҶ **Dolcetto 2005** Deeply coloured and very concentrated; rich black fruits, licorice
and some savoury notes follow the theme of the bouquet; needs time to calm down.
Diam. 12.8° alc. **Rating** 89 **To** 2025 $22

Mt Jagged Wines

Main Victor Harbor Road, Mt Jagged, SA 5211 **Region** Southern Fleurieu
T (08) 8554 9532 **F** (08) 8340 7633 **www**.mtjaggedwines.com.au **Open** Oct–May 7 days
10–5, June–Sept by appt
Winemaker Stephen Pannell, Tom White **Est.** 1989 **Cases** 8500
Jerry White immigrated to Australia in 1970, and after a successful business career, purchased 100
ha at Mt Jagged in 1988. The land is on the main road to Victor Harbor, which he believed would
generate ample cellar door sales demand. Being the first to plant in the region, he planted 28 ha,
thus producing sufficient grapes to supply large companies, and duly entered into a contract with
Penfolds, with semillon, chardonnay, merlot, cabernet sauvignon and shiraz all being sold. The first
Mt Jagged wine appeared in 1996, more and more fruit has since been diverted to the Mt Jagged
label. The cool, maritime environment was described by John Gladstones as 'what appears to be

the best climate in mainland SA for making table wines'. The white wines are exemplary; the red wines, however, seem to struggle for ripeness. Exports to the US and Canada.

♀♀♀♀♀ **Single Vineyard Reserve Southern Fleurieu Shiraz 2004** Medium-bodied; blackberry and mulberry fruit together with splashes of apricot and spice (viognier at work) are supported by quality French oak and soft tannins. Screwcap. 14° alc. **Rating** 93 **To** 2024 $35

Single Vineyard Reserve Southern Fleurieu Chardonnay 2005 Light straw-green; an attractive wine developing slowly; citrussy minerality gives life and zip; subtle oak; 200 dozen. Screwcap. 13° alc. **Rating** 91 **To** 2015 $35

Single Vineyard Southern Fleurieu Shiraz 2004 Clean and aromatic with sweet fruit on the bouquet and likewise on the palate, then fine, savoury tannins; a neat book end. Screwcap. 15° alc. **Rating** 91 **To** 2012 $20

♀♀♀♀ **Bullock Road Cabernet Shiraz 2004** Has far more substance and weight than its price and regional description might suggest; ripe blackberry, blackcurrant and spice fruit; controlled oak and tannins. Will improve. Amazingly a 60/40 blend from declassified Mt Jagged vineyard wine. Screwcap. 14.5° alc. **Rating** 89 **To** 2015 $14

Southern Fleurieu Adelaide Hills Semillon Sauvignon Blanc 2006 Pale straw-green; a spotlessly clean, tight, crisp style offering delicate herb, snow pea and asparagus fruit; dry finish. Screwcap. 12.5° alc. **Rating** 88 **To** 2012 $15

Single Vineyard Southern Fleurieu Merlot Cabernet Sauvignon 2004 Medium red-purple; mint, leaf, earth and berry aromas and flavours; notwithstanding the alcohol, light- to medium-bodied, with fine tannin support. Screwcap. 15° alc. **Rating** 88 **To** 2010 $20

Mt Lofty Ranges Vineyard ★★★★☆

Harris Road, Lenswood, SA 5240 **Region** Adelaide Hills
T (08) 8389 8339 **F** (08) 8389 8349 **Open** W'ends 11–5, or by appt
Winemaker Nepenthe **Est.** 1992 **Cases** 800
Mt Lofty Ranges Vineyard is owned by Alan Herath and Jan Reed, who have been involved from the outset in planting, training and nurturing the 5.2-ha vineyard. Both had professional careers but are now full-time vignerons. Skilled winemaking by Nepenthe has already brought rewards and recognition to the vineyard.

♀♀♀♀♀ **Lenswood Pinot Noir 2005** Has brilliant hue and clarity, reflected in the flavour and structure of the wine; paradoxically, needs a little more forest floor funk, but is utterly delicious at face value. Screwcap. 14° alc. **Rating** 91 **To** 2010 $20

Five Vines Lenswood Riesling 2006 Fine apple, spice and citrus aromas and flavours; good length and balance, but is slightly down on intensity. Screwcap. 13.5° alc. **Rating** 90 **To** 2013 $16

Lenswood Chardonnay 2005 Typical, delicate elegant style; melon, nectarine and grapefruit are the drivers, with a discreet touch of French oak. Screwcap. 13.5° alc. **Rating** 90 **To** 2011 $16

♀♀♀♀ **Lenswood Sauvignon Blanc 2006** Very pale; light mineral and gooseberry flavours; has some length, but not overmuch depth. Screwcap. 12.5° alc. **Rating** 89 **To** 2008 $18

Mt Samaria Vineyard ★★★☆

3231 Midland Highway, Lima South, Vic 3673 **Region** Upper Goulburn
T (03) 5768 2550 **www.**mtsamaria.com.au **Open** By appt
Winemaker Roger Cowan, Delatite, Auldstone Cellars **Est.** 1992 **Cases** 600
The 3-ha Mt Samaria Vineyard, with shiraz (1.7 ha) and tempranillo (0.8 ha) having the lion's share, accompanied by a little cabernet and pinot gris, is owned and operated by Judy and Roger Cowan. Plantings took place over an 8-year period, and in the early days the grapes were sold to Delatite until the Cowans ventured into wine production in 1999. Striking labels are a distinct plus, although wombats are not normally welcome visitors in vineyards.

ŸŸŸŸ **Shiraz Cabernet 2005** Good depth to the colour and flavour; blackcurrant, blackberry and a touch of mint, with good length and finish. Cork. 13.5° alc. **Rating** 89 **To** 2015 $18

Riesling 2006 A solid wine, with plenty of soft varietal flavours, and doesn't rely on residual sugar. Screwcap. 12.5° alc. **Rating** 88 **To** 2010 $16

Shiraz 2005 Well-made, light- to medium-bodied wine with red and black fruit flavours, limited by lack of depth. Screwcap. 14° alc. **Rating** 87 **To** 2011 $16

Mt Surmon Wines

Scarlattis Cellar Door Gallery, Basham Road, Stanley Flat, SA 5453 **Region** Clare Valley
T (08) 8842 1250 **F** (08) 8842 4064 **www**.mtsurmon.com.au **Open** 7 days 10–5
Winemaker Various contract **Est.** 1995 **Cases** 1000

The Surmon family has established just under 20 ha of vineyard, half to shiraz, the remainder to cabernet sauvignon, nebbiolo, chardonnay, pinot gris and viognier. Most of the grapes are sold to other wineries (some on a swap basis for riesling and merlot), but small quantities are contract-made and sold through Scarlattis Gallery and a few local hotels.

Mt Toolleen

103 High Street, Glen Iris, Vic 3146 (postal) **Region** Barossa Valley/Heathcote
T (03) 9885 1367 **F** (03) 9885 1367 **www**.mttoolleen.com.au **Open** Not
Winemaker James Irvine, Dominic Morris, Krystina Morris (Contract) **Est.** 2000 **Cases** 2000

Mt Toolleen is owned by a group of Melbourne investors by a somewhat complicated joint venture scheme which gives Mt Toolleen permanent access to 4.6 ha of shiraz grown in the Ebenezer area of the Barossa Valley, and 6.9 ha of shiraz from a Heathcote vineyard, the latter still coming into production; in the meantime, grapes are purchased from the Heathcote region. The venture achieved early prominence when the 2002 Ebenezer Vineyard Shiraz won the George Mackey Trophy for Best Wine Exported from Australia in the 2004–05 year.

ŸŸŸŸŸ **Heathcote Shiraz 2004** Voluminous, rich and velvety; yes, it's partly alcohol-driven, but it has great flavour (no dead fruit) and – improbably – a degree of elegance. Screwcap. 15° alc. **Rating** 96 **To** 2029 $35

Mt Vincent Estate

1139 Leggetts Drive, Mount Vincent, NSW 2323 **Region** Lower Hunter Valley
T (02) 4938 0078 **F** (02) 4938 0048 **www**.mvewines.com.au **Open** By appt
Winemaker Monarch Winemaking Services **Est.** 1999 **Cases** 1000

If you drive from Sydney to the Hunter Valley by the most conventional and quickest route, Mt Vincent Estate is the first vineyard you will come to, at the foot of Mt Vincent in the Mulbring Valley. The 50-ha property includes a 2-ha lake stocked with fish and yabbies, a 5-bedroom accommodation retreat, and a sign which normally says closed. The range of wines extends from Orange to the Hunter Valley to Tasmania, the common factor contract winemaking of the highest order.

ŸŸŸŸŸ **Regional Range Orange Shiraz 2005** Clean bouquet; medium to full red-purple; powerful and focused, entirely different to the Awaba; blackberry, licorice, spice and subtle oak; long finish. Screwcap. **Rating** 94 **To** 2020 $25

ŸŸŸŸŸ **Cockle Creek Hunter Valley Chardonnay 2003** Faint reduction evident on the bouquet; tangy, intense grapefruit and nectarine flavours holding on tight to the palate; long, lively, citrussy acidity. Screwcap. **Rating** 90 **To** 2012 $25

Regional Range Orange Cabernet Sauvignon 2005 Spotlessly clean blackcurrant aromas; a light- to medium-bodied, silky smooth palate with controlled oak and alcohol. Screwcap. **Rating** 90 **To** 2015 $25

ŸŸŸŸ **Awaba Hunter Valley Shiraz 2005** Spotless bouquet, with no hint of reduction; a light- to medium-bodied mix of red cherry, plum and blackberry fruit flavours, although not particularly complex in texture or structure. Screwcap. **Rating** 89 **To** 2013

Fassifern Hunter Valley Merlot 2002 Holding hue quite well; spicy, savoury, earthy aromas and flavours, red fruit a cellar-dweller, but can be felt. Quality cork. 13° alc. **Rating** 89 **To** 2010 $25

Regional Range Orange Sangiovese 2005 Light- to medium-bodied; savoury, spicy sour cherry flavours; undoubtedly varietal, and grown in an appropriate climate. Screwcap. **Rating** 88 **To** 2010 $25

Toronto Hunter Valley Verdelho 2004 Again a touch of reduction, the palate compensating with complex bottle-developed flavours in a rich and hearty mould. Screwcap. 13.9° alc. **Rating** 87 **To** 2008 $18

Mudgee Growers

Henry Lawson Drive, Mudgee, NSW 2580 **Region** Mudgee
T (02) 6372 2855 **F** (02) 6372 2811 **www.**mudgeegrowers.com.au **Open** 7 days 10–5
Winemaker David Lowe, Jane Wilson **Est.** 2004 **Cases** 1200
After closing their operation in the Hunter Valley, David Lowe and Jane Wilson have set up a new business in Mudgee, using grapes from various vineyards in the region. The cellar door is in the heritage winery at Fairview (formerly known as Platt's), which has been returned to working order, once more housing tanks, oak casks and barrels.

Mulyan

North Logan Road, Cowra, NSW 2794 **Region** Cowra
T (02) 6342 1336 **F** (02) 6341 1015 **Open** W'ends & public hols 10–5, or by appt
Winemaker Contract **Est.** 1994 **Cases** 2000
Mulyan is a 1350-ha grazing property purchased by the Fagan family in 1886 from Dr William Redfern, a leading 19th-century figure in Australian history. The current-generation owners, Peter and Jenni Fagan, began planting in 1994, and intend the vineyard area to be 100 ha in all. Presently there are 29 ha of shiraz, 14.5 ha of chardonnay, and 4.6 ha each of merlot and viognier. The label features a statue of the Roman god Mercury which has stood in the homestead garden since being brought back from Italy in 1912 by Peter Fagan's grandmother. Exports to the UK and China.

Block 7 Cowra Chardonnay 2005 Light-bodied; pleasantly ripe melon, peach and tropical fruit with a gentle echo of barrel ferment oak. Screwcap. 14° alc. **Rating** 88 **To** 2008 $20

Cabernet Merlot 2005 Medium-bodied, with clean, fresh fruit; good length and balance. Screwcap. 14.3° alc. **Rating** 88 **To** 2013 $20

Block 9 Shiraz Viognier 2005 Bright colour; fresh, clear, lively light- to medium-bodied wine; cherry, plum and some blackberry fruit; slightly sharp finish. Screwcap. 14° alc. **Rating** 87 **To** 2011 $20

Munari Wines

Ladys Creek Vienyard, 1129 Northern Highway, Heathcote, Vic 3523 **Region** Heathcote
T (03) 5433 3366 **F** (03) 5433 3905 **www.**munariwines.com **Open** 7 days 11–5
Winemaker Adrian Munari, Deborah Munari **Est.** 1993 **Cases** 2500
Adrian and Deborah Munari made a singularly impressive entry into the winemaking scene, with both their initial vintages winning an impressive array of show medals, and have carried on in similar vein since then. With a little under 8 ha of estate vines, production is limited, but the wines are well worth seeking out. Exports to Singapore, Malaysia, Indonesia and France.

Mundoonen ★★★★

1457 Yass River Road, Yass, NSW 2582 **Region** Canberra District
T (02) 6227 1353 **www.**mundoonen.com.au **Open** Sun & public hols, or by appt
Winemaker Terry O'Donnell **Est.** 2003 **Cases** 700
Jenny and Terry O'Donnell released their first wines in 2003. The winery is situated beside the Yass River, behind one of the oldest settlers' cottages in the Yass River Valley, dating back to 1858.

Estate plantings of shiraz and viognier are supplemented by contract-grown riesling, sauvignon blanc and cabernet sauvignon. The barrel shed has been created by refurbishing and insulating a 140-year-old building on the property.

Murchison Wines   ★★★★☆

105 Old Weir Road, Murchison, Vic 3610 **Region** Goulburn Valley
T (03) 5826 2294 **F** (03) 5826 2510 **www**.murchisonwines.com.au **Open** Fri–Mon & public hols 10–5, or by appt
Winemaker Guido Vazzoler **Est.** 1975 **Cases** 4000
Sandra (ex kindergarten teacher turned cheesemaker) and Guido Vazzoler (ex Brown Brothers) acquired the long-established Longleat Estate vineyard in 2003, renaming it Murchison Wines, having lived on the property (as tenants) for some years. The wines are estate-grown. Exports to Hong Kong.

ⓘⓘⓘⓘⓘ **Longleat Estate Riesling 2006** Clean and firm apple, pear and citrus aromas; similar flavours run through to a particularly long finish, the latter the high point of the wine. Screwcap. 12.5° alc. **Rating** 92 **To** 2015 $15
Longleat Estate Twins Semillon 2006 A clean and crisp bouquet; the flavours wander part of the way towards riesling with quite evident lemon and citrus flavours; good length and, like the Riesling, even better value. Screwcap. 12° alc. **Rating** 92 **To** 2015 $15

ⓘⓘⓘⓘ **Longleat Estate Cabernet Sauvignon 2005** A powerful, medium- to full-bodied wine, full-flavoured but in need of a bit more polishing. Very different to the elegant '04 which preceded it. Screwcap. 14.5° alc. **Rating** 89 **To** 2019 $18.50

Murdoch Hill   ★★★★★

Mappinga Road, Woodside, SA 5244 **Region** Adelaide Hills
T (08) 8389 708119 **F** (08) 8389 799112 **www**.murdochhill.com.au **Open** By appt
Winemaker Brian Light (Contract) **Est.** 1998 **Cases** 2600
A little over 21 ha of vines have been established on the undulating, gum-studded countryside of the Downer family's Erinka property, 4 km east of Oakbank. In descending order of importance, the varieties established are sauvignon blanc, shiraz, cabernet sauvignon and chardonnay.

ⓘⓘⓘⓘⓘ **Adelaide Hills Sauvignon Blanc 2006** No reduction on the bouquet; an intense but not aggressive bouquet and palate, with lingering passionfruit and citrus tied together with a bow of minerally acidity. Screwcap. 13.5° alc. **Rating** 94 **To** 2008 $19

Murdock   ★★★★★

Riddoch Highway, Coonawarra, SA 5263 **Region** Coonawarra
T (08) 8737 3700 **F** (08) 8737 2107 **www**.murdockwines.com **Open** By appt
Winemaker Balnaves **Est.** 1998 **Cases** 4000
The Murdock family has established 10.4 ha of cabernet sauvignon, 2 ha of shiraz, 1 ha of merlot, and 0.5 ha each of chardonnay and riesling, and produces small quantities of an outstanding Cabernet Sauvignon, contract-made by Pete Bissell. A second vineyard has been added in the Barossa Valley, with 5.8 ha of shiraz and 2.1 ha each of semillon and cabernet sauvignon. The labels, incidentally, are ultra-minimalist, no flood of propaganda here. Plans to open a cellar door/café in the Barossa Valley. Exports to the US and Asia.

ⓘⓘⓘⓘⓘ **Coonawarra Cabernet Sauvignon 2002** Starting to move into its secondary phase, with cedary/earthy Coonawarra cabernet characters emerging on the bouquet and palate. Will continue its slow development, becoming more complex for at least a decade, and live for much longer. Cork. 14.5° alc. **Rating** 95 **To** 2022 $45

ŸŸŸŸŸ **Coonawarra Riesling 2006** Light straw-green; typical floral/blossom delicacy of young Coonawarra riesling, but the palate has considerably more intensity and power than the bouquet suggests; good balance and length. Screwcap. 12.2° alc. **Rating** 93 **To** 2015 $16.50

ŸŸŸŸ **Barossa Rose 2006** Firm red fruits and an almost painfully dry (in the context of most roses) finish; true food wine. Screwcap. 14.2° alc. **Rating** 87 **To** 2008 $16.50

Murdup Wines ★★★★

Southern Ports Highway, Mount Benson, SA 5275 **Region** Mount Benson
T (08) 8768 6190 **F** (08) 8768 6190 **www**.murdupwines.com.au **Open** 7 days 10–4
Winemaker Steve Grimley **Est.** 1996 **Cases** 4000
Andy and Melinda Murdock purchased Murdup in 1996, retaining the name of the property which was first settled as a grazing property in the 1860s. They began by planting 10.5 ha of vineyard, the lion's share going to cabernet sauvignon and shiraz, with smaller patches of chardonnay and sauvignon blanc, most of the wine going to the UK. Ten years later they dramatically upped the ante by purchasing the Mildara Black Wattle Vineyard across the road, lifting their vineyards to 65 ha. The also commenced reworking portions of the newly acquired vineyard, removing 6 ha of poorly performing shiraz, replacing it with equal quantities of sauvignon blanc and pinot gris. They have also substantially upped their wine marketing, and introduced a second label, Soaring Kite. Exports to the UK.

ŸŸŸŸŸ **Sauvignon Blanc 2005** Clean; the full range of tropical fruit flavours, the fruit sweetness lingering in the mouth. Screwcap. 12.8° alc. **Rating** 90 **To** 2008 $17
Shiraz 2004 A light- to medium-bodied palate, with a fresh array of blackberry and raspberry fruit; good acidity. Screwcap. 14.2° alc. **Rating** 90 **To** 2012 $20

ŸŸŸŸ **Cabernet Sauvignon 2004** A touch of reduction on the bouquet; a savoury palate offering blackcurrant, earth, leaf and mint flavours; lingering tannins. Screwcap. 14.8° alc. **Rating** 88 **To** 2010 $20
Soaring Kite Mount Benson Sauvignon Blanc 2006 Subdued aromas, with hints of tropical/gooseberry fruit setting the pace for the palate until a lift of crisp acidity on the finish. Screwcap. 13° alc. **Rating** 87 **To** 2008 $17
Soaring Kite Mount Benson Chardonnay 2006 Straightforward unoaked style; peachy fruit and moderate length. Screwcap. 13° alc. **Rating** 87 **To** 2008 $17

Murray Street Vineyard ★★★★★

Lot 723, Murray Street, Greenock, SA 5360 **Region** Barossa Valley
T (08) 8562 8373 **F** (08) 8562 8414 **Open** 7 days 10–4.30
Winemaker Andrew Seppelt **Est.** 2003 **Cases** 2000
Andrew and Vanessa Seppelt have moved with a degree of caution in setting up Murray Street Vineyard, possibly because of inherited wisdom. Andrew Seppelt is a direct descendant of Benno and Sophia Seppelt, who built Seppeltsfield and set the family company bearing their name on its path to fame. They have 46 ha of vineyards, one block at Gomersal, the other at Greenock, with the lion's share going to shiraz, followed by grenache, mourvedre, viognier, marsanne, semillon and zinfandel. Most of the grapes are sold, with a small (but hopefully increasing) amount retained for the Murray Street Vineyard brand. The Benno Shiraz Mataro is the icon tribute on the masculine side; the Sophia Shiraz the feminine icon. Unusually good point of sale/propaganda material. Exports to the UK, the US, Canada and Denmark.

ŸŸŸŸŸ **Greenock Barossa Valley Shiraz 2005** Excellent hue; greater elegance on the bouquet, more vibrancy of sweet fruits in the red, rather than black, spectrum; minimal tannins, and excellent oak balance. Screwcap. 14° alc. **Rating** 95 **To** 2025 $40
Gomersal Barossa Valley Shiraz 2005 The colour is deep, but with an even better hue than the Barossa Valley Shiraz; intense and highly focused blackberry, mocha, chocolate and licorice flavours carry the alcohol with ease; flow through to a long finish. Screwcap. 15° alc. **Rating** 94 **To** 2025 $40

ŸŸŸŸŸ **The Barossa 2005** Superb colour; the percentages of the varieties (Shiraz/Grenache/Cinsaut/Mataro) are not stated, but shiraz plays the major role; a luscious, sweet array of red and black fruits, with no dead fruit or excess alcohol issue. Well-priced. Screwcap. 14.5° alc. **Rating** 93 **To** 2020 $25
Benno 2004 Rich, ripe and luscious, the later picking and higher alcohol appealing to many; for me, just misses the mark, especially at this price. Do remember, however, that the alcohol number can mislead as much as inform (witness the Gomersal Shiraz). Shiraz/Mataro. Cork. 15° alc. **Rating** 92 **To** 2015 $50
Barossa Valley Shiraz 2005 Deep, dense colour; a touch of reduction on the bouquet quickly gives way to a plush, rich, velvety tapestry of dark fruit flavours on the palate. Screwcap. 14.5° alc. **Rating** 91 **To** 2028 $25

Murrindindi   ★★★★

Cummins Lane, Murrindindi, Vic 3717 **Region** Upper Goulburn
T (03) 5797 8448 **F** (03) 5797 8448 **www**.murrindindivineyards.com **Open** At Marmalades Café, Yea
Winemaker Alan Cuthbertson **Est.** 1979 **Cases** 5000
Situated in an unequivocally cool climate, which means that special care has to be taken with the viticulture to produce ripe fruit flavours. In more recent vintages, Murrindindi has succeeded handsomely in so doing.

ŸŸŸŸŸ **Family Reserve Yea Valley Cabernet Sauvignon 2003** Fragrant varietal aromas; fine-grained, cedary palate with blackcurrant fruit and tannins seamlessly interwoven; excellent length. Screwcap. 14° alc. **Rating** 94 **To** 2018 $28

ŸŸŸŸ **Don't Tell Dad Yea Valley Riesling 2005** Light straw-green; an attractive, spotless bouquet leads into a firm, mineral palate with some tropical notes. Screwcap. 13° alc. **Rating** 89 **To** 2010 $18

Mylkappa Wines   ★★★★

Mylkappa Road, Birdwood, SA 5234 **Region** Adelaide Hills
T (08) 8568 5325 **www**.mylkappawines.com.au **Open** W'ends & public hols 10–5
Winemaker Contract **Est.** 1998 **Cases** 850
Having left the Adelaide Hills in 1988 with their 3 children, Patricia and Geoff Porter returned 10 years later to purchase an old dairy farm at Birdwood. Since then the entire family has worked tirelessly to progressively establish a large vineyard planted to chardonnay (12.3 ha), sauvignon blanc (8.4 ha), shiraz (3.9 ha), 2 clones of pinot noir (4 ha), merlot (1.9 ha) and pinot gris (1.8 ha). Almost all of the grape production is sold to other Adelaide Hills makers, with small quantities of wines contract-made.

Myrtaceae   ★★★★

53 Main Creek Road, Main Ridge, Vic 3928 **Region** Mornington Peninsula
T (03) 5989 2045 **F** (03) 5989 2845 **Open** 1st w'end of month, public hols & Jan w'ends
Winemaker Julie Trueman **Est.** 1985 **Cases** 250
The development of the Myrtaceae vineyard began with the planting of 0.7 ha of cabernet sauvignon, cabernet franc and merlot intended for a Bordeaux-style red blend. It became evident that these late-ripening varieties were not well suited to the site, the vineyard was converted to 0.5 ha each of pinot noir and chardonnay. John Trueman (viticulturist) and Julie Trueman (winemaker) are the proprietors. Part of the property is devoted to the Land for Wildlife Scheme.

ŸŸŸŸŸ **Main Ridge Mornington Peninsula Chardonnay 2005** A fine, elegant wine with a long, linear and crisp palate constructed around nectarine and citrus; oak merely a zephyr blowing across the fruit. Screwcap. 13.5° alc. **Rating** 92 **To** 2013 $25

ỶỶỶỶ   **Main Ridge Mornington Peninsula Pinot Noir 2005** Very light colour; light strawberry and cherry fruit, halfway to rose, and ideal for a summer lunch. Screwcap. 13.5° alc. **Rating** 88 **To** 2009 $28.50

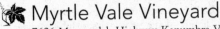 # Myrtle Vale Vineyard ★★★

7626 Maroondah Highway, Kanumbra, Vic 3719 **Region** Upper Goulburn
T (03) 5773 4310 **F** (03) 5773 4312 **Open** By appt
Winemaker Peter Beckingham (Contract) **Est.** 1990 **Cases** 300
Robyn Dickens and Leigh Coleman have established Myrtle Vale Vineyard on a property between Yea and Mansfield at 330 m. The name comes from a sheep station selected in the mid-1800s, of which the vineyard now forms a small part. One ha each of chardonnay and cabernet sauvignon (and a tiny patch of viognier) are used to make the wines, surplus grape production is sold.

ỶỶỶỶ   **Chardonnay 2004** Light- to medium-bodied, clean, firm and quite fresh nectarine flavours, with good acidity. Cork. 14.4° alc. **Rating** 89 **To** 2010 $19
Viognier 2005 Clean; still quite fresh, with apricot fruit salad flavours; crisp acidity on the finish works well to cut back the oily phenolics the variety often displays. Cork. 14.4° alc. **Rating** 87 **To** 2008 $20

Naked Range Wines ★★★☆

125 Rifle Range Road, Smiths Gully, Vic 3760 **Region** Yarra Valley
T (03) 9710 1575 **F** (03) 9710 1655 **www**.nakedrangewines.com **Open** By appt
Winemaker Kate Goodman, Simon Wightwick (Contract) **Est.** 1996 **Cases** 2500
Mike Jansz has established 6.2 ha of vineyard, one-third sauvignon blanc, a small patch of pinot noir and the remainder cabernet sauvignon (predominant), merlot and chardonnay. The wines are made at Punt Road and marketed under the striking Naked Range label, with a second label for overseas markets using grapes from other Vic regions. Exports to Indonesia.

 # Nalbra Estate Wines ★★★☆

225 Whitcombes Road, Drysdale, Vic 3222 **Region** Geelong
T (03) 5253 2654 **F** (03) 5253 2414 **Open** By appt
Winemaker Dick Simonsen, Ray Nadeson, maree Collis (Contract) **Est.** 2001 **Cases** NA
Terri and Leigh Robinson began the establishment of their vineyard, perched on Mt Bellarine and overlooking Port Phillip Bay, in 2001. Shiraz and pinot gris were planted in that year, followed by sauvignon blanc and viognier in 2003. In all, there are 2.8 ha under vine, and the Robinsons are progressively moving from being grapegrowers to wine producers.

ỶỶỶỶ   **Shiraz 2005** Cool climate style with spicy/sappy/leafy characters, but good length and mouthfeel. **Rating** 89 **To** 2011

Nangwarry Station ★★★★

PO Box 1, Nangwarry, SA 5277 **Region** Mount Gambier
T (08) 8739 7274 **F** (08) 8739 7009 **www**.nangwarrystation.com.au **Open** Not
Winemaker Peter Douglas **Est.** 1999 **Cases** 2000
Nangwarry Station was purchased by Ian McLachlan in 1964, variously a high profile President of the National Farmers Federation and Federal Minister of Defence. The property is now managed by Ian's son Dugald and wife Sophie, ardent supporters of the family's philosophy of long term sustainability. One example is the wetlands and conservation areas which have created natural habitats for over 100 species of birds. In what is a large business, the establishment of 9 ha of vineyard (4 ha of cabernet sauvignon, 3 ha of pinot noir and 1 ha each of chardonnay and sauvignon blanc) is a small diversification, but it has been a very successful one. The immensely experienced (and equally likeable) Peter Douglas, for many years a winemaker in Coonawarra, has produced some lovely wines which hold much promise for the future as the vines mature.

Nardone Baker Wines   ★★★

PO Box 386, McLaren Vale, SA 5171 **Region** McLaren Vale
T (08) 8445 8100 **F** (08) 8445 8200 **www**.nardonebaker.com **Open** Not
Winemaker Brian Light (Contract) **Est.** 1999 **Cases** 23 000

Italian-born Joe Nardone and English-born John Baker were brought together by the marriage of Joe's daughter and John's son. Both were already in the wine industry, John studying at Roseworthy Agricultural College and establishing a vineyard. The second generation of Frank Nardone and Patrick Baker, the latter having also studied at Roseworthy, now run what is a significant virtual winery, sourcing grapes from all over SA, with contract winemaking by Brian Light at the Boar's Rock winemaking facility. There are 5 ranges, headed by The Wara Manta Reserve, followed by the Nardone Baker, Blaxland's Legacy, Treeview Selection and Wara Manta (non-reserve). Exports to various markets including the UK and the US.

999 **The Wara Manta Reserve Shiraz 2001** Medium-bodied; pleasant bottle-developed savoury edges to the fruit and mocha chocolate; finishes with fine tannins. At this price point deserved far better than the stained mid-range cork. Langhorne Creek/McLaren Vale. 13.5° alc. **Rating** 89 **To** 2010 $78
Riesling 2005 An aromatic, passionfruit bouquet is followed by a lighter palate with a mix of citrussy acidity and a touch of sweetness on the finish. Screwcap. 12.5° alc. **Rating** 88 **To** 2009 $13.95

Narkoojee   ★★★★★

170 Francis Road, Glengarry, Vic 3854 **Region** Gippsland
T (03) 5192 4257 **F** (03) 5192 4257 **www**.narkoojee.com **Open** 7 days 10.30–4.30
Winemaker Harry Friend, Axel Friend **Est.** 1981 **Cases** 3000

Narkoojee Vineyard (originally a dairy farm owned by the Friend family) is within easy reach of the old gold mining town of Walhalla and looks out over the Strzelecki Ranges. The wines are produced from a little over 10 ha of estate vineyards, with chardonnay accounting for half the total. Former lecturer in civil engineering and extremely successful winemaker Harry Friend changed horses in 1994 to take control of the family vineyard and winery, and hasn't missed a beat since; his skills show through with all the wines, none more so than the Chardonnay. Small amounts are exported.

9999 **Gippsland Pinot Noir 2005** Deep, almost impenetrable colour; varietal character initially obscured by the depth of the fruit, but progressively expresses itself on retasting Central Otago-style, promising a long life. Trophy Gippsland Wine Show '07. Diam. 14° alc. **Rating** 94 **To** 2015 $19
The Athelstan Gippsland Merlot 2004 Medium-bodied; attractive cassis, black olive and spice mix, supported by ripe tannins; high-quality merlot. Diam. 13.5° alc. **Rating** 94 **To** 2014 $30

9999 **Gippsland Cabernet Sauvignon 2004** Lively, fresh and clean blackcurrant fruit, again with touches of spice; fully ripe at its moderate alcohol; fine tannins do have a slight green nuance. Diam. 13.5° alc. **Rating** 92 **To** 2019 $30
Lily Grace Gippsland Chardonnay 2005 Gently ripe peach and nectarine fruit supported by subtle oak. Diam. 14.5° alc. **Rating** 90 **To** 2008 $19
Myrtle Point Gippsland Shiraz 2005 Medium to full-bodied; spice, licorice and blackberry; good tannins and length. Diam. 15.8° alc. **Rating** 90 **To** 2012 $20

9999 **Trafalgar Chardonnay 2005** A complex wine; lots of winemaker inputs evidenced throughout the peachy wine, though it (the fruit) does reassert itself on the finish. Diam. 14.5° alc. **Rating** 88 **To** 2012 $19

Nazaaray   ★★★★

266 Meakins Road, Flinders, Vic 3929 **Region** Mornington Peninsula
T (03) 9585 1138 **www**.nazaaray.com.au **Open** 1st w'end of each month, or by appt
Winemaker Paramdeep Ghumman **Est.** 1996 **Cases** 900

Paramdeep Ghumman is, as far as I am aware, the only Indian-born winery proprietor and winemaker in Australia. He and his wife migrated from India over 20 years ago, and purchased the Nazaaray vineyard property in 1991. An initial trial planting of 400 vines in 1996 was gradually expanded to the present level of 1.6 ha of pinot noir, 0.4 ha of pinot gris and 0.15 ha of chardonnay. Notwithstanding the micro size of the estate, all the wines are made and bottled onsite. Exports to Singapore.

ΨΨΨΨ゚ **Mornington Peninsula Sauvignon Blanc 2006** A clean, bright and lively mix of herbaceous, gooseberry and passionfruit flavours; good length and balance, closing with crisp acidity. Screwcap. 13.5° alc. **Rating** 90 **To** 2008 $25
Mornington Peninsula Pinot Noir 2006 A light-bodied, fresh and lively palate; not complex, but has length. Fully priced. Screwcap. 13.7° alc. **Rating** 90 **To** 2010 $30

ΨΨΨΨ **Reserve Mornington Peninsula Pinot Noir 2004** Savoury/foresty/earthy aromas and flavours; light- to medium-bodied; good structure, though the tannins are still to finally resolve themselves. Screwcap. 13.5° alc. **Rating** 89 **To** 2010 $30
Mornington Peninsula Pinot Noir 2004 Very light colour, with surprising retention of a purple-red hue; strong similarity to the '06, despite 2 years difference in the vintage. Screwcap. 13.5° alc. **Rating** 89 **To** 2009 $35
Mornington Peninsula Pinot Gris 2006 Well-made; some pear and musk, with appropriate balance and length. Not easy to do more. Screwcap. 13.5° alc. **Rating** 88 **To** 2009 $22
Mornington Peninsula Merlot 2004 Savoury, leafy minty aspects, but enough redcurrant to offset those characters; light- to medium-bodied. ProCork. 13.7° alc. **Rating** 87 **To** 2010 $15

Neagles Rock Vineyards ★★★★★

Lot 1 & 2 Main North Road, Clare, SA 5453 **Region** Clare Valley
T (08) 8843 4020 **F** (08) 8843 4021 **www.**neaglesrock.com **Open** Mon–Sat 10–5, Sun 11–4
Winemaker Steve Wiblin, John Trotter (Consultant) **Est.** 1997 **Cases** 10 000
Owner-partners Jane Willson and Steve Wiblin have taken the plunge in a major way, simultaneously raising a young family, resuscitating 2 old vineyards, and – for good measure – stripping a dilapidated house to the barest of bones and turning it into a first-rate, airy restaurant-cum-cellar door. They bring decades of industry experience, gained at all levels of the wine industry, to Neagles Rock, and built upon this by the 2003 acquisition of the outstanding and mature vineyards of Duncan Estate, adding another level of quality to their wines, which now draw on a total of 25 ha. Exports to the UK, the US and other major markets.

ΨΨΨΨΨ **Clare Valley Riesling 2006** Bright green-yellow; a powerful bouquet and palate exuding lime, lemon, mineral and spice; a wine of considerable authority; no phenolics, long finish. Screwcap. 12.5° alc. **Rating** 95 **To** 2020 $18
Clare Valley Shiraz 2005 A delicious array of ripe plum, blackberry, licorice, spice and dark chocolate aromas and flavours; fine tannins. ProCork. 14.5° alc. **Rating** 94 **To** 2020 $22
Clare Valley Sangiovese 2005 Bright colour; classic sour cherry fruit with wild herbs and spices; considerable length, and crystal clear varietal character. Continues the brilliant form of the '04. Screwcap. 14.5° alc. **Rating** 94 **To** 2015 $22

ΨΨΨΨ゚ **Mr Duncan Clare Valley Cabernet Shiraz 2005** Attractive medium-bodied wine with good mouthfeel and balance; black fruits and touches of spice, licorice, chocolate and mocha; soft, balanced tannins and oak. Great value. Screwcap. 14.5° alc. **Rating** 93 **To** 2015 $18
One Black Dog Reserve Clare Valley Cabernet Shiraz 2004 Concentrated and powerful; lashings of black fruits, sweet earth, dark chocolate and tannins; needs a decade at least; would slightly less have been better? Quality cork. 15° alc. **Rating** 93 **To** 2019 $50

Clare Valley Semillon Sauvignon Blanc 2006 More plush and exotic sauvignon blanc influences than expected; ripe gooseberry and passionfruit, almost as if the semillon was only a minor component. Screwcap. 13.5° alc. **Rating** 91 To 2008 $18

ỸỸỸỸ **Misery Clare Valley Grenache Shiraz 2005** Very distinctive confit/jam/ cosmetic varietal expression of grenache typical of the Clare Valley; love it or leave it. Screwcap. 15° alc. **Rating** 88 To 2008 $18

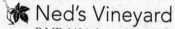 Ned's Vineyard   ★★★

RMB 1404, Ararat, Vic 3377 (postal) **Region** Pyrenees
T (03) 5356 9337 **F** (03) 5356 9337 **www.nedsvineyard.com.au Open** Not
Winemaker Michael Unwin (Contract) **Est.** 1995 **Cases** 135
In 1994 Michael (Mick) Hobson purchased his property situated in the foothills of the Pyrenees on the southern boundary of the region. Planting of shiraz began the following year with advice from Southcorp viticulturists Kym Ludvigsen and Stuart McNab. The first few years production was sold to Southcorp, and in 2002 to Mount Langi Ghiran. Most of the grapes are still sold, but the ultimate aim is to use all of the grapes for the Ned's Vineyard label.

ỸỸỸỸ **Shay's Flat Pyrenees Shiraz 2005** Unconvincing colour; light- to medium-bodied, with both bouquet and palate in the savoury/spicy spectrum; needs more fruit focus and concentration, but is balanced. Screwcap. 14° alc. **Rating** 87 To 2010 $25
Shay's Flat Pyrenees Shiraz 2004 Slightly dull colour; light- to medium-bodied, spicy/earthy overtones to black fruit; young vines? Screwcap. 14° alc. **Rating** 87 To 2010 $26.50

Neilson Estate Wines   ★★★

63 Logue Road, Millendon, WA 6056 **Region** Swan Valley
T (08) 9296 4849 **F** (08) 9396 4849 **Open** By appt
Winemaker John Griffiths, Jim Neilson **Est.** 1998 **Cases** 275
Jim and Jenny Neilson planted their 2-ha vineyard of shiraz and merlot in 1998. Jim has completed 2 years of the 3-year viticulture and oenology degree course at Curtin University, but handed the winemaking reins to John Griffiths at Faber Wines for the 2006 vintage, an arrangement which will continue into the future. The aim is to produce the highest possible quality Swan Valley wines using regulated deficit irrigation and concentration techniques in the winemaking.

ỸỸỸỸ **Swan Valley Shiraz 2006** Medium red-purple; lifted cherry and raspberry aromas flow through into the palate; very fine tannins, the oak inconsequential, the overall flavour very good. Diam. **Rating** 89 To 2011
Swan Valley Merlot 2006 Light- to medium-bodied; well-made, but gather ye rosebuds because the record cool vintage of '06 was tailor-made for merlot; normally flavour and colour such as this simply won't be found in the Swan Valley – as the '05 shows. Diam. **Rating** 88 To 2010

Nelwood Wines   ★★★

PO Box 237, Paringa, SA 5340 **Region** Riverland
T (08) 8595 8042 **F** (08) 8595 8182 **www.nelwood.com Open** Not
Winemaker Boar's Rock (Mike Farmilo) **Est.** 2002 **Cases** 10 000
The wines (released under the Red Mud label) come from 45-ha plantings of shiraz, chardonnay, petit verdot and cabernet sauvignon near Nelwood, 32 km east of Renmark near the SA border. The grapegrowers who are shareholders in the company have been growing grapes for up to 3 generations in the Riverland. Exports to the US.

ΨΨΨΨ **RM Reserve Red Mud Nelwood Petit Verdot 2004** Typical Riverland petit verdot retaining colour and flavour; plum, cherry and licorice; the back label proclaims the wine is 'for the disconcerting wine lover'. Cork. 14.5° alc. **Rating** 89 **To** 2010 **$25**
Red Mud Shiraz 2004 While a no-frills wine, has a more convincing palate presentation of black cherry and blackberry supported by fine tannins. Diam. 14.5° alc. **Rating** 87 **To** 2008 **$15**
Nelwood Station Bulldozer 2004 Has enough red and black fruits to quality as a bargain at the price, and likewise to qualify for your next barbecue. Screwcap. **Rating** 87 **To** 2008 **$8**

Nepenthe Vineyards ★★★★☆

Jones Road, Balhannah, SA 5242 **Region** Adelaide Hills
T (08) 8398 8888 **F** (08) 8388 1100 **www**.nepenthe.com.au **Open** 7 days 10–4
Winemaker Michael Paxton **Est.** 1994 **Cases** 80 000
The Tweddell family has established a little over 110 ha of close-planted vineyards in the Adelaide Hills since 1994, with an exotic array of varieties. In late 1996 it obtained the second licence to build a winery in the Adelaide Hills (Petaluma was the only prior successful applicant, back in 1978). Nepenthe quickly established its reputation as a substantial producer of high-quality wines. Founder Ed Tweddell died unexpectedly in 2006; in March 2007 son James announced McGuigan Simeon had purchased the winery, a move which caused most industry observers to scratch their heads. Exports to all major markets.

ΨΨΨΨΩ **Adelaide Hills Sauvignon Blanc 2006** Pale straw-green; clean, fresh and correct, but not especially expressive; touches of gooseberry and apple, then a dry, crisp finish. Screwcap. 13° alc. **Rating** 90 **To** 2008 **$23**

ΨΨΨΨ **Adelaide Hills Pinot Gris 2006** Some pinking to the colour quite acceptable for the variety; crisp apple and pear, with a hint of musk; clean finish. Screwcap. 14° alc. **Rating** 88 **To** 2008 **$22.99**
Tryst Adelaide Hills Sauvignon Blanc Semillon Pinot Gris 2006 Not surprisingly, sauvignon blanc (70%) drives the wine, but the semillon (25%), in particular, also contributes; delicate, flowery tropical fruits and a touch of citrussy/grassy acidity. Screwcap. 13° alc. **Rating** 88 **To** 2008 **$15.95**
Tryst Adelaide Hills Cabernet Tempranillo Zinfandel 2005 'An eclectic blend of vibrant, well-structured Cabernet Sauvignon (70%), with ripe, fragrant Tempranillo (25%) and a dollop of Zinfandel (5%) for richness and spice.' That's what the back label says, and who am I to say nay. Screwcap. 14.5° alc. **Rating** 88 **To** 2008 **$15.95**
Adelaide Hills Unoaked Chardonnay 2006 Scented white peach and citrus; crisp and fresh. Screwcap. 13.5° alc. **Rating** 87 **To** 2008 **$19.50**

Neqtar Wines ★★★

Campbell Avenue, Irymple, Vic 3498 **Region** Murray Darling
T (03) 5024 9999 **F** (03) 5024 6605 **www**.neqtar.com.au **Open** Mon–Sat 10–4.30, Sun 12–4
Winemaker Donna Stephens, Marnie Roberts **Est.** 1998 **Cases** 400 000
This is yet another Australian–UK joint venture in similar vein to Willunga 100 Wines. The UK end is distributor HwCg, while the Australian components include the former Evans & Tate-owned Salisbury Winery at Irymple, and Roberts Estate at Merbein. A $2 million upgrade of the Salisbury Winery was completed prior to the 2007 vintage. The wines come in 3 price levels: at the bottom under the Roberts Estate brand (sub $10 in Australia); the Commissioner's Block next (sub $14) and, at the top, Calder Grove (sub $15). Space has precluded the inclusion of tasting notes for all wines submitted.

ΨΨΨΨ **Commissioner's Block Sauvignon Blanc 2006** Light- to medium-bodied; well-made and quite crisp, with wisps of apple, guava and passionfruit; nice citrussy finish. A major surprise. Screwcap. 12.5° alc. **Rating** 88 **To** 2008 **$14**

Calder Grove Semillon Sauvignon Blanc 2006 Well-made with some grip; touches of herb and grass to the minerally structure. Screwcap. 11.5° alc. **Rating** 87 To 2008 $15

Commissioner's Block Chardonnay 2005 A cunningly made wine; stone fruit augmented by a touch of oak and a little twist of viognier. Screwcap. 14° alc. **Rating** 87 To 2008 $14

Roberts Estate Chardonnay 2005 Well above the average unoaked chardonnay at this price; attractive melon, citrus and stone fruit; good balance. Screwcap. 13.5° alc. **Rating** 87 To 2008 $10

Commissioner's Block Viognier 2006 Glowing yellow-green; abundant canned yellow peach and apricot flavours; not phenolic. Screwcap. 13.5° alc. **Rating** 87 To 2008 $14

Roberts Estate Cabernet Merlot 2004 Excellent value; has some real depth to the red fruit flavours, and a hint of sweetness doesn't detract overmuch, and will appeal to most consumers of wine at this price point. Screwcap. 13.5° alc. **Rating** 87 To 2008 $10

Calder Grove Cabernet Merlot 2004 Bright colour; light- to medium-bodied, but still fresh, with juicy red and blackcurrant fruit; fine tannins to close. Screwcap. 13.5° alc. **Rating** 87 To 2011

New Era Vineyards   NR

PO Box 391, Woodside SA 5244 **Region** Adelaide Hills
T (08) 8389 7714 **F** (08) 8389 7714 www.neweravineyards.com.au **Open** Not
Winemaker Robert Baxter, Reg Wilkinson **Est.** 1988 **Cases** NA

Newbridge Wines   ★★★☆

18 Chelsea Street, Brighton, Vic 3186 (postal) **Region** Bendigo
T (03) 9591 0660 www.newbridgewines.com.au **Open** At Newbridge Hotel, Newbridge
Winemaker Greg Dedman (Contract), Andrew Simpson **Est.** 1996 **Cases** 350
The Newbridge property was purchased by Ian Simpson in 1979 partly for sentimental family history reasons, and partly because of the beauty of the property situated on the banks of the Loddon River. It was not until 1996 that he decided to plant 1 ha of shiraz, and up to and including the 2002 vintage the grapes were sold to several local wineries. He decided to retain the grapes and make wine in 2003, and Ian lived to see that and the following 2 vintages take shape before his death. The property is now run by his son Andrew and wife Kayleen, the wines contract-made by Greg Dedman with enthusiastic support from Andrew Simpson.

ŢŢŢŢŢ **Loddon River Bendigo Shiraz 2004** Medium-bodied, with much better fruit and varietal expression than the '05; black cherry and blackberry with a sprinkle of spice and fine tannins. Screwcap. 14.2° alc. **Rating** 91 To 2017 $18

ŢŢŢŢ **Loddon River Bendigo Shiraz 2005** Light- to medium-bodied; with savoury/spicy overtones to the mix of red and black fruits; minimal tannins and oak. Screwcap. 14.2° alc. **Rating** 87 To 2012 $18

Loddon River Bendigo Shiraz 2003 Ripe, sweet, slightly confit/jam overtones to the fruit, but not to the finish, which is dry. Ageing nicely. Screwcap. 14.2° alc. **Rating** 87 To 2010 $18

Newtons Ridge   ★★★☆

1170 Cooriemungle Road, Timboon, Vic 3268 **Region** Geelong
T (03) 5598 7394 **F** (03) 5598 7396 **Open** 7 days 11–5 Nov–Apr, or by appt
Winemaker David Newton **Est.** 1998 **Cases** 1200
David and Dot Newton say that after milking cows for 18 years, they decided to investigate the possibility of planting a northeast-facing block of land which they also owned. Their self-diagnosed mid-life crisis also stemmed from a lifelong interest in wine. They planted 2 ha of chardonnay and pinot noir in 1998, and another 2 ha of pinot gris, pinot noir and sauvignon blanc

the following year. Having done a short winemaking course at Melbourne University (Dookie campus), the Newtons completed a small winery in 2003. Originally called Heytesbury Ridge, a large legal stick waved in their direction led to a speedy name change to Newton Ridge.

ŶŶŶŶŶ **Shiraz 2005** Medium- to full-bodied; an array of licorice, black cherry and blackberry; firm but fine tannins underwrite the structure and length. Screwcap. 13.5° alc. **Rating** 90 **To** 2020 $25

ŶŶŶŶ **Sauvignon Blanc 2006** Light straw-green; very positive, ripe gooseberry and kiwifruit with some underlying herbaceous notes; slightly thick finish. Screwcap. 13.2° alc. **Rating** 88 **To** 2008 $18
Chardonnay 2006 Solid stone fruit flavours and some French oak influence; similar texture to the Sauvignon Blanc on the finish. Screwcap. 13.6° alc. **Rating** 87 **To** 2010 $20

Nicholson River

Liddells Road, Nicholson, Vic 3882 **Region** Gippsland
T (03) 5156 8241 **F** (03) 5156 8433 **www**.nicholsonriverwinery.com.au **Open** 7 days 10–4
Winemaker Ken Eckersley **Est.** 1978 **Cases** 2000
The fierce commitment to quality in the face of the temperamental Gippsland climate and frustratingly small production has been handsomely repaid by some massive Chardonnays and quixotic red wines (from 8 ha of estate plantings). Ken Eckersley refers to his Chardonnays not as white wines but as gold wines, and lists them accordingly in his newsletter. Exports to the UK, the US and Thailand.

Nightingale Wines

1239 Milbrodale Road, Broke, NSW 2330 **Region** Lower Hunter Valley
T (02) 6579 1499 **F** (02) 6579 1477 **www**.nightingalewines.com.au **Open** 7 days 10–4
Winemaker Nigel Robinson, Paul Nightingale **Est.** 1997 **Cases** 18 000
Paul and Gail Nightingale have wasted no time since establishing their business in 1997. They have planted 3 ha each of verdelho and merlot, 2 ha of shiraz, 1.5 ha each of chardonnay and cabernet sauvignon and 1 ha of chambourcin. Exports to NZ.

Nillahcootie Estate

RMB 1637, Lima South, Vic 3673 **Region** Upper Goulburn
T (03) 5768 2685 **F** (03) 5768 2678 **www**.nillahcootieestate.com.au **Open** Mon–Thurs by appt, Fri 12–4, Sat 11–11, Sun 12–5
Winemaker Plunkett Wines (Sam Plunkett), Kilchurn Wines (David Cowburn), Victor Nash **Est.** 1988 **Cases** 1500
Karen Davy and Michael White decided to diversify their primary business of beef cattle production on their 280-ha property in 1988. Between then and 2001 they planted a little over 8 ha of grapes, initially content to sell the production to other local wineries, but in 2001 they retained a small proportion of the grapes for winemaking, increasing it the following year to its current level. In 2001 they also purchased a 20-ha property overlooking Lake Nillahcootie, on which they have built a strikingly designed restaurant and cellar door.

ŶŶŶŶŶ **Strathbogie Sauvignon Blanc 2006** A clean but potent herbaceous, green bean/gooseberry mix of aromas; a crisp and long palate follows. Screwcap. 13° alc. **Rating** 90 **To** 2008 $20
Reserve Merlot 2004 Light to medium-bodied, with good varietal character with a mix of red fruits, spice and black olive. Screwcap. 13.5° alc. **Rating** 90 **To** 2012 $25

ŶŶŶŶ **Shiraz 2004** Medium-bodied; quite firm savoury/earthy/bramble/dark chocolate surrounds to the core of black fruits. Screwcap. 13.5° alc. **Rating** 89 **To** 2011 $22

Maggies Paddock Cabernet Merlot 2004 An attractive, straightforward, no frills, medium-bodied blend of red and blackcurrant fruit; fine tannins, light oak. Screwcap. 13.5° alc. **Rating** 89 **To** 2010 $22

Limited Release Sparkling Shiraz 2004 Fresh, light and lively and, blessedly, neither sweet nor oaky. 13.5° alc. **Rating** 88 **To** 2009 $28

Shiraz Cabernet Merlot 2004 A smooth, supple light to medium-bodied, easy style with fine tannins. Screwcap. 13.5° alc. **Rating** 87 **To** 2008 $20

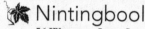

Nintingbool ★★★★★

56 Wongerer Lane, Smythes Creek, Vic 3351 (postal) **Region** Ballarat
T (03) 5342 4393 **F** (03) 5342 4393 **www**.nintingbool.com **Open** Not
Winemaker Peter Bothe **Est.** 1998 **Cases** 110

Peter and Jill Bothe purchased the Nintingbool property in 1982, building the home in which they now live in 1984, using old bluestones gathered from the local area and dating back to the goldrush period. They simultaneously established an extensive Australian native garden and home orchard, but in 1998 diversified with the planting of pinot noir, a further planting the following year lifting the total to 2 ha. A small amount of property remains to be planted with pinot gris. This is one of the coolest mainland regions, and demands absolute attention to detail (and a warm growing season) for success. In 2002 and '03 the grapes were sold to Ian Watson, the wine made and released under the Tomboy Hill label, but with the Nintingbool Vineyard shown on the label. The 2002 was a quite beautiful wine. In 2004 they decided to make the wines themselves, the opening vintage producing a tiny 44 cases.

🍷🍷🍷🍷🍷 **Pinot Noir 2005** Bright, clear colour; a lovely combination of black cherry, plum and spicy fruit; super-fine tannins, and good oak. Screwcap. 13.8° alc. **Rating** 95 **To** 2012 $30

No Regrets Vineyard ★★★★

40 Dillons Hill Road, Glaziers Bay, Tas 7109 **Region** Southern Tasmania
T (03) 6295 1509 **Open** By appt, also at Salamanca Market (Hobart) most Saturdays
Winemaker Hood Wines **Est.** 2000 **Cases** 300

Having sold Elsewhere Vineyard, Eric and Jette Phillips have planted the former flower gardens around the old Elsewhere homestead, where they still live, exclusively to pinot noir, and renamed this 1-ha 'retirement' vineyard No Regrets.

🍷🍷🍷🍷 **Pinot Noir 2005** Fragrant nuances of flowers and violets on the bouquet; delicate, fresh and lively red fruits are appealing, but the overall style is more to rose than conventional pinot. Screwcap. 13° alc. **Rating** 89 **To** 2008 $30

Nookamka Estate Vineyard NR

PO Box 180, Barmera, SA 5345 **Region** Riverland
T (08) 8588 1588 **F** (08) 8588 1011 **www**.nookamkaestate.com.au **Open** Not
Winemaker Bill Kanakaris **Est.** 2002 **Cases** NA

Nookamka Estate Vineyard brings 2 disparate cultures together. Nookamka was the name given by local Aboriginals to what is now known as Lake Bonney. Nookamka was also the name given to the subdivision in the region created for returned soldiers from the First World War. Bill Kanakaris' parents moved from Greece to the Riverland in the early 1960s, gradually establishing a wine grape and table grape production business. Son Bill Kanakaris followed in the footsteps both of his parents and grandfather (the largest wine producer and merchant in his village, Levidi, in Greece) when he started his own vineyard in the 1980s, initially selling grapes, but commencing wine production in 2002, and the wines were quickly rewarded with a string of bronze medals.

Noorilim Estate Vineyard   NR

PO Box 115, Murchison, Vic 3610 **Region** Goulburn Valley
T (03) 5826 2444 **F** (03) 5826 2132 **www**.noorilimestate.com.au **Open** Not
Winemaker Contract **Est.** NA **Cases** NA
Noorilim Estate is a particularly historic property. Built in 1879, the homestead was one of the
showpieces of Vic at the time of the 1888 Centennial Exhibition in Melbourne. It thereafter
fell into disrepair, but has been restored to its former glory by Rod and Carolyn Menzies. They
have also planted a substantial vineyard, with 11.5 ha of shiraz, 5.8 ha of merlot, 5.3 ha of
chardonnay, 4.2 ha of cabernet sauvignon and 4 ha of viognier. While the lion's share of the
grapes are sold, there is significant production of Sauvignon Blanc, Chardonnay, Shiraz,
Cabernet Merlot and Viognier. Barrel samples of the 2006 Viognier, '06 Shiraz Viognier and '06
Cabernet Merlot were crammed with flavour and full of promise.

 # Noorinbee Selection Vineyards

53 Monaro Highway, Cann River, Vic 3890 **Region** Gippsland
T (03) 5158 6500 **F** (03) 5158 3150 **Open** Wed–Sun & public hols 10.30–5
Winemaker Ken Eckersley (Contract) **Est.** 1992 **Cases** 400
Ronald and Elaine Luhrs have 2.5 ha of vines, mostly planted back in 1992. The principal varieties
are cabernet sauvignon, merlot, malbec, cabernet franc and petit verdot (hence their wines
modelled on those of the Medoc in Bordeaux) with a little pinot noir and shiraz. In 2006 they
made 2 interesting blends: a Harslevelu Sauvignon Blanc, and a Mammolo Merlot, I suspect from
purchased grapes. They have built a mudbrick cellar door, restaurant and gallery complex.

ᵠᵠᵠᵠ   **Mammolo Nebbiolo Merlot 2006** An interesting wine, with nice sweet red
fruits, and neither too green nor too oaky. ProCork. 12.5° alc. **Rating** 89
To 2012 $23.50
Pinot Noir 2005 Very good colour; strong plummy fruit presence, though not
over-much finesse. ProCork. 12° alc. **Rating** 87 To 2011 $24.50
Cabernet Sauvignon Cabernet Franc Merlot Malbec Petit Verdot 2005
Medium-bodied; has some cedar and cigar box characters, but has aged quickly.
ProCork. 13° alc. **Rating** 87 To 2008 $23.50

Norfolk Rise Vineyard

Limestone Coast Road, Mount Benson, SA 5265 **Region** Mount Benson
T (08) 8768 5080 **F** (08) 8768 5083 **www**.norfolkrise.com.au **Open** Mon–Fri 9–5
Winemaker Kristen McGann **Est.** 2000 **Cases** 85 000
This is by far the largest and most important development in the Mount Benson region. It is
ultimately owned by a privately held Belgian company, G & C Kreglinger, established in 1797. In
early 2002 it acquired Pipers Brook Vineyard; it will maintain the separate brands of the 2 ventures.
The Mount Benson development commenced in 2000, with a 160-ha vineyard and a 2000-tonne
winery, primarily aimed at the export market. Exports to the UK, the US and other major markets.

ᵠᵠᵠᵠ   **Cabernet Sauvignon 2005** Savoury, medium-bodied style with some herb and
olive offset by quite a deal of oak. Screwcap. 14.5° alc. **Rating** 87 To 2011 $16

Normanby Wines

Rose-Lea Vineyard, 178 Dunns Avenue, Harrisville, Qld 4307 **Region** Queensland Zone
T (07) 5467 1214 **www**.normanbywines.com.au **Open** 7 days Winter 10–5, Summer 10–7
Winemaker Golden Grove Estate (Ray Costanzo) **Est.** 1999 **Cases** 500
Normanby Wines, about 50 km due south of Ipswich, fills in more of the Qld viticultural jigsaw
puzzle. The vineyard has just under 3 ha planted to verdelho, shiraz, merlot, viognier, chambourcin,
durif and grenache.

ᵠᵠᵠᵠ   **Chambourcin 2005** Typical brilliant colour; within the inherent limitations of
the variety (especially the lack of structure), has lively, juicy red fruits with a
squeeze of lemon. Screwcap. 14.8° alc. **Rating** 87 To 2008 $24

Durif 2005 Strong colour as always; however, flavour is achieved at the cost of fairly aggressive tannins, and the wine has to be given several years to start the softening process. Screwcap. 13.1° alc. **Rating** 87 **To** 2015 $24

Norton Estate

758 Plush Hannan Road, Lower Norton, Vic 3400 **Region** Western Victoria Zone
T (03) 5384 8235 **F** (03) 5384 8235 **Open** Wed–Sun 10–5
Winemaker Best's Wines (Contract) **Est.** 1997 **Cases** 1250
Donald Spence worked for the Victorian Department of Forests for 36 years before retiring. In 1996 he and his family purchased a farm at Lower Norton, and, instead of farming wool, meat and wheat, trusted their instincts and planted vines on the lateritic buckshot soil. The vineyard is 6 km northwest of the Grampians GI, and will have to be content with the Western Victoria Zone until a sufficient number of others follow suit and plant on the 1000 ha of suitable soil in the area.

ΨΨΨΨΨ **Arapiles Run Shiraz 2005** An aromatic bouquet with blackberry, black cherry and sundry spices leading into a lively, medium-bodied palate, the flavours tracking the bouquet. Refreshing alcohol. Screwcap. 13.8° alc. **Rating** 94 **To** 2025 $35

ΨΨΨΨΨ **Sauvignon Blanc 2006** Bright and clean; gentle tropical gooseberry fruit, a touch of sweetness on the finish is just what the market wants, apparently. Screwcap. 12.5° alc. **Rating** 90 **To** 2008 $16
Family Reserve Cabernet Sauvignon 2003 Deep colour; dense, drought-concentrated blackberry and earth fruit supported by potent tannins. Will never aspire to elegance, but time and patience should reward. Cork. 14° alc. **Rating** 90 **To** 2020 $25

Norton Summit Vineyards

59 Nicholls Road, Norton Summit, SA 5136 **Region** Adelaide Hills
T (08) 8390 1986 **F** (08) 8390 1986 **www**.nsv.net.au **Open** By appt
Winemaker Dr Kenn Fisher **Est.** 1998 **Cases** 450
Dr Kenn Fisher and partner Meredyth Taylor planted the 1.5 ha of pinot noir and 0.3 ha of chardonnay in 1998. The vineyard has 4 blocks, each with its own meso-climate, orientation and soil type. To add further complexity, 4 clones have been utilised. Up to and including 2003 only old oak was used, but as the vines have gained age and strength, 30% new oak was introduced in 2004 and subsequent vintages. Kenn Fisher makes the wines using traditional Burgundian methods of open fermenters and a basket press.

ΨΨΨΨΨ **Adelaide Hills Pinot Noir 2004** Much fresher and tighter than the '05, with more red fruit flavours; still vibrant. Screwcap. 14° alc. **Rating** 90 **To** 2011

ΨΨΨΨ **Adelaide Hills Chardonnay 2005** Medium- to full-bodied; a solid peach/fig/nut mix of fully ripe flavours; no need to wait. Screwcap. 13.5° alc. **Rating** 89 **To** 2009
Adelaide Hills Pinot Noir 2005 Distinct development in hue, the purples disappearing rapidly; an extremely foresty/stalky/earthy/spicy mix; complex, but again suggesting early consumption. Screwcap. 14° alc. **Rating** 88 **To** 2009

Nova Vita Wines

GPO Box 1352, Adelaide, SA 5001 **Region** Adelaide Hills
T (08) 8356 0454 **F** (08) 8356 1472 **www**.novavitawines.com.au **Open** Not
Winemaker O'Leary Walker Wines **Est.** 2005 **Cases** 2000
Mark and Jo Kozned spent months of painstaking research before locating the property on which they have now established their substantial vineyard. Situated 4 km outside of Gumeracha, it has gentle slopes, plenty of water, and, importantly, moderately fertile soils. The vineyard has 25.6 ha of chardonnay, 3.8 ha of sauvignon blanc and 0.7 ha of shiraz. The name Nova Vita reflects the beginning of the Kozned's new life, the firebird on the label coming from the Kozned's Russian ancestry. It is a Russian myth that only a happy or lucky person may see the bird or hear its song.

ŸŸŸŸŸ **Firebird Adelaide Hills Chardonnay 2006** Clean, fresh and lively; intense citrus, nectarine, apple and pear mix supported by a touch of barrel ferment oak. Screwcap. 13.5° alc. **Rating** 94 **To** 2013 $20
Firebird Adelaide Hills Shiraz 2005 A particularly deep and rich palate for the Adelaide Hills; impressive blackberry, licorice and spice fruit; does show the alcohol, but carries it, except for a slight shortening of the fruit on the finish. Screwcap. 15° alc. **Rating** 94 **To** 2025 $25

ŸŸŸŸŸ **Firebird Adelaide Hills Sauvignon Blanc 2006** Spotlessly clean bouquet with no sweaty reduction; gentle citrus and tropical fruit; good balance and mouthfeel in a non-effusive fashion. Screwcap. 12.5° alc. **Rating** 90 **To** 2008 $20
Firebird McLaren Vale Rose 2006 Well-made; grenache makes quality roses if handled the right way, and this is one such; fruit flavour, with balanced acidity and residual sugar. Screwcap. 12.5° alc. **Rating** 90 **To** 2008 $20
Firebird Adelaide Hills Shiraz 2004 A spicy, tangy, elegant light to medium-bodied wine, with a gentle skein of juicy red berry fruit and controlled oak. Good aftertaste, not forced Screwcap. 13.8° alc. **Rating** 90 **To** 2008 $20

ŸŸŸŸ **Firebird Adelaide Hills Sauvignon Blanc 2005** A more herbal style than the '06, has a degree of punch to the mineral/slate/pebble component accompanying the sweet apple/citrus fruit. Screwcap. 13° alc. **Rating** 89 **To** 2008 $18

Nowhere Creek Vineyard   ★★★
19 Nowhere Creek Road, Elmhurst, Vic 3469 **Region**
T (03) 5354 8319 **F** (03) 5354 8319 **Open** By appt
Winemaker Mount Langi Ghiran **Est.** 1996 **Cases** 500
In 1996 farmers Julian and Kaaren Kaye joined with Melbourne-based investors Robert and Ann Johnson, to plant 4 ha of shiraz. Since then they planted a further 33 ha of shiraz, and thereafter purchased an equivalent area of predominantly cabernet sauvignon planted on an adjoining property. The grapes are sold to Mount Langi Ghiran, which speaks for itself in terms of the quality of the fruit, and a small amount is made for Nowhere Creek by Mount Langi Ghiran.

ŸŸŸŸ **Elmhurst Shiraz 2004** Big, powerful, slightly extractive wine, with robust tannins. A question about low level aldehydes, too. **Rating** 88 **To** 2014 $20
Elmhurst Cabernet Sauvignon 2004 Light- to medium-bodied; a fresh and lively mix of cassis and blackcurrant, with touches of spice and earth; subtle oak. Cork. 14° alc. **Rating** 88 **To** 2014

Nugan Estate   ★★★★★
60 Banna Avenue, Griffith, NSW 2680 **Region** Riverina
T (02) 6962 1822 **F** (02) 6962 6392 **www**.nuganestate.com.au **Open** Mon–Fri 9–5
Winemaker Darren Owers **Est.** 1999 **Cases** 400 000
Nugan Estate arrived on the scene like a whirlwind. It is an offshoot of the Nugan Group headed by Michelle Nugan, inter alia the recipient of an Export Hero Award in 2000. In the mid-1990s the company began developing vineyards, and is now a veritable giant, with 310 ha at Darlington Point, 52 ha at Hanwood and 120 ha at Hillston (all in NSW), 100 ha in the King Valley, and 10 ha in McLaren Vale. In addition, it has contracts in place to buy 1000 tonnes of grapes per year from Coonawarra. It sells part of the production as grapes, part as bulk wine and part under the Cookoothama and Nugan Estate labels. Both brands are having considerable success in wine shows, large and small. Not all tasting notes have been included due to space limitations. Exports to the UK, the US and other major markets.

ŸŸŸŸŸ **McLaren Parish Vineyard McLaren Vale Shiraz 2003** Good hue and depth for the vintage; a full-bodied, no compromise wine offering rich, sweet fruit, more towards red than normal for the region, and perhaps a little less chocolate; tannins cut back what would otherwise have been a too-sweet wine. Cork. 14.5° alc. **Rating** 94 **To** 2020 $24

Manuka Grove Durif 2004 Brilliant winemaking has invested the wine with elegance rarely encountered with durif, without taking away the dark chocolate, spice and blackberry varietal fruit. Gold medal National Wine Show '06. Screwcap. 14.5° alc. **Rating** 94 **To** 2021 $23

♟♟♟♟♀ **McLaren Parish Vineyard McLaren Vale Shiraz 2004** Has excellent texture and structure; medium-bodied; black fruits, chocolate, and unusual, but seductive, slightly grainy tannins. Screwcap. 14.5° alc. **Rating** 92 **To** 2019 $22.95

Cookoothama Darlington Point Cabernet Merlot 2005 Strong red-purple; equally strong and positive flavours of blackcurrant and cassis; good tannin structure and length. Surprise packet. Value. Screwcap. 14° alc. **Rating** 92 **To** 2010 $14.95

Alcira Vineyard Coonawarra Cabernet Sauvignon 2004 Medium-bodied; smooth, supple blackcurrant/cassis and a touch of chocolate; fine tannins add to the length, oak to the complexity. Gold medal Adelaide Wine Show '06. Cork. 14° alc. **Rating** 92 **To** 2015 $24

Cookoothama Darlington Point Botrytis Semillon 2005 Rich, mouthfilling, apricot/candied lemon peel/marmalade/butterscotch flavours; good balancing acidity. Cork. 11.5° alc. **Rating** 92 $19.95

Alfredo Frasca's Lane Vineyard King Valley Sangiovese Merlot 2005 Distinctive aroma very much reflecting the 2 varieties; medium-bodied, with fine-grained tannins running throughout in best Italian fashion; attractive sour cherry fruit flavours. Screwcap. 14° alc. **Rating** 91 **To** 2010 $23

Cookoothama Darlington Point Chardonnay 2004 Full golden green; the screwcap has done a great job, the flavour development still with acid freshness running through ripples of flavour of peach and nectarine, plus a touch of oak support. 13.5° alc. **Rating** 90 **To** 2008 $15

♟♟♟♟ **Frasca's Lane Vineyard King Valley Sauvignon Blanc 2006** Crisp and refreshing; mineral and a touch of grass, the structure good although the fruity side of sauvignon blanc is somewhat suppressed. Screwcap. 13° alc. **Rating** 89 **To** 2008 $19.95

Frasca's Lane King Valley Pinot Grigio 2006 Beats the odds with some distinctive spice and ripe pear aromas and flavours; finishes crisp and clean, with lemony acidity, and no reliance on residual sugar. Screwcap. 13.5° alc. **Rating** 89 **To** 2008 $20

Cookoothama Pigeage Merlot 2003 Excellent colour; an abundance of blackberry/cassis fruit and soft tannins; remarkable given its warm climate origins. Quality cork. 14° alc. **Rating** 89 **To** 2011 $24

Frasca's Lane Vineyard King Valley Sauvignon Blanc 2005 Light minerally structure, with a mix of asparagus and citrus flavours; good length and acidity. Screwcap. 13° alc. **Rating** 88 **To** 2008 $20

Cookoothama King Valley Sauvignon Blanc Semillon 2006 A clean bouquet, with plenty of tropical fruit flavours, the touch of residual sugar balanced by acidity. Screwcap. 13° alc. **Rating** 88 **To** 2008 $15

Frasca's Lane Vineyard King Valley Chardonnay 2005 Positive peach, stone fruit and melon set off against well-balanced and integrated oak. Screwcap. 13.8° alc. **Rating** 88 **To** 2010 $19.95

Cookoothama Darlington Point Merlot 2004 Attractive medium-bodied wine; predominantly red fruits; soft tannins and oak. Cork. 14° alc. **Rating** 88 **To** 2012 $22.95

Manuka Grove Durif 2003 Still has masses of dark fruits, but there are signs the fruit may be softening faster than the tannins; I simply don't know which way the cat will jump over the next few years. Cork. 14° alc. **Rating** 88 **To** 2012 $24

Cookoothama Darlington Point Shiraz 2005 A powerful wine, utterly unexpected, with robust tannins on black fruits, time needed. Screwcap. 14° alc. **Rating** 87 **To** 2013 $14.95

Nuggetty Vineyard

280 Maldon-Shelbourne Road, Nuggetty, Vic 3463 **Region** Bendigo
T (03) 5475 1347 **F** (03) 5475 1647 **www**.nuggettyvineyard.com.au **Open** W'ends &
public hols 10–4, or by appt
Winemaker Greg Dedman, Jackie Dedman **Est.** 1993 **Cases** 1000
The family-owned vineyard was established in 1993 by Greg and Jackie Dedman. Greg is a
Charles Sturt University graduate, while Jackie (having spent 18 months at Bowen Estate in
1997/8) has simultaneously undertaken the winemaking degree at Charles Sturt University and
the wine marketing degree at the Adelaide University. They share the vineyard and winery tasks
(including contract winemaking for others); these include 6.5 ha of estate plantings (shiraz,
cabernet sauvignon and semillon).

Barrel Club Reserve Shiraz 2004 Solid, savoury, dark fruited wine; dips
fractionally on the mid- to back-palate, but then comes again with spicy,
sweeter fruit on the finish. Screwcap. 14° alc. **Rating** 90 **To** 2015 $30
Shiraz 2004 A light- to medium-bodied version of the Barrel Club Reserve; a
mix of fresh, red and black fruits; lesser tannins help lift the profile of the fruit,
and the virtues of each cancel each other out. Screwcap. 13.8° alc. **Rating** 90
To 2012 $25

Barrel Fermented Semillon 2006 Oak has been well-balanced and integrated
with the fruit; not phenolic, and will reward medium-term development. Screwcap.
12.5° alc. **Rating** 89 **To** 2010 $18
Shiraz 2003 Rich, ripe, sweet blackberry, with some confit/jam notes on the way
through, but the wine tightens up nicely on a long finish. Cork. 13.5° alc. **Rating** 88
To 2012 $25

Nurihannam Wines   NR

1 Penrice Road, Nuriootpa, SA 5355 (postal) **Region** Barossa Valley
T (08) 8562 2022 **F** (08) 8562 1029 **www**.barossaclass.sa.edu.au **Open** Not
Winemaker Kevin Hoskin **Est.** 1992 **Cases** NA
The Nurihannam wines are made at the Nuriootpa High School by what must be the largest
winemaking team in the world per bottle of wine produced. Each year 75–100 Year 10 students
assist agriculture teachers with the viticulture and winemaking. Made and sold under the
Barossa Class and Barossa Scholar labels, they are available at the Nuriootpa Vine Inn, Kaeslers
and Chateau Tanunda.

Nyora Vineyard & Winery

Cnr Peacock & Williams Roads, The Gurdies, Vic 3984 **Region** Gippsland
T (03) 5997 6205 **Open** Wed–Mon 10–6
Winemaker Klaus Griese, Denise Griese **Est.** 1995 **Cases** 600
Klaus and Denise Griese have established a Joseph's Coat of varieties since 1995; in descending
order shiraz, chardonnay, cabernet sauvignon, sauvignon blanc, colombard, semillon, pinot noir,
pinot gris, merlot, riesling and verdelho totalling a little under 5 ha in all. The vineyard is planted
on a northeast slope near the top of the ridge overlooking the Bass River Valley, and a 3-storey
winery (the bottom floor underground) has been built. All of the wines are, to a lesser or greater
degree, sweet, and aimed at the cellar door.

O'Donohoe's Find ★★★☆

PO Box 460, Berri, SA 5343 **Region** Riverland
T 0414 765 813 **F** (08) 8583 2228 **www**.tomsdrop.com.au **Open** Not
Winemaker Michael O'Donohoe **Est.** 2002 **Cases** 600
Michael O'Donohoe pays tribute to his Irish grandfather, Thomas O'Donohoe, and 6 great-
uncles, who arrived from Ireland in 1881 to search for gold, ending up distilling salty bore water
into fresh water. A century later Michael O'Donohoe runs a small vineyard in the Riverland

which was certified organic in 1990, receives very little water, and crops at around 2 tonnes per acre. The wines (released under the Tom's Drop label) are made using a tiny crusher, a small hand-operated basket press, and open fermenters. They deserve to be taken seriously.

ŸŸŸŸ   **Tom's Drop Shiraz 2006** Medium red-purple; fresh red and black fruit flavours, with spicy notes to provide counterbalance. Is there a whisper of brett? Screwcap. 14° alc. **Rating** 89 **To** 2016 $25
Tom's Drop Mourvedre Shiraz 2005 The savoury, fine tannins of mourvedre set the tone for the wine; light- to medium-bodied, with gentle earthy/spicy/savoury flavours; distinctly European in feel. Screwcap. 14.5° alc. **Rating** 88 **To** 2013 $25

O'Leary Walker Wines

Main Road, Leasingham, SA 5452 (PO Box 49, Watervale, SA 5452) **Region** Clare Valley
T (08) 8843 0022 www.olearywalkerwines.com **Open** Mon–Fri 10–7, w'ends by appt
Winemaker David O'Leary, Nick Walker **Est.** 2001 **Cases** 15 000
David O'Leary and Nick Walker together have more than 30 years' experience as winemakers working for some of the biggest Australian wine groups. They then took the plunge, and backed themselves to establish their own winery and brand. Their main vineyard is at Watervale in the Clare Valley, with over 36 ha of riesling, shiraz, cabernet sauvignon, merlot and semillon. In the Adelaide Hills they have established 14 ha of chardonnay, cabernet sauvignon, pinot noir, shiraz, sauvignon blanc and merlot. Exports to the UK, the US, Canada, Indonesia and Singapore.

ŸŸŸŸŸ   **Watervale Riesling 2006** Slate, mineral and citrus run through a tight and focused palate, great acidity investing the wine with exceptional length. Screwcap. 12.5° alc. **Rating** 94 **To** 2019 $20
Polish Hill River Riesling 2006 A mix of citrus blossom and tropical aromas, then a generous and rich palate, abundantly flavoured, but not heavy; good acidity. Screwcap. 12.5° alc. **Rating** 94 **To** 2015 $20

ŸŸŸŸŸ   **Adelaide Hills Sauvignon Blanc 2006** Attractive ripe tropical fruit with splashes of gooseberry; long, dry finish. Screwcap. 12° alc. **Rating** 91 **To** 2008 $22

O'Reilly's Canungra Valley Vineyards

Lamington National Park Road, Canungra Valley, Qld 4275 **Region** Queensland Coastal
T (07) 5543 4011 www.canungravineyards.com.au **Open** 7 days 10–4.30
Winemaker Symphony Hill (Mike Hayes) **Est.** 1997 **Cases** 7000
Canungra Valley Vineyards has been established in the hinterland of the Gold Coast with a clear focus on broad-based tourism. Vines (8 ha) have been established around the 19th-century homestead (relocated to the site from its original location in Warwick), but these provide only a small part of the wine offered for sale. In deference to the climate, 70% of the estate planting is chambourcin, the rain and mildew-resistant hybrid; the remainder is semillon.

ŸŸŸŸ   **Platypus Play Semillon 2006** No reduction on the bouquet; relatively soft and fruity young semillon, picked at the right time; no oak adornment. Screwcap. 11.6° alc. **Rating** 88 **To** 2010 $20
Viola Reserve Cabernet Sauvignon 2003 Light- to medium-bodied; savoury/minty overtones to cassis fruit; slightly green tannins, but well-made. Diam. 14.5° alc. **Rating** 87 **To** 2011 $26

O'Shea & Murphy Rosebery Hill Vineyard   NR

Rosebery Hill, Pastoria Road, Pipers Creek, Vic 3444 **Region** Macedon Ranges
T (03) 5423 5253 **F** (03) 5423 5253 www.osheamurphy.com **Open** By appt
Winemaker Barry Murphy, John O'Shea **Est.** 1984 **Cases** NA

Oak Valley Estate

3055 Deakin Avenue, Sturt Highway, Mildura South, Vic 3502 **Region** Murray Darling
T (03) 5021 2379 **F** (03) 5022 7283 www.oakvalleyestate.com.au **Open** 7 days 10–5
Winemaker Ferdinando DeBlasio **Est.** 2000 **Cases** 940
Ferdinando DeBlasio left Italy bound for Australia when he was 13 years old, with both grandfather and father having made wine for home consumption every year. In 1963 he purchased a 20-ha paddock on Oak Avenue (near Mildura Airport) with 4 ha of established vines. With the help of wife Joanne the plantings were slowly expanded, and completed by 1972. In 1980 a 4-ha property on Deakin Avenue was purchased, and by 1999 a little under 3 ha of shiraz had been planted, the onsite winery built the following year.

ỸỸỸỸ **Late Harvest Muscatel Blanc 2006** Well-made and balanced; sweet, but not sickly sweet as some can be; good acidity helps. Screwcap. 13.5° alc. **Rating** 87 To 2008 $18

Oakdene Vineyards

255 Grubb Road, Wallington, Vic 3221 **Region** Geelong
T (03) 5256 3886 **F** (03) 5256 3881 www.oakdene.com.au **Open** Wed–Sun 12–5
Winemaker Ray Nadeson, Robin Brockett (Contract) **Est.** 2001 **Cases** 1500
Bernard and Elizabeth Hooley purchased Oakdene in 2001. Bernard focused on planting 5.4 ha of shiraz, chardonnay and pinot noir in that year, followed by 2.4 ha of sauvignon blanc in 2002, while his wife worked to restore the 1920s homestead. In 2004 they opened the Oakdene restaurant, through which much of the wine is sold. Ray Nadeson of Lethbridge Wines makes Chardonnay, Pinot Noir and Shiraz, Robin Brocket of Scotchmans Hill makes the Sauvignon Blanc.

ỸỸỸỸỸ **Shiraz 2005** Medium-bodied; attractive spicy/cedary notes to the red and black fruits of the mid-palate; silky tannins, good length. **Rating** 93 To 2015 $24
Pinot Noir 2005 Light- to medium-bodied; good fruit weight ranging through plum and black cherry, with additional spice and forest notes. **Rating** 90 To 2010 $24

Oakover Wines

14 Yukich Close, Middle Swan, WA 6056 **Region** Swan Valley
T (08) 9250 7533 **F** (08) 9250 7544 www.oakoverwines.com.au **Open** 7 days 11–4
Winemaker Rob Marshall **Est.** 1990 **Cases** 25 000
Owned by the Yukich family, and part of the Dalmatian Coast/Croatian cultural group in the Swan Valley, whose roots go back to the early 1900s. However, Oakover Estate is very much part of the new wave in the area, with a very large vineyard holding of 100 ha, planted predominantly to chardonnay, shiraz, chenin blanc and verdelho. Part of the production is sold to others, with increasing amounts made under the Oakover label, selling (among the other usual ways) at the large café/restaurant and function centre in the heart of the vineyard. Exports to Ireland, Indonesia, Malaysia and Singapore.

ỸỸỸỸỸ **Merlot 2003** Origin unstated; quite firm cassis, with some olive; a long finish, with tannins just within bounds. Screwcap. 14.5° alc. **Rating** 90 To 2018 $26

ỸỸỸỸ **Margaret River Shiraz 2005** Light- to medium-bodied; good texture with a mix of red and black fruits; minimal oak, but has length, finishing with fine tannins. Excellent value. Screwcap. 13.1° alc. **Rating** 89 To 2015 $16
White Label Margaret River Cabernet Merlot 2005 Bright colour; fresh flavours, but the wine is a little unfinished/underworked. At the price, hardly surprising. Screwcap. 14° alc. **Rating** 88 To 2011 $13
Semillon Sauvignon Blanc 2006 Well-made; moderately low alcohol a good response to the climate, keeping some delicacy and structure. Seafood on a summer day Screwcap. 11.8° alc. **Rating** 87 To 2008 $16

White Label Swan Valley Shiraz 2005 Light- to medium-bodied; fresh blackberry and cherry fruit; balanced tannins and another bargain. Screwcap. 14.2° alc. **Rating** 87 **To** 2013 $13

Oakridge   ★★★★★

864 Maroondah Highway, Coldstream, Vic 3770 **Region** Yarra Valley
T (03) 9739 1920 **F** (03) 9739 1923 **www.**oakridgeestate.com.au **Open** 7 days 10–5
Winemaker David Bicknell **Est.** 1978 **Cases** NFP
The long, dark shadow of Evans & Tate's ownership is now totally dispelled. Life is never easy, but David Bicknell is proving his worth time and again as an extremely talented, even if diffident, winemaker. At the top of the brand tier is 864, all Yarra Valley vineyard selections, and only released in the best years (Chardonnay, Shiraz, Cabernet Sauvignon, Riesling); next is the Oakridge core label (Chardonnay, Pinot Noir, Shiraz, Cabernet Sauvignon); and the Over the Shoulder range, drawn from all of the sources available to Oakridge (Sauvignon Blanc, Pinot Grigio, Pinot Noir, Shiraz Viognier, Cabernet Sauvignon).

ṬṬṬṬṬ **864 Yarra Valley Chardonnay 2005** A complex bouquet and palate, very
different in style to the varietal; intense fruit interplays with oak, wild yeast and lees, but at the end of the day, retains its integrity and purity. Single Vineyard Upper Yarra Valley. Screwcap. 13.5° alc. **Rating** 96 **To** 2017 $50
Yarra Valley Shiraz 2005 A fragrant mix of red and black fruits, the former dominant on the bouquet; cherry, plum and a touch of blackberry are supported by fine, almost powdery, tannins, and quality French oak. Screwcap. 14.5° alc. **Rating** 94 **To** 2017 $30
864 Yarra Valley Cabernet Merlot 2004 A fascinating reversal of alcohol roles; this only 13° versus 14.5° for Over the Shoulder. Here blackcurrant, licorice and dark flavours lead the way in a profound wine; most remarkable is the way David Bicknell has avoided green tannins or any other green flavours. Screwcap. 13° alc. **Rating** 94 **To** 2024 $50

ṬṬṬṬṬ **Yarra Valley Chardonnay 2006** Super-fine and elegant, reflecting the restrained
alcohol and use of new French oak; nectarine and strong citrus flavours; long palate. Screwcap. 13° alc. **Rating** 93 **To** 2012 $30
Yarra Valley Cabernet Sauvignon 2005 Abundant cassis and blackcurrant fruit on both bouquet and palate; fine tannins and integrated French oak (15 months maturation) sustain good length. Screwcap. 14.5° alc. **Rating** 93 **To** 2025 $30
Yarra Valley Pinot Noir 2006 A fragrant bouquet; more substance than Over the Shoulder, but still pure and linear, rather than complex; light- to medium to medium-bodied, demanding time to build complexity. Screwcap. 13.5° alc. **Rating** 91 **To** 2012 $30
Over the Shoulder Cabernet Merlot 2005 Delicious mouthfeel – and mouthful; a supple, smooth cascade of cherry, raspberry, cassis and blackcurrant; fine, polished tannins, oak a bit player. Enticing prices for the Over the Shoulder wines. Screwcap. 14.5° alc. **Rating** 91 **To** 2008 $18
Over the Shoulder Sauvignon Blanc 2006 Fresh, lively, clean and tangy, both on the bouquet and palate; gooseberry, kiwifruit and lychee flavours; good mouthfeel and length. Screwcap. 13° alc. **Rating** 90 **To** 2008 $18

ṬṬṬṬ **Over the Shoulder Pinot Noir 2006** Light- to medium-bodied; fresh and
vibrant cherry and strawberry fruit, linear and long; best sooner than later. Screwcap. 13.5° alc. **Rating** 88 **To** 2010 $18

Oakvale   ★★★★★

Broke Road, Pokolbin, NSW 2320 **Region** Lower Hunter Valley
T (02) 4998 7088 **F** (02) 4998 7077 **www.**oakvalewines.com.au **Open** 7 days 10–5
Winemaker Steve Hagan **Est.** 1893 **Cases** 10 000
All the literature and promotional material emphasises the fact that Oakvale has been family-owned since 1893. What it does not mention is that 3 quite unrelated families have been the

owners: first, and for much of the time, the Elliott family; then former Sydney solicitor Barry Shields; and, since 1999, Richard and Mary Owens, who also own the separately run Milbrovale winery at Broke. Be that as it may, the original slab hut homestead of the Elliott family which is now a museum, and the atmospheric Oakvale winery, are in the 'must visit' category. Exports to the US, Mexico and Japan.

ŦŦŦŦŦ **Semillon 2006** Spotlessly clean; an extra level of flavour and intensity with grass, citrus and lemon nuances giving the wine real presence; likely relatively early-developing wine. Gold medal Hunter Valley Wine Show '06. Terrific value. Screwcap. 12° alc. **Rating** 94 **To** 2011 $13

Barrel Select Shiraz 2003 Good hue and depth for the region; medium-bodied; very attractive red cherry and plum fruit on the supple palate finishing with fine tannins. Still varietal rather than regional, but has plenty of time to develop the latter. Gold medal Hunter Valley Wine Show '06. Cork. 13.5° alc. **Rating** 94 **To** 2020 $30

ŦŦŦŦ **Peppercorn Shiraz 2005** Excellent depth, texture and structure; still primary blackberry/plum fruit, but will develop Hunter character given time. Screwcap. 14° alc. **Rating** 92 **To** 2017 $29.50

Sparkling Shiraz 2002 A very rich wine; another 5 years on lees and another 5 years thereafter on cork would make a wonderful wine; as it is, has far more to offer than most; good balance. 13.5° alc. **Rating** 90 **To** 2015 $33

ŦŦŦŦ **Botrytis Semillon NV** Light- to medium-bodied; fresh peach, cumquat and apricot; good balancing acidity; not over the top in any way. 10.5° alc. **Rating** 89 **To** 2008 $29.50

Old Liqueur Muscat NV If sourced from the Hunter Valley, a pretty remarkable wine; has obvious age, but also varietal raisin fruit and rancio. 18° alc. **Rating** 88 **To** 2008 $29

Oakway Estate ★★★☆

575 Farley Road, Donnybrook, WA 6239 **Region** Geographe
T (08) 9731 7141 **F** (08) 9731 7190 **www**.oakwayestate.com.au **Open** Opening Sept '07
Winemaker Sharna Kowalc.zak **Est.** 1998 **Cases** 1500
Ria and Wayne Hammond run a combined blue gum tree plantation, beef cattle and vineyard property. It has a history of apple and stone fruit orchards, which suggested to the Hammonds that it would be suitable for grapes, and hence they planted a little under 2 ha of chardonnay, merlot, cabernet sauvignon and shiraz in 1998. The wines have won a number of bronze medals in local wine shows.

ŦŦŦŦŦ **Blue Gum Ridge Geographe Merlot 2005** A medium-bodied, well-structured wine; redcurrant fruit is tempered by notes of black olive and spice; good length and balance. Value. Screwcap. 13.7° alc. **Rating** 90 **To** 2011 $16

ŦŦŦŦ **Blue Gum Ridge Margaret River Semillon Sauvignon Blanc 2006** A relatively muted bouquet; citrus and gooseberry flavours come through on the palate providing excellent value. Screwcap. 12.5° alc. **Rating** 88 **To** 2009 $13

Oatley Wines ★★★☆

Craigmoor Road, Mudgee, NSW 2850 **Region** Mudgee
T (02) 6372 2208 **F** (02) 9433 0456 **www**.oatleywines.com.au **Open** Mon–Sat 10–4.30, Sun & public hols 10–4
Winemaker James Manners **Est.** 2006 **Cases** NFP
Oatley Wines, with Wild Oats its main brand, is the latest venture of the Oatley family, previously best known as the owners of Rosemount Estate until it was sold to Southcorp. The founder of both businesses is chairman Bob Oatley, and the new venture is run by son Sandy, with considerable hitting power added by deputy executive chairman Chris Hancock. Wild Oats, as anyone with the remotest interest in yachting and the Sydney-Hobart Yacht Race will know, has

been the name of Bob Oatley's racing yachts. The most recent is Wild Oats XI, which in 2005 and '06 broke more records than any prior yacht. The family has long-owned vineyards in Mudgee, but the new business has been rapidly expanded by the acquisition of the Montrose winery, the Craigmoor cellar door and restaurant, and 7 vineyards spread across the Mudgee region. It's a highly competitive market scene for new wineries, but the executive team assembled for Oatley Wines covers every base, and success will surely follow.

ŸŸŸŸŸ **Robert Oatley Barossa Valley Shiraz Viognier 2005** Slightly hazy colour, not expected; aromas and flavours, however, have plenty of life and zest in medium-bodied style; subtle oak and a long finish. Screwcap. 14.5° alc. **Rating** 90 **To** 2015 $24.95

ŸŸŸŸ **Robert Oatley Mudgee Chardonnay 2006** Melon, stone fruit and citrus of moderate intensity; a light touch of oak. Screwcap. 13.4° alc. **Rating** 89 **To** 2010 $24.95

Wild Oats Rose 2006 Precisely made for the broadest possible appeal; fresh cherry fruits, a hint of sweetness, but with a brisk finish. Screwcap. 13.4° alc. **Rating** 88 **To** 2008 $18.95

Wild Oats Shiraz Viognier 2005 Similar colour to the Robert Oatley; light-to medium-bodied; fresh, vibrant cherry/plum fruit, again belying the colour; nice wine. Screwcap. 14.8° alc. **Rating** 88 **To** 2012 $18.95

Wild Oats Sauvignon Blanc Semillon 2006 Fresh, crisp and delicate; gentle grassy fruit, with a touch of gooseberry. Screwcap. 12.3° alc. **Rating** 87 **To** 2008 $18.95

Wild Oats Mudgee Chardonnay 2006 Not complex, but fresh and lively, cleverly balanced by subliminal residual sugar. Screwcap. 13.8° alc. **Rating** 87 **To** 2010 $18.95

Wild Oats Pinot Grigio 2006 Cleverly made and balanced; pear and citrus, the latter balanced by a flick of residual sugar. Screwcap. 13.5° alc. **Rating** 87 **To** 2008 $18.95

Observatory Hill Vineyard   ★★★

107 Centauri Drive, Mt Rumney, Tas 7170 **Region** Southern Tasmania
T (03) 6248 5380 **Open** By appt
Winemaker Andrew Hood, Alain Rousseau **Est.** 1991 **Cases** 600
Glenn and Chris Richardson's Observatory Hill Vineyard has been developing since 1991 when Glenn and his late father-in-law Jim Ramsey planted the first of the 8500 vines that now make up the estate. Together with the adjoining property owned by Chris' brother Wayne Ramsey and his wife Stephanie, the vineyard now covers 3 ha with new plantings having been made each year. The name 'Observatory Hill' comes from the state's oldest observatory that is perched on the hill above the vineyard.

ŸŸŸŸ **Riesling 2006** Slightly advanced colour, but plenty of punch and drive; big on flavour, less on finesse. Screwcap. 13.1° alc. **Rating** 89 **To** 2011 $22

Chardonnay 2005 Gentle citrus and stone fruit; good balance, in no way relying on sweetness. Screwcap. 13.1° alc. **Rating** 89 **To** 2011 $22

Chardonnay 2006 Clean and fresh; typical cool climate grapefruit and nectarine flavours. Screwcap. 13.5° alc. **Rating** 88 **To** 2010 $22

Pinot Noir 2006 An abundance of flavour is compromised to a degree by heavy extract; may settle down with time. Screwcap. 13.85° alc. **Rating** 87 **To** 2011 $28

Occam's Razor   ★★★★★

c/- Jasper Hill, Drummonds Lane, Heathcote, Vic 3523 **Region** Heathcote
T (03) 5433 2528 **F** (03) 5433 3143 **Open** By appt
Winemaker Emily Laughton **Est.** 2001 **Cases** 400
Emily Laughton has decided to follow in her parents' footsteps after first seeing the world and having a range of casual jobs. Having grown up at Jasper Hill, winemaking was far from strange, but she decided to find her own way, buying the grapes from a small vineyard owned by Jasper

Hill employee Andrew Conforti and his wife Melissa. She then made the wine 'with guidance and inspiration from my father'. The name comes from William of Ockham (also spelt Occam) (1285–1349), a theologian and philosopher responsible for many sayings, including that appearing on the back label of the wine: 'what can be done with fewer is done in vain with more'. Exports to the US, Canada and Singapore.

ΨΨΨΨΨ **Shiraz 2005** Powerful, concentrated, savoury blackberry fruit; a fascinating alcohol contrast to Jasper Hill of the same vintage; spice and oak back up the persistent tannins. Cork. 15° alc. **Rating** 94 **To** 2025 $39

Ocean Eight Vineyard & Winery

271 Tucks Road, Shoreham, Vic 3916 **Region** Mornington Peninsula
T (03) 5989 6471 **F** (03) 5989 6630 **www**.oceaneight.com **Open** By appt
Winemaker Michael Aylward **Est.** 2003 **Cases** 1000
Chris, Gail and Michael Aylward were involved in the establishment of Kooyong vineyard and winery, and after selling Kooyong in 2003, retained their 5-ha pinot gris vineyard at Shoreham. After careful investigation, they purchased another property, where they have now planted 10 ha of pinot noir and 5 ha of chardonnay, 4 ha now in production, the rest soon to follow. A small winery has been set up, and the focus will always be on quality.

ΨΨΨΨ **Mornington Peninsula Pinot Gris 2005** Crisp, clean, fresh and light, but not a lot of personality; simply reflects the usual limitations of the variety, for there can be no complaint about the winemaking. Diam. 13.5° alc. **Rating** 87 **To** 2008 $30

Oddfellows Wines   ★★★★

PO Box 88, Langhorne Creek, SA 5255 **Region** Langhorne Creek
T (08) 8537 3326 **F** (08) 8537 3319 **www**.oddfellowswines.com.au **Open** At Bremer Place, Langhorne Creek 7 days 11–5
Winemaker Greg Follett, David Knight **Est.** 1997 **Cases** 2000
Oddfellows is the name taken by a group of 5 individuals who decided to put their expertise, energy and investments into making premium wine. Greg Follett leads the winemaking side, David Knight the viticultural side, the others the financial and marketing side. Exports to the UK, the US and other major markets.

ΨΨΨΨΨ **Langhorne Creek Shiraz 2003** A powerful wine with black fruits, bitter chocolate and savoury tannins; will always demand a hearty steak, but does creep up on you. Cork. **Rating** 90 **To** 2015 $25
Langhorne Creek Shiraz Cabernet 2004 An attractive blend of blackberry and blackcurrant with a coating of dark chocolate and wafts of mocha; medium-bodied, with ripe tannins providing good support. Cork. **Rating** 90 **To** 2015 $18

ΨΨΨΨ **Langhorne Creek Cabernet Sauvignon 2004** Licorice, prune, blackcurrant and chocolate intermingle; however, cabernet sauvignon at this alcohol level is inflammable. Cork. 15.5° alc. **Rating** 88 **To** 2015 $25

Old Kent River   ★★★★★

1114 Turpin Road, Rocky Gully, WA 6397 **Region** Frankland River
T (08) 9855 1589 **www**.oldkentriver.com.au **Open** At Kent River, Denmark
Winemaker Alkoomi (Michael Staniford) **Est.** 1985 **Cases** 3000
Mark and Debbie Noack have done it tough all their lives but have earned respect from their neighbours and from the other producers to whom they sell more than half the production from the 16.5-ha vineyard on their sheep property. The quality of their wines has gone from strength to strength, Mark having worked particularly hard with his pinot noir. Exports to the UK, the US, Canada, Hong Kong, Malaysia and Singapore.

ΨΨΨΨΨ **Burls Reserve Pinot Noir 2006** Good hue; pretty, seductive cherry, strawberry and plum fruit offset by a faint touch of stem/forest floor. Diam. 12.6° alc. **Rating** 94 **To** 2011 $60

ﾠﾠﾠﾠﾠ **Backtrack Pinot Noir 2005** Light but bright hue; tangy, foresty notes overhang small red fruits; long, intense and stylish, finishing on fruit, not forest. Terrific value. Screwcap. 13° alc. **Rating** 93 **To** 2020 $15

Frankland River Sauvignon Blanc 2006 Highly aromatic citrus, apple and cut grass; a fresh, lively and pure light- to medium-bodied palate; good length. Screwcap. 12° alc. **Rating** 92 **To** 2008 $20

Backtrack Shiraz 2005 Bright red-purple hue, brilliantly clear; a faint tickle on the bouquet gives way to a fine, intense medium-bodied palate; red fruits, spices and good length. Value. Screwcap. 14° alc. **Rating** 92 **To** 2020 $15

Frankland River Shiraz 2005 Denser colour than the Backtrack, but less bright; again there is something on the bouquet which is hard to pin down (is it reduction or something else?); a strongly structured and framed palate; a pity. Screwcap. 14.5° alc. **Rating** 90 **To** 2020 $22

Old Loddon Wines

5 Serpentine Road, Bridgewater, Vic 3516 **Region** Bendigo
T (03) 5437 3197 **F** (03) 5438 3502 **Open** W'ends 12–5, Mon–Fri by appt
Winemaker Passing Clouds **Est.** 1995 **Cases** 5000
A boutique winery overlooking the scenic Loddon River in Bridgewater, owned and managed by Jill Burdett. The 6-ha vineyard is planted to cabernet franc, merlot, cabernet sauvignon and shiraz. The first vintage was in 1995, and the winery produces full-bodied wines.

ﾠﾠﾠﾠ **Merlot 2004** Promisingly deep colour; powerful, ripe black fruits; lots of presence and flavour, rather less varietal character. Diam. **Rating** 88 **To** 2014 $18

Old Plains

6 Britton Street, Gawler, SA 5118 (postal) **Region** Adelaide Plains
T (08) 8523 2824 **F** (08) 8523 1877 **www.**oldplains.com **Open** Not
Winemaker Domenic Torzi **Est.** 2003 **Cases** NFP
Old Plains is a partnership between Tim Freeland and Domenic Torzi who have located small parcels of old vine grenache, shiraz and cabernet sauvignon in the Adelaide Plains region. A large portion of the consistently high-quality wines, sold under the Old Plains and Longhop labels, are exported to an enthusiastic US market.

ﾠﾠﾠﾠﾠ **Power of One 2005** Medium-bodied; ripe, rich blackberry and plum fruit; soft tannins run through the length of the palate; controlled oak, and a long finish. Vines planted in the 1950s. Shiraz. Screwcap. 14.5° alc. **Rating** 93 **To** 2020 $30

Longhop Old Vine Reserve 2005 An attractive array of soft, gently spicy black fruits; gentle extraction, the oak in a pure support role. Cabernet Sauvignon (65%)/Shiraz (35%). Screwcap. 14.5° alc. **Rating** 91 **To** 2010 $30

Longhop Boomerang Shiraz 2005 Deep, dense colour; abundant blackberry fruit with notes of dark chocolate and licorice; shows what the Adelaide Plains can do; excellent value. Screwcap. 15.5° alc. **Rating** 90 **To** 2013 $13

Longhop Old Vine Grenache 2005 A complex array of spices surround the sweet berry fruits; 25% whole bunch fermentation and open fermenters plus 50-year-old vines produce great results. Screwcap. 15° alc. **Rating** 90 **To** 2013 $18

Olivers Taranga Vineyards

Seaview Road, McLaren Vale, SA 5171 **Region** McLaren Vale
T (08) 8323 8498 **www.**oliverstaranga.com **Open** Mon–Fri 10–4, w'ends 11–4
Winemaker Corrina Rayment **Est.** 1841 **Cases** 3000
1839 was the year in which William and Elizabeth Oliver arrived from Scotland to settle at McLaren Vale. Six generations later, members of the family are still living on the Whitehill and Taranga farms. The Taranga property has 12 varieties planted on 92 ha; grapes from the property have been sold, but since 1994 some of the old vine shiraz has been made under the Olivers Taranga label. Since 2000 the wine has been made by Corrina Rayment (the Oliver family's first

winemaker and a sixth-generation family member). Exports to the UK, the US and other major markets.

ŸŸŸŸŸ **McLaren Vale Shiraz 2004** Lovely weight and mouthfeel; rich, supple black-berry/blackcurrant fruit; supple tannins. Cork. 14.5° alc. **Rating** 94 **To** 2024 $28

ŸŸŸŸŸ **Corrina's 2004** Blackcurrant, blackberry, plum and dark chocolate in a medium-to full-bodied frame; built-in tannins and moderate length. McLaren Vale Cabernet Sauvignon/Shiraz co-fermented. Screwcap. 14.5° alc. **Rating** 91 **To** 2019 $28

Olsen ★★★☆

RMB 252 Osmington Road, Osmington, WA 6285 **Region** Margaret River
T (08) 9757 4536 **F** (08) 9757 4114 **www**.olsen.com.au **Open** By appt
Winemaker Bernard Abbott, Jarrad Olsen **Est.** 1986 **Cases** 5000
Steve and AnnMarie Olsen have planted 11.5 ha of cabernet sauvignon, shiraz, merlot, verdelho, shiraz, semillon and chardonnay, which they tend with the help of their 4 children. It was the desire to raise their children in a healthy, country environment that prompted the move to establish the vineyard, coupled with a long-standing dream to make their own wine. Not to be confused with Olsen Wines in Melbourne. Exports to Canada and Singapore.

ŸŸŸŸŸ **Margaret River Semillon Sauvignon Blanc 2006** Clean and brisk, semillon (60%) very much the dominant flavour and texture partner; has power and length, but the semillon is still to open its full flavour wings. Value plus. Screwcap. 11.9° alc. **Rating** 90 **To** 2011 $14

ŸŸŸŸ **Charlotte's Dance Margaret River Cabernet Sauvignon 2004** Firm, with ripe but persistent tannins running throughout the length of the medium-bodied blackcurrant palate; needs a few years to soften. Cork. 14.5° alc. **Rating** 89 **To** 2019 $25
Margaret River Cabernet Merlot 2004 Good red-purple; clean and fresh, with bracing acidity which tends to accentuate the slightly green tannins; a difficult proposition at this stage. Cork. 14° alc. **Rating** 87 **To** 2014 $14

Olsen Wines ★★★★

131 Koornang Road, Carnegie, Vic 3163 **Region** Port Phillip Zone
T (03) 9569 2188 **www**.vin888.com **Open** Mon–Thurs 10.30–8, Fri–Sat 10.30–9
Winemaker Glenn Olsen **Est.** 1991 **Cases** 55 000
Glenn Olsen, a science and engineering graduate of the University of Melbourne, has been involved in the wine industry since 1975, initially importing wines and spirits from Europe, then moving into retailing. In 1991, he started Olsen Wines, claiming to be Melbourne's first inner suburban winery. Several others may dispute this claim, but that is perhaps neither here nor there. Most of the wines come either from grapes grown on the Murray River in Northeast Victoria, or from the Yarra Valley. Not to be confused with Olsen in the Margaret River. A flood of 28 tasting notes pared back to 14. Exports to Canada.

ŸŸŸŸŸ **Personal Reserve Shiraz 2002** Medium- to full-bodied; a smooth and supple abundance of black fruits, licorice, ripe tannins and good oak. Cork. 14.9° alc. **Rating** 93 **To** 2012 $26.95
Glenn's Special Blend Superior 17 Year Old Tokay NV The age is obvious, and has brought the wine into good balance; classic Christmas cake, malt and toffee flavours. Cork. 18.5° alc. **Rating** 92 $24.95
Personal Reserve Shiraz 1999 Showing just the right amount of development; secondary, earthy/leathery characters, but with plenty of red and black fruits remaining. Barossa Valley/Central Victoria/Riverina. Cork. 14.2° alc. **Rating** 91 **To** 2008 $26.95
Yarra Valley Riesling 2004 Bright green-yellow; floral mandarin, orange and lime aromas; has developed well, with plenty of flavour but no coarseness. Cork. 12.5° alc. **Rating** 90 **To** 2010 $16.95

Personal Reserve Mornington Peninsula Chardonnay 2004 Well-made; good intensity and length; powerful stone fruit and citrus mix supported by plenty of oak. Cork. 14° alc. **Rating** 90 **To** 2012 $25.95

Botrytis Semillon 2002 Extremely luscious and rich cumquat, mandarin and peach; balancing acidity. Cork. 11° alc. **Rating** 90 **To** 2009 $16.95

ΥΥΥΥ **Big Fella Shiraz 2003** Medium-bodied; good texture and structure; fine, ripe tannins combine with gently sweet black fruits; harmonious. Cork. 14.5° alc. **Rating** 89 **To** 2013 $18.95

Big Fella Shiraz 2002 Medium-bodied; surprisingly similar to the warmer '03 vintage, presumably relying on different regions to provide riper fruit; nice mouthfeel and balance. Cork. 15.4° alc. **Rating** 89 **To** 2012 $19.95

Yarra Valley Cabernet Sauvignon 2004 Medium-bodied; not a show-stopper, but has been nicely put together, with gentle blackcurrant fruit and fine tannins. It has been 'genuinely hand-made', whatever that may mean. Cork. 14° alc. **Rating** 88 **To** 2014 $16.95

Personal Reserve Yarra Valley Cabernet Sauvignon 2003 Medium-bodied, with good structure, the blackcurrant fruit balanced by tannins; none of the concerns about the bacterial status of the '04. Cork. 14.1° alc. **Rating** 88 **To** 2012 $28.95

Big Fella Petit Verdot 2003 Usual strong colour; likewise, the usual strength of black fruits; controlled tannins. Cork. 14.6° alc. **Rating** 88 **To** 2011 $18.95

Glenn's Special Blend Superior 10 Year Old Tokay NV Good varietal character but is far too luscious and simply sweet, notwithstanding the age and the spirit. Cork. 18.5° alc. **Rating** 88 **To** 2008 $16.95

Yarra Valley Pinot Noir 2004 A tangy, savoury style, albeit with some red fruits still lurking; fair length and balance. Twin top. **Rating** 87 **To** 2008 $19.95

Big Fella Cabernet Sauvignon 2003 Light- to medium-bodied; clean, with cassis and raspberry supported by just enough tannins. Cork. 13.7° alc. **Rating** 87 **To** 2008 $18.95

Olssens of Watervale   ★★★★☆

Sollys Hill Road, Watervale, SA 5452 **Region** Clare Valley
T (08) 8843 0065 **F** (08) 8843 0065 **Open** Thurs–Sun & public hols 11–5, or by appt
Winemaker Contract **Est.** 1994 **Cases** 4000
Kevin and Helen Olssen first visited the Clare Valley in 1986. Within 2 weeks they and their family decided to sell their Adelaide home and purchased a property in a small, isolated valley 3 km north of the township of Watervale. As a result of the acquisition of the Bass Hill Vineyard, estate plantings have risen to more than 32 ha, including unusual varieties such as carmenere and primitivo di Gioia. The Bass Hill project is a joint venture between parents Kevin and Helen and children David and Jane Olssen. Exports to Norway and Canada.

ΥΥΥΥΩ **Clare Valley Late Harvest Riesling 2006** Light straw-green; lovely lime juice flavours, long, bright and well-balanced; part of a growing bandwagon of low alcohol, off-dry rieslings. Screwcap. 11.5° alc. **Rating** 93 **To** 2016 $20

Clare Valley Shiraz 2004 Medium-bodied; ripe, but not jammy/dead fruit; flavours of plum, blackberry and touches of mocha; restrained regional style. Screwcap. 14° alc. **Rating** 92 **To** 2016 $25

Clare Valley Riesling 2006 Firm and powerful lime, mineral and spice flavours flow through to the finish. Screwcap. 12.5° alc. **Rating** 90 **To** 2014 $20

Clare Valley Cabernet Sauvignon 2004 Distinctly briary/earthy/savoury characters surround the cassis/blackcurrant fruit which breaks through on the finish. Screwcap. 14.5° alc. **Rating** 90 **To** 2019 $20

ΥΥΥΥ **Bass Hill Vineyard Primitivo 2005** Light- to medium-bodied; a spicy, savoury style of zinfandel (the other name for primitivo) which reflects the multiple styles found in California. That said, the price is surely determined by the label than the intrinsic quality of the wine. Screwcap. 14.5° alc. **Rating** 88 **To** 2008 $35

Orange Mountain Wines ★★★

Cnr Forbes Road/Radnedge Lane, Orange, NSW 2800 **Region** Orange
T (02) 6365 2626 **www**.orangemountain.com.au **Open** W'ends & public hols 9–5
Winemaker Terry Dolle **Est.** 1997 **Cases** 2500
Terry Dolle has a total of 6 ha of vineyards, part at Manildra (established 1997) and the
remainder at Orange (in 2001). The Manildra climate is distinctly warmer than that of Orange,
and the plantings reflect the climatic difference, with pinot noir and sauvignon blanc at Orange,
shiraz, cabernet sauvignon, merlot and viognier at Manildra.

 Manildra Viognier 2006 Rich wine with plenty of flavour, with the clever use
of a touch sweetness to augment the varietal flavour. Screwcap. 14° alc. **Rating** 88
To 2009 $22

Oranje Tractor Wine/Lincoln & Gomm Wines ★★★★☆

198 Link Road, Albany, WA 6330 **Region** Albany
T (08) 9842 5175 **F** (08) 9842 5175 **www**.oranjetractor.com **Open** Sunday, or by appt
Winemaker Rob Diletti (Contract) **Est.** 1998 **Cases** 1000
The name tells part of the story of the vineyard owned by Murray Gomm and Pamela Lincoln.
Murray was born next door, but moved to Perth to work in physical education and health
promotion. Here he met nutritionist Pamela, who completed the wine science degree at Charles
Sturt University in 2000, before being awarded a Churchill Fellowship to study organic grape and
wine production in the US and Europe. When the partners established their 3-ha vineyard, they
went down the organic path, with the aid of a 1964 vintage Fiat tractor, which is orange.

 Oranje Tractor Albany Riesling 2005 Clean, fresh, crisp and firm; a lovely
mix of citrus and more minerally notes, developing surely but slowly; its best
years are in front of it. Screwcap. 12.5° alc. **Rating** 93 **To** 2013 $18
Oranje Tractor Albany Sauvignon Blanc 2005 Spotlessly clean; fresh,
delicate grass and gooseberry flavours; has good length and aftertaste. Screwcap.
12.5° alc. **Rating** 92 **To** 2008 $18
Oranje Tractor Albany Cabernet Merlot 2005 Light- to medium-bodied; a
lively and fresh mix of cassis, blackberry and plum; sweet, but not confected,
fruit, and ripe, fine tannins; remarkable achievement at this alcohol level.
Screwcap. 12.5° alc. **Rating** 90 **To** 2012 $20

Organic Vignerons Australia ★★★★

Section 395 Derrick Road, Loxton North, SA 5333 **Region** South Australia
T (08) 8541 3616 **F** (08) 8541 3616 **www**.ova.com.au **Open** Not
Winemaker David Bruer **Est.** 2002 **Cases** 9000
Organic Vignerons Australia is a very interesting winemaking business. It consists of the owners
of 5 certified organic SA properties: Claire and Kevin Hansen at Padthaway, Bruce and Sue
Armstrong at Waikerie, Brett and Melissa Munchenberg at Loxton, Terry Markou at Adelaide
Plains and David and Barbara Bruer at Langhorne Creek. The wines are made by David Bruer at
Temple Bruer, which is itself a certified organic producer. Exports to the UK, Germany, Hong
Kong, Taiwan, Singapore, Philippines and NZ.

 Chardonnay 2006 Light- to medium-bodied, but has elegance, length and the
archetypal regional grapefruit characters of Padthaway; good length and
minimal oak. Screwcap. 13.6° alc. **Rating** 90 **To** 2013 $16
Bin 621 Mataro Shiraz Grenache 2004 Light- to medium-bodied fresh,
vibrant raspberry, mulberry and blackberry fruit; firm but fine tannins.
Screwcap. 13.8° alc. **Rating** 90 **To** 2012 $18

 Shiraz Cabernet Sauvignon 2004 A firm mix of blackberry, blackcurrant and
spice fruit; minimal oak, fine tannins. Screwcap. 13.5° alc. **Rating** 88 **To** 2010 $18

Viognier 2006 Slight straw tinge to the colour; has viognier varietal character in full battle dress; distinctly confronting layers of flavour. Screwcap. 13.4° alc. **Rating** 87 **To** 2008 $16

Orlando

Jacob's Creek Visitor Centre, Barossa Valley Way, Rowland Flat, SA 5352 **Region** Barossa Valley
T (08) 8521 3000 **F** (08) 8521 3003 **www**.jacobscreek.com **Open** 7 days 10–5
Winemaker Philip Laffer, Bernard Hicken **Est.** 1847 **Cases** NFP
Orlando is the parent which has been divorced by its child, Jacob's Creek (see separate entry). Orlando is 160 years old, Jacob's Creek little more than 34 years. For what are doubtless sound marketing reasons, Orlando aided and abetted the divorce, but the average consumer is unlikely to understand the logic, and – if truth be known – care about it even less.

ＹＹＹＹＹ **Gramp's Shiraz 2004** Medium- to medium-full-bodied wine, with perfect fruit ripeness, and, likewise, oak balance; fine, long tannins. Gold medal National Wine Show '06. Cork. 14.5° alc. **Rating** 95 **To** 2020 $16
Jacaranda Ridge Cabernet Sauvignon 2000 Good colour; still in ascendance; big, rich blackcurrant fruit with good balancing tannins. Cork. 13.8° alc. **Rating** 95 **To** 2020

ＹＹＹＹＹ **Reeves Point Chardonnay 2004** Showing expected development; medium- to full-bodied, with a complex palate, showing both barrel ferment and mlf inputs to the nectarine and melon fruit; oak less prominent. From 'SA's finest regions'. Cork. **Rating** 92 **To** 2011 $31.95

ＹＹＹＹ **Gramp's Barossa Chardonnay 2005** Well-made; plenty of peachy fruit, with a waft of oak; controlled alcohol adds freshness. Cork. 13° alc. **Rating** 88 **To** 2008 $15.95
Gramp's Barossa Grenache 2005 Typical Barossa grenache, with slightly jammy fruit, but does have some structure and tannins which head off the otherwise soapy finish. Cork. 15° alc. **Rating** 88 **To** 2011 $15.95
Gramp's Cabernet Merlot 2004 Unexpectedly robust – if not downright rustic – tannins dominate the back palate and finish after good fruit on entry to the mouth. Cork. 14.5° alc. **Rating** 87 **To** 2015 $15.95

Otway Estate ★★★

20 Hoveys Road, Barongarook, Vic 3249 **Region** Geelong
T (03) 5233 8400 **www**.otwayestate.com.au **Open** Mon–Fri 11–4.30, w'ends 10–5
Winemaker Ian Deacon **Est.** 1983 **Cases** 3000
The history of Otway Estate dates back to 1983, when the first vines were planted by Stuart and Eileen Walker. The current group of 6 family and friends, including winemaker Ian Deacon, have substantially expanded the scope of the business: there are now 6 ha of vineyard, planted primarily to chardonnay (3 ha) and pinot noir (2 ha) with small patches of riesling, semillon, sauvignon blanc and cabernet making up the remainder. The wines made from these plantings are sold under the Otway Estate label; wines made from contract-grown grapes in the region are marketed under the Yahoo Creek label. Exports to Canada.

ＹＹＹＹＹ **Chardonnay 2005** Attractive wine, with plenty of melon and fig fruit; good barrel ferment balance, likewise length. **Rating** 90 **To** 2011 $22

Outlook Hill ★★★★

97 School Lane, Tarrawarra, Vic 3777 **Region** Yarra Valley
T (03) 5962 2890 **F** (03) 5962 2890 **www**.outlookhill.com.au **Open** Fri–Sun 11–4.45
Winemaker Dixons Creek Winery (Al Fencaros) **Est.** 2000 **Cases** 2200
After several years overseas, former Melbourne professionals Peter and Lydia Snow returned in 1997 planning to open a wine tourism business in the Hunter Valley. However, they had second

thoughts, and in 2000 returned to the Yarra Valley, where they have now established 2 tourist B&B cottages, 5.3 ha of vineyard, a terrace restaurant and adjacent cellar door outlet, backed by a constant temperature wine storage cool room. Exports to Denmark and China.

ŸŸŸŸŸ **Yarra Valley Chardonnay 2005** Citrus, green apple and nectarine fruit providing plenty of mid-palate weight and length; power with finesse. Screwcap. 14° alc. **Rating** 94 **To** 2012 $24

ŸŸŸŸŸ **Yarra Valley Pinot Noir 2005** Bright red-purple; a pure, fruit-driven plum, cherry and strawberry palate; clean, fresh finish; unforced, and should grow. Screwcap. 13.5° alc. **Rating** 90 **To** 2011 $24

ŸŸŸŸ **Yarra Valley Pinot Gris 2006** A light mix of pear, apple and spice then an attractively dry finish. Doesn't pretend to be more than it is. Screwcap. 13° alc. **Rating** 87 **To** 2008 $19

Outram Estate

39 Coora Road, Westleigh, NSW 2120 **Region** Lower Hunter Valley
T 0439 909 818 **F** (02) 9481 7879 **www.**outramestate.com **Open** By appt
Winemaker Peter Howland, Scott Stephens (Contract) **Est.** 1995 **Cases** 1000
Dr Geoff Cutter says his inspiration to start Outram Estate came from Max Lake, a visit to St Emilion/Pomerol in Bordeaux, and my account of the establishment of Coldstream Hills, which he read in one of my books. His aim is to produce quality, not quantity, and with Peter Howland in charge of winemaking, there is no reason why he should not do so. He has 5.5 ha of merlot on rich red volcanic basalt, and 13 ha of verdelho and chardonnay on the sandy grey alluvial soils of Wollombi Creek. Exports to the UK, the US, Fiji and Taiwan.

Padthaway Estate

Riddoch Highway, Padthaway, SA 5271 **Region** Padthaway
T (08) 8734 3148 **F** (08) 8734 3188 **www.**padthawayestate.com **Open** 7 days 10–4
Winemaker Ulrich Grey-Smith **Est.** 1980 **Cases** 6000
For many years, until the opening of Stonehaven, this was the only functioning winery in Padthaway, set in the superb grounds of the estate in a large and gracious old stone wool shed; the homestead is in the Relais et Chateaux mould, offering luxurious accommodation and fine food. Sparkling wines are the speciality. Padthaway Estate also acts as a tasting centre for other Padthaway-region wines.

ŸŸŸŸŸ **Sparkling Chardonnay 2004** Clear chardonnay fruit in a citrus/passionfruit spectrum offset by gentle toasty and opposing creamy notes; 18 months on lees. 12.5° alc. **Rating** 90 **To** 2008 $35
Eliza Pinot Chardonnay 2002 Good mousse; nutty brioche and melon flavours; nice length and balance. **Rating** 90 **To** 2008
Sparkling Rose 2004 Vivid pale-pink; elegant, well-balanced strawberry and quince flavours; has not fallen into the sugar trap; 18 months on lees. Pinot Noir/Pinot Meunier. 12.5° alc. **Rating** 90 **To** 2008 $35

ŸŸŸŸ **Eliza Sparkling Chardonnay 2004** Plenty of citrus and stone fruit flavour, but slightly suppressed mousse. **Rating** 89 **To** 2008 $35
Sparkling Shiraz 2004 Plenty of flavour, and the base wine is not too oaky; however, the dosage shows the wine needs much longer on lees, which would reduce the need for sweetness. 13° alc. **Rating** 87 **To** 2008 $25

Pages Creek

624 Middle Teatree Road, Teatree, Tas 7017 **Region** Southern Tasmania
T (03) 6260 2311 **F** (03) 6331 9884 **www.**pagescreekwine.com.au **Open** By appt
Winemaker Winemaking Tasmania (Julian Alcorso) **Est.** 1999 **Cases** 1600

In 1999 Peter and Sue Lowrie planted a 4-ha vineyard on their 20-ha Pages Creek property named after the creek that runs through it. They have 1.6 ha of cabernet sauvignon, 1 ha each of pinot noir and chardonnay and 0.4 ha of merlot. The tiny first vintage (2002) was consumed at their wedding; the first full vintage was 2003, and the Pages Creek label was launched in 2004.

♀♀♀♀♀ **Pinot Noir 2005** Powerful black fruits, with a slightly rustic mid-palate, but surging again on the long and appealing finish. Diam. 13.9° alc. **Rating** 91 **To** 2012 $22

♀♀♀♀ **Chardonnay 2005** Pleasant flavours and good balance, simply lacking the fruit intensity of the best wines from the vintage. Diam. 13.6° alc. **Rating** 87 **To** 2009 $22

Palandri Wines   ★★★★

Bussell Highway, Cowaramup, WA 6284 **Region** Margaret River
T (08) 9755 5711 **F** (08) 9755 5722 **www.**palandri.com.au **Open** 7 days 10–5
Winemaker Sarah Siddons **Est.** 1999 **Cases** 250 000
A state-of-the-art winery completed in 2000 now has a capacity of 2500 tonnes. The vineyards, which are scheduled to supply Palandri Wines with 50% of its intake, are situated in the Frankland River subregion of the Great Southern. In 1999, 150 ha of vines were planted at Frankland River; the major varieties are shiraz, merlot, cabernet sauvignon, riesling, chardonnay and sauvignon blanc. A further 60 ha were planted in 2000; a second block has been purchased south of the Frankland River vineyard, and a further 140 ha are being developed there. Makes some well-priced, good wines, and rather more indifferent ones. Exports to all major markets.

♀♀♀♀♀ **Frankland River Riesling 2005** Fine, lively and fresh aromas; a highly focused and vibrant palate; long finish. Screwcap. 12.5° alc. **Rating** 93 **To** 2015 $17
Frankland River Riesling 2006 Aromas of apple, newly-mown grass and citrus, moving to more tropical flavours on the palate; well-made. Screwcap. 12.5° alc. **Rating** 90 **To** 2015 $17

♀♀♀♀ **Baldivis Estate Classic White 2006** Driven primarily by its acidity, which is cleansing rather than searing; citrus flavours, presumably from the semillon/sauvignon blanc components, are pleasant. Screwcap. 12.8° alc. **Rating** 87 **To** 2008 $11.95

Palmer Wines   ★★★★

Caves Road, Dunsborough, WA 6281 **Region** Margaret River
T (08) 9756 7388 **F** (08) 9756 7399 **Open** 7 days 10–5
Winemaker Naturaliste Vintners (Bruce Dukes) **Est.** 1977 **Cases** 7000
Stephen and Helen Palmer planted their first ha of vines way back in 1977, but a series of events (including a cyclone and grasshopper plagues) caused them to lose interest and instead turn to thoroughbred horses. But with encouragement from Dr Michael Peterkin of Pierro, and after a gap of almost 10 years, they again turned to viticulture and now have 15 ha planted to the classic varieties.

Pankhurst   ★★★☆

Old Woodgrove, Woodgrove Road, Hall, NSW 2618 **Region** Canberra District
T (02) 6230 2592 **www.**pankhurstwines.com.au **Open** W'ends, public hols, or by appt
Winemaker Lark Hill (Dr David Carpenter, Sue Carpenter), Brindabella Hills (Dr Roger Harris) **Est.** 1986 **Cases** 4000
Agricultural scientist and consultant Allan Pankhurst and wife Christine (with a degree in pharmaceutical science) have established a 5.7-ha split-canopy vineyard. The first wines produced showed considerable promise. In recent years Pankhurst has shared success with Lark Hill in the production of good Pinot Noir. Says Christine Pankhurst, 'the result of good viticulture here and great winemaking at Lark Hill', and she may well be right.

ƟƟƟƟ **Canberra District Cabernet Merlot 2005** Cabernet (80%) is very much the dominant partner with its blackcurrant fruit, not letting much else in; ripe tannins. Screwcap. 13.1° alc. **Rating** 89 **To** 2015 $20
Canberra District Pinot Noir 2005 Light colour; varietal character is, as usual, present, but the wine is very light-bodied, closer to a top-class rose. Screwcap. 13.3° alc. **Rating** 88 **To** 2012 $28

Panorama

1848 Cygnet Coast Road, Cradoc, Tas 7109 **Region** Southern Tasmania
T (03) 6266 3409 **www.**panoramavineyard.com.au **Open** Wed–Mon 10–5
Winemaker Michael Vishacki **Est.** 1974 **Cases** 5500
Michael and Sharon Vishacki purchased Panorama from Steve Ferencz in 1997, and have since spent considerable sums in building a brand new winery and an attractive cellar door sales outlet, and in trebling the vineyard size (7 ha pinot noir, 3 ha chardonnay and 1 ha sauvignon blanc). Exports to Singapore, China, Japan and Taiwan.

ƟƟƟƟƟ **Estate Chardonnay 2005** Powerful, ripe, peachy fruit, almost into fruit salad; lots of presence, but would have been even better if slimmed down a little. Screwcap. 13° alc. **Rating** 91 **To** 2012 $32
Estate Chardonnay 2004 Amazingly, still pale straw-green; crisp wet pebble, citrus and herb flavours à la Chablis; still opening up, the oak invisible. Screwcap. 13° alc. **Rating** 90 **To** 2015 $32
Estate Pinot Noir 2006 A complex bouquet, and has length and complexity on the palate, all in a stemmy/savoury mould. Screwcap. 13.9° alc. **Rating** 90 **To** 2013 $39

ƟƟƟƟ **Estate Pinot Noir 2005** Dense, blockbuster black cherry and plums; almost a distillation of the vintage. Screwcap. 13.9° alc. **Rating** 89 **To** 2013 $39
Wooded Sauvignon Blanc 2006 Certainly has flavour, but this derives as much from sweetness as it does from oak; a crowd pleaser nonetheless. Screwcap. 12° alc. **Rating** 87 **To** 2008 $25
Reserve 2003 A very complex wine, entering the mouth with stalky/savoury edges to the dark plum fruit; if the dry tannins on the finish and aftertaste ever soften, will be a good bottle of pinot noir, but, right now, they sabotage it. We can but live in hope. Cork. 13.8° alc. **Rating** 87 **To** 2015 $180
Noble Sauvignon Blanc 2004 A complex and interesting wine; succeeds much better than any mainland example. Screwcap. 11° alc. **Rating** 87 **To** 2008 $25

Panthers Paw

1925 Melba Highway, Dixons Creek, Vic 3775 **Region** Yarra Valley
T (03) 5965 2205 **F** (03) 9848 3664 **www.**pantherspaw.com.au **Open** Fri–Sun 10–10
Winemaker Rob Dolan, Al Fencaros (Contract) **Est.** 1999 **Cases** 3800
The Pratt family has established just over 5 ha of sauvignon blanc, chardonnay, pinot noir, merlot and cabernet sauvignon since planting began in 1999. All of the wines made to date have been of good quality, promising more as the vines mature.

ƟƟƟƟ **Yarra Valley Chardonnay 2006** Plenty of flavour and impact; melon and stone fruit embellished by obvious lees contact; controlled oak and good length. Screwcap. 14° alc. **Rating** 89 **To** 2012
The Legend Stalks Yarra Valley Cabernet Merlot 2005 Attractive, sweet berry fruit aromas; tightens up somewhat on the finish; may have benefited from more time in barrel. Screwcap. 14° alc. **Rating** 89 **To** 2015
Yarra Valley Pinot Noir 2006 Light-bodied plum and spice; fresh, rather than complex or long; best now. Screwcap. 13° alc. **Rating** 88 **To** 2008 $16.50
The Legend Stalks Yarra Valley Pinot Noir 2005 Light- to medium-bodied; clean plum and red cherry fruit; the tannins just a little abrasive for the light, juicy fruit. Screwcap. 13.8° alc. **Rating** 88 **To** 2011 $16.50

The Legend Stalks Yarra Valley Sauvignon Blanc 2006 Light straw-green; fresh, clean, light grass, apple and a touch of tropical fruit; length, not depth. Screwcap. 13.5° alc. **Rating** 87 **To** 2008 $16.50

The Legend Stalks Yarra Valley Sauvignon Blanc 2005 Has barely developed; very similar fruit register to the '06; interesting portents. Screwcap. 13.5° alc. **Rating** 87 **To** 2008 $16.50

The Legend Stalks Yarra Valley Cabernet Sauvignon 2003 Some minty/leafy/savoury notes an inevitable consequence of the low alcohol, but the wine is fresh, and the oak has not been overplayed. Twin top. 12.4° alc. **Rating** 87 **To** 2011 $16.50

Panton Hill Winery ★★★☆

145 Manuka Road, Panton Hill, Vic 3759 **Region** Yarra Valley
T (03) 9719 7342 **F** (03) 9719 7362 **www.**pantonhillwinery.com.au **Open** W'ends & public hols 11–5, or by appt
Winemaker Dr Teunis AP Kwak **Est.** 1988 **Cases** 700
Melbourne academic Dr Teunis Kwak has a 4-ha fully mature vineyard, part planted in 1976, the remainder in 1988. The vineyard, established on a fairly steep hillside, is picturesque, and there is a large stone hall available for functions. Part of the production is sold to others.

♈♈♈♈ **Yarra Valley Chardonnay 2004** Full yellow-green; a nice wine, with abundant stone fruit and melon with well-integrated French oak; good balance. Diam. 13° alc. **Rating** 89 **To** 2011 $28

Paracombe Wines ★★★★★

Main Road, Paracombe, SA 5132 **Region** Adelaide Hills
T (08) 8380 5058 **F** (08) 8380 5488 **www.**paracombewines.com **Open** By appt
Winemaker Paul Drogemuller **Est.** 1983 **Cases** 6500
Paul and Kathy Drogemuller established Paracombe following the devastating Ash Wednesday bushfires in 1983. It has become a very successful business, producing a range of wines from the 13-ha vineyard which are never less than good, often very good. The wines are made onsite in the 250-tonne winery with every part of the production process through to distribution handled from the winery. Exports to the UK, the US and other major markets.

♈♈♈♈♈ **Holland Creek Adelaide Hills Riesling 2006** A highly aromatic passionfruit, apple and citrus bouquet; the flavours live up to the promise of the bouquet, long and lingering. Screwcap. 12.5° alc. **Rating** 94 **To** 2016 $19

Adelaide Hills Sauvignon Blanc 2006 Spotlessly clean, gentle gooseberry/tropical/passionfruit aromas intensify on the long and balanced palate, with a very attractive finish. Screwcap. 13.5° alc. **Rating** 94 **To** 2008 $21

♈♈♈♈♈ **Adelaide Hills Shiraz 2003** A lively and fresh array of red and black fruits on both bouquet and palate; fine, ripe tannins and controlled oak, then a long finish. Carries its alcohol with aplomb. Cork. 15.5° alc. **Rating** 93 **To** 2018 $21

The Reuben 2003 A lively, sweet but understandably complex array of fruit flavours; remarkably, doesn't show the dead fruit characters of many '03s; good length, balance and structure. Cabernet Sauvignon (59%, 6 clones)/Shiraz (12%)/Merlot (12%)/Cabernet Franc (10%)/Malbec (7%). Cork. 15° alc. **Rating** 92 **To** 2018 $21

♈♈♈♈ **Adelaide Hills Pinot Gris 2006** Solidly constructed and flavoured with the four-square walls of the variety; good balance. Screwcap. 13° alc. **Rating** 88 **To** 2008 $19

Somerville Shiraz 2003 Utterly and totally dominated by alcohol; why on earth do this? Flavour and impact not in dispute, but setting records isn't the be all and end all. A stained and fractured ProCork. 17° alc. **Rating** 87 **To** 2015 $69

Paradigm Hill

26 Merricks Road, Merricks, Vic 3916 **Region** Mornington Peninsula
T (03) 5989 9000 **F** (03) 5989 8555 **www**.paradigmhill.com.au **Open** Every w'end Jan;
first w'end of month, public hols or by appt
Winemaker Dr George Mihaly **Est.** 1999 **Cases** 1000
Dr George Mihaly (with a background in medical research, then thereafter biotech and
pharmaceutical industries) and wife Ruth (a former chef and caterer) have realised a 30-year
dream of establishing their own vineyard and winery, abandoning their previous careers to do so.
George had all the necessary scientific qualifications, and built on those by making the 2001
Merricks Creek wines, moving to home base at Paradigm Hill for the 2002 vintage, all along
receiving guidance and advice from Nat White from Main Ridge Estate. The vineyard, under
Ruth's control with advice from Shane Strange, is planted to 2.1 ha of pinot noir, 1 ha of shiraz,
0.9 ha of riesling and 0.4 ha of pinot gris. Exports to the UK, Canada, China and Singapore.

ŸŸŸŸŸ **Col's Block Mornington Peninsula Shiraz 2005** Medium-bodied, but with
all the depth one could ask for, and great tannin balance, the flavours rollicking
through black fruits, licorice, cracked pepper and French oak. One of the
innumerable pieces of information on the back label is its Resveratrol content
of 4.6 mg per litre. For advice on this ask your physician. Diam. 14° alc.
Rating 94 **To** 2020 $35

ŸŸŸŸŸ **L'ami Sage Mornington Peninsula Pinot Noir 2005** Light colour; a light to
medium-bodied palate with a very fine and long silky texture; an assemblage of red
and black fruit flavours plus fine tannins. Diam. 13.9° alc. **Rating** 93 **To** 2012 $40
Mornington Peninsula Riesling 2006 A well-made and balanced mix of citrus
and apple fruit aromas and flavours; quite long, but does tail off slightly on the finish.
Screwcap. 13.3° alc. **Rating** 90 **To** 2010 $24
Mornington Peninsula Pinot Gris 2006 As always, way out on left field with a
mix of barrel fermentation in new oak and open fermentation; an exercise in texture
and mouthfeel rather than flavour, balance the strong point. Screwcap. 14° alc.
Rating 90 **To** 2011 $35

Paramoor Wines

439 Three Chain Road, Carlsruhe via Woodend, Vic 3442 **Region** Macedon Ranges
T (03) 5427 1057 **F** (03) 5427 3927 **www**.paramoor.com.au **Open** W'ends & public
hols 10–5, or by appt
Winemaker William Fraser, Keith Brien **Est.** 2003 **Cases** 400
Paramoor Wines is the retirement venture of Will Fraser, formerly Managing Director of Kodak
Australasia. To be strictly correct, he is Dr Will Fraser, armed with a PhD in chemistry from the
Adelaide University. Very much later he added a Diploma of wine technology from the University
of Melbourne, Dookie Campus, to his degrees. Paramoor's winery is set on 17 ha of beautiful
country not far from Hanging Rock, originally a working Clydesdale horse farm, leaving a
magnificent heritage-style barn which is now used for cellar door sales and functions. Will has
planted 1.3 ha each of pinot noir and pinot gris, and intends to supplement the product range by
purchasing varieties more suited to warmer climates than the chilly hills of the Macedon Ranges.
He shares the winery with Keith Brien of Silver Wings Winemaking.

ŸŸŸŸŸ **Joan Picton Pinot Noir 2005** More weight and substance than many pinots
from the Macedon region; dark briary plum fruit with sundry spices; real
character. Screwcap. 12.5° alc. **Rating** 91 **To** 2012 $28
Joan Picton Pinot Noir 2004 Healthy colour; a clean bouquet, then gently
sweet plummy fruit followed by a spicy, dry finish. Screwcap. 13° alc. **Rating** 90
To 2010 $28

ŸŸŸŸ **Riesling 2006** Distinctly off-dry, but has enough fruit and acidity to sustain the
style; indeed, more residual sugar and lower alcohol might have made an even better
wine. Screwcap. 12.5° alc. **Rating** 89 **To** 2012 $18

Kathleen Shiraz 2005 Mint and spice overtones to the red cherry and blackberry fruit; medium-bodied; just that undertone of struggle for complete flavour ripeness. Cork. 14.5° alc. **Rating** 89 **To** 2011 $22

Rose 2004 Bone-dry style, with strawberries and citrus flavours; good length. Screwcap. 13° alc. **Rating** 87 **To** 2008 $14

Paringa Estate   ★★★★★

44 Paringa Road, Red Hill South, Vic 3937 **Region** Mornington Peninsula
T (03) 5989 2669 **F** (03) 5931 0135 **www**.paringaestate.com.au **Open** 7 days 11–5
Winemaker Lindsay McCall **Est.** 1985 **Cases** 12 000
Schoolteacher-turned-winemaker Lindsay McCall has shown an absolutely exceptional gift for winemaking across a range of styles, but with immensely complex Pinot Noir and Shiraz leading the way. The wines have an unmatched level of success in the wine shows and competitions Paringa Estate is able to enter, the limitation being the relatively small size of the production. His skills are no less evident in contract winemaking for others. Exports to the UK, South Korea, Singapore and Hong Kong.

ŸŸŸŸŸ Reserve Special Barrel Selection Pinot Noir 2005 Introduces some darker fruit notes, especially plum; again, that peacock's tail expanding finish. Screwcap. 15° alc. Rating 96 To 2014 $90

Reserve Special Barrel Selection Shiraz 2005 A highly aromatic and very complex bouquet; a hint of viognier underscores both the aromas and flavours, making precise description an even more difficult task. American winewriters would need a page to cover the black pepper, plum, cherry, spice, licorice and apricot that I can detect; then there is the oak. I am a babe in arms compared to Americans when it comes to florid descriptions. Screwcap. 14.5° alc. Rating 96 To 2025 $80

Estate Pinot Noir 2005 A silky but vibrant array of red and black fruits of every description; an extremely long and intense palate. Screwcap. 15° alc. Rating 95 To 2012 $55

Estate Riesling 2006 An aromatic lime and blossom bouquet; elegant, long and intense; Paringa Estate breaks all the rules making a riesling of this quality from a coastal climate; the citrus fruit line goes on and on. Screwcap. 13.5° alc. Rating 94 To 2012 $15

Estate Chardonnay 2005 Clean, fresh grapefruit and melon flavours supported by crisp acidity and subtle oak; attractively tight structure and length. Screwcap. 15° alc. Rating 94 To 2012 $35

Peninsula Chardonnay 2005 Fine, elegant and intense; all the hallmarks of Paringa Estate, the emphasis on fruit driving a long, lingering finish. Absurdly underpriced, even if for a third label; 100% barrel ferment in used barriques; 20% mlf. Screwcap. 15° alc. Rating 94 To 2012 $18

Peninsula Pinot Noir 2006 Perfect, brilliantly clear, colour; yet another immaculate pinot noir; it is positively indecent that it should be the fourth level below Estate, Reserve and Barrel Selection at the top. Screwcap. 14° alc. Rating 94 To 2011

Estate Shiraz 2005 Ripe and powerful black cherry and blackberry fruit aromas lead into a supple and round palate, spicy notes on the ascendant on the finish together with fine, lingering tannins. Screwcap. 14.5° alc. Rating 94 To 2019 $45

ŸŸŸŸŸ Peninsula Shiraz 2005 Light to medium red-purple; a tangy, lively mix of red and black fruits, spice and mint; ripe tannins and minimal oak. Screwcap. 14° alc. Rating 91 To 2013 $25

Estate Pinot Gris 2006 Classic pear/pear drop/apple/apple skin aromas and flavours; once again, a magician at work, even if his talents would be better employed on more rewarding varieties. Screwcap. 15° alc. Rating 90 To 2008 $20

Parker Coonawarra Estate ★★★★☆

Riddoch Highway, Coonawarra, SA 5263 **Region** Coonawarra
T (08) 8737 3525 **www**.parkercoonawarraestate.com.au **Open** 7 days 10–4
Winemaker Pete Bissell (Contract) **Est.** 1985 **Cases** 5000
Parker Coonawarra Estate is at the southern end of Coonawarra, on rich terra rossa soil over limestone. Cabernet sauvignon is the predominant variety (17.45 ha), with minor plantings of merlot and petit verdot. Acquired by the Rathbone family in 2004. Exports to the UK, the US and other major markets.

🍷🍷🍷🍷🍷 Terra Rossa Cabernet Sauvignon 2004 Fractionally hazy colour; a tight, classic cabernet with earth and blackcurrant combining in a slightly savoury mould; restrained tannins and quality French oak to tip the scales in its favour. Screwcap. 14° alc. **Rating** 94 **To** 2025 $35

🍷🍷🍷🍷 Terra Rossa Merlot 2004 Interesting wine with clear varietal character coupled with depth and length. Screwcap. 14° alc. **Rating** 90 **To** 2012 $39

Parnassus Vineyard ★★★★

180 Lardners Track, Drouin East, Vic 3818 **Region** Gippsland
T (03) 5626 8522 **www**.parnassus.com.au **Open** Fri–Sun & public hols by appt
Winemaker Mal Stewart **Est.** 1998 **Cases** 600
Gary and Judy Surman bought Parnassus Guest House in 1989, developing a function centre specialising in weddings and conferences. Wishing to take further advantage of the great views, the Surmans planted 1 ha each of pinot noir and chardonnay in 1998. In 2005 they purchased Wild Dog Winery, where their son Luke and Japanese wife Kunie manage the 12 ha vineyard, the cellar door and assist in the winery. Mal Stewart has the same wide-ranging brief for Parnassus as he has for Wild Dog.

🍷🍷🍷🍷🍷 Delphi Chardonnay 2005 Excellent green-yellow; beautifully harmonious and balanced nectarine and citrus fruit; seamless oak, with considerable line and length. Screwcap. 13° alc. **Rating** 94 **To** 2012 $22

🍷🍷🍷🍷 Unoaked Chardonnay 2006 Full, ripe, nectarine and peach fruit with what appears to be a subtle touch of oak, even though the wine is described as unwooded. Screwcap. 13° alc. **Rating** 90 **To** 2010 $20

🍷🍷🍷🍷 Liqueur Chardonnay 2005 Quite well-made for a niche cellar door market, the fortifying spirit not too hot. Screwcap. 18° alc. **Rating** 87 **To** 2008 $22

Parri Estate ★★★★☆

Sneyd Road, Mount Compass, SA 5210 **Region** Southern Fleurieu/McLaren Vale
T (08) 8554 9660 **F** (08) 8554 9694 **www**.parriestate.com.au **Open** 7 days 11–5
Winemaker Linda Domas **Est.** 1998 **Cases** 10 000
Alice, Peter and John Phillips have established a substantial business with a clear marketing plan and an obvious commitment to quality. The 33-ha vineyard is planted to chardonnay, viognier, sauvignon blanc, semillon, pinot noir, cabernet sauvignon and shiraz, using modern trellis and irrigation systems. In 2004 a 9-ha property on Ingoldby Road, McLaren Vale was acquired, with a modern warehouse and shiraz, grenache and cabernet sauvignon up to 60 years old. A new cellar door has also been built on the property. Exports to the UK, the US and other major markets.

🍷🍷🍷🍷🍷 Southern Fleurieu Peninsula Shiraz Viognier 2005 Spicy black and red cherry fruit with that lilt of viognier showing in particular on the long finish; ripe, soft and supple tannins. Screwcap. 14.5° alc. **Rating** 94 **To** 2020 $20

🍷🍷🍷🍷 McLaren Vale Cabernet Sauvignon 2005 Strongly regional, leading in with bitter chocolate before quite powerful blackcurrant fruit makes its presence felt; lots of structure and potential. Cork. 15° alc. **Rating** 93 **To** 2020 $20

Southern Fleurieu Peninsula Sauvignon Blanc 2006 Apple, spice, citrus and passionfruit aromas and flavours; plenty of weight intensity. Screwcap. 12° alc. Rating 91 To 2012 $18

Pangkarra Southern Fleurieu Chardonnay 2006 Light yellow-green; complex and mouthfilling, driven by ripe stone fruit flavours, oak present but not dominating; early maturing. Screwcap. 13° alc. Rating 90 To 2008 $20

Pangkarra McLaren Vale Shiraz 2005 Good texture, but less than expected fruit intensity; savoury and chocolate notes, rather than red or black fruits. Cork. 14.5° alc. Rating 90 To 2012 $24

Pangkarra McLaren Vale Grenache 2005 Above average structure and finesse; fresh red fruits and a touch of chocolate; fine tannins. Cork. 15° alc. Rating 90 To 2012 $24

♟♟♟♟ **Southern Fleurieu Viognier Chardonnay 2006** Very rich and ripe notwithstanding apparently low alcohol; tropical canned fruits, with yellow peach and apricot; a nice twist of lemony acidity on the finish. Screwcap. 13° alc. Rating 89 To 2008 $18

Southern Fleurieu Peninsula Cabernet Sauvignon 2004 Savoury, earthy style reflecting the cooler climate; black fruits, firm tannins, and a faint touch of green. Cork. 13.5° alc. Rating 89 To 2015 $24

Sticky Noble Semillon 2005 Does show botrytis, but at a relatively low level, the wine a spatlese equivalent at best; nonetheless, has a nice array of citrus and lemon cake flavours, balanced by acidity. Cork. 11.5° alc. Rating 89 To 2008 $14

Southcote Southern Fleurieu Cabernet Shiraz 2005 A leafy, savoury, minty mix of cool-grown fruit; does have some length and persistence. Screwcap. 13.5° alc. Rating 87 To 2009 $13

Salmon Brut Pinot Noir Chardonnay 2005 Fresh, lively and zesty; low dosage; has good length, and may benefit with further time under cork; 70%/30%. 12° alc. Rating 87 To 2010 $24

Passing Clouds
★★★★☆

RMB 440 Kurting Road, Kingower, Vic 3517 **Region** Bendigo
T (03) 5438 8257 **www**.passingclouds.com.au **Open** W'ends 12–5, Mon–Fri by appt
Winemaker Graeme Leith **Est.** 1974 **Cases** 4000

Graeme Leith and Sue Mackinnon planted the first vines at Passing Clouds in 1974, 60 km northwest of Bendigo. Graeme Leith is one of the great personalities of the wine industry, with a superb sense of humour, and makes lovely regional reds with cassis, berry and mint fruit. Sheltered by hills of ironbark forest, the valley offers an ideal growing climate for premium red wine. The main varieties planted on the 6-ha vineyard are shiraz, cabernet sauvignon, and pinot noir. Additional varieties are sourced from local grapegrowers. Wines from the Three Wise Men joint venture also available (see separate entry). Exports to the UK and the US.

♟♟♟♟♟ **Graeme's Blend Shiraz Cabernet 2005** Clean, fragrant red and black fruits; supple and smooth texture to the medium-bodied palate offering blackberry, plum and blackcurrant; soft supporting tannins and oak. Diam. Rating 93 To 2018 $30

The Angel 2004 A fragrant array of sweet raspberry, cherry and redcurrant fruits on the bouquet with similar flavours on the palate, but backed up by substantial tannins. Screwcap. Rating 93 To 2020 $30

Pinot Noir 2005 Although light-bodied, has long and intense red fruit flavours, followed by a savoury twist balanced by sweet spices on the finish; no argument regarding varietal character. Diam. Rating 92 To 2011 $23

Reserve Bendigo Shiraz 2005 Medium-bodied, well-balanced and structured; a gentle array of black fruits with tannins and oak in the background chorus; good length, and will develop further in bottle. Diam. Rating 91 To 2015 $35

Paterson's Gundagai Vineyard

474 Old Hume Highway Road, Tumblong, NSW 2729 **Region** Gundagai
T (02) 6944 9227 **F** (02) 9410 1466 **Open** 7 days 9.30–5
Winemaker Celine Rousseau (Contract) **Est.** 1996 **Cases** 700
The Paterson family began developing the 23-ha vineyard in 1996, with 12 ha shiraz, 6 ha cabernet sauvignon and 5 ha chardonnay. It is a powerful team: Robert Paterson (M.Ec. – Sydney, PMD – Harvard) was a Senior Vice-President of Coca Cola and his wife Rhondda was a teacher, before both turned to cattle farming in the early 1980s and grapegrowing in the mid-1990s. Son Stuart Paterson has a PhD in Chemical Engineering from the University of NSW, and has studied viticulture and wine science at Charles Sturt University in Wagga; wife Rainny is an architect. Most of the grapes grown elsewhere in Gundagai are sold to major wine companies for blended wines; Paterson's is one of the few estate-based operations.

ȲȲȲȲ   **Shiraz 2005** As solidly built and constructed as always; very ripe blackberry fruit, the tannins in balance; food-friendly. Screwcap. 15° alc. **Rating** 89 **To** 2020 $18

 # Patina

109 Summerhill Lane, Orange, NSW 2800 **Region** Orange
T (02) 6362 8336 **F** (02) 6361 2949 **www**.patinawines.com.au **Open** By appt
Winemaker Gerald Naef **Est.** 1999 **Cases** NFP
Gerald Naef's family home in Woodbridge in the Central Valley of California was surrounded by the vast vineyard and winery operations of Gallo and Robert Mondavi. It would be hard to imagine a more different environment than that provided by Orange. Gerald Naef and wife Angie left California in 1981, initially establishing an irrigation farm in the northwest of NSW, but 20 years later moved to Orange, and by 2006 Gerald Naef was a final-year student of wine science at Charles Sturt University. He set up a micro-winery at the Orange Cool Stores, and his first wine was a 2003 Chardonnay, made from vines planted by him in 1999. At its first show entry it won the trophy for Best White Wine of Show at the Orange Wine Show '06, of which I was Chairman. Dream starts seldom come better than this.

ȲȲȲȲȲ   **Orange Chardonnay 2003** A complex wine with excellent bottle-developed flavour; rich stone fruit, supple and sumptuous. Trophy and gold medal winner Orange Wine Show '06. Screwcap. **Rating** 94 **To** 2010 $27

ȲȲȲȲȲ   **Orange Merlot 2002** While only medium-bodied, has both flavour and structure complexity; fine-grained, cedary tannins; good varietal fruit and weight. Cork. 13.1° alc. **Rating** 92 **To** 2012 $27
Orange Cabernet Sauvignon 2002 A medium-bodied mix of blackcurrant and mint; soft, almost silky, tannins; controlled oak. Like the Merlot, ageing nicely. Cork. 13.6° alc. **Rating** 90 **To** 2012 $27

ȲȲȲȲ   **Orange Riesling 2005** Clean and fresh; lively, sweet citrus and a touch of tropical fruit promise much, but tend to stumble over each other on the slightly congested finish. Screwcap. 12.9° alc. **Rating** 89 **To** 2012 $19
Orange Sauvignon Blanc 2005 Clean, with plenty of tropical fruit flavours, but soft, rather than crisp. Do not delay in drinking. Screwcap. 13.8° alc. **Rating** 87 **To** 2008 $19

Patrick T Wines

Cnr Ravenswood Lane/Riddoch Highway, Coonawarra, SA 5263 **Region** Coonawarra
T (08) 8737 3687 **F** (08) 8737 3689 **www**.patricktwines.com **Open** 7 days 10–4.30
Winemaker Pat Tocaciu **Est.** 1996 **Cases** 10 000
Patrick Tocaciu is a district veteran, setting up Patrick T Winemaking Services after prior careers at Heathfield Ridge Winery and Hollick Wines. He and his partners have almost 55 ha of vines at Wrattonbully, and another 2 ha of cabernet sauvignon in Coonawarra. The Wrattonbully plantings cover all the major varieties, while the Coonawarra plantings give rise to the Home Block Cabernet Sauvignon. Also carries out contract winemaking for others. Exports to the US, South America and Hong Kong.

ΨΨΨΨΨ **The Caves Vineyard Riesling 2004** A clean and crisp bouquet, the palate flooded with lime and passionfruit from start to finish. A lovely riesling to drink over the next 5 years. Screwcap. 12° alc. **Rating** 94 **To** 2012 $15

ΨΨΨΨΨ **Joanna Wrattonbully Shiraz 2003** Has the sweet fruit elements missing from many Limestone Coast wines in '03; a mix of red cherry and damson plum, plus blackberry and black cherry. The tannins are fine and ripe, the oak harmonious and balanced. Screwcap. 14° alc. **Rating** 93 **To** 2023 $18
Joanna Wrattonbully Riesling 2006 Spotlessly clean flowery lime and apple aromas; the palate is much more intense and powerful than the bouquet would suggest; quite striking. Screwcap. 12° alc. **Rating** 92 **To** 2014 $16

ΨΨΨΨ **Toccas Game Set Match Riesling Sauvignon Blanc 2005** Perhaps a blend of convenience, but works well in providing generous fruit flavours driven by the riesling component. Cork. 12° alc. **Rating** 88 **To** 2008 $13
Toccas Oaks Day Cabernet Rose 2005 Vibrant pink; lively, bright red fruits; has real flavour and good length, the balance spot on. Zork. 12° alc. **Rating** 88 **To** 2008 $13
The Caves Vineyard Joanna Rose 2004 Like the Oaks Day Rose, has good fruit flavour at its core and length, but is simply not quite as fresh. Zork. 11.5° alc. **Rating** 87 **To** 2008 $15

Patrick's Vineyard ★★★

Croziers Road, Cobaw via Mount Macedon, Vic 3441 (postal) **Region** Macedon Ranges
T 0419 598 401 **F** (03) 9521 6266 **Open** Not
Winemaker Alan Cooper (Contract) **Est.** 1996 **Cases** 400
Noell and John McNamara and Judy Doyle planted 2 ha of pinot noir in 1996 and 1997. The vineyard stands high on the southern slopes of the Cobaw Ranges with an 1862 settler's cottage still standing. At an altitude of 600 m, even pinot ripens very late in the season, typically at the end of April or early May, but in the right years the results can be impressive.

ΨΨΨΨ **Macedon Ranges Pinot Noir 2005** Light- to medium- red; light-bodied but clear varietal character; red cherry, strawberry fruit; crisp acidity aids the length. Cork. 13.5° alc. **Rating** 87 **To** 2008 $17

Patritti Wines ★★★★★

13–23 Clacton Road, Dover Gardens, SA 5048 **Region** Adelaide Zone
T (08) 8296 8261 **F** (08) 8296 5088 **Open** Mon–Sat 9–5
Winemaker G Patritti, J Mungall **Est.** 1926 **Cases** 100 000
A traditional, family-owned business offering wines at modest prices, but with impressive vineyard holdings of 10 ha of shiraz in Blewitt Springs and 6 ha of grenache at Aldinga North.

ΨΨΨΨΨ **Old Gate Shiraz 2004** Attractive wine with a lovely marriage of ripe fruit, dark chocolate, tannins and oak. Benchmark McLaren Vale. The price is enough to create a great thirst. **Rating** 94 **To** 2014 $15

Paul Bettio Wines ★★★☆

34 Simpsons Lane, Moyhu, Vic 3732 **Region** King Valley
T (03) 5727 9308 **F** (03) 5727 9344 **www**.paulbettiowines.com.au **Open** 7 days 10–5
Winemaker Daniel Bettio **Est.** 1995 **Cases** 7000
The Bettio family, with Paul and Daniel at the helm, have established 27.5 ha of vines in the King Valley. The plantings are of sauvignon blanc, chardonnay, merlot and cabernet sauvignon, and the wines, including a range of back vintages, are chiefly sold through the cellar door. A new cellar door and café is being constructed on King Valley Road, expected to open at the end of 2007.

♥♥♥♥ **King Valley Chardonnay 2006** A clean bouquet; white peach and citrus fruit is supported by just a touch of subtle oak; the finish is a fraction bitter, and I am not sure why. Screwcap. 13.5° alc. **Rating** 87 **To** 2010 $16

King Valley Sauvignon Blanc Chardonnay 2006 Cleverly made for the cellar door; much, but not all, of the flavour comes from residual sugar; a fleeting hint of bitterness difficult to pin down. At the price, there can be no complaint. Screwcap. 13° alc. **Rating** 87 **To** 2008 $11

Paul Conti Wines

529 Wanneroo Road, Woodvale, WA 6026 **Region** Greater Perth Zone
T (08) 9409 9160 **F** (08) 9309 1634 **www.**paulcontiwines.com.au **Open** Mon–Sat 9.30–5.30, Sun by appt
Winemaker Paul Conti, Jason Conti **Est.** 1948 **Cases** 8000
Third-generation winemaker Jason Conti has now assumed day-to-day control of winemaking, although father Paul (who succeeded his father in 1968) remains interested and involved in the business. Over the years Paul Conti challenged and redefined industry perceptions and standards; the challenge for Jason Conti was to achieve the same degree of success in a relentlessly and increasingly competitive market environment, and he is doing just that. Plantings at the Carabooda Vineyard have been expanded with 1 ha of tempranillo, petit verdot and viognier, and both pinot noir and merlot are purchased from Manjimup. Exports to the UK, Indonesia and Japan.

♥♥♥♥♀ **Mariginiup Shiraz 2004** Medium-bodied; supple, smooth, blackberry, cherry and plum, with touches of sweet leather; good oak. The old faithful for Paul Conti, now coming from vines of distinct seniority. Cork. 14.5° alc. **Rating** 92 **To** 2019 $27

The Tuarts Chardonnay 2006 Nicely balanced and focused; nectarine and a drizzle of citrus; good structure and subtle French oak impact. Screwcap. 14° alc. **Rating** 90 **To** 2012 $19

♥♥♥♥ **Medici Ridge Pinot Noir 2005** Distinct varietal character with notes of ripe plum held within a herbal/stemmy earthy spectrum. Good varietal presentation. Cork. 14° alc. **Rating** 89 **To** 2010 $19

Fronti's Late Harvest Muscat 2006 Lively, fresh, grapey, lemony aromas and flavours; bright sweetness is balanced by crisp acidity; 20 years practise makes perfect, the low alcohol especially commendable. The ultimate spring/summer/autumn refresher. Screwcap. 10° alc. **Rating** 89 **To** 2008 $15

Old Vine Grenache Shiraz 2005 Light to medium-bodied; a ripe mix of red and black fruits; some confit character, but not dramatically so. Easy style. Screwcap. 14° alc. **Rating** 87 **To** 2008 $15

Paulett

Polish Hill Road, Polish Hill River, SA 5453 **Region** Clare Valley
T (08) 8843 4328 **F** (08) 8843 4202 **www.**paulettwines.com.au **Open** 7 days 10–5
Winemaker Neil Paulett **Est.** 1983 **Cases** 13 000
The Paulett story is a saga of Australian perseverance, commencing with the 1982 purchase of a property with 1 ha of vines and a house, promptly destroyed by the terrible Ash Wednesday bushfires of the following year. Son Matthew has joined Neil and Alison Paulett as a partner in the business, responsible for viticulture, and the plantings now total 25 ha on a much-expanded property holding of 147 ha. The winery and cellar door have wonderful views over the Polish Hill River region, the memories of the bushfires long gone. Exports to the UK.

♥♥♥♥♥ **Antonina Polish Hill River Riesling 2005** Intense, bright, but still firm, palate; undertones of citrus, mineral and slate on the palate; very long finish. Will be very long-lived. Screwcap. 12.5° alc. **Rating** 95 **To** 2025 $38

Andreas Shiraz 2003 Medium red-purple; very generously proportioned, ripe plum, blackberry and licorice mix; ripe tannins, good oak. Screwcap. 14° alc. **Rating** 94 **To** 2023 $42

ΨΨΨΨ♀ **Polish Hill River Riesling 2006** Light straw-green; a clean, fresh bouquet; attractive apple, lime and lemon palate; generous, but not the least flabby. Slim price. Screwcap. 12.5° alc. **Rating** 93 **To** 2016 $18

ΨΨΨΨ **Polish Hill River Cabernet Merlot 2003** Medium red-purple; a medium-bodied palate, with blackcurrant, black olive and some spice; savoury tannins and fractionally grippy overall. Screwcap. 14.5° alc. **Rating** 89 **To** 2013 $22

Paulmara Estate   ★★★★☆

47 Park Avenue, Rosslyn Park, SA 5072 (postal) **Region** Barossa Valley
T 0417 895 138 **F** (08) 8364 3019 **www**.paulmara.com.au **Open** Not
Winemaker Paul Georgiadis, Neil Pike **Est.** 1999 **Cases** 250
Born to an immigrant Greek family, Paul Georgiadis grew up in Waikerie, where his family owned vineyards and orchards. His parents worked sufficiently hard to send him first to St Peters College in Adelaide and then to do a marketing degree at Adelaide University. He became the whirlwind grower relations manager for Southcorp, and one of the best-known faces in the Barossa Valley. Paul and wife Mara established a 10.9-ha vineyard in 1995, planted to semillon, shiraz, sangiovese, merlot and cabernet sauvignon. Part of the production is sold, and the best shiraz goes to make the Syna Shiraz ('syna' being Greek for together). Exports to the UK and the US.

ΨΨΨΨΨ **Syna Barossa Valley Shiraz 2002** Great colour, still holding purple tinges; elegant, firm and remarkably fresh; blackberry and cherry fruit on a long and sinuous palate. Cork. 14° alc. **Rating** 94 **To** 2015 $18

ΨΨΨΨ♀ **Syna Barossa Valley Shiraz 2004** Medium-bodied, nicely focused and elegant, with blackberry and spice fruit, the oak integrated and balanced. A quality substitute for the '02, and equally well-priced. Cork. 14.6° alc. **Rating** 91 **To** 2014 $18

ΨΨΨΨ **Syna Barossa Valley Shiraz 2003** Dense and ripe; a dramatic contrast in vintage conditions giving prune, plum and blackberry fruit, with a faint bitterness on the finish. Cork. 15.5° alc. **Rating** 89 **To** 2013 $18

Paxton   ★★★★☆

Wheaton Road, McLaren Vale, SA 5171 **Region** McLaren Vale
T (08) 8323 8645 **www**.paxtonvineyards.com **Open** Thurs–Sun 10–5, pub hols by appt
Winemaker Michael Paxton **Est.** 1979 **Cases** 5000
David Paxton is one of Australia's best-known viticulturists and consultants. He founded Paxton Vineyards in McLaren Vale with his family in 1979, and has since been involved in various capacities in the establishment and management of vineyards in various leading regions across the country. Sons Ben (general manager) and former Flying Winemaker Michael (with 14 years' experience in Spain, South America, France and Australia) are responsible for making the wines. There are 5 vineyards in the 67.87-ha family holdings: the Thomas Block, the Jones Block, Quandong Farm and Landcross Farm Settlement and Homestead. Here an underground barrel store has been completed and a cellar door opened in the original shearing shed. Exports to the US, Canada, Denmark and Sweden.

ΨΨΨΨΨ **AAA Mclaren Vale Shiraz Grenache 2005** Has the richness and texture which is largely unique to McLaren Vale for this blend; blackberry shiraz, red cherry grenache; very good balance and finish. Screwcap. 14° alc. **Rating** 94 **To** 2013 $23

ΨΨΨΨ♀ **McLaren Vale Chardonnay 2005** Elegant style for the region; nectarine, peach and fig with a nice touch of lemony acidity; controlled barrel ferment oak. Screwcap. 14° alc. **Rating** 91 **To** 2012 $29

Peacetree Estate

Harmans South Road, Wilyabrup, WA 6280 **Region** Margaret River
T (08) 9755 5170 **F** (08) 9755 9275 **www**.peacetreeestate.com **Open** 7 days 10–6
Winemaker Paul Green, Severine Maudoux (Contract) **Est.** 1995 **Cases** 1400
Three generations of the Tucker family were involved in the first plantings at Peacetree Estate in 1995; however, it was of olive trees, not vines. One ha each of sauvignon blanc and cabernet sauvignon followed, 0.8 ha viognier coming later. For the first 3 vintages the grapes were sold, and in 2001 the Tuckers decided to take the plunge and have the wine bottled under the Peacetree Estate label.

Peacock Hill Vineyard

29 Palmers Lane, Pokolbin, NSW 2320 **Region** Lower Hunter Valley
T (02) 4998 7661 **F** (02) 4998 7661 **www**.peacockhill.com.au **Open** Thurs–Mon, public & school hols 10–5, or by appt
Winemaker George Tsiros, Bill Sneddon, Rod Russell (Contract) **Est.** 1969 **Cases** 1500
The Peacock Hill Vineyard was first planted in 1969 as part of the Rothbury Estate, originally owned by a separate syndicate but then moving under the direct control and ownership of Rothbury. After several further changes of ownership as Rothbury sold many of its vineyards, George Tsiros and Silvi Laumets acquired the 8-ha property in 1995. Since that time they have rejuvenated the vineyard and seen an improvement in the wines, as well as introducing Methode Champenoise Blanc de Blanc.

♟♟♟♟ **Jaan Hunter Valley Shiraz 2005** Medium-bodied, bright fruits with incipient regional leather and earth notes; however, acidity is very high, and it is doubtful the wine will come into balance. Cork. 14° alc. **Rating** 87 **To** 2015 $35

Peel Estate

Fletcher Road, Baldivis, WA 6171 **Region** Peel
T (08) 9524 1221 **F** (08) 9524 1625 **www**.peelwine.com.au **Open** 7 days 10–5
Winemaker Will Nairn, Maark Morton **Est.** 1974 **Cases** 6500
The icon wine is the Shiraz, a wine of considerable finesse and with a remarkably consistent track record. Every year Will Nairn holds a Great Shiraz Tasting for 6-year-old Australian Shirazs, and pits Peel Estate (in a blind tasting attended by 100 or so people) against Australia's best. It is never disgraced. The wood-matured Chenin Blanc is another winery speciality, although not achieving the excellence of the Shiraz. Exports to the UK, the US, Malaysia, Japan and Singapore.

♟♟♟♟♟ **Cabernet Sauvignon 2002** A solid wine; plenty of blackcurrant and blackberry fruit; warm oak and ripe tannins; has developed well and will continue. Cork. 14.5° alc. **Rating** 93 **To** 2012 $30
Chardonnay 2004 An attractive wine with an abundance of melon/peach/stone fruit; subtle oak; good acidity and length. Partial barrel fermentation. Screwcap. 13.5° alc. **Rating** 92 **To** 2010 $20
Shiraz 2001 Holding hue well; ripe plum, prune and blackberry fruit; soft, lingering tannins support the finish, as does the mocha oak. Cork. 14.5° alc. **Rating** 90 **To** 2014 $33

♟♟♟♟ **Wood Matured Chenin Blanc 2002** Excellent colour for age; a potent wine, but the French oak is very evident, possibly coopered in Australia; slightly green characters give a touch of bitterness. Cork. 14.5° alc. **Rating** 87 **To** 2008 $21
Verdelho 2006 Delicate, fresh and lively fruit salad in a precise varietal mould; good length. Screwcap. 13.5° alc. **Rating** 87 **To** 2010 $17
Rose Sec 2006 Has some length, intensity and character without in any way relying on residual sugar. Screwcap. 14° alc. **Rating** 87 **To** 2008 $15

Peerick Vineyard

Wild Dog Track, Moonambel, Vic 3478 **Region** Pyrenees
T (03) 5467 2207 **www**.peerick.com.au **Open** W'ends & public hols 11–4
Winemaker Chris Jessup, Mount Langhi Ghiran (Dan Buckle) **Est.** 1990 **Cases** 2000
Peerick is the venture of Chris Jessup and wife Meryl. They have mildly trimmed their Joseph's
Coat vineyard by increasing the plantings to 5.6 ha and eliminating the malbec and semillon, but
still grow cabernet sauvignon, shiraz, cabernet franc, merlot, sauvignon blanc and viognier. Quality
has improved as the vines have reached maturity. Exports to NZ.

ŢŢŢŢŢ **Pyrenees Cabernet Merlot 2004** A firm, medium-bodied wine, cabernet
sauvignon takes the lead with lively blackcurrant and cassis; has the vibrancy
of the other '04 Peerick wines, but with greater depth and conviction. Cork.
14° alc. **Rating** 93 **To** 2024 $23.50
Pyrenees Shiraz Viognier 2005 The usual excellent hue; a clean, fresh blend
of blackberry, cherry and plum; less intense than other Central Victorian shiraz
viogniers, but does have length, and restrained alcohol. Screwcap. 14° alc. **Rating** 92
To 2012 $25
Pyrenees Shiraz 2003 Typical big, ripe, rich flavours of the drought in Central
Victoria in 2003. Does, however, have a polished sheen to the texture which is as
unusual as it is appealing. Stained cork. Cork. 14.5° alc. **Rating** 90 **To** 2013 $23.50
Pyrenees Merlot 2004 Different, vibrant flavours appear progressively; first red
cherry, then notes of mint and thyme; medium-bodied, with fine tannins and good
texture. Cork. 13.5° alc. **Rating** 90 **To** 2014 $21
Pyrenees Cabernet Sauvignon 2004 Medium-bodied; fresh, bright crisp
flavours of redcurrant and blackcurrant; the balance and extract good, the tannins
fine. Cork. 14.5° alc. **Rating** 90 **To** 2015 $23.50

ŢŢŢŢ **Pyrenees Shiraz 2004** A medium-bodied wine, with a very fresh and aromatic
bouquet; a supple mouthfeel to the red and black fruits on the palate; all the
appearances suggest relatively recent bottling, though the oak is limited. Cork.
13.5° alc. **Rating** 89 **To** 2012 $23
Pyrenees Cabernet Sauvignon 2003 Some earthy/savoury secondary cabernet
sauvignon characters; more to it than at first sight, particularly its length and sweet
tannins. Diam. 14° alc. **Rating** 89 **To** 2013 $23.50
Pyrenees Sauvignon Blanc 2006 Well-made; a solid wine with the flavours in
a grassy/chalky spectrum, but not a lot of lift. Screwcap. 13.5° alc. **Rating** 88
To 2008 $17
Pyrenees Merlot 2003 Has developed rapidly in both colour and flavour terms,
due partly to vintage conditions, no doubt. Here olive and briar dominate, although
within varietal expectations. Diam. 14° alc. **Rating** 88 **To** 2010 $21

Pelican's Landing Maritime Wines

PO Box 1143, Stirling, SA 5152 **Region** Southern Fleurieu
T 0411 552 077 **F** (08) 8370 9208 **www**.plmwines.com **Open** At Boccabella's, w'ends &
public hols 9–5, school hols Thurs–Sun 9–5
Winemaker Helen Marzola **Est.** 2001 **Cases** 240
Helen Marzola is the owner and winemaker of Pelican's Landing, the second vineyard to be
established on Hindmarsh Island. The 32-ha property was previously a cattle farm; it now has 7.3
ha of cabernet sauvignon, chardonnay and viognier in production, the first vintage in 2004.

Pembroke

191 Richmond Road, Cambridge, Tas 7170 **Region** Southern Tasmania
T (03) 6248 5139 **F** (03) 6234 5481 **www**.pembrokewines.com **Open** By appt
Winemaker Hood Wines (Andrew Hood) **Est.** 1980 **Cases** 350
The 2.3-ha Pembroke vineyard was established in 1980 by the McKay and Hawker families and
is still owned by them. It is predominantly planted to pinot noir and chardonnay, with tiny
quantities of riesling and sauvignon blanc.

♀♀♀♀ Pinot Noir 2005 Light- to medium-bodied sappy, savoury edges to the fruit are challenging; has length. **Rating** 88 **To** 2011

Penbro Estate ★★★☆

Cnr Melba Highway/Murrindindi Road, Glenburn, Vic 3717 **Region** Upper Goulburn
T 0408 548 717 **F** (03) 9215 2346 **www**.penbroestate.com.au **Open** At Glenburn Pub
Winemaker Scott McCarthy (Contract) **Est.** 1997 **Cases** 3000
Since 1997 the Bertalli family has established 40 ha of premium cool-climate vineyards on their highly regarded Black Angus cattle farm. The vineyards are high up in the rolling hills of the Great Dividing Range, flanked by the Toolangi Forest and the alluvial plains of the Yea River, halfway between Yarra Glen and Yea. Part of the grape production is sold. Exports to Italy and China.

♀♀♀♀♀ Merlot 2004 Good purple-red; light- to medium-bodied with gently ripe cassis and plum fruit supported by soft, fine tannins; has the focus and concentration missing from the other '04 wines, where the big berries and bunches of the season have tended to dilute flavour. Screwcap. 13.1° alc. **Rating** 90 **To** 2012 $21

Pendarves Estate NR

78 Old North Road, Belford, NSW 2335 **Region** Lower Hunter Valley
T (02) 9913 1088 **F** (02) 9970 6152 **www**.winedoctor.info **Open** Not
Winemaker Serenella Wines **Est.** 1986 **Cases** NA

Penfolds ★★★★★

Tanunda Road, Nuriootpa, SA 5355 **Region** Barossa Valley
T (08) 8568 9389 **F** (08) 8568 9489 **www**.penfolds.com.au **Open** Mon–Fri 10–5, w'ends & public hols 11–5
Winemaker Peter Gago **Est.** 1844 **Cases** 1.4 million
Senior among the numerous wine companies or stand-alone brands of Fosters and undoubtedly one of the top wine companies in the world in terms of quality, product range and exports. The consistency of the quality of the red wines and their value for money is recognised worldwide; the white wines, headed by the ultra-premium Yattarna Chardonnay, are steadily improving in quality. Exports to the UK and the US.

♀♀♀♀♀ Yattarna Chardonnay 2004 No question this is the jewel in the crown of the Penfolds chardonnays; nothing has been taken away from it for any of the lesser brands, including the Reserve Bin; exquisitely fine, yet intense, nectarine, white peach and citrus are seamlessly integrated with quality French oak and perfectly balanced acidity. Screwcap. 13.5° alc. **Rating** 97 **To** 2012 $120
Grange 2002 As hoped and expected; beautiful colour; a wonderful bouquet, with black fruits of various kinds the engine, oak in tow. Impeccable texture and balance in the mouth; again, a wonderful array of seamless blackberry, licorice and high-quality oak; destined to become recognised as one of the great Granges. Cork. 14.5° alc. **Rating** 97 **To** 2050 $500
Bin 707 Cabernet Sauvignon 2004 Much more generous and appealing than Bin 407 at first acquaintance; luscious blackcurrant fruit, and seamless oak and tannins; great mouthfeel. Cork. 13.5° alc. **Rating** 96 **To** 2034 $150
Great Grandfather Rare Old Liqueur Tawny NV Rich, but by no means heavy; great balance rancio and fruit; long and very fine; superbly balanced. Cork. 19° alc. **Rating** 96 **To** 2008 $325.95
RWT Barossa Shiraz 2004 While the toasty, charry oak is evident; the wine comes together on the medium- to full-bodied palate which has outstanding line and length. Gold medal National Wine Show '06. Cork. 14.5° alc. **Rating** 95 **To** 2029 $150
St Henri 2003 Intense, savoury black fruits with spicy notes on the bouquet; fine tannins are like built-in cupboards on the palate, evenly distributing themselves through its length. Cork. 14.5° alc. **Rating** 95 **To** 2025 $75

Cellar Reserve Coonawarra Barossa Valley Cabernet Shiraz 2005 Based on the famous show wines started by the late Max Schubert in the 1960s, and forgotten in the '70s, before being unearthed in the '80s and '90s. By Penfolds standards, elegant, supple and fleshy; is delicious now, and will be nectar in 10 years as the sweet fruit, fine tannins and oak all coalesce. Screwcap. 14.3° alc. **Rating** 95 **To** 2020 $100

Cellar Reserve Barossa Cabernet Sauvignon 2005 Outstanding red-purple; powerful, blackcurrant and cassis fruit in abundance; the tannins are a fraction chunky, but there is no doubt which way the cat will jump as those tannins settle down. Screwcap. 14° alc. **Rating** 94 **To** 2025 $100

Bin 407 Cabernet Sauvignon 2004 Proclaims its variety immediately the glass is lifted; this is 100% about cabernet sauvignon, and nothing about terroir; absolutely classic cabernet as the old school would have recognised and understood it; great length and Etonian tannins. Multi-region/multi-vineyard selection. Cork. 14° alc. **Rating** 94 **To** 2024 $35.95

Bin 389 Cabernet Shiraz 2004 Built in the fashion of Bin 389s of yesteryear; massive beams of fruit and oak to keep it going for decades; black fruits (no red) earth and a touch of licorice; tannins under control. Not a wine show style. Cork. 14.5° alc. **Rating** 94 **To** 2024 $49.95

Grandfather Fine Old Liqueur Tawny NV The colour almost indistinguishable from Great Grandfather, but on the one hand has more power, yet on the other, less of the silky smoothness of the older wine. Cork. 19.5° alc. **Rating** 94 **To** 2008 $86.95

ҮҮҮҮҮ **Cellar Reserve Eden Valley Gewurztraminer 2006** Positive varietal character, but not as dramatic as that of '05; nonetheless, has strong spice, lychee and ripe apple varietal fruit, and a long, dry finish. A rare breed in Australia. Screwcap. 13.5° alc. **Rating** 93 **To** 2011 $24.95

Reserve Bin Chardonnay 2005 Bin 05A. A superfine, elegant, understated style; many inputs including barrel fermentation, lees stirring and mlf, but the end result is a message of restraint; needs and will repay further time in bottle. Screwcap. 13.5° alc. **Rating** 93 **To** 2014 $84.95

Bin 311 Tumbarumba Chardonnay 2006 Light straw-green; cool climate grapefruit, citrus and nectarine fruit on both bouquet and palate, with minimal oak influence; a delicate, effortless wine. Screwcap. 13.5° alc. **Rating** 92 **To** 2012 $40

Thomas Hyland Shiraz 2005 Medium-bodied; a balanced and harmonious profusion of red and black fruits which drive both bouquet and palate; oak and tannins are in the background; the best yet under this label. Screwcap. 13.5° alc. **Rating** 92 **To** 2017 $19.95

Bin 128 Coonawarra Shiraz 2004 Solid, medium- to full-bodied blackberry fruit; good structure and length; ripe tannins and controlled oak. Cork. 14° alc. **Rating** 91 **To** 2015 $28.95

Bin 51 Eden Valley Riesling 2006 A generously proportioned wine, previously known as the Reserve Bin Eden Valley Riesling; lemon and lime zest with nuances of herb, spice and mineral; substantial alcohol balanced by a touch of CO_2 spritz. Screwcap. 13° alc. **Rating** 90 **To** 2015 $24

Cellar Reserve Adelaide Hills Sauvignon Blanc 2006 Plenty of relatively soft fruit; the flavours are indeterminate, with bits of everything from mineral to tropical, but none drop out. Screwcap. 13° alc. **Rating** 90 **To** 2008 $24.95

Koonunga Hill Shiraz 2004 Medium-bodied, supple, smooth and round; an attractive mix of red and black fruits, super-fine tannins and minimal oak. The history of this wine tells you it will develop wonderfully well in bottle. Screwcap. 13.5° alc. **Rating** 90 **To** 2015 $14.95

Kalimna Bin 28 Shiraz 2004 Firm, savoury, tightly structured black fruits; needs time to unwind and express itself. Cork. 14.5° alc. **Rating** 90 **To** 2024 $27.95

Koonunga Hill Shiraz Cabernet 2004 A medium-bodied, elegant wine showing the vintage to full effect; blackberry, blackcurrant, spice and touches of chocolate; fine tannins and subtle oak. Drink now or much later. Screwcap. 13.5° alc. **Rating** 90 **To** 2019 $14.95

Bin 138 Old Vine Barossa Grenache Shiraz Mourvedre 2005 Lots of muscle from persistent tannins which are sitting on top of the fruit at the moment; will come around, I think, but there are better bets at better odds. Screwcap. 14.5° alc. **Rating** 90 **To** 2020 $29.95

Thomas Hyland Cabernet Sauvignon 2004 Once again, shows the quality of the vintage; bright cassis and blackcurrant fruit, fine tannins and good length and balance; just a smidgeon of oak. Screwcap. 13.5° alc. **Rating** 90 **To** 2019 $19.95

♥♥♥♥ **Rawson's Retreat Shiraz Cabernet 2006** A fresh array of blackberry, cherry and dark chocolate on the light- to medium-bodied, supple palate; such oak as there is an incidental extra. Synthetic. 13.5° alc. **Rating** 89 **To** 2008 $9.99

Koonunga Hill Semillon Sauvignon Blanc 2006 Light-bodied, but with an appropriate depth of varietal fruit inputs; herb and touches of citrus and gooseberry. Screwcap. 13° alc. **Rating** 88 $16

Koonunga Hill Cabernet Sauvignon 2005 Light- to medium-bodied; clean, fresh blackcurrant fruit with touches of cassis and spice; good balance. Screwcap. 13.5° alc. **Rating** 88 **To** 2010 $16

Koonunga Hill Cabernet Sauvignon 2004 A medium-bodied wine reflecting the high quality of the vintage; ripe blackcurrant fruit and good tannins. Screwcap. 13.5° alc. **Rating** 88 **To** 2014 $14.95

Koonunga Hill Chardonnay 2006 Light-bodied, clean and fresh stone fruit flavour; dry, crisp finish. No obvious oak. Screwcap. 13.5° alc. **Rating** 87 **To** 2008 $16

Thomas Hyland Chardonnay 2006 Plenty of stone fruit and melon supported by some oak; flavoursome, but tends to plod along. Screwcap. 13° alc. **Rating** 87 **To** 2008 $19.95

Koonunga Hill Shiraz 2005 Light- to medium-bodied; pleasant, fresh, black cherry fruit; crisp finish. Screwcap. 13.5° alc. **Rating** 87 **To** 2010 $16

Koonunga Hill Cabernet Merlot 2004 Well-made and balanced blackcurrant fruits, controlled oak and fine tannins; dry finish. Screwcap. 13.5° alc. **Rating** 87 **To** 2014 $14.95

Penfolds Magill Estate ★★★★★

78 Penfold Road, Magill, SA 5072 **Region** Adelaide Zone
T (08) 8301 5400 **F** (08) 8301 5544 **www.**penfolds.com **Open** 7 days 10.30–4.30
Winemaker Peter Gago **Est.** 1844 **Cases** 3 million
The birthplace of Penfolds, established by Dr Christopher Rawson Penfold in 1844, his house still part of the immaculately maintained property. It includes 5.2 ha of precious shiraz used to make Magill Estate; the original and subsequent winery buildings, most still in operation or in museum condition; and the much-acclaimed Magill Restaurant, with panoramic views of the city, a great wine list and fine dining. All this is a 20-mins drive from Adelaide's CBD.

♥♥♥♥♥ **Shiraz 2004** Intense, tight and firm; high-quality blackberry fruit; balanced tannins and oak; the best potential since '02; has more structure than normal. Cork. 14° alc. **Rating** 94 **To** 2025 $95

Penley Estate ★★★★☆

McLeans Road, Coonawarra, SA 5263 **Region** Coonawarra
T (08) 8736 3211 **F** (08) 8736 3124 **www.**penley.com.au **Open** 7 days 10–4
Winemaker Kym Tolley **Est.** 1988 **Cases** 35 000
Owner winemaker Kym Tolley describes himself as a fifth-generation winemaker, the family tree involving both the Penfolds and the Tolleys. He worked 17 years in the industry before establishing Penley Estate and has made every post a winner since, producing a succession of rich, complex, full-bodied red wines and stylish Chardonnays. These are made from 91 precious ha of estate plantings. Exports to all major markets.

ΨΨΨΨΨ **Ausvetia Shiraz 2004** Very good purple-red; smooth, supple blackberry and plum fruit with seamlessly woven vanilla oak and fine, ripe tannins; 24 months American oak; ominously stained cork. McLaren Vale (88%)/Coonawarra (12%) Cork. 15° alc. **Rating** 94 **To** 2015 $50

ΨΨΨΨΨ **Hyland Shiraz 2005** Very good balance and structure; fine polish and finesse. The brevity of this note matches the price. Cork. 15° alc. **Rating** 93 **To** 2014 $19
Phoenix Cabernet Sauvignon 2005 Sweet cassis fruit runs through a long, supple palate, oak in restraint. Cork. 15° alc. **Rating** 93 **To** 2015 $19
Reserve Coonawarra Cabernet Sauvignon 2004 Medium-bodied; clearly delineated cabernet sauvignon; a gentle mix of blackcurrant, earth and cassis with seamless tannins and oak; not quite enough concentration notwithstanding its alcohol. Cork. 15° alc. **Rating** 93 **To** 2017 $50
Special Select Coonawarra Shiraz 2004 Powerful, rich blackberry fruits with some sweetness; ample structure, ripe tannins and just a little too much oak for comfort. Cork. 15° alc. **Rating** 90 **To** 2014 $50
Gryphon Coonawarra Merlot 2005 Spicy, leafy with a hint of mint on the bouquet; medium-bodied, with a firm, savoury structure to black olive, spice and leaf; good length courtesy of savoury tannins Cork. 15° alc. **Rating** 90 **To** 2012 $19
Chertsey 2004 Medium-bodied; complex blackcurrant and redcurrant; smooth tannin and extract. Cabernet Sauvignon/Merlot/Shiraz/Cabernet Franc. Cork. 15° alc. **Rating** 90 **To** 2013 $50

ΨΨΨΨ **Coonawarra Chardonnay 2005** Clean, medium-bodied, with gentle peach, fig and a touch of citrus; partial barrel ferment notes are in the background. Screwcap. 14.5° alc. **Rating** 89 **To** 2011 $19
Condor Shiraz Cabernet 2005 Medium-bodied; a pleasing blend of black fruits, chocolate and mocha/vanilla. Cork. 15° alc. **Rating** 89 **To** 2012 $19
Traditional Method Pinot Noir Chardonnay 2001 The 85% pinot component makes for a spicy style; despite is age, still very fresh and crisp, with low dosage. 12.5° alc. **Rating** 89 **To** 2010 $25

Penmara
★★★☆

Suite 42, 5-13 Larkin Street, Camperdown, NSW 2050 (postal) **Region** Upper Hunter Valley/Orange
T (02) 9517 4429 **F** (02) 9517 4439 **www**.penmarawines.com.au **Open** Not
Winemaker Hunter Wine Services (John Horden) **Est.** 2000 **Cases** 25 000
Penmara was formed with the banner '5 Vineyards: 1 Vision'. In fact a sixth vineyard has already joined the group, the vineyards pooling most of their grapes, with a central processing facility, and marketing focused exclusively on exports. The members are Lilyvale Vineyards, in the Northern Slopes Zone near Tenterfield; Tangaratta Vineyards at Tamworth; Birnam Wood, Rothbury Ridge and Martindale Vineyards in the Hunter Valley; and Highland Heritage at Orange. In all, these vineyards give Penmara access to 128 ha of shiraz, chardonnay, cabernet sauvignon, semillon, verdelho and merlot, mainly from the Hunter Valley and Orange. Exports to the UK, the US and other major markets.

ΨΨΨΨΨ **Reserve Orange Chardonnay 2005** Concentrated nectarine, grapefruit and melon fruit supported by subtle oak; does show the alcohol a little, but is a polished wine. Screwcap. 14° alc. **Rating** 90 **To** 2012 $17

ΨΨΨΨ **Reserve Orange Shiraz 2004** Light- to medium-bodied; a mix of gently spicy black fruits and sweeter oak; gentle tannins. Screwcap. 14° alc. **Rating** 89 **To** 2015 $20
Reserve Hunter Valley Sangiovese 2005 Light red; light- to medium-bodied; cedary, cherry-accented aromas and flavours; easy trattoria style. Screwcap. 13° alc. **Rating** 89 **To** 2010 $20

Reserve Orange Sauvignon Blanc 2006 Clean and soft; medium- to full-bodied in sauvignon blanc terms, with tropical fruit leading the way; not sweet, but a little heavy on its feet. Screwcap. 13.5° alc. **Rating** 88 **To** 2008 $17.95

Reserve Orange MCP 2004 Full red-purple; enters the mouth quietly but then the more astringent/savoury aspects of the cabernet franc and petit verdot take over; may come together with time. Merlot/Cabernet Franc/Petit Verdot. Screwcap. 14° alc. **Rating** 88 **To** 2015 $20

Penna Lane Wines ★★★★★

Lot 51, Penna Lane, Penwortham via Clare, SA 5453 **Region** Clare Valley
T (08) 8843 4364 **F** (08) 8843 4349 **www**.pennalanewines.com.au **Open** Thurs–Sun & public hols 11–5, or by appt
Winemaker Paulett **Est.** 1998 **Cases** 3000

Ray and Lynette Klavin purchased their 14-ha property in the Skilly Hills in 1993. It was covered with rubbish, Salvation Jane, a derelict dairy and a tumbledown piggery, and every weekend they travelled from Waikerie to clean up the property, initially living in a tent and thereafter moving into the dairy, which had more recently been used as a shearing shed. Planting began in 1996, and in 1997 the family moved to the region, Lynette to take up a teaching position and Ray to work at Knappstein Wines. Ray had enrolled at Roseworthy in 1991, and met Stephen Stafford-Brookes, another mature-age student. Both graduated from Roseworthy in 1993, having already formed a winemaking joint venture for Penna Lane. Exports to the US.

🍷🍷🍷🍷🍷 **The Willsmore Shiraz 2005** Deep, dense colour; a rich and complex bouquet exuding berry fruit and quality French oak; silky power to the blackberry and black cherry fruit; ripe tannins, and again that quality oak; 20 months in new French oak; unfiltered. Barossa Valley/Clare Valley. Cork. 14.5° alc. **Rating** 96 **To** 2025 $40

Clare Valley Cabernet Sauvignon 2004 Powerful, concentrated but controlled and balanced wine; intense blackcurrant fruit, balanced tannins and integrated oak. Conservative price. Screwcap. 14° alc. **Rating** 94 **To** 2024 $22

🍷🍷🍷🍷½ **Clare Valley Shiraz 2004** Clean, brightly articulated blackberry and plum fruit; supple mouthfeel thanks to good oak and tannin management. Screwcap. 14° alc. **Rating** 93 **To** 2019 $22

Clare Valley Riesling 2006 Citrus aromas with touches of herb and mineral lead into a long, cleansing palate; good acidity and line, albeit not overly effusive. Screwcap. 12.5° alc. **Rating** 91 **To** 2016 $19

🍷🍷🍷🍷 **Clare Valley Sauvignon Blanc Semillon 2006** A solidly-built wine in the grassy/herbal end of the spectrum, especially with the semillon component; firm finish. Screwcap. 13° alc. **Rating** 88 **To** 2009 $18

Clare Valley Rambling Rose 2006 Cherry and plum fruit sufficiently positive to carry the hint of residual sugar; good style. Cabernet/Shiraz saignee. Screwcap. 14° alc. **Rating** 88 **To** 2008 $18

Penny's Hill ★★★★☆

Main Road, McLaren Vale, SA 5171 **Region** McLaren Vale
T (08) 8556 4460 **F** (08) 8556 4462 **www**.pennyshill.com.au **Open** 7 days 10–5
Winemaker Ben Riggs **Est.** 1988 **Cases** 10 000

Penny's Hill is owned by Adelaide advertising agency businessman Tony Parkinson and wife Susie. The vineyard is 43.5 ha and, unusually for McLaren Vale, is close-planted with a thin vertical trellis/thin vertical canopy, the work of consultant viticulturist David Paxton. The innovative red dot packaging was the inspiration of Tony Parkinson, recalling the red dot sold sign on pictures in an art gallery and giving rise to the Red Dot Art Gallery at Penny's Hill. Exports to all major markets, particularly via the Woop Woop joint venture between Ben Riggs and Penny's Hill.

ŸŸŸŸŸ **McLaren Vale Shiraz 2005** Excellent balance and composition; black fruits, integrated oak and good length; has elegance, promising much for the '05 vintage as a whole. Cork. 15° alc. **Rating** 95 To 2019 $27

ŸŸŸŸŸ **Footprint McLaren Vale Shiraz 2004** Medium-bodied and elegant; good line, length and focus, nice tannins and equally attractive regional chocolate. Cork. 15° alc. **Rating** 93 To 2019 $50

The Black Chook Shiraz Viognier 2005 Vivid, deep colour; a rich, luscious and complex mix of blackberry, dark chocolate and the sweet impact of viognier; soft tannins and subdued oak. Screwcap. 15° alc. **Rating** 92 To 2018 $18

Timbuktu Deluxe Shiraz 2005 A rich, ripe and luscious array of black fruits; oak and tannins purely incidental; clever winemaking with grapes from McLaren Vale and Langhorne Creek. Screwcap. 15° alc. **Rating** 91 To 2018 $18

McLaren Vale Grenache 2005 A powerful, medium- to full-bodied example of the variety, a McLaren Vale forté; grainy tannins and a dash of chocolate. Cork. 15° alc. **Rating** 90 To 2013 $22

ŸŸŸŸ **The Black Chook VMR 2006** Light- to medium-bodied; an elegant fusion of the varieties, though the major input comes from the always-aromatic and fruity viognier. Viognier (68%)/Marsanne (16%)/Roussanne (16%). Screwcap. 14° alc. **Rating** 89 To 2008 $18

Red Dot Shiraz Viognier 2005 A lively, medium-bodied, attractive mix of blackberry and cherry fruit, the viognier under control. Good value. Screwcap. 14.5° alc. **Rating** 89 To 2015 $17

Woop Woop Cabernet Sauvignon 2005 Deep red-purple; abundant, ripe black-currant fruit; soft tannins, excellent value. Zork. 15° alc. **Rating** 89 To 2010 $13

McLaren Vale Cabernet Sauvignon 2005 A quite powerful mix of varietal blackcurrant and regional dark chocolate; the tannins need to soften. Cork. 15° alc. **Rating** 89 To 2020 $22

McLaren Vale Chardonnay 2006 Generous ripe peach flavours; a hint of oak adds as much to the texture as to the flavour. Cork. 13.5° alc. **Rating** 88 To 2010 $22

Specialized McLaren Vale Shiraz Cabernet Merlot 2004 Medium- to full-bodied; ripe fruit and high alcohol plus lots of McLaren Vale chocolate are reminiscent of a wine designed and made by a committee without a chairman; the cabernet and merlot are wondering what their role is. Cork. 15° alc. **Rating** 88 To 2015 $22

Red Dot Chardonnay Viognier 2006 Plenty of flavour across a range of stone fruits; avoids phenolics, and has length. Screwcap. 13.5° alc. **Rating** 87 To 2008 $17

Woop Woop Verdelho 2006 Has more length and fruit intensity than expected from the variety and at this price; fruit salad and a twist of lemon. Screwcap. 13.5° alc. **Rating** 87 To 2008 $13

Timbuktu Big Block Red 2005 Strong colour; honest, unsophisticated and flavoursome outdoors red. Shiraz/Cabernet Sauvignon/Petit Verdot/Malbec. Screwcap. 14.5° alc. **Rating** 87 To 2008 $15

Pennyfield Wines   ★★★

Pennyfield Road, Berri, SA 5343 **Region** Riverland
T (08) 8582 3595 **F** (08) 8582 3205 **www**.pennyfieldwines.com.au **Open** Not
Winemaker David Smallacombe **Est.** 2000 **Cases** 3500
Pennyfield Wines is named in memory of the pioneering family which originally developed the property, part of which is now owned by the Efrosinis family. Pennyfield draws on 17.7 ha of estate vineyards (principally planted to cabernet sauvignon and shiraz) but is also supplied with chardonnay, merlot, petit verdot, touriga and viognier by 4 local growers. Exports to the US, Canada, Denmark, Hong Kong, China and Japan.

ⵣⵣⵣⵣ Basket Pressed Petit Verdot 2003 A typically generous wine, but with the sweet fruit now starting to soften, leaving the tannins exposed. Cork. 14.5° alc. **Rating** 88 **To** 2009 $22
Basket Pressed Shiraz 2003 A medium-bodied, traditional style, showing blackberry fruit, a twist of vanilla oak and soft tannins. Cork. **Rating** 87 **To** 2013 $22

Pennyweight Winery ★★★

Pennyweight Lane, Beechworth, Vic 3747 **Region** Beechworth
T (03) 5728 1747 **F** (03) 5728 1704 **www.**pennyweight.com.au **Open** 7 days 10–5
Winemaker Stephen Newton Morris, Stephen MG Morris, Frederick Morris **Est.** 1982
Cases 1000
Pennyweight was established by Stephen Morris, great-grandson of GF Morris, founder of Morris Wines. The 4 ha of vines at Beechworth and 2 ha at Rutherglen are not irrigated and are organically grown. The business is run by Stephen, together with his wife Elizabeth and assisted by their 3 sons; Elizabeth Morris says, 'It's a perfect world', suggesting that Pennyweight is more than happy with its lot in life.

ⵣⵣⵣⵣ Beechworth Riesling 2005 Very developed colour; has abounding lime and toast flavour, normally achieved with 5–10 years' cellaring; for immediate consumption. Cork. 12° alc. **Rating** 88 **To** 2008 $25

Peos Estate ★★★★

Graphite Road, Manjimup, WA 6258 **Region** Manjimup
T (08) 9772 1378 **F** (08) 9772 1372 **www.**peosestate.com.au **Open** 7 days 10–4
Winemaker Shane McKerrow (Contract) **Est.** 1996 **Cases** 3000
The Peos family has farmed the West Manjimup district for 50 years, the third generation of 4 brothers commencing the development of a substantial vineyard in 1996; there is a little over 33 ha of vines, with shiraz (10 ha), merlot (7 ha), chardonnay (6.5 ha), cabernet sauvignon (4 ha) and pinot noir, sauvignon blanc and verdelho (2 ha each). Exports to Denmark.

Pepper Tree Wines ★★★★★

Halls Road, Pokolbin, NSW 2321 **Region** Lower Hunter Valley
T (02) 4998 7539 **www.**peppertreewines.com.au **Open** Mon–Fri 9–5, w'ends 9.30–5
Winemaker Jim Chatto **Est.** 1993 **Cases** 50 000
The Pepper Tree winery is part of a complex which also contains The Convent guesthouse and Roberts Restaurant. In 2002 it was acquired by a company controlled by Dr John Davis, who owns 50% of Briar Ridge. The appointment of Jim Chatto as chief winemaker in March 2007 brings the talents of the best young wine judge on the Australian wine show circuit, with winemaking talents to match. Sources the majority of its Hunter Valley fruit from its Tallavera Grove vineyard at Mt View, but also has premium vineyards at Orange, Coonawarra and Wrattonbully, which provide its Grand Reserve and Reserve (single region) wines. Exports to the US, Canada, Denmark, Germany, Switzerland, Brazil, Indonesia, Singapore, Malaysia and NZ.

ⵣⵣⵣⵣⵣ Grand Reserve Orange Chardonnay 2005 Sophisticated winemaking and high-quality grapes; intense citrus, melon and nectarine mix, oak in the back seat; excellent acidity. Cork. 13.5° alc. **Rating** 94 **To** 2010 $35
Grand Reserve Coonawarra Cabernet Sauvignon 2000 An elegant, medium-bodied wine with cedary/spicy overtones to classic blackcurrant fruit. A curious decision to include a full-sized conventional cork under the screwcap. 14° alc. **Rating** 94 **To** 2025 $95

ⵣⵣⵣⵣ Limited Release Hunter Valley Viognier 2006 Viognier has more inherent interest and quality than verdelho, but is harder to handle and make. This wine has been well-done, with apricot, pear and melon, good acidity and no oily phenolics. Cork. 13° alc. **Rating** 89 **To** 2008 $25

Limited Release Cabernet Sauvignon 2003 Medium-bodied blackcurrant and earth flavours; overall, quite supple. **Rating** 87 **To** 2011

Pepperilly Estate Wines ★★★☆

18 Langham Street, Nedlands, WA 6009 (postal) **Region** Geographe
T 0401 860 891 **F** (08) 9325 8228 **www**.pepperilly.com **Open** Not
Winemaker Di Miller, David Crawford (Contract) **Est.** 1999 **Cases** 1500
Partners Geoff and Kaaren Cross, and Warwick Lavis, planted their substantial vineyard in 1991 with a total of 10 ha, cabernet sauvignon and shiraz leading the way with 2 ha each, then 1 ha each of semillon, sauvignon blanc, chardonnay, viognier, merlot and grenache. The vineyard has views across the Ferguson Valley to the ocean, with sea breezes providing good ventilation.

ΨΨΨΨΨ **Geographe Shiraz 2005** A concentrated, medium- to full-bodied range of black fruits plus red cherry accompanied by spice, cracked pepper and licorice; fine tannins, good length. Screwcap. 14° alc. **Rating** 91 **To** 2020 $16

ΨΨΨΨ **Sauvignon Blanc Semillon 2006** Clean, crisp and lively; more grassy/mineral than tropical flavours; fair balance and length. Screwcap. 12.5° alc. **Rating** 88 **To** 2008 $13

Peppin Ridge ★★★★

Peppin Drive, Bonnie Doon, Vic 3720 **Region** Upper Goulburn
T (03) 5778 7430 **F** (03) 5778 7430 **Open** 7 days 11–5
Winemaker Don Adams **Est.** 1997 **Cases** 400
Peppin Ridge is planted on the shores of Lake Eildon; the land forms part of a vast station property established in 1850, and now partly under Lake Eildon. The property was acquired by the Peppin family, who developed the Peppin Merino sheep, said to be the cornerstone of the Australian wool industry. The plantings of marsanne, verdelho, shiraz and merlot cover 4 ha.

Pertaringa ★★★★☆

Cnr Hunt Road/Rigle Range Road, McLaren Vale, SA 5171 **Region** McLaren Vale
T (08) 8323 8125 **F** (08) 8323 7766 **www**.pertaringa.com.au **Open** Mon–Fri 10–5, w'ends & public hols 11–5
Winemaker Ben Riggs **Est.** 1980 **Cases** 15 000
While Pertaringa remains closely associated with the Geoff Hardy business, it is in fact a separate entity, with separate owners (Geoff Hardy and Ian Leask) and has a separate address from which it sells its own Pertaringa-labelled wines. Hence a Siamese twin operation has taken place, and Pertaringa now stands on its own. Exports to the UK and other major markets.

ΨΨΨΨΨ **Over The Top McLaren Vale Shiraz 2005** An ultimate regional style, with blackberry, dark chocolate and mocha seamlessly welded to and through each other; carries its alcohol well. ProCork. 14.5° alc. **Rating** 94 **To** 2025 $39
Rifle & Hunt Adelaide Cabernet Sauvignon 2005 Medium- to full-bodied, rich and round; abundant, ripe blackcurrant fruit; excellent texture and structure thanks to ripe tannins. Just needs a kangaroo to eat with it. ProCork. 14.5° alc. **Rating** 94 **To** 2025 $35

ΨΨΨΨ **Undercover McLaren Vale Shiraz 2005** Medium- bodied; less rich and baroque than Over the Top, precisely as one would expect; attractive red and black fruits, and overall control of extract; easy drinking style. Screwcap. 14.5° alc. **Rating** 89 **To** 2012 $20
Two Gentlemens McLaren Vale Grenache 2005 Medium red-purple; slightly heavier than typical Barossa grenache, but still lacks the concentration and structure McLaren Vale can achieve; redeemed in part by its sweet fruit. The Two Gentlemens (we are told) are Mr Ian Leask Esq and Mr Geoff Hardy Esq. You are either a mr, or an esquire, but you are not both. Screwcap. 14.5° alc. **Rating** 89 **To** 2012 $20

Scarecrow Adelaide Sauvignon Blanc 2006 Interesting floral apple blossom aromas; gentle balanced fruit, nearing but not quite tropical; clean finish. Screwcap. 12.5° alc. **Rating** 88 **To** 2008 $15

Understudy McLaren Vale Cabernet Petit Verdot 2005 As befits the 70%/30% blend, firm and austere. This is not a wine for immediate consumption. Screwcap. 14.5° alc. **Rating** 87 **To** 2010 $18

Petaluma ★★★★★

Spring Gully Road, Piccadilly, SA 5151 **Region** Adelaide Hills
T (08) 8339 9300 **www**.petaluma.com.au **Open** At Bridgewater Mill, Bridgewater
Winemaker Andrew Hardy **Est.** 1976 **Cases** 30 000

The Petaluma empire comprises Knappstein Wines, Mitchelton, Stonier and Smithbrook, since 2001 part of the Lion Nathan group. The range has been expanded beyond the core group of Croser Sparkling, Clare Valley Riesling, Piccadilly Chardonnay and Coonawarra (Cabernet Sauvignon/Merlot). Newer arrivals of note include Adelaide Hills Viognier and Adelaide Hills Shiraz. Bridgewater Mill is the second label, which consistently provides wines most makers would love to have as their top label. Exports to all major markets.

🍷🍷🍷🍷🍷 **Hanlin Hill Clare Valley Riesling 2006** Bright straw-green; immensely precise and authoritative, a clarion call of terroir speaking; a firm and classic mix of lime, lemon spice, with a lingering, dry minerally finish. Screwcap. 13° alc. **Rating** 96 **To** 2026 $25

Adelaide Hills Viognier 2005 Fermented with indigenous/wild yeast in older barriques; attains the richness and opulence of the variety, without heavy phenolics. Cork. 14° alc. **Rating** 95 **To** 2011 $40

Croser Picadilly Valley Pinot Noir Chardonnay 1996 A mix of minerally, bready, creamy biscuity and fruity characters magically welded together into a coherent and tightly structured palate. Melon, apple and mineral flavours are also to be found. 12.5° alc. **Rating** 95 **To** 2000 $45

🍷🍷🍷🍷½ **Bridgewater Mill Adelaide Hills Chardonnay 2004** Nicely proportioned and balanced; nectarine and melon woven with controlled inputs from barrel fermentation. Screwcap. 13° alc. **Rating** 92 **To** 2011 $18.95

Croser Picadilly Valley Pinot Noir Chardonnay 2004 Fragrant flowery blossom and brioche aromas; a long, citrussy/tangy palate; dry finish. 13° alc. **Rating** 92 **To** 2014 $36

Bridgewater Mill Adelaide Hills Sauvignon Blanc 2005 Lively, fresh, mineral, herb, asparagus and apple aromas and flavours all intermingle; bone-dry finish. Screwcap. 13° alc. **Rating** 90 **To** 2008 $18

🍷🍷🍷🍷 **Bridgewater Mill Adelaide Hills Sauvignon Blanc 2006** Spotlessly clean, with correct length and balance; absolutely won't frighten the horses, and will welcome shellfish. Screwcap. 13.5° alc. **Rating** 88 **To** 2008 $20

Peter Howland Wines ★★★★★

2/14 Portside Crescent, Wickham, NSW 2293 **Region** Lower Hunter Valley
T (02) 4920 2622 **F** (02) 4920 2699 **www**.peterhowlandwines.com **Open** By appt
Winemaker Peter Howland **Est.** 2001 **Cases** 4000

Peter Howland graduated from Adelaide University in 1997 with a first-class Honours degree in oenology. He has worked in the Hunter Valley, Margaret River, Hastings Valley, Macedon Ranges and Puglia in Italy. Newcastle may seem a strange place for a winery cellar door, but this is where his insulated and refrigerated barrel shed is located. From 2004 he has fermented his wines at Serenella Estate, where he also acts as contract winemaker. His wines are sourced from both sides of the continent: Great Southern and the Hunter Valley.

Peter Lehmann

Para Road, Tanunda, SA 5352 **Region** Barossa Valley
T (08) 8563 2100 **F** (08) 8563 3402 **www**.peterlehmannwines.com **Open** Mon–Fri
9.30–5, w'ends & public hols 10.30–4.30
Winemaker Andrew Wigan, Leonie Lange, Ian Hongell, Kerry Morrison **Est.** 1979
Cases 200 000

After one of the more emotional and intense takeover battles in the latter part of 2003, Peter
Lehmann fought off the unwanted suit of Allied Domecq, and is now effectively controlled by the
Swiss/Californian Hess Group. The takeover has reinforced the core business, and protected the
interests of employees, and of Peter Lehmann's beloved Barossa Valley grapegrowers. Exports to
the UK, the US and other major markets.

Stonewell Shiraz 2002 Excellent colour; much firmer and more concentrated
than Eight Songs; classy blackberry fruit, equally classy oak, and tannins which
have more authority, the last still to fully soften into the wine. This is, and will
be for many years, a classic. Cork. 14.5° alc. **Rating** 96 **To** 2025 $100
The Black Queen Barossa Sparkling Shiraz 1999 Shows precisely what
you can do with base wine from 40-year-old vines, and 6 years on yeast lees;
elegant, yet full of flavour; no oak to be covered by sugar. Cork. 14° alc.
Rating 95 **To** 2015 $35
Eden Valley Riesling 2006 Ultra-classic lemon/lime aromas and flavours; a
long, fine palate, fresh and lingering; a cellaring special particularly given its
moderate alcohol. Outstanding value. Screwcap. 12° alc. **Rating** 94 **To** 2016 $16
Barossa Rose 2006 Fresh, almost juicy, red fruits; good balance and a long,
clear finish. Gold medal National Wine Show '06. Screwcap. 11.9° alc.
Rating 94 **To** 2008 $15
Stockwell Road Barossa Valley Shiraz 2004 At the heart of the move by
Peter Lehmann to French oak and to lower alcohol for all his wines. Far more
elegant wines are now the order of the day, here with fresh and vibrant shiraz,
fine tannins and subtle, quality oak, matched to the style. Screwcap. 14° alc.
Rating 94 **To** 2024 $30
Eden Valley Shiraz 2002 Terroir speaks loud and clear in the context of the
cool '02 vintage; blackberry, cracked pepper, and touches of licorice and spice;
fine tannins and a long finish. Cork. 14° alc. **Rating** 94 **To** 2017 $28
Eight Songs Shiraz 2002 Some complexity showing, of course; a complex
interplay of secondary fruit characters, tannins and French oak, the fermentation
having been finished in that oak. Silky smooth, but with the vibrancy of the best
'02 wines; drink any time over the next 5–10 years. Cork. 14.5° alc. **Rating** 94
To 2017 $40

The Mudflat Shiraz Muscadelle 2003 Supple, round and smooth; medium-
bodied, complex flavours appealing for their restraint as much as their exuberance;
lovely texture. Cork. 14.5° alc. **Rating** 93 **To** 2015 $25
Mentor Cabernet Merlot Shiraz Malbec 2002 The colour is still diffuse,
possibly shaken by transport shortly prior to tasting; the cool vintage accentuates the
Bordeaux make-up; this is a wine to challenge rather than soothe you, but is
certainly as varietally correct as possible. Cork. 14° alc. **Rating** 93 **To** 2015 $40
Peppers Marananga Cabernet Sauvignon 2004 Medium-bodied; carefully
constructed and balanced, early-picked to preserve varietal character, then restrained
oak and tannin extract. Impressive. Cork. 13° alc. **Rating** 90 **To** 2014 $30

Barossa Semillon 2005 Clean and fresh; nicely weighted and balanced
lemon/citrus fruit; has length (and good value). Screwcap. 11.5° alc. **Rating** 89
To 2010 $13
Barossa Shiraz 2004 As honest as they come; not too jammy, nor burdened by
sweet alcohol, simply offering generous black fruits in best Barossa fashion. Screwcap.
14.5° alc. **Rating** 89 **To** 2012 $18

Southern Flinders Shiraz 2003 Ripe and luscious, with the suspicion of some dead fruit characters, though no shortage of flavour. Cork. 15° alc. **Rating** 89 To 2013 $25

Barossa GSM 2005 Nicely modulated assemblage of a wide spread of red and black fruit flavours; fine tannins and good length. Cork. 14.5° alc. **Rating** 89 To 2010 $16

Barossa Chardonnay 2005 Fresh, bright nectarine and melon fruit; good balance, length and acidity; subliminal oak. Screwcap. 13° alc. **Rating** 88 **To** 2008 $15

Barossa Merlot 2004 Sweet, plummy fruit with a light kiss of French oak; fine tannins. Easy drinking style. Cork. 13.5° alc. **Rating** 87 **To** 2008 $15

Cabernet Merlot 2004 Mr Reliable shows how to do it once again; light- to medium-bodied, and while not complex, the flavours are correct, the balance good; 70%/30%. Screwcap. 14° alc. **Rating** 87 **To** 2009 $19

Petersons

Mount View Road, Mount View, NSW 2325 **Region** Lower Hunter Valley
T (02) 4990 1704 www.petersonswines.com.au **Open** Mon–Sat 9–5, Sun 10–5
Winemaker Colin Peterson, Gary Reed **Est.** 1971 **Cases** 15 000
Ian and Shirley Peterson were among the early followers in the footsteps of Max Lake, contributing to the Hunter Valley renaissance which has continued to this day. Grapegrowers since 1971 and winemakers since 1981, the second generation of the family, headed by Colin Peterson, now manages the business. It has been significantly expanded to include 16 ha at Mount View, a 42-ha vineyard in Mudgee (Glenesk), and an 8-ha vineyard near Armidale (Palmerston).

ΨΨΨΨΨ **Glenesk Shiraz 2001** Has that extra degree of vinosity and generosity of flavour which demarcates it so much from the Hunter Valley; has matured and changed slowly, with much time to run on the plateau of its form. Cork. 14° alc. **Rating** 94 To 2021 $80

ΨΨΨΨΨ **Botrytis Semillon 2004** Rich and luscious; citrus, cumquat, mandarin and honey; balanced acidity. Screwcap. 9.5° alc. **Rating** 92 To 2008 $35
Old Block Shiraz 2004 Fractionally hazy colour; has strong regional terroir already with earth and leather overtones to blackberry and fine tannins; controlled oak. Cork. 14.5° alc. **Rating** 91 To 2016 $38

ΨΨΨΨ **Semillon 2005** Plenty of varietal flavour and length, even if in a slightly soft profile. **Rating** 89 To 2011 $23

Pettavel

65 Pettavel Road, Waurn Ponds, Vic 3216 **Region** Geelong
T (03) 5266 1120 **F** (03) 5266 1140 www.pettavel.com **Open** 7 days 10–5.30
Winemaker Peter Flewellyn **Est.** 2000 **Cases** 20 000
This is a major landmark in the Geelong region. Mike and wife Sandi Fitzpatrick sold their large Riverland winery and vineyards, and moved to Geelong, where, in 1990, they began developing vineyards at Sutherlands Creek. Here they have been joined by daughter Robyn (who has overseas management of the business) and son Reece (who coordinates the viticultural resources). A striking and substantial winery/restaurant complex was opened in 2002. Exports to the UK, the US, and other major markets.

ΨΨΨΨΨ **Evening Star Geelong Chardonnay 2005** A complex wine; strong barrel ferment inputs, but the fruit carries the oak; ripe melon and fig, with some stone fruit; generous, not heavy. Screwcap. 13.5° alc. **Rating** 94 To 2012 $18
Evening Star Late Harvest Riesling 2006 Very well-made and balanced; abundant lime juice, with supple mouthfeel and lingering acidity. Trophy and gold medal Geelong Wine Show '06. Great value. Screwcap. 9.5° alc. **Rating** 94 To 2011 $18

♀♀♀♀♀ **Evening Star Riesling 2006** Excellent colour; a light tropical/lime juice combination, with pleasing length. Screwcap. 12.5° alc. **Rating** 90 **To** 2010 $18

♀♀♀♀ **Platina Geelong Merlot Petit Verdot 2004** An almost proprietary blend by Pettavel, and always an odd conjunction, with sappy merlot and gritty petit verdot inputs; partially reconciles the seemingly unreconcilable. Cork. 13.5° alc. **Rating** 88 **To** 2012 $27

Evening Star Geelong Sauvignon Blanc 2006 Clean; a gentle mix of tropical, gooseberry and apple flavours; moderate length. Does shorten on the finish. Screwcap. 13.5° alc. **Rating** 87 **To** 2008 $18

Platina Geelong Pinot Noir 2004 Developed medium red; savoury, spicy, foresty varietal fruit, but the tannins are far too aggressive. Screwcap. 13.5° alc. **Rating** 87 **To** 2010 $27

Pewsey Vale
★★★★★

Browns Road, Eden Valley, SA 5353 (postal) **Region** Eden Valley
T (08) 8561 3200 **F** (08) 8561 3393 **www.pewseyvale.com** **Open** At Yalumba
Winemaker Louisa Rose **Est.** 1847 **Cases** 20 000
Pewsey Vale was a famous vineyard established in 1847 by Joseph Gilbert, and it was appropriate that when S Smith & Son (Yalumba) began the renaissance of the Adelaide Hills plantings in 1961, they should do so by purchasing Pewsey Vale and establishing 40 ha of riesling and 2 ha each of gewurztraminer and pinot gris. The Riesling has also finally benefited from being the first wine to be bottled with a Stelvin screwcap in 1977. While public reaction forced the abandonment of the initiative for almost 20 years, Yalumba/Pewsey Vale never lost faith in the technical advantages of the closure. A quick taste (or better, a share of a bottle) of 5–7-year-old Contours Riesling will tell you why. Exports to all major markets.

♀♀♀♀♀ **Individual Vineyard Selection Eden Valley Gewurztraminer 2006** Bright green-straw; clearly articulated varietal aromas of spice, lychee and rose petal carry through onto the palate; a rare example of high-quality gewurztraminer. Screwcap. 14° alc. **Rating** 94 **To** 2010 $23

♀♀♀♀♀ **Eden Valley Riesling 2006** Highly floral blossom aromas; marries elegance with power from the alcohol, but does seem to shorten fractionally. Screwcap. 13° alc. **Rating** 91 **To** 2015 $17

Individual Vineyard Selection Eden Valley Pinot Gris 2006 Has good texture and layers of flavour; pear and baked apple; uncompromising food style. Screwcap. 14° alc. **Rating** 90 **To** 2008 $23

Pfeiffer Wines
★★★★

167 Distillery Road, Wahgunyah, Vic 3687 **Region** Rutherglen
T (02) 6033 2805 **www.pfeifferwines.com.au** **Open** Mon–Sat 9–5, Sun 10–5
Winemaker Christopher Pfeiffer, Jen Pfeiffer **Est.** 1984 **Cases** 20 000
Ex-Lindeman fortified winemaker Chris Pfeiffer occupies one of the historic wineries (built 1880) which abound in Northeast Victoria and which is worth a visit on this score alone. The fortified wines are good, and the table wines have improved considerably over recent vintages, drawing upon 28 ha of estate plantings. Exports to the UK, the US and other major markets (under the Carlyle and Three Chimneys labels).

♀♀♀♀♀ **Carlyle Marsanne 2005** Tight and crisp, with aromas and flavours revolving around talc., slate, citrus and honeysuckle; good length and overall balance. Screwcap. 13.5° alc. **Rating** 90 **To** 2013 $16

Shiraz 2004 Good purple-red; firm, focused blackberry and black cherry fruit with nicely controlled tannins and oak. Screwcap. 14° alc. **Rating** 90 **To** 2017 $19.20

Cabernet Sauvignon 2004 A powerful wine, showing unexpected cabernet definition and style; cassis supported by fine, ripe tannins. Screwcap. 14° alc. **Rating** 90 **To** 2019 $19.20

ŸŸŸŸ Riesling 2006 More citrus florals than the Carlyle; positive citrus flavour, the acidity particularly well-balanced; good length. Screwcap. 12° alc. **Rating** 89 To 2012 $16.50

Carlyle Shiraz 2004 Ripe black fruits with some confit aromas; medium-bodied texture and structure. Screwcap. 14° alc. **Rating** 89 To 2014 $18.50

The Piper 1992 Fully developed, but holding its form, structure and balance; most fascinating is the cabernet sanzey component which was bred in Russia to withstand extreme winter freezing at -15°C or more. It is, without doubt, the most obscure varietal I have ever come across. Cabernet Sauvignon/Cabernet Franc/Cabernet Sanzey/Merlot. Cork. 13.5° alc. **Rating** 89 To 2009 $37.50

Carlyle Riesling 2006 Aromas of talc and cut apple; essentially dry flavours, ie not particularly fruity, but clean. Screwcap. 12° alc. **Rating** 88 To 2010 $16.50

Gamay 2006 Light, vivid purple; has both flavour and structure interest; cherry and plum fruit in a nice shroud of acidity; 20% pigeage in open vessels. Screwcap. 13.5° alc. **Rating** 88 To 2008 $16

Carlyle Cabernet Merlot 2004 A mix of blackcurrant, cassis, mint and leaf is varietal, but the wine does not have enough textural complexity for higher points. Screwcap. 14° alc. **Rating** 88 To 2012 $18.50

Pfitzner ★★★★★

PO Box 1098, North Adelaide, SA 5006 **Region** Adelaide Hills
T (08) 8390 0188 **F** (08) 8390 0188 **Open** Not
Winemaker Petaluma **Est.** 1996 **Cases** 1500
The subtitle to the Pfitzner name is Eric's Vineyard. The late Eric Pfitzner purchased and aggregated a number of small, subdivided farmlets to protect the beauty of the Piccadilly Valley from ugly rural development. His 3 sons inherited the vision, with a little under 6 ha of vineyard planted principally to chardonnay and pinot noir, plus small amounts of sauvignon blanc and merlot. Half the total property has been planted, the remainder preserving the natural eucalypt forest. Roughly half the production is sold in the UK, no surprise given the bargain basement prices asked for these lovely wines.

ŸŸŸŸŸ Adelaide Hills Sauvignon Blanc 2005 Spotlessly clean apple, gooseberry and passionfruit flavours finishing with gently lemony acidity; excellent overall elegance, line and length. Screwcap. 14° alc. **Rating** 94 To 2008 $15

Adelaide Hills Chardonnay 2004 Still very fresh and vibrantly fruit-driven; grapefruit, nectarine and oak are seamlessly welded; especially meritorious for its age, more like 1-year-old than 3. Screwcap. 13.6° alc. **Rating** 94 To 2013 $20

ŸŸŸŸ♀ Adelaide Hills Merlot 2004 Bright colour; savoury olive edges to medium-bodied cassis and spice fruit; a firm finish, but not unduly so. Screwcap. 14.5° alc. **Rating** 91 To 2015 $12

Phaedrus Estate ★★★★☆

220 Mornington-Tyabb Road, Moorooduc, Vic 3933 **Region** Mornington Peninsula
T (03) 5978 8134 **F** (03) 5978 8134 **www.**phaedrus.com.au **Open** W'ends & public hols 11–5
Winemaker Ewan Campbell, Maitena Zantvoort **Est.** 1997 **Cases** 2000
Ewan Campbell and Maitena Zantvoort established Phaedrus Estate in 1997. At that time both had already had winemaking experience with large wine companies, and were at the point of finishing their wine science degrees at Adelaide University. They decided they wished to (in their words) 'produce ultra-premium wine with distinctive and unique varietal flavours, which offer serious (and light-hearted) wine drinkers an alternative to mainstream commercial styles'. Campbell and Zantvoort believe that quality wines involve both art and science, and I don't have any argument with that. Exports to Hong Kong.

PHI

Lusatia Park Vineyard, Owens Road, Woori Yallock, Vic 3139 **Region** Yarra Valley
T (03) 5964 6070 **www**.phiwines.com **Open** By appt
Winemaker Steve Webber **Est.** 1985 **Cases** NFP
This is a joint venture between 2 very influential wine families: that of De Bortoli and
Shelmerdine. The key executives are Stephen Shelmerdine and Steve Webber (and their respective
wives). It has a sole viticultural base: the Lusatia Park vineyard of the Shelmerdine family.
Unusually, however, it is of specific rows of vines, not even blocks, although the rows are
continuous. They are pruned and managed quite differently to the rest of the block, with the
deliberate aim of strictly controlled yields. While the joint venture was only entered into in 2005,
De Bortoli had been buying grapes from the vineyard since 2002, and had had the opportunity
to test the limits of the grapes. The outcome has been wines of the highest quality, and a joint
venture which will last for many years. The name, incidentally, is derived from the 21st letter of
the ancient Greek alphabet, symbolising perfect balance and harmony. Courageous pricing for a
new kid on the block, but reflects the confidence the families have in the wines.

ΨΨΨΨΨ **Chardonnay 2005** Elegant and restrained; the absence of new oak emphasises
the European touch to the wine; texture, structure and excellent acidity are the
highlights of a lovely wine. Screwcap. 13° alc. **Rating** 96 **To** 2012 $50
Pinot Noir 2005 Light- to medium-bodied, but seriously good, with outstanding
line, length, focus and balance. Again texture is the moving force, although the wine
retains fragrance and balance. Screwcap. 13.5° alc. **Rating** 95 **To** 2010 $50
Sauvignon 2006 Interesting texture and structure; some flavour intervention
which works very well; richness without sweatiness; supple, round and tropical,
with a lingering flavour. Sauvignon Blanc. Screwcap. 13.5° alc. **Rating** 94
To 2010 $45

Philip Shaw   ★★★☆

Koomooloo Vineyard, Caldwell Lane, Orange, NSW 2800 **Region** Orange
T (02) 6365 2334 **www**.philipshaw.com.au **Open** W'ends 12–5, or by appt
Winemaker Philip Shaw **Est.** 1989 **Cases** 10 000
Philip Shaw, former chief winemaker of Rosemount Estate and then Southcorp Wines, first
became interested in the Orange region in 1985. In 1988 he purchased the Koomooloo
Vineyard, and began the planting of sauvignon blanc, chardonnay, shiraz, merlot, cabernet franc
and cabernet sauvignon. Wine quality has, quite frankly, disappointed after the first releases,
which sold out quickly.

ΨΨΨΨ **No. 19 Orange Sauvignon Blanc 2006** Herb, mineral and citrus; a long,
intense palate and a minerally finish. Slight sweatiness on the bouquet is the issue
for some. Screwcap. 12.8° alc. **Rating** 89 **To** 2008 $23
No. 11 Orange Chardonnay 2005 Well-made, supple, medium-bodied wine,
with nectarine and melon fruit supported by balanced oak. Screwcap. **Rating** 89
To 2009 $30

Phillip Island Vineyard   ★★★★★

Berrys Beach Road, Phillip Island, Vic 3922 **Region** Gippsland
T (03) 5956 8465 **F** (03) 5956 8465 **www**.phillipislandwines.com.au **Open** 7 days 11–5
Winemaker David Lance, James Lance **Est.** 1993 **Cases** 3000
1997 marked the first harvest from the 2.5 ha of the Phillip Island Vineyard, which is totally
enclosed in the permanent silon net which acts both as a windbreak and protection against birds.
The quality of the wines across the board make it clear that this is definitely not a tourist-trap
cellar door; it is a serious producer of quality wine. Exports to Southeast Asia.

ΨΨΨΨΨ **Pinot Noir 2005** Very good colour; elegant but quite powerful plummy fruit
has retained its freshness and vigour; very well-made, with excellent length.
Screwcap. 14° alc. **Rating** 94 **To** 2012 $50

𝟵𝟵𝟵𝟵𝟵 **The Pinnacles Botrytis Riesling 2006** Excellent botrytis influence, which has given complexity and intensity without subverting the riesling varietal character. Screwcap. 11.5° alc. **Rating** 93 **To** 2010 $19

Sauvignon Blanc 2006 Abundant flavour; ripe gooseberry fruit offset by attractive grassy elements. Considerable length. Screwcap. 13.5° alc. **Rating** 92 **To** 2008 $28

Riesling 2005 Spotlessly clean; generous flavours with ripe fruit and a touch of sweetness on the finish; betwixt and between. Screwcap. 12.5° alc. **Rating** 90 **To** 2015 $19

Phillips Brook Estate

118 Redmond-Hay River Road, Redmond, WA 6332 **Region** Albany
T (08) 9845 3124 **F** (08) 9845 3124 **Open** Wed–Sun 12–4
Winemaker Harewood Estate (James Kellie) **Est.** 1975 **Cases** NA

Pialligo Estate ★★★★

18 Kallaroo Road, Pialligo, ACT 2609 **Region** Canberra District
T (02) 6247 6060 **www**.pialligoestate.com.au **Open** Thurs–Sun & public hols 10–5
Winemaker Andrew McEwin, Greg Gallagher (Contract) **Est.** 1999 **Cases** 1500
Sally Milner and John Nutt planted their 4-ha vineyard (0.6 ha of merlot, 1.5 ha riesling, 0.4 ha sangiovese, and 0.5 ha each of shiraz, cabernet sauvignon and pinot grigio) in 1999. The cellar door sales area and café opened 2002, with views of Mt Ainslie, Mt Pleasant, Duntroon, the Telstra Tower, Parliament House and the Brindabella Ranges beyond. The property, which has a 1-km frontage to the Molonglo River, is only 5 mins drive from the centre of Canberra.

𝟵𝟵𝟵𝟵𝟵 **Chardonnay 2006** Bright straw-green; crisp, clean, with good intensity and length; melon and grapefruit, with no oak obvious, but the wine has personality and length, aided by minerally acidity. Screwcap. 13.7° alc. **Rating** 91 **To** 2010 $22

𝟵𝟵𝟵𝟵 **Shiraz 2004** A touch of sharpness to the mouthfeel suggests a low pH, and elevates the freshness of the fruit flavours. Screwcap. 14° alc. **Rating** 89 **To** 2012 $20

Merlot 2004 Slightly hazy colour; red and black fruits with a mix of black olive and spice provide yet another face of merlot. Screwcap. 13.9° alc. **Rating** 89 **To** 2011 $20

Sangiovese 2005 Good hue; light- to medium-bodied; a lively and crisp marriage of sour cherry, cigar box and fresh acidity. True Blue food style. Screwcap. 12.8° alc. **Rating** 89 **To** 2010 $25

Pinot Grigio 2006 Plenty of aroma; the flavours and texture are headed to Alsace rather than Italy; ends with a somewhat tough finish. Screwcap. 13.5° alc. **Rating** 87 **To** 2010 $22

Rose 2006 Clean and light-bodied; the clever use of a touch of residual sugar which is (just) carried by the red fruit smorgasbord of Merlot/Cabernet Sauvignon/Shiraz/Cabernet Franc. Screwcap. 13° alc. **Rating** 87 **To** 2008 $20

Cabernet Sauvignon 2004 Relatively light colour for the variety; a light to medium-bodied mix of berry, mint and leaf; needs more depth. Screwcap. 14.6° alc. **Rating** 87 **To** 2010 $20

Piano Gully

Piano Gully Road, Manjimup, WA 6258 **Region** Manjimup
T (08) 9772 3140 **F** (08) 9316 0336 **www**.pianogully.com.au **Open** By appt
Winemaker Ashley Lewkowski **Est.** 1987 **Cases** 4000
The 5-ha vineyard was established in 1987 on rich Karri loam, 10 km south of Manjimup, with the first wine made from the 1991 vintage. The name of the road (and the winery) commemorates the shipping of a piano from England by one of the first settlers in the region. The horse and cart carrying the piano on the last leg of the long journey were within sight of their destination when the piano fell from the cart and was destroyed.

ŸŸŸŸ **Cabernet Merlot 2005** Good purple-red; medium-bodied, with attractive blackcurrant aromas and flavours together with touches of spice and cedar; light tannins. Screwcap. 13.5° alc. **Rating** 89 **To** 2015 $18

Cabernet Sauvignon 2004 Savoury/cedary/spicy/earthy notes juxtaposed against some sweet berry fruit. Less convincing than the Cabernet Merlot. Cork. 13° alc. **Rating** 88 **To** 2012 $25

Picardy   ★★★★★

Cnr Vasse Highway/Eastbrook Road, Pemberton, WA 6260 **Region** Pemberton
T (08) 9776 0036 **F** (08) 9776 0245 **www**.picardy.com.au **Open** By appt
Winemaker Bill Pannell, Dan Pannell **Est.** 1993 **Cases** 5000
Picardy is owned by Dr Bill Pannell, wife Sandra and son Daniel; Bill and Sandra founded Moss Wood winery in Margaret River in 1969. Picardy reflects Bill Pannell's view that the Pemberton area has proved to be one of the best regions in Australia for Pinot Noir and Chardonnay, but it is perhaps significant that the wines include a Shiraz, and a Bordeaux-blend of Merlot/Cabernet Franc/Cabernet Sauvignon. Time will tell whether Pemberton has more Burgundy, Rhône or Bordeaux in its veins. Exports to the UK, the US and other major markets.

ŸŸŸŸŸ **Pannell Family Pemberton Chardonnay 2005** A beautifully crafted wine; melon, stone fruit and grapefruit in a fine silken web of quality oak; long finish. Cork. 14° alc. **Rating** 96 **To** 2014 $30

Pannell Family Tete de Cuvee Pinot Noir 2005 Fragrant and flowery lush red fruit aromas; rich and mouthfilling, in no way a copy of Burgundy; long life ahead. Cork. 14° alc. **Rating** 94 **To** 2015 $40

Pemberton Shiraz 2004 An aromatic bouquet of fresh red fruits flows into a palate where red and black cherry plus spice lead the band; silky mouthfeel with very good oak and tannin balance. Cork. 14° alc. **Rating** 94 **To** 2020 $20

Pannell Family Merlimont 2003 Some of the same oak as in the '04, but much more fruit to justify it; cassis, blackcurrant and a touch of raspberry; good tannin structure, and a lovely juicy finish. Merlot/Cabernet Sauvignon/Cabernet Franc. Diam. 13.5° alc. **Rating** 94 **To** 2023 $30

ŸŸŸŸŸ **Pemberton Merlot Cabernet Sauvignon Cabernet Franc 2004** Strong smoky bacon oak aromas; medium-bodied, with an attractive array of red fruits, soft and round; cassis, raspberry and blackcurrant. Cork. 14° alc. **Rating** 92 **To** 2014 $20

Pannell Family Trial Batch No. 1 Pemberton Sauvignon Blanc 2006 Elegant, lively and fresh thanks in part to the moderate alcohol; an appealing mix of flavours starts herbaceous and ends with tropical passionfruit. Made from grapes purchased from a neighbour and hence not estate, nor, said the background sheet, is it a Picardy wine. A convoluted label, because if it was not made at Picardy by the Pannell Family, it was the subject of immaculate conception. Cork. 12.5° alc. **Rating** 91 **To** 2008 $14

Pannell Family Pemberton Pinot Noir 2005 The influence of cork (not TCA, just cork wood) evident; powerful plum and black cherry fruit; the finish a touch tannic/hard needing time. Cork. 14° alc. **Rating** 91 **To** 2013 $25

Piedmont Wines   ★★☆

3430 Yarra Junction-Noojee Road, Noojee, Vic 3833 **Region** Gippsland
T (03) 9733 0449 **www**.piedmontwines.com.au **Open** W'ends & public hols 10–5
Winemaker Ivan Juric **Est.** 1991 **Cases** 1000
Quite where the name Piedmont Wines came from, I do not know, but Ivan and Ljubica Juric started the venture as a hobby, with only 360 vines planted in 1991. Since that time they have expanded twice, the vineyard now comprising 1 ha each of chardonnay, sauvignon blanc and shiraz.

Pierro ★★★★☆

Caves Road, Wilyabrup via Cowaramup, WA 6284 **Region** Margaret River
T (08) 9755 6220 **F** (08) 9755 6308 **www**.pierro.com.au **Open** 7 days 10–5
Winemaker Dr Michael Peterkin **Est.** 1979 **Cases** 10 000
Dr Michael Peterkin is another of the legion of Margaret River medical practitioners; for good measure, he married into the Cullen family. Pierro is renowned for its stylish white wines, which often exhibit tremendous complexity. The Chardonnay can be monumental in its weight and complexity. Exports to the UK, the US, Japan and Indonesia.

♇♇♇♇♇ **Margaret River Chardonnay 2005** Light straw-green; an elegant mix of fig, stone fruit and ripe melon, the oak judged to perfection. Screwcap. 13.5° alc. **Rating** 94 **To** 2015 $67

♇♇♇♇♀ **Margaret River Semillon Sauvignon Blanc LTC 2006** Typical Pierro style; a complex, rich and layered wine moving towards white Bordeaux in style; tropical nectarine plus herbs and that little touch of chardonnay (LTC stands for 'little touch of chardonnay'.) The touch on one's wallet is rather less than for the main Pierro brands. Cork. 13.5° alc. **Rating** 92 **To** 2011 $26
Cabernet Sauvignon Merlot 2003 Fragrant fruit aromas, then pronounced tannins run through the length of the palate, presently enveloping the fruit. Patience should reward. Cork. 13.5° alc. **Rating** 90 **To** 2015 $34
Reserve Margaret River Cabernet Sauvignon Merlot 2003 An elegant wine, but again with some of the olive/herbal notes which diminish the sweet fruit. Cork. 13.5° alc. **Rating** 90 **To** 2013 $60

♇♇♇♇ **Margaret River Cabernet Sauvignon Merlot LTCf 2004** Light- to medium-bodied; tending austere, with some olive, earth notes along with blackcurrant; subtle oak. (LTCf stands for 'little touch of cabernet franc.) Screwcap. 12.5° alc. **Rating** 89 **To** 2012 $32
Margaret River Pinot Noir 2003 Very well-made; savoury earthy style with good structure, but the region simply takes away true varietal expression. Screwcap. 14° alc. **Rating** 88 **To** 2009 $45

Piggs Peake ★★★★★

697 Hermitage Road, Pokolbin, NSW 2321 **Region** Lower Hunter Valley
T (02) 6574 7000 **F** (02) 6574 7070 **www**.piggspeake.com **Open** 7 days 10–5
Winemaker Steve Langham, Hugh Jorgen **Est.** 1998 **Cases** 3000
The derivation of the name remains a mystery to me; if it is a local landmark, I have not heard of it. It sources its grapes from a wide variety of places, to make a range of wines which are well outside the straight and narrow. Piggs Peake has secured listings at a number of leading Sydney metropolitan and NSW country restaurants. The arrival of Steve Langham (having previously worked 4 vintages at Allandale) has seen a marked increase in quality.

Pike & Joyce ★★★★☆

Mawson Road, Lenswood, SA 5240 (postal) **Region** Adelaide Hills
T (08) 8843 4370 **F** (08) 8843 4353 **www**.pikeandjoyce.com.au **Open** Not
Winemaker Neil Pike, John Trotter **Est.** 1998 **Cases** 4000
This is a partnership between the Pike family (of Clare Valley fame) and the Joyce family, related to Andrew Pike's wife, Cathy. The Joyce family have been orchardists at Lenswood for over 100 years, but also have extensive operations in the Riverland. Together with Andrew Pike (formerly chief viticulturist for the Southcorp group) they have established 1 ha of vines; the lion's share to pinot noir, sauvignon blanc and chardonnay, followed by merlot, pinot gris and semillon. The wines are made at Pikes Clare Valley winery. Exports to the UK, the US and other major markets.

♇♇♇♇♀ **Adelaide Hills Sauvignon Blanc 2006** The fruit latent in the bouquet comes through strongly on the palate; a mix of citrus, passionfruit and kiwifruit; well-balanced and fetching flavours. Screwcap. 13° alc. **Rating** 93 **To** 2008 $20

ỴỴỴỴ   **Adelaide Hills Pinot Gris 2006** Strongly structured through minerally/green apple acidity; bright, dry finish. Screwcap. 12° alc. **Rating** 89 **To** 2008 $20
The Bleedings Adelaide Hills Pinot Noir Rose 2006 Pale salmon; bright flavours of spice and strawberry; dry finish and good length. When the Burgundians run off some of the juice immediately the grapes are crushed, it is called saignee, or bleeding the remaining must, thereby concentrating it. Screwcap. 13° alc. **Rating** 89 **To** 2008 $18

Pikes   ★★★★★

Polish Hill River Road, Sevenhill, SA 5453 **Region** Clare Valley
T (08) 8843 4370 **F** (08) 8843 4353 **www.pikeswines.com.au Open** 7 days 10–4
Winemaker Neil Pike, John Trotter **Est.** 1984 **Cases** 35 000
Owned by the Pike brothers: Andrew was for many years the senior viticulturist with Southcorp, Neil was a winemaker at Mitchell. Pikes now has its own winery, with Neil Pike presiding. In most vintages its white wines, led by Riesling, are the most impressive. Exports to the UK, the US and other major markets.

ỴỴỴỴỴ   **The Merle Clare Valley Riesling 2006** Elegant, fine citrus and apple blossom aromas; a long and intense palate with particularly good acidity, lemony and long. Screwcap. 12° alc. **Rating** 96 **To** 2021 $35
Traditionale Clare Valley Riesling 2006 A clean, floral bouquet; supple, smooth and flavoursome citrus and lime fruit; gentle acidity on a long finish. Screwcap. 12° alc. **Rating** 94 **To** 2016 $21

ỴỴỴỴỴ   **The Dogwalk Cabernet Merlot 2004** Medium red-purple; a rich, generous but not over the top array of blackcurrant and cassis fruit flavours; nice touch of oak, and ripe tannins. Screwcap. 14.5° alc. **Rating** 91 **To** 2014 $18
Luccio Pinot Gris Sauvignon Blanc Semillon 2005 An unlikely blend which in fact works very well, with lively, juicy, tangy flavours and good length; 59%/38%/3%. Screwcap. 13° alc. **Rating** 90 **To** 2008 $15
Eastside Clare Valley Shiraz 2004 Not entirely convincing colour; a pleasant, medium-bodied palate with a mix of red and black fruits; fine tannins, gentle oak. Screwcap. 14.5° alc. **Rating** 90 **To** 2014 $22

ỴỴỴỴ   **Luccio Sangiovese Merlot Cabernet Sauvignon 2004** Light but bright red-purple; a supple and smooth light- to medium-bodied palate, with a mix of cherry, raspberry and redcurrant flavours. Screwcap. 14° alc. **Rating** 89 **To** 2008 $15
The Red Mullet Clare Valley Red Blend 2004 Much lighter and more spicy/savoury than the alcohol would suggest. Sangiovese, merlot and tempranillo dragging the shiraz along perhaps; some small red fruits lurk in the blend. Fairly priced. Screwcap. 14.5° alc. **Rating** 88 **To** 2008 $15

🍇 Pindarie Wines   ★★★☆

PO Box 341, Tanunda, SA 5352 **Region** Barossa Valley
T (08) 8524 9019 **F** (08) 8524 9090 **www.pindarie.com.au Open** Not
Winemaker Mark Jamieson **Est.** 2005 **Cases** 1000
Owners Tony Brooks and Wendy Allan met while studying at Roseworthy College in 1985, but had very different family backgrounds. Tony Brooks was the sixth generation of farmers in SA and WA, and was studying agriculture, while NZ-born Wendy Allan was studying viticulture. On graduation Tony worked overseas managing sheep feedlots in Saudi Arabia, Turkey and Jordan, while Wendy worked for the next 12 years with Penfolds, commencing as a grower liaison officer and working her way up to become a senior viticulturist. She also found time to study viticulture in California, Israel, Italy, Germany, France, Portugal, Spain and Chile, working vintages and assessing vineyards for wine projects. In 2001 she completed a graduate diploma in wine business. Today they are renovating the original bluestone homestead and outbuildings, while managing the vineyards, mixed farm enterprises, a wine business and raising 3 children. Small wonder they have retained Mark Jamieson as executive winemaker.

ŶŶŶŶŶ **Barossa Valley Shiraz 2005** Deep purple-red; clear, clean blackberry, plum and black cherry fruit; a touch of mocha oak. Screwcap. 15° alc. **Rating** 90 To 2015 $18

ŶŶŶŶ **Bar Rossa Tempranillo Sangiovese Shiraz 2006** Bright, clear purple-red; spotlessly clean, the tangy tempranillo fruit (70%) understandably dominates; overall distinctly savoury. Tempranillo/Sangiovese/Shiraz. A blend of convenience, perhaps. Screwcap. 14.5° alc. **Rating** 89 To 2012 $19

Pipers Brook Vineyard ★★★★☆

1216 Pipers Brook Road, Pipers Brook, Tas 7254 **Region** Northern Tasmania
T (03) 6382 7527 **F** (03) 6382 7226 **www.**pipersbrook.com **Open** 7 days 10–5
Winemaker Rene Bezemer **Est.** 1974 **Cases** 90 000
The Pipers Brook Tasmanian empire has over 185 ha of vineyard supporting the Pipers Brook and Ninth Island labels, with the major focus, of course, being on Pipers Brook. Fastidious viticulture and winemaking, immaculate packaging and enterprising marketing create a potent and effective blend. Pipers Brook operates 2 cellar door outlets, one at headquarters, the other at Strathlyn. In 2001 it became yet another company to fall prey to a takeover, in this instance by Belgian-owned sheepskin business Kreglinger, which has also established a large winery and vineyard at Mount Benson in SA. Exports to all major markets.

ŶŶŶŶŶ **Ninth Island Chardonnay 2005** Has intensity and thrust to the long, lingering palate; not complex, but nor is it sweet. Most impressive at the price. Screwcap. 13.5° alc. **Rating** 93 To 2011 $22.50
The Lyre Pinot Noir 2003 Bright and clear red-purple; fragrant black cherry and plum fruit, the highly focused palate with considerable length. Price is in the eye of the beholder. Cork. 13.6° alc. **Rating** 93 To 2010 $95
Ninth Island Pinot Grigio 2006 Lively, fresh and tangy, with notes of citrus, apple and pear; has much more flavour interest than most grigios. Screwcap. 13.5° alc. **Rating** 90 To 2008 $21
Estate Pinot Gris 2006 Pale pink; appealing, light-bodied musk and pear flavours; fine, long and strongly varietal even if essentially delicate. Screwcap. 13.5° alc. **Rating** 90 To 2008 $27.50
Estate Pinot Noir 2005 Complex winemaking, with an array of black fruits, spice and some stem; good length. Cork. 13.5° alc. **Rating** 90 To 2012 $36.95

Pirie Estate ★★★★★

17 High Street, Launceston, Tas 7250 (postal) **Region** Northern Tasmania
T (03) 6334 7772 **F** (03) 6334 7773 **www.**andrewpirie.com **Open** Not
Winemaker Andrew Pirie **Est.** 2004 **Cases** 8000
After a relatively short break, Andrew Pirie has re-established his winemaking activities in Tas. He has leased the Rosevears winery, where he will oversee the production of wines for the Rosevears group, for his own brands, and for others on a contract basis. His main responsibility, however, is now his role as CEO of Tamer Ridge, where he will also oversee winemaking.

ŶŶŶŶŶ **Chardonnay 2005** Elegant and intense nectarine and grapefruit supported by subtle oak; has exceptional length, the acidity pronounced but balanced. Screwcap. 13.5° alc. **Rating** 94 To 2012 $37.20
Reserve Pinot Noir 2005 Lovely texture and mouthfeel are the first impression, then a panoply of soft fruits with a strong dash of spice. Screwcap. **Rating** 94 To 0213 $64.30
Pinot Noir 2003 Fragrant red fruits; supple cherry and plum flavours, super-smooth, yet not simple, mouthfeel; good length. Screwcap. 14° alc. **Rating** 94 To 2012 $35.90

ŶŶŶŶŶ **Pirie South Pinot Noir 2005** Bright red-purple; a light- to medium-bodied wine with red cherry and plum fruit; fine tannins appear on the back palate and finish; good length. Screwcap. 13.5° alc. **Rating** 91 To 2008 $22

Riesling 2005 Bright, light straw-green; citrus, spice and mineral characters all intermingle; a delicate wine in the mouth, dipping a little on the mid- to back-palate. Screwcap. 13° alc. **Rating** 90 **To** 2013 $37.20

Pinot Noir 2005 Very good balance, line and length; plenty of black and red cherry fruits on the mid-palate, faltering ever so slightly on the finish. Screwcap. 14° alc. **Rating** 90 **To** 2011 $37.20

Pinot Noir 2004 Very deep colour; powerful, plummy fruit; curiously, not extractive; ripeness may have been an issue. Screwcap. 14° alc. **Rating** 90 **To** 2011 $35.90

ΨΨΨΨ **Pirie South Chardonnay 2005** Overall, an exercise in restraint; melon and nectarine fruit, some traces of cashew from partial mlf. Screwcap. 12.9° alc. **Rating** 89 **To** 2009 $22

Pirie South Rose 2006 Light-bodied; spicy cherry flavours; has some length, and does not rely on residual sugar. Screwcap. 13.9° alc. **Rating** 89 **To** 2008 $23.70

South Sauvignon Blanc 2006 Clean, fresh and crisp in full-on, cool-climate style; herb, grass and a touch of asparagus. Screwcap. 13° alc. **Rating** 88 **To** 2008 $23.70

Pirie South Riesling 2006 Some development to the colour; a big, bold style outside the usual tight Tasmanian structure, heading off towards Alsace. Screwcap. 12.8° alc. **Rating** 87 **To** 2010 $23.70

Estelle 2006 Has good balance, but no particularly distinctive fruit flavour. Riesling/Gewurztraminer/Pinot Gris. Screwcap. 12.8° alc. **Rating** 87 **To** 2008 $22.90

Piromit Wines   ★★★★

113 Hanwood Avenue, Hanwood, NSW 2680 **Region** Riverina
T (02) 6963 0200 **F** (02) 6963 0277 **www**.piromitwines.com.au **Open** Mon–Fri 10–4
Winemaker Sam Mittiga **Est.** 1998 **Cases** 50 000
I simply cannot resist quoting directly from the background information kindly supplied to me. 'Piromit Wines is a relatively new boutique winery situated in Hanwood, NSW. The 1000-tonne capacity winery was built for the 1999 vintage on a 14-acre site which was until recently used as a drive-in. Previous to this, wines were made on our 100-acre vineyard. The winery site is being developed into an innovative tourist attraction complete with an Italian restaurant and landscaped formal gardens.' It is safe to say this extends the concept of a boutique winery into new territory, but then it is a big country. Exports to Canada, Sweden and Italy.

ΨΨΨΨΨ **Chardonnay 2005** Good varietal flavour; nectarine and peach fruit balanced by acidity, oak barely visible; has surprising length. Shows what can be done in this region. Screwcap. 13.5° alc. **Rating** 90 **To** 2009 $12.50

Botrytis Semillon 2005 Golden yellow; an abundance of peach, butterscotch, cumquat and good acidity shows once again how effortlessly Riverina produces this style. Screwcap. 11.5° alc. **Rating** 90 **To** 2008 $14

ΨΨΨΨ **Pinot Grigio 2005** Crisp and clean; not a lot of varietal character (an oxymoron if ever there was one) but citrussy acidity drives the length and finish. Screwcap. 12° alc. **Rating** 87 **To** 2008 $12

Cabernet Merlot 2005 Medium-bodied; has more fine tannins contributing to the structure than expected; savoury, olive flavours from the merlot; good value. Screwcap. 14.5° alc. **Rating** 87 **To** 2008 $12

Sangiovese 2005 Bright, light red; light-bodied, but nonetheless clear varietal expression with a touch of sour cherry fruit and a brisk finish. Screwcap. 13° alc. **Rating** 87 **To** 2008 $12

Pirramimma   ★★★★☆

Johnston Road, McLaren Vale, SA 5171 **Region** McLaren Vale
T (08) 8323 8205 **F** (08) 8323 9224 **www**.pirramimma.com.au **Open** Mon–Fri 9–5,
Sat 11–5, Sun, public hols 11.30–4
Winemaker Geoff Johnston **Est.** 1892 **Cases** 50 000

A long-established, family-owned company with outstanding vineyard resources. It is using those resources to full effect, with a series of intense old-vine varietals including Semillon, Sauvignon Blanc, Chardonnay, Shiraz, Grenache, Cabernet Sauvignon and Petit Verdot, all fashioned without over-embellishment. There are 2 quality tiers, both offering excellent value, the packaging recently significantly upgraded. Exports to the UK, the US and other major markets.

ҮҮҮҮҮ **McLaren Vale Petit Verdot 2004** Typical deep colour; blackcurrant, spice and earth aromas; very concentrated and powerful, but not over-extracted; lingering tannins. One of the veterans with this variety. Cork. 14° alc. **Rating** 93 **To** 2014 $26.50

Pirra McLaren Vale Sauvignon Blanc Semillon 2006 Very vibrant, fresh and lively; delicious lemonade/lime juice flavours; low alcohol a big winner. Screwcap. 9.5° alc. **Rating** 92 **To** 2008 $15

McLaren Vale Shiraz 2004 Strong red-purple; a classic McLaren Vale mix of blackberry, dark plum and bitter chocolate, with overall restraint; firm, fine tannins and good length. Cork. 14° alc. **Rating** 92 **To** 2015 $26.50

Stock's Hill McLaren Vale Cabernet Sauvignon 2003 Some colour development; savoury, earthy, dark chocolate surrounds to the blackcurrant fruit; not spongy or sweet as are many '03s; good tannins. Screwcap. 14° alc. **Rating** 90 **To** 2013 $15

ҮҮҮҮ **McLaren Vale Tannat 2004** A very interesting wine; Pirramimma has tamed the famous tannins of tannat, showing a nice carpet of red and black fruits; well worth a look. It was the ferocious tannins of tannat in its French home region of Madeiran which led to the development of micro-oxygenation by local winemaker Patrick Ducournau. Cork. 14° alc. **Rating** 89 **To** 2014 $26.50

Stock's Hill McLaren Vale Cabernet Sauvignon 2004 Medium-bodied; an appealing mix of varietal blackcurrant fruit and McLaren Vale regional chocolate; the apparent use of older American oak, however, hasn't helped a potentially very good wine. Screwcap. 14° alc. **Rating** 88 **To** 2012 $15

Pirra McLaren Vale Sparkling Chardonnay 2006 Jazzy and lively green apple flavours; very clever winemaking; not sweet, the cleverness lying in the low alcohol. 9.5° alc. **Rating** 88 **To** 2008 $15

Stock's Hill Rose 2005 Good flavour, weight and structure; indistinct cabernet sauvignon style, with a convincing, dry finish. Screwcap. 12° alc. **Rating** 87 **To** 2008 $15

Stock's Hill McLaren Vale Shiraz 2004 Elegant, light- to medium-bodied wine; everything present is correct; just not quite enough of it. Screwcap. 14° alc. **Rating** 87 **To** 2010 $15

Pirra McLaren Vale Grenache Shiraz Merlot 2005 A light-bodied mix of spicy/savoury/juicy fruits; clean, fresh bistro style. Smart new labels and packaging for the Pirra range. Screwcap. 11.5° alc. **Rating** 87 **To** 2008 $15

Pizzini   ★★★★☆

Lano-Trento Vineyard, 175 King Valley Road, Whitfield, Vic 3768 **Region** King Valley
T (03) 5729 8278 **F** (03) 5729 8495 **www**.pizzini.com.au **Open** 7 days 10–5
Winemaker Alfred Pizzini, Joel Pizzini **Est.** 1980 **Cases** 14 000
Fred and Katrina Pizzini have been grapegrowers in the King Valley for over 25 years, with over 50 ha of vineyard. Grapegrowing (rather than winemaking) still continues to be the major focus, but their move into winemaking has been particularly successful, and I can personally vouch for their Italian cooking skills. It is not surprising, then, that their wines should span both Italian and traditional varieties. Exports to Japan.

ҮҮҮҮҮ **King Valley Shiraz 2004** Impressive wine for the region; abundant black fruits and spice, with good structure and texture; gentle oak support. Screwcap. 14° alc. **Rating** 92 **To** 2019 $20

King Valley Sangiovese 2005 A clear mix of black cherry, sour cherry, plum and spice; appropriate medium-bodied wine with fine tannins; impressive. Screwcap. 14.2° alc. **Rating** 90 **To** 2015 $24

ÏÏÏÏ   **King Valley Merlot 2004** Strong colour; equally emphatic varietal expression; black olives and some spicy/earthy notes. Better than many far more expensive versions. Screwcap. 13.5° alc. **Rating** 89 **To** 2015 $16

Il Barone 2002 Powerful, smoky, spicy, leathery wine concentrated and tannic in best Italian tradition. Will the tannins soften before the fruit dies? Cabernet Sauvignon/Shiraz/Sangiovese/Nebbiolo. Cork. 14.2° alc. **Rating** 88 **To** 2022 $43

King Valley Rosetta 2006 Multi-spice aromas twisted with red cherries which come through on the palate, gets away with residual sugar on the finish. Sangiovese. Screwcap. 13.8° alc. **Rating** 87 **To** 2008 $15

 # Plan B

Harman's South Road, Wilyabrup, WA 6284 **Region** Margaret River
T 0413 759 030 **F** (08) 9755 6267 **www**.planbwines.com **Open** At Arlewood Estate
Winemaker Bill Crappsley, Garry Gosatti **Est.** 2005 **Cases** 6000
This is a joint venture between Bill Crappsley, a 43-year veteran winemaker/consultant; Martin Miles, with a wine distribution business in the southwestern part of the state; Gary Gosatti, who acquired Arlewood Estate in 1999; and Terry Chellappah, wine consultant and now also in partnership with Gary Gosatti. The shiraz is sourced from Bill Crappsley's Calgardup Vineyard, the remaining wines from Arlewood, all are single-vineyard releases. The plan is to extend the range with Gold Label limited releases of Barrel Fermented Semillon, Shiraz Tempranillo and IV SKINS. Exports to the UK, the US, Switzerland, Singapore, Hong Kong and Vietnam.

ÏÏÏÏÏ   **Margaret River Semillon Sauvignon Blanc 2006** A generous wine; good depth and complexity yet not extending itself into territory beyond its capacity. Screwcap. 13.5° alc. **Rating** 90 **To** 2009 $17

Margaret River Semillon Sauvignon Blanc 2005 Clean, correct varietal aromas, sauvignon blanc contributing the overt fruit, semillon providing the palate structure. Excellent value. Screwcap. 13.5° alc. **Rating** 90 **To** 2008 $16

IV SKINS 2005 Quite assertive, yet not green or bitter; just where this wine will head I don't know, but given some benefit of the doubt, particularly given the precedent of the '04. Cabernet Sauvignon/Nebbiolo/Petit Verdot/Merlot. Screwcap. 13.5° alc. **Rating** 90 **To** 2015 $35

ÏÏÏÏ   **Barrel Selection Margaret River Semillon 2004** Oak tends to poke its nose out from the start to the finish; has ample overall flavour, but is under-fruited. Screwcap. 14° alc. **Rating** 89 **To** 2010 $25

Margaret River Tempranillo Shiraz 2004 Fresh, zippy, slightly tangy/lemony juicy fruit flavours; not over-much structure. Screwcap. 14° alc. **Rating** 89 **To** 2010 $23

Margaret River Cabernet Merlot 2005 Good colour, with slightly more depth than the Merlot; similarly, a touch more weight from the blackcurrant/blackberry fruits; good value for Margaret River. Screwcap. 14° alc. **Rating** 89 **To** 2013 $15

Margaret River Tempranillo Shiraz 2005 Has the tangy/lemony bite seen in so many young tempranillos from all over Australia; difficult to know whether this is young vines or clones or simply terroir speaking. Theoretically, the Margaret River climate should suit. Screwcap. 13.5° alc. **Rating** 89 **To** 2013 $35

IV SKINS 2004 Bright, clear red-purple; a medium-bodied array of fruit flavours from the unusual blend; something of a tug of war between petit verdot and nebbiolo. Cabernet Sauvignon/Petit Verdot/Nebbiolo/Merlot. Screwcap. 14° alc. Rating 89 **To** 2015 $23

Margaret River Merlot 2004 Bright clear colour; light- to medium-bodied; fresh black olive and savoury nuances to the red fruit core; minimal oak inputs. Screwcap. 14° alc. **Rating** 88 **To** 2010 $15

Plantagenet

Albany Highway, Mount Barker, WA 6324 **Region** Mount Barker
T (08) 9851 3111 **F** (08) 9851 1839 **www**.plantagenetwines.com **Open** 7days 9–5
Winemaker John Durham **Est.** 1974 **Cases** 100 000

The senior winery in the Mount Barker region, making superb wines across the full spectrum of variety and style: highly aromatic Riesling, tangy citrus-tinged Chardonnay, glorious Rhône-style Shiraz and ultra-stylish Cabernet Sauvignon. Exports to all major markets.

ŶŶŶŶŶ **Great Southern Shiraz 2004** Distinguished, medium-bodied wine; spicy notes are woven through blackberry and black cherry fruit; fine, but ripe, tannins and quality oak. Screwcap. 14.5° alc. **Rating** 95 **To** 2020 $40
Great Southern Riesling 2006 Apple and citrus aromas, with a subliminal hint of spice; very pure and long; excellent intensity builds on the finish and aftertaste; citrussy acidity at work. Screwcap. 12° alc. **Rating** 94 **To** 2016 $19

ŶŶŶŶŶ **Omrah Sauvignon Blanc 2006** A whisper of reduction doesn't affect the palate; passionfruit and gooseberry are backed by minerally acidity giving good length; a Curate's egg if ever there was one, the reduction diminishing what might have been something special at the price. Screwcap. 12° alc. **Rating** 90 **To** 2008 $17
Mount Barker Cabernet Sauvignon 2004 Medium red-purple; gently sweet blackcurrant fruit woven through cedary oak. A distinctly user-friendly style. Screwcap. 14° alc. **Rating** 90 **To** 2015 $35

ŶŶŶŶ **Omrah Unoaked Chardonnay 2006** Honest wine; light- to medium-bodied with solid yellow peach flavours, but fully priced. Screwcap. 13.5° alc. **Rating** 87 **To** 2009 $17
Omrah Pinot Noir 2006 Vivid red-purple; an upjumped rose, with cherry, strawberry and plum; simple, but does have length. Screwcap. 13° alc. **Rating** 87 **To** 2008 $17
Omrah Cabernet Sauvignon 2004 Slightly hazy colour; earthy, savoury overtones to blackcurrant fruit; fine tannins. Screwcap. 14.5° alc. **Rating** 87 **To** 2010 $17

Plum Hill Vineyard   NR

45 Coldstream West Road, Chirnside Park, Vic 3116 **Region** Yarra Valley
T (03) 9735 0985 **F** (03) 9735 4109 **Open** By appt
Winemaker Rachel Gore **Est.** 1998 **Cases** NA

Plunkett Fowles   ★★★★★

Cnr Hume Highway/Lambing Gully Road, Avenel, Vic 3664 **Region** Strathbogie Ranges
T (03) 5796 2150 **F** (03) 5796 2147 **www**.plunkettfowles.com.au **Open** 7 days 9–5
Winemaker Sam Plunkett, Victor Nash, Lindsay Brown, Michael Clayden **Est.** 1968
Cases 20 000
This sizeable operation is the result of a merger between Plunkett Wines, Dominion Wines and Strathbogie Vintners. The Fowles family purchased Dominion Wines (which was effectively in receivership), the large winery being the major asset. After considerable to-ing and fro-ing, it was decided the Plunkett and Fowles families would form a joint venture to handle all of the brands within the group. The brands are Stonedwellers (icon), then Upton Run, next Plunkett, and finally Blackwood Ridge. The venture has got away to a dream start.

ŶŶŶŶŶ **Reserve Strathbogie Ranges Shiraz 2004** While the wine has had plenty of exposure to new oak, it has been a prolific gold medal and trophy winner, the intense cool-climate shiraz carrying the oak. Cork. 14.5° alc. **Rating** 95 **To** 2024 $39
Blackwood Ridge Sauvignon Blanc 2006 Positive fruit in herb, grass and asparagus spectrum; good length and mouthfeel, the flavours persisting on the aftertaste but without unwelcome phenolics. Trophy Strathbogie Ranges Wine Show '06. Screwcap. 13° alc. **Rating** 94 **To** 2008 $15
Strathbogie Ranges Chardonnay 2005 Light-bodied, but has clear varietal fruit, excellent length, and judiciously restrained use of oak. Trophy Best White Strathbogie Ranges Wine Show '06. Screwcap. 14° alc. **Rating** 94 **To** 2012 $20

Upton Run Reserve Shiraz 2005 A dense wine, crammed with blackberry and black cherry fruit plus touches of dark chocolate, finished off with good oak. Cork. 14.5° alc. **Rating** 94 **To** 2020 $49

Stonedwellers Shiraz 2004 Rich licorice, blackberry, plum and spice fruit; a long, concentrated palate and positive oak. Cork. 14.5° alc. **Rating** 94 **To** 2019 $100

Upton Run Fence Sitter Cabernet Sauvignon 2004 Powerful, complex dark fruits, with great character compared to some of the lighter-bodied wines in the Strathbogie Ranges Wine Show. Cork. 14.5° alc. **Rating** 94 **To** 2019 $29.95

ŸŸŸŸŸ **Blackwood Ridge Shiraz 2004** Generous blackberry and black cherry fruit on a medium-bodied, smooth and supple palate; finishes with soft tannins. Great value. Screwcap. 14.5° alc. **Rating** 90 **To** 2015 $15

ŸŸŸŸ **Blackwood Ridge Traminer Riesling 2005** Pronounced traminer varietal character on both bouquet and palate with lychee dominant; slightly oily as always on the off-dry finish; a touch more acidity needed, perhaps; Gewurztraminer (80%)/Riesling (20%). Screwcap. 10° alc. **Rating** 89 **To** 2010 $15

Blackwood Ridge Unwooded Chardonnay 2006 Stone fruit and a touch of citrus; while light-bodied, has good length; good example of unwooded chardonnay style. Screwcap. 14° alc. **Rating** 88 **To** 2010 $15

Vinus Semillon Sauvignon Blanc 2006 Well-made; good balance, mineral and herb notes with a hint of oak; fair length. Screwcap. 12.5° alc. **Rating** 87 **To** 2009 $13

Poacher's Ridge Vineyard   ★★★★☆

163 Jersey Street, Wembley, WA 6014 (postal) **Region** Mount Barker
T (08) 9387 5003 **F** (08) 9387 5503 **www**.prv.com.au **Open** Not
Winemaker Robert Diletti (Contract) **Est.** 2000 **Cases** 1600

Alex and Janet Taylor purchased the Poacher's Ridge property in 1999; before then it had been used for cattle grazing. In 2000, 7 ha of vineyard (shiraz, cabernet sauvignon, merlot, riesling, marsanne and viognier) were planted. The first small crop came in 2003, a larger one in 2004, together making an auspicious debut. A cellar door and café are planned. Exports to the US and Canada.

ŸŸŸŸŸ **Louis' Block Great Southern Merlot 2005** Very good hue; merlot of the highest quality; a mix of cassis, blackcurrant and plum; perfect medium-bodied structure and balance; long finish. ProCork. 14.3° alc. **Rating** 95 **To** 2018 $18

ŸŸŸŸŸ **Louis' Block Great Southern Riesling 2005** Pungently crisp and bright lime, lemon and apple flavours; a long, dry, finish. Screwcap. 13° alc. **Rating** 91 **To** 2015 $15

Sophie's Yard Great Southern Shiraz 2005 Firm, clean blackberry with a touch of raspberry fruit; fine-grained tannins add to the long finish. ProCork. 15.3° alc. **Rating** 91 **To** 2015 $18

Louis' Block Great Southern Cabernet Sauvignon 2005 A medium-bodied wine, with some of the structural characteristics of the Merlot, but altogether more savoury, and not quite enough sweet fruit on the mid-palate. ProCork. 14° alc. **Rating** 90 **To** 2015 $18

Louis' Block Great Southern Cabernet Sauvignon 2004 Elegant, light- to medium-bodied wine with gentle red fruits, and fine tannins and oak. No suggestion of greenness. ProCork. 13° alc. **Rating** 90 **To** 2010 $17

ŸŸŸŸ **Louis' Block Great Southern Riesling 2006** A faint touch of reduction on the bouquet is followed by a crisp and firm palate, flavours of herb and mineral, finishing with lemony acidity; a pity about the bouquet. Screwcap. 12.2° alc. **Rating** 89 **To** 2013 $18

Louis' Block Great Southern Marsanne 2005 Fresh and unadorned; some honeysuckle plus gentle citrus tones; good balance. Screwcap. 12.8° alc. **Rating** 88 **To** 2010 $15

Louis' Block Great Southern Marsanne 2006 Very light-bodied; quite crisp, with faint chalk and honeysuckle varietal character; may surprise with time in bottle. Screwcap. 12° alc. **Rating** 87 **To** 2012 $13

Point Leo Road Vineyard

214 Point Leo Road, Red Hill South, Vic 3937 **Region** Mornington Peninsula
T 0406 610 815 **F** (03) 9882 0327 **www**.pointleoroad.com.au **Open** By appt
Winemaker Phillip Kittle, Andrew Thomson, David Cowburn, Anthony Miceli **Est.** 1996
Cases 1000
John Law and family planted 2 ha of pinot noir and 1.6 ha of chardonnay in 1996 as contract growers for several leading Mornington Peninsula wineries. They subsequently planted 1 ha of pinot gris and 0.6 ha of lagrein. These have in turn been followed by 1.4 ha of gewurztraminer and sauvignon blanc, lifting total plantings to 6.6 ha, although the latest additions will not come into bearing until 2008. They have decided to have part of the grapes contract-made, and now have 2 labels: Point Leo Road for premium wines, Point Break is the second label.

ŸŸŸŸŸ **Mornington Peninsula Pinot Noir 2005** Clear but deeper colour than the Point Break Pinot; complex but highly focused and pure pinot noir flavours; black cherry and a touch of plum; excellent development potential. Screwcap. 13.5° alc. **Rating** 94 **To** 2013 $29

ŸŸŸŸŸ **Point Break Mornington Peninsula Chardonnay 2005** Medium-bodied; typical Mornington Peninsula creamy overlay to stone fruit, citrus and melon; minimal oak. Screwcap. 13.5° alc. **Rating** 90 **To** 2012 $16

ŸŸŸŸ **Point Break Mornington Peninsula Pinot Noir 2005** Brilliantly clear and bright colour; a firm, simple, one-dimensional pinot best enjoyed young. Screwcap. 13.5° alc. **Rating** 87 **To** 2010 $19

Pokolbin Estate

McDonalds Road, Pokolbin, NSW 2321 **Region** Lower Hunter Valley
T (02) 4998 7524 **F** (02) 4998 7765 **www**.pokolbinestate.com.au **Open** 7 days 10–6
Winemaker Andrew Thomas (Contract) **Est.** 1980 **Cases** 2500
If you go to the lengths that Pokolbin Estate has done to hide its light under a bushel, you end up with something like 7 vintages of Semillon, 6 of Riesling, 7 of Shiraz, 3 of Tempranillo, 2 each of Nebbiolo and Sangiovese and sundry other wines adding up to more than 30 in total. Between 1998 and 2000 Neil McGuigan and Gary Reid shared the winemaking tasks; since 2001 Andrew Thomas has skilfully made the wines from vineyards over 25 years old.

ŸŸŸŸŸ **Ken Bray Semillon 2006** Bright green-straw; a lovely wine, with intense varietal fruit, already mouthfilling but not the least coarse or heavy. Screwcap. 11° alc. **Rating** 94 **To** 2020 $20

ŸŸŸŸŸ **Hunter Valley Shiraz 2005** A vibrant palate with black cherry/blackberry fruit and a twist of earthy spice; good acidity. Hard to resist at the price. Screwcap. 14.7° alc. **Rating** 92 **To** 2018 $25

Reserve Hunter Valley Shiraz 2005 Firm, powerful and focused; excellent length and potential, even if, as yet, a little oaky. Screwcap. 14.5° alc. **Rating** 90 **To** 2017 $80

Reserve Hunter Valley Shiraz 2004 Has developed earthy regional characteristics around a sweet fruit core. However, has years in front of it if you wish to cellar it. Cork. 14° alc. **Rating** 90 **To** 2010 $48

Belebula Hunter Valley Nebbiolo 2005 Similar colour to the Sangiovese, outstanding for the variety in Australia; fresh fruit aromas, the flavours far more serious in a black fruit spectrum; authority without excessive tannins; one of the best nebbiolos going. Screwcap. 13.8° alc. **Rating** 90 **To** 2014 $25

ﾖﾖﾖﾖ   **Hunter Valley Chardonnay 2006** Tangy, citrussy fruit, the oak well-integrated; good length. Screwcap. 13.4° alc. **Rating** 89 **To** 2009 $20
Belebula Hunter Valley Sangiovese 2005 Fresh colour, still with some purple tints; more varietal sour cherry fruit than many; fresh acidity; vibrant example. Screwcap. 14.3° alc. **Rating** 89 **To** 2011 $25
Belebula Hunter Valley Tempranillo 2005 Colour not entirely convincing; tangy red fruits, fresh and breezy; presumably young vines. Cork. 13.6° alc. **Rating** 87 **To** 2009 $32

Polin & Polin Wines

Mistletoe Lane, Pokolbin, NSW 2230 **Region** Upper Hunter Valley
T (02) 9969 9914 www.polinwines.com.au **Open** W'ends & public hols 11–4
Winemaker Peter Orr, Patrick Auld **Est.** 1997 **Cases** 2000
The 6-ha vineyard was established by Lexie and Michael Polin (and family) in 1997. It is not named for them, as one might expect, but to honour Peter and Thomas Polin, who migrated from Ireland in 1860, operating a general store in Coonamble. Limb of Addy has a distinctly Irish twist to it, but is in fact a hill immediately to the east of the vineyard.

ﾖﾖﾖﾖﾗ   **Limb of Addy Hunter Valley Shiraz 2003** Shows the generous fruit flavours of the '03 Hunter vintage to full advantage; black fruits, earth and spice all flow together; has many years in front of it. Screwcap. 14° alc. **Rating** 90 **To** 2015 $26

ﾖﾖﾖﾖ   **Bell's Lane Hunter Valley Verdelho 2006** A scented, aromatic bouquet which delivers on the promise in the mouth; within the confines of the variety, excellent wine. Screwcap. 13° alc. **Rating** 89 **To** 2009 $18
Hunter Valley Rose 2005 Light, clean, fresh small red fruit flavours; the main feature is the well-balanced acidity. Screwcap. 14° alc. **Rating** 87 **To** 2008 $18

Polleters   ★★★★★

80 Polleters Road, Moonambel, Vic 3478 **Region** Pyrenees
T (03) 9569 5030 www.polleters.com **Open** W'ends 10–5
Winemaker Mark Summerfield **Est.** 1994 **Cases** 1500
Pauline and Peter Bicknell purchased the 60-ha property on which their vineyard now stands in 1993, at which time it was part of a larger grazing property. The first vines were planted in 1994, and there are now 6 ha of shiraz, cabernet sauvignon, cabernet franc and merlot. In the first few years the grapes were sold, but since 2001 part of the production has been used to produce the impressively rich and powerful wines. The grapes are hand-picked, fermented in open vats with hand-plunging, and matured for 18 months in American oak.

ﾖﾖﾖﾖﾖ   **Pyrenees Cabernet Sauvignon 2005** Full purple-red; serious cabernet sauvignon, with pristine blackcurrant aromas and flavours; perfect alcohol and extract, oak likewise; fine tannins. Screwcap. 13.5° alc. **Rating** 96 **To** 2030 $25
Morgans Choice 2005 Has the same succulent, fine, lingering palate structure as the other Polleter '05 wines; a mix of all black fruits imaginable; needs time. Screwcap. 14.5° alc. **Rating** 94 **To** 2025 $25

ﾖﾖﾖﾖﾗ   **Pyrenees Merlot 2005** A complex, ultra-concentrated wine; smooth and supple, and will be very long-lived. As ever, varietal expression is muted. Screwcap. 14.5° alc. **Rating** 93 **To** 2020 $25
Moonambel Shiraz 2005 Bright purple-red; a full-bodied mix of blackberry, plum and nuances of mocha and spice; good balance and structure; simply needs time. Screwcap. 15° alc. **Rating** 92 **To** 2020 $25

Pollocksford Vineyards

Level 3, 68 Myers Street, Geelong, Vic 3221 (postal) **Region** Geelong
T 0419 888 700 **F** (03) 5229 9869 **Open** Not
Winemaker Scott Ireland **Est.** 1991 **Cases** 200

Drew Hewson and Craig Scott purchased the Pollocksford property in 1991 and planted a little under 2 ha of pinot noir, shiraz, chenin blanc and cabernet franc between 1992 and 1994. It is on the typical regional chocolate clay-loam from weathered basalt over powdery limestone, with a northerly aspect to the Barwon River, and was the site of a distinguished winery 150 years ago until phylloxera led to the compulsory removal of all vines from the Geelong district.

 # Ponda Estate ★★★★☆

150 Rhinds Road, Wallington, Vic 3221 **Region** Geelong
T (03) 5250 5300 **F** (03) 5250 5300 **Open** W'ends & public hols 10–5, or by appt
Winemaker St Regis (Peter Nicol) **Est.** 2000 **Cases** 300
Each year owners Greg Blair and Helen Gannon are joined by friends and family to help pick the grapes from the 1.4 ha of pinot noir they have planted and carefully tend, only using irrigation where absolutely necessary. They also source a small amount of chardonnay from local growers.

ΨΨΨΨΨ **Bellarine Peninsula Pinot Noir 2005** Light-bodied, but fragrant and vibrant in a spicy/savoury spectrum; good length. Screwcap. 14° alc. **Rating** 92 To 2011 $22
Bellarine Peninsula Pinot Noir 2004 An abundance of deliciously ripe plum and cherry fruit, but no hint of jamminess; needs more time to maximise the complexity, but still a very attractive price. Screwcap. 14° alc. **Rating** 91 To 2012 $18

ΨΨΨΨ **Bellarine Peninsula Chardonnay 2005** Clean, firm, fresh fruit-driven style with tangy/citrussy acidity. Screwcap. 12.5° alc. **Rating** 89 To 2010 $15
G&H Pinot Noir 2003 Big, ripe, almost licorice/spice flavours; teeters on the edge of dry red, but certainly offers plenty of flavour. **Rating** 88 To 2013

Pondalowie Vineyards ★★★★★

6 Main Street, Bridgewater-on-Loddon, Vic 3516 **Region** Bendigo
T (03) 5437 3332 **www.**pondalowie.com.au **Open** W'ends 12–5, or by appt
Winemaker Dominic Morris, Krystina Morris **Est.** 1997 **Cases** 2500
Dominic and Krystina Morris both have strong winemaking backgrounds, gained from working in Australia, Portugal and France. Dominic has worked alternate vintages in Australia and Portugal since 1995, and Krystina has also worked at St Hallett, and at Boar's Rock. They have established 5.5 ha of shiraz, 2 ha each of tempranillo and cabernet sauvignon, and a little viognier and malbec. Incidentally, the illustration on the Pondalowie label is not a piece of barbed wire, but a very abstract representation of the winery kelpie dog. Exports to the UK.

ΨΨΨΨΨ **Special Release Cabernet Sauvignon 2004** Great intensity of classic blackcurrant fruit supported by fine, ripe tannins and very good oak; overall, a silky, supple mouthfeel to a lovely wine. Screwcap. 14° alc. **Rating** 95 To 2024 $30
Shiraz Viognier 2005 Typical deep colour; blackberry, spice, licorice and the autosuggestion of apricot; a potent wine, yet retains a soft mouthfeel thanks to fine tannins and almost invisible oak. Screwcap. 14.5° alc. **Rating** 94 To 2025 $30

ΨΨΨΨΨ **Shiraz 2005** An elegant, medium-bodied wine with a multitude of flavours neatly woven into a harmonious whole. Simply delicious. Screwcap. 14.5° alc. **Rating** 93 To 2019 $25
MT Tempranillo 2006 Exceptional concentration, power and dark fruit flavours; should be very long-lived. 'MT' stands for Minya Terra, a Portuguese term roughly equivalent to terroir. Screwcap. 13.5° alc. **Rating** 93 To 2026 $24
Vineyard Blend 2005 Quite aromatic, ripe blackberry and plum offset by spicy/savoury notes on the medium-bodied palate, all 3 varieties contributing at various stages but without tripping over each other. Shiraz/Cabernet Sauvignon/Tempranillo. Screwcap. 14.5° alc. **Rating** 90 To 2012 $20

ΨΨΨΨ   **MT Tempranillo 2005** A powerful wine, with lots of black cherry fruit, together with notes of spice and sarsaparilla; entirely fruit-driven. Screwcap. 14° alc. **Rating** 89 **To** 2009 $24

Poole's Rock/Cockfighter's Ghost   ★★★★☆

De Beyers Road, Pokolbin, NSW 2321 **Region** Lower Hunter Valley
T (02) 4998 7356 **F** (02) 4998 6866 **www**.poolesrock.com.au **Open** 7 days 9.30–5
Winemaker Patrick Auld, Usher Tinkler **Est.** 1988 **Cases** NFP
Sydney merchant banker David Clarke has had a long involvement with the wine industry. The 18-ha Poole's Rock vineyard, planted purely to chardonnay, is his personal venture; it was initially bolstered by the acquisition of the larger, adjoining Simon Whitlam Vineyard. However, the purchase of the 74-ha Glen Elgin Estate, upon which the 2500-tonne former Tulloch winery is situated, takes Poole's Rock (and its associated brands, Cockfighter's Ghost and Firestick) into another dimension. Exports to the UK, the US and other major markets.

ΨΨΨΨΨ   **Cockfighter's Ghost Clare Valley Riesling 2006** Bright green-yellow, but slightly advanced; potent aromas and flavours of crushed citrus leaves, some spice and lemon zest; early-drinking style. Screwcap. 12.7° alc. **Rating** 92 **To** 2010 $22.95
Cockfighter's Ghost Hunter Valley Semillon 2006 Bright straw-green; despite the relatively high alcohol, has plenty of line and tension on the palate; lemon and lemongrass fruit, with a clean finish. Screwcap. 12° alc. **Rating** 90 **To** 2016 $17.95
Poole's Rock Hunter Valley Chardonnay 2005 Attractive white and yellow peach fruit; subtle barrel ferment inputs; unforced and well-made. Screwcap. 13.6° alc. **Rating** 90 **To** 2010 $29.99
Poole's Rock Hunter Valley Chardonnay 2003 Rich and complex; a hint of reduction not objectionable, although the peachy fruit has a slightly congested finish. Screwcap. 13.5° alc. **Rating** 90 **To** 2010 $29.95
Cockfighter's Ghost McLaren Vale Shiraz 2004 A relatively restrained style for the region; red and black fruits with a touch of chocolate, oak and tannins in balance. Screwcap. 14.5° alc. **Rating** 90 **To** 2014 $24.95
Cockfighter's Ghost Reserve Coonawarra Cabernet Sauvignon 2002 Going down the path towards full secondary flavour development; earthy, briary black fruits are accompanied by savoury tannins and integrated oak. Cork. 14.5° alc. **Rating** 90 **To** 2014 $29.95

ΨΨΨΨ   **Poole's Rock Hunter Valley Semillon 2003** Extremely light and crisp notwithstanding the higher than usual alcohol; minerally/chalky flavours and a bone-dry finish; extreme patience required. Screwcap. 12° alc. **Rating** 89 **To** 2013 $25
Cockfighter's Ghost Hunter Valley Unwooded Chardonnay 2006 Early picking pays off, investing the wine with citrussy acidity not unlike sauvignon blanc; clean finish. Screwcap. 12.5° alc. **Rating** 89 **To** 2008 $17.95
Cockfighter's Ghost Limestone Coast Merlot 2003 Soft, fine tannins provide good mouthfeel and augment the cedary oak; merlot fruit flavour is partially incidental, but is there. Cork. 14.5° alc. **Rating** 89 **To** 2012 $24.95
Poole's Rock Hunter Valley Shiraz 2002 Is slightly reductive and needed more aeration before being bottled; a savoury style, with strong Hunter earthy overtones. Does have length and regional style; may come around with age. Screwcap. 13° alc. **Rating** 88 **To** 2015 $34.95
Firestick Chardonnay 2005 Light- to medium-bodied; clean melon and stone fruit plus a hint of oak; doesn't have a great deal of drive or intensity, but is fairly priced. Screwcap. 13.6° alc. **Rating** 87 **To** 2008 $14.95
Cockfighter's Ghost Langhorne Creek Cabernet Sauvignon 2003 Savoury chocolatey/earthy/spicy notes dominate the light- to medium-bodied palate; needs more fruit focus. Screwcap. 13.7° alc. **Rating** 87 **To** 2010 $25

Pooley Wines

Cooinda Vale Vineyard, Barton Vale Road, Campania, Tas 7026 **Region** Southern Tasmania
T (03) 6260 2895 **F** (03) 6260 2895 **www**.pooleywines.com.au **Open** 7 days 10–5
Winemaker Matt Pooley, Andrew Hood (Contract) **Est.** 1985 **Cases** 2600
Three generations of the Pooley family have been involved in the development of Pooley Wines,
although the winery was previously known as Cooinda Vale. Plantings have now reached 6.4 ha
in a region which is substantially warmer and drier than most people realise. In 2003 the family
planted 1 ha of pinot noir at Richmond on a heritage property with an 1830s Georgian home
(and 28 ha in all) which will be known as the Belmont Vineyard, and will have a cellar door in
an old sandstone barn on the property.

ŶŶŶŶŶ **Coal River Riesling 2006** Lime zest aromas; has power and length, with great
persistence to the flavour line. Screwcap. 13° alc. **Rating** 91 **To** 2016 $22
Coal River Late Harvest Riesling 2006 Clean, soft, citrus flavours still
developing; needs more time, and, perhaps, a touch more acidity. Screwcap. 10.3° alc.
Rating 90 **To** 2015 $28

ŶŶŶŶ **Coal River Pinot Gris 2006** Pear and quince aromas; light- to medium-
bodied, with good length and varietal character; has elegance, not sweetness.
Screwcap. 13.3° alc. **Rating** 89 **To** 2008 $26

Poonawatta Estate

PO Box 340, Angaston, SA 5353 **Region** Eden Valley
T (08) 8564 1036 **F** (08) 8564 1036 **www**.poonawatta.com **Open** Not
Winemaker Reid Bosward, Jo Irvine, Andrew Holt **Est.** 1880 **Cases** 400
The Poonawatta Estate story is complex, stemming from 1.8 ha of shiraz planted in 1880. When
Andrew Holt's parents purchased the Poonawatta property, the vineyard had suffered decades of
neglect, and a slow process of restoration began. While that was underway, the strongest canes
available from the winter pruning of the 1880s block were slowly and progressively dug into the
stony soil of the site. It took 7 years to establish the matching 1.8 ha, and the yield is even lower
than that of the 1880s block. In 2004 Andrew and wife Michelle were greeted with the same high
yields that were obtained right across southeast Australia, and this led to declassification of part of
the production. This gave rise to a second label, Monties Block, which sits underneath The
Cuttings (from the 'new' vines planted between 1980 and 1987) and, at the top, The 1880. In 2005
a Riesling was introduced, produced from a single vineyard of 2 ha hand planted by the Holt
family in the 1970s. The 2007 drought and frosts mean there will be no riesling from that year, a
Ratafia from 2006 filling the gap.

ŶŶŶŶŶ **The Eden Riesling 2006** Aromatic lime, apple and wild herb aromas; crisp,
lively and intense lime and mineral flavours running through to a long finish.
Screwcap. 12° alc. **Rating** 95 **To** 2016 $24
The 1880 Shiraz 2005 Full-bodied, rich and luscious layers of flavour; the finish
does heat up somewhat, but it really is hard to take too much issue from the remaining 0.8 ha of vines planted in 1880. Cork. 15.5° alc. **Rating** 95 **To** 2025 $80
The Eden Riesling 2005 Amazing aromas of intense apple blossom; a fine,
crisp and delicate palate moving back into a more conventional lime and apple
spectrum. Screwcap. 11.5° alc. **Rating** 94 **To** 2015 $24
The Cuttings Shiraz 2005 Spicy black fruits run through the medium-bodied
palate; alcohol is evident, but, paradoxically, gets away with it better than The
1880. Cork. 15.5° alc. **Rating** 94 **To** 2020 $49
The 1880 Shiraz 2003 Massively powerful full-bodied style; 100% from 1880
vines in their 123rd season; is balanced, and will be long-lived, though the alcohol is
there forever. Cork. 15.5° alc. **Rating** 94 **To** 2025 $80

ŶŶŶŶŶ **Monties Block Shiraz 2004** Fragrant and quite sweet fruit; blackberry and black
cherry, with some confit characters, supple mouthfeel and tannins. Less than 300
cases made, effectively declassified from The 1880 Shiraz. Cork. 15° alc. **Rating** 90
To 2020 $29

Port Phillip Estate

261 Red Hill Road, Red Hill, Vic 3937 **Region** Mornington Peninsula
T (03) 5989 2708 **F** (03) 5989 3017 **www**.portphillip.net **Open** W'ends & public hols 11–5
Winemaker Sandro Mosele **Est.** 1987 **Cases** 4000
Established by leading Melbourne QC Jeffrey Sher, who, after some prevarication, sold the estate to Giorgio and Dianne Gjergja in 2000. The Gjergjas are rightly more than content with the quality and style of the wines; the main changes are enhanced cellar door facilities and redesigned labels. The ability of the site (enhanced, it is true, by the skills of Sandro Mosele) to produce outstanding Syrah, Pinot Noir, Chardonnay, and very good Sauvignon Blanc, is something special. Whence climate change? Quite possibly the estate may have answers for decades to come. Exports to the UK.

♟♟♟♟♟ **Rimage Tete de Cuvee Mornington Peninsula Syrah 2005** Gleaming purple-red; super-fragrant and elegant bouquet, the palate likewise; a prime example of less is more; great length, and the finest imaginable tannins. Diam. 14° alc. **Rating** 96 **To** 2025 $37
Mornington Peninsula Chardonnay 2005 Subtle, yet complex and powerful, with an interplay between citrus, stone fruit, mlf and barrel ferment influences; very good mouthfeel and balance. Diam. 14° alc. **Rating** 94 **To** 2012 $30
Mornington Peninsula Pinot Noir 2005 The deep colour is true to the estate style, as are the powerful black fruits; the tannins need time to soften, but will. Diam. 14° alc. **Rating** 94 **To** 2013 $35
Mornington Peninsula Shiraz 2005 Expected strong purple-red colour; firm and highly focused blackberry and plum fruit, the oak playing a perfectly judged support role. Cork. 14° alc. **Rating** 94 **To** 2020 $30

♟♟♟♟♟ **Mornington Peninsula Sauvignon Blanc 2006** Light straw-green; clean and fresh, with a gentle tropical/herbaceous mix; bright, dry finish. Diam. 13.5° alc. **Rating** 91 **To** 2008 $23

Portree

72 Powells Track via Mount William Road, Lancefield, Vic 3455 **Region** Macedon Ranges
T (03) 5429 1422 **www**.portreevineyard.com.au **Open** W'ends & public hols 11–5
Winemaker Ken Murchison **Est.** 1983 **Cases** 1000
Owner Ken Murchison selected his 5-ha Macedon vineyard after studying viticulture at Charles Sturt University and being strongly influenced by Dr Andrew Pirie's doctoral thesis. All the wines show distinct cool-climate characteristics, the Quarry Red having clear similarities to the wines of Chinon in the Loire Valley. However, Portree has done best with Chardonnay, its principal wine (in terms of volume). Exports to Hong Kong.

♟♟♟♟♟ **Pinot Noir 2004** Fresh red fruits on a light- to medium-bodied palate; good line and length. **Rating** 90 **To** 2010

Possums Vineyard

31 Thornber Street, Unley Park, SA 5061 (postal) **Region** McLaren Vale
T (08) 8272 3406 **F** (08) 8272 3406 **www**.possumswines.com.au **Open** Not
Winemaker Mariana Ranftl **Est.** 2000 **Cases** 8000
Possums Vineyard is owned by Dr John Possingham and Carol Summers. They have 22 ha of shiraz, 17 ha of cabernet sauvignon, 18 ha of chardonnay, 1 ha of viognier and 0.5 ha of grenache established in 2 vineyards (at Blewitt Springs and Willunga). In 2007 they completed construction of a 500-tonne winery at Blewitt Springs and will sell both bottled and bulk wine. Exports to the US, the UK and other markets.

♟♟♟♟♟ **Cabernet Sauvignon 2004** Strong, clear colour; star-bright cabernet varietal character; luxuriant cassis, blackcurrant and dark chocolate supported by fine, ripe tannins; has completely absorbed 22 months in oak; lovely wine. Cork. 14.5° alc. **Rating** 95 **To** 2024 $25

🍷🍷🍷🍷🍷 **Willunga Shiraz 2005** Elegant, light- to medium-bodied, with more spicy, cool-climate red fruit characters than normal for McLaren Vale, even Willunga. Fine, satin-smooth tannins. Cork. 14.5° alc. **Rating** 90 **To** 2012 $16

 # Poverty Hill Wines   ★★★★★

PO Box 76, Springton, SA 5235 **Region** Eden Valley
T (08) 8568 2220 **F** (08) 8568 2220 **www.**povertyhillwines.com.au **Open** Not
Winemaker Colin Forbes **Est.** 2002 **Cases** 3000

I'm not sure whether there is a slight note of irony in the name, but Poverty Hill Wines brings together 4 men who have had a long connection with the Eden Valley. Colin Forbes has been making wine there for over 30 years, establishing Craneford Wines at the end of the 1970s, though having long sold that particular business. Robert Buck owns a small vineyard on the ancient volcanic soils east of Springton, producing both shiraz and cabernet sauvignon. Next is Stuart Woodman, who owns the vineyard which has supplied Craneford Wines with the riesling which produced glorious wines in the early 1990s, and also has high-quality, mature-vine cabernet sauvignon. Finally, there is John Eckert, who worked with Colin Forbes at Saltram, and followed him to Craneford. He not only works as assistant winemaker at Poverty Hill, but manages Rob Buck's vineyard and his own small block of young riesling in the Highlands of Springton. The wheel has turned full circle, and the quality of the wines is - quite simply - inspiring.

🍷🍷🍷🍷🍷 **Cellar Matured Eden Valley Riesling 2001** Brilliant, glowing yellow-green; intense, coruscating, classic lime and toast aromas; abundant flavour on the palate, halfway to its best-by date. Buy one of each of the 3 vintages of Riesling and watch the development for yourself. Screwcap. 11.1° alc. **Rating** 95 **To** 2011 $20
Eden Valley Cabernet Sauvignon 2002 Strongly scented aromatic cassis and blackcurrant fruit, with superfine tannins running through the long and immaculately balanced palate. Screwcap. 13.9° alc. **Rating** 94 **To** 2017 $20

🍷🍷🍷🍷🍷 **Eden Valley Riesling 2006** A floral blossom bouquet followed by a delicate, crisp palate; perfect balance and length, and a bright, citrussy edge to the acidity on the finish. Buy a dozen; drink half, keep half. Screwcap. 12.5° alc. **Rating** 93 **To** 2016 $17
Eden Valley Shiraz 2004 Strong purple-red; richly robed blackberry and licorice fruit from start to finish; medium-bodied, supple and smooth, benefiting from 2 years in old oak. The alcohol comes as a surprise; it didn't show up in the tasting. Screwcap. 16° alc. **Rating** 93 **To** 2024 $25
Eden Valley Cabernet Sauvignon 2005 Abundant ripe blackcurrant and cassis fruit, the tannins and oak playing a pure support role in a generous, well-priced wine. Screwcap. 15° alc. **Rating** 93 **To** 2022 $20
Eden Valley Riesling 2004 Light straw-green; good length and focus; lots of regional lime/lemon flavours starting to move into the secondary phase; an absolute bargain. Screwcap. 12.3° alc. **Rating** 92 **To** 2013 $15
Eden Valley Shiraz 2002 Holding hue well, though not deep; the transition from the high alcohol of the '04 to the much more moderate alcohol of this wine (tasted second) came as a shock; licorice, spice and earth dominant over underlying black fruits. Screwcap. 14.1° alc. **Rating** 90 **To** 2012 $22

🍷🍷🍷🍷 **Eden Valley Merlot 2004** Medium-bodied spice, olive and cassis; I remain to be convinced that the wine needed 14 months in oak. Screwcap. 14.5° alc. **Rating** 89 **To** 2010 $20
Cabernet Sauvignon 2002 Good hue, still retaining tinges of purple; light- to medium-bodied; has elegance, though is not particularly powerful or intense, hardly surprising at the giveaway price. Screwcap. 14.3° alc. **Rating** 89 **To** 2012 $15
Eden Valley Merlot 2005 Good purple-red; merlot varietal character is evident on the bouquet, but subverted and over-sweetened by the alcohol. Screwcap. 16° alc. **Rating** 88 **To** 2011 $20

Prancing Horse Estate

39 Paringa Road, Red Hill South, Vic 3937 **Region** Mornington Peninsula
T (03) 5989 2602 **F** (03) 9827 1231 **www**.prancinghorseestate.com **Open** By appt
Winemaker Sergio Carlei, Pascal Marchand **Est.** 1990 **Cases** 600
Anthony and Catherine Hancy acquired the Lavender Bay Vineyard in early 2002, renaming it the Prancing Horse Estate, and embarking on a radical upgrade of the existing plantings of 1 ha each of chardonnay and pinot noir. They will progressively extend the plantings by 2.5 ha, planted equally to chardonnay, pinot gris and pinot noir, using selected clones. The Hancys avoid the use of pesticides, herbicides and fungicides. Having appointed Sergio Carlei as winemaker, the following year they became joint owners with Sergio in Carlei Wines. Exports to the US and France.

🍷🍷🍷🍷🍷 **Mornington Peninsula Chardonnay 2005** White peach and citrus flavours; has excellent structure, controlled oak and crisp acidity all providing balance and length. Diam. 13.5° alc. **Rating** 94 **To** 2013 $40

🍷🍷🍷🍷🍷 **Mornington Peninsula Pinot Noir 2005** Bright colour; clear, firm black cherry and plum; the mouthfeel is crisp and crunchy; overall, a suggestion the pH may have been a little on the low side. Cork. 13.5° alc. **Rating** 92 **To** 2015 $49

Preston Peak

31 Preston Peak Lane, Toowoomba, Qld 4352 **Region** Darling Downs
T (07) 4630 9499 **F** (07) 4630 9499 **www**.prestonpeak.com **Open** Wed–Sun 10–5
Winemaker Rod MacPherson **Est.** 1994 **Cases** 5000
Dentist owners Ashley Smith and Kym Thumpkin have a substantial tourism business. The large, modern cellar door can accommodate functions of up to 150 people, and is often used for weddings and other events. It is situated less than 10 mins drive from the Toowoomba city centre, with views of Table Top Mountain, the Lockyer Valley and the Darling Downs.

🍷🍷🍷🍷 **Verdelho 2005** Well-made; bright and lively fruit salad with a drizzle of lemon juice. Screwcap. 13° alc. **Rating** 87 **To** 2008 $17
Leaf Series Merlot 2003 Light- to medium-bodied herb, spice and olive varietal flavours; distinctly savoury and slightly green. Screwcap. 12.8° alc. **Rating** 87 **To** 2008 $19

Pretty Sally Estate

PO Box 549, Kilmore East, Vic 3764 **Region** Central Victoria Zone
T (03) 5783 3082 **F** (03) 5783 2027 **www**.prettysally.com **Open** Not
Winemaker Hanging Rock **Est.** 1996 **Cases** 1000
The McKay, Davies and Cornew families have joined to create the Pretty Sally business. It is based on estate plantings of 11.7 ha of shiraz, 23.8 ha of cabernet sauvignon and a splash of sauvignon blanc. The wines are chiefly exported to the US, where Pretty Sally has a permanent office.

🍷🍷🍷🍷 **Shiraz 2004** Light- to medium-bodied; a tight palate with some mint/eucalypt, then a bright, fresh finish; despite the alcohol, not entirely flavour-ripe. ProCork. 14.8° alc. **Rating** 87 **To** 2012 $24.95

Preveli Wines

Bessell Road, Rosa Brook, Margaret River, WA 6285 **Region** Margaret River
T (08) 9757 2374 **F** (08) 9757 2790 **www**.preveliwines.com.au **Open** At Prevelly
General Store, 7 days 10–8
Winemaker John Durham (Consultant), Sharna Kowalczak **Est.** 1998 **Cases** 5000
Andrew and Greg Home have turned a small business into a substantial one, with 15 ha of vineyards at Rosabrook (supplemented by contracts with local growers), and winemaking spread among a number of contract makers. The wines are of consistently impressive quality. The Prevelly General Store (owned by the Homes) is the main local outlet.

ŶŶŶŶŶ Margaret River Semillon Sauvignon Blanc 2006 Crisp, clean and long; precise flavours of citrus, gooseberry and passionfruit linger in the mouth without cloying. Multiple show awards. Screwcap. 12.1° alc. **Rating** 94 To 2009 $18.95

Margaret River Semillon Sauvignon Blanc 2005 Spotlessly clean; the semillon provides a minerally backbone to the structure, sauvignon blanc giving tropical fruit overtones to a synergistic blend. Gold medal Sheraton Wine Awards '05. Screwcap. 13° alc. **Rating** 94 To 2008 $19

Margaret River Chardonnay 2005 Intense, archetypal top-class Margaret River chardonnay; crystal clear varietal character, with the usual Margaret River depth; nectarine and white peach fruit, subtle oak and good length. Screwcap. 13.6° alc. **Rating** 94 To 2014 $24.95

ŶŶŶŶŶ Margaret River Merlot 2003 A distinctive varietal example; spicy, savoury black olive fruit which is in no sense bitter or green. Screwcap. 13.7° alc. **Rating** 93 To 2011 $23.95

Margaret River Sauvignon Blanc 2005 Pale green-straw; a clean bouquet; notwithstanding the alcohol, good overall delicacy and balance to the gooseberry fruits and fresh finish. Screwcap. 13° alc. **Rating** 90 To 2008 $19

Margaret River Pinot Noir 2006 Very impressive for the region, following in the footsteps of the '03; good texture and mouthfeel of red fruits and touches of spice; possibly picked before the rain. Screwcap. 13.9° alc. **Rating** 90 To 2011 $25.95

ŶŶŶŶ Margaret River Merlot 2002 Similar to the '03, with very clear varietal character, but not the same degree of ripeness. Screwcap. 13.5° alc. **Rating** 89 To 2008 $25.95

Margaret River Cabernet Merlot 2004 Light- to medium-bodied; a supple mix of red fruits and forest/black olive notes; thins out fractionally on the finish. Screwcap. 14° alc. **Rating** 89 To 2012 $21.95

Margaret River Cabernet Sauvignon 2003 Once again, a precise varietal expression with cassis and blackcurrant fruit supported by the finest imaginable tannins, its Achilles heel being the minty/green tannins reflected by the alcohol. Screwcap. 12.8° alc. **Rating** 89 To 2010 $25.95

Margaret River Shiraz 2004 Light-bodied; quite elegant and well-balanced but nowhere near enough weight or vinosity. Screwcap. 14° alc. **Rating** 87 To 2010 $24.95

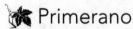

Primerano ★★★☆

480 Upper King River Road, Cheshunt, Vic 3678 **Region** King Valley
T (03) 5729 8367 **F** (03) 5729 8367 **www**.primerano.com.au **Open** 7 days 10–5
Winemaker Warren Proft (Contract) **Est.** 1995 **Cases** 500
The Primerano vineyard was established by Antonio and Caterina Primerano with a background of winemaking in Antonio's birthplace of Monsoreto, in Calabria, Italy. They now have 10 ha of vines, with 4 ha of merlot, 1.5 ha each of sauvignon blanc, pinot grigio and cabernet sauvignon, and 0.75 ha each of shiraz and chardonnay.

ŶŶŶŶŶ King Valley Chardonnay 2003 Light straw-green; intense stone fruit and citrus; a long, lingering finish; very impressive at 4 years old. A radical contrast to the oxidised '02 with a twin top cork. Screwcap. 13.1° alc. **Rating** 91 To 2010

Primo Estate

Old Port Wakefield Road, Virginia, SA 5120 **Region** Adelaide Plains
T (08) 8380 9442 **F** (08) 8380 9696 **www**.primoestate.com.au **Open** June–Aug
Mon–Sat 10–4, Sept–May Mon–Fri 10–4
Winemaker Joseph Grilli **Est.** 1979 **Cases** 25 000
Roseworthy dux Joe Grilli has risen way above the constraints of the hot Adelaide Plains to produce innovative and always excellent wines. The biennial release of the Joseph Sparkling Red

(in its tall Italian glass bottle) is eagerly awaited, the wine immediately selling out. Also unusual and highly regarded are the vintage-dated extra virgin olive oils. However, the core lies with the La Biondina (Colombard), the Il Briccone Shiraz Sangiovese and the Joseph Cabernet Merlot. The business has expanded to take in both McLaren Vale and Clarendon, with 36.3 ha of cabernet sauvignon, colombard, shiraz, merlot, riesling, nebbiolo, sangiovese, riesling, sauvignon blanc and pinot grigio. Exports to all major markets.

ŢŢŢŢŢ **Joseph Pinot Grigio d'Elena 2006** Has much more fruit character than most pinot gris, notes of blossom and honeysuckle; a clean, long finish and good balance. As good as they come. Screwcap. 13° alc. **Rating** 94 **To** 2008 $28

ŢŢŢŢŢ **La Biondina Colombard Sauvignon Blanc 2006** Light straw-green; a tight structure with mineral, herb and lemon, then a chalky, bone-dry finish. The annual summer seafood drink. Screwcap. 12° alc. **Rating** 90 **To** 2008 $15

ŢŢŢŢ **Joseph Angel Gully Shiraz 2004** Good hue; a medium-bodied, quite savoury/earthy style; long finish. Cork. 15° alc. **Rating** 89 **To** 2011 $45
Il Briccone Shiraz Sangiovese 2004 While light- to medium-bodied, is very savoury; tobacco, cherry and earth flavours with ripe but pronounced dusty tannins. Screwcap. 14° alc. **Rating** 89 **To** 2010 $21
Merlot Merlesco 2006 Vibrant colour; light- to medium-bodied, with an uncompromising blend of herb, black olive and red berry fruit; deliberately early-picked for early consumption. Screwcap. 13° alc. **Rating** 88 **To** 2008 $15
Merlot Merlesco 2005 Light- to medium-bodied, with a fresh and lively interesting mix of red fruits, spice and black olive. Screwcap. 13° alc. **Rating** 87 **To** 2008 $15

Prince Albert ★★★

100 Lemins Road, Waurn Ponds, Vic 3216 **Region** Geelong
T (03) 5241 8091 **F** (03) 5241 8091 **Open** By appt
Winemaker Bruce Hyett **Est.** 1975 **Cases** 300
Australia's true pinot noir specialist (it has only ever made the one wine), which also made much of the early running with the variety: the wines always show good varietal character and have rebounded after a dull patch in the second half of the 1980s. In 1998 the vineyard and winery were certified organic by OVAA Inc. Apart from the mailing list, the wine is sold through fine wine retailers in Sydney and Melbourne, with a little finding its way to the UK. At the age of 83, and suffering ill health, Bruce Hyett has put Prince Albert on the market.

Prince of Orange ★★★

'Cimbria', The Escort Way, Borenore, NSW 2800 **Region** Orange
T (02) 6365 2396 **F** (02) 6365 2396 **www**.princeoforangewines.com.au **Open** Sat & long w'ends 10–5, or by appt
Winemaker Monarch Winemaking Services **Est.** 1996 **Cases** 3000
Harald and Coral Brodersen purchased the 40-ha Cimbria property in 1990, and planted 3 ha of sauvignon blanc and 2 ha of cabernet sauvignon in 1996, followed by more recent and smaller plantings of merlot, viognier, shiraz and semillon. The name and label design were inspired by the link between Thomas Livingstone Mitchell, Surveyor-General of NSW, who served in the British Army during the Peninsular Wars against Napoleon alongside Willem, Prince of Orange, who was aide-de-camp to the Duke of Wellington. It was Mitchell who named the town Orange in honour of his friend, who had by then been crowned King Willem II of The Netherlands.

ŢŢŢŢ **Blend 1813 2005** An attractive mix of red and black fruits supported by fine-grained tannins. Screwcap. 14° alc. **Rating** 89 **To** 2012 $23

Principia ★★★★☆

139 Main Creek Road, Red Hill, Vic 3937 (postal) **Region** Mornington Peninsula
T (03) 5931 0010 **www**.principiawines.com.au **Open** Not
Winemaker Rebecca Gaffy **Est.** 1995 **Cases** 400

Darren and Rebecca Gaffy spent their honeymoon in SA, and awakened their love of wines. In due course they gravitated to Burgundy, and began the search in Australia for a suitable cool-climate site to grow pinot noir and chardonnay. In 1995 they began to develop their vineyard, with 2.6 ha of pinot noir, and 0.8 ha of chardonnay. Darren continues to work full-time as a toolmaker (and in the vineyard on weekends and holidays), while Rebecca's career as a nurse took second place to the Bachelor of Applied Science (Wine Science) course at Charles Sturt University. She graduated in 2002. Along the way she worked at Red Hill Estate, Bass Phillip, Virgin Hills and Tuck's Ridge, and as winemaker at Massoni Homes. A cellar door is planned.

ΨΨΨΨΨ **Mornington Peninsula Chardonnay 2005** Light straw-green; super-intense, with beautiful line and length; grapefruit, nectarine and French oak are seamlessly woven. Diam. 14° alc. **Rating** 96 To 2013 $29

ΨΨΨΨΨ **Mornington Peninsula Pinot Noir 2005** Not entirely bright or clear colour; very spicy/savoury/foresty aromas, flavours running down the same track; in a particular style, the fruit needing a little more protection. Diam. 13.5° alc. **Rating** 91 To 2009 $35

Printhie Wines

Yuranigh Road, Molong, NSW 2866 **Region** Orange
T (02) 6366 8422 **F** (02) 6366 9328 **www**.printhiewines.com.au **Open** Mon–Sat 10–4
Winemaker Robert Black **Est.** 1996 **Cases** 16 000
Jim and Ruth Swift have planted 33 ha of viognier, cabernet sauvignon, merlot and shiraz, and built the largest winery in the region. As well as making the Printhie wines, full-time winemaker Robert Black oversees contract winemaking for others. Adding further weight, Printhie supplements the estate-grown grapes with grapes purchased from growers in the region. The wines are modestly priced, and will gain weight as the vines age. Exports to the US and Fiji.

ΨΨΨΨΨ **Swift Family Heritage Orange Cabernet Shiraz 2004** A very elegant and supple wine; attractive red and black fruits run through the length of the palate; finishes with fine, ripe tannins and quality oak. Screwcap. 13.7° alc. **Rating** 94 To 2019 $32

ΨΨΨΨΨ **Orange Cabernet Sauvignon 2004** Medium- to full-bodied; good varietal expression from abundant blackcurrant and earth fruit; positive oak management, and good tannins. Screwcap. 14.1° alc. **Rating** 93 To 2019 $32
Orange Shiraz Viognier 2005 Light- to medium-bodied; a complex mix of aromatic fruit, positive oak and a touch of spice; good mouthfeel and walletfeel. Screwcap. 13.3° alc. **Rating** 92 To 2014 $15
Orange Pinot Noir 2006 Light, crystal-clear red-purple; fresh red cherry and strawberry flavours; entirely fruit-driven, but a delicious summer lunch red. Screwcap. 14° alc. **Rating** 90 To 2009 $15
Orange Shiraz 2005 Bright purple-red; a light- to medium-bodied, fresh and lively wine with a mix of red fruits, spice and oak, albeit minimal tannins. Screwcap. 13° alc. **Rating** 90 To 2010 $15

ΨΨΨΨ **Orange Chardonnay 2006** Clean peach, fig and stone fruit flavours do the work, the oak subtle. Screwcap. 14° alc. **Rating** 88 To 2009 $15
Shiraz Cabernet 2005 Firm red and black fruits; still very tight, and needs to loosen up. Screwcap. 13.2° alc. **Rating** 87 To 2015 $15
Orange Cabernet Merlot 2005 Light- to medium-bodied; a fresh mix of leaf and olive on the one hand, and sweet red berry and spice on the other; minimal tannin and oak influence. Screwcap. 13.7° alc. **Rating** 87 To 2010 $15
Cabernet Shiraz 2005 A medium-bodied mix of minty and riper fruit flavours; fair length. Screwcap. 13° alc. **Rating** 87 To 2014 $15

Provenance Wines

870 Steiglitz Road, Sutherlands Creek, Vic 3331 **Region** Geelong
T (03) 5281 2230 **F** (03) 5281 2205 **www**.provenancewines.com.au **Open** By appt
Winemaker Scott Ireland, Kirilly Gordon **Est.** 1995 **Cases** 3000
A joint venture between Scott Ireland and Pam and Richard Austin of Austin's Wines has resulted
in a new winery being built on land owned by the Austins at Sutherlands Creek, and leased to
winemaker Scott Ireland. Here he makes the Provenance wines, Austin's wines and provides
contract winemaking services for small companies in the region. Naturally, the Provenance brand
is closest to the hearts, minds and hands of winemakers Scott Ireland and Kirilly Gordon. Exports
to the UK.

ΨΨΨΨΨ **Geelong Chardonnay 2005** Still very youthful, fresh and elegant; gentle
stone fruit, with citrussy acidity on a long finish, the oak seamlessly integrated.
Radically different style to the '04. Screwcap. 13.9° alc. **Rating** 94 **To** 2013 $27

ΨΨΨΨΨ **Kismet Pinot Noir 2005** Light-bodied, elegant, spicy/savoury style; has length
and finesse. Screwcap. 13.5° alc. **Rating** 91 **To** 2011 $14.95
Geelong Pinot Noir 2005 Light- to medium-bodied; a clean bouquet, with
good varietal aroma and flavour throughout; good length, nice savoury tannins.
Screwcap. 13.5° alc. **Rating** 90 **To** 2012 $32
Geelong Shiraz 2004 Powerful black fruits, with a touch of bitter chocolate;
needing time to build fluency, but will get there. Screwcap. 13.9° alc. **Rating** 90
To 2015 $32

ΨΨΨΨ **Pinot Gris 2006** Some pear drop and musk varietal character; the balance is
good, not too sweet, and not too much flavour. The price parity with the
Chardonnay is little short of bizarre, but should please the bank manager.
Screwcap. 13.9° alc. **Rating** 88 **To** 2008 $27

Providence Vineyards ★★★★★

236 Lalla Road, Lalla, Tas 7267 **Region** Northern Tasmania
T (03) 6395 1290 **F** (03) 6395 2088 **www**.providence.com.au **Open** 7 days 10–5
Winemaker Hood Wines (Andrew Hood, Alain Rousseau), Riverview Wines (Guy
Wagner) **Est.** 1956 **Cases** 1000
Providence incorporates the pioneer vineyard of Frenchman Jean Miguet, now owned by the
Bryce family, who purchased it in 1980. The original 1.3-ha vineyard has been expanded to a little
over 3 ha, and unsuitable grenache and cabernet (left from the original plantings) have been
grafted over to chardonnay, pinot noir and semillon. Miguet called the vineyard 'La Provence',
reminding him of the part of France he came from, but after 40 years the French authorities
forced a name change. The cellar door offers 70 different Tasmanian wines.

ΨΨΨΨΨ **Madame Miguet Reserve Chardonnay 2005** A beautifully composed and
controlled wine; nectarine and grapefruit are interwoven with a fine skein of
quality French oak; outstanding length. In memory of Madame Cecile Miguet
who died in '05, just weeks short of her century. Top gold Tas Wine Show '06.
Screwcap. 14° alc. **Rating** 96 **To** 2025 $28
Miguet Reserve Chardonnay 2004 Did not show its true quality in the Tas
Wine Show '06, but certainly did in '07, lively and fresh, with perfect balance
and length. Screwcap. 13.3° alc. **Rating** 95 **To** 2010 $26

ΨΨΨΨΨ **Miguet Reserve Pinot Noir 2005** Significantly more colour than the '04
varietal; pure, pristine and understated, but beautifully poised; reminiscent of
Burgundy a la Armand Rousseau. Disappointing in the Tas Wine Show '07,
not sure why. Screwcap. 13.7° alc. **Rating** 90 **To** 2008 $36

Puddleduck Vineyard ★★★★☆

992 Richmond Road, Richmond, Tas 7024 **Region** Southern Tasmania
T (03) 6260 2301 **F** (03) 6260 2301 **www**.puddleduckvineyard.com.au **Open** 7 days 10–5
Winemaker Hood Wines (Andrew Hood) **Est.** 1997 **Cases** 1000

Puddleduck Vineyard is owned and run by Darren and Jackie Brown. Darren's career began at Moorilla Estate, mowing lawns (aged 16), eventually ending up as assistant winemaker to Julian Alcorso. With the changing of the guard at Moorilla Darren left to become vineyard manager of both Craigow and 572 Richmond Road in the Coal Valley. Jackie moved to Craigow when its cellar door opened, then worked in the restaurant and cellar door at Coal Valley Vineyard (formerly Treehouse). In the meantime, they had purchased a house with a block of land suitable for viticulture. So far, they have planted 1 ha of pinot noir, 0.5 ha of riesling, 0.3 ha chardonnay and sauvignon blanc; they are sourcing grapes from other vineyards in the region (particularly those managed by Darren) until they have sufficient vineyards of their own.

ŸŸŸŸŸ **Rose 2006** Bright pink; good balance, and not too sweet; keeps the focus firmly on the pinot noir origin. Lovely rose. Gold medal Tas Wine Show '07. Screwcap. 14.4° alc. **Rating** 94 **To** 2008 $22

ŸŸŸŸŸ **Chardonnay 2006** A complex wine, with lots of barrel ferment inputs; the fruit is there to carry the winemaker's fingerprints. Screwcap. 14.3° alc. **Rating** 93 **To** 2011 $28

ŸŸŸŸ **Riesling 2006** Clean, pure and classic; has balance, line and length, finishing with citrussy acidity. Screwcap. 12.8° alc. **Rating** 89 **To** 2012 $26
Sauvignon Blanc 2006 A gentle tropical entry to the mouth, then traces of herb and cut grass on the finish take it a little too far on the green side. Screwcap. 12.7° alc. **Rating** 88 **To** 2008 $26

Punch ★★★★★

2130 Kinglake Road, St Andrews, Vic 3761 (postal) **Region** Yarra Valley
T (03) 9710 1155 **F** (03) 9710 1369 **www**.punched.com.au **Open** Not
Winemaker James Lance **Est.** 2004 **Cases** 335
In the wake of Graeme Rathbone taking over the brand (but not the real estate) of Diamond Valley, the Lances' son James and wife Claire leased the vineyard and winery from David and Catherine Lance including the 0.25-ha block of close-planted pinot noir. In all Punch has 2.25 ha of pinot noir (including the close planted), 0.8 ha of chardonnay and 0.4 ha of cabernet sauvignon. To have all 4 wines rated outstanding is an exceptional achievement.

ŸŸŸŸŸ **Yarra Valley Close Planted Pinot Noir 2005** Slightly denser colour and more purple than the standard Pinot; flows and fills the mouth with perfect varietal character; has an extra dimension of structure. Screwcap. 14° alc. **Rating** 97 **To** 2017 $50
Yarra Valley Pinot Noir 2005 Excellent pinot varietal flavour from the first moment to the last; silky mouthfeel with flavours of satsuma plum and spice; long, lingering finish. Screwcap. 14° alc. **Rating** 97 **To** 2012 $80
Yarra Valley Chardonnay 2005 Bright yellow-green; superfine, intense and elegant aromas and flavours; melon and grapefruit subtly interwoven with barrel ferment oak; extra length. Screwcap. 14° alc. **Rating** 95 **To** 2018 $40
Yarra Valley Cabernet Sauvignon 2005 A fragrant bouquet flows into the very pure cassis and blackcurrant fruit on the palate; perfect poise and ripeness. Screwcap. 14° alc. **Rating** 94 **To** 2025 $40

Punt Road ★★★★☆

10 St Huberts Road, Coldstream, Vic 3770 **Region** Yarra Valley
T (03) 9739 0666 **F** (03) 9739 0633 **www**.puntroadwines.com.au **Open** 7 days 10–5
Winemaker Kate Goodman **Est.** 2000 **Cases** 12 000
Punt Road was originally known as The Yarra Hill, a name abandoned because of the proliferation of wineries with the word 'Yarra' as part of their name. The wines are made from the best parcels of fruit grown on 100 ha of vineyards owned by members of the Punt Road syndicate, and represent the tip of the iceberg. The winery produces the Punt Road wines, as well as undertaking substantial contract winemaking for others. Exports to the US and other major markets.

ioio Yarra Valley Cabernet Sauvignon 2004 Medium-bodied; shows very pure cabernet varietal fruit in a conventional cassis/blackcurrant spectrum; fine tannins and gentle French oak. Screwcap. 13.5° alc. **Rating** 92 **To** 2024 $25

Yarra Valley Sauvignon Blanc 2006 Clean, minerally aromas; has good intensity, though quite restrained in varietal fruit expression; good length. Screwcap. 12° alc. **Rating** 91 **To** 2010 $20

Yarra Valley Chardonnay 2005 Light- to medium-bodied; a fruit-driven style the oak adding more to structure than flavour; gentle stone fruit and melon; dry finish. Screwcap. 13.5° alc. **Rating** 90 **To** 2010 $22

Yarra Valley Pinot Gris 2006 Clear varietal character courtesy of pear, musk and honeysuckle aromas and flavours; good length and balance, and not obviously sweet. Screwcap. 13.5° alc. **Rating** 90 **To** 2008 $20

Yarra Valley Pinot Noir 2005 A relatively subdued bouquet; plum and spice fruit, scoring for its considerable length and persistence of flavour. Screwcap. 13° alc. **Rating** 90 **To** 2011 $25

Yarra Valley Shiraz 2004 Medium purple-red; a medium-bodied, appealing mix of spice, pepper, black cherry and licorice; good length. Screwcap. 13.5° alc. **Rating** 90 **To** 2014 $25

Little Rebel Cabernet Merlot 2004 Good purple-red; medium-bodied, with attractive redcurrant and blackcurrant fruit supported by ripe tannins. Enticing price. Screwcap. 13.5° alc. **Rating** 90 **To** 2014 $16

Botrytis Semillon 2005 Soft cumquat, tropical and peach flavours, the oak subliminal. Single vineyard/Riverland. Diam. 11.5° alc. **Rating** 90 **To** 2008 $30

ioi **Little Rebel Pinot Noir 2005** Clear-cut varietal character, albeit in a light to medium-bodied frame; spice, black cherry and plum together with some forest floor, savoury notes. Screwcap. 13.5° alc. **Rating** 88 **To** 2008 $16

Little Rebel Chardonnay 2005 Light straw-green; light-bodied melon and ripe apple fruit; minimal oak influence. Screwcap. 13.5° alc. **Rating** 87 **To** 2008 $16

Punters Corner

Cnr Riddoch Highway/Racecourse Road, Coonawarra, SA 5263 **Region** Coonawarra **T** (08) 8737 2007 **F** (08) 8737 3138 **www.**punterscorner.com.au **Open** 7 days 10–5 **Winemaker** Balnaves (Pete Bissell) **Est.** 1988 **Cases** 8000

Punters Corner started off life in 1975 as James Haselgrove, but in 1992 was acquired by a group of investors who evidently had few delusions about the uncertainties of viticulture and wine making, even in a district as distinguished as Coonawarra. The arrival of Pete Bissell as winemaker at Balnaves paid immediate (and continuing) dividends. Sophisticated packaging and label design add to the appeal of the wines. Exports to the UK, the US, Canada, China, Hong Kong, Singapore and Malaysia.

ioioi **Sovereign Reserve Cabernet Sauvignon 2004** Strong, deep colour; considerably more texture, structure and concentration than the standard varietal version; a very long palate built around blackcurrant fruit and balance tannins. A triumph for the vintage. The first reserve release from Punters Corner. ProCork. 14.5° alc. **Rating** 96 **To** 2026 $59.50

Coonawarra Shiraz 2004 Excellent varietal character and mouthfeel; spice, licorice and blackberry fruit; very good tannin structure; a favourite at long odds. Screwcap. 14.5° alc. **Rating** 95 **To** 2019 $20

Single Vineyard Coonawarra Chardonnay 2005 Pale straw-green; sophisticated winemaking, the complex barrel ferment and maturation not compromising the dominance of the chardonnay varietal fruit; has good length and intensity. ProCork. 13.5° alc. **Rating** 94 **To** 2012 $26

Coonawarra Cabernet Sauvignon 2004 Lots of juicy black fruit flavours; good balance and length provided by tannin and oak support. ProCork. 14.5° alc. **Rating** 94 **To** 2021 $30

ŶŶŶŶŶ **Triple Crown 2004** Strong hue; powerful line and structure to the dark fruit flavours, with a briary/savoury undertaste; not quite the same silky smoothness of most Punters Corner wines. Cabernet Sauvignon/Shiraz/Merlot. Screwcap. 14.5° alc. **Rating** 91 **To** 2019 $24

Purple Hen Wines   ★★★☆

96 McFees Road, Rhyll, Vic 3923 **Region** Gippsland
T (03) 5956 9244 **F** (03) 5956 9234 **www**.purplehenwines.com.au **Open** Fri–Mon 11–5.30
Winemaker Marcus Satchell **Est.** 2002 **Cases** 1500
This is the family-owned business of Rick Lacey and wife Maira Vitols. They purchased the property, situated on a small peninsula that is part of Phillip Island, in 2001, and planted the first 2 ha of vines in 2002. Subsequent plantings have increased the area to 4.7 ha of pinot noir, chardonnay, cabernet sauvignon, merlot, shiraz, sauvignon blanc and viognier. Rick Lacey had a horticultural background, and his professional life prior to Purple Hen was as an agricultural economist; he is completing degrees in wine science and viticulture at Charles Sturt University.

ŶŶŶŶ **Gippsland Chardonnay 2006** Obvious barrel ferment characters on the bouquet, but the fruit comes through on the well-balanced and integrated palate. **Rating** 89 **To** 2010 $24

Gippsland Pinot Noir 2005 Very briary, stemmy style, but with considerable length; needed just a touch more sweet pinot fruit. **Rating** 89 **To** 2012 $26

Gippsland Sauvignon Blanc 2006 Crisp, clean, mineral-accented, with some grass and asparagus characters; long finish. Screwcap. 13° alc. **Rating** 88 **To** 2008 $20

Gippsland Shiraz 2006 Medium weight; good varietal expression, still building complexity. **Rating** 87 **To** 2011 $26

Pycnantha Hill Estate   ★★★★

Benbournie Road, Clare, SA 5453 (postal) **Region** Clare Valley
T (08) 8842 2137 **F** (08) 8842 2137 **www**.pycnanthahill.com.au **Open** Not
Winemaker Jim Howarth **Est.** 1997 **Cases** 800
The Howarth family progressively established 2.4 ha of vineyard from 1987, and made its first commercial vintage in 1997. *Acacia pycnantha* is the botanic name for the golden wattle which grows wild over the hills of the Howarth farm, and they say it was 'a natural choice to name our vineyards Pycnantha Hill'. I am not too sure that marketing gurus would agree, but there we go.

ŶŶŶŶŶ **Clare Valley Riesling 2006** Fresh and clean; moderately intense citrus and lime; not as focused and powerful as the best from the region, but a nice wine nonetheless. Screwcap. 12.5° alc. **Rating** 90 **To** 2012 $16
Clare Valley Chardonnay 2005 The reverse of the riesling, with more focus and intensity than many Clare Valley chardonnays; nectarine and melon have been subjected to neatly judged barrel fermentation and oak maturation. Vine age may have something to do with it. Screwcap. 13.5° alc. **Rating** 90 **To** 2010 $18

ŶŶŶŶ **Clare Valley Cabernet Merlot 2005** A big, solid slightly rustic wine; full flavour despite the restrained alcohol; black fruits, olive, earth and a touch of mint. Screwcap. 13.8° alc. **Rating** 89 **To** 2013 $18

Pyramid Gold   NR

Cnr Mologa Road/Durham Ox Road, Yarrawalla South, Vic 3575 **Region** Bendigo
T (03) 5455 7337 **Open** By appt
Winemaker Robert Zagar **Est.** 2000 **Cases** NA
The 7.7-ha vineyard (6.3 ha of shiraz and 0.7 ha each of mourvedre and brown muscat) was planted in 2000, conceived by Michael and Mia Ponjican. Both the Shiraz and Mataro (as it is labelled) are worthy wines.

Pyramid Hill Wines

194 Martindale Road, Denman, NSW 2328 **Region** Upper Hunter Valley
T (02) 6547 2755 **F** (02) 6547 2735 **www**.pyramidhillwines.com **Open** 7 days 10–5
Winemaker First Creek Winemaking Services **Est.** 2002 **Cases** 5000

Pyramid Hill is a partnership between the Adler and Hilder families. Richard Hilder is a veteran viticulturist who oversaw the establishment of many of the Rosemount vineyards. Nicholas Adler and Caroline Sherwood made their mark in the international film industry before moving to Pyramid Hill in 1997. There are now 72 ha of chardonnay, semillon, verdelho, shiraz, merlot, cabernet sauvignon and ruby cabernet, with a computer-controlled irrigation system backed up by a network of radio-linked weather and soil moisture sensors which constantly relay data detailing the amount of available moisture at different soil depths to a central computer, thus avoiding excess irrigation and preventing stress. Most of the grapes are sold, but a small amount has been vinified, with cautious expansion planned. Exports to the UK, Canada, Japan and Singapore.

ꭞꭞꭞꭞꭞ **Semillon 2005** The extra squeeze of lemon juice so typical of the '05 vintage; excellent balance and length; developing surely. Gold medals no surprise. Screwcap. 11° alc. **Rating** 94 **To** 2015 $17

ꭞꭞꭞꭞ **Chardonnay 2005** Bright straw-green; light-bodied, elegant melon, fig and apple; balanced and integrated oak. Screwcap. 13.5° alc. **Rating** 89 **To** 2008 $20
Shiraz 2004 Light- to medium-bodied, with a gently earthy regional overlay; good texture and mouthfeel to savoury fruit characters; controlled oak and tannins. Cork. 13° alc. **Rating** 89 **To** 2010 $22
Hunter Valley Merlot 2005 Bright, light red; brisk, fresh small berry red fruits in a correct varietal spectrum; minimal tannins and oak. Cork. 13.5° alc. **Rating** 89 **To** 2012 $22
Hunter Valley Verdelho 2006 Has more flavour and presence than most of the verdelho nonentities; fruit salad and nice lemony acidity. Screwcap. 13.5° alc. **Rating** 87 **To** 2008 $17
Hunter Valley Verdelho 2005 Pleasant fruit salad flavours; has some length and a clean finish. Screwcap. 13° alc. **Rating** 87 **To** 2008 $17
Hunter Valley Merlot 2004 Light- to medium red-purple; earth, olive, leaf, spice and bramble varietal character; the sweetness on the finish is distracting. Cork. 13° alc. **Rating** 87 **To** 2008 $22

Pyramids Road Wines   **NR**

Pyramids Road, Wyberba via Ballandean, Qld 4382 **Region** Granite Belt
T (07) 4684 5151 **F** (07) 4684 5151 **www**.pyramidsroad.com.au **Open** Thurs–Mon, school & public hols 10–4.30
Winemaker Warren Smith **Est.** 1999 **Cases** NA

Pyren Vineyard

22 Errard Street North, Ballarat, Vic 3350 (postal) **Region** Pyrenees
T (03) 5467 2352 **F** (03) 5021 0804 **www**.pyrenvineyard.com **Open** Not
Winemaker Mount Avoca Winery, Pyrenees Ridge **Est.** 1999 **Cases** 3000

This is a substantial venture. Martin and Kevyn Joy have planted 25 ha of shiraz, 3 ha each of cabernet sauvignon and viognier, 1 ha of durif and 2 ha comprising cabernet franc, malbec and petit verdot on the slopes of the Warrenmang Valley near Moonambel. The initial releases in 2005 were of Shiraz, a Cabernet blend followed in 2006, and Durif and Viognier will follow in the future as the vines mature. Yield is restricted to between 1.5 and 2.5 tonnes per acre.

ꭞꭞꭞꭞꭞ **Broken Quartz Pyrenees Shiraz 2005** Slightly deeper colour than Block E; more spicy/savoury/earthy aspects to both bouquet and palate; despite its lower alcohol and price, is better balanced, with sweeter tannins. Screwcap. 13.5° alc. **Rating** 91 **To** 2020 $16

Block E Pyrenees Shiraz 2005 Good hue; a bright and brisk array of red fruits and spicy notes; charry oak largely irrelevant. Twin top. 13.7° alc. **Rating** 90 **To** 2013 $26

Pyrenees Ridge ★★★★★

532 Caralulup Road, Lamplough via Avoca, Vic 3467 **Region** Pyrenees
T (03) 5465 3710 **www.**pyreneesridge.com.au **Open** Thurs–Mon & public hols 10–5
Winemaker Graeme Jukes **Est.** 1998 **Cases** 2500
Notwithstanding the quite extensive winemaking experience (and formal training) of Graeme Jukes, this started life as small-scale winemaking in the raw version of the French garagiste approach. Graeme and his wife, Sally-Ann, now have another 10 ha of shiraz, cabernet sauvignon and chardonnay; the grape intake is supplemented by purchases from other growers in the region. Contract winemaking for others will also be expanded. Exports to the US, Canada, Germany, Macau, China and Hong Kong.

ŸŸŸŸŸ **Reserve Shiraz 2005** Deep, impenetrable colour; masses of flavour, and does admit the textural complexity not so apparent in the varietal version, thanks to gently ripe tannins. I do wonder how the wines will compare in 10 years' time. Cork. 14.8° alc. **Rating** 94 **To** 2018 $45

ŸŸŸŸŸ **Shiraz 2005** Dense, rich, mouthfilling black fruits, dark chocolate and licorice; despite its density, not extractive or tannic, nor is the alcohol excessive. Nonetheless, doesn't admit much light or shade. Screwcap. 14.6° alc. **Rating** 93 **To** 2018 $25
Chardonnay 2006 A clean bouquet, with quite intense melon and citrus fruit, the palate has good length and balance, the kiss of French oak is entirely appropriate. Screwcap. 14° alc. **Rating** 90 **To** 2010 $20
Ridge Red 2005 Strong colour; layer-upon-layer of blackberry, blackcurrant, plum and chocolate fruit; a blend of Shiraz (75%)/Cabernet Sauvignon (25%), the structure coming from the cabernet. The ultimate quality barbecue red. Screwcap. 14.1° alc. **Rating** 90 **To** 2020 $16

Quoin Hill Vineyard **NR**

Quoin Hill Road, Waubra, Vic 3352 **Region** Pyrenees
T (03) 5343 5365 **www.**quoinhill.com.au **Open** Mon–Fri 11–5, w'ends & public hols 10–5
Winemaker Steve Coleman **Est.** 1997 **Cases** NA
The Coleman family, headed by Steve and Trish, purchased 10 ha of volcanic soil at an elevation of 520 m on what is the southernmost extension of the Pyrenees region. They have a little over 3 ha of shiraz, chardonnay, pinot gris, tempranillo and pinot noir, the first vintage following in 2001. A chaff mill and stables built approximately 100 years ago have now been renovated and transformed into the winery and tasting rooms. The wines so far made have had consistent show success.

Racecourse Lane Wines

PO Box 215, Balgowlah, NSW 2093 **Region** Lower Hunter Valley
T 0408 242 490 **F** (02) 9949 7185 **www.**racecourselane.com.au **Open** Not
Winemaker David Fatches (Contract) **Est.** 1998 **Cases** 1000
Mike and Helen McGorman purchased their 15-ha property in 1998. They have established 5.2 ha of shiraz, sangiovese, semillon, verdelho and viognier. Consultancy viticultural advice from Brian Hubbard, and winemaking by David Fatches, a long-term Hunter Valley winemaker (who also makes wine in France each year), has paid dividends. Exports to the UK.

ŸŸŸŸ **Basket Press Hunter Valley Shiraz 2005** Earthy regional aromas followed by a firm palate; fairly brisk acidity needs to settle down, but should do so. Cork. 12.5° alc. **Rating** 87 **To** 2013

Radford Dale

RSD 355, Eden Valley, SA 5235 (postal) **Region** Eden Valley
T (08) 8565 3256 **F** (08) 8565 3244 www.radfordwines.com **Open** Not
Winemaker Ben Radford, Gillian Radford **Est.** 2003 **Cases** 900

I first met Ben Radford when he was working as a head winemaker at the Longridge/Winecorp group in Stellenbosch, South Africa. A bevy of international journalists grilled Ben, a French winemaker and a South African about the wines they were producing for the group. The others refused to admit there were any shortcomings in the wines they had made (there were), while Ben took the opposite tack, criticising his own wines even though they were clearly the best. He and Gillian Radford are now the proud owners of a 4-ha vineyard in the Eden Valley, with 1.2 ha of riesling planted in 1930, 1.1 ha planted in 1970, and 1.7 ha of shiraz planted in 2000. Ben also acts as a contract winemaker for a number of other Barossa Zone businesses. Exports to the UK, the US, Denmark, Sweden and Malaysia.

 Old Vines Eden Valley Riesling 2006 Aromatic floral blossom bouquet; great balance, line and flow to the gently ripe citrus, and an appropriately long finish. Screwcap. 12.5° alc. **Rating** 94 **To** 2016 $18

Rahona Valley Vineyard ★★★☆

PO Box 256, Red Hill South, Vic 3937 **Region** Mornington Peninsula
T (03) 5989 2924 **F** (03) 5989 2924 www.rahonavalley.com.au **Open** Not
Winemaker John Salmons, Rebecca Gaffy (Consultant) **Est.** 1991 **Cases** 200

John and Leonie Salmons have one of the older and more interesting small vineyards on the Mornington Peninsula, on a steep north-facing slope of a small valley in the Red Hill area. The area takes its name from the ancient red basalt soils. In all there are 1.2 ha of pinot noir planted to 5 different clones and a few hundred vines each of pinot meunier and pinot gris.

 Red Hill Pinot Noir 2005 Very light colour; slightly deceptive, as is the very light initial impact, but red berry flavour does come up a little on retasting, as does the length. Screwcap. 14.3° alc. **Rating** 88 **To** 2010 $26
Red Hill Pinot Rose 2006 Fresh strawberry flavours and a hint of spice, the touch of sweetness well-balanced. Screwcap. 13.7° alc. **Rating** 87 **To** 2008 $18
Red Hill Pinot Meunier 2005 Rose-pink, bright and cheerful; similar flavours and weight; this really is no more than a rose, albeit a nice one. Cork. 14.3° alc. **Rating** 87 **To** 2008 $22

Ralph Fowler Wines ★★★☆

Limestone Coast Road, Mount Benson, SA 5275 **Region** Mount Benson
T (08) 8768 5000 **F** (08) 8768 5008 www.ralphfowlerwines.com.au **Open** 7 days 10–5
Winemaker Sarah Squires **Est.** 1999 **Cases** 4000

Established in 1999 by the Fowler family, headed by well-known winemaker Ralph Fowler, with wife Deborah and children Sarah (Squires) and James all involved in the 40-ha property. Ralph Fowler began his winemaking career at Tyrrell's, moving to the position of chief winemaker before moving to Hungerford Hill, then the Hamilton/Leconfield group. In 2005 he passed on the operation of the business to Sarah. Exports to Europe and Asia.

Ramsay's Vin Rose ★★★☆

30 St Helier Road, The Gurdies, Vic 3984 **Region** Gippsland
T (03) 5997 6531 **F** (03) 5997 6158 **Open** 7 days 11–5
Winemaker Dianne Ramsay **Est.** 1995 **Cases** 400

The slightly curious name (which looks decidedly strange in conjunction with Riesling and Cabernet Sauvignon) stems from the original intention of Alan and Dianne Ramsay to grow roses on a commercial scale on their property. Frank Cutler, at Western Port Winery, persuaded them to plant wine grapes instead; they established the first 2 ha of riesling and cabernet sauvignon in 1995. They opened their micro-winery in 1999, and have 4 self-contained units set around their 800-bush rose garden.

🍷🍷🍷🍷🍷 **Cabernet Sauvignon 2004** Deep red-purple; medium- to full-bodied; has plenty of depth and concentration to the blackcurrant varietal fruit; the tannins firm and persistent but ripe. Best yet from Ramsay's. Cork. 13.5° alc. **Rating** 90 To 2019 $20

Random Valley Organic Wines   ★★★★☆

PO Box 11, Karridale, WA 6288 **Region** Margaret River
T (08) 9758 6707 **F** (08) 9758 6743 **www.**randomvalley.com **Open** Not
Winemaker Naturaliste Vintners (Bruce Dukes) **Est.** 1995 **Cases** 1000
The Little family has established 7 ha of sauvignon blanc, semillon, shiraz and cabernet sauvignon, with a no-holds-barred organic grapegrowing program. No chemical-based fertilisers, pesticides or herbicides are used in the vineyard, building humus and biological activity in the soil. Given that the 7 ha produce 50 tonnes per year, it is evident that the approach has worked well.

🍷🍷🍷🍷🍷 **Margaret River Semillon Sauvignon Blanc 2006** A seamless fusion of Semillon/Sauvignon Blanc; long and intense, without sacrificing the delicacy of the grass and citrus flavours. Screwcap. 12.4° alc. **Rating** 92 To 2010 $17.50
Margaret River Sauvignon Blanc 2006 A clean and fragrant bouquet; a crisp and clean entry to the mouth, then tropical fruit and a glimmer of sweetness on the mid to back-palate. Cork. 12.6° alc. **Rating** 90 To 2008 $18.50

Ravens Croft Wines   ★★★★

274 Spring Creek Road, Stanthorpe, Qld 4380 **Region** Granite Belt
T (07) 4683 3252 **www.**ravenscroftwines.com.au **Open** Fri–Sun 10–4, or by appt
Winemaker Mark Ravenscroft **Est.** 2002 **Cases** 500
Mark Ravenscroft was born in South Africa, and studied oenology there. He moved to Australia in the early 1990s, and in 1994 became an Australian citizen. He makes 500 cases of wine under the Ravens Croft label, with limited quantities of grapes purchased from other growers in the Granite Belt to supplement the estate-grown fruit. In addition to his winemaking for Robert Channon, he makes wines for 10 other clients.

🍷🍷🍷🍷🍷 **Chardonnay 2005** Finely crafted and fresh, with the winemaker inputs precisely balanced with the capacity of the fruit to stand up to them; stone fruit and citrus, long finish. Screwcap. 12.5° alc. **Rating** 90 To 2012 $24

🍷🍷🍷🍷 **Verdelho 2006** A delicate, fresh wine, a speciality of Ravens Croft; does have length and balance, good acidity a plus. Screwcap. 13.5° alc. **Rating** 88 To 2010 $18
Petit Verdot 2005 Powerful, full-bodied; takes no prisoners in its emphatic statement of black fruits and tannins; great barbecue wine. Screwcap. 14° alc. **Rating** 88 To 2015 $30

Ravensworth   ★★★★

312 Patemans Lane, Murrumbateman, ACT 2582 **Region** Canberra District
T (02) 6226 8368 **F** (02) 6262 2161 **www.**ravensworthwines.com.au **Open** Not
Winemaker Bryan Martin **Est.** 2000 **Cases** 1500
Winemaker, vineyard manager and partner Bryan Martin (with dual wine science and winegrowing degrees from Charles Sturt University) has a background of wine retail, food and beverage in the hospitality industry, and teaches part-time in that field. He is also assistant winemaker to Tim Kirk at Clonakilla, after 7 years at Jeir Creek. Judging at wine shows is another arrow to his bow. Ravensworth has 7 ha of vineyards spread over 2 sites: Rosehill planted in 1998 to cabernet sauvignon, merlot and sauvignon blanc, and Martin Block (planted 2000/01) to shiraz, viognier, marsanne and sangiovese.

🍷🍷🍷🍷🍷 **Canberra District Shiraz Viognier 2005** Typical bright colour; light- to medium-bodied, with vigorous plum and blackberry fruit plus that twist which viognier gives; soft tannins. Screwcap. 14° alc. **Rating** 90 To 2011 $28

Raydon Estate

Lake Plains Road, Langhorne Creek, SA 5255 **Region** Langhorne Creek
T (08) 8537 3158 **F** (08) 8537 3158 **Open** At Bremer Place, Langhorne Creek
Winemaker Wayne Dutschke (Contract) **Est.** 1999 **Cases** 1200
The establishment date of any winery can have a wide number of meanings. In this instance it is
the date of the first vintage, but Colleen and Joe Borrett planted 8 ha each of shiraz and cabernet
sauvignon many years ago, selling the majority of the grapes to Bleasdale and others. A small parcel
of shiraz not under contract gave them the opportunity to move into the winemaking business,
now extended with a little cabernet sauvignon. Exports to the UK and the US.

RBJ   ★★★★

PO Box 34, Tanunda, SA 5352 **Region** Barossa Valley
T (08) 8563 0080 **F** (08) 8563 0080 **www**.rbjwines.com **Open** Not
Winemaker Chris Ringland **Est.** 1991 **Cases** 1000
The name comes from the 3 owners of this venture: Ringland, Bruce and Johnstone. They have
1 ha each of old, dry-grown grenache and mourvedre, and have quietly gone about their work
over the past 15 years, secure in the knowledge that there would always be more demand than
supply. Their stated aim 'is to work with this great fruit and make wines that are driven by the
vineyard with little influence of oak'. Microscopic quantities are released in Sydney through
Ultimo Wines, in Melbourne through Rathdowne Cellars, in Perth through Chateau Gilford and
in Adelaide East End, Edinburgh and Melbourne Street Cellars.

Red Earth Estate Vineyard

18L Camp Road, Dubbo, NSW 2830 **Region** Western Plains Zone
T (02) 6885 6676 **F** (02) 6882 8297 **www**.redearthestate.com.au **Open** Thurs–Tues 10–5
Winemaker Ken Borchardt **Est.** 2000 **Cases** 2500
Ken and Christine Borchardt look set to be the focal point of winegrowing and making in the
future Macquarie Valley region of the Western Plains Zone. They have planted 1.3 ha each of
riesling, verdelho, frontignac, grenache, shiraz and cabernet sauvignon plus 0.5 ha of torrentes. The
winery has a capacity of 14 000 cases, and the Borchardts also contract winemaking facilities for
others in the region.

ꙮꙮꙮꙮ   **Riesling 2006** A pleasant wine, with just a splash of residual sugar, not surprising
given the low alcohol; well-made; estate-grown. Screwcap. 9.3° alc. **Rating** 87
To 2008 $18

Red Edge

Golden Gully Road, Heathcote, Vic 3523 **Region** Heathcote
T (03) 9337 5695 **F** (03) 9337 7550 **Open** By appt
Winemaker Peter Dredge, Judy Dredge **Est.** 1971 **Cases** 1500
Red Edge is a relatively new name on the scene, but the vineyard dates back to 1971, and the
renaissance of the Vic wine industry. In the early 1980s it produced the wonderful wines of Flynn
& Williams and has now been rehabilitated by Peter and Judy Dredge, producing 2 quite lovely
wines in their inaugural vintage and has continued that form in succeeding vintages. They now
have a little under 15 ha under vine. Exports to the UK, the US and Canada.

ꙮꙮꙮꙮꙮ   **Heathcote Shiraz 2005** A medium- to full-bodied assemblage of black fruits,
licorice, leather and spice; controlled oak, though the alcohol does poke through a
little. Screwcap. 14.9° alc. **Rating** 93 To 2025 $45
Degree Heathcote Shiraz 2005 Interesting spice, forest and briar aromas
followed by spicy black fruits, good structure and ripe tannins. The usual Red
Edge exotic blend of 85% Shiraz/12% Mourvedre/3% Riesling. Screwcap.
14.5° alc. **Rating** 90 To 2012 $25
Heathcote Cabernet Sauvignon 2005 Medium red-purple, not dense; nicely
ripened cassis/blackcurrant fruit, then a palpable delay before tannins bite; will come
together very well with patience. Screwcap. 14.4° alc. **Rating** 90 To 2012 $45

Red Hill Estate

53 Shoreham Road, Red Hill South, Vic 3937 **Region** Mornington Peninsula
T (03) 5989 2838 **F** (03) 5931 0143 **www**.redhillestate.com.au **Open** 7 days 11–5
Winemaker Michael Kyberd, Luke Curry **Est.** 1989 **Cases** 30 000
Red Hill Estate was established by Sir Peter Derham and family, and has 3 vineyard sites: Range
Road, with a little over 31 ha, Red Hill Estate (the home vineyard) with 10 ha, and The Briars
with 2 ha. Taken together, the vineyards make Red Hill Estate one of the larger producers of
Mornington Peninsula wines. The tasting room and ever-busy restaurant have a superb view
across the vineyard to Westernport Bay and Phillip Island. In 2007 it (somewhat surprisingly)
merged with Arrowfield Estate in the Hunter Valley; one can only assume marketing synergies are
expected to drive the new InWine Group Australia. Exports to the US, Canada, the UK and
Sweden.

ΨΨΨΨΨ **Classic Release Pinot Noir 2004** Fruit aromas, then a complex palate with
built-in tannins; plenty of ripe, plummy fruit; will continue to develop. Diam.
14.5° alc. **Rating** 94 **To** 2011 $35

Red Nectar Wines

Stonewell Road, Marananga, SA 5355 **Region** Barossa Valley
T 0409 547 478 **F** (08) 8563 3624 **www**.rednectar.com.au **Open** By appt
Winemaker Troy Kalleske **Est.** 1997 **Cases** 3000
Tammy Pfeiffer may be a sixth-generation grapegrower, but she was only 19 when she purchased
the 27-ha property now known as Red Nectar Estate in 1997. At that time there were 2.4 ha
shiraz plantings, the remainder grazing land with a beautiful view towards the Seppeltsfield palm
avenue. The existing shiraz had been sourced from 80-year-old vines grown in the Moppa district,
and Tammy has since established another 5.3 ha of shiraz and 2 ha of cabernet sauvignon. She
carries out much of the work on the vineyards herself, using sustainable vineyard practices
wherever possible. The Stonewell area, in which the vineyard is situated, is well-known for its
high-quality shiraz fruit. The winemaking is done by her good friend and cousin Troy Kalleske.

ΨΨΨΨΨ **Barossa Valley Shiraz 2005** Flooded with soft blackberry, chocolate and vanilla
flavours; controlled alcohol a plus. Cork. 14.5° alc. **Rating** 90 **To** 2012 $25
Barossa Valley Cabernet Sauvignon 2005 Very sweet, soft, voluptuous black
fruits; velvety texture. An unusual manifestation of cabernet sauvignon. Cork.
14.5° alc. **Rating** 90 **To** 2013 $25

Redbank Victoria

Whitfield Road, King Valley, Vic 3678 **Region** King Valley
T (03) 5729 3604 **F** (08) 8561 3411 **www**.redbankwines.com **Open** Fri–Mon 11–11
Winemaker Natalie Fryar **Est.** 2005 **Cases** 75 000
The Redbank brand was for decades the umbrella for Neill and Sally Robb's Sally's Paddock. In
2005 long-term distributor of Redbank, the Yalumba Wine Group, acquired the Redbank brand
from the Robbs, leaving them with the Redbank Winery and Sally's Paddock. Yalumba is most
unhappy with the continued designation of the winery as Redbank, the Robbs saying it is simply
the name of the winery as shown in district maps, district signposts and at the gate, but is in no
sense a brand. Redbank Victoria now draws almost all its grapes from the King Valley, purchasing
viognier from the Taylor's vineyard, and pinot gris from the Cavedon Vineyard.

Redbox Vineyard & Winery

2 Ness Lane, Kangaroo Ground, Vic 3097 **Region** Yarra Valley
T (03) 9712 0440 **F** (03) 9712 0422 **www**.redboxvineyard.com.au **Open** W'ends &
public hols 11–6, or by appt
Winemaker Phil Kelly (Contract) **Est.** 2004 **Cases** 3000
Colin and Clayton Spencer have moved quickly since establishing their business, with a
kaleidoscopic array of wines, partly from the Yarra Valley, and partly from the Perricoota region

north of the Murray River .The wines are released under the Redbox,Wildfell Estate and Murray Flyer labels, with all of the red wines (other than Pinot Noir) coming from Perricoota.Their estate plantings in the Yarra comprise 2 ha of cabernet sauvignon, 0.8 ha of chardonnay and 0.4 ha of riesling; they also purchase pinot gris from the Yarra Valley region.

Redden Bridge Wines   ★★★★

PMB 147, Naracoorte, SA 5271 (postal) **Region** Wrattonbully
T (08) 8764 7494 **F** (08) 8764 7501 **www**.reddenbridge.com **Open** Not
Winemaker Rob Moody (Contract) **Est.** 2002 **Cases** 800
This is the venture of Greg and Emma Koch, Greg with a quarter of a century of viticultural experience first in Coonawarra (17 years) and thereafter turning his attention to Wrattonbully, buying land there in 1995 and setting up Terra Rossa Viticultural Management to assist growers across the Limestone Coast. Greg and Emma now have 24 ha of cabernet sauvignon and 22 ha of shiraz, and in 2002 retained the services of the immensely experienced Robin Moody to oversee the making of the Redden Bridge wines at Cape Jaffa Estate.The first wines were released from the 2002 vintage, and the following vintage won the trophy for Best Individual Vineyard Wine at the Limestone Coast Wine Show '05.

ΨΨΨΨΨ Gully Shiraz 2003 Elegant medium-bodied style with good texture and
          structure; notes of spice and mocha to plum and blackberry fruit. Trophy
          Limestone Coast Wine Show '05. Screwcap. 14.1° alc. **Rating** 94 **To** 2013 $30

ΨΨΨΨΨ **The Crossing Cabernet Sauvignon 2003** A strongly savoury/earthy style with
          black fruits, black olive and a lingering tannin finish; patience needed. Screwcap.
          13.8° alc. **Rating** 90 **To** 2018 $30

ΨΨΨΨ Gully Shiraz 2002 Strong colour; powerful, savoury/briary complexity, and a tangy
          finish; shows the cool vintage. Screwcap. 14.1° alc. **Rating** 89 **To** 2010 $30

Redesdale Estate Wines   ★★★★☆

North Redesdale Road, Redesdale,Vic 3444 **Region** Heathcote
T (03) 5425 3236 **F** (03) 5425 3122 **www**.redesdale.com **Open** By appt
Winemaker Tobias Ansted (Contract) **Est.** 1982 **Cases** 860
Planting of the Redesdale Estate vines began in 1982 on the northeast slopes of a 25-ha grazing property, fronting the Campaspe River on one side.The rocky quartz and granite soil meant the vines had to struggle for existence, and when Peter Williams and wife Suzanne Arnall-Williams purchased the property in 1988 the vineyard was in a state of disrepair.They have rejuvenated the vineyard, planted an olive grove, and, more recently, erected a 2-storey cottage surrounded by a garden which is part of the Victorian Open Garden Scheme (and cross-linked to a villa in Tuscany).

ΨΨΨΨΨ Heathcote Shiraz 2004 Strong purple-red; medium-bodied, clean and fresh,
          somewhat lighter than the alcohol would suggest; black fruits and fine tannins.
          Continues to evolve slowly and convincingly. Screwcap. 15° alc. **Rating** 92
          To 2013 $40

          Heathcote Cabernet Sauvignon Cabernet Franc 2004 Firm, bracing fruit;
          blackcurrant, cedar and cigar box, lemony acidity allied with powerful tannins. Still
          fairly formidable, but the softening changes will eventuate. Screwcap. 14.5° alc.
          Rating 90 **To** 2014 $40

Redfin   ★★★★☆

80 Vancouver Street, Albany, WA 6330 (postal) **Region** Warehouse
T (08) 8554 2894 **F** (08) 8554 2493 **www**.redfinwines.com.au **Open** Not
Winemaker Plantagenet **Est.** 2002 **Cases** 1500
Given the approach of owners Caroline and Jonathan O'Neill to the creation of Redfin, it comes as no surprise to find that Jonathan has been Plantagenet Wines' marketing manager for 8 years, and in fact continues in that role.Wife Caroline (a pharmacist) also brings some expertise into the

technical side of the venture. That said, they have neither vineyards nor winery, using contract growers in the Mount Barker region, and Plantagenet to make the wines. They have set themselves goals which any new winery venture could well adopt, number one being 'only produce what you can sell to make sure the brand doesn't become compromised'. They also believe that a little bit of fun should be part of the formula. Being true to the region, there are only 2 wines in the portfolio: Shiraz and Riesling.

Redgate ★★★★★

Boodjidup Road, Margaret River, WA 6285 **Region** Margaret River
T (08) 9757 6488 **F** (08) 9757 6308 www.redgatewines.com.au **Open** 7 days 10–5
Winemaker Simon Keall **Est.** 1977 **Cases** 5000
Founder and owner of Redgate, Bill Ullinger, chose the name not simply because of the nearby eponymous beach, but also because – so it is said – a local farmer (with a prominent red gate at his property) had run an illegal spirit still 100 or so years ago, and its patrons would come to the property and ask whether there was any 'red gate' available. True or not, Ullinger was one of the early movers in the Margaret River, and there is now a little over 21 ha of mature estate plantings (the majority to sauvignon blanc, semillon, cabernet sauvignon, cabernet franc, shiraz and chardonnay). Exports to the US, Switzerland, The Netherlands and Singapore.

♆♆♆♆♆ **Margaret River Sauvignon Blanc Semillon 2006** Expressive varietal fruit trembles on the brink of reduction, but avoids it; a lively and fresh palate with passionfruit and tropical flavours balanced by lemony acidity; deliciously fresh finish and great value. Screwcap. 12.5° alc. **Rating** 94 **To** 2008 $18.50
Margaret River Chardonnay 2005 Light- to medium-bodied; crisp, lively and very elegant; stone fruit, grapefruit and citrus married with subtle oak and fine acidity. Very different to the usual more muscular Margaret River style. Screwcap. 14° alc. **Rating** 94 **To** 2015 $35
Margaret River Shiraz 2004 Very good purple-red; excellent balance and composition from the bouquet through to the finish; a mix of blackberry, plum, cherry and spice; fine tannins and oak on a long finish. Screwcap. 14° alc. **Rating** 94 **To** 2020 $25

♆♆♆♆♆ **Reserve Oak Matured Margaret River Sauvignon Blanc 2005** A complex wine; oak has been well-handled, integrated with and not obscuring the gooseberry and ripe citrus fruit. Screwcap. 12.5° alc. **Rating** 92 **To** 2008 $22.50
Margaret River Rose 2006 Fresh cherry, strawberry and raspberry flavours; fruit-not sugar-driven. Cabernet Franc. Screwcap. 13° alc. **Rating** 90 **To** 2008 $17
WW Ullinger Reserve Margaret River Cabernet Merlot 2004 An elegant, restrained style, barely medium-bodied; earthy overtones to blackcurrant fruit supported by subtle oak and fine tannins. Screwcap. 13° alc. **Rating** 90 **To** 2013 $40
Margaret River Cabernet Sauvignon 2004 Fresh, medium-bodied, clearly articulated cassis blackcurrant varietal fruit; fine-boned tannins; good length. Screwcap. 13.5° alc. **Rating** 90 **To** 2015 $30

♆♆♆♆ **Bin 588 2004** Fresh, bright and clean, driven as much by the cabernet sauvignon and cabernet franc as shiraz; zesty fruits on the crisp finish. Shiraz (48%)/Cabernet Sauvignon (32%)/Cabernet Franc (19%). Screwcap. 14° alc. **Rating** 89 **To** 2013 $22.50
Margaret River Cabernet Franc 2004 Savoury, cedary, spicy, even tobacco leaf – all varietal markers, but what is the inherent charm? Screwcap. 14° alc. **Rating** 87 **To** 2010 $40

Redman ★★★

Riddoch Highway, Coonawarra, SA 5263 **Region** Coonawarra
T (08) 8736 3331 www.redman.com.au **Open** Mon–Fri 9–5, w'ends 10–4
Winemaker Bruce Redman, Malcolm Redman **Est.** 1966 **Cases** 17 000

After a prolonged period of mediocrity, the Redman wines are showing sporadic signs of improvement, partly through the introduction of modest amounts of new oak, even if principally American. It would be nice to say the wines now reflect the potential of the fully mature vineyard, but there is still some way to go.

TTTT **Shiraz 2004** Medium-bodied, smooth and subtle, with good fruit and oak balance; just a little short on intensity. Cork. 13° alc. **Rating** 88 **To** 2011 $20
Coonawarra Cabernet Sauvignon Merlot 2004 Some green fruit characters to both bouquet and palate, but does have length. Cork. 14.4° alc. **Rating** 87 **To** 2012 $31

Rees Miller Estate

5355 Goulburn Highway, Yea, Vic 3717 **Region** Upper Goulburn
T (03) 5797 2101 **F** (03) 5797 3276 **www**.reesmiller.com **Open** 7 days 10–6
Winemaker David Miller **Est.** 1996 **Cases** 3000
Partners Sylke Rees and David Miller purchased the 64-ha property in 1998 with 7 ha of vines already planted to pinot noir, cabernet sauvignon, merlot and shiraz, all of which came into production in 2002. The entire property, including the vineyard, is undergoing organic and biodynamic certification and they deliberately irrigate sparingly, the upshot being yields typically 5 tonnes per ha. Some of the wines are named after the original owners of the property, Daniel Joseph and Wilhelmina Therese Sier. Exports to Canada and Germany.

TTTTT **Thousand Hills Upper Goulburn Shiraz 2004** Deep, impenetrable colour; licorice, smoke, leather and blackberry aromas; full-bodied and very powerful, but happily the tannins have been controlled, and are ripe. Diam. 14.5° alc. **Rating** 92 **To** 2030 $18

TTTT **Wilhelmina Upper Goulburn Pinot Noir 2004** A powerful, almost abrasive, palate with plum and black cherry fruit encircled by somewhat rough, dry tannins. Diam. 13.5° alc. **Rating** 87 **To** 2010 $18
Sier's Field Upper Goulburn Cabernet Sauvignon 2004 Medium-bodied; persistent earthy/savoury tannins run through and around the core of blackcurrant fruit. Diam. 14.5° alc. **Rating** 87 **To** 2012 $18

Reilly's Wines

Cnr Hill Street/Burra Street, Mintaro, SA 5415 **Region** Clare Valley
T (08) 8843 9013 **F** (08) 8843 9013 **www**.reillyswines.com **Open** 7 days 10–4
Winemaker Justin Ardill **Est.** 1994 **Cases** 25 000
Cardiologist Justin and Julie Ardill are no longer newcomers in the Clare Valley, with 10 or so vintages under their belt. An unusual sideline of Reilly's Cottage is the production of extra virgin olive oil, made from wild olives found in the Mintaro district of the Clare Valley. Justin Ardill also does some contract making for others. In 2005 a second cellar door opened in Adelaide, which also holds wine classes. Exports to the US, Ireland, Malaysia and Singapore.

TTTTT **Dry Land Shiraz 2002** Abundant black fruit aromas and flavours, but not over the top in any way; notes of spice and attractive oak; ripe tannins. Cork. 15° alc. **Rating** 94 **To** 2014 $27

TTTTT **Watervale Riesling 2005** Lively and lissome, with bright, fresh apple, citrus and mineral flavours; long finish. Screwcap. 12° alc. **Rating** 93 **To** 2015 $17
Old Bush Vine Grenache 2005 Fragrant, almost flowery cherry blossom aromas; much more weight and concentration than most other Clare Valley grenache, but can't get away from those distracting cosmetic nuances. From a block planted in 1919. Screwcap. 15° alc. **Rating** 92 **To** 2015 $22
Watervale Riesling 2006 Far more elegant than the Barking Mad; does take its time to open up its floral aromas, which lead into a mix of citrus and apple on the palate. Screwcap. 12.5° alc. **Rating** 91 **To** 2016 $19

Watervale Riesling 2004 Bright green-straw; abundant depth and richness; has already developed into a very different style. Who says screwcaps prevent development? 12° alc. **Rating** 91 **To** 2012 $19

Old Bush Vine Grenache 2004 Clear and bright colour; sweet varietal confit fruit, but has both freshness and elegance not always found with Clare grenache. Screwcap. 15° alc. **Rating** 90 **To** 2010 $22

ΨΨΨΨ **Stolen Block Shiraz 2003** Unconvincing colour; ripe, sweet blackberry fruit and some dark chocolate; somewhat lacking in structure; 80-year-old vines. Cork. 14.5° alc. **Rating** 89 **To** 2011 $27

Dry Land Cabernet Sauvignon 2002 Very ripe fruit flavours despite the moderate alcohol; blackberry, bitter chocolate, spice and earth; just a fraction short. Cork. 14.5° alc. **Rating** 89 **To** 2010 $27

Barking Mad Riesling 2006 Considerable depth of ripe citrus flavours, the balance correct. Screwcap. 12.5° alc. **Rating** 88 **To** 2011

Barking Mad Adelaide Hills Sauvignon Blanc 2005 Relatively soft and rich, with ample tropical fruit, and good balance; no frills. Screwcap. 12.5° alc. **Rating** 88 **To** 2008 $13

Barking Mad Clare Valley Shiraz 2004 A big, somewhat rustic, red; lots of extract and tannins around the ripe blackberry fruit. Good value. Screwcap. 14.5° alc. **Rating** 87 **To** 2010 $13

Late Picked Watervale Riesling 2005 Delicate, clean and crisp, barely off-dry; simple now, but will develop some complexity with extended bottle development. Screwcap. 12° alc. **Rating** 87 **To** 2013 $18

Remarkable View Wines   NR

Main North Road, Murray Town, SA 5481 **Region** Southern Flinders Ranges
T (08) 8667 2223 **www.**remarkableview.com.au **Open** W'ends & public hols 11–4.30, or by appt
Winemaker Contract **Est.** 1997 **Cases** NA
Karen and the late Malcolm Orrock (and their family) began the establishment of the vineyard in 1997, and over the next 4 years planted shiraz, cabernet sauvignon, sangiovese, grenache, tempranillo and petit verdot. There are now a little under 20 ha of vines, the bulk of the production being sold to Peter Lehmann Wines, with limited amounts made for sale under the Remarkable View brand label.

Renewan Murray Gold Wines   ★★★

Murray Valley Highway, Piangil, Vic 3597 **Region** Swan Hill
T (03) 5030 5525 **F** (03) 5030 5695 **Open** 7 days 9–5
Winemaker Hanging Rock **Est.** 1989 **Cases** 220
In 1990 former senior executive at Nylex Corporation in Melbourne, Jim Lewis, and artist wife Marg, retired to what is now Renewan, set on the banks of the Murray River. It is a small business, based on 2 ha of estate plantings.

ΨΨΨΨ **Durif 2004** As always, potent black fruits in colour, bouquet and palate. Custom-made for a 500 g barbecue T-bone. Diam. 14° alc. **Rating** 88 **To** 2012 $20

Riesling 2006 Nicely made Riesling, especially given the region; ripe citrus fruit braced by good acidity. Altogether unexpected. Screwcap. 11° alc. **Rating** 87 **To** 2009 $12

Shiraz 2004 Plenty of ripe fruit flavours, and slightly rustic tannins and mouthfeel; the vintage virtue shines through. Screwcap. 13.5° alc. **Rating** 87 **To** 2010 $16

Reschke Wines   NR

Level 1, 183 Melbourne Street, North Adelaide, SA 5006 (postal) **Region** Coonawarra
T (08) 8239 0500 **F** (08) 8239 0522 **www.**reschke.com.au **Open** Not
Winemaker Peter Douglas (Contract) **Est.** 1998 **Cases** NA

Restif

64 Parker Road, Wandin East, Vic 3139 (postal) **Region** Yarra Valley
T (03) 5964 2341 **F** (03) 5964 3651 **Open** Not
Winemaker Gary Mills **Est.** 1990 **Cases** 250

Val Diamond and Professor John Funder (of Prince Henrys Institute at the Monash Medical Centre) purchased the vineyard in 2003, when the chardonnay vines were already 13 years old. Thus both the 2005 and 2006 Restif Chardonnay came off the Front Block (as it is known). The first Cabernet Sauvignon (from younger plantings) to merit the label will be the '06, not to be released for some time.

ŸŸŸŸŸ **Yarra Valley Chardonnay 2005** Excellent structure; vibrant and intense nectarine and grapefruit in a web of subtle oak. Just a fraction green on the finish as a trade-off for the low alcohol freshness. Screwcap. 12.8° alc. **Rating** 92 **To** 2013 $25

Yarra Valley Chardonnay 2006 Pale straw-green; elegant, tightly structured and thus understated fruit; good balance and length; needs 2-3 years. Screwcap. 12.6° alc. **Rating** 91 **To** 2012 $27.50

Richard Hamilton

Cnr Main Road/Johnstone Road, Willunga, SA 5172 **Region** McLaren Vale
T (08) 8323 8830 **F** (08) 8323 8881 **www**.leconfieldwines.com **Open** Mon–Fri 10–5, w'ends & public hols 11–5
Winemaker Paul Gordon **Est.** 1972 **Cases** 27 000

Richard Hamilton has outstanding estate vineyards, some of great age, all fully mature. The arrival (in 2001) of former Rouge Homme winemaker Paul Gordon has allowed the full potential of those vineyards to be expressed. His move to lower alcohol wines (without sacrificing flavour) is to be commended. Exports to all major markets.

ŸŸŸŸŸ **Gumpr's McLaren Vale Shiraz 2004** Medium-bodied, with excellent balance and mouthfeel, likewise regional-varietal fruit expression; fine tannins, good length. Screwcap. 14° alc. **Rating** 94 **To** 2019 $17

ŸŸŸŸŸ **Gumpr's McLaren Vale Shiraz 2005** The moderate alcohol immediately manifests itself in the fresh bouquet and palate; black fruits, with notes of spice, dark chocolate and savoury nuances; crisp finish. Screwcap. 14° alc. **Rating** 91 **To** 2015 $16.95

Hut Block McLaren Vale Cabernet Sauvignon 2005 The aromatic fruit of the bouquet is seemingly riper than the analysis suggests; medium-bodied, with supple blackcurrant fruit, then balanced tannins on the back-palate and finish. Screwcap. 14° alc. **Rating** 90 **To** 2018 $16.95

ŸŸŸŸ **Hut Block McLaren Vale Cabernet Sauvignon 2004** A certain amount of astringency seems to have been emphasised by the closure; certainly a very earthy and austere wine which will benefit from both age and aeration. Screwcap. 14° alc. **Rating** 89 **To** 2015 $17

Lot 148 McLaren Vale Merlot 2005 Regional chocolate aromas make their presence felt before anything else has a chance; red fruits come next; and in the final phase, olives and savoury tannins. Screwcap. 13.5° alc. **Rating** 88 **To** 2013

Almond Grove McLaren Vale Chardonnay 2005 Yellow peach and fig; a soft palate of moderate length, and no pretensions to complexity. Screwcap. 13.5° alc. **Rating** 87 **To** 2008 $14

Richfield Estate

Bonshaw Road, Tenterfield, NSW 2372 **Region** New England
T (02) 6737 5488 **F** (02) 6737 5598 **www**.richfieldvineyard.com.au **Open** 7 days 10–4
Winemaker John Cassegrain **Est.** 1997 **Cases** 15 000

Singapore resident Bernard Forey is the Chairman and majority shareholder of Richfield Estate. The 500-ha property, at an altitude of 720 m, was selected after an intensive survey by soil specialists. Just under 30 ha of shiraz, cabernet sauvignon, merlot, semillon, chardonnay and verdelho have been planted, the first vintage being made in 2000. Winemaker John Cassegrain is a shareholder in the venture, and it is expected that the bulk of the sales will come from the export markets of South-East Asia and Japan.

Richmond Grove ★★★★★

Para Road, Tanunda, SA 5352 **Region** Barossa Valley
T (08) 8563 7303 **www**.richmondgrovewines.com **Open** 7 days 10.30–4.30
Winemaker Steve Clarkson, John Vickery (Consultant) **Est.** 1983 **Cases** 150 000
Richmond Grove, owned by Orlando Wyndham, draws its grapes from diverse sources. The Richmond Grove Barossa Valley and Watervale Rieslings made by the team directed by consultant winemaker John Vickery represent excellent value for money (for Riesling) year in, year out. Exports to the UK.

ＹＹＹＹＹ **Limited Release Barossa Vineyards Shiraz 2002** Holding hue very well; a very elegant wine reflecting the cool, high quality vintage; restrained black fruits, and long, silky tannins; 2 trophies, 3 gold medals. Ridiculous price. Cork. 14.5° alc. **Rating** 95 **To** 2016 $19
Limited Release Watervale Vineyards Riesling 2006 A quintessential floral bouquet; beautifully balanced flavours on the palate, primarily sweet lime with a touch of passionfruit; excellent length. Screwcap. 13° alc. **Rating** 94 **To** 2020 $18.95
Limited Release Watervale Vineyards Riesling 2005 A clean bouquet leads into a firm, reserved wine with tight but good structure; will develop slowly but absolute certainty on the basis of its classic mineral and citrus foundation; 4 gold medals. Screwcap. 12.5° alc. **Rating** 94 **To** 2015 $16

ＹＹＹＹＹ **Padthaway Vineyards Chardonnay 2005** Fine and elegant; an excellent example of Padthaway terroir and ensuring varietal character, with classic grapefruit and stone fruit; sensitive use of French oak. I suspect few will associate the Richmond Grove label with chardonnay of this quality and style. Screwcap. **Rating** 91 **To** 2012 $18.95

Rickety Gate ★★★★

RMB 825, Scotsdale Road, Denmark, WA 6333 **Region** Denmark
T (08) 9840 9504 **F** (08) 9840 9502 **www**.ricketygate.com.au **Open** Fri–Mon & hols 11–4
Winemaker John Wade **Est.** 2000 **Cases** 2600
The 3-ha vineyard of Rickety Gate is situated on north-facing slopes of the Bennet Ranges, in an area specifically identified by Dr John Gladstones as highly suited to cool-climate viticulture. The property was purchased by Russell and Linda Hubbard at the end of 1999, and 1.8 ha of merlot, 0.8 ha of riesling and 0.5 ha of chardonnay and pinot noir were planted in 2000. John Wade contract-makes the wines at the small onsite winery.

Riddells Creek Winery

296 Gap Road, Riddells Creek, Vic 3431 **Region** Macedon Ranges
T (03) 5428 7222 **www**.riddellscreekwinery.com.au **Open** Wed–Sun 11–5, or by appt
Winemaker John Ellis, Trefor Morgan, Peter Evans **Est.** 1998 **Cases** 2300
Partners Peter Evans, Sonia Mailer, Craig Wellington and Susan Wellington commenced planting the 18.5-ha vineyard in 1998; the varieties chosen were riesling, chardonnay, cabernet sauvignon, shiraz and merlot. While it is situated at the extreme southern end of the Macedon Ranges, the partners correctly anticipated that achieving full ripeness with the red varieties might be difficult in cooler vintages. However, winemakers John Ellis and Trefor Morgan, with input from Peter Evans, have done an excellent job with the white wines since the inaugural vintage of 2001.

🍷🍷🍷🍷 **Amee Alyce Riesling 2006** Lively and fresh, still with some CO_2 spritz; built for the long haul. **Rating** 88 **To** 2014

Ridgeback Wines

87 The Boulevard, Warrandyte, Vic 3113 **Region** Yarra Valley
T (03) 9844 1645 **www**.ridgebackwines.com.au **Open** By appt
Winemaker MasterWineMakers, Rob Dolan **Est.** 2000 **Cases** 1000
Ron and Lynne Collings purchased their Panton Hill property in 1990, clearing the land and making it ready for the first vine planting in 1992; there are now a little over 4 ha on the hillside slopes beneath their house. Most of the grapes were sold, but Ron Collings made small batches of wine himself each year, which ultimately led to the decision to establish the Ridgeback label. The winery was sold to Sean Dixon and Kylie Dunscombe in 2006. Exports to the UK, Indonesia and Fiji.

🍷🍷🍷🍷🍷 **Yarra Valley Cabernet Merlot 2005** Clear varietal expression in a blackcurrant and cassis spectrum; curiously, free of the dry, grippy tannins of the '05 Merlot, though there is plenty of structure. Diam. **Rating** 90 **To** 2020 $23

🍷🍷🍷🍷 **Yarra Valley Merlot 2003** Has improved over the past 2 years, with more red fruits; now close to its zenith. Cork. 13.5° alc. **Rating** 89 **To** 2010 $29
Yarra Valley Cabernet Merlot 2004 Medium-bodied; firm, fresh blackcurrant and a touch of cassis, green tannins lurking in the background. Screwcap. 13.5° alc. **Rating** 88 **To** 2014 $23

Ridgeline

PO Box 695, Healesville, Vic 3777 **Region** Yarra Valley
T 0421 422 154 **F** (03) 5962 2670 **Open** By appt
Winemaker Mark Haisma **Est.** 2001 **Cases** 800
Mark Haisma has established 2 ha of dry-grown pinot noir, shiraz, cabernet sauvignon and merlot on a small hillside vineyard on Briarty Road; his neighbours include such well-known producers as Yarra Yering and Giant Steps, and 2 substantial vineyards, one owned by Coldstream Hills, the other by Malcolm Fell.

🍷🍷🍷🍷🍷 **Single Vineyard Yarra Valley Shiraz 2004** Savoury, spicy overtones to blackberry fruit on the medium-bodied palate; touches of licorice and cracked pepper; restrained oak, the tannins in balance. Diam. 13.5° alc. **Rating** 90 **To** 2019 $35
Single Vineyard Yarra Valley Cabernet Merlot 2004 Medium-bodied, with a touch of austerity, perhaps stemming from a conviction that control of alcohol is of paramount importance. On the other hand, there is some lovely cabernet fruit to be found if you work on the wine. Diam. 13.5° alc. **Rating** 90 **To** 2019 $35

🍷🍷🍷🍷 **Single Vineyard Yarra Valley Shiraz Rose 2006** Firm texture and bone dry; a serious rose to accompany cold food or Asian of almost any description. Diam. 12.5° alc. **Rating** 89 **To** 2008 $18

Ridgemill Estate

218 Donges Road, Severnlea, Qld 4352 **Region** Granite Belt
T (07) 4683 5211 **F** (07) 4683 5211 **www**.ridgemillestate.com **Open** Thurs–Mon 10–5
Winemaker Martin Cooper, Peter McGlashan, Jim Barnes (Consultant) **Est.** 1998
Cases 800
Martin Cooper and Dianne Maddison acquired what was then known as Emerald Hill Winery in 2004. In 2005 they expanded the existing 2 ha of vineyard (planted to chardonnay, tempranillo, shiraz, merlot and cabernet sauvignon) by adding 0.2 ha each of saperavi, lagrein and viognier, firmly setting a course down the alternative variety road. The 2005 Chardonnay is said to be the only Qld wine to win an international gold medal (at the International Chardonnay Challenge '05 in Gisborne, NZ). Its best wines are part of the Qld charge to recognition against all-comers.

ŶŶŶŶŶ **Black Dog Cabernet Sauvignon 2005** Good colour, and not too hazy for an unfiltered wine; medium-bodied, with sweet cassis/blackcurrant fruit right in the varietal slot. Impressive. Screwcap. 14° alc. **Rating** 91 **To** 2018 $25

ŶŶŶŶ **Sinister Cabernet Sauvignon 2005** Light- to medium-bodied; has varietal character, but without the depth or conviction of Black Dog; nonetheless, nice savoury/cedar notes. Screwcap. 14° alc. **Rating** 88 **To** 2011 $18

The Spaniard Tempranillo 2006 Clean, fresh red fruits; light- to medium-bodied, with good mouthfeel and balance; not especially complex, but well-made. Screwcap. 12.8° alc. **Rating** 88 **To** 2008 $16

Shiraz 2005 Light- to medium-bodied; predominantly black with some red fruit flavours; no frills, but well-balanced. Screwcap. 13.5° alc. **Rating** 87 **To** 2010 $18

RidgeView Wines ★★★

273 Sweetwater Road, Rothbury, NSW 2335 **Region** Lower Hunter Valley
T (02) 9534 5391 **F** (02) 9534 5468 **www**.ridgeview.com.au **Open** Fri–Sun 10–5
Winemaker Cameron Webster, Darren Scott **Est.** 2000 **Cases** 1500
Darren and Tracey Scott (plus their 4 children and extended family) have transformed a 40-ha timbered farm into a 10-ha vineyard together with self-contained accommodation and cellar door. The lion's share of the plantings are 4.5 ha of shiraz, with cabernet sauvignon, chambourcin, merlot, pinot gris, viognier and traminer making up a somewhat eclectic selection of varieties.

ŶŶŶŶ **Shiraz 2005** Firm, and still quite oaky, but with the potential to develop more complexity. Screwcap. 13° alc. **Rating** 87 **To** 2015

Rimfire Vineyards ★★★

Bismarck Street, Maclagan, Qld 4352 **Region** Darling Downs
T (07) 4692 1129 **F** (07) 4692 1260 **www**.rimfirewinery.com.au **Open** 7 days 10–5
Winemaker Louise Connellan **Est.** 1991 **Cases** 6000
The Connellan family (Margaret and Tony and children Michelle, Peter and Louise) began planting the 12-ha, 14-variety Rimfire Vineyards in 1991 as a means of diversification of their large cattle stud in the foothills of the Bunya Mountains, northeast of Toowoomba. They produce a kaleidoscopic array of wines, the majority without any regional claim of origin. The wine (and variety) simply called 1893 is made from a vine brought to the property by a German settler in about 1893; the vineyard ceased production in the early 1900s, but a single vine remained, and DNA testing has established that the vine does not correspond to any vine cultivar currently known in Australia. Rimfire propagated cuttings, and a small quantity is made each year.

Riposte ★★★★☆

PO Box 256, Lobethal, SA 5241 **Region** Adelaide Hills
T (08) 8389 8149 **F** (08) 8389 8178 **Open** Not
Winemaker Tim Knappstein **Est.** 2006 **Cases** 1500
It's never too late to teach an old dog new tricks where the old dog in question is Tim Knappstein. With 40 years of winemaking and more than 500 wine show awards under his belt, Tim has started yet another new wine life with Riposte, a subtle response to the various vicissitudes he has suffered in recent years. While neither he nor his former wife, Annie, have any continuing financial interest in the Lenswood Vineyards they established so many years ago, Tim is sourcing the grapes for Riposte from that Lenswood Vineyard.

ŶŶŶŶŶ **The Foil Adelaide Hills Sauvignon Blanc 2006** Opens quietly but correctly on the clean bouquet, then has masses of flavour bursting from the palate in a classic mineral/gooseberry/tropical mix. Screwcap. 13° alc. **Rating** 94 **To** 2008 $19

ŶŶŶŶŶ **The Sabre Adelaide Hills Pinot Noir 2005** No hint of reduction; elegant, unforced style allowing the delicate varietal red fruits to fully express themselves. Screwcap. 14° alc. **Rating** 91 **To** 2010 $27

The Rapier Adelaide Hills Traminer 2006 Spicy scents of bramble and wild flowers, the palate nicely balanced with flavour building on the finish. Screwcap. 13° alc. **Rating** 90 **To** 2010 $19

Rivendell ★★★★

Wildwood Road, Yallingup, WA 6282 **Region** Margaret River
T (08) 9755 2090 **www**.rivendellwines.com.au **Open** Thurs–Tues 10.30–5
Winemaker James Pennington **Est.** 1987 **Cases** 3000
Rivendell was established in 1987 by a local family and became recognised for its gardens, restaurant and wines. The property has recently been purchased by private investors who have renovated the restaurant and cellar door. The new owners also wish to lift wine quality and have employed James Pennington to oversee the improvements to the winery and its production.

ŸŸŸŸŸ **Margaret River Shiraz 2005** While only medium-bodied, does have above-average texture and structure for Margaret River shiraz; quite luscious black cherry fruit, and fine tannins. Screwcap. **Rating** 92 **To** 2018 $18
Margaret River Cabernet Merlot 2005 Strong purple-red; abundant blackcurrant fruits and equally abundant tannins; it will be a race to the finish line to determine the ultimate winner. Screwcap. 14° alc. **Rating** 90 **To** 2020 $20

ŸŸŸŸ **Margaret River Sauvignon Blanc 2006** A hint of reduction on the bouquet; a lively grassy, herbal palate, finishing with crisp acidity and not affected by reduction. Screwcap. 12° alc. **Rating** 89 **To** 2008
Pennington Margaret River Cabernet Sauvignon 2004 Light- to medium-bodied; an austere, savoury style, though within the bounds of varietal expectation; lingering tannins do have slightly green edges. Cork. 14° alc. **Rating** 89 **To** 2015 $28
Margaret River Semillon Sauvignon Blanc 2006 A neatly tied together bunch of herbaceous flavours; good length and acidity, perhaps just a touch austere. Screwcap. 12.5° alc. **Rating** 87 **To** 2009 $15

RiverBank Estate ★★★★

126 Hamersley Road, Caversham, WA 6055 **Region** Swan Valley
T (08) 9377 1805 **F** (08) 9377 2168 **www**.riverbankestate.com.au **Open** 7 days 10–5
Winemaker Robert James Bond **Est.** 1993 **Cases** 5000
Robert Bond, a graduate of Charles Sturt University and a Swan Valley viticulturist for 20 years, established RiverBank Estate in 1993. He draws upon 11 ha of estate plantings and, in his words, 'The wines are unashamedly full bodied, produced from ripe grapes in what is recognised as a hot grapegrowing region'. Several back vintages are available at the cellar door. Bond conducts 8-week wine courses affiliated with the Wine Industry Association of WA. Exports to Poland.

ŸŸŸŸŸ **Riesling 2006** In fact from a single Mount Barker vineyard; delicate apple blossom aromas, the low baume reflected not in residual sugar, but in the crisp, delicate citrus and apple flavours and balanced acidity. Very unusual to find a riesling so low in alcohol without significant residual sugar. Screwcap. 10° alc. **Rating** 92 **To** 2015 $18
Bindoon Shiraz 2002 Medium- to full-bodied, and retains significant tannins, but 36 months in new French oak is an awfully long time; it has certainly added to total flavour and will greatly appeal to those who like a lot of oak, and the points partially reflect that view. Cork. 15° alc. **Rating** 90 **To** 2015 $25

ŸŸŸŸ **Padlock Paddock Cabernets 2003** Has above-average weight and structure; sweet mocha and black fruits; fine and ripe tannins; 24 months in oak. Cabernet Sauvignon (80%)/Cabernet Franc (20%). Screwcap. 14.2° alc. **Rating** 89 **To** 2013 $20

Padlock Paddock Chardonnay 2006 I'm not convinced the wine handles the winemaker inputs; creamy/nutty characters don't have enough fruit behind them; brave effort in the coolest vintage on record. Screwcap. 12.6° alc. **Rating** 87 To 2009 $20

Rivergate Wines

580 Goornong Road, Axedale, Vic 3551 **Region** Bendigo
T (03) 5439 7367 **www**.rivergatewines.com.au **Open** W'ends 10–5, or by appt
Winemaker Greg Dedman, Geoff Kerr **Est.** 1999 **Cases** 700
Geoff and Ann Kerr have lived in the Campaspe River Valley, north of Axedale, for 25 years. It was not until the late 1990s that they took the decision to plant 2 ha of shiraz; while the vines were establishing themselves, Geoff Kerr completed the viticulture and winemaking courses at Bendigo TAFE, studying successively under Vince Lakey, Mal Steward and Lindsay Ross. Rivergate continues to use the contract winemaking facilities of the TAFE to crush, ferment and press the grapes bringing the fermented juice back to Rivergate for barrel maturation, bottling and packaging. When conditions permit (2002, 2003, 2004) a small amount of Reserve is made, spending 2 years in oak, rather than the 12 months for the standard Shiraz.

Bendigo Shiraz 2004 A mix of ripe blackberry, plum and cherry fruit; the tannin support is strong, but in balance; just needs time. Cork. 14.6° alc. **Rating** 93 To 2018 $22
Bendigo Shiraz 2005 Strong colour; blackberry, licorice and spice aromas; rich, ripe, plush fruit and strong tannins; heroic Henry VIII style. The wine will live, the stained cork a serious worry, however. **Rating** 92 To 2020 $22

Reserve Bendigo Shiraz 2003 Very ripe fruit flavours have gone that bit too far, though they do carry the tannins better. Cork. 15.5° alc. **Rating** 89 To 2015 $35
Bendigo Shiraz 2003 Overall more savoury than the younger wines, the tannins tougher and not as ripe as those of the '04, but it does have plenty of flavour. Cork. 14.3° alc. **Rating** 87 To 2015 $22

Robert Channon Wines ★★★★

32 Bradley Lane, Stanthorpe, Qld 4380 **Region** Granite Belt
T (07) 4683 3260 **F** (07) 4683 3109 **www**.robertchannonwines.com **Open** 7 days 10–5
Winemaker Ravens Croft Wines **Est.** 1998 **Cases** 3500
Peggy and Robert Channon have established 8 ha of chardonnay, verdelho, shiraz, merlot and cabernet sauvignon under permanent bird protection netting. The initial cost of installing permanent netting is high, but in the long term it is well worth it: it excludes birds and protects the grapes against hail damage. Also, there is no pressure to pick the grapes before they are fully ripe. The winery has established a particular reputation for its Verdelho.

Reserve Chardonnay 2005 Elegant, fine and complex, the barrel ferment influences judged to perfection; melon, nectarine and gently creamy/nutty overlay from the barrel fermentation and possible mlf; a calm understatement. Screwcap. 13.5° alc. **Rating** 94 To 2011 $35
Shiraz 2005 Medium-bodied, with quasi-Hunter Valley characters courtesy of the earthy/savoury edge to the black fruits. Screwcap. 14° alc. **Rating** 88 To 2012 $18
Verdelho 2006 Spotlessly clean; technically very well-made and balanced; simply lacks the zest which marks the very best verdelhos, and which Robert Channon does achieve in some years. Screwcap. 14° alc. **Rating** 87 To 2009 $24

Robert Johnson Vineyards

PO Box 6708 Halifax Street, Adelaide, SA 5000 **Region** Eden Valley
T (08) 8227 2800 **F** (08) 8227 2833 **Open** Not
Winemaker Robert Johnson **Est.** 1997 **Cases** 2500

The home base for Robert Johnson is a 12-ha vineyard and olive grove purchased in 1996, with 0.4 ha of merlot (previously sold to Irvine Wines for Grand Merlot) and 5 ha of dilapidated olive trees. The olive grove has been rehabilitated, and 2.1 ha of shiraz, 1.2 ha of merlot and a small patch of viognier have been established. Wines made from the estate-grown grapes are released under the Robert Johnson label; these are supplemented by Alan & Veitch wines purchased from the Sam Virgara vineyard in the Adelaide Hills, and named after Robert Johnson's parents.

Robertson of Clare Wines

3/2 Niangala Close, Austlink Corporate Park, Belrose, NSW 2085 (postal) **Region** Clare Valley
T (02) 9479 7188 **F** (02) 9450 0808 **www**.rocwines.com.au **Open** Not
Winemaker Simon Gilbert, Leigh Eldredge **Est.** 2004 **Cases** 1800
This is the new venture of Simon Gilbert, established after he ceased to have an executive position with Simon Gilbert Wines in Mudgee. He has joined with Clare Valley vigneron Leigh Eldredge to produce limited quantities of Clare Valley wines. The first release, MAX V, was sourced from 3 growers in the Clare Valley, utilising the 5 grapes of Bordeaux: cabernet sauvignon, cabernet franc, merlot, malbec and petit verdot. The wine was made by conducting the entire primary fermentation and malolactic fermentation in French barrels from a range of forests and coopers at Sevenhill Cellars. Exports to the US.

ΨΨΨΨΨ **MAX V 2005** Powerful and concentrated, but in the best way; blackcurrant leads the charge, quality oak also very much part of the equation; lingering tannins. Exceptionally complex oak treatment: one-third fermented in oak vats, two-thirds fermented in old Mintaro slate fermenters. Cabernet Sauvignon (66%)/Malbec/Merlot/Cabernet Franc/Petit Verdot. Cork. 14.5° alc. **Rating** 95 To 2020 $75

Robinsons Family Vineyards

Curtin Road, Ballandean, Qld 4382 **Region** Granite Belt
T (07) 4684 1216 **www**.robinsonswines.com.au **Open** Sat–Wed 10–5, Thurs–Fri by appt
Winemaker Craig Robinson **Est.** 1969 **Cases** 2000
One of the pioneers of the Granite Belt, with the second generation of the family Robinson now in control. One thing has not changed: the strongly held belief of the Robinsons that the Granite Belt should be regarded as a cool, rather than warm, climate. It is a tricky debate, because some climatic measurements point one way, others the opposite. Embedded in all this are semantic arguments about the meaning of 'cool' and 'warm'. Suffice it to say that shiraz and (conspicuously) cabernet sauvignon are the most suitable red varieties for the region; semillon, verdelho and chardonnay are the best white varieties.

Robinvale ★★★

Sea Lake Road, Robinvale, Vic 3549 **Region** Murray Darling
T (03) 5026 3955 **www**.organicwines.com.au **Open** 7 days 9–5
Winemaker Bill Caracatsanoudis **Est.** 1976 **Cases** 15 000
Robinvale was one of the first Australian wineries to be fully accredited with the Biodynamic Agricultural Association of Australia. Most, but not all, of the wines are produced from organically grown grapes, with some made preservative-free. Production has grown dramatically, no doubt reflecting the interest in organic and biodynamic viticulture and winemaking. Exports to the UK, Japan, Belgium, Canada and the US.

ΨΨΨΨ **Chardonnay Chenin Blanc Sauvignon Blanc 2005** Driven by ripe, yellow peach chardonnay fruit; medium- to full-bodied, rather rustic, but creditworthy. Here vegan/vegetarians can drink easily. Screwcap. 13° alc. **Rating** 87 To 2008 $15
Demeter Madeleine Elizabeth Rose Reserve Shiraz 2004 Very rich, super-ripe, prune flavours; nice fruit under, but simply over the top. Screwcap. 16° alc. **Rating** 87 To 2014

Robyn Drayton Wines

Cnr Pokolbin Mountain Road/ McDonalds Road, Pokolbin, NSW 2321 **Region** Lower Hunter Valley
T (02) 4998 7523 **F** (02) 4998 7523 **www.**robyndraytonwines.com.au **Open** 7 days 10–5
Winemaker Tish Cecchini, Robyn Drayton **Est.** 1989 **Cases** 5500

Reg and Pam Drayton were among the victims of the Seaview/Lord Howe Island air crash in 1984, having established Reg Drayton Wines after selling their interest in the long-established Drayton Family Winery. Their daughter Robyn (a fifth-generation Drayton and billed as the Hunter's first female vigneron) and husband Craig continue the business, which draws chiefly upon the Pokolbin Hills Estate but also takes fruit from the historic Lambkin Estate vineyard.

ΨΨΨΨΨ **Lambkin Estate Semillon 2004** Glorious golden-yellow; elegant lemony fruit still there; great balance and length. Thoroughly deserved gold medal Hunter Valley Wine Show '06. **Rating** 94 **To** 2008

ΨΨΨΨ **Pokolbin Hills Chardonnay Semillon 1998** A very toasty bouquet, then sweet, luscious, peachy fruit, no doubt driven by the chardonnay component. **Rating** 88 **To** 2008
Justin Reserve Chardonnay 2006 A quite aromatic and elegant bouquet, the palate, however, a little simple. **Rating** 87 **To** 2008

Roche Wines

Broke Road, Pokolbin, NSW 2320 **Region** Lower Hunter Valley
T (02) 4998 7600 **F** (02) 4998 7706 **www.**hvg.com.au **Open** 7 days 10–5
Winemaker Tempus Two Wines **Est.** 1999 **Cases** 10 000

Roche Wines, with its 45.77 ha of semillon, shiraz and chardonnay (plus a few bits and pieces), is but the tip of the iceberg of the massive investment made by Bill Roche in the Pokolbin subregion. He has transformed the old Hungerford Hill development on the corner of Broke and McDonalds roads, and built a luxurious resort hotel with extensive gardens and an Irish pub on the old Tallawanta Vineyard, as well as resuscitating the vines on Tallawanta. The wines are all sold through the various outlets in the overall development; excess grapes are sold to other makers.

ΨΨΨΨΨ **Tallawanta Rose 2006** Bright red-purple; attractive wine with good balance and length; fresh fruit and not sweet. Shiraz. **Rating** 90 **To** 2008

ΨΨΨΨ **Premium Chardonnay 2005** A complex bouquet and a palate generous to a fault, with ripe yellow peach and soft acid. **Rating** 88 **To** 2008

Rochford Wines

Cnr Maroondah Highway/Hill Road, Coldstream, Vic 3770 **Region** Yarra Valley
T (03) 5962 2119 **F** (03) 5962 5319 **www.**rochfordwines.com **Open** 7 days 10–5
Winemaker David Creed **Est.** 1988 **Cases** 30 000

Following the acquisition of the former Eyton-on-Yarra by Helmut and Yvonne Konecsny, major changes have occurred. Most obvious is the renaming of the winery and brand, slightly less so the move of the winemaking operations of Rochford to the Yarra Valley. The large restaurant is open 7 days for lunch and Rochford is well-known for the numerous concerts it stages in its lakeside amphitheatre. Exports to the UK, Canada, Singapore, Hong Kong and China.

ΨΨΨΨΨ **Macedon Ranges Chardonnay 2005** Spotlessly clean and quite aromatic; clean, intense citrus and nectarine on a long palate, the finish impressively powerful and long; oak and lees in the back seat. Cork. 13.5° alc. **Rating** 94 **To** 2015 $27
Macedon Ranges Pinot Gris 2006 Bright green-straw; beautifully made, with plenty of fruit, even if it is not distinctively varietal; as good as they come. Gold medal Macedon Ranges Wine Exhibition '06. Screwcap. 13.5° alc. **Rating** 94 **To** 2009 $27
Yarra Valley Pinot Noir 2005 A pretty, light- to medium-bodied wine; predominantly red fruits; fine, elegant texture and structure; considerable length with the peacock's tail opening on the finish. Screwcap. 14° alc. **Rating** 94 **To** 2012 $30

Reserve Yarra Valley Shiraz 2005 Elegant, cool-grown spicy black cherry and licorice fruit; lively mouthfeel, and rides over the alcohol. Screwcap. 15° alc. **Rating** 94 **To** 2030 $44

ŢŢŢŢŢ **Yarra Valley Sauvignon Blanc 2006** High quality varietal aromas; a long palate which progressively gains intensity leading to a bracing finish. Screwcap. 13.5° alc. **Rating** 93 **To** 2008 $23

Yarra Valley Cabernet Sauvignon 2004 Medium red-purple; medium-bodied; tangy, lively, multi-flavours of blackcurrant, cassis, bitter chocolate and oak; fine tannins to close. Screwcap. 14° alc. **Rating** 93 **To** 2014 $27

Latitude Macedon Ranges Pinot Noir 2004 More savoury, spicy, briary aromas; the developed flavours follow down the same track, but will please some greatly. Screwcap. 14° alc. **Rating** 90 **To** 2009 $17

ŢŢŢŢ **Latitude Victoria Chardonnay 2005** Clean, crisp citrus and stone fruit; partial barrel fermentation in old oak plus lees contact; still very direct and relatively simple, but good value. Sourced from a single Yarra Valley vineyard rather than all over Victoria. Quixotic labelling. Screwcap. 14° alc. **Rating** 88 **To** 2011 $17

Yarra Valley Shiraz 2004 Light- to medium-bodied; some attractive spicy/peppery components in the sweet fruit, but lacks fruit density/intensity. Screwcap. 14.8° alc. **Rating** 87 **To** 2011 $27

RockBare   ★★★★☆

PO Box 63, Mt Torrens, SA 5244 **Region** McLaren Vale
T (08) 8389 5192 **F** (08) 8389 5193 **Open** Not
Winemaker Tim Burvill **Est.** 2000 **Cases** 10 000
A native of WA, Tim Burvill moved to SA in 1993 to do the winemaking course at the Adelaide University Roseworthy campus. Having completed an Honours degree in oenology, he was recruited by Southcorp, and quickly found himself in a senior winemaking position, with responsibility for super-premium whites including Penfolds Yattarna. He makes the RockBare wines under lend-lease arrangements with other wineries. Exports to all major markets.

ŢŢŢŢŢ **McLaren Vale Shiraz 2005** Medium-bodied, sharing the same finesse and elegance with the other RockBare wines; also has focus and intensity to the blackberry and dark chocolate fruit; fine, persistent tannins; very good length, balance and finish. Screwcap. 15° alc. **Rating** 94 **To** 2020 $22

ŢŢŢŢŢ **Mojo Shiraz 2005** Medium-bodied; elegant and fresh, perfectly ripened shiraz, with blackberry and black cherry fruit; good acidity, fine tannins and subtle oak. Great value. Barossa Valley. Screwcap. 14.5° alc. **Rating** 92 **To** 2020 $15

Mojo Sauvignon Blanc 2006 Light, clean and crisp passionfruit/kiwifruit and citrus flavours; particularly good finish and aftertaste – and cheap. Adelaide Hills. Screwcap. 12° alc. **Rating** 90 **To** 2008 $15

McLaren Vale Chardonnay 2006 Light straw-green; an elegant, medium-bodied wine with sophisticated winemaking techniques, lees stirring and other tricks of the trade giving the illusion of a touch of oak when (apparently) none is there; very good balance. Screwcap. 13.5° alc. **Rating** 90 **To** 2011 $18

Rockfield Estate   ★★★★☆

Rosa Glen Road, Margaret River, WA 6285 **Region** Margaret River
T (08) 9757 5006 **www.**rockfield.com.au **Open** Wed–Sun & hols 11–5, or by appt
Winemaker Andrew Gaman Jr, John Durham (Consultant) **Est.** 1997 **Cases** 8000
Rockfield Estate Vineyard is very much a family affair. Dr Andrew Gaman wears the hats of chief executive officer, assistant winemaker and co-marketing manager; wife Anne Gaman is a director; Alex Gaman is the viticulturist; Andrew Gaman Jr is winemaker; and Anna Walter (née Gaman) helps with the marketing. Chapman Brook meanders through the property, the vines running from its banks up to the wooded slopes above the valley floor. Exports to the UK.

ϷϷϷϷϙ **Semillon 2006** Quite aromatic for young semillon; citrus, herb and apple come through strongly on both bouquet and palate; vibrant finish. Screwcap. 13° alc. **Rating** 91 **To** 2012 $22

Semillon Sauvignon Blanc 2006 There is the barest whiff of sweatiness from the sauvignon blanc; then a remarkably intense, almost fierce, palate with grass, lemon rind and apple flavours. Where to next, I wonder? Screwcap. 13° alc. **Rating** 90 **To** 2009 $17

Reserve Cabernet Sauvignon 2004 Complex, with most of that complexity coming from the earthy/savoury/minty side of cabernet sauvignon; black fruits and dark chocolate, but no cassis; firm, lingering tannins. Screwcap. 14° alc. **Rating** 90 **To** 2019 $39

ϷϷϷϷ **Cabernet Merlot 2004** Well-balanced and structured; the fruit flavours are restrained rather than effusive, as are the ripe tannins; best described – not unkindly – as a food wine. Screwcap. 14° alc. **Rating** 89 **To** 2015 $24

Rockford ★★★★★

Krondorf Road, Tanunda, SA 5352 **Region** Barossa Valley
T (08) 8563 2720 **F** (08) 8563 3787 **Open** 7 days 11–5
Winemaker Robert O'Callaghan, Ben Radford **Est.** 1984 **Cases** NFP
Rockford can only be described as an icon, no matter how over-used that word may be. It has a devoted band of customers who buy most of the wine through the cellar door or mail order (Rocky O'Callaghan's entrancing annual newsletter is like no other.) Some wine is sold through restaurants, and there are 2 retailers in Sydney, and 1 each in Melbourne, Brisbane and Perth. Whether they will have the Basket Press Shiraz available is another matter; it is as scarce as Henschke Hill of Grace (and less expensive). Exports to the UK, the US, Canada, Switzerland, Singapore and NZ.

ϷϷϷϷϷ **Basket Press Barossa Valley Shiraz 2004** A complete Barossa traditional shiraz; moderate alcohol, oak and tannins, yet full of flavour and character. Has taken full advantage of a very good vintage. In its own-branded, high-shouldered brown bottle. Cork. 14.5° alc. **Rating** 96 **To** 2019 $46

Rifle Range Barossa Valley Cabernet Sauvignon 2004 Great colour and hue; this is a quite beautiful expression of cabernet sauvignon in the Barossa Valley; great purity of line and fruit flavour; blackcurrant and cassis fruit, with positively silky tannins. Cork. 14.5° alc. **Rating** 95 **To** 2019 $33

Handpicked Eden Valley Riesling 2004 A lovely wine, sliding through towards secondary flavours and aromas, but without closing down; classic regional lime, the low alcohol adding freshness. I suppose you can't complain about cork if they all taste and look like this. 11.5° alc. **Rating** 94 **To** 2012 $18

Rod & Spur Barossa Valley Shiraz Cabernet 2004 The same strong colour as the Basket Press Shiraz; aromatic; more sweet (in the best sense) fruit than usual; perfect ripening of fine tannins. Cork. 14.5° alc. **Rating** 94 **To** 2019 $28

Black Shiraz NV Big, round and rich, smooth and sexy, but just a little less dosage would have been even better. Regardless, just join the queue waiting to get on the mailing list. 13.5° alc. **Rating** 94 **To** 2015 $54

ϷϷϷϷϙ **Rod & Spur Barossa Valley Shiraz Cabernet 2003** A medium-bodied array of blackberry, blackcurrant, dark chocolate, spice and a faint touch of vanilla; good tannins and balance. Cork. 14.8° alc. **Rating** 90 **To** 2011 $28

Rifle Range Barossa Valley Cabernet Sauvignon 2003 Bright red-purple; fresh and lively cassis and blackcurrant fruit is a particularly good outcome for a difficult cabernet year. Stained cork. Cork. 13.5° alc. **Rating** 90 **To** 2013 $33

ϷϷϷϷ **Local Growers Semillon 2003** Full-bodied dry white; a peachy, toasty, thoroughly and deliberately old-fashioned style. Cork. 11.5° alc. **Rating** 89 **To** 2008 $17

Moppa Springs 2002 I would have thought this should be released earlier rather than later, but there you go. Pleasant Southern Rhone blend; light- to medium-bodied, but from an outstanding vintage. Grenache (74%)/Mataro (15%)/Shiraz 11%). Cork. 14.5° alc. **Rating** 89 **To** 2010 $22

Moppa Springs 2001 Starting to develop brick tones to the colour; medium-bodied, and now fully mature spicy/earthy overtones to gently sweet red fruits. Grenache/Shiraz/Mataro. Cork. 14.5° alc. **Rating** 89 **To** 2008 $22

White Frontignac 2005 Delicate flowery grapey aromas; some passionfruit flavours; seductive drink now style. Don't delay. Synthetic. 9.5° alc. **Rating** 89 **To** 2008 $13

Alicante Bouchet 2005 Vivid crimson-purple; no-holds-barred residual sugar in ultimate cellar door style; very sweet, though perhaps stemming from the low alcohol. Synthetic. 9.2° alc. **Rating** 87 **To** 2008 $16

Rocky Passes Wines

1590 Highlands Road, Seymour, Vic 3660 **Region** Upper Goulburn
T (03) 5796 9366 **F** (03) 5796 9366 **www**.rockypasseswines.com.au **Open** W'ends 10–5
Winemaker Vitto Oles **Est.** 2000 **Cases** 800

Vitto Oles and Candida Westney run this tiny, cool-climate vineyard situated at the southern end of the Strathbogie Ranges which in fact falls in the Upper Goulburn region. They have planted 1.6 ha of shiraz and 0.4 ha of viognier, growing the vines with minimal irrigation and preferring organic and biodynamic soil treatments. Vitto Oles is also a fine furniture designer and maker, with a studio at Rocky Passes.

ΨΨΨΨΨ **Upper Goulburn Syrah 2005** Intense blackberry, plum, licorice and prune on both bouquet and palate; excellent structure with ripe tannins and good length. Top-quality biodynamically grown wine. Diam. 13.8° alc. **Rating** 94 **To** 2025 $16.50

Rocland Estate ★★★★☆

PO Box 679, Nuriootpa, SA 5355 **Region** Barossa Valley
T (08) 8562 2142 **F** (08) 8562 2182 **Open** Not
Winemaker Simon Adams, Sam Scott **Est.** 2000 **Cases** 1000

Rocland Wines is primarily a bulk winemaking facility for contract work, but Frank Rocca does have 6 ha of shiraz which is used to make Rocland Wines, largely destined for export markets, but with retail distribution in Adelaide.

Rogues Lane Vineyard

370 Lower Plenty Road, Viewbank, Vic 3084 (postal) **Region** Heathcote
T 0409 202 103 **F** (03) 9457 2811 **www**.rogueslane.com.au **Open** Not
Winemaker Hanging Rock (John Ellis) **Est.** 1998 **Cases** 600

Pauline and Eric Dowker have planted 4 ha of shiraz (including a smattering of malbec), the first vintage coming in 1998. 'Dowker' is an ancient word meaning 'herder of ducks and geese', making the location of the vineyard on Wild Duck Creek doubly appropriate.

Rojo Wines ★★★

34 Breese Street, Brunswick, Vic 3056 **Region** Port Phillip Zone
T (03) 9386 5688 **F** (03) 9386 5699 **Open** W'ends 10–6
Winemaker Graeme Rojo **Est.** 1999 **Cases** 600

Rojo Wines is part of Melbourne's urban winery at Brunswick. Core production is cool-climate wines from the Strathbogie Ranges (Sauvignon Blanc, Chardonnay, Shiraz and Merlot). Fruit is also sourced from various regions in Vic. Production is low, allowing maximum time to be spent with each wine through its development.

ΨΨΨΨ **Terip Sauvignon Blanc 2006** Solid wine; mineral, herb and grass flavours; fair length. **Rating** 87 **To** 2008

Terip Chardonnay 2006 Pleasant, gentle melon and stone fruit aromas and flavours; not complex, but may develop with time. **Rating** 87 **To** 2010

Rokewood Junction ★★★★☆

123 Georges Road, Cambrian Hill, Vic 3352 (postal) **Region** Ballarat
T (03) 5342 0307 **F** (03) 5342 0307 www.rokewoodjunction.com.au **Open** Not
Winemaker Graham Jacobsson **Est.** 1995 **Cases** 180
Western District farmer Graham Jacobsson planted 0.5 ha of pinot noir on a steep north-facing slope in 1995. There are vertical slabs of shaley rock both under and on the surface, and the roots of the vines penetrate the fissures. With no top soil and a very windy, exposed site, the vineyard is basically devoid of diseases, and minimal vineyard intervention is needed. For a period of time, Jacobsson sold his grapes to Tomboy Hill, but since 2005 has made wine under his own label.

Pinot Noir 2005 A powerful, stylish wine; dark fruits, plums and spice; excellent length and structure. Screwcap. 13.7° alc. **Rating** 94 **To** 2010 $30

Pinot Noir 2004 Fragrant; strongly spicy/foresty but not green aromas; allspice and black cherry fruit on the palate, with a long, silky finish. Cork. 13° alc. **Rating** 93 **To** 2011 $30

Shiraz 2005 Considerable intensity, weight and persistence; faint olive and leaf characters, but of minor consequence in the overall context. It's a brave decision to grow shiraz in a climate as cool as this. Stained Diam. 13.5° alc. **Rating** 89 **To** 2013 $30

Rolf Binder ★★★★☆

Cnr Seppeltsfield Road/Stelzer Road, Tanunda, SA 5352 **Region** Barossa Valley
T (08) 8562 3300 www.rolfbinder.com **Open** Mon–Fri 10–4.30, Saturdays 11–4
Winemaker Rolf Binder, Christa Deans, Kym Teusner **Est.** 1955 **Cases** 25 000
The change of name from Veritas to Rolf Binder came with the 50th anniversary of the winery, established by Rolf's and sister Christa Deans' parents. The growth in production and sales is due to the quality of the wines rather than the (hitherto) rather laid-back approach to marketing.

Hanisch Barossa Valley Shiraz 2004 By the standards of modern Barossa Valley shiraz, positively elegant, the emphasis on moderately ripe fruit, rather than on alcohol and oak; some savoury/spicy notes extend the flavour spectrum. High-quality cork. 14.5° alc. **Rating** 94 **To** 2024 $95

Eden Valley Riesling 2006 Lemon blossom and apple aromas; has an intense and long fruit line right through to the finish. Screwcap. 12.5° alc. **Rating** 92 **To** 2015 $17
Heinrich Barossa Valley Shiraz Mataro Grenache 2005 Medium red-purple; strongly regional juicy berry/confit/jammy fruit aromas and flavours, counterbalanced on the finish by fine, sustained tannins. Screwcap. 14.5° alc. **Rating** 91 **To** 2020 $25
Binder's Bull's Blood Shiraz Mataro Pressings 2004 Strong colour; lives up to its name in every way, lush yet structured, power without the encumbrance of finesse; the tannins, while strong, have a leg rope in place. Cork. 14.5° alc. **Rating** 90 **To** 2014 $40

Christa Rolf Barossa Valley Semillon 2006 A nicely balanced hint of French oak adds to, rather than detracts from, grass and lemon fruit; good balance and mouthfeel. Screwcap. 13.5° alc. **Rating** 89 **To** 2010 $15

Rookery Wines ★★★★★

PO Box 132, Kingscote, Kangaroo Island, SA 5223 **Region** Kangaroo Island
T (08) 8553 9099 **F** (08) 8553 9201 www.rookerywines.com.au **Open** Not
Winemaker Garry Lovering, Geoff Weaver (Consultant) **Est.** 1999 **Cases** 4200

Garry and Gael Lovering have established a total of 8.4 ha of vines, with 3.6 ha of cabernet sauvignon and 1.6 ha of shiraz, the remainder divided between sauvignon blanc, tempranillo, saperavi, sangiovese, chardonnay, merlot, petit verdot and riesling. The wines are made under the watchful eye of Geoff Weaver, as experienced as he is skilled.

ŦŦŦŦŦ **Cabernet Sauvignon 2004** Dense red-purple; flooded with blackcurrant and cassis; ample structure and ripe tannins; good length and balance. Screwcap. 14° alc. **Rating** 94 **To** 2019 $30
Rookery Peak Cabernet Shiraz 2004 Good focus, line and length to a mix of blackcurrant, black cherry and blackberry fruit; excellent oak, tannin and extract control. Screwcap. 14.5° alc. **Rating** 94 **To** 2024 $50

ŦŦŦŦ **Shiraz 2004** Some reduction on the bouquet; medium- to full-bodied; sweet red and black fruits drive the flavours, although alcohol impacts. Screwcap. 14.8° alc. **Rating** 89 **To** 2014 $30
Sangiovese 2005 Light to medium red; a mix of cigar box and sour cherry aromas and flavours; fine cedary/savoury tannins. Screwcap. 14.5° alc. **Rating** 89 **To** 2010 $25
Cabernet Sauvignon 2003 Savoury, earthy, cedary style, lacking the ripeness of '04, but is far from a bad wine. Screwcap. 13° alc. **Rating** 87 **To** 2009 $17
Sangiovese 2004 Minty, leafy, savoury, and some cherry, notes; overall, light- to medium-bodied; silver medal Alternative Varieties Show '05. Screwcap. 14° alc. **Rating** 87 **To** 2008 $17

Rosabrook Estate   ★★★★★

Rosa Brook Road, Margaret River, WA 6285 **Region** Margaret River
T (08) 9757 2286 **F** (08) 9757 3634 **www.rosabrook.com Open** 7 days 10–4
Winemaker Bill Crappsley **Est.** 1980 **Cases** 4000
The 14-ha Rosabrook Estate vineyards were established progressively between 1984 and 1996, with sauvignon blanc, semillon, chardonnay, shiraz, merlot, cabernet sauvignon and petit verdot. The cellar door is housed in what was Margaret River's first commercial abattoir, built in the early 1930s, hence the icon red is named Slaughterhouse Block. Exports to the UK, Canada and Vietnam.

Rosby   ★★★

122 Strikes Lane, Mudgee, NSW 2850 **Region** Mudgee
T (02) 6373 3856 **F** (02) 6373 3109 **www.rosby.com.au Open** By appt
Winemaker Tim Stevens, Lesley Robertson (Contract) **Est.** 1997 **Cases** 500
Gerald and Kaye Norton-Knight have 4 ha of shiraz and 2 ha of cabernet sauvignon established on what is truly a unique site in Mudgee. Many new vignerons like to think that their vineyard has special qualities, but in this instance the belief is well-based. It is situated in a small valley, with unusual red basalt over a quartz gravel structure, encouraging deep root growth, and making the use of water far less critical than normal. Tim Stevens of Abercorn and Huntington Estate has purchased much of the production, and has no hesitation in saying it is of the highest quality (it formed an important part of his multi trophy-winning A Reserve range).

ŦŦŦŦ **Mudgee Shiraz 2004** Rich, fully ripe and sensuous plum, blackberry, prune and chocolate; ripe tannins and controlled oak; needs time. Diam. **Rating** 89 **To** 2019 $18

Rosebrook Estate   ★★★★☆

1092 Maitlandvale Road, Rosebrook, NSW 2320 **Region** Lower Hunter Valley
T (02) 4930 6961 **F** (02) 4930 6963 **www.rosebrookestatewines.com.au Open** At Morpeth Wine Cellar, tel (02) 4933 2612
Winemaker Graeme Levick **Est.** 2000 **Cases** 2000
Graeme and Tania Levick run Rosebrook Estate and Hunter River Retreat as parallel operations. They include self-contained cottages, horse-riding, tennis, canoeing, swimming, bushwalking, fishing, riverside picnic area, recreation room and minibus for winery tours and transport to

functions or events in the area. Somewhere in the middle of all this they have established 2.5 ha each of chardonnay and verdelho, purchasing shiraz and muscat to complete the product range.

ŸŸŸŸŸ **Chardonnay 2004** Excellent green-yellow; tightly focused citrus and nectarine supported by well-balanced and perfectly integrated oak. Top gold Hunter Valley Wine Show '06. Screwcap. **Rating** 94 **To** 2012 $13

ŸŸŸŸŸ **Chardonnay 2005** Crisp, lively and minerally; Chablis-like with restrained oak, not common in the Hunter. Screwcap. 15° alc. **Rating** 90 **To** 2011 $13

Roselea Vineyard   NR

310 Princes Highway, Gerringong, NSW 2534 (postal) **Region** Shoalhaven Coast
T (02) 4234 0340 **F** (02) 4234 0340 **www**.roseleavineyard.com.au **Open** Not
Winemaker Contract **Est.** 1998 **Cases** NA
Jeff and Margaret Lester have established their vineyard on a north-facing slope overlooking Rose Valley and Werri Beach. Planting began in 1998, and now extends to chardonnay, verdelho, sauvignon blanc, chambourcin, ruby cabernet and nebbiolo. Cellar door sales are not available as there is no public access from the Princes Highway.

Rosemount Estate (Hunter Valley)

Rosemount Road, Denman, NSW 2328 **Region** Upper Hunter Valley
T (02) 6549 6400 **F** (02) 6549 6499 **www**.rosemountestates.com **Open** 7 days 10–4
Winemaker Matthew Koch **Est.** 1969 **Cases** 3 million
Rosemount Estate achieved a miraculous balancing act, maintaining wine quality while presiding over an ever-expanding empire and dramatically increasing production. The wines were consistently of excellent value; all had real character and individuality, and more than a few were startlingly good. The outcome was the merger with Southcorp in 2001; what seemed to be a powerful and synergistic merger turned out to be little short of a disaster. Southcorp lost more than its market capitalisation and more than half of its most effective and talented employees. Now part of Fosters. Exports to all major markets.

ŸŸŸŸ **Traminer Riesling 2006** In time-honoured style, but suddenly fashionable, with spicy lime juice flavours and appreciable sweetness, balanced by acidity; tailor-made for Chinese restaurants. Screwcap. 11° alc. **Rating** 89 **To** 2008 $10.95
Diamond Label Shiraz 2005 A medium-bodied wine with positive varietal blackberry, licorice and plum fruit supported by balanced oak and tannins; good length, and the best of the Diamond Label range. Screwcap. 13.5° alc. **Rating** 89 **To** 2010 $16
Diamond Label Sauvignon Blanc 2006 Clean varietal character, in middle-of-the-road style; workmanlike making. For all these wines discounting to $13.99 seems more probable than not. Screwcap. 13° alc. **Rating** 88 **To** 2008 $16
Diamond Cellars Semillon Sauvignon Blanc 2006 Has more character and intensity than expected; pleasant grassy/citrus/mineral aromas and flavours; dry finish. Screwcap. 13° alc. **Rating** 88 **To** 2009 $11.95
Diamond Cellars Grenache Shiraz 2006 Clean, fresh and virtually entirely fruit-driven; has selected grenache with skill, not mushy or cosmetic; good balance and flavour. Screwcap. 14° alc. **Rating** 88 **To** 2008 $10.95
Diamond Label Cabernet Sauvignon 2005 Plenty of cabernet flavour in the mid spectrum between warm and cool-grown influences; what you see is what you get. Screwcap. 14° alc. **Rating** 88 **To** 2011 $16
Diamond Label Riesling 2006 Pleasant, full-flavoured wine with a combination of lime, tropical and stone fruit flavours; shortens somewhat on the finish. **Rating** 87 **To** 2008
Diamond Cellars Semillon Chardonnay 2005 A nice wine; good, lively fruit flavours, chardonnay giving nectarine and peach, the semillon lemon. Synthetic. 13.5° alc. **Rating** 87 **To** 2008 $11

Diamond Label Pinot Noir 2006 Has some varietal flavour and structure; light to medium-bodied, and not enough to excite overmuch, but does show definite varietal character. Screwcap. 13.5° alc. **Rating** 87 **To** 2009 $15.95

Diamond Cellars Shiraz Cabernet 2005 More than sufficient blackberry, blackcurrant and plum fruit; a ghost of sweetness, perhaps, likely a plus for most buyers. Screwcap. 11° alc. **Rating** 87 **To** 2009 $11.95

Diamond Cellars Cabernet Merlot 2006 Bright cassis, plum and cherry fruitshake; a definite style runs through this group of wines. Screwcap. 13.5° alc. **Rating** 87 **To** 2009 $11.95

Rosemount Estate (McLaren Vale)

Chaffeys Road, McLaren Vale, SA 5171 **Region** McLaren Vale
T (08) 8323 8250 **F** (08) 8323 9308 **www**.rosemountestate.com.au **Open** Mon–Sat 10–5, Sun & public hols 11–4
Winemaker Charles Whish **Est.** 1888 **Cases** 3 million
The specialist red wine arm of Rosemount Estate, responsible for its prestigious Balmoral Syrah, Show Reserve Shiraz and GSM, as well as most of the other McLaren Vale-based Rosemount brands. These wines come in large measure from 325 ha of estate plantings.

Show Reserve Coonawarra Cabernet Sauvignon 2003 Medium-bodied; a very earthy/savoury wine, with tannins doing much of the talking, the fruit already seeming somewhat diminished. A small, indifferent quality, cork has not helped. 14° alc. **Rating** 88 **To** 2010 $28

Rosenthal Wines

PO Box Y3110, East St Georges Terrace, Perth, WA 6832 **Region** Blackwood Valley
T 0407 773 966 **www**.rosenthalwines.com.au **Open** Not
Winemaker Dr Diane Miller (Contract) **Est.** 1997 **Cases** 800
Perth medical specialist Dr John Rosenthal heads Rosenthal Wines, which is a small part of the much larger 180-ha Springfield Park cattle stud situated between Bridgetown and Manjimup. He acquired the property from Gerald and Marjorie Richings, who in 1997 had planted a small vineyard as a minor diversification. The Rosenthals extended the vineyard to just under 5 ha, equally divided between shiraz, cabernet sauvignon and cabernet franc. The wines, especially the Sparkling Shiraz, have had significant show success.

The Cabernets 2004 A very nice wine; rich, supple and smooth blackcurrant fruit supported by round, soft tannins; good oak; great finish and aftertaste. Cork. 14.5° alc. **Rating** 94 **To** 2015 $18.50

Richings Shiraz 2004 Bright and clear colour; a vibrant, fresh, medium-bodied palate with predominantly red cherry and plum fruit; engaging and unforced. Cork. 14.8° alc. **Rating** 90 **To** 2012 $18.50

Shiraz Cabernet 2002 Maturing attractively; spicy/earthy overtones to the still substantial foundations of red and black fruits; good tannins and oak. Cork. 13.5° alc. **Rating** 89 **To** 2010 $18.50

Sparkling Shiraz 2003 Plenty of flavour; good balance to the spice and black cherry fruit; a longer time on lees would have produced an even better wine. 13.5° alc. **Rating** 89 **To** 2010 $25

Rosenvale Wines   ★★★★★

Lot 385 Railway Terrace, Nuriootpa, SA 5355 **Region** Barossa Valley
T 0407 390 788 **F** (08) 8565 7206 **www**.rosenvale.com.au **Open** By appt
Winemaker James Rosenzweig, Mark Jamieson **Est.** 2000 **Cases** 3500
The Rosenzweig family has 80 ha of vineyards, some old and some new, planted to riesling, semillon, pinot noir, grenache, shiraz and cabernet sauvignon. Most of the grapes are sold to other

producers, but since 1999 select parcels have been retained and vinified for release under the Rosenvale label. Exports to the UK, the US, Canada, Denmark, Korea and Hong Kong.

ŸŸŸŸŸ **Reserve Barossa Valley Shiraz 2004** Medium-bodied, but with finesse rather than power; a twist of sweet fruit on the mid-palate with clearly articulated varietal character; fine tannins and good length. Diam. 14.5° alc. **Rating** 94 To 2024 $33
Reserve Barossa Valley Cabernet Sauvignon 2004 Rich and bursting with cassis and blackcurrant fruit; ripe, but not the least jammy or extractive; controlled oak. Cork. 14.5° alc. **Rating** 94 To 2024 $33

ŸŸŸŸŸ **Estate Barossa Valley Shiraz 2005** Rich, ripe warm-grown, faintly stewed, fruit aromas; the palate brings the wine together, flavoursome, and with good structure. Diam. 14.5° alc. **Rating** 91 To 2018 $22

ŸŸŸŸ **Estate Barossa Valley Semillon 2006** A clean, fresh bouquet; plenty of flavour with ripe citrus, but lacks the sparkle of lower alcohol versions; 11.5° better than 13.5°; 1940s plantings. Screwcap. 13.5° alc. **Rating** 88 To 2010 $16
Estate Barossa Valley Grenache 2005 Soft, spicy, juicy berry flavours; utterly typical; early drinking. Diam. 15° alc. **Rating** 87 To 2008 $22

Rosily Vineyard ★★★★☆

Yelveton Road, Wilyabrup, WA 6284 **Region** Margaret River
T (08) 9755 6336 www.rosily.com.au **Open** W'ends 10–5, 7 days Christmas
Winemaker Mike Lemmes, Dan Pannell (Consultant) **Est.** 1994 **Cases** 6500
The partnership of Mike and Barb Scott and Ken and Dot Allan acquired the Rosily Vineyard site in 1994. Under the direction of consultant Dan Pannell (of the Pannell family) 12 ha of vineyard were planted over the next 3 years: sauvignon blanc, semillon, chardonnay, cabernet sauvignon, merlot, shiraz and a little grenache and cabernet franc. The first crops were sold to other makers in the region, but in 1999 Rosily built a winery with a 120-tonne capacity, and is now moving to fully utilise that capacity. Exports to the UK, Hong Kong and Singapore.

ŸŸŸŸŸ **Margaret River Sauvignon Blanc 2006** Spotlessly clean, no reduction; abundant passionfruit/tropical aromas and flavours, but balanced and sharpened by a twist of minerally acidity. Quite different to the '05. Screwcap. 12.6° alc. **Rating** 94 To 2008 $18

ŸŸŸŸŸ **Margaret River Semillon Sauvignon Blanc 2006** Fine, elegant, long and fresh; a seamless flow of fruit and a light touch of barrel ferment French oak. Top class, and great value; 65%/35%. Screwcap. 12.9° alc. **Rating** 93 To 2010 $18
Margaret River Merlot 2004 Star-bright colour; fragrant red fruits, warm spices, and a hint of snow peas; admirable varietal character. Screwcap. 14° alc. **Rating** 92 To 2014 $20
Reserve Semillon Sauvignon Blanc 2005 Complex and powerful; has largely soaked up the French oak in which it was fermented, but, in doing so, has somewhat diminished fruit expression. Screwcap. 13.8° alc. **Rating** 90 To 2009 $25
Chardonnay 2005 Ripe and relatively full peach/stone fruit flavours with some smoky/nutty characters; solid finish. Screwcap. 13.5° alc. **Rating** 90 To 2011 $20

ŸŸŸŸ **Margaret River Cabernet Sauvignon 2003** Bright, deep red-purple; full-bodied and powerful blackcurrant and cassis fruit within a very firm tannin structure needing years to soften. Cork. 13.9° alc. **Rating** 89 To 2015 $23

Rosnay Organic Wines ★★☆

Rivers Road, Canowindra, NSW 2804 **Region** Cowra
T (02) 6344 3215 **F** (02) 6344 3229 www.organicfarms.com.au **Open** By appt
Winemaker Various contract **Est.** 2002 **Cases** 3000

Rosnay Organic Wines is an interesting business venture, with the Statham and Gardner families at its centre. There are 36 ha of vineyard on the 140-ha property, part of which has been divided into 12 blocks along with 10 housing blocks, each of 5000 m². The viticulture is organic, and the management company provides active growers or absentee investors with a range of specialist organic farming machinery and contract management. Winemaking is split between John Cassegrain of Cassegrain Wines, Kevin Karstrom of Botobolar and Rodney Hooper of Windowrie, each one of whom has expertise in organic grapegrowing and organic winemaking.

Cowra Chardonnay Semillon 2004 Has flavour and character; peach with a touch of butterscotch balanced by acidity, the blend working well. Screwcap. 13° alc. **Rating** 87 **To** 2008 $14

Ross Estate Wines

Barossa Valley Way, Lyndoch, SA 5351 **Region** Barossa Valley
T (08) 8524 4033 **www**.rossestate.com.au **Open** Mon–Fri 10–4.30, w'ends 11–4.30
Winemaker Neville Falkenberg, Alex Peel **Est.** 1999 **Cases** 25 000
Darius and Pauline Ross laid the foundation for Ross Estate Wines when they purchased 43 ha of vines which included 2 blocks of 75- and 90-year-old grenache. Also included were blocks of 30-year-old riesling and semillon, and 13-year-old merlot. Chardonnay, sauvignon blanc, cabernet sauvignon, cabernet franc and shiraz followed. Neville Falkenberg has moved from Chain of Ponds to take the place of Rod Chapman, who has retired. Exports to all major markets.

Lynedoch Cabernet Sauvignon Cabernet Franc Merlot 2004 Perfumed and elegant; the quality of the vintage allows the varieties to flower and meld together in a fluid line of fragrant berry fruits; tannins and oak are there but not obvious. Cork. 13.5° alc. **Rating** 94 **To** 2019 $25

Tempranillo Grenache Cabernet Franc 2006 More complex and mouthfilling than the varietal Tempranillo, with a fine web of flavours, and an equally fine textural web, but without the purity of the varietal. Both lovely in their own way. Screwcap. 13.5° alc. **Rating** 93 **To** 2011 $19
ROSS Tempranillo 2006 Youthful purple; a delicious wine, aromatic and juicy, but with textured black cherries, hints of lemon zest and fruit cake spices, then a clean, fresh finish. A freakishly old planting of tempranillo, present when the Ross family purchased the property in '93, and subsequently identified by a French ampelographer. Screwcap. 13.5° alc. **Rating** 93 **To** 2008 $18
ROSS Shiraz 2004 Amazingly youthful purple-red hue; a medium-bodied palate, with a fresh and lively array of predominantly red and black cherry fruit; fine tannins and a nice splash of oak. Counter-cultural in the extreme. Screwcap. 13.5° alc. **Rating** 91 **To** 2014 $18
ROSS Cabernet Merlot 2004 Firm and muscular; it is certainly cabernet sauvignon which sets the pace. A touch of mint is a small pay-off for the excellent alcohol control. Cork. 13.5° alc. **Rating** 91 **To** 2019 $18
Old Vine Grenache 2004 Raspberry, red cherry and spice; old vines (up to 90 years old) do, in this instance, suppress the cosmetic characters, and give good structure. Cork. 14.5° alc. **Rating** 90 **To** 2014 $19

Estate Barossa Valley Riesling 2006 An honest wine, with plenty of traditional Barossa Valley flavour and structure; ripe citrus and stone fruit flavours; good balance. Screwcap. 13° alc. **Rating** 89 **To** 2012 $16

Ross Hill Vineyard

62 Griffin Road, via Ammerdown, Orange, NSW 2800 **Region** Orange
T (02) 6360 0175 **F** (02) 6363 1674 **www**.rosshillwines.com.au **Open** Sat 11–5, or by appt
Winemaker David Lowe, Stephen Doyle (Contract) **Est.** 1994 **Cases** 3000
Peter and Terri Robson began planting 10 ha of vines in 1994. Chardonnay, sauvignon blanc, merlot, cabernet sauvignon, shiraz and cabernet franc have been established on north-facing, gentle slopes at an elevation of 800 m. No insecticides are used in the vineyard, the grapes are

hand-picked and the vines are hand-pruned. Ross Hill also has an olive grove with Italian and Spanish varieties and a free-range organic snail production business. Exports to the UK.

ŸŸŸŸŸ **Orange Sauvignon Blanc 2006** A clean, minerally bouquet; lively lemon/citrus/gooseberry fruit flows through to the back palate and finish. Screwcap. 13° alc. **Rating** 90 **To** 2008 $20

Isabelle Cabernet Shiraz 2004 Rather more fruit weight than the blend would lead one to expect; dark fruits have some sweetness, but also the touches of tobacco leaf of the cabernet franc. Cork. 14.5° alc. **Rating** 90 **To** 2015 $24

Jack's Lot Limited Release Cabernet Franc 2005 Obviously picked at a higher baume, the fruit sweetness shows through; much better than the majority of cabernet francs in Australia, although the varietal expression is not entirely convincing. Cork. 14.8° alc. **Rating** 90 **To** 2017 $24

ŸŸŸŸ **Lily Sauvignon Blanc 2006** Mineral, citrus and passionfruit aromas and flavours; generous mouthfeel and total flavour; just a touch sweet. Screwcap. **Rating** 89 **To** 2008 $20

The Griffin Line Chardonnay 2005 Rich, textured and quite complex; needs a touch more acid to carry the fruit and alcohol richness. Screwcap. **Rating** 89 **To** 2010 $20

Orange Cabernet Sauvignon 2005 Full-bodied, rich blackcurrant fruit; a fraction rustic, and a little more work on the tannins and texture would have paid big dividends; time will help, nonetheless. Cork. 14.1° alc. **Rating** 89 **To** 2015 $24

Mick's Lot Shiraz 2005 Medium-bodied; hints of earth and animal on the bouquet; spicy fruit, and again a hint of bitterness on the finish; is this climate or something else at work? Cork. 14.5° alc. **Rating** 87 **To** 2010 $24

Rothvale Vineyard   ★★★☆

223 Deasy's Road, Pokolbin NSW 2320 **Region** Lower Hunter Valley
T (02) 4998 7290 **F** (02) 4998 7926 **www.**rothvale.com.au **Open** 7 days 10–5
Winemaker Max Patton, Luke Patton **Est.** 1978 **Cases** 10 000
Owned and operated by the Patton family, headed by Max Patton, who has the fascinating academic qualifications of BVSc, MSc London, BA Hons Canterbury – the scientific part has no doubt been useful for winemaking. The wines have accumulated an impressive array of medals. Exports to China.

ŸŸŸŸŸ **Luke's Hunter Valley Shiraz 2003** Still very youthful indeed; is this earthy regional character or a touch of reduction on the bouquet? The wine does have great length, and it is likely simply regional character, with years in front of it. Screwcap. 13° alc. **Rating** 91 **To** 2023 $25

ŸŸŸŸ **Lightly Oaked Hunter Valley Chardonnay 2005** Soft peach and melon fruit barely kissed by 10 weeks in French oak; an easy style, but the great colour may hint there is more to come as it ages. Screwcap. 14° alc. **Rating** 89 **To** 2010 $16

Georgia Hunter Valley Vintage Port 2006 A dense, rich melange of blackberry, dark chocolate and raspberries; fine spirit, and nicely balanced baume. Cork. 19.4° alc. **Rating** 89 **To** 2016 $20

Angus Lightly Oaked Hunter Valley Semillon Chardonnay 2006 Considerable colour development; complex but soft peachy chardonnay does most of the work without overmuch jabbing from the semillon; 50/50 blend. Screwcap. 12.5° alc. **Rating** 88 **To** 2010 $15

Roundstone Winery & Vineyard   ★★★★☆

54 Willow Bend Drive, Yarra Glen, Vic 3775 **Region** Yarra Valley
T (03) 9730 1181 **F** (03) 9730 1151 **www.**roundstonewine.com.au**Open** Wed–Sun & public hols 10–5, or by appt
Winemaker John Derwin **Est.** 1998 **Cases** 4000

John and Lynne Derwin have moved quickly since establishing Roundstone, planting 8 ha of vineyard (half to pinot noir with a mix of the best clones), building a small winery and opening a cellar door and restaurant. The Derwins tend the vineyard, enlisting the aid of friends to pick the grapes; John makes the wine with advice from Rob Dolan and Kate Goodman; Lynne is the chef and sommelier. Her pride and joy is a shearer's stove which was used at the Yarra Glen Grand Hotel for 100 years before being abandoned. The restaurant has established itself as one of the best winery restaurants in the valley. Exports to Ireland.

ΨΨΨΨΨ **Charmed Reserve Yarra Valley Chardonnay 2005** Like the Connemara, delicate and fresh; does have greater fruit weight and the added bonus of some barrel ferment notes. Cork. 13° alc. **Rating** 92 **To** 2011 $25
Connemara Yarra Valley Chardonnay 2005 A crisp, direct, minerally substrate to light citrus fruit has distinct Chablis connotations; no oak evident. Screwcap. 13° alc. **Rating** 90 **To** 2010 $18
Yarra Valley Shiraz Viognier 2005 A substantial wine; black fruits with lingering tannins offset by the moderating/lifting impact of viognier on the bouquet rather than the palate. Screwcap. 13° alc. **Rating** 90 **To** 2015 $25

ΨΨΨΨ **Yarra Valley Gamay 2006** Bright colour; light- to medium-bodied, but has plenty of drive with its dark cherry and blueberry fruit flavours; balanced acidity a plus. Screwcap. 13° alc. **Rating** 89 **To** 2008 $20
Rubies Reserve Yarra Valley Pinot Noir 2005 Very light colour; fragrant and fresh; the red fruit flavours are pretty, but doesn't have enough weight and concentration for higher points. Cork. 13° alc. **Rating** 89 **To** 2010 $25
Yarra Valley Basket Pressed Viognier 2005 Basket pressing is not a great method for white wines, but never mind; does have some apricot and peach fruit and fair acidity, but the pricing is somewhat ambitious. Cork. 13° alc. **Rating** 87 **To** 2008 $35
Yarra Valley Pinot Noir 2005 Slightly more stemmy notes and less vibrant fruit; just above rose in weight. Screwcap. 13° alc. **Rating** 87 **To** 2009 $18
Yarra Valley Cabernet Merlot 2004 Has abundant weight and structure but the flavours are too green and savoury; needed a longer hang-time. Screwcap. 13° alc. **Rating** 87 **To** 2012 $25

Rowans Lane Wines   ★★★

40 Farnham Road, Dennington, Vic 3280 **Region** Henty
T (03) 5565 1586 **F** (03) 5565 1586 **www**.rowanslanewines.com.au **Open** W'ends & public hols 10.30–5, or by appt
Winemaker Ted Rafferty **Est.** 2003 **Cases** 370
Ted and Judy Rafferty expanded their lifetime interest in wine by establishing an experimental 0.8-ha vineyard at their Rowans Lane property in 1999, making their first Pinot Noir in 2003. This encouraged them to expand their plantings to 3.6 ha at a second site at Dennington, on the banks of the Merri River. To supplement their own production, they have purchased grapes from other leading Henty grapegrowers, each with an impressive track record.

ΨΨΨΨ **Chardonnay 2005** Bright nectarine/peach aromas and flavours; subtle oak; crisp acidity tightens the wine up to its advantage, showing none of the reduction in the Unwooded '06. Cork. 13° alc. **Rating** 88 **To** 2010 $18

Rowanston on the Track

2710 Burke & Wills Track, Glenhope, Vic 3444 **Region** Macedon Ranges
T (03) 5425 5492 **F** (03) 5425 5493 **Open** Fri–Sun 9–5, or by appt
Winemaker John Frederiksen **Est.** 2003 **Cases** 800
John (a social worker) and Marilyn (a former teacher turned viticulturist) Frederiksen are no strangers to grapegrowing and winemaking in the Macedon Ranges. They founded Metcalfe Valley Vineyard in 1995, planting 5.6 ha of shiraz, going on to win gold medals at local wine shows. They sold the vineyard in early 2003, moving to their new property in the same year,

which has 4 ha of shiraz, 2 ha of merlot (planted between 1998 and 2000), and 2 ha of pinot noir and 1.3 ha of riesling (planted between 2000 and 2002).

ŸŸŸŸŸ **Macedon Ranges Riesling 2006** Striking aromas of wild herb, lavender and lime; a tighter and more conventional palate, precise and focused, with a long finish and aftertaste. Screwcap. 12.5° alc. **Rating** 95 **To** 2016 $15
Macedon Ranges Riesling 2005 Some of the same herbs as the '06 plus citrus and apple aromas; excellent palate, with impeccable balance, line and length. Screwcap. 12.5° alc. **Rating** 94 **To** 2014 $15

Rubicon   ★★★★

186 Blue Range Road, Rubicon, Vic 3172 **Region** Upper Goulburn
T (03) 9802 2174 **Open** By appt
Winemaker Robert Zagar **Est.** 2004 **Cases** 1000
Douglas Gordan and wife Lillian purchased Rubicon in 2004 intending to expand their cattle enterprise. The property included a 5.4-ha vineyard planted in 1992 to chardonnay, pinot noir and cabernet sauvignon by the original owners. When the sale of the grapes fell through, Douglas Gordan decided to have the wines made. Douglas is studying viticulture/wine production at Swinburne TAFE, and manages the vineyard using minimal intervention techniques with the help of his family.

Rusticana   ★★★★☆

Lake Plains Road, Langhorne Creek, SA 5255 **Region** Langhorne Creek
T (08) 8537 3086 **F** (08) 8537 3220 **www.**rusticanawines.com.au **Open** 7 days 10–5
Winemaker Bremerton Wines **Est.** 1998 **Cases** 2400
Brian and Anne Meakins are also owners of Newman's Horseradish, which has been on the SA market for over 80 years. Increasing demand for the horseradish forced them to move from Tea Tree Gully to Langhorne Creek in 1985. It wasn't until 1997 that they succumbed to the urging of neighbours and planted 5 ha each of shiraz and cabernet, adding 1 ha each of durif and zinfandel several years later. In a slightly unusual arrangement, the premium Black Label wines are made at Bremerton, the White Label range at the Langhorne Creek winery.

ŸŸŸŸŸ **Black Label Shiraz 2004** A medium-bodied, supple and round palate with sweet red and black fruits on the middle, then a long finish with fine tannins; minimal oak inputs. Screwcap. 14° alc. **Rating** 92 **To** 2019 $25

Rutherglen Estates   ★★★★☆

Cnr Great Northern Road/Murray Valley Highway, Rutherglen, Vic 3685 **Region** Rutherglen
T (02) 6032 7999 **F** (02) 6032 7998 **www.**rutherglenestates.com.au **Open** 7 days 10–6,
Tuileries Building, Drummond Street, Rutherglen
Winemaker Nicole Esdaile, Ricky James **Est.** 2000 **Cases** 50 000
Rutherglen Estates is an offshoot of a far larger contract crush and make business, with a winery capacity of 4000 tonnes (roughly equivalent to 280 000 cases). Rutherglen is in a declared phylloxera region, which means all the grapes grown within that region have to be vinified within it, itself a guarantee of business for ventures such as Rutherglen Estates. It also means that some of the best available material can be allocated for the brand, with an interesting mix of varieties. Exports to the UK, the US and other major markets.

ŸŸŸŸŸ **Durif 2005** Typical inky-purple; absolutely typical full-bodied wine, steeped in black fruits, licorice and some spice; 5% of this wine would go a remarkable distance in blends. Screwcap. 14.5° alc. **Rating** 92 **To** 2015 $20
Viognier 2006 Fresh and lively citrus blossom/honeysuckle aromas, the palate following suit though adding a touch of apricot; partial barrel ferment merely a whisper; very good length and winemaking. Screwcap. 14.5° alc. **Rating** 91 **To** 2011 $20

The Alliance Marsanne Viognier 2006 The blend (70/30) works well, the viognier lifting the fruit flavour complexity; true synergy; well-made. Screwcap. 14.5° alc. **Rating** 90 **To** 2010 $15

ΥΥΥΥ   **Marsanne 2006** Has plenty of weight and presence in the mouth thanks to the touch of barrel ferment, even if the slate and lemon flavours are presently fleeting; well-made and should develop. Screwcap. 14.5° alc. **Rating** 89 **To** 2013 $18

Shiraz 2005 Medium red-purple; black and red fruits on the medium-bodied palate, which almost aspires to elegance; certainly not over-ripe. Screwcap. 14.5° alc. **Rating** 89 **To** 2012 $18

Red 2005 A powerful, if somewhat rustic wine, with an abundance of red and black fruits, then slightly raw tannins needing to soften with time. Shiraz/Durif. Screwcap. 14.5° alc. **Rating** 88 **To** 2015 $13

Sangiovese 2005 Excellent colour; a big, bold style, with sultry red fruits, the tannins just a little too robust. Screwcap. 14.5° alc. **Rating** 88 **To** 2013 $18

Nebbiolo 2005 Respectable colour for this temperamental variety; likewise for the palate, which receives 99 points for effort, and 87 for the wine in the glass. Screwcap. 14.5° alc. **Rating** 87 **To** 2008 $18

Rymill Coonawarra

Riddoch Highway, Coonawarra, SA 5263 **Region** Coonawarra
T (08) 8736 5001 **F** (08) 8736 5040 **www**.rymill.com.au **Open** 7 days 10–5
Winemaker John Innes, Sandrine Gimon **Est.** 1974 **Cases** 50 000
The Rymills are descendants of John Riddoch and have long owned some of the finest Coonawarra soil, upon which they have grown grapes since 1970; present plantings are 150 ha. The output from the modern winery is substantial, the quality dependable rather than exciting. Quite why this should be so is an interesting question without an obvious answer. Exports to all major markets.

ΥΥΥΥΥ   **Cabernet Sauvignon 2004** Medium-bodied; strong blackcurrant and cassis fruit drive the wine, although there is doubtless French oak in the background. Cork. 14° alc. **Rating** 90 **To** 2014 $28

ΥΥΥΥ   **Sauvignon Blanc 2006** A clean, fresh light-bodied palate, with tropical fruits in a soft, crowd pleaser style. Screwcap. 12° alc. **Rating** 88 **To** 2008 $17

June Traminer (375 ml) 2005 Richer and more textured than most prior releases; not much varietal character, but has good balance and mouthfeel. Screwcap. 12.5° alc. **Rating** 88 **To** 2008 $16

The Yearling Cabernet Sauvignon 2005 Light- to medium-bodied, but good value; has attractive cabernet fruit, albeit just a little callow with slightly edgy tannins. Screwcap. 13° alc. **Rating** 87 **To** 2008 $13

S Kidman Wines

Riddoch Highway, Coonawarra, SA 5263 **Region** Coonawarra
T (08) 8736 5071 **F** (08) 8736 5070 **www**.kidmanwines.com.au **Open** 7 days 10–5
Winemaker John Innes (Contract) **Est.** 1984 **Cases** 8000
One of the district pioneers, with a 16-ha estate vineyard which is now fully mature. Limited retail distribution in Melbourne and Adelaide; exports through Australian Prestige Wines.

ΥΥΥΥ   **Coonawarra Shiraz 2003** Light- to medium-bodied; juicy red berry fruits, with more life and style than some of the prior releases; drink for pleasure. ProCork. 13.5° alc. **Rating** 89 **To** 2011 $18

Coonawarra Sauvignon Blanc 2006 Tight, firm and crisp; quite good mineral structure with a touch of herb. Screwcap. **Rating** 88 **To** 2008 $15

Saddlers Creek

Marrowbone Road, Pokolbin, NSW 2320 **Region** Lower Hunter Valley
T (02) 4991 1770 **F** (02) 4991 2482 www.saddlerscreekwines.com.au **Open** 7 days 9–5
Winemaker John Johnstone **Est.** 1989 **Cases** 20 000
Made an impressive entrance to the district with consistently full-flavoured and rich wines, and has continued on in much the same vein, with good wines across the spectrum. Exports to Canada, NZ and Mauritius.

🍷🍷🍷🍷🍷 **Reserve Chardonnay 2005** Tangy, crisp, vibrant and fresh; citrus and nectarine on a long palate. Cork. **Rating** 90 **To** 2010 $30

🍷🍷🍷🍷 **Classic Hunter Semillon 2005** A big, powerful chunky palate, with citrus offset by some mineral. Screwcap. **Rating** 88 **To** 2014 $18

Salena Estate

Bookpurnong Road, Loxton, SA 5333 **Region** Riverland
T (08) 8584 1333 **F** (08) 8584 1388 www.salenaestate.com.au **Open** Mon–Fri 8.30–4.30
Winemaker Robert Patynowski **Est.** 1998 **Cases** 480 000
This business encapsulates the hectic rate of growth across the entire Australian wine industry. Its 1998 crush was 300 tonnes, and by 2001 it was processing around its present level of 7000 tonnes. This was in part produced from over 200 ha of estate vineyards, supplemented by grapes purchased from other growers. It is the venture of Bob and Sylvia Franchitto, the estate being named after their daughter Salena. Exports to the US, the UK and other major markets.

🍷🍷🍷🍷 **South Australia Shiraz 2004** Light- to medium-bodied, with excellent fruit definition expressed by plum, black cherry and blackberry; minimal oak and tannin inputs, but not needed. Great value. Screwcap. 13.5° alc. **Rating** 89 **To** 2008 $12

🍇 Salet Wines

PO Box 19, Currarong, NSW 2540 **Region** Warehouse
T (02) 4448 3999 **F** (02) 4448 3999 www.salet.com.au **Open** Not
Winemaker Michael Salecich **Est.** 2002 **Cases** 700
Michael Salecich hails from Croatia, where his family has made wine for many generations. His winemaking methods are strongly influenced by the practices of his Croatian family, which he visits each year. He buys his grapes from SA, bringing them to his onsite winery by refrigerated trucks. Here the wines are crushed and fermented, and then matured in shaved hogsheads for 3 to 3.5 years, in the style of Barolo made the traditional way.

🍷🍷🍷🍷 **Shiraz 2004** Much better colour than the '05; likewise, deeper and rounder flavours; blackberry and chocolate, with some confit/jam notes, but not over the top. Screwcap. 13.9° alc. **Rating** 88 **To** 2012
Shiraz 2003 Soft, rich and round; obvious vanillin American oak influence, gentle red fruits, and soft tannins; well-made. Screwcap. 14.6° alc. **Rating** 88 **To** 2012

Salitage

Vasse Highway, Pemberton, WA 6260 **Region** Pemberton
T (08) 9776 1771 **F** (08) 9776 1772 www.salitage.com.au **Open** 7 days 10–4
Winemaker Patrick Coutts, Greg Kelly **Est.** 1989 **Cases** 20 000
Salitage is the showpiece of Pemberton. If it had failed to live up to expectations, it is a fair bet the same fate would have befallen the whole of the Pemberton region. The quality and style of Salitage did vary substantially, presumably in response to vintage conditions and yields, but since 1999 has found its way, with a succession of attractive wines. Exports to the UK, the US and other major markets.

Sally's Paddock

Redbank Winery, 1 Sally's Lane, Redbank, Vic 3478 **Region** Pyrenees
T (03) 5467 7255 **www.**sallyspaddock.com.au **Open** Mon–Sat 9–5, Sun 10–5
Winemaker Neill Robb **Est.** 1973 **Cases** 4000
The Redbank brand and stocks (Long Paddock, etc) were acquired by the Hill Smith Family
Vineyards (aka Yalumba) several years ago. The winery and surrounding vineyard which produces
Sally's Paddock were retained by Neill and Sally Robb, and continue to produced (and sell) this
single-vineyard, multi-varietal red wine and the new Sally's Hill range. There is some disagreement
on the use of the Redbank Winery name (see Redbank Victoria entry), but there is no dispute
about Sally's Paddock. Exports to the US, Germany and Asia.

Sally's Hill Shiraz 2005 Some questions on the bouquet give way to the tangy,
medium-bodied mix of spice, licorice, earth and blackberry fruit on the palate; fine,
lingering tannins. From vineyards surrounding Sally's Paddock. Cork. 13.5° alc.
Rating 89 **To** 2015 $19.90
Sally's Hill Cabernet Franc 2005 Very full-bodied, particularly for cabernet
franc; black, rather than red, fruits; unusual, particularly given the controlled alcohol.
Cork. 14° alc. **Rating** 88 **To** 2014 $19.90

Salomon Estate

PO Box 829, McLaren Vale, SA 5171 **Region** Southern Fleurieu
T 0417 470 590 **F** (08) 8323 8668 **Open** Not
Winemaker Bert Salomon, Boar's Rock (Mike Farmilo) **Est.** 1997 **Cases** 6000
Bert Salomon is an Austrian winemaker with a long-established family winery in the Kremstal
region, not far from Vienna. He became acquainted with Australia during his time with import
company Schlumberger in Vienna; he was the first to import Australian wines (Penfolds) into
Austria in the mid-1980s, and later became head of the Austrian Wine Bureau. He was so
taken by Adelaide that he moved his family there for the first few months each year, sending
his young children to school and setting in place an Australian red winemaking venture. He
has now retired from the Bureau, and is a full-time travelling winemaker, running the family
winery in the northern hemisphere vintage, and overseeing the making of the Salomon Estate
wines at Boar's Rock in the first half of the year. The circle closes as Mike Farmilo, former
Penfolds chief red winemaker, now makes Salomon Estate wines. Exports to the UK, the US,
and other major markets.

Finniss River Shiraz 2004 Medium- to full-bodied, supple and mouthfilling;
rich but not heavy or jammy blackberry, plum and licorice fruit; fully
representative of the '04 vintage where the crop has been thinned; seamless oak
and tannins. Cork. 14.5° alc. **Rating** 94 **To** 2020 $38
Finniss River Cabernet Sauvignon 2004 A very pure and correct cabernet
from the start of the bouquet to the finish of the palate; picked at optimum
ripeness, it has that delicious cassis/blackcurrant fruit and fine, ripe tannins in
support. Cork. 14.5° alc. **Rating** 94 **To** 2020 $38

Fleurieu Peninsula Syrah Viognier 2004 The usual highly perfumed aromas
of shiraz viognier; a supple, smooth texture also reflecting the viognier impact
on the black fruits, and associated touches of chocolate and earth; super-fine
tannins. One of the pioneers in Australia of the glass stopper VinoLock. 14° alc.
Rating 91 **To** 2014 $30
Bin 4 Baan Homage to Asia Shiraz Petit Verdot 2004 Powerful, but quite
supple, medium- to full-bodied dark fruits; the petit verdot percentage is not stated,
but is likely to be relatively low. Nonetheless I'm not sure about its suitability to Thai
food. Cork. 14.5° alc. **Rating** 90 **To** 2019 $20

 Salt Collins   **NR**

Locked Mail Bag No 6, Sydney, NSW 2000 **Region** Warehouse
T (02) 9958 3373 **F** (02) 9958 3373 **www.**saltcollins.com.au **Open** Not
Winemaker Various contract **Est.** 2005 **Cases** NA
This is a full-blown virtual winery, owning neither vineyards nor winery. Gary Collins is a 22-year veteran of the wine industry in Sydney, and CEO Peter Salt, who works in the recruitment industry, has turned a consumer's love of wine into a business enterprise. The partners seek out premium parcels of grapes, and then employ winemakers such as James Kellie (in Great Southern, WA) to make the wines.

Saltram   ★★★★★

Nuriootpa Road, Angaston, SA 5355 **Region** Barossa Valley
T (08) 8561 0200 **F** (08) 8561 0232 **www.**saltramwines.com.au **Open** Mon–Fri 9–5, w'ends & public hols 10–5
Winemaker Nigel Dolan **Est.** 1859 **Cases** 190 000
There is no doubt that Saltram has taken giant strides towards regaining the reputation it held 30 or so years ago. Under Nigel Dolan's stewardship, grape sourcing has come back to the Barossa Valley for the flagship wines, a fact of which he is rightly proud. The red wines, in particular, have enjoyed great show success over the past few years, with No. 1 Shiraz, Mamre Brook and Metala leading the charge. Exports to the UK, the US and other major markets.

🍷🍷🍷🍷🍷 **Pepperjack Barossa Shiraz Viognier 2005** Deeply coloured; a huge shiraz viognier, stacked with round, voluptuous flavour, oak and tannins somewhere in the background. Gold medal National Wine Show '06. Screwcap. 14.5° alc. **Rating** 95 **To** 2025 $23.95
No. 1 Barossa Shiraz 2004 Deep, dark fruits led by blackberry and a touch of prune, but no dead fruit; an icon Barossa wine from a great vintage with a virtually unlimited life; tannins and oak spot-on, and bravo for the screwcap. **Rating** 95 **To** 2029
Mamre Brook Barossa Shiraz 2004 Excellent purple hue; an attractive medium-bodied array of licorice, black cherry and blackberry fruit with neatly integrated and balanced vanilla oak; fine tannins, long finish. Cork. 14.5° alc. **Rating** 94 **To** 2015 $26
Metala Langhorne Creek Shiraz Cabernet 2005 Excellent wine; very good length and texture; gently savoury edges to the black fruits, finishing with fine tannins. Gold medal National Wine Show '06. Cork. 14.5° alc. **Rating** 94 **To** 2013 $21.95
Mamre Brook Barossa Cabernet Sauvignon 2004 Strong blackcurrant fruit on the medium- to full-bodied palate; evident but balanced tannins. It's only in very good and relatively cool vintages that the Barossa is suited to cabernet. Cork. 14° alc. **Rating** 94 **To** 2020 $26
Winemakers Selection Barossa Valley Cabernet Sauvignon 2002 Ultra-powerful, concentrated and focused emblem of a great vintage; blackcurrant with touches of cedar and earth. Cork. 14.5° alc. **Rating** 94 **To** 2022 $65

🍷🍷🍷🍷🍷 **Pepperjack Barossa Shiraz Viognier 2004** Typical deep purple-red; carries the alcohol without blinking; supple damson plum with typical varietal lift; subtle oak. Screwcap. 15° alc. **Rating** 93 **To** 2014 $22
Metala Langhorne Creek Shiraz Cabernet 2004 Replete with masses of luscious and spicy black fruits; excellent tannin structure, soft but lingering. Cork. 14.5° alc. **Rating** 93 **To** 2019
Winemakers Selection Barossa Valley Cabernet Sauvignon 2004 A vintage which helped cabernet sauvignon retain personality and typicity in the Barossa; the wine is flush with cassis and blackcurrant, soft, ripe tannins, and good oak. Cork. 14.5° alc. **Rating** 93 **To** 2024 $55

Pepperjack Barossa Shiraz 2005 Deep, dense purple-red; abundant blackberry and prune fruit coupled with some licorice; overall tannin and oak extract well-handled. Cork. 14.5° alc. **Rating** 91 **To** 2012 $23

Mamre Brook Barossa Chardonnay 2005 A generous wine in typical Barossa full-throated style, though the oak handling and lees management have been carefully controlled; clean, fresh finish. Screwcap. 13.5° alc. **Rating** 90 **To** 2010 $20.95

Pepperjack Barossa Grenache Rose 2006 Vivid fuchsia; lots of red cherry and raspberry fruit, no significant sweetness involved. Long finish. Screwcap. 13.5° alc. **Rating** 90 **To** 2008 $23.95

Pepperjack Barossa Shiraz Grenache Mourvedre 2005 Shiraz sets the tune, and calls the shots, providing the backbone for the other varieties, and the synergy for the overall red fruit flavours. Cork. 14.5° alc. **Rating** 90 **To** 2013 $23.95

 \u0001\u0001\u0001\u0001 **The Eighth Maker Barossa Shiraz 2003** A very powerful wine, and an achievement for the troubled vintage. However, the tannins pose a major question mark: will they soften before the fruit dies? Cork. **Rating** 89 **To** 2012

Mr Pickwick's Limited Release Particular Port NV The sweetest of the 12-year-old tawny styles on the market, making it a distinctly different style; whether you prefer the drier more biscuity alternatives is a simple question of preference. Cork. 18° alc. **Rating** 89 **To** 2008 $55

Pepperjack Barossa Viognier 2006 Aromas and flavours are decidedly amorphous; the rich texture is the varietal marker, and the maker has cleverly avoided phenolics on the finish. Screwcap. 14° alc. **Rating** 88 **To** 2009 $23.95

Maker's Table Unwooded Chardonnay 2006 Surprise; an Australia-wide supply source, but actually tastes of chardonnay and doesn't rely on sweetness. Cork. 13° alc. **Rating** 87 **To** 2008 $9.95

Next Chapter Barossa Chardonnay 2005 Appealing mineral, citrus and nectarine fruit with a ghost of oak; good balance. Cork. 13.5° alc. **Rating** 87 **To** 2008 $15

Sam Miranda of King Valley ★★★★☆

Cnr Snow Road/King Valley Road, Oxley, Vic 3678 **Region** King Valley
T (03) 5727 3888 **F** (03) 5727 3851 **www**.sammiranda.com.au **Open** 7 days 10–5
Winemaker Sam Miranda **Est.** 2004 **Cases** 10 000
Sam Miranda, grandson of Francesco Miranda, joined the family business in 1991, striking out on his own in 2004 after Miranda Wines was purchased by McGuigan Simeon. The High Plains Vineyard is in the Upper King Valley at an altitude of 450 m; 13 ha of vines are supplemented by some purchased grapes. In 2005 Sam Miranda purchased the Symphonia Wines business, and intends to keep its identity intact and separate from the Sam Miranda brand. Exports to China.

\u0001\u0001\u0001\u0001\u0001 **Sangiovese Barbera 2005** Smooth, supple cherry fruits, with good length and intensity; far more authority than usual, and lives up to its stylish packaging. Cork. 14° alc. **Rating** 91 **To** 2010 $28

High Plains Cabernet Sauvignon 2004 A well-balanced and composed medium-bodied wine, with firm blackcurrant varietal fruit the cornerstone; fine tannins back up the finish, as does the price. Cork. 13.5° alc. **Rating** 90 **To** 2014 $18

King Valley Chardonnay Pinot 2004 An attractive mix of strawberry and citrus fruits; just a touch of creamy lees from 18 months on lees; good balance and length. 13° alc. **Rating** 90 **To** 2010 $25

\u0001\u0001\u0001\u0001 **High Plains Shiraz 2005** Light- to medium-bodied; distinctly savoury/earthy nuances to the fruit which has unexpected length and a bright finish. Screwcap. 14° alc. **Rating** 88 **To** 2012 $18

King Valley Late Harvest Verdelho 2005 Lovely pale green colour; soft, demonstrably sweet, tropical fruit salad balanced by acidity on the finish. Screwcap. 10.5° alc. **Rating** 88 **To** 2008 $20

Samuel's Gorge

Lot 10 Chaffeys Road, McLaren, SA 5171 **Region** McLaren Vale
T (08) 8323 8651 **F** (08) 8323 8673 www.gorge.com.au **Open** First w'end of spring
until sold out, or by appt
Winemaker Justin McNamee **Est.** 2003 **Cases** 1250

After a wandering winemaking career in various parts of the world, Justin McNamee became a winemaker at Tatachilla in 1996, where he remained until 2003, leaving to found Samuel's Gorge. He has established his winery in a barn built in 1853, part of a historic property known as the old Seaview Homestead. The property was owned by Sir Samuel Way, variously Chief Justice of the SA Supreme Court and Lieutenant Governor of the State. The grapes come from small contract growers spread across the ever-changing (unofficial) subregions of McLaren Vale, and are basket-pressed and fermented in old open slate fermenters lined with beeswax.

 McLaren Vale Shiraz 2004 A medium- to full-bodied wine, with abundant ripe, though not jammy, black fruits; fine, soft tannins make the wine harmonious. **Rating** 94 **To** 2019 $35
McLaren Vale Grenache 2004 Typical top-quality McLaren Vale grenache; a complete wine with ample structure and supple, not jammy, black fruits; good oak handling. Cork. 14.8° alc. **Rating** 94 **To** 2014 $40

 McLaren Vale Tempranillo 2005 Fragrant aromas, and a light- to medium-bodied, spicy, elegant palate, the tannins tending to linger. Radically different to the '04. Cork. 13.8° alc. **Rating** 88 **To** 2010 $40

Sanctuary Hill Vineyard

PO Box 103, Harcourt, Vic 3453 **Region** Bendigo
T (03) 5474 3127 **F** (03) 5474 3127 **Open** Not
Winemaker Simon Moten **Est.** 1999 **Cases** 500

Sanctuary Hill takes its name from the koala sanctuary situated on Mt Alexander above the vineyard. (Koalas have a very specific eucalypt tree diet, and unlike kangaroos and wallabies present no threat to the vineyard.) It has been a long way round for Simon Moten and Karen Abe; Simon's exposure to wine began at 13 when his father established the Asher boutique vineyard and winery in Geelong. Having graduated from Deakin University with a Bachelor of Science degree majoring in biochemistry, Simon commenced work with Lindemans in Karadoc. He thereafter moved to Fosters, at one stage being head brewer of Matilda Bay Brewery in WA. Winemaking remained in his blood, however, and in 1999 he and Karen began the establishment of a little over 4 ha of shiraz, cabernet sauvignon, merlot, and tiny blocks of cabernet franc and semillon. High-density planting and a number of other viticultural techniques are designed to maximise flavour and quality. The Savage Dog Cabernet Sauvignon is a relic of university days when one of the students (whose father was a grapegrower in Robinvale) tried to convince everyone that sauvignon was French for 'savage dog', and the term has stuck.

Shiraz 2004 Fragrant spice and herb overlay to red fruits on the bouquet; cool-grown flavours, but not too green, rather intense and long. Nonetheless, won't appeal to Barossa Valley lovers. Screwcap. 14.2° alc. **Rating** 88 **To** 2014 $19

Sandalford ★★★★☆

3210 West Swan Road, Caversham, WA 6055 **Region** Margaret River
T (08) 9374 9374 **F** (08) 9274 2154 www.sandalford.com **Open** 7 days 10–5
Winemaker Paul Boulden **Est.** 1840 **Cases** 80 000

Some years ago the upgrading of the winery and the appointment of Paul Boulden as chief winemaker resulted in far greater consistency in quality, and the proper utilisation of the excellent vineyard resources of Sandalford in Margaret River and Mount Barker. Things have continued on an even keel since, with the entry level Element range (from various parts of WA), Protege (from Margaret River) at the mid-level, and Single Vineyard Estate (Margaret River) at the top level. Exports to the UK, the US and other major markets.

ŸŸŸŸŸ **Prendiville Reserve Margaret River Cabernet Sauvignon 2003** A powerful, concentrated wine; earthy cabernet fruit has absorbed all the French oak; long and distinguished. From the oldest vines, and the best 20 new French oak barrels. Screwcap. 14.5° alc. **Rating** 94 **To** 2028 $90

ŸŸŸŸŸ **Margaret River Riesling 2006** A flowery and fruity bouquet which diminishes somewhat on the palate; on the plus side has a long finish, driven by acidity. Screwcap. 11.5° alc. **Rating** 90 **To** 2013 $22
Element Chardonnay 2006 Clean stone fruit aromas; the palate adds a touch of grapefruit, and there is a whisper of oak. Top value. Screwcap. 12.5° alc. **Rating** 90 **To** 2010 $13

ŸŸŸŸ **Element Classic White 2006** Lively and fresh fruit salad flavours with touches of tropical fruit ranging through to more herbal notes; good acidity and length. Chenin Blanc/Verdelho. Screwcap. 12° alc. **Rating** 89 **To** 2008 $13
Element Shiraz Cabernet 2005 Like the Chardonnay, over-delivers at the price; bright, fresh black and red fruits drive the wine; tannins and oak lurk in the background; ready now, but will hold. Screwcap. 14° alc. **Rating** 89 **To** 2011 $13
Element Merlot 2005 Completes a range of Element wines which all over-deliver; clearly articulated varietal character in a light- to medium-bodied palate; long, savoury finish. Screwcap. 14° alc. **Rating** 89 **To** 2011 $13
Margaret River Sauvignon Blanc Semillon 2006 No reduction; quite soft and ripe fruit, particularly given the vintage and alcohol; in a tropical spectrum, not enough drive, however. Screwcap. 12° alc. **Rating** 88 **To** 2008 $22
Margaret River Verdelho 2006 The most surprising feature of the wine is its price; no frills, fair varietal character, good length and acidity, but where is the excitement? Screwcap. 13.5° alc. **Rating** 88 **To** 2010 $25

Sandalyn Wilderness Estate ★★☆

162 Wilderness Road, Rothbury, NSW 2321 **Region** Lower Hunter Valley
T (02) 4930 7611 **F** (02) 4930 7611 www.huntervalleyboutiques.com.au **Open** 7 days 10–5
Winemaker Lindsay Whaling **Est.** 1988 **Cases** 6000
Sandra and Lindsay Whaling preside over the picturesque cellar door building of Sandalyn on the evocatively named Wilderness Road, where you will find a one-hole golf range and views to the Wattagan, Brokenback and Molly Morgan ranges. The estate has 9 ha of vineyards planted to chardonnay, pinot noir, verdelho and semillon. Exports to Ireland.

Sandhurst Ridge ★★★★★

156 Forest Drive, Marong, Vic 3515 **Region** Bendigo
T (03) 5435 2534 www.sandhurstridge.com.au **Open** Wed–Mon 11–5, or by appt
Winemaker Paul Greblo, George Greblo **Est.** 1990 **Cases** 2500
The Greblo brothers (Paul and George), with combined experience in business, agriculture, science and construction and development, began the establishment of Sandhurst Ridge in 1990 with the planting of the first 2 ha of shiraz and cabernet sauvignon. Plantings have now been increased to over 7 ha, principally cabernet and shiraz, but also a little merlot and nebbiolo. As the business has grown, the Greblos have supplemented their crush with grapes grown in the region. Exports to Canada and Hong Kong.

ŸŸŸŸŸ **Bendigo Shiraz 2005** Clean and rich fruit aromas; a rich layered palate with blackberry, blood plums and dark chocolate; good American and French oak use. Hail reduced the crop. Screwcap. 15.5° alc. **Rating** 94 **To** 2025 $28
Reserve Shiraz 2004 A very interesting and most elegant wine with lesser alcohol and adorned by French (not American) oak. Medium-bodied blackberry and plum fruit; silky texture and good length. Diam. 14° alc. **Rating** 94 **To** 2019 $38

ϒϒϒϒϒ **Heathcote Shiraz 2005** American oak makes an impact on both bouquet and
palate; however, the focused fruit handles it, with ripples of prune, plum and
blackberry jam. Screwcap. 16° alc. **Rating** 93 **To** 2025 $25

Bendigo Shiraz 2004 Deep colour; significantly more complex and rich than
the Reserve, but does not have its elegance; full-bodied blackberry, vanilla and dark
chocolate; abundant tannins and American oak (14 months). Diam. 14.5° alc.
Rating 92 **To** 2020 $32

Fringe Bendigo Shiraz 2004 A clean bouquet with no hint of reduction;
medium-bodied, supple, round and ripe (not jammy) fruit; gentle tannins;
12 months American oak. Screwcap. 14.5° alc. **Rating** 92 **To** 2019 $22

Bendigo Cabernet Sauvignon 2004 A medium- to full-bodied mix of
blackcurrant and a dash of blackberry; ripe tannins in balance, as is the French oak.
Cork. 13.5° alc. **Rating** 92 **To** 2019 $32

Bendigo Merlot 2005 Deep colour for the variety; distinct savoury varietal
characters, albeit in typical Sandhurst heroic mould; black olive, earth and
blackcurrant. Screwcap. 14.5° alc. **Rating** 91 **To** 2016 $28

Bendigo Cabernet Sauvignon 2005 Similar to the Fringe Cabernet; perhaps
just that little bit sweeter, but still has some slight green olive flavours on the finish.
Will appeal to some. Screwcap. 14.5° alc. **Rating** 90 **To** 2015 $28

Fringe Bendigo Cabernet Sauvignon 2004 Medium-bodied; a soft, supple
palate with blackcurrant and cassis fruit; well-balanced and integrated French oak.
Screwcap. 14° alc. **Rating** 90 **To** 2015 $22

ϒϒϒϒ **Fringe Bendigo Shiraz 2005** Far lighter in colour than the Bendigo Shiraz;
more spicy red fruits, the slightly lower alcohol evident, and, indeed, tastes lower than
it states. Screwcap. 15° alc. **Rating** 89 **To** 2015 $20

Fringe Bendigo Cabernet Sauvignon 2005 A pretty useful wine; medium-
bodied, with attractive blackcurrant/redcurrant fruit, and controlled oak and tannins;
just a twist of green on the very finish. Screwcap. 14° alc. **Rating** 89 **To** 2012 $20

Sandstone   ★★★☆

Cnr Johnson Road/Caves Road, Wilyabrup, WA 6280 **Region** Margaret River
T (08) 9755 6271 **F** (08) 9755 6292 **Open** 7 days 11–4
Winemaker Jan McIntosh **Est.** 1988 **Cases** 4000
There have been a number of changes at Sandstone over recent years, Jan McIntosh is now
winemaker and runs the business. It will eventually be estate-based following the planting of
9 ha (semillon and cabernet sauvignon).

Sanguine Estate   ★★★★☆

77 Shurans Lane, Heathcote, Vic 3523 (postal) **Region** Heathcote
T (03) 9646 6661 **F** (03) 9646 1746 **www.**sanguinewines.com.au **Open** Not
Winemaker Mark Hunter, Peter Dredge, Ben Riggs (Contract) **Est.** 1997 **Cases** 4000
The Hunter family, with parents Linda and Tony at the head, and their children, Mark and Jodi,
with their respective partners Melissa and Brett, began establishing the vineyard in 1997. From a
starting base of 4 ha of shiraz planted that year, it has now grown to 20.23 ha of shiraz, and 2 ha
of 8 different varieties, including chardonnay, viognier, merlot, tempranillo, zinfandel, petit verdot,
cabernet sauvignon, merlot and cabernet franc. Low-yielding vines and the magic of the
Heathcote region have produced Shiraz of exceptional intensity, which has received rave reviews
in the US, and led to the 'sold out' sign being posted almost immediately upon release. With the
ever-expanding vineyard, Mark Hunter has become full-time vigneron, and Jodi Marsh part-time
marketer and business developer. Exports to the UK, the US, Canada, Singapore and Hong Kong.

ϒϒϒϒϒ **Heathcote Shiraz 2005** Extremely rich, dense and concentrated in the main
Heathcote style; blackberry, licorice, plum and spice; fine but lingering tannins;
hard to deny. Screwcap. 14.8° alc. **Rating** 94 **To** 2030 $35

ΨΨΨΨ **Heathcote Tempranillo 2005** Black cherry, feijoa, rhubarb and citrus; lively but supple mouthfeel; good length, and starting to show the way for the variety. Cork. 14.5° alc. **Rating** 91 **To** 2015 $25

Classic Quattro 2005 A masculine, muscular, earthy wine but not on steroids; blackcurrant, blackberry and cedar; has length, and the tannins are controlled. Cabernet Sauvignon/Cabernet Franc/Petit Verdot/Merlot. Cork. 14.8° alc. **Rating** 90 **To** 2018 $25

Saracen Estates ★★★★★

3487 Caves Road, Wilyabrup, WA 6280 **Region** Margaret River
T (08) 9221 4955 **F** (08) 9221 4966 **www**.saracenestates.com.au **Open** By appt
Winemaker Naturaliste Vintners (Bruce Dukes), Bob Cartwright (Consultant) **Est.** 1998
Cases 5000
The Cazzolli and Saraceni families have established 17 ha of vines on their 80-ha property, with a striking restaurant and cellar door opened in 2007. The name not only echoes one of the founding families, but also pays tribute to the Saracens, one of the most advanced races in cultural and social terms at the time of the Crusades. Exports to the UK, Singapore, Malaysia, Hong Kong, India and Denmark.

ΨΨΨΨΨ **Margaret River Sauvignon Blanc Semillon 2006** Very well-made; lovely interplay between barrel-fermented semillon and stainless steel-fermented sauvignon blanc; intense passionfruit and grass flavours without heaviness, and a long, fine finish. Screwcap. 12.9° alc. **Rating** 94 **To** 2011 $18

Margaret River Shiraz 2005 Elegant, perfectly balanced and proportioned; blackcurrant and complex spicy notes, some sweet, some savoury, some simply peppery; fine, lingering tannins. Screwcap. 14.2° alc. **Rating** 94 **To** 2020 $30

ΨΨΨΨ **Margaret River Cabernet Sauvignon 2004** Elegance is the key word for the Saracen style, here in medium-bodied mode, with cassis, raspberry and blackcurrant; fine tannins and good oak management; creeps up on you. Screwcap. 14.2° alc. **Rating** 92 **To** 2018 $30

Margaret River Sauvignon Blanc 2006 The 50% barrel fermentation subdues the varietal aroma in the short-term, but on the well-balanced palate flavours run from the grassy end to riper, richer notes; a rare sauvignon blanc needing time. Screwcap. 13.1° alc. **Rating** 90 **To** 2010 $22

Sarsfield Estate ★★★★☆

345 Duncan Road, Sarsfield, Vic 3875 **Region** Gippsland
T (03) 5156 8962 **F** (03) 5156 8970 **www**.sarsfieldestate.com.au **Open** By appt
Winemaker Dr Suzanne Rutschmann **Est.** 1995 **Cases** 1200
Owned by Suzanne Rutschmann, who has a PhD in Chemistry, a Diploma in Horticulture and and a BSc (Wine Science) from Charles Sturt University, and Swiss-born Peter Albrecht, a civil and structural engineer who has also undertaken various courses in agriculture and viticulture. For a part-time occupation, these are exceptionally impressive credentials. Their 2-ha vineyard was planted between 1991 and 1998; the first vintage made at the winery was 1998, the grapes being sold to others in previous years. High-quality packaging is a plus. Exports to Ireland.

ΨΨΨΨΨ **Pinot Noir 2005** Well-balanced plum, cherry and spice with touches of forest floor and stem; good length and impressive style. Gold medal Gippsland Wine Show '07. **Rating** 94 **To** 2013 $22.50

ΨΨΨΨ **Cabernet Shiraz Merlot 2004** Bright colour; generous flavour and ample structure to the cassis and black fruit flavours; fine tannins to close. Cork. 13.7° alc. **Rating** 92 **To** 2019 $20

Pinot Noir 2004 Lively plum and cherry fruit with good balance and mouthfeel. Cork. 13.9° alc. **Rating** 90 **To** 2010 $22.50

❦❦❦❦ **Cabernet Shiraz Merlot 2005** Has flavour in a green, spice and herb spectrum; more red fruit needed. **Rating** 87 **To** 2010
Rose 2006 Has good structure, and an array of red fruit flavours; doesn't simply rely on residual sugar. Cork. 12.8° alc. **Rating** 87 **To** 2008 $17.50
Mourvedre 2005 Unusual variety for Gippsland; however, has varietal character, and, in particular, the mourvedre tannins which one expects. **Rating** 87 **To** 2011 $22.50

SC Pannell

14 Davenport Terrace, Wayville, SA 5034 (postal) **Region** McLaren Vale
T (08) 8299 9256 **F** (08) 8299 9274 **Open** Not
Winemaker Stephen Pannell **Est.** 2004 **Cases** 2500
The only surprising piece of background is that it took (an admittedly still reasonably youthful) Stephen Pannell (and wife Fiona) so long to cut the painter from Constellation/Hardys and establish their own winemaking and consulting business. Steve Pannell radiates intensity, and extended experience backed by equally long experimentation and thought has resulted in wines of the highest quality right from the first vintage. At present the focus of their virtual winery (they own neither vineyards nor winery) is grenache and shiraz grown in McLaren Vale. This is a label which is quite certain to become thoroughly iconic in the years ahead.

❦❦❦❦❦ **McLaren Vale Grenache 2004** Grenache simply doesn't come better than this. Has all the structure one could wish for, with highly expressive red fruits, silky tannins and perfect oak. Cork. 14° alc. **Rating** 96 **To** 2019 $40
McLaren Vale Shiraz 2004 A particularly elegant example of 90-year-old McLaren Vale shiraz; bright and clear aromas and flavours of cherry and blackberry; controlled oak, fine tannins. High-quality cork. 14° alc. **Rating** 95 **To** 2024 $40
McLaren Vale Shiraz Grenache 2004 Another lovely wine with great texture and structure; expressive fruit without a hint of jamminess; perfect finish and mouthfeel. Cork. 14.5° alc. **Rating** 95 **To** 2024 $40
Adelaide Hills Sauvignon Blanc 2006 Spotlessly clean; lively, clean, zingy passionfruit, ripe apple and gooseberry; crisp acidity to close. Screwcap. 13° alc. **Rating** 94 **To** 2008 $25

❦❦❦❦❦ **McLaren Vale Grenache Rose 2006** Pale, bright fuchsia; has abundant flavour and length, and a bone-dry finish; serious lunch/food style. Screwcap. 13.5° alc. **Rating** 91 **To** 2008 $22

Scaffidi Wines

Talunga Cellars, Adelaide-Mannum Road, Gumeracha, SA 5233 **Region** Adelaide Zone
T (08) 8389 1222 **www.**talunga.com.au **Open** Wed–Sun & public hols 10.30–5
Winemaker Vince Scaffidi **Est.** 1994 **Cases** 2000
Owners Vince and Tina Scaffidi have a one-third share of the 80-ha Gumeracha Vineyards, and it is from these vineyards that the wines are sourced. The cellar door and restaurant is named Talunga Cellars. The wines are exceptionally well-priced given their quality.

❦❦❦❦❦ **St Vincent Gulf One Tree Hill Shiraz 2004** Good purple-red; plenty of intensity, focus and concentration; blackberry, bitter chocolate and licorice flavours; ripe tannins, controlled oak. Cork. 14° alc. **Rating** 93 **To** 2015 $19.50
Hard Rock One Tree Hill Shiraz 2002 An extremely focused and potent wine; blackberry and spice fruit, with firm, but not harsh, tannins; long finish, controlled oak. Cork. 14.5° alc. **Rating** 92 **To** 2015 $19.50

❦❦❦❦ **Gulf Breeze One Tree Hill Sangiovese 2005** Good colour for the variety; simply too much extract to allow sangiovese to speak with a clear voice; cherry jam reduction fruit; all hard to reconcile with the relatively low alcohol. Interesting, nonetheless. Screwcap. 13.5° alc. **Rating** 89 **To** 2015 $13.50

Scarborough

179 Gillards Road, Pokolbin, NSW 2320 **Region** Lower Hunter Valley
T (02) 4998 7563 **F** (02) 4998 7786 www.scarboroughwine.com.au **Open** 7 days 9–5
Winemaker Ian Scarborough, Jerome Scarborough **Est.** 1985 **Cases** 15 000
Ian Scarborough honed his white winemaking skills during his years as a consultant, and has brought all those skills to his own label. He makes 3 different styles of Chardonnay: the Blue Label in a light, elegant, Chablis style for the export market and a richer barrel-fermented wine (Yellow Label) primarily directed to the Australian market, the third is the White Label, a cellar door-only wine made in the best vintages. However, the real excitement for the future lies with the portion of the old Lindemans Sunshine Vineyard which he has purchased (after it lay fallow for 30 years) and planted with semillon and (quixotically) pinot noir. The first vintage from the legendary Sunshine Vineyard was made in 2004. Exports to the UK, the US and Singapore.

ŸŸŸŸŸ **Shiraz 2003** Firm, but good texture and structure; balanced red/black fruits and Hunter leather; has all the requisites for long ageing. Screwcap. 13° alc. **Rating** 94 **To** 2028 $25
Late Harvest Semillon 2006 Lovely tangy, citrussy edge to the lushly sweet fruit; late harvest, but with alcohol ending up at 10°, pointing to the substantial amount of unfermented sugar. Screwcap. 10° alc. **Rating** 94 **To** 2010 $18

ŸŸŸŸŸ **Hunter Valley Semillon 2006** Classic style; crisp lemon/lemongrass/grass flavours; a long, balanced and precise finish. Screwcap. 11° alc. **Rating** 93 **To** 2016 $22

ŸŸŸŸ **White Label Hunter Valley Chardonnay 2005** Complex, ripe melon and peach fruit; generous flavour for immediate consumption. Screwcap. 13° alc. **Rating** 89 **To** 2009 $25

Scarpantoni Estate

Scarpantoni Drive, McLaren Flat, SA 5171 **Region** McLaren Vale
T (08) 8383 0186 **F** (08) 8383 0490 www.scarpantoni-wines.com.au **Open** Mon–Fri 9–5, w'ends & public hols 11–5
Winemaker Michael Scarpantoni, Filippo Scarpantoni **Est.** 1979 **Cases** 30 000
With 20 ha of shiraz, 11 ha of cabernet sauvignon, 3 ha each of chardonnay and sauvignon blanc, 1 ha each of merlot and gamay, and 0.5 ha of petit verdot, Scarpantoni has come a long way since Domenico Scarpantoni purchased his first property of 5.6 ha in 1958. He was working for Thomas Hardy at its Tintara winery; he subsequently became vineyard manager for Seaview Wines, responsible for the contoured vineyards which were leading-edge viticulture in the 1960s. In 1979 his sons, Michael and Filippo, built the winery, which has now been extended to enable all the grapes from the estate plantings to be used to make wine under the Scarpantoni label. As the vines have matured, quality has improved. Exports to the US, the UK and other major markets.

ŸŸŸŸŸ **Block 3 McLaren Vale Shiraz 2005** Medium-bodied; excellent line and length for the blackberry, licorice, plum and bitter chocolate fruit; the finish is particularly impressive, thanks to fine, ripe tannins. Screwcap. 15° alc. **Rating** 94 **To** 2025 $25

ŸŸŸŸŸ **Sauvignon Blanc 2006** Considerable vivacity and bright fruit; fine but intense citrussy nuances to the tropical fruit salad palate; a major achievement for McLaren Vale. Screwcap. 12° alc. **Rating** 92 **To** 2008 $18
Ceres Rose 2006 Remarkably fresh fruit; canned strawberries balanced by good acidity; has character and length. Gamay (the grape of Beaujolais) is rarely planted in Australia, and this wine suggests there should be more for the rose category. Screwcap. 12° alc. **Rating** 90 **To** 2008 $14

ŸŸŸŸ **Estate Reserve Shiraz Cabernet 2003** Medium red-purple; very rich and ripe; bordering on dead fruit/confit fruit, the regional chocolate present as always; alcohol adds to the sweetness. Cork. 15° alc. **Rating** 89 **To** 2010 $36

The Brother's Block McLaren Vale Cabernet Sauvignon 2004 Light- to medium-bodied; fresh black fruits with a touch of cassis; fine tannins add to the length though not to the weight. Screwcap. 14° alc. **Rating** 89 **To** 2014 $25

Block 3 McLaren Vale Shiraz 2004 Plenty of activity with lifted aromas, then sweet fruit on the palate, and then a burst of tannins. Screwcap. 14.5° alc. **Rating** 88 **To** 2010 $25

School Block McLaren Flat Shiraz Cabernet Merlot 2004 A bright assemblage of red and black fruits set off against crisp acidity; lively, but not particularly friendly. Needs to leave school and mature. Screwcap. 14.5° alc. **Rating** 88 **To** 2014 $15

School Block McLaren Flat Shiraz Cabernet Merlot 2003 Medium red; a sweet array of strongly regional flavours, the red fruit wrapped in a chocolate overcoat. Screwcap. 15° alc. **Rating** 87 **To** 2009 $15

Black Tempest NV Blackberry and black cherry, the oak contribution less than ideal, the nice dry finish a plus. **Rating** 87 **To** 2008 $28

Schild Estate Wines

Cnr Barossa Valley Way/Lyndoch Valley Road, Lyndoch, SA 5351 **Region** Barossa Valley **T** (08) 8524 5560 **F** (08) 8524 4333 **www**.schildestate.com.au **Open** 7 days 10–5 **Winemaker** Wine Wise (Jo Irvine) **Est.** 1998 **Cases** 20 000

Ed Schild is a Barossa Valley grapegrower who first planted a small vineyard at Rowland Flat in 1952, steadily increasing his vineyard holdings over the next 50 years to their present 150 ha. Currently 12% of the production from these vineyards (now managed by son Michael Schild) is used to produce Schild Estate Wines, and the plan is to increase this percentage. The flagship wine is made from 150-year-old shiraz vines on the Moorooroo Block. The cellar door is in the old ANZ Bank at Lyndoch, and provides the sort of ambience which can only be found in the Barossa Valley. Exports to the UK, the US and other major markets.

ŸŸŸŸŸ **Barossa Riesling 2006** Highly aromatic spice and blossom; bursting with fruit flavour in a sweet citrus/tropical spectrum, but a dry finish. Great value, but best now. Screwcap. 12.9° alc. **Rating** 94 **To** 2009 $15

Moorooroo Limited Release Barossa Valley Shiraz 2002 Ultra-concentrated, rich and ripe, but not jammy, blackberry, prune, licorice and plum fruit supported by mocha/vanilla oak. Just a touch of alcohol-derived sweetness has to be accepted; 150-year-old vines. Cork. 15° alc. **Rating** 94 **To** 2017 $85

ŸŸŸŸŸ **Ben Schild Reserve Barossa Shiraz 2005** Powerful, dense and concentrated; a no-holds-barred Barossa shiraz tailored for the palate of Robert Parker and the US; some heat, but certainly masses of flavour. Cork. 15° alc. **Rating** 92 **To** 2015 $35

Barossa Shiraz 2005 Blackberry, black cherry and chocolate; medium- to full-bodied, the alcohol largely contained; finishes with supple tannins. Screwcap. 14.5° alc. **Rating** 90 **To** 2015 $20

ŸŸŸŸ **Barossa Semillon Sauvignon Blanc 2006** Spotlessly clean; very well-made, with a nice balance of tropical and more grassy notes; a totally unexpected surprise. Screwcap. 13.2° alc. **Rating** 89 **To** 2008 $15

Alma Schild Reserve Barossa Chardonnay 2005 Golden yellow; opulent, fleshy and rich yellow peach flavours; early drinking. Diam. 13.5° alc. **Rating** 89 **To** 2008 $20

Barossa Frontignac 2006 Sweet, grapey, spicy aromas and flavours; a cellar door flytrap, but might have been better with a touch higher acidity. Screwcap. 13° alc. **Rating** 87 **To** 2008 $14

Barossa Grenache Mataro Shiraz 2006 Light- to medium-bodied; fresh, juicy berry fruit; simple structure; 70-year-old vines. Screwcap. 15° alc. **Rating** 87 **To** 2008 $17

Schindler Northway Downs

437 Stumpy Gully Road, Balnarring, Vic 3926 **Region** Mornington Peninsula
T (03) 5983 1945 **www.**northwaydowns.com.au **Open** First w'end of month
Winemaker Tammy Schindler-Hands **Est.** 1996 **Cases** 250
The Schindler family planted the first 2 ha of pinot noir and chardonnay in 1996. A further 4 ha
of pinot noir was planted on an ideal north-facing slope in 1999, and the first vintage followed
in 2000. The cellar door offers Austrian food and live Austrian music on Sundays.

Mornington Peninsula Chardonnay 2006 Aromatic and light- to medium-bodied, with vibrant nectarine and grapefruit flavours, the oak all but invisible on the long finish. Diam. 13.5° alc. **Rating** 93 **To** 2014 $18
Mornington Peninsula Chardonnay 2005 Light- to medium-bodied; seamless white peach, nectarine, fig and oak flavours; good acidity. Diam. 14.2° alc. **Rating** 92 **To** 2012 $20

Mornington Peninsula Pinot Noir 2005 Light-bodied, with strawberry/cherry fruit and harmonious, silky tannins; a rose substitute if you want something with better quality and character. Cork. 15.4° alc. **Rating** 89 **To** 2010 $24

Schubert Estate

Roennfeldt Road, Marananga, SA 5355 **Region** Barossa Valley
T (08) 8562 3375 **F** (08) 8562 4338 **www.**schubertestate.com.au **Open** Not
Winemaker Steve Schubert **Est.** 2000 **Cases** 460
Steve and Cecilia Schubert are primarily grapegrowers, with 13 ha of shiraz and 2 ha of viognier.
They purchased the 25-ha property in 1986, when it was in such a derelict state that there was
no point trying to save the old vines. Both were working in other areas, so it was some years before
they began replanting, at a little under 2 ha per year. Almost all the production is sold to Torbreck.
In 2000 they decided to keep enough grapes to make a barrique of wine for their own (and
friends') consumption. They were sufficiently encouraged by the outcome to venture into the
dizzy heights of 2 hogsheads a year (since increased to 4 or so). The wine is made with wild yeast,
open fermentation, basket pressing and bottling without filtration. Exports to the US, Canada,
Denmark and Japan.

Goose-yard Block Barossa Valley Shiraz 2005 Strong red-purple; a ripe cascade of blackberry, prune and plum, positive tannins cutting back what might otherwise have been simple fruit; a long finish; needs time. High-quality cork. 15° alc. **Rating** 94 **To** 2025 $60

The Gosling Barossa Valley Shiraz 2005 Plenty of power and concentration; lively and focused, with touches of licorice and spice; good fruit and oak balance. Screwcap. 14.5° alc. **Rating** 92 **To** 2020 $22

Schulz Vignerons

PO Box 121, Nuriootpa, SA 5355 **Region** Barossa Valley
T (08) 8565 6257 **F** (08) 8565 6257 **Open** By appt
Winemaker David Powell (Contract) **Est.** 2003 **Cases** 1450
Marcus and Roslyn Schulz are the fifth generation of one of the best known wine families (or,
rather, extended families) in the Barossa Valley. Five generations of grapegrowing and winemaking
precede them, but they have gone down a totally new path since initiating biological farming in
2002. They have moved from irrigation and extensive spraying to the situation where the vines
are now virtually dry-grown, producing generous yields of high-quality grapes, using natural
nitrogen created by the active soil biology, and minimal chemical input. They have a 58-ha
vineyard with 12 varieties planted, shiraz (18.9 ha), mourvedre (7.2 ha), grenache (6.3 ha) and
cabernet sauvignon (6.2 ha) leading the band. As might be imagined, the lion's share of the grapes
are sold to other producers (some, no doubt, finding its way to Torbreck).

ΨΨΨΨ♀ **Marcus Barossa Valley Old Shiraz 2003** A rich, plush wine; ripe plum, blackberry and prune flavours with persistent but soft tannins; very much in-house style; vines planted 1950s. Screwcap. 15° alc. **Rating** 92 **To** 2017 $70
Benjamin Barossa Valley Shiraz 2004 Medium-bodied; neatly fruit-driven with blackberry, plum, prune and spice flavours plus soft tannins. Screwcap. 14° alc. **Rating** 90 **To** 2014 $25

ΨΨΨΨ **Julius Barossa Valley Merlot 2004** Medium-bodied; savoury black olive and spice varietal nuances on a gentle cassis/redcurrant base. Screwcap. 14° alc. **Rating** 89 **To** 2011 $25
Johann Barossa Valley Zinfandel 2004 One of the innumerable faces of zinfandel, with lots of sweet, juicy berry fruit, but not so much structure; work in progress. Screwcap. 14° alc. **Rating** 88 **To** 2010 $20

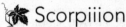 # Schwarz Wine Company   ★★★★☆

PO Box 182, Tanunda, SA 5352 **Region** Barossa Valley
T 0417 881 923 **F** (08) 8562 3534 **www**.schwarzwineco.com.au **Open** Not
Winemaker Jason Schwarz **Est.** 2001 **Cases** 940
The economical name is appropriate for a business which started with 1 tonne of grapes making 2 hogsheads of wine in 2001. The shiraz was purchased from Jason Schwarz's parents' vineyard in Bethany; the following year half a tonne of grenache was added, once again purchased from the parents, the vines planted 60 years ago. Production remained static until 2005, when the grape sale agreements to another (larger) winery were terminated, freeing up 1.8 ha of shiraz, and 0.8 ha of grenache. From this point on things moved a little more quickly: in 2006 Jason Schwarz worked with Peter Schell of Spinifex which led to the formation of a partnership (Biscay Road Vintners) with Peter Schell giving each total control over production. Using grapes purchased from other growers, Jason Schwarz hopes to eventually increase production to 3000–4000 cases.

ΨΨΨΨ♀ **Nitschke Block Barossa Valley Shiraz 2005** Intense purple-red; floods the mouth with full-on confit black fruits, sufficiently luscious to largely carry the alcohol; heroic style, but a good one, particularly in 20 years or so. Screwcap. 15° alc. **Rating** 92 **To** 2030 $32
Thiele Road Barossa Valley Grenache 2005 Lots of appealing cherry and raspberry red fruit flavours, and no cosmetic characters; good tannins and length; impressive. Screwcap. 15° alc. **Rating** 91 **To** 2015 $26

Scorpiiion   ★★★★☆

32 Waverley Ridge Road, Crafers, SA 5152 (postal) **Region** Warehouse
T 0409 551 110 **F** (08) 8353 1562 **www**.scorpiiionwines.com.au **Open** Not
Winemaker Peter Schell (Spinifex) **Est.** 2002 **Cases** 1500
Scorpiiion Wines was the concept of Mark Herbertt who decided to buy a small quantity of McLaren Vale and Barossa grapes in 2002 and have the wine made for himself, friends and family. In 2004 Paddy Phillips and Michael Szwarcbord, like Mark Herbertt sharing the Scorpio birth sign, joined the partnership. It is a virtual winery, with the grapes purchased, and the wines contract-made by various winemakers including the brilliant Peter Schell. They say 'We share a number of likes and dislikes in relation to Australian red wines – apart from that, we don't really agree on anything...We aim for a fruit-driven style with elegant oak, rather than a big, oak-driven style.' Oh, and they are united in their insistence on using screwcaps rather than corks.

ΨΨΨΨΨ **Barossa Valley Shiraz 2004** Bright purple-red; luscious blackberry, plum and a touch of prune tempered by good acidity; fine tannins and exceptional length. Screwcap. 14.5° alc. **Rating** 94 **To** 2024 $27

ΨΨΨΨ **Barossa Valley Grenache Shiraz Mataro 2005** Light to medium-bodied; the juicy berry fruit is strongly regional, almost lemony; good length. Cork. 14.5° alc. **Rating** 89 **To** 2013 $20
Barossa Valley Rose 2006 Has flavour without sweetness or phenolics; spicy notes through the palate and finish. Screwcap. 13.5° alc. **Rating** 88 **To** 2008 $16

Scorpo Wines

23 Old Bittern-Dromana Road, Merricks North, Vic 3926 **Region** Mornington Peninsula
T (03) 5989 7697 **F** (03) 9813 3371 **www**.scorpowines.com.au **Open** By appt
Winemaker Paul Scorpo, Sandro Mosele (Contract) **Est.** 1997 **Cases** 2600
Paul Scorpo has a 27-year background as a horticulturist/landscape architect, and has worked in
major projects ranging from private gardens to golf courses in Australia, Europe and Asia. His
family has a love of food, wine and gardens, all of which led to them buying a derelict apple and
cherry orchard on gentle rolling hills between Port Phillip and Westernport Bay. Part of a ridge
system which climbs up to Red Hill, it offers north and northeast-facing slopes on red-brown,
clay loam soils. They have established 4.5 ha of pinot noir, chardonnay, pinot gris and shiraz.

Scotchmans Hill

190 Scotchmans Road, Drysdale, Vic 3222 **Region** Geelong
T (03) 5251 3176 **F** (03) 5253 1743 **www**.scotchmanshill.com.au **Open** 7 days 10.30–5.30
Winemaker Robin Brockett **Est.** 1982 **Cases** 70 000
Situated on the Bellarine Peninsula, southeast of Geelong, with a well-equipped winery and first-
class vineyards. It is a consistent performer with its Pinot Noir and has a strong following in
Melbourne and Sydney for its astutely priced, competently made wines. The second label, Swan
Bay, has been joined at the other end of the spectrum with top-end individual vineyard wines.
Exports to the UK and other major markets.

ỸỸỸỸ **Sutton Vineyard Chardonnay 2004** An extra degree of concentration to the
nectarine, peach and melon fruit; evident but restrained use of French oak and
lees contact, though no mlf. One wonders whether the price is simply inspired
by the old adage 'if you don't ask, you don't get'. Screwcap. 13.2° alc. **Rating** 94
To 2015 $75
Norfolk Vineyard Pinot Noir 2004 Light colour; a similar style to the
Geelong Pinot, but does move up a step with all the characters evident and in
balance; overall, commanding more than charming. Screwcap. 13.5° alc.
Rating 94 **To** 2012 $75
Geelong Shiraz 2005 High-toned, multi-spice and crushed black pepper
notes are sustained and balanced by abundant black fruits, the oak and tannin
handling providing yet further support and, ultimately, balance. Clearly, you pay
the money and take your choice. Screwcap. 14.5° alc. **Rating** 94 **To** 2020 $29
Geelong Shiraz 2004 Unconvincing colour; the bouquet promises a little
more, but not the elegant and intense spray of red fruits of every description,
plus a dusting of spice, which the palate provides. Jekyll and Hyde, if there ever
was one. Screwcap. 14.5° alc. **Rating** 94 **To** 2019 $29

ỸỸỸỸ♀ **Geelong Chardonnay 2005** Well-made; the focus is on nectarine, melon and
citrus fruit which underline the length of the palate; winemaking inputs of barrel
ferment, etc are well-controlled. Screwcap. 13.5° alc. **Rating** 92 **To** 2011 $27
Geelong Cabernet Sauvignon 2005 Medium-bodied; strongly focused
blackcurrant fruit, with just a hint of earth; good oak and tannin management, and
has length. Screwcap. 14° alc. **Rating** 92 **To** 2017 $29
Geelong Pinot Noir 2005 Light- to medium-bodied, but has intensity and
complexity strongly expressed through forest floor and spice notes; fine tannins carry
on the impression; good length. Screwcap. 14° alc. **Rating** 91 **To** 2010 $29
The Hill Chardonnay 2006 Fragrant grapefruit/stone fruit aromas, the
flavours tracking the bouquet; good length, with no apparent oak. Screwcap.
13.5° alc. **Rating** 90 **To** 2011 $12

ỸỸỸỸ **Geelong Riesling 2005** Firm lime and mineral aromas and flavours, but tails away
rather than accelerates on the finish. Screwcap. 13° alc. **Rating** 89 **To** 2010 $27
Geelong Sauvignon Blanc 2006 Faintly sweaty/reductive aromas are, as so
often, joined with abundant sauvignon blanc fruit on the palate; attractive, citrussy
finish. Screwcap. 13.5° alc. **Rating** 89 **To** 2010 $22

Swan Bay Pinot Noir 2006 Medium-bodied, with clear-cut varietal character; plum, cherry, multi-spice notes and some stem; firm finish, better in 1–2 years. Excellent value. Screwcap. 14° alc. **Rating** 89 **To** 2010 $17.50
Swan Bay Shiraz 2005 Light- to medium-bodied peppery/spicy red and black fruits; mainly cool-grown fruit, with minimal oak and tannin inputs, but still has length. Screwcap. 14° alc. **Rating** 89 **To** 2010 $17

Scotts Brook

Scotts Brook Road, Boyup Brook, WA 6244 **Region** Blackwood Valley
T (08) 9765 3014 **F** (08) 9765 3015 **Open** 7 days 10–5
Winemaker Vasse River **Est.** 1987 **Cases** 1000
The Scotts Brook winery at Boyup Brook (equidistant between the Margaret River and Great Southern regions) has been developed by local schoolteachers Brian Walker and wife Kerry. There are 15 ha of vineyards, but the majority of the production is sold to other winemakers, with limited quantities being made by contract.

Seaforth Vineyard

520 Arthurs Seat Road, Red Hill, Vic 3937 **Region** Mornington Peninsula
T (03) 5989 2362 **www.**seaforthwines.com.au **Open** Spring & summer w'ends 11–5
Winemaker Contract (Phillip Kittle) **Est.** 1994 **Cases** 2000
Andrew and Venetia Adamson planted their 3.6 ha vineyard to chardonnay (2.2 ha), pinot noir (1 ha) and pinot gris (0.4 ha) in 1994. At 300 m, it is one of the highest on the Mornington Peninsula, and is always amongst the last to pick. The wines are 100% estate-grown, and all of the standard vineyard operations are carried out personally by Andrew and Venetia, with only picking bringing in outside contractors.

ŸŸŸŸŸ **Mornington Peninsula Pinot Noir 2005** Rich, ripe black fruits with spicy/foresty nuances adding complexity; oak plays a background role. Screwcap. 13.6° alc. **Rating** 93 **To** 2012 $28

ŸŸŸŸ **Mornington Peninsula Pinot Gris 2005** Powerful varietal musk and spice, but has some heat to the finish. Screwcap. 13.8° alc. **Rating** 88 **To** 2008 $24
Mornington Peninsula Wild Rose 2005 A fresh, virtually dry, strawberry/cherry mix; good alcohol and acid balance. Screwcap. 12.8° alc. **Rating** 87 **To** 2008 $18

Secret Garden Wines

251 Henry Lawson Drive, Mudgee, NSW 2850 **Region** Mudgee
T (02) 6373 3874 **F** (02) 6373 3854 **Open** Fri–Sun & public hols 9–5
Winemaker Ian MacRae **Est.** 2000 **Cases** NA
Secret Garden Wines is owned by Ian and Carol MacRae, and is a sister operation to their main business, Miramar Wines. Estate plantings consist of 10 ha of shiraz and around 2 ha each of cabernet sauvignon and chardonnay. The wines are made at Miramar, the cellar door is at Secret Garden. The property is only 5 km from Mudgee, and also fronts Craigmoor Road, giving it a prime position in the so-called 'golden triangle'.

ŸŸŸŸŸ **Chardonnay 2002** Light straw-green; elegant and fresh as a daisy; very good balance of melon fruit and subtle oak; touches of cashew; impressive. Screwcap. 13° alc. **Rating** 93 **To** 2012 $18

Sedona Estate ★★★★☆

182 Shannons Road, Murrindindi, Vic 3717 **Region** Upper Goulburn
T (03) 9730 2883 **F** (03) 9730 2583 **Open** By appt
Winemaker Paul Evans **Est.** 1998 **Cases** 1500
The Sedona Estate vineyard was chosen by Paul and Sonja Evans after a long search for what they considered to be the perfect site. Situated on north-facing and gently undulating slopes, with

gravelly black soils, it is planted (in descending order) to 4 ha of shiraz, cabernet sauvignon, merlot and sangiovese. Paul Evans (former Oakridge winemaker) also contract-makes wines for a number of other small Yarra Valley producers.

ŸŸŸŸŸ **Yea Valley Cabernet Sauvignon 2004** Medium- to full-bodied; abundant blackcurrant fruit and touches of dark chocolate; good structure and mouthfeel; total contrast to the Merlot. Diam. 13.5° alc. **Rating** 94 **To** 2024 $22

ŸŸŸŸ **Yea Valley Riesling 2006** Lime, citrus and mineral aromas; a fairly tight though light palate needing to loosen/open up; needs more fruit depth. Diam. 13° alc. **Rating** 89 **To** 2013 $20

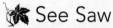 # See Saw ★★★

PO Box 611, Manly, NSW 1655 **Region** Lower Hunter Valley
T (02) 8966 9020 **www.**seesawwine.com **Open** Not
Winemaker Hamish MacGowan, Andrew Margan, Sarah-Kate Dineen **Est.** 2006
Cases 2000
This is another venture of Hamish MacGowan, the winemaker-cum-marketer who was responsible for Angus the Bull. While working in the Hunter Valley he met Andrew Margan and Sarah-Kate Dineen, then winemaker at Tempus Two. She has now returned to NZ (with winemaker husband Dan Dineen) to make sauvignon blanc, and Andrew Margan remains in the Hunter with his own substantial winery and business. See Saw is a blend of 85% Hunter Valley Semillon and 15% Marlborough Sauvignon Blanc.

ŸŸŸŸ **Hunter Valley & Marlborough Semillon Sauvignon Blanc 2006** Glowing yellow-green; an abundance of tropical sauvignon blanc flavour, the semillon in the background; fractionally phenolic. Screwcap. 15° alc. **Rating** 89 **To** 2008 $18

Seppelt ★★★★★

1 Seppeltsfield Road, Seppeltsfield via Nuriootpa, SA 5355 **Region** Barossa Valley
T (08) 8568 6217 **www.**seppelt.com.au **Open** Mon–Fri 10–5, w'ends & public hols 11–5
Winemaker James Godfrey **Est.** 1851 **Cases** 150 000
A multimillion-dollar expansion and renovation program by Southcorp saw the historic Seppeltsfield winery become the production centre for the Seppelt fortified and SA table wines, adding another dimension to what was already the most historic and beautiful major winery in Australia. It is now home to some of the world's great fortified wines, nurtured and protected by the passionate James Godfrey. However, to the great dismay of many, it is being sold by Fosters; at the time of going to print, the sale had not been finalised. One can only hope the utterly irreplaceable stocks of very old wines will not be scattered to the 4 winds.

ŸŸŸŸŸ **100 Year Old Para Liqueur 1907** The usual honey, treacle consistency, the olive-green/brown wine staining the sides of the glass as it is swirled; offers cinnamon stick, every spice known to man, grandma's Christmas pudding and a hundred other things; the senses almost go into free-fall, so intense and complex is the wine. The length is extraordinary, and all the components (including volatile acidity) are exactly as they should be. In prior years I have given the wine 98 points, which is clearly wrong. This is the one and only 100-point wine made in Australia. Cork. 23° alc. **Rating** 100 **To** 2100 $1000
Amontillado DP116 NV Marvellous balance and intensity of nutty rancio with penetrating acidity; flavour-packed, fleetingly sweet and nutty, then a dry finish. Screwcap. 22° alc. **Rating** 96 **To** 2008 $19.95
Oloroso DP38 NV NV Mid-brown, with a hint of green on the rim; nutty rancio complexity, with just a touch of sweetness; finely balanced with a constant interplay between nutty, honeyed sweetness and drier, rancio characters. The finish lingers in the mouth for minutes, without any hint of alcohol heat. Screwcap. 21° alc. **Rating** 95 **To** 2008 $19.95

Para Liqueur Aged Tawny Bin 125 Tawny Port NV Like the vintage version, has a real streak of elegance; sweet and immensely complex, yet no unwelcome bite on the finish; dry and long. Cork. 19° alc. **Rating** 94 To 2008 $19.95

ᵀᵀᵀᵀᵀ **Fino DP117 NV** The alcohol is less than many Barossa Valley red wines; finesse and grace so well-constructed you do not think it is dry until the aftertaste, which is as clear as a spring day. Along the way you meet cut green apple and nutty characters, adding to a wine which comes second only to freshly imported Spanish manzanilla. Screwcap. 15.5° alc. **Rating** 93 To 2008 $19.95
Para Liqueur 1986 Well on its way to full golden-tawny colour; very intense, raisiny, nutty and spicy palate, the acidity cutting across like a beacon. Cork. 20.5° alc. **Rating** 93 To 2008 $40.95

Seppelt (Great Western)   ★★★★★

Moyston Road, Great Western, Vic 3377 **Region** Grampians
T (03) 5361 2222 **F** (03) 5361 2200 **www.**seppelt.com.au **Open** 7 days 10–5
Winemaker Emma Wood **Est.** 1865 **Cases** 150 000
Australia's best-known producer of sparkling wine, always immaculate in its given price range but also producing excellent Great Western-sourced table wines, especially long-lived Shiraz and Australia's best Sparkling Shirazs. The glitzy labels of the past have rightly been consigned to the rubbish bin, and the product range has been significantly rationalised. Paradoxically, this arm of Seppelt is being retained by Fosters (so we are told). Exports to the UK, the US and other major markets.

ᵀᵀᵀᵀᵀ **St Peters Grampians Shiraz 2004** Great colour; elegant and long, with black pepper, spice and blackberry; literally sings on its lovely finish; 40% new oak, wild yeast, etc. Screwcap. 13.8° alc. **Rating** 96 To 2024 $60
Show Sparkling Shiraz 1996 A beautifully complex wine, with sweetness coming from the fruit rather than by dosage; spice, blackberry and nut cake flavours. A big base drum of elegance. Crown seal. 13° alc. **Rating** 96 To 2016 $65
Benno Bendigo Shiraz 2004 Plusher, riper and rounder than the St Peters; sophisticated winemaking with a similar approach, though the regional influence provides fuller, albeit rounded, tannins. Screwcap. 13.5° alc. **Rating** 95 To 2024 $50.95
Drumborg Riesling 2006 Considerable weight and structural intensity; builds lime, passionfruit and apple flavours throughout, the finish particularly powerful. Great pedigree. Screwcap. 12.5° alc. **Rating** 94 To 2016 $29.95
Chalambar Grampians Bendigo Pyrenees Shiraz 2005 Medium- to full-bodied; a rich tapestry of blackberry, plum and licorice fruits which would have gained the immediate approval of the late Colin Preece; has the structure to age gracefully for up to 30 years or more. Screwcap. 13.5° alc. **Rating** 94 To 2035 $25.95
Mount Ida Heathcote Shiraz 2004 Bigger again and fleshier; fermented in the Yarra Valley, and matured in the Barossa Valley; French oak adds a dimension to previous vintages of Mt Ida, which were not under the Seppelt label. Screwcap. 14.5° alc. **Rating** 94 To 2019 $50
Moyston Cabernet Merlot 2004 Very good purple-red; exceptionally good structure and balance; blackcurrant with touches of cedar and spice; long finish. Screwcap. 14° alc. **Rating** 94 To 2019 $30

ᵀᵀᵀᵀᵀ **Jaluka Drumborg Vineyard Chardonnay 2006** Beautifully fashioned, delicate and elegant; a classic example of how more restrained wines can be ignored in wine shows (as this one was at the Sydney Wine Show '07); cool-climate chardonnay perfectly married with the right amount of high quality French oak; perhaps does tail off a fraction on the back palate. Screwcap. 13° alc. **Rating** 93 To 2012 $25.95

Bellfield Marsanne Roussanne 2005 Has very distinct similarities to the White Hermitage of the northern Rhone Valley; mineral, spice and talc; a sotto voce whisk of oak. Needs time. Screwcap. 13.5° alc. **Rating** 90 **To** 2015 $30

♟♟♟♟ **Coborra Drumborg Vineyard Pinot Gris 2006** Has consistently shown more structure and texture than the majority of wines in this amazingly loved category; minerally musk, apple and pear; dry finish. Screwcap. 13.5° alc. **Rating** 89 **To** 2008 $25.95

Serafino Wines

McLarens on the Lake, Kangarilla Road, McLaren Vale, SA 5171 **Region** McLaren Vale **T** (08) 8323 0157 **F** (08) 8323 0158 **Open** Mon–Fri 10–5, w'ends & public hols 10–4.30 **Winemaker** Scott Rawlinson **Est.** 2000 **Cases** 20 000
In the wake of the sale of Maglieri Wines to Beringer Blass in 1998, Maglieri founder Steve Maglieri acquired the McLarens on the Lake complex originally established by Andrew Garrett. The accommodation has been upgraded and a larger winery was commissioned prior in 2002. The operation draws upon 40 ha each of shiraz and cabernet sauvignon, 7 ha of chardonnay, 2 ha each of merlot, semillon, barbera, nebbiolo and sangiovese, and 1 ha of grenache. Part of the grape production is sold to others. Exports to the UK, the US, Asia, Italy and NZ.

♟♟♟♟♟ **Sharktooth McLaren Vale Shiraz 2004** Excellent colour; has all the flavour of the standard version, and also all the structure and discipline partly missing from that wine. Totally delicious, with perfect line and structure. Cork. 14.5° alc. **Rating** 96 **To** 2029 $40

Sorrento McLaren Vale Cabernet Sauvignon Cabernet Franc Merlot 2004 Medium red-purple; very elegant, perfectly balanced, medium-bodied wine, with the seamless winemaking at which Scott Rawlinson excels, making what is a very difficult task at this level seem easy. Caresses the mouth, unfolding its flavours progressively, and always luring you back for more. Trophy Best Bordeaux Blend McLaren Vale Wine Show '06. Screwcap. 14° alc. **Rating** 96 **To** 2024 $15

McLaren Vale Cabernet Sauvignon 2004 Strong purple-red, holding its hue well; a very pure expression of cabernet varietal character on both bouquet and palate; oak and soft, ripe tannins are seamlessly integrated. Another delicious wine. Trophy Best Cabernet McLaren Vale Wine Show '06. Cork. 14° alc. **Rating** 95 **To** 2025 $24

McLaren Vale Semillon Sauvignon Blanc 2006 A restrained bouquet, but an explosively intense palate, predominantly in a citrus/herb/grass spectrum, gooseberry appearing on the finish. Screwcap. 12.5° alc. **Rating** 94 **To** 2010 $18

Sharktooth Wild Ferment McLaren Vale Chardonnay 2005 Takes the many qualities of the Reserve, but lifts the intensity; oak is again evident (Perle Blanche barriques) but is in balance with the nectarine, fig and melon fruit; good length. You also know the barrel no. was 5F684, bottle no. 788. Screwcap. 13.5° alc. **Rating** 94 **To** 2011 $30

Reserve McLaren Vale Chardonnay 2004 Light straw-green; attractive white peach and grapefruit flavours plus classy barrel ferment oak inputs; long, tangy finish. A tribute to the vintage. Screwcap. 13.5° alc. **Rating** 94 **To** 2010 $18

Goose Island McLaren Vale Shiraz 2004 Soft, medium-bodied, velvety black fruits within a dark chocolate wrapper; soft tannins, great balance and good length round off a really nice wine. Screwcap. 14° alc. **Rating** 94 **To** 2014 $12

♟♟♟♟♟ **Reserve McLaren Vale Chardonnay 2005** Has plenty of presence and grip; the fruit has largely soaked up the Never (doubtless Nevers) oak; a nice touch of acidity on the finish. Screwcap. 13.5° alc. **Rating** 92 **To** 2009 $18

McLaren Vale Shiraz 2004 A rich, super-generous and unequivocally ripe style in both fruit and tannin terms; seems higher than 14.5° alcohol. Gold medal Adelaide Wine Show '06. Cork. 14.5° alc. **Rating** 92 **To** 2015 $24

McLaren Vale Merlot 2004 The region comes through with greater authority than the varietal expression of merlot, but has been well-made. A Cherry Ripe mix of red fruits and chocolate. Quality cork. 13.5° alc. **Rating** 90 **To** 2010 $18

Vintage McLaren Vale Fortified Shiraz 2005 In traditional style, with massive blackberry fruit and licorice; a quite high baume, and slightly fiery spirit, plus a long finish. I would steer clear of it for 7 or 8 years. Cork. 20° alc. **Rating** 90 **To** 2020 $25

♟♟♟♟ **Goose Island McLaren Vale Unwooded Chardonnay 2006** Fresh, bright and unusually intense citrus and stone fruit mix; good length. Screwcap. 13° alc. **Rating** 89 **To** 2009 $12

Dry Grown Bushvine McLaren Vale Grenache 2005 A pleasant, medium-bodied wine; spicy, soft red fruit flavours with just a hint of chocolate; lunch wine for red meats. Cork. 14.5° alc. **Rating** 89 **To** 2015 $22

McLaren Vale Tempranillo 2005 A somewhat quixotic tilt at the tempranillo window, in best Don Quixote fashion. Rawlinson tells us we can find passionfruit, quince paste, frangipani, blueberry, blood plum, prune, fruit pastille, a touch of citrus and spice. No wonder I've had trouble putting my finger on tempranillo. Cork. 14.5° alc. **Rating** 89 **To** 2012 $22

McLaren Vale Tempranillo 2003 Light- to medium-bodied; spicy black fruits with hints of licorice and good length. Quality cork. 13.5° alc. **Rating** 88 **To** 2008 $22

Serrat

★★★★☆

PO Box 478, Yarra Glen, Vic 3775 **Region** Yarra Valley
T (03) 9730 1439 **F** (03) 9730 1579 **www**.serrat.com.au **Open** Not
Winemaker Tom Carson **Est.** 2001 **Cases** 300

Serrat is the family business of Tom Carson (celebrated winemaker at Yering Station) and partner Nadege Suné. They have close-planted (at 8800 vines per ha) 1 ha of pinot noir, 0.7 ha of shiraz, and lesser amounts of chardonnay, viognier and grenache. The intention is to make pinot noir, chardonnay and, likely, a blend of shiraz, viognier and grenache.

♟♟♟♟♟ **Yarra Valley Close Planted Chardonnay 2004** Highly aromatic nectarine blossom leads into a more restrained and delicate palate; a very complex wine, but with no single component dominant, especially oak. Screwcap. 13.5° alc. **Rating** 94 **To** 2011 $25

♟♟♟♟♟ **Yarra Valley Close Planted Pinot Noir 2005** Lots of character, with dark fruits and touches of forest floor; a fractionally grippy finish which will settle down in a year or so. Screwcap. 13.5° alc. **Rating** 91 **To** 2010 $25

Yarra Valley Close Planted Late Harvest Viognier 2005 A unique approach (to viognier); late harvest, then partially ferment the wine leaving substantial residual sugar and balancing acidity, with no trace of phenolics. Screwcap. 12° alc. **Rating** 91 **To** 2009 $20

Serventy Organic Wines

★★★

Rocky Road, Forest Grove, WA 6286 **Region** Margaret River
T (08) 9757 7534 **F** (08) 9757 7272 **www**.serventy.com **Open** 7 days 10–5
Winemaker Frank Kittler **Est.** 1984 **Cases** 1700

In 2003 a small group of wine enthusiasts from Perth acquired the business from the famous naturalist Serventy family (one of the early movers in organic viticulture and winemaking). Substantial investments have been made to both vineyard and winery, and the house on the property has been restored for short-term holiday stays. The quality of the wines has improved significantly, without losing the original identity. Exports to the UK.

Setanta Wines

RSD 43 Williamstown Road, Forreston, SA 5233 (postal) **Region** Adelaide Hills
T (08) 8380 5516 **F** (08) 8380 5516 www.setantawines.com.au **Open** Not
Winemaker Rod Chapman, Rebecca Wilson **Est.** 1997 **Cases** 5000
Setanta is a family-owned operation involving Sheilagh Sullivan, her husband Tony, and brother
Bernard; the latter is the viticulturist, while Tony and Sheilagh manage marketing, administration
and so forth. Of Irish parentage (they are first-generation Australians), they chose Setanta, Ireland's
most famous mythological hero, as the brand name. The beautiful and striking labels tell the
individual stories which give rise to the names of the wines. Exports to Ireland, of course; also to
the UK, Dubai, Singapore, Hong Kong and Japan.

ŶŶŶŶŶ **Cuchulain Adelaide Hills Shiraz 2005** Medium to full purple-red; elegant,
perfectly proportioned and balanced, with very good flow and line; polished
black cherry, plum and blackberry fruit, finishing with fine, silky tannins. Cork.
14.5° alc. **Rating** 96 **To** 2020 $32
Emer Adelaide Hills Chardonnay 2005 Gently aromatic; fine nectarine,
grapefruit and melon supported by subtle oak; well above-average length and
intensity on the palate. Cork. 13.7° alc. **Rating** 94 **To** 2012 $29
Black Sanglain Adelaide Hills Cabernet Sauvignon 2005 Clearly defined
blackcurrant/cassis cabernet fruit, fully ripe, but not jammy; the tannins are
entirely in balance, as is the oak. Cork. 15.3° alc. **Rating** 94 **To** 2022 $32

ŶŶŶŶŶ **Diachmid Adelaide Hills Sauvignon Blanc 2005** Has considerable power
and intensity to the range of aromas and flavours; tropical fruit rides the mid-palate,
but the wine fines up on the long, crisp, dry finish. Cork. 13° alc. **Rating** 93
To 2008 $22
Speckled House Adelaide Hills Riesling 2005 Light- to medium-bodied;
clean, good balance, with gentle lime/lemon/citrus flavours; going into the transition
phase between youth and maturity. Cork. 11.8° alc. **Rating** 90 **To** 2012 $22

Settlement Wines

Cnr Olivers Road/Chalk Hill Road, McLaren Vale, SA 5171 **Region** McLaren Vale
T (08) 8323 7344 www.settlementwines.com.au **Open** Mon–Fri 10–5, w'ends 11–5
Winemaker Vincenzo Berlingieri **Est.** 1992 **Cases** 3500
Vincenzo Berlingieri, one of the great characters of the wine industry, arrived in Sydney with
beard flowing and arms waving in the 1960s, and gained considerable publicity for his then
McLaren Vale winery. Fortune did not follow marketing success for this research scientist, who
had arrived to work in plant genetics at Melbourne University's Botany Department in 1964,
armed with a doctorate in agricultural science from Perugia University, Italy. However, after
various moves he is in business again with his children – Jason, John and Annika – sourcing most
of the grapes from Langhorne Creek and McLaren Vale.

Settlers Rise Montville

249 Western Avenue, Montville, Qld 4560 **Region** Queensland Coastal
T (07) 5478 5558 **F** (07) 5478 5655 www.settlersrise.com.au **Open** 7 days 10–5
Winemaker Peter Scudamore-Smith MW (Contract) **Est.** 1998 **Cases** 3500
Settlers Rise is located in the beautiful highlands of the Blackall Range, a 75-mins drive north of
Brisbane and 20 mins from the Sunshine Coast. A little over 1 ha of chardonnay, verdelho, shiraz
and cabernet sauvignon have been planted at an elevation of 450 m on the deep basalt soils of the
property. First settled in 1887, Montville has gradually become a tourist destination, with a
substantial local arts and crafts industry and a flourishing B&B and lodge accommodation.

ŶŶŶŶ **Queensland Classic Semillon Sauvignon Blanc 2006** A nicely made and
balanced wine, with positive tropical fruit from the sauvignon blanc and structure
courtesy of the semillon. Screwcap. 11° alc. **Rating** 88 **To** 2009 $18.50

Verdelho 2006 Has more going for it than the average; good length, with a touch of citrus to the fruit salad lifting and brightening the finish. Screwcap. 14° alc. **Rating** 87 **To** 2008 $18.50

Reserve Shiraz 2003 Curious cosmetic aromas and flavours, possibly from the oak, are distractions from a pleasant, medium-bodied Granite Belt shiraz which spent 24 months in oak. Cork. 13.5° alc. **Rating** 87 **To** 2010 $28.50

 # Seven Ochres Vineyard

PO Box 202, Dunsborough, WA 6281 **Region** Margaret River
T (08) 9755 2030 **F** (08) 9755 2030 **www**.sevenochres.com.au **Open** Not
Winemaker Chris Harding **Est.** 1998 **Cases** 100
Chris and Alice Harding have taken a roundabout route to the Margaret River, Chris' interest in wine blossoming while working at the Royal Sydney Yacht Squadron in the late 1970s, before moving to Scotland. He and wife Alice returned to Australia in 1994, immediately settling in the Margaret River with their young family. They established the Viticlone Supplies Grapevine Nursery, and now have 60 grape varieties and over 120 clones available. Some of the more exotic varieties in propagation are vermentino, fiano, mondeuse, lagrein, sagrantino, cilliegiolo and sangiovese brunello di montalcino. They have established 1 ha of viognier, encouraged by the early results from this variety. They have also purchased cabernet sauvignon, petit verdot and merlot from a single-vineyard site in the northern part of the Margaret River.

Cabernet Sauvignon Petit Verdot Merlot 2005 A powerful wine, with abundant blackcurrant, cassis and olive tapenade flavours; good control of tannins and oak. Twin top. 14° alc. **Rating** 90 **To** 2012 $28

Sevenhill Cellars

College Road, Sevenhill, SA 5453 **Region** Clare Valley
T (08) 8843 4222 **F** (08) 8843 4382 **www**.sevenhillcellars.com.au **Open** Mon–Fri 9–5, w'ends & public hols 10–5
Winemaker Brother John May, Liz Heidenreich **Est.** 1851 **Cases** 35 000
One of the historical treasures of Australia; the oft-photographed stone wine cellars are the oldest in the Clare Valley, and winemaking is still carried out under the direction of the Jesuitical Manresa Society, and in particular Brother John May. Quality is very good, particularly of the powerful Shiraz; all the wines reflect the estate-grown grapes from old vines. Exports to the UK, Switzerland, Norway and NZ.

Shiraz 2004 Good length and flavour to the black fruits, but is fractionally austere on the finish and aftertaste. **Rating** 88 **To** 2014 $19

Seville Estate

65 Linwood Road, Seville, Vic 3139 **Region** Yarra Valley
T (03) 5964 2622 **F** (03) 5964 2633 **www**.sevilleestate.com.au **Open** 7 days 10–5
Winemaker Dylan McMahon **Est.** 1970 **Cases** 4000
Dr Peter McMahon and wife Margaret commenced planting Seville Estate in 1972 as part of the resurgence of the Yarra Valley. Peter and Margaret retired in 1997, selling to Brokenwood. Graham and Margaret Van Der Meulen acquired the property in 2005, bringing it back into family ownership. Graham and Margaret are hands-on in the vineyard and winery, working closely with winemaker Dylan McMahon who is the grandson of Peter and Margaret. The philosophy is to capture the fruit expression of the vineyard in styles that reflect the cool climate.

Reserve Old Vine Yarra Valley Shiraz 2004 Saturated with delicious red fruits, plums and spice, intense yet refined. All class. Screwcap. 14° alc. **Rating** 95 **To** 2024 $60

Reserve Yarra Valley Chardonnay 2004 A complex wine, whole bunch-pressed, with strong barrel ferment and lees inputs; the fruit is not submerged on the palate, offering sweet nectarine and citrus through to a long finish. Screwcap. 14.5° alc. **Rating** 94 **To** 2014 $40

ŶŶŶŶỌ The Barber Yarra Valley Chardonnay 2005 Fine, elegant melon, nectarine and citrus; seamless oak and good acidity; will grow. Screwcap. 14.5° alc. Rating 92 To 2015 $19

Yarra Valley Pinot Noir 2005 Bright, clear colour; has immediate varietal expression, with cherry, plum, spice and a touch of stalk; delicate French oak support. Screwcap. 14.5° alc. Rating 92 To 2011 $27

Yarra Valley Shiraz 2004 Smooth, sweet, supple fruit; medium-bodied, opening with red cherry fruit, moving through to plum; fine, ripe tannins. Screwcap. 13.5° alc. Rating 92 To 2017 $27

Yarra Valley Chardonnay 2004 A radically different wine to the Reserve; here fruit is to the fore; ripe stone fruit, melon and a touch of citrussy acidity; subtle French oak. Screwcap. 14.5° alc. Rating 91 To 2013 $27

Reserve Yarra Valley Cabernet Sauvignon 2003 A powerful wine crossing a number of different registers from cassis to black olive; robust tannins. Screwcap. 14.5° alc. Rating 90 To 2015 $35

ŶŶŶŶ The Barber Beechworth Pinot Gris 2006 A mix of spice, pear, apple and honeysuckle on both bouquet and palate, but fades slightly on the finish. Screwcap. 14.5° alc. Rating 89 To 2008 $21

The Barber Late Picked Riesling 2006 Headed in the right direction, but needs more acidity and/or less alcohol. Screwcap. 11.5° alc. Rating 89 To 2012 $21

The Barber Yarra Valley Shiraz 2004 More spicy and savoury than the other Seville '04s; still medium-bodied, but doesn't have the sweet fruit of the varietal or Reserve versions. Screwcap. 13.5° alc. Rating 88 To 2013 $19

The Barber Rose 2006 Slightly more structure than usual, the juice run-off from the early stages of a shiraz fermentation; plum and cherry flavours. Screwcap. 14° alc. Rating 87 To 2008 $16

Seville Hill   ★★★★

8 Paynes Road, Seville, Vic 3139 **Region** Yarra Valley
T (03) 5964 3284 **F** (03) 5964 2142 **www**.sevillehill.com.au **Open** 7 days 10–6
Winemaker Dom Bucci, John D'Aloisio **Est.** 1991 **Cases** 3000
John and Josie D'Aloisio have had a long-term involvement in the agricultural industry, which ultimately led to the establishment of the Seville Hill vineyard in 1991. There they have 2.4 ha of cabernet sauvignon and 1.3 ha each of merlot, shiraz and chardonnay. John D'Aloisio makes the wines with Dominic Bucci, a long-time Yarra resident and winemaker.

ŶŶŶŶỌ Yarra Valley Sauvignon Blanc 2005 Plenty of flavour; strong mineral/grass/ asparagus/gooseberry flavours, with a long finish; imposes itself on your palate. Diam. 13.7° alc. Rating 91 To 2008 $19

Reserve Yarra Valley Chardonnay 2005 A complex wine; barrel ferment oak dominant on both bouquet and palate, but there is plenty of stone fruit, nectarine and peach providing a round finish. Diam. 14° alc. Rating 90 To 2011 $25

Yarra Valley Merlot 2004 Fragrant red fruit/cassis aromas; light- to medium-bodied with fresh cherry and raspberry flavours; fine tannins; enjoyable style. Diam. 14.5° alc. Rating 90 To 2012 $22

ŶŶŶŶ Yarra Valley Unoaked Chardonnay 2006 Has bright and lively nectarine and citrus fruit; excellent handling in the winery, the alcohol not showing itself. Diam. 14.5° alc. Rating 89 To 2010 $18

Yarra Valley Cabernet Sauvignon 2002 Despite the slightly dull colour and cool vintage, is holding onto its varietal fruit well. Light- to medium-bodied, with cedary notes along with blackcurrant; long finish. Cork. 14° alc. Rating 89 To 2012 $22

Yarra Valley Rose 2006 Fragrant cherry blossom; good red fruit, just a little unnecessarily sweet. Diam. 13.7° alc. Rating 87 To 2008 $15

Shadowfax

K Road, Werribee, Vic 3030 **Region** Geelong
T (03) 9731 4420 **F** (03) 9731 4421 **www**.shadowfax.com.au **Open** 7 days 11–5
Winemaker Matt Harrop **Est.** 2000 **Cases** 15 000
Shadowfax is part of an awesome development at Werribee Park, a mere 20 mins from Melbourne. The truly striking winery, designed by Wood Marsh architects, built in 2000, is adjacent to the extraordinary 60-room private home built in the 1880s by the Chirnside family and known as The Mansion. It was then the centrepiece of a 40 000-ha pastoral empire, and the appropriately magnificent gardens were part of the reason why the property was acquired by Parks Victoria in the early 1970s. The Mansion is now The Mansion Hotel, with 92 rooms and suites. Exports to the UK, Japan, NZ and Singapore.

ΨΨΨΨΨ **One Eye Heathcote Shiraz 2004** Quite fragrant and spicy; medium-bodied, with the spicy/savoury aspects of the palate following the bouquet, but there is also intense fruit underneath, supported by fine, silky tannins and quality oak. Screwcap. 14.2° alc. **Rating** 96 **To** 2026 $65
Pink Cliffs Heathcote Shiraz 2004 Clear-cut varietal aromas; medium-bodied, but full of black fruits, spice and licorice; long finish with very fine tannins; alcohol to be wholly commended. Screwcap. 14° alc. **Rating** 96 **To** 2026 $65
Adelaide Hills Sauvignon Blanc 2006 Highly skilled winemaking; spotlessly clean, it opens with some tropical and apple fruit, then builds intensity right through the length of the palate, with a sunburst of crisp acidity on the finish. Screwcap. 13° alc. **Rating** 94 **To** 2008 $18
Chardonnay 2005 An elegant wine, slowly building complexity courtesy of its screwcap; melon, nectarine and some grapefruit supported by subtle oak and a long finish. Geelong/Macedon/Beechworth/Cardinia. Screwcap. 13.7° alc. **Rating** 94 **To** 2012 $28
Landscape Shiraz 2004 Bright purple-red; a medium-bodied mix of attractive black fruits, bitter chocolate and fine, persistent tannins giving length. Screwcap. 14° alc. **Rating** 94 **To** 2015 $29
Argyle Heathcote Shiraz 2003 Medium red-purple, not especially dense; a very restrained and elegant wine by Heathcote standards; plum, raspberry, blackberry, spice and chocolate all intermingle; fine, silky tannins run through the finish. Screwcap. 14.6° alc. **Rating** 94 **To** 2015 $65

ΨΨΨΨΨ **Adelaide Hills Pinot Gris 2006** Matt Harrop has teased that bit extra out of pinot gris, partly thanks to Adelaide Hills fruit quality, partly whole-bunch pressing, and part extended lees contact in tank à la Muscadet Sur Lie. Screwcap. 13.5° alc. **Rating** 90 **To** 2008 $22

ΨΨΨΨ **Shiraz 2004** Light- to medium-bodied; pleasant dark fruits with a touch of chocolate; showing some early signs of development. Tallarook/Heathcote/Werribee. Screwcap. 14° alc. **Rating** 88 **To** 2010 $18

Shantell ★★★★

1974 Melba Highway, Dixons Creek, Vic 3775 **Region** Yarra Valley
T (03) 5965 2155 **F** (03) 5965 2331 **www**.shantellvineyard.com.au **Open** 7 days 10.30–5
Winemaker Shan Shanmugam, Turid Shanmugam **Est.** 1980 **Cases** 1800
The substantial and fully mature Shantell vineyards provide the winery with a high-quality fruit source; part is sold to other Yarra Valley makers, the remainder vinified at Shantell. Chardonnay, Semillon and Cabernet Sauvignon are its benchmark wines, sturdily reliable, sometimes outstanding. Exports to the UK and Singapore.

Sharmans ★★★

Glenbothy, 175 Glenwood Road, Relbia, Tas 7258 **Region** Northern Tasmania
T (03) 6343 0773 **F** (03) 6343 0773 **www**.sharmanswines.com **Open** W'ends 10–5
Winemaker Tamar Ridge (Andrew Pirie) **Est.** 1987 **Cases** 1000

Mike Sharman pioneered one of the more interesting wine regions of Tas, not far south of Launceston but with a distinctly warmer climate than (say) Pipers Brook. Ideal north-facing slopes are home to a vineyard now approaching 4 ha. This additional warmth gives the red wines greater body than most Tas counterparts.

ΨΨΨΨΨ Pinot Noir 2005 Very deep colour; full-bodied, extremely rich; rape, not seduction. **Rating** 90 **To** 2015 $23

Sharpe Wines of Orange ★★★☆

Stagecoach Road, Emu Swamp, Orange, NSW 2800 **Region** Orange
T (02) 6361 9046 **F** (02) 6361 1645 www.sharpewinesoforange.com.au **Open** By appt
Winemaker Margot Sharpe, Rob Black **Est.** 1998 **Cases** 1000
When Margot and Tony Sharpe began planting their 4-ha vineyard, predominantly to cabernet sauvignon, with lesser amounts of merlot and cabernet franc, the wheel turned in a somewhat wayward full circle. Sharpe Bros Cordials was established in 1868 by strict Methodists to give the working man something to drink other than the demon alcohol. Says Margot Sharpe, 'I do believe there might be some serious grave turning over the product.' The Rose and Single Barrel Cabernet Sauvignon were made by the Sharpes in a tiny winery established in small stables at the back of their house; the Jack Demmery Cabernet Sauvignon was named in honour of Margot Sharpe's late father, who died just as planting of the vineyard was completed.

ΨΨΨΨ   Shattered Margot Merlot 2005 Medium- to full-bodied; plenty of rich blackcurrant fruit with some varietal black olive notes. Cork. **Rating** 89 **To** 2012 $20
Gentleman's Claret 2004 A powerful wine, with abundant black fruits, albeit slightly extractive. Cork. **Rating** 89 **To** 2020 $16

Shaw & Smith ★★★★★

Lot 4 Jones Road, Balhannah, SA 5242 **Region** Adelaide Hills
T (08) 8398 0500 **F** (08) 8398 0600 www.shawandsmith.com **Open** W'ends 11–4
Winemaker Martin Shaw, Darryl Catlin **Est.** 1989 **Cases** 35 000
Has progressively moved from a contract grape-grown base to estate production with the development of a 51.5-ha vineyard at Balhannah, followed in 2000 by a state-of-the-art, beautifully designed and executed winery, which ended the long period of tenancy at Petaluma. From a single wine (Sauvignon Blanc) operation, now makes at least 4 wines, all of the highest quality, but each has only been officially introduced after several trial vintages. Exports to all major markets.

ΨΨΨΨΨ M3 Vineyard Chardonnay 2005 Glowing yellow-green, the winemaker inputs simply serve to frame the fig, melon and nectarine fruit running through to a long finish. Screwcap. 13.5° alc. **Rating** 95 **To** 2012 $35
Adelaide Hills Shiraz 2005 An unusually powerful wine for the region; highly focused and intense blackberry, licorice and spice flavours, yet no heat, over-extraction or dead fruit. Quality cork. 14° alc. **Rating** 95 **To** 2030 $38
Adelaide Hills Sauvignon Blanc 2006 A super-fine, elegant and precise sauvignon blanc; passionfruit, spice, mineral and apple notes come and go repeatedly; a long, dry finish. Screwcap. 13° alc. **Rating** 94 **To** 2008 $25

ΨΨΨΨΨ Adelaide Hills Riesling 2006 Clean, crisp, fresh and firm; apple, pear, citrus and mineral; good length and attractively dry finish. Screwcap. 13° alc. **Rating** 92 **To** 2016 $20

Shaw Vineyard Estate ★★★★★

Isabelle Drive, Murrumbateman, NSW 2582 **Region** Canberra District
T (02) 6227 5827 www.shawvineyards.com.au **Open** Wed–Sun & public hols 9.30–5
Winemaker Bill Calabria, Ken Helm (Contract) **Est.** 1999 **Cases** 3000

Graeme and Michael Shaw have established 32 ha of vineyard, planted to semillon, riesling, shiraz, merlot and cabernet sauvignon. Production has grown; quality is up in leaps and bounds. The winery, cellar door and restaurant opened in 2005. Exports to Singapore.

ȲȲȲȲȲ **Canberra Riesling 2006** Green-straw; abundant power to the focused and long palate, a convincing mix of citrus (dominant) and tropical fruit. Screwcap. 12.5° alc. **Rating** 94 **To** 2018 $22
Canberra Cabernet Shiraz 2004 Strong colour; a perfectly ripened and delicious mix of red and black fruits; long, silky tannins; oak in the background. Screwcap. 14° alc. **Rating** 94 **To** 2020 $22

ȲȲȲȲȲ **Murrumbateman Semillon 2006** Pale straw-green; clean and crisp, with surprising overall delicacy given its alcohol; has all the ingredients to develop. Screwcap. 12.5° alc. **Rating** 90 **To** 2013 $20
Murrumbateman Cabernet Sauvignon 2004 Medium- to full-bodied; abundant blackcurrant and cassis fruit within a solid frame; carries itself with grace; good finish and aftertaste. Screwcap. 14° alc. **Rating** 90 **To** 2016 $20

ȲȲȲȲ **Murrumbateman Cabernet Merlot 2004** Strong purple-red; a big, concentrated, chewy wine; the flavours are good but it needed a little more barrel work and/or fining. Screwcap. 14° alc. **Rating** 89 **To** 2015 $20

Shays Flat Estate

482 Shays Flat-Malakoff Road, Landsborough, Vic 3384 **Region** Pyrenees
T 0417 589 136 **F** (03) 9826 6191 **www**.shaysflat.com **Open** Not
Winemaker Michael Unwin Wines **Est.** 1999 **Cases** 500
With advice from leading viticultural consultant Di Davidson, Rob and Isabella Burns have planted 11 ha of shiraz, 3.5 ha of cabernet sauvignon, 3.1 ha of merlot and 0.9 ha of sangiovese on the western slopes of the Pyrenees Ranges. Since the arrival of Glenlofty Vineyard in 1995, almost 1000 ha of vines have been planted in the valley. The Shays Flat soil has a thin layer of loam over a red-orange duplex clay heavily dispersed with quartz particles, the quartz providing favourable water holding and draining properties. At an altitude of 300–330 m on gently rising ridges, the property is situated at the end of the Great Dividing Range, and is slightly warmer than most of the Pyrenees and Grampians vineyards. The 2 wines come as a disappointment after the performance in the 2007 edition. Exports to Singapore.

ȲȲȲȲ **Pyrenees Shiraz 2005** Slightly cloudy colour; sweet and sour aspects through ripe fruits and green tannins; may or may not resolve the issue with time. Screwcap. 13.5° alc. **Rating** 87 **To** 2011 $20
Pyrenees Sangiovese 2004 Tangy sour cherry varietal fruit, with some spice and length. Screwcap. 13° alc. **Rating** 87 **To** 2009 $18

Sheep's Back

PO Box 441, South Melbourne, Vic 3205 **Region** Barossa Valley
T (03) 9696 7018 **F** (03) 9686 4015 **Open** Not
Winemaker Dean Hewitson **Est.** 2001 **Cases** 3000
Sheep's Back is a joint venture between Neil Empson (with 30 years' experience as an exporter to Australia and elsewhere of Italian wines) and Dean Hewitson. They decided to produce a single estate-grown shiraz after an extensive search found a 6-ha vineyard of 75-year-old vines. Exports to the US and Canada.

ȲȲȲȲȲ **Old Vine Barossa Valley Shiraz 2003** Blackberry, spice and a touch of chocolate; round, silky/velvety mouthfeel; classy oak, fine tannins; 75-year-old vines; 22 months French oak; no filtration; all things bright and beautiful except for a creased, stained cork. 14.3° alc. **Rating** 94 **To** 2019 $40

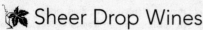 Sheer Drop Wines

207 Faraday–Sutton Grange Road, Faraday, Vic 3451 (postal) **Region** Bendigo
T 0417 244 410 **F** (03) 5474 3277 **www**.sheerdropwines.com.au **Open** Not
Winemaker Garth Doolan **Est.** 1995 **Cases** 5000
This is quite a story. Jo Clifford and Garth Doolan ask the rhetorical question, 'So how does a couple with 4 young children stay sane while juggling 2500 fine wool merinos, 120 ha of grapes, and 100 000 litres of premium, cool-climate wine? In a town such as Castlemaine, the answer is obvious: you just create your own circus troupe!' They might have added they enlisted the talents of painter Katharina Rapp to design the striking labels. If all this were not enough, their NV Sheer Drop Sparkling Shiraz NV won a gold medal at the Victorian Wines Show '06.

ＹＹＹＹ **Sparkling Shiraz NV** Light- to medium-bodied; well-balanced, the gentle spicy base wine not over-oaked; the dosage is low, the wine having some finesse. 14° alc. **Rating** 89 **To** 2010 $20
Shiraz 2004 Light- to medium-bodied; fresh red and black fruit, predominantly cherry; some spice appears on the lively finish; drink now while it retains its freshness. Screwcap. 14.3° alc. **Rating** 88 **To** 2008 $20
Riesling 2004 Still very youthful colour; soft tropical/apple/citrus aromas and flavours, which needed fining. The double entendre of the label painting by Katharina Rapp entitled 'My indoor garden' will amuse some. Screwcap. 12.9° alc. **Rating** 87 **To** 2010 $18.50
Cabernet Sauvignon 2004 Very savoury, briary edges to light- to medium-bodied cabernet fruit, which retains just enough blackcurrant to sustain the finish. Screwcap. 14.3° alc. **Rating** 87 **To** 2008 $18.50

Shelmerdine Vineyards ★★★★★

Merindoc Vineyard, Lancefield Road, Tooborac, Vic 3522 **Region** Heathcote
T (03) 5433 5188 **F** (03) 5433 5118 **www**.shelmerdine.com.au **Open** 7 days 10–5
Winemaker De Bortoli (Yarra Valley) **Est.** 1989 **Cases** 10 000
Stephen Shelmerdine has been a major figure in the wine industry for well over 20 years, like his family before him (who founded Mitchelton Winery), and has been honoured for his many services to the industry. The venture has 130 ha of vineyards spread over 3 sites: Lusatia Park in the Yarra Valley and Merindoc Vineyard and Willoughby Bridge in the Heathcote region. Substantial quantities of the grapes produced are sold to others; a small amount of high-quality wine is contract-made. Exports to the UK and NZ.

ＹＹＹＹＹ **Merindoc Vineyard Heathcote Shiraz 2004** Deeply coloured; extremely potent and focused blackberry and bitter chocolate fruit supported by ripe tannins and high-quality oak. Radically different style to the standard Heathcote. Screwcap. 15.5° alc. **Rating** 95 **To** 2030 $62
Yarra Valley Sauvignon Blanc 2006 Attractive bouquet, flavour and balance from start to finish; gentle tropical fruit with touches of guava and passionfruit; good acidity. Screwcap. 13° alc. **Rating** 94 **To** 2008 $20

ＹＹＹＹＹ **Yarra Valley Rose 2006** Pale salmon rather than shocking pink; off on its own, as much about texture as about flavour; 100% whole-bunch pressed and then 100% barrel-fermented in old oak; definite food style highly commendable. Screwcap. 13.5° alc. **Rating** 93 **To** 2008 $18
Heathcote Shiraz 2005 Bright colour; in typical Shelmerdine style, brighter, lighter and fresher than most of the wines from Heathcote; plum and black cherry fruit with supple tannins and oak. Screwcap. 14.5° alc. **Rating** 93 **To** 2018 $30
Yarra Valley Chardonnay 2005 Light- to medium-bodied and elegant; melon and nectarine fruit with good length and controlled oak; will develop with time in bottle. Screwcap. 13.3° alc. **Rating** 92 **To** 2012 $25
Yarra Valley Pinot Noir 2005 Fragrant spiced cherry and plum aromas; light- to medium-bodied, with good length and balance, varietal character not threatened by over-extraction. Screwcap. 13.5° alc. **Rating** 92 **To** 2010 $28

Heathcote Cabernet Sauvignon 2005 A medium-bodied, fine and elegant style, with bright cassis and blackcurrant fruit; long finish. Screwcap. 14.9° alc. **Rating** 92 **To** 2015 $30

Heathcote Viognier 2006 Lighter on its feet than many, though still has varietal expression, and a particularly good, lingering finish. Screwcap. 13.9° alc. **Rating** 91 **To** 2009 $25

Heathcote Merlot 2005 Shows varietal character in both structure (medium-bodied, fine tannins) and flavour (red fruits and touches of olive). Hangs together nicely. Screwcap. 14.2° alc. **Rating** 91 **To** 2012 $25

ŶŶŶŶ　**Heathcote Riesling 2006** Clean and correct; delicate blossom aromas, then a palate with good balance but not a lot of mid-palate intensity; may build. Screwcap. 13° alc. **Rating** 89 **To** 2012 $18

Shepherd's Hut ★★★☆

PO Box 194, Darlington, WA 6070 **Region** Porongurup
T (08) 9299 6700 **F** (08) 9299 6703 **www**.shepherdshutwines.com **Open** Not
Winemaker Rob Diletti **Est.** 1996 **Cases** 1600
The shepherd's hut which appears on the wine label was one of 4 stone huts used in the 1850s to house shepherds tending large flocks of sheep. When WA pathologist Dr Michael Wishart (and family) purchased the property in 1996, the hut was in a state of extreme disrepair. It has since been restored, and still features the honey-coloured Mt Barker stone. A total of 18 ha of riesling, chardonnay, sauvignon blanc, shiraz and cabernet sauvignon have been established; the daily running of the vineyard is the responsibility of son Philip, who also runs a large farm of mainly cattle; son William helps with marketing and sales. Most of the grapes are sold to other makers in the region. Exports to the UK.

ŶŶŶŶ　**Porongurup Cabernet Sauvignon 2004** Medium-bodied; savoury notes with some cedar developing; fine structure around gentle blackcurrant and blackberry fruit. Screwcap. 14.5° alc. **Rating** 89 **To** 2008 $19

Porongurup Sauvignon Blanc 2006 Strongly varietal and slightly sweaty aromas; grassy fruit flavours; one to divide opinions. Screwcap. 12.5° alc. **Rating** 87 **To** 2008 $18

Shepherd's Moon ★★★☆

Barwang Ridge, 1 Barwang Road, via Young, NSW 2594 **Region** Hilltops
T (02) 6382 6363 **F** (02) 6382 6363 **Open** By appt
Winemaker Canberra Winemakers (Greg Gallagher) **Est.** 1979 **Cases** 1500
Rick and Julie Hobba purchased the Hansen Hilltops property in 2002. They have since engaged in an extensive rehabilitation program in the vineyard, which is starting to pay dividends. The plantings are 2 ha of cabernet sauvignon, 1.5 ha riesling, and 1 ha each of chardonnay, shiraz and semillon.

ŶŶŶŶŶ　**Cabernet Sauvignon 2005** Vibrant, lively cassis/blackcurrant fruit drives the wine; fine tannin and oak support. Screwcap. 13.1° alc. **Rating** 90 **To** 2015 $22

ŶŶŶŶ　**Shiraz 2005** Highly fragrant cherry, spice, clove and licorice aromas; medium-bodied, with fine tannins, oak making inroads into the cherry fruit. Screwcap. 13° alc. **Rating** 89 **To** 2015 $22

Shingleback

1 Main Road, McLaren Vale, SA 5171 **Region** McLaren Vale
T (08) 8323 7388 **F** (08) 8323 7336 **www**.shingleback.com.au **Open** 7 days 10–4
Winemaker John Davey, Dan Hills **Est.** 1995 **Cases** 100 000
Shingleback has 100 ha of vineyards in McLaren Vale, all of which is vinified for the Shingleback labels. Originally a specialist export business, but now the wines are also available in Australia. Quality has risen greatly, as has total production. Which is the chicken, which is the egg? It doesn't really matter is the best answer. Exports to the UK, the US, and other major markets.

ŸŸŸŸŸ　McLaren Vale Shiraz 2004 A more fragrant and elegant face of McLaren Vale; bright black and red fruits, with fine but persistent tannins; good length. Cork. 14.5° alc. **Rating** 94 **To** 2017 $25

D Block Reserve McLaren Vale Cabernet Sauvignon 2004 Strong McLaren Vale dark chocolate opens the batting, then cassis and blackcurrant take over, supported by fine tannins and sensitive oak use. Cork. 14.5° alc. **Rating** 94 **To** 2024 $59.95

ŸŸŸŸŸ　**D Block Reserve McLaren Vale Shiraz 2004** Medium-bodied, with abundant red and black fruits, supple and smooth; just 'too easy on the gums', an expression first used by Sir James Hardy (universally Jim to his friends) many years ago. Cork. 14.5° alc. **Rating** 93 **To** 2024 $59.95

D Block Reserve McLaren Vale Shiraz 2003 Retains full red-purple colour; a medium- to full-bodied, strongly regional, style; dark chocolate never far from the surface, along with blackberry and spice; good oak and tannins; excellent outcome for the vintage. Cork. 14.5° alc. **Rating** 93 **To** 2018 $65

Red Knot McLaren Vale Cabernet Sauvignon 2005 Abundant cassis and blackcurrant aromas, then lots of flesh and flavour with dark chocolate prominent on the palate; top-value barbecue red. Cork. 14° alc. **Rating** 93 **To** 2012 $15

McLaren Vale Cabernet Sauvignon 2004 Rich and ripe, flush with juicy blackcurrant fruit and a touch of dark chocolate; soft tannins; just a touch sweet (not from residual sugar). Cork. 14° alc. **Rating** 92 **To** 2019 $24.95

McLaren Vale Chardonnay 2006 Has a certain amount of restraint, and some nectarine, grapefruit and melon more associated with cooler climates; well-balanced and integrated French oak. Screwcap. 13° alc. **Rating** 90 **To** 2011 $19.95

The Gate McLaren Vale Shiraz 2004 Supple, elegant and smooth wine, medium-bodied, but slightly oaky. Cork. 14.5° alc. **Rating** 90 **To** 2014 $35

ŸŸŸŸ　**Red Knot McLaren Vale Shiraz 2005** The bouquet and palate both seem to have higher alcohol than the stated level; certainly generous, rich and ripe confit black fruits and a dash of chocolate. Definitely barbecue red country. Cork. 14° alc. **Rating** 89 **To** 2010 $14.95

McLaren Vale Grenache 2005 Light but bright hue; fresh juicy raspberry and redcurrant fruits; minimal tannins. Cork. 14.5° alc. **Rating** 89 **To** 2008 $25

Red Knot Cadenzia Grenache Shiraz Mourvedre 2005 A succulent, smooth cascade of red and black fruits, spice and regional chocolate. Ready now. Cork. 14° alc. **Rating** 89 **To** 2010 $14.95

Shottesbrooke　★★★★★

Bagshaws Road, McLaren Flat, SA 5171 **Region** McLaren Vale
T (08) 8383 0002 **F** (08) 8383 0222 **www.**shottesbrooke.com.au **Open** Mon–Fri 10–4.30, w'ends & public hols 11–5
Winemaker Nick Holmes, Hamish Maguire **Est.** 1984 **Cases** 12 000
For many years now the full-time business of former Ryecroft winemaker Nick Holmes (now with stepson Hamish Maguire), drawing primarily on estate-grown grapes at his Myoponga vineyard. He has always stood out for the finesse and elegance of his wines compared with the dam-buster, high-alcohol reds for which McLaren Vale has become famous (or infamous, depending on one's point of view). Now the wheel has started to turn full circle, and finesse and elegance are much more appreciated. Exports to all major markets.

ŸŸŸŸŸ　**Punch McLaren Vale Cabernet Sauvignon 2005** Has an extra dimension of complexity and power without in any way succumbing to the alcohol or extract trap; beautifully balanced cabernet fruit, oak and ripe tannins. Punch was a long-serving Clydesdale horse. Screwcap. 14.5° alc. **Rating** 95 **To** 2025 $38

Eliza McLaren Vale Shiraz 2004 Medium to full red-purple; delicious red and black fruits with a dusting of dark chocolate; excellent oak and tannin balance, likewise length and finish. ProCork. 14.5° alc. **Rating** 94 **To** 2016 $38

McLaren Vale Cabernet Sauvignon 2005 In typical Shottesbrooke style; medium-bodied and elegant; supple, smooth cassis and blackcurrant fruit; integrated oak and fine tannins. Gold medal Sydney Wine Show '07. Screwcap. 14° alc. **Rating** 94 **To** 2018 $19.95

ŸŸŸŸŸ McLaren Vale Chardonnay 2005 Clean and fresh, showing the very judicious use of a touch of French oak leaving the nectarine and citrus fruit to do most of the talking; fresh finish, with gently lemony acidity. Screwcap. 14° alc. **Rating** 92 **To** 2010 $20

McLaren Vale Shiraz 2005 Bright, deep purple-red; more weight and extract than prior vintages, though the moderate alcohol keeps the Shottesbrooke elegance with the blackberry, spice and dark chocolate flavours. Screwcap. 14.5° alc. **Rating** 92 **To** 2015 $20

Adelaide Hills Fleurieu Sauvignon Blanc 2006 Light straw-green; a quite complex array of aromas and flavours ranging through apple to gooseberry to tropical; attractive mix. Screwcap. 13.5° alc. **Rating** 91 **To** 2008 $18

ŸŸŸŸ Merlette McLaren Vale Merlot Rose 2006 Lots of sweet red berry fruit, and no green characters notwithstanding the low alcohol. Some sophisticated winemaking (reverse osmosis). Screwcap. 10° alc. **Rating** 89 **To** 2008 $15

The Proprietor 2005 The choc mint aromas of the bouquet flow through in part to the palate; has nice texture and structure, but doesn't quite come off. Cabernet Sauvignon/Merlot/Malbec. Screwcap. 14.5° alc. **Rating** 89 **To** 2013 $27.95

Sieber Road Wines

Sieber Road, via Tanunda, SA 5352 **Region** Barossa Valley
T (08) 8562 8038 **F** (08) 8562 8681 **www.**sieberwines.com **Open** 7 days 11–4
Winemaker Tim Geddes **Est.** 1999 **Cases** 4500
Richard and Val Sieber are the third generation to run Redlands, the family property, traditionally a cropping/grazing farm. They have diversified into viticulture with a total of 18 ha of vines, shiraz (14 ha) with the lion's share, the remainder viognier, grenache and mourvedre. Son Ben Sieber is a viticulturist.

ŸŸŸŸŸ Redlands Barossa Valley Shiraz 2002 Holding hue very well; an elegant, medium-bodied wine, reflecting the restrained alcohol; a fragrant fruit profile and fine, lingering tannins. Cork. 14° alc. **Rating** 94 **To** 2012 $20

ŸŸŸŸŸ Ernest Barossa Valley Shiraz 2004 Medium-bodied; attractive blackberry, black cherry and plum fruit supported by fine tannins and controlled oak. Cork. 14.5° alc. **Rating** 92 **To** 2014 $20

Barossa Valley Shiraz Grenache 2005 An interesting light- to medium-bodied wine; fresh raspberry and blackberry fruits, but no cosmetic notes from the grenache; fine tannins. Screwcap. 15.5° alc. **Rating** 90 **To** 2010 $16

Barossa Valley Grenache Shiraz Mourvedre 2005 Similar fruit flavours and profile to the Shiraz Grenache except for an additional touch of spicy/savoury tannins from the mourvedre. Screwcap. 15.5° alc. **Rating** 90 **To** 2010 $18

ŸŸŸŸ Barossa Valley Shiraz Viognier 2005 Typical deep, bright colour; an array of black fruits with spicy/savoury notes; the relatively high viognier (8%) doesn't help the mid-palate or finish. Screwcap. 14.5° alc. **Rating** 89 **To** 2012 $18

Barossa Valley Grenache Shiraz Mourvedre 2004 Firmer than the '05, with a touch of reduction evident which will probably dissipate; fine tannins and texture. Screwcap. 15.5° alc. **Rating** 89 **To** 2008 $18

Sienna Estate

Canal Rocks Road, Yallingup, WA 6282 **Region** Margaret River
T (08) 9755 2028 **F** (08) 9755 2101 **www.**siennaestate.com.au **Open** W'ends & hols 10–5
Winemaker Egidijus Rusilas **Est.** 1978 **Cases** 2000

The 3.7-ha vineyard, planted to semillon, sauvignon blanc, riesling and cabernet sauvignon, was established by David Hunt in 1978. It has now passed into the ownership of the Rusilas family, which has enhanced its legacy.

♀♀♀♀♀ Momentum of Growth Margaret River Cabernet Sauvignon 2004 Youthful purple-red; spotlessly clean; medium-bodied cassis, blackcurrant and mulberry fruit; fine, ripe tannins and good length. Screwcap. 13.5° alc. **Rating** 94 **To** 2016 $19

♀♀♀♀♀ Momentum of Youth Margaret River Semillon 2006 Ghostly pale; pristine cut grass and wild herb aromas; a fresh palate following the pattern of the bouquet; will develop well, and it's easy to afford to watch that development. Screwcap. 12.5° alc. **Rating** 90 **To** 2016 $14

♀♀♀♀ Momentum of Gratitude Geographe Merlot 2005 Small red fruit aromas, then unexpected strength in the mouth, particularly the tannins, which needed fining. Screwcap. 14.5° alc. **Rating** 88 **To** 2014 $20
Momentum of Passion Margaret River Semillon Sauvignon Blanc 2006 Slight reduction haunts the wine throughout; however, it does have length, and the flavours grow on retasting. Would have been outstanding without that reduction. Screwcap. 13° alc. **Rating** 87 **To** 2008 $15

Silk Hill

324 Motor Road, Deviot, Tas 7275 **Region** Northern Tasmania
T (03) 6394 7385 **F** (03) 6394 7392 **Open** By appt
Winemaker Gavin Scott **Est.** 1989 **Cases** 500
Pharmacist Gavin Scott has been a weekend and holiday viticulturist for many years, having established the Glengarry Vineyard, which he sold, and then establishing the 1.5-ha Silk Hill (formerly Silkwood Vineyard) in 1989, planted exclusively to pinot noir.

♀♀♀♀♀ The Supply Pinot Noir 2005 Strong colour; rich, ripe, abundant black plum fruit, with soft, fine tannins and quality oak. There is just a trace of mint which will distract some discriminating tasters. Diam. **Rating** 93 **To** 2013 $30

♀♀♀♀ Pinot Noir 2005 A pretty wine, with a supple and smooth mix of plum and cherry; perhaps a tad simple. Diam. **Rating** 88 **To** 2010 $25

Silkwood Wines   **NR**

5204/6249 Channybearup Road, Pemberton, WA 6260 **Region** Pemberton
T (08) 9776 1584 **F** (08) 9776 1540 **www**.silkwoodwines.com.au **Open** 7 days 10–5
Winemaker Hugh Murray **Est.** 1998 **Cases** NA

Silver Wings Winemaking   ★★★★☆

Paramoor Farm, 439 Three Chain Road, Carlsruhe, Vic 3442 **Region** Central Victoria Zone
T (03) 5429 2444 **F** (03) 5429 2442 **Open** By appt
Winemaker Keith Brien **Est.** 2003 **Cases** 1500
This is the new venture of Keith Brien, formerly of Cleveland. After a brief shared occupation with Goona Warra Winery in Sunbury, he has moved Silver Wings to a little winery at Carlsruhe, near Lancefield. Here he offers contract winemaking and export consulting, as well as making the Silver Wings wines from 4 ha of contract-grown grapes (3 ha of mourvedre, 1 ha of shiraz) coming from 50-year-old vines.

 # Silverstream Wines   ★★★☆

2365 Scotsdale Road, Denmark, WA 6333 **Region** Great Southern
T (08) 9840 9119 **F** (08) 9384 5657 **Open** W'ends & public hols 11–4
Winemaker James Kellie (Harewood Estate), John Wade (Contract) **Est.** 1999 **Cases** 500

Tony and Felicity Ruse have 9 ha of chardonnay, merlot and cabernet franc in their vineyard 23 km from Denmark. The wines are contract-made, and after some hesitation, the Ruses decided their very pretty garden and orchard more than justified their recently opened cellar door, a decision supported by the quality on offer at very reasonable prices.

ŸŸŸŸŸ **Denmark Merlot Cabernet Franc 2005** An elegant, light- to medium-bodied wine offering cassis, red cherry and raspberry fruit flavours; fine tannins and good length. Screwcap. 13.5° alc. **Rating** 90 **To** 2015 $22

ŸŸŸŸ **Denmark Unwooded Chardonnay 2005** Still very fresh and relatively tight; stone fruit with a touch of grapefruit; good length and balance. Screwcap. 13.5° alc. **Rating** 89 **To** 2008 $18
Denmark Unwooded Chardonnay 2006 Flavoursome tropical passionfruit flavours, with a dash of market-led sweetness on the finish. Screwcap. 13.5° alc. **Rating** 88 **To** 2008 $18
Denmark Cabernet Franc Rose 2006 Fragrant and lively cherry flavours, the residual sugar offset (partially) by brisk acidity. Screwcap. 13.2° alc. **Rating** 87 **To** 2008 $17

Silverwaters Vineyard

PO Box 41, San Remo, Vic 3925 **Region** Gippsland
T (03) 5678 5230 **F** (03) 5678 5989 **Open** Not
Winemaker Paul Evans (Contract) **Est.** 1995 **Cases** 1000
Lyn and Lionel Hahn planted 0.5 ha each of chardonnay, pinot gris, pinot noir, shiraz and cabernet sauvignon in 1995. The first commercial vintage followed 5 years later, and the wines have gone from strength to strength, the 2003 Pinot Noir winning the trophy and gold medal for Pinot Noir at the International Cool Climate Wine Show '05.

ŸŸŸŸŸ **Cabernet Sauvignon 2004** Better colour than the '05, in both hue and depth; the bouquet and palate are radically better; deeper, more classic cabernet varietal fruit; nicely balanced ripe tannins. Diam. 13.5° alc. **Rating** 94 **To** 2024

ŸŸŸŸŸ **Shiraz 2004** Full-bodied, powerful black fruits, licorice and plum; flashes of spice and black pepper; should be long-lived. Diam. 13.5° alc. **Rating** 93 **To** 2019
Pinot Noir 2005 Strong dark plum and black cherry fruit, the spicy lift on the finish tipping the scales away from dry red to pinot noir; given this, an impressive wine. Diam. 14.5° alc. **Rating** 92 **To** 2012
Shiraz 2005 Medium-bodied; very different to the '04, here more to a red and black fruit mix, the spice and pepper more obvious; fine tannins. Diam. 14.5° alc. **Rating** 91 **To** 2017

ŸŸŸŸ **Chardonnay 2006** Intense citrus and nectarine fruit proclaiming the cool-grown environment; fairly high acidity, and oak is not obvious. Diam. 13.51° alc. **Rating** 88 **To** 2013
Pinot Gris 2006 The faintly pink colour is perfectly acceptable; enters the mouth well, with ripe pear and a touch of strawberry, then a dry but fractionally hard finish. Diam. 14° alc. **Rating** 87 **To** 2008
Cabernet Sauvignon 2005 Quite developed colour; light- to medium-bodied with savoury/earthy overtones; will likely continue its rapid development. Diam. 14° alc. **Rating** 87 **To** 2010

Silverwood Wines

66 Bittern-Dromana Road, Balnarring, Vic 3926 **Region** Mornington Peninsula
T 0419 890 317 **F** (03) 8317 6642 **www.**silverwoodwines.com.au **Open** Not
Winemaker Paul Dennis, Phillip Kittle **Est.** 1997 **Cases** 1000

Paul and Denise Dennis were inspired to establish Silverwood by living in France for a year. They, with members of their family, did much of the establishment work on the vineyard, which is meticulously maintained. All of the grapes are now used for Silverwood (in earlier years some were sold), not surprising given that the 2005 Pinot Noir topped the class of 48 '05 pinots at the strictly judged Winewise Small Vignerons Awards '06 in Canberra.

ŶŶŶŶŶ **The Reserve 2004** Complex spicy, savoury, forest floor aromas; the flavours follow down the same track with considerable length, but with red fruits coming through strongly on the finish and aftertaste. Pinot Noir. Screwcap. 13.7° alc. **Rating** 94 **To** 2013 $50

ŶŶŶŶŶ **Mornington Peninsula Pinot Noir 2005** Clear cherry and plum varietal character on the mid-palate; good line and length, and obvious potential for development. Screwcap. 13.9° alc. **Rating** 90 **To** 2012 $31.20

ŶŶŶŶ **Mornington Peninsula Chardonnay 2005** Light- to medium-bodied; very easy-going style, with gentle peach and melon fruit supported by appropriately subtle oak. Screwcap. 13.9° alc. **Rating** 89 **To** 2010 $25

Simon Gilbert Wines   ★★★★☆

1220 Sydney Road, Mudgee, NSW 2850 **Region** Mudgee
T (02) 6373 1245 **F** (02) 6373 1350 www.simongilbertwines.com.au **Open** 7 days 9–5
Winemaker Andrew Ewart, David Darlow **Est.** 1993 **Cases** 35 000
The arrival of high-profile, ex-Southcorp senior executives David Coombe as Chairman and Paul Pacino as Chief Executive saw a complete restructuring of this $20-million, 5000-tonne winery. In late 2005 the company merged with Cassegrain, which extends the vineyard resources to include the burgeoning Northern Slopes/New England areas of NSW. There will also be rationalisation of the winemaking business of Cassegrain, albeit with the active and continued involvement of John Cassegrain, who has become a shareholder in Simon Gilbert. The wines, with new products being introduced, continue to be predominantly sourced from the Central Ranges regions of NSW, including Orange, Mudgee and Cowra. In 2007 changes at the top of the executive management team, and a sagging share price, strongly suggest all is not well. Exports to all major markets.

ŶŶŶŶŶ **Five Shillings Mudgee Shiraz 2005** Smooth and supple; a rich array of black and red fruits; excellent tannin and oak handling; a genuine selection of the best barrels of Prince Hill. Cork. 14.5° alc. **Rating** 94 **To** 2020 $35

ŶŶŶŶŶ **Eighty Links Mudgee Chardonnay 2005** A very well-made wine; unusually intense and fine melon and nectarine fruit; balanced oak, long citrussy finish. Cork. 14° alc. **Rating** 93 **To** 2014 $35
Prince Hill Mudgee Sangiovese 2005 Unusually full-flavoured; abundant red fruits ranging from cherry to plum; ripe tannins. Not particularly varietal, but is nonetheless enjoyable. Screwcap. 13.5° alc. **Rating** 90 **To** 2018 $25

ŶŶŶŶ **Prince Hill Mudgee Merlot 2005** Plenty of substance and texture to the fruit, oak and tannins; black fruit flavours overall, merlot varietal character slipping through the cracks. Screwcap. 14.5° alc. **Rating** 88 **To** 2015 $25
Prince Hill Mudgee Chardonnay 2005 Pleasant light- to medium-bodied peach and nectarine aromas and flavours; oak (if any) irrelevant. Screwcap. 13.5° alc. **Rating** 87 **To** 2008 $25
Prince Hill Mudgee Shiraz 2005 Not surprisingly, a (very) junior version of Five Shillings; pleasant, but a touch of sweetness for the commercial market. Screwcap. 14.5° alc. **Rating** 87 **To** 2012 $25

Simon Hackett   ★★★☆

Budgens Road, McLaren Vale, SA 5171 **Region** McLaren Vale
T (08) 8323 7712 **F** (08) 8323 7713 **Open** Wed–Sun 11–5
Winemaker Simon Hackett **Est.** 1981 **Cases** 20 000

In 1998 Simon Hackett acquired the former Taranga winery in McLaren Vale, which has made his winemaking life a great deal easier. He has 8 ha of estate vines, and has contract growers in McLaren Vale and the Barossa Valley, with another 32 ha of vines.

 ## Sinclair of Scotsburn   ★★★★★

256 Wiggins Road, Scotsburn, Vic 3352 **Region** Ballarat
T 0419 885 717 **F** (03) 8699 7550 **www.**sinclairofscotsburn.com.au **Open** By appt
Winemaker Scott Ireland **Est.** 1997 **Cases** 260
David and Barbara Sinclair purchased their property in 2001. At that time 1.2 ha of chardonnay and 0.8 ha of pinot noir had been planted, but had struggled, the pinot noir yielding less than 0.25 tonnes in 2002. With the aid of limited drip irrigation, cane pruning, low crop levels and bird netting, limited quantities of high-quality chardonnay and pinot have since been produced. Since 2003 the grapes have gone to Tomboy Hill, but in 2005 half were made into wine for the Sinclair of Scotsburn label.

ŶŶŶŶŶ **Wallijak Chardonnay 2005** Glowing yellow-green; a lovely wine, textured and rich; nectarine, melon and grapefruit balanced by perfect acidity and quality oak; 90 dozen made. Screwcap. 13.5° alc. **Rating** 95 **To** 2015 $21
Manor House Pinot Noir 2005 Fragrant red fruits and spices; beautiful poised and constructed; a silky fine line through to the peacock's tail on the finish. Screwcap. 13.5° alc. **Rating** 94 **To** 2011 $21

Sinclair Wines   ★★★★☆

Graphite Road, Glenoran, WA 6258 **Region** Manjimup
T (08) 9335 6318 **F** (08) 9433 5489 **www.**sinclairwines.com.au **Open** By appt
Winemaker Brenden Smith (Contract) **Est.** 1994 **Cases** 2800
Sinclair Wines is the child of Darelle Sinclair, a science teacher, wine educator and graduate viticulturist from Charles Sturt University, and John Healy, a lawyer, traditional jazz musician and graduate wine marketing student of Adelaide University, Roseworthy campus. The 5 ha of estate plantings underpin high-quality wines at mouth-watering prices. Looking at the range as a whole, one cannot help but wonder how anyone thought that pinot noir would be the most suitable variety for this part of the world. Exports to the UK, The Netherlands and Japan.

ŶŶŶŶŶ **Jezebel Manjimup Cabernet Merlot 2005** Despite its modest alcohol has all the weight and flesh one could wish for; seductive cassis and blackcurrant fruit runs the full length of the palate; fine tannins and oak. Great value. Screwcap. 13° alc. **Rating** 94 **To** 2020 $20

ŶŶŶŶŶ **Ricardo Shiraz 2005** Fragrant and lively aromas; excellent cool-grown bright cherry, spice and cracked pepper aromas and flavours; fine tannins, good length. Screwcap. 14.5° alc. **Rating** 92 **To** 2017 $20
Giovanni Manjimup Cabernet Sauvignon 2005 Curiously lighter in flavour impact than the Shiraz or Cabernet Merlot; pretty cassis/redcurrant flavours; does have length, though. Screwcap. 13° alc. **Rating** 90 **To** 2013 $20
Jeremy Cabernet Shiraz 2006 Softer than the Cabernet Sauvignon, but has many of the same red fruit characters, and the fruit is allowed to express itself without being pumped up by oak; appealing light- to medium-bodied wine. Screwcap. 13° alc. **Rating** 90 **To** 2012 $20

ŶŶŶŶ **Swallow Hill Manjimup Sauvignon Blanc 2006** Plenty of ripe tropical fruit flavours, freshened up with citrussy acidity on the finish. Screwcap. 13° alc. **Rating** 89 **To** 2008 $16
Jezebel Manjimup Cabernet Merlot 2004 Medium-bodied; immediately savoury olive/earth/blackcurrant flavours attest to the blend; finishes with silky, fine tannins. Screwcap. 13° alc. **Rating** 88 **To** 2014

Sinclair's Gully

Lot 3 Colonial Drive, Norton Summit, SA 5136 **Region** Adelaide Hills
T (08) 8390 1995 **www**.sinclairsgully.com **Open** Wed–Sun 12–4 Aug–May, or by appt
Winemaker Contract **Est.** 1998 **Cases** 600

Sue and Sean Delaney purchased their 10.5 ha property at Norton Summit in 1997. The property
had a significant stand of remnant native vegetation, with a State Conservation Rating, and since
acquiring the property much energy has been spent in restoring 8 ha of pristine bushland, home
to 130 species of native plants and 66 species of native birds, some recorded as threatened or rare.
It has been a DIY venture for the Delaneys (supported by family and friends) with Sue Delaney
hand-pruning the 0.4 ha each of chardonnay and sauvignon blanc planted in 1998.

Adelaide Hills Sauvignon Blanc 2006 Extremely pale colour; crisp, crunchy
mineral, herb, grass and apple aromas and flavours, then a touch of lemony
acidity. Screwcap. 13° alc. **Rating** 90 **To** 2008 $22

Adelaide Hills Chardonnay 2006 Light-bodied; clean and crisp, with touches of
stone fruit; delicate, unforced style. Screwcap. 13° alc. **Rating** 87 **To** 2009 $20

Sir Paz Estate

384 George Street, Fitzroy, Vic 3065 (postal) **Region** Yarra Valley
T (03) 9417 9337 **F** (03) 9417 3981 **www**.sirpaz.com **Open** Not
Winemaker Gary Mills, John Zapris **Est.** 1997 **Cases** 4900

The Zapris family established Sir Paz Estate in 1997, planting just under 11 ha of shiraz; the first
release of 2001 scored an emphatic gold medal at the Victorian Wines Show '03 as the highest
scored entry. Subsequent vintages have not disappointed, and the success led to the planting of
an additional 7 ha of merlot (even though the original intention was to simply make one wine).
It is not hard to see the anagrammatic derivation of of the name. Exports to Sri Lanka, China
and Cyprus.

Blocks A, B & D Shiraz 2005 Vibrant and elegant; light- to medium-bodied
blackberry, cherry and dark chocolate fruit; fine, ripe, silky tannins. Cork.
14.2° alc. **Rating** 93 **To** 2015 $32

Block E Merlot 2005 Fragrant and savoury; light- to medium-bodied, but intense
raspberry, cassis, black olive and spice flavours are wholly merlot. Cork. 14.5° alc.
Rating 92 **To** 2015 $27

Sirromet Wines

850-938 Mount Cotton Road, Mount Cotton, Qld 4165 **Region** Queensland Coastal
T (07) 3206 2999 **F** (07) 3206 0900 **www**.sirromet.com **Open** 7 days 10–5
Winemaker Adam Chapman, Craig Stevenson, Velten Tiemann **Est.** 1998 **Cases** 66 500

This was an unambiguously ambitious venture, which has succeeded in its aim of creating Qld's
premier winery. The founding Morris family, retained a leading architect to design the striking
state-of-the-art winery with an 80 000-case production capacity; the state's foremost viticultural
consultant to plant the 4 major vineyards (in the Granite Belt) which total over 100 ha; and the
most skilled winemaker practising in Qld, Adam Chapman, to make the wine. It has a 200-seat
restaurant, a wine club offering all sorts of benefits to its members, and is firmly aimed at the
domestic and international tourist market, taking advantage of its situation, halfway between
Brisbane and the Gold Coast. Exports to the UK, the US and The Netherlands.

TM Viognier 2005 A very respectable first vintage; plenty of mouthfeel and
weight to ripe, yellow peach and apricot fruit; not phenolic. Screwcap.
13.3° alc. **Rating** 90 **To** 2009 $30

Seven Scenes Granite Belt Shiraz Viognier 2005 Typical colour; rich
blackberry fruit and viognier lift on the bouquet, followed by spice and
black fruits on the palate with fine, ripe tannins and controlled oak. Screwcap.
13.8° alc. **Rating** 90 **To** 2015 $22

♥♥♥♥ **Seven Scenes Chardonnay 2003** Significant development in colour and flavour; stone fruit and fig; controlled oak. The suspicion is of premature development/oxidation. Cork. 13.5° alc. **Rating** 88 **To** 2008 $28

Sittella Wines

100 Barrett Road, Herne Hill, WA 6056 **Region** Swan Valley
T (08) 9296 2600 **F** (08) 9296 0237 **www.**sittella.com.au **Open** Tues–Sun & public hols 11–5
Winemaker Matthew Bowness, John Griffiths (Consultant) **Est.** 1998 **Cases** 7000
Perth couple Simon and Maaike Berns acquired a 7-ha block (with 5 ha of vines) at Herne Hill, making the first wine in 1998 and opening a most attractive cellar door facility later in the year. They also own the 10-ha Wildberry Springs Estate vineyard in the Margaret River region.

♥♥♥♥♀ **Berns Reserve 2005** Fine texture courtesy of the Margaret River cabernet component, but with even more going for it, thanks to the synergistic Swan Valley shiraz; perfect balance, and a very good finish. Cork. 14.5° alc. **Rating** 91 **To** 2020 $32

♥♥♥♥ **Margaret River Cabernet Sauvignon 2005** Textured and supple courtesy of fine, ripe tannins running through black fruits, with sweet earth and oak notes; a complex wine. Screwcap. 14° alc. **Rating** 89 **To** 2015 $20

Skillogalee

Off Hughes Park Road, Sevenhill via Clare, SA 5453 **Region** Clare Valley
T (08) 8843 4311 **F** (08) 8843 4343 **www.**skillogalee.com.au **Open** 7 days 10–5
Winemaker Dave Palmer, Daniel Palmer **Est.** 1970 **Cases** 10 000
David and Diana Palmer purchased the small hillside stone winery from the George family at the end of the 1980s and have fully capitalised on the exceptional fruit quality of the Skillogalee vineyards. All the wines are generous and full-flavoured, particularly the reds. In 2002 the Palmers purchased next-door neighbour Waninga Vineyards, with 30 ha of 30-year-old vines, allowing a substantial increase in production without any change in quality or style. Exports to the UK, Switzerland, the US, Malaysia and Hong Kong.

♥♥♥♥♀ **Clare Valley Riesling 2006** Tropical lime and citrus aromas; generously flavoured, with lots of similar tropical/citrus nuances; as often, marches to the tune of its own drum. Screwcap. 12.5° alc. **Rating** 90 **To** 2010 $20
Clare Valley Shiraz 2004 Medium-bodied; smooth and supple blackberry and black cherry fruit; fine tannins, controlled oak and a long finish. Screwcap. 14° alc. **Rating** 90 **To** 2019 $27.50

Smallfry Wines

13 Murray Street, Angaston, SA 5353 **Region** Barossa Valley
T (08) 8564 2182 **F** (08) 8564 2182 **www.**smallfrywines.com.au **Open** Fri–Sun & public hols 12–4.30, or by appt tel 0412 153 243
Winemaker Wayne Ahrens, Colin Forbes, Tim Smith **Est.** 2005 **Cases** 1500
The engagingly-named Smallfry Wines is the venture of Wayne Ahrens and partner Suzi Hilder. Wayne comes from a fifth-generation Barossa family, Suzi is the daughter of well-known Upper Hunter viticulturist Richard Hilder and wife Del, partners in Pyramid Hill Wines. Both have degrees from Charles Sturt University, and both have extensive experience; Wayne's track record includes 7 vintages as a cellar hand at Orlando Wyndham and other smaller Barossa wineries. They have 5.5 ha of cabernet sauvignon, 2.3 ha of riesling, 1.5 ha of shiraz and a few vines of mataro/mourvedre, and purchase small lots of interesting grapes which become available – hence wines such as Grenache and Bordeaux blends including cabernet franc, merlot and petit verdot.

♥♥♥♥♥ **Eden Valley Cabernet Sauvignon 2005** A convincing mix of blackcurrant, dark chocolate, spice, licorice and earth; good oak and tannins; a cabernet with attitude. No small fry here. Screwcap. 14.5° alc. **Rating** 94 **To** 2020 $28

🍷🍷🍷🍷♀ **Eden Valley Riesling 2006** Tighter, more elegant and more minerally than the Barossa Riesling, reflecting the different terroir; delicate and refreshing, as is the price. Screwcap. 12.5° alc. **Rating** 93 **To** 2016 $18

Barossa Valley Riesling 2006 Spotless lemon blossom aromas; abundant lime-accented flavour, with some tropical notes; good length. Screwcap. 11.5° alc. **Rating** 92 **To** 2014 $18

Barossa Valley Grenache 2005 Excellent hue; full-bodied by Barossa standards, and gets away with the alcohol thanks to the fruit density; raisin and prune flavours fit into the varietal profile. Screwcap. 16° alc. **Rating** 90 **To** 2015 $28

🍷🍷🍷🍷 **Barossa Valley Cabernet Grenache Rose 2006** Attractive rose, even if slightly sweet on the finish; has lots of fragrant red fruits; serve fully chilled. Screwcap. 12° alc. **Rating** 89 **To** 2008 $18

Eden Valley Shiraz Cabernet 2005 Some slightly dead/desiccated fruit flavours on entry to the mouth are at odds with the moderate alcohol, and the wine does pick up a little on the finish. Screwcap. 14.5° alc. **Rating** 87 **To** 2013 $28

Smithbrook ★★★★★

Smith Brook Road, Pemberton, WA 6260 **Region** Pemberton
T (08) 9772 3557 **www**.smithbrook.com.au **Open** Mon–Fri 9–4, w'ends by appt
Winemaker Michael Symons, Ashley Lewkowski **Est.** 1988 **Cases** 8000
Smithbrook is a major player in the Pemberton region, with over 60 ha of vines in production. Owned by Petaluma/Lion Nathan, but continues its role as a contract grower for other companies, as well as supplying Petaluma's needs and making relatively small amounts of wine under its own label. Perhaps the most significant change has been the removal of Pinot Noir from the current range of products, and the introduction of Merlot. The 2 vintages of Yilgarn Cabernet Merlot Petit Verdot are certain pointers for the future. Exports to the UK, Canada and Japan.

🍷🍷🍷🍷🍷 **Yilgarn Pemberton Cabernet Merlot Petit Verdot 2004** Strong red-purple; abundant blackcurrant, cassis and olive fruit; fine, ripe tannins and good French oak; exemplary length. Cork. 14.5° alc. **Rating** 94 **To** 2014 $35

Yilgarn Pemberton Cabernet Merlot Petit Verdot 2005 A successful medium-bodied marriage of the 3 varieties which ought to always work, but sometimes don't. Here the components are deftly blended in terms of structure and flavour. Shows the '04 was no fluke. Cork. **Rating** 94 **To** 2020 $35

🍷🍷🍷🍷 **Pemberton Merlot 2004** Clear and bright purple-red; a mix of olive and bright red fruits on the bouquet, then savoury olive flavours take control of the palate; so hard to get the balance right. Screwcap. **Rating** 89 **To** 2013 $24

Pemberton Sauvignon Blanc 2006 A clean, crisp and correct, but very light-bodied wine, with just a few nuances of gooseberry, apple and citrus. Screwcap. 12.5° alc. **Rating** 88 **To** 2008 $19

Smiths Vineyard ★★★★★

27 Croom Lane, Beechworth, Vic 3747 **Region** Beechworth
T 0412 475 328 **F** (03) 5728 1603 **www**.smithsvineyard.com.au **Open** W'ends & public hols 10–5, or by appt
Winemaker Jeanette Henderson, Will Flamsteed **Est.** 1978 **Cases** 600
Pete Smith established the first vineyard in Beechworth in 1978, with the encouragement of John Brown Jr of Brown Brothers. Most of the production of the Smiths' 2.5 ha of chardonnay, cabernet sauvignon and merlot is sold to Shadowfax, the remainder being made and sold under the Smiths Vineyard and Flamsteed labels. The winery is now owned by Will Flamsteed (the highly regarded winemaker at Giant Steps) and wife Sarah, daughter of Pete and Di Smith.

🍷🍷🍷🍷🍷 **Beechworth Chardonnay 2005** A beautifully made, discreet and elegant style; stone fruit, melon and cashew with perfectly integrated and balanced oak; long finish. Screwcap. 13.9° alc. **Rating** 94 **To** 2012 $32

Snobs Creek Wines

486 Goulburn Valley Highway, via Alexandra, Vic 3714 **Region** Upper Goulburn
T (03) 5774 2017 **www**.snobscreekvineyard.com.au **Open** W'ends 11–5, closed in winter
Winemaker MasterWineMakers **Est.** 1996 **Cases** 3500
The vineyard is situated where Snobs Creek joins the Goulburn River, 5 km below the Lake
Eildon wall. Originally planted in 1996, the vineyard has recently been increased to 16 ha. The
varieties grown are pinot gris, pinot noir, shiraz, viognier, chardonnay, merlot and dolcetto.

Somerled

7 Heath Road, Crafers, SA 5152 (postal) **Region** McLaren Vale
T (08) 8339 2617 **F** (08) 8339 2617 **Open** Not
Winemaker Rob Moody **Est.** 2001 **Cases** 1000
This is the venture of Robin and Heather Moody, and daughters Emma and Lucinda. The quietly
spoken Robin Moody (with a degree in oenology) joined Penfolds in 1969, and remained with
Penfolds/Southcorp until 2001. This is a classic negociant business in the strict sense of that term:
it produces only full-bodied McLaren Vale Shiraz, selected by Robin from exceptional parcels of
young wine, during or soon after fermentation. The wines are blended and matured at Boar's
Rock Winery at McLaren Vale. The name, incidentally, comes from the bay gelding which Robin's
grandfather raced to victory in the amateur steeplechase at the famous Oakbank Picnic Races in
1908, which in turn took its name from the Scottish king who defeated the Vikings in 1156. So
there you are.

Somerset Hill Wines ★★★★☆

891 McLeod Road, Denmark, WA 6333 **Region** Denmark
T (08) 9840 9388 **F** (08) 9840 9394 **www**.somersethillwines.com.au **Open** 7 days 11–5
summer, 11–4 winter
Winemaker Harewood Estate (James Kellie) **Est.** 1995 **Cases** 3000
Graham Upson commenced planting 11 ha of pinot noir, chardonnay, semillon, merlot and
sauvignon blanc in 1995, on one of the coolest and latest-ripening sites in WA. The limestone
cellar door sales area has sweeping views out over the ocean and to the Stirling Ranges, with
everything from Belgian chocolates to farm-grown mushrooms for sale (and, of course, wine).
Exports to Denmark, Russia, Poland and China.

ŶŶŶŶŶ **Semillon 2006** Spotlessly clean; no reduction; lively, vibrant lemongrass and
citrus fruit flow into a precisely pitched acidity on a very long finish. Wait
5 years minimum. Screwcap. 11.5° alc. **Rating** 94 **To** 2026 $21

ŶŶŶŶŶ **Sauvignon Blanc 2006** Laser-like precision from the vineyard to the glass;
a tangy, vibrant lemon, citrus, passionfruit and tropical progression. Screwcap.
12° alc. **Rating** 93 **To** 2008 $19
Harmony Classic White 2006 Lively unoaked style; an array of aromas and
flavours through tropical, stone fruit and citrus range, sauvignon blanc making
its mark. Screwcap. 12° alc. **Rating** 90 **To** 2009 $17

ŶŶŶŶ **Constellation Pinot Noir Chardonnay 2004** Elegant, fine and citrussy; good
length and balance, but not particularly complex. Relatively simple, extended age on
lees not apparent. 11.5° alc. **Rating** 89 **To** 2010 $39
Pinot Noir 2004 Quite developed colour; bramble, leaf, spice, forest aromas and
flavours; fully priced if nothing else. Cork. 13.5° alc. **Rating** 87 **To** 2008 $30

Songlines Estates

PO Box 221, Cessnock, NSW 2325 **Region** Southeast Australia
T (02) 4934 3214 **F** (02) 4934 3214 **www**.songlinesestates.com **Open** Not
Winemaker David Fatches, John Duval **Est.** 2002 **Cases** 3500
This is yet another of the multi-national, multi-talented boutique wine operations springing up
like mushrooms after autumn rain. The English end is represented by Martin Krajewski and Esme

Johnstone (very big names in the UK) and by David Fatches and John Duval as McLaren Vale winemakers. It becomes a little more complicated when one finds the vineyard address is Gabriel's Paddocks in the Hunter Valley, and that Bylines Hunter Valley Chardonnay is one of several wines produced. The majority come from old-vine vineyards in McLaren Vale and from Coonawarra.

ŸŸŸŸŸ **Bylines McLaren Vale Shiraz 2005** Classic McLaren Vale blackberry and dark chocolate driving all else before them (and there is plenty); alcohol is not the issue one might expect, and the oak is good. Cork. 15° alc. **Rating** 94 To 2025 $70

McLaren Vale Shiraz 2005 Well-structured, textured and balanced; medium-bodied, with the usual suspects of blackberry fruit plus elements of spice, licorice and chocolate; the oak is positive, the tannins ripe but not aggressive. I am unlikely to be killed in the rush to buy it. Cork. 15° alc. **Rating** 94 To 2020 $110

ŸŸŸŸŸ **McLaren Vale Shiraz 2004** A solid, medium- to full-bodied very typical McLaren Vale shiraz; abundant blackberry and dark chocolate; persistent but balanced tannins; classy French oak. Priced, I assume, for the American market. Cork. 15° alc. **Rating** 93 To 2014 $100

Leylines McLaren Vale Shiraz 2005 Bright red-purple; a clean, nicely balanced medium-bodied wine; black fruits and hints of licorice and spice, plus, of course, chocolate; fine tannins and judicious oak. This one priced for the domestic market. Cork. 14.5° alc. **Rating** 90 To 2015 $20

ŸŸŸŸ **Bylines Hunter Valley Chardonnay 2005** Very developed, although the colour change is to green-yellow, rather than straw-brown; broad peachy fruit seems overworked, although some acidity on the finish helps. Either the price is wrong, or I am, or this is a case of sporadic oxidation. Cork. 13.5° alc. **Rating** 88 To 2008 $50

Sorby Adams Wines   ★★★★

Lot 18, Gawler Park Road, Angaston, SA 5353 **Region** Eden Valley
T (08) 8564 2744 **F** (08) 8564 2437 **www**.sorbyadamswines.com **Open** 7 days 10–5
Winemaker Simon Adams **Est.** 2004 **Cases** 3500
Simon Adams and wife Helen purchased a 3.2-ha vineyard in 1996, which had been planted by Pastor Franz Julius Lehmann (none other than Peter Lehmann's father) in 1932. Peter Lehmann always referred to it as 'Dad's Block'. They have added 0.25 ha of viognier which, as one might expect, is used in a shiraz viognier blend. Nonetheless, the top wines, The Family Shiraz and The Thing Shiraz, need no assistance from viognier. Only 6 barrels of The Thing are made each year, using the best grapes from Dad's Block. The name Sorby Adams has overtones of a chameleon: it comes from a female ancestor of long-serving Yalumba winemaker Simon Adams, whose full name is Simon David Sorby Adams.

ŸŸŸŸŸ **The Thing Eden Valley Shiraz 2004** Excellent purple-red; a totally delicious wine, bursting with an array of supple, ripe fruit flavours; flavour without alcohol and excessive extraction, quality cork used for export one assumes. 14° alc. **Rating** 95 To 2015 $48

ŸŸŸŸŸ **The Family Eden Valley Clare Valley Shiraz 2004** Very good structure and mouthfeel; fruit-driven with blackberry, spice and licorice, though there is oak in support. Controlled alcohol a plus. Screwcap. 14° alc. **Rating** 92 To 2019 $31.75

ŸŸŸ **Morticia Sparkling Shiraz NV** Abundant flavour from the quality base wine, but, as yet, relatively little complexity; bottle age will help. 14° alc. **Rating** 88 To 2012 $19

Sorrenberg   ★★★★

Alma Road, Beechworth, Vic 3747 **Region** Beechworth
T (03) 5728 2278 **www**.sorrenberg.com **Open** Mon–Fri & most w'ends 1–5 by appt
Winemaker Barry Morey **Est.** 1986 **Cases** 1200

Barry and Jan Morey keep a low profile, but the wines from their 2.5-ha vineyard at Beechworth have a cult following not far removed from that of Giaconda; chardonnay, sauvignon blanc, cabernet sauvignon and gamay are the principal varieties planted on the north-facing, granitic slopes. Gamay and Chardonnay are the winery specialties.

ŸŸŸŸŸ **Beechworth Cabernet Sauvignon Cabernet Franc Merlot 2004** Good red-purple; excellent texture and structure to a medium-bodied palate; ripe blackcurrant, cassis and a touch of black olive; high-quality cork. 14° alc. **Rating** 92 **To** 2014 $41

Soul Growers   ★★★★★

34 Maria Street, Tanunda, SA 5352 (postal) **Region** Barossa Valley
T 0417 851 317 **Open** By appt
Winemaker James Lindner, Paul Lindner, David Cruickshank **Est.** 1998 **Cases** 240
James Lindner is a fifth-generation Barossan, working in every area of the wine industry since he left school. In 1998 he acquired a small property on the hills of Seppeltsfield, planting 1.6 ha of shiraz, 0.8 ha of grenache, 0.3 ha of mourvedre, and a little cabernet sauvignon and black muscat. The first 3 varieties are separately open-fermented and given 2 years barrel age before the wine is blended and bottled (without filtration or fining). Exports to the UK and Singapore.

ŸŸŸŸŸ **Barossa Valley Shiraz Cabernet Sauvignon 2004** More structure and better overall balance; blackberry, blackcurrant and some licorice; 69%/31%. Cork. 14.5° alc. **Rating** 94 **To** 2019 $28
Barossa Valley Shiraz Grenache Mourvedre 2004 Elegant, medium-bodied shiraz is holding the structure, the 3 flavour streams coalesce convincingly; good balance and finish. Cork. 15.5° alc. **Rating** 94 **To** 2015 $28

ŸŸŸŸŸ **Barossa Valley Shiraz 2004** Powerful black fruits with a strong lick of licorice; the alcohol doesn't show up until the finish, and detracts from an otherwise great wine. Cork. 15.5° alc. **Rating** 92 **To** 2019 $45

Southern Highland Wines   ★★★

Oldbury Road, Sutton Forest, NSW 2577 **Region** Southern Highlands
T (02) 4868 2300 **F** (02) 4868 1808 **www.**southernhighlandwines.com **Open** 7 days 10–5
Winemaker Eddy Rossi **Est.** 2003 **Cases** 10 000
The venture is owned by its 5 directors, who together have 50 years of experience in the wine industry and in commerce. John Gilbertson ran Ericsson in NZ and then in China between 1983 and 2000. Darren Corradi and Eddy Rossi, respectively in charge of viticulture and winemaking, both had lengthy careers in various Griffith wineries, also the training ground for production director Frank Colloridi. NZ-born Simon Gilbertson graduated from Lincoln University with a degree in agriculture, and after 13 years in corporate life, purchased 3 vineyards in Hawke's Bay, NZ; he is de facto general manager and sales director. There are 41 ha of vines, a veritable fruit salad of pinot gris, riesling, gewurztraminer, sauvignon blanc, chardonnay, viognier, nebbiolo, sangiovese, pinot noir, shiraz and cabernet sauvignon.

Spence

760 Burnside Road, Murgheboluc, Vic 3221 **Region** Geelong
T (03) 5264 1181 **F** (03) 5265 1181 **Open** By appt
Winemaker Peter Spence **Est.** 1997 **Cases** 700
Peter and Anne Spence were sufficiently inspired by an extended European holiday, which included living on a family vineyard in Provence, to purchase a small property specifically for the purpose of establishing a vineyard and winery. It remains a part-time occupation; Peter is an engineering manager at the Ford product development at Geelong, Anne a teacher, but presently full-time mother looking after 2 young children. They have planted 3.2 ha on a north-facing slope in a valley 7 km south of Bannockburn; the lion's share to 3 clones of shiraz (1.83 ha), the remainder to chardonnay, pinot noir and fast-diminishing cabernet sauvignon (which is being grafted over to viognier for use in the Shiraz). It seems to me Peter has had access to some friendly winemaking advice; if this is really cold turkey, great wines will be on their way.

ŶŶŶŶŶ **Oakbough Geelong Shiraz 2005** Aromatic spicy red and blackcurrant fruit aromas; black cherry, blackberry and pronounced spice; has elegance and length; a fresh fruit-driven finish. Screwcap. 13.5° alc. **Rating** 94 **To** 2018 $25

ŶŶŶŶŶ **Oakbough Geelong Shiraz 2004** Supple blackberry/black fruits; good oak and tannins. Would be improved by viognier, but doing it easily without the viognier jockey on board. **Rating** 93 **To** 2012 $25

Oakbough Geelong Cabernet Sauvignon 2005 Bright red-purple; medium-bodied; gentle cassis blackberry fruit with cedary overtones; fine tannins and good length. Screwcap. 13.5° alc. **Rating** 90 **To** 2018 $25

Spinifex   ★★★★★

PO Box 511, Nuriootpa, SA 5355 **Region** Barossa Valley
T (08) 8562 1914 **F** (08) 8562 1409 **www.**spinifexwines.com.au **Open** Not
Winemaker Peter Schell **Est.** 2001 **Cases** 2500

Peter Schell and Magali Gely are a husband and wife team from NZ who came to Australia in the early 1990s to study oenology and marketing respectively at Roseworthy College. Together they have spent 4 vintages making wine in France, mainly in the south where Magali's family were vignerons for generations near Montpellier. The focus at Spinifex is the red varieties which dominate in the south of France: mataro (more correctly mourvedre), grenache, shiraz and cinsaut. The wine is made in open fermenters, basket-pressed, partial wild (indigenous) fermentations, and relatively long post-ferment maceration. This is at once a very old approach, but nowadays à la mode. The wines are made at Spinifex's winery in Vine Vale, where Peter also makes wines for a number of clients to whom he consults. So far as I am concerned Spinifex out-Torbrecks Torbreck. Exports to the UK, the US, Canada, Belgium, The Netherlands and Singapore.

ŶŶŶŶŶ **Eden Valley Shiraz Viognier 2005** The leader of the band, with significantly richer and more overtly powerful fruit than Esprit or Indigene, but without losing any of their elegance and perfect balance. Polished to a lustrous sheen, it is able to convince you to drink it now, when it really needs another 5 years minimum, and decades thereafter. Very high-quality cork. 14.8° alc. **Rating** 97 **To** 2025 $44

Indigene 2005 Beautifully rounded and proportioned plum and black cherry fruit picked at perfect ripeness, with a gossamer web of silken tannins and, as with all the Spinifex wines, precisely integrated and balanced oak. Very high-quality cork. Barossa Valley Mataro (55%)/Shiraz (45%). 14.5° alc. **Rating** 96 **To** 2025 $44

Esprit 2005 A fragrant bouquet with multiple oriental spices defying precise description; light- to medium-bodied, with silky mouthfeel, bright red fruits running through to a long finish uncluttered by tannins. Barossa Valley Grenache/Shiraz/Cinsaut/Mataro/Carignan. Screwcap. 14.9° alc. **Rating** 94 **To** 2015 $28

ŶŶŶŶŶ **Papillon 2006** Either the Southern Rhone's or Australia's answer to Beaujolais, take your pick; vivid colour and equally vividly fresh red fruits to be slightly chilled and drunk right now; 800 dozen made. Grenache/Cinsaut/Carignagne. Screwcap. 13.9° alc. **Rating** 92 **To** 2008 $25

Lola 2006 Classic Southern Rhone white blend, albeit with more vibrancy and character to the fruit than you would find in the Rhone; lingering, lemony acidity a major plus; 166 dozen made. Marsanne/Semillon/Vermentino/Viognier/Grenache Gris. Screwcap. 13° alc. **Rating** 91 **To** 2010 $25

Barossa Valley Rose 2006 Light, bright pink; comes together very well, with warm oriental spice, red fruits, and a dry finish with just the right acidity; 350 dozen made. Serious rose. Grenache/Cinsaut/Mourvedre/Shiraz. Screwcap. 13° alc. **Rating** 90 **To** 2008 $23

Splitters Swamp Vineyards   **NR**

Craigielee, Bolivia via Tenterfield, NSW 2372 **Region** Northern Slopes Zone
T (02) 6737 3640 **F** (02) 6737 3640 **Open** By appt
Winemaker Ravens Croft Wines **Est.** 1997 **Cases** NA

Spring Ridge Wines

880 Darbys Falls Road, Cowra, NSW 2794 **Region** Cowra
T (02) 6341 3820 **F** (02) 6341 3820 **Open** W'ends, public hols, or by appt
Winemaker Contract **Est.** 1997 **Cases** NA
Peter and Anne Jeffery have established 12.5 ha of shiraz, chardonnay, semillon, cabernet sauvignon
and merlot. They sell the greatest part of the grape production, having only a small amount made
under the Spring Ridge Wines label.

Spring Vale Vineyards

130 Spring Vale Road, Cranbrook, Tas 7190 **Region** East Coast Tasmania
T (03) 6257 8208 **www**.springvalewines.com **Open** Mon–Fri 10–5, or by appt
Winemaker Kristen Cush, David Cush **Est.** 1986 **Cases** 5000
Rodney Lyne progressively established 1.5 ha each of pinot noir and chardonnay and then added
0.5 ha each of gewurztraminer and pinot gris; the latter produced its first crop in 1998. Spring
Vale produces first-class wines when the frost stays away. Exports to the UK.

ΨΨΨΨΨ Pinot Noir 2005 Big, rich, full-bodied style; highly structured, and plenty
of ripe fruit. A more-than-welcome return to form. Screwcap. 13.5° alc.
Rating 94 **To** 2013 $35

ΨΨΨΨΨ Gewurztraminer 2006 Floral, rose petal, lychee aromas; a lovely wine, with
good varietal character, acidity and length. Screwcap. 14.2° alc. **Rating** 90
To 2009 $23

St Aidan

754 Ferguson Road, Dardanup, WA 6236 **Region** Geographe
T (08) 9728 3007 **www**.saintaidan.com **Open** Mon–Fri 10–3, w'ends & public hols 10–5
Winemaker Mark Messenger (Contract) **Est.** 1996 **Cases** 1500
Phil and Mary Smith purchased their property at Dardanup in 1991, 20-mins drive from the
Bunbury hospitals for which Phil Smith works. They first ventured into Red Globe table grapes,
planting 1 ha in 1994–05, followed by 1 ha of mandarins and oranges. With this experience, and
with Mary completing a TAFE viticulture course, they extended their horizons by planting 1 ha
each of cabernet sauvignon and chardonnay in 1997. A little muscat followed in 2001.

St Hallett

St Hallett Road, Tanunda, SA 5352 **Region** Barossa Valley
T (08) 8563 7000 **F** (08) 8563 7001 **www**.sthallett.com.au **Open** 7 days 10–5
Winemaker Stuart Blackwell, Di Ferguson, Matt Gant **Est.** 1944 **Cases** 100 000
Nothing succeeds like success. St Hallett merged with Tatachilla to form Banksia Wines, which
was then acquired by NZ's thirsty Lion Nathan. St Hallett understandably continues to ride the
Shiraz fashion wave, but all its wines are honest and well priced. Exports to all major markets.

ΨΨΨΨΨ Old Block Barossa Shiraz 2003 Medium red-purple; a complex, multifaceted
wine, very good red fruits for the vintage; elegant, long and fine; good tannins.
Cork. 14.5° alc. **Rating** 94 **To** 2013 $70

ΨΨΨΨΨ Eden Valley Riesling 2006 Spotlessly clean aromas; fine, delicate mineral,
citrus and flowery flavours; long finish. Screwcap. 12.5° alc. **Rating** 93
To 2016 $19

Barossa Semillon 2004 Very well-made; has flavour, depth and complexity without the clumsy phenolics commonly encountered in traditional Barossa semillons. Screwcap. 11.5° alc. **Rating** 93 **To** 2011 $19

Poacher's Blend Barossa Semillon Sauvignon Blanc 2006 Distinctly sweet, much more so than in prior vintages; however, attractive lemony acidity partly restores balance. Screwcap. 12° alc. **Rating** 93 **To** 2016 $13

Blackwell Barossa Shiraz 2004 Dense, almost opaque, purple-red; stuffed full with neatly ripened blackberry fruit in classic Barossa style; good balance of fruit, oak and tannins. Cork. 14.5° alc. **Rating** 93 **To** 2014 $30

Faith Barossa Shiraz 2005 Deep, bright red-purple; a medium- to full-bodied, complex mix of ripe, sweet blackberry fruit, oak and soft tannins; all come together well. Screwcap. 14.5° alc. **Rating** 90 **To** 2015 $19

Barossa GST Grenache Shiraz Touriga 2005 Fresh, lively juicy berry fruit; spice and touches of jam ex the grenache; fine tannins; subtle oak. Cork. 14.5° alc. **Rating** 90 **To** 2010 $24

ŸŸŸŸ **Barossa GST Grenache Shiraz Touriga 2006** Some clever winemaking to have this in bottle prior to the end of '06; no shortage of fruit flavour, the 3 varieties combining synergistically. Screwcap. 14.5° alc. **Rating** 89 **To** 2010 $25

Gamekeeper's Reserve Barossa Shiraz Grenache 2006 Bright colour and flavours, at their best 9 months old; it is a rose drinkers' red wine, or perhaps the other way around. Whatever, supple, smooth red fruits, zero tannins and oak give maximum pleasure if you don't want to think or talk about it. Screwcap. 14.5° alc. **Rating** 88 **To** 2008 $13

Gamekeeper's Reserve Barossa Shiraz Grenache 2005 Attractive early-drinking style; fresh red and black fruits; minimal tannin and oak influence, but works well. Screwcap. 14.5° alc. **Rating** 88 **To** 2008 $13

St Huberts   ★★★★☆

St Huberts Road, Coldstream, Vic 3770 **Region** Yarra Valley
T (03) 9739 1118 **www**.sthuberts.com.au **Open** Mon–Fri 9–5, w'ends 10.30–5.30
Winemaker Damian De Castella **Est.** 1966 **Cases** 10 000
A once famous winery (in the context of the Yarra Valley) which is now part of Fosters. The wines are very reliable, and the cellar door – if somewhat humble – is well situated.

ŸŸŸŸŸ **Yarra Valley Cabernet Sauvignon 2005** Elegant, medium-bodied wine, with a mix of blackcurrant and more cedary/earthy notes; good tannins and finish. Cork. 14.5° alc. **Rating** 93 **To** 2020 $26

Yarra Valley Cabernet Merlot 2005 Good structure, texture and balance; the flavours of the varieties are seamlessly joined in a delicious blackcurrant spectrum; positive oak a plus. Cork. 14.5° alc. **Rating** 92 **To** 2015 $23

Yarra Valley Cabernet Sauvignon 2004 Typical St Huberts high-quality cabernet; shows the cool climate, yet no green notes, simply cassis and blackcurrant supported by good tannins and appropriate oak. Cork. 13.5° alc. **Rating** 92 **To** 2024 $26.95

ŸŸŸŸ **Yarra Valley Roussanne 2005** Not a variety that says much in its youth; this is well-balanced and structured, and its latent honeysuckle/citrus/orange peel characters will develop given time. Screwcap. 12° alc. **Rating** 89 **To** 2015 $26.95

Yarra Valley Pinot Noir 2005 A mix of red fruits and darker foresty/savoury characters; medium-bodied, and has length, but doesn't thrill. Screwcap. 13° alc. **Rating** 89 **To** 2011 $26.95

St Ignatius Vineyard   ★★★★☆

5434 Sunraysia Highway, Lamplough, Vic 3352 **Region** Pyrenees
T (03) 5465 3542 **F** (03) 5465 3542 **www**.stignatiusvineyard.com.au **Open** 7 days 10–5
Winemaker Enrique Diaz **Est.** 1992 **Cases** 2000

Silvia and husband Enrique Diaz began establishing their vineyard, winery and restaurant complex in 1992. They have planted 8 ha of shiraz, chardonnay, cabernet sauvignon, sauvignon blanc, merlot and sangiovese. The vineyard has received 3 primary production awards. Wines are released under the Hangmans Gully label. Exports to the UK.

ΨΨΨΨΨ **Hangmans Gully Founder's Collection Pyrenees Shiraz 2004** Medium-bodied, with silky tannins and supple texture, the alcohol spot-on; black cherry and blackberry merge with attractive French oak. Twin top. 14.5° alc. **Rating** 94 To 2015

ΨΨΨΨ♀ **Hangmans Gully Founder's Collection Pyrenees Merlot 2005** Strongly varietal; savoury/foresty/black olive notes dominate the base of black fruits; food style. Twin top. 14° alc. **Rating** 90 To 2012 $35

ΨΨΨΨ **Hangmans Gully Founder's Collection Pyrenees Shiraz Merlot 2005** A medium-bodied supple blend, with both varieties contributing significantly, particularly the savoury olive characters from the merlot; oak in a support role. Twin top. 14.5° alc. **Rating** 89 To 2012 $35

St John's Road

PO Box 286, Rundle Mall, SA 5000 **Region** Barossa Valley
T (08) 8342 9070 **F** (08) 8342 9007 **www.stjohnsroad.com Open** Not
Winemaker Biscay Rd Vintners (Peter Schell), Rolf Binder (Christa Deans) **Est.** 2002
Cases 3500
Martin Rawlinson (with a background of politics and defence) and wife Vivienne (journalism and music) were running a small B&B (equivalent) in France surrounded by vineyards. One thing led to another, and in 2002 they purchased a small vineyard in the Eden Valley, planted to 30-year-old riesling on lean, rocky soils. The following year they purchased a much larger property at Greenock, established by the Helbig family in the 1880s. In all, they had 24 ha of riesling, semillon, chardonnay, grenache, cabernet sauvignon and shiraz. Out of the blue Martin was diagnosed with motor neurone disease, dying in 2005. Says Vivienne, 'I am grateful that Martin had a chance to see and taste the realisation of his dream with the bottling of our 2003 Julia (named after their young daughter) and the other wines of the 2004 vintage'. Exports to the US, Canada, Indonesia, Malaysia and NZ.

ΨΨΨΨΨ **Blood and Courage Greenock Shiraz 2005** Dense purple-red; extremely rich and powerful, well-named indeed; all the ingredients are there; simply needs 20 years. Screwcap. 14.5° alc. **Rating** 94 To 2029 $21
Julia Barossa Valley Shiraz 2005 Dense colour; exotic ripe licorice, anise black fruit aromas; powerful and complex, but just when you think it has gone over the top, it pulls back. A long life ahead. Screwcap. 14.8° alc. **Rating** 94 To 2030 $30

ΨΨΨΨ♀ **Peace of Eden Riesling 2006** A generous mix of fleshy lime and citrus fruit around a core of mineral; solidly flavoured and structured. Screwcap. 12.5° alc. **Rating** 92 To 2016 $20
The Dog Walker Greenock Cabernet Sauvignon 2004 Elegant, medium-bodied cabernet sauvignon with blackcurrant and black olive fruit; no concessions to alcohol or oak sweetening. Screwcap. 14.5° alc. **Rating** 92 To 2024 $24
First Crush Greenock Rose 2006 Pale fuchsia; dry, fresh, crisp spice and red berry grenache; good acidity and length. Screwcap. 13° alc. **Rating** 90 To 2008 $18

St Leonards Vineyard

St Leonards Road, Wahgunyah, Vic 3687 **Region** Rutherglen
T (02) 6033 1004 **F** (02) 6033 3636 **www.stleonardswine.com.au Open** 7 days 10–5
Winemaker Dan Crane **Est.** 1860 **Cases** 20 000
An old favourite, relaunched in late 1997 with a range of premium wines cleverly marketed through a singularly attractive cellar door and bistro at the historic winery on the banks of the Murray. All Saints and St Leonards were wholly owned by Peter Brown, tragically killed in a road

accident in late 2005. Ownership has passed to Peter Brown's children, Eliza, Angela and Nicholas, and it is the intention to keep the business in the family.

ŸŸŸŸ **Rutherglen Muscat NV** A genuine touch of age and rancio, though youthful raisiny muscat is still at the core; good value and likewise typicity. Cork. 18° alc. **Rating** 89 **To** 2008 $19
Semillon Sauvignon Blanc 2006 Clean, light and fresh, with touches of lemon rind, and a crisp finish. Screwcap. 12.9° alc. **Rating** 88 **To** 2010 $17
Rose 2006 Brilliant puce-pink; plenty of fresh red fruits; off-dry, but not cloyingly sweet. Screwcap. 13.5° alc. **Rating** 87 **To** 2008 $16
Shiraz Viognier 2005 Unconvincing colour; a wine at war with itself, and needing to soften and settle down. Screwcap. 14.2° alc. **Rating** 87 **To** 2011 $22

St Matthias

113 Rosevears Drive, Rosevears, Tas 7277 **Region** Northern Tasmania
T (03) 6330 1700 **F** (03) 6330 1975 **www**.moorilla.com.au **Open** 7 days 10–5
Winemaker Michael Glover (former) **Est.** 1983 **Cases** 16 000
After an uncomfortable period in the wilderness following the sale of the vineyard to Moorilla Estate, and the disposal of the wine made by the previous owners under the St Matthias label, Moorilla has re-introduced the label, and markets a full range of competitively priced wines which are in fact made at Moorilla Estate.

ŸŸŸŸŸ **Single Vineyard Chardonnay 2005** Sophisticated winemaking, in particular avoiding the mlf, retaining fruit brightness, but also managing to avoid excess acidity; nectarine, peach and grapefruit flavours supported by subtle oak. Screwcap. 13.5° alc. **Rating** 90 **To** 2010 $34

St Mary's

V & A Lane, via Coonawarra, SA 5277 **Region** Penola
T (08) 8736 6070 **F** (08) 8736 6045 **www**.stmaryswines.com **Open** 7 days 10–4
Winemaker Barry Mulligan **Est.** 1986 **Cases** 4000
The Mulligan family has lived in the Penola/Coonawarra region since 1909. In 1937 a 250-ha property 15 km west of Penola, including an 80-ha ridge of terra rossa over limestone, was purchased for grazing. The ridge was cleared, the remainder of the property was untouched and is now a private wildlife sanctuary. In 1986 Barry and Glenys Mulligan planted shiraz and cabernet sauvignon on the ridge, followed by merlot in the early 1990s. Exports to the UK, the US, Canada, Singapore, Belgium and Switzerland.

St Michael's Vineyard

503 Pook Road, Toolleen, Vic 3521 **Region** Heathcote
T (03) 5433 2580 **F** (03) 5433 2612 **Open** By appt
Winemaker Mick Cann **Est.** 1994 **Cases** 300
Owner/winemaker Mick Cann has established just over 4 ha of vines on the famous deep red Cambrian clay loam on the east face of the Mt Camel Range. Planting began in 1994, continued in 1995, with a further extension in 2000. Shiraz (2.5 ha), merlot (1.25 ha) and petit verdot (0.3 ha) are the main varieties, with a smattering of cabernet sauvignon and semillon. Part of the production is sold to David Anderson of Wild Duck Creek, the remainder made by Mick Cann, using open fermentation, hand-plunging of skins and a basket press, a low-technology but highly effective way of making high-quality red wine. The period poster-style labels do the wines scant justice.

ŸŸŸŸ **Heathcote Shiraz 2004** Rich and ripe, but not jammy or dead, fruit; black and red cherry flavours, good acidity counterbalancing the alcohol. Screwcap. 15.1° alc. **Rating** 91 **To** 2019 $23
Heathcote Merlot 2004 An expressive wine; the fruit flavours are clear and bright, and hit before the notes of earth and olive; a smooth and slippery finish. Diam. 15.2° alc. **Rating** 90 **To** 2016 $25

Heathcote Cabernet Merlot 2004 Abundant flavours, rich and deep; black fruits, spices, licorice and earth, with the faintest touch of green tannins. Diam. 14.5° alc. **Rating** 90 To 2016 $25

St Regis

35 Princes Highway, Waurn Ponds, Vic 3216 **Region** Geelong
T (03) 5241 8406 **F** (03) 5241 8946 **www**.stregis.com.au **Open** 7 days 11–6
Winemaker Peter Nicol **Est.** 1997 **Cases** 600
St Regis is a family-run boutique winery focusing on estate-grown Shiraz, Chardonnay and Pinot Noir. Each year the harvest is hand-picked by members of the family and friends, with Peter Nicol (assisted by wife Viv) the executive, onsite winemaker. While Peter has a technical background in horticulture, he is a self-taught winemaker, and has taught himself well.

ΨΨΨΨ **Wild Reserve Geelong Pinot Noir 2005** Light colour; very complex foresty/ stemmy characters on both bouquet and palate; no shortage of varietal character, but really needed more sweet fruit. Screwcap. 14.8° alc. **Rating** 89 To 2011 $30
The Reg Geelong Shiraz 2005 A slightly muffled bouquet, but has distinctly more ripe fruit; licorice, spice and black cherry fruit in an elegant, light- to medium-bodied mould. Screwcap. 13.8° alc. **Rating** 89 To 2012 $30
Geelong Shiraz 2005 Light but bright red-purple; unexpected stemmy and green characters detract from the palate. Screwcap. 13.5° alc. **Rating** 87 To 2008 $20

 # Staindl Wines

63 Shoreham Road, Red Hill South, Vic 3937 (postal) **Region** Mornington Peninsula
T (03) 9813 1111 **Open** Not
Winemaker Phillip Jones (Contract) **Est.** 1982 **Cases** 500
As often happens, the establishment date for a wine producer can mean many things. In this instance it harks back to the planting of the vineyard by the Ayton family, and the establishment of what was thereafter called St Neots. Juliet and Paul Staindl acquired the property in 2002, and, with the guidance of Phillip Jones, have since extended the plantings of pinot noir. In all there are now 1.5 ha of pinot noir, 1 ha of chardonnay and 0.5 ha of riesling. The vineyard is run on a low chemical regime, headed towards biodynamic viticulture. Paul Staindl says, 'It's all good fun and lots of learning'. I would add it's also more than slightly demanding.

ΨΨΨΨΨ **Pinot Noir 2004** Very deep colour; a complex, rich, mouthfilling style, which belies its low alcohol; attractive spicy plum flavours, although the quality of the cork is a real concern for a high-quality wine. 13° alc. **Rating** 93 To 2011 $32.50

Stanley Lambert Wines ★★★☆

Barossa Valley Way, Tanunda, SA 5352 **Region** Barossa Valley
T (08) 8563 3375 **F** (08) 8563 3758 **www**.stanleylambert.com.au **Open** Mon–Fri 10–5, w'ends & public hols 11–5
Winemaker Lindsay Stanley **Est.** 1994 **Cases** 15 000
Former Anglesey winemaker and industry veteran Lindsay Stanley established his own business in the Barossa Valley when he purchased (and renamed) the former Kroemer Estate in late 1994. As one would expect, the wines are competently made, although often very light-bodied. The 21 ha of estate plantings have provided virtually all the grapes for the business. Exports to the UK, the US and other major markets.

ΨΨΨΨΨ **The Family Tree Individual Vineyard Barossa Valley Shiraz 2004** The generosity of the blackberry and plum fruit carries the vanillin American oak with ease; fine tannins; a Group One wine. Diam. 14.5° alc. **Rating** 93 To 2018 $45

ΨΨΨΨ **August Barossa Valley Shiraz 2001** Light- to medium-bodied; savoury/earthy/ spicy edges to blackberry fruit; fine tannins and minimal oak. Cork. 14° alc. **Rating** 89 To 2013 $22

Black Sheep Shiraz Malbec Merlot 2002 A savoury, spicy wine, prolonged but fine tannins giving some critical structure. Diam. 14° alc. **Rating** 87 **To** 2011 $15

Stanton & Killeen Wines   ★★★★★

Jacks Road, Murray Valley Highway, Rutherglen, Vic 3685 **Region** Rutherglen
T (02) 6032 9457 **www.**stantonandkilleenwines.com.au **Open** Mon–Sat 9–5, Sun 10–5
Winemaker Chris Killeen **Est.** 1875 **Cases** 20 000
Chris Killeen has skilfully expanded the portfolio of Stanton & Killeen but without in any way compromising its reputation as a traditional maker of smooth, rich reds, some of Australia's best Vintage Ports, and attractive, fruity Muscats and Tokays. All in all, deserves far greater recognition. Exports to the UK, the US and NZ.

ooooo **Rutherglen Vintage Port 2002** Excellent hue, still red-purple; a totally delicious vintage port style, with an elegance no other young Australian vintage ports approach; spicy black fruits, and a long finish. Cork. 18.1° alc. **Rating** 96 **To** 2022 $27
Rutherglen Durif 2005 Deep colour; it is impossible not to be impressed with the power of this variety, especially when made by winemakers as skilled as Chris Killeen. The secret is to control the extract, and give the wines the freedom to fully express themselves. Diam. 15° alc. **Rating** 94 **To** 2020 $30

oooo **Jack's Block Rutherglen Shiraz 2005** Medium-bodied; an attractive combination of spicy/earthy overtones to blackberry fruit; good tannin and oak handling. Diam. 14.5° alc. **Rating** 91 **To** 2015 $30
Rutherglen Merlot Cabernet Franc Cabernet Sauvignon 2005 Impressive red-purple colour; an equally impressive ability to bring out the varietal expression of varieties theoretically needing a far cooler climate. Diam. 14.5° alc. **Rating** 90 **To** 2012 $22

oooo **Rutherglen Shiraz Durif 2005** The colour is quite developed, perhaps reflecting the shiraz component; spicy/savoury/earthy flavours, best enjoyed younger than older. Diam. 14.5° alc. **Rating** 89 **To** 2010 $18
Rutherglen Cabernet Sauvignon 2005 As with the merlot blend, shows clear varietal character; blackcurrant with some savoury/earthy/olive nuances; oak and tannin management spot-on. Diam. 14° alc. **Rating** 89 **To** 2015 $22

Stanton Estate   NR

135 North Isis Road, Childers, Qld 4660 **Region** Queensland Zone
T (07) 4126 1255 **F** (07) 4126 1255 **Open** 7 days 10–5
Winemaker Clovelly Estate **Est.** 2000 **Cases** NA

Steels Creek Estate   ★★★★

1 Sewell Road, Steels Creek, Vic 3775 **Region** Yarra Valley
T (03) 5965 2448 **F** (03) 5965 2448 **www.**steelsckestate.com.au **Open** W'ends & public hols 10–6, or by appt
Winemaker Simon Peirce **Est.** 1981 **Cases** 400
A 1.7-ha vineyard, family-operated since 1981, is located in the picturesque Steels Creek Valley with views towards to the Kinglake National Park. Red wines are made onsite, white wines with the assistance of consultants. Visitors can view the winemaking operations from the cellar door.

ooooo **Yarra Valley Chardonnay 2005** Bright green-yellow; highly aromatic; tangy melon/citrus fruit is the primary driver on a clear-cut palate; excellent length and acidity. Screwcap. 14° alc. **Rating** 93 **To** 2015 $22
Yarra Valley Cabernet Sauvignon 2004 Plenty of depth to the texture and structure, the blackcurrant fruit with just a touch of earth; good length and finish. ProCork. 13.5° alc. **Rating** 93 **To** 2014 $20

�♙ **Yarra Valley Shiraz 2004** Light- to medium-bodied; quite sweet plum, cherry and blackberry fruit bolstered by savoury/spicy tannins. ProCork. 13.5° alc. **Rating** 89 **To** 2012 $25
Yarra Valley Cabernet Franc 2004 Has flavours ranging through tobacco leaf to red berry to mint to green tannins. A difficult mistress. ProCork. 13.5° alc. **Rating** 87 **To** 2009 $20

Stefani Estate ★★★★★

389 Heathcote–Rochester Road, Heathcote, Vic 3523 **Region** Heathcote
T (03) 9570 8750 **F** (03) 9579 1532 **Open** By appt
Winemaker Mario Marson **Est.** 2002 **Cases** 1100
Stefano Stefani came to Australia in 1985. Business success has allowed Stefano and wife Rina to follow in the footsteps of Stefano's grandfather, who had a vineyard and was an avid wine collector. The first property they acquired was at Long Gully Road in the Yarra Valley, with pinot grigio, cabernet sauvignon, chardonnay and pinot noir. The next was in Heathcote, where he acquired a property adjoining that of Mario Marson, and built a winery and established 8.5 ha of vineyard, planted predominantly to shiraz, then cabernet sauvignon and merlot and a mixed block of cabernet franc, malbec and petit verdot. In 2003 a second Yarra Valley property was purchased where Dijon clones of chardonnay and pinot noir have been planted. Mario Marson (ex Mount Mary) oversees the operation of all the vineyards and is also the winemaker. He is also able to use the winery to make his own brand wines, completing the business link.

♙♙♙♙♙ **The View Yarra Valley Chardonnay 2005** At once elegant, subtle yet very complex; barrel ferment, mlf and lees all contribute to the texture and mouthfeel, and are seamlessly married with nectarine, fig and cream; ageing slowly but surely. Diam. 14.5° alc. **Rating** 96 **To** 2015 $54
The Gate Yarra Valley Pinot Noir 2005 Gently foresty overtones to red fruits on the bouquet lead into a long palate which, while savoury, is not bitter, just complex. A pinot drinkers' pinot. Diam. 14° alc. **Rating** 94 **To** 2012 $39

♙♙♙♙♙ **The Estate Heathcote Vineyard Shiraz 2004** Strong colour; has infinitely seductive and opulent plum and blackberry fruit; rich without over-emphasis, with further complexity added by the notes of bitter chocolate and fine tannins; 774 cases made. Diam. 14.5° alc. **Rating** 92 **To** 2020 $39
The Gate Yarra Valley Cabernet Sauvignon Merlot 2005 Classic cabernet sauvignon with fine tannins running through from the start of the palate to the finish, almost Italianate in its structure. Needs time to settle down and allow the cabernet currant and cassis fruit to express itself. Diam. 14° alc. **Rating** 92 **To** 2020 $39

♙♙♙♙ **The View Yarra Valley Pinot Gris 2005** Apple, pear and a touch of musk; builds flavour and character progressively through the palate to the finish. Diam. 14° alc. **Rating** 89 **To** 2009 $29

Stefano Lubiana ★★★★★

60 Rowbottoms Road, Granton, Tas 7030 **Region** Southern Tasmania
T (03) 6263 7457 **www**.slw.com.au **Open** Sun–Thurs 11–3 (closed some public hols)
Winemaker Steve Lubiana **Est.** 1990 **Cases** NFP
When Stefano (Steve) Lubiana moved from the Riverland to Tas, he set up a substantial contract sparkling winemaking facility to help cover the costs of the move and the establishment of his new business. Over the years, he has steadily decreased the amount of contract winemaking, now focusing on his estate-grown wines from 18 ha of beautifully located vineyards sloping down to the Derwent River. Exports to Italy, Sweden, Korea, Indonesia and Japan.

♙♙♙♙♙ **Prestige Pinot Noir Chardonnay 1995** A remarkable wine; extremely long and fresh, the fine, minerally flavours in no way drying the wine out. 12.5° alc. **Rating** 95 **To** 2010 $125

Collina Chardonnay 2003 Light- to medium-bodied; while nectarine/citrus fruit is dominant, there are notes of toast and grilled nuts which appear at various points, then promptly disappear. A complex wine with overall elegance. An expensive bottle with an ominously wet cork. 13.5° alc. **Rating** 94 **To** 2013 $60
Vintage Brut 1999 The extra degree of complexity from the time on lees works very well without compromising the stone fruit flavours in any way. 12.5° alc. **Rating** 94 **To** 2010 $47

ŶŶŶŶŶ Tasmania Chardonnay 2003 Nectarine, peach and grapefruit guide the intense, fruit-driven palate; very different in style to Collina. Cork. 13.5° alc. **Rating** 93 **To** 2012 $37
NV Brut NV Very elegant and long; fine stone fruit with a hint of creaminess; the acidity is perfectly handled and balanced. 12.5° alc. **Rating** 92 **To** 2010 $30

ŶŶŶŶ Sauvignon Blanc 2006 A clean but closed bouquet; good mouthfeel and balance; gentle tropical fruit on entry, then more grassy/minerally flavours on the finish. Screwcap. 13° alc. **Rating** 89 **To** 2008 $24
Pinot Grigio 2006 Lemon and honeysuckle blossom aromas outside the norm; fresh and crisp texture; has length without resort to sugar. Screwcap. 14° alc. **Rating** 89 **To** 2009 $26
Tasmania Merlot 2004 Varietal character is clear enough, but savoury tannins take hold the moment the wine enters the mouth, and don't really let go. Whether time will cure the problem is problematical. Cork. 13.5° alc. **Rating** 87 **To** 2011 $28

Stella Bella Wines ★★★★★

PO Box 536, Margaret River, WA 6285 **Region** Margaret River
T (08) 9757 6377 **F** (08) 9757 6022 **www**.stellabella.com.au **Open** Not
Winemaker Janice McDonald **Est.** 1997 **Cases** 50 000
Stella Bella was established by 2 well-known Margaret River winemakers who, in deference to their employers, did not identify themselves on any of the background material or the striking front and back labels of the wines. In the wake of increased financial backing, Janice McDonald has (oenologically) come out. Production has increased dramatically in the wake of deserved market success, with exports to the UK, the US and other major markets.

ŶŶŶŶŶ Sauvignon Blanc 2006 Light straw-green, voluminous floral (but not the least bit sweaty) aromas lead into a silky smooth, sensual palate with just enough minerally acidity to tighten and freshen the finish. Screwcap. 12.5° alc. **Rating** 96 **To** 2008 $21

Semillon Sauvignon Blanc 2006 Classic, elegant and restrained, with perfect balance and structure to the mix of herbs, grass and small green fruits. Screwcap. 12.5° alc. **Rating** 95 **To** 2008 $20
Cabernet Sauvignon Merlot 2004 Spotlessly clean and aromatic, immaculately crafted throughout; a perfect balance between red (cassis) and black (blackcurrant, spice) fruit components, oak and tannins. Screwcap. 14.5° alc. **Rating** 95 **To** 2024 $25
Chardonnay 2005 Complex, sophisticated winemaking; barrel ferment, lees and some notes suggest mlf for part of the wine; nectarine and grapefruit plus a gloss of gently creamy/nutty characters; long and balanced. Screwcap. 13° alc. **Rating** 94 **To** 2015 $25
Shiraz 2005 Deep purple-red; a medium-bodied, complex array of red and black fruits, licorice and spice, the oak and tannins suitably restrained. Screwcap. 14° alc. **Rating** 94 **To** 2020 $24
Suckfizzle Cabernet Sauvignon 2004 Medium purple-red; a silky smooth entry of cassis-accented fruit, next blackcurrant, and finally lingering, savoury tannins on the finish, the oak subservient; simply needs time. Screwcap. 14° alc. **Rating** 94 **To** 2024 $45

ŶŶŶŶŶ **Suckfizzle Sauvignon Blanc Semillon 2006** Spotless bouquet; crisp, clean, light- to medium-bodied passionfruit and stone fruit; lemony acidity gives added length. Has a touch of chardonnay for good measure. Screwcap. 12.5° alc. **Rating** 90 **To** 2008 $16
Viognier 2005 Plenty of varietal fruit, with apricot, baked apple and spice on both bouquet and palate, but fails to find a finish to enthral as did the '04. Screwcap. 13° alc. **Rating** 90 **To** 2010 $25
Sangiovese Cabernet 2005 Lifted savoury, earthy, spicy red fruit aromatics courtesy of the sangiovese; medium-bodied; firm but not green, and has excellent length. Screwcap. 14° alc. **Rating** 90 **To** 2018 $27

ŶŶŶŶ **Skuttlebutt Shiraz Merlot Rose 2006** In typical winery fashion, comes up with that little bit extra; sweet small red fruits on the mid-palate, then a dry, crisp finish. Screwcap. 13.5° alc. **Rating** 89 **To** 2008 $16
Pink Muscat 2005 Very clever winemaking; a brilliant balance of fruit, alcohol, acidity and residual sugar, all leaving the mouth fresh yet satisfied. Screwcap. 8° alc. **Rating** 89 **To** 2008 $17
Tempranillo 2005 Typically strong colour; the intriguing touch of lemon, herb and thyme seems to be the mark of the variety in Australia; red fruit flavours at the core, but the texture seems inadequate. Screwcap. 14° alc. **Rating** 88 **To** 2009 $27
Pink Muscat 2006 At the outer edge of grapey sweetness, but hauled back by crisp acidity; very clever winemaking. Note 7.5° alcohol. Screwcap. **Rating** 88 **To** 2008 $16
Skuttlebutt Shiraz Cabernet 2005 Ripe fruit, doesn't have the typical texture or structure of the winery, but at the price that is hardly surprising. Screwcap. 13.5° alc. **Rating** 87 **To** 2010 $16

Step Road Winery   ★★★★☆

Davidson Road, Langhorne Creek, SA 5255 (postal) **Region** Langhorne Creek
T (08) 8537 3342 **F** (08) 8537 3357 **www**.steprd.com **Open** Not
Winemaker Rob Dundon, Scott McIntosh **Est.** 1998 **Cases** 160 000
Step Road has 100 ha of vineyard at Langhorne Creek, and 40 ha in the Adelaide Hills. In a sign of the times, it is an environmentally aware winery: all liquid waste is stored in plastic-lined dams, treated to remove chemicals and salinity and then recycled as irrigation for the vineyard. All solid waste from the grapes (skins, stalks and seeds) is mulched and returned to the vineyards, reducing irrigation requirements by up to 25%. Exports to the UK, the US, Denmark, Hong Kong and NZ.

ŶŶŶŶŶ **Langhorne Creek Cabernet Sauvignon 2004** An elegant, medium-bodied wine with black fruits, fine tannins and a nice touch of oak; has finesse and length. Screwcap. 14° alc. **Rating** 93 **To** 2015 $20

Stephen John Wines   ★★★★★

Sallys Hill Road, Watervale, SA 5452 **Region** Clare Valley
T (08) 8843 0105 **F** (08) 8843 0105 **www**.stephenjohnwines.com **Open** 7 days 11–5
Winemaker Stephen John **Est.** 1994 **Cases** 10 000
The John family is one of the best-known in the Barossa Valley, with branches running Australia's best cooperage (AP John & Sons) and providing the chief winemaker of Lindemans (Philip John) and the former chief winemaker of Quelltaler (Stephen John). Stephen and Rita John have now formed their own family business in the Clare Valley, based on a 6-ha vineyard overlooking Watervale, and supplemented by modest intake from a few local growers. The cellar door is a renovated 80-year-old stable full of rustic charm. Exports to the UK, the US, Malaysia and Singapore.

ŶŶŶŶŶ **Watervale Riesling 2006** Bright green-yellow; intense flavours, with sweet citrus on the mid-palate, then a long finish with no obvious residual sugar. Part from a block planted in 1926. Screwcap. 12° alc. **Rating** 94 **To** 2020 $20

VI Generations Shiraz Cabernet 2004 Strong red-purple; medium to full-bodied blackberry, black plum, blackcurrant and spice; fine but persistent tannins on the long finish. Cork. 14° alc. **Rating** 94 **To** 2015 $50

♀♀♀♀♀ **Dry Grown Shiraz 2005** Dense colour; prune, blackberry and plum aromas and flavours; not overly extracted or tannic. Cork. 13° alc. **Rating** 90 **To** 2015 $20

Sticks ★★★★

Glenview Road, Yarra Glen, Vic 3775 **Region** Yarra Valley
T (03) 9739 0666 **F** (03) 9739 0633 **www**.sticks.com.au **Open** 7 days 10–5
Winemaker Rob Dolan **Est.** 2000 **Cases** 25 000
In 2005 the former Yarra Ridge winery, with a 3000-tonne capacity, and 24 ha of vineyards planted mainly in 1983, was acquired by a partnership headed by Rob 'Sticks' Dolan. He is making all the Sticks wines here, and also provides substantial contract-making facilities for wineries throughout the Yarra Valley.

♀♀♀♀♀ Chardonnay Viognier 2006 A highly aromatic and totally unexpected bouquet; a neat fusion of the varieties, although the chardonnay dominates the citrus, nectarine and apricot palate. Fresh and lively, the finish without phenolics. Great value. Screwcap. 13.5° alc. **Rating** 90 **To** 2010 $13.95

♀♀♀♀ Yarra Valley Sauvignon Blanc 2006 A clean bouquet with no reduction/sweatiness; moderate intensity, with tropical, apple, gooseberry and grass flavours; not particularly long. Screwcap. 12.5° alc. **Rating** 89 **To** 2008 $17.95
Shiraz Viognier 2006 A robust style, more so than for most shiraz viogniers; plenty of black and red fruits with controlled tannins. Good value. Screwcap. 13.5° alc. **Rating** 89 **To** 2016 $13.95
Yarra Valley Pinot Noir 2005 Light-bodied; savoury elements run through the light red cherry fruit; unforced, but not riveting. Screwcap. 13.5° alc. **Rating** 87 **To** 2010 $19.95
Yarra Valley Cabernet Sauvignon 2004 Savoury hedgerow aromas; a medium-bodied palate, overall tight and a little green and mean; just gets across the line. Screwcap. 13.5° alc. **Rating** 87 **To** 2012 $18.95

Stonebrook Estate ★★★☆

RSM 361, Busselton, WA 6280 **Region** Margaret River
T (08) 9755 1104 **F** (08) 9755 1001 **www**.stonebrookestate.com **Open** By appt
Winemaker John Durham (Consultant) **Est.** 1997 **Cases** 900
Perth lawyer Jonathan Meyer decided on a sea change in 1992, moving with his family to their beach house at Dunsborough. From the outset, the intention was to establish a vineyard, and a property was selected in 1996; planting of 7.4 ha of chardonnay, cabernet sauvignon and merlot began in 1997. Most of the production is sold, part made under the Stonebrook Estate label, and a small amount under the second label, Station Gully.

Stonehaven ★★★★★

Riddoch Highway, Padthaway, SA 5271 **Region** Padthaway
T (08) 8765 6166 **F** (08) 8765 6177 **www**.stonehavenvineyards.com.au **Open** 7 days 10–4
Winemaker Susanne Bell, Gary Stokes **Est.** 1998 **Cases** 200 000
It is, to say the least, strange that it should have taken 30 years for a substantial winery to be built at Padthaway. However, when Hardys took the decision, it was no half measure: $20 million has been invested in what is the largest greenfields winery built in Australia for more than 20 years. Exports to the US, Canada and the UK.

♀♀♀♀♀ Stepping Stone Padthaway Shiraz 2004 Medium red-purple; as often, punches way above its price weight; beautifully supple plum, cherry and blackberry fruit supported by fine tannins and little or no oak. Screwcap. 13.5° alc. **Rating** 94 **To** 2014 $13

ŸŸŸŸ℧ Limited Vineyard Release Padthaway Chardonnay 2001 First tasted Oct '02; now, still incredibly youthful in every aspect: colour, bouquet and palate; nectarine and grapefruit flavours perfectly balanced by oak. Several gold medals. Cork. 13.5° alc. **Rating** 92 **To** 2011 $26.50
Stepping Stone Padthaway Chardonnay 2006 An aromatic bouquet; light- to medium-bodied citrussy stone fruit; good length. Screwcap. 13.5° alc. **Rating** 90 **To** 2009 $13

ŸŸŸŸ Stepping Stone Padthaway Chardonnay 2005 Typical fresh Padthaway flavours in a grapefruit/citrus spectrum; attractive unwooded style. Screwcap. 13° alc. **Rating** 89 **To** 2008 $13
Hidden Sea Limestone Coast Chardonnay 2005 Pronounced regional grapefruit and nectarine aromas and flavours, but also showing a less welcome touch of green bean; if oaked, only a light touch. Screwcap. 14° alc. **Rating** 89 **To** 2011 $15.95
Hidden Sea Shiraz 2004 Supple medium-bodied palate with blackberry fruit and good, ripe tannins. Cork. 14.7° alc. **Rating** 89 **To** 2012 $15.95
Hidden Sea Limestone Coast Cabernet Sauvignon 2003 Medium-bodied; elegant, understated; some earthy spicy notes add to the main core of blackcurrant fruit; fine tannins a plus. Cork. 13.5° alc. **Rating** 89 **To** 2015 $15.95
Hidden Sea Sangiovese 2004 Excellent colour for the variety; savoury, spicy fruits with hints of rose and cherry; good length. Cork. 13.5° alc. **Rating** 89 **To** 2012 $15.95
Stepping Stone Coonawarra Cabernet Sauvignon 2005 Austere style with earthy black fruits and firm tannins. Screwcap. 14.3° alc. **Rating** 87 **To** 2013 $13
Stepping Stone Coonawarra Cabernet Sauvignon 2004 Fairly modest and, one suspects, high-yielding vines make for a pleasant wine which doesn't out-perform the field. Screwcap. 13.5° alc. **Rating** 87 **To** 2008 $13

Stonehurst Cedar Creek ★★★

Wollombi Road, Cedar Creek, NSW 2325 **Region** Lower Hunter Valley
T (02) 4998 1576 **F** (02) 4998 0008 **www.**cedarcreekcottages.com.au **Open** 7 days 10–5
Winemaker Monarch Winemaking Services **Est.** 1995 **Cases** 3500
Stonehurst (subtitled Cedar Creek) has been established by Daryl and Phillipa Heslop on a historic 220-ha property in the Wollombi Valley, underneath the Pokolbin Range. They have 6.5 ha of vineyards, planted to chambourcin, semillon, chardonnay and shiraz. A substantial part of the business, however, is the 6 self-contained cottages on the property.

Stonewell Vineyards ★★★★☆

Stonewell Road, Tanunda, SA 5352 **Region** Barossa Valley
T (08) 8563 3624 **F** (08) 8563 3624 **www.**stonewell.com.au **Open** By appt
Winemaker Troy Kalleske **Est.** 1965 **Cases** 360
Owners John and Yvonne Pfeiffer, together with daughters Lisa and Tammy, represent the fifth and sixth generations of this Barossa winegrowing family. John and Yvonne transformed what was an unviable mixed fruit and farming property into 50 ha of mainstream varieties. The vineyard has a common boundary with the vineyard which produces Peter Lehmann's renowned Stonewell Shiraz, which may or may not cause confusion with the names. The successful conversion owes much to John, who has been growing grapes since he was 17 years old. The grapes from the vineyard have been sold to local growers for decades, but in 2004 a decision was taken to have specially selected parcels contract-made under the Daughters of the Valley brand, the derivation of the name being self-evident.

ŸŸŸŸ℧ Daughters of the Valley Shiraz 2005 Strong colour; a traditional but very well-made Barossa Valley style with an array of black fruits offset by mocha/vanilla American oak; soft, ripe tannins; not over-cooked. Cork. 14.5° alc. **Rating** 92 **To** 2015 $22

Daughters of the Valley Cabernet Sauvignon 2005 Rich, full-bodied blackcurrant fruit with hints of bitter chocolate; good extract, length and balance; quality French oak; 40-year-old vines. Cork. 14.5° alc. **Rating** 91 To 2013 $22

Stoney Rise ★★★☆

Hendersons Lane, Gravelly Beach, Tas 7276 **Region** Northern Tasmania
T (03) 6394 3678 **F** (03) 6394 3684 **Open** 7 days 11–5
Winemaker Joe Holyman **Est.** 2000 **Cases** 2000
Changes came fast at Stoney Rise in 2004. Surf- and sun-loving Joe Holyman has gone back to his native Tas, having purchased one of the State's most distinguished vineyard sites, Rotherhythe. Though small, this Tamar Valley vineyard has produced magnificent Pinot Noir and Cabernet Sauvignon (the latter to be replaced by Chardonnay) in the past. The SA wines in the Stoney Rise portfolio (Sauvignon Blanc, Shiraz and Hey Hey Rose) are still produced; 2005 was the first vintage from the Tamar Valley. Exports to the US.

ᵀᵀᵀᵀ **Holyman Chardonnay 2005** A fragrant, aromatic, early-picked style; just a fraction too fresh for some palates. **Rating** 88 To 2012
Tamar Valley Pinot Noir 2005 Extremely powerful and ripe, the touch of volatile acidity diminishing the overall appeal. **Rating** 88 To 2010

Stonier Wines ★★★★★

Cnr Thompson's Lane/Frankston-Flinders Road, Merricks, Vic 3916
Region Mornington Peninsula
T (03) 5989 8300 **F** (03) 5989 8709 **www**.stoniers.com.au **Open** 7 days 11–5
Winemaker Geraldine McFaul **Est.** 1978 **Cases** 22 000
One of the most senior wineries on the Mornington Peninsula, now part of the Petaluma group, which is in turn owned by Lion Nathan of NZ. Wine quality is assured, as is the elegant, restrained style of the majority of the wines. Exports to all major markets.

ᵀᵀᵀᵀᵀ **Reserve Mornington Peninsula Chardonnay 2005** Typically restrained and refined Stonier style, the iron fist in a velvet glove cliche almost unavoidable. Has great length, and the more it is tasted, the more characters emerge; creamy and nutty texture with bright nectarine and grapefruit flavours; exemplary oak. Screwcap. 14° alc. **Rating** 95 To 2013 $39
Mornington Peninsula Chardonnay 2005 Light straw-green; a spotlessly clean bouquet leads into a light- to medium-bodied, attractive palate with attractive stone fruit, melon and cashew flavours; perfectly balanced oak. Screwcap. 14° alc. **Rating** 94 To 2012 $23
KBS Vineyard Chardonnay 2004 Light straw-green; supple, gently ripe melon and white peach fruit with quality oak inputs; good length and finish. Cork. 14° alc. **Rating** 94 To 2011 $55
Reserve Mornington Peninsula Pinot Noir 2005 The hue is good, though slightly light; excellent texture and structure; elegant, filigreed fruit and tannins, the hint of stalk adding interest. Screwcap. 14.5° alc. **Rating** 94 To 2012 $45
Cuvee Mornington Peninsula 2000 Pale green-straw; good mousse; very tight and fine, with crystalline purity emphasised by the low dosage; citrus, rather than red fruits, and will benefit from further time on cork. 12.5° alc. **Rating** 94 To 2010 $45

ᵀᵀᵀᵀ♀ **Windmill Vineyard Pinot Noir 2004** More savoury and foresty than the KBS, but again there isn't quite the fruit intensity needed for top points. Cork. 13.5° alc. **Rating** 93 To 2012 $55
KBS Vineyard Pinot Noir 2004 Light red-purple; elegant, though obvious oak pushes a light-bodied wine that little bit too far. Cork. 14° alc. **Rating** 92 To 2011 $55

Mornington Peninsula Pinot Noir 2005 Light- to medium-bodied; savoury, foresty, spicy style; has undoubted varietal fruit, but is a little shy. Screwcap. 13.5° alc. **Rating** 90 **To** 2009 $25

Mornington Peninsula Pinot Noir Chardonnay 2004 Typical very pure and lancing fruit line; uncompromisingly low dosage; 18 months on yeast lees. The hotter the day, the better the wine (provided, of course, that it's fully chilled). 12.5° alc. **Rating** 89 **To** 2012 $28

Stringy Brae of Sevenhill

Sawmill Road, Sevenhill, SA 5453 **Region** Clare Valley
T (08) 8843 4313 **F** (08) 8843 4319 **www.**stringybrae.com.au **Open** 7 days 11–5
Winemaker O'Leary Walker **Est.** 1991 **Cases** 3500
Donald and Sally Willson began planting their vineyard in 1991, having purchased the property in 1983. In 2004 daughter Hannah Rantanen took over day-to-day management from father Donald. A slip of the finger last year increased plantings from 10 ha to 70 ha – the former figure was correct, and Stringy Brae is still of modest proportions, with 2.8 ha riesling and 3.6 ha each of shiraz and cabernet sauvignon. Exports to the UK, the US, Canada and Singapore.

Clare Valley Riesling 2006 Speaks of its region and variety from the first whiff of citrus through to the aftertaste of the palate; tight as can be, with a firm mineral framework to build on. Screwcap. 11.5° alc. **Rating** 93 **To** 2017 $21
Clare Valley Shiraz 2004 Colour not entirely convincing; however, there are plenty of red and black fruits, dark chocolate and ripe tannins; good length and acidity. Screwcap. 14.5° alc. **Rating** 90 **To** 2019 $21

Clare Valley Cabernet Sauvignon 2004 Has attractive varietal fruit in a classic blackcurrant spectrum, but needs more intensity. Screwcap. 14.5° alc. **Rating** 89 **To** 2012 $21

Stringybark

2060 Chittering Road, Chittering, WA 6084 **Region** Perth Hills
T (08) 9571 8069 **F** (08) 9561 6547 **www.**stringybarkwinery.com.au **Open** Wed–Sat 12–late, Sun 9–8
Winemaker Lilac Hill Estate (Steven Murfitt) **Est.** 1985 **Cases** 660
Bruce and Mary Cussen have a vineyard dating back to 1985, but the development of the cellar door and restaurant complex is far more recent. The vineyard consists of 2 ha of verdelho, chardonnay and cabernet sauvignon. Impressive contract winemaking makes its mark.

Chittering Chardonnay 2006 Aromatic and complex fruit aromas and flavours ranging from ripe stone fruit to pineapple/tropical, but with an edge of citrus; very much the product of a cool vintage. Screwcap. 13.5° alc. **Rating** 90 **To** 2010 $21.90
Chittering Rose 2006 Fuchsia colour; well above-average fruit flavour, with excellent balancing acidity to the subliminal sweetness. From cabernet and merlot. Screwcap. 12.6° alc. **Rating** 90 **To** 2008 $22.50

Chittering Cabernet Shiraz 2006 Light- to medium-bodied; fresh red and black fruits; light tannins and oak; well-made, early-drinking style. Diam. 13.5° alc. **Rating** 87 **To** 2010 $21.90

Stuart Range ★★★

67 William Street, Kingaroy, Qld 4610 **Region** South Burnett
T (07) 4162 3711 **F** (07) 4162 4811 **www.**stuartrange.com.au **Open** 7 days 9–5
Winemaker Heulwen Dixon **Est.** 1997 **Cases** 3000
Stuart Range has had a turbulent history since 1997, when a newly-equipped winery was established in part of a large, old butter factory in Kingaroy. Since then there has been a change of ownership, but business as usual (3 growers with 50 ha supply the winery) continues. The prior history of the business is reflected in cheese-making and olive oil-processing on site.

ŢŢŢŢ **Goodger Cabernet Merlot 2005** Plenty of depth and structure; blackcurrant, spice and some cassis; good length. Well-made. Cork. 14.2° alc. **Rating** 88 To 2011 $24

Stuart Wines

93A Killara Road, Gruyere, Vic 3770 (postal) **Region** Yarra Valley
T (03) 5964 9000 **F** (03) 5964 9313 **www**.stuartwinesco.com.au **Open** Not
Winemaker Peter Wilson **Est.** 1999 **Cases** 100 000
The Indonesian Widjaja family have major palm oil plantations in Java, with downstream refining. Under the direction of Hendra Widjaja it has decided to diversify into the Australian wine business, establishing 2 very significant vineyards, one in the Yarra Valley planted to no less than 12 varieties, and an even larger one in Heathcote, with 7 varieties – shiraz, nebbiolo, tempranillo, merlot, cabernet sauvignon, viognier and chardonnay. Between them the 2 vineyards cover 128 ha. Since 2004 all the wines have been made at a new winery at Heathcote. While the major part of the production will be exported, there are also direct sales in Australia. Wines are released under the Cahillton, White Box and Buddha's Wine labels; 50c per bottle of the proceeds of sales of all of the Buddha's Wine are donated to the Buddha's Global Childrens Fund, www.buddhaswine.com.au. Exports to Germany, The Netherlands, Indonesia, China and NZ.

ŢŢŢŢŢ **Cahillton Yarra Valley Chardonnay 2005** Melon, nectarine, white peach and barrel ferment oak aromas; the complex palate follows suit, with excellent depth and mouthfeel from the well-judged use of mlf; long and well-balanced. Cork. 15° alc. **Rating** 94 **To** 2014 $30
White Box Heathcote Shiraz 2005 Generous medium- to full-bodied with quite lush, but in no sense over-ripe or jammy, blackberry, spice and chocolate fruit. The tannins are fully ripe, the oak subtle; really pleasurable mouthfeel. Screwcap. 14.8° alc. **Rating** 94 **To** 2019 $18
Cahillton Yarra Valley Cabernet Merlot 2005 Well-constructed and balanced, the grapes picked at optimum ripeness; a lovely mix of blackcurrant and cassis; long, fine tannins and subtle oak. Cork. 14.3° alc. **Rating** 94 **To** 2020 $30
Cahillton Yarra Valley Cabernet Merlot 2004 A classically framed and weighted wine, with black fruits, oak and tannins all in balance and seamlessly interwoven. No green characters, but, on the other side, not over-ripe. Cork. 14.5° alc. **Rating** 94 **To** 2025 $30

ŢŢŢŢŢ **White Box Yarra Valley Chardonnay 2005** Light- to medium-bodied, clean, elegant and fresh; precise stone fruit, melon and citrus flavours, with good line and length; barrel-fermented and part mlf, the oak not too obvious. Cork. 14.6° alc. **Rating** 92 **To** 2011 $18
White Box Yarra Valley Sauvignon Blanc 2006 Clean; quite intense, the flavours predominantly in the grassy/asparagus/capsicum spectrum, but also taking in touches of passionfruit. Screwcap. 12.2° alc. **Rating** 91 **To** 2008 $18
White Box Yarra Valley Chardonnay 2004 Complexity developing on the bouquet; has also gained complexity and weight on the palate, though full mlf has played a role in creating a quite different style. Cork. 13.9° alc. **Rating** 90 **To** 2010 $18
Buddha's Wine Yarra Valley Sangiovese 2004 A more than useful sangiovese; all the correct characters, fruit weight, structure, balance and length; needless to say, light- to medium-bodied. Do the charity and yourself a favour by buying a bottle (or 2). Cork. 13.7° alc. **Rating** 90 **To** 2011 $17.50

ŢŢŢŢ **Cahillton Yarra Valley Viognier 2005** Has good weight and mouthfeel featuring apricot, peach and melon (no single flavour dominant) augmented by an airbrush of French oak. Cork. 14° alc. **Rating** 89 **To** 2010 $30
Buddha's Wine Yarra Valley Merlot 2005 High-toned juicy red fruit flavours of cherry, raspberry and cassis course through both bouquet and palate; its Achilles heel is the lack of structure. Cork. 14.3° alc. **Rating** 89 **To** 2011 $16.50

Buddha's Wine Yarra Valley Cabernet Merlot 2004 Elements of mint and green leaf on the bouquet suggest the fruit was not 100% ripe; the trade-off is freshness, and the light- to medium-bodied weight; the tannins are fine, and not green; abstemious use of oak. Cork. 13.7° alc. **Rating** 89 **To** 2012 $18.50

White Box Heathcote Cabernet Merlot 2004 Medium-bodied; some spicy, savoury, earthy notes to the core of blackcurrant fruit; the tannins are fine, but are also fractionally savoury. Cork. 14.6° alc. **Rating** 89 **To** 2013 $18

White Box Heathcote Merlot Cabernet 2005 Distinctly more minty and savoury than the Cabernet Merlot; since merlot ripens earlier than cabernet, not easy to understand why this should be so; overall texture and weight is quite good. Cork. 14.2° alc. **Rating** 89 **To** 2013 $18

Buddha's Wine Yarra Valley Tempranillo 2006 Has more structure and texture than average, although the tannins are light; the flavours, melding tangy citrus with sweeter cherry fruit, are also correct. Cork. 13.3° alc. **Rating** 89 **To** 2012 $18.50

Buddha's Wine Yarra Valley Sauvignon Blanc 2005 Much more user-friendly than White Box, higher alcohol pointing to riper grapes with more tropical fruit components. Screwcap. 13.1° alc. **Rating** 88 **To** 2008 $15.50

Cahillton Yarra Valley Shiraz 2004 Shares many things with Buddha's Shiraz, and has developed rather quickly for a wine at this price-point; soft, light- to medium-bodied sweet fruit; fine, ripe tannins. Cork. 14.5° alc. **Rating** 88 **To** 2010 $30

Buddha's Wine Yarra Valley Shiraz Mataro Viognier 2005 Light-bodied; as one might expect, a fragrant and complex bouquet; spicy notes dominate both the bouquet and palate, mocha and chocolate joining in on the mid-palate and finish. Cork. 14.8° alc. **Rating** 88 **To** 2015 $17.50

Buddha's Wine Yarra Valley Tempranillo 2005 Similar to the '06, likewise with some texture to the spice, cherry and plum fruit; well-balanced. Cork. 13.5° alc. **Rating** 88 **To** 2008 $16.50

White Box Heathcote Shiraz Viognier 2005 The normal colour intensity is missing; light- to medium-bodied, and in every way denies its alcohol and varietal parentage; quite strange. Don't look a gift horse in the mouth. Screwcap. 14.8° alc. **Rating** 87 **To** 2012 $18

Buddha's Wine Yarra Valley Shiraz 2004 Light- to medium-bodied; not particularly concentrated, complex or rich (despite the alcohol) but does have quite sweet fruit flavours; easy-access tyle, no cellaring required. Cork. 14.9° alc. **Rating** 87 **To** 2008 $18.50

Huma Yarra Valley Cabernet Merlot 2004 The $10 price is not easy to understand; light- to medium-bodied, to be sure, but there is no fault, the wine representative of both the region and varieties. Screwcap. 14° alc. **Rating** 87 **To** 2010 $10

Stumpy Gully

1247 Stumpy Gully Road, Moorooduc, Vic 3933 **Region** Mornington Peninsula
T (03) 5978 8429 **F** (03) 5978 8419 **www**.stumpygully.com.au **Open** W'ends 11–5
Winemaker Wendy Zantvoort, Maitena Zantvoort, Ewan Campbell **Est.** 1988
Cases 7500

When Frank and Wendy Zantvoort began planting their first vineyard in 1988 there were no winemakers in the family: now there are 3, plus 2 viticulturists. Mother Wendy was first to obtain her degree from Charles Sturt University. She was followed by daughter Maitena, who married Ewan Campbell, also a winemaker. Father Frank and son Michael look after the vineyards. The original vineyard has 9 ha of vines, but in establishing the 20-ha Moorooduc vineyard (first harvest 2001) the Zantvoorts have deliberately gone against prevailing thinking, planting it solely to red varieties, predominately cabernet sauvignon, merlot and shiraz. They believe they have one of the warmest sites on the Peninsula, and that ripening will in fact present no problems. In all they now have 10 varieties planted on 40 ha, producing 18 different wines (Peninsula Panorama is their second label). Exports to all major markets.

$\bar{Y}\bar{Y}\bar{Y}\bar{Y}\hat{Y}$ **Mornington Peninsula Riesling 2006** An attractive multi-blossom bouquet, the abundant fruit flavours ranging through sweet citrus, apple and passionfruit; early-developing style. Screwcap. 13.6° alc. **Rating** 92 **To** 2008 $22

Mornington Peninsula Sauvignon Blanc 2006 Good texture, flavour and length; grass, asparagus and gooseberry followed by a clean, brisk finish. Undeniably good value. Screwcap. 13.2° alc. **Rating** 90 **To** 2008 $18

Peninsula Panorama Shiraz 2005 Impressive aromas with black fruits and wafts of spice; light- to medium-bodied but has good balance and mouthfeel, the flavours tracking the bouquet. Outstanding value for a Mornington Peninsula wine. Screwcap. 15.2° alc. **Rating** 90 **To** 2012 $15

Mornington Peninsula Merlot 2005 Medium-bodied; black olive, cassis and blackberry flavours; very fine, gently savoury, tannins; controlled oak. Screwcap. 14.4° alc. **Rating** 90 **To** 2010 $25

$\bar{Y}\bar{Y}\bar{Y}\bar{Y}$ **Mornington Peninsula Cabernet Sauvignon 2005** Has more sweet fruit than usually encountered on the Peninsula, but still having notes of mint and wintergreen. Screwcap. 13.6° alc. **Rating** 88 **To** 2012 $25

Mornington Peninsula Pinot Grigio 2006 Well-made; though light-bodied, does have apple, pear and musk nuances, followed by a crisp finish. Screwcap. 14.4° alc. **Rating** 87 **To** 2008 $22

Sugarloaf Creek Estate ★★★★☆

20 Zwars Road, Broadford, Vic 3658 **Region** Goulburn Valley
T (03) 5784 1291 **F** (03) 5784 1291 www.sugarloafcreek.com **Open** First Sun of the month 10–5, or by appt
Winemaker Munari Wines **Est.** 1998 **Cases** 600
The 2-ha vineyard, planted exclusively to shiraz, was established by the Blyth and Hunter families in the 1990s, the first vintage in 2001. While situated in the Goulburn Valley, it is in fact near the boundary of the Upper Goulburn, Goulburn Valley and Macedon Ranges regions, and the climate is significantly cooler than that of the major part of the Goulburn Valley. Adding the skilled winemaking by Adrian Munari, it became immediately apparent that this is a distinguished producer of Shiraz.

Sugarloaf Ridge ★★★

336 Sugarloaf Road, Carlton River, Tas 7173 **Region** Southern Tasmania
T (03) 6265 7175 **F** (03) 6266 7275 www.sugarloafridge.com **Open** Fri–Mon 10–5 Oct–May
Winemaker Winemaking Tasmania (Julian Alcorso) **Est.** 1999 **Cases** 300
Dr Simon and wife Isobel Stanley are both microbiologists, but with thoroughly unlikely specialities: he in low-temperature microbiology, taking him to the Antarctic, and she in a worldwide environmental geosciences company. Sugarloaf Ridge is an extended family business, with daughter Kristen and husband Julian Colvile partners. Since 1999, multiple clones of pinot noir, sauvignon blanc, pinot gris, viognier and lagrein have been planted, and 1580 native trees, 210 olive trees and 270 cherry trees have also helped transform the property from bare, sheep grazing pasture.

$\bar{Y}\bar{Y}\bar{Y}\bar{Y}$ **Chardonnay 2005** Some colour development; a powerful wine which lacks focus on the mid-palate, before coming through strongly on the finish. **Rating** 89 **To** 2010

Summerfield ★★★★★

5967 Stawell-Avoca Road, Moonambel, Vic 3478 **Region** Pyrenees
T (03) 5467 2264 **F** (03) 5467 2380 www.summerfieldwines.com **Open** 7 days 9–5.30
Winemaker Mark Summerfield **Est.** 1979 **Cases** 8000
A specialist red wine producer, the particular forte of which is Shiraz. The red wines are consistently excellent: luscious and full-bodied and fruit-driven, but with a slice of vanillin oak to top them off. Founder Ian Summerfield has now handed over the winemaking reins to son Mark,

who, with consulting advice, produces consistently outstanding and awesomely concentrated Shiraz and Cabernet Sauvignon, both in varietal and Reserve forms. The red wines are built for the long haul, and richly repay cellaring. Exports to the US and the UK.

ＹＹＹＹＹ **Shiraz 2005** Slightly lighter than the Reserve (just medium- to full-bodied), and with a touch more spiciness to the aromas and flavours; good tannin structure. Screwcap. 14.5° alc. **Rating** 94 **To** 2020 $27

Reserve Shiraz 2005 Archetypal, full-bodied, deep, dense, rich and ripe fruit, with no holds barred; blackberry, prune and licorice; the tannins ripe and not abrasive; all achieved without undue reliance on alcohol. Cork. 14.5° alc. **Rating** 94 **To** 2030 $50

Reserve Shiraz 2004 Medium red-purple; richer, riper and chunkier than the varietal; blackberry fruit with dashes of sweet chocolate, and more oak influence. Odd choice of closure, presumably dictated by export markets. Cork. 14.5° alc. **Rating** 94 **To** 2015 $50

Reserve Cabernet 2004 Medium-bodied; riper fruit than the varietal, but by no means over the top; lush blackcurrant flavours with controlled new oak and ripe tannins. Cork. 14° alc. **Rating** 94 **To** 2015 $50

Tradition 2005 The most conventionally balanced and structured of all the Summerfield wines; you don't have to draw up your courage to take a mouthful (or a glass) or even 2. No shortage of flavour or mouthfeel. A roughly equal blend of Shiraz/Cabernet Sauvignon/Merlot/Cabernet Franc. Screwcap. 14.5° alc. **Rating** 94 **To** 2025 $27

ＹＹＹＹＹ **Shiraz 2004** Medium red-purple; abundant fruit aromas of plum and blackberry; soft round tannins; gentle oak, and gentle price. Screwcap. 14.1° alc. **Rating** 93 **To** 2019 $23

Reserve Cabernet Sauvignon 2005 The reverse of the Shiraz; here the wine, while of gargantuan proportions, has a little more texture than the varietal; shiraz seems better able to perform in these specifications. Cork. 14.6° alc. **Rating** 93 **To** 2025 $50

Cabernet Sauvignon 2005 Hyper-concentrated, almost viscous, and very ripe confit cabernet fruit; these wines continue to defy conventional wisdom (only 14.6° alcohol), unless, of course, they have been deliberately concentrated in the winery. Screwcap. 14.6° alc. **Rating** 92 **To** 2035 $27

Cabernet Sauvignon 2004 Light- to medium-bodied; crisp, fresh blackcurrant fruit with touches of mint; light tannins, attractive wine. Screwcap. 13.1° alc. **Rating** 90 **To** 2015 $23

ＹＹＹＹ **Merlot 2005** Lush, rich medium- to full-bodied dry red, which just happens to be made from merlot, a variety which is very hard to please. Cork. 13.9° alc. **Rating** 89 **To** 2018 $27

Tradition 2004 Medium red-purple; a medium-bodied array of predominantly red fruits with some foresty/savoury edges. Cabernet Sauvignon/Cabernet Franc/Merlot/Shiraz. Screwcap. 13.9° alc. **Rating** 89 **To** 2014 $27

Summerhill Wines

65 Dandenong-Hastings Road, Somerville, Vic 3912 **Region** Mornington Peninsula
T (08) 9884 5687 **Open** By appt
Winemaker Robert Zagar **Est.** 1998 **Cases** 1000
Since the latter part of the 1990s, Summerhill Wines has successfully gone through various crises. Having started with 6 tonnes of grapes in 1998 producing a mix of multi-regional wines, vintage doubled each succeeding year, reaching 80 tonnes in 2002. Since then they have largely focused on their Mornington Peninsula vineyard and winery, with pinot noir and shiraz grown on the sandy soils of the Somerville area. The overwhelming percentage is sold on-premise, and Summerhill also provides contract winemaking services for (among others) Rubicon, Pyramid Gold, Oakdale and Corniola. Exports to Malaysia.

Summit Estate ★★★

291 Granite Belt Drive, Thulimbah, Qld 4377 **Region** Granite Belt
T (07) 4683 2011 **F** (07) 4683 2600 **www**.summitestate.com.au **Open** 7 days 9–5
Winemaker Paòla Cabezas Rhymer **Est.** 1997 **Cases** 2500
Summit Estate is the public face of the Stanthorpe Wine Co, owned by a syndicate of
10 professionals who work in Brisbane, and share a love of wine. They operate the Stanthorpe
Wine Centre, which offers wine education as well as selling wines from other makers in the
region (and, of course, from Summit Estate). The 17-ha vineyard is planted to chardonnay,
marsanne, pinot noir, shiraz, merlot, tempranillo, petit verdot and cabernet sauvignon, and they
have set up a small, specialised contract winemaking facility. Exports to the UK.

ŶŶŶŶ **Single Vineyard Granite Belt Petit Verdo 2005** Medium-bodied, with some
attractive blackcurrant fruit before slightly green tannins; pity about the
phonetic spelling of the variety on the label; from 720 vines. Cork. 13.2° alc.
Rating 88 **To** 2009 $35
Single Vineyard Granite Belt Tempranillo 2005 Lively fruit; red berries with
the touch of citrus often seen in Australian tempranillo; nonetheless, well-made and
an interesting variety; from 1100 vines. Cork. 13.2° alc. **Rating** 87 **To** 2009 $35

Surveyor's Hill Winery ★★★★☆

215 Brooklands Road, Wallaroo, NSW 2618 **Region** Canberra District
T (02) 6230 2046 **www**.survhill.com.au **Open** W'ends & public hols, or by appt
Winemaker Brindabella Hills Winery (Dr Roger Harris) **Est.** 1986 **Cases** 1000
Following the sale of the Kamberra winery, grape sales to it have ceased, and the wines are now
made by Dr Roger Harris in place of Kamberra.

ŶŶŶŶŶ **Riesling 2006** Clean and crisp aromas, with no reduction; citrus, apple and
mineral flavours; good length. Screwcap. 11.6° alc. **Rating** 90 **To** 2013 $25
Semillon Sauvignon Blanc 2006 Very well-made; shows the synergy which
can be obtained from these varieties, sauvignon blanc with tropical fruits, and
structure from the semillon. Screwcap. 12.4° alc. **Rating** 90 **To** 2009 $18
Cabernet Franc Cabernet Sauvignon Merlot 2004 Light- to medium-
bodied, with a lovely range of cherry, raspberry and rhubarb red fruit flavours,
and just a hint of blackcurrant; fine, silky tannins, and ready now, though will
hold for another 5 years. Screwcap. 13.9° alc. **Rating** 90 **To** 2008 $15
Autumn Gold 2004 Very late-harvested sauvignon blanc and semillon; no
botrytis, but the fermentation stopped at 8°; only moderately sweet, and has
very good balancing acidity. Clever winemaking and good value. Cork. 8° alc.
Rating 90 **To** 2008 $10

ŶŶŶŶ **Sweet Touriga NV** Once called port, but no more thanks to the EU; a blend
of '97 and '00 vintages, described on the back label as tawny, but is closer to
late-bottled vintage, as the colour is still red, the primary fruit still strong. Cork.
20.5° alc. **Rating** 89 **To** 2008 $12

Sutherland Estate

2010 Melba Highway, Dixons Creek, Vic 3775 **Region** Yarra Valley
T 0402 052 287 **F** (03) 9762 1122 **Open** 7 days 10–5 summer, or Thurs–Sun & public hols
Winemaker Alex White (Contract) **Est.** 2000 **Cases** 2000
The Phelan family (father Ron, mother Sheila, daughter Catherine and partner Angus Ridley)
established Sutherland Estate in 2000, when they acquired a mature 2-ha vineyard at Dixons
Creek. Later that year they planted another 3.2 ha, including a small amount of tempranillo.
Catherine and Angus are in the final year of the part-time viticulture and oenology course at
Charles Sturt University; in the meantime, Angus is gaining further experience as a winemaker at
Coldstream Hills. The DHV range is estate-grown on Daniel's Hill Vineyard.

ŶŶŶŶŶ **Chardonnay 2004** Very youthful green-yellow; attractive melon and citrus fruit does most of the talking, oak only a whisper; crisp, fresh finish. Screwcap. 13° alc. **Rating** 92 **To** 2014 $20

ŶŶŶŶ **Tempranillo 2005** A clean and fragrant array of red fruits; more approachable than many, with good balance and length. Screwcap. 13.5° alc. **Rating** 89 **To** 2013 $30

Sutton Grange Winery

Carnochans Road, Sutton Grange, Vic 3448 **Region** Bendigo
T (03) 5474 8277 **www**.suttongrangewines.com **Open** Mon–Fri 9–4, w'ends by appt
Winemaker Gilles Lapalus **Est.** 1998 **Cases** 2200
The 400-ha Sutton Grange property is a thoroughbred stud acquired in 1996 by Peter Sidwell, a Melbourne-based businessman with horse racing and breeding among his activities. A lunch visit to the property by long-term friends Alec Epis and Stuart Anderson led to the decision to plant 14 ha of syrah, merlot, cabernet sauvignon, viognier and sangiovese, and to the recruitment of French winemaker Gilles Lapalus, who just happens to be the partner of Stuart Anderson's daughter. The winery, built from WA limestone, was completed in 2001. Exports to the UK and Switzerland.

Swan Valley Wines ★★★★

261 Haddrill Road, Baskerville, WA 6065 **Region** Swan Valley
T (08) 9296 1501 **www**.swanvalleywines.com.au **Open** Fri–Sun & public hols 10–5
Winemaker Julie White (Consultant) **Est.** 1999 **Cases** 6600
Peter and Paula Hoffman, with sons Paul and Thomas, acquired their 6-ha property in 1989. It had a long history of grapegrowing, and the prior owner had registered the name Swan Valley Wines back in 1983. In 1999 the family built a new winery to handle the grapes from 5.5 ha of chenin blanc, grenache, semillon, malbec, cabernet sauvignon and shiraz. Exports to Japan.

ŶŶŶŶŶ **Chenin Blanc 2006** Has a freshness and brightness not often encountered with this workhorse variety; gentle citrus overtones to white peach fruit, then a long finish. Screwcap. 12.4° alc. **Rating** 90 **To** 2010 $14
Raw Power Reserve Shiraz 2005 No doubt deliberately made in precisely this old-fashioned style, demanding a 3-inch-thick barbecued T-bone steak. Screwcap. 15.7° alc. **Rating** 90 **To** 2025 $35

ŶŶŶŶ **Blush Rose 2006** Classic cabernet rose style with redcurrant fruit and a crisp finish; no reliance on residual sugar. Screwcap. 12.4° alc. **Rating** 88 **To** 2008 $15
The Roadbull Grenache Cabernet 2005 An utterly odd conjunction of flavour and texture, with drying tannins on the finish and aftertaste. Patience may be rewarded, but I wouldn't want to put my house on the proposition. Cork. 14.5° alc. **Rating** 88 **To** 2020 $30
Tawny Port NV Deep, youthful, colour. An interesting wine, with black fruits and touches of dark chocolate and not overly sweet. Cork. 17.5° alc. **Rating** 87 **To** 2008 $15
Amphisbaena Red NV In similar style to the Tawny Port, slightly lighter and fresher. Cork. 17.5° alc. **Rating** 87 **To** 2008 $20

Swinging Bridge ★★★

'Belubula', Fish Fossil Drive, Canowindra, NSW 2804 **Region** Cowra
T (02) 6344 3212 **F** (02) 6344 3232 **Open** By appt
Winemaker Tom Ward, Chris Derrez (Contract) **Est.** 1995 **Cases** 700
The Ward (Mark and Anne, Tom and Georgie) and Patten (Michael and Helen) families commenced the development of a large vineyard in Cowra in 1995. In all there are 45 ha of chardonnay, 18 ha of shiraz, 8 ha of merlot and 6 ha of cabernet sauvignon. Most of the grapes are sold, with small amounts of Shiraz and Chardonnay made under the Swinging Bridge label. Swinging Bridge had a moment of glory with its 2004 Chardonnay being one of 2 gold medals in a class in a class of over 200 wines entered in the Cowra Wine Show '05. Those entries come

from all over Australia, the region of origin unknown to the judges. It is one of the most recent testimonies to the suitability of the region for chardonnay, which first came to prominence when Brian Croser made the first Petaluma Chardonnay from Cowra grapes.

ŶŶŶŶ **Canowindra Shiraz 2005** Soft plum, black cherry and blackberry fruit; more substance than usual from this region. Good value. Screwcap. 13.8° alc. **Rating** 88 **To** 2011 $12

Swings & Roundabouts ★★★★

Caves Road, Wilyabrup, WA 6280 **Region** Margaret River
T (08) 9756 6640 **F** (08) 9286 1933 www.swings.com.au **Open** 7 days 10–5
Winemaker Mark Lane **Est.** 2004 **Cases** NA
The winemaking skills of Mark Lane and the marketing skills of Ian Latchford have come together to create 3 ranges: the super-premium Swings & Roundabouts (Chardonnay, Semillon Sauvignon Blanc, Shiraz and Cabernet Merlot); the varietal Laneway series of The Italian, Tempranillo and Shiraz, targeted at on-premises sales, and with exceptionally striking labels; and the premium Kiss Chasey range.

ŶŶŶŶŶ **Margaret River Sauvignon Blanc Semillon 2006** Light-bodied; crisp, clean apple, passionfruit and grass all in cameo proportions; well-balanced, and no residual sugar. Screwcap. 12.5° alc. **Rating** 90 **To** 2008 $17

ŶŶŶŶ **Kiss Chasey Cabernet Shiraz Merlot 2005** Plenty of cassis, black cherry and blackcurrant fruit all tumbling together, then some persistent tannins; excellent value. Screwcap. 14° alc. **Rating** 89 **To** 2012 $14
Tempranillo 2005 Clean aromas, then a highly expressive juicy, mulberry, cherry palate, the savoury tannins on the finish just a touch assertive. Screwcap. 14.5° alc. **Rating** 88 **To** 2010 $19
Life of Riley Chenin Blanc 2006 Well-made; gentle fruit salad, a touch of lemony acidity and not too sweet. Screwcap. 13° alc. **Rating** 87 **To** 2009 $16

Swooping Magpie ★★★★☆

860 Commonage Road, Yallingup, WA 6282 **Region** Margaret River
T 0417 921 003 **F** (08) 9756 6222 www.swoopingmagpie.com.au **Open** By appt
Winemaker Mark Standish (Contract) **Est.** 1998 **Cases** 2000
Neil and Leann Tuffield have established their 2-and-a-bit-ha vineyard in the hills behind the coastal town of Yallingup. The name, they say, 'was inspired by a family of magpies who consider the property part of their territory'. One ha each of semillon and cabernet franc is supplemented by purchased sauvignon blanc, chenin blanc and merlot to produce the wines.

ŶŶŶŶŶ **Margaret River Semillon 2006** Lively and intense, the fruit having absorbed the French oak in which two-thirds was fermented and matured; mineral, green apple, citrus and spice; long finish. Screwcap. 13.1° alc. **Rating** 93 **To** 2012 $20
Margaret River Cabernet Merlot 2003 This is not, as one would suppose, a blend of cabernet sauvignon and merlot, but is Cabernet Franc (46%)/Merlot (40%)/Cabernet Sauvignon (14%). Whatever, it is light- to medium-bodied, with fresh, nicely balanced red and black berry fruits; fine tannins and gentle vanilla/mocha oak. Screwcap. 13.5° alc. **Rating** 92 **To** 2019 $16
Margaret River Cabernet Franc 2004 Emphasises the worth of cabernet franc in the Margaret River. Generous, polished black fruits and super-fine, almost sweet, tannins. Screwcap. 14.5° alc. **Rating** 92 **To** 2019 $20

Symphonia Wines ★★★★☆

RMB 1760, Myrrhee, Vic 3732 (postal) **Region** King Valley
T (03) 5727 3888 **F** (03) 5727 3851 www.sammiranda.com.au **Open** At Sam Miranda
Winemaker Sam Miranda **Est.** 1998 **Cases** 4000

Peter Read and his family were veterans of the King Valley, commencing the development of their vineyard in 1981 to supply Brown Brothers. As a result of extensive trips to both Western and Eastern Europe, Peter Read embarked on an ambitious project to trial a series of grape varieties little known in this country. The process of evaluation and experimentation produced a number of wines with great interest and no less merit. In 2005 Rachel Miranda (wife of Sam Miranda), with parents Peter and Suzanne Evans, purchased the business, and intends to keep its identity intact and separate from the Sam Miranda brand. Exports to the UK.

ΨΨΨΨΨ **King Valley Petit Manseng 2006** Not a hint of reduction; lively, zesty, fresh surprise packet; citrus and lemon in abundance; both balance and mouthfeel very good. Wow! It's hard to agree with the back label that this is a noble variety, however good the wine may be. Screwcap. 13° alc. **Rating** 93 **To** 2009 $24

King Valley Pinot Grigio 2006 Spotlessly clean; attractive pear drop and lemon skin aromas and flavours; lively and long; way above the average. Screwcap. 12.5° alc. **Rating** 92 **To** 2008 $24

La Solista King Valley Tempranillo 2006 Attractive juicy, ripe and vibrant fruit without any of the green/lemon notes often encountered in Australia. Screwcap. 14° alc. **Rating** 91 **To** 2014 $19

Las Triadas Winemaker's Reserve King Valley Tempranillo 2005 More complex than the La Solista in flavour terms; notes of spice and heather to go with the sweet fruits; good length. Screwcap. 14° alc. **Rating** 91 **To** 2014 $24

King Valley Saperavi 2005 Deep, dense colour typical of the variety; suitably black fruit, dark/bitter chocolate and earth; plenty of tannins; needs patience. From Russia with love. (Saperavi is a Russian variety, the name literally meaning dyer.) Screwcap. 14° alc. **Rating** 90 **To** 2017 $24

ΨΨΨΨ **King Valley Arneis 2006** A pleasant, well-balanced and well-made wine though not a lot of positive fruit; suggestions of ripe apple and pear. Screwcap. 13° alc. **Rating** 87 **To** 2008 $24

Symphony Hill Wines ★★★★

2017 Eukey Road, Ballandean, Qld 4382 **Region** Granite Belt
T (07) 4684 1388 **F** (07) 4684 1399 **www**.symphonyhill.com.au **Open** 7 days 10–4
Winemaker Mike Hayes **Est.** 1999 **Cases** 3000
Ewen and Elissa Macpherson purchased what was then an old table grape and orchard property in 1996. In partnership with Ewen's parents, Bob and Jill Macpherson, they have developed 4 ha of vineyards, while Ewen has completed his Bachelor of Applied Science in viticulture (in 2003). The vineyard has been established using state-of-the-art technology; vineyard manager and winemaker Mike Hayes has a degree in viticulture and is a third-generation viticulturist in the Granite Belt region. Between Hayes and Ewen Macpherson, a trial block of 50 varieties has been established, including such rarely encountered varieties as picpoul, tannat and mondeuse.

ΨΨΨΨΨ **Premium Shiraz 2005** Elegantly framed and crafted medium-bodied wine; classic shiraz, with gentle blackberry fruits and a touch of spice; harmonious. Screwcap. **Rating** 94 **To** 2018 $25

ΨΨΨΨ **Pinot Gris 2006** Crisp and crunchy in grigio style, rather than gris; pear and green apple fruit, and a mercifully dry finish. Outlandish price. Screwcap. **Rating** 88 **To** 2008 $30

Rose 2006 Tangy, spicy, classic dry cabernet-based style; fresh finish. Screwcap. 12° alc. **Rating** 88 **To** 2008 $18

Tempranillo 2006 Bright colour; fresh red berry fruits on entry, then persistent, drying tannins. Screwcap. **Rating** 87 **To** 2012 $25

Syrahmi ★★★★☆

PO Box 438, Heathcote, Vic 3523 **Region** Heathcote
T 0407 057 471 **Open** Not
Winemaker Adam Foster **Est.** 2004 **Cases** 350

Adam Foster worked as a chef in Vic and London before moving to the front of house and becoming increasingly interested in wine. He then worked as a cellar hand with a who's who in Australia and France, including Torbreck, Chapoutier, Mitchelton, Domaine Ogier, Heathcote Winery, Jasper Hill and Domaine Pierre Gaillard. He became convinced that the Cambrian soils of Heathcote could produce the best possible shiraz, and since 2004 has purchased grapes (rising from 1.5 tonnes in 2004 to 4 tonnes in 2006) from Heathcote Winery, using the full bag of open ferment techniques, co-fermenting 3.4% viognier with the 2 separate clonal batches of shiraz. The wine spends 14 months in French oak (25% new) and is neither fined nor filtered. The wine, Syrahmi SV2, has 2 separately fermented clones, each with 3.4% viognier, which are subsequently blended.

🍷🍷🍷🍷 **V2 Heathcote Shiraz 2005** Light but bright red-purple; an elegant light- to medium-bodied wine; a very fresh array of cherry, blackberry and plum fruit, although it does trail away a little bit on the finish. V2 signifies old vines, a somewhat elastic definition at the best of times. Screwcap. 14° alc. **Rating** 91 To 2015 $38

T'Gallant

1385 Mornington-Flinders Road, Main Ridge, Vic 3928 **Region** Mornington Peninsula
T (03) 5989 6565 **F** (03) 5989 6577 **www.tgallant.com.au Open** 7 days 10–5
Winemaker Kevin McCarthy **Est.** 1990 **Cases** 40 000
Husband-and-wife winemakers Kevin McCarthy and Kathleen Quealy carved out such an important niche market for the T'Gallant label that in 2003, after protracted negotiations, it was acquired by Beringer Blass. The acquisition of a 15-ha property, and the planting of 10 ha of pinot gris gives the business a firm geographic base, as well as providing increased resources for its signature wine. The yearly parade of new (usually beautiful and striking) labels designed by Ken Cato do not make my life at all easy. La Baracca Trattoria is open 7 days for lunch and for specially booked evening events. Kathleen Quealy has now retired to look after her large family.

🍷🍷🍷🍷 **Chardonnay 2004** Nicely balanced and sculptured wine through a mix of barrel ferment and stainless steel fermentation and maturation; good lees and mlf components. Screwcap. 13.5° alc. **Rating** 92 To 2011 $18.95
Tribute Mornington Peninsula Pinot Gris 2005 Scented, almost spicy, in the Imogen gris spectrum, more powerful and intense; good length. Screwcap. 14.5° alc. **Rating** 91 To 2008 $27.95
Pinot Grigio 2006 Much more precise and pointed than the Imogen; more tangy, green apple and citrus notes. Screwcap. 13.5° alc. **Rating** 90 To 2008 $18.95

🍷🍷🍷 **Juliet Mornington Peninsula Pinot Noir 2005** Bright, fresh, crisp and unadorned, all the more allowing pinot noir varietal character to express itself, the oak well-restrained; one level up from a top-class rose, one level down in price. Screwcap. 13° alc. **Rating** 89 To 2008 $14
Imogen Pinot Gris 2006 A powerful rich wine with masses of flavour, although hard to pinpoint outside of the general pear/pear skin/musk varietal descriptors. Screwcap. 14.5° alc. **Rating** 88 To 2008 $18.95

Tahbilk ★★★★★

Goulburn Valley Highway, Tabilk, Vic 3608 **Region** Nagambie Lakes
T (03) 5794 2555 **F** (03) 5794 2360 **www.tahbilk.com.au Open** Mon–Sat 9–5, Sun 11–5
Winemaker Alister Purbrick, Neil Larson, Alan George **Est.** 1860 **Cases** 120 000
A winery steeped in tradition (with National Trust classification), which should be visited at least once by every wine-conscious Australian, and which makes wines – particularly red wines – utterly in keeping with that tradition. The essence of that heritage comes in the form of the tiny quantities of Shiraz made entirely from vines planted in 1860. In 2005 Tahbilk opened its substantial wetlands project, with a series of walks connected (if you wish) by short journeys on a small punt. Exports to the UK and the US.

ŢŢŢŢŢ 1860 Vines Shiraz 2001 The colour (as is usual) is not strong, but the hue is good; an elegant medium-bodied, finely boned and structured wine; more to do with what it does not say than what it does, ie moderate alcohol and restrained oak. For all that, this is one of the great wines for classicists. All the vines were planted in 1860, and there has been no replacement of dead vines with young vines, not even using cuttings from the old; 275 dozen made. Cork. 13.5° alc. **Rating** 96 **To** 2020 $120

Reserve Shiraz 2001 Deeper hue, though not as brilliant and bright as that of the 1860 Vines; medium- to full-bodied, with the strongest structure of the 3 Shirazs, though not the finesse of the 1860 Vines; the tannins are strong in typical Tahbilk fashion, the wine with years in front of it. Cork. 14° alc. **Rating** 94 **To** 2031 $70

ŢŢŢŢŢ Marsanne 2006 Aromas of cake, honey, melon and spice, then a long, harmonious palate, with a gold-plated guarantee to develop honeysuckle and gentle toast as it ages over the next 10+ years. Screwcap. 13.5° alc. **Rating** 93 **To** 2016 $12.95

Cabernet Sauvignon 2003 Powerfully built and framed in the best Tahbilk tradition, and not unduly marked by the drought; rich blackcurrant fruit and tannins are neatly balanced, the oak incidental. Cork. 14.5° alc. **Rating** 92 **To** 2018 $21

Shiraz 2003 Medium-bodied, but with more mid-palate fruit than some recent releases; tannins ripe and balanced. Cork. 14.5° alc. **Rating** 91 **To** 2015 $21

Cabernet Franc 2005 An interesting wine, the flavours running from red fruits and raspberries through to savoury, tobacco leaf, all positive varietal characteristics; has good structure and length; a bargain. Screwcap. 13.5° alc. **Rating** 90 **To** 2008 $12.95

ŢŢŢŢ Reserve Cabernet Sauvignon 2001 Medium-bodied; earthy notes are starting to come through along with black fruits and tannins; obviously, I am not totally convinced by the wine. Cork. 14° alc. **Rating** 89 **To** 2015 $70

Talijancich   ★★★☆

26 Hyem Road, Herne Hill, WA 6056 **Region** Swan Valley
T (08) 9296 4289 **F** (08) 9296 1762 **Open** Sun–Fri 11–5
Winemaker James Talijancich **Est.** 1932 **Cases** 10 000
A former fortified wine specialist (with old Liqueur Tokay) now making a select range of table wines, with particular emphasis on Verdelho – in November each year there is a tasting of fine 3-year-old Verdelho table wines from both Australia and overseas. James Talijancich is an energetic and effective ambassador for the Swan Valley as a whole. Exports to China, Japan and Hong Kong.

Tallarook   ★★★★☆

2 Delaney's Road, Warranwood, Vic 3134 (postal) **Region** Upper Goulburn
T (03) 9876 7022 **F** (03) 9876 7044 **www**.tallarook.com **Open** Not
Winemaker MasterWineMakers **Est.** 1987 **Cases** 1200
Tallarook has been established on a property between Broadford and Seymour at an elevation of 200–300m. Since 1987, 14 ha of vines have been planted, mainly to chardonnay, shiraz and pinot noir. The retaining of MasterWineMakers in 1998 brought a substantial change in emphasis, and the subsequent releases of impressive Chardonnays and other good wines. Subsequently, the second label Terra Felix was sold. Exports to the UK and Europe.

ŢŢŢŢŢ Chardonnay 2004 Glowing yellow-green; medium- to full-bodied with peach, fig and melon fruit supported by subtle oak and mlf inputs; full wild yeast treatment; carries the alcohol very well. Screwcap. 14° alc. **Rating** 92 **To** 2016 $23.50

Roussanne 2005 Light straw-green; another very complex wine with a range of winemaking inputs, yet quite restrained and with very good structure; there is a minerally substrate to spicy pear, honeyed stone fruit and citrus. Screwcap. 13.5° alc. **Rating** 91 **To** 2017 $27.50

Marsanne 2004 Bright straw-green; an interesting, very complex wine, with honey/honeysuckle/nutmeg and spice; has absorbed the oak. A wine of real character. Screwcap. 14.5° alc. **Rating** 90 **To** 2015 $27.50

 Viognier 2006 Bright straw-green; appealing balance and mouthfeel, yet lacks positive varietal character; always a difficult variety to handle. Screwcap. 14° alc. **Rating** 89 **To** 2010 $23.50

Tallis Wine ★★★☆

PO Box 10, Dookie, Vic 3646 **Region** Central Victoria Zone
T (03) 5823 5383 **F** (03) 5828 6532 **www.talliswine.com.au Open** Not
Winemaker Richard Tallis, Gary Baldwin (Consultant) **Est.** 2000 **Cases** 2000
Richard, Mark and Alice Tallis have a substantial vineyard, with 16 ha of shiraz, 5 ha of cabernet sauvignon, 2 ha of viognier and 1 ha of merlot. While most of the grapes are sold, they have embarked on winemaking with the aid of Gary Baldwin, and have had considerable success. The philosophy of their viticulture and winemaking is to create a low-input and sustainable system; all environmentally harmful sprays are eliminated.

The Silent Showman Shiraz Viognier 2004 Medium-bodied; very lively, the viognier lift making its presence felt early; vibrant flavours provide the pleasure, rather than any tannin contribution. Cork. 14.2° alc. **Rating** 90 **To** 2024 $27

Dookie Hills Rose 2006 Vivid red-purple; lively red cherry and strawberry running through to a lingering, dry finish. Shiraz. Screwcap. 13° alc. **Rating** 89 **To** 2008 $16

Dookie Hills Viognier 2006 Has some interesting varietal character without heavy phenolics; ripe tropical and apricot fruit, but typically does not leave the mouth thirsting for more. Screwcap. 13.4° alc. **Rating** 88 **To** 2010 $19

Dookie Hills Sangiovese 2005 Fairly typical spicy cherry/sour cherry aromas and flavours; light- to medium-bodied, and those faintly dusty tannins of the variety. Screwcap. 13.6° alc. **Rating** 88 **To** 2008 $19

Taltarni ★★★★☆

339 Taltarni Road, Moonambel, Vic 3478 **Region** Pyrenees
T (03) 5459 7900 **F** (03) 5467 2306 **www.taltarni.com.au Open** 7 days 10–5
Winemaker Loic Le Calvez **Est.** 1972 **Cases** 80 000
After a hiatus of 2 years or so following the departure of long-serving winemaker and chief executive Dominique Portet, Taltarni gathered momentum and inspiration with a new wine-making team. Major changes in the approach to the vineyards; major upgrading of winery equipment and investment in new oak barrels; a long-term contract for the purchase of grapes from the Heathcote region; and the release of a flagship wine, Cephas, are the visible signs of the repositioning of the business. Exports to all major markets.

Cephas 2004 A full-bodied wine, stacked with black fruits; abundant tannins and structure. Shiraz (70%)/Cabernet Sauvignon (30%). Gold medal National Wine Show '06. Cork. 14° alc. **Rating** 93 **To** 2024 $49

Lalla Gully Sauvignon Blanc 2006 Clean, fresh, light-bodied flavours ranging through apple, passionfruit and gooseberry; finishes with fresh acidity. Screwcap. 13° alc. **Rating** 90 **To** 2009 $22

Pyrenees Shiraz 2003 Noticeably finer and more elegant, notwithstanding the drought, than some prior vintages; clear-cut black and red fruits; fine but persistent tannins and integrated oak. Cork. 14.5° alc. **Rating** 90 **To** 2018 $32

 Sauvignon Blanc 2006 Lively, lemony overtones to gentle gooseberry and passionfruit flavours; light- to medium-bodied, and needs a touch more intensity. Screwcap. 13° alc. **Rating** 89 **To** 2008 $20

T Series Shiraz 2005 Medium-bodied; plenty of blackberry and earth fruit; good tannin structure, controlled oak. Better value than many others in the range. Pyrenees/Heathcote. Screwcap. 14° alc. **Rating** 89 **To** 2012 $15.95

Three Monks Fume Blanc 2006 Typically firm and relatively austere; has length; for those who prefer sauvignon blanc sotto voce, the oak likewise. Screwcap. 13° alc. **Rating** 88 **To** 2009 $21.95

T Series Sauvignon Blanc Semillon 2006 Doesn't have enough fruit aromas for a sauvignon blanc–dominant blend, but judged as if it were semillon-predominant, has length and development potential. An Irish tasting note, if you will. Screwcap. 13° alc. **Rating** 88 **To** 2012 $16

T Series Rose 2006 Has good balance and length; red fruits, good acidity and, above all else, not sweet. Shiraz/Cabernet Sauvignon saignee. Screwcap. 13° alc. **Rating** 88 **To** 2008 $15.95

T Series Sauvignon Blanc Semillon 2005 Light straw-green; plenty of flavour and attitude; an intermediate style, showing some bottle development, ready for immediate consumption. Screwcap. 13° alc. **Rating** 87 **To** 2008 $15.95

Lalla Gully Pinot Gris 2006 Water white; won't frighten the horses, more likely to tranquillise them; delicate in the extreme. Screwcap. 14° alc. **Rating** 87 **To** 2008 $24

Lalla Gully Pinot Noir 2005 Leaner and more spicy/slatey than most of the wines from the vintage in Tas, but does have length. 13° alc. **Rating** 87 **To** 2008 $28

Pyrenees Cabernet Sauvignon 2002 Quite developed, as one would expect; a light- to medium-bodied wine with elegant cedary/earthy/bottle-developed cabernet aromas; earthy/leathery notes are just too pronounced, needing more sweet fruit at the word go. Cork. 13.5° alc. **Rating** 87 **To** 2009 $32

Brut 2005 A nicely balanced wine; crisp fruit flavours with enough intensity to make one regret it didn't spend more time on lees before disgorgement. 13° alc. **Rating** 87 **To** 2010 $22

Tamar Ridge   ★★★★★

Auburn Road, Kayena, Tas 7270 **Region** Northern Tasmania
T (03) 6394 1111 **F** (03) 6394 1126 **www.**tamarridge.com.au **Open** 7 days 10–5
Winemaker Andrew Pirie, Tom Ravech, Matt Lowe **Est.** 1994 **Cases** 60 000
In 2003 Gunns Limited, a large, publicly listed Tasmanian forestry and agribusiness entity, purchased Tamar Ridge. With the retention of Dr Richard Smart as viticultural advisor, the largest expansion of Tasmanian plantings is now underway, with 137 ha of wines, 72.5 in bearing, in the vicinity of the winery. A further development at Coombend, on the east coast, is also underway. Dr Andrew Pirie became CEO and chief winemaker in 2005, adding further lustre to the brand. Tasting notes for lesser quality wines trimmed. Exports to the UK, the US and other major markets.

ⵟⵟⵟⵟⵟ **Chardonnay 2004** Classy barrel-ferment inputs to a complex wine built around stone fruit flavours; excellent line, length and balance. Top gold Tas Wine Show '06 and again in '07, still superbly complex. Screwcap. 13° alc. **Rating** 96 **To** 2011 $21

Reserve Pinot Noir 2005 Intense and focused, at the top end of the great Tasmanian vintage; all it needs is time to unfold its magic; long, penetrating red and black fruits. Screwcap. 14° alc. **Rating** 95 **To** 2018 $40

Pinot Noir 2005 Bright purple-red; smooth, supple and extremely elegant; perfect varietal expression, and great length. Gold medal Tas Wine Show '07. Screwcap. 14° alc. **Rating** 94 **To** 2013 $26.95

Limited Release Botrytis Riesling 2005 Bright green-yellow; a complex bouquet showing obvious botrytis influence, continuing unabated into the palate; has length and persistence. Screwcap. 9° alc. **Rating** 94 **To** 2020 $25

ⵟⵟⵟⵟⵎ **Chardonnay 2005** Clean, smooth and supple; stone fruit complexed by carefully targeted oak and mlf inputs; good length. Screwcap. 13° alc. **Rating** 91 **To** 2012 $24.95

Pinot Gris 2006 Has more interest than expected; a touch of lemon blossom as well as pear and quince; comment on the slightly hot finish is a trifle unfair. Screwcap. 14.5° alc. **Rating** 91 **To** 2009 $24.95

Devils Corner Pinot Noir 2005 Altogether charming; a light- to medium-bodied, pure pinot with delicate but intense varietal character flowing from start to finish. Screwcap. 14° alc. **Rating** 91 **To** 2012 $16.90

Riesling 2005 A light bouquet, with hints of spice and lanolin; unusual stone fruit flavours; then typical varietal crisp acidity on the finish. Contentious. **Rating** 90 **To** 2013

Gewurztraminer 2005 A compelling wine with good line, length and balance; citrus and spice flavours, and a lack of clear varietal character can't spoil the wine. Screwcap. 14.5° alc. **Rating** 90 **To** 2010 $19.95

Sauvignon Blanc 2006 Gentle passionfruit/gooseberry/tropical fruit; well-balanced, and good acidity. Screwcap. 13.5° alc. **Rating** 90 **To** 2008 $22

9 Degrees Riesling 2005 Still very shy, but has all the right ingredients, and good balance. All that is required is patience. Screwcap. 9° alc. **Rating** 89 **To** 2012 $16.90

Devils Corner Pinot Noir 2006 Savoury, with some slightly bitter notes on the finish, but does express the variety. Screwcap. 14° alc. **Rating** 87 **To** 2010 $16.95

Reserve Riesling 2005 The bouquet is quiet, but the palate expressive, even slightly raspy, with touches of apple. **Rating** 87 **To** 2012

Devils Corner Sauvignon Blanc 2003 A mix of tropical and passionfruit, with offsetting mineral notes. **Rating** 87 **To** 2008

Pinot Noir 2004 Attractive wine, albeit somewhat simple and direct; clean red pinot fruit flavours. **Rating** 87 **To** 2008

Tambo Estate ★★★★

96 Pages Road, Bumberrah, Vic 3902 **Region** Gippsland
T (03) 5156 4921 **F** (03) 5156 4291 **Open** W'ends by appt
Winemaker Bill Williams, David Coy **Est.** 1994 **Cases** NFP

Bill and Pam Williams returned to Australia in the early 1990s after 7 years overseas, and began the search for a property which met the specific requirements for high-quality table wines established by Dr John Gladstones in his masterwork *Viticulture and Environment*. They chose a property in the foothills of the Victorian Alps on the inland side of the Gippsland Lakes, with predominantly sheltered, north-facing slopes. They planted a little over 5 ha of chardonnay (the lion's share of the plantings with 3.44 ha), sauvignon blanc, pinot noir, cabernet sauvignon and a splash of merlot. Until 1999 the grapes were sold to other producers in the region, and part continues to be sold. They have been rewarded with high-quality Chardonnay and Pinot Noir.

Tamborine Estate Wines ★★☆

32 Hartley Road, North Tamborine, Qld 4272 **Region** Queensland Coastal
T (07) 5545 1711 **F** (07) 5545 3522 **www**.tamborineestate.com.au **Open** 7 days 10–4
Winemaker John Cassegrain **Est.** 1990 **Cases** 4000

Tamborine Estate is a joint venture between the well-known John Cassegrain (of Cassegrain Wines at Port Macquarie) and French-born entrepreneur Bernard Forey (owner of the large Richfield Vineyard at Tenterfield in northern NSW). They have acquired the former Mount Tamborine Winery and its 2.5 ha of merlot, cabernet franc and malbec, planted adjacent to the winery. Exports to Switzerland, Singapore and Thailand.

Tamburlaine ★★★★★

358 McDonalds Road, Pokolbin, NSW 2321 **Region** Lower Hunter Valley
T (02) 4998 7570 **F** (02) 4998 7763 **www**.mywinery.com **Open** 7 days 9.30–5
Winemaker Mark Davidson, Simon McMillan **Est.** 1966 **Cases** 70 000

A thriving business which, notwithstanding the fact that it has doubled its already substantial production in recent years, sells over 90% of its wine through the cellar door and by mailing list (with an active tasting club members' cellar program offering wines which are held and matured at Tamburlaine). The maturing of the estate-owned Orange vineyard has led to a dramatic rise in quality across the range. Both the Hunter Valley and Orange vineyards are now Australian Certified Organic. Exports to the US, Japan and China.

ᵀᵀᵀᵀᵀ **Members Reserve Orange Syrah 2005** Very deep purple-red; strong multi-layered flavours show the impact of alcohol on fruit density, yet the wine isn't hot nor does it show dead fruit character; blackberry, spice and prune, then balancing acidity. Screwcap. 15.8° alc. **Rating** 94 To 2025 $32

Reserve Orange Shiraz 2004 A complex wine, with good structure and depth; spicy, peppery notes to black fruits; good oak balance and integration. Screwcap. 14.7° alc. **Rating** 94 To 2018 $28

Reserve Orange Shiraz 2005 A powerful wine, with layers of dark fruits; excellent oak/extract/tannins, and well-handled oak. Screwcap. 15.8° alc. **Rating** 94 To 2020 $36

Members Orange Vineyard Cabernet Sauvignon 2004 A powerful, tightly focused medium to full-bodied palate, with good varietal expression; cassis, blackcurrant and spice fruit, with firm but balanced tannins. Screwcap. 14.9° alc. **Rating** 94 To 2025 $32

ᵀᵀᵀᵀᵀ **Members Reserve Hunter Valley Semillon 2006** Pale green-straw; plenty of flavour and mouthfeel, the grass and citrus flavours finishing crisp and long. Screwcap. 11.5° alc. **Rating** 93 To 2016 $26

Members Hunter Syrah 2004 Light- to medium red-purple; a fresh bouquet of red fruits, the palate belying the alcohol, quite silky and fresh. Screwcap. 14.7° alc. **Rating** 92 To 2014 $28

Members Reserve Orange Merlot 2004 Fragrant, spicy varietal aromas; an elegant but intense wine which carries its alcohol with seeming ease; cassis/berry fruit, fine tannins. Screwcap. 15.4° alc. **Rating** 92 To 2014 $28

Members Reserve Orange Cabernet Sauvignon 2005 Very ripe blackcurrant, prune and plum, with some dead fruit; seems to be part of a winemaking philosophy, but less might be better. Screwcap. 15.5° alc. **Rating** 91 To 2010 $32

Reserve Orange Riesling 2005 Floral herb, spice and blossom aromas; a firm, long palate, with elegance. Screwcap. 14° alc. **Rating** 90 To 2015 $26

Orange Marsanne 2004 Yellow-gold; good varietal character, and starting to show bottle development much in the same way as semillon. Screwcap. 15.1° alc. **Rating** 90 To 2011 $30

Reserve Orange Merlot 2005 Light- to medium-bodied; a savoury, spicy, earthy wine with a mix of gentle cassis and olive; varietal, though not to everyone's taste. Screwcap. 14.8° alc. **Rating** 90 To 2012 $32

Reserve Orange Malbec 2004 Attractive example of the variety; sweet but not jammy fruit; good texture and structure. Screwcap. 14.3° alc. **Rating** 90 To 2012 $30

ᵀᵀᵀᵀ **Members Reserve Hunter Valley Verdelho 2006** Good balance and length; citrussy acidity adds authority and interest to the normally bland fruit salad verdelho offering. Screwcap. 13.7° alc. **Rating** 89 To 2008 $26

Reserve Hunter Cabernet Merlot 2004 The hallmark elegance of Tamburlaine, which has its winemaking down pat; a savoury/earthy wine verging on outright austerity, but undeniably varietal. Screwcap. 13.4° alc. **Rating** 89 To 2012 $28

Reserve Orange Petit Verdot 2004 An exceptionally powerful and ripe wine, even in this climate, offering amazing blending opportunities in future vintages. Screwcap. 16.1° alc. **Rating** 89 To 2020 $30

Members Hunter Chambourcin 2004 Light- to medium-bodied; juicy, jammy red fruits, without much structure, but then that's almost always the case. Screwcap. 13.1° alc. **Rating** 87 To 2009 $28

Taminick Cellars   ★★★☆

339 Booth Road, Taminick via Glenrowan, Vic 3675 **Region** Glenrowan
T (03) 5766 2282 **www**.taminickcellars.com.au **Open** Mon–Sat 9–5, Sun 10–5
Winemaker Peter Booth, James Booth **Est.** 1904 **Cases** 4000

Peter Booth is a member of the fourth-generation of the family owners of the winery started when Esca Booth purchased the property in 1904. He makes massively flavoured and very long-lived red wines, most sold to long-term customers and through the cellar door.

ŶŶŶŶ **Premium Shiraz 2004** A big wine, with rich, ultra-ripe prune and confit black fruits, the tannins not over-extracted. The high alcohol and slightly resinous oak don't help. Cork. 15.2° alc. **Rating** 89 **To** 2014 $16

Centenary Port NV Rich, Northeast Vic version of tawny port; big-shouldered and quite complex, rape rather than seduction. Cork. 18.1° alc. **Rating** 89 **To** 2008 $55

Durif 2005 Deep colour; not as powerful as most, but that is no loss; nice black fruits with spicy touches. Cork. 15.8° alc. **Rating** 88 **To** 2012 $15

Alicante Rose 2006 Bright fuchsia-red; vibrant and lively, with fresh, tingling acidity; well-made. Cork. 12° alc. **Rating** 87 **To** 2008 $14

Cliff Booth Glenrowan Shiraz 2004 Masses of stuffing and flavour but a slightly disconcerting edge to the bouquet, then luscious confit fruit reflecting the alcohol. For heroes on a dark night. Cork. 15.7° alc. **Rating** 87 **To** 2008 $14

Tandou Wines

Nixon Road, Monash, SA 5342 **Region** Riverland
T (08) 8583 6500 **F** (08) 8583 6599 www.tandou.com.au **Open** Mon–Fri 10–4
Winemaker Stuart Auld, John Lempens **Est.** 2001 **Cases** 30 000
Tandou is a subsidiary of a diversified public company which has 17 000 ha of land 142 km southeast of Broken Hill and 50 km from Mildura. At its Millewa vineyard, 450 ha of vines have been planted to chardonnay, verdelho, cabernet sauvignon, merlot, shiraz and sangiovese. A winery with a 21 000-tonne capacity has been built, and produces a range of wine sold in bulk, as cleanskin bottles and under the proprietary Broken Earth and Wontanella brands (the latter is a cheaper, second label). Purchased by Champagne Indage in May 2007.

Tanglewood Estate

Bulldog Creek Road, Merricks North, Vic 3926 **Region** Mornington Peninsula
T (03) 5974 3325 **F** (03) 5974 4170 www.tanglewoodestate.com.au **Open** Sun–Mon 12–5
Winemaker Ken Bilham, Wendy Bilham **Est.** 1984 **Cases** 400
One of the smaller and lower-profile wineries on the Mornington Peninsula, with Ken Bilham quietly doing his own thing on 2 ha of estate plantings. Lunch and dinner are available by arrangement.

ŶŶŶŶŶ **Chardonnay 2005** Light- to medium-bodied; gentle melon and stone fruit; good balance, though lower acidity than many Mornington Peninsula wines. Cork. 12.5° alc. **Rating** 90 **To** 2012

ŶŶŶŶ **Reserve Cabernet Shiraz 2004** Medium-bodied; distinctly earthy/spicy notes partly from oak, but surprisingly no green characters given the low alcohol. Cork. 12.8° alc. **Rating** 89 **To** 2015 $29

Tanjil Wines

1171 Moe Road, Willow Grove, Vic 3825 (postal) **Region** Gippsland
T (03) 9773 0378 **F** (03) 9773 0378 www.tanjilwines.com **Open** Not
Winemaker Robert Hewet, Olga Garot **Est.** 2001 **Cases** 1000
Robert Hewet and Olga Garot planted 4 ha of pinot noir and pinot grigio on a north-facing slope at an altitude of 200 m between the Latrobe and Tanjil valleys. The cool climate allows the vines to grow without irrigation, yields are kept low and the wines are made onsite using traditional methods and minimal intervention. The prices do not reflect the quality of the wines.

ŶŶŶŶŶ **Gippsland Pinot Noir 2006** A very pure, elegant and well-balanced wine, needing just a fraction more complexity. Screwcap. 13.8° alc. **Rating** 91 **To** 2013 $15

Gippsland Pinot Noir 2005 Generous sweet plum and black cherry fruit; smooth and supple; combines complexity and finesse, although charry oak is a little obvious. Screwcap. 13.2° alc. **Rating** 91 **To** 2009 $15

Pinot Gris 2006 Very fragrant; a totally superior pinot gris, with real flavour, character and attitude; lime juice, pear, apple and melon; good length. **Rating** 90 **To** 2010 $18

Tapanappa ★★★★★

PO Box 174, Crafers, SA 5152 **Region** Wrattonbully

T 0418 818 223 **F** (08) 8370 8374 **www.**tapanappawines.com.au **Open** Not

Winemaker Brian Croser **Est.** 2002 **Cases** 2000

The Tapanappa partners are Brian Croser (formerly of Petaluma), Jean-Michel Cazes of Chateau Lynch-Bages in Pauillac and Societe Jacques Bollinger, the parent company of Champagne Bollinger. Presently the partnership is restricted to 2 vineyard sites in Australia, the 8-ha Whalebone Vineyard at Wrattonbully (planted to cabernet sauvignon, shiraz and merlot 30 years ago) and the 3 ha of Tiers Vineyard (chardonnay) at Piccadilly in the Adelaide Hills (the remainder of the Tiers Vineyard chardonnay continues to be sold to Petaluma). Exports to the UK, the US and other major markets.

ɥɥɥɥɥ **Tiers Vineyard Chardonnay 2005** Pale straw-green; a study in reserved composition, all the elements of melon, fig, nectarine, oak and mlf so seamlessly interwoven they are all but invisible on a one-by-one basis; less is more. Cork. 13.5° alc. **Rating** 96 **To** 2012 $79.95

Tapestry ★★★★★

Olivers Road, McLaren Vale, SA 5171 **Region** McLaren Vale

T (08) 8323 9196 **F** (08) 8323 9746 **www.**tapestrywines.com.au **Open** 7 days 11–5

Winemaker Jon Ketley **Est.** 1971 **Cases** 15 000

After a relatively brief period of ownership by Brian Light, the former Merrivale Winery was acquired in 1997 by the Gerard family, previously owners of Chapel Hill. It has 40 ha of 30-year-old vineyards, 6.5 ha in McLaren Vale and 33.5 ha in Bakers Gully. Less than half the grapes are used for the Tapestry label. Exports to the UK, the US, Canada, Singapore, Hong Kong and NZ.

ɥɥɥɥɥ **The Vincent Shiraz 2004** The colour is already fractionally more developed thanks to the cork; an extremely luscious and concentrated version of the varietal wine, with more fruit, more chocolate, more depth and more alcohol – the latter a guess, for it is nowhere specified on either front or back label. 14.5° alc. **Rating** 94 **To** 2029 $45

McLaren Vale Shiraz 2004 Mocha, chocolate and black fruit aromas; medium-bodied, with excellent texture and structure; fine, ripe tannins woven through the fruit flavours promised by the bouquet. Screwcap. 14.5° alc. **Rating** 94 **To** 2024 $25

Fifteen Barrels Cabernet Sauvignon 2004 Fragrant, berry-driven aromas, but with oak in attendance; a fine, silky medium-bodied palate with cassis, blackcurrant and fine tannins; long finish. Cork. 14° alc. **Rating** 94 **To** 2020 $45

ɥɥɥɥɥ **Bakers Gully McLaren Vale Shiraz 2005** Typical of the best of McLaren Vale; a mix of black fruits, bitter chocolate and fine tannins; good length, great value. Cork. 14.5° alc. **Rating** 93 **To** 2015 $15

McLaren Vale Shiraz Viognier 2005 Strong purple-red; the aromatic, tangy contribution of viognier is immediately evident; medium-bodied, with supple fruit, and soft, fine tannins. Screwcap. 14.5° alc. **Rating** 92 **To** 2015 $25

McLaren Vale Cabernet Sauvignon 2004 Strong colour; powerful, more earthy, chocolatey blackberry fruit aromas, then a rich palate with lots of blackcurrant fruit and relatively gentle tannins. Cork. 14.5° alc. **Rating** 91 **To** 2017 $25

ŸŸŸŸ   **McLaren Vale Sauvignon Blanc 2006** No frills, but ample varietal fruit on both bouquet and palate; better still, not sweet. Screwcap. 11.5° alc. **Rating** 88 To 2008 $18

McLaren Vale Chardonnay 2005 The oak stands as a surly guard over the stone fruit and citrus, investing the wine with a slightly hard finish. Screwcap. 14° alc. **Rating** 88 To 2012 $18

Adelaide Hills Viognier 2006 Has some freshness and drive, largely courtesy of citrussy acidity surrounding the peach and apricot fruit; clean finish. Screwcap. 13° alc. **Rating** 88 To 2009 $18

Tarrawarra Estate ★★★★★

Healesville Road, Yarra Glen, Vic 3775 **Region** Yarra Valley
T (03) 5962 3311 **F** (03) 5962 3887 **www**.tarrawarra.com.au **Open** 7 days 11–5
Winemaker Clare Halloran, Bruce Walker **Est.** 1983 **Cases** 18 000

Clare Halloran has lightened the Tarrawarra style, investing it with more grace and finesse, but without losing complexity or longevity. The opening of the large art gallery (and its attendant café/restaurant) in early 2004 added another dimension to the tourism tapestry of the Yarra Valley. The gallery is open Wed–Sun, and as the *Michelin Guide* says, it is definitely worth a detour. Tin Cows is the second label, with most of the grapes for the Chardonnay and Pinot Noir estate-grown. The ratings for the Tin Cows range speak for themselves. Exports to the UK, the US, Canada, France, Denmark, Slovakia, Hong Kong, Malaysia and Singapore.

ŸŸŸŸŸ   **Reserve Chardonnay 2005** Elegant and refined, but with no shortage of flavour; nectarine, melon and oak are seamlessly woven together; great line and length. Screwcap. 13.5° alc. **Rating** 96 To 2017 $50

Yarra Valley Pinot Noir 2004 A complex, powerful wine in flavour, textural and structural terms; dark fruits; forest will develop, although the cork throws in an element of uncertainty. 13.8° alc. **Rating** 94 To 2012 $50

ŸŸŸŸŸ   **Tin Cows Chardonnay 2005** A pure wine; a lighter version of the Reserve, with melon and citrus in distinctive regional parameters, the length of palate being its major strength. Great value. Screwcap. 13.8° alc. **Rating** 93 To 2011 $22

Tin Cows Shiraz 2004 Fresh, spicy and vibrant black fruits are supported by supple tannins; a really enjoyable wine. Screwcap. 14.3° alc. **Rating** 92 To 2019 $22

ŸŸŸŸ   **John Olson Pinot Noir Rose 2006** Has good structure and length; spicy, small red fruits, and a long, dry finish. Screwcap. 13° alc. **Rating** 89 To 2008 $17

Tin Cows Merlot 2005 Incisive varietal character, with olive and bramble surrounded by light- to medium-bodied red fruits, tannins tying the bundle together. Screwcap. 14° alc. **Rating** 89 To 2012 $22

Tin Cows Pinot Noir 2005 Light-bodied, fresh and spicy red cherry and plum fruit; gentle tannins; for immediate consumption. Screwcap. 13.8° alc. **Rating** 88 To 2008 $22

Tarrington Vineyards ★★★★★

Hamilton Highway, Tarrington, Vic 3301 **Region** Henty
T (03) 5572 4509 **F** (03) 5572 4509 **www**.tarrington.com.au **Open** By appt
Winemaker Tamara Irish, Dianne Nagorcka **Est.** 1993 **Cases** 400

The grapegrowing and winemaking practices of Burgundy permeate every aspect of Tarrington Vineyards. While its establishment began in 1993, there has been no hurry to bring the vineyard into production. Two varieties only have been planted: pinot noir and chardonnay, with a planting density varying between 3333 and 8170 vines per ha. There are no less than 9 clones in the 2 ha of pinot noir, and 4 clones in the 0.5 ha of chardonnay. The approach to making the Pinot Noir is common in Burgundy, while the unoaked Chardonnay is kept in tank on fine lees for 9 months, the traditional method of making Chablis. Everything about the operation speaks of a labour of love, with a high standard of packaging and presentation of all background material. The exemplary wines are to be found on a thoroughly impressive collection of Vic's top restaurant wine lists. Miniscule exports to the UK.

❦❦❦❦❦ **Artemisia Shiraz 2005** Great colour; distinct Cote Rotie overtones to the blackberry fruit, which has eaten up the year the wine spent in new Francois Freres oak. Long finish. Cork. 13.7° alc. **Rating** 95 **To** 2015 $37

Tassell Park Wines   ★★★★☆
Treeton Road, Cowaramup, WA 6284 **Region** Margaret River
T (08) 9755 5440 **F** (08) 9755 5442 www.tassellparkwines.com **Open** 7 days 10.30–5
Winemaker Peter Stanlake (Consultant) **Est.** 2001 **Cases** 3000
One of the light brigade of newcomers to the Margaret River region. Ian and Tricia Tassell have 7 ha of sauvignon blanc, chenin blanc, semillon, cabernet sauvignon, merlot, shiraz and petit verdot. Their white wines have proved so successful that some of the red varieties are being grafted over to white varieties.

❦❦❦❦❧ **Margaret River Cabernet Sauvignon Merlot 2004** Bright colour; highly aromatic red fruits with flow through onto the cassis and blackcurrant flavours of the palate; fresh acidity to close. Screwcap. 14° alc. **Rating** 92 **To** 2015 $20
Margaret River Sauvignon Blanc Semillon 2006 Bright, lively, zesty surrounds to the tropical fruit; good length and focus; clever use of oak. Screwcap. **Rating** 91 **To** 2008 $20
Margaret River Cabernet Sauvignon 2004 Light but bright purple hue; light- to medium-bodied; fragrant cassis, raspberry and blackcurrant fruit; a slightly strange gold medal in the tough school of the Winewise Small Winemakers Competition '06. Screwcap. 14° alc. **Rating** 91 **To** 2016 $25
Margaret River Sauvignon Blanc 2006 A slightly reduced bouquet; abundant juicy tropical citrus flavours and a long finish; pity about the reduction. Screwcap. 11.5° alc. **Rating** 90 **To** 2008 $22

❦❦❦❦ **Margaret River Shiraz 2005** Light- to medium-bodied, with fresh cherry, raspberry and plum fruit flavours; nice fresh finish. Screwcap. 14.2° alc. **Rating** 89 **To** 2013 $23
Margaret River Chenin Blanc 2006 Has a lively touch of citrus along with more gentle fruit salad flavours, and doesn't rely on residual sugar. Screwcap. 12° alc. **Rating** 87 **To** 2008 $18

Tatachilla   ★★★★★
151 Main Road, McLaren Vale, SA 5171 **Region** McLaren Vale
T (08) 8323 8656 **F** (08) 8323 9096 www.tatachillawines.com.au **Open** Mon–Fri 12–5, Sat & public hols 11–5
Winemaker Fanchon Ferrandi **Est.** 1903 **Cases** 50 000
Tatachilla was reborn in 1995 but has had an at-times tumultuous history going back to 1903. Between 1903 and 1961 the winery was owned by Penfolds. It was closed in 1961 and reopened in 1965 as the Southern Vales Co-operative. In the late 1980s it was purchased and renamed The Vales but did not flourish; in 1993 it was purchased by local grower Vic Zerella and former Kaiser Stuhl chief executive Keith Smith. After extensive renovations, the winery was officially reopened in 1995 and won a number of tourist awards and accolades. It became part of Banksia Wines in 2001, in turn acquired by Lion Nathan in 2002. Exports to all major markets.

❦❦❦❦❦ **Keystone McLaren Vale Shiraz Viognier 2004** Deep purple-red; the viognier immediately announces its presence in a medium-bodied wine with a complex, rich and satisfying cascade of black fruits; good balance and finish. Screwcap. 14.5° alc. **Rating** 94 **To** 2015 $18
Foundation Shiraz 2002 Layer-upon-layer of cool-vintage McLaren Vale shiraz: blackberry, then dark chocolate, then more blackberry, and finally a thin slice of licorice and earth. Will be very long-lived. Cork. 14.5° alc. **Rating** 94 **To** 2022 $50

ŢŢŢŢ McLaren Vale Cabernet Sauvignon 2004 Medium- to full-bodied; rich and ripe, but not the least jammy or alcoholic; simply has the usual ladle of dark chocolate, then ripe tannins and balanced oak. Screwcap. 14.5° alc. **Rating** 91 To 2019 $23

ŢŢŢ Keystone McLaren Vale Grenache Shiraz 2004 Good line; light- to medium-bodied, with fresh juicy red grape flavours and fine tannins in support; minimal oak, but a long finish. Screwcap. 14.5° alc. **Rating** 89 To 2010 $18
Keystone McLaren Vale Cabernet Sangiovese 2004 Red-purple; a medium-bodied blend which works very well, even if cabernet sauvignon does most of the talking, a wild, slightly tangy, edge from the sangiovese. Screwcap. 14.9° alc. **Rating** 89 To 2013 $18
Clarendon Vineyard Merlot 2001 Savoury, earthy fruit, the back label explaining 'a long silky finish is defined by grippy oak tannin'. Hmm. Cork. 13.5° alc. **Rating** 88 To 2008 $45

Tatler Wines ★★★★★

477 Lovedale Road, Lovedale, NSW 2321 **Region** Lower Hunter Valley
T (02) 4930 9139 **F** (02) 4930 9145 **www**.tatlerwines.com **Open** 7 days 9.30–5.30
Winemaker Monarch Winemaking Services, Ross Pearson, Alasdair Sutherland, Jenny Bright (Contract) **Est.** 1998 **Cases** 2500
Tatler Wines is a family-owned company headed by Sydney hoteliers Theo and Spiro Isak (Isakidis). The name comes from the Tatler Hotel on George Street, Sydney, which was purchased by James (Dimitri) Isak from the late Archie Brown, whose son Tony is general manager of the wine business. Together with wife Deborah (whom he met at the Tatler Hotel many years ago) he now runs the vineyard, cellar door, café and accommodation. The 40-ha property has 13 ha of shiraz, semillon and chardonnay.

ŢŢŢŢŢ Nigel's Hunter Valley Semillon 2006 Wild herbs and grass aromas; a lively, multifaceted palate, introducing touches of sweet citrus and orange peel; very good finish. Screwcap. 10° alc. **Rating** 94 To 2017 $20
Dimitri's Paddock Chardonnay 2005 A very elegant, well-made wine; attractive nectarine and citrus fruit; quality oak is well integrated and balanced. Screwcap. 13.5° alc. **Rating** 94 To 2012 $20
The Nonpariel Hunter Valley Shiraz 2005 Medium red-purple; an elegant, medium-bodied wine, with fine black fruits, earth and silky but persistent tannins; a great expression of Hunter shiraz. Screwcap. 13.6° alc. **Rating** 94 To 2020 $40

ŢŢŢŢŢ The Sticky 2006 Green-yellow; fresh, clean and lively, with good length and acidity. Screwcap. 10° alc. **Rating** 93 To 2010 $22
Over the Ditch Hunter Valley Marlborough Semillon Sauvignon Blanc 2006 A cleverly conceived and executed blend; interesting how the semillon imposes its will (via structure) on Marlborough sauvignon blanc, though the latter undoubtedly adds to flavour. Screwcap. 11.3° alc. **Rating** 92 To 2010 $24

ŢŢŢŢ Archie's Paddock Shiraz 2004 Clear, bright red-purple; light- to medium-bodied with fresh, red and black fruits in an unforced style; fair length and balanced oak. Screwcap. 13.1° alc. **Rating** 89 To 2012 $22
McLaren Vale Shiraz 2005 A chameleon, at one moment generous and flowing, the next with a slightly smoky/vegetal character, possibly from oak, possibly something else. Screwcap. 14° alc. **Rating** 88 To 2015 $20

Tawonga Vineyard ★★★

2 Drummond Street, Tawonga, Vic 3697 **Region** Alpine Valleys
T (03) 5754 4945 **F** (03) 5754 4925 **www**.tawongavineyard.com **Open** By appt
Winemaker John Adams **Est.** 1994 **Cases** 500

Diz and John Adams' vineyard is at the head of the Kiewa Valley, looking out the mountains of the area. It is on a northeast slope with a mixture of deep, red loam/clay and shallow red loam over ancient river stone soils, at an altitude of 1200 ft. Over the years, the Shiraz has won many wine show medals, not surprising given the extensive Flying Winemaker experience of John Adams; he has spent 10 weeks in each of the last 4 years as a consultant senior winemaker in France, overseeing the production of wines for the UK market.

Taylors ★★★★★

Taylors Road, Auburn, SA 5451 **Region** Clare Valley
T (08) 8849 1111 **F** (08) 8849 1199 **www**.taylorswines.com.au **Open** Mon–Fri 9–5, Sat & public hols 10–5, Sun 10–4
Winemaker Adam Eggins, Helen McCarthy **Est.** 1969 **Cases** 580 000
The family-founded and owned Taylors continues to flourish and expand, its vineyards now total over 500 ha, by far the largest holding in Clare Valley. There have also been substantial changes both in terms of the winemaking team and in terms of the wine style and quality, particularly through the outstanding St Andrews range. With each passing vintage, Taylors is managing to do the same for the Clare Valley as Peter Lehmann is doing for the Barossa Valley. Exports (under the Wakefield brand due to trademark reasons) to all major markets.

🍷🍷🍷🍷🍷 **St Andrews Clare Valley Riesling 2001** Glowing yellow-green; a complex bouquet and palate; has built layers of richness, with citrus peel and touches of petrol; very good length. Vividly demonstrates wines do develop normally under screwcap. Screwcap. 13° alc. **Rating** 95 **To** 2014 $35
St Andrews Cabernet Sauvignon 2002 A pure expression of Clare cabernet sauvignon, variety and terroir twinned from birth. Dark fruits, cedar/cigar box, and long tannins; great balance and length. Screwcap. 14.5° alc. **Rating** 95 **To** 2022 $60
St Andrews Clare Valley Riesling 2002 Glowing yellow-green; has fine restraint to the mineral, spice and citrus flavours supported by perfect acidity; still only halfway to its optimum. Screwcap. 12.5° alc. **Rating** 94 **To** 2012 $35
St Andrews Clare Valley Shiraz 2002 Starting to enter the second phase of maturity; blackberry fruit and vanillin American oak coming together well, supported by ripe tannins; will stay on the plateau of its development for many years. Cork. 15° alc. **Rating** 94 **To** 2015 $60
Jaraman Clare Valley Coonawarra Cabernet Sauvignon 2004 Big, rich and ripe cassis and blackcurrant fruit solidly supported by integrated oak. Gold medal National Wine Show '06. Screwcap. 14.6° alc. **Rating** 94 **To** 2019 $29

🍷🍷🍷🍷🍷 **Jaraman Clare Valley Eden Valley Riesling 2005** Classic restraint, still in first gear; firm mineral/spice/apple/lime/lemon flavours. Screwcap. 13° alc. **Rating** 93 **To** 2020 $25
Clare Valley Riesling 2006 Delicacy and purity mark both the bouquet and entry to the palate; citrus and apple feature on the long finish with more power than expected from the bouquet. Screwcap. 13° alc. **Rating** 92 **To** 2013 $17
Jaraman Clare Valley McLaren Vale Shiraz 2004 A potent and powerful union of 2 forces of approximately equal strength; masses of black fruits, a twist of chocolate and pleasing acidity on the finish. Screwcap. 14.5° alc. **Rating** 92 **To** 2024 $30
Clare Valley Shiraz 2005 Far more fruit richness and weight than normally encountered at this price and volume (discounting is almost inevitable); abundant round, supple blackberry fruits and a hint of oak. Screwcap. 14.5° alc. **Rating** 91 **To** 2020 $17
Clare Valley Riesling 2005 Light straw-green; mainstream Clare style, with a mix of citrus and mineral; good balance and length. Give it time. Screwcap. 13° alc. **Rating** 90 **To** 2015 $18
Clare Valley Cabernet Sauvignon 2004 Plenty of substance to the black fruits and ripe tannins; controlled oak, good length. Screwcap. 14.5° alc. **Rating** 90 **To** 2011 $18

ΨΨΨΨ **Adelaide Hills Sauvignon Blanc 2006** Slightly suppressed bouquet; flavours in a gentle, tropical fruit spectrum; good balance and finish. Screwcap. 13° alc. **Rating** 89 To 2008 $17

Jaraman Clare Valley Adelaide Hills Chardonnay 2004 Complex melon and stone fruit aromas and flavours; the Adelaide Hills component helps tighten focus and structure; subtle oak. Screwcap. 13.5° alc. **Rating** 89 To 2011 $25

St Andrews Chardonnay 2002 Glowing yellow-green; a powerful, developed wine, with plenty of flavour, but rather less finesse. Screwcap. 14.8° alc. **Rating** 89 To 2008 $35

Clare Valley Merlot 2005 Not for the first time, confounds terroir and climate by producing merlot with positive varietal character; the tannins are obvious, but are in balance. Screwcap. 14.5° alc. **Rating** 89 To 2014 $17

Clare Valley Cabernet Sauvignon 2005 Good depth and structure; sweet, but not jammy, cabernet varietal fruit; good tannins and balance. Screwcap. 14.5° alc. **Rating** 89 To 2013 $17

Promised Land White Cabernet 2006 Closer to red wine than rose colour; abundant cassis and red cherry fruit, likewise just within rose bounds; interesting wine. Screwcap. 12° alc. **Rating** 87 To 2008 $14

Promised Land Shiraz Cabernet 2004 A powerful wine given its price; a trace of reduction, though not critical; blackberry and earth flavours, controlled extract. Screwcap. 14.5° alc. **Rating** 87 To 2012 $14

Jaraman Clare Valley Coonawarra Cabernet Sauvignon 2003 Relatively light colour; minty/leafy/savoury flavours; hasn't aged convincingly notwithstanding its gold medal at the Melbourne Wine Show '05. Screwcap. 14.5° alc. **Rating** 87 To 2008 $30

Te-aro Estate

Lot 501 Fromm Square Road, Williamstown, SA 5351 **Region** Barossa Valley
T (08) 8524 6116 **F** (08) 8524 7289 **www**.te-aroestate.com **Open** By appt
Winemaker Rod Chapman, Mark Jamieson **Est.** 1919 **Cases** 2000
Te-aro Estate has been in the Fromm family since 1895, when Carl Hermann Fromm purchased the land and married Elizabeth Minnie Kappler. In 1919, with the aid of a crowbar, they planted 2 ha of Madeira clone semillon and a shiraz block of 1.2 ha, both of which remain in production to this day. Te-aro is not a Maori name, nor are the Fromms related to the Marlborough (NZ) Fromm family. It is a latin-derived phrase meaning 'to plough'. With a second family-developed property now also owned by Te-aro Estate, the Fromms' main occupation is grape production for others from the 56 ha of estate vines, some of which are dry-grown. Exports to the UK, the US, Singapore and Japan.

ΨΨΨΨΨ **Two Charlies Barossa Valley GSM 2004** Highly aromatic but more focused than the '05, the structure firmer without sacrificing fruit; excellent length, carrying the alcohol with ease. A top example of the style. Grenache (45%)/ Shiraz (40%, 1919 plantings)/Mourvedre (15%). Screwcap. 15° alc. **Rating** 94 To 2015 $22

ΨΨΨΨΨ **Harold's Creek Barossa Valley Shiraz 2005** Fresh; no aldehydic characters; plum, blackberry and cherry fruit; medium-bodied, with fine tannins. Screwcap. 15° alc. **Rating** 92 To 2018 $20

Two Charlies Barossa Valley GSM 2005 An aromatic spice, herb and pine needle bouquet; lively, bright and fresh, quite distinct from the usual run of Barossa blends such as this; a synergistic blend, the structure from the shiraz. Grenache (45%)/Shiraz (40%, 1919 plantings)/Mourvedre (15%). Screwcap. 15° alc. **Rating** 92 To 2013 $22

Crocket's Block Dry Grown Barossa Valley Cabernet Sauvignon 2005 Strong purple hue; scented red and black fruits, the palate slightly more austere than the bouquet suggests, with fine but persistent tannins. Patience will be rewarded. Screwcap. 14.5° alc. **Rating** 91 To 2025 $27

ϓϓϓϓ **Crocket's Block Barossa Valley Grenache 2004** Light red, with just a tinge of purple; clear varietal character in Barossa mould, but juicy berry rather than confection, notwithstanding the alcohol. Enjoyable early drinking. Screwcap. 15.5° alc. **Rating** 89 **To** 2008 $25
Harold's Creek Barossa Valley Shiraz 2004 Attractive fruit marred by a touch of aldehyde; fine plum and blackberry underneath; a pity. Vines planted 1919. Screwcap. 15° alc. **Rating** 88 **To** 2013 $20
Saddleback Barossa Valley Merlot 2005 A clean, aromatic red fruit bouquet; more savoury olive varietal character on the palate, then a fairly tart finish. Screwcap. 15° alc. **Rating** 88 **To** 2011 $18
1919 Old Vine Barossa Valley Botrytis Semillon 2005 A low level of botrytis infection, with sweet banana/tropical flavours; neither fish nor fowl. Screwcap. 11.5° alc. **Rating** 87 **To** 2010 $23

Temple Bruer

Milang Road, Strathalbyn, SA 5255 **Region** Langhorne Creek
T (08) 8537 0203 **www.templebruer.com.au Open** Mon–Fri 9.30–4.30
Winemaker David Bruer, Vanessa Altmann **Est.** 1980 **Cases** 10 000
Always known for its eclectic range of wines, Temple Bruer (which also carries on a substantial business as a vine propagation nursery) has seen a sharp lift in wine quality. Clean, modern redesigned labels add to the appeal of a stimulatingly different range of red wines. Part of the production from the 19.2 ha of estate vineyards is sold to others, the remainder made under the Temple Bruer label. The vineyard is now certified organic and organic wines are an increasingly important part of the business. Exports to the US and Japan.

ϓϓϓϓϓ **Langhorne Creek Grenache Shiraz Viognier 2004** Fragrant, fresh and lively, juicy rather than jammy, literally dancing in the mouth; a lovely summer red. Screwcap. 14° alc. **Rating** 93 **To** 2008 $17
Reserve Merlot 2001 Very good colour for age; sweet red berry fruits on entry, then more spicy, savoury varietal nuances emerge; French oak makes a positive contribution. Cork. 13.3° alc. **Rating** 90 **To** 2010 $25

ϓϓϓϓ **Organically Grown Langhorne Creek Riesling 2005** Straw-green; good varietal aroma and flavour, with gentle tropical fruit; just a little heavy. Screwcap. 12.1° alc. **Rating** 89 **To** 2010 $15
Preservative Free Organic Langhorne Creek Cabernet Merlot 2006 Medium purple-red; firm, very youthful (not unexpected) red and black fruits; good acidity and presumably no oak. Screwcap a fine closure for preservative-free wines. Screwcap. 13.5° alc. **Rating** 87 **To** 2008 $17

Tempus Two Wines

Broke Road, Pokolbin, NSW 2321 **Region** Lower Hunter Valley
T (02) 4993 3999 **F** (02) 4993 3988 **www.tempustwo.com.au Open** 7 days 9–5
Winemaker Sarah-Kate Dineen **Est.** 1997 **Cases** 50 000
Tempus Two is the name for what was once Hermitage Road Wines. It is a mix of Latin (Tempus means time) and English; the change was forced on the winery by the EU Wine Agreement and the prohibition of the use of the word 'hermitage' on Australian wine labels. Occupies a controversial new winery on Broke Road (I like it). Exports to the UK.

ϓϓϓϓ **Copper Moscato 2006** An interesting version of Italian moscato; fresh and lively fruits with crisp acidity balancing the sweetness. At this level of alcohol you get 2 glasses for 1. Crown seal. 7° alc. **Rating** 88 **To** 2008 $20

Ten Minutes by Tractor Wine Co

1333 Mornington-Flinders Road, Main Ridge, Vic 3928 **Region** Mornington Peninsula
T (03) 5989 6455 **F** (03) 5989 6433 **www.tenminutesbytractor.com.au Open** 7 days 11–5
Winemaker Richard McIntyre, Alex White (Contract) **Est.** 1999 **Cases** 5200

Ten Minutes by Tractor was sold to Martin Spedding in early 2004, but the same 3 families (Judd, McCutcheon and Wallis), with their vineyards 10 mins by tractor from each other, continue to supply the fruit, and the contract winemaking continues. There are now 3 wine ranges: Individual Vineyard at the top; Reserve in the middle; and 10X, with its striking label graphics, the base range. There are strong elements of The Da Vinci Code in the new labels for the Reserve and Individual Vineyard, but I suppose a $65 bottle of Pinot is not an impulse buy. There are few underpriced wines on the Peninsula, and certainly none here. Exports to the UK, Hong Kong and Singapore.

ΨΨΨΨΨ **Mornington Peninsula Chardonnay 2005** Super-fine Chablis-like restraint; nectarine, citrus and mineral, with oak a mere bystander. Screwcap. 13.8° alc. **Rating** 95 **To** 2015 $47

10X Mornington Peninsula Chardonnay 2005 Has matured beautifully in bottle; complete and balanced; nectarine and melon with touches of fig and cream. Screwcap. 13.5° alc. **Rating** 94 **To** 2012 $30

Mornington Peninsula Pinot Noir 2005 Very good hue, slightly deeper than the other pinots; a powerful wine, with lots of texture and structure to the intense fruit; needs time to settle down. Screwcap. 13.5° alc. **Rating** 94 **To** 2011 $58

McCutcheon Vineyard Pinot Noir 2005 Bright, brilliant red-purple; delicate, perfumed and elegant, radically different to the Mornington Peninsula, with Burgundian finesse. I wonder what a blend of the 2 would have been like. Screwcap. 13.5° alc. **Rating** 94 **To** 2011 $65

ΨΨΨΨΨ **10X Mornington Peninsula Pinot Noir 2005** Very good purple-red hue; fragrant, spicy, stemmy notes intermingle with small red fruits; good length. Screwcap. 13.5° alc. **Rating** 93 **To** 2012 $34

10X Mornington Peninsula Sauvignon Blanc 2006 Quite delicate, but has excellent length and balance; passionfruit and kiwifruit, with a fresh finish. Screwcap. 12.5° alc. **Rating** 92 **To** 2008 $23

10X Mornington Peninsula Rose 2006 Fresh, lively, flowery strawberry; needed just a little jab more of fruit from the vineyard, but well-made. Pinot Noir ex McCutcheon Vineyard. Screwcap. 13.8° alc. **Rating** 90 **To** 2008 $20

ΨΨΨΨ **10X Mornington Peninsula Pinot Gris 2006** A well-made but largely featureless wine except for acidity on the finish. This is what you get with pinot gris. Don't expect me to buy it at this price (or any other). Screwcap. 14° alc. **Rating** 87 **To** 2008 $30

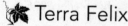

Terra Felix   ★★★★

PO Box 2029, Wattletree Road, Malvern East, Vic 3134 **Region** Upper Goulburn
T (03) 9509 1662 **www.**terrafelix.com.au **Open** Not
Winemaker Trina Smith **Est.** 1985 **Cases** 15 000

Terra Felix was for many years a brand of Tallarook Wines, jointly owned by the Riebl family and by Peter Simon, Stan Olszewski and John Nicholson. In 2005 it was decided to separate the businesses, with Luis Riebl now solely concerned with the production of the Tallarook wines. Peter Simon and Stan Olszewski had run the Stanley Wine Company in Clare over 20 years ago, leaving it in the early '80s, but always harbouring a desire to be involved in the industry as owners. They have worked hard to establish export markets as well as on-premise distribution in Australia, with one-third of the 15 000 case production exported to the UK, Holland and the US. Grapes continue to be sourced from Tallarook, and also supplemented by other local growers.

ΨΨΨΨΨ **Shiraz Viognier 2005** A highly fragrant bouquet with viognier inputs obvious; plenty of grunt to the palate, particularly on the grainy tannin finish. Screwcap. 14.3° alc. **Rating** 92 **To** 2015 $15

ΨΨΨΨ **Marsanne Roussanne 2005** A complex texture and rich mouthfeel; dried fruit aromas and flavours, with just enough acidity to cleanse the finish. Truly original. Wild yeast, lees contact, no oak and reserve wine (older than '05) added as with sparkling wine (quite legal as long as no more than 15% by volume). Screwcap. 13.6° alc. **Rating** 88 **To** 2009 $15

Chardonnay 2006 Light-bodied; gentle melon and stone fruit with a touch of citrus; subliminal oak influence; nicely put together. Screwcap. 13.3° alc. **Rating** 87 To 2009 $15

Chardonnay 2005 Smooth nectarine and peach fruit; supple mouthfeel and good length; minimal, if any, oak. Screwcap. 13.6° alc. **Rating** 87 To 2008 $13

Terrace Vale

Deasys Road, Pokolbin, NSW 2321 **Region** Lower Hunter Valley
T (02) 4998 7517 **F** (02) 4998 7814 **www.terracevale.com.au Open** 7 days 10–4
Winemaker Alain Leprince **Est.** 1971 **Cases** 14 000
In 2001, the Batchelor family (headed by former AMP chief executive Paul Batchelor) acquired Terrace Vale. In late 2004 Terrace Vale (and its various second labels and brands) was merged with Cheviot Bridge/The Long Flat Wine Co, of which Paul Batchelor is now non-executive chairman. Marketing in Australia and overseas is being undertaken by Cheviot Bridge.

La Vie Pinot Noir Chardonnay NV More elegance than expected; long palate, with pleasing citrus and melon fruit flavours. 12.5° alc. **Rating** 87 To 2008

Tertini Wines

PO Box 445, Chester Hill, NSW 2162 **Region** Southern Highlands
T 0419 220 435 **F** (02) 4878 5162 **www.tertiniwines.com.au Open** Not
Winemaker Nick Spencer **Est.** 2000 **Cases** 3000
When Julian Tertini began the development of Tertini Wines in 2000, he followed in the footsteps of Joseph Vogt 145 years earlier. History does not relate the degree of success that Joseph Vogt had, but the site he chose then was, as it is now, a good one. Tertini has 1.8 ha each of riesling and pinot noir, 1 ha each of arneis, chardonnay and cabernet sauvignon, and 0.6 ha of merlot and 0.2 ha of lagrein. It is early days, but the indications are that the earlier ripening varieties – notably riesling – will be most suited. That said, the 1855 Cabernet Sauvignon suggests that, with mature vines, and a bit of help from climate change, anything may be possible.

Tertini & Knight Private Cellar Collection Arneis 2006 A distinct almond and pear bouquet; a well-handled touch of (partial) barrel fermentation; peach, ripe apple, almond and just a twist of oak drive the palate; no sweetness issues; a really interesting, high-quality wine. Screwcap. **Rating** 93 To 2009 $25

T Riesling 2005 A clean but shy bouquet; an elegant palate, like the bouquet, spotlessly clean, but reluctant to release its flavours of apple, pear and citrus; good length and balance. Screwcap. 11° alc. **Rating** 91 To 2010 $19.95

Eighteen 55 Arneis 2006 Clean and well-made; spiced apple, peach and stone fruit; sweetness on the finish a pity. Screwcap. 12.8° alc. **Rating** 87 To 2008 $20

Eighteen 55 Berrima Valley Cabernet Sauvignon 2005 Medium-bodied; gentle mint, leaf and blackcurrant fruit, finishing with soft tannins; has largely achieved ripeness in the context of the other wines, but the struggle hasn't been easy. Screwcap. 12.9° alc. **Rating** 87 To 2012 $21.95

Teusner

29 Jane Place, Tanunda, SA 5352 (postal) **Region** Barossa Valley
T (08) 8563 0898 **F** (08) 8563 0898 **www.teusner.com.au Open** Not
Winemaker Kym Teusner **Est.** 2001 **Cases** 10 000
Teusner is a partnership between former Torbreck winemaker Kym Teusner and brother-in-law Michael Page, and is typical of the new wave of winemakers determined to protect very old, low-yielding, dry-grown Barossa vines. The winery approach is based on lees ageing, little racking, no fining or filtration, and no new American oak. The reasonably priced wines are made either from 100% shiraz or from Southern Rhône blends. Limited exports to the US, Canada and the UK.

Albert 2004 A rich tapestry of black and red fruits, with colourful splashes of licorice and chocolate; very good length and balance. Shiraz. Cork. 14.5° alc. **Rating** 95 To 2019 $45

The Riefke Ebenezer Road Barossa Valley Shiraz 2005 Powerful and rich, but not the least jammy or overripe; ripples of black fruits supported by good tannins and oak. Fantastic value. Cork. 14.5° alc. **Rating** 94 **To** 2025 $19

ŶŶŶŶŶ **Joshua 2006** Light- to medium-bodied, but no confection sweetness, simply restraint and tannin balance on the dry, lingering finish. Grenache/Mataro/Shiraz. Cork. 14.5° alc. **Rating** 91 **To** 2011 $24

The Blok Estate

Riddoch Highway, Coonawarra, SA 5263 **Region** Coonawarra
T (08) 8737 2734 **F** (08) 8737 2994 **www**.blok.com.au **Open** 7 days 10–5
Winemaker Kopparossa Wines (Gavin Hogg) **Est.** 1999 **Cases** 2000
The Trotter family (Luke, Rebecca, Gary and Ann) purchased The Blok Estate in 2005, and have significantly increased production. The cellar door is in a renovated, old stone home surrounded by gardens.

The Carriages Vineyard ★★★

549 Kotta Road, Echuca, Vic 3564 **Region** Goulburn Valley
T (03) 5483 7767 **F** (03) 5483 7767 **Open** By appt
Winemaker Plunkett Wines (Sam Plunkett) **Est.** 1996 **Cases** 1000
David and Lyndall Johnson began the development of The Carriages in 1996, planting 2 ha of cabernet sauvignon, 1 ha of merlot and 0.5 ha each of chardonnay and semillon. The wines are made at Plunkett, where David Johnson was previously employed. The name and the extremely innovative packaging stems from 4 old railway carriages which the Johnsons have painstakingly rehabilitated, and now live in. Each bottle is identified with a cardboard rail ticket which is strikingly similar to the tickets of bygone years. The ticket manages to show the brand name, the vintage, the variety, the number of standard drinks, the alcohol and the bottle number (which is in fact the ticket number, or vice versa). The ticket is fixed to the label with fine twine, so it can be removed either as a memento or for further orders.

ŶŶŶŶ **Chardonnay 2006** Clean and well-made; gentle stone fruit on the mid-palate, with a touch of citrus enlivening the finish. Cork. 12.9° alc. **Rating** 88 **To** 2010 $15

 # The Colonial Estate   **NR**

PO Box 85, Nuriootpa, SA 5355 **Region** Barossa Valley
T (08) 8562 1244 **F** (08) 8562 1288 **www**.colonialwine.com.au **Open** Not
Winemaker Jonathan Maltus **Est.** 2002 **Cases** NA
The brand names of the wines produced by The Colonial Estate tell part of the story: Exile, Emigre, Exodus, Explorateur, Etranger, Envoy, Expatrie, Evangeliste and Enchanteur. It will come as no surprise, then, to find that this is a French-managed business with an extensive export program to many parts of the world including France and other European countries. Thoroughly European winemaking methods are used, most obviously being 2 sorting tables, one for the bunches before they pass through the destemmer, and other for individual berries after the destemming process. While there is no cellar door, the company runs an active membership program for direct sales.

The Cups Estate

269 Browns Road, Fingal, Vic 3939 **Region** Mornington Peninsula
T 1300 131 741 **F** (03) 9886 1254 **www**.thecupsestate.com **Open** 7 days 10–5
Winemaker Moorooduc Estate, Pfeiffer, Kilchurn Wines **Est.** 1999 **Cases** 2500
Joe Fisicaro has returned to his roots after a career as a financial executive, establishing The Cups Estate near Rye. The name comes from the rolling dune region of the Peninsula known as 'the cups country'; the soils are light, with relatively low fertility, but drainage is excellent. Wind and frost have been problems, and the composition of the 6.15-ha vineyard has been somewhat modified by a grafting program placing more emphasis on early ripening varieties. Exports to Japan.

ŶŶŶŶŶ **Raimondo Reserve Mornington Peninsula Pinot Noir 2005** Similar modest alcohol to the standard Pinot, but substantially richer; first-class structure, line and length; lovely cherry, plum and spice fruit. Diam. 13.5° alc. **Rating** 95 **To** 2013 $35
Mornington Peninsula Pinot Noir 2005 Excellent attack with intensity and line; slightly more savoury than the Raimondo Reserve, but is a high-class wine, as recognised by its gold medal at the Sydney Wine Show '07. Diam. 13.5° alc. **Rating** 94 **To** 2011 $25

ŶŶŶŶŶ **Mornington Peninsula Shiraz 2005** Abundant weight and texture to the black cherry, blackberry, licorice and pepper flavours of the palate; good tannins. Cork. 13.5° alc. **Rating** 91 **To** 2015 $25

ŶŶŶŶ **Mornington Peninsula Blanc de Noir 2005** A lively wine; like a fresh rose with a spray of mist; does have considerable pinot noir fruit length; pleasant surprise. 13.5° alc. **Rating** 88 **To** 2011 $25
Mornington Peninsula Pinot Port 2006 Has achieved the impossible, partly because of the perfect fortifying spirit. Even for Australians, it's hard to imagine pinot noir from a single producer spanning everything from sparkling wine to port, and I'm not too sure that it's not a case of the dog preaching. Cork. 18.5° alc. **Rating** 88 **To** 2012 $20

The Deanery Vineyards ★★★☆

PO Box 1172, Balhannah, SA 5242 **Region** Adelaide Hills
T (08) 8390 1948 **F** (08) 8390 0321 **Open** Not
Winemaker Duncan Dean, Phil Christiansen, Petaluma **Est.** 1995 **Cases** 500
The Dean family – Pat and Henry, and sons Duncan, Nick and Alan – purchased a 30-ha dairy farm at Balhannah in late 1994, and planted 6.5 ha of chardonnay, sauvignon blanc and semillon in the spring of 1995, subsequently adding 0.67 ha of shiraz. Pinot noir and a tiny block of sangiovese were also planted at a property at Piccadilly. A further 8 ha are now being developed on a third property, adjacent to the original Balhannah holding. Alan Dean, a Charles Sturt University-trained viticulturist and former Petaluma vineyard manager, is in charge of the vineyards, working alongside brother Duncan, and with part-time help from the third generation. The primary aim of the business is contract grapegrowing, the purchasers including Petaluma, Tower Estate and Jeffrey Grosset.

The Duke Vineyard ★★★

38 Paringa Road, Red Hill South, Vic 3937 **Region** Mornington Peninsula
T (03) 5989 2407 **F** (03) 5989 2407 **Open** W'ends, public & summer hols 12–5
Winemaker Geoff Duke **Est.** 1989 **Cases** 600
Geoff and Sue Duke run a tiny, low-key winery with a 1.6-ha vineyard equally divided between chardonnay and pinot noir. Its establishment goes back to 1989; 1994 marked the first commercial Chardonnay and 1997 the first Pinot Noir. The wines are made in an onsite micro-winery and back vintages are available; none of the wines are sold until they are 2 years old.

The Islander Estate Vineyards ★★★★★

PO Box 96, Parndana, SA 5220 **Region** Kangaroo Island
T (08) 8553 9008 **F** (08) 8553 9228 **www**.iev.com.au **Open** By appt
Winemaker Jacques Lurton **Est.** NA **Cases** 5000
Established by one of the most famous Flying Winemakers in the world, Bordeaux-born, trained and part-time resident Jacques Lurton, who has established 10 ha of close-planted vineyard. The principal varieties are sangiovese and cabernet franc; then lesser amounts of semillon, viognier, grenache, malbec and merlot. The wines are made and bottled at the onsite winery, in true estate style. The flagship wine (The Yakka Jack) is an esoteric blend of sangiovese and cabernet franc. Exports to the US, France, Denmark, Sweden, Norway, China and Japan.

ŶŶŶŶŶ **Wally White Kangaroo Island Semillon Viognier 2005** A complex wine with obvious cellaring future; excellent texture and structure in no way imperilled by the alcohol; a particularly impressive finish devoid of the expected phenolics. Don't be put off by the name and memories of Wallaby White. Screwcap. 13.5° alc. **Rating** 94 **To** 2015 $44
Yakka Jack Cabernet Franc Sangiovese 2004 Fragrant, spicy aromas; an elegant, particularly fine and supple, texture to a long, sustained palate; controlled oak. Cork. 14.5° alc. **Rating** 94 **To** 2010 $72

ŶŶŶŶŶ **Bark Hut Road 2004** Medium red; light- to medium-bodied, with a spicy, savoury melange of flavours; fine, ripe tannins and controlled oak. Screwcap. 14.5° alc. **Rating** 92 **To** 2019 $37
Majestic Plough Malbec 2004 Dark, spicy fruits with some confit characters; the mid-palate seems to dip structurally before fine tannins on the finish. Screwcap. 14.5° alc. **Rating** 92 **To** 2013 $44

The Lake House Denmark   ★★★☆

106 Turner Road, Denmark, WA 6333 **Region** Denmark
T (08) 9848 2444 **F** (08) 9848 3444 **www**.lakehousedenmark.com.au **Open** Thurs–Sun, public hols & school hols (7 days) 11–4
Winemaker Harewood Estate (Jamie Kellie) **Est.** 1995 **Cases** 3000
When Gary Capelli and partner Leanne Rogers purchased the vineyard (formerly known as Jindi Creek) in 2005, it had 5.2 ha planted 10 years earlier to no less than 8 mainstream varieties, headed by chardonnay (2 ha) and pinot noir and merlot (0.8 ha each). They have since moved to incorporate biodynamic principles into the vineyard.

ŶŶŶŶŶ **Semillon Sauvignon Blanc 2006** Zesty, lively, sea breeze-fresh; a delicate passion-fruit and citrus mix; bright finish. Screwcap. 12° alc. **Rating** 94 **To** 2009 $22.50

ŶŶŶŶ **Unwooded Chardonnay 2006** Stone fruit, melon and grapefruit aromas and flavours; light-bodied, but fresh and lively. Screwcap. 13.5° alc. **Rating** 88 **To** 2008 $19.95
Shiraz 2005 Light- to medium-bodied; raspberry, cherry and plum fruits with spice and pepper; fine tannins, and not at all extractive; altogether belies the alcohol. Screwcap. 14.5° alc. **Rating** 88 **To** 2012 $23.50
Classic White 2006 A please-everyone style; best consumed when thinking about other things, and not wanting to be distracted. Sauvignon Blanc/Chardonnay/Semillon. Screwcap. 12° alc. **Rating** 87 **To** 2008 $16.95

The Lane   ★★★★

Ravenswood Lane, Hahndorf, SA 5245 **Region** Adelaide Hills
T (08) 8388 1250 **F** (08) 8388 7233 **www**.thelane.com.au **Open** 7 days 10–4.30
Winemaker Robert Mann **Est.** 1993 **Cases** 8000
With their sales and marketing background, John and Helen Edwards opted for a major lifestyle change when they began establishing the first of the present 28.1 ha of vineyards in 1993. Initially, part of the production was sold to Hardys, but now some of the wine is made for release under The Lane label (until 2003, Ravenswood Lane). A joint venture with Hardys has been terminated, which has resulted in the Starvedog Lane brand being owned by Hardys, and a revamped Ravenswood Lane label (and a new, cheaper Off The Leash label) carrying the flag for The Lane. John Edwards has applied to build a 500-tonne winery, and plans to open a cellar door and café. Exports to all major markets.

The Minya Winery   **NR**

Minya Lane, Connewarre, Vic 3227 **Region** Geelong
T (03) 5264 1397 **F** (03) 5264 1097 **www**.theminya.com.au **Open** Public hols, or by appt
Winemaker Susan Dans **Est.** 1974 **Cases** NA

The Poplars Winery

NR

Riddoch Highway, Coonawarra, SA 5263 **Region** Coonawarra
T (08) 8736 3130 **F** (08) 8736 3163 **www.chardonnaylodge.com.au Open** 7 days 9–6
Winemaker Gavin Hogg, Jonathon Luestner **Est.** 2006 **Cases** NA
A new name in Coonawarra, but in fact a long-term and highly successful cornerstone of the region. It is part of Coonawarra Developments Pty Ltd, which is in turn the owner of Chardonnay Lodge, the only large-scale (and ever-growing) accommodation complex in the heart of Coonawarra. Founded by the Yates family 21 years ago, it remains in that ownership, now offering 38 large suites and a deservedly popular restaurant. Most recently, and in a way most significantly, Coonawarra Developments has also purchased the former Jamiesons Run Winery from Fosters. The adjacent 4 ha of vineyard opposite the winery, and adjacent to Chardonnay Lodge, will underpin one of the most diverse tourism developments in SA on the 22-ha property. As if this were not enough, Coonawarra Developments has also put in place a major cheesemaking operation, which will be initiated under the direction of Tarago River Cheese Company, but with a resident cheesemaker, Craig Sceney, who in 2003 was acclaimed maker of the world's best cheese at the International Cheese Competition in Wisconsin, US.

The Ritual

★★★☆

233 Haddrill Road, Baskerville, WA 6056 (postal) **Region** Peel
T 0438 124 087 **F** (08) 9296 0681 **Open** Not
Winemaker John Griffiths **Est.** 2005 **Cases** 600
The Ritual is the product of a partnership between Perth wine identities covering the field from winemaking to the rather harder task of wine selling. John Griffiths is winemaker, Bill Healy owns Orondo Farm Vineyard in Dwellingup, where John Griffiths obtains much of his grapes for his own (Faber) and other labels, while Alex Hudak has been involved in wine wholesaling and retailing for many years. The modest line-pricing and simplicity of the product range reflect no more than sober experience.

ＹＹＹＹＹ **Shiraz Viognier 2006** Intensely fragrant and lifted red and black cherry fruit aromas, with vibrant flavours underlining the bouquet; the viognier influence very evident, and to the benefit of the wine. Screwcap. 14° alc. **Rating** 90 **To** 2008 $17

ＹＹＹＹ **Viognier 2006** Well-made, but lacks positive varietal character; some apricot and musk, with good acidity. Screwcap. 13.5° alc. **Rating** 87 **To** 2008 $17
Grenache Mourvedre Shiraz 2006 A light summer red to be served on the rocks if you so incline. Screwcap. 14° alc. **Rating** 87 **To** 2008 $17

The Rothbury Estate

NR

Broke Road, Pokolbin, NSW 2321 **Region** Lower Hunter Valley
T (02) 4998 7363 **F** (02) 4993 3559 **Open** Not
Winemaker Mike de Garis **Est.** 1968 **Cases** NA

The Standish Wine Company

★★★★☆

PO Box 498, Angaston, SA 5353 **Region** Barossa Valley
T (08) 8564 3634 **F** (08) 8564 3634 **www.standishwineco.com Open** Not
Winemaker Dan Standish **Est.** 1999 **Cases** 800
Dan Standish is an extremely experienced winemaker, adding work in the Napa and Sonoma valleys in California, La Rioja in Spain and the Rhone Valley in France to his domestic winemaking. In 1999 he was able to negotiate a small parcel of 96-year-old shiraz from his parents' vineyard in the Vine Vale subregion of the Barossa Valley. This produces 300 cases of The Standish, a wild yeast, open-fermented and basket-pressed shiraz matured in French oak for 30 months. The Standish, which uses his Rhone Valley experience led to the creation of The Relic, Shiraz (93%)/Viognier (7%) co-fermented, otherwise made with similar techniques.

The Tiers Wine Co

Chalk Hill Road/Foggo Road, McLaren Vale, SA 5171 **Region** McLaren Vale
T (08) 8323 9773 **www**.tierswines.com.au **Open** Mon–Fri & public hols 10–5
Winemaker Claudio Curtis, Phillip Reschke **Est.** 1990 **Cases** 50 000
In 1956 the Curtis family emigrated from Italy to Australia, and purchased its first vineyard land
from one Clarence William Torrens Rivers. They renamed it Clarence Hill. Further land was
acquired in the 1980s and 1990s, establishing the Landcross Estate and California Rise vineyards,
which, together with Clarence Hill, now have over 100 ha in production. Claudio Curtis (who
has a science degree from the Adelaide University) manages wine production and sales. Wines are
released under the Clarence Hill, Landcross Estate and Martins Road labels. Exports to the UK,
the US and other major markets.

¶¶¶¶¶ **Clarence Hill McLaren Vale Shiraz 2004** Rich, archetypal regional style; lots
of sweet black fruits in a swathe of dark chocolate; balanced tannins; best yet.
Diam. 14.5° alc. **Rating** 93 **To** 2019 $20
Clarence Hill McLaren Vale Cabernet Sauvignon 2004 Regional dark
chocolate comes rocketing through regardless of the variety; here with strong
blackcurrant fruit and good tannins. Diam. 14.5° alc. **Rating** 91 **To** 2010 $25
Clarence Hill Carina Botrytis Semillon 2004 The blend of Riverina/McLaren
Vale material works well; elegant but flavoursome, with gentle citrus, apricot and
peach. Cork. 12.5° alc. **Rating** 91 **To** 2009 $25
Clarence Hill McLaren Vale Cabernet Sauvignon Merlot 2004 The
cabernet dominates through a mix of blackcurrant and dark chocolate, a lesser
influence from the olive tones of the merlot; good tannin base; a surprise packet.
Cork. 14.5° alc. **Rating** 90 **To** 2014 $25

¶¶¶¶ **Clarence Hill McLaren Vale Chardonnay 2004** Light- to medium-bodied;
clean peach, melon and fig fruit; subtle oak, and good length. Nice wine, the
recipient of a gold medal at the Chardonnay du Monde '05 competition. Screwcap.
14° alc. **Rating** 89 **To** 2008 $16

The Wanderer

2850 Launching Place Road, Gembrook, Vic 3783 **Region** Yarra Valley
T (03) 5968 1622 **F** (03) 5968 1699 **Open** By appt
Winemaker Andrew Marks **Est.** 2005 **Cases** 1000
Andrew Marks is the son of Ian and June Marks, owners of Gembrook Hill, and after graduating
from Adelaide University with a degree in oenology he joined Southcorp, working for 6 years with
Penfolds in the Barossa Valley and Seppelt at Great Western, as well as undertaking vintages in
Coonawarra and France. Since then he has worked in the Hunter Valley, Great Southern, Sonoma
County in the US and Costa Brava in Spain – hence the name of his business. He made the
2005 wines at Gembrook Hill, lending a hand with the Gembrook Hill vintage while doing so.

¶¶¶¶¶ **Yarra Valley Gewurztraminer 2006** No reduction; gentle varietal expression
on both bouquet and palate, with fleeting notes of spice, rose petal and musk;
well-made. Screwcap. 12.8° alc. **Rating** 91 **To** 2012 $23

The Willow Lane Vineyard   **NR**

Eurunderee Lane, Mudgee, NSW 2850 **Region** Mudgee
T (02) 6373 3131 **www**.thewillowlane.com.au **Open** Fri–Mon & public hols 11–5
Winemaker Contract **Est.** 1995 **Cases** NA
Peter and Ann Wormald took over 10 years for their dream of owning a vineyard in Mudgee
to become a reality. It came true when they purchased a property in Eurunderee Lane, which
had an 1870s house and soil that seemed suited to viticulture. But it also involved Peter
spending 6 years part-time studying for his degree in viticulture (while working full-time) and
Ann going back into a pharmacy shop after many years in the pharmaceutical industry. A little
over 2 ha of chardonnay was planted in 1996, and 3.5 ha of shiraz in 1997 (replanted in 1998).
The first vintage followed in 2000, and in 2002 the Wormalds left Sydney to live in the old

house that had been renovated and extended. The cellar door, which opened in 2004, was made in part from the sections of the old house removed for the extension.

The Willows Vineyard ★★★★★

Light Pass Road, Light Pass, Barossa Valley, SA 5355 **Region** Barossa Valley
T (08) 8562 1080 **F** (08) 8562 3447 **www.thewillowsvineyard.com.au Open** Wed–Mon 10.30–4.30, Tues by appt
Winemaker Peter Scholz, Michael Scholz **Est.** 1989 **Cases** 6500
The Scholz family have been grapegrowers for generations and have almost 40 ha of vineyards, selling part and retaining the remainder of the crop. Current generation winemakers Peter and Michael Scholz make smooth, well-balanced and flavoursome wines under their own label, all marketed with bottle age. Exports to the UK, the US, Canada, NZ and Singapore.

♀♀♀♀♀ Bonesetter Barossa Shiraz 2004 Although the alcohol is the same as the Barossa Valley Shiraz, the wine has another dimension of richness to the strong blackberry and plum fruit; silky, persistent tannins, the oak in admirable restraint. From the oldest vines. Cork. 14.5° alc. **Rating** 96 **To** 2021 $56
Barossa Valley Shiraz 2004 Fine and elegant by normal Barossa Valley standards; blackberry, plum and black cherry are supported by fine tannins and quality oak. Screwcap. 14.5° alc. **Rating** 94 **To** 2024 $25
Barossa Valley Shiraz 2003 Youthful hue, notwithstanding the vintage; a fresh array of red and black fruits; fine tannins and judicious oak; great outcome for the year. Screwcap. 14.5° alc. **Rating** 94 **To** 2018 $26

♀♀♀♀♀ Bonesetter Barossa Shiraz 2003 A rich amalgam of licorice, leather, blackberry and plum fruit; fine tannins; mocha and vanilla oak. Cork. 14.5° alc. **Rating** 93 **To** 2015 $45
Barossa Valley Cabernet Sauvignon 2004 Good purple-red; ripe cassis and blackcurrant fruit with no hint of green characters whatsoever, but on the other hand, is not jammy nor does it show any dead fruit characters. Screwcap. 14.5° alc. **Rating** 93 **To** 2019 $25
Single Vineyard Barossa Valley Semillon 2004 A good wine, almost in Adelaide Hills style; the percentage barrel-fermented in French oak is not obvious, and the acidity gives both length and freshness; unexpectedly successful. Screwcap. 12° alc. **Rating** 90 **To** 2012 $15

♀♀♀♀ Barossa Valley Riesling 2006 A neutral bouquet, but more expression on the palate; quite tight, with citrus and apple flavours. Screwcap. 12.5° alc. **Rating** 89 **To** 2012 $14
Barossa Valley Cabernet Sauvignon 2003 Medium-bodied; distinctly earthy/savoury edges to the black fruits; gentle oak and tannin inputs. Screwcap. 14° alc. **Rating** 89 **To** 2010 $26

The Wine & Truffle Co ★★★★☆

PO Box 1538, Osborne Park, WA 6916 **Region** Pemberton
T (08) 9777 2474 **F** (08) 9204 1013 **www.wineandtruffle.com.au Open** Wed–Sun 10–4.30
Winemaker Mark Aitken **Est.** 1997 **Cases** 10 000
Owned by a group of investors from various parts of Australia who share the common vision of producing fine wines and black truffles. The winemaking side is under the care of Mark Aitken, who, having graduated as dux of his class in applied science at Curtin University in 2000, joined Chestnut Grove as assistant winemaker in 2002. He now is contract maker for the Wine & Truffle Company, as well as working for Chestnut Grove. The truffle side of the business is under the care of former CSIRO scientist Dr Nicholas Malajcsuk. He has overseen the planting of 13 000 truffle-inoculated hazelnut and oak trees on the property, which has now produced truffles, some of prodigious size. Exports to the US, Denmark and Singapore.

♀♀♀♀♀ Pemberton Riesling 2005 Lime and apple blossom aromas; a precise and long palate with good intensity and a lingering finish. Screwcap. 13° alc. **Rating** 92 **To** 2013 $18

Icon Series Pemberton Shiraz Cabernet 2004 Keeps the elegant theme going; dark fruits and fine tannins; there is a question on ripeness, but the wine has very good structure. Screwcap. 14° alc. **Rating** 91 **To** 2017 $35

Pemberton Chardonnay 2005 Lively and flavoursome; rich nectarine and peach fruit complexed by toasty oak and brisk acidity on the finish. Screwcap. 13.5° alc. **Rating** 90 **To** 2011 $18

Pemberton Shiraz 2005 Elegant cool climate style; a light- to medium-bodied palate with spice and pepper dusted on red and black cherry fruit; supple and smooth. Screwcap. 14.6° alc. **Rating** 90 **To** 2015 $18

ŶŶŶŶ **Pemberton Cabernet Merlot 2005** Minty, leafy red berry fruits; minimal tannins; here the struggle for ripeness is self-evident. Screwcap. 14.1° alc. **Rating** 87 **To** 2010 $18

🍂 Third Child ★★★

134 Mt Rumney Road, Mt Rumney, Tas 7170 (postal) **Region** Southern Tasmania
T 0419 132 184 **F** (03) 6223 8042 **Open** Not
Winemaker John Skinner, Rob Drew **Est.** 2000 **Cases** 250
John and Marcia Skinner planted 2.5 ha of pinot noir and 0.5 ha of riesling in 2000. It is very much a hands-on operation, the only concession being the enlistment of Rob Drew (on an adjoining property) to help John Skinner with the winemaking. When the first vintage (2004) was reaching the stage where it was to be bottled and labelled, the Skinners could not come up with a name and asked their daughter Claire. 'Easy,' she said. 'You've got 2 kids already; considering the care taken and time spent at the farm, it's your third child.'

ŶŶŶŶ **Benjamin Daniel Pinot Noir 2006** A multi-clone blend as opposed to the single clone 2051 wine, supporting the French point that a mixture of clones will always be better than a single clone; there is strong black cherry fruit and green, stemmy notes needing to integrate; nonetheless an impressive achievement. Screwcap. 13° alc. **Rating** 89 **To** 2012 $25

Thistle Hill ★★★

74 McDonalds Road, Mudgee, NSW 2850 **Region** Mudgee
T (02) 6373 3546 **F** (02) 6373 3540 **www**.thistlehill.com.au **Open** Mon–Sat 9.30–4.30, Sun & public hols 9.30–4
Winemaker Lesley Robertson, Robert Paul (Consultant) **Est.** 1976 **Cases** 2500
The Robertson family owns and operates Thistle Hill. The estate-grown wines are made onsite with the help of Robert Paul. Whatever additional assistance is needed is happily provided by the remaining wine community of Mudgee. The vineyard, incidentally, is registered by the National Association for Sustainable Agriculture Australia (NASAA), which means no weedicides, insecticides or synthetic fertilisers – the full organic system. Exports to the UK, Canada and Japan.

ŶŶŶŶŶ **Mudgee Riesling 2005** Much finer, more intense and longer than the '06; driven by pure citrus fruit, finishing with good acidity. Screwcap. 11° alc. **Rating** 93 **To** 2014 $16

ŶŶŶŶ **Basket Press Mudgee Shiraz 2003** Traditional savoury/earthy blackberry fruit; soft but sufficient tannins and oak; has good balance and will continue to develop. Screwcap. 13.6° alc. **Rating** 89 **To** 2015

Mudgee Riesling 2006 Clean, fresh and well-made; gentle apple, spice and citrus flavours, needing just a little more focus and precision. Screwcap. 13° alc. **Rating** 88 **To** 2011

Mudgee Chardonnay 2005 Slightly funky oak is not, one assumes, deliberate; pleasant peachy fruit finishing with a touch of lemony acidity. Screwcap. 12.5° alc. **Rating** 87 **To** 2008

Basket Press Mudgee Cabernet Sauvignon 2003 Earthy/savoury/olive overtones to the bouquet and palate; needed more aerative handling before being screwcapped. 13.5° alc. **Rating** 87 **To** 2012

Thomas Vineyard Estate   ★★★★☆

PO Box 490, McLaren Vale, SA 5171 **Region** McLaren Vale
T (08) 8557 8583 **F** (08) 8557 8583 **www**.thomasvineyard.com.au **Open** Not
Winemaker Trevor Tucker **Est.** 1998 **Cases** 2000
Merv and Dawne Thomas thought long and hard before purchasing the property on which they
have established their vineyard. It is 3 km from the coast of the Gulf of St Vincent on the Fleurieu
Peninsula, with a clay over limestone soil known locally as 'Bay of Biscay'. They had a dream start
to the business when the 2004 Shiraz won the trophy for Best Single Vineyard Wine (red or white)
at the McLaren Vale Wine Show '05, the Reserve Shiraz also winning a gold medal.

♥♥♥♥♥ **Estate Reserve McLaren Vale Shiraz 2005** Impenetrable purple, verging on
black; hyper-concentrated regional style swollen with bitter chocolate,
blackberry and plum; carries the alcohol without apparent sweetness; a heroic
Henry VIII style. Diam. 15.5° alc. **Rating** 94 **To** 2028 $35

♥♥♥♥♀ **McLaren Vale Shiraz 2005** Deep purple-red; like the Reserve, unashamedly
full-bodied, concentrated and intense; black fruits have literally devoured the
French oak as with the Reserve. You either find the alcohol acceptable or not,
a purely personal decision. Diam. 15.5° alc. **Rating** 93 **To** 2025 $20
Estate Reserve McLaren Vale Shiraz 2004 Abundant black fruits with touches
of regional chocolate and mocha; plenty of texture and depth. Cork. 14.5° alc.
Rating 93 **To** 2024 $50

Thomas Wines

c/- The Small Winemakers Centre, McDonalds Road, Pokolbin, NSW 2321 **Region**
Lower Hunter Valley
T (02) 6574 7371 **F** (02) 6574 7371 **www**.thomaswines.com.au **Open** 7 days 10–5
Winemaker Andrew Thomas **Est.** 1997 **Cases** 3000
Andrew Thomas came to the Hunter Valley from McLaren Vale, to join the winemaking team at
Tyrrell's. After 13 years with Tyrrell's, he left to undertake contract work and to continue the
development of his own winery label, a family affair run by himself and his wife, Jo. To date the
Semillon has come from the renowned vineyard of Ken Bray, but the plan is to add other single
vineyard wines, simply to underline the subtle differences between the various subregions of the
Hunter. Exports to Canada, Singapore and Japan.

♥♥♥♥♥ **Braemore Hunter Valley Semillon 2006** A beautiful young semillon, bursting
with youthful varietal flavour; intense lemon and grass, the lingering aftertaste
going on and on. Screwcap. 10.4° alc. **Rating** 96 **To** 2026 $24
The OC Hunter Valley Semillon 2006 Pale straw-green; vibrant, fresh and
pure aromas; delicate but intense citrus/lemon fruit on the palate; very good
balance. Screwcap. 10.2° alc. **Rating** 94 **To** 2016 $20

♥♥♥♥ **Kiss Hunter Valley Shiraz 2005** Deep colour; densely packed blackberry fruits
with a long finish; needs time to soften. **Rating** 89 **To** 2015 $45

Thompson Estate   ★★★★★

Harmans Road South, Wilyabrup, WA 6284 **Region** Margaret River
T (08) 9386 1751 **F** (08) 9386 1708 **www**.thompsonestate.com **Open** Wed–Sun 10–5
Winemaker Various contract **Est.** 1998 **Cases** 4000
Cardiologist Peter Thompson planted the first vines at Thompson Estate in 1994, inspired by his
and his family's shareholdings in the Pierro and Fire Gully vineyards, and by visits to many of the
world's premium wine regions. A total of 15 ha has been established: cabernet sauvignon, cabernet
franc, merlot, chardonnay and pinot noir. The Thompsons have split the winemaking between
specialist winemakers: Cabernet Merlot by Mark Messenger of Juniper Estate (previously of Cape
Mentelle), Pinot Noir by Flying Fish Cove, and Pinot Chardonnay by Harold Osborne of Fraser
Woods. Exports to the UK, the US and other major markets.

ŢŢŢŢŢ **Margaret River Chardonnay 2005** Fresh and clean; tight and elegant but intense nectarine and melon fruit; oak background scenery; very good length. Screwcap. 13.5° alc. **Rating** 94 **To** 2015 $35

Margaret River Cabernet Sauvignon 2003 Excellent colour; flooded with cassis and blackcurrant supported by quality oak and ripe tannins. Cork. 14° alc. **Rating** 94 **To** 2020 $35

ŢŢŢŢŢ **Margaret River Chardonnay Pinot Noir 2002** Fine, elegant and balanced; good mousse; gentle citrus and nectarine fruit; fine acidity and length. 13.6° alc. **Rating** 90 **To** 2010 $35

ŢŢŢŢ **Margaret River Semillon Sauvignon Blanc 2006** Fragrant grass, herb, citrus and apple aromas; the light- to medium-bodied palate follows the bouquet, but not with quite the same intensity, falling away slightly on the finish. Screwcap. 11.5° alc. **Rating** 89 **To** 2010 $22

Thorn-Clarke Wines   ★★★★★

Milton Park, Gawler Park Road, Angaston, SA 5353 **Region** Barossa Valley
T (08) 8564 3036 **F** (08) 8564 3255 **www**.thornclarkewines.com **Open** Mon–Fri 10–4
Winemaker Derek Fitzgerald **Est.** 1997 **Cases** 90 000
Established by David and Cheryl Clarke (née Thorn), and son Sam. Thorn-Clarke is one of the largest Barossa grapegrowers, with 270 ha across 4 vineyard sites. Shiraz (136 ha), cabernet sauvignon (49 ha) and merlot (20 ha) are the principal plantings, with lesser amounts of petit verdot, cabernet franc, nebbiolo, chardonnay, riesling and pinot gris. As with many such growers, most of the grape production is sold, but the best is retained for the Thorn-Clarke label. Thorn-Clarke has become a serial trophy and gold medal winner, with a wholly enviable track record. Exports to the US, Europe, Canada and NZ.

ŢŢŢŢŢ **Shotfire Ridge Barossa Valley Shiraz 2005** A full-bodied wine, with layers of black fruits; tannins and oak in appropriate support. Gold medal National Wine Show '06. Screwcap. 14° alc. **Rating** 94 **To** 2025 $22.95

Shotfire Ridge Barossa Valley Quartage 2005 Has great fragrance, and a beautifully fine, silky palate with a mix of cherry, cassis and spice. Unlucky not to win a gold at the National Wine Show '06. Screwcap. 14° alc. **Rating** 94 **To** 2015 $22.95

ŢŢŢŢŢ **William Randell Barossa Valley Shiraz 2004** Dense red-purple; blackberry, licorice and leather fruit; excellent texture and structure, with well-balanced and integrated French and American oak. Cork. 14.5° alc. **Rating** 93 **To** 2014 $49.95

Sandpiper Barossa Shiraz 2005 Powerful, medium- to full-bodied wine with abundant fresh and juicy blackberry fruit, yet has length. A bargain by any standards. Screwcap. 14° alc. **Rating** 92 **To** 2018 $16

Sandpiper Eden Valley Chardonnay 2006 A powerful wine, with nectarine, ripe apple and a touch of citrus; subliminal French oak. Screwcap. 14° alc. **Rating** 90 **To** 2010 $16

Sandpiper Barossa Cabernet Sauvignon 2005 Distinctly varietal cassis and blackcurrant fruit which is very fresh; perhaps a little more structure needed, but at this price that is not a valid complaint. Screwcap. 14° alc. **Rating** 90 **To** 2014 $16

ŢŢŢŢ **Sandpiper Eden Valley Riesling 2006** Generous, sweet citrus in regional style; voluminous flavour, though lacks focus. Screwcap. 12.5° alc. **Rating** 89 **To** 2010 $16

Sandpiper The Blend 2005 Light- to medium-bodied; herbal/green notes partly obscure the red fruit components; at least the tannin and oak inputs are controlled. Shiraz/Petit Verdot/Cabernet Sauvignon/Cabernet Franc. Screwcap. 14° alc. **Rating** 87 **To** 2010 $16

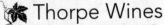 Thorpe Wines

NR

PO Box 720, McLaren Vale, SA 5171 **Region** McLaren Vale
T (08) 8556 4237 **F** (08) 8556 4287 **www.**thorpewines.com **Open** Not
Winemaker Linda Domas **Est.** 1997 **Cases** NA

Craig and Nicole Thorpe purchased 8 ha of land in 1996, mainly to buy a house and shedding to help the expansion of Craig's water-drilling business. Leaving the remainder of the land bare made no sense, and a vineyard was planted in 1997 backed by a 5-year contract with Geoff Merrill. In the lead up to the fifth vintage in 2003, the Thorpes had a chance meeting with Linda Domas who was looking for opportunities after a Flying Winemaking stint overseas (which had followed big company winemaking). Making small quantities of high-quality wines for a number of small clients was an opportunity too good to miss.

3 Drops

PO Box 1828, Applecross, WA 6953 **Region** Mount Barker
T (08) 9315 4721 **F** (08) 9315 4724 **www.**3drops.com **Open** Not
Winemaker Robert Diletti (Contract), John Wade (Consultant) **Est.** 1998 **Cases** 4000

The 3 Drops are not the 3 owners (John Bradbury, Joanne Bradbury and Nicola Wallich), but wine, olive oil and water, all of which come from the property, a substantial vineyard at Mount Barker. The 16 ha are planted to riesling, sauvignon blanc, semillon, chardonnay, cabernet sauvignon, merlot, shiraz and cabernet franc. The business expanded significantly in 2007 with the purchase of the 14.7-ha Patterson's Vineyard. Exports to the UK, Japan and Canada.

Mount Barker Merlot 2005 Medium red-purple; a very attractive wine, with clear-cut varietal fruit ranging through cassis, black olive and spice; classic texture and medium-bodied weight. Screwcap. 14.5° alc. **Rating** 94 **To** 2015 $22

Mount Barker Sauvignon Blanc 2006 Pale straw-green; the aromas verge on the edge of sweaty, but strongly varietal flavours build through the length of the palate and aftertaste; good wine. Screwcap. 12.5° alc. **Rating** 92 **To** 2008 $19

Mount Barker Riesling 2006 Apple, pear, citrus and spice aromas and flavours; moderate length and good balance. Screwcap. 12° alc. **Rating** 90 **To** 2012 $20

Mount Barker Chardonnay 2005 Light straw-green; plenty of mouthfeel with gentle white peach/stone fruit flavours; subtle oak dressing; good finish. Screwcap. 14° alc. **Rating** 90 **To** 2010 $22

Three Willows Vineyard

46 Montana Road, Red Hills, Tas 7304 **Region** Northern Tasmania
T 0438 507 069 **www.**threewillowsvineyard.com.au **Open** By appt
Winemaker Philip Pares **Est.** 2002 **Cases** 50

Philip Pares and Lyn Prove have planted a micro-vineyard, with 1.4 ha of pinot noir, pinot gris, baco noir (a hybrid) and chardonnay. It is 50 km west of Launceston near Deloraine on a gentle north-facing slope at an elevation of 220–250 m. The present tiny production will peak at around 250 cases, sold to in-house guests at the B&B accommodation, and by mail and phone order.

Three Wise Men

Woongarra Estate, 95 Hayseys Road, Narre Warren East, Vic 3804 **Region** Port Phillip Zone
T (03) 9796 8886 **www.**threewisemen.com.au **Open** Thurs–Sun 9–5 by appt
Winemaker Graeme Leith **Est.** 1994 **Cases** 800

The Three Wise Men label was conceived to make a top-quality single-vineyard Pinot Noir grown at Woongarra Estate, a well-drained, cool and moist site close to the Yarra Valley. An agreement between the Jones's of Woongarra and Passing Clouds (see separate entries) winemaker Graeme Leith means that the wine is made at Passing Clouds at Kingower, near Bendigo. A variety of winemaking techniques are used, varying according to vintage conditions. Each of the partners takes half of the resulting wine and sells it through their respective cellar doors.

ŸŸŸŸ♀ Pinot Noir 2005 Complex savoury, stemmy style of pinot, the tannins underpinning and running through the palate and long finish; cerebral style. Diam. **Rating** 91 **To** 2020 $35

Three Wishes Vineyard   ★★★★☆

604 Batman Highway, Hillwood, Tas 7252 **Region** Northern Tasmania
T (03) 6331 2009 **F** (03) 6331 0043 **www**.threewishesvineyard.com.au **Open** W'ends & public hols 11–5, or by appt
Winemaker Bass Fine Wines **Est.** 1998 **Cases** 500
Peter and Natalie Whish-Wilson began the establishment of their vineyard in 1998 while they were working in Hong Kong, delegating the management tasks to parents Rosemary and Tony Whish-Wilson until 2003. Peter and Natalie took a year's sabbatical to do the first vintage, with their children aged 6 and 4 also involved in tending the vines. The seachange became permanent, Peter completing his wine growing degree from Charles Sturt University in 1996. The original 2.8 ha of pinot noir, chardonnay and riesling are being extended by the planting of a further ha of pinot noir.

ŸŸŸŸŸ Riesling 2006 Intense, fine, long, swelling a little on the mid-palate, but tightening up once again on the finish. Screwcap. 12.7° alc. **Rating** 93 **To** 2016 $27
Pinot Noir 2005 Very deep purple-red colour; of heroic proportions, with masses of dark plum and spice fruit, reminiscent of some Central Otago pinots. A 10-year pinot. Screwcap. 13.5° alc. **Rating** 92 **To** 2015 $30
Chardonnay 2005 Light straw-green; a spotless, super-elegant wine with nectarine and grapefruit; has absorbed 9 months maturation in 50% new French oak. Screwcap. 13° alc. **Rating** 90 **To** 2011 $25

Tibooburra Wines   ★★★★☆

Stringybark Lane, off Beenak Road, Yellingbo, Vic 3139 (postal) **Region** Yarra Valley
T 0418 367 319 **F** (03) 5964 8577 **www**.tibooburra.com **Open** Not
Winemaker Paul Evans, Timo Mayer (Contract) **Est.** 1996 **Cases** 1500
The Kerr family has done much with Tibooburra since they began assembling their 1000-ha property in 1967. They have established a champion Angus herd, planted a 32.5-ha vineyard in 1996 on elevated northern and northwest slopes, established a trufffliere in 2001 to supply Japanese and northern hemisphere restaurants with black truffles, and launched the Tibooburra Wines label in 2002. Four generations have been, and are now, involved in the business. Most of the grapes are sold under long-term contract to Oakridge, Yering Station and Yarra Burn. Plantings (in descending order) are pinot noir, chardonnay, shiraz, sauvignon blanc, merlot and cabernet sauvignon, and the quality of the early releases is all one could possibly ask for.

ŸŸŸŸŸ Yarra Valley Shiraz 2005 An aromatic, almost flowery cherry blossom bouquet; lovely balance and line, with fine, smooth, supple tannins to support the fruit, the oak perfectly judged. Diam. 13.5° alc. **Rating** 94 **To** 2020 $25

ŸŸŸŸ♀ Yarra Valley Chardonnay 2005 A neatly sculptured, fruit-forward style with a typical Yarra Valley melon, stone fruit and citrus mix supported by neatly judged barrel ferment oak. Screwcap. 13.5° alc. **Rating** 93 **To** 2012 $22
Yarra Valley Sauvignon Blanc 2006 A highly aromatic and flowery passion-fruit blossom bouquet; latent citrus and mineral flavours add another dimension to the palate; good length. Screwcap. 12.5° alc. **Rating** 92 **To** 2008 $19
Yarra Valley Merlot 2005 Complex fruit falling into 2 parts: on the one hand, spice and olive, and on the other, rich, sweet and ripe cassis. Much to suggest significant improvement over the next 7 years. Diam. 13.5° alc. **Rating** 92 **To** 2015 $25

ŸŸŸŸ Yarra Valley Pinot Noir 2005 Bright, clear colour; fresh, clean and light-bodied; pure fruit, but needs more depth and texture. Screwcap. 13° alc. **Rating** 89 **To** 2010 $25

Tidswell Wines ★★★★

PO Box 94, Kensington Park, SA 5068 **Region** Limestone Coast Zone
T (08) 8363 5800 **F** (08) 8363 1980 **www**.tidswellwines.com.au **Open** Not
Winemaker Wine Wise Consultancy **Est.** 1997 **Cases** 7000
The Tidswell family has 2 large vineyards in the Limestone Coast Zone near Bool Lagoon; in total
there are 114 ha, the lion's share planted to shiraz and cabernet sauvignon, with smaller plantings
of merlot, chardonnay and sauvignon blanc. Wines are released under the Jennifer, Heathfield
Ridge and Caves Rd labels. Exports to Canada and Japan.

♀♀♀♀♀ **Heathfield Ridge Sauvignon Blanc 2006** Tropical/passionfruit aromas;
particularly good balance and length; not sweet. Screwcap. **Rating** 90 **To** 2008
$17.50

Tiger Ranch Wines ★★☆

116 Allisons Road, Lower Barrington, Tas 7306 (postal) **Region** Northern Tasmania
T (03) 6492 3339 **F** (03) 6492 3356 **www**.tigerranch.com.au **Open** Not
Winemaker Neil Colbeck **Est.** 2000 **Cases** NFP
Neil Colbeck developed a fascination with fine wine during his time as sommelier at Hayman
Island between 1987 and 1990. At that time the Island was at its zenith, with a cellar of over
38 000 bottles worth $750 000. All good things have to come to an end, and when he returned
to Tasmania in 1990, he planted his first vineyard. In 2000 Tiger Ranch was relocated to Lower
Barrington and a new vineyard established. While this was coming into bearing, grapes were
purchased from Lake Barrington Estate; it has to be said that Neil Colbeck's DIY winemaking
has not been entirely successful, although it is early days. Tiger Ranch not only produces wine; it
has an Arabian horse stud, breeds border collie working dogs and is home to Brian Colbeck's very
beautiful watercolour and ink bird paintings, which Gould would not be ashamed of.

Tilbrook ★★★★★

17/1 Adelaide Lobethal Road, Lobethal, SA 5241 **Region** Adelaide Hills
T (08) 8389 5315 **F** (08) 8389 5318 **Open** Fri–Sun 11–5 & public hols, or by appt
Winemaker James Tilbrook **Est.** 2001 **Cases** 2000
James and Annabelle Tilbrook have 4.4 ha of multi-clone chardonnay and pinot noir, and 0.4 ha
of sauvignon blanc at Lenswood. The winery and cellar door are in the old Onkaparinga Woollen
Mills building in Lobethal; this not only provides an atmospheric home, but also helps meet the
very strict environmental requirements of the Adelaide Hills in dealing with winery waste water.
English-born James Tilbrook came to Australia in 1986, aged 22; a car accident led to his return
to England. Working for Oddbins and passing the WSET diploma set his future course. He
returned to Australia, met wife Annabelle, purchased the vineyard and began planting the vineyard
in 1999. Plantings are continuing for the Tilbrook label, and for the moment the major part of
the 1999 plantings of chardonnay and pinot noir is sold to Fosters. Exports to the UK.

♀♀♀♀♀ **Adelaide Hills Sauvignon Blanc 2006** A powerful, clean bouquet, the power
continuing through the palate with gooseberry, snow peas, kiwifruit and a touch
of passionfruit. Takes no prisoners. Diam. 13.5° alc. **Rating** 94 **To** 2008 $18
Reserve Adelaide Hills Chardonnay 2004 Restrained complexity; gentle
stone fruit, fig and citrus, with creamy notes from partial mlf; fruit and oak
balance perfect. Whole bunch-pressed; one-third new French oak; one-third
mlf. Diam. 14° alc. **Rating** 94 **To** 2012 $25
Reserve Adelaide Hills Shiraz 2005 Luscious cool-grown blackberry and
licorice fruit flavours; lingering, fine tannins; controlled oak; very good finish
and aftertaste. Diam. 14.5° alc. **Rating** 94 **To** 2025 $25
**Reserve Adelaide Hills Cabernet Sauvignon Cabernet Franc Merlot
2005** Good purple-red; a luscious, but not in the least jammy, cascade of red
and black fruits; supple and slurpy, with seamless tannins and oak. Diam. 14° alc.
Rating 94 **To** 2020 $25

ΨΨΨΨΫ **Reserve Adelaide Hills Chardonnay 2003** Developing very well; ripe, but not overripe, stone fruit and fig flavours; good oak integration and balance. Cork. 13.5° alc. **Rating** 93 **To** 2010 $22

Adelaide Hills Pinot Gris 2006 Abundant character, with ripe pear, apple, musk and quince; has more flavour depth than most. Diam. 14° alc. **Rating** 90 **To** 2008 $20

Adelaide Plains Barossa Valley Cabernet Sauvignon 2004 Medium to full-bodied, with nicely ripened black fruits; an unlikely provenance for wine of this style and quality, the vintage doubtless helping; ripe tannins and good oak. Diam. 14.5° alc. **Rating** 90 **To** 2015 $25

Reserve Adelaide Hills Late Harvest Pinot Gris 2005 An interesting wine, not quite Vendage Tardive by the reckoning of Alsace, but does have intensified varietal character. Cork. 12.5° alc. **Rating** 90 **To** 2008 $20

ΨΨΨΨ **Adelaide Plains Barossa Valley Shiraz 2004** Deep red-purple; luscious, ripe blackberry, prune and plum fruit, suggesting even higher alcohol than is the case; could surprise with age. Diam. 14.5° alc. **Rating** 89 **To** 2015 $18

Reserve Cabernet Merlot 2003 Shows some colour development; an interesting wine, with savoury/earthy notes offset by mocha oak and soft tannins. Adelaide Hills. Cork. 14° alc. **Rating** 89 **To** 2012 $25

Adelaide Hills Sauvignon Blanc 2005 A very reserved, tight style; predominantly grassy, with some citrus and mineral. Diam. 14° alc. **Rating** 88 **To** 2008 $18

Reserve Adelaide Hills Late Harvest Pinot Gris 2004 Apricot and dried fruit characters; a super-long ferment over winter, unusual in Australia; some errant characters, but interesting nonetheless. Cork. 13.5° alc. **Rating** 87 **To** 2008 $18

Tim Adams

★★★★☆

Warenda Road, Clare, SA 5453 **Region** Clare Valley
T (08) 8842 2429 **F** (08) 8842 3550 **www**.timadamswines.com.au **Open** Mon–Fri 10.30–5, w'ends 11–5
Winemaker Tim Adams **Est.** 1986 **Cases** 35 000
After almost 20 years slowly and carefully building the business, based on 11 ha of the Clare Valley classic varieties of riesling, semillon, grenache, shiraz and cabernet sauvignon, Tim and Pat Adams have decided to more than double their venture. Like their move to a total reliance on screwcaps, there is nothing unexpected in that. However, the makeup of the new plantings is anything but usual: they will give Tim Adams more than 10 ha of tempranillo and pinot gris, and about 3.5 ha of viognier, in each case with a very clear idea about the style of wine to be produced. Exports to the UK, the US, Canada, Singapore and Sweden.

ΨΨΨΨΨ **Reserve Clare Valley Riesling 2006** A clean bouquet, with some minerally overtones; very tight and very classic in the mouth, with extremely intense, lingering citrussy acidity; to keep for your wake. Screwcap. 10.5° alc. **Rating** 96 **To** 2031 $35

The Aberfeldy Clare Valley Shiraz 2004 Strong red-purple; a firm, tightly focused wine; intense black fruits; a full-bodied wine which still has a few sharp edges to soften, but should develop superbly over time. Screwcap. 15° alc. **Rating** 94 **To** 2025 $55

ΨΨΨΨΫ **Clare Valley Cabernet 2004** Medium- to full-bodied, with intense black fruits sustained by ripe tannins and balanced oak. Screwcap. **Rating** 93 **To** 2024 $26

Clare Valley Riesling 2006 Multiple aromas and flavours of apple, citrus and spice; good length and balance. Screwcap. 12° alc. **Rating** 92 **To** 2016 $22

Reserve Clare Valley Tempranillo 2005 The varietal character is clearly defined, and the fruit does all the talking, notwithstanding 16 months in new French oak. Strawberry, plum and spice (says Adams); what about the Rawlinson/Scarpantoni lexicon? Screwcap. 13.5° alc. **Rating** 92 **To** 2017 $35

Clare Valley Semillon 2006 Aggressive winemaking inputs (12 hours skin contact and 7 months in oak) certainly change the character of the wine, but are neatly stitched together, along with the alcohol. Screwcap. 13.5° alc. **Rating** 90 To 2011 $22

Reserve Clare Valley Merlot 2004 Excellent purple-red hue; quite intense and focused savoury/earthy/olive notes seamlessly interwoven with dark blackcurrant fruit. The farewell is at the savoury end; uncompromisingly varietal. Screwcap. 14.5° alc. **Rating** 90 **To** 2015 $35

ΨΨΨΨ **Clare Valley Semillon 2005** A big, bold Adams style, the flavour maximised by 12 hours of skin contact, then barrel ferment and 5 months in oak. Don't cellar it. Screwcap. 13° alc. **Rating** 89 **To** 2008 $22

Clare Valley Pinot Gris 2006 Pale blush pink; a trace of residual sugar helps the wine's personality. Screwcap. 13.5° alc. **Rating** 89 **To** 2008 $23

Clare Valley Shiraz 2005 Slightly hazy colour; medium-bodied, with spicy/earthy overtones to black fruits; an altogether savoury wine which comes as an antidote to rich, sweet monsters. Screwcap. 14.5° alc. **Rating** 89 **To** 2014 $26

Botrytis Affected Riesling 2006 Good material, but has ended up neither one thing or the other, neither particularly sweet and complex, but certainly not dry. Could well surprise with time in the bottle. Screwcap. 12° alc. **Rating** 89 To 2013 $20

Tim Gramp

Mintaro/Leasingham Road, Watervale, SA 5452 **Region** Clare Valley
T (08) 8344 4079 **www.**timgrampwines.com.au **Open** W'ends & hols 10–4
Winemaker Tim Gramp **Est.** 1990 **Cases** 6000
Tim Gramp has quietly built up a very successful business and by keeping overheads to a minimum, provides good wines at modest prices. The operation is supported by 2 ha of cabernet sauvignon around the cellar door. Exports to the UK, the US, Malaysia and NZ.

ΨΨΨΨΨ **Watervale Riesling 2006** Both the bouquet and palate are flush with ripe citrus, passionfruit and apple flavours, but avoid heaviness; excellent length. Screwcap. 12.5° alc. **Rating** 94 **To** 2020 $18

ΨΨΨΨΨ **Gilbert Valley Shiraz Cabernet 2004** Medium- to full-bodied black berry fruits, spice and touches of bitter chocolate supported by ripe tannins; the fruit has swallowed the 23 months of American oak maturation. Screwcap. 14.5° alc. **Rating** 91 **To** 2015 $21

Tim Smith Wines ★★★★★

PO Box 446, Tanunda, SA 5352 **Region** Barossa Valley
T (08) 8563 0939 **F** (08) 8563 0939 **Open** Not
Winemaker Tim Smith **Est.** 2001 **Cases** 1000
Tim Smith aspires to make wines in the mould of the great producers of Cote Rotie and Chateauneuf du Pape, but using a New World approach. It is a business in its early stages, with only 3 wines, a Shiraz, Botrytis Semillon and Grenache/Shiraz/Mourvedre. Exports to the UK and the US.

ΨΨΨΨΨ **Barossa Shiraz 2005** Blackberry, plum, licorice and prune define the bouquet and the flavours of the complex, textured palate; overall, does seem riper than 14.5°, which might explain Tim Smith's cryptic note to me hoping I will enjoy my 1000th overripe Barossa shiraz (which I did). Screwcap. 14.5° alc. **Rating** 94 **To** 2025 $31

Timmins Wines

7 Durham Street, Hunters Hill, NSW 2110 (postal) **Region** Hunter Valley/Orange
T (02) 9816 1422 **F** (02) 9816 1477 **www.**timminswines.com.au **Open** Not
Winemaker John Timmins **Est.** 2001 **Cases** 500

Unusually, this is a micro-wine operation without its own vineyard. Pharmacist John Timmins completed his Bachelor of Applied Science (Wine Science) degree in 2003, and is using his qualifications to make wines in small volumes from grapes grown in the Hunter Valley and Orange. Exports to Singapore.

Tin Shed Wines   ★★★★☆

PO Box 504, Tanunda, SA 5352 **Region** Eden Valley
T (08) 8563 3669 **F** (08) 8563 3669 www.tinshedwines.com **Open** Not
Winemaker Andrew Wardlaw, Peter Clarke **Est.** 1998 **Cases** 3000
Tin Shed proprietors Andrew Wardlaw and Peter Clarke weave all sorts of mystique in producing and marketing the Tin Shed wines. They say, 'our wines are handmade so we can only produce small volumes; this means we can take more care at each step of the winemaking process ... most bizarre of all we use our nose, palette (sic) and commonsense as opposed to the safe and reliable formula preached by our University's and peers'. The Tin Shed newsletter continues with lots of gee-whizz, hayseed jollity, making one fear the worst, when the reality is that the wines (even the Wild Bunch Riesling, wild-fermented without chemicals) are very good. Exports to the UK, the US, NZ and Japan.

ΨΨΨΨΨ **Wild Bunch Eden Valley Riesling 2006** A classic citrus mix of lemon and lime aromas, the medium-bodied palate having plenty of flavour and length. Screwcap. 12° alc. **Rating** 93 **To** 2016 $18
Single Wire Eden Valley Shiraz 2003 Powerful, intense and focused blackberry fruits with touches of spice and licorice from the cooler Eden Valley climate; persistent tannins; very good outcome for a challenging vintage. Cork. 14.9° alc. **Rating** 93 **To** 2015 $50

ΨΨΨΨ **Three Vines Barossa Mourvedre Shiraz Grenache 2003** Jammy, slushy fruit flavours accentuated by the vintage; the fruit finishes somewhat abruptly, leaving alcohol in the mouth. Definitely needs food; 40%/30%/30%. Screwcap. 14.9° alc. **Rating** 88 **To** 2010 $28

Tinderbox Vineyard   ★★★★

Tinderbox, Tas 7054 **Region** Southern Tasmania
T (03) 6229 2994 **F** (03) 6229 2994 **Open** By appt
Winemaker Hood Wines (Andrew Hood) **Est.** 1994 **Cases** 185
Liz McGown is a Hobart nurse who has established her vineyard on the slope beneath her house, overlooking the entrance to the Derwent River and the D'Entrecasteaux Channel, doubling the size from 1 to 2 ha in 2003. The attractive label was designed by Barry Tucker, who was so charmed by Liz McGown's request that he waived his usual (substantial) fee.

 ## Tinkers Hill Vineyard   ★★★★★

84 Sugarloaf Lane, Beechworth, Vic 3747 **Region** Beechworth
T (03) 5728 3327 www.tinkershillwines.com.au **Open** Fri–Mon 11–5, or by appt
Winemaker David O'Leary **Est.** 2000 **Cases** NA
James and Rhonda Taylor have established 0.2 ha each of chardonnay and cabernet sauvignon, and 0.8 ha of shiraz. The cellar door is situated in the Chiltern Mt Pilot National Park, close to the Woolshed Falls, one of Beechworth's main natural attractions. Small quantities of Barbera are sourced from within the region, the Merlot coming from their daughter's Cirko V winery (see separate entry). Classy packaging is a feature.

ΨΨΨΨΨ **Shiraz 2004** Very elegant medium-bodied style; fresh plum and blackberry fruit, super-fine tannins and controlled oak. Cork. 13.9° alc. **Rating** 94 **To** 2019 $22

Tinklers Vineyard   ★★★★

Pokolbin Mountains Road, Pokolbin, NSW 2330 **Region** Lower Hunter Valley
T (02) 4998 7435 **F** (02) 4998 7469 www.tinklers.com.au **Open** 7 days 10–5
Winemaker Usher John Tinkler **Est.** 1997 **Cases** 1000

Three generations of the Tinkler family have been involved with the property since 1942. Originally a beef and dairy farm, vines have been both pulled out and replanted at various stages along the way, and part of the adjoining old Ben Ean Vineyard acquired, the net result being a little over 41 ha of vines. The major part of the production is sold as grapes to McWilliam's, but when Usher John Tinkler returned from Charles Sturt University in 2001, he turned the tractor shed into a winery, and since then the wines have been made onsite. The wines have had significant show success.

Tintagel Wines

Sebbes Road, Forest Grove, WA 6286 **Region** Margaret River
T (08) 9386 2420 **F** (08) 9386 2420 **www.**tintagelwines.com.au **Open** By appt
Winemaker Mark Messenger (Contract) **Est.** 1993 **Cases** 750
The Westphal family began establishing their 9-ha vineyard in 1993, which now has 2 ha each of chardonnay, shiraz and cabernet sauvignon, and 1 ha each of semillon, sauvignon blanc and merlot. It is just south of the township of Margaret River, rubbing shoulders with names such as Leeuwin Estate and Devil's Lair. Part of the crop is sold to other makers. Exports to Malaysia.

ȲȲȲỴ̄ **Margaret River Semillon 2005** So different from Hunter Valley semillon; full of aroma and flavour in a crossover towards riesling; shows no sign of alcohol heat; good length, balance and intensity. Screwcap. 13° alc. **Rating** 91 **To** 2012 $18

Tintilla Wines ★★★★★

725 Hermitage Road, Pokolbin, NSW 2320 **Region** Lower Hunter Valley
T (02) 6574 7093 **F** (02) 9767 6894 **www.**tintilla.com.au **Open** 7 days 10.30–6
Winemaker James Lusby **Est.** 1993 **Cases** 3000
The Lusby family has established a 25-ha vineyard (including 1 ha of sangiovese) on a northeast-facing slope with red clay and limestone soil. They have also planted an olive grove producing 4 different types of olives, which are cured and sold from the estate.

ȲȲȲȲȲ **Pebbles Brief Hunter Valley Chardonnay 2006** Lots of colour, yet no skin contact used; a complex wine with abundant flavour and character; long and intense, with tangy/citrussy acidity. High-class winemaking. Screwcap. 13° alc. **Rating** 94 **To** 2011 $25
Reserve Hunter Valley Shiraz 2005 A particularly potent and powerful Hunter shiraz reflecting the dry vintage; ripe but not jammy blackberry fruit and supporting tannins; will be long-lived. Screwcap. 13.5° alc. **Rating** 94 **To** 2025 $26

ȲȲȲỴ̄ **Angus Semillon 2006** A powerful wine; good drive and length; focused lemon and grass. Screwcap. 10.5° alc. **Rating** 90 **To** 2016 $20
Justine Hunter Valley Merlot 2005 Fragrant and flavoursome; a particularly good wine from a region basically unsuited to merlot; supple mouthfeel and finish. Screwcap. 13.5° alc. **Rating** 90 **To** 2015 $26

ȲȲȲȲ **Rosato di Jupiter 2006** Bright, lively and fresh; light, but has length, and is not sweet. Screwcap. 11.5° alc. **Rating** 89 **To** 2008 $20

Tipperary Estate

167 Tipperary Road, Moffatdale via Murgon, Qld 4605 **Region** South Burnett
T (07) 4168 4802 **F** (07) 4168 4839 **www.**tipperaryestate.com.au **Open** Mon–Tues & Thurs–Fri 12–3, w'ends & public hols 10–4
Winemaker Clovely Estate (Luke Fitzpatrick) **Est.** 2002 **Cases** 500
The 2.5-ha vineyard of Tipperary Estate, planted to shiraz, verdelho and chardonnay, has been established high on the northern slopes overlooking the Barambah Valley. Additional grapes are purchased from other growers in the South Burnett region.

Tipperary Hill Estate

Alma-Bowendale Road, Alma via Maryborough, Vic 3465 **Region** Bendigo
T (03) 5461 3312 **F** (03) 5461 3312 **Open** W'ends 10–5, or by appt
Winemaker Paul Flowers **Est.** 1986 **Cases** 250
Paul Flowers says production depends 'on the frost, wind and birds', which perhaps explains why this is very much a part-time venture. Situated 7 km west of Maryborough, Tipperary Hill Estate is the only winery operating in the Central Goldfields Shire. Paul built the rough-cut pine winery and the bluestone residential cottage next door with the help of friends.

Tisdall Wines

19–29 Cornelia Creek Road, Echuca, Vic 3564 **Region** Goulburn Valley
T (03) 5482 1911 **F** (03) 5482 2516 **www.**tisdallwines.com.au **Open** 7 days 9.30–5
Winemaker Robin Querre, John Mackley **Est.** 1971 **Cases** 60 000
Tisdall Wines is not so much a new winery, as a reborn one. The vineyard, with 96 ha of most of the mainstream varieties, has been in continuous production and is managed by the Lummis family, originally appointed by Dr Peter Tisdall, founder of Tisdall Wines. Under the ownership of the Ballande Groupe, which acquired the business in 1998, the focus has been on export markets, with exports to the UK, Europe, Asia and Canada. A considerable number of tasting notes of lesser wines have been dropped from this edition due to space constraints.

Chardonnay 2004 Surprising elegance, flavour and intensity at this price point; nectarine and stone fruit; minimal oak, developing slowly. Screwcap. 13.5° alc. **Rating** 89 **To** 2009 $13
Cabernet Merlot 2003 Distinctly savoury/earthy overtones to the black fruits; fine-grained tannins; nice length and balance. Cork. 13.5° alc. **Rating** 88 **To** 2010 $13
Sauvignon Blanc 2004 A clean bouquet; gentle tropical fruit aromas and flavours; slightly simple but well-balanced. Screwcap. 11° alc. **Rating** 87 **To** 2008 $13
Shiraz 2003 A solid wine; earthy black fruits, and quite firm tannins; good value, though beware the dodgy cork. 14.5° alc. **Rating** 87 **To** 2010 $13

TK Wines   NR

c/- Kilikanoon Wines, Penna Lane, Penwortham, SA 5453 **Region** Adelaide Hills
T (08) 8843 4377 **F** (08) 8843 4246 **www.**tkwines.com.au **Open** Not
Winemaker Tim Knappstein **Est.** 1991 **Cases** NA

Tobin Wines

34 Ricca Road, Ballandean, Qld 4382 **Region** Granite Belt
T (07) 4684 1235 **F** (07) 4684 1235 **www.**tobinwines.com.au **Open** 7 days 10–5
Winemaker Adrian Tobin, David Gianini **Est.** 1964 **Cases** 1300
In the early 1960s the Ricca family planted table grapes, planting shiraz and semillon in 1964/6, which are said to be the oldest vinifera vines in the Granite Belt region. The Tobin family (headed by Adrian and Frances Tobin) purchased the vineyard in 2000 and have substantially increased plantings. There are now nearly 10 ha planted to semillon, verdelho, chardonnay, sauvignon blanc, shiraz, merlot, cabernet sauvignon and tempranillo, with some remaining rows of table grapes. The emphasis has changed towards quality bottled wines, with some impressive wines leading the way.

Isabella Semillon 2006 Clean and well-made; a crisp, minerally mouthfeel with touches of grass and lemon. Screwcap. 11.4° alc. **Rating** 89 **To** 2013 $20
Semillon Sauvignon Blanc 2006 Crisp, clean, grassy notes plus touches of lemon; an attractive dry, lingering finish. Screwcap. 11.4° alc. **Rating** 89 **To** 2010 $18

Tokar Estate

6 Maddens Lane, Coldstream, Vic 3770 **Region** Yarra Valley
T (03) 5964 9585 **F** (03) 5964 9587 **www.**tokarestate.com.au **Open** 7 days 10–5
Winemaker Paul Evans **Est.** 1996 **Cases** 4700
Leon Tokar is one of the number of new arrivals on Maddens Lane, having established 12.4 ha of
pinot noir, shiraz, cabernet sauvignon and tempranillo. Part of the grape production is sold to
Fosters, the remainder contract-made.

TTTTT **The Reserve Pinot Noir 2003** Fragrant and spicy, with touches of stem and
forest on the bouquet; the palate has ripe, rich and velvety fruit, very much at the
big end of town. French oak for 2 years. Diam. 14° alc. **Rating** 90 **To** 2011 $50
Shiraz 2004 Powerful, full-bodied wine in typical Tokar style; luscious ripe
blackberry fruit, some licorice and smooth tannins. Diam. 13.5° alc. **Rating** 90
To 2024 $28
Tempranillo 2004 The variety is starting to establish itself within varying
climatic bounds; red cherry and a squeeze of lemon juice are well-balanced,
the wine clean and long. Diam. 13.5° alc. **Rating** 90 **To** 2017 $29
Joie de Vie Methode Traditional 2000 Inconsistent mousse; full-flavoured
ripe and citrus, almost tropical; length and balance on the rich side. Spent
5 years on lease, hand-riddled, and disgorged late '05. Pinot Noir/Pinot
Meunier/Chardonnay. 12.5° alc. **Rating** 90 **To** 2010 $30

TTTT **Chardonnay 2005** A medium- to full-bodied style within the Yarra, with an
abundance of ripe stone fruit; oak also pushes the envelope. Diam. 14° alc.
Rating 89 **To** 2009 $24
Pinot Noir 2005 Very full-bodied; powerful plum fruit, nowhere near ready,
again outside the Yarra mainstream. Should develop. Screwcap. 14° alc.
Rating 89 **To** 2016 $24
Cabernet Sauvignon 2004 Ripe aromas and flavours, very much in the black
fruit spectrum, tending to tail off on the mid- to back-palate. Diam. 14° alc.
Rating 89 **To** 2015 $30

Tollana

Tanunda Road, Nuriootpa, SA 5355 **Region** Barossa Valley
T (08) 8568 9389 **F** (08) 8568 9489 **www.**australianwines.com.au/tollana **Open** Not
Winemaker Andrew Baldwin **Est.** 1888 **Cases** 10 000
Tollana survived a near-death experience during the turbulent days of the Rosemount
management of Southcorp; where it will ultimately fit in the Fosters scheme of things remains to
be seen, but in the meantime, Tollana is back in business producing Riesling, Viognier, Shiraz and
Cabernet Sauvignon.

TTTTT **Bin TR16 Adelaide Hills Eden Valley Shiraz 2005** One of the most
powerful and rich TR16s ever made; redolent with blackberry, licorice and
cracked pepper fruit, with ripe tannins in support, oak likewise; has the
requisite balance for prolonged ageing. Screwcap. 14.5° alc. **Rating** 95
To 2030 $18.95

TTTTT **Reserve Bin Barossa Shiraz 2002** Light- to medium-bodied; an immaculately
balanced and elegant shiraz reflecting the cool vintage. Screwcap. 14° alc. **Rating** 92
To 2019 $44.95
Cellar Door Reserve Barossa Valley Shiraz 2005 Elegant; has long fruit
flavour and persistence, as well as good balance; blackberry with touches of
leather, earth and chocolate. Screwcap. 15° alc. **Rating** 91 **To** 2015 $19.95

Tom's Waterhole Wines ★★★

Felton, Longs Corner Road, Canowindra, NSW 2804 **Region** Cowra
T (02) 6344 1819 **F** (02) 6344 2172 www.tomswaterhole.com.au **Open** W'ends &
public hols 10–4, or by appt
Winemaker Graham Kerr **Est.** 1997 **Cases** 800

Graham Timms and Graham Kerr started the development of Tom's Waterhole Wines in 1997,
progressively establishing 6 ha of shiraz, cabernet sauvignon, semillon and merlot, completing the
planting program in 2001. They have decided to bypass the use of irrigation, so the yields will
always be low.

Tomboy Hill ★★★★★

204 Sim Street, Ballarat, Vic 3350 (postal) **Region** Ballarat
T (03) 5331 3785 **Open** Not
Winemaker Scott Ireland (Contract) **Est.** 1984 **Cases** 1200

Former schoolteacher Ian Watson seems to be following the same path as Lindsay McCall of
Paringa Estate (also a former schoolteacher) in extracting greater quality and style than any other
winemaker in his region, in this case Ballarat. Since 1984 Watson has slowly and patiently built up
a patchwork quilt of small plantings (most from 0.33 ha to 2 ha). In the better years, the single-
vineyard wines of Chardonnay and/or Pinot Noir are released; Rebellion Chardonnay and Pinot
Noir are multi-vineyard blends, but all 100% Ballarat. Exports to Canada.

ΨΨΨΨΨ **Rebellion Ballarat Goldfields Chardonnay 2005** A very complex wine; fully
ripened melon, stone fruit and fig fruit; good oak handling, and a long finish.
Screwcap. 13.5° alc. **Rating** 94 **To** 2018 $30

Harry's Picking Chardonnay 2005 A seamless union between white peach,
grapefruit and oak flavours; faintly nutty/creamy notes, presumably from mlf.
Screwcap. 13.8° alc. **Rating** 94 **To** 2012 $45

Rebellion Ballarat Goldfields Pinot Noir 2005 Excellent hue, still purple-
tinged; an aromatic bouquet with spicy/flowery red fruit; lovely balance and
mouthfeel, with a perfectly presented array of cherry and plum fruit, silky
tannins and discreet oak. Screwcap. 13.5° alc. **Rating** 94 **To** 2011 $35

Tomich Hill Wines ★★★★

87 King William Road, Unley, SA 5061 (postal) **Region** Adelaide Hills
T (08) 8272 9388 **F** (08) 8373 7229 www.tomichhill.com.au **Open** Not
Winemaker John Tomich, Tim Knappstein (Contract) **Est.** 2002 **Cases** 2200

There is an element of irony in this family venture. Patriarch John Tomich was born on a vineyard
near Mildura, where he learnt firsthand the skills and knowledge required for premium
grapegrowing. He went on to become a well-known Adelaide ear, nose and throat specialist. He
has taken the wheel full circle with post-graduate studies at the University of Adelaide, resulting
in a diploma in winemaking in 2002, and now venturing on the Master of Wine revision course
from the Institute of Masters of Wine. His son Randal is a cutting from the old vine
(metaphorically speaking), having invented new equipment and techniques for tending the
family's 80-ha vineyard in the Adelaide Hills near Woodside; resulting in a 60% saving in time and
fuel costs. Most of the grapes are sold, but the amount of wine made under the Tomich Hill brand
is far from a hobby.

ΨΨΨΨΨ **Adelaide Hills Riesling 2006** Attractive spice, herb and citrus aromas; positive
flavours build through the length of the palate. Screwcap. 13° alc. **Rating** 92
To 2014 $17

Lenswood Pinot Noir 2005 Has more flavour intensity and complexity than the
colour (or the bouquet) would suggest; red fruits, with ripe stemmy characters, the
wine progressively creeping up on you. Screwcap. 13.5° alc. **Rating** 90 **To** 2011 $20

ΨΨΨΨ **Adelaide Hills Gewurztraminer 2006** Shy, spicy, lychee nuances on the
bouquet; some rose petal and spice add to the flavours; will develop with a little
more time. Screwcap. 12.8° alc. **Rating** 88 **To** 2012 $17

Adelaide Hills Sauvignon Blanc 2006 Light- to medium-bodied; gentle tropical/gooseberry fruit, with moderate length; clean and well-made. Screwcap. 13° alc. **Rating** 88 **To** 2008 $16
Adelaide Hills Pinot Gris 2006 Mainstream aromas of apple, pear and musk; the palate has a catch on the finish akin to that of grenache blanc; subliminal sweetness. Screwcap. 13° alc. **Rating** 88 **To** 2008 $24.50

Toms Cap Vineyard

322 Lays Road, Carrajung Lower, Vic 3844 **Region** Gippsland
T (03) 5194 2215 **www**.tomscap.com.au **Open** Fri–Sun & public hols, or by appt
Winemaker Owen Schmidt (Contract) **Est.** 1994 **Cases** 570
Graham Morris began the development of the vineyard in 1992 on a 40-ha property surrounded by the forests of the Strzelecki Ranges, the 90-mile beach at Woodside, and the Tarra Bulga National Park, one of the 4 major areas of cool temperature rainforest in Vic. The vineyard has 2.4 ha of cabernet sauvignon, chardonnay, sauvignon blanc and riesling.

 Gippsland Sauvignon Blanc 2006 Well-made; clean, crisp herb, cut grass and gooseberry aromas and flavours; bright, dry finish. Screwcap. 12.8° alc. **Rating** 88 **To** 2008
Cabernet Sauvignon 2004 Surprisingly sweet and ripe fruit given the low alcohol, the flavours ranging through cassis, raspberry and blackcurrant; finishes with soft tannins. Cork. 12.6° alc. **Rating** 88 **To** 2012
Gippsland Chardonnay 2005 Some echoes of barrel fermentation giving a touch of funky complexity; savoury/citrussy flavours; fair length. Screwcap. 13.5° alc. **Rating** 87 **To** 2010
Botrytis Sauvignon Blanc 2004 Bronze colour; exceptionally rich, and also has good acidity; simply lost or used its available free SO_2 before, during or after bottling. Cork. **Rating** 87 **To** 2008

Toogoolah Wines ★★★

4602 Mitchell Highway, Lucknow, NSW 2800 **Region** Orange
T (02) 6365 5200 **F** (02) 6365 5545 **www**.toogoolah.com.au **Open** 7 days 11–5
Winemaker Chris Derrez, Lucy Maddox (Contract) **Est.** 1995 **Cases** 1500
Local business owners, Laurence and Susan Mockler, began the development of their vineyard 12 km east of Orange in 1995. Typical of many such properties in the area, it was once a cherry orchard, at an elevation of 935 m on rich, red volcanic soils. The 8 ha of vines include sauvignon blanc, pinot gris, riesling, shiraz and pinot noir, part of the production sold as grapes and part competently contract-made.

Riesling 2006 Big, slightly phenolic/heavy flavours in full-on Alsace style. Screwcap. **Rating** 88 **To** 2013

Toolangi Vineyards ★★★★★

PO Box 5046, Glenferrie South, Vic 3122 **Region** Yarra Valley
T (03) 9822 9488 **F** (03) 9804 3365 **www**.toolangi.com **Open** Not
Winemaker Various contract **Est.** 1995 **Cases** 10 000
Garry and Julie Hounsell acquired their property in the Dixons Creek subregion of the Yarra Valley, adjoining the Toolangi State Forest, in 1995. Plantings have taken place progressively since then, with 13 ha now in the ground. The primary accent is on pinot noir and chardonnay, accounting for all but 2.8 ha, which is predominantly shiraz, and a few rows of merlot. As only half the vineyards are in bearing, production is supplemented by chardonnay and pinot noir from the Coldstream subregion, cropped at 2 tonnes per acre. Winemaking is by Tom Carson of Yering Station, Rick Kinzbrunner of Giaconda and Matt Harrop of Shadowfax, as impressive a trio of winemakers as one could wish for. A 24-ha property was acquired in late 2005 on which a cellar door will be built, and further chardonnay planted.

ŶŶŶŶŶ **Reserve Yarra Valley Chardonnay 2005** Far more depth and texture than most Yarra chardonnays, almost headed into Margaret River territory; perhaps the Rick Kinzbrunner touch, given major winemaking inputs which augment every flavour nuance. Screwcap. 14° alc. **Rating** 94 **To** 2013 $70

ŶŶŶŶŶ **Yarra Valley Chardonnay 2005** An elegant, medium-bodied wine with melon and citrus fruit, then a minerally finish; still very tight and closed, and will flourish with time in bottle. Screwcap. 13.5° alc. **Rating** 90 **To** 2015 $22

Toolleen Vineyard

2004 Gibb Road, Toolleen, Vic 3551 (postal) **Region** Heathcote
T (03) 5433 6397 **F** (03) 5433 6397 **Open** Not
Winemaker Dominque Portet **Est.** 1996 **Cases** 1500
Owned by Mr KC Huang and family, Toolleen's 14.7 ha of shiraz, cabernet sauvignon, merlot, cabernet franc and durif are planted on the western slope of Mt Camel, 18 km north of Heathcote. The lower Cambrian red soils are now well recognised for their suitability for making full-bodied and strongly structured red wines. Most of the wine (80%) is exported to Taiwan, Malaysia, Singapore, Hong Kong and the US.

Toorak Wines

Farm 279 Toorak Road, Leeton, NSW 2705 **Region** Riverina
T (02) 6953 2333 **F** (02) 6953 4454 **www**.toorakwines.com.au **Open** Mon–Sat 10–5
Winemaker Robert Bruno **Est.** 1965 **Cases** 400 000
A traditional, long-established Riverina producer with a strong Italian-based clientele around Australia. Production has been increasing significantly, utilising 150 ha of estate plantings and grapes purchased from other growers, both in the Riverina and elsewhere. Wines are released under the Willandra Estate, Toorak Estate and Amesbury Estate labels.

ŶŶŶŶ **Willandra Premium Shiraz 2005** Medium-bodied blackberry, plum and black cherry fruit; soft tannins. Like all the Willandra wines, good value. Langhorne Creek. Screwcap. 15° alc. **Rating** 87 **To** 2010 $8

Top-Paddock Winery

Elard Farm, Lot 9 Fleay Road, Harvey, WA 6220 **Region** Geographe
T (08) 9729 3240 **F** (08) 9729 1569 **www**.top-paddock.com **Open** 7 days 12–5
Winemaker Peter Stanlake **Est.** 2003 **Cases** 700
Richard Warren and Elaine George have planted 3 ha of cabernet sauvignon on a property high in the Darling Ranges, forming part of Elard Farm. The grapes are hand-picked and basket-pressed, but are then made into no less than 4 different styles: White Cabernet Sauvignon, Cabernet Rose, Carbonic Macerated Cabernet Sauvignon and traditional Cabernet Sauvignon, designed, says Richard Warren, 'to suit all tastes'.

Topper's Mountain Vineyard ★★★☆

13 Mirrabook Street, Bilgola Plateau, NSW 2107 (postal) **Region** New England
T (02) 6723 3506 **F** (02) 6723 3222 **www**.toppers.com.au **Open** Not
Winemaker Contract **Est.** 2000 **Cases** NFP
This is yet another New England venture, owned by the Kirkby and Birch families, with Mark Kirkby having the primary management responsibilities. Planting began in the spring of 2000, with 1.1 ha, the remaining 8.9 ha following in the spring of 2002. Varieties planted include chardonnay, gewurztraminer, sauvignon blanc, semillon, riesling, tempranillo and shiraz.

ŶŶŶŶ **Chardonnay 2005** Skilled winemaking inputs, with touches of malolactic, lees and barrel ferment characters which do not compromise the varietal fruit; creamy mouthfeel. **Rating** 92 **To** 2010 $24

Torambre Wines   NR

Balfour Ogilvy Avenue, Loxton North, SA 5333 **Region** Riverland
T (08) 8584 1530 **www.torambre.com.au Open** Fri–Sun 10–4
Winemaker Tony Saunders, Marino Gregoric **Est.** 2000 **Cases** NA
This is an unusual business, to say the least. Tony Saunders and Marino and Deb Gregoric have
set up a cellar door in a World War II Nissen hut, much refurbished and air-conditioned, but
nonetheless a reminder of the hellish conditions soldiers in the Second World War had to endure
even when not in battle. It is also unusual in being an estate-based operation, with 24.5 ha
of chardonnay, verdelho, grenache, cabernet sauvignon, merlot, shiraz and mataro, this in a region
noted for broadacre farming and vast wineries.

Torbreck Vintners   ★★★★★

Roennfeldt Road, Marananga, SA 5352 **Region** Barossa Valley
T (08) 8562 4155 **F** (08) 8562 4195 **www.torbreck.com Open** 7 days 10–6
Winemaker David Powell **Est.** 1994 **Cases** 50 000
Of all the Barossa Valley wineries to grab the headlines in the US, with demand pulling prices up
to undreamt of levels, Torbreck stands supreme. David Powell has not let success go to his head,
or subvert the individuality and sheer quality of his wines, all created around very old, dry-grown,
bush-pruned vineyards. The top trio are led by The RunRig (Shiraz/Viognier); then The Factor
(Shiraz) and The Descendant (Shiraz/Viognier); next The Struie (Shiraz) and The Steading
(Grenache/Shiraz). Notwithstanding the depth and richness of the wines, they have a remarkable
degree of finesse.

ΨΨΨΨΨ **The Factor 2004** Deep red-purple; rich, multi-layered palate both in texture
and flavour terms; silky black fruits, super-fine tannins, and a long, harmonious
finish. Shiraz. Cork. 14.5° alc. **Rating** 96 **To** 2019 $135
The Gask 2005 Typical, dense purple-red; equally typical dense layers of
blackberry and licorice fruit, although a distinctively new regional style for
Torbreck; supple and rich, backed by the requisite tannins and oak. Eden Valley
Shiraz. Cork. 15° alc. **Rating** 95 **To** 2030 $75
The Struie 2005 Both the bouquet and palate sing the same song; blackberry,
spice and quality oak woven together with ripe, balanced tannins. It is so
difficult to fault these wines within the parameters, particularly at 14.5° alcohol.
Barossa Valley Shiraz. Cork. **Rating** 95 **To** 2025 $48.50

ΨΨΨΨΨ **Barossa Valley Viognier 2006** Certainly demonstrates that oak and viognier are
compatible, having been barrel-fermented and spent 9 months in new French oak.
Whether the fermentation and maturation was over-enthusiastic is another matter.
Rich and mouthfilling, nonetheless. Cork. 13.5° alc. **Rating** 90 **To** 2010 $48.50
Cuvee Juveniles 2006 Fresh and lively red fruit flavours; Torbreck is on the
ball releasing the wine as an early-drinking style. Barossa Valley Grenache/
Mataro/Shiraz. Screwcap. 14.5° alc. **Rating** 90 **To** 2008 $27.50
The Steading 2004 Typical raspberry/cherry jam flavours ex grenache, but given
more complexity by the other components; fine, gentle, savoury tannins.
Grenache/Mataro/Shiraz. Cork. 14.5° alc. **Rating** 90 **To** 2010 $42

ΨΨΨΨ **Cuvee Juveniles 2005** Light red-purple; light-bodied, clean, fresh juicy berry
grenache seemingly playing a bigger role than the shiraz. Shiraz/Grenache/Mataro.
Screwcap. 14.6° alc. **Rating** 88 **To** 2008 $26

Torzi Matthews Vintners   ★★★★★

Cnr Eden Valley Road/Sugarloaf Hill Road, Mount McKenzie, SA 5353 **Region** Eden
Valley
T (08) 8565 3393 **F** (08) 8565 3393 **www.edenvalleyshiraz.com.au Open** By appt
Winemaker Domenic Torzi **Est.** 1996 **Cases** 1900
Domenic Torzi and Tracey Matthews, former Adelaide Plains residents, searched for a number of
years before finding a 6-ha block at Mt McKenzie in the Eden Valley. The block they chose is in

a hollow and the soil is meagre, and they were in no way deterred by the knowledge that it would be frost-prone. The result is predictably low yields, concentrated further by drying the grapes on racks and reducing the weight by around 30% (the Appassimento method is used in Italy to produce Amarone-style wines). Two wines are made, both under the Frost Dodger label: Eden Valley Riesling and Eden Valley Shiraz, the Shiraz wild yeast-fermented and neither fined nor filtered. Exports to the UK, the US, Denmark and Singapore.

⟡⟡⟡⟡⟡ **Frost Dodger Eden Valley Shiraz 2004** Medium red-purple; a complex array of aromas and flavours ranging through sweet plum, blackberry, touches of dark chocolate, and spice; fine-grained tannins; Amarone style. Screwcap. 14.5° alc. **Rating** 94 **To** 2025 $30

⟡⟡⟡⟡⟡ **Frost Dodger Eden Valley Riesling 2006** Tightly structured and focused; lemon, citrus and spice with a strong, minerally backbone; refreshing, bone-dry finish. Screwcap. 12° alc. **Rating** 93 **To** 2018 $18

Tower Estate

Cnr Broke Road/Hall Road, Pokolbin, NSW 2320 **Region** Lower Hunter Valley
T (02) 4998 7989 **F** (02) 4998 7919 **www**.towerestatewines.com.au **Open** 7 days 10–5
Winemaker Scott Stephens, Jeff Byrne **Est.** 1999 **Cases** 10 000
Tower Estate was founded by the late Len Evans, with the 5-star Tower Lodge accommodation and convention centre part of the development. It is anticipated there will be little day-to-day change in either part of the business. Tower Estate will continue to draw upon varieties and regions which have a particular synergy, the aim being to make the best possible wines in the top sector of the wine market. Exports to the UK, Denmark, Russia, Singapore, Hong Kong, Japan and Canada.

⟡⟡⟡⟡⟡ **Yarra Valley Pinot Noir 2004** Fragrant and clear varietal character, with a mix of red fruits and some savoury notes ex whole bunches; perfect structure, texture and balance. Dijon clones. Cork. 13.5° alc. **Rating** 95 **To** 2013 $45

⟡⟡⟡⟡⟡ **Hunter Valley Shiraz 2004** Medium red-purple; juicy berry fruit, bright acidity and sober oak influence; will flower with more time in bottle. High-quality cork. 13° alc. **Rating** 93 **To** 2019 $42
Adelaide Hills Sauvignon Blanc 2006 Spotlessly clean; generous flavours oscillating around a tropical core; good finish and length. Cork. 13.5° alc. **Rating** 92 **To** 2008 $32

⟡⟡⟡⟡ **Hunter Valley Verdelho 2006** Clean, well-made and balanced; the limitations lie with the variety, not the winemaking; simply designed not to frighten the horses. Cork. 14° alc. **Rating** 88 **To** 2008 $22

Trafford Hill Vineyard ★★★☆

Lot 1 Bower Road, Normanville, SA 5204 **Region** Southern Fleurieu
T (08) 8558 3595 **www**.geocities.com/traffordhill **Open** Thurs–Mon & hols 10.30–5
Winemaker John Sanderson **Est.** 1996 **Cases** 650
Irene and John Sanderson have established 1 ha of vineyard on the coast of the Fleurieu Peninsula, near to its southern extremity. Irene carries out all the viticulture, and John makes the wine with help from district veteran Allan Dyson.

⟡⟡⟡⟡⟡ **Monique Family Reserve Southern Fleurieu Red 2003** Attractive spicy, cedary wine; lots of texture and flavour within its medium-bodied frame; fine, ripe tannins. Shiraz/Cabernet Sauvignon/Grenache. Cork. 14.5° alc. **Rating** 90 **To** 2014 $22

⟡⟡⟡⟡ **Master Liam Southern Fleurieu Riesling 2006** Only one of a dozen rieslings tasted in that flight closed with a cork, the others screwcap; the unmistakable taste of cork (not TCA or any other fault) blurred the flavour, although the structure is good. 13° alc. **Rating** 88 **To** 2009 $16.50

Train Trak

957 Healesville-Yarra Glen Road, Yarra Glen, Vic 3775 **Region** Yarra Valley
T (03) 9730 1314 **F** (03) 9427 1510 **www.**traintrak.com.au **Open** Thurs–Mon
Winemaker Contract **Est.** 1995 **Cases** 10 000
The unusual name comes from the Yarra Glen to Healesville railway, which was built in 1889 and abandoned in 1980 – part of it passes by the Train Trak vineyard. The 15.95-ha vineyard is planted (in descending order) to pinot noir, cabernet sauvignon, chardonnay and shiraz. The restaurant makes exceptional pizzas in a wood-fired oven. Exports to Japan.

Yarra Valley Cabernet Sauvignon 2004 Attractive cassis and blackcurrant fruit belies the low alcohol which, however, leaves no green notes; controlled oak and ripe, fine tannins. In bygone decades 12.5% alcohol would have been considered a sign of perfect maturing. Cork. **Rating** 94 **To** 2019 $25

Yarra Valley Pinot Noir 2004 Spicy, toasty oak and fresh cherry and plum fruit; light- to medium-bodied, good acidity making up for some lack of flesh. Screwcap. **Rating** 90 **To** 2010 $25

Yarra Valley Chardonnay 2005 Light- to medium-bodied; similar to the '06 Sojourn except for an obvious touch of barrel ferment oak; well-made within its limitations. Screwcap. 13° alc. **Rating** 89 **To** 2010 $25
Sojourn Yarra Valley Chardonnay 2006 A pleasant, light- to medium-bodied wine, with melon, apple and citrus; not particularly complex; little or no oak, perhaps. Screwcap. 13° alc. **Rating** 87 **To** 2009 $18

Tranquil Vale

325 Pywells Road, Luskintyre, NSW 2321 **Region** Lower Hunter Valley
T (02) 4930 6100 **www.**tranquilvalewines.com.au **Open** Thurs–Mon 10–5, or by appt
Winemaker Phil Griffiths **Est.** 1996 **Cases** 2000
Phil and Lucy Griffiths purchased the property sight unseen from a description in an old copy of the *Weekend Australian* found in the High Commission Office in London. The vineyard they established is on the banks of the Hunter River, opposite Wyndham Estate, on relatively fertile, sandy clay loam. Competent winemaking has resulted in good wines, some of which have already had show success. Exports to the UK.

Hunter Valley Semillon 2006 Water-white; tight, vibrant and crisp, but the elevated acidity is distracting. Screwcap. 11° alc. **Rating** 88 **To** 2013 $17
Hunter Valley Shiraz 2005 A medium-bodied, understated, sotto voce style; while not deep, it does have length to the plum and black cherry fruit, the oak sensibly restrained. Screwcap. 13.5° alc. **Rating** 87 **To** 2013 $25
Old Luskie NV Extremely rich and luscious peach, honey and cream; to adequately sustain the richness needed longer maturation and higher acidity. **Rating** 87 **To** 2006 $21

Trappers Gully

Lot 6 Boyup Road, Mount Barker, WA 6324 **Region** Mount Barker
T (08) 9851 2565 **F** (08) 9851 3565 **Open** By appt
Winemaker Clea Candy, James Kellie (Consultant) **Est.** 1998 **Cases** 1000
The Lester and Candy families began the development of Trappers Gully in 1998, bringing varied backgrounds with them. Clea Candy has the most directly relevant CV, as a qualified viticulturist and practised winemaker, and, according to the official history, 'mother, daughter and wife, and pretty much the instigator of all heated discussions'. The families have progressively planted 1.2 ha each of chenin blanc, sauvignon blanc, cabernet sauvignon and shiraz, and slightly less than 1 ha of cabernet sauvignon.

Treeton Estate ★★★☆

North Treeton Road, Cowaramup, WA 6284 **Region** Margaret River
T (08) 9755 5481 **F** (08) 9755 5051 **www.**treetonestate.com.au **Open** 7 days 10–6
Winemaker David McGowan **Est.** 1984 **Cases** 6000
In 1982 David McGowan and wife Corinne purchased the 30-ha property upon which Treeton
Estate is established, planting the 7.1-ha vineyard 2 years later. David has done just about
everything in his life, and in the early years was working in Perth, which led to various setbacks
for the vineyard. The wines are light and fresh, sometimes rather too much so.

Trentham Estate ★★★★

Sturt Highway, Trentham Cliffs, NSW 2738 **Region** Murray Darling
T (03) 5024 8888 **F** (03) 5024 8800 **www.**trenthamestate.com.au **Open** 7 days 9.30–5
Winemaker Anthony Murphy, Shane Kerr **Est.** 1988 **Cases** 60 000
Remarkably consistent tasting notes across all wine styles from all vintages attest to the expertise
of ex-Mildara winemaker Tony Murphy, making the Trentham wines from his family vineyards.
All the wines offer great value for money. Exports to the US, the UK, Belgium and NZ.

 La Famiglia Pinot Gris 2006 A extra degree of perfumed fragrance and
flavour; citrus blossom and honeysuckle give the wine personality. Screwcap.
12° alc. **Rating** 89 **To** 2008 $14
Sauvignon Blanc 2006 Expressive, flowery bouquet; the palate light but with
clear sauvignon blanc varietal character; impressive achievement for the region
and the price. Screwcap. 12.5° alc. **Rating** 88 **To** 2008 $12
Cabernet Sauvignon Merlot 2004 Fresh and firm blackcurrant, mulberry and
cassis fruit; good length. Screwcap. 13.5° alc. **Rating** 88 **To** 2010 $14
Two Thirds Semillon Sauvignon Blanc 2006 An interesting attempt at a wine
with two-thirds of the normal alcohol; gentle tropical fruit and good balance; points
for the idea. Screwcap. 8.5° alc. **Rating** 87 **To** 2008 $12
Pinot Noir 2005 Once again flies in the face of all reason, producing pinot
from such a warm climate which retains some varietal expression in a sweet
cherry and spice spectrum. Screwcap. 13.5° alc. **Rating** 87 **To** 2008 $14.50
Shiraz 2003 Fresh and youthful; a mix of earthy/spicy berry fruit, but not
especially fleshy; fair balance and length. Screwcap. 14° alc. **Rating** 87 **To** 2008 $15
Merlot 2005 Predominantly blackcurrant and some cassis; perhaps closer to
cabernet sauvignon, but doesn't have any savoury characters (good or bad), the warm
region prevailing. Screwcap. 13.5° alc. **Rating** 87 **To** 2012 $12.50

Trevelen Farm ★★★★☆

Weir Road, Cranbrook, WA 6321 **Region** Great Southern
T (08) 9826 1052 **www.**trevelenfarmwines.com.au **Open** Thurs–Mon 10–4.30, or by appt
Winemaker Harewood Estate (James Kellie) **Est.** 1993 **Cases** 3000
John and Katie Sprigg, together with their family, operate a 1300-ha wool, meat and grain-
producing farm, run on environmental principles with sustainable agriculture at its heart. As a
minor, but highly successful, diversification they established 5 ha of sauvignon blanc, riesling,
chardonnay, cabernet sauvignon and merlot in 1993, adding 1.5 ha of shiraz in 2000. The quality
of the wines is as consistent as the prices are modest, and visitors to the cellar door have the added
attraction of both garden and forest walks, the latter among 130 ha of remnant bush home to
many different orchids. Exports to the UK, Hong Kong, Malaysia and Japan.

 Riesling 2006 Lime/grapefruit/apple aromas and flavours; mid-palate
sweetness balanced by acidity on the finish; overall delicacy. Screwcap. 11° alc.
Rating 94 **To** 2014 $18

Chardonnay 2005 Still very youthful and slow-developing; stone fruit and
grapefruit flavours, the oak seamlessly balanced and integrated; citrus/mineral
acidity to close. Great value. Screwcap. 13.5° alc. **Rating** 93 **To** 2011 $18

Tunney Cabernet Sauvignon 2005 Clear-cut cabernet sauvignon varietal character; blackcurrant aromas, with cassis joining in on the palate; medium-bodied, but has considerable length and persistence; perfect ripeness. Screwcap. 14° alc. **Rating** 93 **To** 2020 $20

Reserve Frankland Shiraz 2005 An aromatic wine, seemingly just a little late-picked; blackberry, raspberry and spice, with the paradox of a brisk finish. Screwcap. 15.5° alc. **Rating** 90 **To** 2015 $25

♱♱♱♱ **Reserve Frankland Merlot 2005** Fragrant red berry and olive bouquet; plenty of flavour, and supple tannins. Screwcap. 15° alc. **Rating** 89 **To** 2014 $23

Katie's Kiss Soft Sweet Riesling 2006 One of the many Mosel-style wines with low alcohol and appreciable sweetness, in this instance the sweetness well and truly balanced by acidity. Screwcap. 9.5° alc. **Rating** 89 **To** 2008 $14

Trevor Jones/Kellermeister   ★★★★★

Barossa Valley Highway, Lyndoch, SA 5351 **Region** Barossa Valley
T (08) 8524 4303 **F** (08) 8524 4880 **www**.kellermeister.com.au **Open** 7 days 9–6
Winemaker Trevor Jones, Matthew Reynolds **Est.** 1996 **Cases** 26 000
Trevor Jones is an industry veteran, with vast experience in handling fruit from the Barossa Valley, Eden Valley and the Adelaide Hills. His business operates on 2 levels: Kellermeister was founded in 1979 with the emphasis on low-cost traditional Barossa wine styles. In 1996 he expanded the scope by introducing the ultra-premium Trevor Jones range, with a strong export focus. Exports to the US, France, Switzerland, Macau, Singapore and Japan.

♱♱♱♱♱ **Trevor Jones Wild Witch Reserve Barossa Valley Shiraz 2003** Dense red-purple; a concentrated and layered palate, with many levels of blackberry, prune, plum and licorice; has easily dealt with 2.5 years in French and American oak. Cork. 14.5° alc. **Rating** 96 **To** 2033 $72

Kellermeister Black Sash Barossa Valley Shiraz 2004 Fragrant, spicy overtones to black fruit aromas; elegant, perfectly balanced and structured medium-bodied wines; fruit-driven, but with sufficient oak and tannin support for top quality. Screwcap. 14.5° alc. **Rating** 95 **To** 2025 $32.50

Trevor Jones Boots Eden Valley Riesling 2006 Tight, classic mineral/slate lime and lemon aromas and flavours; acidity is particularly good, adding length and vibrancy. Screwcap. 12.5° alc. **Rating** 94 **To** 2016 $17.50

Trevor Jones Dry Grown Barossa Shiraz 2004 Medium-bodied; at once elegant and complex, with fruit, oak and tannins intertwined from start to finish; a finish which is remarkably supple. Screwcap. 14.8° alc. **Rating** 94 **To** 2024 $38

Trevor Jones Dry Grown Barossa Shiraz 2003 A very generous and rich '03 wine, with lots of black fruits; nicely ripe, but not jammy; good length and balance. Screwcap. 14.9° alc. **Rating** 94 **To** 2024 $40

♱♱♱♱♀ **Kellermeister Fragrant Fruity Eden Valley White Gewurztraminer 2006** Relatively full-bodied; Eden Valley is one of the few regions to work with the variety; strongly spiced in oriental mode; has length. Screwcap. 13.8° alc. **Rating** 90 **To** 2010 $16

Trevor Jones Boots Grenache 2004 Typical light- to medium-bodied juicy Barossa style, but not too much confection; good acidity and considerable length. Screwcap. 14.5° alc. **Rating** 90 **To** 2009 $17

♱♱♱♱ **Trevor Jones Boots Cebo Barossa Valley Rose 2006** Lots of fresh juicy berry flavours balanced by long, but not aggressive, acidity. Screwcap. 13.5° alc. **Rating** 89 **To** 2008 $15

Trevor Jones Methode Champenoise Sparkling Shiraz NV Reserve wines up to 10 years old are blended with current vintage; not oaky or too sweet; better than many, though the high alcohol a minor handicap. 14.8° alc. **Rating** 89 **To** 2015 $23

Trevor Jones Boots Barossa Valley Sticky 2002 Not complex, but easy to drink; canned tropical fruit characters with a touch of lemony acidity to provide balance. Screwcap. 11.5° alc. **Rating** 89 **To** 2008 $15

Trevor Jones Virgin Chardonnay 2005 Attractive unwooded style made from free-run juice and no oak; is still crisp, and has good length. Screwcap. 13.5° alc. **Rating** 88 **To** 2010 $17

Trevor Jones Boots Barossa Shiraz 2005 A medium-bodied, pleasant wine with just enough fruit and tannins to give length; cellaring not really required. Screwcap. 14.5° alc. **Rating** 88 **To** 2011 $19

Trevor Jones Methode Champenoise Chardonnay Pinot NV Distinct rose tint; dry and crisp, with a long finish marked by cleansing acidity; 18 months on lees. 12° alc. **Rating** 88 **To** 2009 $23

Trevor Jones A/T Liqueur Shiraz NV A very rich and sweet mix of older and younger material; in full-on sweet Australian tawny port style. Has a remarkably incoherent back label. Screwcap. 18.5° alc. **Rating** 88 **To** 2008 $17

Kellermeister Windsong Barossa Valley Crisp Dry White 2005 Has some stony, wet pebble, minerality and a touch of citrus; serve well-chilled with cold seafood. Screwcap. 10.2° alc. **Rating** 87 **To** 2008 $15.50

Trevor Jones Sparkling Red NV Not too heavy or sweet, though tending simple at this stage; time on cork might work miracles. 14° alc. **Rating** 87 **To** 2012 $12

Trust

81 Horace Street, Bendigo, Vic 3550 (postal) **Region** Central Victoria Zone
T 0427 310 214 **www**.trustwines.com.au **Open** Not
Winemaker Don Lewis, Narelle King **Est.** 2004 **Cases** 500
Trust is the venture of Don Lewis and Narelle King; the fact that it is a virtual winery, with neither vineyards nor winery of its own, should not fool you. Don Lewis was the chief winemaker at Mitchelton almost from the word go, with over 25 years' experience. This has given him the knowledge to source parcels of high-quality grapes from vineyards in Central Victoria, and it goes without saying that the winemaking is of the highest quality.

Shiraz 2004 Naturally, in very similar style to the '05, but with a little more focus and length; stylish and age-worthy. Screwcap. 14.5° alc. **Rating** 94 **To** 2023 $35

Shiraz 2005 An elegant, medium-bodied, lively array of red and black fruits, with fine tannins supporting the long finish; oak sotto voce. Screwcap. 14.9° alc. **Rating** 93 **To** 2020 $35

Tscharke Wines/Glaymond Wines   ★★★☆

PO Box 657, Greenock, SA 5360 **Region** Barossa Valley
T 0438 628 178 **F** (08) 8562 4920 **www**.glaymondwines.com **Open** Not
Winemaker Damien Tscharke **Est.** 2001 **Cases** 1500
Damien Tscharke grew up in the Barossa Valley among the vineyards at Seppeltsfield and Marananga. In 2001 he began the production of 4 estate-grown wines based on what he calls the classic varieties (following the contemporary trend of having catchy, snappy names) followed by 4 wines under the Tscharke brand using the alternative varieties of tempranillo, graciano, zinfandel, montepulciano and albarino. Like the Glaymond wines (made from traditional varieties), these are estate-grown, albeit in very limited quantities.

Tuart Ridge

344 Stakehill Road, Baldivis, WA 6171 **Region** Peel
T (08) 9524 3333 **F** (08) 9524 2168 **www**.tuartridgewines.com **Open** W'ends 10–4
Winemaker Phil Franzone **Est.** 1996 **Cases** 2000

Phil Franzone has established 5 ha of chardonnay, verdelho, shiraz, cabernet sauvignon, grenache and merlot on the coastal tuart soils. Phil Franzone also acts as contract winemaker for several of the many new ventures springing up in the Peel region.

ᵞᵞᵞᵞᵞ Peel Chardonnay 2005 The bouquet doesn't enthral, but the palate is far better; abundant, ripe stone fruit flavours ranging through yellow peach to passionfruit; oak is somewhere in the mix, but not obvious; good quality/price ratio for this part of the world. Screwcap. 12.6° alc. **Rating** 90 **To** 2010 $14

ᵞᵞᵞᵞ Reserve Peel Shiraz 2004 Medium-bodied; savoury black fruits shiraz, with flecks of spice and licorice; quality tannins add to both length and texture. Screwcap. 13° alc. **Rating** 89 **To** 2013 $15
Peel Shiraz Grenache 2005 Light, fresh, crisp shiraz keeping the grenache in line, and under control; minimum tannin and oak support. Screwcap. 12.6° alc. **Rating** 87 **To** 2008 $14

Tuck's Ridge ★★★★★

37 Shoreham Road, Red Hill South, Vic 3937 **Region** Mornington Peninsula
T (03) 5989 8660 **F** (03) 5989 8579 **www.**tucksridge.com.au **Open** 7 days 11–5
Winemaker Peninsula Winemakers **Est.** 1985 **Cases** 4000
Tuck's Ridge has changed focus significantly since selling its large Red Hill vineyard. Estate plantings are now an eclectic mix of pinot noir (3 ha), 1 ha each of chardonnay and albarino, and contract grape purchases have been reduced. Quality, not quantity, is the key; the Callanans Road label offers great value for money. Exports to the US, Hong Kong and Singapore.

ᵞᵞᵞᵞᵞ Hurley Vineyard Pinot Noir 2005 Outstanding colour; opulently luscious and rich, normally impossible at this alcohol; pure and vibrant red fruits, with great length. Screwcap. 13.3° alc. **Rating** 97 **To** 2015 $60
Mornington Peninsula Chardonnay 2005 Most attractive, fine grapefruit, melon and nectarine flavours; excellent balance, line and length; subtle barrel ferment oak inputs. Top gold medal Winewise '06. Screwcap. 14° alc.
Rating 95 **To** 2010 $29
Turramurra Vineyard Chardonnay 2005 No reduction whatsoever; excellent length and intensity, well above the norm; melon and grapefruit supported by stylish oak handling; will be very long-lived. Screwcap. 14.5° alc. **Rating** 95 **To** 2018 $60
Mornington Peninsula Pinot Noir 2005 A spotlessly clean, fragrant red fruit bouquet; abundant cherry, plum and spice flavours with seamless oak and tannins. Screwcap. 13.8° alc. **Rating** 95 **To** 2012 $35
Mornington Peninsula Pinot Noir 2003 Exceptional colour retention, still purple-dominated; as the colour promises, still very fresh and youthful; plum and black cherry fruit with firm acidity, will be long-lived (cork permitting). 13.5° alc. **Rating** 94 **To** 2011 $28

ᵞᵞᵞᵞᵞ Callanans Road Pinot Noir 2004 Medium red-purple; very good varietal bouquet and palate with spice, plum and black cherry fruit; lingering finish. Screwcap. 13° alc. **Rating** 93 **To** 2011 $20
Callanans Road Chardonnay 2004 High-quality Mornington Peninsula fruit; intense melon and grapefruit flavours drive across the palate from start to finish. Screwcap. 13° alc. **Rating** 92 **To** 2010 $20
Mornington Peninsula Sangiovese 2005 Light red-purple; fragrant and fresh red cherry fruit; a really delicious wine; none of the earthy, almost hairy, characters of many Australian sangioveses. Screwcap. 14.5° alc. **Rating** 91 **To** 2010 $28
Mornington Peninsula Pinot Rose 2006 Fresh and crisp; given the alcohol, likely made by bleeding off juice (saignee); faint herbal, stalk and spice twist to the finish; good length, not sweet, and gets away with the alcohol. Screwcap. 14.2° alc. **Rating** 90 **To** 2008 $20

Tulley Wells

Lot 4, RMB 33 Tulley Road, Lima South, Vic 3673 (postal) **Region** North East Victoria Zone
T (03) 9723 4353 **F** (03) 9720 1855 **Open** Not
Winemaker Roz Ritchie **Est.** 1997 **Cases** 375
When Dan and Margaret Mary Zaal purchased the Tulley Wells vineyard in 1998, they came with
a background of owning and running restaurants. The vineyard had 0.75 ha of (then) 17-year-old
grenache, and in 1999 they extended the plantings with 1 ha of shiraz. In 2002 they planted 350
grenache vines, grown in the traditional bush vine fashion, without any trellising.

Tulloch

'Glen Elgin', 638 De Beyers Road, Pokolbin, NSW 2321 **Region** Lower Hunter Valley
T (02) 4998 7580 **F** (02) 4998 7226 **www.tulloch.com.au Open** 7 days 10–5
Winemaker Jay Tulloch, Monarch Winemaking Services **Est.** 1895 **Cases** 50 000
The revival of the near-death Tulloch brand continues apace, production up from 30 000 cases.
Angove's, the national distributors for the brand, have invested in the business, the first time the
Angove family has taken a strategic holding in any business other than its own. Inglewood
Vineyard (aka Two Rivers) also has a shareholding in the new venture, and will be the primary
source of grapes for the brand. A lavish new cellar door and function facility has opened, and Jay
Tulloch is in overall control, with his own label, JYT Wines, also available at the cellar door. The
return of the classic Dry Red and Private Bin Dry Red labels (only slightly rejigged) brings back
memories of the great wines of the 1950s and '60s, and is a sign of the continuing resurgence of
this brand. Exports to Canada, Germany, Poland, Malaysia and Singapore.

🍷🍷🍷🍷🍷 **JYT Julia Hunter Valley Semillon 2005** Light straw-green; a more delicate,
yet more intensely fruit-flavoured wine; sweet lemon juice, bone-dry finish.
Screwcap. 10° alc. **Rating** 95 **To** 2018 $28
Hunter Valley Semillon 2006 An extra dimension of flavour without
sacrificing elegance, varietal character or regional character; that said, almost
strays into young riesling territory, so delicious is the fruit. Gold medal Hunter
Valley Wine Show '06. Screwcap. 10.5° alc. **Rating** 94 **To** 2016 $14

🍷🍷🍷🍷🍷 **Private Bin Pokolbin Dry Red Shiraz 2005** More purple-red colour and
more flavour than the standard wine; elegant, clean red fruits; good acidity and
tannins; may well surprise with its tenacity. A commemorative release in
memory of Hector John Tulloch. Screwcap. 13.5° alc. **Rating** 90 **To** 2020 $35

🍷🍷🍷🍷 **Hector of Glen Elgin Shiraz 2003** Firm, fresh, savoury/earthy regional fruit;
may have had a little too rigorous acid adjustment, which on the other hand may
serve it well in the long term. Screwcap. 13° alc. **Rating** 89 **To** 2015 $38
Creme de Liqueur Muscat NV Based on a 1972 solera; rich and complex,
though the spirit is somewhat fiery. Cork. 18.5° alc. **Rating** 89 **To** 2008 $30
Hunter Valley Chardonnay 2006 Tangy citrus, melon and nectarine flavours;
good balance and length; good regional example. Screwcap. 13.5° alc. **Rating** 88
To 2008 $15
Hunter Valley Verdelho 2006 A clean bouquet; has some life and bite from
citrus notes both on the mid-palate and finish; still anchored on varietal fruit salad,
and a good example of the variety. Screwcap. 13.5° alc. **Rating** 88 **To** 2010 $14
Sweetie NV Unlike many, has sufficient acidity to balance the extremely sweet
array of citrus, apricot and honey; long finish. Semillon. Screwcap. 9° alc. **Rating** 87
To 2008 $20

Tumbarumba Wine Estates

Glenroy Hills Road, Tumbarumba, NSW 2653 **Region** Tumbarumba
T (02) 6948 8326 **F** (02) 6948 8326 **www.mannuswines.com.au Open** 7 days by appt
Winemaker Monarch Winemaking Services **Est.** 1989 **Cases** 2000

Within sight of the Snowy Mountains, Tumbarumba Wine Estates' Mannus Vineyard was established by a group of Sydney businessmen, all wine enthusiasts, with the aim of producing high-quality cool-climate wines. The vineyard is currently undergoing some refinement, with some cabernet sauvignon being grafted to more suited varieties (sauvignon blanc and chardonnay). The major part of the production from the 21 ha of vineyard (principally chardonnay and sauvignon blanc) is sold to other producers.

ꟿꟿꟿꟿ **Mannus Reserve Pinot Noir 2005** Very light-bodied, but does have surprising length; bramble, spice and light plum fruit flavours; well-made and not forced to be something it is not. Screwcap. 12.7° alc. **Rating** 89 **To** 2010 $19

Mannus Sauvignon Blanc 2006 Spotlessly clean; balanced, but curiously lacking in positive varietal character,although there certainly are some grass, herb and citrus notes. Screwcap. 12.5° alc. **Rating** 88 **To** 2008 $18

Mannus Cabernet Merlot 2005 Light but fragrant and spicy aromas; leaf, berry, mint, and fairly brisk acidity. An obvious battle for full flavour ripeness. Screwcap. 13.5° alc. **Rating** 87 **To** 2009 $19

Turkey Flat   ★★★★★

Bethany Road, Tanunda, SA 5352 **Region** Barossa Valley
T (08) 8563 2851 **F** (08) 8563 3610 **www**.turkeyflat.com.au **Open** 7 days 11–5
Winemaker Julie Campbell **Est.** 1990 **Cases** 25 000

The establishment date of Turkey Flat is given as 1990 but it might equally well have been 1870 (or thereabouts), when the Schulz family purchased the Turkey Flat vineyard, or 1847, when the vineyard was first planted to the very shiraz which still grows there today. In addition there are 8 ha of very old grenache and 8 ha of much younger semillon and cabernet sauvignon, together with a total of 7.3 ha of mourvedre, dolcetto and (a recent arrival) marsanne. Exports to the UK, the US and other major markets.

ꟿꟿꟿꟿꟿ **Barossa Valley Shiraz 2005** Bright purple-red; replete with dark fruits ranging through blackberry, plum, prune and a dash of licorice; very focused and controlled; no artifice or exaggeration, simply classic restraint. Cork. 14.5° alc. **Rating** 95 **To** 2020 $45

The Last Straw Marsanne 2005 Golden colour utterly appropriate to the nectar-like aromas and honey/honeysuckle flavours, the sweetness perfectly balanced by acidity. ProCork. 14° alc. **Rating** 94 **To** 2015 $40

Butchers Block Barossa Valley Shiraz Grenache Mourvedre 2005 Strong colour; a fragrant array of black and red fruits, spices, plum and prune; the medium-bodied, elegant palate has ripples of cherry, plum and blackberry; no baggage at all from the alcohol. Part emanates from the original vines planted in 1847. Screwcap. 15° alc. **Rating** 94 **To** 2015 $30

Barossa Valley Cabernet Sauvignon 2005 Rich, almost velvety, with blackcurrant to the fore backed by touches of licorice and the French oak in which it spent 20 months; delicious and luscious. Cork. 14.5° alc. **Rating** 94 **To** 2022 $40

Barossa Valley Mourvedre 2005 Unusual finesse, delineation and line for this variety; no more than medium-bodied, with the finest imaginable tannins, French oak somewhere in the mix, but not easy to pinpoint. Cork. 14.5° alc. **Rating** 94 **To** 2015 $35

ꟿꟿꟿꟿꟿ **Butchers Block Barossa Valley Marsanne Viognier 2006** Medium- to medium-full-bodied complex array of honey/honeysuckle/nutty/tropical/apricot aromas and flavours; fermentation and ageing in old French oak barrels imparts considerable texture, but much less – if any – discernible flavour. Screwcap. 14° alc. **Rating** 93 **To** 2012 $23

Barossa Valley Rose 2006 A mix of small red fruits and more minerally nuances; carefully calibrated sweetness and lemony acidity. Grenache/ Shiraz/Cabernet Sauvignon/Dolcetto. Screwcap. 12.5° alc. **Rating** 90 **To** 2008 $20

Turner's Crossing Vineyard ★★★★★

747 Old Bridgewater Serpentine Road, Serpentine, Vic 3517 **Region** Bendigo
T (03) 5944 4599 **www.turnerscrossing.com Open** W'ends by appt
Winemaker Sergio Carlei **Est.** 2002 **Cases** 10 000

The name of this outstanding vineyard comes from local farmers crossing the Loddon River in the mid to late 1800s on their way to the nearest town. The 40-ha vineyard was planted in 1999 by former corporate executive and lecturer in the business school at La Trobe University, Paul Jenkins. However, Jenkins' experience as a self-taught viticulturist dates back to 1985, when he established his first vineyard at Prospect Hill, planting all the vines himself. The grapes from both vineyards have gone to a who's who of winemakers in Central Victoria, but an increasing amount is being made under the Turner's Crossing label, not surprising given the exceptional quality of the wines. Phil Bennett and winemaker Sergio Carlei have joined Paul Jenkins as co-owners of the vineyard, with Sergio putting his money where his winemaking mouth is.

ΨΨΨΨΨ **The Cut Shiraz 2004** Comes in what seems to be the biggest and heaviest bottle in captivity, but the wine is not dwarfed by it. This is distilled power, but without rough edges or extract; a seriously long palate and an equally long and distinguished future. Diam. 14.5° alc. **Rating** 96 **To** 2030 $75
Bendigo Shiraz Viognier 2005 Medium purple-red; medium-bodied, fragrant and elegant; seems to have achieved maximum flavour with a minimum of effort, especially the alcohol; red and black cherry fruit, with splashes of spice, has exemplary length. Cork. 14.5° alc. **Rating** 95 **To** 2020 $26

ΨΨΨΨΨ **Bendigo Cabernet Sauvignon 2004** Medium-bodied, with a slightly savoury/earthy twist to the core of firm blackcurrant fruit; good tannin and oak management. Cork. 14.3° alc. **Rating** 93 **To** 2025 $24

Turramurra Estate ★★★★☆

295 Wallaces Road, Dromana Vic 3936 **Region** Mornington Peninsula
T (03) 5987 1146 **F** (03) 5987 1286 **www.turramurraestate.com.au Open** W'ends 11–5
Winemaker David Leslie **Est.** 1989 **Cases** 4500

Dr David Leslie gave up his job as a medical practitioner after completing the Bachelor of Applied Science (Wine Science) at Charles Sturt University, to concentrate on developing the family's 10-ha estate at Dromana; wife Paula is the viticulturist. They have also established what is described as the first purpose-built cooking school in an Australian vineyard. Exports to the UK, the US and Hong Kong. The Leslies are reluctantly seeking to sell Turramurra Estate as the physical demands of viticulture and winemaking have become too great.

Two Hands Wines ★★★★★

Neldner Road, Marananga, SA 5355 **Region** Various
T (08) 8562 4566 **www.twohandswines.com Open** Wed–Fri 11–5, w'ends 10–5
Winemaker Matthew Wenk **Est.** 2000 **Cases** 20 000

The 'Hands' in question are those of SA businessmen Michael Twelftree and Richard Mintz, Twelftree in particular having extensive experience in marketing Australian wine in the US (for other producers). On the principle that if big is good, bigger is better, and biggest is best, the style of the wines has been aimed fairly and squarely at the palate of Robert Parker Jr and the *Wine Spectator*'s Harvey Steiman. Grapes are sourced from the Barossa Valley, McLaren Vale, Clare Valley, Langhorne Creek and Padthaway, and each of the wines is made in microscopic quantities (down to 50 dozen). Exports to the US, Canada and the UK.

ΨΨΨΨΨ **Bella's Garden Barossa Valley Shiraz 2005** Rich, fleshy fruit in abundance, but not the least jammy; indeed, borders on outright elegance; good balance and structure. Cork. 14.8° alc. **Rating** 95 **To** 2020 $55
Harry & Edward's Garden Langhorne Creek Shiraz 2005 Complex black fruit flavours accompanied by spice and licorice; fine tannins, and great length. Cork. 14.8° alc. **Rating** 95 **To** 2020 $55

Ares Barossa Valley Shiraz 2004 Dense colour; ultra-powerful and concentrated, and somewhat bound up in itself, albeit with sumptuous dark fruits; needs much patience. Cork. 15° alc. **Rating** 95 **To** 2024 $120

Sophie's Garden Padthaway Shiraz 2005 Very dense, deep colour; much the most dense and rich wine in the group, achieved at least in part through higher alcohol; US, here we come. Cork. 15.2° alc. **Rating** 94 **To** 2015 $55

Lily's Garden McLaren Vale Shiraz 2005 Deep colour, though slightly less purple than Bella's Garden; powerful, strongly regional style, dark chocolate and earth intermingling with blackberry fruit; firm but not rough tannins. Cork. 14.5° alc. **Rating** 94 **To** 2025 $55

Bad Impersonator Barossa Valley Shiraz 2005 Spotlessly clean aromas; abundant ripe, fleshy black fruits in a plum and blackberry spectrum; soft tannins, good oak. Screwcap. 14.8° alc. **Rating** 94 **To** 2020 $45

The Bull and The Bear Barossa Valley Shiraz Cabernet 2005 Masses of luscious blackberry and blackcurrant fruit; while at the top of the alcohol comfort zone, stays within it; very clever making; 67%/33%. Screwcap. 15° alc. **Rating** 94 **To** 2024 $45

The Bull and The Bear Barossa Valley Shiraz Cabernet 2004 Excellent bright, deep purple-red; fresh, vibrant flavours, carrying the alcohol with ease; vivid black fruits, controlled oak and a long finish. Screwcap. 15° alc. **Rating** 94 **To** 2024 $45

ㅜㅜㅜㅜ♀ **Samantha's Garden Clare Valley Shiraz 2005** Most developed colour of the Two Hands' shirazs; spicy, earthy blackberry aromas and flavours; good tannin balance. Cork. 14.5° alc. **Rating** 93 **To** 2015 $55

Angel's Share McLaren Vale Shiraz 2005 A big, bold, rich, ripe and round style, but not jammy or extractive, and carries the alcohol quite well, expressing itself as sweetness. Screwcap. 15° alc. **Rating** 92 **To** 2018 $28

Max's Garden Heathcote Shiraz 2005 Good hue, though less depth than the other shirazs in the portfolio; a fragrant, light- to medium-bodied wine, perhaps reflecting younger vines; fresh fruit flavours. Cork. 14.5° alc. **Rating** 92 **To** 2015 $55

Aerope Barossa Valley Grenache 2004 Some development; very fragrant and spicy; light- to medium-bodied, but a strong expression of the region and variety; an almost lemony tang to the fruit. Cork. 14.5° alc. **Rating** 92 **To** 2015 $95

Aphrodite Barossa Valley Cabernet Sauvignon 2004 Every bit as concentrated as Ares, again raising the possibility of some juice run-off; the essency blackcurrant fruit has a faint fish oil aroma, curious rather than unpleasant. Cork. 14.5° alc. **Rating** 92 **To** 2015 $120

Brave Faces Barossa Valley Shiraz Grenache 2005 Abounds with flavour, the juicy, jammy grenache component coming through strongly with raspberry and plum flavours. Screwcap. 15° alc. **Rating** 90 **To** 2014 $28

ㅜㅜㅜㅜ **Gnarly Dudes Barossa Shiraz 2004** Strong red-purple; blackberry/prune/confit fruit, alcohol making its mark. If I had a vine(s) like that depicted on the label, I wouldn't be featuring it. Screwcap. 15° alc. **Rating** 89 **To** 2014 $28

Yesterday's Hero Barossa Valley Grenache 2005 Light red-purple; encapsulates the difference between Barossa Valley and McLaren Vale grenache; sweet, feminine red fruits, largely unburdened by structure or tannins. Screwcap. 15° alc. **Rating** 89 **To** 2012 $35

Aerope Barossa Valley Grenache 2005 Smooth, sweet simple red fruits and spices; has length, but seemingly little structure. The price strongly suggests I am missing the boat. Cork. 15° alc. **Rating** 89 **To** 2012 $90

The Wolf Clare Valley Riesling 2006 A closed, though not reduced, bouquet; the palate is firm, the fruit still to develop with minerally acidity dominating early in its life. Screwcap. 11.5° alc. **Rating** 88 **To** 2010 $20

Gnarly Dudes Barossa Shiraz 2005 Ripe fruit – some might say dead fruit – is immediately obvious; the high alcohol and lesser quality grapes tell the tale; does have flavour, but so it would at 14° alcohol. Screwcap. 15.5° alc. **Rating** 88 **To** 2015 $25

For Love or Money Cane Cut Barossa Valley Semillon 2006 Intensely sweet banana and apricot fruit and flavour, and an absolute lack of complexity. The price is ludicrously high. Cork. 12.7° alc. **Rating** 88 **To** 2008 $50

Brilliant Disguise Barossa Valley Moscato 2006 A brilliant disguise indeed, the seemingly normal cork hiding the fact that the wine has considerable CO_2 mousse; fragrant apple and passionfruit, with crisp acidity; you barely register the alcohol. Cork. 6.5° alc. **Rating** 87 **To** 2008 $18

Two Rivers

2 Yarrawa Road, Denman, NSW 2328 (postal) **Region** Upper Hunter Valley
T (02) 6547 2556 **F** (02) 6547 2546 **www.**tworiverswines.com.au **Open** By appt
Winemaker Monarch Winemaking Services **Est.** 1988 **Cases** 15 000
A significant part of the viticultural scene in the Upper Hunter Valley, with almost 170 ha of vineyards established, involving a total investment of around $7 million. Part of the fruit is sold under long-term contracts, and part is made for the expanding winemaking and marketing operations of Two Rivers, the chief brand of Inglewood Vineyards. The emphasis is on Chardonnay and Semillon, and the wines have been medal winners on the wine show circuit. It is also a partner in the Tulloch business, together with the Tulloch and Angove families.

Stones Throw Semillon 2005 Has literally transformed itself since '05; now has considerable weight and intensity; with almost explosive flavour on the back-palate and finish. Semillon's ever-present ability to surprise. Screwcap. 11° alc. **Rating** 91 **To** 2012 $13

Lightning Strike Chardonnay 2006 Abundant barrel ferment oak is just carried by the fruit; shortens slightly. **Rating** 88 **To** 2008

Twofold

142 Beulah Road, Norwood, SA 5067 (postal) **Region** Clare Valley/Heathcote
T 0418 544 001 **Open** Not
Winemaker Neil Pike, Sergio Carlei (Contract) **Est.** 2002 **Cases** 800
This is the venture of brothers Nick and Tim Stock, both of whom have had a varied background in the wine industry (primarily at the marketing end, whether as sommeliers or in wholesale) and both of whom have excellent palates. Their contacts have allowed them to source a single-vineyard riesling from Sevenhill in the Clare Valley, and a single-vineyard shiraz from Heathcote, both under ongoing arrangements. As one might expect, the quality of the wines is excellent.

Heathcote Shiraz 2004 Spicy black fruit aromas, then a palate of exceptional richness and depth; masses of ripe (in no sense over the top) black fruits, supported by ripe tannins and quality oak. Shows just what can be achieved at this moderate alcohol level. Diam. 13.5° alc. **Rating** 95 **To** 2029 $38

Clare Valley Riesling 2006 Aromatic green apple and lime aromas; unfolds with lime and apple on the palate; a clean, crisp lemony finish with lemony acidity. Screwcap. 12° alc. **Rating** 94 **To** 2018 $24

Tyler Wines

PO Box 244, Rosedale, Vic 3847 **Region** Gippsland
T (03) 5199 2788 **www.**tylerwines.com.au **Open** Not
Winemaker Ben Tyler **Est.** 2004 **Cases** 1500
This is the business of Ben Tyler and his father Peter, initially established on the family farm at Willung, but moving to a much larger unused facility in Rosedale (also in Gippsland) prior to the 2005 vintage. Ben graduated with a degree in Applied Science (Winemaking) from Charles Sturt University; during his time at the university he was offered and accepted the position of trainee winemaker. The following year he was employed as assistant winemaker, before returning to Vic. In 2000 he became the winemaker at Clyde Park, producing a series of excellent wines over the following years. He now works full-time for Tyler Wines, developing the estate label, and also providing contract winemaking services for other clients.

Tyrrell's ★★★★★

Broke Road, Pokolbin, NSW 2321 **Region** Lower Hunter Valley
T (02) 4993 7000 **F** (02) 4998 7723 **www.**tyrrells.com.au **Open** Mon–Sat 8–5
Winemaker Andrew Spinaze, Mark Richardson **Est.** 1858 **Cases** 500 000
One of the most successful family wineries, a humble operation for the first 110 years of its life
which grew out of all recognition over the past 40 years. In 2003 it cleared the decks by selling
its Long Flat range of wines for an 8-figure sum, allowing it to focus on its premium, super-
premium and ultra-premium wines: Vat 1 Semillon is one of the most dominant wines in the
Australian show system, and Vat 47 Chardonnay is one of the pace-setters for this variety. It has
an awesome portfolio of single-vineyard Semillons released when 5–6 years old. Exports to all
major markets.

🍷🍷🍷🍷🍷 **Reserve HVD Hunter Valley Semillon 1999** Superb green-yellow; still shows
remarkable youth, with a lovely balance between citrus and more honeyed com-
ponents; fantastic length; 8 gold medals. Cork. 10.5° alc. **Rating** 97 **To** 2015 $30
Vat 1 Semillon 2001 The usual immaculate balance and length, still
remarkably fresh and crisp; only gold medal in 55 entries in its class National
Wine Show '06. Cork. **Rating** 96 **To** 2015
Reserve Stevens Hunter Valley Semillon 2002 Very pale green-straw;
spotlessly clean; super-intense and long, with a great finish. Cork. 10° alc.
Rating 95 **To** 2017 $25
Lost Block Semillon 2006 Typically for young semillon with only the slightest
touch of colour; very precise lemon and cut grass aromas and flavours run
through to a lingering, fruit-driven, but dry finish. Screwcap. 11° alc. **Rating** 94
To 2016 $16.99
Vat 47 Chardonnay 2005 An element of finesse and elegance rare in the
Hunter Valley outside of Tyrrell's, Lake's Folly and Keith Tulloch; a seamless
marriage of stone fruit and oak; despite the screwcap, best earlier than later.
Screwcap. 12.5° alc. **Rating** 94 **To** 2010 $45
Rufus Stone McLaren Vale Shiraz 2004 Strong red-purple; medium-bodied,
with excellent balance and structure; blackberry and dark chocolate on a supple
palate with a long finish and restrained alcohol. Screwcap. 14.2° alc. **Rating** 94
To 2020 $20
Reserve Stevens Hunter Valley Shiraz 2003 An extra dimension of
intensity, length and flavour; particularly good acidity is built into the wine; will
age very well. Screwcap. 13.5° alc. **Rating** 94 **To** 2023 $30

🍷🍷🍷🍷 **DB24 McLaren Vale Shiraz 2003** It's not entirely clear why this wine was
selected for double oaking, 12 months in new oak, then another 12 months in
another set of new oak barrels; mixture of black fruits, chocolate and vanilla, with
soft tannins and lots of oak. Diam. 14.5° alc. **Rating** 92 **To** 2015 $75
Rufus Stone McLaren Vale Cabernet Sauvignon Malbec 2004 Rollicking,
rich, ripe cassis, blackcurrant and raspberry fruit, sustained tannins. Screwcap.
14.5° alc. **Rating** 91 **To** 2014 $20

🍷🍷🍷🍷 **Vat 9 Hunter Valley Shiraz 2005** Good hue, though not especially deep;
medium-bodied cherry, plum and blackberry fruit; fine tannins and gentle oak.
Cork. 13.5° alc. **Rating** 89 **To** 2010 $45
Rufus Stone Heathcote Shiraz 2004 Does not have the usual colour density
of shiraz from Heathcote; ripe fruit flavours plus alcohol give the impression of
sweetness on the palate, but not on the aftertaste; slightly schizophrenic. Screwcap.
15° alc. **Rating** 89 **To** 2014 $20
Brokenback Hunter Valley Shiraz 2004 Fresh and lively; light- to medium-
bodied red and black fruits, supported by fine tannins and subtle oak. Not especially
complex. Screwcap. 13.2° alc. **Rating** 88 **To** 2011 $20
Moon Mountain Hunter Valley Chardonnay 2006 Green-straw; melon and
ripe stone fruit; modest intensity and length, but well-made. Screwcap. 13° alc.
Rating 87 **To** 2008 $20

Uleybury Wines

Uley Road, Uleybury, SA 5114 **Region** Adelaide Zone
T (08) 8280 7335 **F** (08) 8280 7925 **www.**uleybury.com **Open** 7 days 10–5
Winemaker Tony Pipicella **Est.** 1995 **Cases** 15 500
The Pipicella family – headed by Italian-born Tony – has established nearly 45 ha of vineyard near
One Tree Hill in the Mt Lofty Ranges; 10 varieties have been planted, with more planned.
Daughter Natalie Pipicella, who has completed the wine marketing course at the University of
SA, was responsible for overseeing the design of labels, the promotion and advertising, and the
creation of the website. Exports to the UK, Canada, Denmark, China and Japan.

ＹＹＹＹＹ **La Vipera Shiraz Viognier 2004** Impenetrable inky purple; massively rich in
texture and flavour; fills every corner of the mouth, yet is not tannic or abrasive. It is
a little soupy, but this is a carping criticism. Would live forever with a screwcap; if the
heavily stained cork is typical, monitor the fill level as the wine matures. 15° alc.
Rating 94 **To** 2024 $25

ＹＹＹＹＹ **Nasello Unwooded Chardonnay 2006** Abundant nectarine and peach aromas;
backs off a little on entry to the mouth, but has length and personality. A good
example of the style. Screwcap. 12.5° alc. **Rating** 90 **To** 2008 $19.50

ＹＹＹＹ **Maritimo Semillon 2006** Surprisingly crisp and crunchy given its alcohol; grassy
flavours dominate, with a light touch of citrus. Screwcap. 13.2° alc. **Rating** 89
To 2012 $35

Ulithorne

The Middleton Mill, Mill Terrace, Middleton, SA 5213 **Region** McLaren Vale
T (08) 8382 5528 **www.**ulithorne.com.au **Open** Fri–Sun 8 am–midnight, or by appt
Winemaker Brian Light, Natasha Mooney (Contract) **Est.** 1971 **Cases** 800
The changes have continued apace for Ulithorne. Sam Harrison and partner Rose Kentish have
sold the vineyard (but with the right to select and buy part of the production each vintage) and
have purchased the Middleton Mill on the south coast of the Fleurieu Peninsula. It is now their
home, and Sam has resumed full-time painting while Rose is running a wine bar in the
Middelton Mill with Ulithorne and other local wines, beers and platters of regional food on offer.
Exports to the UK, the US and other major markets.

ＹＹＹＹＹ **Frux Frugis McLaren Vale Shiraz 2005** Strong purple-red; a medium-bodied
palate, with blackberry, plum and a mixture of chocolate and spice; ripe tannins
are in balance, as is the oak; overall, supple mouthfeel. Cork. 14.5° alc.
Rating 94 **To** 2025 $42

Unavale Vineyard

10 Badger Corner Road, Flinders Island, Tas 7255 **Region** Northern Tasmania
T (03) 6359 3632 **F** (03) 6359 3632 **Open** By appt
Winemaker Andrew Hickinbotham (Contract) **Est.** 1999 **Cases** 100
Roger and Bev Watson have pioneered viticulture on Flinders Island, planting 1 ha of pinot noir,
and 0.5 ha each of chardonnay, sauvignon blanc, riesling and cabernet sauvignon. The windswept
environment has slowed the development of the vines, and will always keep yields low, but
production will rise over the next few years. Two quite lovely wines from 2006 will hopefully
point the way for the future given the struggle the Watsons have to grow and protect the grapes.

ＹＹＹＹＹ **Flinders Island Sauvignon Blanc 2006** Spicy French oak on the bouquet,
but the sauvignon blanc all but obliterates the oak on the palate; powerful,
intense and focused in a grass/herb/citrus spectrum; long finish. Screwcap.
13° alc. **Rating** 94 **To** 2009 $22

ＹＹＹＹ **Flinders Island Riesling 2006** Crisp, clean, mineral, citrus and apple aromas
and flavours; lively and bright; fresh finish and good acidity. Screwcap. 13° alc.
Rating 91 **To** 2016 $22

Upper Reach Vineyard ★★★★

77 Memorial Avenue, Baskerville, WA 6056 **Region** Swan Valley
T (08) 9296 0078 **F** (08) 9296 0278 **www**.upperreach.com.au **Open** Thurs–Mon 11–5
Winemaker Derek Pearse **Est.** 1996 **Cases** 3000

This 10-ha property on the banks of the upper reaches of the Swan River was purchased by Laura Rowe and Derek Pearse in 1996. The original vineyard was 4 ha of 12-year-old chardonnay, which has been expanded by 1.5 ha of shiraz, 1 ha of cabernet sauvignon, 0.5 ha each of verdelho and merlot and 0.2 ha of graciano. All wines are estate-grown. The fish on the label, incidentally, is black bream, which can be found in the pools of the Swan River during the summer months. Exports to the UK.

Shiraz 2005 Medium to full-bodied blackberry, earth and spice; controlled tannins and good length. Top quality Swan Valley red. Screwcap. 14° alc. **Rating** 92 **To** 2020 $25

Verdelho 2006 Lively and fresh, with freshly squeezed lemon juice over fruit salad; crisp finish; excellent varietal example. Screwcap. 13° alc. **Rating** 88 **To** 2010 $16

Ursa Major ★★★★☆

105 Tucks Road, Main Ridge, Vic 3928 **Region** Mornington Peninsula
T (03) 5989 6500 **F** (03) 5989 6501 **www**.yrsasvineyard.com **Open** By appt
Winemaker Michael Kyberd, Judy Gifford (Contract) **Est.** 1994 **Cases** 1500

Ursa Major is named after the lady from whom Steven and Marianne Stern acquired the property. She, in turn, was named after Queen Yrsa of Sweden, born in 565 AD, whose story is told in the Norse sagas. Well-known patent and trademark attorney Steven Stern (whose particular area of expertise is in the wine and liquor business) and wife Marianne have established around 2.75 ha each of pinot noir and chardonnay, and initially marketed the wines only in the UK. The 2004 Pinot Noir was awarded Victoria's Best Dry Red at the annual Federation Square Wine Awards in '06.

Vale Wines ★★★☆

2914 Frankston-Flinders Road, Balnarring, Vic 3926 **Region** Mornington Peninsula
T (03) 5983 1521 **F** (03) 5983 1942 **www**.valewines.com.au **Open** 7 days 11–5
Winemaker John Vale **Est.** 1991 **Cases** 500

After a lifetime in the retail liquor industry, John and Susan Vale took a busman's retirement by purchasing a grazing property at Balnarring in 1991. They planted a little under 0.5 ha of cabernet sauvignon (since grafted over to gewurztraminer), and John Vale undertook what he describes as 'formal winemaking training' before building a 20-tonne winery in 1997. In 2000 they extended the plantings with 1.4 ha of tempranillo, riesling and durif, seeking to move outside the square. In the meantime the wine range has been extended by the purchase of chardonnay and pinot grigio from local growers.

Valley View Vineyard ★★★

21 Boundary Road, Coldstream, Vic 3770 (postal) **Region** Yarra Valley
T (03) 9739 1692 **F** (03) 9739 0430 **Open** Not
Winemaker Contract **Est.** 2000 **Cases** 200

Judy and John Thompson purchased their property in 1998, and with the unanimous advice of various contacts in the wine industry they planted 2.2 ha of pinot noir on a north and northwest-facing rocky slope.

Everest Yarra Valley Pinot Noir 2005 A light-bodied and fresh blend of plum cherry and strawberry fruit; a little firm and one-dimensional, and wouldn't seem to have the depth for long-term development. Screwcap. 13.5° alc. **Rating** 89 **To** 2009 $35

Yarra Valley Pinot Noir 2005 Shows obvious development in colour; light-bodied, in similar style to the '06 Everest, with foresty/savoury notes evident and adding interest; an early easy-drinking style. Screwcap. 13.5° alc. **Rating** 88 **To** 2008 $26

Vardon Lane/Kanta   ★★★★☆

22-26 Vardon Lane, Adelaide, SA 5000 (postal) **Region** Adelaide Hills
T (08) 8232 5300 **F** (08) 8232 2055 **Open** Not
Winemaker Egon Muller **Est.** 2005 **Cases** NA
This is the ultimate virtual winery, a joint venture between famed Mosel-Saar-Ruwer winemaker (and proprietor) Egon Muller, Michael Andrewartha from Adelaide's East End Cellars, and Armenian-born vigneron and owner of La Corte from Italy's Puglia region, Vahe Keushguerian. A 3-year search for the perfect riesling site ended almost where the journey began, at the Shaw & Smith Adelaide Hills vineyard. Muller arrived on the day of picking to oversee the whole production, carried out at Shaw & Smith with input from Steve Pannell and Shaw & Smith's winemaker, Daryl Catlin. The grapes were crushed and cold-soaked for up to 16 hours, the juice settled without enzyme and kept at 12°C until spontaneous fermentation began. Small wonder that the wine is so different from other Australian Rieslings, and even more different from the gloriously fine wines which Muller makes at home.

♥♥♥♥♀ **Kanta Riesling 2006** A spotless bouquet, with no hint of reduction, but nor is it particularly expressive; springs to life on the palate, with a firm, pure mineral overlay to apple, citrus and lime fruit; bone-dry finish; needs 5 years at least. Screwcap. 13.5° alc. **Rating** 92 **To** 2016 $28

Varrenti Wines   NR

'Glenheather', Blackwood Road, Dunkeld, Vic 3294 **Region** Grampians
T (03) 5577 2368 **F** (03) 5577 2367 **Open** 7 days 12–5
Winemaker Ettore Varrenti **Est.** 1999 **Cases** NA

Vasse Felix   ★★★★★

Cnr Caves Road/Harmans Road South, Cowaramup, WA 6284 **Region** Margaret River
T (08) 9756 5000 **F** (08) 9755 5425 **www.**vassefelix.com.au **Open** 7 days 10–5
Winemaker David Dowden, Virginia Willcock **Est.** 1967 **Cases** 1500 000
In 1999 the production of Vasse Felix wines moved to a new 2000-tonne winery; the old winery is now dedicated entirely to the restaurant and tasting rooms. A relatively new 140-ha vineyard at Jindong in the north of the Margaret River region supplies a large part of the increased fruit intake. Exports to all major markets.

♥♥♥♥♥ **Heytesbury Margaret River Chardonnay 2005** A highly aromatic and striking bouquet; the depth and content of the palate are wholly remarkable at this alcohol level; nutty almond/creamy flavours seamlessly welded with melon and grapefruit. Screwcap. 13.5° alc. **Rating** 96 **To** 2025 $40
Margaret River Semillon 2006 Light-bodied; bright, intense, fresh lemony aromas and flavours; oak all but invisible, simply adding a gloss of texture to the lingering, spotlessly clean finish; has phenomenal drive. Screwcap. 12.5° alc. **Rating** 95 **To** 2011 $25
Margaret River Chardonnay 2005 Medium-bodied; sophisticated winemaking with whole-bunch pressing, wild yeasts, solids and lees stirring successfully bring out the multiple nuances in the fruit; nectarine, melon, fig and grapefruit, finishing with citrussy acidity. Screwcap. 13.5° alc. **Rating** 95 **To** 2017 $25
Margaret River Shiraz 2005 Vivid purple-red; an elegant, spicy mix of black and red fruits plus a dash of chocolate; fine, silky, smooth mouthfeel, the tannins perfectly ripe and balanced. Cork. 14.8° alc. **Rating** 95 **To** 2020 $35
Margaret River Shiraz 2004 Much more weight, density and structure than most Margaret River shiraz, and confounds the critics who decried the Jindong

subregion; plum, blackberry and spice, augmented by the astute use of oak. Cork. 14.5° alc. **Rating** 95 **To** 2015 $35

Heytesbury 2004 Intensely fragrant and exuberant aromas with a seamless mix of multi-berry fruits and high-quality French oak, the palate a mirror image; long finish. High-quality cork. 14.5° alc. **Rating** 95 **To** 2025 $65

Margaret River Sauvignon Blanc Semillon 2006 Very complex wine with wild yeast and barrel ferment inputs; tropical passionfruit flavours, long and intense; French oak again plays a deliberately low-key role. Great finish. Screwcap. 12° alc. **Rating** 94 **To** 2010 $25

Margaret River Cabernet Sauvignon 2005 Deep colour; potent, brooding, multi-layered aromas and flavours, the structure provided by ripe cabernet tannins and, to a lesser degree, French oak. High-quality cork. 14.5° alc. **Rating** 94 **To** 2020 $35

ΨΨΨΨΨ **Margaret River Cabernet Merlot 2005** Floral, fragrant touches of leaf, mint, cassis and cherry follow through from the bouquet to the medium-bodied palate; light, but persistent, savoury tannins. Screwcap. 14.5° alc. **Rating** 93 **To** 2015 $25

Cane Cut Margaret River Semillon 2006 Vibrant aromas and flavours as much in the citrus spectrum as tropical; perfectly integrated and balanced acidity. Screwcap. 12.5° alc. **Rating** 93 **To** 2016 $20

Margaret River Cabernet Merlot 2004 Medium- to full-bodied with plenty of structure and texture; predominantly black fruits with gently savoury, fine tannins giving length. Cork. 14.5° alc. **Rating** 91 **To** 2014 $25

Margaret River Classic Dry White 2006 Crisp, zesty, lively and long; citrus/herb/grass components; long, clean finish, though not especially complex. Screwcap. 12° alc. **Rating** 90 **To** 2009 $20

Vasse River Wines   ★★★★

c/- Post Office, Carbunup, WA 6280 **Region** Margaret River
T (08) 9755 1111 **F** (08) 9755 1011 **www.vasseriver.com.au Open** Not
Winemaker Sharna Kowalazuh **Est.** 1993 **Cases** 2500
This is a major and rapidly growing business owned by the Credaro family; 90 ha of chardonnay, semillon, verdelho, sauvignon blanc, cabernet sauvignon, merlot and shiraz have been planted on the typical gravelly red loam soils of the region. The wines are released under 2 labels: Vasse River for the premium, and Carbunup Estate (not to be confused with Carbunup Crest) for the lower-priced varietals.

Velo Wines   ★★★☆

755 West Tamar Highway, Legana, Tas 7277 **Region** Northern Tasmania
T 0418 526 858 **F** (03) 6330 2321 **Open** Wed–Sun 10–6
Winemaker Micheal Wilson, Winemaking Tasmania (Julian Alcorso) **Est.** 1966 **Cases** 1000
The story behind Velo Wines is fascinating, wheels within wheels. The 0.9 ha of cabernet sauvignon and 0.5 ha of pinot noir of the Legana Vineyard were planted in 1966 by Graham Wiltshire, legitimately described as one of the 3 great pioneers of the Tasmanian wine industry. Fifteen years ago Micheal and Mary Wilson returned to Tasmania after living in Italy and France for a decade. Micheal was an Olympic cyclist, following which he joined the professional ranks, racing in all of the major European events. Imbued with a love of wine and food, they spent '7 long hard years in the restaurant game'. Somehow, Micheal found time to become a qualified viticulturist, and was vineyard manager for Moorilla Estate based at St Matthias. Wife Mary spent 5 years working in wine wholesaling for leading distributors. In 2001 they purchased the Legana Vineyard planted so long ago, and have painstakingly rehabilitated the 40-year-old vines. They have built a small winery where Micheal makes the red wines, Julian Alcorso makes the white wines, sourced in part from 0.6 ha of estate riesling and from grapes grown on the East Coast.

ΨΨΨΨΨ **Unwooded Chardonnay 2006** Elegant but nicely modulated; light- to medium-bodied, with an array of nectarine, grapefruit and melon flavours. Screwcap. 12.9° alc. **Rating** 92 **To** 2012 $20

♟♟♟♟ **Riesling 2006** A fairly subdued bouquet, but a palate with nice bite and length. Screwcap. 12.5° alc.**Rating** 88 **To** 2012 $22
Pinot Gris 2006 Lemony acidity gives the wine some grigio-like grip, even though it has the pinot gris name. Screwcap. 13.4° alc. **Rating** 87 **To** 2008 $24
Rose 2006 A fresh bright colour introduces a wine with voluminous fruit, but needlessly sweet. Diam. 13.5° alc. **Rating** 87 **To** 2008 $20
Reserve Cabernet Sauvignon 2005 Some minty/herbal overtones attesting to the cool climate, but has good structure and mouthfeel. Diam. 13.5° alc. **Rating** 87 **To** 2010 $35

Vercoe's Vineyard   ★★★★

PO Box 145, Cessnock, NSW 2325 **Region** Lower Hunter Valley
T 0410 541 663 **F** (02) 6574 7352 **www.**vercoesvineyard.com.au **Open** Not
Winemaker Monarch Winemaking Services **Est.** 2002 **Cases** 700
In the mid-1960s a young John Vercoe toyed with the idea of establishing a wine bar, but it took another 30 years for his interest in wine to translate itself into Vercoe's Vineyard. Together with wife Elizabeth, and adult children, the property on the evocatively-named Sweetwater Ridge was purchased in 1999. After 3 years of soil preparation, 1.8 ha of verdelho was planted in 2002, followed by merlot (1.3 ha) and semillon and chardonnay (0.8 ha each).

Veronique   ★★★★

PO Box 599, Angaston, SA 5353 **Region** Barossa Valley
T (08) 8565 3214 **Open** Not
Winemaker Domenic Torzi **Est.** 2004 **Cases** 1500
Peter Manning, general manager of Angas Park Fruits, and wife Vicki, moved to Mt McKenzie in the 1990s. His wine consumption soon focused on Barossa shiraz, and he quickly became a close drinking partner of all things shiraz with Domenic Torzi. By 2004 the Mannings decided it was high time to produce a Barossa shiraz of their own, and, with the help of Torzi, sourced grapes from 3 outstanding blocks. The vineyards include mataro and grenache (thoroughly excusable in the context) and sauvignon blanc, the last seeming to have an inexhaustible demand, wherever it is grown and made.

♟♟♟♟♟ **Shiraz 2005** A very attractive palette of flavours have come together merging black cherry, spice, blackberry and licorice, oak playing incidental music. Screwcap. 14.5° alc. **Rating** 93 **To** 2025 $23

Victory Point Wines   ★★★★☆

121 Rosalie Street, Shenton Park, WA 6008 (postal) **Region** Margaret River
T (08) 9381 5765 **F** (08) 9388 2449 **www.**victorypointwines.com **Open** Not
Winemaker Keith Mugford, Ian Bell (Contract) **Est.** 1997 **Cases** 2500
Judith and Gary Berson (the latter a partner in the Perth office of a national law firm) have set their aims high. With viticultural advice from Keith and Clare Mugford of Moss Wood, they have established their 12-ha vineyard without irrigation, emulating those of the Margaret River pioneers (including Moss Wood). The plantings comprise 4.47 ha chardonnay, the remainder the Bordeaux varieties, with cabernet sauvignon accounting for 6 ha, merlot for 2 ha, cabernet franc 1.5 ha and malbec and petit verdot 0.3 ha each. There will thus be 2 wines each year: a Chardonnay and a Cabernet blend.

♟♟♟♟♟ **Margaret River Chardonnay 2006** A complex bouquet showing barrel ferment and intense, albeit ripe, fruit; fruit drives the palate with ripe peach, nectarine and melon. Made from the French Dijon clones 76, 95, 96 and 2007, plus Mendoza. The French clones are performing exceptionally well across Australia. Screwcap. 14.5° alc. **Rating** 94 **To** 2012 $33

♟♟♟♟♟ **Margaret River Cabernet Sauvignon Malbec Cabernet Franc Petit Verdot 2004** Good though relatively light hue; light- to medium-bodied, elegant, smooth and supple; the fruit flavours have meshed well; good balance and length, simply needing a little more depth for maximum points. Screwcap. 13.3° alc. **Rating** 91 **To** 2012 $33

The Mallee Root Margaret River Cabernet Franc Malbec 2005 A blend of opposites, but not the only one in the Margaret River; sweet juicy fruit flavours, with fine, soft tannins and a long finish certainly establishes the blend is a valid one. Screwcap. 13.4° alc. **Rating** 91 **To** 2015 $22.50

Viking Wines

RSD 108 Seppeltsfield Road, Marananga, SA 5355 **Region** Barossa Valley
T (08) 8562 3842 **F** (08) 8562 4266 **www.**vikingwines.com **Open** 7 days 11–5
Winemaker Rolf Binder, Kym Teusner (Contract) **Est.** 1995 **Cases** 1500
Based on 50-year-old, dry-grown and near-organic vineyards yielding of 1–1.5 tonnes per acre, Viking Wines has been 'discovered' by Robert Parker with inevitable consequences for the price of its top Shiraz. There are 5 ha of shiraz and 3 ha of cabernet sauvignon. The Odin's Honour wines (made by sister company Todd-Viking Wines) also come from old (20–100 years) dry-grown vines around Marananga and Greenoch. Exports to the US, the UK, Singapore and France.

Royal Reserve Barossa Valley Shiraz 2004 Deep colour; massively concentrated prune, plum and confit fruit; undoubtedly impressive, but was it taken just a little too far? Cork. 15° alc. **Rating** 90 **To** 2019 $40

Villa Caterina Wines

4 Wattletree Road, Drumcondra, Geelong, Vic 3215 (postal) **Region** Geelong
T (03) 5278 2847 **F** (03) 5278 4884 **Open** Not
Winemaker Ernesto Vellucci **Est.** 2001 **Cases** 300
Ernesto Vellucci was born in Italy where his parents brought him up in the traditional and cultural way of Italian winemaking. He is a qualified as an industrial chemist, with years of working with laboratory equipment and techniques. He offers the only wine laboratory services in Geelong with microbiological testing facilities and gas chromatography, directed to the detection of brettanomyces/dekkera yeasts. His small production is made from purchased grapes.

Pinot Noir 2005 Fine and elegant; gently spicy/savoury/foresty characters throughout; good structure and balance; likewise overall flavour. Diam. 13° alc. **Rating** 93 **To** 2012 $18

Geelong Shiraz 2005 Medium-bodied red and black cherry fruit with some spicy notes; fine tannins; good mouthfeel. Diam. 14.5° alc. **Rating** 89 **To** 2012 $18

Villa d'Esta Vineyard

2884 Wallambah Road, Dyers Crossing, NSW 2429 **Region** Northern Rivers Zone
T (02) 6550 2236 **F** (02) 6550 2236 **www.**villadesta.com.au **Open** 7 days 9–5
Winemaker Zoltan Toth **Est.** 1997 **Cases** 1000
Zolton Toth and Maria Brizuela have 5.5 ha of chardonnay, verdelho, chasselas dore, pinot noir, cabernet sauvignon, merlot, shiraz, muscat, hamburg and chambourcin. They make the wines onsite.

Full Moon 2005 Fruit-driven, crisp and lively, with good acidity. The chasselas influence is obvious. Chardonnay/Chasselas. Cork. 12.2° alc. **Rating** 87 **To** 2008 $12

Villa Tinto

Krondorf Road, Tanunda, SA 5352 **Region** Barossa Valley
T (08) 8563 3044 **F** (08) 8563 0460 **www.**villatinto.com.au **Open** W'ends & public hols 10–5, Mon–Fri by appt
Winemaker Albert Di Palma **Est.** 2001 **Cases** 900

Albert and Dianne Di Palma began the development of their business in 1987, planting a little under 2 ha of cabernet sauvignon and 0.7 ha of shiraz. They were content to sell their grapes until 1999, but they are now making an increasing amount of wine at their small winery. The wines are also available at the Barossa Small Winemakers Centre at Chateau Tanunda. I can't work out why the 2004 wines were so mediocre, hopefully an aberration. Prior vintages were much better.

Vinden Estate

17 Gillards Road, Pokolbin, NSW 2320 **Region** Lower Hunter Valley
T (02) 4998 7410 **F** (02) 4998 7175 **www.**vindenestate.com.au **Open** 7 days 10–5
Winemaker Guy Vinden, John Baruzzi (Consultant) **Est.** 1998 **Cases** 3500
Sandra and Guy Vinden have a beautiful home and cellar door, with landscaped gardens, and 3.6 ha of merlot, shiraz and alicante bouschet, with the Brokenback mountain range in the distance. The winemaking is done onsite, using estate-grown red grapes; semillon and chardonnay are purchased from other growers. The reds are open-fermented, hand-plunged and basket-pressed.

ᵺᵺᵺᵺ **Hunter Valley Late Harvest Semillon 2006** Well-made; not especially complex, but has nicely balanced sweet fruit and acidity; cumquat and vanilla. Screwcap. 11° alc. **Rating** 89 **To** 2010 $22
Hunter Valley Chardonnay 2005 Light- to medium-bodied; clean, gentle stone fruit and melon, with equally gentle French oak; easy access style. Screwcap. 13° alc. **Rating** 88 **To** 2008 $22
Hunter Valley Alicante Bouschet 2006 Pale blush; crisp and lively reflecting its low alcohol; flavours of cherry and citrus, then a dry finish. Screwcap. 10° alc. **Rating** 88 **To** 2008 $22
Hunter Valley Verdelho 2006 Typical Hunter Valley verdelho; quite rich and full; flavour without distraction. Screwcap. 13.5° alc. **Rating** 87 **To** 2008 $22
Basket Press Hunter Valley Shiraz 2004 Typical light- to medium-bodied regional style with distinct earthy overtones to the fruit; fine tannins. Cork. 13° alc. **Rating** 87 **To** 2012 $23

Vinea Marson

PO Box 222, Heathcote, Vic 3523 **Region** Heathcote
T (03) 5433 2768 **F** (03) 5433 2768 **www.**vineamarson.com **Open** Not
Winemaker Mario Marson **Est.** 2000 **Cases** NFP
Owner-winemaker Mario Marson spent many years as the winemaker viticulturist with the late Dr John Middleton at the celebrated Mount Mary. He purchased the Vinea Marson property in 1999, on the eastern slopes of the Mt Camel Range, and in 2000 planted syrah and viognier, plus Italian varieties, sangiovese, nebbiolo and barbera. Since leaving Mount Mary, he has undertaken vintage work at Isole e Olena in Tuscany, worked as winemaker at Jasper Hill vineyard, and as consultant and winemaker for Stefani Estate.

ᵺᵺᵺᵺᵺ **Syrah 2004** Bright purple-red; an elegant wine despite the alcohol; blackberry and multi-spices; soft, fine, ripe tannins lead to very good mouthfeel and texture. Diam. 15° alc. **Rating** 95 **To** 2014 $33

ᵺᵺᵺᵺᵹ **Sangiovese 2004** More colour than most; has substance, authority and balance; spice, cedar and black cherry all showing what can be done with the variety. Cork. 14° alc. **Rating** 90 **To** 2010 $27

ᵺᵺᵺᵺ **Rose 2005** Salmon pink; some floral aromas from small red fruits; bone-dry style with good structure. Diam. 13° alc. **Rating** 89 **To** 2008 $17

Vinecrest

Cnr Barossa Valley Way/Vine Vale Road, Tanunda, SA 5352 **Region** Barossa Valley
T (08) 8563 0111 **F** (08) 8563 0444 **www.**vinecrest.com.au **Open** 7 days 11–5
Winemaker Mos Kaesler **Est.** 1999 **Cases** 5000

The Mader family has a long connection with the Barossa Valley. Ian Mader is a fifth-generation descendant of Gottfried and Maria Mader, who immigrated to the Barossa Valley in the 1840s, and his wife, Suzanne, is the daughter of a former long-serving vineyard manager for Penfolds. In 1969 Ian and Suzanne established their Sandy Ridge Vineyard, and more recently the Turrung Vineyard (together a total of 30 ha), a few mins from Tanunda. Having been grapegrowers for 30 years, in 1999 they established Vinecrest, using a small portion of the production from their vineyards. Exports to Hong Kong and Singapore.

ΥΥΥΥΥ **Myths & Memories Barossa Valley Merlot 2005** Medium red-purple; quite sweet cassis/redcurrant fruit with the counterpoint of low alcohol keeping the profile and mouthfeel appropriately elegant; sweet, fine tannins. Screwcap. 13° alc. **Rating** 91 **To** 2012 $22

Fifth Generation Barossa Valley Shiraz 2004 Restrained fruit and extract; medium-bodied, with elements of earth, leaf, spice and licorice; good balance and length. Screwcap. 14° alc. **Rating** 90 **To** 2014 $21

A Capital C Barossa Valley Cabernet Sauvignon 2004 Cassis and blackcurrant aromas, then a more restrained palate; notes of black olive and herb; firm, but balanced, tannins. Screwcap. 14.5° alc. **Rating** 90 **To** 2014 $21

ΥΥΥΥ **One Colour White Barossa Valley Semillon 2006** A big, rich traditional style; no oak, but plenty of alcohol (for the variety) and the suggestion of some skin contact. A gold medal at the Barossa Valley Wine Show '06 is a tribute to the past, not the future. Screwcap. 13° alc. **Rating** 89 **To** 2008 $16

Two Colours White Barossa Valley Semillon Sauvignon Blanc 2006 Flavoursome; a pleasant surprise from the contribution of the tropical/gooseberry sauvignon blanc component; presumably a very cool spot in the Barossa. Screwcap. 13.5° alc. **Rating** 88 **To** 2008 $16

Late Harvest 2004 Pale green-gold; the low alcohol works well, providing a delicate and fresh palate with lemon and lime juice flavours. Great with chilled fresh fruit. Screwcap. 10.5° alc. **Rating** 88 **To** 2008 $12

Vineyard 28   ★★☆

270 Bagieau Road, Harvey, WA 6220 **Region** Geographe
T (08) 9733 5605 **F** (08) 9733 4500 **Open** 7 days 10–5
Winemaker Contract **Est.** 1998 **Cases** 700
In 1997 Mark and Pippa Cumbers decided to leave Melbourne (where they had worked and become wine lovers) and return to Mark's home state of WA. They chose a 4-ha property on coastal tuart sands, and have planted cabernet sauvignon (0.8 ha) and nebbiolo, sauvignon blanc and chenin blanc (0.4 ha each). Nebbiolo was planted as a point of difference, but has so far proved as difficult to come to terms with here as elsewhere.

Vinifera Wines   ★★★☆

194 Henry Lawson Drive, Mudgee, NSW 2850 **Region** Mudgee
T (02) 6372 2461 **F** (02) 6372 6731 **www.**viniferawines.com.au **Open** 7 days 10–5.30
Winemaker Tony McKendry, Frank Newman **Est.** 1997 **Cases** 2000
Having lived in Mudgee for 15 years, Tony McKendry (a regional medical superintendent) and wife Debbie succumbed to the lure; they planted their small (1.5-ha) vineyard in 1995. In Debbie's words, 'Tony, in his spare 2 mins per day, also decided to start Wine Science at Charles Sturt University in 1992.' She continues, 'His trying to live 27 hours per day (plus our 4 kids!) fell to pieces when he was involved in a severe car smash in 1997. Two months in hospital stopped full-time medical work, and the winery dreams became inevitable.' Financial compensation finally came through and the small winery was built. The vineyard is now 11 ha, including 2 ha of tempranillo and 1 ha of graciano.

ΥΥΥΥΥ **Easter Semillon 2005** Very rich and sweet; banana, cumquat and citrus flavours; needed a touch more acidity to give it longevity. Screwcap. 12° alc. **Rating** 90 **To** 2008 $25

ŸŸŸŸ **Tempranillo 2005** Bright and clear; firm and quite crisp, that twist of tempranillo citrus and tamarillo; precise line and length; all that is missing (as so often) is structure. Screwcap. **Rating** 89 **To** 2012 $25

Mudgee Cabernet Sauvignon 2005 Earthy foresty notes, but also a good volume of blackcurrant fruits, the tannins ripe. Screwcap. **Rating** 88 **To** 2013 $23

Gran Tinto 2005 Slightly hazy but deep colour; a blend of Tempranillo/Grenache/Graciano/Cabernet Sauvignon giving rise to a genuine note of Spain; a medium-bodied wine finishing with gently savoury tannins. Screwcap. **Rating** 88 **To** 2011 $23

Vinrock

23 George Street, Thebarton, SA 5031 (postal) **Region** McLaren Vale
T (08) 8234 8288 **F** (08) 8234 8266 www.vinrock.com **Open** Not
Winemaker Serafino (Scott Rawlinson) **Est.** 2004 **Cases** 5000
Owners Don Luca, Marco Iannetti and Anthony De Pizzol all have a background in the wine industry, none more than Don Luca, a former board member of Tatachilla. He also planted the 30-ha Luca Vineyard in 1999. The majority of the grapes are sold, but since 2004 limited quantities of wine have been made from the best blocks in the vineyard.

ŸŸŸŸŸ **McLaren Vale Shiraz 2005** Medium-bodied; skilful winemaking has resulted in good texture and structure; fine tannins surround perfectly ripened black fruits and regional dark chocolate, plus engaging vanilla American oak. Cork. 14.5° alc. **Rating** 93 **To** 2020 $22

McLaren Vale Grenache 2005 Yet another wine to underline the McLaren Vale superiority of grenache; has real structure and an exotic array of cherry and raspberry fruits; good tannins hold the wine together. Cork. 14.5° alc. **Rating** 90 **To** 2013 $19

Vintner's Nest Wines

692 Rowella Road, Rowella, Tas 7270 **Region** Northern Tasmania
T (03) 6394 7179 www.vintnersnestwines.com **Open** Sep–May 7 days 11–5
Winemaker Chris Beanlands, Kristen Cush **Est.** 1996 **Cases** 650
Chris and Judy Beanlands have established a typical Tasmanian micro vineyard with 0.75 ha each of chardonnay and pinot noir, and 0.25 ha each of cabernet sauvignon and merlot. The chardonnay was planted in 1996, the pinot noir and cabernet in the next year and the merlot in 2000.

ŸŸŸŸŸ **Pinot Noir 2005** Strong, clear purple-red; flooded with ripe plum and black cherry fruit, strongly varietal; fruit-driven and minimal oak; some may be distracted by what appears to be some brettanomyces. Twin top. 13.5° alc. **Rating** 94 **To** 2012 $19

ŸŸŸŸŸ **Chardonnay 2004** Toasty nutty aromas; extremely intense and long palate, with uncompromising Tasmanian acidity. Cork. 13.2° alc. **Rating** 93 **To** 2010 $18

Pinot Noir 2004 Holding hue well; complex savoury/spicy/tangy fruit; an almost lemony cast to its vibrant flavours. Twin top. 13.2° alc. **Rating** 93 **To** 2010 $19

Chardonnay 2005 Spotlessly clean aromas; light but tangy and long grapefruit flavours; subtle oak, good balance and a long finish. Screwcap. 13.5° alc. **Rating** 92 **To** 2012 $18

Virgara Wines

Lot 11 Heaslip Road, Angle Vale, SA 5117 **Region** Adelaide Plains
T (08) 8284 7688 **F** (08) 8284 7666 www.virgarawines.com.au **Open** Mon–Fri 9–5, w'ends & public hols 10–5
Winemaker Tony Carapetis **Est.** 2001 **Cases** 10 000

In 1962 the Virgara family, with father Michael, mother Maria and 10 children ranging from 1 to 18 years old, migrated to Australia from southern Italy. Through the hard work so typical of many such families, in due course they became market gardeners on land purchased at Angle Vale (1967) and in the early 1990s acquired an existing vineyard in Angle Vale. This included 25 ha of shiraz, the plantings since expanded to over 68 ha of alicante, cabernet sauvignon, grenache, malbec, merlot, riesling, sangiovese, and sauvignon blanc. In 2001 the Virgara brothers purchased the former Barossa Valley Estates winery, but used it only for storage and maturation, as the first wine (made in '02 from 40-year-old shiraz) was made by the Glaetzer family. The death of Domenic Virgara in a road accident led to the employment of former Palandri winemaker (and, before that, Tahbilk winemaker) Tony Carapetis, and the full commissioning of the winery.

♟♟♟♟♀ **Adelaide Hills Riesling 2006** Light straw-green; lively apple blossom and lime aromas; one of a growing number of lovely sweet but food-friendly wines; note the 10° alcohol and you will not be surprised when you taste it. Screwcap. **Rating** 91 **To** 2011 $15
Adelaide Hills Cabernet Sauvignon 2003 Attractive rich, ripe cassis and blackcurrant fruit, alcohol actually having a positive contribution; good length and balance. Screwcap. 15° alc. **Rating** 91 **To** 2012 $18

♟♟♟♟ **Barossa Adelaide Hills Cabernet Sauvignon 2004** Medium-bodied; distinctly earthy/savoury characters with a nice touch of black olive; good length, and doesn't really show its alcohol. Screwcap. 15° alc. **Rating** 89 **To** 2010 $18

Voyager Estate　★★★★★

Lot 1 Stevens Road, Margaret River, WA 6285 **Region** Margaret River
T (08) 9757 6354 **F** (08) 9757 6494 **www.**voyagerestate.com.au **Open** 7 days 10–5
Winemaker Cliff Royle **Est.** 1978 **Cases** 35 000
Voyager Estate has come a long way since it was acquired by Michael Wright (of the mining family) in 1991. It now has a high-quality 103-ha vineyard which means it can select the best parcels of fruit for its own label, and supply surplus (but high-quality) wine to others. The Cape Dutch-style tasting room and vast rose garden are a major tourist attraction. Exports to the UK, the US and other major markets.

♟♟♟♟♟ **Margaret River Chardonnay 2006** Again shows why the golden triangle of Margaret River (Leeuwin Estate, Devil's Lair and Voyager Estate) make such superb chardonnay; there is a taught intensity to the fabric of the wine, allowing the nectarine, grapefruit and melon to play at will with new French oak and come out on top. Superb balance and length. Screwcap. 13.4° alc. **Rating** 96 **To** 2016 $42
Margaret River Sauvignon Blanc Semillon 2006 A spotless fragrant grass and lemon through to gentle passionfruit bouquet and palate; immaculate line and balance; 55%/45%. Screwcap. 12.5° alc. **Rating** 94 **To** 2010 $24
Margaret River Shiraz 2005 Medium-bodied; fragrant black fruits; a strong structure underpinned by tannins, but by no means ferocious; in fact the balance is very good, as is the length; predominantly blackberry and black cherry fruit with well-integrated quality oak. Screwcap. 14° alc. **Rating** 94 **To** 2027 $32
Girt by Sea Margaret River Cabernet Merlot 2005 Medium- to full-bodied; clear-cut cassis, blackcurrant, black fruits in a firmly delineated frame; perfect balance of oak and tannins guarantee the slow, long-term development of a classy wine. Screwcap. 14.1° alc. **Rating** 94 **To** 2027 $24

♟♟♟♟♀ **Girt by Sea Margaret River Cabernet Merlot 2004** Medium to full purple-red; supple, sweet blackcurrant and cassis on an evenly flowing palate; good oak and tannin balance. Screwcap. 14° alc. **Rating** 93 **To** 2019 $24

Walden Woods Farm

469 Donald Road, Armidale, NSW 2350 (postal) **Region** New England
T (02) 6772 8966 **Open** Not
Winemaker Scott Wright (Contract), Doug Hume **Est.** 2001 **Cases** 85
Doug Hume and Nadine McCrea have established 0.3 ha of close-planted pinot gris, using
certified organic growing and management techniques from the outset. The necessarily small
production sells out quickly by word of mouth, phone and mail orders.

Wallaroo Wines

PO Box 272, Hall, ACT, 2618 **Region** Canberra District
T (02) 6230 2831 **F** (02) 6230 2830 **www**.wallaroowines.com.au **Open** Not
Winemaker Roger Harris (Contract) **Est.** 1996 **Cases** 800
Leading international reporters and journalists Carolyn Jack and Philip Williams purchased the
property on which they have subsequently established Wallaroo Wines in 1996, after a 5-year
sojourn in Japan led to a desire for space. They retained leading viticultural consultant Di Davidson
to evaluate the property and recommend varieties, and she quickly encouraged them to proceed.
In 1997 they planted 2 ha of riesling, 4 ha of cabernet sauvignon and 6 ha of shiraz, leading to
the first vintage in 2000. Approximately 80% of the production is sold to Kamberra winery, and
is used in Kamberra's Meeting Place gold medal-winning wines. Much of the production has
been done by remote control, as they lived in the UK from 2000 to 2005, Philip as the European
correspondent for the ABC covering the Iraq war, the Madrid bombing and the Beslan Siege, all
making the return to Wallaroo and its elegant house especially rewarding.

Wandin Valley Estate

Wilderness Road, Lovedale, NSW 2320 **Region** Lower Hunter Valley
T (02) 4930 7317 **F** (02) 4930 7814 **www**.wandinvalley.com.au **Open** 7 days 10–5
Winemaker Matthew Burton **Est.** 1973 **Cases** 5000
After 15 years in the wine and hospitality business, owners Phillipa and James Davern have
decided to offer the property as a going concern, with vineyard, winery, accommodation, function
centre, cricket ground and restaurant in the package, aiming to keep its skilled staff as part of the
business, and ensure that all existing contracts are ongoing. Ironically, being offered for sale just as
the overall quality has increased. Exports to Denmark and Japan.

Shiraz 2004 Strong purple-red; a powerful wine, with the Barossa Valley
component leading the way; intense and focused blackberry and plum/dark
chocolate fruit; good length and much potential. Barossa Valley/Hunter Valley.
Screwcap. 13.5° alc. **Rating** 93 **To** 2015 $18
Single Vineyard Hunter Valley Semillon 2006 Very pale straw-green; a clean,
grassy bouquet, the palate with delicate structure, but plenty of flavour in a
grass/lemon/spice spectrum, the finish lengthened by citrussy acidity. Screwcap.
10.5° alc. **Rating** 92 **To** 2015 $20
Bridie's Reserve Hunter Valley Shiraz 2004 Elegant, regional style; sweet
plum and blackberry fruit with just a hint of earth; fine tannins. Cork. 13.5° alc.
Rating 92 **To** 2014 $35
Reserve Hunter Valley Semillon 2006 Water white; vibrant green apple,
grass and lemongrass flavours with a bright, lively finish. Screwcap. 10.5° alc.
Rating 90 **To** 2016 $20
Reserve Hunter Valley Chardonnay 2005 Fragrant nectarine and citrus aromas
lead into a bright, fresh fruit-driven palate; good length and finish. Screwcap. 14° alc.
Rating 90 **To** 2008 $30
Fatso's Revenge Red 2005 Surprisingly rich, vibrant and full of luscious, but
not jammy, red fruits; totally delicious. Cabernet Sauvignon/Shiraz/Merlot.
Screwcap. 13.5° alc. **Rating** 90 **To** 2011 $15

Fatso's Revenge White 2006 Fresh, lively and vibrant, the flavours of Hunter
semillon and Orange sauvignon blanc coming together very well, with a mix

of citrus and gentle tropical fruit; long finish. Screwcap. 12° alc. **Rating** 89
To 2010 $15
Pavilion Hunter Valley Rose 2006 Bright red-purple; neatly composed and
balanced, with subliminal sweetness running through to the long finish. Screwcap.
13.5° alc. **Rating** 88 **To** 2008 $20
Riley's Reserve Wrattonbully Cabernet Sauvignon 2003 Some brown
tinges; blackberry, briar, bramble and coffee flavours, the tannins quite grippy. Cork.
14° alc. **Rating** 87 **To** 2012 $35

Wangolina Station

Cnr Southern Ports Highway/Limestone Coast Road, Kingston SE, SA 5275 **Region**
Mount Benson
T (08) 8768 6187 **F** (08) 8768 6149 **www**.wangolina.com.au **Open** 7 days 10–5
Winemaker Anita Goode **Est.** 2001 **Cases** 3000
Four generations of the Goode family have been graziers at Wangolina Station, but now Anita
Goode has broken with tradition by becoming a vigneron. She has planted a total of 9 ha of vines,
with a little over 3 ha of shiraz, 2.6 ha sauvignon blanc, and 1.6 ha each of cabernet sauvignon
and sauvignon blanc.

99999 **Mount Benson Shiraz 2005** Medium-bodied but quite intense and focused
blackberry fruit, with touches of earth, licorice and spice; good structure and length.
Screwcap. 14.5° alc. **Rating** 90 **To** 2018 $20

9999 **Mount Benson Semillon 2006** Clean, quite aromatic lemongrass aromas; a fresh
palate, with light touches of citrus and lemon; good length; needs to build with time.
Screwcap. 11° alc. **Rating** 89 **To** 2013 $15

Wanted Man

c/- Jinks Creek Wines, Tonimbuk Road, Tonimbuk, Vic 3815 (postal) **Region** Heathcote
T (03) 5629 8502 **F** (03) 5629 8551 **www**.wantedman.com.au **Open** Not
Winemaker Andrew Clarke, Peter Bartholomew **Est.** 1996 **Cases** 2000
The Wanted Man vineyard was planted in 1996, and managed by Andrew Clarke since 2000,
producing Jinks Creek's Heathcote Shiraz. That wine was sufficiently impressive to lead Andrew
Clarke and partner Peter Bartholomew (a Melbourne restaurateur) to purchase the vineyard in
2006, and give it its own identity. It is a substantial vineyard, with 6 ha of shiraz, 1.5 ha each of
merlot and marsanne, 1 ha of viognier and 0.3 ha of dolcetto. The quirky Ned Kelly label is the
work of Mark Knight, cartoonist for the *Herald Sun*.

9999 **Marsanne Viognier 2006** A synergistic blend, the marsanne providing spine, the
viognier plenty of stone fruit/apricot flavour; good length, clean finish. Screwcap.
13° alc. **Rating** 89 **To** 2010

Wantirna Estate

Bushy Park Lane, Wantirna South, Vic 3152 **Region** Yarra Valley
T (03) 9801 2367 **F** (03) 9887 0225 **www**.wantirnaestate.com.au **Open** Not
Winemaker Maryann Egan, Reg Egan **Est.** 1963 **Cases** 800
Situated well within the boundaries of the Melbourne metropolitan area, Wantirna Estate is an
outpost of the Yarra Valley. It was one of the first established in the rebirth of the valley. Maryann
Egan has decided it is time to come in from the cold, and have the wines rated, self-evidently a
very sensible decision. Exports to Hong Kong, Singapore and Japan.

99999 **Isabella Yarra Valley Chardonnay 2005** Nectarine and apple blossom aromas; a
fine, elegant, fruit-driven palate, with more citrussy tones evident; barrel ferment oak
seamlessly integrated. Diam. 14° alc. **Rating** 94 **To** 2013 $48

99999 **Amelia Yarra Valley Cabernet Merlot 2004** Very well-structured and balanced
fruit, ripe, but not excessively so; a fine tannin backbone and harmonious French
oak. Diam. 14° alc. **Rating** 92 **To** 2019 $50

Lily Yarra Valley Pinot Noir 2005 Crystal clear, but very light colour; fresh, delicious cherry and strawberry flavours; no forcing, and the oak is subtle. Diam. 14° alc. **Rating** 91 **To** 2010 $50

Waratah Hills Vineyard

Promontory Road, Fish Creek, Vic 3959 **Region** Gippsland
T (03) 5683 2441 **www**.waratahhills.com.au **Open** Wed–Sun 11–4 (summer 10–5)
Winemaker Various contract **Est.** 1995 **Cases** 1000
Peter and Liz Rushen acquired Waratah Hills Vineyard in 2001; it had been established with advice from Phillip Jones (of Bass Phillip) on a northeast slope in a beautifully domed valley formed by the Battery Creek. There are 3 ha of pinot noir and 1 ha of chardonnay, together with a sprinkle of merlot. The vines have developed slowly, the first vintage coming in 2004, but Phillip Jones has had no involvement in the winemaking since the Rushens purchased the vineyard.

Waratah Vineyard   **NR**

11852 Gladstone Road, Mungungo via Monto, Qld 4630 **Region** Queensland Zone
T (07) 4166 5100 **www**.waratahvineyard.com.au **Open** Tues–Sun & public hols 10–5
Winemaker Peter Scudamore-Smith MW (Consultant) **Est.** 1998 **Cases** NA

Warburn Estate

700 Kidman Way, Griffith, NSW 2680 **Region** Riverina
T (02) 6963 8300 **www**.warburnestate.com.au **Open** Mon–Fri 9–5, Sat 10–4
Winemaker Sam Trimboli, Moreno Chiappin, Carmelo D'Aquino **Est.** 1969 **Cases** 1.25 million
Warburn Estate, doubtless drawn in part by the success of Casella's yellowtail, has seen its production soar to 1.25 million cases. It draws on 1000 ha of vineyards, and produces an encyclopaedic range of wines exported to all major markets. The wines tasted are a tiny part of its large number of wines.

🍷🍷🍷🍷🍷 **1164 Family Reserve Barossa Valley Merlot 2003** Medium red-purple; a medium-bodied, elegant, well-balanced wine driven by cassis/red fruits, supported in turn by fine, lingering tannins. Gold and trophy, International Wine Challenge '06. Cork. 14° alc. **Rating** 91 **To** 2012 $25

🍷🍷🍷🍷 **Premium Merlot 2005** Considerable weight and concentration to the red and black fruits; varietal character is not obvious, but a very good red wine at the price. Curiously, entered twice in the Queensland Wine Show '06, winning golds and the Chairman's Choice for Best Dry Red Merlot. (In almost all wine shows a single wine can only be entered once in any given show.) Screwcap. 14° alc. **Rating** 89 **To** 2015 $9
1164 Family Reserve Shiraz 2003 Is in part a victim of the '03 vintage, with a strongly earthy/savoury array of flavours. **Rating** 88 **To** 2012 $20

Warrabilla

Murray Valley Highway, Rutherglen, Vic 3685 **Region** Rutherglen
T (02) 6035 7242 **F** (02) 6035 7298 **www**.warrabillawines.com.au **Open** 7 days 10–5
Winemaker Andrew Sutherland Smith **Est.** 1990 **Cases** 10 000
Andrew Sutherland Smith and wife Carol have built a formidable reputation for their wines, headed by the Reserve trio of Durif, Cabernet Sauvignon and Shiraz, quintessential examples of Rutherglen red wine at its best. Their 18.5-ha vineyard has been extended with the planting of some riesling and zinfandel. Andrew spent 15 years with All Saints, McWilliam's, Yellowglen, Fairfield and Chambers before setting up Warrabilla, and his accumulated experience shines through in the wines. The red wines at the core of Warrabilla's production were not tasted this year (why I don't know, probably Murphy's Law at work).

ŸŸŸŸŸ **Reserve Vintage Port 2004** Technically, might not have needed much fermentation, but in fact fermented through to a relatively low baume, which is to be commended. Clean spirit and pristine black fruit flavours. Cork. 19° alc. **Rating** 90 **To** 2034 $22
Reserve Muscat NV Super-rich; moderately aged; strong raisin plum pudding flavours; needed a little more time in barrel to highlight the rancio. Cork. 18.5° alc. **Rating** 90 **To** 2008 $35

ŸŸŸŸ **Reserve Marsanne 2006** An injection of new oak is still to integrate and settle down; honeysuckle and a touch of citrus are on target, and time will help. Cork. 14° alc. **Rating** 89 **To** 2012 $15

Warramate

27 Maddens Lane, Gruyere, Vic 3770 **Region** Yarra Valley
T (03) 5964 9219 **F** (03) 5964 9219 **www**.warramatewines.com.au **Open** 7 days 10–6
Winemaker David Church **Est.** 1970 **Cases** 1500
A long-established and perfectly situated winery reaping the full benefits of its 37-year-old vines; recent plantings have increased production. All the wines are well-made, the Shiraz providing further proof (if such be needed) of the suitability of the variety to the region.

ŸŸŸŸŸ **White Label Shiraz 2005** Extremely elegant; a faithful reflection of its terroir; medium-bodied cherry, blackberry, spice and licorice. Vines planted in the 1970s. Screwcap. 13.5° alc. **Rating** 94 **To** 2020 $42

ŸŸŸŸŸ **Black Label Shiraz 2005** Considerable richness and flavour; blackberry and ripe plum; a very different expression to the White Label Shiraz. Screwcap. 13.5° alc. **Rating** 90 **To** 2020 $19
Black Label Cabernet Sauvignon 2005 Attractive, sweet cabernet fruit; medium-bodied, with gentle, ripe tannins and good balance. Screwcap. 13.5° alc. **Rating** 90 **To** 2017 $19

ŸŸŸŸ **White Label Cabernet Merlot 2004** Strongly earthy/savoury overtones to the blackcurrant fruit; fine tannins and controlled oak. Screwcap. 13.5° alc. **Rating** 89 **To** 2014 $32
Riesling 2006 Clean, fresh and well-made; lacks the penetration and precision of continental climate riesling, and is showing some early signs of development. Screwcap. 12.5° alc. **Rating** 88 **To** 2010 $25
White Label Pinot Noir 2005 Relatively light; sweet strawberry and cherry fruit; in no small measure a consequence of young vines. White Label is normally used for the old vines, Black Label for the young. Screwcap. 13.5° alc. **Rating** 87 **To** 2008 $19

Warraroong Estate

247 Wilderness Road, Lovedale, NSW 2321 **Region** Lower Hunter Valley
T (02) 4930 7594 **F** (02) 4930 7199 **www**.warraroongestate.com **Open** Thurs–Mon 10–5
Winemaker Andrew Thomas **Est.** 1978 **Cases** 3500
'Warraroong' is an Aboriginal word for 'hillside', reflecting the southwesterly aspect of the property, which looks back towards the Brokenback Range and Watagan Mountains. The label design is from a painting by Aboriginal artist Kia Kiro who, while coming from the NT, is now living and working in the Hunter Valley. The mature vineyard plantings were extended in 2004 with a little over 1 ha of verdelho. Exports to Japan.

ŸŸŸŸŸ **Hunter Valley Semillon 2006** Classic, intense and powerful Hunter Valley semillon with an extra dimension of flavour running well into citrus; great now or much later. Screwcap. 9.6° alc. **Rating** 95 **To** 2016 $20

ŸŸŸŸŸ **Claremont Methode Champenoise 2002** Excellent mousse; very fine, elegant and long; a minor miracle, but Andrew Thomas provides plenty of these. 10.9° alc. **Rating** 90 **To** 2008 $35

ŦŦŦŦ **Hunter Valley Verdelho 2006** Labrador-friendly; will wag its gentle fruit salad tail at anyone showing interest and with $25 to invest. Screwcap. 13.9° alc. **Rating** 87 **To** 2008 $25
Long Lunch White 2006 Lovely fresh and crisp white with as much to offer as the Verdelho at a much lower price. Screwcap. 13° alc. **Rating** 87 **To** 2008 $17

Warrego Wines

9 Seminary Road, Marburg, Qld 4306 **Region** Queensland Coastal
T (07) 5464 4400 **F** (07) 5464 4800 **www**.warregowines.com.au **Open** 7 days 10–4
Winemaker Kevin Watson **Est.** 2000 **Cases** 31 500
Kevin Watson has completed his wine science degree at Charles Sturt University, and the primary purpose of his business is custom winemaking for the many small growers in the region, including all the clients of Peter Scudamore-Smith MW. In 2001, the Marburg Custom Crush company developed a state-of-the-art winery (as the cliché goes), cellar door and restaurant. $500 000 in government funding, local business investment and significant investment from China provided the funds, and the complex opened in 2002. Since then, the business has expanded further with a public share raising. The 3500-case own-brand Warrego wines come from 0.5 ha of estate chambourcin, plus grapes purchased in various regions. Exports to the US and Canada.

ŦŦŦŦŦ **Reserve Shiraz 2002** Supple, rich plum and black cherry fruit; fine, ripe tannins plus integrated oak; a generous wine with a hint of sweetness. Cork. 13.5° alc. **Rating** 90 **To** 2012 $35

ŦŦŦŦ **Fiona's Folly 2006** Very early-picked; an interesting style fermented near to dryness; the tangy, citrus fruit offset by a touch of residual sugar, making it impossible to dislike. Extremely clever winemaking. Chardonnay. Screwcap. 10.5° alc. **Rating** 88 **To** 2008 $13.50
Organic Opulence Shiraz Rose 2006 Strong colour; considerable depth to the cherry fruit on bouquet and palate; in a crossover to light dry red style. Cork. **Rating** 87 **To** 2008 $20.50
Organic Opulence Shiraz 2006 Plenty of bright flavour, but early picking and/or excess addition of tartaric acid leaves the wine anything but opulent. Cork. **Rating** 87 **To** 2013 $24
Seminary Shiraz 2005 Clean, light- to medium-bodied blackberry and plum fruit; milky tannins distract somewhat, but the wine does have pleasant overall flavour. Screwcap. 13.5° alc. **Rating** 87 **To** 2012 $22.50

Warrenmang Vineyard & Resort

Mountain Creek Road, Moonambel, Vic 3478 **Region** Pyrenees
T (03) 5467 2233 **F** (03) 5467 2309 **www**.bazzani.com.au **Open** 7 days 10–5
Winemaker Chris Collier **Est.** 1974 **Cases** 11 000
The proposed merger of Warrenmang with other wine interests in 2004 failed to eventuate, through no fault of Luigi and Athalie Bazzani, who resumed full control of the business in 2005, securing a number of large export orders to the US and Singapore. However, the desire to retire led to the property being placed on the market once again in 2007.

ŦŦŦŦŦ **Black Puma Pyrenees Shiraz 2005** Impenetrable colour; an exceptionally intense and powerful wine, well-balanced within its terms of reference. A rare exception made to taste a final tank sample. If the wine makes it safely to bottle will merit higher points still. Cork. 15° alc. **Rating** 94 **To** 2020 $80

ŦŦŦŦŦ **Estate Pyrenees Shiraz 2005** Dense, inky wine; extremely rich and layered, with more light and shade than the Black Puma. Likewise a tank sample; likewise headed to higher points. Cork. 14.5° alc. **Rating** 93 **To** 2025 $60
Grand Pyrenees 2002 Powerful, dense and concentrated; blackberry, blackcurrant, chocolate and mocha sustained by persistent but balanced tannins. Cabernet Sauvignon/Cabernet Franc/Shiraz. Cork. 14.5° alc. **Rating** 92 **To** 2014 $35

Estate Pyrenees Chardonnay 2005 Obvious barrel ferment oak on the bouquet, but the oak and fruit coalesce on the palate; creamy/nutty/figgy notes join stone fruit and a touch of citrus. Screwcap. 14.5° alc. **Rating** 91 **To** 2012 $25
Torchio Aged Pressings NV A most unusual wine; a blend of cabernet and shiraz basket pressings from the best vintages of the past decade, and kept in barrel until being bottled. Has succeeded in keeping sufficient fruit freshness and power to tame the tannins; not an easy task. Cork. 14.5° alc. **Rating** 90 **To** 2012 $60

ŸŸŸŸ **Bazzani Pyrenees Shiraz Cabernet 2005** Very generously flavoured; red and black fruits with a touch of chocolate; soft tannins and a hint of sweetness; terrific value. Screwcap. 14.5° alc. **Rating** 89 **To** 2010 $13
Pyrenees Sauvignon Blanc 2005 The light touch of oak adds texture to a very delicate, minerally palate; crisp finish. Cork. 14° alc. **Rating** 87 **To** 2010 $25

Watchbox Wines

Indigo Creek Road, Indigo Valley, Vic 3688 **Region** Rutherglen
T (02) 6026 9299 **www.**watchboxwines.com.au **Open** Wed–Fri 10–4, Sat & public hols 10–5
Winemaker Alan Clark **Est.** 2001 **Cases** NA
Alan and Lisa Clark have established an 11-ha vineyard in the Indigo Valley, planted to sauvignon blanc, chardonnay, cabernet sauvignon, merlot, shiraz, durif and muscat. The wines are made onsite and sold through mail order and through the cellar door and café.

Water Wheel

Bridgewater-on-Loddon, Bridgewater, Vic 3516 **Region** Bendigo
T (03) 5437 3060 **F** (03) 5437 3082 **www.**waterwheelwine.com **Open** Mon–Fri 9–5, w'ends & public hols 12–4
Winemaker Peter Cumming, Bill Trevaskis **Est.** 1972 **Cases** 45 000
Peter Cumming, with more than 2 decades of winemaking under his belt, has quietly built on the reputation of Water Wheel year by year. The winery is owned by the Cumming family, which has farmed in the Bendigo region for 50+ years, with horticulture and viticulture special areas of interest. The wines are of remarkably consistent quality and modest price. Exports to the UK, the US and other major markets.

ŸŸŸŸŸ **Bendigo Cabernet Sauvignon 2005** Gently sweet cassis blackcurrant fruit framed by firm but balanced tannins. No frills, just rock-solid value. Screwcap. 14.8° alc. **Rating** 91 **To** 2015 $18
Bendigo Shiraz 2005 Classic Water Wheel style, as honest as the day is long; blackberry and dark plum fruit with some spicy notes; the tannins fine but persistent, oak a bit player. Screwcap. 15.5° alc. **Rating** 90 **To** 2015 $18
Memsie Bendigo Shiraz Cabernet Sauvignon Malbec 2006 First released less than 12 months old, chock-full of blackberry and blackcurrant fruit, backed by firm tannins. Great now or later proposition; small wonder it often appears in Qantas business class. Screwcap. 14.5° alc. **Rating** 90 **To** 2012 $12

Watershed Wines

Cnr Bussell Highway/Darch Road, Margaret River, WA 6285 **Region** Margaret River
T (08) 9758 8633 **F** (08) 9757 3999 **www.**watershedwines.com.au **Open** 7 days 10–5
Winemaker Severine Logan **Est.** 2002 **Cases** 76 000
Watershed Wines has been established by a syndicate of investors, and no expense has been spared in establishing the vineyard and building a striking cellar door, and a 200-seat café and restaurant. Situated towards the southern end of the Margaret River region, its neighbours include Voyager Estate and Leeuwin Estate. Exports to the UK, the US and other major markets.

ŸŸŸŸŸ **Awakening Margaret River Chardonnay 2006** Subtle complexity from 70% barrel fermentation in new and used oak with the usual lees contact; harmonious, with no overt flavours, just the marriage of melon and citrus fruit, with nutty oak and a long finish. Screwcap. 13.5° alc. **Rating** 94 **To** 2016 $32.95

ŸŸŸŸŸ **Awakening Margaret River Sauvignon Blanc 2006** Crisp, clean and fresh; the varietal fruit is not particularly intense, perhaps toned down by the percentage of barrel fermentation; long palate, and lingering finish. Screwcap. 12.5° alc. **Rating** 90 **To** 2009 $32.95

Shades Sauvignon Blanc Semillon 2006 Bounteous flavour starting with tropical/gooseberry moving (slightly unusually) into stone fruit; easy, drink now style. Screwcap. 12.5° alc. **Rating** 90 **To** 2008 $18

Margaret River Cabernet Merlot 2004 Fresh red and black fruits, still with firm edges although the wine is only medium-bodied; good length, and will improve with cellaring. Cork. 14° alc. **Rating** 90 **To** 2019 $24.95

ŸŸŸŸ **Awakening Margaret River Cabernet Sauvignon 2005** A minty, eucalypt overlay is very pronounced in a light- to medium-bodied wine with just enough varietal fruit to carry those characters. Cork. 13.5° alc. **Rating** 87 **To** 2012 $32.95

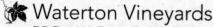 # Waterton Vineyards

PO Box 141, Exeter, Tas 7275 **Region** Northern Tasmania
T (03) 6394 7214 **F** (03) 6394 7614 **Open** Not
Winemaker Julian Alcorso (Contract) **Est.** 2006 **Cases** 140
Jennifer Baird and Peter Cameron purchased this remarkable property in 2002. Waterton Hall was built in the 1850s, and modified extensively by well-known neogothic architect Alexander North in 1910. The property was owned by the Catholic church from 1949 to 1996, variously used as a school, a boys home and retreat. Following its sale the new owners planted 1 ha of riesling at the end of the 1990s, and Jennifer and Peter extended the vineyard with 1 ha of shiraz, electing to sell the riesling until 2006, when part was made under the Waterton label. The plans are to use the existing buildings to provide a restaurant, accommodation and function facilities.

ŸŸŸŸ **Riesling 2006** Good weight and balance; ripe citrus fruit, perhaps needing a touch more authority on the finish. **Rating** 88 **To** 2010

Watson Wine Group   ★★★★

PO Box 6243, Halifax Street, Adelaide, SA 5000 **Region** Coonawarra
T (08) 8338 3200 **F** (08) 8338 3244 **www.**wwgwines.com **Open** Not
Winemaker Roger Harbord **Est.** 1997 **Cases** NFP
After he sold his highly successful industrial services business to Brambles Group in 1998, Rex Watson decided to build on the core of a small 10-ha vineyard he had acquired in Coonawarra the year before. The business rapidly expanded, and today owns and manages almost 400 ha over 3 vineyards all within the Coonawarra region, and acquires additional grapes for the Limestone Coast range. The wines are made by industry veteran Roger Harbord at the Russet Ridge winery. Current releases are under the Gum Bear and Rex Watson labels, the latter from Coonawarra. Exports to the US, Canada, Singapore, Malaysia, India, Sri Lanka, Taiwan, China and NZ.

ŸŸŸŸŸ **Rex Watson Three Sons Cabernet Sauvignon 2005** Good balance and structure; restrained fruit with black olive and some oak sweetening; good mouthfeel and texture. Screwcap. **Rating** 91 **To** 2015 $19

Rex Watson Three Sons Coonawarra Shiraz 2005 Light- to medium-bodied; an elegant, well-balanced mix of black and red fruits supported by appropriate vanilla oak and tannins. Screwcap. 14.5° alc. **Rating** 90 **To** 2015 $19

Rex Watson Cabernet Sauvignon 2005 A complex wine, with good fruit and oak balance and integration; good structure, the oak handling a definite plus. Screwcap. **Rating** 90 **To** 2013 $15

ŸŸŸŸ **Rex Watson Cabernet Shiraz Merlot 2005** Pleasant, smooth medium-bodied wine with attractive tannin structure. Screwcap. **Rating** 89 **To** 2012 $15

Rex Watson Three Sons Coonawarra Sauvignon Blanc 2005 Clean, honest, light- to medium-bodied sauvignon, with tropical/passionfruit flavours; ready to roll. Screwcap. 12.5° alc. **Rating** 88 **To** 2008 $19

Rex Watson Coonawarra Unwooded Chardonnay 2005 The screwcap still has the wine 100% fresh; attractive, sweet stone fruit flavours, although inevitably simple. Screwcap. 14° alc. **Rating** 87 **To** 2008 $15

Wattle Ridge Vineyard

Loc 11950 Boyup-Greenbushes Road, Greenbushes, WA 6254 **Region** Blackwood Valley
T (08) 9764 3594 **www**.wattleridgewines.com.au **Open** Thurs–Mon 10–4
Winemaker Contract **Est.** 1997 **Cases** 1500
James and Vicky Henderson have established 6.25 ha of vines at their Nelson Vineyard, planted to riesling, verdelho, merlot and cabernet sauvignon. The wines are sold by mail order and through the cellar door, which offers light meals, crafts and local produce. Exports to Canada and Japan.

Wattlebrook Vineyard ★★★★

Fordwich Road, Broke, NSW 2330 **Region** Lower Hunter Valley
T (02) 9929 5668 **F** (02) 9929 5668 **www**.wattlebrook.com **Open** Not
Winemaker Andrew Margan (Contract) **Est.** 1994 **Cases** 1000
Wattlebrook Vineyard was founded by NSW Supreme Court Justice Peter McClellan and family in 1994, with a substantial vineyard lying between the Wollemi National Park and Wollombi Brook. The family planted another major vineyard, in 1998, on Henry Lawson Drive at Mudgee, to shiraz, merlot and cabernet sauvignon. The Wollombi Vineyard is planted to chardonnay, semillon, verdelho, cabernet sauvignon and shiraz. The wines have been consistent medal winners at various local wine shows. Exports to Japan.

ᵀᵀᵀᵀᵀ **Bird's Keep Hunter Valley Shiraz 2005** Abundant blackberry and plum fruit; good length and depth with harmonious tannin and oak contributions. Screwcap. 13.6° alc. **Rating** 94 **To** 2020 $22

ᵀᵀᵀᵀ **Semillon 2005** Sweet, gentle lemon/lime/herb flavour; soft and should develop quickly. **Rating** 87 **To** 2010 $14
Hunter Valley Chardonnay 2004 Has some mineral tightness, but not quite enough mid-palate fruit. **Rating** 87 **To** 2009 $17

Wayne Thomas Wines ★★★★

26 Kangarilla Road, McLaren Vale, SA 5171 **Region** McLaren Vale
T (08) 8323 9737 **F** (08) 8323 9737 **Open** Not
Winemaker Wayne Thomas, Tim Geddes **Est.** 1994 **Cases** 5000
Wayne Thomas was a McLaren Vale veteran, having started his winemaking career in 1961, working for Stonyfell, Ryecroft and Saltram before establishing Fern Hill with his late wife Pat in 1975. When they sold Fern Hill in 1994 they started again, launching the Wayne Thomas Wines label, using grapes sourced from 10 growers throughout McLaren Vale. Exports to the UK, the US, Canada and Hong Kong. Wayne Thomas passed away in April 2007.

ᵀᵀᵀᵀᵀ **McLaren Vale Shiraz 2005** Classic McLaren Vale shiraz with black fruits and dark chocolate plus a generous whack of alcohol, presumably for the benefit of the American market. Cork. 15.5° alc. **Rating** 90 **To** 2015 $32
McLaren Vale Cabernet Sauvignon 2005 Rich, archetypal McLaren Vale, with blackcurrant, chocolate, tannins and alcohol all streaming together. Cork. 15.5° alc. **Rating** 90 **To** 2017 $32

ᵀᵀᵀᵀ **McLaren Vale Petit Verdot 2005** Impenetrable colour; impossibly powerful, dense and extractive; 5% in a blend would make a major statement. Cork. 15.5° alc. **Rating** 87 **To** 2027 $35

Wedgetail Estate

40 Hildebrand Road, Cottles Bridge, Vic 3099 **Region** Yarra Valley
T (03) 9714 8661 **F** (03) 9714 8676 **www.**wedgetailestate.com.au **Open** W'ends &
public hols 12–5, or by appt, closed 25 Dec–Australia Day w'end
Winemaker Guy Lamothe **Est.** 1994 **Cases** 1500

Canadian-born photographer Guy Lamothe and partner Dena Ashbolt started making wine in
the basement of their Carlton home in the 1980s. The idea of their own vineyard started to take
hold, and the search for a property began. Then, in their words, 'one Sunday, when we were "just
out for a drive", we drove past our current home. The slopes are amazing, true goat terrain, and
it is on these steep slopes that in 1994 we planted our first block of pinot noir.' While the vines
were growing – they now have 5.5 ha in total – Lamothe enrolled in the wine-growing course
at Charles Sturt University, having already gained practical experience working in the Yarra Valley
(Tarrawarra), the Mornington Peninsula and Meursault. The net result is truly excellent wine.
Exports to the UK, Canada and Singapore.

ΨΨΨΨΨ **Single Vineyard Yarra Valley Pinot Noir 2005** Light to medium red; sappy/
spicy/foresty/earthy aromas lead into a very long palate, adding red and black
cherry to the mix; zesty style. Screwcap. 13.5° alc. **Rating** 94 **To** 2012 $40

ΨΨΨΨΨ **Reserve Pinot Noir 2004** Deep colour; very powerful and concentrated black
cherry and plum fruit, ripe, dense and spicy, but not alcoholic or over the top. The
bottle tasted March '06 was (in retrospect) clearly oxidised, the closure
notwithstanding. Diam. 13.5° alc. **Rating** 93 **To** 2010 $60

Single Vineyard Yarra Valley Chardonnay 2005 A complex bouquet and
palate; figgy/creamy/nutty characters point to oak, when in fact little used;
good mouthfeel. Screwcap. 14° alc. **Rating** 91 **To** 2010 $32

Par 3 Yarra Valley Pinot Noir 2006 A mix of strawberries and cherries with
nuances of stalk and spice; good length. Screwcap. 13.5° alc. **Rating** 90
To 2011 $20

The North Face 2004 Better depth of colour than the '05, and more character
and depth of flavour, all with a certain masculine astringency; commands attention.
Screwcap. 13° alc. **Rating** 90 **To** 2014 $30

ΨΨΨΨ **Single Vineyard Yarra Valley Shiraz 2005** Light- to medium-bodied; cool-
grown spicy/savoury characteristics; red fruits and a touch of mint. Screwcap. 14° alc.
Rating 89 **To** 2011 $38

The North Face 2005 Relatively light colour; light- to medium-bodied; leafy
early-drinking style. Cabernet Sauvignon/Merlot. Screwcap. 13° alc. **Rating** 88
To 2010 $30

Wehl's Mount Benson Vineyards

Wrights Bay Road, Mount Benson, SA 5275 **Region** Mount Benson
T (08) 8768 6251 **F** (08) 8678 6251 **Open** 7 days 10–4
Winemaker Contract **Est.** 1989 **Cases** 2500

Peter and Leah Wehl were the first to plant vines in the Mount Benson area, beginning the
establishment of their 24-ha vineyard (two-thirds shiraz and one-third cabernet sauvignon) in
1989. While primarily grapegrowers, they have moved into winemaking via contract makers, and
plan to increase the range of wines available by grafting 1 ha of merlot and 1.5 ha of sauvignon
blanc onto part of the existing plantings.

ΨΨΨΨΨ **Shiraz 2004** Firm, slightly old-fashioned style; fine tannin structure; may end up
like an old Hunter Valley shiraz. Screwcap. **Rating** 90 **To** 2014 $25

ΨΨΨΨ **Cabernet Sauvignon Merlot 2004** Linear flavours of blackcurrant and
redcurrant within a controlled medium-bodied range; needs to build more
complexity for higher points. Screwcap. 13.5° alc. **Rating** 88 **To** 2014 $20

Wellington Vale Wines

'Wellington Vale', Deepwater, NSW 2371 (postal) **Region** New England
T (02) 6734 5226 **F** (02) 6734 5226 **Open** Not
Winemaker Preston Peak (Rod McPherson) **Est.** 1997 **Cases** 300
David and Dierdri Robertson-Cuninghame trace their ancestry (via David) back to the Duke of
Wellington, with Cuninghame Senior being the ADC to the Duke, and his son, Arthur Wellesley-
Robertson, the godson. Arthur Wellesley migrated to Australia and took up the land upon which
Wellington Vale is situated in 1839. Planting began in 1997 with 0.7 ha of semillon, and continued
with 1 ha of pinot noir and 0.3 ha of riesling. The first vintage was in 2000, and the subsequent
vintages have won bronze medals at the competitive Australian Small Winemakers Show.

ŶŶŶŶ   **Wooded Reserve Semillon 2005** Pale straw-green; little or no development yet
evident; appropriately subtle oak adding more to texture than flavour; curious
pricing parity with the '06 varietal. Screwcap. 12° alc. **Rating** 88 **To** 2011 $12
Semillon 2006 Crisp and minerally, though there is a slightly broken line in the
fruit intensity; may mend. Screwcap. 12° alc. **Rating** 87 **To** 2010 $12

Wendouree

Wendouree Road, Clare, SA 5453 **Region** Clare Valley
T (08) 8842 2896 **Open** By appt
Winemaker Tony Brady **Est.** 1895 **Cases** 2000
The iron fist in a velvet glove best describes these extraordinary wines. They are fashioned with
passion and precision from the very old vineyard with its unique terroir by Tony and Lita Brady,
who rightly see themselves as custodians of a priceless treasure. The 100-year-old stone winery is
virtually unchanged from the day it was built; this is in every sense a treasure beyond price. Even
though I doubted the wisdom of providing tasting notes for current or immediate past releases, I
did not wish Wendouree to slip into the obscurity of NR rating. I could barely believe the beauty
of the wines, the 2002 and 2004 already at the point of which it is not vinicide to open them.

ŶŶŶŶŶ   **Shiraz 2004** More refined and intense than the '03, with great strength of line, and
excellent balance; the breadth of fruit flavours is slightly finer and more supple than
the '02, but not as intense. Cork. **Rating** 96 **To** 2034
Shiraz 2002 Medium- to full-bodied; intense and powerful, but the tannins are
already amazingly well-knit; blackberry fruit; beautiful line and length, and a great
finish. Cork. **Rating** 96 **To** 2032

ŶŶŶŶŶ   **Shiraz 2003** Full-bodied; a masculine wine, with blackberry, earth, and touches of
plum; the tannins do linger, but not over the top or unexpected. Definitely needs
time to evolve. Cork. **Rating** 93 **To** 2025

Wenzel Family Wines

'Glenrowan', Step Road, Langhorne Creek, SA 5255 **Region** Langhorne Creek
T (08) 8537 3035 **F** (08) 8537 3435 **www**.langhornewine.com.au **Open** By appt
Winemaker Greg Follett (Contract) **Est.** 2000 **Cases** 215
The Wenzel family left the Hartz Mountains in Germany in 1846 for Australia, and settled in
Langhorne Creek in 1853. Six generations later Dale and Lisa Wenzel run 2 vineyards, with a little
over 46 ha of chardonnay, merlot, shiraz, cabernet sauvignon and petit verdot. Over 90% of the
grapes are sold to other makers; 'The Old Man's' label is a respectful tribute to Oscar (and Hazel)
Wenzel who planted the first vines in 1968.

ŶŶŶŶ   **The Old Man's Langhorne Creek Shiraz 2004** Light, but quite bright hue;
medium-bodied cassis berry fruit; fair length. Cork. 13.8° alc. **Rating** 88
To 2013 $19

Were Estate

Cnr Wildberry Road/Johnson Road, Wilyabrup, WA 6280 **Region** Margaret River
T (08) 9755 6273 **F** (08) 9755 6273 www.wereestate.com.au **Open** 7 days 10.30–5
Winemaker Jan McIntosh (Contract) **Est.** 1998 **Cases** 5000
Owners Diane and Gordon Davies say, 'We are different. We're original, we're bold, we're innovative.' This is all reflected in the design of the unusual back labels, incorporating pictures of the innumerable pairs of braces which real estate agent Gordon Davies wears on his Perth job; in the early move to screwcaps for both white and red wines; and, for that matter, in the underground trickle irrigation system in their Margaret River vineyard which can be controlled from Perth. Exports to the US, Philippines and Singapore.

ҮҮҮҮҮ **Margaret River Shiraz 2004** Clear red-purple; bright, fresh, fragrant and lively; red and black fruit mix; controlled oak and fine tannins. Screwcap. 14.4° alc. **Rating** 94 **To** 2014 $25

ҮҮҮҮҮ **Margaret River Cabernet Sauvignon 2004** Clear red-purple; medium-bodied; vibrant and fresh in winery style; just a little minty/savoury, but has good length and balance. Screwcap. 14.2° alc. **Rating** 90 **To** 2014 $25

ҮҮҮҮ **Margaret River Shiraz Cabernet 2005** A medium-bodied and fresh array of predominantly red fruits (cherries) and black fruits (plums) plus sundry spices; controlled tannins. Screwcap. 14° alc. **Rating** 89 **To** 2012 $17
Margaret River Semillon Sauvignon Blanc 2006 Light straw-green; a spotlessly clean bouquet leads into a palate with mineral notes offset by tropical fruit and augmented by a touch of sweetness. Uncertain line. Screwcap. 12.9° alc. **Rating** 88 **To** 2009 $17

West Cape Howe Wines

★★★★★

Lot 42 South Coast Highway, Denmark, WA 6333 **Region** Denmark
T (08) 9848 2959 **F** (08) 9848 2903 **Open** 7 days 10–5
Winemaker Gavin Berry, Dave Cleary, Coby Ladwig **Est.** 1997 **Cases** 55 000
After a highly successful 7 years, West Cape Howe founders Brenden and Kylie Smith moved on, selling the business to a partnership including Gavin Berry (until 2004, senior winemaker at Plantagenet) and viticulturist Rob Quenby. As well as existing fruit sources, West Cape Howe now has the 80-ha Lansdale Vineyard, planted in 1989, as its primary fruit source. The focus now will be less on contract winemaking, and more on building the very strong West Cape Howe brand. Exports to the US, Hong Kong, Singapore, Japan, Denmark and The Netherlands.

ҮҮҮҮҮ **Great Southern Riesling 2006** Spotlessly clean; a light, vibrant and crisp palate with touches of apple, citrus and lemon zest; long, dry finish. Screwcap. 11° alc. **Rating** 94 **To** 2016 $19
Great Southern Sauvignon Blanc 2006 A complex, strongly varietal, albeit slightly sweaty, bouquet, then a similarly powerful, multifaceted palate, unusually deep in flavour. My hypersensitivity to sweatiness ignored. Screwcap. 12° alc. **Rating** 94 **To** 2008 $19
Two Steps Great Southern Shiraz Viognier 2005 Fragrant black and red fruits, licorice and spice with the unmistakable viognier lift; a medium-bodied palate with similarly attractive flavours; very good texture and structure. Screwcap. 14.5° alc. **Rating** 94 **To** 2020 $24
Book Ends Great Southern Cabernet Sauvignon 2005 Strong, deep colour; medium- to full-bodied, crammed with blackcurrant and cassis fruit, but in no sense over the top; touches of dark chocolate and French oak; fine tannins. Screwcap. 14° alc. **Rating** 94 **To** 2025 $24
Great Southern Tempranillo 2005 Bright, fresh and lively aromas and flavours; a cascade of red fruits; excellent balance and structure. Screwcap. 14° alc. **Rating** 94 **To** 2010 $19

ℙℙℙℙℙ **Semillon Sauvignon Blanc 2006** Light straw-green; an abundance of soft, gently tropical aromas and flavours; long and rich palate. **Rating** 93 **To** 2008 $16
Styx Gully Chardonnay 2005 A complex bouquet and palate with nutty barrel ferment characters interwoven with fruit on the light-bodied palate; has good finish and aftertaste. Screwcap. 13.5° alc. **Rating** 93 **To** 2012 $19
Book Ends Great Southern Cabernet Sauvignon 2004 Medium-bodied; convincing varietal expression through sweet cassis and blackcurrant fruit, tightening up on the finish as it should with ripe, fine tannins. Cork. 13.5° alc. **Rating** 92 **To** 2015 $24

ℙℙℙℙ **Rose 2006** Cabernet sauvignon, pinot noir and shiraz are strange bedfellows, but here they have enjoyed their union; abundant red fruits and a nice, dry finish. A wine partly forced by a wet red grape vintage. Screwcap. 12.5° alc. **Rating** 89 **To** 2008 $16
Two Steps Great Southern Shiraz Viognier 2004 Colour not as intense as expected; a curious wine, not showing its alcohol; medium-bodied at most, with red and black fruits and spicy notes; may simply be going through awkward adolescence. Cork. 15° alc. **Rating** 89 **To** 2014 $24
Great Southern Tempranillo 2006 Light- to medium red-purple; tangy, juicy, lemony overtones, so typical of much young tempranillo grown around Australia, and which still has a lot to prove. Screwcap. 14.5° alc. **Rating** 88 **To** 2009 $19

Westend Estate Wines   ★★★★

1283 Brayne Road, Griffith, NSW 2680 **Region** Riverina
T (02) 6969 0800 **www**.westendestate.com **Open** Mon–Fri 8.30–5, w'ends 10–4
Winemaker William Calabria, Bryan Currie, Sally Whittaker **Est.** 1945 **Cases** 150 000
Along with a number of Riverina producers, Westend Estate is making a concerted move to lift both the quality and the packaging of its wines. Its leading 3 Bridges range, which has an impressive array of gold medals to its credit since being first released in 1997, is anchored in part on 20 ha of estate vineyards. Bill Calabria has been involved in the Australian wine industry for more than 40 years, and is understandably proud of the achievements both of Westend and the Riverina wine industry as a whole. Exports to all major markets.

ℙℙℙℙℙ **3 Bridges Durif 2004** Dense purple-red; stacked with dark fruit flavours and no bitter extract; easy to see how it enjoyed great success in minor shows. Cork. 15° alc. **Rating** 92 **To** 2011 $20
3 Bridges Cabernet Sauvignon 2004 Medium-bodied, with precise varietal expression through a mix of blackcurrant, cassis and mulberry; good tannin and oak management; a tribute to both vintage and winemaker. Cork. 14.5° alc. **Rating** 91 **To** 2012 $20

ℙℙℙℙ **3 Bridges Shiraz 2004** Firm, clear-cut blackberry shiraz varietal flavour; not overmuch texture, but makes a statement, and is not porty or jammy. Cork. 14.5° alc. **Rating** 88 **To** 2010 $20
Richland Shiraz 2006 Strong colour; rich and concentrated; slightly dusty mouthfeel suggesting some form of concentration has been successfully used. Open-fermented; a bargain at the price. Screwcap. 14.5° alc. **Rating** 87 **To** 2009 $9.95
Richland Cabernet Merlot 2005 Has an extra dimension of weight above the Merlot; rich, black fruits and cassis; flavour rather than complexity, but, again, good value, and underlines the consistency of the quality of the range, which will doubtless be discounted, at times substantially. Screwcap. 14° alc. **Rating** 87 **To** 2009 $9.95

Western Range Wines   ★★★★☆

1995 Chittering Road, Lower Chittering, WA 6084 **Region** Perth Hills
T (08) 9571 8800 **F** (08) 9571 8844 **www**.westernrangewines.com.au **Open** Wed–Sun 10–5
Winemaker Ryan Sudano, John Griffiths (Consultant) **Est.** 2001 **Cases** 40 000

Between the mid-1990s and 2001, several prominent West Australians, including Marilyn Corderory, Malcolm McCusker, Terry and Kevin Prindiville and Tony Rechner, established approximately 125 ha of vines (under separate ownerships) in the Perth Hills, with a kaleidoscopic range of varietals. The next step was to join forces to build a substantial winery. This is a separate venture, but takes the grapes from the individual vineyards and markets the wine under the Western Range brand. In 2004 the releases were rebranded and regrouped at 4 levels: Lot 88, Goyamin Pool, Julimar and Julimar Organic. The label designs are clear and attractive. Exports to the UK, the US and other major markets.

Westgate Vineyard

180 Westgate Road, Armstrong, Vic 3377 **Region** Grampians
T (03) 5356 2394 **F** (03) 5356 2594 **www**.westgatevineyard.com.au **Open** At Garden Gully
Winemaker Bruce Dalkin **Est.** 1997 **Cases** 500
Westgate has been in the Dalkin family ownership since the 1860s, the present owners Bruce and Robyn being the sixth-generation owners of the property, which today focuses on grape production, a small winery and 4-star accommodation. There are 14 ha of vineyards, progressively established since 1969, including a key holding of 10 ha of shiraz; most of the grapes are sold to Mount Langi Ghiran and others, but a small amount of high-quality wine is made under the Westgate Vineyard label. Exports to Singapore.

Riesling 2006 Potent lemon citrus aromas; good intensity and length, very pure and correct, the flavours faithfully tracking the bouquet. Cork. 12.6° alc. **Rating** 93 **To** 2016 $22
Endurance Shiraz 2005 Vibrant, spicy smoky aromas; tangy, bright red and black fruits; good length and fine tannins; 35-year-old vines. Screwcap. 13.5° alc. **Rating** 93 **To** 2020 $50

Wharncliffe ★★★

Summerleas Road, Kingston, Tas 7050 **Region** Southern Tasmania
T 0438 297 147 **F** (03) 6229 2298 **Open** W'ends by appt
Winemaker Andrew Hood **Est.** 1990 **Cases** 125
With total plantings of 0.75 ha, Wharncliffe could not exist without the type of contract-winemaking service offered by Andrew Hood, which would be a pity, because the vineyard is beautifully situated on the doorstep of Mt Wellington, the Huon Valley and the Channel regions of southern Tasmania.

Whinstone Estate

295 Dunns Creek Road, Red Hill, Vic 3937 **Region** Mornington Peninsula
T (03) 5989 7487 **F** (03) 5989 7641 **www**.whinstone.com.au **Open** By appt
Winemaker Ewan Campbell, Maitena Zantvoort (Contract) **Est.** 1994 **Cases** NA
Ken and Leon Wood began the development of their vineyard in 1994, planting 1 ha of chardonnay, 0.8 ha of pinot gris, 0.6 ha of pinot noir, 0.4 ha of sauvignon blanc and a few rows of melon (a grape of Muscadet, France). Initially the grapes were sold to other makers in the region, with a small amount made under the Whinstone label for friends and family. Demand has grown and, with it, production; it is anticipated that in 2008 all the fruit will be used for the Whinstone Estate wines, and that a cellar door will have opened by that time.

Barrel Fermented Mornington Peninsula Chardonnay 2004 Bright straw-green; an attractive wine with plenty of intensity and length to the grapefruit, nectarine and melon flavours; controlled barrel ferment inputs. Screwcap. 13.5° alc. **Rating** 91 **To** 2010 $20

Whispering Brook

Hill Street, Broke, NSW 2330 **Region** Lower Hunter Valley
T (02) 9818 4126 **F** (02) 9818 4156 **www**.whispering-brook.com **Open** By appt
Winemaker Nick Patterson, Susan Frazier **Est.** 2000 **Cases** 1000

Susan Frazier and Adam Bell say the choice of Whispering Brook was the result of a 5-year search to find the ideal viticultural site (while studying for wine science degrees at Charles Sturt University). Some may wonder whether the Broke subregion of the Hunter Valley needed such persistent effort to locate, but the property does in fact have a combination of terra rossa loam soils on which the reds are planted, and sandy flats for the white grapes. The partners have also established an olive grove and accommodation for 6–14 guests in the large house set in the vineyard. Exports to the UK, Japan and South-East Asia.

ŢŢŢŢŢ **Hunter Valley Semillon 2006** Relatively shy and tight on both bouquet and palate; zesty acidity is the main impression at this stage; why use a cork? 10.5° alc. **Rating** 90 **To** 2011 $19
Limited Release Chardonnay 2006 Crisp and lively citrus and stone fruit; light but evident oak, with good length and balance. Cork. 13.2° alc. **Rating** 90 **To** 2010 $25

Whispering Hills   ★★★★

580 Warburton Highway, Seville, Vic 3139 **Region** Yarra Valley
T (03) 5964 2822 **F** (03) 5964 2064 **www**.whisperinghills.com.au **Open** 7 days 10–6
Winemaker Murray Lyons **Est.** 1985 **Cases** 1500
Whispering Hills is owned and operated by the Lyons family (Murray, Marie and Audrey). Murray (with a degree in viticulture and oenology from Charles Sturt University) concentrates on the vineyard and winemaking, Marie (with a background in sales and marketing) and Audrey take care of the cellar door and distribution of the wines. The 3.5-ha vineyard was established in 1985 (riesling, chardonnay and cabernet sauvignon), with further plantings in 1996, and some grafting in 2003. Exports to Japan.

ŢŢŢŢŢ **Shiraz 2004** A medium-bodied, lively mix of black cherry and blackberry; good oak handling, likewise of the tannins; nice wine. Screwcap. 14° alc. **Rating** 92 **To** 2015 $24

ŢŢŢŢ **Yarra Valley Pinot Noir Chardonnay 2005** Attractive fresh fruit flavours of stone fruit and strawberry; good length and balance; will profit from more time on cork, and may surprise. 11° alc. **Rating** 89 **To** 2010 $25
Yarra Valley Cabernet Sauvignon 2004 Light- to medium-bodied; notes of earth and mint plus blackcurrant; just a little on the lean side. Screwcap. 13.5° alc. **Rating** 88 **To** 2013 $24

Whisson Lake   ★★★☆

Lot 2 Gully Road, Carey Gully, SA 5144 **Region** Adelaide Hills
T (08) 8390 1303 **F** (08) 8390 3822 **www**.whissonlake.com **Open** By appt
Winemaker Mark Whisson **Est.** 1985 **Cases** 400
Mark Whisson (a plant biochemist) is primarily a grapegrower, with 5 ha of close-planted, steep-sloped north-facing vineyard on Mt Carey in the Piccadilly Valley. Over the years small portions of the grape production have been vinified under the Whisson Lake label, initially by Roman Bratasiuk, then Dave Powell of Torbreck, but since 2002 by Mark Whisson. The wine has a consistent style, is distinctly savoury, and ages well. His partners in the venture are Bruce Lake (a Perth-based engineer) and Bill Bisset, who has helped broaden the business base to include Pinot Gaz (an early-drinking Pinot), Shiraz from the Adelaide Hills, and Grenache from Blewitt Springs. Tiny quantities are exported to the US and the UK.

Whistle Stop Wines   NR

8 Elk Street, Nanango, Qld 4615 **Region** South Burnett
T (07) 4163 2222 **F** (07) 4163 2288 **www**.whistlestop.com.au **Open** Wed–Sun 10–5
Winemaker Symphony Hill (Mike Hayes) **Est.** 1998 **Cases** NA

Whistler Wines

Seppeltsfield Road, Marananga, SA 5355 **Region** Barossa Valley
T (08) 8562 4942 **F** (08) 8562 4943 **www.**whistlerwines.com **Open** 7 days 10.30–5
Winemaker Troy Kalleske **Est.** 1999 **Cases** 7500
Whistler Wines had a dream start at the Barossa Valley Wine Show '00, when its 2000 Semillon
won trophies for Best Dry White and for Most Outstanding Barossa White Table Wine. Add to
that the distinguished US importer Weygandt-Metzler, and it is no surprise to find the sold out
sign going up on the extremely attractive (modern) galvanised iron cellar door building. The
operation is based on 5 ha of shiraz, 2 ha each of semillon and merlot and 1 ha of cabernet
sauvignon, with an additional 4 ha of grenache, mourvedre and riesling planted in 2001. The hope
is to gradually increase production to match existing demand. Exports to the US, Canada, Russia,
Denmark and Thailand.

ΨΨΨΨΨ **Estate Grown Barossa Shiraz 2004** Medium to full red-purple; a beautifully
crafted wine; lovely blackberry fruit, fine tannins and a long finish. ProCork.
14.5° alc. **Rating** 93 **To** 2019 $18
Estate Grown Barossa Cabernet Sauvignon 2004 Clean, with lots of
blackcurrant/blackberry fruit supported by sweet, ripe tannins. Has spent
20 months in quality oak. Screwcap. 13.6° alc. **Rating** 91 **To** 2019 $22
The Black Piper GSM 2005 While undoubtedly driven by sweet fruit, with some
confection from the grenache and the high alcohol, the shiraz and mourvedre
tighten up and lengthen the palate. Screwcap. 15.5° alc. **Rating** 90 **To** 2015 $21

ΨΨΨΨ **Barossa Riesling 2006** Glowing yellow-green; ripe fruit aromas then a
predictably generous palate with ripe citrus and tropical fruit balanced by good
acidity. Early-drinking style. Screwcap. 12.5° alc. **Rating** 89 **To** 2010 $16
Hubert Irving 2004 A light- to medium-bodied, fresh and vibrant mix of red and
black fruits, with touches of herb and mint. Shiraz/Merlot/Cabernet Sauvignon.
Screwcap. 14.5° alc. **Rating** 89 **To** 2014 $16
Estate Grown Barossa Merlot 2004 A substantial, medium-bodied wine with
a surprising degree of sweetness given the modest alcohol; longer on flavour than
finesse. Screwcap. 14° alc. **Rating** 89 **To** 2017 $22

White Rock Vineyard

1171 Railton Road, Kimberley, Tas 7304 (postal) **Region** Northern Tasmania
T (03) 6497 2156 **F** (03) 6497 2156 **Open** At Lake Barrington Estate
Winemaker Julian Alcorso (Contract), Phil Dolan **Est.** 1992 **Cases** 150
Phil and Robin Dolan have established White Rock Vineyard in the northwest region of
Tasmania, which, while having 13 wineries and vineyards, is one of the least known parts of the
island. Kimberley is 25 km due south of Devonport in the sheltered valley of the Mersey River.
The Dolans have planted 2.4 ha of pinot noir, chardonnay, riesling and pinot gris, the lion's share
going to the first 2 varieties. It has been a low-profile operation not only because of its location,
but because the major part of the production is sold, with only Riesling and Chardonnay being
made and sold through local restaurants and the cellar door at Lake Barrington Estate.

ΨΨΨΨ **Riesling 2005** Lime, apple and citrus aromas and flavours; very much in the
mainstream of '05 style. **Rating** 88 **To** 2012
Riesling 2006 Generous flavour and structure; ripe fruit flavours; ready now.
Rating 87 **To** 2009
Chardonnay 2006 Soft and insidiously appealing, with melon and nectarine fruit;
does not aspire to be complex. **Rating** 87 **To** 2008

Whitechapel Wines

Gerry Semmler Road, Lyndoch, SA 5351 **Region** Barossa Valley
T 0438 822 409 **F** (08) 8342 4028 **www.**whitechapelwines.com.au **Open** By appt
Winemaker Contract **Est.** 1997 **Cases** 950

The Colovic family, headed by Adelaide insolvency lawyer David Colovic, purchased the small, run-down Whitechapel property at Lyndoch in 1997 as a retirement occupation for Tom Colovic. The idea was to renovate the building, but instead most of the time was spent establishing the immaculately tended 4.5 ha shiraz vineyard. The grapes were initially sold to another well-known Barossa winemaker and commencing in 2001 small batches of the grapes were made for the Whitechapel label. The name Tom's Lot for the particular wine was almost inevitable.

TTTTT Tom's Lot Lyndoch Shiraz 2004 Exceptionally generous, mouthfilling and flavoursome for a 14° baume Barossa red; layers of blackberry, plum, black cherry and licorice; ripe tannins and oak are both balanced and integrated. Cork. 14° alc. **Rating** 95 **To** 2019 $24

TTTTT Tom's Lot Lyndoch Shiraz 2003 A good wine with clear shiraz varietal character in the gently sweet, elegant mode of the '04, but without the vibrancy. What a difference a vintage makes. Cork. 14° alc. **Rating** 91 **To** 2013 $24

Whitsend Estate

52 Boundary Road, Coldstream, Vic 3770 **Region** Yarra Valley
T (03) 9739 1917 **F** (03) 9739 0217 **www**.whitsend.com.au **Open** By appt
Winemaker Quercus Oenology (Paul Evans) **Est.** 1998 **Cases** 500
The Baldwin family, headed by Ross and Simone, but with Trish, Tim and Jenny all involved in one way or another, have planted a 13-ha vineyard to pinot noir, shiraz, merlot, viognier and cabernet sauvignon. Most of the production is sold to local wineries; a small amount is retained for the Baldwins. Exports to Canada, Japan and Indonesia.

TTTTT Yarra Valley Chardonnay 2005 Quite complex; light- to medium-bodied, with a touch of oak supporting neat melon and fig fruit; understated; developing slowly. Cork. 13.5° alc. **Rating** 90 **To** 2011 $22

TTTT Yarra Valley Cabernet Sauvignon 2005 Medium to full red-purple; plenty of cassis, blackcurrant and mulberry fruit; soft, ripe tannins; good length. Cork. 14° alc. **Rating** 89 **To** 2014 $24

Wicks Estate Wines

555 The Parade, Magill, SA 5072 (postal) **Region** Adelaide Hills
T (08) 8331 0211 **F** (08) 8431 3300 **www**.wicksestate.com.au **Open** Not
Winemaker Tim Knappstein, Leigh Ratzmer **Est.** 2000 **Cases** 4000
Tim and Simon Wicks had a long-term involvement with orchard and nursery operations at Highbury in the Adelaide Hills prior to purchasing the 54-ha property at Woodside in 1999. They promptly planted fractionally less than 40 ha of chardonnay, riesling, sauvignon blanc, shiraz, merlot and cabernet sauvignon, following this with the construction of a state-of-the-art winery in early 2004. The vast experience of Tim Knappstein, supported by Adelaide University graduate in oenology, Leigh Ratzmer, has predictably produced wines of impressive quality.

TTTTT Adelaide Hills Shiraz 2004 Bright, clear red-purple; lively, fresh spice, black cherry, blackberry, plum and licorice flavours all intermingle; very fine tannin structure; long finish. Screwcap. 14° alc. **Rating** 95 **To** 2019 $18

TTTTT Adelaide Hills Sauvignon Blanc 2006 Fragrant, tropical fruit aromas; generous flavours run-down a similar track to the Riesling, but work fractionally better. Screwcap. 13° alc. **Rating** 91 **To** 2008 $17
Adelaide Hills Riesling 2005 Light straw-green; spotlessly clean aromas, then a gentle, round, mouthfilling palate, verging on outright softness; unusual style, but not unattractive. Screwcap. 13° alc. **Rating** 90 **To** 2010 $15
Adelaide Hills Unwooded Chardonnay 2005 A well above average example of the style; nectarine and grapefruit aromas and flavours, some creamy notes adding to the texture. Screwcap. 13° alc. **Rating** 90 **To** 2008 $16

Adelaide Hills Cabernet Merlot 2004 Typical bright colour; zesty, lively cassis, blackcurrant and redcurrant fruit; subtle oak. Screwcap. 14° alc. **Rating** 90 **To** 2012 $18

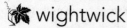 ## wightwick   ★★★★☆

Lot 8 Slatey Creek Road, Invermay, Vic 3352 **Region** Ballarat
T (03) 5332 4443 **F** (03) 9710 1897 www.wightwick.com.au **Open** By appt
Winemaker Simon Wightwick **Est.** 1996 **Cases** 160
wightwick might best be described as an angels on a pinhead exercise. Keith and Ann Wightwick have planted 0.12 ha of chardonnay and 0.29 ha of pinot noir; son Simon Wightwick works as a viticulturist and winemaker in the Yarra Valley, and looks after the vineyards on weekends (using organic principles) and the micro winemaking during the Yarra Valley vintage. The Pinot Noir is hand-plunged, basket-pressed, with racking via gravity, and minimal fining.

♀♀♀♀♀ Ballarat Chardonnay 2005 Bright, intense, super-cool-grown citrus, lime and nectarine flavours; great length, with excellent mouthfeel and aftertaste. Screwcap. 13.9° alc. **Rating** 94 **To** 2015 $27

♀♀♀♀ Ballarat Pinot Noir 2004 Savoury, stemmy, spicy, with relatively little primary fruit flavours remaining; does have length, and is not green. Screwcap. 13.9° alc. **Rating** 89 **To** 2011 $30

Wignalls Wines   ★★★★★

448 Chester Pass Road (Highway 1), Albany, WA 6330 **Region** Albany
T (08) 9841 2848 **F** (08) 9842 9003 www.wignallswines.com.au **Open** 7 days 11–4
Winemaker Rob Wignall, Michael Perkins **Est.** 1982 **Cases** 6000
A noted producer of Pinot Noir which extended the map for the variety in Australia, the 2004 and 2005 Pinots a welcome return to form. The white wines are elegant, and show the cool climate to good advantage. A winery was constructed in 1998 and uses the production from the 16 ha of estate plantings. Exports to Denmark, Indonesia, Japan, Malaysia and Singapore.

♀♀♀♀♀ Albany Sauvignon Blanc 2006 Spotlessly clean, with no hint of sweaty characters; the delicacy and intensity found in top-class sauvignon blanc; passionfruit and kiwifruit, with a long finish. Screwcap. 12.5° alc. **Rating** 94 **To** 2008 $16.80

♀♀♀♀♀ Albany Pinot Noir 2006 Good, clear purple-red; attractive plum and black cherry, with touches of spice; good balance, depth and length; will evolve and improve. Screwcap. 14° alc. **Rating** 93 **To** 2013 $29

♀♀♀♀ Albany Shiraz 2005 Fresh, light- to medium-bodied red fruits, spices and pepper; length, but not a lot of depth. Screwcap. 14° alc. **Rating** 89 **To** 2014 $21

Wild Cattle Creek Winery   ★★★★

473 Warburton Highway, Wandin, Vic 3139 **Region** Yarra Valley
T (03) 5964 4755 www.wildcattlecreek.com **Open** Wed–Sun 11–5, or by appt
Winemaker Jeff Wright **Est.** 1996 **Cases** 800
This is the (much-altered) reincarnation of Langbrook Estate Vineyard, continuing under the ownership of Graeme and Ingrid Smith. It has 10 ha of pinot noir, chardonnay, sauvignon blanc, pinot gris and cabernet sauvignon, and the Sauvignon Blanc, in particular, has had significant show success.

Wild Dog   ★★★★☆

South Road, Warragul, Vic 3820 **Region** Gippsland
T (03) 5623 1117 **F** (03) 5623 6402 www.wilddogwinery.com **Open** 7 days 10–5
Winemaker Mal Stewart **Est.** 1982 **Cases** 3600

An aptly named winery which produces somewhat rustic wines from the 12 ha of estate vineyards; even the Farringtons say that the 'Shiraz comes with a bite', but they also point out that there is minimal handling, fining and filtration. Following the acquisition of Wild Dog by Gary and Judy Surman, Mal Stewart was appointed winemaker with a far-ranging brief to build on the legacy of the previous owners. As the tasting notes indicate, there is much to be confident about.

ΨΨΨΨΨ **Reserve Gippsland Shiraz 2005** The colour suggests slightly later picking than the varietal, although the flavours are similar, simply in greater volume and conviction. A good mix of ripe plum, blackberry and spice. Screwcap. **Rating** 94 **To** 2020 $35

ΨΨΨΨ **Gippsland Riesling 2006** Fragrant citrus blossom aromas; intense, powerful and long. Trophy Gippsland Wine Show '07. Screwcap. 12° alc. **Rating** 93 **To** 2012 $19
Reserve Chardonnay 2005 Complex, rich and ripe stone fruit; well-balanced and integrated oak; lots of winemaker inputs are carried by the wine. Screwcap. **Rating** 93 **To** 2012 $35
Gippsland Shiraz 2005 Strongly spicy/earthy/savoury/peppery flavours run through the medium-bodied palate; has good length, the tannins and oak tightly controlled. Screwcap. 13° alc. **Rating** 90 **To** 2014 $20
Wild Ice Liqueur Riesling 2006 Intense, lively and fresh; good length and varietal character, the sweetness (just) balanced by acidity. The juice was frozen to -4°C to make the wine. Screwcap. 10° alc. **Rating** 90 **To** 2010 $19

ΨΨΨΨ **Gippsland Semillon 2006** Clean and well-made; plenty of depth to the ripe citrus fruit rightly unaided by oak. Screwcap. 13° alc. **Rating** 89 **To** 2010 $14
Sparkling Shiraz 2005 A wine with considerable complexity through spicy fruit; most importantly, not excessively sweet. **Rating** 89 **To** 2010 $25
Wild Rose 2006 Well-named, for it does have rose, bramble and spice flavours; restrained, relatively dry style. Screwcap. 13° alc. **Rating** 88 **To** 2008 $17

Wild Duck Creek Estate ★★★★☆

Spring Flat Road, Heathcote, Vic 3523 **Region** Heathcote
T (03) 5433 3133 **F** (03) 5433 3133 **Open** By appt
Winemaker David Anderson **Est.** 1980 **Cases** 4000
The first release of Wild Duck Creek Estate from the 1991 vintage marked the end of 12 years of effort by David and Diana Anderson. They began planting the 4.5-ha vineyard in 1980, made their first tiny quantities of wine in 1986, the first commercial quantities of wine in 1991, and built their winery and cellar door facility in 1993. Exports to the US (where Duck Muck has become a cult wine), the UK and other major markets.

ΨΨΨΨΨ **Springflat Heathcote Shiraz 2004** Deep purple-red; rich and luscious; very ripe fruit with blackberry confit flavours; soft tannins, and it's easy to see why it has such appeal in the US. This is not to denigrate its appeal in Australia, either. Cork. 15° alc. **Rating** 92 **To** 2024 $36.40

Wild Geese Wines ★★★

PO Box 1157, Balhanna, SA 5242 **Region** Adelaide Hills
T (08) 8388 4464 **F** (08) 8388 4464 **Open** Not
Winemaker Patrick O'Sullivan **Est.** 2000 **Cases** 400
Patrick, a graduate of Charles Sturt University, and Amanda O'Sullivan (and 2 business partners) have established a trial planting of 4 clones of merlot, and have found the difference between each of the clones to be substantial. The Wild Geese name, incidentally, comes from the Irish emigres who fled religious and political persecution in the 18th century to settle elsewhere.

Wild Orchid Wines ★★★★☆

PO Box 165, Boyup Brook, WA 6244 **Region** Blackwood Valley
T (08) 9767 3058 **F** (08) 9767 3058 **www.wildorchidwines.com.au Open** Not
Winemaker Frank Kittler (Contract), Brad Skraha **Est.** 1997 **Cases** 1000

Orest, Robyn and Brad Skraha have established a little under 16 ha of chardonnay, shiraz, merlot and cabernet sauvignon. Most of the grapes are sold, the remainder made by Brad Skraha. Brad completed his bachelor of science in viticulture and oenology at Curtin University after working at the Chappellet winery in the Napa Valley. His time in California has led to a small export market to Canada; in Australia the wines are available through mail order.

Wildwood ★★★★☆

St John's Lane, Wildwood, Bulla, Vic 3428 **Region** Sunbury
T (03) 9307 1118 **F** (03) 9331 1590 **www.**wildwoodvineyards.com.au **Open** 7 days 10–5
Winemaker Dr Wayne Stott **Est.** 1983 **Cases** 2000
Wildwood is just 4 km past Melbourne airport, at an altitude of 130 m in the Oaklands Valley, which provides unexpected views back to Port Phillip Bay and the Melbourne skyline. Plastic surgeon Dr Wayne Stott has taken what is very much a part-time activity rather more seriously than most by completing the wine science degree at Charles Sturt University.

♟♟♟♟♟ **Shiraz 2003** Good depth to the colour; lovely cool climate, warm vintage, shiraz; blackberry, licorice and spice; round, supple, smooth and long; fine tannins. Screwcap. 14.5° alc. **Rating** 96 **To** 2018 $30

♟♟♟♟♟ **Chardonnay 2006** The bouquet is clean, but not particularly expressive; however, the elegant, light- to medium-bodied and finely crafted palate puts matters right; seamless nectarine, melon and oak, with a light but long finish. Screwcap. 13.6° alc. **Rating** 92 **To** 2015 $25
Shiraz 2004 Medium red-purple; the medium-bodied palate has much more weight than the '05; classic regional spicy red and black fruits; good length, fine tannins. Screwcap. 13.5° alc. **Rating** 92 **To** 2014 $30
Chardonnay 2005 An elegant, light-bodied style offering a subtle fusion of stone fruit, melon and cashew flavours; good balance and length. Screwcap. 13.1° alc. **Rating** 91 **To** 2012 $25
The Dunalister 2003 Light- to medium-bodied; mint, spice, leaf and red berry fruits provided by the blend, and the astute exclusion of cabernet sauvignon; balanced oak and tannins. Cabernet Franc/Merlot/Malbec Cork. 13° alc. **Rating** 91 **To** 2015 $40
Pinot Noir 2006 Bountiful aromas and flavours of plum and black cherry; restrained oak. Screwcap. 14° alc. **Rating** 90 **To** 2012 $30
Pinot Noir 2005 Crystal-bright clarity; light-bodied but clear-cut and quite complex varietal fruit probably at its peak now; a lovely drink. Screwcap. 12.7° alc. **Rating** 90 **To** 2008 $30

♟♟♟♟ **Pinot Noir 2004** Attractive plum and spice aromas and flavours, but an unexpectedly short finish. Screwcap. 12° alc. **Rating** 88 **To** 2008 $30
Shiraz 2005 A light- to medium-bodied spicy/earthy wine showing the impact of the drought; however, not forced or tannic, just not enough fruit for the future. Screwcap. 13.8° alc. **Rating** 88 **To** 2008 $30

Will Taylor Wines ★★★★☆

1B Victoria Avenue, Unley Park, SA 5061 **Region** Southeast Australia
T (08) 8271 6122 **F** (08) 8271 6122 **Open** By appt
Winemaker Various contract **Est.** 1997 **Cases** 1500
Will Taylor is a partner in the leading Adelaide law firm Finlaysons, and specialises in wine law. He and Suzanne Taylor have established a classic negociant wine business, having wines contract-made to their specifications. Moreover, they choose what they consider the best regions for each variety; thus Clare Valley Riesling, Adelaide Hills Sauvignon Blanc, Hunter Valley Semillon and Yarra Valley Pinot Noir. Exports to the UK, Canada, Hong Kong and Singapore.

♟♟♟♟♟ **Hunter Valley Semillon 2004** Glowing yellow-green; lovely citrus and lemon cake flavours; long, well-balanced finish; 5 years since its first release (a re-release) makes all the difference. Cork. 10.8° alc. **Rating** 94 **To** 2011 $21

ΨΨΨΨΨ **Adelaide Hills Sauvignon Blanc 2006** Pleasant gently tropical fruit flavours offset by citrussy acidity on a long finish; well-made. Screwcap. 13° alc. **Rating** 91 **To** 2008 $21

Willespie

Harmans Mill Road, Wilyabrup via Cowaramup, WA 6284 **Region** Margaret River
T (08) 9755 6248 **F** (08) 9755 6210 **www**.willespie.com.au **Open** 7 days 10.30–5
Winemaker Kevin Squance **Est.** 1976 **Cases** 7000
Willespie has produced many attractive white wines over the years, typically in brisk, herbaceous Margaret River style; all are fruit- rather than oak-driven. The wines have had such success that the Squance family (which founded and owns Willespie) has substantially increased winery capacity, drawing upon an additional 24 ha of estate vineyards now in bearing. Exports to the UK, the US and other major markets.

William Downie

★★★★★

PO Box 1024, Healesville, Vic 3777 **Region** Yarra Valley
T 0400 654 512 **F** (03) 5962 6630 **Open** Not
Winemaker William Downie **Est.** 2003 **Cases** 300
William Downie spends 6 months each year making wine in Burgundy, the other 6 based in the Yarra Valley with De Bortoli. He uses purchased grapes from older vines to make the wines, avoiding the use of pumps, filtration and fining. The striking label, designed by artist Reg Mombassa, has helped obtain listings at The Prince Wine Store and elsewhere. In the 2006 *Gourmet Traveller Wine* Winemaker of the Year Awards, Bill Downie was awarded the Kemeny's Medal for the Best Young Winemaker 2006. His boss at De Bortoli, Stephen Webber, goes a little further when he says, 'Downie is the best winemaker in Australia'.

ΨΨΨΨΨ **Yarra Valley Pinot Noir 2005** Very spicy/savoury aromas; the complex palate taking in the bouquet, adding restrained plum fruit; impressive length and finish. Not for Beaujolais-lovers. Cork. 13° alc. **Rating** 94 **To** 2013 $45

Willow Bridge Estate

Gardin Court Drive, Dardanup, WA 6236 **Region** Geographe
T (08) 9728 0055 **F** (08) 9728 0066 **www**.willowbridgeestate.com **Open** 7 days 11–5
Winemaker David Crawford **Est.** 1997 **Cases** 40 000
The Dewar family has followed a fast track in developing Willow Bridge Estate since acquiring the spectacular 180-ha hillside property in the Ferguson Valley in 1996: 70 ha of chardonnay, semillon, sauvignon blanc, shiraz and cabernet sauvignon were planted, with tempranillo added in 2000. The winery is capable of handling the 1200–1500 tonnes from the estate plantings. There are few wineries in Australia equalling or bettering the price/value ratio of the mid-range wines of Willow Bridge. Exports to the UK, the US and other major markets.

ΨΨΨΨΨ **Reserve Semillon 2006** Pale colour, especially given the barrel ferment in 1- and 2-year-old oak; likewise, the lively, intense and long palate is fruit-driven, having completely subdued the oak. Great length. The WA Janus face of the variety, that of the Hunter Valley the other. Screwcap. 12° alc. **Rating** 94 **To** 2016 $20
Reserve Sauvignon Blanc 2006 A flowery, aromatic bouquet with tropical/passionfruit overtones; the palate follows the same track, with abundant flavour, a dry finish (the saints be praised) and good acidity. Screwcap. 12.5° alc. **Rating** 94 **To** 2008 $20

ΨΨΨΨΨ **Reserve Shiraz Viognier 2004** Medium purple-red; rich, multi-texture and flavours; blackberry, plum and a slash of viognier; fine tannins. Cork. 14.5° alc. **Rating** 93 **To** 2019 $28
Shiraz 2005 Medium red-purple; a fragrant mix of red and black fruits; a lively, silky, light- to medium-bodied wine with plenty of personality. Great value, and also demonstrates that you don't have to have viognier to create flavour and/or personality. Screwcap. 14.5° alc. **Rating** 90 **To** 2012 $15

Black Dog Shiraz 2004 Medium-bodied; quite elegant, with some sweet red fruits, licorice and spice; does show some signs of overripeness on the palate, however. Is this 4 times as good as the varietal Shiraz? Surely the answer is no. Cork. 15.5° alc. **Rating** 90 **To** 2018 $60

ŶŶŶŶ **Rose 2006** Aromatic red fruits; strawberry/strawberry stem flavours; well-balanced acidity and sweetness. Screwcap. 13.5° alc. **Rating** 89 **To** 2008 $15
Cabernet Merlot 2005 Medium-bodied, with plenty of easily accessed, generous red and black fruits, soft tannins and minimal oak. Like the Shiraz, a bargain. Screwcap. 14.5° alc. **Rating** 89 **To** 2012 $15
Unwooded Chardonnay 2006 Water-white; crisp grapefruit/stone fruit/citrus; length, not depth. Screwcap. 12.5° alc. **Rating** 88 **To** 2010 $15
Sauvignon Blanc Semillon 2006 A distinct change in tempo moving towards the cellar door with ample fruit and a touch of residual sugar. Screwcap. 12.5° alc. **Rating** 87 **To** 2008 $15
Reserve Tempranillo 2005 Light- to medium-bodied weight and texture; typical varietal sweet fruit with a squeeze of lemon, and not much texture. Cork. 14° alc. **Rating** 87 **To** 2010 $20

Willow Creek

166 Balnarring Road, Merricks North, Vic 3926 **Region** Mornington Peninsula
T (03) 5989 7448 **F** (03) 5989 7584 **www**.willow-creek.com.au **Open** 7 days 10–5
Winemaker Phil Kerney **Est.** 1989 **Cases** 7000
A significant presence in the Mornington Peninsula area, with 12 ha of vines planted to cabernet sauvignon, chardonnay, pinot noir and sauvignon blanc. The grape intake is supplemented by purchasing small, quality parcels from local growers. Salix restaurant is out of the ordinary, winning a 'Chef's Hat' from the *Age Good Food Guide*, and with a wine list which includes wines from all 31 of Burgundy's Grand Cru vineyards. The wines from Willow Creek aren't bad, either. Exports to the US and Norway.

ŶŶŶŶŶ **Tulum Mornington Peninsula Chardonnay 2005** A super-elegant wine with all the components finely crafted and woven together; grapefruit and nectarine seamlessly welded with French oak in perfect balance. Screwcap. 13.5° alc. **Rating** 95 **To** 2015 $35
Cistercia Mornington Peninsula Chardonnay 2005 A sophisticated and multi-layered wine; ripe stone fruit and nectarine plus cashew/creamy notes; very good balance and length. First release from an unirrigated block; wild yeast. Diam. 14° alc. **Rating** 95 **To** 2015 $50
Mornington Peninsula Chardonnay 2006 Elegant, intense and long; nectarine, grapefruit and green apple aromas and flavours do most of the talking; sensitive use of oak and a long finish. Screwcap. 13.5° alc. **Rating** 94 **To** 2012 $20
Tulum Mornington Peninsula Pinot Noir 2005 Much more colour than the varietal; from the same stable, but here lovely cherry and plum fruits are the drivers, not the touches of forest floor. Screwcap. 14° alc. **Rating** 94 **To** 2012 $34
Benedictus Mornington Peninsula Pinot Noir 2005 Light to medium red-purple; fine, elegant and intense, with savoury forest floor notes alongside red fruits; a striking wine, albeit that some tasters have some seen what they consider to be the influence of brett. Diam. 14° alc. **Rating** 94 **To** 2013 $50

ŶŶŶŶŶ **Tulum Mornington Peninsula Cabernet Sauvignon 2004** Medium-bodied, with supple cassis and blackcurrant fruit; fine, ripe tannins and quality oak. Peninsula cabernet at its best. Screwcap. 14° alc. **Rating** 93 **To** 2019 $29.95
Mornington Peninsula Shiraz 2005 A typically elegant, light- to medium-bodied, cool-grown shiraz, not forced in the winery to look like something else; silky black cherry fruit; good acidity and minimal oak. Screwcap. 14° alc. **Rating** 91 **To** 2015 $25

Mornington Peninsula Pinot Noir 2005 Light red-purple; an intense tangy/foresty/stemmy style which I personally like; it is, however, a little light-on. Screwcap. 14° alc. **Rating** 90 **To** 2010 $25

ΥΥΥΥ **Mornington Peninsula Pinot Saignee 2006** Very pale pink; crisp, lively strawberry and citrus flavours with a dry finish. Screwcap. 13.5° alc. **Rating** 88 **To** 2008 $18.95

Wills Domain

Cnr Brash Road/Abbey Farm Road, Yallingup, WA 6281 **Region** Margaret River
T (08) 9755 2327 **F** (08) 9756 6072 **www**.willsdomain.com.au **Open** 7 days 10–5
Winemaker Naturaliste Vintners (Bruce Dukes) **Est.** 1992 **Cases** 7000
Has a little over 10 ha of semillon, sauvignon blanc, chardonnay, viognier, cabernet sauvignon, merlot, malbec, shiraz, cabernet franc and petit verdot under the control of Darren Haunold, whose ancestor Ulrich commenced winemaking in 1383 in modern-day Austria. Between 1992 and 2001 the grapes were sold to local winemakers, but since 2002 have been made into a series of good wines (with its map of Australia on the back label inspired by Ulrich). Exports to the UK, the US, Philippines, Singapore and Hong Kong.

ΥΥΥΥΥ **Margaret River Chardonnay 2005** Light- to medium-bodied and elegant, but, at the same time, intense and long; classic melon and grapefruit mix supported by neatly handled French oak; very good aftertaste. Screwcap. 14° alc. **Rating** 94 **To** 2015 $32

ΥΥΥΥ **Margaret River Semillon Sauvignon Blanc 2006** A reasonably complex array of fruit flavours, much seemingly coming from the sauvignon blanc; relatively soft overall flavour and structure. Screwcap. 13° alc. **Rating** 88 **To** 2009 $17
Margaret River Shiraz 2005 Light- to medium-bodied; spicy, lively and bright red fruits; fine tannins, but not a lot of flesh or density. Screwcap. 13.5° alc. **Rating** 88 **To** 2016 $23

Willunga 100 Wines ★★★★★

PO Box 238, McLaren Vale, SA 5171 **Region** McLaren Vale
T (08) 8323 8649 **F** (08) 8323 7622 **www**.libertywine.co.uk **Open** Not
Winemaker Nick Haselgrove, Warren Randall **Est.** 2005 **Cases** 12 000
This is a joint venture between Blackbilly and Liberty Wines UK, the latter a well-known importer of quality wines from Australia. It is a grape-to-retail venture, the foundation being grapes supplied by 400 ha of McLaren Vale vineyards, with a particular emphasis on viognier, shiraz, grenache and cabernet sauvignon. Almost all the wine is exported to the UK and Europe, with limited amounts sold in Australia by mail order; has hit the scene running with outstanding value for money.

ΥΥΥΥΥ **McLaren Vale Shiraz Viognier 2005** Typical deep, bright purple-red conferred by viognier; a medium-bodied array of raspberry, blackberry and plum fruit; controlled oak, fine tannins, subtle oak and a long finish all add up to a delicious wine. Screwcap. 14.5° alc. **Rating** 95 **To** 2020 $18
McLaren Vale Cabernet Shiraz 2005 A blend of blackberry, blackcurrant, dark chocolate and spice flavours braced by savoury tannins and echoes of pine needles; good balance and finish. Screwcap. 14.5° alc. **Rating** 94 **To** 2020 $18

ΥΥΥΥΥ **McLaren Vale Grenache 2005** Vivid red-purple; unusual elegance for grenache, with silky raspberry and cherry red fruit flavours. Fine, ripe tannins; oak merely a maid servant. Screwcap. 14.5° alc. **Rating** 93 **To** 2012 $18

Willunga Creek Wines ★★★★

Lot 361 Delabole Road, Willunga, SA 5172 **Region** McLaren Vale
T (08) 8556 2244 **F** (08) 8556 4660 **www**.willungacreekwines.com.au **Open** By appt
Winemaker Goe De Fabio, Phil Christiansen **Est.** 2002 **Cases** 3500

David and Julie Cheesley purchased the property in the early 1990s, planting 6 ha each of shiraz and cabernet sauvignon in 1994, adding 0.5 ha of merlot in 2000. The vines are planted on terraced sloping hills, the wind exposure helping the Cheesley's organic management of the vineyard. The Willunga name and the Black Duck brand come from the Aboriginal word 'willangga', which means black duck. A new cellar door is scheduled to be open by the time of publication, replacing the one established in 2002 in a refurbished circa 1850 building in the town of Willunga. Exports to the UK, South Korea and Japan.

ŸŸŸŸŸ **Black Duck McLaren Vale Cabernet Sauvignon 2005** Medium-bodied, smooth and supple; attractive cassis and blackcurrant, with just the barest touch of bitter chocolate; very good indeed for the region. Diam. 14.5° alc. **Rating** 93 To 2015 $19

Black Duck McLaren Vale Shiraz 2005 Absolutely classic McLaren Vale shiraz, the dark chocolate hitting before all the other fruit components, of which there are many, mainly in the blackcurrant and licorice spectrum. Diam. 14.5° alc. **Rating** 91 To 2020 $18

ŸŸŸŸ **Black Duck McLaren Vale Merlot 2005** Light- to medium-bodied, with fresh juicy cassis fruit, good acidity and downplayed tannins and oak. Cork. 14.5° alc. **Rating** 89 To 2012 $18.90

Black Duck McLaren Vale Cabernet Merlot 2005 Medium-bodied; slightly grainy/gritty texture; olive and earth flavours dominate. Diam. 14.5° alc. **Rating** 87 To 2010 $18

Willy Bay   ★★★★☆

19 Third Avenue, Mount Lawley, WA 6050 (postal) **Region** Geographe
T (08) 9271 9890 **F** (08) 9271 7771 **www**.willybay.com.au **Open** Not
Winemaker Peter Stanlake **Est.** 2003 **Cases** 700
Willy Bay Wines is jointly owned and run by the Siciliano and Edwards families, who have established 6.5 ha of shiraz, 2.8 ha of cabernet sauvignon and 1.7 ha of chardonnay. While some of the wine names are borrowed from cricket (I suppose I am meant to know why, but don't) there is nothing ambiguous about wine quality, with even higher scores in prospect.

ŸŸŸŸŸ **Fine Leg Chardonnay 2004** Complex barrel ferment inputs; ample stone fruit, fig and melon to carry the oak; lots happening in the best way possible. Screwcap. 13° alc. **Rating** 94 To 2011 $28

ŸŸŸŸŸ **French Cut Semillon Sauvignon Blanc 2005** Light straw-green; clean and fresh, with touches of citrus and passionfruit; light-bodied, but has length; 30% barrel ferment new French oak is well-balanced and integrated. Screwcap. 13° alc. **Rating** 90 To 2010 $24

Wilmot Hills Vineyard   ★★★

407 Back Road, Wilmot, Tas 7310 **Region** Northern Tasmania
T (03) 6492 1193 **F** (03) 6492 1193 **www**.wilmothills.tascom.net **Open** Thurs–Tues 10–6
Winemaker John Cole, Ruth Cole **Est.** 1991 **Cases** 250
The beautiful Wilmot Hills Vineyard is on the western side of Lake Barrington, not far from the Cradle Mountain road, with marvellous views to Mt Roland and the adjacent peaks. It is very much a family affair, and produces both wine and cider. John Cole spent 18 years in Melbourne in engineering design and some graphic art, and Ruth worked in the hospitality industry for 10 years and making fruit wines for 20 years. The neat onsite winery was designed and built by the Coles, as was much of the wine- and cider-making equipment.

Wilson Vineyard   ★★★★★

Polish Hill River, Sevenhill via Clare, SA 5453 **Region** Clare Valley
T (08) 8843 4310 **www**.wilsonvineyard.com.au **Open** W'ends 10–4
Winemaker Dr John Wilson, Daniel Wilson **Est.** 1974 **Cases** 4000

After working at the shoulder of his father John for many years, Daniel Wilson took responsibility for the winemaking in 2003. The Wilson Vineyard of today is a far cry from that of 10 years ago, taking its place in the upper echelon of the Clare Valley. Exports to Norway.

☆☆☆☆☆ **Polish Hill River Riesling 2006** Aromas of spice and citrus lead into a finely braced and structured wine built for the long haul. Mineral and citrus flavours run through the long, dry finish. Screwcap. 13° alc. **Rating** 95 **To** 2021 $22
DJW Clare Valley Riesling 2006 Voluminous aromas and flavours of tropical fruits, sweet citrus and passionfruit; a long palate and good finish. Screwcap. 13° alc. **Rating** 94 **To** 2015 $22
Hand Plunge Shiraz 2004 Focused black fruits provide a lovely fruit line to a medium-bodied, highly focused wine of good length. Screwcap. 15.5° alc. **Rating** 94 **To** 2024 $35
Stonecraft Clare Valley Cabernet Sauvignon 2004 Ripe, almost juicy, blackcurrant/cassis fruit drives the wine; an excellent mid-palate, likewise fine, gently savoury, tannins on the finish. Exceptional achievement for the Clare Valley. Screwcap. 14° alc. **Rating** 94 **To** 2012 $22

☆☆☆☆☆ **Pepperstone Clare Valley Shiraz 2004** A rich combination of ripe black fruits, coffee, mocha, earth and chocolate showing some of the qualities of the Hand Plunge, though of lesser intensity. Screwcap. 14.5° alc. **Rating** 93 **To** 2019 $27
Polish Hill River Merlot 2004 Smoky, savoury aromas; an interesting medium-bodied palate, with a range of cassis, olive, chocolate and blackberry flavours, all with an inherent sweetness. Not easy to pigeonhole. Screwcap. 14° alc. **Rating** 90 **To** 2015 $24

☆☆☆☆ **Polish Hill River Cabernet Sauvignon Cabernet Franc Shiraz 2004** Medium-bodied; a strongly savoury wine as befits the blend; some faintly stemmy characters, but there is also sweet fruit. Screwcap. 14° alc. **Rating** 87 **To** 2009 $17

Wily Trout   ★★★☆

Marakei-Nanima Road, via Hall, NSW 2618 **Region** Canberra District
T (02) 6230 2487 **F** (02) 6230 2211 **www.**wilytrout.com.au **Open** 7 days 10–5
Winemaker Dr Roger Harris, Andrew McEwen (Contract) **Est.** 1998 **Cases** 3000
The 20-ha Wily Trout vineyard shares its home with the Poachers Pantry, a renowned gourmet smokehouse. The quality of the wines is very good, and a testament to the skills of the contract winemakers. The northeast-facing slopes, at an elevation of 720 m, provide some air drainage and hence protection against spring frosts.

☆☆☆☆ **Canberra District Sauvignon Blanc 2006** Bright straw-green; plenty of ripe fruit, tropical, even stone fruit; a touch of sweetness is slightly distracting. Screwcap. 12° alc. **Rating** 88 **To** 2008 $23
Canberra District Merlot 2004 Light- to medium-bodied; savoury, earthy, leafy aromas and flavours, consistent with the other wines, except that it does have good length. Screwcap. 14° alc. **Rating** 88 **To** 2010 $30
Methode Champenoise Sparkling Pinot Noir 2004 Fresh, light, spicy, with touches of strawberry; not complex, but is neither sweet nor oaky, both definite pluses. 12.5° alc. **Rating** 88 **To** 2008 $30
Canberra District Cabernet Merlot 2004 Slightly weak colour; savoury earthy flavours with some black fruits, but not enough vinosity. Screwcap. 14° alc. **Rating** 87 **To** 2011 $30

Wimbaliri Wines   ★★★☆

Barton Highway, Murrumbateman, NSW 2582 **Region** Canberra District
T (02) 6227 5921 **F** (02) 6227 5921 **Open** 7 days 10–5
Winemaker John Andersen **Est.** 1988 **Cases** 700
John and Margaret Andersen moved to the Canberra District in 1987 and began establishing their vineyard at Murrumbateman in 1988; the property borders highly regarded Canberra producers

Doonkuna and Clonakilla. The vineyard is close-planted with a total of 2.2 ha planted to chardonnay, pinot noir, shiraz, cabernet sauvignon and merlot (plus a few vines of cabernet franc).

ŶŶŶŶ **Cabernet Merlot 2004** Medium-bodied, with more fruit sweetness than in prior vintages; cassis and redcurrant as well as more briary savoury characters provide complexity. Diam. **Rating** 89 **To** 2014 $22
Chardonnay 2005 Generous peach and stone fruit flavours; what you see is what you get. Diam. **Rating** 88 **To** 2010 $20

Winbirra Vineyard

173 Point Leo Road, Red Hill South, Vic 3937 **Region** Mornington Peninsula
T (03) 5989 2109 **F** (03) 5989 2109 **www**.winbirra.com.au **Open** 1st w'end of month & public hols 11–5, or by appt
Winemaker Tuerong Winery **Est.** 1990 **Cases** 800
Winbirra is a small, family-owned and run vineyard which has been producing grapes since 1990, between then and 1997 selling the grapes to local winemakers. Since 1997 the wine has been made and sold under the Winbirra label. There is 1.5 ha of pinot noir (with 3 clones) at Merricks and 1.5 ha on a second site at Merricks South.

ŶŶŶŶŶ **Mornington Peninsula Viognier 2005** Bright green-straw; an elegant, medium-bodied wine, supple and smooth, with light peach and apricot nuances. Diam. 13.5° alc. **Rating** 91 **To** 2009 $28

ŶŶŶŶ **The Brigadier Mornington Peninsula Pinot Noir 2005** Light- to medium-bodied, with savoury/forest floor notes to the mix of red and black fruits; a slightly tart finish. Diam. 14° alc. **Rating** 89 **To** 2012
Mornington Peninsula Pinot Gris 2006 Pear, apple and musk; a rich style, the sweetness coming as much from the fruit as from residual sugar. Diam. 14° alc. **Rating** 88 **To** 2008
Mornington Peninsula Pinot Gris 2005 Light straw-green; has some mid-palate flavour, and the texture is as good as it gets with the variety. Diam. 14° alc. **Rating** 88 **To** 2008 $20
Mornington Peninsula Viognier 2006 Gentle peach and apricot fruit; avoids phenolics, but doesn't have much drive. Diam. 14.5° alc. **Rating** 87 **To** 2008

Winburndale

116 Saint Anthony's Creek Road, Bathurst, NSW 2795 **Region** Central Ranges Zone
T (02) 6337 3134 **F** (02) 6337 3106 **www**.winburndalewines.com.au **Open** By appt
Winemaker Mark Renzaglia, David Lowe (Consultant) **Est.** 1998 **Cases** 2500
Michael Burleigh and family acquired the 200-ha Winburndale property in 1998: 160 ha is forest, to be kept as a nature reserve; 3 separate vineyards have been planted under the direction of viticulturist Mark Renzaglia. The winery paddock has 2.5 ha of shiraz facing due west at an altitude of 800–820 m; the south paddock, with north and northwest aspects, varying from 790–810 m, has chardonnay (1.2 ha), shiraz (1 ha) and cabernet sauvignon (3.5 ha). The home paddock is the most level, with a slight north aspect, and with 1.2 ha each of merlot and cabernet franc. The name derives from Lachlan Macquarie's exploration of the Blue Mountains in 1815. Exports to the US and Denmark.

ŶŶŶŶŶ **Solitary Shiraz 2005** Clean and fresh; as the alcohol suggests, the wine has achieved full ripeness without dead fruit characters, and is only medium-bodied at best; spicy black cherry, plum and blackberry fruits; harmonious palate and finish. Screwcap. 15° alc. **Rating** 93 **To** 2020 $25

Winchelsea Estate

248 Flinders Street, Adelaide, SA 5000 (postal) **Region** Geelong
T 0431 709 305 **Open** Not
Winemaker Peter Flewellyn **Est.** NA **Cases** 1000

Winchelsea Estate raises as many questions as it answers: its owner is itself a vineyard, with a Flinders Street, Adelaide, address. It is a chardonnay specialist with 8 ha of vines situated on 3 different terroirs, the grapes being separately harvested, and the identity of each wine likewise protected. Thus there is Warri Chardonnay, said to be the leanest of the 3, closest to Chablis; Alkira, said to be an Australian interpretation of fine White Burgundy; and Karalla, being the 'fat boy' of the trio, the red wine drinkers chardonnay. There is also a Pinot Gris and Pinot Noir.

ƔƔƔƔ **Pinot Gris 2006** A powerful bouquet; an abundance of pear/musk and apple aromas; the palate would be much better with less sugar. **Rating** 87 **To** 2008 $22.50

Windance Wines ★★★★★

Lot 12, Loc 589, Caves Road, Yallingup, WA 6282 **Region** Margaret River
T (08) 9755 2293 **F** (08) 9755 2293 **www**.windance.com.au **Open** 7 days 10–5
Winemaker Janice McDonald, Damon Eastaugh, Harry Clegg **Est.** 1998 **Cases** 4000
Drew and Rosemary Brent-White own this family business, situated 5 km south of Yallingup. A little over 7 ha of cabernet sauvignon, shiraz, sauvignon blanc, semillon and merlot have been established, incorporating sustainable land management and organic farming practices where possible. The wines are exclusively estate-grown, pricing fairly reflecting quality.

ƔƔƔƔƔ **Margaret River Cabernet Merlot 2004** A beautifully proportioned and weighted wine with deliciously ripe cassis and blackcurrant fruit supported by soft, ripe tannins. Quality oak is balanced and integrated. Screwcap. 14.2° alc. **Rating** 95 **To** 2019 $30
Reserve Cabernet Sauvignon 2005 Excellent wine; medium to medium-full-bodied; supple mouthfeel, with a harmonious blend of cassis/blackcurrant fruit, fine, ripe tannins, and classy oak handling. Screwcap. **Rating** 95 **To** 2025 $40
Margaret River Semillon Sauvignon Blanc 2005 Spotlessly clean aromas; a mix of piercing citrus and less powerful minerally characters; good length, bright finish. Gold medal Winewise '06. Screwcap. 12.5° alc. **Rating** 94 **To** 2008 $18

ƔƔƔƔꝊ **Reserve Shiraz 2005** Ample spice, licorice, blackberry and plum fruit plus savoury tannins to give authority; good oak balance. Screwcap. **Rating** 93 **To** 2025 $40

ƔƔƔƔ **Shiraz 2005** Deep, dense purple-red; fully ripe and sweet blackberry and plum fruit, vanilla oak and soft tannins. Screwcap. 14° alc. **Rating** 89 **To** 2015 $20
Margaret River Cabernet Merlot 2005 Medium-bodied; cassis, blackcurrant and spice flavours; slightly furry tannins on the finish. Screwcap. 14.2° alc. **Rating** 87 **To** 2009 $20

Windows Margaret River ★★★★☆

Location 775 Caves Road, Yallingup, WA 6282 (postal) **Region** Margaret River
T (08) 9755 2719 **F** (08) 9755 2719 **Open** Not
Winemaker Christopher Davies, Barbara Davies **Est.** 1996 **Cases** 2500
Len and Barbara Davies progressively established 1.5 ha of cabernet sauvignon, 1 ha each of chenin blanc and shiraz, and 0.5 ha each of semillon and merlot, selling the grapes. In 2006 the decision was taken to move to winemaking. Since Barbara Davies is a qualified winemaker and works with her son Chris (as assistant winemaker and vineyard manager) the decision wasn't hard to make. It has been rewarded with considerable show success for its consistently good, enticingly priced, wines.

WindshakeR Ridge

PO Box 106, Karrinyup, WA 6921 **Region** Swan District
T (08) 6241 4100 **F** (08) 9240 6220 **www**.windshaker.com.au **Open** Not
Winemaker Ryan Sudano **Est.** 2003 **Cases** 4000

The Moltoni family has owned a 2000-ha farming property for 3 generations. Robert Moltoni is the driving force, establishing WindshakeR Ridge in 2003. The 25-ha vineyard (carnelian, semillon, shiraz and verdelho) is 9 km north of Gingin, and looks out over the hills to the sea. Moltoni is an accomplished poet, and I cannot help but quote one of his poems: 'Easterlies whistle through the gums; Crashing over silent ridges; Bathing vines in Namatjira Crimson; WindshakeR, WindshakeR, WindshakeR; The ghost winds whisper down; Off the red plains to the sea.'

Windy Ridge Vineyard & Winery ★★☆

Foster-Fish Creek Road, Foster, Vic 3960 **Region** Gippsland
T (03) 5682 2035 **www**.windyridgewinery.com.au **Open** Holiday w'ends 10–5
Winemaker Graeme Wilson **Est.** 1978 **Cases** 300
The 2.6-ha Windy Ridge Vineyard was planted between 1978 and 1986, with the first vintage taking place in 1988. Graeme Wilson favours prolonged maturation, part in stainless steel and part in oak, before bottling his wines, typically giving the Pinot Noir 3 years and the Cabernet 2 years. One gets the feeling the wines would be far better if bottled earlier, the Pinot 2 years earlier.

wine by brad ★★★★

PO Box 475, Margaret River, WA 6285 **Region** Margaret River
T 0409 572 957 **F** (08) 9757 1897 **www**.winebybrad.com.au **Open** Not
Winemaker Brad Wehr, Clive Otto **Est.** 2003 **Cases** 2600
Brad Wehr says that wine by brad 'is the result of a couple of influential winemakers and shadowy ruffians deciding that there was something to be gained by putting together some pretty neat parcels of wine from the region, creating their own label, and releasing it with minimal fuss'. This, therefore, is another version of the virtual winery, with sales through the website at enticing prices.

 Margaret River Semillon Sauvignon Blanc 2006 Grassy, minerally aromas; fresh, crisp and lively grass, slate and a nice line of lemony acidity. Screwcap. 13° alc. **Rating** 90 **To** 2010 $18
Margaret River Cabernet Merlot 2004 A chunky wine with plenty of weight and texture; blackcurrant rather than cassis; good tannins and length. Screwcap. 14° alc. **Rating** 90 **To** 2014 $18

Winetrust Estates ★★★★

PO Box 541, Balgowlah, NSW 2093 **Region** Southeast Australia
T (02) 9949 9250 **F** (02) 9907 8179 **www**.winetrustestates.com **Open** Not
Winemaker Various contract **Est.** 1999 **Cases** 32 000
Mark Arnold is the man behind Winetrust Estates, drawing on a lifetime of experience in wine marketing. It is a virtual winery operation, drawing grapes from 3 states and 5 regions using contract winemakers according to the origin of the grapes. The top-of-the-range Picarus red wines come from the Limestone Coast; the other ranges are Ocean Grove and Firebox, covering all the major varietal wines plus a few newcomers. Exports to the US, Canada, China, Japan, Singapore and Thailand.

 Picarus Wrattonbully Shiraz 2005 Medium- to full-bodied, with abundant blackberry fruit and well-chosen oak; good tannins and length. Screwcap. 14.5° alc. **Rating** 93 **To** 2018 $19.95

♀♀♀♀ **Firebox Vineyard Selection Barossa Valley Cabernet Sauvignon 2005** Has more weight and structure than the others in this range; attractive cassis fruit plus blackcurrant and a touch of vanilla oak. Screwcap. 14° alc. **Rating** 89 **To** 2015 $14
Picarus Coonawarra Chardonnay 2004 A powerful and rich wine with ripe stone fruit and obvious barrel ferment oak; some sweetness apparent not necessarily from residual sugar. Cork. 13.5° alc. **Rating** 88 **To** 2008 $19.95
Firebox Victorian Chardonnay 2006 Soft, peach, fig and nectarine with an airbrush of oak; has presumably developed quickly prior to bottling given the screwcap closure. Screwcap. 13.5° alc. **Rating** 87 **To** 2008 $13

Firebox Victorian Shiraz 2005 A pleasant, nicely balanced medium-bodied wine, with red fruits and fine tannins all making for early, easy drinking. Screwcap. 14.5° alc. **Rating** 87 **To** 2011 $13

Winstead

75 Winstead Road, Bagdad, Tas 7030 **Region** Southern Tasmania
T (03) 6268 6417 **F** (03) 6268 6417 **Open** By appt
Winemaker Neil Snare **Est.** 1989 **Cases** 350
The good news about Winstead is the outstanding quality of its extremely generous and rich Pinot Noirs, rivalling those of Freycinet for the abundance of their fruit flavour without any sacrifice of varietal character. The bad news is that production is so limited, with only 0.8 ha of pinot noir and 0.4 ha riesling being tended by fly-fishing devotee Neil Snare and wife Julieanne.

Pinot Noir 2005 Red cherry and raspberry; a fraction sweet in fruit terms, but does have some balancing tannins. **Rating** 89 **To** 2011
Ensnared Riesling 2005 Soft, rich and luscious; crystallised lemon flavours; once again, however, the hard acid on the finish needs to resolve itself. **Rating** 87 **To** 2010
Reserve Pinot Noir 2005 A very stemmy, complex style, but does not have quite enough fruit to carry the winemaking inputs. **Rating** 87 **To** 2009

Winter Creek Wine

PO Box 170, Williamstown, SA 5351 **Region** Barossa Valley
T (08) 8524 6382 **F** (08) 8524 6382 **www.**wintercreekwine.com.au **Open** Not
Winemaker David Cross **Est.** 2000 **Cases** 1200
David and Pam Cross acquired their small vineyard at Williamstown in the cooler foothills of the southern Barossa Valley in 2000, in time for their first vintage that year. There are 2 ha of shiraz, and 1 ha of grenache, the latter 70 years old. More recently they have added a Sauvignon Blanc and a Chardonnay to the Winter Creek range, the grapes purchased from the Adelaide Hills. Until recently (late 2006) most of the wine was exported to the US, where it has received strong support from leading wine writers, notwithstanding that the emphasis is on elegance rather than alcohol.

Barossa Valley Shiraz 2004 Elegant, smooth and supple; a medium-bodied mix of predominantly black fruits, though some red fruit flavours are also present; enhanced by 16 months in French oak. Screwcap. 14° alc. **Rating** 93 **To** 2019 $30
Adelaide Hills Sauvignon Blanc 2006 Some hints of herb and grass on the bouquet, the palate swinging to a nice mix of citrus, passionfruit and tropical flavours; good acidity and length. Screwcap. 12.5° alc. **Rating** 92 **To** 2008 $18
Vintage Barossa Valley Fortified Shiraz 2005 Impenetrable black-purple; almost as impenetrable flavours, with licorice, blackberry and spice; good spirit. Gold medal Barossa Valley Wine Show '06. Did the alcohol get out of hand? (Fortification tables for calculating the end-point are notoriously difficult.) Screwcap. 20° alc. **Rating** 92 **To** 2030 $20
Adelaide Hills Chardonnay 2005 Fruit-driven; citrus, nectarine and melon, with just a little French oak; good length. Screwcap. 13° alc. **Rating** 90 **To** 2012 $18
Barossa Valley Shiraz 2005 A mix of black fruits, and touches of leaf and earth on the bouquet; the medium-bodied palate has a similar complex web of flavours; slightly off the beaten track, but none the worse for that. Screwcap. **Rating** 90 **To** 2020 $30
Old Barossa Blend 2004 Interesting; while not having the weight of McLaren Vale, avoids the cosmetic/jammy nuances the Barossa often has; instead, bright red cherry and raspberry fruits plus fine, silky tannins; good length. Grenache/Shiraz. Screwcap. 14° alc. **Rating** 90 **To** 2014 $25

Wirilda Creek

NR

Lot 11, 173 Port Road, Old Aldinga, SA 5173 **Region** McLaren Vale
T 0407 100 922 **F** (08) 8231 8842 **Open** 7 days 10–5
Winemaker Kerry Flanagan **Est.** 1993 **Cases** NA

Wirra Wirra

★★★★★

McMurtie Road, McLaren Vale, SA 5171 **Region** McLaren Vale
T (08) 8323 8414 **www**.wirrawirra.com **Open** Mon–Sat 10–5, Sun & public hols 11–5
Winemaker Samantha Connew, Alexia Roberts **Est.** 1969 **Cases** 120 000
Long respected for the consistency of its white wines, Wirra Wirra has now established an equally
formidable reputation for its reds. Right across the board, the wines are of exemplary character,
quality and style, The Angelus Cabernet Sauvignon and RSW Shiraz battling with each other for
supremacy. Long may the battle continue under the direction of new managing director Andrew
Kay following the retirement of highly respected Tim James, particularly in the wake of the death
of the universally loved co-founder/owner Greg Trott in early 2005. Exports to all major markets.

▽▽▽▽▽ **RSW Shiraz 2004** A fragrant and elegant marriage of fruit and oak, with
elements of spice on the intense and very long palate. All in all, a superb
exercise in restraint. Diam. 14.7° alc. **Rating** 96 **To** 2024 $55
The Angelus Cabernet Sauvignon 2004 Very regional, with masses of earthy
dark chocolate, together with blackcurrant fruit, giving it opulence without
imperilling its finesse. Diam. 14.7° alc. **Rating** 95 **To** 2024 $50
Hand Picked Riesling 2006 Ultra-clean, clear and crisp aromas and flavour;
mineral and grapefruit/lime flavours on the palate; fresh finish, and good
length. Adelaide Hills. Screwcap. 12.5° alc. **Rating** 94 **To** 2016 $16
Woodhenge Shiraz 2004 A very attractive medium-bodied regional style;
luscious black and red fruits with a strong skein of chocolate; confident oak
handling, and a long finish. Cork. 14.5° alc. **Rating** 94 **To** 2019 $29

▽▽▽▽▽ **Catapult McLaren Vale Shiraz Viognier 2005** Typical, bright purple-red; full-
on regional dark chocolate shapes the wine far more than the small touch of
viognier; medium- to full-bodied, but not extractive; good texture, structure and
length. Screwcap. 14.5° alc. **Rating** 93 **To** 2020 $20
Woodhenge Shiraz 2005 Medium-bodied, but with abundant power from the
blackberry, licorice and dark chocolate fruit; fine tannins and good oak. Screwcap.
14.5° alc. **Rating** 91 **To** 2020 $27.50
Adelaide Hills Chardonnay 2005 Fresh, lively and crisp aromas; light- to
medium-bodied, with restrained winemaker inputs to the nectarine and citrus fruit;
subtle oak. Screwcap. 13° alc. **Rating** 90 **To** 2012 $25

▽▽▽▽ **Adelaide Hills Sauvignon Blanc 2006** A faintly sweaty bouquet, then a palate
with apple and gooseberry flavours supported by a mineral structure. Screwcap.
13.5° alc. **Rating** 89 **To** 2008 $24
McLaren Vale Mourvedre 2004 Powerful, spicy and intense black fruits; tannins
take a firm hold, and don't relinquish it. Only 150 cases made for cellar door.
Screwcap. 14° alc. **Rating** 89 **To** 2024 $20
Adelaide Hills Arneis 2005 Floral orange blossom aromas with hints of spice,
then a light-bodied palate with pear and citrus flavours, finishing with good acidity.
Screwcap. 13.5° alc. **Rating** 88 **To** 2010 $24
Mrs Wigley Rose 2006 Precisely aimed at the cellar door, with small red fruits
and a closing touch of sweetness. Screwcap. 12.5° alc. **Rating** 87 **To** 2008 $16

Wirruna Estate

★★★☆

RMB 5015A, Bethanga, Vic 3691 (postal) **Region** North East Victoria Zone
T (02) 6040 4808 **F** (02) 6040 6046 **www**.wirrunawines.com **Open** Not
Winemaker John Woodhouse **Est.** 1997 **Cases** 1650

John and Sandra Woodhouse have established 1.5 ha of each of shiraz, durif and marsanne on the banks of Lake Hume. The varieties were chosen because of their compatibility with the hot, dry summers, while the Wirruna name is an Aboriginal word for the sunset depicted on the labels. Son-in-law Manfred Walch works as assistant winemaker during vintage, and John, Sandra and Manfred work on the property in a part-time capacity for most of the year. Picking, done over 3 weekends, is a family and friends affair.

Wise Wine   ★★★★☆

Lot 4 Eagle Bay Road, Dunsborough, WA 6281 **Region** Margaret River
T (08) 9756 8627 **F** (08) 9756 8770 **www.**wisewine.com.au **Open** 7 days 10–5
Winemaker Amanda Kramer, Andrew Bromley **Est.** 1986 **Cases** 18 000
Wise Vineyards, headed by Perth entrepreneur Ron Wise, is going from strength to strength, with 18 ha at the Meelup Vineyard in Margaret River, 10 ha at the Donnybrook Vineyard in Geographe, and leases the Bramley and Bunkers Bay vineyards, with a total of almost 40 ha. Wine quality has taken a leap forward, with a number of excellent wines. Exports to the US, Vietnam, Singapore and Taiwan.

ΨΨΨΨΨ **Reserve Pemberton Chardonnay 2005** Glowing yellow-green; layers of complexity from barrel ferment and stone fruit/grapefruit flavours; has excellent length and balance, retaining elegance in the face of all the flavour. Screwcap. 14° alc. **Rating** 94 **To** 2015 $35

ΨΨΨΨΨ **Semillon Sauvignon Blanc 2006** The bouquet is a touch closed, but hints at the intensity of the fruit delivered by the palate; semillon does dominate, especially in the structure, but there is a flash of tropical sauvignon blanc fruit before a lemony finish. Screwcap. 13° alc. **Rating** 92 **To** 2011 $17

ΨΨΨΨ **Pemberton Unwooded Chardonnay 2006** A lively wine, which has the crispness and attack unwooded chardonnay needs; grapefruit and nectarine, with good length and a clean finish. Screwcap. 13.5° alc. **Rating** 89 **To** 2011 $17
Lot 80 Margaret River Cabernet Sauvignon 2004 Not a lot of depth to the colour; savoury/earthy/lean, but does have some length. Screwcap. 14° alc. **Rating** 87 **To** 2010 $30

Witchcliffe Estate   ★★★★★

Wickham Road, Witchcliffe, WA 6285 **Region** Margaret River
T (08) 9757 6329 **F** (08) 9757 6279 **www.**witchcliffe-estate.com.au **Open** 7 days (summer), Wed–Sun (winter) 11-5
Winemaker Peter Stanlake **Est.** 2003 **Cases** 2000
While the establishment date of Witchcliffe Estate is shown as 2003, the 8-ha vineyard of semillon, sauvignon blanc, chardonnay and shiraz was planted in the early 1990s. Tony and Maureen Cosby acquired the 69-ha property in 2000, at which time it was best known as the Margaret River Marron Farm. The Cosbys still farm marron on a small scale, selling both at the farm gate, and through the cellar door. It has been a very impressive start.

ΨΨΨΨΨ **Chardonnay 2004** Bright green-straw; complex barrel ferment aromas and flavours of fig, cashew, melon and nectarine; retains elegance, with good length and aftertaste. Screwcap. **Rating** 94 **To** 2010 $18
Reserve Shiraz 2004 Strong red-purple; medium- to full-bodied, with good focus and concentration to the black fruits, spice and touches of bitter chocolate; good tannin and oak management. Screwcap. 14.3° alc. **Rating** 94 **To** 2015 $28

ΨΨΨΨ **Semillon Sauvignon Blanc 2005** Bright green-straw; a multifaceted array of fruit aromas and flavours; passionfruit and sweet grapefruit, and even a touch of nectarine; good texture and mouthfeel. Screwcap. **Rating** 93 **To** 2009 $15
Shiraz 2004 Medium to full red-purple; medium-bodied, with good line and length; an expressive array of black and red fruits and fine tannins; long finish. Cork. **Rating** 93 **To** 2014 $19

Sauvignon Blanc 2004 Bright, light green-straw; has a complex fruit spectrum ranging through passionfruit and mandarin; lingering finish and aftertaste; has held together very well. Screwcap. 12° alc. **Rating** 92 **To** 2008 $14

Shiraz 2005 Medium red-purple; a substantial, full-bodied wine with masses of black fruits and a dusting of spice and pepper; good tannins. Screwcap. 13.8° alc. **Rating** 91 **To** 2005 $19

Semillon Sauvignon Blanc 2004 Lower alcohol than the '05 is immediately obvious; bright, crisp, fresh grass, herb and mineral, the semillon component the dominant partner. Screwcap. 12° alc. **Rating** 90 **To** 2010 $14

Chardonnay 2005 An elegant, light- to medium-bodied wine; a touch of pleasantly funky characters on both the bouquet and palate; melon and ripe apple with a touch of cashew. Screwcap. 14.1° alc. **Rating** 90 **To** 2011 $18

Chardonnay 2003 Green-gold; complex and quite rich, with good developed characters albeit in a different register to the screwcap wines; nutty yellow peach and citrus dominate. Cork. 13.9° alc. **Rating** 90 **To** 2008 $19

Shiraz Cabernet 2005 Youthful purple-red; typical expressive Witchcliffe style; abundant blackberry, blackcurrant and cassis; good tannin and oak management. Screwcap. **Rating** 90 **To** 2015 $15

ΨΨΨΨ **Shiraz 2003** Light to medium red-purple; light red fruits and spicy notes; well off the pace of the '04s. Cork. 15.2° alc. **Rating** 87 **To** 2009 $19

Witchmount Estate   ★★★★★

557 Leakes Road, Rockbank, Vic 3335 **Region** Sunbury
T (03) 9747 1188 **F** (03) 9747 1066 **www.**witchmount.com.au **Open** Wed–Sun 10–5
Winemaker Tony Ramunno, Steve Goodwin **Est.** 1991 **Cases** 6800
Gaye and Matt Ramunno operate Witchmount Estate in conjunction with its Italian restaurant and function rooms. Over 20 ha of vines have been established since 1991: varieties include nebbiolo, barbera, tempranillo and the rare northern Italian white grape picolit. The quality of the wines is consistently good, the prices very modest. Exports to Canada and Singapore.

ΨΨΨΨΨ **Sauvignon Blanc 2006** A spotlessly clean bouquet; grass, herb, gooseberry and citrus chase each other along the palate before a cleansing, crisp, dry finish. Screwcap. 13° alc. **Rating** 94 **To** 2008 $20

Shiraz 2004 Medium-bodied, complex, but perfectly fused black fruits, cedar oak and fine tannins; long finish and immaculate balance. Screwcap. 14.5° alc. **Rating** 94 **To** 2019 $26

Cabernet Merlot 2004 Deeply coloured; richly robed and layered blackcurrant fruit, with touches of cedar and mocha; ripe tannins. Trophy Ballarat Wine Show '06. Screwcap. 14.5° alc. **Rating** 94 **To** 2020 $26

ΨΨΨΨΨ **Pinot Gris 2006** A highly aromatic though unusual bouquet; ripe pear and apple flavours, with more impact than most. Screwcap. 13.5° alc. **Rating** 90 **To** 2008 $20

WJ Walker Wines   NR

Burns Road, Lake Grace, WA 6353 **Region** Central Western Australia Zone
T (08) 9865 1969 **Open** 7 days 10–4
Winemaker Porongurup Winery **Est.** 1998 **Cases** NA

Wolf Blass   ★★★★★

Bilyara Vineyards, 97 Sturt Highway, Nuriootpa, SA 5355 **Region** Barossa Valley
T (08) 8568 7300 **F** (08) 8568 7380 **www.**wolfblass.com.au **Open** Mon–Fri 9.15–5, w'ends & public hols 10–5
Winemaker Chris Hatcher (Chief), Caroline Dunn (Red), Kirsten Glaetzer (White)
Est. 1966 **Cases** 4 million
Although merged with Mildara and now under the giant umbrella of Fosters, the brands (as expected) have been left largely intact. The white wines are particularly impressive, none more so

than the Gold Label Riesling. After a short pause, the red wines have improved out of all recognition thanks to the sure touch (and top palate) of Caroline Dunn. All of this has occurred under the leadership of Chris Hatcher, who has harnessed the talents of the team and encouraged the changes in style. Exports to all major markets.

ŸŸŸŸŸ **Black Label Shiraz Cabernet Sauvignon Malbec 2002** 30th Vintage. Flooded with opulent, multi-layered black fruits; a silky, sensual, supple texture, with seamless oak and tannins. This note is for the version under screwcap; there is a vast difference between it and the conventionally closed bottle. 15° alc. **Rating** 96 **To** 2022 $125

Black Label Langhorne Creek Cabernet Sauvignon Shiraz Malbec 2004 Deeply robed colour; the throbbing power of an idling V8 turbo engine; shows the '04 vintage quality, with an array of black fruits of considerable intensity; will be very long-lived, of course. Screwcap. 15° alc. **Rating** 96 **To** 2029 $125

White Label Specially Aged Release Eden Valley Riesling 2001 Glowing but light green-yellow; complex lemon blossom, crushed leaves and herbs intermingle with the toast, lime and mineral flavours of the palate; very good length. Screwcap. 10° alc. **Rating** 94 **To** 2011 $40

Gold Label Mount Gambier Sauvignon Blanc 2006 An intense bouquet, with strong herb, asparagus and grass aromas; the palate follows on, adding just a dash of sweeter tropical fruit; clean and brisk. Further evidence of the potential of Mt Gambier as a distinctly cooler alternative to Coonawarra. Screwcap. 11.5° alc. **Rating** 94 **To** 2008 $21.95

Gold Label Adelaide Hills Chardonnay 2001 Great finesse and elegance; fine and long; subtle oak; only a screwcap could keep the wine so fresh. Gold medal National Wine Show '06. 13.5° alc. **Rating** 94 **To** 2012 $21.95

Gold Label Barossa Shiraz 2005 Bold, rich flavours of blackberry, black plums and licorice seamlessly woven with positive French and American oak; tannins ripe and in perfect balance. Screwcap. 14.5° alc. **Rating** 94 **To** 2020 $21.95

Grey Label McLaren Vale Shiraz 2005 Multi-layered, powerful and focused wine; blackberry, black cherry, dark chocolate and licorice; carries the alcohol (and the oak) with ease. Screwcap. 15° alc. **Rating** 94 **To** 2029 $40

Platinum Label Barossa Shiraz 2004 Extremely powerful, with layers of black fruits sandwiched between layers of tannin and French oak; the fruit will win out, but take 10 years to do so. Screwcap. 14.5° alc. **Rating** 94 **To** 2034 $180

Platinum Label Barossa Shiraz 2003 Deep colour; an impressive achievement for a very difficult vintage, with a cascade of black fruits, dark chocolate and French oak all interwoven. The alcohol does make its mark, however. Screwcap. 15.5° alc. **Rating** 94 **To** 2028 $146.95

Black Label Langhorne Creek Cabernet Sauvignon Shiraz Malbec 2003 A rich, aromatic bouquet with ripe fruit and oak in chorus, then a deeply textured and structured palate, happily with none of the aggressive tannins of the Platinum Label Shiraz; a major success in a difficult vintage. Screwcap. 15° alc. **Rating** 94 **To** 2034 $120

ŸŸŸŸŸ **Gold Label Eden Valley Riesling 2006** Aromatic lime, thyme and apple aromas; the palate follows on with intensity and good length. Screwcap. 12.5° alc. **Rating** 93 **To** 2012 $21.95

Gold Label Barossa Shiraz 2004 Ripe blackberry, prune and plum fruit almost hides the alcohol in this instance; clever oak and soft tannins also at work. Screwcap. 15° alc. **Rating** 93 **To** 2020 $21.95

Grey Label Langhorne Creek Cabernet Sauvignon 2005 Opens with the generosity of fruit typical of Langhorne Creek, but becomes much more serious and tight on the back palate and finish; the Jekyll and Hyde characters should merge with 5 years' cellaring, and a very good wine should be the end result. Pointed now, and not for the long life in front of it. Screwcap. 15° alc. **Rating** 92 **To** 2030 $40

White Label Specially Aged Release Adelaide Hills Chardonnay 2001
Has developed slowly, which is a good thing; has also become more complex which should be a good thing, but does not deliver the expected fruit line. Screwcap. 13.5° alc. **Rating** 91 **To** 2009 $40

Gold Label Adelaide Hills Shiraz Viognier 2005 A very powerful wine, the viognier not easily accommodating the intensity and ripeness of the shiraz. I'm not understanding the philosophy here; perhaps it's the US market. Screwcap. 15° alc. **Rating** 91 **To** 2015 $21.95

Gold Label Pinot Chardonnay 2003 Super-fine and elegant; a long, crisp, citrussy palate with some bready/yeasty characters in the background. 12° alc. **Rating** 91 **To** 2011 $21.95

ŶŶŶŶ **Eaglehawk Chardonnay 2006** A clean, aromatic and fruity bouquet; well above-average intensity and length to its melon, peach and nectarine flavours; just a background whisk of oak. Twin top. 13° alc. **Rating** 89 **To** 2009

Yellow Label Merlot 2005 Has hit the mark with this wine; it does have varietal character; does have appropriately sweet fruit flavour; and is easy to drink. Screwcap. 14° alc. **Rating** 88 **To** 2010 $16.95

Red Label Cabernet Merlot 2005 Well-handled and assembled; a nice mix of black and red fruits; fine tannins, good length. Cork. 14° alc. **Rating** 88 **To** 2011 $13.95

Eaglehawk Rose 2006 Lively red berry fruits and a touch of citrus, the latter possibly from white wine blended in Yellow Label Shiraz. Screwcap. 12.5° alc. **Rating** 87 **To** 2008

Yellow Label Shiraz 2005 Well-made and put together commercial shiraz; introspection not required. Screwcap. 13.5° alc. **Rating** 87 **To** 2010 $16.95

Yellow Label Shiraz 2004 Medium-bodied; a well-made wine especially given the volume made; neatly balanced plum and black cherry fruit with fine tannins, and a whisk of oak. Cork. 14° alc. **Rating** 87 **To** 2009

Red Label Shiraz Cabernet 2005 A commercial red wine made in large quantities, but with more than adequate flavour and structure. Screwcap. 14° alc. **Rating** 87 **To** 2008 $13.95

Wolseley Wines   ★★★☆

1790 Hendy Main Road, Moriac, Geelong, Vic 3240 **Region** Geelong
T 0412 990 638 **www**.wolseleywines.com **Open** W'ends & public hols 11–6
Winemaker Will Wolseley **Est.** 1992 **Cases** 2500
Will Wolseley grew up in Somerset, England, and from an early age made blackberry wine at home. He came to Australia in 1986 and enrolled in wine science at Charles Sturt University, gathering vintage experience at various wineries over the next 5 years. A 2-year search for an ideal vineyard site resulted in the acquisition of property on the gently sloping hills of Paraparap, inland from Bells Beach, Torquay. He established 6.5 ha of vineyard planted to pinot noir, cabernet sauvignon, chardonnay, shiraz, cabernet franc and semillon. Hail storms, frost and drought delayed the first commercial vintage until 1998, but the solar-powered winery is now in full production.

ŶŶŶŶŶ **Geelong Botrytis Semillon 2004** Extremely rich and luscious cumquat/crème brûlée flavours. Colour somewhat advanced. **Rating** 90 **To** 2009 $40

Wonga Estate   ★★★★☆

204 Jumping Creek Road, Wonga Park, Vic 3115 **Region** Yarra Valley
T (03) 9722 2122 **F** (03) 9722 1715 **Open** Mon–Sat 9–5, Sun 10–5 by appt
Winemaker Greg Roberts, Sergio Carlei (Consultant) **Est.** 1997 **Cases** 700
Greg and Jady Roberts developed of their 1.8-ha vineyard in 1997 with a minor expansion in 2002. The wines are made at the onsite micro-winery by Greg Roberts with assistance from Sergio Carlei. Since 2002 the range has been expanded with shiraz grown in the Colbinabbin area of Heathcote, open-fermented and basket-pressed. Limited production has not stopped the listing of the wines at an impressive range of Melbourne, Yarra Valley and Brisbane restaurants.

ΨΨΨΨΨ **Yarra Valley Chardonnay 2005** Fine, elegant and intense; nectarine and citrus fruit has soaked up the 12 months in French oak; admirable Yarra Valley length; 250 cases made; Dijon clones 76 and 95. Diam. 13° alc. **Rating** 94 **To** 2013 $22

ΨΨΨΨϘ **Yarra Valley Pinot Noir 2005** Bright red-purple; light-bodied, elegant and restrained; pure red pinot fruits have absorbed the oak, and the wine has excellent length. The only question is whether vinosity/weight will develop in bottle; 250 cases made; clones 115 and MV6. Diam. 13° alc. **Rating** 93 **To** 2015 $24

Heathcote Shiraz 2004 Spicy, clove and blackberry aromas, the palate medium- to full-bodied, but supple, smooth and ripe, with a slight lift on the finish; 140 cases made; 24 months in French oak. Cork. 14.5° alc. **Rating** 93 **To** 2019 $55

Reserve Pinot Noir 2003 Moderately intense cherry and plum fruit; good acidity and length; not complex, but ageing nicely; 38 cases made, clone 115. Diam. 13° alc. **Rating** 92 **To** 2010 $28

Wood Park

263 Kneebone Gap Road, Markwood, Vic 3678 **Region** King Valley
T (03) 5727 3367 **F** (03) 5727 3682 **www.**woodparkwines.com.au **Open** At Milawa Cheese Factory 7 days 10–5
Winemaker John Stokes **Est.** 1989 **Cases** 9000
John Stokes planted the first vines at Wood Park in 1989 as part of a diversification program for his property at Bobinawarrah, in the hills of the Lower King Valley, east of Milawa. The vineyard is managed with minimal chemical use, winemaking a mix of modern and traditional techniques. In an unusual twist, Stokes acquires his chardonnay from cousin John Leviny, one of the King Valley pioneers, who has his vineyard at Meadow Creek. The quality of the wines made in 2004 and subsequent vintages is very impressive. Exports to the US and other major markets.

ΨΨΨΨϘ **Reserve Cabernet Sauvignon 2004** Very good balance and modulation of earthy blackcurrant fruit and a touch of bitter chocolate; tannins and French oak are spot-on; 22 months in barrel. Screwcap. 13.5° alc. **Rating** 93 **To** 2024 $35

Meadow Creek Chardonnay 2005 Obvious effort has been put into the winemaking courtesy of barrel-ferment in French oak and indigenous/wild yeast; rich texture with good stone fruit flavours and a slightly unexpected touch of apple. Screwcap. 13.5° alc. **Rating** 91 **To** 2010 $22

Sauvignon Blanc 2006 Gentle tropical fruit aromas lead into a palate with an amplitude of passionfruit and mango braced by balancing acidity; good length. Screwcap. 13.5° alc. **Rating** 90 **To** 2008 $18

Myrrhee Merlot 2005 While there is plenty of French oak evident, there is also distinctive merlot varietal character, with a twist of black olive to the sweet red fruit on the medium-bodied palate; fine, savoury tannins add length. Screwcap. 13.5° alc. **Rating** 90 **To** 2012 $20

Cabernet Sauvignon Shiraz 2005 Classic cassis cabernet with notes of plum and cherry from the shiraz; seductive fruit flavours on the mid-palate, savoury tannins to close. Screwcap. 14° alc. **Rating** 90 **To** 2015 $20

ΨΨΨΨ **Kneebones Gap Shiraz 2005** Bright, fresh fruit aromas; generously proportioned, with ripe morello cherry flavours and good supporting tannins. Screwcap. 14° alc. **Rating** 89 **To** 2015 $21

Wild's Gully Shiraz Cabernet 2005 A juicy bundle of freshly squeezed red fruits; lots of flavour, and no sweetness. Excellent value. Screwcap. 13.5° alc. **Rating** 89 **To** 2008 $13

Wild's Gully Semillon Sauvignon Blanc 2006 Light- to medium-bodied; a clean and pleasant mix of tropical and more herbal notes; overall, sauvignon blanc dominates the play. Screwcap. 12.5° alc. **Rating** 87 **To** 2008 $13

Pinot Gris 2006 An anonymous bouquet and largely anonymous palate, but does have some length, the residual sugar balanced by acidity. Screwcap. 13.5° alc. **Rating** 87 **To** 2008 $20

Woodeneye Estate   ★★★

PO Box 893, Irymple, Vic 3498 **Region** Murray Darling
T 0419 518 846 **F** (03) 5024 6126 **www**.woodeneye.com.au **Open** Not
Winemaker Steve Glasson **Est.** 1990 **Cases** 750

Steve and Debi Glasson purchased their 12-ha vineyard at Irymple in 1990. It was largely planted to sultana, and in 1992 they took the decision to remove all but 0.6 ha of 65-year-old grenache. They replanted the vineyard to chardonnay, cabernet sauvignon, shiraz and merlot, leading to the first vintage in 2003. In the meantime Steve Glasson had completed a winemaking course through La Trobe University at Bundoora, and made the wine in an insulated shed on the property. A new winery and cellar door on the property next door, which the Glassons also own, was completed in time for the 2007 vintage.

Woodlands

Cnr Caves Road/Metricup Road, Wilyabrup via Cowaramup, WA 6284
Region Margaret River
T (08) 9755 6226 **F** (08) 9755 6236 **www**.woodlandswines.com **Open** 7 days 10.30–5
Winemaker Stuart Watson, David Watson **Est.** 1973 **Cases** 5500

The quality of the grapes, with a priceless core of 6.8 ha of 30+-year-old cabernet sauvignon, more recently joined by merlot, malbec, cabernet franc, pinot noir and chardonnay, has never been in doubt. Whatever the shortcomings of the 1990s, these days Woodlands is producing some spectacular wines in small quantities. The larger volume Cabernet Sauvignon is also of very high quality. Some behind-the-scenes consultancy advice has played its part, and Woodlands is now a major player in the top echelon of Margaret River producers. Exports to the UK and Asia.

🍷🍷🍷🍷🍷 **Margaret Reserve Cabernet Merlot 2005** Rich and layered, in a different style to the Reserve de la Cave wines; medium-bodied blackcurrant and cassis fruit, then a faint touch of austerity of a young Bordeaux on the finish; very impressive. Screwcap. 13° alc. **Rating** 95 **To** 2025 $39.50

Emily Special Reserve 2005 Spotlessly clean, with no hint of reduction; a supple, velvety array of red and black fruits, the contributions of tannin and oak magically balanced. Merlot/Malbec/Cabernet Sauvignon. Screwcap. 14° alc. **Rating** 95 **To** 2025 $25

Chloe Reserve Margaret River Chardonnay 2005 Retains the elegance of the varietal, but with more power, intensity, complexity and length; ripe peachy/nectarine fruit has absorbed the new oak in which it was fermented and matured. Screwcap. 14° alc. **Rating** 94 **To** 2015 $49.50

Reserve de la Cave Margaret River Merlot 2005 Bright, clear, purple-red; restrained and refined, with elegant red berry fruits, and just a right amount of olive and briar. Cork. 14° alc. **Rating** 94 **To** 2017 $65

Reserve de la Cave Margaret River Malbec 2005 Extravagantly deep colour; very rich and ripe; typical, slightly confit jam characters to the raspberry and blackberry mix; hard to fault within its style. Like all of these Reserve de la Cave wines, only 600 bottles made. Cork. 14° alc. **Rating** 94 **To** 2022 $65

🍷🍷🍷🍷🍷 **Cabernet Sauvignon Merlot 2005** A fresh and elegant wine; a classic cassis-blackcurrant mix, it has silky fine tannins, and restrained alcohol and oak. Screwcap. 13.5° alc. **Rating** 93 **To** 2010 $20

Rachael Cabernet Sauvignon 2004 A medium-bodied, elegant wine with ripe cassis fruit, ripeness without any sense of warmth; good finish, fine tannins. Cork. 14.3° alc. **Rating** 93 **To** 2010 $90

Reserve de la Cave Margaret River Pinot Noir 2005 Goes some distance to exploding the myth that you cannot make a silk purse out of a sow's ear; excellent texture, structure and mouthfeel; early picking has preserved far more than usual varietal character for the region. It's hard to imagine success such as this will be achieved every year, but we shall see. Screwcap. 12.5° alc. **Rating** 92 **To** 2013 $65

Reserve de la Cave Margaret River Cabernet Franc 2005 Marches to the tune of its own drum, but cabernet franc is arguably better in Margaret River than any other part of Australia; a brighter, but somehow thinner mouthfeel and flavour, less complete than the best. Cork. 14° alc. **Rating** 92 **To** 2018 $65

Margaret River Chardonnay 2006 Fragrant, elegant citrus and nectarine; light-bodied, bright and fresh, fully reflecting the deliberately modest alcohol. Screwcap. 12.5° alc. **Rating** 91 **To** 2010 $20

Woodside Valley Estate ★★★★★

PO Box 332, Greenwood, WA 6924 **Region** Margaret River
T (08) 9345 4065 **F** (08) 9345 4541 **www.**woodsidevalleyestate.com.au **Open** Not
Winemaker Kevin McKay **Est.** 1998 **Cases** 500
Woodside Valley has been developed by a small syndicate of investors headed by Peter Woods. In 1998 they acquired 67 ha of land at Yallingup, and have now established 19 ha of chardonnay, sauvignon blanc, cabernet sauvignon, shiraz, malbec and merlot. The experienced Albert Haak is consultant viticulturist, and together with Peter Woods, took the unusual step of planting south-facing in preference to north-facing slopes. In doing so they indirectly followed in the footsteps of the French explorer Thomas Nicholas Baudin, who mounted a major scientific expedition to Australia on his ship The Geographe, and defied established views and tradition of the time in (correctly) asserting that the best passage for sailing ships travelling between Cape Leeuwin and Bass Strait was from west to east. Exports to the US and Japan.

ȲȲȲȲȲ **Baudin Cabernet Sauvignon 2004** Brilliantly clear but strong red-purple; medium-bodied; classic cool-grown cabernet sauvignon, yet with no green aspects at all; beautifully balanced and structured; long finish. Cork. 14° alc. **Rating** 96 **To** 2019 $48

Le Bas Chardonnay 2005 A quality wine, although not overly embellished; discreet fig, melon and grapefruit; subtle oak. Cork. 13° alc. **Rating** 94 **To** 2013 $35

Bissy Merlot 2004 An attractive light to medium-bodied varietal wine, the character of merlot clearly expressed; fine, soft olive, gentle earth and red fruit flavours; fine, soft tannins. Cork. 13.5° alc. **Rating** 94 **To** 2014 $45

ȲȲȲȲȲ **Bonnefoy Shiraz 2004** Medium red-purple; medium-bodied; savoury, spicy cool-grown style; has undoubted elegance, and also length; just a touch more flesh needed. Cork. 14.5° alc. **Rating** 93 **To** 2015 $48

Woodstock ★★★★

Douglas Gully Road, McLaren Flat, SA 5171 **Region** McLaren Vale
T (08) 8383 0156 **www.**woodstockwine.com.au **Open** Mon–Fri 9–5, w'ends, hols 12–5
Winemaker Scott Collett, Ben Glaetzer **Est.** 1974 **Cases** 25 000
One of the stalwarts of McLaren Vale, producing archetypal and invariably reliable full-bodied red wines, spectacular botrytis sweet whites and high-quality (14-year-old) Tawny Port. Also offers a totally charming reception-cum-restaurant, which does a roaring trade with wedding receptions. Has supplemented its 22 ha of McLaren Vale vineyards with 10 ha at its Wirrega Vineyard, in the Limestone Coast Zone. Exports to the UK, Canada, Switzerland, Denmark, Hong Kong and South-East Asia.

ȲȲȲȲȲ **Shiraz 2004** Medium red-purple, bright and clear; the clean, fresh bouquet leads into a very attractive mix of raspberry, blackberry and dark chocolate fruit; a long, supple finish. Screwcap. 14° alc. **Rating** 92 **To** 2014 $20

McLaren Vale Cabernet Sauvignon 2004 Strong red-purple; shows the vintage to full advantage with blackcurrant and dark chocolate flavours; good texture, structure and balance. Screwcap. 14° alc. **Rating** 92 **To** 2014 $20

Fortified McLaren Vale Shiraz 2005 Intense, opaque purple-red; extremely powerful but not abrasive; blackberry fruits, clean spirit and, hallelujah, not too sweet. Screwcap. 18° alc. **Rating** 91 **To** 2025 $20

The Stocks McLaren Vale Shiraz 2004 Medium red-purple; rich, ripe fruit which has some quite sweet/confit characters, and thus not quite the freshness of the cheaper varietal sister. Screwcap. 14.5° alc. **Rating** 90 **To** 2014 $50

McLaren Vale Semillon Sauvignon Blanc 2006 Very light straw-green; light, crisp, mineral, grass and herb all pick up on the finish and aftertaste. Screwcap. 12.5° alc. **Rating** 89 **To** 2009 $15

Five Feet Cabernet Shiraz 2004 A pleasant mix of cassis, blackcurrant, spice and blackberry; abundant flavour. Screwcap. 14.5° alc. **Rating** 89 **To** 2013 $17

Barbera Recioto 2003 Interesting wine; lots of texture and flavour, with dark spices and bitter chocolate, then an almost dry finish. Screwcap. 16° alc. **Rating** 88 **To** 2008 $20

McLaren Vale Chardonnay 2006 Light-bodied; apple with touches of nectarine and pear, with a subliminal touch of oak; somewhat simple. Screwcap. 12.5° alc. **Rating** 87 **To** 2009 $20

McLaren Vale Rose 2006 Bright light purple-red; cherry and raspberry and flavours from the grenache; just enough sugar for cellar door trade. Screwcap. 13° alc. **Rating** 87 **To** 2008 $15

Woolybud ★★★

Playford Highway, Parndana, SA 5220 **Region** Kangaroo Island
T (08) 8559 6031 **F** (08) 8559 6031 **Open** Not
Winemaker Dudley Partners **Est.** 1998 **Cases** 1000
The Denis family moved to their sheep-farming property, Agincourt, west of Parndana, in 1986. Like many others, the downturn in the wool industry caused them to look to diversify their farming activities, and this led to the planting of shiraz and cabernet sauvignon, and to the subsequent release of their Wollombi brand wines. The wines are available by mail order.

Woongarra Estate ★★★★☆

95 Hayseys Road, Narre Warren East, Vic 3804 **Region** Port Phillip Zone
T (03) 9796 8886 **www**.woongarrawinery.com.au **Open** Thurs–Sun 9–5 by appt
Winemaker Bruce Jones, Sergio Carlei **Est.** 1992 **Cases** 3000
Dr Bruce Jones, and wife Mary, purchased their 16-ha property many years ago; it falls within the Yarra Ranges Shire Council's jurisdiction but not within the Yarra Valley wine region. In 1992 they planted 1 ha of sauvignon blanc, a small patch of shiraz and a few rows of semillon. Over 1 ha of sauvignon blanc and pinot noir followed in 1996 (mostly MV6, some French clone 114 and 115) with yet more 114 and 115 pinot noir in 2000, lifting total plantings to 3.2 ha of pinot noir, 1.4 ha of sauvignon blanc and a splash of the other 2 varieties. Spectacular success has come with the Three Wise Men Pinot Noir, (a joint venture between Woongarra and Passing Clouds – see separate entry).

Pinot Noir 2005 Very fragrant aromas, with pine needles and red fruits; good focus, intensity and length, the palate flavours very convincing, building to a peacock's tail on the finish. Diam. **Rating** 94 **To** 2013 $19

Shiraz 2005 Medium-bodied; black fruits with some licorice and spice on the way through; good length. **Rating** 90 **To** 2012 $15

Word of Mouth Wines ★★★★

Campbell's Corner, Pinnacle Road, Orange, NSW 2800 **Region** Orange
T (02) 6362 3509 **www**.wordofmouthwines.com.au **Open** Fri–Sun & public hols 11–5
Winemaker David Lowe, Jane Wilson (Contract) **Est.** 1991 **Cases** 1500
Word of Mouth Wines acquired the former Donnington Vineyard in 2003, with its 10 ha of mature vineyards, planted (in descending order of size) to sauvignon blanc, chardonnay, merlot, cabernet sauvignon, pinot noir, riesling and pinot gris between 1991 and 1996. Since 1996 all the cabernet sauvignon, and most of the merlot, has been removed, with additional plantings of pinot gris, sauvignon blanc and chardonnay taking their place, along with viognier. Thus the focus is on white wines and pinot noir.

ŸŸŸŸŸ **Orange Riesling 2006** Floral blossom aromas; passionfruit, lime juice and apple; elegance and delicacy. Screwcap. 14° alc. **Rating** 93 **To** 2016 $22
Orange Sauvignon Blanc 2006 Fragrant lime and mineral aromas; a long, intense and vibrant palate with a lingering aftertaste; slightly green characters are the Achilles heel. Screwcap. 13.1° alc. **Rating** 90 **To** 2008 $22

ŸŸŸŸ **Pinnacle Pinot Gris 2006** Strong, focused pear aromas and flavours; plenty of fruit without sweetness. Screwcap. 14.9° alc. **Rating** 88 **To** 2008 $22

Wordsworth Wines

Cnr South Western Highway/Thompson Road, Harvey, WA 6220 **Region** Geographe
T (08) 97373 4576 **F** (08) 9733 4269 **www.**wordsworthwines.com.au **Open** 7 days 10–5
Winemaker Lamont's, Western Range Wines **Est.** 1997 **Cases** 5000
David Wordsworth has established a substantial business in a relatively short space of time: 27 ha of vines have been planted, with cabernet sauvignon (10 ha), shiraz (5 ha) and verdelho (4 ha) predominant, and lesser amounts of zinfandel, petit verdot, chardonnay and chenin blanc. The winery features massive jarrah beams, wrought iron and antique furniture, and the tasting room seats 80 people. The wines have had show success. Exports to the US.

ŸŸŸŸŸ **Geographe Shiraz 2005** Attractive aromas of black cherry, raspberry and blackberry, the light- to medium-bodied palate running down the same road; gently spicy/savoury tannins; good mouthfeel and aftertaste. Screwcap. 14.5° alc. **Rating** 90 **To** 2015 $25

Wovenfield

PO Box 1021, Subiaco, WA 6904 **Region** Geographe
T (08) 9481 3250 **F** (08) 9481 3076 **www.**wovenfield.com **Open** Not
Winemaker Martin Buck, Rienne Buck **Est.** 1997 **Cases** NFP
Martin Buck, together with daughter Rienne, purchased an old dairy farm in 1996, and with advice from an experienced local viticulturist, Phil Gumbrell, came up with a 3-stage planting program. Five hectares of shiraz and semillon were planted in 1997; 7.5 ha of merlot and cabernet sauvignon in 1998; and in 2002 a further 3.5-ha, northwest-facing paddock was partially planted with viognier on a trial basis, the planting extended in 2005 after a successful outcome. Nor have they rested there; in 2004 1.85 ha of merlot and cabernet sauvignon were grafted over to sauvignon blanc, and a small amount of tempranillo planted. They have also formed a highly successful winemaking team, the wines made at the small winery established on the property.

ŸŸŸŸŸ **Marguy Shiraz Viognier 2004** Attractive wine; medium-bodied; spicy aromas with touches of licorice and pepper; fine tannins, gentle new French oak and good length. Screwcap. 14.7° alc. **Rating** 90 **To** 2014 $24

Wright Family Wines

'Misty Glen', 293 Deasey Road, Pokolbin, NSW 2320 **Region** Lower Hunter Valley
T (02) 4998 7781 **F** (02) 4998 7768 **www.**mistyglencottage.com.au **Open** 7 days 10–4
Winemaker Contract **Est.** 1985 **Cases** 1200
Jim and Carol Wright purchased their property in 1985, with a small existing vineyard in need of tender loving care. This was duly given, and the semillon, chardonnay and cabernet sauvignon revived. In 2000, 1.5 ha of shiraz was planted; 1.5 ha of chambourcin was added in 2002, lifting total plantings to 7.5 ha. Carol has been involved in the wine industry since the early 1970s, and is now helped by husband Jim (who retired from the coal mines in 2002), and by children and grandchildren. Wines are released under the Misty Glen Cottage label.

ŸŸŸŸŸ **Misty Glen Cottage Hunter Valley Semillon 2006** Light straw-green; herb, citrus and stone aromas, with a remarkable depth of flavours in the same spectrum with an added touch of lime; great early drinking, but has length for the future. Screwcap. 10.4° alc. **Rating** 94 **To** 2013 $23

ŸŸŸŸ♀ **Misty Glen Cottage Hunter Valley Shiraz 2005** Despite the relatively modest alcohol, has unusual power and concentration for the Hunter; black fruits, mocha, sweet leather and earth all waiting to make their presence felt; good oak and tannins. Screwcap. 13° alc. **Rating** 92 **To** 2025 $23

ŸŸŸŸ **Misty Glen Cottage Hunter Valley Cabernet Sauvignon 2005** Once again, above-average for the Hunter Valley, particularly in terms of varietal expression; early picking has worked wonders, providing gentle cassis and blackcurrant fruit supported by fine tannins. Screwcap. 12° alc. **Rating** 89 **To** 2015 $25

Wroxton Wines ★★★★

Flaxman's Valley Road, Angaston, SA 5353 **Region** Eden Valley
T (08) 8565 3227 **F** (08) 8565 3312 **www**.wroxton.com.au **Open** By appt
Winemaker Stephen Henschke, Christian Canute (Contract) **Est.** 1995 **Cases** 90
Ian and Jo Zander are third-generation grapegrowers on the 200-ha Wroxton Grange property, which was established in 1845 in the high country of the Eden Valley. The Zander family purchased the property in 1920, and planted their first vines; since 1973 an extensive planting program has seen the progressive establishment of riesling (15.4 ha), shiraz (10.5 ha), chardonnay (6.9 ha), semillon (2.5 ha) and traminer (2 ha). The majority of the grapes are sold, the best parcels from the mature vineyards retained to produce single vineyard wines.

ŸŸŸŸ♀ **Single Vineyard Eden Valley Riesling 2004** Tightly constructed and textured riesling, only just starting to unfurl its sails; will go from strength to strength. Screwcap. 12° alc. **Rating** 91 **To** 2012 $19.50

Wyanga Park ★★★

Baades Road, Lakes Entrance, Vic 3909 **Region** Gippsland
T (03) 5155 1508 **F** (03) 5155 1443 **Open** 7 days 9–5
Winemaker Damien Twigg **Est.** 1970 **Cases** 3000
Offers a broad range of wines of diverse provenance directed at the tourist trade; one of the Chardonnays, and the Cabernet Sauvignon are estate-grown. Winery cruises up the north arm of the Gippsland Lake to Wyanga Park are scheduled 4 days a week all year.

ŸŸŸŸ **Sauvignon Blanc 2005** An abundance of ripe, rich flavours made for immediate drinking. **Rating** 87 **To** 2008

Wyndham Estate ★★★★

700 Dalwood Road, Dalwood, NSW 2335 **Region** Lower Hunter Valley
T (02) 4938 3444 **www**.wyndhamestate.com **Open** 7 days 10–4.30 except public hols
Winemaker Sam Kurtz **Est.** 1828 **Cases** 1 million
This historic property is now merely a shopfront for the Wyndham Estate label. The Bin wines often surprise with their quality, representing excellent value; the Show Reserve wines, likewise, can be very good. The wines come from various parts of South East Australia, sometimes specified, sometimes not.

ŸŸŸŸŸ **Bin 777 Semillon Sauvignon Blanc 2006** A remarkable wine which appeared in the large-volume commercial class at the National Wine Show '06, taking the only gold and dispatching some very distinguished wines in so doing. Vibrant and crunchy, with great structure and flavour; above all else, did not rely on the residual sugar rampant in the class. Screwcap. 13° alc. **Rating** 94 **To** 2008 $11

ŸŸŸŸ♀ **Black Cluster Hunter Valley Shiraz 2003** Light- to medium-bodied; elegant wine with well-balanced fruit, oak and tannins; single vineyard wine which won a gold medal at the Hunter Valley Wine Show '06. I'm not persuaded the price is justified, however, even if it is a single vineyard. Cork. 13.5° alc. **Rating** 90 **To** 2011 $65

♥♥♥♥ Bin 999 Merlot 2005 An extremely creditable wine at this price point; has genuine varietal character, good balance and length. Said to come from Langhorne Creek/Padthaway/Adelaide Hills, which explains the quality, but not the price. Cork. 14.5° alc. **Rating** 89 **To** 2011 $13.95

Regional Selection Hunter Valley Shiraz 2000 After 7 years, has certainly developed regional character; earthy/leathery/spicy flavours and good length, just a little lacking on the mid-palate. Cork. **Rating** 88 **To** 2010 $29.95

Bin 888 Cabernet Merlot 2004 Plenty of character and varietal typicity, with no apparent use of sugar to soften the impact, or otherwise appeal to the broader public; also has good tannin structure, oak largely absent. Screwcap. **Rating** 88 **To** 2010 $13.95

Bin 444 Cabernet Sauvignon 2004 Continues the theme for these Bin wines; they neither under- nor over-deliver, and can be routinely depended on to present true varietal character in an unostentatious, medium-bodied frame when you have top vintages such as '04. Screwcap. **Rating** 88 **To** 2010 $13.95

Bin 505 Shiraz Rose 2006 Vivid fuchsia; has the broadest possible appeal, offending no-one but thrilling few. Screwcap. 13.5° alc. **Rating** 87 **To** 2008 $14

Bin 333 Pinot Noir 2006 A surprise packet; pinot noir fruit characters are only just there, but the wine has good structure and balance, and is fairly priced. Screwcap. **Rating** 87 **To** 2008 $13.95

Bin 555 Shiraz 2004 Quite fragrant sweet fruits on the bouquet; a similar palate, the seductive touch of sweetness on the finish will please some and displease others. Won a gold medal at the Cairns Wine Show, which has been a happy hunting ground for some pot hunters. Screwcap. **Rating** 87 **To** 2008 $13.95

Wynns Coonawarra Estate

Memorial Drive, Coonawarra, SA 5263 **Region** Coonawarra
T (08) 8736 3266 **F** (08) 8736 3202 **www**.wynns.com.au **Open** 7 days 10–5
Winemaker Sue Hodder **Est.** 1897 **Cases** NFP
Large-scale production has not prevented Wynns from producing excellent wines covering the full price spectrum, from the bargain basement Riesling and Shiraz through to the deluxe John Riddoch Cabernet Sauvignon and Michael Shiraz. Even with steady price increases, Wynns offers extraordinary value for money. Good though that may be, there is even greater promise for the future; the vineyards are being rejuvenated by new trellising or replanting, and a regime directed to quality rather than quantity has been introduced, under the direction of Allen Jenkins. Exports to the UK, the US and other major markets.

♥♥♥♥♥ Michael Limited Release Shiraz 2002 Very good colour; a lovely wine, much more restrained and elegant than prior releases; plum and blackberry fruit; fine tannins, very good oak and restrained alcohol. Cork. 13.5° alc. **Rating** 96 **To** 2017 $75

John Riddoch Cabernet Sauvignon 2004 Richness in terms of the multi-layered texture is the first impression, then complexity in the multifaceted nuances of different levels of ripeness (none extreme) in the cabernet sauvignon; harmony in length and sheer class on the finish. Screwcap. 13.5° alc. **Rating** 96 **To** 2029 $72.95

John Riddoch Cabernet Sauvignon 2003 Much better colour than the Cabernet Sauvignon; classic cassis and blackcurrant fruit in abundance, yet not going over the top. A beautiful wine. Cork. 13.5° alc. **Rating** 96 **To** 2023 $75

Michael Limited Release Shiraz 2004 Powerful, intense and firm black fruits with balanced oak; will be very long-lived. Screwcap. 13.5° alc. **Rating** 95 **To** 2024 $72.95

Riesling 2005 A year ago I wrote 'simply needing time to flower and garner higher points' (then 89 points). Over the ensuing year it has done precisely that; while still very fresh and delicate, it has that unique Coonawarra apple blossom and flavour profile, with a long dry finish. Gold medal Sydney Wine Show '07. Screwcap. 12.5° alc. **Rating** 94 **To** 2013 $16.95

Cabernet Sauvignon 2004 Medium-bodied; but complex; flavours come from black fruits and licorice; from oak, but not over the top; and from tannins (ripe). The wine has considerable length and finesse, and will be long-lived. Gold medal Sydney Wine Show '07. Cork. 13.5° alc. **Rating** 94 **To** 2024 $29.95

ŸŸŸŸŸ **Shiraz 2005** An elegant, medium-bodied wine; the ripe fruit has returned to Coonawarra in '05; blackberry with some spice and cracked pepper; fine, ripe tannins and good oak. Cork. 14° alc. **Rating** 93 **To** 2020 $18.95

Cabernet Shiraz Merlot 2005 Supple, sweet entry to the mouth, ranging through red and black fruits; tightens up somewhat on the finish, simply promising cellaring potential. Cork. 13.5° alc. **Rating** 91 **To** 2020 $18.95

Chardonnay 2005 A medium-bodied wine with obvious barrel-ferment, mlf and lees inputs; creamy, cashew overtones to stone fruit flavours; soft finish and controlled oak. Screwcap. 13.5° alc. **Rating** 90 **To** 2010 $16.95

Cabernet Sauvignon 2003 Developed colour; medium-bodied blackcurrant, mocha and cedar aromas and flavours; good control of extract, the oak balanced. Cork. 13.5° alc. **Rating** 90 **To** 2013 $30

Cabernet Shiraz Merlot 2004 Medium-bodied; an appealing interplay of cedary/earthy/spicy flavours on the medium-bodied palate. Cork. 13.5° alc. **Rating** 90 **To** 2012 $18.95

Wyuna Park ★★☆

105 Soho Road, Drysdale, Vic 3222 (postal) **Region** Geelong
T (03) 5253 1348 **F** (03) 5253 2801 **Open** Not
Winemaker Bill Sawyer, Curlewis **Est.** 1998 **Cases** 150
Former professor of biochemistry and molecular biology at the University of Melbourne Bill Sawyer, and wife Diana, planted 1.6 ha of pinot noir and 0.4 ha of pinot gris between 1998 and 1999. The intention was to sell the grapes to other wineries, but in 2004 they could not resist the temptation to start making Pinot Noir at the estate. Bill Sawyer teaches biochemistry in the wine course at Dookie College, his winemaking at the estate putting theory into practice. The Pinot Gris is made by Rainer Breit at Curlewis. An unusual application of the pinot noir is partly as a saignee rose and partly as a fortified wine, although the main portion is made conventionally.

Xabregas ★★★☆

Cnr Spencer Road/Hay River Road, Narrikup, WA 6326 **Region** Mount Barker
T (08) 9321 2366 **F** (08) 9327 9393 **www**.xabregas.com.au **Open** By appt
Winemaker Dr Diane Miller, Greg Jones, Mike Garland (Contract) **Est.** 1996 **Cases** 15 000
In 1996 stockbrokers Terry Hogan and Eve Broadley, the major participants in the Spencer Wine Joint Venture, commenced a viticulture business which has now grown into 3 vineyards totalling 120 ha on sites 10 km south of Mount Barker. The varieties planted are riesling, chardonnay, sauvignon blanc, cabernet sauvignon, cabernet franc, merlot and shiraz. As well as being contract growers to Houghton, Howard Park and Forest Hill, they act as contract managers to surrounding vineyards. Fifteen thousand cases of wine are made for the Xabregas label. The wines are modestly priced. Exports to NZ and China.

ŸŸŸŸŸ **Mount Barker Shiraz 2005** A substantial wine; savoury/spicy edges to the core of blackberry fruit; good control of extract and tannins. Screwcap. 14.2° alc. **Rating** 90 **To** 2020 $14

ŸŸŸŸ **Rose 2006** Light-bodied but well-balanced; light fruit flavours without excessive sweetness make for a pleasant lunch rose. Screwcap. 12.6° alc. **Rating** 87 **To** 2008 $14

Mount Barker Shiraz 2004 Medium red-purple; sweet red and black fruits on entry, then assertive tannins take over, breaking the line of the wine. Screwcap. 14° alc. **Rating** 87 **To** 2010 $14

Xanadu Wines

Boodjidup Road, Margaret River, WA 6285 **Region** Margaret River
T (08) 9757 2581 **F** (08) 9757 3389 **www**.xanaduwines.com **Open** 7 days 10–5
Winemaker Glenn Goodall **Est.** 1977 **Cases** 65 000
Xanadu fell prey to over-ambitious expansion and to the increasingly tight trading conditions in 2005 as wine surpluses hit hard. The assets were acquired by the Rathbone Group, completing the Yering Station/Mount Langi Ghiran/Parker Coonawarra Estate/Xanadu group. The prime assets were (and are) the 130 ha of vineyards and a winery to match. The increasing production is matched by exports to 18 markets, led by the UK and the US.

ΨΨΨΨΨ **Margaret River Chardonnay 2005** Quite aromatic, with some blossom aromas; light citrus, apple and stone fruit, with minimal oak; good length and finish. Screwcap. 14° alc. **Rating** 91 **To** 2013 $25

ΨΨΨΨ **Dragon Margaret River Cabernet Merlot 2005** Aromatic red and black spicy fruits on the bouquet; soft tannins provide the texture and mouthfeel of a very nice wine. 14° alc. **Rating** 89 **To** 2012 $16
Dragon Margaret River Sauvignon Blanc Semillon 2006 Clean, tangy aromas; crisp, fresh and lively, with a mix of tropical and more grassy flavours. Screwcap. 12.5° alc. **Rating** 88 **To** 2008 $16
Dragon Margaret River Unoaked Chardonnay 2006 Has enough life, freshness and citrussy acidity to lift it from the ruck, and invest it with length. Screwcap. 12.5° alc. **Rating** 87 **To** 2009 $16

Yabby Lake Vineyard ★★★★★

1 Garden Street, South Yarra, Vic 3141 (postal) **Region** Mornington Peninsula
T (03) 9251 5375 **F** (03) 9639 1540 **www**.yabbylake.com **Open** Not
Winemaker Tod Dexter, Larry McKenna **Est.** 1998 **Cases** 3350
This high-profile wine business is owned by Robert and Mem Kirby (of Village Roadshow) who have been landowners in the Mornington Peninsula for decades. In 1998 they established Yabby Lake Vineyard, under the direction of vineyard manager Keith Harris; the vineyard is on a north-facing slope, capturing maximum sunshine while also receiving sea breezes. The main focus is the 21 ha of pinot noir, 10 ha of chardonnay and 5 ha of pinot gris; the 2 ha each of shiraz and merlot take a back seat. Tod Dexter (former long-term winemaker at Stonier) and Larry McKenna (ex Martinborough Vineyards and now the Escarpment in NZ) both have great experience.

ΨΨΨΨΨ **Mornington Peninsula Chardonnay 2005** A totally harmonious and seamless fusion of melon/nectarine fruit and oak in a continuous line and flow; long finish. Diam. 13.5° alc. **Rating** 95 **To** 2020 $43
Mornington Peninsula Pinot Noir 2005 Very richly upholstered pinot noir, with plush and velvety plummy fruit; good balance and length; could be something special with enough time in the bottle. Diam. 14° alc. **Rating** 95 **To** 2015 $60

Yacca Paddock Vineyards

PO Box 824, Kent Town, SA 5071 **Region** Adelaide Hills
T (08) 8362 3397 **F** (08) 8363 3797 **www**.yaccapaddock.com **Open** Not
Winemaker Mr Riggs Wine Company **Est.** 2000 **Cases** 500
Filmmakers Kerry Heysen-Hicks and husband Scott Hicks have left little to chance in establishing Yacca Paddock Vineyards. The vineyards (22 ha) have been established under the direction of leading viticulturist Geoff Hardy, and the wines are made by equally illustrious winemaker Ben Riggs. The vineyard is at an altitude of 350 m in the Adelaide Hills, and all of the vines are netted. In descending order of size the rainbow selection of varieties is chardonnay, pinot noir, tempranillo, merlot, cabernet sauvignon, riesling, sauvignon blanc, shiraz, arneis, dolcetto, tannat and durif.

TTTT **Adelaide Hills Tempranillo 2005** Deep colour; packs a ferocious flavour bite of pickled cherries; demands attention (and food). Screwcap. 15° alc. **Rating** 89 To 2015 $25

Yaccaroo Wines ★★★

PO Box 201, Yankalilla, SA 5203 **Region** Southern Fleurieu
T (08) 8558 3218 **Open** Not
Winemaker Justin Lane **Est.** 2004 **Cases** 260
Gavin and Julianne Schubert planted 2 ha of shiraz in 1998, followed by 2.2 ha of cabernet sauvignon in 1999. The original intention was to simply sell the grapes, but oversupply in the grape market has led to part of the production being made for the Yaccaroo wines.

TTTT **Northern Fleurieu Shiraz 2004** Soft, spicy red and black fruits have been overcome by too much vanilla American oak, which is a pity, though some will simply love it. Diam. 14.8° alc. **Rating** 88 To 2014 $18

Yalumba

Eden Valley Road, Angaston, SA 5353 **Region** Barossa Valley
T (08) 8561 3200 www.yalumba.com **Open** Mon–Fri 8.30–5, Sat 10–5, Sun 12–5
Winemaker Louisa Rose (chief), Brian Walsh, Alan Hoey, Peter Gambetta **Est.** 1849
Cases 950 000
Family-owned and run by Robert Hill Smith; much of its prosperity in the late 1980s and early 1990s turned on the great success of Angas Brut in export markets, but the company has always had a commitment to quality and shown great vision in its selection of vineyard sites, new varieties and brands. It has always been a serious player at the top end of full-bodied (and full-blooded) Australian reds, and was the pioneer in the use of screwcaps (for Pewsey Vale Riesling). While its 940 ha of estate vineyards are largely planted to mainstream varieties, it has taken marketing ownership of Viognier. Exports to all major markets.

TTTTT **Eden Valley Viognier 2005** Abundant aromas and flavours of peach, apricot and spice, with a typical full-bodied texture and structure, but which avoids phenolics on the powerful finish. Screwcap. 14.5° alc. **Rating** 94 To 2008 $21.95
Hand Picked Shiraz Viognier 2004 Typical bright, deep colour; bursting with vibrant black fruits, spice and the lift of viognier; tannins, oak and alcohol all under tight control. Dreadnought bottle and a very ordinary stained cork. 14.5° alc. **Rating** 94 To 2014 $29
The Octavius Old Vine Barossa Shiraz 2003 In hallmark Octavius style, immensely powerful and deep, with chunky black fruits, yet not extractive and with no porty/jammy characters. Gold medal National Wine Show '06. Cork. 14° alc. **Rating** 94 To 2023 $89.95
The Signature Cabernet Shiraz 2003 Medium-bodied; balanced fruit is supported by distinctly savoury/earthy lingering tannins. Gold medal National Wine Show '06; 54%/44%. Cork. 14° alc. **Rating** 94 To 2015 $42.95

TTTTT **Limited Release Sangiovese Rose 2006** The fresh, light pink colour announces flowery, vibrant cherry blossom aromas, cherry persisting on a palate with excellent length, and balanced by a delicious touch of acidity on the finish. Screwcap. 13° alc. **Rating** 93 To 2008 $12
Y Series Sauvignon Blanc 2006 Pale straw-green, it has pristine varietal aromas of cut grass and spice, the light but vibrant palate with citrus fruit and a clean, brisk, dry finish. Screwcap. 11° alc. **Rating** 91 To 2008 $12
Ringbolt Margaret River Cabernet Sauvignon 2004 Clear varietal character to the medium-bodied palate; blackcurrant, cedar and earth; positive tannin and oak contributions. Cork. 14.5° alc. **Rating** 91 To 2014 $23
Hand Picked Barossa Tempranillo Grenache Viognier 2005 An aromatic, lifted red fruit bouquet; light- to medium-bodied, the fresh fruit in a sour cherry spectrum; fine tannins. The varieties are co-fermented. Screwcap. 13.5° alc. **Rating** 90 To 2015 $29

🍷🍷🍷🍷 Oxford Landing Sauvignon Blanc 2006 Once again shows an ability to rise above its region and status in life; tropical varietal fruit in abundance. Screwcap. 11° alc. **Rating** 88 To 2008 $8
Oxford Landing Merlot 2005 Bright, fresh fruit; terrific value at the price; light- to medium-bodied raspberry and redcurrant fruit; fine, soft tannins. Screwcap. 14° alc. **Rating** 88 To 2008 $8

Yalumba The Menzies (Coonawarra)   ★★★★☆

Riddoch Highway, Coonawarra, SA 5263 **Region** Coonawarra
T (08) 8737 3603 **F** (08) 8737 3604 **www**.yalumba.com **Open** 7 days 10–4.30
Winemaker Peter Gambetta **Est.** 2002 **Cases** 5000
Like many SA companies, Yalumba had been buying grapes from Coonawarra and elsewhere in the Limestone Coast Zone long before it became a landowner there. In 1993 it purchased the 20-ha vineyard which had provided the grapes previously purchased, and a year later added a nearby 16-ha block. Together, these vineyards now have 22 ha of cabernet sauvignon and 4 ha each of merlot and shiraz. The next step was the establishment of 82 ha of vineyard in the Wrattonbully region, led by 34 ha of cabernet sauvignon, the remainder equally split between shiraz and merlot. The third step was to build The Menzies Wine Room on the first property acquired – named Menzies Vineyard – and to offer the full range of Limestone Coast wines through this striking rammed-earth tasting and function centre. Exports to all major markets.

🍷🍷🍷🍷🍷 **Mawson's Wrattonbully Sauvignon Blanc 2006** Highly aromatic, with just a hint of sweatiness; positive varietal flavour and character throughout. Screwcap. 11.5° alc. **Rating** 90 To 2008 $14.95
Smith & Hooper Reserve Wrattonbully Merlot 2004 Big, powerful wine with dark fruits, more to cabernet in style, but you can't deny the flavour. Cork. 14° alc. **Rating** 90 To 2015 $36.95

🍷🍷🍷🍷 **Mawson's Bridge Block 7A Wrattonbully Sauvignon Blanc 2006** A clean but subdued bouquet; lemon and gooseberry fruit supported by crunchy, yet fruity, acidity; good value. Screwcap. 11.5° alc. **Rating** 89 To 2008 $15
Smith & Hooper Wrattonbully Cabernet Merlot 2004 Medium-bodied; supple structure and mouthfeel; well-balanced spice and black fruits; fractionally dilute. Cork. 14° alc. **Rating** 88 To 2012 $16.95

Yangarra Estate   ★★★★☆

Kangarilla Road, McLaren Vale, SA 5171 **Region** McLaren Vale
T (08) 8383 7459 **F** (08) 8383 7518 **www**.yangarra.com **Open** By appt
Winemaker Peter Fraser **Est.** 2000 **Cases** 12 000
This is the Australian operation of Kendall-Jackson, one of the leading premium wine producers in California. In 2000 Kendall-Jackson acquired the 172-ha Eringa Park vineyard from Normans Wines (97 ha are under vine, the oldest dating back to 1923). The renamed Yangarra Estate is the estate base for the operation, which has, so it would seem, remained much smaller than originally envisaged by Jess Jackson. Exports to the US and Europe.

Yarra Brook Estate   ★★★☆

Yarraview Road, Yarra Glen, Vic 3775 **Region** Yarra Valley
T (03) 9763 7066 **F** (03) 9763 8757 **www**.yarrabrook.com.au **Open** By appt
Winemaker Timo Mayer, Charlie Brydon (Contract) **Est.** 1997 **Cases** 2000
Since 1997 Yarra Brook Estate has established 26 ha of vineyard, planted (in descending order) to pinot noir, chardonnay, cabernet sauvignon, sauvignon blanc, shiraz and merlot. While most of the grapes are sold to other producers, production under the Yarra Brook label has increased.

Yarra Burn

Settlement Road, Yarra Junction, Vic 3797 **Region** Yarra Valley
T (03) 5967 1428 **F** (03) 5967 1146 **www**.yarraburn.com.au **Open** 7 days 10–5
Winemaker Mark O'Callaghan **Est.** 1975 **Cases** 15 000
Acquired by Hardys in 1995 and, for the time being, the headquarters of Hardys' very substantial Yarra Valley operations, the latter centring on the large production from its Hoddles Creek vineyards. The new brand direction has largely taken shape. Exports to the UK and the US.

ɪɪɪɪɪ Yarra Valley Chardonnay Pinot Noir Pinot Meunier 2004 Super-fine, elegant and harmonious; excellent balance and length, with lovely flavours. Perhaps lacks the complexity of extended lees contact, but what is there is irresistible. 13° alc. **Rating** 94 **To** 2010 $21.99

ɪɪɪɪↄ Yarra Valley Chardonnay Pinot Noir Pinot Meunier 2002 Fine and elegant, with intense citrussy fruit, then a long finish, dry and refreshing. 13° alc. **Rating** 93 **To** 2008 $21
Pinot Noir 2004 An aromatic plum, forest and spice bouquet; an elegant light-to medium-bodied wine with good varietal definition and length. Cork. 13° alc. **Rating** 91 **To** 2010 $24
Pinot Noir Chardonnay Rose 2003 Blush pink; strangely, less developed than the '04 Pinot Noir Chardonnay Pinot Meunier; an easy style with good balance. 13° alc. **Rating** 90 **To** 2010 $21.99

ɪɪɪ Third Light Sauvignon Blanc 2006 Clean, chiselled, flavours and structured; slate, green pea, asparagus and citrus, the last lingering on the finish. Screwcap. 13° alc. **Rating** 89 **To** 2008 $15.95
Chardonnay 2004 Amazingly pale; still a baby, with bright, crisp citrus and nectarine fruit; controlled oak; demands time, but a tatty cork is a worry. 13° alc. **Rating** 89 **To** 2010 $21
Third Light Shiraz 2004 Attractive, light- to medium-bodied wine; spicy black cherry fruit; fine, supple tannins. Well-priced. Screwcap. 13.5° alc. **Rating** 89 **To** 2010 $15

Yarra Ridge

Fosters, GPO Box 753F, Melbourne Vic 3001 **Region** Yarra Valley
T (03) 8626 3300 **www**.yarraridge.com.au **Open** Not
Winemaker Joanna Marsh **Est.** 1983 **Cases** 37 000
Yarra Ridge wines will continue to be made in the Yarra Valley, and aged at Seppelt (Great Western) under the guidance of Joanna Marsh. The white wines will be crushed and pressed in the Yarra Valley, and fermented at Seppelt; the reds will be pressed and fermented at Sticks, and sent to Great Western for mlf and finishing.

ɪɪɪ Pinot Noir 2005 Excellent wine at the price; what it lacks in intensity it makes up in style, and, to a degree, complexity; a nice blend of spicy/stemmy notes and typical Yarra Valley red fruits. Screwcap. 13° alc. **Rating** 89 **To** 2010 $16
Eye Spy Cabernet Merlot 2004 Medium-bodied; a core of sweet cassis fruit with savoury/olive surrounds; good varietal expression. Screwcap. 14° alc. **Rating** 88 **To** 2009 $16
Unwooded Chardonnay 2005 Stone fruit, melon fruit typical of the variety and region; good balance and length, even at this level. Screwcap. 13° alc. **Rating** 87 **To** 2009 $20.95

Yarra Track Wines

518 Old Healesville Road, Yarra Glen, Vic 3775 **Region** Yarra Valley
T (03) 9730 1349 **F** (03) 9730 1910 **www**.yarratrackwines.com.au **Open** 7 days 10–5.30
Winemaker Al Fencaros, Jeff Wright **Est.** 1989 **Cases** 600

Jim and Diana Viggers began establishing their vineyard back in 1989; it now has 3.1 ha of chardonnay and 3.5 ha of pinot noir. The Viggers intend to increase wine production progressively, and sell part of the grape production in the meantime.

ΨΨΨΨΨ **Hamish's Pinot Noir 2005** An elegant, smooth and supple light- to medium-bodied wine; silky texture to a display of red and black fruits; some tannins on the back palate need to soften. Screwcap. 13.9° alc. **Rating** 93 **To** 2012 $27

Yarra Vale

Paynes Road, Seville, Vic 3139 **Region** Yarra Valley
T (03) 9735 1819 **F** (03) 9737 6565 **Open** Not
Winemaker Domenic Bucci **Est.** 1982 **Cases** 1500
This is the second time around for Domenic Bucci, who built the first stage of Eyton-on-Yarra (now Rochford) before being compelled to sell the business in the hard times of the early 1990s. He has established 2 ha of cabernet sauvignon and 0.5 ha of merlot, supplemented by chardonnay which is supplied in return for his winemaking services to the grower.

Yarra Valley Gateway Estate

669 Maroondah Highway, Coldstream, Vic 3770 **Region** Yarra Valley
T (03) 9739 0568 **F** (03) 9739 0568 **www**.gatewayestate.com.au **Open** 7 days 9–5
Winemaker Matt Aldridge (Contract) **Est.** 1993 **Cases** 2150
Rod Spurling extended his successful hydroponic tomato-growing business by planting 5 ha of sauvignon blanc, chardonnay and pinot noir in 1993. This is part of the grouping of so-called Micro Masters in the Yarra Valley.

ΨΨΨΨΨ **Spurling Hill Vineyard Sauvignon Blanc 2006** Quite ripe, with some tropical fruit; has seen some older oak barriques; crisp authoritative finish. **Rating** 91 **To** 2008 $17

ΨΨΨΨ **Spurling Hill Vineyard Chardonnay 2006** A firm fruit profile; solidly constructed from start to finish, with 40% new French oak well-balanced and integrated. **Rating** 89 **To** 2012
Spurling Hill Vineyard Pinot Noir 2006 Whole bunch-pressed into older barrels; crisp, clean and well-balanced; attractive food style, with a totally dry finish. **Rating** 87 **To** 2008

Yarra Yarra

239 Hunts Lane, Steels Creek, Vic 3775 **Region** Yarra Valley
T (03) 5965 2380 **F** (03) 5965 2086 **Open** By appt
Winemaker Ian Maclean **Est.** 1979 **Cases** NFP
Despite its small production, the wines of Yarra Yarra found their way onto a veritable who's who of Melbourne's best restaurants, encouraging Ian Maclean to increase the estate plantings from 2 ha to over 7 ha in 1996 and 1997. Demand for the beautifully crafted wines continued to exceed supply, so the Macleans have planted yet more vines and increased winery capacity. Exports to the UK and Singapore.

ΨΨΨΨΨ **Syrah Viognier 2005** Very, very rich, yet reflects its alcohol; classic blackberry and spice with firm tannins, and has swallowed up the viognier; redefines the taste borders of Yarra Valley shiraz. Diam. 13.5° alc. **Rating** 96 **To** 2025 $45
The Yarra Yarra 2004 Tight, elegant and classic, reminiscent of the Mount Mary style; nothing overstated or over-extracted; effortless power and intensity to the dark blackcurrant fruit; great texture and mouthfeel. Cork. 13.5° alc. **Rating** 96 **To** 2019 $70
Reserve Merlot 2004 There is an intensity to the mouthfeel and flavour which is strongly varietal; olive, bracken and potent cassis fruit all interwoven; love it or hate it style. Cork. 13.5° alc. **Rating** 95 **To** 2020 $70

Sauvignon Blanc Semillon 2004 Typical Yarra Yarra style, with a complete fusion of the varieties and oak in the manner of white Bordeaux; has great length, good balance and natural acidity; ambitious pricing. Diam. 13° alc. Rating 94 To 2012 $40

ŢŢŢŢŢ **Cabernets 2004** Unequivocally the lightest-bodied of the Yarra Yarra reds; notes of briar and bush along with black fruits, and fractionally green tannins. Diam. 13° alc. **Rating** 90 To 2014 $50

Yarra Yering ★★★★★

Briarty Road, Coldstream, Vic 3770 **Region** Yarra Valley
T (03) 5964 9267 **F** (03) 5964 9239 **Open** Sat 10–5, Sun 2–5 while stocks last
Winemaker Bailey Carrodus, Mark Haisma **Est.** 1969 **Cases** 10 000
Dr Bailey Carrodus makes extremely powerful, occasionally idiosyncratic, wines from his 40-year-old, low-yielding unirrigated vineyards. Both red and white wines have an exceptional depth of flavour and richness, although my preference for what I believe to be his great red wines is well known. As he has expanded the size of his vineyards, so has the range of wines become ever more eclectic, none more so than the only Vintage Port being produced in the Yarra Valley. Exports to the UK, the US and other major markets.

ŢŢŢŢŢ **Dry Red No. 2 2004** Fragrant red and black fruits on the bouquet; wonderfully fine and silky mouthfeel, with lovely red fruit flavours, the finest tannins and seamless oak. One of the best ever Dry Red No. 2. Shiraz/Viognier/Marsanne. Cork. 14° alc. **Rating** 96 To 2024 $65
Dry Red No. 1 2004 Medium- to medium-full-bodied; an outstanding expression of Bordeaux varieties at perfect ripeness, new oak handling impeccable; fine, ripe tannins; exceptional length of palate and aftertaste. Cork. 13° alc. **Rating** 96 To 2034 $65
Pinot Noir 2004 Spicy, foresty, stemmy aromas; intense flavours with plum and cherry at the epicentre, the aromas tracking through in the background; clean and crisp, with a long finish. Cork. 14° alc. **Rating** 94 To 2013 $65
Portsorts 2004 Inky purple-black; tremendously complex, concentrated and powerful; more suitable for a 50th anniversary/birthday than a 21st; layer-upon-layer of black fruits, and not too sweet. Cork. 22° alc. **Rating** 94 To 2050 $65

ŢŢŢŢŢ **Underhill Shiraz 2004** Medium-bodied; highly spicy/cracked pepper/black cherry/blackberry fruit; fine, persistent tannins, and good length. Cork. 14.5° alc. **Rating** 93 To 2019 $65
Chardonnay 2004 Rich, layered, complex stone fruit, with some citrus; subtle oak; continues the run of stylish wines in recent vintages. Cork. 14° alc. **Rating** 92 To 2013 $65
New Vineyard Dry Red No. 1 2004 Medium red-purple; a light- to medium-bodied mix, predominantly cassis/blackcurrant, with some herb and olive notes. Cork. 13° alc. **Rating** 90 To 2019 $65

Yarrabank ★★★★★

38 Melba Highway, Yarra Glen, Vic 3775 **Region** Yarra Valley
T (03) 9730 0100 **F** (03) 9730 0135 **www**.yering.com **Open** 7 days 10–5
Winemaker Michel Parisot, Tom Carson, Darren Rathbone **Est.** 1993 **Cases** 5000
The 1997 vintage saw the opening of the majestic new winery, established as part of a joint venture between the French Champagne house Devaux and Yering Station. Until 1997 the Yarrabank Cuvee Brut was made under Claude Thibaut's direction at Domaine Chandon, but thereafter the entire operation has been conducted at Yarrabank. There are now 4 ha of dedicated 'estate' vineyards at Yering Station; the balance of the intake comes from other growers in the Yarra Valley and southern Vic. Wine quality has been quite outstanding, the wines having a delicacy unmatched by any other Australian sparkling wines. Exports to all major markets.

♀♀♀♀♀ **Late Disgorged 1998** Full-straw colour but with fine mousse; the late disgorged strategy, with no dosage, has worked brilliantly; a lovely bready/yeasty overlay; absolutely no need of dosage; long and precise. **Rating** 96 **To** 2010 $45

YarraLoch   ★★★★★

36 Mary Street, St Kilda West, Vic 3182 (postal) **Region** Yarra Valley
T (03) 9525 4275 **F** (03) 9534 7539 **www**.yarraloch.com.au **Open** Not
Winemaker Sergio Carlei **Est.** 1998 **Cases** 4500
This is the ambitious project of successful investment banker Stephen Wood. He has taken the best possible advice, and has not hesitated to provide appropriate financial resources to a venture which has no exact parallel in the Yarra Valley or anywhere else in Australia. Twelve ha of vineyards may not seem so unusual, but in fact he has assembled 3 entirely different sites, 70 km apart, each matched to the needs of the variety/varieties planted on that site. The 4.4 ha of pinot noir are on the Steep Hill Vineyard, with a northeast orientation, and a shaley rock and ironstone soil. The 4 ha of cabernet sauvignon have been planted on a vineyard at Kangaroo Ground, with a dry, steep northwest-facing site and abundant sun exposure in the warmest part of the day, ensuring full ripeness of the cabernet. Just over 3.5 ha of merlot, shiraz, chardonnay and viognier are planted at the Upper Plenty vineyard, 50 km from Kangaroo Ground. This has an average temperature 2° cooler and a ripening period 2–3 weeks later than the warmest parts of the Yarra Valley. Add the winemaking skills of Sergio Carlei, and some sophisticated (and beautiful) packaging, and you have a 5-star recipe for success.

♀♀♀♀♀ **Yarra Valley Chardonnay 2005** Elegant perfumed peach blossom aromas; fine and yet very intense nectarine and grapefruit; long finish, the oak a bystander. Screwcap. 13.5° alc. **Rating** 95 **To** 2018 $32
The Collection Shiraz Viognier 2004 Vivid, strong purple-red; potent high-toned plum, spice and blackberry fruit, intense and long; very good oak integration and balance. Cork. 14° alc. **Rating** 95 **To** 2015 $40
Yarra Valley Chardonnay 2004 Supple and smooth; great mouthfeel to the melon and nectarine fruit; long finish; subtle oak throughout. Screwcap. 13° alc. **Rating** 94 **To** 2010 $30
Yarra Valley Pinot Noir 2004 A fragrant and complex mix of spice, forest floor and stem, together with potent black cherry fruit; good length and intensity, finishing with fine tannins. Diam. 13.5° alc. **Rating** 94 **To** 2011 $25

♀♀♀♀♀ **Stephanie's Dream Yarra Valley Cabernet Sauvignon 2003** Bright hue; a light- to medium-bodied, elegant wine with blackcurrant and cassis fruit, quality oak and fine tannins; long finish; refined. Cork. 13.5° alc. **Rating** 92 **To** 2014 $40

♀♀♀♀ **Yarra Valley Arneis 2005** Lacks particular fruit distinction, though it is pleasant, with a light mix of tropical and pear fruit. The limitation of the variety rather than the winemaking. Screwcap. 13° alc. **Rating** 89 **To** 2008 $25

Yarraman Estate   ★★☆

Yarraman Road, Wybong, NSW 2333 **Region** Upper Hunter Valley
T (02) 6547 8118 **F** (02) 6547 8039 **www**.yarramanestate.com **Open** 7 days 10–5
Winemaker Chris Mennie **Est.** 1958 **Cases** 55 000
This is the oldest winery and vineyard in the Upper Hunter, established in 1958 as Penfolds Wybong Estate; it was acquired by Rosemount in 1974, and retained until 1994. During 1999–2001 a new winery and storage area was built; after hitting financial turbulence it was acquired by a small group of Sydney businessmen. Board changes and subsequent strengthening of the management and winemaking team have seen a surge in exports to all major markets.

♀♀♀♀ **Classic Hunter Chardonnay 2006** The tangy fruit is moderately intense and long; has some potential. **Rating** 87 **To** 2010 $22.95

Yarrambat Estate

45 Laurie Street, Yarrambat, Vic 3091 (postal) **Region** Yarra Valley
T (03) 9717 3710 **F** (03) 9717 3712 **Open** Not
Winemaker John Ellis (Contract) **Est.** 1995 **Cases** 1500

Ivan McQuilkin has a little over 2.6 ha of chardonnay, pinot noir, cabernet sauvignon and merlot on his vineyard in the northwestern corner of the Yarra Valley, not far from the Plenty River. It is very much an alternative occupation for McQuilkin, whose principal activity is as an international taxation consultant to expatriate employees. While the decision to make wine was at least in part triggered by falling grape prices, hindsight proves it to have been a good one, because some of the wines have impressed. In 2006 the vineyard-grown grapes were supplemented with shiraz from Heathcote. There are no cellar door sales; the conditions of the licence are that wine sales can only take place by mail or phone order.

ΤΤΤΤς **Pinot Noir 2003** Holding depth and hue well; abundant plum and cherry fruit fill the mouth; promises much for further development. Screwcap. 13.1° alc. **Rating** 92 **To** 2015 $15

ΤΤΤΤ **Chardonnay 2004** Quite sweet peach, nectarine and melon fruit, still 100% fresh thanks to the screwcap; any oak is irrelevant. Screwcap. 13.1° alc. **Rating** 89 **To** 2012 $12.50

Merlot Cabernet 2003 Savoury black olive notes blend well with the cassis of the cabernet sauvignon, although the low alcohol has both pluses and minuses, the latter in the undertow of minty/leafy characters. Cork. 12.5° alc. **Rating** 87 **To** 2010 $17.50

Yarrawalla Wines

PO Box 17, Coldstream, Vic 3770 **Region** Yarra Valley
T (03) 5964 9363 **F** (03) 5964 9363 www.yarrawallawines.com.au **Open** At 132 Auburn Road, Hawthorn, Tues–Sat 12–6
Winemaker Dominique Portet **Est.** 1994 **Cases** 1500

A very prominent vineyard on Maddens Lane, with 23 ha of chardonnay, 13 ha of pinot noir and 7 ha of sauvignon blanc. With the arrival of Dominique Portet (also on Maddens Lane), Yarrawalla has ventured into winemaking under its own label, although the major part of the production continues to be sold as grapes.

 # Yarrawood Estate

1275 Melba Highway, Yarra Glen, Vic 3775 **Region** Yarra Valley
T (03) 9730 2003 **F** (03) 9730 1144 www.yarrawood.com.au **Open** 7 days 10–5
Winemaker Contract **Est.** 1997 **Cases** NFP

Yarrawood Estate has 40 ha of riesling, chardonnay, sauvignon blanc, pinot noir, shiraz, merlot and cabernet sauvignon. The major part of the production is sold, and the Yarrawood Tall Tales wines are contract-made. It does, however, have a café and cellar door on the Melba Highway, 3 km north of Yarra Glen.

ΤΤΤΤ **Tall Tales Yarra Valley Shiraz 2003** Licorice, anise and spice cool-grown black fruits; some curious herbal notes thrown in for good measure. The overall impression of sweetness is slightly unexpected, but I think it comes from the fruit rather than unfermented sugar. Cork. 14° alc. **Rating** 89 **To** 2013 $15.30

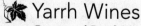 # Yarrh Wines

Greenwood Road, Murrumbateman, NSW 2582 **Region** Canberra District
T (02) 6227 1474 www.yarrhwines.com.au **Open** Sep–June w'ends & public hols 11–5
Winemaker Fiona Wholohan **Est.** 1997 **Cases** 2500

It is probably best to quickly say that Yarrh is Aboriginal for running water, and is neither onomatopoeic nor letters taken from the partners names, the partners being Fiona Wholohan, Neil McGregor and Peta and Christopher Mackenzie Davey. The vineyard was planted in 3 stages between 1997 and 2000, and there are now 6 ha of cabernet sauvignon, shiraz, sauvignon blanc, riesling, pinot noir and sangiovese (in descending order of importance), and all of the wines are estate-grown, and competently made by Fiona Wholohan.

♀♀♀♀ **Canberra District Riesling 2004** Developing nicely; rich tropical fruit with lime acidity; a fraction phenolic suggesting a light fining might have improved it. Screwcap. 13° alc. **Rating** 89 **To** 2011 $16

Canberra District Sauvignon Blanc 2006 Clean, firm and long; powerful flavours ranging from citrus/grapefruit through to melon/tropical. Screwcap. 13° alc. **Rating** 89 **To** 2008 $16

Canberra District Pinot Noir 2005 Has fair varietal expression; light-bodied, but does have texture and structure; a mix of cherry, plum and stalky notes. Screwcap. 13.5° alc. **Rating** 87 **To** 2008 $20

Canberra District Cabernet Sauvignon 2003 Clean, medium-bodied black fruits on entry to the mouth and mid-palate, then fine but persistent tannins swoop on the finish. Cried out to be gently fined. Cork. 13.5° alc. **Rating** 87 **To** 2013 $18

Canberra District Cabernet Shiraz 2004 Medium- to full-bodied; blackcurrant and blackberry, then near-identical structure to the cabernet from fine, persistent tannins. Screwcap. 14° alc. **Rating** 87 **To** 2014 $18

Yarrowlumla Estates

1133 Bungendore Road, Bywong, NSW 2621 (postal) **Region** Canberra District
T (02) 6236 9108 **F** (02) 6236 9508 **www**.yarrowlumla.com.au **Open** Not
Winemaker Lark Hill **Est.** 2004 **Cases** 500
In 2004 Martine and Stuart Gibson-Bode, together with Gary and Dianne Gibson (Stuart's parents) purchased an existing 1.5 ha vineyard planted to chardonnay, sauvignon blanc, merlot and cabernet sauvignon in 1997. The property is located in the hills above Bungendore, and the Aboriginal name means 'where the cry comes back from the mountains' (echo).

Yass Valley Wines

5 Crisps Lane, Murrumbateman, NSW 2582 **Region** Canberra District
T (02) 6227 5592 **F** (02) 6227 5592 **Open** Wed–Sun & public hols 10–5, or by appt
Winemaker Michael Withers **Est.** 1978 **Cases** 500
Michael Withers and Anne Hillier purchased Yass Valley in 1991 and have subsequently rehabilitated the existing run-down vineyards and extended the plantings. Mick Withers is a chemist by profession and has completed a Wine Science degree at Charles Sturt University; Anne is a registered psychologist and has completed a Viticulture diploma at Charles Sturt.

♀♀♀♀♀ **Riesling 2006** Very pale straw-green; a spotlessly clean, though still closed bouquet; the delicate palate has ripe citrus plus touches of apple and pear; will develop well. Screwcap. 11.6° alc. **Rating** 90 **To** 2013 $18

♀♀♀♀ **Traminer 2006** Extremely shy from start to finish; the traminer character is arrived at by eliminating other possibilities; not an easy variety to handle. Screwcap. 13.6° alc. **Rating** 87 **To** 2010 $18

Yaxley Estate

31 Dransfield Road, Copping, Tas 7174 **Region** Southern Tasmania
T (03) 6253 5222 **F** (03) 6253 5222 **Open** 7 days 10–6.30 by appt
Winemaker Hood Wines **Est.** 1991 **Cases** 400
While Yaxley Estate was established back in 1991, it was not until 1998 that it offered each of the 4 wines from its vineyard plantings, which total just under 2 ha. Once again, it is the small batch-handling skills (and patience) of Hood Wines that have made the venture possible.

Yengari Wines

Lot 3 Wangaratta Road, Beechworth, Vic 3747 **Region** Beechworth
T (03) 5833 9295 **F** (03) 5833 9296 **www**.yengari.com **Open** By appt
Winemaker Tony Lacy **Est.** 1998 **Cases** 2000
Tony Lacy and partner Trish Flores run an interesting grape and olive produce business. Painted
candles coloured with wine lees, stationery tinted using the same colour bases, wine soap (shiraz,
chardonnay and cabernet sauvignon) and watercolour paints (shiraz from 100% sun-dried wine
lees and chardonnay from sun-dried wine lees plus traces of natural water colour) are all produced
and sold. Green Ant Wines is the separate venture of Tony Lacy, using contract-grown grapes from
Northeast Victoria. Since 2002 a range of reserve and single vineyard wines has been made from
grapes grown in various parts of SA and Vic.

ΨΨΨΨ **William's Reserve Shiraz 2004** Potent, very ripe, blackberry fruits with lots of
dark chocolate. McLaren Vale. Cork. **Rating** 88 **To** 2014 $18
George & Elaine Reserve Shiraz 2004 Ultra late-picked style; desiccated/dried
fruit/dead fruit characters do add power, as does (I guess) high alcohol. Adelaide
Hills. Cork. **Rating** 88 **To** 2015 $22

Yering Farm

St Huberts Road, Yering, Vic 3770 **Region** Yarra Valley
T (03) 9739 0461 **F** (03) 9739 0467 **www**.yeringfarmwines.com **Open** 7 days 10–5
Winemaker Alan Johns **Est.** 1988 **Cases** 7000
Former East Doncaster orchardist Alan Johns acquired the 40-ha Yeringa Vineyard property in
1980; the property had originally been planted by the Deschamps family in the mid-19th century
and known as Yeringa Cellars. The plantings now extend to 12 ha. Since 1992 all the wines have
been made onsite, and have enjoyed consistent show success.

Yering Station

38 Melba Highway, Yarra Glen, Vic 3775 **Region** Yarra Valley
T (03) 9730 0100 **F** (03) 9739 0135 **www**.yering.com **Open** 7 days 10–5
Winemaker Tom Carson, Darren Rathbone, Caroline Mooney **Est.** 1988 **Cases** 60 000
The historic Yering Station (or at least the portion of the property on which the cellar door sales
and vineyard are established) was purchased by the Rathbone family in 1996 and is now the site
of a joint venture with French Champagne house Devaux. A spectacular and very large winery
has been erected which handles the Yarrabank sparkling wines and the Yering Station and Yarra
Edge table wines. It has immediately become one of the focal points of the Yarra Valley, particularly
as the historic Chateau Yering, where luxury accommodation and fine dining are available, is next
door. Yering Station's own restaurant is open every day for lunch, providing the best cuisine in the
Valley. In 2004 Yering Station, via Tom Carson, was named International Winemaker of the Year
by the International Wine & Spirit Competition in London. Exports to all major markets. The
failure to include tasting notes of the outstanding 2005 Chardonnays is entirely my fault.

ΨΨΨΨΨ **Yarra Valley Shiraz Viognier 2005** Deep but brilliant colour leads into a
wine flush with blackberry, cherry and spice lifted by the unmistakable perfume
of viognier. Ripe, rounded tannins and immaculate oak complete the parcel.
Screwcap. 14.5° alc. **Rating** 96 **To** 2020 $23
Reserve Yarra Valley Shiraz Viognier 2005 Came top of a fiercely contested
and high quality '05 shiraz class at the National Wine Show '06. Perfect texture
and structure based around fine, ripe tannins and vibrant fruit gave the wine
the extra touch of finesse. Screwcap. 14.5° alc. **Rating** 96 **To** 2022 $64
ED Rose 2006 Salmon-pink, it is a complex wine, weaving a spicy web
around cherry and strawberry fruit. Well-balanced, it is by no means painfully
dry or austere, just serious. Screwcap. 12.5° alc. **Rating** 94 **To** 2008 $17.50

Yeringberg

Maroondah Highway, Coldstream, Vic 3770 **Region** Yarra Valley
T (03) 9739 1453 **F** (03) 9739 0048 **www.yeringberg.com Open** By appt
Winemaker Guill de Pury, Sandra de Pury **Est.** 1863 **Cases** 1200
Makes wines for the new millennium from the low-yielding vines re-established on the heart of what was one of the most famous (and infinitely larger) vineyards of the 19th century. In the riper years, the red wines have a velvety generosity of flavour which is rarely encountered, yet never lose varietal character, while the Yeringberg Marsanne Roussanne takes students of history back to Yeringberg's fame in the 19th century. Exports to the UK, the US, Switzerland, Malaysia, Singapore and Hong Kong.

ΨΨΨΨΨ **Yarra Valley Chardonnay 2005** A complex wine; potent melon and grapefruit matched by barrel-ferment oak and lees contact inputs, all of the parts in perfect balance. Cork. 14° alc. **Rating** 94 **To** 2012 $36
Yarra Valley Pinot Noir 2004 Good hue; lively, spicy, slightly foresty bouquet; powerful plum and cherry varietal fruit on the palate, particularly given the relatively high-yielding vintage; has length to match. Cork. 13.5° alc. **Rating** 94 **To** 2012 $55
Yeringberg 2004 A clean, pure, classic Bordeaux blend of Cabernet Sauvignon/Cabernet Franc/Merlot/Malbec; a beautiful mix of blackcurrant and cassis fruit, with fine, ripe tannins and classy oak. Cork. 14° alc. **Rating** 94 **To** 2029 $55

ΨΨΨΨΨ **Yarra Valley Marsanne Roussanne 2005** A clean, but relatively tight and unyielding bouquet; the palate is similar, but prior vintages show how this wine emerges from pupae to shimmering butterfly given enough time; simply buy it and cellar it for reward. Cork. 14° alc. **Rating** 93 **To** 2020 $36
Young Vines Shiraz 2004 A supple, smooth, silky palate, with flavours of cherry and plum predominant; fine but persistent tannins. The 4th vintage from vines around 7 years old. How Guill de Pury must be regretting the decision to remove the original shiraz (planted in the 1960s) in 1981. Cork. 14° alc. **Rating** 93 **To** 2012 $25

Yilgarnia

6634 Redmond West Road, Redmond, WA 6327 **Region** Denmark
T (08) 9845 3031 **F** (08) 9845 3031 **www.yilgarnia.com.au Open** By appt
Winemaker Harewood Estate (James Kellie) **Est.** 1997 **Cases** 2500
Melbourne-educated Peter Buxton travelled across the Nullarbor and settled on a bush block of 405 acres on the Hay River, 6 km north of Wilson Inlet. That was over 40 years ago, and for the first 10 years Buxton worked for the WA Department of Agriculture in Albany. While there, he surveyed several of the early vineyards in WA, and recognised the potential of his family's property. Today there are 10 ha of vines in bearing, with another 6 ha planted in 2002 and 2003. All the vineyard plantings (8 varieties in all) are on north-facing blocks, the geological history of which stretches back 2 billion years.

ΨΨΨΨΨ **Denmark Shiraz 2004** Fine, aromatic black fruits, licorice and cracked pepper; a light- to medium-bodied wine with elegance, finesse, subtlety and balance. Screwcap. 14° alc. **Rating** 93 **To** 2015 $21
Denmark Classic White 2006 Unexpected intensity and length; lifted gooseberry, kiwifruit tied with a bow of lemony acidity; clean as a whistle. Screwcap. 12.5° alc. **Rating** 90 **To** 2009 $15
Denmark Merlot 2005 A strongly varietal expression in a light-bodied frame; savoury, spicy black olive with accompanying sweet cassis fruit. Screwcap. 13.5° alc. **Rating** 90 **To** 2012 $21

ΨΨΨΨ **Denmark Sauvignon Blanc 2006** Green apple and nettle aromas; crisp and firm, basically in a herbaceous spectrum; minerally acidity. Screwcap. 13.5° alc. **Rating** 87 **To** 2008 $16

Zarephath Wines

Moorialup Road, East Porongurup, WA 6324 **Region** Porongurup
T (08) 9853 1152 **www**.zarephathwines.com **Open** Mon–Sat 10–5, Sun 12–4
Winemaker Robert Diletti **Est.** 1994 **Cases** 3000
The 9-ha Zarephath vineyard is owned and operated by Brothers and Sisters of The Christ
Circle, a Benedictine community. They say the most outstanding feature of the location is the
feeling of peace and tranquility which permeates the site, something I can well believe on the
basis of numerous visits to the Porongurups. Exports to the UK and NZ.

ΨΨΨΨΩ **Porongurup Riesling 2006** Fragrant, flowery lime and honeysuckle aromas
and flavours; good balance and length; very different to the '05. Screwcap.
12.5° alc. **Rating** 92 **To** 2016 $20
Chardonnay 2005 Grapefruit and nectarine infused with barrel-ferment
and yeast lees characters; intense, long, lingering finish. Screwcap. **Rating** 91
To 2009 $25

ΨΨΨΨ **Pinot Noir 2005** Some tomato vine aromas, then a firm palate with plum and
spice; an interesting wine which may develop well. Screwcap. **Rating** 89 **To** 2010
$25
Porongurup Cabernet Sauvignon 2003 Cedary, spicy, earthy nuances to
medium-bodied cassis and blackcurrant fruit; doesn't really sing, but may do so with
a few more years in the bottle. Screwcap. 13° alc. **Rating** 88 **To** 2011 $25

Zema Estate

Riddoch Highway, Coonawarra, SA 5263 **Region** Coonawarra
T (08) 8736 3219 **F** (08) 8736 3280 **www**.zema.com.au **Open** 7 days 9–5
Winemaker Greg Clayfield **Est.** 1982 **Cases** 20 000
Zema is one of the last outposts of hand-pruning in Coonawarra, with members of the Zema
family tending a 61-ha vineyard progressively planted since 1982 in the heart of Coonawarra's
terra rossa soil. Winemaking practices are straightforward; if ever there was an example of great
wines being made in the vineyard, this is it. The extremely popular and equally talented former
Lindemans winemaker Greg Clayfield has joined the team, replacing long-term winemaker Tom
Simons. Exports to all major markets.

ΨΨΨΨΩ **Coonawarra Cabernet Sauvignon 2004** Medium-bodied, elegant wine; pure
varietal expression; has good length, though – thanks to the vintage – not quite
as much depth. Cork. 14° alc. **Rating** 90 **To** 2019 $26

ΨΨΨΨ **Cluny 2004** A complex wine; very much in the herb, leaf and earth spectrum, with
some attractive spicy overtones. Screwcap. 14° alc. **Rating** 89 **To** 2012 $26

Zig Zag Road

201 Zig Zag Road, Drummond, Vic 3461 **Region** Macedon Ranges
T (03) 5423 9390 **F** (03) 5423 9390 **Open** W'ends & public hols 10–6, or by appt
Winemaker Alan Stevens, Eric Bellchambers **Est.** 1972 **Cases** 300
Alan Stevens and Deb Orton purchased the vineyard in 1988 when it was 16 years old, having
been established by Roger Aldridge. The dry-grown vines produce relatively low yields, and until
1996 the grapes were sold to Hanging Rock Winery. In 1996 the decision was taken to manage
the property on a full-time basis, and to make the wine onsite, using 0.25 ha each of riesling,
merlot and pinot noir, and 1 ha each of shiraz and cabernet sauvignon.

ΨΨΨΨΨ **Riesling 2005** Lovely green-straw colour; a pure wine, with delicacy and
power a magic combination. Trophy Macedon Ranges Wine Exhibition '06.
Screwcap. 11.5° alc. **Rating** 95 **To** 2015 $22

ΨΨΨΨ **Shiraz 2003** Elegant red and black fruits; jumpy acidity on the finish a pity. Cork.
14.5° alc. **Rating** 89 **To** 2010 $22

Sparkling Shiraz 2004 An interesting play for cool climate shiraz; fresh, and while slightly sweet, still within bounds. 11.5° alc. **Rating** 88 **To** 2008 $25

Zilzie Wines

Lot 66 Kulkyne Way, Karadoc via Red Cliffs, Vic 3496 **Region** Murray Darling
T (03) 5025 8100 **F** (03) 5025 8116 **www.**zilziewines.com **Open** Not
Winemaker Bob Shields, Leigh Sparrow **Est.** 1999 **Cases** NFP
The Forbes family has been farming Zilzie Estate since 1911; it is currently run by Ian and Ros Forbes, and sons Steven and Andrew. A diverse range of farming activities now include grapegrowing with 250 ha of vineyards. Having established a position as a dominant supplier of grapes to Southcorp, Zilzie formed a wine company in 1999 and built a winery in 2000. It has a capacity of 16 000 tonnes, but is designed so that modules can be added to take it to 50 000 tonnes. The business includes contract processing, winemaking and storage. Exports to the UK, the US, Canada, NZ, Singapore and Thailand.

ŶŶŶŶ   **Petit Verdot 2004** Dark colour; full-bodied black fruits, cedar, a touch of bitter chocolate; substantial, savoury tannins. Screwcap. 15° alc. **Rating** 89 **To** 2010 $15
Tempranillo 2004 Intense, slightly lemony/savoury overtones to the red fruits; long palate. Screwcap. 12.5° alc. **Rating** 89 **To** 2011 $15
Pinot Grigio 2006 A faint blush of pink; light aromas of pear before the wine springs into life on the palate, with zingy, zippy, citrussy acidity. Screwcap. 11.5° alc. **Rating** 88 **To** 2006 $15
Sangiovese 2004 Typical light colour; interesting varietal notes of cherry, spice and cedar; fine tannins. Worthy example. Screwcap. 14.5° alc. **Rating** 88 **To** 2008 $15
Selection 23 Shiraz 2005 Fresh, bright and lively light-bodied red fruits; good balance and length, likewise value. Screwcap. 14.5° alc. **Rating** 87 **To** 2009 $10

Zonte's Footstep ★★★☆

Wellington Road/PO Box 53, Langhorne Creek, SA 5255 **Region** Langhorne Creek
T (08) 8537 3334 **F** (08) 8537 3231 **www.**zontesfootstep.com.au **Open** Not
Winemaker Ben Riggs **Est.** 1997 **Cases** 50 000
The 215-ha vineyard of Zonte's Footstep dates back to 1997 when a group of old school mates banded together to purchase the land and established the vineyard under the direction of viticulturist Geoff Hardy and long-term vigneron John Pargeter. Obviously enough, a large percentage of the grapes are sold to others, a small part skilfully made by Ben Riggs. While it is not clear who Zonte was, the footprint on the label is that of Diprotodon or giant wombat, which inhabited the southeastern corner of SA for more than 20 million years until becoming extinct 10–20 000 years ago. The wine quality is as good as the prices are modest.

ŶŶŶŶŶ   **Langhorne Creek Shiraz Viognier 2006** A special synergy with viognier makes smooth and supple Langhorne Creek shiraz even more so; no-one could dislike this gently spicy wine, with lifted red fruits and minimal tannins. Screwcap. 14.5° alc. **Rating** 93 **To** 2012

ŶŶŶŶ   **Langhorne Creek Cabernet Petit Verdot Dry Rose 2006** Adds to the amazing range of base wines using in making rose; annoyingly, works quite well, with lots of flavour and, as promised by the label, dry. Screwcap. 13.5° alc. **Rating** 89 **To** 2008
Langhorne Creek Sangiovese Barbera 2005 Medium-bodied; spicy, gently earthy red and black cherry fruit aromas and flavours; fine, soft tannins; ready now. Screwcap. 14.5° alc. **Rating** 89 **To** 2008 $18
Langhorne Creek Viognier 2006 A similar story to the Verdelho, but here with more conviction; the fruit line is good, the apricot and peach flavour without phenolics. Screwcap. 13.5° alc. **Rating** 88 **To** 2008
Langhorne Creek Verdelho 2006 Has enough weight and mouthfeel to lift it out of the ruck, but not by much; the usual fruit salad flavours. Screwcap. 13.5° alc. **Rating** 87 **To** 2008

Index

McLaren Vale (SA)

Mornington Peninsula (Vic)